41: *Afro-American Poets Since 1955*, edited by Trudier Harris and Thadious M. Davis (1985)

42: *American Writers for Children Before 1900*, edited by Glenn E. Estes (1985)

43: *American Newspaper Journalists, 1690-1872*, edited by Perry J. Ashley (1986)

44: *American Screenwriters*, Second Series, edited by Randall Clark, Robert E. Morsberger, and Stephen O. Lesser (1986)

45: *American Poets, 1880-1945*, First Series, edited by Peter Quartermain (1986)

46: *American Literary Publishing Houses, 1900-1980: Trade and Paperback*, edited by Peter Dzwonkoski (1986)

47: *American Historians, 1866-1912*, edited by Clyde N. Wilson (1986)

48: *American Poets, 1880-1945*, Second Series, edited by Peter Quartermain (1986)

49: *American Literary Publishing Houses, 1638-1899*, 2 parts, edited by Peter Dzwonkoski (1986)

50: *Afro-American Writers Before the Harlem Renaissance*, edited by Trudier Harris (1986)

51: *Afro-American Writers from the Harlem Renaissance to 1940*, edited by Trudier Harris (1987)

52: *American Writers for Children Since 1960: Fiction*, edited by Glenn E. Estes (1986)

53: *Canadian Writers Since 1960*, First Series, edited by W. H. New (1986)

54: *American Poets, 1880-1945*, Third Series, 2 parts, edited by Peter Quartermain (1987)

55: *Victorian Prose Writers Before 1867*, edited by William B. Thesing (1987)

56: *German Fiction Writers, 1914-1945*, edited by James Hardin (1987)

57: *Victorian Prose Writers After 1867*, edited by William B. Thesing (1987)

58: *Jacobean and Caroline Dramatists*, edited by Fredson Bowers (1987)

59: *American Literary Critics and Scholars, 1800-1850*, edited by John W. Rathbun and Monica M. Grecu (1987)

60: *Canadian Writers Since 1960*, Second Series, edited by W. H. New (1987)

61: *American Writers for Children Since 1960: Poets, Illustrators, and Nonfiction Authors*, edited by Glenn E. Estes (1987)

62: *Elizabethan Dramatists*, edited by Fredson Bowers (1987)

63: *Modern American Critics, 1920-1955*, edited by Gregory S. Jay (1988)

64: *American Literary Critics and Scholars, 1850-1880*, edited by John W. Rathbun and Monica M. Grecu (1988)

65: *French Novelists, 1900-1930*, edited by Catharine Savage Brosman (1988)

66: *German Fiction Writers, 1885-1913*, 2 parts, edited by James Hardin (1988)

67: *Modern American Critics Since 1955*, edited by Gregory S. Jay (1988)

68: *Canadian Writers, 1920-1959*, First Series, edited by W. H. New (1988)

69: *Contemporary German Fiction Writers*, First Series, edited by Wolfgang D. Elfe and James Hardin (1988)

70: *British Mystery Writers, 1860-1919*, edited by Bernard Benstock and Thomas F. Staley (1988)

71: *American Literary Critics and Scholars, 1880-1900*, edited by John W. Rathbun and Monica M. Grecu (1988)

72: *French Novelists, 1930-1960*, edited by Catharine Savage Brosman (1988)

73: *American Magazine Journalists, 1741-1850*, edited by Sam G. Riley (1988)

74: *American Short-Story Writers Before 1880*, edited by Bobby Ellen Kimbel, with the assistance of William E. Grant (1988)

75: *Contemporary German Fiction Writers*, Second Series, edited by Wolfgang D. Elfe and James Hardin (1988)

76: *Afro-American Writers, 1940-1955*, edited by Trudier Harris (1988)

77: *British Mystery Writers, 1920-1939*, edited by Bernard Benstock and Thomas F. Staley (1988)

78: *American Short-Story Writers, 1880-1910*, edited by Bobby Ellen Kimbel, with the assistance of William E. Grant (1988)

79: *American Magazine Journalists, 1850-1900*, edited by Sam G. Riley (1988)

(Continued on back endsheets)

Twentieth-Century German Dramatists, 1919-1992

Dictionary of Literary Biography® • Volume One Hundred Twenty-Four

Twentieth-Century German Dramatists, 1919-1992

8892

Edited by
Wolfgang D. Elfe
University of South Carolina

and

James Hardin
University of South Carolina

A Bruccoli Clark Layman Book
Gale Research Inc.
Detroit, London

Printed in the United States of America

Published simultaneously in the United Kingdom
by Gale Research International Limited
(An affiliated company of Gale Research Inc.)

The paper used in this publication meets the minimum requirements
of American National Standard for Information Sciences—Permanence
Paper for Printed Library Materials, ANSI Z39.48-1984. ∞™

Library of Congress Catalog Card Number 92-26833
ISBN 0-8103-5383-0

To Hans-Gert and Anke Roloff

Contents

Plan of the Series

. . . Almost the most prodigious asset of a country, and perhaps its most precious possession, is its native literary product—when that product is fine and noble and enduring.

Mark Twain*

The advisory board, the editors, and the publisher of the *Dictionary of Literary Biography* are joined in endorsing Mark Twain's declaration. The literature of a nation provides an inexhaustible resource of permanent worth. We intend to make literature and its creators better understood and more accessible to students and the reading public, while satisfying the standards of teachers and scholars.

To meet these requirements, *literary biography* has been construed in terms of the author's achievement. The most important thing about a writer is his writing. Accordingly, the entries in *DLB* are career biographies, tracing the development of the author's canon and the evolution of his reputation.

The purpose of *DLB* is not only to provide reliable information in a convenient format but also to place the figures in the larger perspective of literary history and to offer appraisals of their accomplishments by qualified scholars.

The publication plan for *DLB* resulted from two years of preparation. The project was proposed to Bruccoli Clark by Frederick C. Ruffner, president of the Gale Research Company, in November 1975. After specimen entries were prepared and typeset, an advisory board was formed to refine the entry format and develop the series rationale. In meetings held during 1976, the publisher, series editors, and advisory board approved the scheme for a comprehensive biographical dictionary of persons who contributed to North American literature. Editorial work on the first volume began in January 1977, and it was published in 1978. In order to make *DLB* more than a reference tool and to compile volumes

that individually have claim to status as literary history, it was decided to organize volumes by topic, period, or genre. Each of these freestanding volumes provides a biographical-bibliographical guide and overview for a particular area of literature. We are convinced that this organization—as opposed to a single alphabet method—constitutes a valuable innovation in the presentation of reference material. The volume plan necessarily requires many decisions for the placement and treatment of authors who might properly be included in two or three volumes. In some instances a major figure will be included in separate volumes, but with different entries emphasizing the aspect of his career appropriate to each volume. Ernest Hemingway, for example, is represented in *American Writers in Paris, 1920-1939* by an entry focusing on his expatriate apprenticeship; he is also in *American Novelists, 1910-1945* with an entry surveying his entire career. Each volume includes a cumulative index of the subject authors and articles. Comprehensive indexes to the entire series are planned.

With volume ten in 1982 it was decided to enlarge the scope of *DLB*. By the end of 1986 twenty-one volumes treating British literature had been published, and volumes for Commonwealth and Modern European literature were in progress. The series has been further augmented by the *DLB Yearbooks* (since 1981) which update published entries and add new entries to keep the *DLB* current with contemporary activity. There have also been *DLB Documentary Series* volumes which provide biographical and critical source materials for figures whose work is judged to have particular interest for students. One of these companion volumes is entirely devoted to Tennessee Williams.

We define literature as the *intellectual commerce of a nation:* not merely as belles lettres but as that ample and complex process by which ideas are generated, shaped, and transmitted. *DLB* entries are not limited to "creative writers" but extend to other figures who in their time and in their way influenced the mind of a people. Thus the series encompasses historians, journalists, publishers, and screenwriters. By this means

*From an unpublished section of Mark Twain's autobiography, copyright © by the Mark Twain Company

readers of *DLB* may be aided to perceive literature not as cult scripture in the keeping of intellectual high priests but firmly positioned at the center of a nation's life.

DLB includes the major writers appropriate to each volume and those standing in the ranks immediately behind them. Scholarly and critical counsel has been sought in deciding which minor figures to include and how full their entries should be. Wherever possible, useful references are made to figures who do not warrant separate entries.

Each *DLB* volume has a volume editor responsible for planning the volume, selecting the figures for inclusion, and assigning the entries. Volume editors are also responsible for preparing, where appropriate, appendices surveying the major periodicals and literary and intellectual movements for their volumes, as well as lists of further readings. Work on the series as a whole is coordinated at the Bruccoli Clark Layman editorial center in Columbia, South Carolina, where the editorial staff is responsible for accuracy of the published volumes.

One feature that distinguishes *DLB* is the illustration policy—its concern with the iconography of literature. Just as an author is influenced by his surroundings, so is the reader's understanding of the author enhanced by a knowledge of his environment. Therefore *DLB* volumes include not only drawings, paintings, and photographs of authors, often depicting them at various stages in their careers, but also illustrations of their families and places where they lived. Title pages are regularly reproduced in facsimile along with dust jackets for modern authors. The dust jackets are a special feature of *DLB* because they often document better than anything else the way in which an author's work was perceived in its own time. Specimens of the writers' manuscripts are included when feasible.

Samuel Johnson rightly decreed that "The chief glory of every people arises from its authors." The purpose of the *Dictionary of Literary Biography* is to compile literary history in the surest way available to us—by accurate and comprehensive treatment of the lives and work of those who contributed to it.

The *DLB* Advisory Board

Introduction

Dictionary of Literary Biography, volume 124, *Twentieth-Century German Dramatists, 1919-1992*, presents fifty German, Austrian, and Swiss-German writers, most of whom had their first significant work published or performed after World War I; its companion volume is *DLB 118, Twentieth-Century German Dramatists, 1889-1918*. The editors divided the volumes chronologically because of the wrenching political, social, economic, and cultural changes that occurred in central Europe in 1918-1919; to choose a literary movement as a structural principle seemed less useful because many dramatists in the first half of the twentieth century belonged to more than one literary movement in the course of their productive years. In addition to these two volumes, the reader should also consult *DLB* volumes 56, 66, 69, 75, 81, and 85, which deal with writers of prose fiction; many of the dramatists in volumes 118 and 124 were also significant fiction writers and thus have already been treated in *DLB* entries for that genre.

Each entry in volumes 118 and 124 starts with the rubric PLAY PRODUCTIONS, which lists the first performances of the author's dramas. In the case of some authors, this information can be found in no other reference work. PLAY PRODUCTIONS is followed by the primary bibliography of the author's works, the most important part of which is the listing of the author's book publications, including the first British or American translations. The entry discusses the author's life and dramatic works and "places" him or her in the history of German drama and theater. A secondary bibliography and, where applicable, a statement about the author's papers concludes the entry. The entries are written for English-speaking readers who are not necessarily familiar with the German language; quotations, as well as titles and words not readily understandable are followed by English translations.

In German-speaking countries, theater since the time of Johann Wolfgang von Goethe and Friedrich Schiller has been more than a place for entertainment; rather, as one of the contributors puts it, theater "holds a special and honorable place as the site of moral education for an enlightened public." Municipal and state governments provide substantial financial support for theaters in Germany, thus making it possible for every good-sized city to have a well-equipped, well-staffed theater with professional actors and actresses. Given the opportunities for fame and income, it is not surprising that many writers—including most of the illustrious ones—were attracted to drama. From the stature of the theater it also follows that a study of German drama and theater will reveal more than just superficial information about the societies and cultures of the German-speaking countries.

From the end of World War I until 1923 expressionism, the movement in literature and the arts that had started around 1910, dominated German drama. It was a time of economic hardship and political unrest, when the young dramatists, with their noisy rejection of prewar traditions and their antimilitarist and anticapitalist stance, could still draw large audiences. As a rule, expressionists rejected a realistic, photographic representation of reality in favor of presenting an inner reality: their mostly negative vision of the existing world or their positive vision of a new, utopian world. To portray these visions required nontraditional stage effects, including the innovative use of color, light, sound, and choreography. Rational discourse was generally absent from the expressionist dramas; instead, there was a high intensity of emotion and pathos, often verging on bathos. Rejection of traditional reality also meant a rejection of traditional language patterns in favor of linguistic innovation and, frequently, a telegraphic style. Expressionism was stark and abstract; it portrayed its world in bold, primary colors.

Expressionist dramatists covered in *DLB 118* include Ernst Barlach, Reinhard Goering, Paul Kornfeld, Heinrich Mann, Reinhard Johannes Sorge, and Fritz von Unruh; among those treated in this volume are Arnolt Bronnen, Hanns Johst, Georg Kaiser, Oskar Kokoschka, Else Lasker-Schüler, Ernst Toller, and Franz Werfel. It should be remembered, however, that the label *expressionist* does not describe the entire oeuvre of most of these authors but, in most instances, only their early periods.

In several cases the literary, cultural, and philosophical radicalism of the authors was combined with political radicalism. Toller, for example, was a Marxist, while Johst supported the extreme political Right.

The beginning of relative economic and political stability in the Weimar Republic in 1924 marked the end of expressionism and the beginning of Neue Sachlichkeit (New Realism or New Objectivity), a literary movement characterized by sobriety and matter-of-factness as well as an intense interest in all aspects of contemporary culture. Neue Sachlichkeit constituted a rejection of the subjectivity of expressionism and of its revolutionary and visionary concepts. Even the expressionist dramatists for the most part turned to a more objective and less emotional representation of reality after 1923. New dramatists who emerged during the period of Neue Sachlichkeit include Ferdinand Bruckner, Marieluise Fleißer, Ödön von Horváth, Friedrich Wolf, and Carl Zuckmayer. Fleißer, Horváth, and Zuckmayer also gave literary respectability to the Volksstück (folk play), traditionally a light comedy for and about common people, by making it a vehicle for portraying unresolved contemporary political, economic, and social problems. From the onset of the Great Depression in 1929 until the Nazi takeover in 1933 an increased politicization of the drama can be observed in the works of Toller, Bertolt Brecht, Wolf, Hans José Rehfisch, and many others. Especially on the political Left, drama was brought into the political struggle of the day; the major issues treated were social injustice, abuses in the criminal justice system that favored the wealthy classes, the plight of women, militarism, and war.

While expressionism and Neue Sachlichkeit were the dominant modern movements in the theater of the Weimar years, they were by no means the only ones. Well-known dramatists of earlier periods, such as Hugo von Hofmannsthal, Arthur Schnitzler, Carl Sternheim, and Gerhart Hauptmann, continued to write during the 1920s. Demand for entertainment untouched by the turbulent times produced Curt Goetz's drawing-room comedies and mysteries. Even Germany's foremost expressionist dramatist, Kaiser, wrote plays in the 1920s that fit into the category of light entertainment.

The Nazi takeover of Germany in 1933 and of Austria in 1938 resulted in an exodus of writers and artists. Among the exiled dramatists were Brecht, Bruckner, Goetz, Horváth, Kaiser, Lasker-Schüler, Hermann Broch, Elias Canetti, Bruno Frank, Leonhard Frank, Heinrich Mann, Robert Musil, Toller, Unruh, Werfel, Wolf, Zuckmayer and Stefan Zweig. The exodus from Germany and Austria also included some of the most renowned theater directors, such as Max Reinhardt, Erwin Piscator, Leopold Jessner, and Viktor Barnowsky, as well as actors. Most of the writers continued to be productive in exile, but the working conditions for the dramatists were particularly difficult: in addition to the material hardships and legal problems in often inhospitable host countries, most of the exiled dramatists were unable to have their plays performed; thus the interplay between creative writing and stage work was missing. Even though stylistic and thematic continuity can be observed in their works, none of these writers could ignore the struggle against National Socialism. In Bruckner's *Die Rassen* (performed, 1933; published, 1934; translated as *Races*, 1934), Wolf's *Der gelbe Fleck: Doktor Mamlocks Ausweg* (The Yellow Spot: Doctor Mamlock's Remedy; performed, 1934; published as *Doktor Mamlocks Ausweg*, 1935; translated as *Professor Mamlock*, 1935), and Brecht's *Furcht und Elend des Dritten Reiches* (performed as *99%*, 1938; published, 1941; translated as *The Private Life of the Master Race*, 1944), to mention just a few of the best-known examples, drama was used as a tool in the anti-Nazi struggle. Brecht, whose best plays were written in exile, also dealt with the political issues of those years in his "parable" plays.

In Germany the Nazis favored dramatists who had a nationalist and racist message. Johst's pro-Nazi stand, which was a departure from the humanist-pacifist sentiments and the anti-bourgeois outcries of his expressionist period, was generously rewarded by the regime. The rural Austrian setting and themes of Richard Billinger's dramas were promoted by the authorities as Blut- und Boden (blood and soil) literature that glorified the German racial heritage and the presumed values of the German and Austrian countryside. Hans Rehberg's nationalistic historical plays were hailed by the Nazi cultural functionaries, and Erwin Guido Kolbenheyer's works advocating a greater German nation and displaying racism and biologism were officially favored and propagated.

While no drama of lasting value emerged from the pro-Nazi writers, the Nazis did not destroy theatrical traditions in Germany. Intent on placating or winning over the nonpolitical majority of the middle class, the Nazis kept the theater—that class's most cherished cultural institution—more or less intact. State-subsidized theaters continued to exist, and pro-Nazi dramas by no means dominated their repertoires. Major German dramas of eighteenth- and nineteenth-century authors, such as Goethe, Schiller, and Friedrich Hebbel, as well as nonpolitical plays providing light entertainment, could still be performed. Missing were dramas by German-Jewish dramatists, socialist and communist plays of the 1920s, and modern avant-garde dramas. In general, the repertoires of major theaters in big cities changed more noticeably during the Nazi years than did those of provincial theaters.

With Germany's defeat in 1945 and the onset of the Cold War shortly thereafter, a distinctly different political, economic, and cultural development commenced in the two parts of Germany. In the Western zones of occupation, which became the Federal Republic of Germany in 1949, there was a great demand for modern Western drama. Having been culturally isolated from 1933 until 1945, German readers and theatergoers showed a great interest in the plays of Jean Anouilh, Paul Claudel, T. S. Eliot, Christopher Fry, Jean Giraudoux, Arthur Miller, Eugene O'Neill, Jean-Paul Sartre, Thornton Wilder, and Tennessee Williams. Of the exiled German dramatists only Zuckmayer was highly successful. As a result of the Cold War, Brecht's leftist plays were not popular in West Germany. Exile literature in general did not fare well in West Germany, and it was not until the late 1960s that a reintegration of exile writings into German literature began.

The dominance of foreign modern dramatists at the time would have been felt even more strongly had it not been for the Swiss-Germans Friedrich Dürrenmatt and Max Frisch, the leading living dramatists from the early 1950s until the early 1960s. Their success can primarily be attributed to their ability to produce brilliant—often grotesque—satire; in addition, they were writing in German and were close to the situation in postwar Germany without having been compromised by previous accommodation with the Nazi regime. During the Nazi years they had been able to stay in contact with the development of modern drama, including German exile drama, that had found a haven at the Zurich Schau-

spielhaus. Plays by Brecht, Bruckner, Horváth, Wolf, and Zuckmayer were first performed in Zurich, and the Schauspielhaus was an ideal place for Frisch and Dürrenmatt to learn their craft.

The strong influence of modern foreign dramatists in West Germany also extends to the theater of the absurd. From the mid 1950s to the mid 1960s plays of Samuel Beckett, Eugène Ionesco, and Harold Pinter were widely read and performed. Some German dramatists joined in this trend, most notably Wolfgang Hildesheimer and Günter Grass.

The increased politicization of intellectual life in West Germany in the 1960s can also be observed in the drama. Influenced by Brecht but even more by Piscator's political theater of the 1920s, dramatists such as Tankred Dorst, Rolf Hochhuth, Heinar Kipphardt, and Peter Weiss wrote highly political documentary dramas which incorporated historical source materials. A world-famous example of this genre is *Der Stellvertreter* (1963; translated as *The Representative*, 1963, and as *The Deputy*, 1964), in which Hochhuth accuses Pope Pius XII of silence and inaction during the Holocaust.

In the 1970s and 1980s new German and Austrian dramatists emerged whose work still awaits classification. Martin Sperr, Peter Turrini, and Felix Mitterer attempted to renew the Volksstück. Herbert Achternbusch, Wolfgang Bauer, Thomas Bernhard, Peter Handke, and Gerhard Roth resorted to extensive formal experimentation; rebellious, self-centered, and unconventional in their life-styles, they tried to shock their readers and audiences by presenting chaotic and often distasteful works about a senseless world of death, disease, violence, and madness.

In the Soviet zone of Germany, which became the German Democratic Republic (GDR) in 1949, cultural life was under the tight control of the Communist authorities. Drama and theater were used to propagate Communist ideology and to support the transformation of the eastern part of Germany into a Soviet Communist dictatorship. The history of GDR drama begins with the return of leftist pre-World War II dramatists to East Germany, with Brecht and Wolf the most notable examples. In the mid 1950s a new generation of dramatists emerged in East Germany. For twenty years, until the mid 1970s, the political and ideological demands of the Socialist Unity (Communist) party and the formal requirements of "socialist realism" left little room for artistic creativity and originality. After that, relatively more freedom was granted to artists and writers, and dramas and dramatists began to emerge that received public recognition beyond East Germany. Taken together, the entries in this volume on Volker Braun, Peter Hacks, Christoph Hein, and Heiner Müller provide an overview of the history of drama in the former GDR, which ceased to exist in 1989.

Until the breakthrough of television in central Europe in the 1960s, public radio played an important role in the cultural life of German-speaking countries. The opportunities for income and recognition in this area led many dramatists to write radio plays in the post-World War II period. The heyday of German radio occurred in the 1950s and early 1960s, when radio plays by serious writers were listened to by large audiences. The German radio plays—as Professor Wulf Koepke's article in the appendix to this volume shows—bore little resemblance to American radio shows of the 1940s and 1950s, which were intended to amuse or to horrify in a cozy way and to sell the products of their advertisers. German radio, like German drama, usually aimed to give moral and spiritual instruction.

—*Wolfgang D. Elfe and James Hardin*

Acknowledgments

This book was produced by Bruccoli Clark Layman, Inc. Karen L. Rood is senior editor for the *Dictionary of Literary Biography* series. Philip B. Dematteis was the in-house editor.

Production coordinator is James W. Hipp. Projects manager is Charles D. Brower. Photography editors are Edward Scott and Timothy C. Lundy. Layout and graphics supervisor is Penney L. Haughton. Copyediting supervisor is Bill Adams. Typesetting supervisor is Kathleen M. Flanagan. Mary Scott Dye is editorial associate. Systems manager is George F. Dodge. The production staff includes Rowena Betts, Steve Borsanyi, Teresa Chaney, Patricia Coate, Rebecca Crawford, Margaret McGinty Cureton, Denise Edwards, Sarah A. Estes, Robert Fowler, Brenda A. Gillie, Bonita Graham, Avril E. Gregory, Jolyon M. Helterman, Ellen McCracken, Kathy Lawler Merlette, John Myrick, Pamela D. Norton, Thomas J. Pickett, Patricia Salisbury, Maxine K. Smalls, Deborah P. Stokes, Jennifer C. J. Turley, and Wilma Weant.

Walter W. Ross and Samuel Bruce did library research. They were assisted by the following librarians at the Thomas Cooper Library of the University of South Carolina: Jens Holley and the interlibrary-loan staff; reference librarians Gwen Baxter, Daniel Boice, Faye Chadwell, Cathy Eckman, Rhonda Felder, Gary Geer, Jackie Kinder, Laurie Preston, Jean Rhyne, Carol Tobin, Virginia Weathers, and Connie Widney; circulation-department head Thomas Marcil; and acquisitions-searching supervisor David Haggard.

Twentieth-Century German Dramatists, 1919-1992

Dictionary of Literary Biography

Herbert Achternbusch
(23 November 1938 -   )

Linda C. DeMeritt
Allegheny College

PLAY PRODUCTIONS: *Ella*, Stuttgart, Württembergisches Staatstheater, 27 January 1978;

Susn, Bochum, Schauspielhaus, 23 October 1980;

Kuschwarda City, Bochum, Schauspielhaus, 23 October 1980;

Plattling, Frankfurt, Kammerspiele, 20 March 1982;

Der Frosch, Bochum, Schauspielhaus, 5 June 1982;

Mein Herbert, Graz, Vereinigte Bühnen, 24 September 1983;

Gust, Caen, France, Comédie de Caen, 6 March 1984; German opening, Munich, Residenztheater, 12 April 1985;

Sintflut, Bochum, Schauspielhaus, 15 September 1984;

Weg, Munich, Kammerspiele, 22 November 1985;

Linz, Munich, Kammerspiele, 13 February 1987;

Weißer Stier, Bonn, Schauspielhaus, 19 March 1987;

An der Donau, music by Heiner Goebbels, Vienna, Akademietheater, 3 June 1987;

Auf verlorenem Posten, Munich, Kammerspiele, 5 April 1990.

BOOKS: *Sechs Radierungen* (Stierstadt im Taunus: Eremiten-Presse, 1964);

Südtyroler Gedichte und Siebdrucke (Munich: Maistraßenpresse, 1966);

Zigarettenverkäufer; Hülle; Rita (Frankfurt am Main: Suhrkamp, 1969);

Die Macht des Löwengebrülls (Frankfurt am Main: Suhrkamp, 1970);

Das Kamel (Frankfurt am Main: Suhrkamp, 1970)—comprises *Tibet, Indio, Afganistan, 2. Mai 69;*

Herbert Achternbusch (photograph by Gunter Freyse)

Die Alexanderschlacht (Frankfurt am Main: Suhrkamp, 1971; revised, 1978);

L'Etat c'est moi (Frankfurt am Main: Suhrkamp, 1972);

Der Tag wird kommen: Roman (Frankfurt am Main: Suhrkamp, 1973);

Happy oder Der Tag wird kommen: Roman (Frankfurt am Main: Suhrkamp, 1975)—includes *Der Neger Erwin*;

Die Stunde des Todes: Roman (Frankfurt am Main: Suhrkamp, 1975)—includes *Herz aus Glas*, translated and adapted by Alan Greenberg and Werner Herzog as *Heart of Glass* (Munich: Skellig, 1976);

Servus Bayern (Gauting: Kirchheim, 1977); revised as *Servus Bayern: Filmbuch* (Frankfurt am Main: Suhrkamp, 1978);

Land in Sicht: Roman (Frankfurt am Main: Suhrkamp, 1977);

1969 (Frankfurt am Main: Suhrkamp, 1978);

Die Atlantikschwimmer (Frankfurt am Main: Suhrkamp, 1978)—includes *Ella*;

Der Komantsche (Heidelberg: Das Wunderhorn, 1979);

Es ist ein leichtes beim Gehen den Boden zu berühren (Frankfurt am Main: Suhrkamp, 1980)—includes *Susn, Gust, Kuschwarda City*;

Der Neger Erwin: Filmbuch (Frankfurt am Main: Suhrkamp, 1981);

Das Haus am Nil (Frankfurt am Main: Suhrkamp, 1981)—includes *Der Frosch* and *Das letzte Loch*;

Revolten (Frankfurt am Main: Suhrkamp, 1982);

Mein Herbert (Frankfurt am Main: Suhrkamp Theaterverlag, 1982);

Das letzte Loch: Filmbuch (Frankfurt am Main: Suhrkamp, 1982);

Die Olympiasiegerin: Filmbuch (Frankfurt am Main: Suhrkamp, 1982);

Die Olympiasiegerin (Frankfurt am Main: Suhrkamp, 1982)—includes *Plattling*;

Wellen (Frankfurt am Main: Suhrkamp, 1983)—includes *Sintflut*;

Das Gespenst: Filmbuch bei Zweitausendeins (Frankfurt am Main: Suhrkamp, 1983);

Der Depp: Filmbuch (Frankfurt am Main: Suhrkamp, 1983);

Wind (Frankfurt am Main: Zweitausendeins, 1984);

Wanderkrebs (Frankfurt am Main: Zweitausendeins, 1984);

Weg (Frankfurt am Main: Suhrkamp, 1985);

Die Föhnforscher (Frankfurt am Main: Zweitausendeins, 1985);

1969: Schriften 1968-69 (Frankfurt am Main: Suhrkamp, 1986);

Die Alexanderschlacht: Schriften 1963-71 (Frankfurt am Main: Suhrkamp, 1986);

Die Atlantikschwimmer: Schriften 1973-79 (Frankfurt am Main: Suhrkamp, 1986);

Breitenbach (Cologne: Kiepenheuer & Witsch, 1986);

Reden über das eigene Land: Deutschland 4, by Achternbusch, Cordelia Edvardson, Daniel Cohn-Bendit, and Stephan Hermlin (Munich: Bertelsmann, 1986);

Das Ambacher Exil (Cologne: Kiepenheuer & Witsch, 1987)—includes *Weißer Stier* and *Linz*;

Die blaue Blume (Frankfurt am Main: Zweitausendeins, 1987);

Das Haus am Nil: Schriften 1980-81 (Frankfurt am Main: Suhrkamp, 1987);

Wohin? (Cologne: Kiepenheuer & Witsch, 1988);

Akira Kurosawa (Munich: Hanser, 1988);

Duschen: 20 Tuschen (Munich: Scaneg, 1988);

Wind: Schriften 1982-83 (Frankfurt am Main: Suhrkamp, 1989);

Mixwix (Cologne: Kiepenheuer & Witsch, 1990)—includes *Auf verlorenem Posten*.

OTHER: *Anthologie 1*, contributions by Achternbusch (Munich: Maistraßenpresse, 1965);

Peter Härtling, ed., *Leporello fällt aus der Rolle: Zeitgenössische Autoren erzählen das Leben von Figuren der Weltliteratur weiter*, contribution by Achternbusch (Frankfurt am Main: Fischer, 1971);

Karl Valentin, *Karl Valentins Filme: Alle 29 Filme, 12 Fragmente, 342 Bilder, Texte, Filmographie*, edited by Michael Schulte and Peter Syr, introduction by Achternbusch (Munich: Piper, 1978);

Heimat deine Sterne: Künstler aus Ostbayern, contributions by Achternbusch (Regensburg: Städtische Galerie, Regensburg, 1984);

Liebes Leben: Anleitung zum Liebesbriefschreiben, contributions by Achternbusch (Heidelberg: Das Wunderhorn, 1985).

SELECTED PERIODICAL PUBLICATIONS—
UNCOLLECTED: "Neues von Ambach," *Filmkritik*, 236 (1976): 338-341;

"Unter diesen Leuten darf ich ein Gesicht haben: Leserbrief," *Der Spiegel*, 31 (20 June 1977): 14-15;

An der Donau: Libretto, in *manuskripte*, 76 (1982): 70-79;

"Es ist ein Leichtes, beim Gehen den Boden zu berühren: Innerer Monolog zu den Gesammelten Theaterstücken," *Süddeutsche Zeitung*, 22/23 June 1991, p. 3.

Due in part to the controversy which seems to spring forth in his wake and in part to the chaotic and at times incomprehensible nature of his literary production, Herbert Achternbusch is considered by many to be Bavaria's, and perhaps even Germany's, most infamous and interesting enfant terrible. He is certainly one of Germany's most prolific writers, in terms both of sheer volume and of versatility. His oeuvre includes more than forty works encompassing a wide variety of genres: poetry, novels, short stories, commentaries, dramas, radio plays, film scripts, and even paintings and sculptures. Yet there is a unity among these individual pieces. In the first place, they contain repeated autobiographical references; second, many of Achternbusch's dramas and film scripts are based on his prose works; finally, and perhaps most important, Achternbusch writes from a consistent stance of rebellion or resistance. He defines art not as "Können" (a process of perfecting technique) but as "Kontern" (an act of protest). It is in this context that one must understand critics' frequent charges of dilettantism, solipsism, and anarchy: Achternbusch's message is that all preformulated and institutionalized ideologies must be destroyed. His writing is a rebellion against the rules of contemporary technocratic society, including standardized writing conventions; his goal is to prevent the disappearance of the individual subject.

Achternbusch objects to any attempt to categorize his work as "Heimatliteratur" (regional literature), claiming that his home, Bavaria, serves merely as a backdrop against which he illuminates universal problems. Nevertheless, the people, places, and dialect of the region where he was raised and still lives figure prominently in all of his major works. Born on 23 November 1938 as the illegitimate son of Louise Schild and Adolf Achternbusch, Herbert Schild lived with his mother in Munich until 1943, when his grandmother, Anna Muckenthaler, took him to Breitenbach, a small town in the Bavarian Forest. After completing primary school in Mietraching, he entered secondary school in Deggendorf in 1948. In 1959 he was dismissed from school for impregnating a classmate; he completed his studies the following year at a high school in Cham. It was also in 1960 that he assumed the last name of his father through formal adoption proceedings.

Encouraged by his mother, an amateur painter, Achternbusch initially channeled his cre-

ative energies into the fine arts. He enrolled at the Art Academy in Nuremberg, where he married Gerda Oberpaul in 1962; he transferred to the Art Academy in Munich in 1963. While Gerda pursued her formal training as an art teacher, Achternbusch supported his growing family—Gerda and he eventually had four children: Rut, Andreas, Rita, and Judit—with various temporary jobs. One of these jobs was as a cigarette vendor during the Munich Oktoberfest, an experience that provided material for his first collection of fiction, *Zigarettenverkäufer*; *Hülle*; *Rita* (Cigarette Vendor; Cover; Rita, 1969). After the publication of the widely acclaimed *Die Alexanderschlacht* (The Battle of Alexander) in 1971 Achternbusch turned exclusively to writing; not until the mid 1980s would his interest in painting and sculpture be rekindled.

Achternbusch's growing reputation as a writer of prose was recognized by the Ludwig Thoma Medal of the city of Munich in 1975 and the prestigious Petrarca Prize in 1977. It was during the 1970s that Achternbusch began writing screenplays and dramas. The decision to become involved with the theater was prompted not by love of the stage but by financial exigencies: Achternbusch has made it clear that he writes dramas only to raise money to finance his films. Achternbusch faults the theater for being too commercial and the theatergoing public for being too passive and accepting. Nevertheless, Achternbusch continues to write dramas, some of which have played to enthusiastic audiences throughout Europe.

Achternbusch's first drama, *Ella* (published, 1978), premiered in Stuttgart on 27 January 1978 under the dramatist's direction. This dramatic monologue is taken from the novel *Der Tag wird kommen* (The Day Will Come, 1973). *Ella* relates the story of a life of physical and mental abuse; it describes the systematic destruction of an individual through societal pressure to conform. For two hours the audience listens to an account of the broken and tortured life of the title character. Her birth was accompanied by a paternal curse, and her father continued to beat and victimize her during childhood and adolescence, finally marrying her off to a brutal cattle dealer. The degrading marriage lasted only a few years, and Ella found herself on a downward spiral of catastrophe leading through several pregnancies, syphilis, and incarceration in a variety of mental wards and prisons. And yet, in the midst of this oppression, Ella continued to pursue minute sparks

Scene from the German premiere of Achternbusch's Gust *at the Residenztheater in Munich, 1985, with Sepp Bierbichler in the title role and Robert Spitz as his dying wife, Lies (photograph by Winfried Radanus)*

of happiness—going to the movies, exchanging warm glances with a fellow inmate, even escaping. Although the system interns her as aberrant, the drama makes it clear that it is the system, not Ella, that is insane.

The stage set consists of a huge chicken coop, complete with wire netting and live chickens. Inside it sits Ella, curlers in her hair, wearing earphones, incessantly watching television. Her son, Josef, wearing a wig, an apron, and a false bosom, relates Ella's story in the first person. This role switch is necessary because Ella has been stripped of her identity and is no longer aware enough to be able to express herself. In Stuttgart, Sepp Bierbichler breathed life into the demanding role of Josef; it was to his performance that many critics credited the success of the play. In the written version, and in subsequent productions, the drama concludes with Ella's scream as she realizes that her son has poisoned himself. At the premiere Achternbusch, dressed in white underwear, bleeding from the forehead, and brandishing a large weapon, appeared onstage after Josef's suicide. What this apparition was supposed to mean and how it fit

into Ella's story remain unclear. More than likely it was intended as a protest against the kind of societal norms that victimized Ella.

Achternbusch's second and third dramas, *Susn* and *Kuschwarda City*, both published in 1980, premiered together at the Bochum Playhouse on 23 October 1980. *Susn*, like *Ella*, depicts a woman unable to fulfill herself in the face of a society controlled by men. Five episodes, separated by approximately ten years, unfold before the audience. In the first episode Susn is a girl in a small Bavarian village confessing to the parish priest. With all the naiveté and youthful defiance of a sixteen-year-old first confronting the world, Susn spouts forth about her girl- and boyfriends, her sexual awakening, and her decision to leave the church. The next episode portrays Susn as a student confiding her dreams, wishes, and fears to her diary. The vibrancy and hopeful will of the schoolgirl are still apparent but are undermined by her increasingly trancelike state, by the seven men vying to be the first to rape her, and by the menacing Pink Floyd song "Careful with That Axe, Eugene" at the end of the scene. In the third episode Susn is married to an author named Achternbusch who uses his wife only as the source of his writings; his productivity is dependent on her surrender of self. Susn's dreams of a life of love and purpose have been disappointed, and in the fourth episode she turns for comfort to drink. The final scene shows an old woman crouching in a wasteland, smoking and pleading for whiskey. The writer is present, reading from his book about Susn's life. She takes his gun, props it up in the desert sand against her forehead, and pulls the trigger.

In *Susn* the aspirations of a young woman are inexorably annihilated; her voice—initially so full of life—is gradually silenced and then usurped by a masculine voice. Susn herself, however, never completely gives up. Her defiance in the face of a desperate and hopeless situation is sustained throughout the drama, from her original decision to leave the church to her suicide. Her diary, alcohol, a brief affair with a foreign worker, and even the gun are all "Rettungsringe" (life-belts), attempts to save herself. Susn's courageous dignity was particularly emphasized in the Hamburg production of the play in May 1981. But even in the more pessimistic version directed at Bochum by Vera Sturm, in which Susn was played by five actresses so as to underline the impossibility of a unified female identity, her final action must be seen as her ultimate refusal to be co-opted and misused by society.

After the bleak silence closing *Susn*, Achternbusch's *Kuschwarda City*, directed by Alfred Kirchner, was greeted at first with a sense of relief. In contrast to the droning monologues and isolated twosomes of the earlier drama, this play begins with a lively and humorous dialogue. An irreverent schoolteacher kidnaps the son of Lower Bavaria's head of state. Transformed into an Indian named Kuschwarda City, he eventually scalps the son and a policeman and then shoots the sun, snuffing out its reddish glow. The play is difficult to understand, and the plot is frequently interrupted by seemingly irrelevant outbursts, such as a long tirade about the "Badewannenmensch" (bathtub person) and home movies of Achternbusch's family. Critics charge that although the drama points to impending societal and environmental catastrophes, no reasons for the disaster are given and, accordingly, no possibility of averting it is acknowledged. Achternbusch might argue that change is possible only if societal authority is "scalped"—that is, radically questioned.

Achternbusch's *Plattling* (published, 1982) opened in Frankfurt on 20 March 1982 under the direction of Wilfried Minks. The drama takes place on an expressway leading to Plattling, a Bavarian village that has disappeared under concrete. The straight and sterile expressway, in contrast to the natural and purposeless meanderings of a stream, represents the death of individuality. The expressway is occupied by Herbert, who engages in exchanges with Death in the guise of a policeman, a reporter, and a lady. In the second of four scenes, the policeman has anyone who refuses to assume without question the anonymity of his or her role decapitated. In the next scene Herbert sits on his expressway and sabotages political demonstrations by throwing banana peels in front of the demonstrators. When asked why, he replies that the sole motivation of the demonstrators is to slip on his banana peels. Achternbusch is ridiculing as ineffectual any attempt to better the world through political engagement. For Achternbusch, the potential for change lies in art: in the writer asserting his or her individuality despite overwhelming pressure to conform and in the reader or viewer irritated and frustrated by the unconventional, unexpected, and at times incomprehensible work with which he or she is confronted.

The premiere of *Der Frosch* (The Frog; published, 1981) on 5 June 1982 in Bochum was directed by Walter Bockmayer. It is a fantastic and grotesque fairy tale with only the barest outline of a plot. The main figure, Herbert, assumes that he became a frog by drinking excessively and attempts to reverse the condition by more heavy drinking. In the meantime, the frog's alienated perspective reveals the cold functionality of the modern world. At the conclusion of the drama all the characters are transformed into frogs and jump happily into the Nile. For some critics, the play reveals an ultimate faith in the individual's ability to overcome an alienated condition; others regard it merely as one additional example of the chaotic frolics typical of Achternbusch.

Sintflut (The Flood; published, 1983) was directed by Axel Manthey at its Bochum premiere on 15 September 1984. At the beginning of this verse drama Noah and his partner, Noahin, are gathering couples into their ark, depicted here as a sailboat. In this case, however, pairs are understood as rhymes. Thus the "Autor" (author) arrives with his "Auto" (auto), the "Schwalbe" (swallow) and the "Halbe" (glass of beer) are considered a perfect match, and the "Wasserhahn" (faucet) and "Wasserhuhn" (coot) are to enjoy connubial bliss. Such partners make sense only in a reality reduced to words. During the voyage these pairs pass their time in unsuccessful and sometimes deadly attempts to consummate their relationships. The antics of Noah's pairs are interrupted by a long monologue titled "C'est la vie Sellerie" (That's Life Celery) detailing impending atomic annihilation. Here, and through descriptions rendered by the Autor, the audience learns of the precariousness of the world situation. The possibility of a remedy is questioned by the whimsical and frequently absurd wordplays as well as by the Autor's ultimate response to imminent catastrophe: as soon as he leaves the ark he goes off to find the nearest bar. Although Achternbusch has been criticized for overly taxing the audience, in particular with the lengthy monologue, he is praised for his creative and critical use of language and farce.

The autobiographical *Mein Herbert* (My Herbert; published, 1982) premiered in Graz on 24 September 1983 under the direction of Kitty Buchhammer. Herbert, born illegitimate and sent to live with his grandmother at the age of three, experiences mixed feelings toward his mother: incomprehension at being sent away, anger at having no name, longing for closeness, and fear of rejection. His mother, Luise, also yearns for a loving relationship but repels anyone who intrudes on her private sphere. Thus, she expresses love and tenderness for Herbert while awaiting his return home but forbids him from using her freshly cleaned bathroom; she offers him money but resents the time his visit has cost. These conflicts remain unresolved, and Luise commits suicide. In *Weg* (Away; published, 1985), directed by Achternbusch at its opening in Munich on 22 November 1985, homage is paid to the person who raised and cared for Herbert. At his prompting the grandmother relates scenes from her past, a history dominated by hard work and poverty and mastered by her tenacity and ingenuity. The autobiographical nature of the plays has led to charges of narcissism on Achternbusch's part. Georg Hensel finds *Weg* not only socially irrelevant but, with its long monologues and concluding half-hour death scene, excruciatingly boring. On the other hand, defenders of the play say that the situation portrayed is applicable to a whole social class. A production in Berlin that combined *Mein Herbert* and *Weg*, inserting scenes with the grandmother into the mother/son frame-

work, created a powerful statement about the status of women in modern society.

Gust, first published in the collection *Es ist ein leichtes beim Gehen den Boden zu berühren* (It Is an Easy Matter to Touch the Floor when Walking, 1980), contributes one further piece to Achternbusch's family saga. Gust is Herbert's eighty-three-year-old uncle; the play consists of the random reminiscences of this poor, uneducated farmer and beekeeper from Bavaria. He tells of the daily drudgery and dangers of life as a hired thresher, of the death of his first wife, of his struggles with officials during and after the Nazi period, and of his battle with tetanus. His is a biography of suffering and hardship, but it is also testimony to his will to survive. In many ways Gust is the male counterpart to Ella: he always manages, through cunning or sheer determination, to overcome the catastrophes that threaten his life. The harsh personality he has had to develop to withstand such conditions affects Gust's relations with others, especially with his second wife, Lies, who is dying. Her final plea for at least one sweet word elicits from Gust a helplessly inadequate "Honig" (honey)—referring to the honey produced by his bees, the all-important source of his beer money. Lies's death throes highlight Gust's determination to live. His flow of words can be seen as one further act of self-assertion, ebbing only after Lies dies.

Gust premiered in Caen, France, on 6 March 1984. For its German opening at Munich's Residenztheater on 12 April 1985 the play was directed by Achternbusch. Bierbichler played Gust, and, as with *Ella*, at least some of the success of the play must be credited to his masterful interpretation of this difficult role. Gust talks for nearly two hours without intermission, interrupting his monologue only to drink beer, take snuff tobacco, or respond to the call of nature. His words are directed to Lies and to the audience. He is involved in a never-ending and sometimes fruitless effort to make his heavy Bavarian dialect comprehensible. Silence greets his monologue, underlining his isolation. In Munich, Bierbichler improvised in response to audience reactions: he asked a departing couple why they were leaving and baited audience members who dared to protest the performance. The set, designed by Gunter Freyse, was a shed piled high with massive, light brown, wooden beehives. Lies's deathbed was at the bottom of a ladder propped up against the hives. Freyse alienated the realism of the setting through various grotesque additions,

Annamirl Bierbichler, Klaus Schwarzkopf, and Richard Beek in a scene from the February 1987 premiere of Achternbusch's Linz
at the Munich Kammerspiele (photograph by Winfried Rabanus)

such as a huge crucifix next to Lies's bed and a phalliclike, almost defoliated tree trunk. Further alienation was assured through the casting of a male actor, Robert Spitz, in the role of Lies.

Gust is considered by many critics to be Achternbusch's finest play. It was one of only seven plays produced during the 1985 Berlin Theater Festival, and it was awarded the Drama Prize of the city of Mülheim in 1986. *Gust* has been praised for its successful integration of the private and public: Achternbusch's hatred of the hierarchy of church and state is reflected in Gust's struggle to live in the face of those authorities, who would condemn him to servitude; and the slice of life portrayed is considered a realistic representation of the Bavarian farmer during and after World War II. Achternbusch would undoubtedly object to any accolade based on the political relevance or realism of his play: he insists that his work has no political message to convey but celebrates life in the face of adversity; and he rejects realism as an ignominious capitulation to and reinforcement of the status quo. Achternbusch ignores or deliberately violates theatrical conventions so as to provoke the audience and enliven

the German theater scene.

If provocation is one of Achternbusch's main literary goals, he has been highly successful at generating it. In 1977 he refused to accept the twenty thousand marks that came with the Petrarca Prize to protest the pretentiousness of the ceremony and the fact that broken equipment prevented the screening of his films. In May 1981 his film *Servus Bayern* (Bye Bye Bavaria; published, 1977) was deemed to be in violation of Bavarian broadcasting laws and was banned from being shown on television in the state. The following year his film *Das letzte Loch* (The Last Hole; published, 1982) was awarded the Film Journalists' Study Group Prize, the West German Film Prize, and the Special Prize of the Locarno Film Festival. The three thousand marks accompanying the Locarno Prize was intended to finance future movie productions, and Achternbusch applied it toward his subsequent film *Das Gespenst* (The Ghost; published, 1983). This film, however, was banned in West Germany by the Office of Voluntary Censorship because of its attacks on the church. In addition, the minister of the interior, Friedrich Zimmermann, withheld the third and final installment of the Locarno Prize on the basis that state funds should not support a film so inimical to public sensitivities. Eventually the film was released in West Germany, Austria, and Switzerland; the ironic consequence of the West German government's censorship effort was that *Das Gespenst* has become Achternbusch's most widely viewed film. In 1985 Achternbusch was voted Playwright of the Year by the journal *Theater heute* (Theater Today).

Three Achternbusch dramas premiered in 1987. *Linz* (published, 1987), which opened in Munich on 13 February under the playwright's direction, deals with the alleged Nazi past of Austrian president Kurt Waldheim and with past and present anti-Semitism in that country. *Weißer Stier* (White Bull; published, 1987), directed by David Mouchtar-Samorai, premiered in Bonn on 19 March. It portrays a man who frantically searches for a white ox so as to collect the finder's fee of fifty thousand marks but reaps only repeated blows and setbacks. The autobiographical reference to Achternbusch's unsuccessful attempts to collect the final installment of his Locarno Prize and to his confrontations with the Christian Democratic government of West Germany is only too obvious. *An der Donau* (On the Danube; published, 1982) is a loose collection of scenes of decline and meaninglessness; the text was set to music by Heiner Goebbels for its premiere in Vienna on 3 June under the direction of Alfred Kirchner. Three gods, a couple, twenty Negroes, two Chinese men, workers, apes, and elephants parade onstage in a kaleidoscope of absurdity and confusion. All three dramas have been criticized for excessive subjectivity, and it is claimed that the humorous and pointed ingenuity of Achternbusch's farce has degenerated into boring banality. Critics express the fear that Achternbusch is more interested in quantity than quality due to his economic situation, and the author admits as much through his stage double in *Weißer Stier*: if his film work had been financed, the character says, the public would no longer be tormented by plays such as this one.

In 1989 Achternbusch was awarded the Tukan Prize of Munich. A new drama, *Auf verlorenem Posten* (Last Stand; published, 1990), opened in Munich on 5 April 1990 under the direction of the author. The play takes place from 20 December to 26 December 1989 and portrays a man from the former East Germany who takes advantage of the recently breached Berlin Wall to travel to Italy, where he fulfills his lifelong dream of seeing the Alps. Eventually he is joined by two other East Germans. In typical Achternbusch fashion, their monologues and dialogues are frequently chaotic streams of consciousness and associations. Several political themes are repeated throughout the play, however, and lend it more coherence and unity than some of the playwright's immediately preceding pieces. The most important of these themes is the brutal suppression of the Romanian uprising at Temesvar during the days preceding Christmas 1989. This topic leads to discussions of related issues such as the East German uprising, the fates of communism and capitalism, and the nature of happiness.

References:

Peter von Becker, "Genie und Blödsinn: Achternbusch inszeniert Achternbusch: *Linz* an den Münchner Kammerspielen," *Theater heute*, 28 (April 1987): 37;

Becker, "Die Stadt, das Land und der Tod: Kroetz und Achternbusch inszenieren Kroetz und Achternbusch in München: *Bauern sterben* und *Gust*," *Theater heute*, 26 (July 1985): 22-27;

Thomas Beckermann and Michael Töteberg, "Herbert Achternbusch," in *Kritisches Lexikon zur deutschsprachigen Gegenwartsliteratur*, edited by Heinz Ludwig Arnold (Munich: Edition text + kritik, 1978), n.pag.;

Anne Betten, "Der Monolog als charakteristische Form des deutschsprachigen Theaters der achtziger Jahre: Anmerkungen zu Thomas Bernhards und Herbert Achternbuschs dramatischer Schreibweise," *Cahiers d'études germaniques*, 20 (1991): 37-48;

Stefanie Carp, "Diese Susn geht mit Mut kaputt," *Theater heute*, 22 (July 1981): 28-31;

Carp, "Vom Unglück der beschißnen Unterdrückung und vom Zorn darauf," *Theater heute*, 21 (December 1980): 21-22;

Sabina Dhein, " 'Sepp, spiel mal wie im Film, spiel nicht Theater': Sabina Dhein beobachtete, wie Herbert Achternbusch seinen *Gust* inszenierte," *Theater heute*, 26 (July 1985): 28-31;

Jörg Drews, ed., *Herbert Achternbusch* (Frankfurt am Main: Suhrkamp, 1982);

Peter Hamm, "Ichsüchtig ohne Spur von Eitelkeit," *Der Spiegel*, 36 (30 July 1984): 116-118;

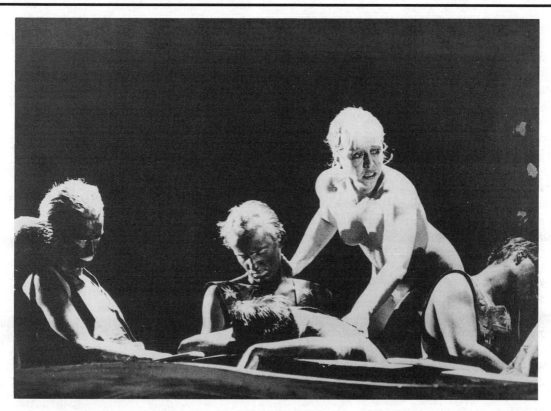

Hilke Ruthner as "Sie" (She) and other actors in a scene from the premiere of Achternbusch's An der Donau *at the Akademietheater in Vienna, June 1987 (photograph by Matthias Horn)*

Benjamin Henrichs, "Gust und Frust oder: Deutschlands Jammer, Bayerns Stolz," *Die Zeit*, 26 April 1985, p. 17;

Henrichs, "Schnarche Noah: Achternbuschs *Sintflut* in Bochum," in *Deutsche Literatur 1984: Ein Jahresüberblick*, edited by Volker Hage (Stuttgart: Reclam, 1985), pp. 97-101;

Georg Hensel, "Laß dir was von Oma erzählen: *Weg* von Herbert Achternbusch," in *Deutsche Literatur 1985: Jahresüberblick*, edited by Hage (Stuttgart: Reclam, 1986), pp. 131-135;

Herbert Achternbusch: Mit Beiträgen von Wolfgang Jacobsen, Peter W. Jansen, Hans Günther Pflaum, Helmut Schödel, Wolfram Schütte (Munich: Hanser, 1984);

Wend Kässens, "Eine Radikale, eine Frau: Über *Susn*, das neue Theaterstück von Herbert Achternbusch," *Theater heute*, 20 (September 1979): 38-39;

Isabel Keilig, "Bemerkungen zu Herbert Achternbuschs Sublimierungsversuchen gestörter Kommunikation," in *Aufbrüche—Abschiede: Studien zur deutschen Literatur seit 1968*, edited by Michael Zeller (Stuttgart: Klett, 1979), pp. 70-82;

Roy Kift, "Blight on Berlin," *Drama*, 161 (1986): 31-32;

Heinz Klunker, "*Der Frosch* in Bochum," *Theater heute*, 23 (August 1982): 22-23;

Paul Lifton, "The Frog: By Herbert Achternbusch," *Theatre Journal*, 39 (October 1987): 383-384;

Wolfgang Limmer, "Bayrisches Dichterleben," *Der Spiegel*, 32 (6 February 1978): 181-185;

Limmer, "'Bazon, was sollen wir denken?,'" *Der Spiegel*, 31 (13 June 1977): 174-176;

Limmer, "Sprachschlachten," *Der Spiegel*, 39 (6 May 1985): 209-212;

Timothy McFarland, "Freerange Drama: *Ella*," *Times Literary Supplement*, 3 July 1981, p. 755;

Rolf Michaelis, "Literatur, daß die Fetzen fliegen," *Die Zeit*, 17 June 1977, pp. 13-15;

Johannes G. Pankau, "Figurationen des Bayrischen: Sperr, Fassbinder, Achternbusch," in *Der Begriff "Heimat" in der deutschen Gegenwartsliteratur: The concept of "Heimat" in contemporary German literature*, edited by Helfried W. Seliger (Munich: Iudicium, 1987), pp. 133-147;

Eric Rentschler, "Herbert Achternbusch: Celebrating the Power of Creation," in *New German Filmmakers*, edited by Klaus Phillips (New York: Ungar, 1984), pp. 1-19;

Henning Rischbieter, "Was Neues im Westen?," *Theater heute*, 25 (October 1984): 4-6;

Michael Schindlbeck, " 'Früher ist hier Bayern gewesen': Achternbuschs neue Stücke *Plattling* und *Der Frosch* sowie die Frankfurter *Plattling*-Uraufführung," *Theater heute*, 23 (May 1982): 40-41;

Marina Schneede and Matthias Klein, eds., *Herbert Achternbusch: Der Maler* (Munich: Universitätsdruckerei, 1988);

Helmut Schödel, "Ausgezählt," *Die Zeit*, 3 April 1987, p. 72;

Schödel, "Die Eroberung des Tempels," *Die Zeit*, 3 February 1978, p. 40;

Winfried Georg Sebald, "Die Kunst der Verwandlung: Achternbuschs theatralische Sendung," in *Patterns of Change: German Drama and the European Tradition*, edited by Dorothy James and Silvia Ranawake (New York: Lang, 1990), pp. 297-306;

Sebald, "Die weiße Adlerfeder am Kopf: Versuch über den Indianer Herbert Achternbusch," *manuskripte*, 79, no. 23 (1983): 75-79;

Jürgen Serke, "Gibt es ein Leben vor dem Tod?,' *Der Stern*, 14 (14 April 1977): 141-153;

Michael Skasa, "*Ella* in Berlin," *Theater heute*, 19 (May 1978): 11;

Skasa, "Der wilde Mann von Feldafing: Herbert Achternbusch inszeniert sein erstes Stück *Ella*," *Theater heute*, 19 (March 1978): 6-10;

Thomas Thieringer, "Entsetzensherrliche Alpträume," *Theater heute*, 29 (November 1988): 6-8;

Chris Wickham, "Heart and Hole: Achternbusch, Herzog and the Concept of Heimat," *Germanic Review*, 64 (Summer 1989): 112-120;

Franz Wille, "Berlin: Valentins Bruder und Liesl Karlstadts Schwestern: Herbert Achternbuschs *Mein Herbert* und *Weg* (Schillertheater-Werkstatt)," *Theater heute*, 30 (April 1989): 52.

Wolfgang Bauer

(18 March 1941 -   )

Jürgen Koppensteiner
University of Northern Iowa

PLAY PRODUCTIONS: *Der Schweinetransport*, Graz, Forum Stadtpark, 10 February 1962;

Maler und Farbe, Graz, Forum Stadtpark, 10 February 1962;

Zwei Fliegen auf einen Gleis, Graz, Forum Stadtpark, 24 November 1962;

Katharina Doppelkopf, Graz, Theater im Keller, 23 January 1964;

Die Menschenfresser, Graz, Schauspielhaus/Probebühne, 4 April 1967;

Party for Six: Volksstück, Innsbruck, Landestheater Kammerspiele, 9 May 1967;

Magic Afternoon, Hannover, Landestheater Studio im Künstlerhaus, 12 September 1968;

Change, Vienna, Volkstheater, 26 September 1969;

Film und Frau, Hamburg, Schauspielhaus, 16 April 1971;

Silvester oder Das Massaker im Hotel Sacher, Vienna, Volkstheater, 24 September 1971;

Gespenster, Munich, Kammerspiele, 5 June 1974;

Magnetküsse, Vienna, Akademietheater, 31 March 1976;

Memory Hotel, Graz, Schauspielhaus, 12 April 1980;

Batyscaphe 17-26 oder Die Hölle ist oben, Graz, Theater im Keller, 27 October 1982;

"Woher kommen wir? Was sind wir? Wohin gehen wir?," Bonn, Kammerspiele Bad Godesberg, 28 October 1982;

Ein fröhlicher Morgen beim Friseur, Graz, Schauspielhaus, 25 September 1983;

Das kurze Leben der Schneewolken, Stuttgart, Württembergisches Staatstheater, Schauspielhaus, 28 October 1983;

Der Tod des Ingenieurs Leo Habernik aus Linz, Vienna, Ateliertheater, 3 March 1984;

Pfnacht, Graz, Schauspielhaus, 13 April 1985;

Herr Faust spielt Roulette, Vienna, Akademietheater, 25 January 1987;

Ach, armer Orpheus, Vienna, Schauspielhaus, 2 May 1991;

Das Lächeln des Brian de Palma, Graz, Schauspielhaus, 1 December 1991.

Wolfgang Bauer in 1990 (photograph by Jürgen Koppensteiner)

BOOKS: *Mikrodramen* (Berlin: Fietkau, 1964); translated by Rosemarie Waldrop as *Microdramas, Dimension*, 5, no. 1 (1972): 106-131;

Der Fieberkopf: Roman in Briefen (Frankfurt am Main: Bärmeier & Nikel, 1967);

Das stille Schilf: Ein schlechtes Meisterwerk. Schlechte Texte mit schlechten Zeichnungen und einer schlechten Schallplatte (Frankfurt am Main: Bärmeier & Nikel, 1969; revised edition, Vienna: Verlag der Österreichischen Staatsdruckerei, Edition S, 1985);

Magic Afternoon; Change; Party for Six: Drei Stücke (Cologne & Berlin: Kiepenheuer & Witsch, 1969); *Magic Afternoon* translated and adapted by Herb Greer, *Change* and *Party for Six* translated by Martin and Renata Esslin, in *Change and Other Plays* (New York: Hill & Wang, 1973); translation republished as *All Change and Other Plays* (London: Calder & Boyars, 1973);

Romeo und Julia: Drama in 5 Bildern (Munich: Hanser, 1969);

Katharina Doppelkopf und andere Eisenbahnstücke (Dornbirn: Vorarlberger Verlagsanstalt, 1973)—comprises *Katharina Doppelkopf, Die Menschenfresser, Zwei Fliegen auf einem Gleis*;

Gespenster; Silvester oder Das Massaker im Hotel Sacher; Film und Frau: Drei Stücke (Cologne: Kiepenheuer & Witsch, 1974); *Gespenster* translated by Karl-Heinz Bauer as *Ghosts: A Play*, M.A. thesis, Bowling Green State University, 1978; *Film und Frau* translated by Renata and Martin Esslin as *Shakespeare the Sadist*, in *Shakespeare the Sadist; Bremen Coffee; My Foot My Tutor; Stallerhof*, by Bauer, Rainer Werner Fassbinder, Peter Handke, and Franz Xaver Kroetz, translated by Renata and Martin Esslin, Anthony Vivis, Michael Roloff, and Katharina Helm (London: Eyre Methuen, 1977), pp. 7-26;

Die Sumpftänzer: Dramen, Prosa, Lyrik aus zwei Jahrzehnten (Cologne: Kiepenheuer & Witsch, 1978);

Pfnacht: Komödie in 3 Akten (Graz: Droschl, 1980);

Batyscaphe 17-26 oder Die Hölle ist oben: Einakter (Graz: Droschl, 1980);

Woher kommen wir? Was sind wir? Wohin gehen wir?: Stück (Vienna & Munich: Sessler, 1981);

Das Herz: Gedichte (Salzburg & Vienna: Residenz, 1981);

Woher kommen wir? Wohin gehen wir?: Dramen und Prosa mit bisher unveröffentlichten und neuen Stücken (Munich: Heyne, 1982)—includes *Der Tod des Ingeniuers Leo Habernik aus Linz; Memory Hotel*, translated under the same title by Renata and Martin Esslin and adapted by John Lion (New York: Theatre Communications Group, 1981);

Ein fröhlicher Morgen beim Friseur: Text, Materialien, Fotos, edited by Gerhard Melzer and Michael Muhr (Graz: Droschl, 1983);

In Zeiten wie diesen: Ein Drehbuch (Salzburg & Vienna: Residenz, 1984);

Werke in sieben Bänden, 6 volumes published, edited by Gerhard Melzer, volume 2: *Schauspiele 1967-1973: Magic Afternoon; Change; Film und Frau; Silvester oder Das Massaker im Hotel Sacher; Gespenster* (Graz: Droschl, 1986); volume 3: *Schauspiele 1975-1986: Magnetküsse; Memory Hotel; Woher kommen wir? Was sind wir? Wohin gehen wir?; Das kurze Leben der Schneewolken; Ein fröhlicher Morgen beim Friseur; Herr Faust spielt Roulette* (Graz: Droschl, 1986); volume 4: *Der Fieberkopf: Ein Roman in Briefen* (Graz: Droschl, 1986); volume 1: *Einakter und frühe Dramen* (Graz: Droschl, 1987); volume 6: *Kurzprosa, Essays und Kritiken* (Graz: Droschl, 1989); volume 5: *Gedichte* (Graz: Droschl, 1992);

Das Lächeln des Brian de Palma: Stück (Vienna: Sessler, 1988).

RECORDINGS: *Das stille Schilf* (Frankfurt am Main: Bärmeier & Nikel, 1969);

Wolfgang Bauer liest Mikrodramen von Wolfgang Bauer (Stuttgart: Intercord, 1975);

Hirn mit Ei: Lyrik und Jazz, by Bauer and H. C. Artmann (Graz: Droschl, 1981).

VIDEO: *Über das absurde Theater* (Graz: Droschl, 1990).

SELECTED PERIODICAL PUBLICATIONS—
UNCOLLECTED: "Ach, armer Orpheus!," *manuskripte*, 106 (1989): 121-140;

"Insalata mista"—Gemischter Salat: Boulevard-Komödie, *manuskripte*, 116 (1992): 83-95.

Dubbed "Magic Wolfi" by his fans, Wolfgang Bauer has been one of Austria's most talked-about writers since the early 1960s. He has also helped change the image of his hometown, Graz. Traditionally considered staid, conservative, bourgeois, and rather provincial, in the 1960s, Graz became a center of avant-garde literature when the Forum Stadtpark, an abandoned café in the city park, opened as a cultural center. Literature soon dominated the Forum's activities, and Bauer played a major role in establishing the reputation of Graz as the "secret capital" of German-language literature. One of the Forum's most noteworthy accomplishments is the sponsorship of the avant-garde journal *manuskripte*, edited by Bauer's colleague and friend Alfred Kolleritsch. Bauer's first creative activity was with the Forum Stadtpark, and many of his plays were first published in *manuskripte*.

Born in Graz on 18 March 1941, the only child of Rolf and Edith Maidl Bauer, both of whom were respected teachers, Bauer attended the Lichtenfelsgasse gymnasium. Following his graduation in 1959 he studied law at the University of Graz; but after two semesters he switched to French and geography, planning to become a schoolteacher. He soon decided against a teaching career and went to Vienna to study drama. After a few semesters he returned to Graz to try to establish himself as a playwright. Although many of the citizens of Graz despised him for rejecting their traditional life-style, for his drinking, and for the scandals he provoked, Bauer has remained fiercely loyal to his hometown and has repeatedly said that he would not want to live anywhere else. He travels regularly, however, having developed a fondness for the United States in particular. In California he has found a following among directors and actors in avant-garde theaters. "I consume America like a drug," he commented during a brief stay in Santa Monica in 1990, adding that he loved American theater audiences because of their unpretentiousness and the openness with which they approached his plays.

While he still does not enjoy universal esteem among his fellow townspeople, Bauer's days as the enfant terrible of Graz are over. Father of a son, Jack, born in 1971 from a previous marriage, he married Adelheid Schrumm in 1983 and lives a rather secluded life. With the exception of one novel, *Der Fieberkopf: Roman in Briefen* (The Fever Head: Epistolary Novel, 1967); two volumes of poetry, *Das stille Schilf* (The Quiet Reed, 1969) and *Das Herz* (The Heart, 1981); and occasional short prose works, Bauer has limited himself to drama.

Bauer's early plays are in the tradition of the theater of the absurd. In November 1961 he attended a performance in Graz of Eugène Ionesco's *Rhinoceros* (1959) which impressed him so much that he spontaneously decided to become a writer. The inspiration he received from Ionesco resulted in several one-act plays. In *Der Schweinetransport* (Shipment of Hogs; published, 1987) Ionesco's rhinoceroses are replaced by foul-smelling pigs. Bauer's theme is the conformism prevalent in modern society. Two characters are traveling together in a cattle car—a metaphor for humanity's situation in modern civilization, according to Bauer. *Der Schweinetransport* premiered in 1962 together with *Maler und Farbe* (Painter and Color; published, 1987) in the Forum Stadtpark, with Bernd Fischerauer directing. *Maler und Farbe*, a play within a play, is an attack on traditional theater. Taking a seemingly sense-

less, provocative, and subversive approach, it defies interpretation.

Batyscaphe 17-26 oder Die Hölle ist oben (Bathyscaphe 17-26 or Hell Is Above) was written as early as 1961 but was not published until 1980 and was not performed until 1982, after Bauer had become an established playwright. In this short play the influence of Jean-Paul Sartre's *Huis clos* (No Exit, 1944) is obvious. Six living corpses are in a small bathyscaphe which is on its way to hell; they are accompanied by a journalist who moderates a radio show titled "Reporter from the Other World." The reporter falls in love with one of the dead women and commits suicide so that he can marry her. For him, hell is now up above.

Zwei Fliegen auf einen Gleis (Two Flies on a Railroad Track; performed, 1962; published, 1973), *Katharina Doppelkopf* (Katharina the Doubleheaded; performed, 1964; published, 1973), and *Die Menschenfresser* (The Cannibals; performed, 1967; published, 1973) constitute Bauer's "Eisenbahntrilogie" (Railroad Trilogy). All three plays are set in a train compartment. The setting is a symbol of the unknown: one usually does not know one's fellow passengers on a train. Individuals in the plays fail because of their inability to adjust to new situations. In *Die Menschenfresser* the cannibals look for their victims not in the bush but in a first-class compartment of an Austrian train. In *Zwei Fliegen auf einen Gleis* Count Raffaelo is on his way to a duel; the train engineer is about to take revenge on a former colleague by arranging a collision. The men find themselves in a dilemma: if the engineer stops the train, Raffaelo will reach the duel site on time; in this case, however, the engineer will not succeed in his act of revenge. They agree to let a game of cards decide the matter. While playing, they fail to notice that the train has picked up speed so that the collision has become unavoidable. Even so, it turns out that both accomplish their goals: since Raffaelo's opponent is on the train, the collision fulfills a double purpose. "Two flies on one track" is a reference to the Grimm fairy tale "Das tapfere Schneiderlein" (The Brave Little Tailor), in which the hero's motto is "Sieben auf einen Streich" (Seven at one blow [hence Bauer's faulty accusative in the title]) —referring to flies he has killed and not to enemies, as everyone in the story assumes. In Bauer's play both men become victims of a situation they thought they could control. The message is that the individual lives in an absurd situation and is totally powerless.

Katharina Doppelkopf, first performed in 1964 under the direction of Bauer and Horst Zankl in a small basement theater in Graz, is another example of Bauer's theater of the absurd. A gentleman from Lower Austria and one from Mexico are traveling by train through Austria on their way to visit their respective brides. Each fantasizes about his ideal woman, a combination of the two nationalities with two heads. This vision signifies a rejection of all restraints of marriage. But the two men reject their dream once reality sets in and the double-headed woman, Katharina, actually appears; in spite of their previous desires, they are not ready to abandon convention and marry the monster. The train's engineer and the conductor trade places with the two travelers, but their involvement with Katharina ends in catastrophe: the engineer fails to observe the signals, and the train wrecks. Bauer is saying that willingness to open up to the unknown results in the breakdown of order; we are all trapped and there is no escape.

Completed in 1963, *Pfnacht* was not published until 1980; its first performance was five years later at the Graz Schauspielhaus (Playhouse), in a production directed by Kurt Josef Schildknecht. This delay is surprising because, unlike Bauer's other early dramas, *Pfnacht* has all the ingredients that make for a successful play: a clear story line, witty dialogue, and humor. Pfnacht, an eccentric poet, becomes the dictator of the small town where he lives: he buys up businesses and forces children to memorize his poems. The townspeople try to get rid of him by accusing him of murder, but the ploy does not work. Pfnacht, much to the citizens' surprise, readily confesses to the crime: he has found out that the "victim" murdered 365 women and that there is a large reward for his capture, dead or alive. In the end, nobody is willing to believe an eyewitness who comes forward with the truth: it was not Pfnacht but a brick falling from a roof during a storm that killed the murderer. *Pfnacht* was the hit of the 1985 Graz theater season.

The themes of Bauer's early plays—the disjuncture of self and world, the obliteration of the border between reality and fiction, the conflict between nature and civilization—can also be found in his *Mikrodramen* (1964; translated as *Microdramas*, 1972). Never intended to be performed, these plays average only one and a half pages in length and require technically impossible sets and props. *Franz Xaver Gabelsberger: Erfinder der Schnellschrift* (translated as *Franz Xaver Gabelsberger: Inventor of Shorthand*) takes place in a swimming pool full of floating noodles, *Die drei Musketiere* (translated as *The Three Musketeers*), in a DC-6, and *Rasputin* in a factory with one thousand workers. The stage directions in *Richard Wagner* call for ten thousand Apaches, in *Haydn* for three-foot waves on Lake Neusiedl, and in *Ramses* for a fire that fills the theater.

Party for Six (performed, 1967; published, 1969) drew negative reviews from most critics, and the theater public felt cheated when the play did not deliver what its title seemed to promise. The action of *Party for Six* takes place in a vestibule which is dark most of the time. In the first act the host of the party, a sixteen-year-old student, receives his guests and frequently comes out of the living room—which is behind the set, hence invisible to the audience—to get drinks from the bar. When the door to the living room is open, light is seen coming from there, and the sound of dissonant music and glasses clinking can be heard. The second act consists largely of guests making their way through the vestibule to and from the bathroom. The repeated flushing of the toilet is the principal sound in this act. A kind of dramatic conflict does develop when two young men make passes at the same girl; one is so drunk that he soon falls asleep. He does not react when some of the guests pour wine on him. All hope of getting at least a glimpse of the party vanishes in the third act. The vestibule is fully lit; as there are no longer any coats hanging on the racks, the party is apparently over. A rooster crows every thirty seconds for four minutes before the curtain falls. The fourth and final act is even shorter: two girls straighten up the apartment; the noise of a vacuum cleaner can be heard.

Party for Six forms a bridge between Bauer's early and later dramas. With its four acts, it has the structure of a conventional play; despite the absence of a plot in the usual sense, it has at least the rudiments of dramatic tension; the action appears to take place on a realistic level. The play's English title and its subtitle, *Volksstück* (Folk Play), however, are incongruous: a Volksstück would hardly have an English title. And in 1967 most Austrian theatergoers would expect a Volksstück to be an easily understandable, probably sentimental play with a rural setting and comic situations. Ödön von Horváth's socially critical Volksstücke, which do not at all fit this pattern, had not yet be-

Scene from Bauer's Pfnacht

come popular. The English title is reinforced by English or American pop music played at top volume; for Bauer, English represents the world outside Austria, where exciting things happen. The contradiction in the title permeates the entire play: for example, the use of dialect by the characters would be appropriate in a traditional Volksstück but not for the urban students in *Party for Six*. Bauer uses dialects to emphasize the limitations of Austrian society. There is clearly a discrepancy between the conventional structure and the lack of a plot. Bauer uses such contradictions to undermine, even destroy, the audience's concept of what is "realistic" and "surrealistic." He wants to demonstrate that the theater cannot present total reality but only a slice of life.

Bauer's short play *Der Tod des Ingenieurs Leo Habernik aus Linz* (The Death of the Engineer Leo Habernik from Linz; published, 1982), written in 1965, was first performed at Vienna's Ateliertheater under the direction of Peter Janisch in 1984 and was received quite favorably. The play satirizes Austria's tourist industry. The resort where Habernik is spending his vacation has expanded to the point where it has lost its identity, but it desperately tries to preserve its whole-

some image. During carnival season Habernik attends a masked ball there dressed as the devil. The ball turns rowdy, and the guests decide to crucify Habernik; they tie him to a cross in the mountains and disperse. To protect their community, the village priest and the local policeman attempt a cover-up. But it turns out that Habernik has survived the cold winter night. He is not willing to see the matter as a joke and keep quiet, and the policeman shoots him.

Magic Afternoon (published, 1969), which Zankl directed at its premiere in Hannover in 1968, appears to present none of the problems of *Party for Six*. While *Party for Six* had only a surface appearance of realism, here verisimilitude seems to abound. The stage directions call for a disorderly, smoke-filled room; contributing to the illusion of reality are the colloquial Austrian language, references to the Austrian cultural scene, and pop music played on a stereo. In addition, the play takes place in "real time": the performance is supposed to last two hours and fifteen minutes, the exact time it would take in real life to perform the actions in it. As *Magic Afternoon* begins, two young people, Birgit and Charly, are so bored that they begin to scuffle.

They leave the stage and are replaced by Monika and Joe, who are in a similar mood. Joe breaks Monika's nose; while he takes her to the hospital, Birgit and Charly return, their aggressiveness undiminished. An argument ensues, which, after Joe comes back, turns into a brutal fight. Then the men smoke marijuana and attack Birgit. She fatally stabs Joe with a kitchen knife; then, sexually aroused, she seduces the benumbed and frightened Charly. She exits abruptly, and the play ends as Charly rolls Joe's body into a rug.

In the 1969-1970 theater season *Magic Afternoon* was among the six plays most frequently presented in German-speaking countries. Translated into many languages, it has been performed throughout the world. With *Magic Afternoon* Bauer established himself both as a literary star and as "the wild man from Graz," a reputation he has not been able to shed despite many years as a writer of mostly philosophical plays. Much of the success of *Magic Afternoon* has been attributed to Bauer's having captured in it the spirit of the youth culture of the 1960s. Furthermore, the play is entertaining, and it satisfies the audience's voyeuristic tendencies. Like Bauer's early works, *Magic Afternoon* is a study of cultural alienation. The play's revival in the late 1980s shows that it transcends time and place and can be understood as a parable for human isolation, loneliness, and the feeling expressed by many young people worldwide that they have no future.

Change (published, 1969) was first performed under Fischerauer's direction at Vienna's Volkstheater in 1969—the first premiere of a Bauer play in a major theater in his native Austria. It is considered by many to be Bauer's first truly significant work because of its larger cast and scope of action and its structured plot. Instead of being set in a single room, *Change* takes place in a kitchen, a boutique, a sleazy bar, the salon of a wealthy art patron, a hospital ward, and two artists' studios. As in Bauer's other plays, a toilet is present throughout, at least acoustically.

The plot of *Change* is similar to that of a play outlined by Charly in *Magic Afternoon*. Fery, a painter frustrated by failure, decides to build up Blasi, a moderately talented amateur painter, to be a star. At the height of Blasi's career, Fery will let him fall and watch him commit suicide out of despair. Playing with life rather than with words or paint is to become a new art form. Blasi, however, upsets Fery's plans in every respect. First he steals Fery's girlfriend, Guggi, and

impregnates her. Blasi then turns his attention to Guggi's mother, who is starved for affection. When Guggi catches the two on the kitchen floor, she calls her demented father, who has a stroke and dies on the spot. Shortly thereafter, Blasi marries the widow. At the wedding reception Fery becomes obstreperous and is asked to leave. A fight breaks out and a policeman is called. Fery threatens the policeman with a knife, is shot, and is taken to the hospital. The drunken wedding guests visit him there. Guggi provokes Fery with her gibes; he hits her, she gives birth, and the baby dies. At the end Blasi gives a reconciliation party at which a change-dance game is played. Blasi requires of his guests total change, not just an exchange of clothing: each participant must slip into the skin of another; Fery becomes Blasi and vice versa. Bauer seems to be saying that society dictates our roles; a personal identity based on free determination is an illusion. When Fery hears words he had previously spoken coming from Blasi's lips, it undoes him. Hurrying to the toilet, he hangs himself.

Bauer's one-act play *Film und Frau* (Film and Woman; published, 1974) premiered at Hamburg's Schauspielhaus in 1971 under Zankl's direction. Under the title *Shakespeare the Sadist* (published, 1977), an English version by Martin and Renata Esslin was performed at the Almost Free Theatre in London on 31 October 1972, with Prunella Scales directing; it was performed at the Magic Theater in San Francisco in 1978. Four young people—three men and a woman—kill time by talking about movies. After Senta reads the movie listings aloud, two of the men decide to go see *Shakespeare the Sadist*, a pornographic film. Senta stays home with the third man, Bruno. The stage now becomes the movie theater where the porno film is being shown; Senta and Bruno perform the action in the film behind a scrim. Bruno, as Shakespeare, tears off Senta's clothes; binds, gags, and beats her; then puts out his cigarette on her skin. While he cuts off her hair, she is forced to recite his sonnets to him. After they engage in sex, Shakespeare cuts off Senta's head and throws it into the wastebasket. The play then returns to "real life." The two men come back from the movie and describe to Senta and Bruno the events that have just been shown on the stage. Then the "real" events are fused into a western film, in which Bruno, after an argument over a card game, guns down the other men. Senta brings him his horse; as the music swells to a crescendo, there are pledges of

Scene from the premiere of Bauer's Ein fröhlicher Morgen beim Friseur *at the Graz Schauspielhaus, 1983 (photograph by Wolfgang Veit)*

love and farewells, followed by the words "The End" projected on the scrim to signal that both the film and the play are over.

In *Film und Frau* Bauer again presents problems of alienated identity and self-realization. Although reality is boring to the characters in the play, their escape from it does not result in self-realization; they remain in an artificial world of dreams, movies, and music. In real life Bruno is illiterate and is also ineffectual as a lover. At the movies he experiences what reality has denied him: he is a fearsome stud, a writer of sonnets, and a gunfighter. The more miserable his reality is, the more desperate are his dreams and compensations. Senta feels isolated because of the men's indifference toward her; the depersonalization she experiences is illustrated in an exaggerated way by the porno movie and compensated for by

her fantasy that she is the sweetheart of a western hero. Both Bruno and Senta suffer because of the discrepancy between their private misery and the utopia they glimpse in the movies. What they consider to be self-realization is exposed by Bauer as being but a substitute for fulfillment.

Bauer's next play, *Silvester oder Das Massaker im Hotel Sacher* (New Year's Eve; or, The Massacre in the Sacher Hotel; published, 1974), was a major flop; directed by Fischerauer at Vienna's Volkstheater, it had only one performance, on 24 September 1971. No theater in Austria or Germany would take a second chance on the play. Bauer was attacked for his lack of imagination and was accused of copying himself. Wolfram Bersenegger, the protagonist, is a formerly successful writer who has run out of ideas. But he has promised to deliver a new play by the end of the year, and that time has arrived. He hits on the idea of making a play out of a New Year's Eve party he is arranging at the elegant Sacher Hotel in Vienna. Besides the theater manager, to whom he has promised the play, the guests include an author, an actor, playboys and their girlfriends, a group of activists, and a psychopath called Robespierre. He plans to record their conversations on a hidden tape recorder; at midnight he will present the tape—his new play—to the theater manager.

The party is reminiscent of the one depicted offstage in *Magic Afternoon*. The guests chatter, laugh, drink, make telephone calls, take bubble baths, go to the toilet, exchange clothes, and engage in sex games. The actors do a scene from *Romeo and Juliet*; then the activists stage a reenactment of the My Lai Massacre, during which they wreck the furniture and spray red paint all around. The other guests join in, totally demolishing the room. To celebrate the end of the old year, Robespierre recites a crazy monologue. At midnight, as the radio plays "The Blue Danube Waltz"—an Austrian tradition—the guests embrace and Robespierre shoots himself. The theater manager has his play: life has written it for him.

Silvester, like Bauer's other plays, deals with the transformation of reality into fiction. The play's characters, representatives of the culture industry, all have an indirect relationship to life. On this evening they do not see themselves as actors but merely as guests. Like their counterparts in *Change*, they are not conscious of their role playing; nonetheless, they are role players without recognizable individuality, and their behavior amounts to a series of clichés. The only one able to recognize the lack of identity in the others is the psychopath. He rejects the name Robespierre, foisted on him by the others apparently to label him as an insane outsider. He pokes fun at them for their role playing, and his suicide brings an end to the game which transforms life and art into a lie. His death can therefore be understood as the highest form of authenticity. Contrary to what many viewers saw as a celebration of the life-style of the play's characters, Bauer repudiates their self-indulgence.

In the early 1970s Bauer's name appeared more often in gossip columns than in theater programs. His stormy divorce from Sylvia Brodner, whom he had married only a year earlier, made headlines in 1972. While press and public overreacted in their fascination with Bauer the hard-drinking Bohemian and neglected the author of philosophical plays, Bauer contributed to his reputation as a bad boy. He never missed an opportunity to provoke his countrymen. His casual remark in 1973 that his native state of Styria was extremely ugly caused an uproar; in 1970 he had been awarded the Peter Rosegger Literature Prize, the state's major literary prize.

Gespenster (published, 1974; translated as *Ghosts*, 1978), first performed in Munich's Kammerspiele (Intimate Theater) in 1974, received much attention when it was produced during the 1975 "Styrian Autumn," an annual avant-garde arts festival in Graz. An unproductive writer, his friend, and their wives and girlfriends bore one another, drink, and change partners so frequently that they are not always sure who belongs to whom. Their conversations are full of obscenities and discussions of all imaginable sexual activities. The writer and his friend create for themselves a "game of life," the rules of which are known only to them and can be changed or dispensed with at will. They can assume or discard roles according to their needs; at any time they can distance themselves from any role they happen to be playing through the use of alcohol, to which they turn at the slightest threat to their sense of reality.

At first glance, the title of *Gespenster* seems unrelated to its content. Originally Bauer had planned to rework Henrik Ibsen's *Ghosts* (1881) in such a way that during the performance the characters would gradually lose their identities; later he confessed his inability to carry out the plan. But the characters' nihilism, instability, and

dehumanization do indeed turn them into ghosts.

The premiere of *Magnetküsse* (Magnetic Kisses; published, 1986) at Vienna's prestigious Akademietheater in 1976 was directed by Fritz Zecha. Most critics admitted that they did not understand the play, and most theatergoers suspected that it was a bad joke on Bauer's part. Bauer admitted that the play evolved from a paranoid episode he had experienced after taking LSD. Ernst Ziak, a writer of detective stories, murders his pregnant girlfriend, Iris, because he suspects her of holding time constant by means of a magnet in her stomach. The viewer does not realize until the end of the play that Ziak is insane; only then does it become clear that the first ten scenes present a single moment as experienced by the protagonist. In the eleventh and last scene Ziak, sleeping in his bed, awakens after the telephone rings ten times. The final scene is the only "real" one and it is only from its perspective that the first ten scenes make sense. Only now is it clear why time in the first ten scenes has stood still, with the clock stopped at 3:15; only now does the audience understand why the telephone rings at the end of every scene. The first ten scenes are a series of nightmares in which Ziak experiences the events leading up to the murder. He suffers from jealousy and delusions of persecution; the images in his mind center around Iris's pregnancy, a topic continually reintroduced and surrealistically distorted until it reaches a climax in a grotesque birth scene. *Magnetküsse* was produced at San Francisco's Magic Theater in 1979. Translated by Martin Esslin as *Magnetic Kisses*, the play was directed by John Lion.

Memory Hotel (published, 1982; translated, 1981) was performed at the Graz Schauspielhaus in 1980 with Bauer directing. It is in many ways reminiscent of *Magnetküsse*. The heroes of both plays are writers of detective stories, and most of the action in each occurs within the mind of the protagonist. In *Memory Hotel* Toni's attempts to recall the recent past permeate the action. Toni, a millionaire, has been told by his wife and her physician-lover, who want to inherit his money, that he has terminal cancer. Toni's unexpected reaction is to use his remaining time to take a trip to Jamaica with his lover and a friend. At his hotel he meets all kinds of questionable characters who engage in every imaginable scheme to trick him out of his money. When he refuses to sign any papers, they try to rob him. Toni is the sole survivor of the ensuing massacre. Covered

Scene from the premiere of Bauer's Herr Faust spielt Roulette *at the Akademietheater, Vienna, January 1987*
(photograph by Keglevic)

with blood, he awakens in his bed just as his wife and her lover arrive; they have come out of fear that he will squander his money, leaving nothing for them. To ascertain where the money is, they try to make him recall the events of the past few days. Unable to endure the pressure they are putting on him, Toni jumps into the ocean and is killed by a shark. In the final scene Toni reappears, carrying his own corpse and that of the shark. This conclusion is an indication that a meaningful life and happiness, which were denied to the characters in Bauer's earlier plays, are possible after all.

As its title suggests, Bauer's play *"Woher kommen wir? Was sind wir? Wohin gehen wir?"* (Where Do We Come from? What Are We? Where Are We Going?; published, 1981) clearly has philosophical implications. The play was written in the fall of 1980 and premiered in 1982 at the Kammerspiele Bad Godesberg under Karl-Heinz Kubik's direction. In a translation by Renata and Martin Esslin, the play was performed at San Francisco's Magic Theater in 1983. For its American premiere, which was directed by Geoffrey Reeves, the play was titled *Sin-*

gapore Sling. Singapore Sling was received enthusiastically in San Francisco—in contrast to its reception in Bad Godesberg six months earlier, when many theatergoers walked out. Critics in both countries almost unanimously rejected the play. The play's German title is a reference to Paul Gauguin's painting *D'où venons-nous? Que sommes-nous? Où allons-nous?* (Where Do We Come From? What Are We? Where Are We Going?, 1897-1898). At one point Gauguin appears onstage with his friend Vincent van Gogh, to whom he offers one of the many human ears he is carrying in a shopping bag. Three couples who are invisible to each other are locked in a hotel room in Singapore. They are trying to escape a war that has broken out in Europe, but when they open the window of their room they hear the noise of battle. In the end God appears in the guise of van Gogh and chases them away. They resist but a marabou with a giant beak drags them to their death, which is simultaneously their birth: when the play ends, the crying of babies accompanies the death knells.

Bauer's next play, *Ein fröhlicher Morgen beim Friseur* (A Happy Morning in the Barber Shop;

published, 1983), was written in 1982 and directed by the author in Graz in 1983. A thoroughly enjoyable celebration of nonsense, it involves a neo-Gothic cathedral being cemented into the hero's skull by his barber and a train conductor who is transformed into a stewed pear; all the characters regress into baffling infantilism when the play closes. *Ein fröhlicher Morgen beim Friseur* can best be understood as a parable of the senselessness of the world.

Das kurze Leben der Schneewolken (The Short Life of the Snow Clouds; published, 1986) was written in 1982 and premiered in Stuttgart in 1983. It deals with the inability to share one's life with another person. Lilly and Balduin have retreated to a snowed-in mountain chalet to revitalize their relationship. But they continue to torment each other. Lilly kills a former lover and finally sucks Balduin's blood until he dies. Bauer's technique of letting his characters voice their innermost thoughts and secrets adds to the viewers' confusion: they do not always know whether they are witnessing a real conversation or interior monologues.

Herr Faust spielt Roulette (Mr. Faust Plays Roulette; published, 1986), written in 1985, premiered at Vienna's prestigious Akademietheater in 1987; Bauer directed the production. As in previous plays, the action in *Herr Faust spielt Roulette* takes place in the mind of the protagonist. Faust is a seventy-year-old mathematician who ponders the eternal return of numbers; Mephisto is the director of the casino. Gretl, Faust's wife, serves goulash made out of Faust himself—who, simultaneously, is a dinner guest. Needless to say, Bauer's play has little to do with Johann Wolfgang von Goethe's *Faust* (1808, 1832).

In *"Ach, armer Orpheus!"* ("Oh, Poor Orpheus!"), published in *manuskripte* in 1989 and first performed in Vienna's Schauspielhaus in 1991 under the direction of Hans Gratzer, a writer reminiscent of those in previous plays is in a state of crisis but is able to manipulate his dreams. The literary award he receives in a dream turns out to be a real cash inheritance from his psychiatrist friend.

Das Lächeln des Brian de Palma (The Smile of Brian de Palma), published in 1988 and first performed in Graz in 1991 under the direction of Bauer himself, is another realistic as well as surrealistic play. Ada and Odo, an elderly couple, both of whom are archaeologists, take tablets in a suicide attempt and go on a hallucinatory trip to

Egypt. There they meet Brian de Palma, who is directing a movie.

"Insalata mista"—Gemischter Salat (Tossed Salad; published, 1992), set in New York City, is a parable stating that life is—philosophically, politically, and socially—a "tossed salad." The world's chaos and confusion are interconnected and must, according to Henrik, a Broadway theater manager, be shown onstage.

All of Bauer's plays are based on the same presupposition: human existence is defined by a lack of purpose, lethargy, emptiness, and alienation. People find themselves in a vacuum which they fill with sex, drugs, alcohol, rebellion, and violence. In his major plays written before 1973 he seems to present his message "realistically," although the realism actually camouflages an underlying surrealism. In his later plays Bauer attempts to show the vacuum from the inside, revealing the instantaneous associations that the mind makes. The normal rules of logic are suspended; only the logic of dreams carries weight.

Bauer is one of the major exponents of the contemporary Austrian theater and has an international reputation. The seven-volume collection of his works (1986-), edited by Gerhard Melzer and published by Droschl in Graz, bears witness to his status. In a ceremony at the governor's palace in Graz in 1988 Bauer accepted the Manuskripte Prize, a coveted literary award of the state of Styria.

Interviews:
Hiide Schmölzer, "Wolfgang Bauer," in her *Das böse Wien: Gespräche mit österreichischen Künstlern* (Munich: Nymphenburger Verlagshandlung, 1973), pp. 39-52;

Paul Stefanek, "Aus einem Gespräch mit Wolfgang Bauer (Graz) über Kritik, Stückeschreiben, Theater, Regie und Publikum," *Modern Austrian Literature*, 18, no. 2 (1985): 79-89;

Rudiger Wischenbart, "Akademietheater: Gespräch mit Wolfgang Bauer zur Uraufführung seines jüngsten Stückes 'Herr Faust spielt Roulette,'" *Bühne*, no. 340 (January 1987): 21-23;

"Heinz Hartwig spricht mit Wolfgang Bauer," in *Mitschnitt 4: Literatur aus dem ORF-Studio Steiermark 1988*, edited by Heinz Hartwig and Walter Grond (Graz: Droschl, 1989), p. 61;

"Wolfgang Bauer im Gespräch," in *Die Tiefe der Tinte*, edited by Harald Friedl (Salzburg: Ver-

Bauer and his wife, Adelheid Schrumm Bauer, at the ceremony where Bauer received the Manuskripte Prize, 2 March 1988
(photograph © by Photoreport, Helmut Utri)

lag Grauwerte im Institut für Alltagskultur, 1990), pp. 10-26.

Bibliography:
Günter Peters and Michael Töteberg, "Werkverzeichnis," in *Kritisches Lexikon der deutschsprachigen Gegenwartsliteratur*, edited by Heinz Ludwig Arnold (Munich: Edition text + kritik, 1978), n.pag.

References:
Roger Bauer, "Die Poeten der Wiener Gruppe und die Herren Vettern aus Steiermark," in his *Laßt sie koaxen: Die kritischen Frösch' in Preußen und Sachsen! Zwei Jahrhunderte Literatur in Österreich* (Vienna: Europaverlag, 1977), pp. 219-234;

Anne Betten, "Die Dramensprache von Wolfgang Bauer," in her *Sprachrealismus im deutschen Drama der siebziger Jahre* (Heidelberg: Winter, 1985), pp. 81-144;

Gerald Bisinger, "Wolfgang Bauer: Mikrodramen," *Neue Deutsche Hefte*, 105 (1965): 128-129;

Gotthard Böhm, "Wolfgang Bauer: 'Die Wölt is nämlich unhamlich schiach,' " in *Die zeitgenössische Literatur Österreichs*, edited by Hilde Spiel (Zurich & Munich: Kindler, 1976), pp. 614-619;

Charles A. Carpenter, "The Plays of Bernhard, Bauer, and Handke: A Checklist of Major Critical Studies," *Modern Drama*, 23, no. 4 (1981): 484-491;

Regine Friedrich, "Wolfgang Bauer: Dichter," in *Wie die Grazer auszogen, die Literatur zu erobern: Texte, Porträts, Analysen und Dokumente junger österreichischer Autoren*, edited by Peter Laemmle and Jörg Drews (Munich: Edition text + kritik, 1975), pp. 76-87;

Paul M. Haberland, "Duality, the Artist, and Wolfgang Bauer," *Modern Austrian Literature*, 11, no. 2 (1978): 73-86;

Volker Hage, "Auf der Bühne steht eine DC-6: Zu den frühen Theaterstücken Wolfgang Bauers," *protokolle*, 2 (1972): 15-18;

Hellmuth Karasek, "Der Bauer im Bauer," *Der Spiegel*, 28 (10 June 1974): 130-131;

Jürgen Koppensteiner, "Wolfgang Bauer," in *Major Figures of Contemporary Austrian Literature*, edited by Donald G. Daviau (New York: Lang, 1987), pp. 67-88;

Koppensteiner, "Wolfgang Bauer: Portrait of a Controversial Writer," *Austria Today*, 3 (1985): 49-51;

Koppensteiner, "Wolfgang Bauers Dramen-Versuch einer Synthese," in *Die österreichische Literatur: Ihr Profil von der Jahrhundertwende bis zur Gegenwart (1880-1980)*, edited by Her-

bert Zeman (Graz: Akademische Druck-
und Verlagsanstalt, 1989), pp. 927-938;

Jutta Landa, *Bürgerliches Schocktheater: Entwicklungen im österreichischen Drama der sechziger und siebziger Jahre* (Frankfurt am Main: Athenäum, 1988);

Dorothea Leitner, "Wolfgang Bauer: Erfolg in den USA," *Kleine Zeitung* (Graz), 26 July 1983, p. 16;

Gerhard Melzer, "Bundeskanzler wird Briefträger: Wolfgang Bauers neues Bühnenstück 'Herr Faust spielt Roulette,'" *Die Presse* (Vienna), 29/30 November 1986, p. iv;

Melzer, "Geburtsweh: Zu Wolfgang Bauers Stück 'Woher kommen wir? Was sind wir? Wohin gehen wir?,'" *manuskripte*, 85 (1984): 79-86;

Melzer, "Von der Rolle, eine Rolle zu spielen: Bemerkungen zu einigen Schwerpunkten in der publizistischen und wissenschaftlichen Auseinandersetzung mit Wolfgang Bauer," *manuskripte*, 58 (1977/1978): 28-33;

Melzer, "Ein Wintermärchen: Zu Wolfgang Bauers Stück *Das kurze Leben der Schneewolken*," *manuskripte*, 91 (1986): 56-60;

Melzer, *Wolfgang Bauer: Eine Einführung in das Gesamtwerk* (Königstein: Athenäum, 1981);

Melzer, "Wolfgang Bauers 'Mikrodramen,'" in *Österreich in amerikanischer Sicht: Das Österreichbild im amerikanischen Schulunterricht*, volume 4, edited by Maria Luise Caputo-Mayr and Herbert Lederer (New York: Austrian Institute, 1988), pp. 28-33;

Hugh Rorrison, "The 'Grazer Gruppe', Peter Handke and Wolfgang Bauer," in *Modern Austrian Writing: Literature and Society after 1945*, edited by Alan Best and Hans Wolfschütz (London: Wolff / Totowa, N.J.: Barnes & Noble, 1980), pp. 252-266;

Karol Sauerland, "Das österreichische Drama in jüngster Zeit," *Literatur und Kritik*, 96/97 (1975): 341-353;

Grete Scheuer, "Das Forum Stadtpark und anderes," in *Literatur in der Steiermark von 1945-1976* (Graz: Steiermärkische Landesregierung, n.d.), pp. 81-136;

Botho Strauß, "Melodrama und Mikropsychologie: Wolfgang Bauers 'Change,'" *Theater heute*, 10, no. 11 (1969): 39-40;

text + kritik, special issues on Bauer, 59 (July 1978);

Erika E. Theobald, "Das österreichische Drama der Gegenwart," *Modern Austrian Literature*, 4, no. 1 (1971): 7-22;

Thomas Trenkler, "Der Doppelbewegungssurfer: Wolfgang Bauer inszeniert in Graz 'Das Lächeln des Brian de Palma,'" *Wochenpresse-WirtschaftsWoche*, no. 48 (28 November 1991): 67;

Peter Vujica, "Dichter und Bauer," *Der Standard*, 2 May 1991, p. 9;

Ulrich Weinzierl, "Herr Faust: Eine Uraufführung in Wien," *Frankfurter Allgemeine Zeitung*, 27 January 1987, p. 25;

Jürgen Wertheimer, "'Indianer und Wölfe suchen lachend das Weite': Comic und Komik im Theater des Grazers Wolfgang Bauer," *Austriaca*, 14 (1982): 187-198.

Thomas Bernhard

(9 or 10 February 1931 - 12 February 1989)

Steve Dowden
Yale University

See also the Bernhard entry in *DLB 85: Austrian Fiction Writers After 1914*.

PLAY PRODUCTIONS: *Ein Fest für Boris*, Hamburg, Deutsches Schauspielhaus, 29 June 1970;

Der Ignorant und der Wahnsinnige, Salzburg, Festspiele, 29 July 1972;

Die Jagdgesellschaft, Vienna, Burgtheater, 4 May 1974;

Die Macht der Gewohnheit, Salzburg, Festspiele, 27 July 1974;

Der Präsident, Vienna, Burgtheater, 17 May 1975;

Die Berühmten, Vienna, Theater an der Wien, 8 June 1976;

Minetti: Porträt des Künstlers als alter Mann, Stuttgart, Staatstheater, 1 September 1976;

Immanuel Kant, Stuttgart, Staatstheater, 15 April 1978;

Vor dem Ruhestand, Stuttgart, Württembergisches Staatstheater, 29 June 1979;

Der Weltverbesserer, Bochum, Schauspielhaus, 6 September 1980;

Maiandacht, *Freispruch*, and *Eis*, Bochum, Schauspielhaus, 7 November 1981;

Der Schein trügt, Bochum, Schauspielhaus, 21 January 1984;

Der Theatermacher, Salzburg, Festspiele, 17 August 1985;

Einfach kompliziert, West Berlin, Schiller-Theater, 28 February 1986;

Claus Peymann verläßt Bochum und geht als Burgtheaterdirektor nach Wien, Bochum, Schauspielhaus, 8 June 1986;

Ritter, Dene, Voss, Salzburg, Festspiele, 18 August 1986;

Match, Vienna, Burgtheater, 23 October 1987;

Heldenplatz, Vienna, Burgtheater, 4 November 1988;

Elisabeth II: Keine Komödie, Berlin, Schiller-Theater, 5 November 1989.

BOOKS: *Auf der Erde und in der Hölle: Gedichte* (Salzburg: Müller, 1957);

Thomas Bernhard (photograph by Oliver Hermann)

In hora mortis (Salzburg: Müller, 1958);

Unter dem Eisen des Mondes: Gedichte (Cologne & Berlin: Kiepenheuer & Witsch, 1958);

die rosen der einöde: fünf sätze für ballett, stimmen, und orchester (Frankfurt am Main: Fischer, 1959);

Frost (Frankfurt am Main: Insel, 1963); excerpt translated by Helene Scher as "Frost," in *Postwar German Culture*, edited by Charles McClelland and Steven Scher (New York: Dutton, 1974), pp. 238-242;

Amras (Frankfurt am Main: Insel, 1964);

Prosa (Frankfurt am Main: Suhrkamp, 1967);

Verstörung (Frankfurt am Main: Insel, 1967); translated by Richard and Clara Winston as *Gargoyles* (New York: Knopf, 1970);

Ungenach: Erzählung (Frankfurt am Main: Suhrkamp, 1968);

Ein Fest für Boris (Frankfurt am Main: Suhrkamp, 1968); translated by Peter Jansen and Kenneth Northcott as *A Party for Boris*, in *Histrionics: Three Plays* (Chicago & London: University of Chicago Press, 1990), pp. 1-71;

An der Baumgrenze: Erzählungen (Salzburg: Residenz, 1969); "An der Baumgrenze" translated by Sophie Wilkins as "At the Timberline," in *Anthology of Modern Austrian Literature*, edited by Adolf Opel (Atlantic Heights, N.J.: Humanities Press, 1981; London: Wolff, 1981);

Ereignisse (Berlin: Literarisches Kolloquium, 1969);

Watten: Ein Nachlaß (Frankfurt am Main: Suhrkamp, 1969);

Das Kalkwerk (Frankfurt am Main: Suhrkamp, 1970); translated by Wilkins as *The Lime Works* (New York: Knopf, 1973);

Der Italiener (Salzburg: Residenz, 1971);

Midland in Stilfs: Drei Erzählungen (Frankfurt am Main: Suhrkamp, 1971);

Gehen (Frankfurt am Main: Suhrkamp, 1971);

Der Ignorant und der Wahnsinnige (Frankfurt am Main: Suhrkamp, 1972);

Die Jagdgesellschaft (Frankfurt am Main: Suhrkamp, 1974), translated by Gitta Honegger as *The Hunting Party*, in *Performing Arts Journal*, 5, no. 1 (1980): pp. 101-131;

Die Macht der Gewohnheit: Komödie (Frankfurt am Main: Suhrkamp, 1974); translated by Neville and Stephen Plaice as *The Force of Habit: A Comedy* (London: Heinemann, 1976);

Der Kulterer: Eine Filmgeschichte (Salzburg: Residenz, 1974);

Der Präsident (Frankfurt am Main: Suhrkamp, 1975); translated by Honegger as *The President*, in *The President & Eve of Retirement* (New York: Performing Arts Journal Publications, 1982), pp. 17-114;

Die Ursache: Eine Andeutung (Salzburg: Residenz, 1975); translated by David McLintock as "An Indication of the Cause," in *Gathering Evidence: A Memoir* (New York: Knopf, 1985), pp. 75-141;

Korrektur: Roman (Frankfurt am Main: Suhrkamp, 1975); translated by Wilkins as *Correction* (New York: Knopf, 1979;

Der Wetterfleck: Erzählungen (Stuttgart: Reclam, 1976);

Die Berühmten (Frankfurt am Main: Suhrkamp, 1976);

Minetti: Porträt des Künstlers als alter Mann (Frankfurt am Main: Suhrkamp, 1976);

Der Keller: Eine Entziehung (Salzburg: Residenz, 1976); translated by McLintock as "The Cellar: An Escape," in *Gathering Evidence*, pp. 142-213;

Der Atem: Eine Entscheidung (Salzburg & Vienna: Residenz, 1978); translated by McLintock as "Breath: A Decision," in *Gathering Evidence*, pp. 215-275;

Die Kälte: Eine Isolation (Salzburg: Residenz, 1978); translated by McLintock as "In the Cold," in *Gathering Evidence*, pp. 277-340;

Ja (Frankfurt am Main: Suhrkamp, 1978); translated by Ewald Osers as *Yes* (London: Quartet, 1991);

Der Stimmenimitator (Frankfurt am Main: Suhrkamp, 1978);

Immanuel Kant: Komödie (Frankfurt am Main: Suhrkamp, 1978);

Die Erzählungen (Frankfurt am Main: Suhrkamp, 1979);

Vor dem Ruhestand (Frankfurt am Main: Suhrkamp, 1979); translated by Honegger as *Eve of Retirement*, in *The President & Eve of Retirement*, pp. 115-207;

Der Weltverbesserer (Frankfurt am Main: Suhrkamp, 1979);

Die Billigesser (Frankfurt am Main: Suhrkamp, 1980); translated by Osers as *The Cheap-Eaters* (London: Quartet, 1990);

Über allen Gipfeln ist Ruh: Ein deutscher Dichtertag um 1980. Komödie (Frankfurt am Main: Suhrkamp, 1981);

Am Ziel (Frankfurt am Main: Suhrkamp, 1981);

Ave Vergil: Gedicht (Frankfurt am Main: Suhrkamp, 1981);

Wittgensteins Neffe: Eine Freundschaft (Frankfurt am Main: Suhrkamp, 1982); translated by McLintock as *Wittgenstein's Nephew: A Friendship* (New York: Knopf, 1989);

Ein Kind (Salzburg: Residenz, 1982); translated by McLintock as "A Child," in *Gathering Evidence*, pp. 1-73;

Beton (Frankfurt am Main: Suhrkamp, 1982); translated by McLintock as *Concrete* (New York: Knopf, 1984; London: Dent, 1984);

Der Schein trügt (Frankfurt am Main: Suhrkamp, 1983); translated by Honegger as *Appearances are Deceiving*, in *Theater* (Yale University), 15 (Winter 1983): 31-51;

Der Untergeher (Frankfurt am Main: Suhrkamp, 1983); translated by Jack Dawson as *The Loser: A Novel* (New York: Knopf, 1991);

Der Theatermacher (Frankfurt am Main: Suhrkamp, 1984); translated by Jansen and Northcott as *Histrionics*, in *Histrionics*, pp. 179-282;

Holzfällen: Eine Erregung (Frankfurt am Main: Suhrkamp, 1984); translated by McLintock as *Woodcutters* (New York: Knopf, 1987);

Ritter, Dene, Voss (Frankfurt am Main: Suhrkamp, 1984); translated by Jansen and Northcott as *Ritter, Dene, Voss* in *Histrionics*, pp. 73-178;

Alte Meister: Komödie (Frankfurt am Main: Suhrkamp, 1985); translated by Osers as *Old Masters* (London: Quartet, 1989);

Einfach kompliziert (Frankfurt am Main: Suhrkamp, 1986);

Auslöschung: Ein Zerfall (Frankfurt am Main: Suhrkamp, 1986);

Elisabeth II. (Frankfurt am Main: Suhrkamp, 1987);

Der deutsche Mittagstisch: Dramolette (Frankfurt am Main: Suhrkamp, 1988)—includes *Maiandacht, Freispruch, Eis, Match*; translated by Honegger as *The German Lunch Table*, in *Performing Arts Journal*, 6, no. 1 (1981): 26-29;

Stücke, 4 volumes (Frankfurt am Main: Suhrkamp, 1988);

Heldenplatz (Frankfurt am Main: Suhrkamp, 1988);

Die Irren; Die Häftlinge (Frankfurt am Main: Insel, 1988);

In der Höhe: Rettungsversuch, Unsinn (Salzburg: Residenz, 1989); translated by Russell Stockman as *On the Mountain* (Marlboro, Vt.: Marlboro Press, 1991);

Claus Peymann kauft sich eine Hose und geht mit mir essen: Drei Dramolette (Frankfurt am Main: Suhrkamp, 1990).

OTHER: "Großer, unbegreiflicher Hunger," in *Stimmen der Gegenwart 1954*, edited by Hans Weigel (Vienna: Dürer, 1954), pp. 138-143;

"Der Schweinehüter," in *Stimmen der Gegenwart 1956* (Vienna & Munich: Herold, 1956), pp. 158-179;

"Ein Frühling," in *Spektrum des Geistes 1964: Literaturkalender* (Ebenhausen: Voss, 1963), p. 36;

"Der Italiener," in *Insel-Almanach auf das Jahr 1965* (Frankfurt am Main: Insel, 1964);

"Mit der Klarheit nimmt die Kälte zu," in *Jahresring 65/66* (Stuttgart: DVA, 1965), pp. 243-245;

"Nie und mit nichts fertig werden," in *Deutsche Akademie für Sprache und Dichtung: Jahrbuch 1970* (Heidelberg & Darmstadt: Schneider, 1971), pp. 83-84.

SELECTED PERIODICAL PUBLICATIONS—
UNCOLLECTED: "Eine Zeugenaussage," *Wort in der Zeit*, 10 (1964): 38-43;

"Ein junger Schriftsteller," *Wort in der Zeit*, 11 (1965): 56-59;

"Politische Morgenandacht," *Wort in der Zeit*, 12 (1966): 11-13;

"Unsterblichkeit ist unmöglich: Landschaft der Kindheit," *Neues Forum*, 169/170 (1968): 95-97;

"Der Wahrheit und dem Tod auf der Spur: Zwei Reden," *Neues Forum*, 173 (1968): 347-349;

Ein Fest für Boris, in *Theater heute*, 11 (January 1970): 39-47;

"Der Berg," *Literatur und Kritik*, 46 (1970): 330-352;

"Vor der Akademie," *Frankfurter Allgemeine Zeitung*, 19 October 1970, p. 22;

"Als Verwalter in Asyl: Fragment," *Merkur*, 24 (1970): 1163-1164;

"Protest," *Theater heute*, 13 (September 1972): 14;

Der Ignorant und der Wahnsinnige, in *Theater heute*, 13 (September 1972): 34-47;

Die Jagdgesellschaft, in *Spectaculum*, 20 (1974): 15-79;

Die Macht der Gewohnheit, in *Theater heute*, 15 (September 1974): 37-52;

"Die Komödie der Eitelkeit," *Die Zeit*, 27 February 1976, p. 55;

"Was Österreich nicht lesen soll: Die Kleinbürger auf der Heuchelleiter," *Die Zeit*, 17 February 1978, p. 40;

Der deutsche Mittagstisch: Eine Tragödie für ein Burgtheatergastspiel in Deutschland, in *Die Zeit*, 29 December 1978, p. 33;

Der Weltverbesserer, in *Theater* (1978): 88-102;

"Der doppelte Herr Bernhard," *Die Zeit*, 31 August 1979, pp. 43-44;

Vor dem Ruhestand: Eine Komödie von deutscher Seele, in *Theater heute*, 20 (August 1979): 33-49;

"Zu meinem Austritt," *Frankfurter Allgemeine Zeitung*, 7 December 1979, p. 25;

*A Doda: Für zwei Schauspielerinnen und eine Land-
straße*, in *Die Zeit*, 12 December 1980, p. 40;

"Der pensionierte Salonsozialist," *profil*, 26 January 1981, pp. 5-9;

Alles oder nichts: Ein deutscher Akt, in *Theater heute*,
22 (May 1981): 5-9;

"Am Ziel," *Theater heute*, 22 (October 1981):
35-53;

"Verfolgungswahn?," *Die Zeit*, 11 January 1982,
p. 32;

"Goethe schtirbt," *Die Zeit*, 19 March 1982, pp.
41-42;

"Montaigne: Eine Erzählung in 22 Fortsetzun-
gen," *Die Zeit*, 8 October 1982, pp. 1-22;

"Der Schein trügt," *Spectaculum*, 39 (1984): 17-77;

"Vranitzky: Eine Erwiderung," *Die Presse*, 13 September 1985;

*Claus Peymann verläßt Bochum und geht als Burgthea-
terdirektor nach Wien*, in *Die Zeit*, 9 May 1986,
p. 51;

"Claus Peymann kauft sich eine Hose und geht
mit mir essen," *Theater* (1986): 6-10;

"Claus Peymann und Hermann Beil auf der Sulz-
weise," *Die Zeit*, 11 September 1987, pp.
53-54;

"Mein glückliches Österreich," *Die Zeit*, 11 March
1988, p. 75;

"Einfach kompliziert," *Spectaculum*, 46 (1988):
7-42;

"Zwei Briefe an Claus Peymann," *Die Zeit*, 3
March 1989, p. 14.

From the production of his first dramas in
the early 1970s until his death in 1989, Thomas
Bernhard was one of the most prominent and controversial playwrights composing for the German-
language theater. His grimly comic works for the
stage confront the audience with death, madness,
hatred, contempt, and disease. The role of plot,
character, and psychology in his dramas is thin;
Bernhard concentrates his gift on language. He
was a virtuoso in his unique and highly musical
prose style, which, though it was more dependent on charismatic stage performers than most
theatrical idioms, earned him a substantial international reputation in Europe. Virtuosity of language is all that remains of the dramatic art in
Bernhard's vision of the stage. The more humane aspects of theater and acting are allowed to
wither: "die Schauspieler müssen Talent haben
und müssen eine Maschine sein" (the actors have
to have talent and have to be a machine), he
once said. Empty virtuosity is also one of his favorite themes.

Bernhard's drama is satirical and anti-
psychological. His protagonists are individuals isolated beyond recall to the human community,
which is only a dim memory to them. The course
of modernity, especially World War II, has
eroded the spiritual vitality of Austria. And theater, which in the German tradition holds a special and honorable place as the source of moral education for an enlightened public, has not
escaped the ravages of modern degeneration.
Bernhard's works for the stage embody an idea
of theater as a mutilated cadaver bearing little resemblance to the living institution envisioned by
Gotthold Ephraim Lessing and Friedrich Schiller,
by Franz Grillparzer and Hugo von Hofmannsthal. His idea of theater must be understood as
an ironic comment on theirs.

Bernhard's predilection for metaphors of
death and disease is partly biographical in origin.
Plagued by heart and lung problems from the
age of eighteen, Bernhard's life was difficult and
unhappy. He was born on 9 or 10 February 1931
to Hertha Bernhard in a Dutch home for unwed
mothers in Heerlen, near Maastricht. He never
met his father, an itinerant Austrian carpenter
named Alois Zuckerstätter. Hertha Bernhard
soon returned to Austria, where she married in
1935 and raised her family mostly in Henndorf,
a village near Salzburg. Her father, Johannes
Freumbichler, a novelist of local reputation who
never managed to earn a living as a professional
writer, was probably the most significant influence on Bernhard's childhood.

Life was arduous for Bernhard's poverty-
stricken clan. He records the details of the hard
times in his memoirs, which have been collected
and translated under the title *Gathering Evidence*
(1985). He spent time at a home for maladjusted
children; he did not do well in his Nazi-
administered boarding school, nor did he fare
well at the hands of the school's Catholic administration after the war. At fifteen he dropped out
to become a grocer's apprentice at a store in one
of Salzburg's saddest postwar housing projects.
He was studying voice on the side and hoped to
make a career for himself in music; but in 1949
hard work and poor nutrition caught up with
him, and he came down with pneumonia. His doctors did not expect him to recover, and they committed him to a gruesome ward for the terminally ill. Bernhard did not die, but he did
contract tuberculosis. During the next few years
he was in and out of sanatoriums, and his lungs
were scarred for life. The disease put an end to

A scene from the premiere of Bernhard's first play, Ein Fest
für Boris, *at the Deutsches Schauspielhaus in Berlin, June
1970, with Judith Holzmeister (in wheelchair) as "die Gute"
and Angela Schmid (in pig mask) as her servant Johanna (photograph by Rosemarie Clausen)*

his hope for a singing career. During this same
period he lost his mother to cancer and his beloved grandfather to old age. These experiences
of disease and death, together with a pessimistic
outlook that he learned from his grandfather,
shaped Bernhard's literary imagination.

In the course of his slow convalescence
Bernhard became increasingly interested in reading literature and in writing poetry. After his release from the public health system he studied
music and drama in Vienna and then at
Salzburg's Mozarteum, from which he was graduated in 1957 with a qualifying examination on
Antonin Artaud and a thesis on Bertolt Brecht.
During the 1950s he had some short prose works
and three books of verse published, followed by librettos in 1959 and 1960. He did not achieve substantial recognition until the publication of his
first novel, *Frost*, in 1963.

His first published work for the theater, *Ein
Fest für Boris* (translated as *A Party for Boris*, 1990),
appeared as a book in 1968 and premiered two
years later. It begins his lifelong assault on the
complacent assumptions of modern German theater. Bernhard aims to shock, to confront his audience with "truths" that most people would prefer
not to see. An alarmingly tasteless farce, *Ein Fest
für Boris* concentrates on several legless and demented invalids who use and abuse one another.
Foremost among them is "die Gute" (the Good
Woman), a monstrous hypocrite who is bent on hu-
miliating everyone around her. The macabre situation embodies Bernhard's vision of modernity: a
morally, spiritually, and physically twisted humanity. The play ends with the sudden death of
Boris at his birthday party and the raving laughter of the Good Woman. For Bernhard, death defines the human condition; a joke played by nature, death is both comic and tragic, a brute fact
against which all else is measured. Bernhard's subsequent dramatic work hardly deviates from the
underlying theme of *Ein Fest für Boris*, that
human beings are wretched creatures and death
is a certainty. His dramas constitute series of variations on this basic premise and explore two issues: the loss of genuine art (especially theater)
in modernity; and the Austrian historical experience, which Bernhard understands to be a moral
and intellectual catastrophe.

By the time his second drama, *Der Ignorant
und der Wahnsinnige* (The Ignoramus and the Mad-
man; published, 1972), made its way to the stage
in 1972, Bernhard's prestige as a novelist was established. He had begun to accumulate literary
awards: the Julius Campe Prize in 1964; the
Bremen Prize in 1965; the Austrian State Prize
for Literature, the Presentation of the Culture Circle of the Federated League of German Industry,
and the Anton Wildgans Prize of the Austrian
Industrialists' Association in 1967; the Georg
Büchner Prize in 1970; and the Grillparzer Prize,
the Franz Theodor Csokor Prize of the Austrian
PEN Club, and the Adolf Grimme Prize in 1972.
More prizes were to come, in spite of Bernhard's
reputation for heaping contempt on his benefac-
tors: the Hannover Dramatists Prize and the Prix
Séguier in 1974, the Literature Prize of the Austrian Chamber of Commerce in 1976, the Premio
Prato in 1982, the Premio Modello in 1983, and
the Prix Medicis in 1988. It was no doubt due to
Bernhard's extraordinary prestige that the Salzburg Festival, though in general an aesthetically
conservative undertaking, staged *Der Ignorant und*

der Wahnsinnige, a parody on the value and meaning of high culture.

The play revolves around a production of Wolfgang Amadeus Mozart's *Die Zauberflöte* (The Magic Flute, 1791) and the figure called the Queen of the Night: she is so steeped in the aria that has made her famous that she has adopted its name. But her celebrated virtuosity is empty and mechanical; and she is tired of Mozart, *Die Zauberflöte*, opera, and theater and is filled with scorn for her audience:

> Wir kennen alle Opern
> alle Schauspiele
> wir haben alles gelesen
> und wir kennen die schönsten Gegenden auf der
>   Welt
> und insgeheim hassen wir das Publikum
> nicht wahr
> unsere Peiniger
> wir treten auf
> und verabscheuen was
> wir kennen
>
> (We know all the operas
> all the plays
> we have read it all
> and we know the world's most beautiful spots
> and secretly we hate the audience
> isn't it so
> our tormentors
> we go on stage
> and despise what
> we know).

The visual image of broken lines on the page suggests that even poetry is crippled; Bernhard withholds from his disabled verse even the modest support of punctuation. There is no rhyme or recurrence of stress patterns to suggest the character of traditional prosody; only repetition remains as a grotesque vestige of lyric and dramatic verse forms. Bernhard uses monotonously recurring phrases to irritate his audience and expresses contempt for theater and for poetry itself.

The director of *Der Ignorant und der Wahnsinnige* was Claus Peymann, one of West Germany's established avant-gardists. Peymann staged the premieres of most of Bernhard's plays, including his next, *Die Jagdgesellschaft* (published, 1974; translated as *The Hunting Party*, 1980), which opened on 4 May 1974 at Vienna's Burgtheater, Austria's most venerable stage. An aging general has gathered a hunting party at his remote lodge; the forest around the lodge is in-

fested with insects and, like the general, is dying. What is diseased here is history itself, personified in the authoritarian, vaguely Austro-Balkan figure of "der General." History has shaped or—more exactly—misshaped him. The general is a veteran of Stalingrad, where his arm (as he constantly reminds everyone) was ripped from his body; the carcasses of frozen game in the forest remind him of the frozen corpses of his soldiers. His antagonist is the voice of art and literature, embodied in "der Schriftsteller" (the writer), who offers a running commentary on death, disease, and ruination: "Das Unheil kommt / wie wir wissen / aus allen menschlichen Naturen / und die ganze Geschichte / ist nichts als Unheil / Und wenn wir in die Zukunft hineinschauen / sehen wir nichts anderes" (Ruination stems / as we know / from all human natures / and all of history / is nothing but ruination / And if we look into the future / we see nothing else). By the end of the piece the general has committed suicide, and the woodcutters, in an allusion to the end of Anton Chekhov's *The Cherry Orchard* (1904), have begun to raze the diseased forest.

In the same way that *Der Ignorant und der Wahnsinnige* defined Bernhard's sense of art's place in the order of things, *Die Jagdgesellschaft* registers his apocalyptic sense of history. His next play, *Die Macht der Gewohnheit* (1974; translated as *The Force of Habit*, 1976) returns to the futility of art in a comic mode. Written for the Salzburg Festival, *Die Macht der Gewohnheit* indirectly mocks that grand and solemn enterprise in the image of a second-rate family circus. Its tyrannical director, Herr Caribaldi, is obsessed with forcing his unmusical troupe to perform Franz Schubert's *Trout Quintet* (1819) flawlessly. He tortures them with his obsession, and they do all they can to sabotage the daily ritual of rehearsing the piece. His motto, "Wir hassen das Forellenquintett / aber es muß gespielt werden" (We hate the Trout Quintet / but it has to be played), expresses the play's idea that empty ritual has driven out true art. It is nothing but force of habit that, from Bernhard's cantankerous viewpoint, motivates the pretentious middle-class aspirations to Bildung (culture) which, in turn, fuel the empty ritual of high culture in places such as Salzburg. His satirical play *Die Berühmten* (The Big Names, 1976), also commissioned by the Salzburg Festival, reveals an intent similar to that of *Die Macht der Gewohnheit*. But this time the satire was not oblique. When the administrators discovered that it openly lampooned "the big names" (and their

Bernhard Minetti (left) and Fritz Lichtenhahn in a scene from the premiere of Bernhard's Die Macht der Gewohnheit *at the Salzburg Festival, July 1974 (photograph by PSF/Steinmetz)*

lesser successors) on which the festival's reputation and tradition were based, they refused to produce it.

The idea that drives *Die Macht der Gewohnheit* and *Die Berühmten* recurs in Bernhard's dramas and prose with heavy emphasis: in this fallen era, true art is lost forever. *Über allen Gipfeln ist Ruh* (O'er All Mountain Peaks Is Repose, 1981 [the title is an ironic citation of a well-known poem by Johann Wolfgang von Goethe]) and *Der Theatermacher* (published, 1984; performed, 1985; translated as *Histrionics*, 1990) proceed in a similar vein. Yet Bernhard's plays do not claim to recover the squandered patrimony; they merely attempt to call attention to the catastrophe. *Minetti: Porträt des Künstlers als alter Mann* (Minetti: A Portrait of the Artist as Old Man, 1976), written for and about one of Bernhard's favorite stage stars, Bernhard Minetti, deals with a senescent actor banished from the limelight because he refuses to compromise his artistic vision. His suicide embodies the extinction of art. Minetti appeared in the premieres of *Der Schein trügt* (published, 1983; performed, 1984; translated as *Appearances Are Deceiving*, 1983) and *Einfach kompliziert* (Simply Complicated, 1986),

both of which are similar in theme to *Minetti*. Bernhard also wrote a play for three favorite actors from Peymann's troupe in Bochum: Gert Voss, Kirsten Dene, and Ilse Ritter. *Ritter, Dene, Voss* (published, 1984; performed, 1986; translated, 1990) satirizes the sterile elegance of the Viennese upper middle class.

Vor dem Ruhestand (1979; translated as *Eve of Retirement*, 1982) brought a previously latent concern to the forefront of Bernhard's dramatic imagination: the history and politics of Germany and Austria. An earlier work, *Der Präsident* (1975; translated as *The President*, 1982) had mocked the vanity of political power, but it was an indirect critique with a vaguely Austro-Balkan setting. In contrast, *Vor dem Ruhestand* savagely attacks the afterlife of Nazism in Germany and Austria. Rudolf Höller, a former concentration-camp commandant, is retiring as chief justice of a German court. He and his sister Vera annually celebrate the birthday of Heinrich Himmler. In honor of the occasion Höller dons his old SS uniform, which Vera lovingly cares for, and the two reminisce over a meal. As a final tribute to Himmler, Rudolf and Vera go to bed together. The two monsters are opposed by their paraplegic sister Clara,

31

Minetti in the title role at the premiere of Bernhard's Minetti *at the Stuttgart Staatstheater, September 1976 (photograph by Abisag Tüllman)*

a leftist. They torment her, shaving her head and forcing her into the role of a concentration-camp victim.

Vor dem Ruhestand was Bernhard's response to a scandal that involved Peymann, who directed its premiere in Stuttgart. The archconservative prime minister of Baden-Württemberg, Hans Filbinger, who was also a likely candidate for president of the Federal Republic of Germany, had severely criticized Peymann's work at the Staatstheater (State Theater) in Stuttgart and was instrumental in forcing Peymann from his post as artistic director. But before Peymann left, it was discovered that Filbinger had concealed a sordid Nazi past. Rolf Hochhuth worked out the details of Filbinger's case in his documentary play *Juristen* (Lawyers; published, 1979; performed, 1980). The difference between Hochhuth's approach and Bernhard's is significant. Characteristically, Bernhard sought not to review and analyze the facts of the Filbinger case but to explore satirically the sensibility that underlay Filbinger's prestige and prosperity in a booming postwar Germany.

In a similar spirit Bernhard's final drama, *Heldenplatz*, offers a histrionic vision of postwar Austria. The play was his offering on the occa-

sion of the Burgtheater's one hundredth anniversary. But 1988 was also the fiftieth anniversary of Austria's union with Nazi Germany. Against the background of the scandal surrounding the Austrian president, Kurt Waldheim, but with little direct reference to it, Bernhard pokes into the sore wound of Austrian anti-Semitism and complicity in Nazism. Professor Josef Schuster, a Jew who had fled Vienna for Oxford in 1938 and had returned in 1955, has committed suicide. His brother, Professor Robert Schuster, who has returned from English exile, is one of Bernhard's most fully achieved misanthropes. He rants artfully and at great length against Austria's politicians and pretensions, against the lowered standards of art and intellect in modern Austria, and above all against Austrian anti-Semitism, symbolized by the Heldenplatz: on 15 March 1938 the Heldenplatz had been the scene of Adolf Hitler's speech to masses of jubilant Viennese shortly after the annexation of Austria to Germany.

The premiere of *Heldenplatz* at the Burgtheater fomented an acrimonious public debate over questions of taste, patriotism, art, self-indulgence, and national conscience. Bernhard and Peymann, who had become artistic director of the Burgtheater in 1986, were denounced by outraged politicians and citizens. But Bernhard advocates no political or social agenda other than absolute resignation. The intention that drives Bernhard's theater is not revolution or social reform or even constructive criticism; it is personal outrage at the course of modern Austrian history. Bernhard, the misanthrope, was an uncompromising moralist.

On 12 February 1989 Bernhard died at his home in Ohlsdorf, near Gmunden in Upper Austria; a lifetime of heart and lung disease had finally claimed him at the age of fifty-eight. He was buried in Vienna's Grinzinger Cemetery on 15 February, before the news of his death was made public. At his request only three close relatives were in attendance. In a posthumous demonstration of his contempt for Austria, Bernhard specified in his will—prepared three days before his death—that none of his novels or plays could be published, produced, or recited in that country for the duration of his copyright, seventy years. The will also forbids access to his private papers, letters, and unpublished manuscripts, which are reported to include two presumably unfinished plays and a novel, "Neufundland" (Newfoundland).

Interviews:

"Je remplis le vide avec des phrases," *Nouvelles littéraires*, 22-29 (June 1978): 18;

André Müller, "Thomas Bernhard," in his *Entblößungen* (Munich: Goldmann, 1979), pp. 59-102;

"Ich könnte auf dem Papier jemand umbringen," *Der Spiegel*, 34 (23 June 1980): 172-182;

"Ansichten eines unverbesserlichen Weltverbesserers," *Stern*, 24 (4 June 1981): 160-162;

"Aveux et paradoxes de Thomas Bernhard," *Le Monde*, 7 January 1983, p. 15;

"Ich behaupte nicht, mit der Welt gehe es schlechter: Aus einem Gespräch mit Thomas Bernhard," *Frankfurter Allgemeine Zeitung*, 24 February 1983, p. 23;

" 'Es ist eh alles positiv,' Thomas Bernhard über seine Bücher, seine Feinde und sich selbst," *Die Presse*, 22/23 September 1984, "Spektrum" supplement;

"Von einer Katastrophe in die andere," *Süddeutsche Zeitung*, 17/18 January 1987, pp. 169-170;

"Eine groteske Phantomedebatte," *profil*, 17 October 1988;

Kurt Hofmann, ed., *Aus Gesprächen mit Thomas Bernhard* (Vienna: Löcker, 1988);

"Letzte Worte aus der Einsamkeit," *Der Spiegel*, 44 (29 January 1990): 160-170;

Interviews (Frankfurt am Main: Suhrkamp, 1992).

Bibliographies:

Charles A. Carpenter, *Modern Drama Scholarship and Criticism 1966-1980: An International Bibliography* (Toronto: University of Toronto Press, 1986), p. 318;

Donald Daviau, "The Reception of Thomas Bernhard in the United States," *Modern Austrian Literature*, 21, nos. 3/4 (1988): 267-276;

Jens Dittmar, *Thomas Bernhard Werkgeschichte*, revised edition (Frankfurt am Main: Suhrkamp, 1990);

Bernhard Sorg and Michael Töteberg, "Thomas Bernhard," in *Kritisches Lexikon sur deutschsprachigen Gegenwartsliteratur*, edited by Heinz Ludwig Arnold (Munich: Edition text + kritik, n.d.), n. pag.

References:

Mark Anderson, "Notes on Thomas Bernhard," *Raritan*, 7 (1987): 81-96;

Arnold Barthofer, "Das Cello und die Peitsche: Beobachtungen zu Bernhards *Die Macht der Gewohnheit*," *Sprachkunst*, 7 (1976): 294-331;

Barthofer, "King Lear in Dinkelsbühl: Historisch-biographisches zu Thomas Bernhards Theaterstück *Minetti*," *Maske und Kothurn*, 23 (1977): 158-172;

Barthofer, "The Plays of Thomas Bernhard—A Report," *Modern Austrian Literature*, 11, no. 1 (1978): 21-48;

Barthofer, "Vorliebe für die Kömodie: Todesangst; Anmerkungen zum Kömodienbegriff bei Thomas Bernhard," *Vierteljahresschrift des Adalbert-Stifter-Instituts*, 31 (1982): 77-100;

Peter von Becker, "Bei Bernhard: Eine Geschichte in 15 Episoden," *Theater heute*, supplement 1977/1978, 19 (1978): 80-87;

Becker, "Die Unvernünftigen sterben nicht aus: Über Thomas Bernhards *Vor dem Ruhestand*," *Theater heute*, 20 (August 1979): 4-11;

Alexander von Bormann, ed., *Sehnsuchtsangst: Zur österreichischen Literatur der Gegenwart*, Kolloquium an der Universität von Amsterdam (Amsterdam: Rodopi, 1987);

Anneliese Botond, ed., *Über Thomas Bernhard* (Frankfurt am Main: Suhrkamp, 1970);

Denis Calandra, *New German Dramatists* (New York: Grove, 1983), pp. 139-161;

Robert Craft, "Comedian of Horror," *New York Review of Books*, 27 September 1990, pp. 40-48;

Gordon Craig, *The Germans* (New York: Putnam's, 1982), pp. 229-230;

Michel Demet, "Le Théâtre de Thomas Bernhard," *Etudes germaniques*, 31 (1976): 58-66;

Peter Demetz, "Thomas Bernhard: The Dark Side of Life," in his *After the Fires: Recent Writing in the Germanies, Switzerland, and Austria* (New York: Harcourt Brace Jovanovich, 1986), 199-212;

A. P. Dierick, "Thomas Bernhard's Austrian Neurosis," *Modern Austrian Literature*, 12, no. 1 (1979): 73-93;

Josef Donnenberg, "Thomas Bernhard und Österreich," *Österreich in Geschichte und Gegenwart*, 14 (1970): 237-251;

Heinz Ehrig, "Probleme des Absurden: Vergleichende Bemerkungen zu Bernhard und Beckett," *Wirkendes Wort*, 29 (1978): 44-64;

Nicholas Eisner, "Theatertheater/Theaterspiele: The Plays of Thomas Bernhard," *Modern Drama*, 30 (March 1987): 104-114;

Ria Endres, *Am Ende angekommen: Dargestellt am wahnhaften Dunkel der Männerporträts des Thomas Bernhard* (Frankfurt am Main: Fischer, 1980);

Martin Esslin, "Beckett and Bernhard: A Comparison," *Modern Austrian Literature*, 18, no. 2 (1985): 67-78;

Esslin, "Contemporary Austrian Playwrights," *Performing Arts Journal*, 3 (Spring/Summer 1978): 93-98;

Esslin, "A Drama of Disease and Derision: The Plays of Thomas Bernhard," *Modern Drama*, 23 (January 1981): 367-384;

Betty Falkenberg, "Thomas Bernhard," *Partisan Review*, 47, no. 2 (1980): 269-277;

Joseph Federico, "Millenarianism, Legitimation, and the National Socialist Universe in Thomas Bernhard's *Vor dem Ruhestand*," *Germanic Review*, 59 (Fall 1984): 142-148;

Ulrich Gaier, "*Ein Fest für Boris* oder das Ende der Hermeneutik," *Deutschunterricht*, 36 (1984): 31-40;

Herbert Gamper, *Thomas Bernhard* (Munich: Deutscher Taschenbuch Verlag, 1977);

Rüdiger Görner, "Thomas Bernhard," in *A Radical Stage*, edited by W. G. Sebald (Oxford: Berg, 1988), pp. 161-173;

Görner, "Thomas Bernhard as Dramatic Writer," *Neue Rundschau*, 99 (1988): 157-171;

Robert Gross, Jr., "The Perils of Performance in Thomas Bernhard's *Der Ignorant und der Wahnsinnige*," *Modern Drama*, 23 (January 1981): 385-392;

Götz Großklaus, "Österreichische Mythen: Zu zwei Filmen von Bernhard und Handke," *Lili*, 29 (1978): 40-62;

Bruno Hannemann, "Satirisches Psychogramm der Mächtigen: Zur Kunst der Provokation in Thomas Bernhards *Der Präsident*," *Maske und Kothurn*, 23 (1977): 147-158;

Hannemann, "Totentanz der Marionetten: Monotonie und Manier bei Thomas Bernhard," *Modern Austrian Literature*, 13, no. 2 (1980): 123-150;

Hannemann, "Vernunft und Irrfahrt: Zu Thomas Bernhards Komödie *Immanuel Kant*," *Maske und Kothurn*, 27 (1981): 346-359;

"*Heldenplatz*-Skandal: Stille Post," *Wochenpresse* (Vienna), 20 January 1989, pp. 43-44;

Benjamin Henrichs, "Heldenplatz, die Schlacht ums Wiener Burgtheater," *Die Zeit*, 21 October 1988, pp. 67-68;

Henrichs, "Ein Toter wird ermordet: *Elisabeth II.*, die letzte Thomas Bernhard Uraufführung," *Die Zeit*, 10 November 1989, p. 80;

Hannes Höller, "Die Form der Sprache und die Form der Gesellschaft: Zu Bernhards *Ein Fest für Boris*," *Acta Universitatis Wratislaviensis*, 26 (1976): 203-219;

Gitta Honegger, "Acoustic Masks: Strategies of Language in the Theater of Canetti, Bernhard, and Handke," *Modern Austrian Literature*, 18, no. 2 (1985): 57-66;

Honegger, "How German Is It? Thomas Bernhard at the Guthrie," *Performing Arts Journal*, 6, no. 1 (1981): 7-25;

Honegger, "Wittgenstein's Children: The Writings of Thomas Bernhard," *Theater*, Yale University, 15 (Winter 1983): 58-62;

Werner Jung, "Die Anstrengung des Erinnerns," *Neue Deutsche Hefte*, 35 (1988): 96-104;

Manfred Jurgensen, ed., *Bernhard: Annäherungen* (Bern & Munich: Francke, 1981);

Dieter Kafitz, "Die Problematisierung des individualistischen Menschenbildes im deutschsprachigen Theater der Gegenwart," *Basis*, 10 (1980): 93-126;

Ulrich Klingemann, "Begriff und Struktur des Komischen in Thomas Bernhards Dramen," *Wirkendes Wort*, 34 (1984): 78-87;

Gerhard Knapp, "Der Prozeß hat kaum begonnen: Thomas Bernhard und die Literaturwissenschaften," *Österreich in Geschichte und Gegenwart*, 15 (1971): 347-350;

Wolfgang Kralicek, "Sein Wille geschehe: Thomas Bernhards letzter Text sorgt posthum für Erregung," *Wochenpresse* (Vienna), 24 February 1989, pp. 42-43;

Renate Latimer, "Thomas Bernhard's Image of Woman," *Germanic Notes*, 8, no. 1 (1977): 25-27;

Hans Lietzau, "Zum Tod von Thomas Bernhard," *Theater heute*, 30 (April 1989): 17-20;

Caroline Markolin, *Die Großväter sind die Lehrer: Johannes Freumbichler und sein Enkel Thomas Bernhard* (Salzburg: Müller, 1988);

Terrill May, "Thomas Bernhard's *Der Ignorant und der Wahnsinnige*: An Analysis of Dramatic Style," *Modern Language Studies*, 9 (Winter 1978-1979): 60-72;

Siegfried Melchinger, "Das Material ist die Wahrheit der Welt: *Die Jagdgesellschaft*," *Theater heute*, 15 (June 1974): 8-9;

Franz N. Mennemeier, "Nachhall des absurden Dramas: Thomas Bernhard," in *Modernes deutsches Drama: Kritiken und Charakteristiken*, volume 2, edited by Mennemeier (Munich: Fink, 1975), pp. 307-320;

Michael Merschmeier, "Heldenspatz: Thomas Bernhards *Heldenplatz* am Wiener Burgtheater: Anmerkungen zu einem Theaterskandal," *Theater heute*, 29 (December 1988): 1-4;

Nicholas J. Meyerhofer, *Thomas Bernhard*, Köpfe des 20. Jahrhunderts, 104 (Berlin: Colloquium, 1985);

Rolf Michaelis, "Mein Salzburg—eine Todesstadt: Das Neueste vom Dauerkrach Thomas Bernhards mit den Salzburger Festspielen," *Die Zeit*, 29 August 1975, p. 33;

Modern Austrian Literature, special Bernhard issue, 21, nos. 3/4 (1988);

Ingrid Petrasch, *Die Konstitution von Wirklichkeit in der Prosa Thomas Bernhards* (Frankfurt am Main: Lang, 1987);

Alfred Pittertschatscher, ed., *Literarisches Kolloquium Linz '84 Thomas Bernhard*, Schriftenreihe literarisches Kolloquium Linz, 1 (Linz: Land Oberösterreich, 1985);

Henning Rischbieter, "Salzburg/Strehler/Bernhard: Die Festspielkrise," *Theater heute*, 15 (September 1974): 31-36;

Amity Schlaes, "Thomas Bernhard and the German Literary Scene," *New Criterion*, 5 (January 1982): 26-32;

Wendelin Schmidt-Dengler, *Der Übertreibungskünstler: Studien zu Thomas Bernhard*, revised edition (Vienna: Sonderzahl, 1989);

Schmidt-Dengler and Martin Huber, eds., *Statt Bernhard: Über Misanthropie im Werk Thomas Bernhards* (Vienna: Edition S, 1987);

Helmut Schödel, "Wenn ihr nicht brav seid, kommt der Bernhard: Ohlsdorf nach dem Tod des Dichters," *Die Zeit*, 11 August 1989, pp. 15-16;

Zdenko Škreb, "Weltbild und Form bei Thomas Bernhard," in *Literatur aus Österreich, österreichische Literatur*, edited by Karl Konrad Polheim (Bonn: Bouvier, 1981), pp. 145-166;

Bernhard Sorg, *Thomas Bernhard*, Autorenbücher, 7 (Munich: Beck, 1977);

Hilde Spiel, "Das Dunkel ist Licht genug: Die Salzburger Festspiele 1972," *Theater heute*, 13 (September 1972): 8-14;

Botho Strauß, "Komödie aus Todesangst: Thomas Bernhard *Ein Fest für Boris* in Berlin," *Theater heute*, 11 (August 1970): 30-32;

Text und Kontext, special Bernhard issue, 14 (1987);

text + kritik, special Bernhard issue, 43 (1974);

Erika Tunner, "Absolutheitsstreben oder Vernichtungsdrang," *Revue d'Allemagne*, 8 (October/December 1976): 584-600;

Tunner, "Thematik der Regression bei Thomas Bernhard," *Austriaca* (Rouen), 7 (November 1978): 23-36;

Albrecht Weber, "Wittgensteins Gestalt und Theorie und ihre Wirkung im Werk Thomas Bernhards," *Österreich in Geschichte und Literatur*, 25 (1981): 86-104;

Ernst Wendt, "Krankheit als musikalisches Problem," *Theater heute*, 13 (September 1972): 33-34;

Benno von Wiese, "Thomas Bernhard," in *Otium et Negotium*, edited by Folke Sandgren (Stockholm: Kungl, 1972), pp. 632-646.

Richard Billinger

(20 July 1890 - 7 June 1965)

Michael Mitchell
University of Stirling

PLAY PRODUCTIONS: *Das Spiel vom Knecht*, Vienna, Konzerthaus, 14 October 1924;

Das Perchtenspiel, Salzburg, Salzburg Festival, 26 July 1928;

Rauhnacht, Munich, Kammerspiele, 10 October 1931;

Das Verlöbnis, Rottach am Tegernsee, Ludwig-Ganghofer-Bühne, 12 August 1932;

Lob des Landes, Leipzig, Altes Theater, 25 January 1933;

Rosse, Berlin, Staatstheater, 1 March 1933;

Stille Gäste, Leipzig, Altes Theater, 5 December 1933;

Die Hexe von Passau, Augsburg and Regensburg, Staatstheater, 13 November 1935;

Die Windsbraut, Gießen, Staatstheater, 4 October 1937;

Der Gigant, Berlin, Staatstheater, 21 October 1937;

Am hohen Meer, Berlin, Staatstheater, 16 February 1939;

Melusine, Leipzig, Altes Theater, 13 October 1941;

Das Spiel vom Erasmus Grasser, Munich, Alter Rathaussaal, 12 September 1942;

Die Fuchsfalle, Munich, Bayrisches Staatsschauspiel; Hamburg, Schauspielhaus; Linz, Landestheater, 23 October 1942;

Der Galgenvogel, Munich, Bayrisches Staatstheater, 7 December 1942;

Das Haus, Linz, Landestheater, 21 June 1949;

Traube in der Kelter, Vienna, Burgtheater, 16 June 1951;

Das nackte Leben, Hamburg, Schauspielhaus, 18 December 1951;

Ein Tag wie alle, Mannheim, Nationaltheater, 27 March 1952;

Der Plumpsack, Munich, Bayrisches Staatstheater, 17 November 1954;

Das Augsburger Jahrtausendspiel, Augsburg, Freilichttheater am Roten Tor, 2 July 1955;

Viktoria, Vienna, Akademietheater, 10 September 1955;

Richard Billinger

Donauballade, Vienna, Volkstheater, 31 August 1959;

Bauernpassion, Bad Hersfeld Festival, 9 July 1960;

Die Schafschur, Kaiserslautern, Staatstheater, 12 September 1964.

BOOKS: *Lob Gottes* (Vienna: Haybach, 1922);

Über die Äcker: Gedichte (Berlin: Rowohlt, 1923);

Grete Wiesenthal und ihre Schule: Gedichte (Vienna: Haybach, 1923);

Das Perchtenspiel: Tanz- und Zauberspiel vom törichten Bauern, von der Windsbraut und den Heiligen, in einem Akte (Leipzig: Insel, 1928);

Gedichte (Leipzig: Insel, 1929); revised and enlarged as *Sichel am Himmel: Der Gedichte dritte, vermehrte Auflage* (Leipzig: Insel, 1931);

Die Asche des Fegefeuers: Eine Dorfkindheit (Munich: Müller, 1931);

Rosse; *Rauhnacht: Zwei Dramen* (Leipzig: Insel, 1931);

Zwei Spiele: Spiel vom Knechte; Reise nach Ursprung (Munich: Langen-Müller, 1932);

Lob des Landes: Komödie (Munich: Langen-Müller, 1933);

Der Pfeil im Wappen: Gedichte (Munich: Langen-Müller, 1933);

Das Verlöbnis: Schauspiel (Munich: Langen-Müller, 1933);

Stille Gäste: Komödie (Berlin: Fischer, 1934);

Das Tagewerk: Chorzyklus mit Soli und Orchester, music by A. Piechler (Berlin: Transmare, 1934);

Das Schutzengelhaus: Roman (Berlin: Fischer, 1934);

Die Hexe von Passau: Schauspiel in sechs Aufzügen und einem Vorspiel (Berlin: Fischer, 1935);

Lehen aus Gottes Hand: Roman (Berlin: Keil, 1935);

Nachtwache: Lieder und Gedichte (Berlin: Fischer, 1935);

Der Gigant: Schauspiel (Berlin: Fischer, 1937);

Das verschenkte Leben (Berlin: Fischer, 1937);

Am hohen Meer: Schauspiel in fünf Aufzügen (Berlin: Bloch, 1939);

Die Windsbraut: Oper, music by Winfried Zillig (Mainz: Schott, 1941);

Die Hexe von Passau: Oper in vier Bildern, music by Ottmar Gerster (Mainz: Schott, 1941);

Drei Dramen: Gabriele Dambrone; *Melusine*; *Die Fuchsfalle* (Vienna: Andermann, 1942);

Holder Morgen: Lieder und Gedichte (Vienna: Andermann, 1942);

Paracelsus: Ein Salzburger Festspiel (Vienna: Andermann, 1943);

Das Spiel vom Erasmus Grasser: Eine Münchener Legende (Vienna: Andermann, 1943);

Das Haus: Spiel in drei Akten (Munich: Desch, 1949?);

Das nackte Leben: Schauspiel in vier Aufzügen (Vienna: Braumüller, 1953);

Lobgesang: Gedichte (Linz: Kulturamt der Stadt Linz, 1953);

Ein Strauß Rosen: Erzählung (Vienna & Stuttgart: Wancura, 1954);

Das Augsburger Jahrtausendspiel (Augsburg: Industrie- und Handelskammer, 1955);

Gesammelte Werke, 12 volumes, edited by Heinz Gerstinger (Graz & Vienna: Stiasny, 1955-1960);

Würfelspiel, edited by Viktor Suchy (Graz & Vienna: Stiasny, 1960);

Gesammelte Werke, edited by Wilhelm Bortenschlager (volumes 1-5, Wels: Kellner & Pliseis; volumes 6-8, Wels: Ovilava-Libri, 1979-1984).

OTHER: "Der Altar: Erzählung," in *Buch des Dankes für Hans Carossa* (Leipzig: Insel, 1928), pp. 64-74;

"Triumph des Gotles," in *Erzähler unserer Zeit*, edited by R. Ramlow (Berlin: Franke, 1934);

Alfred Kubin, *Schemen: 60 Köpfe aus einer verklungenen Zeit*, foreword by Billinger (Königsberg: Kanter, 1943);

Wir reisen nach Oberösterreich, contributions by Billinger (Linz: Oberösterreichischer Landesverlag, 1959).

Richard Billinger's peasant background is reflected in the settings and themes of his best plays, which conjure up the powerful elemental forces that he saw as still present in peasant life. These forces are revealed in Christian images and pagan myths and can be both life-giving and savagely destructive. The Nazis, possibly influenced by the saccharine film versions of his plays, promoted him as a Blut und Boden (blood and soil) writer. Although this designation misrepresented his work, he accepted the commissions and honors it brought; and after World War II he had to endure the suspicion his reputation caused.

Billinger was born on 20 July 1890 to Alois and Maria Billinger (née Pucher), farmers who also ran a small shop in the little town of Sankt Marienkirchen bei Schärding in Upper Austria. Originally intended for the priesthood, he was moved to a state high school when his lack of vocation became apparent. In 1910 he went to the University of Innsbruck, but in 1912 he began the life of a wandering student. In Kiel, Berlin, and Vienna his "studies" were carried on in the coffeehouses as much as in the lecture halls. He was called up for military service in 1914 but was released because of a deformed finger. During and after World War I he lived mainly in Vienna.

In these early years Billinger had no clear idea of what career he wanted to pursue; at one point he even thought of becoming a circus strong man. His literary career began with poetry; but he had an aversion to writing his poems down, feeling that once they were on the page they no longer truly belonged to him. In 1920 the dancer Grete Wiesenthal was sitting behind him in a Vienna café and overheard him reciting his verses to himself. She and her husband, Erwin Lang, introduced Billinger to Hugo von Hofmannsthal, who encouraged him to develop his talent as a dramatist. Billinger's second volume of poems, *Über die Äcker* (Over the Fields, 1923), was dedicated to Wiesenthal.

His first play to be performed was *Das Spiel vom Knecht* (The Laborer's Play; published, 1932), which was produced in Vienna in 1924, the year he was awarded the Literature Prize of the City of Vienna. It is written in a style that has been called his "woodcut manner," with short, rhymed lines in irregular rhythms, crude characterization, and violent action. Rosa, a beautiful peasant girl, is wooed by a laborer with whom she is in love, a forester who can offer her security, and an old farmer who can offer her wealth. She goes to live with the forester but continues to see the laborer, who shoots the forester. She then marries the rich farmer, but in the end elemental passion proves stronger than material greed: she strangles her husband and goes off with the laborer. As in the plays that were to follow, strong passions and the physical violence they generate are neither approved of nor condemned; they are portrayed as facts of life.

Das Perchtenspiel (The Play of the Sprites, published, 1928) was commissioned by Hofmannsthal, who asked for a play that could alternate with his own *Jedermann* (1911; translated as *The Salzburg Everyman*, 1911) at the Salzburg Festival. It was produced there by Max Reinhardt in 1928, and in that year Billinger moved to Salzburg. *Das Perchtenspiel* contains much movement and dance, reflecting the influence of Wiesenthal, who took the role of the Perchtin, the beautiful sprite. Her daring costume—one breast was exposed—aroused the anger of the bishop, who had the play, which was performed outside the cathedral, closed. The central figure, Peter, is a peasant farmer who has tired of life on the land and gone out into the world. At the start of the play he returns to the farm, but he cannot settle back into the old life. He seduces the Perchtin, then abandons her for his former wife. In revenge, a band of nature demons sets fire to Peter's farm. When Peter decides to sell the land and stock, his grandfather kills him with an ax. The play ends on a positive note: the maid gives birth to Peter's child, and Peter's mother accepts

it as a token of new life. A procession of saints appears and blesses the child. The language of *Das Perchtenspiel* is that of all Billinger's plays up to *Rosse* (Horses; published, 1931; performed, 1933): it is powerful, concise, and concrete, making poetic and not naturalistic use of dialect; there is much internal rhyme within the prose, giving the country folk a pithy, sententious mode of expression; and frequent use is made of verse in songs, hymns, prayers.

Billinger's next play, *Rauhnacht* (Yule Night, 1931), is set on 23 December, the evening on which, in the area of Upper Austria from which Billinger came, peasants dress up in grotesque masks representing nature demons and whirl around the villages in a wild dance, finishing with a bonfire. Simon, who has returned to the village after many years in Africa, and Kreszenz, a girl who has been at school in the city, observe the rural customs as outsiders. The saturnalia release their sexuality in a sadomasochistic outburst that culminates with Simon murdering Kreszenz and setting fire to his own house. By exposure to civilization, Simon and Kreszenz have become "denatured"; thus, for them the excitement of the Rauhnacht becomes twisted into a destructive perversion. The wide gap between the well-off and the poor farmers is a frequent motif in Billinger; arrogance and hard-heartedness are as common as humility and charity, and violence is always lurking below the surface and threatening to break out. (Billinger's first title for the play was "Verfluchtes Dorf " [Cursed Village].)

Rauhnacht was one of Billinger's most widely performed plays. The first production, directed in Munich by Otto Falkenberg and starring Käthe Gold, Ewald Balser, and Therese Giese, was a wild success. It brought Billinger the Kleist Prize in 1932 (he shared it with Else Lasker-Schüler). That year he moved from Salzburg to Munich.

About the same time as *Rauhnacht* Billinger wrote *Rosse*, which was given a reading in the Residenz-Theater in Munich in 1931, although it was not produced onstage until 1933 in Berlin; that same year it became Billinger's first play to be produced at the Burgtheater in Vienna. The play examines the mechanization of agriculture and the destruction of old ways that such progress entails. The protagonist is a stableman whose life centers around the horses in his care; for him, the new machinery is a menace that undermines his whole existence. He opposes the farm owners at a public meeting that threatens to turn into revolution as landless laborers and villagers

Scene from a performance of Billinger's Rauhnacht *at the Staatsschauspielhaus in Berlin*

who had gone to the city and been thrown out of work by technology gather in his support. But in a mixture of pride and hopelessness, he draws back from physical resistance. He squanders his life savings on a feast for the poor, and the act ends in an orgy of music, song, and dance as he goes off to hang himself.

Billinger's autobiographical novel *Die Asche des Fegefeuers: Eine Dorfkindheit* (The Ashes of Purgatory: A Village Childhood, 1931) contains the story of his next play, *Das Verlöbnis* (The Betrothal; performed, 1932; published, 1933). It is a tale, presented with a mixture of bloody horror and dark, brooding lyricism, of sexual violence culminating in a double murder. As in *Das Spiel vom Knecht*, though not quite as successfully this time, Billinger presents the violence with which elemental passion erupts and tries neither to condemn nor to glorify it.

Billinger's next two plays—*Lob des Landes* (Praise of Rural Life, 1933) and *Stille Gäste* (Silent Visitors; performed, 1933; published, 1934)—are comedies in which the humor derives largely from the contrast between city ways and rural life. Thus, these plays are comic variations on the basic themes in his early plays—in *Lob des Landes* there is even a comic attempted murder involv-

ing a poisoned shaving bowl. The central character of *Stille Gäste*, Hedwig Bachstelzer, is a type Billinger returned to repeatedly: the plain, even ugly girl who radiates inner beauty. She is contrasted on the one hand with her mother's materialism and aggressive sexuality and on the other with the sophistication of the shallow city flirt who tries to seduce the man Hedwig loves. The "silent visitors" of the title are ghosts in a baroque hunting lodge who perform a play within the play, acting out a tragedy from the past, and are finally exorcised by the victory of Hedwig's love. Billinger loved to use such devices, and his plays are full of ballad singers, mummers, strolling players, dancers, and the like. *Stille Gäste* was said to be Billinger's own favorite play. It is rather sentimental and has a meandering plot, but it also has great charm.

In 1935, for reasons which have never been established, Billinger was arrested. His friends persuaded Heinrich Himmler and Hermann Göring to intervene, and he was released, apparently having promised never to comment on the matter. That year he moved to Berlin, where he rented a room in the house of the widow of the publisher Samuel Fischer.

Die Hexe von Passau (The Witch of Passau, 1935) is the first of Billinger's historical plays. The "witch" is the leader of a troupe of strolling players who want to perform in Passau a play about Mary Magdalene. She falls afoul of the religious authorities because of her profession and of the secular authorities because she hides a peasant who killed a soldier for trying to requisition his corn. The count is bewitched by her beauty, frees her when she is arrested by the vicar-general, allows her to perform her play, and releases the leaders of the peasant rebellion. When she is retaken by the religious authorities and condemned to be burned as a witch, the count leads the peasants in their revolt.

Der Gigant (The Giant, 1937) was directed in Berlin by Jürgen Fehling and was an enormous success. It is Billinger's first play to be set outside his native Upper Austria, taking place in Moravia and Prague, but the peasant values that underlie it are much the same as in his earlier works. These values are embodied in the massive figure of Melchior Dub (*dub* is Czech for oak). His daughter, Anuschka, is fascinated by the modern world of the city and runs away to Prague, where she is seduced by her cousin Tony, a shallow ladies' man. She returns home but is rejected by her father. She goes off to seek her death in the marshes that are said to house a demon and that Dub has refused to allow a city company to drain. The play does not present a simplistic contrast between the values of country life and the decadence of the modern world: for example, the engineer Leidwein is a positive figure, while the greatest contrast to the vital Dub is his feeble neighbor, Pelikan. And Dub himself is not an unambiguous figure; his vitality has a demonic aspect that can destroy weaker characters. In the final scene, where he greets his prodigal daughter with massive silence, he is not admirable but has the inevitability of a natural phenomenon.

Der Gigant was treated by directors not only as a portrayal of peasant virtues but as a celebration of German values threatened by the surrounding Slav peoples. This interpretation was even more pronounced in the film version, *Die goldene Stadt* (The Golden City, 1942). Directed by Veit Harlan, it was the second German color film and the most popular film during the Third Reich. It adapted Billinger's play to the more superficial clichés of Blut und Boden art—the good characters are, for example, given German names, the bad ones Czech—and established Billinger's reputation in the Third Reich as well

as bringing him sixteen thousand Reichsmarks for the film rights. Billinger was not a Nazi, and the authorities felt uncomfortable with the unsentimental portrayal of the eruption of elemental forces in some of his other plays; but he allowed his works to be used by the Nazis and earned huge sums of money for doing so. The published version of his 1942 festival play *Das Spiel vom Erasmus Grasser* (The Play of Erasmus Grasser, 1943) says, "Das Spielwurde . . . im Auftrag des Kulturamtes der Hauptstadt der Bewegung geschaffen" (the play was commissioned by the cultural department of the Capital of the [Nazi] Movement [Munich]). One cannot get much closer to being an official Nazi artist. His supporters claim that he was a victim of his own naiveté; if so, it was a naiveté that brought him an income of more than seventy thousand Reichsmarks per year.

Until this point all of Billinger's plays had been peopled by rather similar rough-hewn characters subject to violent elemental passions. With the next three plays—*Am hohen Meer* (By the Open Sea, 1939), *Melusine* (performed, 1941; published, 1942), and *Die Fuchsfalle* (The Fox Trap, 1942)—he moved into Arthur Schnitzler's territory of erotic entanglements among the middle classes, though these plays lack Schnitzler's all-pervading sense of death in the background.

Gabriele Dambrone, the heroine of *Amhohen Meer*, is one of the most attractive of Billinger's put-upon females. She is a sensitive seamstress with a mind receptive to higher things, similar in type to Christine in Schnitzler's *Liebelei* (A Casual Affair; performed, 1895; published, 1896; translated as *The Reckoning*, 1907). She rejects an offer of marriage from a dependable pharmacist and has an affair with a fashionable artist who eventually returns to his wife and children. The ending is not tragic: through the sufferings of her sentimental education Gabriele has matured emotionally so that she is now ready to become the actress she had wanted to be before she became involved with the painter. The play concentrates on mood rather than action and is pleasant rather than deeply moving. There is nothing to replace the elemental power of the early plays, and *Amhohen Meer* has little to offer beyond the charm of the main character.

Melusine, set in a lakeside fishing village that has become a holiday resort, lacks even charm. The main figures are pale clichés, and the attempted intertwining of two strands—the efforts of a local inhabitant to buy back his family home and the erotic entanglements of the woman who now owns it, her daughter, and a summer visitor— does not work. The erotic triangle, in particular, seems to run its course rather mechanically.

Ownership of property is more closely tied up with the love triangle in the comedy *Die Fuchsfalle*. A country estate has been left to Dr. Mauch on the condition that he live on the estate and practice as a country doctor; otherwise the estate falls to the testator's illegitimate son, Fürst. When Mauch eventually decides to accept a professorship in Vienna, he discovers he has also lost his wife to Fürst. Fürst is the true owner of the estate not only because of the conditions of the will but because he belongs there in a way the city academic never can. The plot is more integrated than that in *Melusine*, but the characters' motivation is unconvincing. An orgiastic dance at the end, performed by misshapen figures from the region gathered together by Mauch for research purposes, is grotesquely out of place, as if a page from an early Billinger play had been bound in by mistake.

Billinger had returned to Munich in 1940; when the bombing raids on the city became more frequent, he moved to the village of Niederpöcking on Lake Starnberg, which was to remain his home until his death. In 1942 he was awarded the Literature Prize of the City of Munich, which, in the same year, commissioned the festival play *Das Spiel vom Erasmus Grasser*. Grasser was the sculptor who, toward the end of the fifteenth century, carved the *Morisken* (Moorish dancers) for the Munich Town Hall; the figures are still seen as one of the emblems of the city. The play makes few concessions to the tastes of the Nazi rulers. It is, admittedly, written in Billinger's rather rough-hewn, irregular, and highly expressive "woodcut-style" verse, which fit in with official notions of Germanic art; but it shows the burghers of Munich as intolerant of outsiders, including Grasser and the Moorish dancers he uses as his models. The play is set in a time of plague, for which the citizens blame Grasser and the Moors. Grasser, condemned to execution, is saved by the allegorical figure of Death, who confesses that he was the one who brought in the plague.

The echoes of *Jedermann* are clear; it is not, therefore, surprising that Billinger was asked to write a play for the 1943 Salzburg Festival to replace the Hofmannsthal work, which had been banned because Hofmannsthal was of part Jewish ancestry. For his subject Billinger chose Para-

celsus, the pioneer of the use of drugs in medicine, who settled in Salzburg. Paracelsus's mission is to fight death. He realizes that everyone comes to death in the end, but he distinguishes between a "good" death, which crowns a fulfilled life, and an "evil" death, which prevents a person from achieving such a life. *Paracelsus* (1943) never reached the stage, since in 1943 the Salzburg Festival was canceled for the duration of the war. In that year Billinger was awarded the Raimund Prize.

Billinger had great difficulty in reestablishing himself in the theater after the war, and he never recaptured the position he had enjoyed in the 1930s. In *Das Haus* (The House, 1949), he attempts to give current political developments symbolic representation. The eponymous house is three hundred years old, the home of a patrician family of glassmakers. It symbolizes the solid virtues of tradition and selfless loyalty to family. Those values are confirmed when the latest in the line finally sees through the fashionable fiancée he has brought back from Vienna and marries his distant cousin, who has devoted herself unselfishly to the house. The modern world that threatens to impinge on the bourgeois idyll is represented by a caricature Russian prisoner of war and by the hero's brother, a feckless wanderer who ended up in the United States and now returns as an officer in the American army. It is made clear that there is no place in the house for the newfangled ways the brother represents. In *Das Haus* what Billinger avoids saying is more interesting than the statement he is trying to make: there is no mention of fascism, hardly even of the war. The play's shallow pretense that Austria can go on its way as if nothing had happened did not endear it even to its Austrian audience, and it was not widely performed.

Although Billinger's productivity continued unabated, hardly any of his works made any impression on the stage of the 1950s. *Traube in der Kelter* (Grape in the Winepress; performed, 1951; published in Billinger's *Gesammelte Werke* [Collected Works], 1960) portrays the sensual love of Margarete Maultasch, the fourteenth-century "ugly duchess of the Tirol," for a local innkeeper as a receptiveness to deep natural forces and an expression of her closeness to her native land. Some of the scenes have Billinger's old power, but the plot, in which the innkeeper is revealed as having murdered one of Margarete's noble suitors, is arbitrary and unconvincing.

The central character of *Ein Tag wie alle* (A Day Like Any Other; performed, 1952; published in *Gesammelte Werke*, 1960), Hanna Amon, has the gentle, self-effacing charm of several of Billinger's other heroines. She devotes her life to her work as a schoolteacher and to her brother, Thomas. He is seduced by the sophisticated Frau Dunckl, who mocks him when he asks her to marry him. In his fury he is going to kill her, but Hanna does the deed for him. When she returns from prison seven years later she overhears Thomas arguing with his wife and father-in-law, who want to send her away, and she leaves without being seen.

Das nackte Leben (Bare Life; performed, 1951; published, 1953) is an attempt to re-create the world of *Das Perchtenspiel*. A party for beggars and Gypsies is given by a mysterious peddler; the bustle of grotesque and malformed figures at the beggars' ball has some of Billinger's old vigor, but the action is sensational and sentimental. A blind young man is struck by lightning and recovers his sight; the ugly girl who has been looking after him and who is in love with him is given a beautiful wax mask by the peddler, and when she takes it off her inner beauty has become manifest in her outward appearance.

Der Plumpsack (The Tub of Lard; performed, 1954; published in *Gesammelte Werke*, 1960) is a weak and watery chronicle from the time of the Peasant War; *Viktoria* (performed, 1955; published in *Gesammelte Werke*, 1984) is a similarly tedious, clichéd sequence of scenes taken from a story by Knut Hamsun of the unfulfilled love of a rich girl and a miller's son who becomes a poet. Billinger's loss of dramatic power came to a head with *Donauballade* (Danube Ballad; published in *Gesammelte Werke*, 1960), which was panned by the critics when it was directed by Leon Epp in Vienna in 1959. Set in an old inn on the Danube close to the Hungarian border, it deals with the theme of the Iron Curtain through crude mockery of Communist sympathizers in the West and demonization of the East.

Upper Austria awarded Billinger a pension for life in 1954 and subsidized the publication of his collected works, which began to appear in 1955. In 1960 he received the Grillparzer Prize and was elected to the Bavarian Academy of Sciences, but a production the same year of *Der Gigant* by Heinz Hilpert at the Theater in der Josefstadt in Vienna was another flop. The title of professor awarded by the state in 1962 was a small consolation.

There was one final success, although it could not revive his fortunes. *Bauernpassion* (Peasant Passion; published in *Gesammelte Werke*, 1979) was performed in 1960 at the Bad Hersfeld Festival. An effective short play, it exists in various versions, including one for radio. During the Peasant Wars the peasant leader has wandering players perform their passion play before the townspeople he has condemned to be executed. His intention is to make the townsfolk repent their exploitation of the peasants before they die, but he is himself so moved by the play that he spares them.

When Billinger died on 7 June 1965 he left many unperformed and unpublished plays. Some have been published, thanks to the efforts of Wilhelm Bortenschlager, but they are unlikely to reach the stage. His reputation rests on powerful early plays such as *Das Perchtenspiel* and *Rauhnacht*. Imaginative multimedia productions could secure Billinger the niche in theatrical history that has been obscured by his involvement with the Nazis and by his later repetitions, which almost amount to self-parody.

References:

Klaus Amann, *Der Anschluß österreichischer Schriftsteller an das Dritte Reich* (Frankfurt am Main: Athenäum, 1988);

Wolfgang Johanes Bekh, *Dichter der Heimat: 10 Porträts aus Bayern und Österreich* (Regensburg: Pustet, 1984);

Heinz Gerstinger, "Richard Billinger als Dramatiker," Ph.D. dissertation, Vienna University, 1947;

Karl Maria Grimme, "Der Fall Billinger und seine Aspekte," *Wort in der Zeit*, 5, no. 10 (1959): 20-23;

Edith Rabenstein, *Dichtung zwischen Tradition und Moderne: Richard Billinger. Untersuchungen zur Rezeptionsgeschichte und zum Werk* (Bern: Lang, 1988);

Peter Roessler, *Studien zur Auseinandersetzung mit Faschismus und Krieg in der österreichischen Literatur der Nachkriegszeit und der fünfziger Jahre* (Cologne: Pahl-Rugenstein, 1987), pp. 211-224;

Theodor Sapper, " 'Rustikaler' Expressionismus bei Johannes Lindner und Richard Billinger," in his *Alle Glocken der Erde* (Vienna: Europa, 1974), pp. 132-138;

Viktor Suchy, "Bauer, Hirt und Knecht: Ihre Mythisierung bei drei österreichischen Lyrikern der Zwischenkriegszeit. Ein Interpretations-versuch," in *Marginalien zur poetischen Welt: Festschrift Robert Mühlher zum 60. Geburtstag*, edited by Alois Eder, Hellmuth Himmel, and Alfred Kracher (Berlin: Duncker & Humblot, 1971), pp. 427-480.

Papers:
Richard Billinger's manuscripts are at the Adalbert Stifter Institute in Linz and at Billinger's house in Niederpöcking.

Wolfgang Borchert

(20 May 1921 - 20 November 1947)

Albert E. Gurganus
The Citadel

See also the Borchert entry in *DLB 69: Contemporary German Fiction Writers, First Series*.

PLAY PRODUCTIONS: *Draußen vor der Tür*, Hamburg, Hamburger Kammerspiele, 21 November 1947.

BOOKS: *Laterne, Nacht und Sterne: Gedichte um Hamburg* (Hamburg: Hamburgische Bücherei, 1946);
Die Hundeblume: Erzählungen aus unseren Tagen (Hamburg: Hamburgische Bücherei, 1947);
Draußen vor der Tür: Ein Stück, das kein Theater spielen und kein Publikum sehen will (Hamburg & Stuttgart: Rowohlt, 1947);
An diesem Dienstag: Neunzehn Geschichten (Hamburg & Stuttgart: Rowohlt, 1947);
Hundeblumen-Geschichten, edited by Martin F. Cordes (Horgen: Holunderpresse, 1948);
Im Mai, im Mai schrie der Kuckuck (Leipzig: Akademie für Grafik und Buchkunst, 1948);
Das Gesamtwerk, edited, with a biographical afterword, by Bernhard Meyer-Marwitz (Hamburg & Stuttgart: Rowohlt, 1949)—includes "Dann gibt es nur eins!";
Draußen vor der Tür und ausgewählte Erzählungen, afterword by Heinrich Böll (Hamburg: Rowohlt, 1956);
Schischyphusch oder Der Kellner meines Onkels (Stuttgart: Druckspiegel-Verlag, 1959);
Die traurigen Geranien und andere Geschichten aus dem Nachlaß, edited by Peter Rühmkorf (Reinbek: Rowohlt, 1962); translated by Keith Hamnet as *The Sad Geraniums and*

Other Stories (New York: Ecco Press, 1973; London: Calder & Boyars, 1973).

Editions in English: *The Man Outside: The Prose Works of Wolfgang Borchert*, translated by David Porter (Norfolk, Conn.: New Directions, 1952; London: Calder & Boyars, 1966);
Selected Short Stories, edited by A. W. Hornsey (Oxford: Pergamon Press / New York: Macmillan, 1964);
Selected Readings, edited by Anna Otten (New York: Holt, Rinehart & Winston, 1973).

RADIO: *Draußen vor der Tür*, Nordwestdeutscher Rundfunk, 13 February 1947.

In midwinter 1947 a bedridden actor emerged from near obscurity to become the leading voice of postwar literature, his cry of existential despair a play entitled *Draußen vor der Tür* (Outside the Door; published, 1947; translated as *The Man Outside*, 1952). Its broadcast by the Nordwestdeutscher Rundfunk (Northwest German Radio) on 13 February aroused public acclaim and the interest of producers and publishers throughout Germany. The author, terminally ill from deprivations suffered at the Russian front and in Nazi prisons, died nine months later in Basel, Switzerland, one day before the play's stage premiere in Hamburg. He was twenty-six.

Wolfgang Borchert was born in Hamburg on 20 May 1921, the only child of Fritz and Hertha Salchow Borchert. His father, a public-school teacher in the middle-class Eppendorf quarter, was cultured and reserved, an enlight-

Wolfgang Borchert in 1939

ened and permissive parent. Hertha Borchert, author of popular stories in the dialect of the north German provinces, read regularly from her works for Radio Hamburg. Their circle included prominent journalists, artists, and actors.

Although Borchert showed early promise as a student, he became increasingly disaffected with school life, particularly with the youth organizations that proliferated after the Nazis came to power in 1933. An outsider, Borchert reveled in his eccentricity. His few friends shared with him a disdain for conformity, a penchant for extravagant dress, and an interest in theater. At fifteen he was writing copious verse, which his father, a collaborator on the Dadaist journal *Rote Erde* (Red Earth), critiqued and corrected. Friedrich

Hölderlin and Rainer Maria Rilke served as Borchert's models; for a while he signed his name Wolff Maria Borchert in homage to the latter. His first published poem, "Reiterlied" (Rider's Song), thirteen bombastic lines containing twelve exclamation points, appeared in the *Hamburger Anzeiger* (Hamburg Advertiser) in 1938. That same year Borchert began a cycle of three plays that evince his aversion to the fascist regime: the dramas "Yorick, der Narr" (Yorick, the Jester) and "Granvella! Der schwarze Kardinal" (Granvella! The Black Cardinal); and a black comedy, "Der Käseladen" (The Cheese Shop), coauthored with his friend Günther Mackenthun. Each play deals with a tyrant's downfall. The manuscripts were located in private hands by Alexandre Marius de Sterio and discussed in his 1972 doctoral dissertation at the University of Paris.

In December 1938 Borchert withdrew from the Oberrealschule (vocational high school), hoping for a career as an actor. Skeptical of his prospects, his parents arranged an apprenticeship with the bookseller Heinrich Boysen. In Boysen's storeroom he found works by banned expressionists, including Georg Trakl and Gottfried Benn, copies of which he spirited out to be read and discussed in a literary circle he had organized. He began to study acting, at first without his parents' knowledge, under Helmuth Gmelin (to whom "Granvella!" is dedicated). For six months he rehearsed after work, wrote his plays and poetry, and planned with friends to open a little theater.

His first brush with the Gestapo came in April 1940: letters in which he had written of his love for Rilke had been passed to the secret police. In their ignorance the philistines suspected Borchert of having a homosexual relationship with someone named Rieke. After a night of questioning he was released. In fact, he had fallen in love with the daughter of Dr. C. H. Hager, an attorney and family friend. She politely rebuffed his affections, which he then turned toward others in rapid succession, unable to find the abiding love of which he read in Hölderlin's poems.

In December 1940 Borchert passed his stage test to be licensed as an actor. He left the bookshop to join the Landesbühne Osthannover (East Hannoverian Regional Theater), based in Lüneburg. The ninety-odd days he spent touring with the troupe, acting in comedies of manners to favorable reviews and cultivating a relationship with the actress Heidi Boyes, he would later term the happiest period of his life. His call-up to the army ended it abruptly. Assigned to the Third Armored Signal Reserve, he underwent training as a radioman during the summer and fall at Weimar-Lützendorf, where he chafed under the coarseness of his superiors and the indignities of barracks life.

His unit was sent to the Russian front in November 1941 to join fighting around Kalinin. Within weeks Borchert was suffering from jaundice. Early in 1942 he returned from guard duty with his left middle finger shot away. He maintained under interrogation that his weapon had discharged during a hand-to-hand struggle with a Soviet soldier who had surprised him. At the field hospital he contracted diphtheria and was transported to Germany to convalesce. In May he was formally charged with self-mutilation to avoid duty—an offense for which the punishment was death by firing squad—and placed in solitary confinement in Nuremberg to await court-martial. When the case came to trial three months later, Dr. Hager's skillful defense won Borchert's acquittal. He was nevertheless re-interned to face charges of subversion arising from letters that had come to light during the investigation of the first charge—letters in which he had impugned the Third Reich, the military, and the war. This time the verdict was guilty. The sentence of four months' imprisonment was commuted to six weeks and return to the front.

In December 1942, following his jail term and a temporary posting to Jena, Borchert rejoined his unit near Toropez as a messenger. Fighting and casualties were heavy, yet he was entrusted with only a flare pistol. It was evidently during this action that Borchert had the macabre duty of checking the dimensions of freshly dug graves by lying in them himself, an experience recounted in his short story "Jesus macht nicht mehr mit" (Jesus Won't Go Along with It Anymore), published in *Die Hundeblume* (The Dandelion, 1947). After a few weeks he was in quarantine at Smolensk with recurring jaundice, frostbite, and suspected typhus. He was granted leave in August 1943 and arrived in Hamburg to be horrified at the devastation wrought by Allied bombing: in ten nights in late July and early August half the city had been reduced to rubble. Much of his leave was spent at a bohemian cabaret where guests were welcome to read poetry and perform songs.

Back at Jena in October, Borchert was beset by fever and swelling of the liver; four years later a Swiss pathologist would diagnose the afflic-tion as progressive degeneration of the liver stemming from malnutrition. The medical officers declared him unfit for combat. He was to be assigned to a theater troupe entertaining at the front, but on 30 November, at a party celebrating his transfer, Borchert rashly parodied the crippled propaganda minister, Joseph Goebbels: "Das deutsche Volk kann ruhig sein, Lügen haben kurze Beine . . . " (The German people can rest assured that lies have short legs . . .). Denounced by an informant, he was arrested and charged with undermining national defense.

From January to September 1944 Borchert awaited trial in Berlin's Moabit Prison. This incarceration proved to be much worse than his earlier experience. Conditions were wretched. During bombing raids prisoners were left above in their cells while the guards went to shelters. After the attempt on Adolf Hitler's life on 20 July, Borchert became convinced that his fate as a political prisoner was bleak indeed. He read the works of William Shakespeare and Johann Wolfgang von Goethe and waited. Dr. Hager represented him at the trial on 4 September; pronounced guilty, Borchert was sentenced to nine months' imprisonment, reduced to four for time served. Germany's worsening military position resulted in the sentence being commuted, once again, to reassignment to the front, this time in the west.

In the spring of 1945 Borchert's company surrendered to the French near Frankfurt. While being transported to France, he escaped and began the trek of nearly four hundred miles through Allied lines to Hamburg. Perhaps recalling Hölderlin's walk from Bordeaux to Nürtingen, made in the grip of mental illness, Borchert feigned insanity to avoid detention by the Americans. He reached home on 10 May in a state of exhaustion.

His parents safe and their home intact, Borchert rested and sought to reestablish himself by playing in a cabaret. Together with several fellow thespians he founded a little theater called Die Komödie (Comedy), and with the photographer Rosemarie Clausen, whose romantic portraits of him stare up hauntingly from several works on Borchert, he planned a book celebrating the enduring port city. In November Borchert was asked by Gmelin to assist in directing Gotthold Ephraim Lessing's *Nathan der Weise* (1779; translated as *Nathan the Wise*, 1791) for the Hamburger Schauspielhaus (Hamburg Playhouse), but he was forced by intolerable pain to withdraw from the production. Doctors at two local hospitals were confounded by his symptoms. In late January 1946, despondent and further sickened by radiation treatments, he began to write short stories, a new medium for him, in his lucid hours. The first, "Die Hundeblume," was completed in a day. Confined to bed, the wan twenty-four-year-old based his story on an incident that had occurred during his confinement in Nuremberg: for plucking a flower he was permitted no exercise or contact with fellow prisoners for a week. Before his death twenty-two months later, Borchert, writing like John Keats with the urgency of mortality, would compose the nearly fifty stories and the single play that secure his position in German letters.

He was discharged on Easter 1946 from Saint Elizabeth's Hospital as a hopeless case with at most a year to live. On 30 April "Die Hundeblume" was published in the *Hamburger Freie Presse* (Hamburg Free Press). Working at home, Borchert continued to write stories, served as an editorial reader for Hermes Press, reviewed books for a local newspaper, and selected fourteen of his war poems for a volume entitled *Laterne, Nacht und Sterne* (Streetlamp, Night, and Stars), published in December. *Draußen vor der Tür* was written in eight febrile days in January. He subtitled it *Ein Stück, das kein Theater spielen und kein Publikum sehen will* (A Play that No Theater Wants to Perform and No Audience Wants to See), but after a private reading for friends, word of the play spread quickly. Ernst Schnabel, drama producer for the Nordwestdeutscher Rundfunk, arranged for the premiere broadcast on 13 February 1947. Hans Quest, to whom Borchert would dedicate the published version of the play, read the role of Beckmann. The debilitated author, at his parents' home in a district where electricity was rationed, could not hear the broadcast, which evoked immediate and overwhelming response. Letters from admirers, critics, and would-be publishers were followed by a host of pilgrims who came to meet the spokesman for "a betrayed generation."

In April the Hamburgische Bücherei published a collection of Borchert's stories under the title of the initial work, *Die Hundeblume*. Through the summer Borchert wrote more than twenty stories, mainly late at night, which his father would dutifully type each morning. As his condition worsened, friends and newfound patrons underwrote treatment at Saint Clara's Hospital in Basel in the hope that care in Switzerland would

be better than in devastated Hamburg. The passage by train was excruciating; the patient, however, suffered worse at Saint Clara's from homesickness, the austerity of the nuns, and the general hostility of the Swiss toward Germans. The success of his play—which was being rehearsed in Hamburg, Stuttgart, Heidelberg, Brunswick, Frankfurt, Munich, and Basel—and the frequent visits of devoted German émigrés and sympathetic Swiss were his consolation. In October Borchert wrote a final pacifist appeal, "Dann gibt es nur eins!" (Then There Is Only One Answer!; 1949), in which he admonishes everyone to say no to any future call to arms. He died at Saint Clara's on 20 November.

The day after Borchert's death the Hamburger Kammerspiele (Hamburg Intimate Theater) presented the stage premiere of *Draußen vor der Tür*, under the direction of Wolfgang Liebeneiner. Composed of a prologue, two preludes, and five scenes, the play treats in expressionist style the disquieting, familiar theme of a soldier's return to a home that bears little resemblance to what he left. The language is rich in Hamburg colloquialisms and in compounds of Borchert's own invention such as *hundehundemüde* (dogdog-tired), *Wasserleichenaspirant* (drowning victim aspirant), and *Märchenbuchliebergott* (fairy-tale-Heavenly-Father). It is a work of blackest despair; a fitting epigraph reflecting its timbre could well be lifted from scene 4: "Das soll ein Schrei sein, ein Aufschrei ihrer Herzen" (It should be a scream, a shriek from their hearts).

In a March 1947 letter Borchert had specified that there should be no pause between scenes but that scene changes be delineated by lighting, that there be no backdrop and only such props as were necessary to the action. The characters include God; Death; "die Elbe" (the River Elbe); "der Andere" (the other); "ein Mädchen" (a girl); "ihr Mann" (her husband); "ein Oberst" (a colonel); "ein Kabarett direktor" (a cabaret director); Frau Kramer; and Beckmann, the protagonist, described in the dramatis personae as "einer von denen" (one of those). A brief prose prologue states the play's premise and introduces Beckmann, a haggard, limping twenty-five-year-old veteran exhibiting multiple symptoms of what today would be called posttraumatic stress disorder. He has just returned from a Russian prison camp to Hamburg, under whose rubble his infant son lies buried, to find his wife living with another man. The first prelude opens with Death in his guise as a bloated

"Beerdigungsunternehmer" (undertaker) observing Beckmann's attempt at suicide by leaping into the Elbe. Reflecting on the meaninglessness of death in an age when death has been trivialized by its sheer volume, the undertaker is surprised by an old man, weeping piteously. It is God, who concedes that he has been superseded by Death. In a second prelude, "Der Traum" (The Dream), Beckmann converses with the River Elbe. She mocks his wonder that she is not the pale, young Ophelia type into whose arms he believed he was casting himself but rather a worldly-wise old fishwife. Maternally, she tells him to return only when he has really suffered, then spits him onto the beach at Blankenese.

Scene 1 begins with Beckmann lying in the sand at the river's edge. A presence appears in the dark whom Beckmann recognizes as the other, "die Stimme, die jeder kennt . . . der Optimist, der an den Bösen das Gute sieht" (the voice that everyone knows . . . the optimist who sees the good in the bad). Although Beckmann orders him to leave, the other remains to question gently Beckmann's suicide attempt. While Beckmann contends with his alter ego—his instinct to survive—a girl approaches. She helps Beckmann rise and suggests that he come home with her. As they leave together, the other remarks to the audience, like the chorus in Greek tragedy, on the effect of shapely breasts and soft curls on one bent on self-destruction.

The second scene unfolds in the girl's room. Flirting easily, calling Beckmann "Fisch" (Fish)—the ancient phallic symbol—she removes his cumbersome spectacles issued for wear beneath a gas mask. She presents him with dry clothes belonging to her husband, missing in action since Stalingrad. As she entices him, Beckmann hears the rhythmic crescendo of someone on crutches nearing her door. It opens to reveal the girl's husband, an amputee who bitterly recognizes Beckmann as his former sergeant. Unhinged by his reversed role in the scene that he himself had experienced the night before, Beckmann dashes out to throw himself into the Elbe again. He is met by the other, to whom he confesses that the one-legged man, Corporal Bauer, lost his leg obeying Beckmann's orders. The other dissuades Beckmann from his intent by proposing that they visit Beckmann's former commander, the colonel, to whom Beckmann can hand over responsibility for the men lost under his command.

Hans Quest (front) as Beckmann and Hermann Lenschau as "der Andere" in the premiere of Borchert's Draußen vor der Tür *in Hamburg, 1947 (photograph by Rosemarie Clausen)*

Scene 3 opens with Beckmann interrupting the colonel's supper. The colonel listens as Beckmann, exhausted, recounts his recurring nightmare: a ghastly general—his trousers' stripes two streams of blood, his prosthetic arms two stick grenades—plays a march on a xylophone composed of human bones. To this summons arise dead soldiers, mutilated and putrid. The general commands Beckmann to have the troops fall in and sound off, but rather than obey they form choruses and howl Beckmann's name in accusation. Beckmann attempts to return responsibility for eleven casualties in a squad he had led on patrol on the colonel's orders—eleven men whose widows and orphans haunt Beckmann's dreams. The colonel laughs, praises Beckmann's performance, and suggests that he take his act onstage. The scene ends with Beckmann drunk on the street. He toasts the colonel and resolves to present the absurd tragedy of his existence as a comedy at the circus.

Scene 4 finds Beckmann in an interview with the priggish cabaret director, who explains what German theater needs: courageous, committed young actors at once unromantic and revolutionary, who hold up truth but love the world as it is, who embody the genius of Goethe, Friedrich Schiller, Wolfgang Amadeus Mozart, Shirley Temple, and the prizefighter Max Schmeling. Accompanied by eerie xylophone music, Beckmann auditions a garish parody of "Tapfere kleine Soldatenfrau" (Brave Little Soldier-Wife), concluding with the realization that her vaunted fidelity was a sham. The director offers the critique that although his act rings true, it is not yet polished enough to be art. Beckmann leaves in the direction of the Elbe. Once again the other intercepts and dissuades him, this time evoking the tranquillity of Beckmann's childhood home.

The fifth scene, which constitutes almost half the play, places Beckmann at his parents' door. The building has survived the bombing, but there is a strange name on the doorplate. He rings, and a slovenly, aging housewife, Frau Kramer, opens the door. To Beckmann's confused questions she answers that his parents now reside in Ohlsdorf, the cemetery on the outskirts of town (Borchert's ashes are interred there). When the war ended, Herr and Frau Beckmann were to lose their apartment because of the old man's Nazi sympathies. They "denazified" themselves permanently, Frau Kramer reports grudgingly, by using up enough gas for a month's cooking. In a quiet rage Beckmann tells the woman to shut her door. She marks his murderous tone, shrieks, and slams it in his face.

The other reappears and argues, desperately now, that Beckmann's view of the world is distorted by his gas-mask glasses. But Beckmann, increasingly gaining the upper hand, counters that his vision is the same, it is people who have changed; they have been hardened and embittered by endless casualty lists. He desires now only to sleep dreamlessly and eternally. He sits down at Frau Kramer's door, falls asleep, and dreams that the play's characters pass by: first God, then Death in the guise of ein Straßenfeger (a streetsweeper), der Oberst, der Kabarettdirektor, Frau Kramer, and Beckmann's wife and her lover. Beckmann advises God to find a hiding place, implores Death to take him, and accuses the rest of his murder. The intermittent protests of the other become ever more feeble as

Beckmann's invective against life swells. He chronicles how he and his fellows were betrayed by those pillars of society who clamored for war, glorified it, sent them to it, and now disown them. Only the girl stops and holds out hope. She flees, however, at the appearance of the one-legged-man, who accuses Beckmann of *his* murder: having found Beckmann with his wife, he drowned himself in the Elbe. Beckmann awakens. He recoils at being at once murdered and murderer. He asks why, how, and with whom the betrayed should cling to wretched life. Beckmann is alone on stage. He cries out to the other, to God, to anyone for an answer. There is none. The play ends with his tormented question.

Borchert's friend Bernhard Meyer-Marwitz, who attended the premiere in Hamburg after notice of the playwright's death had come by telegram from Basel, says in his biographical afterword to Borchert's collected works (1949): "Dieser Abend war mehr als eine Premiere, er war ein Requiem für eine verlorene Jugend in einem zerschlagenen Lande" (That evening was more than a premiere, it was a requiem for lost youth in a broken land). The circumstances, he reports, silenced any formal criticism of the opening night. Borchert, in an interview shortly before his death (cited by Peter Rühmkorf), had not anticipated his play's reception: "morgen sieht es keiner mehr an" (tomorrow no one will see it anymore). Despite its nihilistic ending and critics' aversion to its shrillness, repetitiveness, and unevenness, *Draußen vor der Tür* found its resonance in the public, becoming, in the words of the literary historian Karl A. Horst, "der größte Nachkriegserfolg" (the greatest postwar success) and a standard in the repertoire of virtually every major German theater. In 1948 alone there were 32 productions, followed by more than 130 performances between 1949 and 1969. What Erich Maria Remarque's *Im Westen nichts Neues* (1929; translated as *All Quiet on the Western Front*, 1929) had been to one generation of defeated, dispossessed veterans, *Draußen vor der Tür* was to Borchert's own.

The English-language premiere occurred on 29 November 1948 as an evening broadcast of the BBC's Third Programme, produced by E. A. Harding and the translator, David Porter. The Dramatic Workshop of the New School presented the American premiere under the title *Outside the Door* at New York's President Theater on 1 March 1949, with Martin Baum as Beckmann. The director, Erwin Piscator, collaborated on the translation with Zoe Lund-Schiller. The *New York Times* review ventured that while the play was unoriginal in concept and could not be considered great drama, its theme "transcends nationality and ideology" and "there is lyrical brilliance in many of Herr Borchert's lines." Surveying the German theater four years later, Eric Bentley predicted that of the young German playwrights only the best, Wolfgang Borchert, would reach non-German audiences—and rued that he was already dead.

Biography:

Peter Rühmkorf, *Wolfgang Borchert in Selbstzeugnissen und Bilddokumenten* (Reinbek: Rowohlt, 1961).

References:

Eric Bentley, *In Search of Theater* (New York: Knopf, 1953), p. 58;

Heinrich Böll, "Der *Schrei* Wolfgang Borcherts," *Moderna Språk*, 52 (February 1958): 20-23;

Kurt J. Fickert, "The Christ-Figure in Borchert's *Draußen vor der Tür*," *Germanic Review*, 54 (Fall 1979): 165-167;

Karl A. Horst, *Die deutsche Literatur der Gegenwart* (Munich: Nymphenburger Verlag, 1957), p. 268;

Stefan H. Kaszyński, "Expressionistische und existentielle Elemente im Drama *Draußen vor der Tür* von Wolfgang Borchert," *Studia Germanica Posnaniensia*, 2 (1973): 55-65;

Joseph Mileck, "Wolfgang Borchert's *Draußen vor der Tür*: A Young Poet's Struggle with Guilt and Despair," *Monatshefte*, 51 (December 1959): 328-336;

Donald F. Nelson, "To Live or Not to Live: Notes on Archetypes and the Absurd in Borchert's *Draußen vor der Tür*," *German Quarterly*, 48 (May 1975): 343-354;

J. H. Reid, "*Draußen vor der Tür* in Context," *Modern Languages*, 61 (December 1980): 184-190;

Peter Rühmkorf, *Wolfgang Borchert in Selbstzeugnissen und Bilddokumenten* (Reinbek: Rowohlt, 1961);

[J. P. Shanley], "Dramatic Workshop of the New School Presents Borchert's *Outside the Door*," *New York Times*, 2 March 1949, p. 33;

Alexandre Marius de Sterio, "Les oeuvres de jeunesse Wolfgang Borchert," Ph.D. dissertation, University of Paris, 1972;

Sterio, "Wolfgang Borchert: Eine literatursoziologische Interpretation," in *Wolfgang Borchert: Werk und Wirkung*, edited by Rudolf Wolff (Bonn: Bouvier, 1984), pp. 12-37;

Karl S. Weimar, "No Entry, No Exit: A Study of Borchert with Some Notes on Sartre," *Modern Language Quarterly*, 17 (June 1956): 153-165;

Leslie A. Willson, "The Drowning Man: *Draußen vor der Tür*," *Texas Studies in Literature and Language*, 10 (Spring 1968): 119-131;

Rudolf Wolff, ed., *Wolfgang Borchert: Werk und Wirkung* (Bonn: Bouvier, 1984).

Papers:

Wolfgang Borchert's papers are in the Wolfgang-Borchert-Archiv of the Staats- und Universitätsbibliothek (State and University Library), Hamburg.

Volker Braun

(7 May 1939 -   )

H. M. Waidson
University of Wales, Swansea

See also the Braun entry in *DLB 75: Contemporary German Fiction Writers, Second Series.*

PLAY PRODUCTIONS: *Hans Faust*, Weimar, 27 August 1968; revised as *Hinze und Kunze*, Karl-Marx-Stadt, Städtisches Theater, May 1973;
Die Kipper, Magdeburg, Bühnen der Stadt Magdeburg, 1972;
Freunde, 1972;
Hinze und Kunze, Karl-Marx-Stadt, 1973;
Tinka, Karl-Marx-Stadt, Städtisches Theater 1976;
Guevara oder Der Sonnenstaat, Mannheim, 10 December 1977;
Großer Frieden, Berlin, 1979;
Simplex Deutsch, Berlin, Berliner Ensemble, 1980;
Dmitri, Karlsruhe, 1982;
Schmitten, Leipzig, Leipziger Theater, 1982;
Lenins Tod, Berlin, Berliner Ensemble, 25 September 1983;
Transit-Europa: Der Ausflug der Toten, Berlin, Deutsches Theater, 30 January 1988.

BOOKS: *Provokation für mich: Gedichte* (Halle: Mitteldeutscher Verlag, 1965; revised, 1965; revised, 1975); republished as *Vorläufiges* (Frankfurt am Main: Suhrkamp, 1966);
Kriegserklärung (Halle: Mitteldeutscher Verlag, 1967);
Wir und nicht sie: Gedichte (Halle: Mitteldeutscher Verlag, 1970; enlarged, 1979);
Die Kipper: Schauspiel (Berlin & Weimar: Aufbau, 1972);
Das ungezwungene Leben Kasts: Drei Berichte (Berlin & Weimar: Aufbau, 1972; enlarged edition, Frankfurt am Main: Suhrkamp, 1979);
Gedichte, edited by Christel and Walfried Hartinger (Leipzig: Reclam, 1972; enlarged, 1976; enlarged again, 1979);
Gegen die symmetrische Welt: Gedichte (Halle: Mitteldeutscher Verlag, 1974);
Die Kipper; Hinze und Kunze; Tinka: Drei Stücke (Berlin: Henschel, 1975); republished as *Stücke* (Frankfurt am Main: Suhrkamp, 1975);
Es genügt nicht die einfache Wahrheit: Notate (Leipzig: Reclam, 1975);
Poesiealbum 115 (Berlin: Neues Leben, 1977); republished as *Zeit-Gedichte* (Munich: Damnitz, 1977);
Unvollendete Geschichte (Frankfurt am Main: Suhrkamp, 1977; edited by Andy Hollis, Manchester, U.K. & New York: Manchester University Press, 1988);
Der Stoff zum Leben (Pfaffenweiler: Pfaffenweiler Presse, 1977);
Im Querschnitt Volker Braun: Gedichte, Prosa, Stücke, Aufsätze, edited by Holger J. Schubert (Halle: Mitteldeutscher Verlag, 1978);
Training des aufrechten Gangs: Gedichte (Halle & Leipzig: Mitteldeutscher Verlag, 1979);
Gedichte (Frankfurt am Main: Suhrkamp, 1979);
Stücke 2 (Frankfurt am Main: Suhrkamp, 1981)—comprises *Schmitten, Guevara oder Der Sonnenstaat, Großer Frieden, Simplex Deutsch*;
Berichte von Hinze und Kunze (Halle: Mitteldeutscher Verlag, 1983); republished as *Hinze-Kunze-Roman* (Frankfurt am Main: Suhrkamp, 1985);
Stücke (Berlin: Henschel, 1983)—comprises *Die Kipper, Hinze und Kunze, Tinka, Schmitten, Guevara oder Der Sonnenstaat, Großer Frieden, Simplex Deutsch, Dmitri*;
Rimbaud: Ein Psalm der Aktualität (Wiesbaden: Steiner, 1985);
Langsamer knirschender Morgen: Gedichte (Frankfurt am Main: Suhrkamp, 1987);
Verheerende Folgen mangelnden Anscheins innerbetrieblicher Demokratie (Leipzig: Reclam, 1988; Frankfurt am Main: Suhrkamp, 1988);
Stücke 2 (Berlin: Henschel, 1989)—comprises *Lenins Tod, Der Eisenwagen, Totleben, T., Die Übergangsgesellschaft, Siegfried Frauenprotokolle Deutscher Furor, Transit Europa: Der Ausflug der Toten*;

Volker Braun (photograph by Isolde Ohlbaum)

Bodenloser Satz (Frankfurt am Main: Suhrkamp, 1990).

OTHER: Gerhard Wolf, ed., *Sonnenpferde und Astronauten: Gedichte junger Menschen*, contributions by Braun (Halle: Mitteldeutscher Verlag, 1964);

Kipper Paul Bauch, in *Deutsches Theater der Gegenwart*, volume 2, edited by Karlheinz Braun (Frankfurt am Main: Suhrkamp, 1967), pp. 5-104;

Freunde, in *Neue Stücke: Autoren der Deutschen Demokratischen Republik*, edited by Manfred Hocke (Berlin: Henschelverlag, 1971), pp. 367-387;

Hinze und Kunze, in *Spectaculum 19* (Frankfurt am Main: Suhrkamp, 1973), pp. 83-128.

Volker Braun was prominent in the former German Democratic Republic (GDR) as a lyrical poet, writer of fiction, and dramatist. *Die Kipper* (The Dumpers; performed and published, 1972), usually regarded as his first important play, was followed by three further plays concerned with factory life in the GDR, a theme that was officially encouraged at that time. Beginning with *Guevara oder Der Sonnenstaat* (Guevara; or, The Sun State; performed, 1977; published, 1981) Braun's plays embraced wider themes, including historical

ones. One of the principal themes of his writing has been the portrayal of the individualist who rebels against or deviates from society's expectations of him. Braun has described his goal in his early plays as that of promoting a more enthusiastic acceptance of socialism.

One of five brothers, Braun was born in Dresden on 7 May 1939. His father was killed in the war in 1945. Braun took his Abitur (school-leaving examination) in 1957 with the intention of attending a university, but he was not allowed to do so at that time. Instead, he worked for a year as a printer's assistant and then as a machine engineer and underground construction laborer. In 1960 he joined the Socialist Unity party, the Communist party of the GDR. He spent 1960 to 1964 as a student at Leipzig University. He worked as a writer and producer for the Berliner Ensemble in 1965-1966, with the City Theater in Leipzig in 1971-1972, and with the Deutsches Theater in Berlin from 1972 to 1977. He visited Russia, France, Great Britain, Italy, Cuba, and Peru. He was appointed to the committee of the Association of Writers in the GDR in 1973 but was removed when he was one of the first four signatories of a petition protesting the official refusal to allow the poet and singer Wolf Biermann to return to the GDR after a successful tour in West Germany in 1976. But Braun and

Stephan Hermlin were the only supporters of Biermann allowed to take part in the Eighth Writers' Congress of the GDR in 1978. Braun was awarded the Heinrich Heine Prize in 1971 and the Heinrich Mann Prize in 1980. In June 1989 he was awarded a newly established West Berlin prize for his short prose work *Bodenloser Satz* (Groundless Sentiment, 1990). He donated two-thirds of the prize money to support environmental improvement in the GDR. On 29 November 1989 the *Frankfurt Allgemaine Zeitund* (Frankfurt General Newspaper) published a statement by several East German writers, including Braun and Christa Wolf, pleading for the GDR to continue to exist as a socialist alternative to the FRG which would aim to become a humane, idealistic community dedicated to peace, social justice, freedom, and care for the environment.

The final title given to *Die Kipper* indicates Braun's intention to focus on a group of workers, whereas earlier titles—*Kipper Paul Bauch* (published, 1967) and "Der totale Mensch" (The Total Human Being)—emphasized the individual. The Kippers are unskilled laborers who tip trucks of sand by means of a hand lever. There is little future in the work, for the process will soon be replaced by a less cumbersome method. After an evening's drinking and brawling Bauch is summoned before the works manager and party secretary of his factory and made the leader of his brigade of workers. Seized by an ambition to break production records, he tries to motivate his workers by whipping up their enthusiasm. His mismanagement leads to his being removed from his position. His relationship with a young homeless woman, Marinka, ends with his leaving her when she becomes pregnant. The emphasis on a spontaneity that leads to disaster recalls Peter Hacks's play *Moritz Tassow* (1965).

Braun's autobiographical story *Das ungezwungene Leben Kasts* (The Free and Easy Life of Kast, 1972) describes the protagonist's experiences in three types of work: hard labor on a building site; study at Leipzig University, where Kast is particularly affected by a lecture on Johann Wolfgang von Goethe's *Faust* (1808, 1832); and the creative work of being involved in the production of a play which Kast has written and which can be identified as Braun's *Hinze und Kunze* (Hinze and Kunze; performed, 1973; published, 1975). *Hinze und Kunze* consists of twenty-four scenes in which various verse forms as well as prose are used. An early version of the play, with the title *Hans Faust*, was presented in Weimar on

27 August 1968; a revised version was performed in May 1973 in Karl-Marx-Stadt (now Chemnitz). The title, the German equivalent of "Tom, Dick, and Harry," points to the everyday quality of the two protagonists, who meet amid the ruins of Berlin in 1945. Hinze is clearing rubble from the streets and has glimmerings of faith in the newly established communist government. Kunze, a Mephistopheles figure, is attracted by the younger man's potential and conscientiousness. The two enter into a pact which is to enable Hinze to find fulfillment in work which will further the ideals of the new state. (The traditional relationship is reversed; Kunze gives orders to Hinze, whereas Mephistopheles is Faust's servant.) Hinze moves from manual labor to university study in order to be qualified to take on more responsible administrative tasks in factory production. A third figure, Propeller, refuses the tasks offered him by Kunze and advocates free elections; but eventually he comes to appreciate the communist state. Marlies, Hinze's wife, has an abortion so that she, too, can have an executive post.

Tinka (published, 1975; performed, 1976) again treats the theme of factory production, though with more emphasis on the role of women than in the earlier plays. After completing her university course with distinction, Tinka has been posted to a factory in Magdeburg. Although a relationship develops between Tinka and the works manager, Brenner, she criticizes the management as old-fashioned. She and her friend Helga dress up as men and interfere with the management's welcoming of two important visitors from Berlin. Tinka and Brenner sever their relationship; but when Brenner marries another woman, Tinka appears, uninvited, at the wedding and makes a scene. Her taunts provoke Brenner to kill her. A solution to the problems of the factory has been reached well before the end of the play, and in these later scenes personal emotions predominate.

Schmitten (published, 1981; performed, 1982) is similar to *Tinka*. Whereas Tinka is often excessively confident in the rightness of her position, Jutta Schmitten, a single parent with two children, is embarrassed by being publicly recognized as a highly productive worker. Other women are jealous that she should have been singled out; Schmitten is also uneasy because she is pregnant and the father, the technical director of the factory, is unwilling to accept responsibility. Like *Tinka*, *Schmitten* ends with a violent act,

Scene from a performance of Braun's Die Kipper *at the Bühnen der Stadt Magdeburg, 1972 (photograph by Jürgen Banse)*

though this time it is the woman who inflicts it: Schmitten and two other women employees attack Kolb and castrate him. Unlike Tinka, Schmitten is aware of her own limitations and is afraid of the challenge that factory modernization will bring.

Guevara oder Der Sonnenstaat is in blank verse, and the location is Bolivia; the action begins shortly after the death of Che Guevara, and each scene takes place at an earlier time than the one before it. The last scene (which is the first chronologically) presents a dialogue between Guevara and a friend in which Guevara expresses his impatience with the Cuban policy of continuing to use some of the economic features of capitalism, such as profits, credits, prices, and wages; he decides to fight actively against the capitalist enemy. As the guerillas are resting in an orange grove, Guevara says that he is looking forward to violent action and that the hour of violence is the time of truth. In another scene he asks his beloved Tania to return home, but she insists on remaining in the jungle with him. The guerillas are disappointed that the local inhabitants are fatalistic and unwilling to take action. When the guerril-

las kill some of the soldiers pursuing them, it seems inevitable that Guevara and some of his supporters will soon meet death in a similar way. Alternating with the principal action are interludes presented by two clownish figures, an archaeologist and a philosopher. Written in 1975, the play was to premiere at the Deutsches Theater in Berlin; but the production was postponed, reputedly because the Cuban Embassy raised objections. The first performance was on 10 December 1977 in Mannheim.

Großer Frieden (Great Peace; performed, 1979; published, 1981) is set in China two thousand years ago. "Great Peace" was the name given to an ideal society; the reality is grim warfare involving groups of armed marauders until the farmer Gau Dsu establishes himself as emperor. Braun has described the play as depicting a victory for a farmers' revolutionary movement.

Simplex Deutsch (The German Simpleton; performed, 1980; published, 1981) consists of a loose sequence of scenes illustrating the inability of characters to make decisions or the fateful consequences of making the wrong decisions; it goes further than Braun's previous plays in its experimental approach. No one figure links the action together, and the sequence of events is not chronological. The play begins and ends with the collapse of the Third Reich in 1945. Characters from Bertolt Brecht's *Trommeln in der Nacht* (1922; translated as *Drums in the Night*, 1966) are transferred from 1918 to 1945 and to the period of the war in Vietnam; Samuel Beckett's *Waiting for Godot* (1956) provides a context for other action. The death of a German soldier who faces the advancing Russians is thought to refer to the death of Braun's father.

At about the same time that he was working on *Simplex Deutsch,* Braun was composing a large-scale dramatic work portraying the struggles for power in the early years of Soviet Russia to commemorate the 1970 centenary of Lenin's birth; but the work was not performed or published at that time. *Lenins Tod* (Lenin's Death; performed, 1983; published, 1989) shows Lenin's struggle with the illness which was to terminate his life. The major scenes present the discussions, arguments, and aims of Lenin and those close to him in the Politburo and the Central Committee, as well as the intrigues and deviousness of Joseph Stalin and his supporters. Lenin would like to see Leon Trotsky as his deputy, but Trotsky is reluctant to take the post. Lenin's dislike of Stalin is due to the latter's lack of principle; while Trotsky favors democracy and Lenin centralization, Stalin is concerned only for his own personal power. Although the main action involves the political leaders there are street scenes in which two recently demobilized soldiers, Markin and Kusmin, are a vehicle for conveying the loyalty and integrity of the Russian people. The sequel to *Lenins Tod* is *T.* (published, 1989). Without Lenin the opposition groups do not have sufficient authority to halt Stalin's advance; Trotsky is arrested, and Joffe, a member of the opposition group, is shot. The presentation of the early power struggles within the Russian Communist party, and especially the negative assessment of Stalin, made the play unacceptable for performance in the GDR. Although the two dramas are realistic and quasi-documentary, *Lenins Tod* has as a prelude the surrealistic monologue of a dying man who has taken refuge in an old car. The car turns into a tank; the man finds himself inseparable from the vehicle, which he cannot direct. The tank may represent life itself.

Totleben (Dead Life; published, 1989), a one-act play in the style of Brecht's didactic dramas, is subtitled *Straßengericht* (Street Judgment). Two political agitators shoot five starving people.

Dmitri (performed, 1982; published, 1983) has links with *Schmitten* and *Simplex Deutsch* in its experimental features. Braun takes the general shape of his play from Friedrich Schiller's fragment *Demetrius* (1805). Dmitri takes the throne after the death of Ivan the Terrible in 1584. As czar, Dmitri struggles against the reactionary policies of those around him; hope is to be sought in the people, not in court circles.

Die Übergangsgesellschaft (Society in Transition; published, 1989) takes place on an estate at Straussberg, near Berlin, which was formerly the pied-à-terre of an armament manufacturer and is now in a neglected condition. The play portrays a group of East German intellectuals and artists during the early 1980s who feel their lives to be stagnant. Shortly before his death the seventy-six-year-old Wilhelm says "Die Revolution kann nicht als Diktatur zum Ziel kommen" (The revolution cannot fulfill its aim if it is a dictatorship).

Braun treats the myth of the Nibelungen in *Siegfried Frauenprotokolle Deutscher Furor* (Siegfried Women-Agreement German Furor; published, 1989). King Gunter and Siegfried arrange at their convenience to take possession of Brünhild and Krimhild. Brünhild is deeply hurt when she learns of her deception by the two men; she becomes a gray, shadowy figure in contrast to her former confident self. Krimhild appears to be outwardly unaffected by the murder of Siegfried, but she marries Etzel with the aim of avenging her husband's death.

Transit Europa: Der Ausflug der Toten (Transit Europe: The Excursion of the Dead; performed, 1988; published, 1989) indicates by its title the author's literary source: the writings of Anna Seghers, a respected author of the older generation in the GDR. The setting is an obscure hotel in Marseilles where Seidel, a German refugee, is staying. German troops are advancing southward to extend their control of France, and Seidel is given the opportunity to use the visa and tickets that were prepared for a German Communist agent to travel to Mexico. Seidel generously lets two other people use the papers, but the couple dies when their ship sinks off the coast of Martinique.

References:

Heinz Ludwig Arnold, ed., *Volker Braun* (Munich: Edition text + kritik, 1971);

Gerrit-Jan Berendse, "Fünfunzwanzig Jahre politische Praxis von Volker Braun: Von einem heftigen Experimentator, der immer neue

Scene from the premiere of Braun's Schmitten *at the Leipziger Theater in 1982, with (in foreground) Matthias Humnutsch as the engineer and Ellen Hedwig as Schmitten (photograph by Helga Waldmüller)*

Wege sucht," *Wirkendes Wort*, 41, no. 3 (1991): 425-435;

Klaus L. Berghahn, "Den Faust-Mythos zu Ende bringen: Von Volker Brauns *Hans Faust* zu *Hinze und Kunze*," *Amsterdamer Beiträge zur Neueren Germanistik*, 24 (1988): 297-315;

Christine Cosentino, "Der 'unruhige' Held: Utopie und Stagnation in Volker Brauns Stück' *Großer Frieden*," *Neophilologus*, 66 (1982): 259-268;

Cosentino, "Volker Brauns *Geschichten von Hinze und Kunze*: A New Look at an Old Problem," *Studies in GDR Culture and Society*, 4 (1984): 95-106;

Cosentino, "Volker Brauns roter Empedokles: *Guevara oder Der Sonnenstaat*," *Monatshefte für deutschen Unterricht* (1979): 41-48;

Heinz Czechowski, "Volker Brauns *Die Kipper*—Sprache. Stil. Struktur," *Weimarer Beiträge*, 19, no. 7 (1973): 130-152;

Dietmar Goltschnigg, "Utopie und Revolution. Georg Buchner in der DDR-Literatur: Christa Wolf, Volker Braun, Heiner Muller," *Zeit-schrift fur Deutsche Philologie*, 109 (1990): 571-591;

Christel and Walfried Hartinger, "Volker Braun," in *Literatur der DDR in Einzeldarstellungen*, edited by Hans Jürgen Geerdts (Stuttgart: Kröner, 1972), pp. 504-522;

Ursula Heukenkamp, "Die Uneinsichtigen handeln," *Sinn und Form*, 37 (1985): 208-218;

Julian Hilton, "Back to the Future—Volker Braun and the German Theatrical Tradition," in *A Radical Stage: Theatre in Germany in the 1970s and 1980s*, edited by W. E Sebald (Oxford, New York & Hamburg: Berg), pp. 124-144;

Gudrun Klatt, "DDR-Dramatik am Beginn der 70er Jahre: Tendenzen und Schreibweisen," *Weimarer Beiträge*, 10 (1973): 117-130;

Heinz Klunker, *Zeitstücke und Zeitgenossen: Gegenwartstheater in der DDR* (Munich: Deutscher Taschenbuch Verlag, 1975);

Franz Norbert Mennemeier, "Dialektik von Vorgriff und kleinen Schritten," in his *Modernes deutsches Drama: Kritiken und Charakteristiken*, volume 2: *1933 bis zur Gegenwart* (Munich: Fink, 1975), pp. 331-378;

Ulrich Profitlich, "'Härten' im Werk Volker Brauns," *Der Deutschunterricht*, 36, no. 3 (1984): 69-77;

Profitlich, *Volker Braun: Studien zu seinem dramatischen und erzählerischen Werk* (Munich: Fink, 1985);

Ursula Reinhold, "Volker Brauns Konzept und Realisierung einer gesellschafts gestaltenden Dichtung im Sozialismus," in *Weggenossen: Fünfzehn Schriftsteller der DDR*, edited by Klaus Jarmatz und Christel Berger (Leipzig: Reclam, 1975), pp. 448-489;

Jay Rosellini, "Kulturerbe und Zeitgenossenschaft: Volker Braun und Georg Büchner," *German Quarterly*, 60 (Fall 1987): 600-616;

Rosellini, *Volker Braun* (Munich: Beck, 1983);

Silvia Schlenstedt, "Das WIR und das ICH des Volker Braun," *Weimarer Beiträge*, 18, no. 10 (1972): 53-69;

Karl Heinz Schmidt, "Zur Dramaturgie des Volker Braun," *Sinn und Form*, 30, no. 2 (1978): 433-450;

Klaus Schuhmann, "Peter Hacks: *Pandora*—

Volker Braun: *Großer Frieden*. Problemfeld Zukunft," *Weimarer Beiträge*, 29 (1983): 71-75;

Hans-Jürgen Timm, "Geschichte als Erfahrungsraum Zu Aspekten der Dramatik Volker Brauns," *Weimarer Beiträge*, 35 (1989): 1506-1530;

Ian Wallace, "The Pyramid and the Mountain: Volker Braun in the 1970s," in *The GDR under Honecker 1971-1981*, edited by Wallace (Dundee: University of Dundee 1981), pp. 43-62;

Wallace, *Volker Braun: Forschungsbericht* (Amsterdam: Rodopi, 1986);

Wallace, "Volker Braun's *Tinka*," in *The Writer and Society in the GDR*, edited by Wallace (Tayport: Hutton Press, 1984), pp. 120-133;

Heinz-Dieter Weber, "Die Wiederkehr des Tragischen in der Literatur der DDR," *Der Deutschunterricht*, 30, no. 2 (1978): 79-99;

Ilse Winter, "*Dmitri* versus 'Demetrius': Zu Volker Brauns kritischer Adaption von Friedrich Schiller," *German Quarterly*, 60 (Winter 1987): 52-67.

Bertolt Brecht
(10 February 1898 - 14 August 1956)

Herbert Knust
University of Illinois at Urbana-Champaign

See also the Brecht entry in *DLB 56, German Fiction Writers, 1914-1945.*

PLAY PRODUCTIONS: *Trommeln in der Nacht*, Munich, Kammerspiele, 29 September 1922;

Die rote Zibebe, contributions by Brecht, Munich, Kammerspiele, 30 September 1922;

Im Dickicht, Munich, Residenztheater, 9 May 1923;

Baal, Leipzig, Altes Theater, 8 December 1923;

Leben Eduards des Zweiten von England, by Brecht and Lion Feuchtwanger, Munich, Kammerspiele, 18 March 1924;

Mann ist Mann, Darmstadt, Landestheater, 25 September 1926;

Die Hochzeit (Die Kleinbürgerhochzeit), Frankfurt am Main, Städtische Bühnen, Schauspielhaus, 11 December 1926;

Mahagonny, Baden-Baden, Stadttheater, 17 July 1927;

Kalkutta, 4. Mai, by Brecht and Feuchtwanger, Königsberg, Neues Schauspielhaus, 12 November 1927;

Jaroslav Hašek, *Die Abenteuer des braven Soldaten Schwejk*, dramatized by Max Brod and Hans Reimann, adapted by Brecht, Erwin Piscator, and Leo Lania, Berlin, Theater am Nollendorfplatz, 23 January 1928;

Die Dreigroschenoper, music by Kurt Weill, Berlin, Theater am Schiffbauerdamm, 31 August 1928;

Der Ozeanflug, Baden-Baden, Kurhaus, 27 July 1929;

Das Badener Lehrstück vom Einverständnis, music by Paul Hindemith, Baden-Baden, Kurhaus, 28 July 1929;

Happy End, by Brecht and Elisabeth Hauptmann, music by Weill, Berlin, Theater am Schiffbauerdamm, 31 August 1929;

Aufstieg und Fall der Stadt Mahagonny, music by Weill, Leipzig, Opernhaus, 9 March 1930;

Bertolt Brecht in 1953

Der Jasager und der Neinsager, music by Weill, Berlin, Zentralinstitut für Erziehung und Unterricht, 23 June 1930;

Die Maßnahme, music by Hanns Eisler, Berlin, Berliner Philharmonie, 13 December 1930;

Die Mutter, music by Eisler, Berlin, Komödienhaus am Schiffbauerdamm, 15 January 1932;

Die sieben Todsünden der Kleinbürger, music by Weill, Paris, Théâtre des Champs-Elysées, Les Ballets, 7 June 1933;

Die Ballade vom Reichstagsbrand, Moscow, Deutsches Theater Kolonne links im Klub ausländischer Arbeiter, March 1934;

Die Rundköpfe und die Spitzköpfe, music by Eisler, Moscow, Thälmann-Klub, Spring 1935;

Die Gewehre der Frau Carrar, Paris, Salle Adyar, 16 October 1937;

Die Ausnahme und die Regel (in Hebrew), Givat Chaim, Palestine, 1 May 1938;

99% (scenes from *Furcht und Elend des Dritten Reiches*), Paris, Salle d'léna, 21 May 1938;

Vad kostar järnet? (*Was kostet das Eisen*; later called *Dansen II*), Stockholm, Volkshochschule Tollare, August 1939;

Mutter Courage und ihre Kinder, music by Paul Dessau, Zurich, Schauspielhaus, 19 April 1941;

Der gute Mensch von Sezuan, Zurich, Schauspielhaus, 4 February 1943;

Leben des Galilei, Zurich, Schauspielhaus, 9 March 1943;

John Webster, *The Duchess of Malfi*, adapted by Brecht and W. H. Auden, Boston, Schubert Theater, 23 September 1946;

Friedrich Hölderlin, *Die Antigone des Sophokles*, adapted by Brecht, Chur, Stadttheater, 15 February 1948;

The Caucasian Chalk Circle, translated by Eric and Maja Bentley, Northfield, Minn., Nourse Little Theatre, 4 May 1948;

Herr Puntila und sein Knecht Matti, Zurich, Schauspielhaus, 5 June 1948;

J. M. R. Lenz, *Der Hofmeister*, adapted by Brecht, Berlin, Berliner Ensemble, 15 April 1950;

Das Verhör des Lukullus, music by Dessau, Berlin, Deutsche Staatsoper, 17 March 1951;

Herrnburger Bericht, Berlin, Deutsches Theater, 5 August 1951;

Die Verurteilung des Lukullus, music by Dessau, Berlin, Deutsche Staatsoper, 12 October 1951;

Molière, *Don Juan*, adapted by Brecht, Rostock, Volkstheater, 25 May 1952;

Anna Seghers, *Der Prozess der Jeanne d'Arc zu Rouen 1431*, adapted by Brecht, Berlin, Berliner Ensemble, 23 November 1952;

George Farquhar, *Pauken und Trompeten*, adapted by Brecht, Berlin, Berliner Ensemble, 19 June 1955;

Die Tage der Commune, music by Eisler, Karl-Marx-Stadt, Städtisches Theater, 17 November 1956;

Schweyk im zweiten Weltkrieg, translated into Polish by Andrzej Wirth, Warsaw, Theater der polnischen Armee, 15 January 1957;

Die Gesichte der Simone Machard, by Brecht and Feuchtwanger, Frankfurt am Main, Städtische Bühnen, 8 March 1957;

Die Horatier und die Kuriatier, music by Kurt Schwaen, Halle, Theater der jungen Garde, 26 April 1958;

Der aufhaltsame Aufstieg des Arturo Ui, Stuttgart, Württembergisches Staatstheater, 10 November 1958;

Die heilige Johanna der Schlachthöfe, Hamburg, Deutsches Schauspielhaus, 30 April 1959;

William Shakespeare, *Coriolan von Shakespeare*, adapted by Brecht, Frankfurt am Main, Schauspielhaus, 22 September 1961;

Flüchtlingsgespräche, Munich, Kammerspiele, 15 February 1962;

Der Messingkauf, Berlin, Berliner Ensemble, 12 October 1963;

Der Ingwertopf, Heidelberg, Städtische Bühne, 9 February 1965;

Der Fischzug, Heidelberg, Städtische Bühne, 11 January 1967;

Der Brotladen, Berlin, Berliner Ensemble, 13 April 1967;

Der Bettler oder der tote Hund, Berlin, Tribüne, 27 September 1967;

Dansen I; *Dansen II*, Cologne, Kammerspiele der Kölner Bühnen, 4 October 1967;

Turandot oder Der Kongreß der Weißwäscher, music by Eisler, Zurich, Schauspielhaus, 5 February 1969;

Lux in Tenebris, Essen, Städtische Bühnen, 6 December 1969;

Circus-Pantomime, New York, Theatre de Lys, 9 October 1972;

Er treibt einen Teufel aus, Basel, Stadttheater, 3 October 1975;

Der Untergang des Egoisten Johann Fatzer, Berlin, Schaubühne am Halleschen Ufer, 11 March 1976.

SELECTED BOOKS: *Baal* (Potsdam: Kiepenheuer, 1922); translated by Eric Bentley as *Baal* in *Baal, A Man's a Man, and The Elephant Calf* (New York: Grove, 1966);

Trommeln in der Nacht: Drama (Munich: Drei Masken, 1922); edited by Volkmar Sander (Waltham, Mass., Toronto & London: Blaisdell, 1969); translated by Anselm Hollo as *Drums in the Night* in *Jungle of Cities and Other Plays* (New York: Grove, 1966);

*Leben Eduards des Zweiten von England: Nach Mar-
lowe. Historie*, by Brecht and Lion Feuchtwanger (Potsdam: Kiepenheuer, 1924); translated by Bentley as *Edward II: A Chronicle Play*
(New York: Grove, 1966);

*Taschenpostille: Mit Anleitungen, Gesangsnoten und
einem Anhang* (Potsdam: Privately printed,
1926);

*Im Dickicht der Städte: Der Kampf zweier Männer in
der Riesenstadt Chicago. Schauspiel* (Berlin: Propyläen, 1927); translated by Hollo as *Jungle
of Cities* in *Jungle of Cities and Other Plays*;

*Hauspostille: Mit Anleitungen, Gesangsnoten und
einem Anhang* (Berlin: Propyläen, 1927);
translated by Bentley as *Manual of Piety: A Bilingual Edition* (New York: Grove, 1966);

*Mann ist Mann: Die Verwandlung des Packers Galy
Gay in den Militärbaracken von Kilkoa im Jahre
1925: Lustspiel* (Berlin: Propyläen, 1927);
translated by Bentley as *A Man's a Man* in
Baal, A Man's a Man, and The Elephant Calf;

Drei angelsächsische Stücke, by Brecht and Feuchtwanger (Berlin: Propyläen, 1927);

*Aufstieg und Fall der Stadt Mahagonny: Oper in drei
Akten*, text by Brecht, music by Kurt Weill
(Vienna & Leipzig: Universal-Edition, 1929);
translated by Guy Stern as *Rise and Fall of
the City of Mahagonny* (brochure accompanying recorded version, Columbia K3L 243,
1959);

Die Dreigroschenoper, text translated by Elisabeth
Hauptmann from John Gay's *The Beggar's
Opera*, rewritten by Brecht, music by Weill
(Vienna: Universal-Edition, 1929; London:
Malik, 1938); translated by Bentley and Des-
mond Vesey as *The Threepenny Opera* (New
York: Grove, 1964);

Versuche, volume 1, edited by Hauptmann (Berlin: Kiepenheuer, 1930)—comprises *Der
Flug der Lindberghs: "Radiotheorie"; "Geschichten vom Herrn Keuner"; Fatzer, 3*;

Versuche, volume 2, edited by Hauptmann (Berlin: Kiepenheuer, 1930)—comprises *Aufstieg
und Fall der Stadt Mahagonny*, "Über die
Oper, Aus dem Lesebuch für Städtebewoh-
ner," *Das Badener Lehrstück vom Einverständnis; Das Badenar Lehrstück vom Einverständnis*
translated by Lee Baxandall as *The Baden
Play for Learning*, in *Drama Review* (Tulane),
4 (May 1960): 118-133;

Versuche, volume 3, edited by Hauptmann (Berlin: Kiepenheuer, 1931)—comprises *Die Dreigroschenoper, Die Beule: Ein Dreigroschenfilm,
Der Dreigroschenprozess*;

Versuche, volume 4, edited by Hauptmann (Berlin: Kiepenheuer, 1931)—comprises *Der Jasager und Der Neinsager: Schulopern, Die Maßnahme: Lehrstück*; *Der Jasager* translated by
Gerhard Nillhaus as *He Who Said Yes*, in *Accent*, 7 (Autumn 1946): 14-20; *Die Maßnahme*
translated by Carl L. Mueller as *The Measures Taken* in *The Measures Taken and Other
Lehrstücke* (London: Methuen, 1977);

Versuche, volume 5, edited by Hauptmann (Berlin: Kiepenheuer, 1932)—comprises *Die heilige Johanna der Schlachthöfe: Schauspiel*, "Geschichten vom Herrn Keuner"; *Die heilige
Johanna der Schlachthöfe* translated by Frank
Jones as *Saint Joan of the Stockyards* (Bloomington: Indiana University Press, 1969);

Versuche, volume 6, edited by Hauptmann (Berlin: Kiepenheuer, 1932)—comprises "Die
drei Soldaten"; "Ein Kinderbuch;"

Versuche, volume 7, edited by Hauptmann (Berlin: Kiepenheuer, 1933)—comprises *Die Mutter*, "Geschichten aus der Revolution"; *Die
Mutter* translated by Baxandall as *The Mother*
(New York: Grove, 1965);

Ballade vom armen Stabschef + 30. Juni 1934 (N.p.,
1934);

Dreigroschenroman (Amsterdam: De Lange, 1934);
translated by Vesey and Christopher Isherwood as *A Penny for the Poor* (London: Hale,
1937); translation republished as *Threepenny
Novel* (New York: Grove, 1956; London: Gra-
nada, 1981);

Lieder Gedichte Chöre, music by Hanns Eisler
(Paris: Editions du Carrefour, 1934);

Gesammelte Werke, 2 volumes (London: Malik,
1938);

*Svendborger Gedichte; Deutsche Kriegsfibel; Chroni-
ken: Deutsche Satiren für den deutschen Freiheits-
sender* (London: Malik, 1939);

Furcht und Elend des III. Reiches (Moscow: Meshdunarodnaja Kniga, 1941; New York: Aurora,
1945); translated by Bentley as *The Private
Life of the Master Race* (New York: New Directions, 1944);

*Herr Puntila und sein Knecht: Nacherzählungen der
Hella Wuolijoki. Volksstück in 9 Bildern* (Munich: Desch, 1948); republished as *Herr Puntila und sein Knecht Matti*, edited by Margaret
Mare (London: Methuen, 1962); translated
by John Willett as *Mister Puntila and His
Man Matti* (London: Methuen, 1977);

Kalendergeschichten (Halle: Mitteldeutscher Verlag,
1948); translated by Yvonne Kapp and Mi-

chael Hamburger as *Tales from the Calendar* (London: Methuen, 1961);

Versuche, volume 9, edited by Hauptmann (Berlin & Frankfurt am Main: Suhrkamp, 1949)—comprises *Mutter Courage und ihre Kinder: Eine Chronik aus dem Dreißigjährigen Krieg*, "Anmerkungen," "Fünf Schwierigkeiten beim Schreiben der Wahrheit"; *Mutter Courage und ihre Kinder* translated by Bentley as *Mother Courage and Her Children* (New York: Grove, 1966);

Das Zukunftslied: Aufbaulied der FDJ, music by Paul Dessau (Weimar: Thüringer Volksverlag, 1949);

Antigonemodell 1948: Die Antigone des Sophokles, nach der Hölderlinschen Übertragung für die Bühne, bearbeitet (Berlin: Weiss, 1949);

Versuche, volume 10, edited by Hauptmann (Berlin & Frankfurt am Main: Suhrkamp, 1950)—comprises *Herr Puntila und sein Knecht Matti*, "Chinesische Gedichte," *Die Ausnahme und die Regel*; *Die Ausnahme und die Regel* translated by Bentley as *The Exception and the Rule*, in *Chrysalis*, 14, no. 68 (1961);

Versuche, volume 11, edited by Hauptmann (Berlin: Suhrkamp, 1951)—comprises *Der Hofmeister*, by Jakob Michael Reinhold Lenz, revised by Brecht; "Studien: Neue Technik der Schauspielkunst"; *Übungsstücke für Schauspieler*; *Das Verhör des Lukullus*, by Brecht and Margarete Steffin; "Anmerkungen über die Oper *Die Verurteilung des Lukullus*"; *Das Verhör des Lukullus* translated by H. R. Hays as *The Trial of Lucullus* (New York: New Directions, 1943);

Offener Brief an die deutschen Künstler und Schriftsteller (Berlin, 1951);

Die Erziehung der Hirse. Nach dem Bericht von G. Fisch: Der Mann, der das Unmögliche wahr gemacht hat (Berlin: Aufbau, 1951);

Hundert Gedichte, 1918-1950 (Berlin: Aufbau, 1951);

An meine Landsleute (Leipzig: VEB Offizin Haag-Großdrugulin, 1951);

Das Verhör des Lukullus: Oper in zwölf Bildern, music by Dessau (Berlin: Aufbau, 1951);

Die Verurteilung des Lukullus: Oper, music by Dessau (Berlin: Aufbau, 1951);

Versuche, volume 12, edited by Hauptmann (Berlin & Frankfurt am Main: Suhrkamp, 1953)—comprises *Der gute Mensch von Sezuan*, "Kleines Organon für das Theater," "Über reimlose Lyrik mit unregelmäßigen Rhythmen," "Geschichten vom Herrn Keuner";

Der gute Mensch von Sezuan translated by Bentley as *The Good Woman of Setzuan* in *Parables for the Theater: Two Plays by Bertolt Brecht* (Minneapolis: University of Minnesota Press, 1948); translation revised as *The Good Woman of Setzuan* (New York: Grove, 1966); "Kleines Organon für das Theater" translated by Willett as "A Short Organum for the Theatre" in *Brecht on Theatre* (New York: Hill & Wang, 1964);

Versuche, extra volume, edited by Hauptmann (Berlin: Aufbau, 1953)—comprises *Die Gewehre der Frau Carrar*, "Der Augsburger Kreidekreis," "Neue Kinderlieder"; *Die Gewehre der Frau Carrar* translated by Keene Wallis as *Señora Carrar's Rifles*, in *Theatre Workshop*, 2 (April-June 1938): 30-50; retranslated by George Tabori as *The Guns of Carrar* (New York: French, 1971);

Versuche, volume 13, edited by Hauptmann (Berlin & Frankfurt am Main: Suhrkamp, 1954)—comprises *Der kaukasische Kreidekreis*, by Brecht and Ruth Berlau; "Weite und Vielfalt der realistischen Schreibweise"; "Buckower Elegien"; *Der kaukasische Kreidekreis* translated by Bentley and Maja Apleman as *The Caucasian Chalk Circle* in *Parables for the Theater*;

Versuche, volume 14, edited by Hauptmann (Berlin: Suhrkamp, 1955)—comprises *Leben des Galilei*, "Gedichte aus dem Messingkauf," *Die Horatier und die Kuriatier*; *Leben des Galilei* translated by Vesey as *The Life of Galileo* (London: Methuen, 1963); translated by Charles Laughton as *Galileo* (New York: Grove, 1966);

Gedichte, edited by S. Streller (Leipzig: Reclam, 1955);

Kriegsfibel, edited by Berlau (Berlin: Eulenspiegel, 1955);

Gedichte und Lieder, edited by Paul Suhrkamp (Berlin & Frankfurt am Main: Suhrkamp, 1956);

Die Geschäfte des Herrn Julius Cäsar: Romanfragment (Berlin: Aufbau, 1957);

Lieder und Gesänge (Berlin: Henschel, 1957);

Versuche, volume 15, edited by Hauptmann (Berlin & Frankfurt am Main: Suhrkamp, 1957)—comprises *Die Tage der Commune*, "Die Dialektik auf dem Theater," *Zu Leben des Galilei*, "Drei Reden," "Zwei Briefe"; *Die Tage der Commune* translated by Leonard J. Lehrmann as *The Days of the Commune*, in *Dunster Drama Review*, 10, no. 2 (1971);

Schriften zum Theater: Über eine nicht-aristotelische Dramatik, edited by S. Unseld (Berlin & Frankfurt am Main: Suhrkamp, 1957);

Stücke aus dem Exil, 5 volumes (Frankfurt am Main: Suhrkamp, 1957)—includes *Die Rundköpfe und die Spitzköpfe*; *Der aufhaltsame Aufstieg des Arturo Ui*; *Die Gesichte der Simone Machard*, by Brecht and Feuchtwanger; *Schweyk im zweiten Weltkrieg*; *Die Rundköpfe und die Spitzköpfe* translated by N. Goold-Verschoyle as *Roundheads and Peakheads* in *Jungle of Cities and Other Plays*; *Der aufhaltsame Aufstieg des Arturo Ui* adapted by Tabori as *The Resistible Rise of Arturo Ui: A Gangster Spectacle*, music by Hans-Dieter Hosalla (New York: French, 1972); translated by Ralph Manheim as *The Resistible Rise of Arturo Ui* (London: Eyre Methuen, 1976); *Die Gesichte der Simone Machard* translated by Carl Richard Mueller as *The Visions of Simone Machard* (New York: Grove, 1965); *Schweyk im weiten Weltkrieg* translated by Peter Sander as *Schweyk in the Second World War* (Waltham, Mass.: Brandeis University, 1967);

Geschichten vom Herrn Keuner (Berlin: Aufbau, 1958);

Brecht: Ein Lesebuch für unsere Zeit, edited by Hauptmann and Benno Slupianek (Weimar: Volksverlag Weimar, 1958);

Mutter Courage und ihre Kinder: Text; *Aufführung*; *Anmerkungen* (Berlin: Henschel, 1958);

Versuche, volumes 5-8, 1 volume (Berlin & Frankfurt am Main: Suhrkamp, 1959)—comprises *Die heilige Johanna der Schlachthöfe*, "Die drei Soldaten," *Die Mutter, Die Spitzköpfe und die Rundköpfe*;

Der gute Mensch von Sezuan: Parabelstück, by Brecht, Berlau, and Steffin, music by Dessau (Berlin & Frankfurt am Main: Suhrkamp, 1959); edited by Mare (London: Methuen, 1960);

Schweyk im zweiten Weltkrieg (Berlin & Frankfurt am Main: Suhrkamp, 1959);

Die sieben Todsünden der Kleinbürger (Frankfurt am Main: Suhrkamp, 1959); translated by W. H. Auden and Chester Kallmann as *The Seven Deadly Sins of the Lower Middle Class*, in *Drama Review* (Tulane), 6 (September 1961): 123-129;

Bearbeitungen, 2 volumes (Frankfurt am Main: Suhrkamp, 1959)—comprises *Die Antigone des Sophokles, Der Hofmeister, Coriolan, Der Prozeß der Jeanne d'Arc zu Rouen 1431, Don Juan, Pauken und Trompeten*;

Kleines Organon für das Theater: Mit einem "Nachtrag zum Kleinen Organon" (Frankfurt am Main: Suhrkamp, 1960);

Flüchtlingsgespräche (Berlin: Suhrkamp, 1961);

Me-Ti; Buch der Wendungen—Fragment, edited by Uwe Johnson (Frankfurt am Main: Suhrkamp, 1965);

Einakter: Die Kleinbürgerhochzeit; *Der Bettler oder Der tote Hund*; *Er treibt einem Teufel aus*; *Lux in Tenebris*; *Der Fischzug*; *Dansen*; *Was kostet das Eisen?* (Frankfurt am Main: Suhrkamp, 1966); *Lux in Tenebris, Der Fischzug, Dansen,* and *Was kostet das Eisen?* translated by Martin and Rose Kastner as *Lux in Tenebris, The Catch, Dansen,* and *How Much Is Your Iron?*, in *Collected Plays*, 9 volumes, edited by Willett and Manheim (London: Methuen, 1971-1973; New York: Random House, 1971-1973);

Gesammelte Werke, 22 volumes (Frankfurt am Main: Suhrkamp, 1967-1969); volumes 1-7, *Stücke*, translation edited by Willett and Manheim as *Collected Plays*, 9 volumes (London: Methuen, 1971-1973; New York: Random House, 1971-1973); volumes 8-10, *Gedichte*, translated by Willett and Manheim as *Poems 1913-1956* (New York: Methuen, 1976); volume 11, *Prosa I*, translated by Willett and Manheim as *Short Stories 1921-1946* (New York: Methuen, 1983); volumes 15-17, *Schriften zum Theater*, translated by Willett as *Brecht on Theatre* (New York: Hill & Wang, 1964);

Turandot oder Der Kongreß der Weißwäscher (Frankfurt am Main: Suhrkamp, 1968);

Arbeitsjournal 1938-1955, 3 volumes (Frankfurt am Main: Suhrkamp, 1973);

Tagebücher 1920-1922: Autobiographische Aufzeichnungen 1920-1954, edited by Herta Ramthun (Frankfurt am Main: Suhrkamp, 1975); translated by Willett as *Diaries 1920-1922* (New York: St. Martin's Press, 1979);

Werke: Große kommentierte Berliner und Frankfurter Ausgabe, 30 volumes projected, 15 volumes published, edited by Werner Hecht, Jan Knopf, Werner Mittenzwei, and Klaus-Detlev Müller (Berlin: Aufbau / Frankfurt am Main: Suhrkamp, 1988-   )—included in volume 5, *Leben des Galilei*.

OTHER: M. Andersen-Nexö, *Die Kindheit: Erinnerungen*, translated by Brecht (Zurich: Vereinigung "Kultur und Volk," 1945);

Lion Feuchtwanger, *Auswahl*, contributions by Brecht (Rudolstadt: Greifen, 1949);

T. Otto, *Nie wieder: Tagebuch in Bildern*, foreword by Brecht (Berlin: Volk und Welt, 1950);

Wir singen zu den Weltfestspielen: Herrnburger Bericht, edited by Brecht and Paul Dessau (Berlin: Neues Leben, 1951);

Theaterarbeit: Sechs Aufführungen des Berliner Ensembles, edited by Brecht, Ruth Berlau, C. Hubalek, and others (Dresdner: Dresden Verlag, 1952);

Die Kleinbürgerhochzeit, in *Spiele in einem Akt. 35 exemplarische Stücke*, edited by Walter Höllerer (Frankfurt am Main: Suhrkamp, 1961); translated by Martin and Rose Kastner as *The Wedding*, in volume 1 of *Collected Plays*, edited by Ralph Manheim and John Willett (New York: Random House, 1971);

Der Bettler oder Der tote Hund, in *Wer zuletzt lacht: Eine Auswahl heiterer Stücke für Laienspielgruppen*, edited by Carl-Ernst Teichmann and Rosemarie Zimmermann (Berlin, 1965); translated by Peter Hertz as *The Beggar, or The Dead Dog*, in volume 1 of *Collected Plays*, edited by Manheim and Willett (New York: Random House, 1971).

RADIO: *Lindberghflug*, music by Kurt Weill and Paul Hindemith, 29 July 1929;

Die heilige Johanna der Schlachthöfe, Berlin Radio, 11 April 1932;

Das Verhör des Lukullus, Studio Bern, 12 May 1940.

Bertolt Brecht is one of the great names not only of twentieth-century German literature but of modern world literature. His contribution, though varied—it includes lyrical, narrative, dramatic, and theoretical works—has a distinct "Brechtian" quality throughout. It has made a virtue out of provocation in the course of Germany's troubled history from World War I to World War II and beyond. But, although Brecht became increasingly committed to analyses of the sociopolitical scene, he was not just a writer for the day, nor did he put topical subjects above artistic considerations. With a keen eye for hypocrisy and injustice, he addressed fundamental issues of humanity with the fervor of a rebellious idealist and the poetic sensitivity of a great artist of the word. Long a figure of ideological controversy, Brecht has emerged as a classic, and he continues to challenge successive generations to take a close look at their world, to note its contradictions, and

to weigh the options and actions that might change it to the better.

Eugen Berthold Brecht—he later dropped the first name and changed the spelling of the middle name—was born in Augsburg into a fairly well-to-do bourgeois family on 10 February 1898. His father, Friedrich Berthold Brecht, an employee of a paper factory, advanced to the position of business director; Brecht's mother was Sofie Brezing Brecht. Brecht attended elementary and high school in Augsburg. Having failed to educate his teachers (as he put it), he began to write occasional poems. In 1914 he had a short play, *Die Bibel* (The Bible), published in the school journal. This first drama, a kind of Judith story set in the religious wars of the seventeenth century, reflects not only the beginning of a lifelong critical involvement in the conflicting teachings of the Bible (influenced, perhaps, by a Protestant father and a Catholic mother) but also the victimization of a girl by a warring world—a motif Brecht was to take up again in later plays. Although he wrote a few patriotic poems at the outbreak of World War I, Brecht's antiwar sentiments developed early. His criticism of Horace's dictum "Dulce est et decorum pro patria mori" (It is sweet and honorable to die for the fatherland) almost led to his expulsion from school. Various journals and newspapers printed poems and stories by the fledgling author, who liked to play the guitar, pursue love adventures, and roam through countryside, fairs, and pubs with a group of bohemian friends.

In 1917 Brecht moved to Munich, enrolled at the university, devoured books, scouted the theater scene, became increasingly involved in literary circles, and tried his hand at several projects, among them one-act plays and a full-fledged drama, *Baal* (published, 1922; performed, 1923). Even the one-act plays written in 1919 exhibit features that were to become his trademark. *Die Kleinbürgerhochzeit* (performed, 1926; translated as *The Wedding*) is a stinging exposure of petit bourgeois mentality; *Der Bettler oder Der tote Hund* (translated as *The Beggar, or the Dead Dog*) confronts the extreme opposites of the social scale: the world of the emperor and the world of the beggar; *Der Fischzug* (translated as *The Catch*) is a clever parodistic double adaptation of a Homeric and a biblical "catch" (Ares trapping Aphrodite, Saint Peter fishing for souls); and in *Lux in Tenebris* Brecht uses the theme of prostitution on several levels for his attack on what he considers the physical, spiritual, and social corruption of the bourgeoisie, whose perversion of the spirit, language, and action is highlighted by parodistic allusions to the Bible (which was to become one of his major literary sources). In style these interludelike sketches tend toward farcical satire; they show some influence of the Munich comedian Karl Valentin, whose witty dialogue-sketches Brecht admired and with whom he had performed in sideshows at fairs. The first full-fledged play, *Baal*, glorifies unfettered, amoral individualism, reflecting, to some extent, Brecht's bohemianism and his sympathy for such vitalist-sensualist figures as Frank Wedekind, Paul Verlaine, Arthur Rimbaud, and François Villon. It is both a literary and a social protest. As a "Gegenentwurf" (counterplay) to Hanns Johst's drama *Der Einsame* (1917; *The Solitary*), about a misunderstood poet, Brecht's play "corrects" the expressionist pathos and sentimentalizing "spirituality" of a Christlike, suffering "genius" by his own earthbound, materialist, selfish vagabond-genius named after a heathen deity; Baal (like Brecht) plays the guitar, writes poetry, eats, drinks, dances, makes love, and uses and drops people without any scruples. As an affront against a stale society, Baal breaks conventions at every turn, living only for his own pleasure, indulging until the last moment in the sensual experiences of this world which knows no afterworld. The powerful imagery of this balladlike, dramatic biography has strong ties to Brecht's early poetry, blending Baal's lust for life with the cyclical rhythm of vegetative nature. Like an insatiable animal Baal "grazes" off the world, and he as well as his lyrics are finally consumed in life's "digestive" process. Baal's reckless craving for self-assertion, tantamount to self-deification, seems to express Brecht's own hunger for life in the face of nothingness. (Brecht reworked the play repeatedly—there are five versions altogether. Such reworkings in the light of historical developments became characteristic of his habits as playwright.)

Brecht's early dramatic responses to the world indicate that while he had an eye for things he disliked, he had not yet developed a political or moral philosophy. In the absence of a constructive stance critics have called Brecht's literary beginnings "nihilistic"—a somewhat dubious term if one considers the vigor and keenness of his early poetic statements.

Shortly before the end of World War I Brecht, who had enrolled in medical studies to avoid the draft, was called to military service nevertheless. As a hospital orderly he witnessed the suffering of victims of war and disease. He wrote the satiric "Legende vom toten Soldaten" (Legend of the Dead Soldier), in which a corpse is revived to be declared fit for military service again. This antiwar ballad was sung in the fourth act of *Trommeln in der Nacht* (1922; translated as *Drums in the Night*, 1966) and was one of the reasons Brecht was put on the blacklist of the Nazis as early as 1923. After the war Brecht witnessed the turbulent beginning of the Weimar Republic and the power struggle among political parties, the violent suppression of the 1918-1919 revolution (whose cause he then seemed to consider hopeless), and the murders of political figures such as Rosa Luxemburg, Karl Liebknecht, and Kurt Eisner by reactionaries. While working on *Baal*, Brecht wrote *Trommeln in der Nacht*, which captures a drab postwar milieu. A disillusioned soldier, Andreas Kragler, returns from the front to his faithless bride, Anna. He encounters war profiteers—Anna's father and Murk, the father of her unborn child—and supporters of the communist "Spartacus" uprising. The revolution is thus in the background of the play (which was initially titled "Spartacus") but is hardly the issue of a serious political debate. Brecht called the play a comedy; it certainly is a satire of the bourgeois mentality and of art forms dear to such a mentality, such as bourgeois tragedy, operatic scenes, and sentimental songs played on gramophones. Andreas's in-laws, the Balickes, who had been doing a thriving war business manufacturing ammunition boxes, now make baby carriages. They have engineered a profitable liaison between their daughter and Murk after telling her that Andreas has been killed in the war. The engagement is celebrated in a dinner scene titled "Fressen" (Gobbling)—a suggestive image for their brutal, grabbing mentality—that includes sentimental German songs and patriotic slogans typical of a "good" German family. The postwar bourgeois victory feast is disturbed by the returning soldier, who pops up claiming his rights—an exploited survivor wanting his slice of the pie. As a "have-not" he is linked with the revolutionaries by the wary Balicke; and he seems to be drifting that way out of spite when he falls into the company of proletarians in a pub. But the play does not end with his joining the revolution. He does not have that sort of romantic "red moon" in his head but drums up his own antiromantic mood: Why, he asks, should he risk himself a second time for pure ideas, when he is likely to become damaged just like the purity of his pregnant

Scene from the premiere of Brecht's first staged play, Trommeln in der Nacht, *at the Munich Kammerspiele in 1922*

bride? Let's be a stinker in a stinking world, he decides. He throws his drum at the red moon, which is nothing but a stage prop lantern; "moon" and "drum" fall into a river without water, and off he goes to bed with his prize, Anna.

This stark assessment of reality was a slap in the face to all ideology, and the later, political Brecht reviewed it with some embarrassment. But *Trommeln in der Nacht*, the first Brecht play performed, brought rave reviews—especially from the influential theater critic Herbert Ihering, who discovered Brecht as a new talent and was instrumental in his receiving the Kleist Prize. New were Brecht's pithy language, his strategy of disillusionment, his radical unveiling of false fronts and sentiments. The many noble clichés are undercut by the actions of lowly characters: exploiters, cutthroats, cowards, and opportunists of every persuasion. Brecht's theater dissects reality rather than imitating it. Symbols such as the artificial red moon that lights up each time Andreas comes onstage point to the bourgeoisie's fear of the revolutionary who would threaten their smug existence, and placards saying "Glotzt nicht so romantisch" (Don't gape so romantically) were hung in the auditorium as part of the strategy of

disillusionment—early examples of a technique that Brecht would later develop into his dramaturgy of estrangement.

In 1919, while still a student, Brecht had a son by Paula Banholzer, whose parents disliked Brecht and dissuaded their daughter from marrying him. Frank, named after Brecht's idol, Wedekind, was placed in a foster home; he would be killed on the eastern front in 1943. In 1922 Brecht married the actress Marianne Zoff; the following year they had a daughter, Hanne, who would later become an actress as well. While working on his own projects Brecht also wrote stinging theater reviews that indicate his displeasure with fashionable entertainment void of intellectual challenge.

From several trips to the German capital Brecht had learned that Berlin was the cultural metropolis and, especially, the center of the theater scene in Germany, and he made up his mind to move to Berlin. But even before he settled there in 1924 he was engaged in a new project that was obviously influenced by his impression of a cold, chaotic cityscape. Like Upton Sinclair and Johannes Vilhelm Jensen, both of whose works he had read, Brecht set out to portray the city as jungle, filled with struggle and solitude. The result was a confusing play, first titled "Garga," then *Im Dickicht* (In the Jungle; performed, 1923), later *Im Dickicht der Städte* (published, 1927; translated as *Jungle of Cities*, 1966). Set in Chicago, it is Brecht's first American play and an early instance of his practice of addressing the immediate via the distant to allow more objective perceptions. Americanism was fashionable during the 1920s in Berlin; there were many who romanticized American freedom and open spaces as against the drabness and restrictions of German society; and many saw the cities, with skyscrapers, progress, gangsterism, and clashing social extremes, as American models of modern development.

The duel between the two men in the jungle of cities appears to be a duel of principles. Garga, a library clerk, begins as a sensitive individualist who believes in the freedom of the spirit; Shlink, a successful businessman lonely and hardened by the conditions of his profession, challenges Garga to a combat of changing strategies in which they undermine each other's existence. Neither side really wins. Ultimately Garga survives because he is the younger; but in the course of the fight his individualist ideas are compromised and battered. He emerges a changed man: the struggle has made him a thick-skinned city dweller at the expense of his family, which has disintegrated in the process.

Brecht's adaptation of Christopher Marlowe's play *Edward II* (1693), *Leben Eduards des Zweiten von England* (Life of Edward the Second of England, 1924; translated as *Edward II: A Chronicle Play*, 1966), is a bestiary of lusts and passions in which the members of the nobility are at each other's throat during thirteen years of slaughter, leaving the country ravaged and the people starved. Brecht shows that a deep-rooted source of the vicious circle of historical events is the "eye for an eye" obsession posing as justice.

Brecht pushed his criticism of individualism a step further in the comedy *Mann ist Mann* (performed, 1926; published, 1927; translated as *A Man's a Man*, 1966), set in colonial India. Among the motifs he develops are the economic nature of war and the manipulation of the economic nature of the individual. Galy Gay, a plain dock porter who has almost no passions, goes out to buy a fish for supper and is changed, through calculated triggering of his desire for gain, into an insatiable war machine. Galy takes the place of the soldier Jip, who is changed in a similar way: hungry not for a fish but for a beefsteak (*beefsteak* is a sym-

Brecht in 1927

bolic word in Brecht's play, meaning not only food [existence] for the soldiers but also the soldiers themselves as cannon fodder—war turns them into beefsteak tartare) he is turned into a god in a pagoda, where he is used to exploit the faithful. The interchangeability of the men in the roles that they assume as new identities "proves" that "a man's a man." Galy loses his private self in his uniformed function in a collective that may be used for any purpose. Brecht's transition from anarchic individualism through anti-individualism to collectivism is reflected in this first stage of his dramatic production between 1918 and 1924. By turning his plays into demonstrations of social conditions rather than perpetuating, in traditional fashion, dramatic clashes of great individuals, Brecht laid the groundwork for an innovative kind of theater. With naturalists and expressionists Brecht shared a discontent with society. But he considered purely emotional dramatic effects unproductive. To change social conditions, nothing was to be accepted as natural or inevitable. The audience was to be confronted with a theater that was not an illusion of reality but a detached yet provocative portrayal that would challenge the viewers to use their critical faculties.

Brecht's adaptation of John Gay's *The Beggar's Opera* (1728), translated by his collaborator Elisabeth Hauptmann, was a major theatrical event in 1928 and made Brecht and Kurt Weill, who wrote the music for it, famous. Gay's successful play had parodied fashionable pastorals and had satirized aristocrats and respectable members of the bourgeoisie by representing them as underworld types: rogues, harlots, and thieves. Two hundred years later Brecht updated this formula, letting his beggars, thieves, gangsters, and harlots behave like the members of the bourgeoisie. This depiction was part of his estrangement technique, as were the songs that interrupted the action and commented on the goings-on in a corrupt world. But the experiment had unforeseen effects: the bourgeoisie apparently considered what they saw as natural rather than as striking. They did not feel affronted; they loved the play and never stopped whistling the melody of "Mackie Messer" (Mac the Knife). The wit and the music seemed to diffuse the stinging antibourgeois attack rather than to enhance it as intended.

Nevertheless, Brecht's *Die Dreigroschenoper* (published, 1929; translated as *The Threepenny Opera*, 1964) certainly has an aggressive edge. Peachum, king of the beggars, wants to see Macheath, the gentlemanly street robber, hanged because Macheath has married Peachum's alluring daughter Polly. Peachum controls the beggars, whom he trains and exploits, while Mac controls the thieves and burglars in a similar way. During a visit to the brothel Mac is betrayed by Ginny Jenny and jailed, but he is freed by Police Chief Brown's daughter Lucy, who is one of Mac's girlfriends. Peachum puts pressure on Brown, threatening to disrupt the upcoming coronation ceremony with his hordes of beggars. Mac is captured again; his attempts at bribery fail because of lack of money. He is brought to the gallows, and the noose is laid around his neck, when a royal messenger rides up, orders his immediate release, and raises him to the permanent ranks of the nobility.

The trivial operatic story with a happy ending is used as a critical commentary on bourgeois mentality. It is a ravenous mentality: Mac, Brown, and Peachum are the beasts of society, preying on their victims. What is dangerous about them—and Brecht's estrangement technique calls attention to it—is that they cannot be recognized as beasts of prey by sharp teeth, fins, or claws. They hide their true nature under white-gloved manners. They do their preying according to rules: Peachum by the Bible, Mac by bourgeois etiquette, Brown by the law. But while they feast, the poor, living in shacks gnawed by rats, have to eat stone instead of bread. It is a society in which each person lives by maltreating, beating, cheating, or eating someone else. The maxim "Erst kommt das Fressen, dann kommt die Moral" (First comes the belly, then morality) is sung by Macheath and by Jenny, by the bourgeois exploiter and by the tavern harlot—higher and lower circles seem to agree on that fundamental economic issue, and Jenny adds that right and wrong can wait until the stomach of the poor is fed as well. Depending on which side of the double-faced characters speaks, the maxim expresses cynicism or rebellion. The marriage feast in the stable—which is not in Gay's play—unites the trinity: Religion (Reverend Kimball), Law (Brown), and Gangsterism (Mac). A manger in the stable suggests that this society has perverted a gospel of bliss into a gospel of looted blessings. Mac on the gallows parodies Christ on the cross, inverting the message of salvation: Mac, not humanity, is saved, and he will continue to plague mankind as a banker. Brecht later rewrote the play as a novel (1934) and gave a sharper political focus to the subject. But it is *Die Dreigroschenoper*, with its spicy ballads set to Weill's catchy tunes, that has made its mark in the history of modern theater.

Brecht and Weill collaborated on another opera, *Aufstieg und Fall der Stadt Mahagonny* (published, 1929; performed, 1930; translated as *Rise and Fall of the City of Mahagonny*, 1959). Here a fictive American city of pleasure and exploitation is the setting for an indictment of a capitalist world that ends in apocalypse. It is a paradise fed by biblical myth and the myth of the Wild West; but everything hinges on money, turning all value—including freedom—into a commodity. A commercial paradise that knows no mercy becomes hell. Nazi sympathizers disrupted the premiere of this collaboration by a "communist" and a "Jew."

Between 1928 and 1930 Brecht also wrote several brief "Lehrstücke" (didactic plays) as educational practice pieces for actors. The main concerns of these plays—*Der Ozeanflug* (The Flight across the Ocean; performed, 1929; published as *Der Flug der Lindberghs* [Lindbergh's Flight], 1930), *Das Badener Lehrstück vom Einverständ-*

Scene from the 1928 premiere of Brecht's Die Dreigroschenoper *at the Theater am Schiffbauerdamm, with Harald Paulsen as Macheath*

nis (The Baden Didactic Play on Consent; performed, 1929; published, 1930; translated as *The Baden Play for Learning*, 1960), *Die Maßnahme* (performed, 1930; published, 1931; translated as *The Measures Taken*, 1977), *Der Jasager und Der Neinsager* (He Who Says Yes and He Who Says No; performed, 1930; published, 1931; translated as *He Who Said Yes*, 1946), and *Die Ausnahme und die Regel* (performed, 1938; published, 1950; translated as *The Exception and the Rule*, 1961)—are the experimental exploration of human behavior in socioeconomic relationships and the relationship between individual and collective. These experiments were influenced by Marxist doctrine and by questions about the political effectiveness of revolutionary group efforts by the workers.

A full-fledged revolutionary play is *Die Mutter* (performed, 1932; published, 1933; translated as *The Mother*, 1965), derived from Maksim Gorky's novel *Mat'* (Mother, 1907), about the Russian revolution of 1905, which Brecht extends to include the revolution of 1917 against the czarist regime. A loving but apolitical mother, Pelagea Vlassova, is educated by her experiences to join her son and his comrades in the revolution; after

her son is killed she continues the fight. The mother has adopted the children of the revolution, and she carries the flag, leading the striking workers. This was the last Brecht play performed before the takeover by the Nazis, who had increasingly harassed leftist productions.

The most ambitious and powerful political play from Brecht's Berlin period is *Die heilige Johanna der Schlachthöfe* (published, 1932; performed, 1959; translated as *Saint Joan of the Stockyards*, 1969), written under the impact of the Great Depression of 1929, the bloody suppression of workers' demonstrations by the police in Berlin, and his reading of Karl Marx and Friedrich Engels's *Das Kapital* (1867-1895; translated as *Capital*, 1887-1896). The play is a variation on the Jeanne d'Arc theme and alludes to classical German authors, George Bernard Shaw, and Upton Sinclair's *The Jungle* (1906), which Brecht had recommended ten years earlier as an antidote to Friedrich Schiller's idea of freedom. Once again an American city is the setting for a general—but particularly German—reality. The stockyards of Chicago become the battleground between the meat packers, whose king is Pierpont Mauler, and the masses of hungry work-

Brecht's wife, Helene Weigel, with Werner Hinz (left) and Paul Bildt in a scene from Brecht's Mutter Courage und ihre Kinder *(photograph by Willy Saeger)*

ers, victims of engineered economic crises and recoveries serving monopolist interests. Johanna Dark, leading the Black Straw Hats of the Salvation Army, tries to mediate between the two sides by appealing to philanthropy and religion. She is good but naive about economic and political operations, which Brecht exposes by his estrangement technique. One of the strangest effects is that the meat packers strut around like great individuals in classical drama and speak in noble verse expressing (or covering up) their cutthroat business interests. This work is one of Brecht's bitterest counterplays, in which he demonstrates the dehumanizing power of hunger and the machinations of those in power who cause it. In his *Die Jungfrau von Orleans* (1802; translated as *The Maid of Orleans*, 1824) Schiller had idealized the alliance between the king of France and the God of victorious battle brought about by a self-sacrificial "Saint" Johanna. Brecht parodies this notion with the commercial alliance between the king of the slaughterhouses and the "saint" from the Salvation Army who unwittingly helps him to win his battle. In Brecht's imagery, the world is a bloody slaughterhouse. There is not much difference between cattle and people; both become the objects

of consumerism, as symbolically highlighted in the gruesome and grotesque accident of the worker Luckerniddle, who falls into the boiler, is processed through the bacon-maker, and is marketed like the slaughtered oxen, and whose place and coat are desperately grabbed by the next worker.

Johanna wants to help the workers; she preaches religion and feeds them a meager soup. Her actions are useful to the capitalist Mauler, who, "influenced" by her goodness, shows himself as a "humanitarian" and wants to collaborate with the Salvation Army to keep things as they are. When Johanna begins to recognize these machinations she joins the communists; but she fails them because, as a pacifist, she shies away from the use of violence. She cannot prevent the new alliance between the king of the slaughterhouses and the god of the Salvation Army, between capitalism and religion. She was the initiator and becomes victim of this alliance, which provides just enough soup for the poor and hungry to keep them from smashing their tools and rising in rebellion.

Brecht and Marianne Zoff had been divorced in 1927. In 1929 he married the actress Helene Weigel, whom he had met in 1923. Their son, Stefan, had been born in 1924; a daughter, Barbara, was born in 1930. With the Nazis coming into power the exile of the Brecht family began. His works were included in the infamous burning of the books in May 1933, but he had read the signs and escaped one day after the Reichstag fire on 27 February. The stations of his exile, during which he changed countries more often than his shoes (as he once put it), were Czechoslovakia, Austria, Switzerland, France, Denmark, Sweden, Finland, and the United States. Brecht remained active and productive while in exile. He traveled to conferences of writers and emigrants, joined anti-Fascist demonstrations, collaborated on emigrant journals, wrote poems and satires for the German broadcasting station in Moscow, attempted through his publications abroad to strengthen anti-Fascist resolve, and had his works smuggled into Germany for underground circulation. His parable play *Die Rundköpfe und die Spitzköpfe* (performed, 1935; published, 1957; translated as *Roundheads and Peakheads*, 1966) lashes out against Adolf Hitler's racism as a tool of class exploitation. Brecht used more realistic means in the resistance piece *Die Gewehre der Frau Carrar* (performed, 1937; translated as *Señora Carrar's Rifles*, 1938; published,

1953), dedicated to the struggle of the Spanish people against fascism. Beginning in 1935 Brecht worked on a series of one-act sketches about the Nazi terror, which he joined together in the play *Furcht und Elend des III. Reiches* (Fear and Misery of the Third Reich; performed as *99%*, 1938; published, 1941; translated as *The Private Life of the Master Race*, 1944). In 1938 he finished the first version of *Leben des Galilei* (Life of Galileo; performed, 1943). His claim that this play contained no barbs against Germany or Italy was to placate the nervous Danish authorities; its topicality, nevertheless, was apparent. With *Mutter Courage und ihre Kinder* (performed, 1941; published, 1949; translated as *Mother Courage and her Children*, 1966) Brecht warns against imminent war. The one-act plays *Dansen* (performed, 1967; published, 1966; translated, 1971-1973) and *Was kostet das Eisen* (performed as *Vad kostar järnet?*, 1939; published, 1966; translated as *How Much Is Your Iron?*, 1971-1973) criticize, in parabolic form, Scandinavian trade with Nazi Germany. In *Der aufhaltsame Aufstieg des Arturo Ui* (published, 1957; performed, 1958; translated as *The Resistible Rise of Arturo Ui*, 1976) Brecht chose a Chicago gangster story to indict Nazi methods. In American exile Brecht updated, together with Charles Laughton, the Galileo play in view of new political events. He also wrote *Die Gesichte der Simone Machard* (1957; translated as *The Visions of Simone Machard*, 1965) and *Schweyk im zweiten Weltkrieg* (1957; translated as *Schweyk in the Second World War*, 1967), and the frame story of *Der kaukasische Kreidekreis* (published, 1954; translated as *The Caucasian Chalk Circle*, 1948; translation performed, 1948), all of which take issue with the events of the time and raise keen questions about the kind of society in which such events can occur.

Among the anti-Fascist projects he pursued in Scandinavian exile, *Mutter Courage und ihre Kinder*, written on the eve of World War II, sounded the most intense warning about consenting to—and doing business with—war. Mother Courage, a sutler who follows the armies of the Thirty Years' War to make her living, loses all three of her children in the process. The Thirty Years' War, a low point in German history, had been realistically described by Hans Jacob Christoph von Grimmelshausen in his novels *Der abentheuerliche Simplicissimus Teutsch* (1669; translated as *The Adventurous Simplicissimus*, 1912) and *Trutz Simplex: Oder Ausführliche und wunderseltzame Lebensbeschreibung der Ertzbetrügerin und Lanstörtzerin Courasche* (Simple Defiance; or, Detailed and Curious Biography of the Arch-Cozener and Vagabond Courasche, 1669), which were Brecht's major sources of inspiration. Brecht does not show "great" generals of the "religious" war but rather the plain people who are the cannon fodder for "higher" interests. The ups and downs of the fortunes of war are reflected in the alternatingly prosperous and run-down condition of Courage's wagon, which links the twelve scenes. She does business with war to support her children, and she uses her children to support her business. That this practice cannot lead to success is shown by the horrors of war in which her children perish—at the end it is just Mother Courage who pulls her tattered wagon.

The wagon is the center of all kinds of trading for profit or survival: while Courage sells a belt buckle, the recruiter "buys" her son Eilif; a scrawny capon can be sold to the army cook at a high price because the captain has nothing else to offer to Eilif for his heroic deed; a preacher sells out his ideals to the war; a prostitute sells herself to the highest bidder; because Courage's honest son Schweizerkas (Swiss Cheese) does not trade a military cashbox to the enemy, his mother is forced to trade her wagon for his life, which is then lost anyway because she bargains too long for the best deal; a sudden enemy take-over necessitates a hasty trading of Protestant for Catholic insignia and garb. Such give-and-take is highlighted time and again to show that dealing with war, which is the business of those in power, brings nothing but loss to the lower classes. Mother Courage loses each of her children while she tries to drive some bargain, and the virtues she taught them only contribute to their destruction.

Brecht gives both admirable and despicable traits to Courage—he did not see her as a tragic figure. Some critics see her as a split character in an irreconcilable conflict between mother and businesswoman, while others think that she is more the latter than the former. At one point Courage condemns the war; but she is quick to get back into it, as it is her source of business. She does not recognize that her little world of opportunism, aggressiveness, scheming, and outsmarting others is a reflection of the tactics of big business. War is made—it does not just happen—and the common people have to pay the bill.

While for Courage business takes priority over family, for her daughter Kattrin the opposite is true. Victimized by the brutalities of war since she was a child, Kattrin is mute, disfigured, and deprived of hope for personal happiness. Yearning for love and sympathizing with the miserable and helpless, she opposes her mother's cold business tactics. One night she witnesses a sneak attack on a city and thinks of all the people— especially innocent children—about to be murdered; she beats a drum to warn them and is promptly shot to death, but she has awakened the city and saved other lives. She has been seen as a rebel and a martyr, a spontaneous activist in contrast to her calculating opportunist mother. But while Brecht endowed her with the qualities of a heroine, he does not glorify martyrdom per se and points out in considerable detail how the unselfish girl was manipulated, time and again, by the selfish people around her.

Der gute Mensch von Sezuan (performed, 1943; published, 1953; translated as *The Good Woman of Setzuan*, 1948) is Brecht's master parable, considered by many to be his most perfect example of epic theater as the art of estrangement. His first plans for the play date back to 1927; he worked on it intermittently during his exile and completed it in the United States in 1941. In a prologue three gods descend to earth; they will allow the world to go on as it is if they can find enough people who live lives worthy of human beings. No one except the poor prostitute Shen Te is willing to put them up overnight; the gods, happy to have found one good soul, remind her to maintain a good life, and they continue their search. But Shen Te, who earns the nickname "Engel der Vorstädte" (angel of the suburbs) by practicing goodness with the money the gods left her, is about to lose her little tobacco shop because parasites and opportunists have descended on her, exploiting her humanitarianism. She finds no other way out but to disguise herself as her "cousin" Shui Ta, a hard-nosed businessman, whenever she needs him. While Shui Ta provides the means through "his" ruthless bargaining methods and factory employment practices, Shen Te remains good to others. As demands on her goodness increase, Shui Ta has to stay longer and longer. Finally, Shen Te cannot keep up the double front and is unmasked in a trial before the gods, who can neither help her nor tell her why the world cannot be different. They hastily beat a retreat to heaven on their theater clouds and leave behind them a split person, an open-ended play, and an audience urged in the epilogue to find its own happy conclusion. Brecht uses the trial scene to confront the gods' judg-

ment of humans with human judgment of the gods. The open ending challenges the old idea of the "theatrum mundi," according to which God observes and judges individuals in their performance of the roles allotted to them in life. Shen Te recognizes that something is wrong with this world; the spectators and readers have also witnessed the negative experiment demonstrated by the parable. By addressing the audience directly, the speaker of the epilogue links the parable to whatever reality the spectators may find themselves in, a reality they are encouraged to shape toward a good end.

Less strident in its exposure of social injustice and more detached from immediate historical reference is the colorful comedy *Herr Puntila und sein Knecht Matti* (1948; translated as *Mister Puntila and His Man Matti*, 1977), based on a story by Hella Wuolijoki, who hosted Brecht during his Finnish exile. The landowner Puntila is humane and fraternizes with his servants only when he is drunk; when he is sober he is a ruthless exploiter. At the end his servant Matti, who has realized that a worthwhile relationship with the upper class is impossible, leaves to become his own master. Once again the conclusion is open-ended; Brecht challenges his audience to determine the meaning and the method of becoming one's "own master."

During his American exile Brecht lived in a colony of German emigrants in Los Angeles and continued with his anti-Fascist theater in a more direct, realistic style. *Die Gesichte der Simone Machard*, written together with Lion Feuchtwanger, is a modern variant of the Jeanne d'Arc theme. A naive young French servant girl, reading the patriotic legend, becomes a resistance fighter against the Nazi occupation of France; she is victimized by her countrymen, who, to save their possessions, collaborate with the invaders.

In *Schweyk im zweiten Weltkrieg* Brecht uses folk comedy and satire to encourage indirect subversiveness. Apparently he hoped to repeat the success of the 1928 Berlin staging of a dramatization of Jaroslav Hašek's antiwar novel *Osudy dobrého vojáka Svejka* (1920-1923; translated as *The Good Soldier Schweik*, 1930) by Erwin Piscator's political theater, a production in which the satirist George Grosz and Brecht himself had collaborated. A cartoon of Hitler, Hermann Göring, Heinrich Himmler, and Joseph Goebbels by the caricaturist Arthur Szyk, published in *Collier's* (17 January 1942), and reprinted in *Look* (8 September 1942), influenced Brecht's prelude set in

Brecht in the New York apartment of his collaborator Ruth Berlau during his exile from Germany, circa 1943 (photograph by Fred Stein)

the higher regions, where preternaturally large gods with grandiose plans for world power talk about the self-denying virtues of the little people on whose faith, love, and work they must rely. But while the "great ones" proclaim their totalitarian goals, the lowly ones, seemingly fulfilling these plans, actually undermine them. The Good Soldier Schweyk, who has survived World War I, battles to outlive World War II. Brecht sees in him the indestructible vitality of the people: the more oppressive the system, the more devious the defensive tactics. Under the pretense of naiveté, if not idiocy, Schweyk follows orders sometimes to the letter; but by fumbling his assignments he avoids danger. For example, he gives confusing directions to a freight train attendant, who sends a carload of weapons off on the wrong track; his march to the front turns out to be circular, leading him back to base. "Alles hat zwei Seiten" (there are two sides to everything) is Schweyk's motto: he does not accept the absolute or the inevitable but keeps the door open to alternatives. Some see him as an opportunistic fellow traveler, others as a devious opponent. He must

be both, for open resistance is simply clobbered down. Brecht's hope of seeing *Schweyk im zweiten Weltkrieg* performed on Broadway with music by his erstwhile collaborator Weill did not materialize; the play was first staged in Warsaw, with music by Hanns Eisler.

Another Broadway prospect, *The Caucasian Chalk Circle*, was not accepted either—Brecht's epic theater style was too unusual for mainstream American stages, and the play premiered in Northfield, Minnesota. With this new play, Brecht once again elaborated a subject that had interested him earlier. It is based on a Chinese fable about a Solomonic judgment that identifies the "true" mother of a child. The main story is a play within a play that is used to demonstrate the solution to a conflict between two collective farms that have survived Nazi aggression and plan to rebuild their economy. One group proposes to return to its old methods of breeding sheep so that the cheese will taste better (a conservative position); the other proposes to build an irrigation system for growing fruit in the valley (a progressive position aimed at communal good). The latter group wins the day and puts on the play, which consists of two parts: the story of Grusha, a kitchen maid; and the story of Azdak, the judge. The stories, presented one after the other, are parallel in time and converge at the end; in Brechtian fashion, the performance is interspersed with narrative comments and songs. During a revolution in a Caucasian city the governor is overthrown and killed. Grusha saves the child left behind by the escaping governor's wife, and protects and educates him. At the end of the first story all her self-sacrificial effort seems for naught: the soldiers of the "Fat Prince" (the governor's rival) capture the child, who is reclaimed by its biological mother; she hopes that after the return of the grand duke to power her properties will be restored to her by virtue of being the blood relative of the governor's heir. While Grusha saved a child, Azdak, a tramp, saved an old man. The old man turns out to be the grand duke, who, after the rebellion fails, rewards Azdak by making him a judge. Azdak settles law cases in a most unorthodox manner: taking from the rich and giving to the poor, he becomes the hero of the people, who at long last see real justice being done. Azdak's situation, however, becomes more and more precarious: feudal society did not change through the revolution, which was merely a power struggle between feudal lords. Azdak finally fades out of the picture, but not before he has decided the dispute between the two "mothers" by way of the chalk-circle test: the real mother is the one who can pull the child out of the circle. While the biological mother pulls him recklessly, Grusha lets go of his hand so that he will not be torn apart. Azdak declares her the "real" mother. The minstrel-narrator summarizes the message that what there is should belong to those who are good for it—the children to the motherly that they may thrive, the valley to those who water it so that it may bring forth fruit. Some performances of the play exclude the socialistic frame story about the valley. A sensitive audience will not miss the modern relevance of an old parable demonstrating how and why injustices occur in society.

To many, *Leben des Galilei* is the most significant of Brecht's dramas, not only because of its fascinating, complex central character but also because of its examination of the difficult pursuit of truth and the problem of applying truth to the well-being of society. Galileo Galilei, one of the great figures of the Renaissance, founder of modern astronomy and pioneer of empirical scientific inquiry, championed the new heliocentric theory of Nicolaus Copernicus against the old geocentric theory of Ptolemy. As Galileo's teaching appeared to contradict certain passages in the Bible, the Inquisition forced him to recant, put him under house arrest for the rest of his life, and policed his further research. This situation set back the pursuit of scientific truth, and men such as René Descartes ceased publishing "dangerous" findings; but the spread of Galileo's works, which were smuggled out of Italy, could not be stopped. As in *Mutter Courage und ihre Kinder*, the situation remote in time becomes a parable for current political events. The first sketches of the play project Galileo as a popular hero amid social upheaval, a courageous and cunning underground fighter. As resistance was more and more suppressed by the Nazis, the first full version of the play, written in Danish exile in 1938-1939, makes Galileo a more controversial character bending under political pressure in order to survive but continuing to write while under arrest. Those who saw the inaugural performance of this play in Zurich in 1943 were clearly aware of its anti-Fascist thrust.

The second version, *Galileo*, was a collaboration between Brecht, who was then in California, and Charles Laughton, who was to play the title role in an American production. The dropping of the atomic bombs on Japan in early August

Brecht and Paul Dessau, who wrote the music for several of Brecht's plays, in 1955

1945 gave a new meaning to the biography of the founder of modern physics. This version shows more negative traits of the hero; Brecht also left out the last scene, which showed the smuggling of Galileo's work over the border and suggested prospects for a better future. Also, social conflicts are profiled to a larger extent to bring home the message of the scientist's betrayal of society. The most important change, however, is the denial of the ethics of cunning through Galileo's self-accusation, which forms the new conclusion of the play. Galileo is now cast into the role of hero *and* criminal, one who committed the scientist's original sin: selling out truth to the powers that be for irresponsible political use. The play was performed in Beverly Hills in 1947 and later that year in New York, without making a great impression on an audience not used to Brechtian theater.

The third version translated the American version back into German and added material from the first version, including the last (crossing-of-the-border) scene. By this time the race for nuclear weapons had given the arsenals of the superpowers unfathomable potential for destruction. The negative elements in Galileo's character remain and are sharpened by radical additions such as the claim that, if he had held out, scientists might have developed something like the physicians' Hippocratic oath, the vow to use their knowledge only for the good of mankind. But as things stand now, Galileo says to his former student Andrea, the best one can hope for is a generation of inventive dwarfs who can be hired for any purpose. Brecht's molding of distant history into a parable with contemporary relevance, and the autobiographical affinities between Brecht and his Galileo, have elicited critical responses that include indictments of facism, capitalism, and communism, as well as divided opinions about Brecht himself.

In 1947 Brecht returned to Europe. His departure came one day after he and other members of the Hollywood scene were interrogated by the House Committee on Un-American Activities about communist affiliations. The transcript recording of the hearing is a revealing document of the times and of Brecht's cunning performance. After a brief period in Zurich, Brecht settled in 1948 in East Berlin. He and his wife, Weigel, were given a theater and the opportunity to take part in the cultural rebuilding of East Germany—not an easy task for Brecht, who was unwilling to bend to the narrow precepts of socialist realism, the artistic principle dictated by the ruling party. Until his death he was more active as a director than as a playwright. Although he completed such plays as *Die Tage der Commune* (The Days of the Commune; performed, 1956; published, 1957; translated, 1971) and *Turandot oder Der Kongreß der Weißwäscher* (Turandot; or, The Congress of Whitewashers; published, 1968; performed, 1969), many projects remained unfinished. A substantial part of his theater experimentation focused on adaptations of plays by Molière, Shakespeare, and Sophocles. At last Brecht was able to direct his own plays according to principles he had developed over the years in such works as "Kleines Organon für das Theater" (1953; translated as "A Short Organum for the Theatre," 1964), with a troupe of actors that was to become world famous as the Berliner Ensemble. Brecht died in Berlin on 14 August 1956, during rehearsals of *Leben des Galilei*.

Letters:

Briefe, 2 volumes, edited by Günter Glaeser (Frankfurt am Main: Suhrkamp, 1981).

Bibliographies:

Walter Nubel, "Brecht Bibliographie," *Sinn und Form: Sonderheft Bertolt Brecht 2* (1957): 479-623;

Klaus-Dietrich Petersen, *Bertolt-Brecht-Bibliographie* (Bad Homburg: Gehlen, 1968);

Reinhold Grimm, *Bertolt Brecht*, third edition (Stuttgart: Metzler, 1971);

Klaus Völker, "Verzeichnis sämtlicher Stücke," Bearbeitungen und Fragmente zu Stücken von Bertolt Brecht," *text + kritik. Sonderband Bertolt Brecht II* (1973): 210-225;

Jan Knopf, *Bertolt Brecht: Ein kritischer Forschungsbericht* (Frankfurt am Main: Athenäum Taschenbuchverlag, 1974);

Gerhard Seidel, *Bibliographie Bertolt Brecht. Titelverzeichnis Band I: Deutschsprachige Veröffentlichungen aus den Jahren 1913-1972* (Berlin & Weimar: Aufbau, 1975);

Stephan Bock, *Brecht, Bertolt: Auswahl- und Ergänzungs-Bibliographie* (Bochum: Brockmeyer, 1979).

Biographies:

Frederic Ewen, *Bertolt Brecht: His Life, His Art and His Times* (New York: Citadel, 1967);

Werner Frisch and K. W. Obermeier, *Brecht in Augsburg: Erinnerungen, Texte, Photos* (Berlin: Aufbau, 1975);

Klaus Völker, *Bertolt Brecht: Eine Biographie* (Munich: Hanser, 1976); translated by John Nowell as *Brecht: A Biography* (New York: Seabury Press, 1978);

Lion Feuchtwanger, ed., *Bertolt Brecht: Leben und Werk im Bild* (Frankfurt am Main: Insel, 1979);

James K. Lyon, *Bertolt Brecht in America* (Princeton: Princeton University Press, 1980);

Ernst Schumacher and Renate Schumacher, *Leben Brechts in Wort und Bild*, third edition (Berlin: Henschel, 1981);

Ronald Hayman, *Brecht: A Biography* (New York: Oxford University Press, 1983);

Bruce Cook, *Brecht in Exile* (New York: Holt, Rinehart & Winston, 1983);

Ruth Berlau, *Brechts Lai-tu: Erinnerungen und Notate*, edited by Hans Bunge (Darmstadt: Luchterhand, 1985);

Werner Mittenzwei, *Das Leben des Bertolt Brecht*, 2 volumes (Berlin: Aufbau, 1986);

Werner Hecht, ed., *Brecht: Sein Leben in Bildern und Texten* (Frankfurt am Main: Insel, 1988).

References:

Eric Bentley, *The Brecht Commentaries, 1943-1980* (New York: Grove, 1981);

Keith A. Dickson, *Towards Utopia: A Study of Brecht* (Oxford: Clarendon, 1978);

Martin Esslin, *Brecht: A Choice of Evils* (London: Eyre & Spottiswoode, 1959); republished as *Brecht: The Man and His Work* (Garden City, N.Y.: Doubleday, 1960); revised as *Brecht: A Choice of Evils. A Critical Study of the Man, His Work and His Opinions* (London: Methuen, 1984);

Ronald Gray, *Brecht the Dramatist* (Cambridge: Cambridge University Press, 1976);

Reinhold Grimm, *Bertolt Brecht: Die Struktur seines Werkes*, sixth edition (Nuremberg: Carl, 1972);

Claude Hill, *Bertolt Brecht* (Boston: Twayne, 1975);

Walter Hinck, *Die Dramaturgie des späten Brecht*, sixth edition (Göttingen: Vandenhoeck & Ruprecht, 1977);

Walter Hinderer, ed., *Brechts Dramen: Neue Interpretationen* (Stuttgart: Reclam, 1984);

Helmut Jendreiek, *Bertolt Brecht: Drama der Veränderung*, second edition (Düsseldorf: Bagel, 1973);

Jan Knopf, *Brecht-Handbuch: Theater. Eine Ästhetik der Widersprüche* (Stuttgart: Metzler, 1980);

Siegfried Mews, ed., *Critical Essays on Bertolt Brecht* (Boston: G. K. Hall, 1989);

Mews and Herbert Knust, eds., *Essays on Brecht: Theater and Politics* (Chapel Hill: University of North Carolina Press, 1974);

John Milful, *From Baal to Keuner: The "Second Optimism" of Bertolt Brecht* (Bern & Frankfurt am Main: Lang, 1974);

Michael Morley, *Brecht: A Study* (London: Heinemann, 1977);

Klaus-Detlev Müller, ed., *Bertolt Brecht: Epoche—Werk—Wirkung* (Munich: Beck, 1985);

Jan Needle and Peter Thomson, *Brecht* (Chicago: University of Chicago Press, 1981);

Patty Lee Parmalee, *Brecht's America* (Columbus: Ohio State University Press, 1981);

Herta Ramthun, ed., *Bertolt-Brecht-Archiv: Bestandsverzeichnis des literarischen Nachlasses*, 4 volumes (Berlin: Aufbau, 1969-1973);

Karl-Heinz Schoeps, *Bertolt Brecht* (New York: Ungar, 1977);

Ronald Speirs, *Brecht's Early Plays* (Atlantic Highlands, N.J.: Humanities Press, 1982);

Antony Tatlow, *The Mask of Evil: Brecht's Response to the Poetry, Theatre, and Thought of China and Japan* (Bern: Lang, 1977);

Klaus Völker, *Brecht Kommentar zum dramatischen Werk* (Munich: Winkler, 1983);

Betty Nance Weber and Hubert Heinen, eds., *Bertolt Brecht: Political Theory and Literary Practice* (Athens: University of Georgia Press, 1980);

Alfred White, *Bertolt Brecht's Great Plays* (New York: Barnes & Noble, 1978);

John Willett, *The Theater of Bertolt Brecht: A Study from Eight Aspects* (London: Methuen, 1977).

Papers:

Bertolt Brecht's papers are at the Bertolt Brecht Archive, Berlin, administered by the Deutsche Akademie der Künste (German Academy of the Arts).

Hermann Broch

(1 November 1886 - 30 May 1951)

James Hardin
University of South Carolina

See also the Broch entry in *DLB 85, Austrian Fiction Writers After 1914.*

PLAY PRODUCTIONS: . . . *denn sie wissen nicht, was sie tun (Die Entsühnung)*, Zurich, Züricher Schauspielhaus, 15 March 1934;

Aus der Luft gegriffen oder Die Geschäfte des Baron Laborde, Osnabrück, Städtische Bühne, 6 October 1981.

BOOKS: *Die Schlafwandler: Eine Romantrilogie*, 3 volumes (Munich & Zurich: Rhein, 1931-1932); translated by Willa and Edwin Muir as *The Sleepwalkers: A Trilogy* (New York: Little, Brown, 1932; London: Secker, 1932);

Die unbekannte Größe: Roman (Berlin: Fischer, 1933); translated by Willa and Edwin Muir as *The Unknown Quantity* (New York: Viking, 1935; London: Collins, 1935);

James Joyce und die Gegenwart: Rede zu Joyces 50. Geburtstag (Vienna, Leipzig & Zurich: Reichner, 1936); translated by Maria and Eugène Jolas as "James Joyce and the Present Age," in *A James Joyce Yearbook* (Paris: Transition Press, 1949), pp. 68-108;

The City of Man: A Declaration on World Democracy, by Broch, Herbert Agar, and others (New York: Viking, 1940);

Der Tod des Vergil: Roman (New York: Pantheon, 1945); translated by Jean Starr Untermeyer as *The Death of Virgil* (New York: Pantheon, 1945; London: Routledge, 1946);

Die Schuldlosen: Roman in elf Erzählungen (Munich: Weismann, 1950); translated by Ralph Manheim as *The Guiltless* (Boston & Toronto: Little, Brown, 1974);

Gesammelte Werke, 10 volumes (Zurich: Rhein, 1952-1961)—comprises volume 1, *Gedichte: Mit 9 Bildern und 2 Handschriftproben des Autors*, edited by Erich Kahler (1953); volume 2, *Die Schlafwandler: Romantrilogie* (1952); volume 3, *Der Tod des Vergil: Epische Dichtung* (1952); volume 4, *Der Versucher: Roman*, edited by Felix Stössinger (1953); republished as *Deme-*

Hermann Broch circa 1948 (photograph by Sol Libsohn)

ter (Frankfurt am Main: Suhrkamp, 1967); volume 5, *Die Schuldlosen* (1954); volume 6, *Dichten und Erkennen: Essays*, edited by Hannah Arendt (1955); volume 7, *Erkennen und Handeln: Essays*, edited by Arendt (1955); volume 8, *Briefe: Von 1929 bis 1951*, edited by Robert Pick (1957); volume 9, *Massenpsychologie: Schriften aus dem Nachlaß*, edited by Wolfgang Rothe (1959); volume 10, *Die unbekannte Größe und frühe Schriften*, edited by Ernst Schönwiese, and *Mit den Briefen an Willa Muir*, edited by Eric William Herd (1961);

Nur das Herz ist das Wirkliche, edited by Schönwiese (Graz: Stiasny, 1959);

Die Entsühnung: Schauspiel, in der Hörspielfassung, edited by Schönwiese (Zurich: Rhein, 1961);

Die Heimkehr: Prosa und Lyrik. Auswahl aus dem dichterischen Werk ergänzt durch den Vortrag Geist und Zeitgeist, edited by Harald Binde (Frankfurt am Main & Hamburg: Fischer, 1962);

Hermann Broch der Dichter: Eine Auswahl aus dem dichterischen Werk, edited by Binde (Zurich: Rhein, 1964);

Hermann Broch der Denker: Ein Auswahl aus dem essayistischen Werk und aus Briefen, edited by Binde (Zurich: Rhein, 1966);

Short Stories, edited by Herd (London: Oxford University Press, 1966);

Die Idee ist ewig: Essays und Briefe, edited by Binde (Munich: Deutsche Taschenbuch Verlag, 1968);

Zur Universitätsreform, edited by Götz Wienold (Frankfurt am Main: Suhrkamp, 1969);

Bergroman: Die drei Originalfassungen, 4 volumes, edited by Frank Kress and Hans Albert Maier (Frankfurt am Main: Suhrkamp, 1969);

Gedanken zur Politik, edited by Dieter Hildebrandt (Frankfurt am Main: Suhrkamp, 1970);

Barbara und andere Novellen: Eine Auswahl aus dem dichterischen Werk, edited by Paul Michael Lützeler (Frankfurt am Main: Suhrkamp, 1973)—comprises "Eine methodologische Novelle," "Ophelia," "Leutnant Jaretzki," "Hanna Wendling," "Eine leichte Enttäuschung," "Vorüberziehende Wolke," "Ein Abend Angst," "Die Heimkehr," "Der Meeresspiegel," "Esperance," "Barbara," "Die Heimkehr des Vergil," "Die vier Reden des Studienrats Zacharias," "Die Erzählung der Magd Zerline";

Völkerbund-Resolution: Das vollständige politische Pamphlet von 1937 mit Kommentar, Entwurf und Korrespondenz, edited by Lützeler (Salzburg: Müller, 1973);

Kommentierte Werkausgabe, 17 volumes, edited by Lützeler (Frankfurt am Main: Suhrkamp, 1974-1981)—includes volume 1, *Die Schlafwandler: Eine Romantrilogie* (1978); volume 2, *Die unbekannte Größe: Roman* (1977); volume 3, *Die Verzauberung* (1976), translated by H. F. Broch de Rothermann as *The Spell* (New York: Farrar, Straus & Giroux, 1987); volume 4, *Der Tod des Vergil: Roman* (1976); volume 5, *Die Schuldlosen: Roman in elf Erzählungen* (1974); volume 6, *Novellen*; *Prosa*; *Fragmente* (1980); volume 7, *Dramen* (1979); includes *Die Entsühnung*, translated by George E. Wellwarth and Broch de Rothermann as *The Atonement*, in *German Drama be-*

tween the Wars, edited by Wellwarth (New York: Dutton, 1972); *Aus der Luft gegriffen oder Die Geschäfte des Baron Laborde*; and *Es bleibt alles beim Alten: Schwank mit Musik*, by Broch and Broch de Rothermann; volume 8, *Gedichte* (1980); volume 9, part 1, *Schriften zur Literatur: Kritik* (1975); includes "Hugo von Hofmannsthal und seine Zeit," translated by Michael P. Steinberg as *Hugo von Hofmannsthal and His Time: The European Imagination, 1860-1920* (Chicago & London: University of Chicago Press, 1984); volume 9, part 2, *Schriften zur Literatur: Theorie* (1975); volume 10, part 1, *Philosophische Schriften: Kritik* (1977); volume 10, part 2, *Philosophische Schriften: Theorie* (1977); volume 11, *Politische Schriften* (1979); volume 12, *Massenwahntheorie: Beiträge zu Einer Psychologie der Politik* (1979); volume 13, part 1, *Briefe 1913-1938* (1981); volume 13, part 2, *Briefe 1938-1945* (1981); volume 13, part 3, *Briefe 1945-1951* (1981).

OTHER: "Logik einer zerfallenden Welt," in *Wiedergeburt der Liebe: Die unsichtbare Revolution*, edited by Frank Thiess (Berlin: Zsolnay, 1931), pp. 361-380;

"Gedanken zum Problem der Erkenntnis in der Musik," in *Almanach: "Das 48. Jahr"* (Berlin: Fischer, 1934), pp. 53-66;

"Eh ich erwacht," "Über die Felswand," "Helle Sommernacht," "Sommerwiese," "Schon lichtet der Herbst den Wald," "Die Waldlichtung," "Später Herbst," "Nachtgewitter," "Lago Maggiore," "Das Nimmergewesene," in *Patmos: Zwölf Lyriker*, edited by Ernst Schönwiese (Vienna: Johannespresse, 1935), pp. 57-67;

"Mythos und Altersstil," in Rachel Bespaloff, *On the Iliad*, translated by Mary McCarthy (New York: Pantheon, 1947), pp. 9-33;

"Vom Altern," in *Frank Thiess: Werk und Dichter. 32 Beiträge zur Problematik unserer Zeit*, edited by Rolf Italiaander (Hamburg: Krüger, 1950), p. 9.

Hermann Broch has long been considered one of the most significant and formidable Austrian novelists, a profoundly engaged thinker with an essayistic bent, a writer to whom fiction had value only insofar as it could ameliorate humanity's existential or sociopolitical condition. His novels are, in varying degrees, expositions of his eclectic psychological, philosophical, aesthetic, and political view of the world. Novels such as the trilogy *Die Schlafwandler* (1931-1932; translated as *The Sleepwalkers*, 1932) and *Der Tod des Vergil* (1945; translated as *The Death of Virgil*, 1945) are at the same time masterful poetic evocations of epochs that were historic turning points and detailed, subtle interpretations of these periods viewed from the vantage point of Broch's complex Weltanschauung. Broch's dramas have received much less critical attention than his novels, but they deserve analysis because they provide—in the most succinct form of which Broch was capable—interesting dramatic treatments of the basic tenets of his worldview and because at least one of the plays, the tragedy *Die Entsühnung* (performed 1934; published, 1961; translated as *The Atonement*, 1972), is an enthralling, highly effective drama in its own right.

Broch was born in Vienna on 1 November 1886 to Josef Broch, a wealthy flannel merchant, and Johanna Broch (née Schnabel), whose family was also wealthy. Broch's brother, Friedrich, was born three years later. The parents seemed to Broch to favor Friedrich, a perception that galled him into his final years. In Broch's view both his father and mother were highly neurotic, and they had a decidedly negative influence on the mental and physical health of their elder son.

Still, Broch's childhood must have been relatively happy. His summers were spent at the Broch villa in Purkersdorf or in his grandmother Schnabel's villas in Hinterbrühl and Baden. He was enrolled in school in 1892, though he was taught at home and did not actually attend school until 1896. In 1897 he was enrolled in the kaiserlich-königlich Staats-Realschule (Imperial and Royal State Secondary School). It was understood that he would go into the textile business. Broch was an average student at a time and place when "average" represented a high level of achievement, and he was thrown together with bright and industrious boys whose companionship was significant in his intellectual development. His occasional tutor, David Bach, was a childhood friend of Arnold Schoenberg and a former student of the philosopher Ernst Mach; Bach was well versed in philosophy, music, literature, and mathematics and had strong socialist tendencies.

Broch graduated in 1904. From the fall of that year until the summer of 1906 he attended a textile institute in Vienna, and also, against his father's wishes, registered at the University of Vi-

enna for the winter semester 1904-1905 for courses in philosophy and mathematics. There he encountered the neopositivism then blossoming that argued that the great metaphysical questions are not answerable and that metaphysics has no place in science. Broch continued his education as a textile engineer at the Spinning and Weaving School in Mulhouse, Alsace, from 1906 to 1907. At the conclusion of his studies he made a six-week trip to the United States, where he inspected textile mills and attended the International Cotton Growers, Buyers and Spinners convention in Atlanta and visited the New York Cotton Exchange. After his journey to the United States Broch took the position of assistant director of the Teesdorf spinning factory in Lower Austria, in which his father held a majority interest. At about the same time Broch met Franziska von Rothermann, who came from a wealthy family in the sugar business. In part due to the pressure to assimilate but also with a view to marrying Franziska, Broch converted from Judaism to Catholicism in 16 July 1909. Broch gradually won over her family with his wit, charm, diplomacy, and good looks, accompanying them on their holiday on the Riviera. He had joined the Third Ulan Regiment in May 1909; but the shy, gentle Broch did not fit well into this swaggering cavalry regiment and he transferred to an artillery unit. He was released from service 26 October 1909, presumably because of illness, after serving five months of his one-year commitment.

In fall 1909 Broch assumed duties as a director of the Teesdorf textile factory. In October he was engaged to Franziska, and the marriage took place on 11 December in a Catholic chapel near Vienna. On 4 October 1910 the Brochs' only child, Hermann Friedrich Maria (Armand) Broch, was born. The family lived mainly in Teesdorf but also had a residence in Vienna. Broch became increasingly absorbed in philosophical studies, while Franziska enjoyed a rich social life; the two drifted apart, and the result was a divorce that became official on 13 April 1923.

Like many other Viennese intellectuals, Broch felt that the dominant trend of the time was what he termed "Wertzerfall" (the disintegration of values). Much of the age's preoccupation with values was due to the writings of the seminal philosopher-poet Friedrich Nietzsche, whose works had a marked influence on Broch. A sense of decay, even of nearing apocalypse, lay in the air, in the music of Richard Wagner and Richard Strauss, in the cultural pessimism of the Vien-

*Self-caricature by Broch, circa 1917 (from Hans Kaufmann,
ed.,* Geschichte der deutschen Literatur, *1975)*

nese critic and dramatist Karl Kraus, and in much of European fin de siècle art. Broch absorbed these ideas and began writing as yet unpublished articles in 1911. On 1 February 1913 Broch's first published work, "Philistrosität, Realismus, Idealismus der Kunst" (Philistinism, Realism, Idealism of Art), appeared in *Der Brenner* (The Burner); on 1 November his first published poems, "Mathematisches Mysterium" (Mathematical Mystery), appeared in the same periodical. Broch's double career as writer-industrialist was launched. Broch soon began to distance himself from the irrational aspects of the thought of Nietzsche and was drawn to the cooler philosophy and ethics of Immanuel Kant.

When war broke out in 1914 Broch twice volunteered for military duty but was turned down as too old. He was given the assignment of administering a convalescence center that was set up in

one of the buildings in the Teesdorf factory. His brother was in the air force, and his father was less active in the day-to-day operation of the factory, so Broch's business responsibilities increased considerably. The war was good for business—uniforms were in demand—and the Teesdorf factory reached its peak of production around 1915. Forced by business to spend more time in Vienna, Broch associated with coffeehouse intellectuals and literati such as Robert Musil, Franz Blei, and Alfred Polgar, who were grappling with many of the same philosophical and aesthetic issues that occupied him.

When the war ended in November 1918, the collapse of the old Austro-Hungarian regime seemed to promise the birth of a communist government on the Russian model. There was much jubilation among the coffeehouse intellectuals, and expressionist writers such as Franz Werfel greeted workers' uprisings in Vienna with euphoria. Broch wrote in an open letter to Blei that he was "mit jeder Art kommunistischer Wirtschaft von vornherein einverstanden wie sie einzurichten, die Welt für gut findet. Keinerlei Besitz besitzt mich" (from the outset in agreement with any kind of communist economic system that the world is pleased to erect. No possessions possess me). But he goes on to say that he did not share the enthusiasm of most intellectuals for the rioting masses. Broch's cool, distant view of mass movements was an indication of the trends his thought and writing would follow for the rest of his life. Broch apparently did not favor the dictatorial Russian model of communism but accepted the idea of workers' councils that would have parity with management in business and government. When the revolution failed, Broch turned away from political essays until the rise of Nazism, but his concern with the lot of the worker is reflected in his works of the 1930s—especially *Die Entsühnung*.

The Teesdorf factory had come close to bankruptcy at the end of the war, in part because Josef Broch had invested a large sum in the last war bonds issued by Austria. Hermann Broch wanted to sell the factory but was prevented from doing so by his parents and brother. He took courses in the winter semester 1919-1920 at the Technische Hochschule in Vienna in mathematics, finance, and trade law, presumably to enhance his ability to administer the family's business affairs. He was a progressive, liberal force at Teesdorf: he arranged for needy children to receive free lunches and provided money for a library and gymnasium for his workers. In spite of his efforts the workers called him "Großnase" (Big Nose) behind his back.

In November 1925, at age thirty-nine, Broch registered as a student of mathematics and philosophy at the University of Vienna. He studied until 1930, but since he had attended a Realschule rather than the humanistically oriented gymnasium, he could not receive a doctorate unless he made up his deficiency in Latin; he never succeeded in doing so. He continued to move in rarefied intellectual circles and was a frequent guest in the salons of such luminaries as Alma Mahler-Werfel. In 1927 he sold the Teesdorf factory to his friend Felix Wolf for the relatively low sum of a hundred thousand dollars; after the other partners were paid off, sixty thousand dollars went to the Brochs, which was divided into one-third each for Hermann, Friedrich, and their parents. Broch continued to work for the firm until 1928. In 1927 he had come into close contact with Sigmund Freud's Viennese circle, and he underwent regular analysis from then until 1935. In 1929 he broke with his long-time mistress Ea von Allesch and moved in with Anna Herzog, fifteen years his junior; much of *Die Schlafwandler* was written in a villa they shared and was typed by her from his manuscript. His friend Frank Thiess's contacts with publishers and his willingness to print essays on the novel trilogy in his periodical *Literarische Welt* (Literary World) were significant factors in establishing Broch's reputation. In this period literature—especially the novel—enjoyed a new international esteem. Writers such as James Joyce, John Dos Passos, André Gide, Robert Musil, and Thomas Mann popularized philosophical and psychological theories among the broad middle-class readership. Literature could again, as in the Romantic period, enlighten as well as entertain. It is in this light that Broch's turn to literature should be seen, for all his writing is at bottom didactic, profoundly concerned with issues of morality and ethics.

Die Schlafwandler established Broch as a "writer's writer" who enjoyed a small but enthusiastic intellectual following. The book was a failure financially, especially after Adolf Hitler's rise to power in 1933 made its distribution and sale difficult in Germany. Broch had exhausted most of his capital, and for that reason spent considerable time in mountain villages such as Gössl and Altaussee, where the solitude and beauties of nature were as attractive as the low price—a couple of schillings per day for a primitive, poorly heated room. It was in Gössl in 1932 that Broch wrote his first drama, *Die Entsühnung*. By writing for the stage, Broch hoped in vain for the kind of immediate success and financial rewards that prose generally could not offer.

Die Entsühnung, Broch's only play to be performed in his lifetime, was originally conceived as part of a never-completed novel. It premiered on 15 March 1934 at the Zurich Schauspielhaus (playhouse) under a title provided by the director, Gustav Hartung: . . . *denn sie wissen nicht, was sie tun* (. . . for they know not what they do). In *Die Entsühnung* Broch drew on personal experience and possibly also on the novel *Union der festen Hand* (Union of the Firm Hand, 1931), by Erik Reger (pseudonym for Hermann Dennenberger), to portray a cross section of German society around 1930. Combining traditional realistic plot with modern "alienation" technique such as film, lyrical monologues and dialogues, and a chorus, the play aims to reveal the hidden, omnipresent economic forces that underlie not only the financial misery of the industrial world but also the ubiquitous angst and neuroses of the twentieth century. As Ernst Schürer observes in a special Broch issue of *Modern Austrian Literature* (1980), Broch was attempting to link the metaphysical religious realm with the political and economic.

Up to a point *Die Entsühnung* is a realistic portrayal of the economic competition between two companies, the Menck-Kouzern (Menck Concern) and the Durig-Gruppe (Durig Group). In the center of the battle are the Filsmann-Werke (Filsmann Works). Herbert Filsmann attempts through firings, reorganization, and salary cuts to avert bankruptcy; but Menck gains control of the Filsmann factory by means of ruthless and ingenious financial manipulations, and Filsmann commits suicide. Menck is then able to cut wages at both the Filsmann and Durig firms—he has also made the latter a part of the Menck Syndicate—and to raise prices. Menck, the prototype of the twentieth-century manager and businessman, has followed with absolute consistency the logic of his own value system, that of the entrepreneur, which is to use economic means to destroy or absorb all of one's competition. The figures in the play are portrayed as marionettes possessing little will of their own, manipulated by impersonal, inexorable economic forces. As critics have pointed out, even Menck and Martin Durig are

Broch (left) with director Gustav Hartung after the premiere of Broch's . . . denn sie wissen nicht, was sie tun in Zurich, 15 March 1934 (photograph by Trude Geiringer)

puppets dependent on the financial support of American capitalists.

In some respects, the play can be seen as part of a tradition stretching back to the late-nineteenth-century naturalist drama of Gerhart Hauptmann which presents figures who are dependent on little-understood forces—genes and environment—beyond their control. But there is much that is quite specific to the time when the play was written: its social-political spectrum comprises not only factory tycoons and capitalist caricatures but also a Nazi activist and sympathizers, a union organizer, white-collar workers, a revolutionary, a liberal intellectual (possibly based on Broch himself), and women, who represent a more positive side of humanity and provide much of the emotional and even metaphysical content of the drama. What most decisively places the drama outside a realistic-naturalist tradition, however, is Broch's use of Verfremdung (alienation)—most conspicuously practiced by Bertolt Brecht and found in expressionist drama just before and after World War I—to make it clear that the play makes no attempt to provide the illusion of reality. Broch felt that Brecht's Lehrstücke (didactic plays) went too far toward an abstract,

bare propaganda, but he followed the alienation techniques because they permitted him to draw attention to the ideas behind his figures and their actions. In *Die Entsühnung* he uses techniques borrowed from the film, such as a transition from one scene to another in which the lighting is turned off, often with an actor in midsentence, and turned on to reveal another scene in a different area of the stage. For sets that require more time to prepare, Broch calls for the use of film and sound to bridge the gap between scenes. He stresses the message of a climactic scene by using unnatural lighting or by having his figures speak in a sing-song manner. The appearance at the end of *Die Entsühnung* of a Greek chorus of the women characters lamenting their dead in a pathos-laden language that moves from the specific to the prototypical and cosmic strains the dramatic genre to the breaking point. The director of the Zurich premiere excised this and some other lyrical scenes, much to Broch's dismay. But Hartung's New Objectivist rendering probably made the play palatable to audiences, and Broch reported that the performance received applause after every scene. The play was positively reviewed in the 4 April 1934 *Neues Wiener Abendblatt* (New Vienna Evening Paper), but by then it had already closed; the third and final performance was on 21 March. The play's concern with contemporary political issues made it unattractive to German and Austrian theaters during the Nazi period. It was produced as a radio play and broadcast by Austrian Radio and the Swiss Broadcasting Company in 1961; it received its German stage premiere on 3 June 1982 in Osnabrück. It is an effective play, and its lack of success is largely attributable to the hostile environment in which it arose.

Broch completed the novel *Die unbekannte Größe* (translated as *The Unknown Quantity*, 1935) in 1933. Ironically, this relatively short, unambitious work brought its author more money than any other of his books, but it was a critical failure both in the original and in its English translation. Broch was also writing novellas and poetry; but his father died in October 1933, and much of Broch's time was occupied in lawsuits with his brother concerning the inheritance and in moving his mother's household from Teesdorf to Vienna. In 1934 his continued attempts to write popular works for the stage resulted in *Aus der Luft gegriffen oder Die Geschäfte des Baron Laborde* (Out of Thin Air; or, The Business Affairs of Baron Laborde, published, 1979; performed, 1981).

Broch's son Armand provided the main title, the idea for the prologue, and the stage design for *Aus der Luft gegriffen*, which in Lützeler's view is one of the few good comedies in German literature of the period. Armand was also clearly one of the models for the protagonist, André Laborde, an affable confidence man. The setting of the play, a luxury hotel with a shallow air of romance and intrigue, probably owes something to Armand's job at a Viennese travel agency of questionable probity; but hotel life was a favorite literary topos of the time, as seen in Vicki Baum's *Menschen im Hotel* (1929; translated as *Grand Hotel*, 1930) and Joseph Roth's *Hotel Savoy* (1924; translated, 1986). In this satirical variation on themes developed in *Die Entsühnung*, Laborde is a financial sleight-of-hand artist who deals in international capital. The play ends happily when Laborde saves an honest but inept businessman, Ruthart, from his lack of entrepreneurial skill. The play had been written for the actor Oscar Karlweis, who was one of the stars of the Theater in der Josephstadt under the direction of Max Reinhardt. The actor and director were enthusiastic about the play, which was scheduled for production in 1935. But Reinhardt went to Hollywood, and Otto Preminger became director; Preminger found the play too cerebral and ironic and dropped it. After immigrating to the United States in 1941 Armand, who had changed his name to H. F. Broch de Rothermann, translated the play into English with George E. Wellwarth. Reinhardt's son Wolfgang was interested in staging a Broadway production starring Paul Henreid, but the idea came to nothing. The play was produced for the first time at the Städtische Bühne (City Stage) in Osnabrück on 6 October 1981. Since then it has been staged in Vienna, Zurich, Munich, Hamburg, and other cities.

Also in 1934 Broch wrote *Es bleibt alles beim Alten: Schwank mit Musik* (Nothing Ever Changes: Farce with Music; published, 1979), an inconsequential work in Viennese dialect, some of which was written by Broch's son. Armand's own judgment of the play, which was never produced, is that it is "a pretty worthless little bubble, a persiflage of my own life in the early thirties." The play is pleasant if exceedingly trivial; it is unrecognizable as a work of Broch's.

Broch wrote no plays after 1934. After the failure of his ill-starred attempts to alleviate his financial predicament by writing popular literature, he turned again to the novel and the essay to propagate his ideas about Wertzerfall and moral decay. In the remaining years of the decade arose the first versions of his great novel *Der Tod des Vergil* (1945; translated as *The Death of Virgil*, 1945) and of his novel about mass hypnosis and corroded value systems, *Der Versucher* (The Tempter, 1953). Broch was arrested by a group of local ragtag Nazis the day after the annexation of Austria by Germany in March 1938. He was released on 31 March and left for England on 24 July. He arrived in the United States on 9 October 1938. There he continued his studies of mass psychology, made tireless efforts to aid friends and fellow refugees, and advocated world government. His poverty increased due to his failure to obtain a paid academic position, and he died of a heart attack in run-down student housing in New Haven, Connecticut, on 30 May 1951.

Ironically, it is not Broch's plays that have been most successful on the stage but his *Die Schuldlosen* (1950; translated as *The Guiltless*, 1974), a "Roman in elf Erzählungen" (novel in eleven stories) that was dramatized in a French version starring Jeanne Moreau that premiered at the Bouffes du Nord in Paris in December 1986. A dramatic version of the novella "Zerline" from *Die Schuldlosen* was staged as a monologue with Helene Thimig at the Burgtheater in Vienna in the early 1980s, and it took on new life in a French version that enjoyed a long Paris run. In the late 1980s *Zerline* was performed in Bochum, Stuttgart, Milan, Munich, Hamburg, Berlin, Warsaw, and Moscow; the tour went on to Japan, where Broch de Rothermann reports that it had thirty-four performances—in French—in three cities in twenty-one days.

Letters:

Hermann Broch—Daniel Brody: Briefwechsel 1930-1951, edited by Bertold Hack and Marietta Kleiss (Frankfurt am Main: Buchhändler-Vereinigung, 1971);

Hermann Broch: Briefe über Deutschland. Die Korrespondenz mit Volkmarvon Zühlsdorff, edited by Paul Michael Lützeler (Frankfurt am Main: Suhrkamp, 1986).

Biography:

Paul Michael Lützeler, *Hermann Broch: Eine Biographie* (Frankfurt am Main: Suhrkamp, 1985); translated by Janice Furness as *Hermann Broch: A Biography* (London: Quartet, 1987).

References:

Stephen D. Dowden, ed., *Hermann Broch: Literature, Philosophy, Politics. The Yale Broch Symposium* (Columbia, S.C.: Camden House, 1988);

Manfred Durzak, *Hermann Broch: Der Dichter und seine Zeit* (Stuttgart: Kohlhammer, 1968);

Durzak, *Hermann Broch: Dichtung und Erkenntnis* (Stuttgart: Kohlhammer, 1978);

Durzak, ed., *Hermann Broch: Perspektiven der Forschung* (Munich: Fink, 1972);

Die Fähre, special Broch issue, 8 (November 1946);

Erich Kahler, *Die Philosophie von Hermann Broch* (Tübingen: Mohr, 1962);

Kahler, ed., *Dichter wider Willen: Einführung in das Werk von Hermann Broch* (Zurich: Rhein, 1958);

Michael Kessler and Paul Michael Lützeler, eds., *Hermann Broch: Das dichterische Werk: Neue Interpretationen* (Tübingen: Stauffenberg, 1987);

Thomas Koebner, *Hermann Broch: Leben und Werk* (Bern & Munich: Francke, 1965);

Hermann Krapoth, *Dichtung und Philosophie: Eine Studie zum Werk Hermann Brochs* (Bonn: Bouvier, 1971);

Paul Michael Lützeler, ed., *Hermann Broch* (Frankfurt am Main: Suhrkamp, 1983);

Karin Mack and Wolfgang Hofer, eds., *Spiegelungen: Denkbilder zur Biographie Brochs* (Vienna: Sonderzahl, 1984);

Karl Menges, *Kritische Studien zur Wertphilosophie Hermann Brochs* (Tübingen: Niemeyer, 1970);

Modern Austrian Literature, special Broch issue, 13, no. 4 (1980);

Edwin Muir, "Hermann Broch," *Bookman*, 75 (November 1932): 664-668;

Ernestine Schlant, *Hermann Broch* (Boston: Twayne, 1978);

Schlant, *Die Philosophie Hermann Brochs* (Bern & Munich: Francke, 1971);

Joseph Strelka, ed., *Broch heute* (Bern & Munich: Francke, 1978);

Richard Thieberger, ed., *Hermann Broch und seine Zeit* (Bern: Lang, 1980).

Papers:

A large collection of Hermann Broch's papers is in the Beinecke Rare Book Library, Yale University. Broch's correspondence with Daniel Brody is in the Deutsches Literaturarchiv (German Literature Archive), Marbach, Germany.

Arnolt Bronnen
(A. H. Schelle-Noetzel)
(19 August 1895 - 12 October 1959)

Ward B. Lewis
University of Georgia

PLAY PRODUCTIONS: *Vatermord*, Frankfurt am Main, Schauspielhaus, 22 April 1922;

Anarchie in Sillian, Berlin, Deutsches Theater, 6 April 1924;

Katalaunische Schlacht, Frankfurt am Main, Schauspielhaus, 28 November 1924;

Rheinische Rebellen, Berlin, Staatliches Schauspielhaus, 16 May 1925;

Die Exzesse, Berlin, Lessing-Theater, 7 June 1925;

Die Geburt der Jugend, Berlin, Lessing-Theater, 13 December 1925;

Ostpolzug, Berlin, Staatliches Schauspielhaus, 29 January 1926;

Heinrich von Kleist, *Michael Kohlhaas*, adapted by Bronnen, Erfurt, Städtische Bühnen; Frankfurt an der Oder, Stadttheater, 4 October 1929;

Reparationen, Mannheim, Nationaltheater, 30 January 1930;

"N," Linz, Landestheater, 24 April 1948;

Gloriana, Stuttgart, Württembergisches Staatstheater, 8 November 1951;

Die jüngste Nacht, Linz, Volkshochschule-Studio, 6 May 1952;

Die Kette Kolin, Karlsruhe, Badisches Staatstheater, 8 March 1981.

BOOKS: *Vatermord: Schauspiel* (Berlin: Fischer, 1920);

Die Geburt der Jugend (Berlin: Rowohlt, 1922);

Die Exzesse: Lustspiel (Berlin: Rowohlt, 1923);

Die Septembernovelle (Berlin: Rowohlt, 1923);

Anarchie in Sillian: Schauspiel (Berlin: Rowohlt, 1924);

Katalaunische Schlacht: Schauspiel (Berlin: Rowohlt, 1924);

Napoleons Fall (Berlin: Rowohlt, 1924);

Rheinische Rebellen: Schauspiel (Berlin: Rowohlt, 1925);

Ostpolzug: Schauspiel (Berlin: Rowohlt, 1926);

Reparationen: Lustspiel (Berlin: Rowohlt, 1926);

Arnolt Bronnen

Film und Leben, Barbara La Marr: Roman (Berlin: Rowohlt, 1928);

Die Frau von Morgen, wie wir sie wünschen, by Bronnen, Max Brod, Axel Eggebrecht, and others, edited by Friedrich M. Huebner (Leipzig: Seemann, 1929);

O. S.: Roman (Berlin: Rowohlt, 1929);

Roßbach (Berlin: Rowohlt, 1930);

Erinnerung an eine Liebe (Berlin: Rowohlt, 1933);

Sonnenberg: Hörspiel (Berlin: Hobbing, 1934);

Kampf im Äther oder die Unsichtbaren: Roman, as A. H. Schelle-Noetzel (Berlin: Rowohlt, 1935);

arnolt bronnen gibt zu protokoll: beiträge zur geschichte des modernen schriftstellers (Hamburg: Rowohlt, 1954);

Deutschland, kein Wintermärchen: Eine Entdeckungsfahrt durch die Deutsche Demokratische Republik (Berlin: Verlag der Nation, 1956);

Viergespann (Berlin: Aufbau, 1958)—comprises *Gloriana, "N," Die Kette Kolin, Die jüngste Nacht*;

Tage mit Bertolt Brecht: Geschichte einer unvollendeten Freundschaft (Vienna, Munich & Basel: Desch, 1960);

Begegnungen mit Schauspielern: 20 Portraits aus dem Nachlaß, edited by Harald Kleinschmidt (Berlin: Henschel, 1967);

Stücke, edited by Hans Mayer (Kronberg: Athenäum, 1977)—comprises *Vatermord, Die Exzesse, Ostpolzug, Gloriana, Die Kette Kolin*;

Sabotage der Jugend: Kleine Arbeiten 1922-1934, edited by Friedbert Aspetsberger (Innsbruck: Institut für Germanistik, Universität Innsbruck, 1989).

OTHER: Heinrich von Kleist, *Michael Kohlhaas: Für Funk und Bühne bearbeitet*, adapted by Bronnen (Berlin: Rowohlt, 1929);

Kleist, *Michael Kohlhaas: Schauspiel nach der Novelle Heinrich von Kleists*, adapted by Bronnen (Salzburg & Vienna: Pallas, 1948);

Aesop, *Sieben Berichte aus Hellas: Der antike Aisopos-Roman neu übersetzt und nach dokumentarischen Quellen ergänzt*, edited and translated by Bronnen (Hamburg: Rowohlt, 1956).

Arnolt Bronnen's first premiere evoked a great scandal, made his name known overnight, and garnered him a contract with a leading publisher. He moved from one success to the next, his works enjoying premieres in rapid succession and sustaining his status as the enfant terrible of the stage. Although generally characterized as an expressionist, Bronnen in his dramas manifests aspects of naturalism, surrealism, and epic theater and employs techniques of the film.

Bronnen was born Arnold Bronner on 19 August 1895 in Vienna to Martha Schelle Bronner and Ferdinand Bronner, a gymnasium professor and naturalist author. A childhood that was not particularly happy was followed by the study of law and philosophy in Vienna, a pursuit which he eagerly abandoned to enlist in the army during World War I. He served with a unit in the Dolomites until 1916, when he was wounded in the larynx, captured, and interned in Sicily. Unlike many of his generation who went to the front with fervor and quickly converted to pacifism, Bronnen enjoyed the war; he was exhilarated by the experience. He saw defeat as a national humiliation and the loss of the South Tirol to Italy as a cause for shame.

Bronnen returned to Vienna in October 1919 but left within a few months for Berlin, where he hoped the prospects for the publication of his work might be more favorable. There he associated with the literary circles around Alfred Wolfenstein and Otto Zarek and made the acquaintance of the still-unknown Bertolt Brecht and Moriz Seeler. Two dramas written during the war, *Die Geburt der Jugend* (The Birth of Youth; performed, 1925) and *Vatermord* (Parricide) were printed together in Wolfenstein's expressionist journal *Die Erhebung* (The Uprising) in 1920. *Vatermord* was published in book form the same year; *Die Geburt der Jugend* was published in book form two years later.

For the next two years Bronnen was employed as a sales clerk in the Wertheim department store and worked in a bank as well. Then, on 22 April 1922, *Vatermord* premiered at the Schauspielhaus in Frankfurt am Main, creating such a scandal that Bronnen became famous overnight. He received a one-year contract from the publisher Ernst Rowohlt that enabled him to quit his jobs and pursue a career as a free-lance writer. Three weeks after the premiere, at the matinee on 14 May 1922 at the Deutsches Theater, "Die junge Bühne" (The Young Stage)—a group founded by Seeler to foster new antiestablishment dramatists—presented *Vatermord* as its first play.

The one-act drama unfolds among family members and a few passersby from 5:30 to shortly past 9:00 on an evening in late March. The confining space of simple rooms conveys a repressive atmosphere and the suggestion of economic straits. In the background is heard the whine of the mother's sewing machine. Eighteen-year-old Walter Fessel wants to abandon school and learn agriculture; his father demands that Walter become an attorney and spokesman of the working class. The boy is abused both verbally and physically, and the surname Fessel (fetter, shackle) suggests the limitations on his freedom.

Walter's friend Edmund drops by to exercise his corrupting influence. He masturbates Walter and reminds him of his mother's good looks

First page of the manuscript for Bronnen's Vatermord *(Deutsches Literaturarchiv, Marbach am Neckar)* and Walter's confessed sexual desire for her, a feeling that the audience sees reciprocated when mother and son embrace. She is repelled by her husband's brutal domination of the family. Walter's hatred for his father grows with his increasing lust for his mother, and in ecstatic language Walter discloses his intention to kill his father. The mother separates father and son by attempting to entice each of them to bed in turn, and intercourse between mother and son follows. Thereupon Walter fatally stabs his father and rejects his mother's plea to continue their affair. He recognizes that there is no longer anyone in his way; he has achieved sovereignty over himself, and his mother was merely a means to that end.

The Berlin performance prompted a riot among the audience, and the police had to be called in; but the critics responded favorably. Alfred Döblin described the drama as a bold, challenging accomplishment. Herbert Ihering wrote that one had to thank the eruptive energy of a young poet for one of the strongest theatrical impressions of the season. Monty Jacobs counted Bronnen one of the bright new hopes of the theater.

The drama reflects Bronnen's personality: he was obsessed with thoughts of suicide and death, especially in erotic associations. Seeking compensation for his sense of inferiority by provoking others, he was at the same time inflexible and uncompromising, counting each acquaintance as either friend or foe. He felt intensely isolated and longed for a group identity but was at the same time mistrustful and misanthropic.

In late 1922 and early 1923, while living with the actress Gerda Müller, Bronnen further developed his conception of erotically brutal theater and sketched the drama "Verrat" (Betrayal) with her in mind. While working on the play he directed Hans Henny Jahnn's *Pastor Ephraim Magnus* (published, 1919) in its premiere at the private club "Das Theater" in Berlin on 23 August 1923; he and Brecht had reduced the work's playing time from seven hours to two; it was closed by the police after a week. With the help of Brecht's criticism and suggestions, "Verrat" was transformed by October 1923 into *Anarchie in Sillian* (Anarchy in Sillian; published, 1924), which had a sensational premiere at a matinee on 6 April 1924 at the Deutsches Theater in Berlin. The engineer Carrel attempts to preserve the energy-producing capacity of the plant Sillian during a day and night of emotional turmoil and continuous rain. Opposed to Carrel is the machinist and technician Grand, a saboteur who is linked with striking workers whose pay Carrel has purportedly diverted. The engineer is sexually enthralled by his virginal secretary, Vergan, whose presence prevents him from devoting himself to his work. The uncouth Grand also lusts for her. Explicit descriptions of Vergan's body are provided in ecstatic, exclamatory outbursts from the two males. As the generators fail about him, Carrel realizes that his work is threatened by both Grand and Vergan; he decides to eliminate them. He hands Vergan over to Grand as part of a deal, then forces lye down Grand's throat. As the rain ceases and dawn breaks, Carrel celebrates his triumph over lewdness and anarchy. He joins two wires, and the dynamos begin churning dully in the background.

Bronnen's next play, *Katalaunische Schlacht* (Catalaunian Battle; published, 1924) premiered on 28 November 1924 at the Schauspielhaus in Frankfurt am Main. The three-act drama opens during World War I in a bunker at Château-Thierry, where the brothers Karl and Kenned recognize each other with surprise, both having presumed the other dead. Karl's companion is revealed as Hiddie, his wife of three weeks. Although Kenned, the commanding officer, has cowered in the bunker, he threatens to report the desertion of others. Kenned orders Karl to the artillery post and absconds with Hiddie. Karl returns, fatally wounded, as his comrades Margin, Wung, and Mellermann desert. They rob the dead, taking jewelry, valuables, and a phonograph seconds before the French storm in.

After the war Wung, who serves as a loge attendant in a Paris film theater, seats his fellow deserters in a box next to that occupied by Hiddie, whom the three plan to kidnap. Kenned has gone through all his own money as well as hers and implores her to flee their creditors with him on a train to Cologne. She has dreamed that the spirit of the dead Karl is responsible for their misfortune and cannot decide whether to die or continue living; she refuses to accompany the cowardly Kenned, while at the same time confessing that she is aroused by him. Just as Hiddie discovers Karl's wedding ring and wristwatch where they were placed by the deserters, these three enter the box. Afraid of dying and confronting Karl, Hiddie draws her revolver and shoots Kenned as he tries to protect her from the lustful attack which threatens her. She flees with the three men close on her heels. The final act takes place on board an ocean steamer bound for South America. The three men corner Hiddie like a hunted beast. She teases them and bids them play the phonograph they have brought with them from the bunker; she will dance with them before they take her. From the apparatus come the chords of Kurt Weill and the reproachful voice of Karl in one of the drama's monotonous soliloquies, and Hiddie poisons herself.

Hiddie shares some qualities of Frank Wedekind's Lulu as a devourer of men and the embodiment of the power of female sexuality. Bronnen has, however, endowed her with characteristics from his own fevered creative imagination. She is more lustful than Lulu, given to sadomasochistic eroticism and sexual death wishes expressed in extended soliloquies of egoistic bathos.

The work was a catastrophe by any measure. Nationalist fervor incited by the dishonorable representation of German soldiers plundering the dead fanned protest in the press to the extent that the director, Richard Weichert, struck the scene. The play's run was shortened, and some theaters turned down the work outright. After two intoxicating successes Bronnen had created a flop; but he was quick to recover.

Rheinische Rebellen (Rhenish Rebels; published, 1925), which premiered at the Staatliches Schauspielhaus in Berlin on 16 May 1925, was Bronnen's most widely acclaimed play. Bronnen availed himself of a current political topic to serve as the backdrop for an erotic struggle: the uprising of fall 1923 inspired by the desire for separation of the Rhineland from Germany, which had agreed in the Treaty of Versailles to French occupation of the region. Each of the five acts of the work is set in a different principal city of the Rhineland during the uprising. The separatists are led by Charles Occc and his mistress Pola. Occc is consumed by passion for Gien Vonhagen, who is pursued, arrested, and harassed for her underground activities. The successful putsch establishes a Rhenish Republic, which is short-lived when Gien betrays to the provincial parliament a secret agreement Occc has entered into with the French. Occc confesses his love to Gien and thereby puts his fate in her hands. She demands that he take her to Aachen, the last holdout of the separatists. He does so, and a scene ensues which is characteristically Bronnen in its representation of the tension between the sexes. Gien describes her body and Occc's burning lust for her, thereby inflaming him to seize her. In disgust,

she slaps him in the face with leather straps; she then raises the German flag over that of the separatists while crying out ecstatically: "Sonne über Aachen! Sonne über Deutschland!" (Sun over Aachen! Sun over Germany!). The director, Leopold Jessner, used techniques of Erwin Piscator's political theater to appeal to the right. The names of the cities where the work unfolds—Koblenz, Aachen, and so on—were projected on a dark curtain in a green, shimmering light. At the conclusion the black, red, and gold flag of Germany floated down over the stage.

Bronnen's *Die Exzesse* (The Excesses; published, 1923) premiered three weeks after *Rheinische Rebellen* at the Lessing-Theater in Berlin. It had developed from sketches made during the author's days as a prisoner of war and manifests Bronnen's negative attitudes toward capitalism as well as his patriotic chauvinism. The play is a comedy consisting of sixteen scenes ranging from the Italian South Tirol to Northern Germany. A bank with branches in Bolzano and Stralsund employs the two central figures, Hildegard Paul and Lois Raffl, who, during a chance meeting on a Berlin railroad platform in the opening scene, are struck with love at first sight. They part wordlessly for different ends of the country at the behest of their employer until they are drawn to this platform again in the final scene and exchange their first words after the curtain falls. In the meantime, they are subjected to sexual onslaught by secondary figures to whom they gladly surrender. It is Hildegard, however, who enjoys the most lascivious adventures; in one scene she sexually embraces a ram in the grass and celebrates the union before the eyes of a young goatherd. The critic Alfred Kerr characterized *Die Exzesse* as banal and meaningless. Ihering, on the other hand, said that Bronnen had given drama a new form and faulted the director, Heinz Hilpert, for failing to develop the author's humor.

Bronnen was hot, and Seeler was not one to let an opportunity pass him by. "Die Junge Bühne" sponsored *Die Geburt der Jugend* in a matinee at the Lessing-Theater on 13 December 1925 directed by Friedrich Neubauer. Written when Bronnen was nineteen, the work reflects his early dramatic development; considered together with *Vatermord*, it provides a complementary statement on the subject of rebellious adolescence. *Die Geburt der Jugend* is a short work set near a school; the action unfolds over the course of a day. The final act is an expressionist choreo-

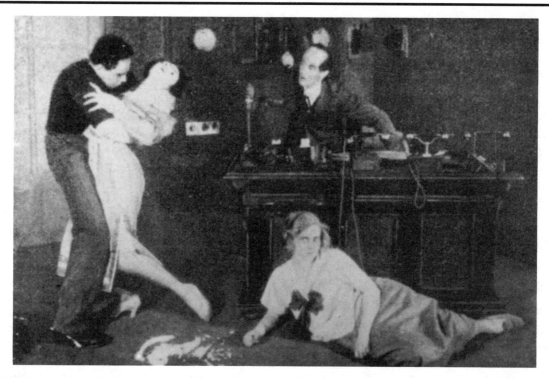

Scene from the premiere of Bronnen's Anarchie in Sillian *in Berlin in 1924, with (clockwise, from left) Walter Frank, Maria Eis, H. H. von Twardowski, Franziska Kinz*

graphic vision. The drama deals with the revolt of adolescents against the school system and their parents. Ulrich Kröll, a weak student who has skipped classes, is denied the opportunity to graduate. When his fellow students show support for him by refusing to return to class, the teacher Bruck imposes house arrest on them. The punishment means that they are deprived of attendance at the school dance that evening. Karl, a ringleader among the students, calls for a student strike. Breaking out of the room in which he has been confined, Karl leads the students in an uprising—an expression of self-assertion and the realization of their youth. In ecstatic language he calls forth the destroying fire of revenge, which will bring death upon that shame represented by old age. The other children follow, forsaking their homes. At the dance the girls pour from the building into the night, where the boys are waiting and drinking. Together they stream out onto the meadows. The final act is an anarchic vision during which the birth of youth is achieved. On the meadow and in the woods the young sing and dance with animals, drive off police authorities and indignant peasants, embrace and celebrate their unity as anonymous individuals in a collective body growing toward divinity.

Given Bronnen's political history there has been an overwhelming temptation among critics and literary historians to find elements of fascism in his early works. Sadism and the glorification of youth are most often emphasized. But *Die Geburt der Jugend* and *Vatermord* were written at a time when the same themes were being treated by other dramatists, notably by Wedekind in *Frühlings Erwachen* (1891; translated as *The Awakening of Spring*, 1909) and by Walter Hasenclever in *Der Sohn* (The Son, 1914).

Five weeks after the premiere of *Die Geburt der Jugend*, Bronnen's *Ostpolzug* (East Pole Expedition; published, 1926) received its stormy premiere at the Staatliches Schauspielhaus in Berlin. The monodrama presents Alexander the Great on an expedition to reach the East Pole, as he calls the summit of Mount Everest. The nine short scenes are linked in that the final line of each is repeated, with a slight variation, as the first line of the succeeding scene. The Alexander of classical antiquity fails to conquer the world; the modern Alexander, however, fires a rocket from the summit of Everest announcing his accomplishment to the world. The play was singled out by Brecht as the best example of epic theater to date. Explanatory text was projected on a screen before each scene, and a map illustrated Alexan-

Scene from the premiere of Bronnen's Katalaunische Schlacht *at the Schauspielhaus in Frankfurt am Main in 1924*

der's route from Greece across central Asia to the Himalayas.

The publication of the novel *O. S.* in 1929 marked Bronnen's identification with the radical right. The abbreviation stands for Oberschlesien (Upper Silesia), an area of Germany contested with Poland after World War I and now part of Poland.

Bronnen became fascinated with the techniques of mass communication: film, radio, and ultimately television. He served as dramaturge for the film studio Ufa (Universum Film AG.), and from 1928 until 1933 he functioned in the same capacity for radio with the Dramatische Funkstunde (Dramatic Radio Hour) in Berlin. His adaptation for radio of Heinrich von Kleist's novella *Michael Kohlhaas* was first broadcast in April 1929; the work was also recast as a stage drama, which premiered simultaneously in Erfurt and Frankfurt an der Oder in October of the same year. Both scripts were published together in 1929.

On 30 January 1930 Bronnen's satire *Reparationen* (Reparations; published, 1926) premiered in Mannheim. The gentlemen Pound and Franc extort from old Mark his last means, and

his astronomic debt falls on the shoulders of his young son Pfennig.

Bronnen's novel *Roßbach* (1930) glorified Adolf Hitler's attempted putsch in Munich. After the appearance of this work Bronnen made the acquaintance of National Socialist propaganda chief Joseph Goebbels, whom he introduced to the intellectual circle representing the Conservative Revolution. About this time Bronnen began trying unsuccessfully to establish his status as an Aryan. He represented himself to Goebbels as illegitimate; and his mother is supposed to have sworn under oath that he was not the son of Ferdinand Bronner, a Jew, but of Wilhelm Andreas Schmidt, the minister who had joined her and Bronner in marriage.

Bronnen's failure to prove himself an Aryan had consequences. In June 1935 he was fired from his position with the state radio broadcasting company. On 13 May 1937 he was excluded from the Reichschrifttumskammer, the academy of acceptable authors, and his works were banned from publication. His work as a program director for a television studio ended in the summer of 1939 when he collapsed with ulcers of the stomach and small intestine. On 27 April 1940 he was declared politically unreliable, and two years later all his works, including drama productions, were prohibited.

In the summer of 1943 Bronnen fled Berlin with his family to the Salzkammergut area of Austria, where he became acquainted with members of the resistance. In August of the following year he was inducted into the army and after a few days was arrested for high treason because of remarks he had made. Incarcerated in Vienna until October, he was then sent back to his unit. At the end of the war he was in the town of Bad Goisern, Upper Austria, where he was installed by the occupation forces as the mayor for two months. Moving to Linz, Bronnen served as cultural editor of the communist newspaper *Neue Zeit* (New Time) for five years.

During the postwar period several of Bronnen's dramas were produced that were written during the Third Reich as he moved from National Socialism to communism. *"N"* (published, 1958) premiered at the Landestheater in Linz on 24 April 1948. Written in 1935 and 1936, the work would have premiered in Kassel in the fall of 1942 but had been suppressed by the general prohibition of Bronnen's works. Ostensibly a historical drama about Napoleon, *"N"* is actually a veiled attack on Hitler.

Another historical drama, *Gloriana* (published, 1977), premiered at the Württembergisches Staatstheater in Stuttgart on 8 November 1951. Written in 1940 and 1941, it is an amusing and confusing comedy dealing with Queen Elizabeth I and the execution of her favorite, the Earl of Essex, in 1601. One character is a combination of Francis Bacon, William Shakespeare, and Edward VI.

In 1951 Bronnen became the director of the communist Neues Theater in der Scala in Vienna, where he also served as dramaturge. He also wrote for the party paper *Der Abend* (The Evening).

The most clearly political and ideological of Bronnen's dramas premiered three decades after its conception: *Die Kette Kolin* (The Kolin Chain; published, 1958) premiered in March 1981 in Karlsruhe. Four concentration camp inmates constitute a resistance group, or "chain," which takes its name from a victory of Frederick the Great in 1757. They escape and capture the camp commandant, Greyll, who is in flight from the advancing Russians. The former inmates try him for his crimes; he remains obstinate in his lack of repentance, citing his obedience to the law, his duty,

his oath, and orders. The woman, Ricki, is inclined toward mercy until Greyll's son attempts to kill her; then all unite in sentencing Greyll to death. Bronnen structures the work both as a drama and an antidrama. The action onstage remains self-contained, and the theatrical illusion of reality is preserved; but in the audience the "theater director" points out the moral issues involved in an exchange with a disgruntled "spectator" who wants only to be entertained and threatens to leave.

Die jüngste Nacht (The Last Night; published, 1958) premiered in Linz on 6 May 1952. The title is an allusion to Judgment Day ("der jüngste Tag"), when the Third Reich, upon its demise, is held accountable for its actions. The work is a burlesque in which the chauffeur Gamserl cunningly prevents his boss, the mayor of Roith in the Salzkammergut, from absconding with the village's flour during the last night of National Socialism. The next day, 8 May 1945, Gamserl is elected mayor; but the occupying American officer gets the facts backwards. The moral, in an inversion of standard Marxist ideology, is the necessity of changing the human being as a precondition to changing society.

The atmosphere became less favorable for communists in Austria after the enactment of the Austrian state treaty in 1955. In response to the invitation of the cultural minister of the German Democratic Republic, Johannes R. Becher, Bronnen moved to East Berlin and became a publicist and theater critic for the *Berliner Zeitung* (Berlin Newspaper). He found a hostile environment in East Berlin, where he was considered bourgeois, decadent, and politically suspect. He died on 12 October 1959 in an East Berlin hospital.

References:

Alfred Döblin, *Ein Kerl muß eine Meinung haben: Berichte und Kritiken 1921-1924* (Olten & Freiburg: Walter, 1976), pp. 81-84, 244-245;

Herbert Ihering, *Der Kampf ums Theater*, edited by the Akademie der Künste der DDR (Berlin: Henschel, 1974), pp. 216-217, 226-228, 293-295;

Ihering, *Von Reinhardt bis Brecht*, edited by Rolf Badenhausen (Reinbek bei Hamburg: Rowohlt, 1967);

Edwin Klingner, *Arnolt Bronnen: Werk und Wirkung* (Hildesheim: Gerstenberg, 1974);

Ursula Münch, *Weg und Werk Arnolt Bronnens: Wandlungen seines Denkens* (Frankfurt am

Main, Bern, New York & Nancy: Lang, 1985);
Günther Rühle, *Theater für die Republik 1917-1933: In Spiegel der Kritik* (Frankfurt am Main: Fischer, 1967);
Alfred Stögmüller, "Arnolt Bronnen," *Adalbert Stifter Institut des Landes Oberösterreich*, 34, nos. 3-4 (1985): 151-155.

Papers:
Arnolt Bronnen's papers are at the Archiv der Akademie der Künste (Archive of the Academy of the Arts) in Berlin and the Deutsches Literaturarchiv (German Literature Archive) in Marbach am Neckar.

Elias Canetti
(25 July 1905 -   )

Thomas H. Falk
Michigan State University

See also the Canetti entry in *DLB 85: Austrian Fiction Writers After 1914.*

PLAY PRODUCTIONS: *The Numbered (Die Befristeten)*, translated by Carol Stewart, Oxford, Playhouse Theatre, 5 November 1956;
Die Komödie der Eitelkeit, Brunswick, Staatstheater, 6 February 1965;
Hochzeit, Brunswick, Staatstheater, 3 November 1965;
Die Befristeten, Vienna, Theater in der Josefstadt, 17 November 1967.

BOOKS: *Die Blendung: Roman* (Vienna, Leipzig & Zurich: Reichner, 1936); translated by C. V. Wedgwood as *Auto-da-Fé* (London: Cape, 1946); republished as *The Tower of Babel* (New York: Knopf, 1947);
Komödie der Eitelkeit: Drama (Munich: Weismann, 1950); translated by Gitta Honegger as *Comedy of Vanity* (New York: Performing Arts Journal Publications, 1983);
Fritz Wotruba (Vienna: Rosenbaum, 1955);
Masse und Macht (Hamburg: Claassen, 1960); translated by Carol Stewart as *Crowds and Power* (London: Gollancz, 1962; New York: Viking, 1962);
Welt im Kopf, edited by Erich Fried (Graz & Vienna: Stiasny, 1962);
Hochzeit: Drama (Munich: Hanser, 1964); translated by Honegger as *The Wedding* (New York: Performing Arts Journal Publications, 1986);

Elias Canetti in Stockholm to receive the 1981 Nobel Prize for Literature (photograph by Lüfti Özkök)

Die Befristeten: Drama (Munich: Hanser, 1964); translated by Honegger as *Life-Terms* (New York: Performing Arts Journal Publications,

1983); translated by Stewart as *The Num-bered* (London: Calder & Boyars, 1984);

Dramen (Munich: Hanser, 1964)—comprises *Hochzeit, Komödie der Eitelkeit, Die Befristeten;*

Aufzeichnungen 1942-1948 (Munich: Hanser, 1965);

Die Stimmen von Marrakesch: Aufzeichnungen nach einer Reise (Munich: Hanser, 1967); trans-lated by J. A. Underwood as *The Voices of Mar-rakesh: A Record of a Visit* (London: Calder & Boyars, 1978; New York: Seabury Press, 1978);

Der andere Prozeß: Kafkas Briefe an Felice (Munich: Hanser, 1969); translated by Christopher Middleton as *Kafka's Other Trial: The Letters to Felice* (London: Calder & Boyars, 1974; New York: Schocken, 1974);

Alle vergeudete Verehrung: Aufzeichnungen 1949-1960 (Munich: Hanser, 1970);

Die gespaltene Zukunft: Aufsätze und Gespräche (Mu-nich: Hanser, 1972);

Macht und Überleben: Drei Essays (Berlin: Literari-sches Colloquium, 1972);

Die Provinz des Menschen: Aufzeichnungen 1942-1972 (Munich: Hanser, 1973); translated by Joachim Neugroschel as *The Human Province* (New York: Seabury Press, 1978);

Der Ohrenzeuge: Fünfzig Charaktere (Munich: Han-ser, 1974); translated by Neugroschel as *Ear-witness: Fifty Characters* (New York: Seabury Press, 1979);

Das Gewissen der Worte (Munich: Hanser, 1975; en-larged, 1976); translated by Neugroschel as *The Conscience of Words* (New York: Seabury Press, 1979);

Der Überlebende (Frankfurt am Main: Suhrkamp, 1975);

Der Beruf des Dichters (Munich: Hanser, 1976);

Die gerettete Zunge: Geschichte einer Jugend (Mu-nich: Hanser, 1977); translated by Neugro-schel as *The Tongue Set Free: Remembrance of a European Childhood* (New York: Continu-um, 1979);

Die Fackel im Ohr: Lebensgeschichte 1921-1931 (Mu-nich: Hanser, 1980); translated by Neugro-schel as *The Torch in My Ear* (New York: Far-rar, Straus & Giroux, 1982);

Das Augenspiel: Lebensgeschichte 1931-1937 (Mu-nich: Hanser, 1985); translated by Ralph Manheim as *The Play of the Eyes* (New York: Farrar, Straus & Giroux, 1986);

Das Geheimherz der Uhr: Aufzeichnungen 1973-1985 (Munich: Hanser, 1987); translated by Joel Agee as *The Secret Heart of the Clock: Notes,* *Aphorisms, Fragments 1973-1985* (New York: Farrar, Straus & Giroux, 1989).

TRANSLATIONS: Upton Sinclair, *Leidweg der Liebe* (Berlin: Malik, 1930);

Sinclair, *Das Geld schreibt: Eine Studie über die ameri-kanische Literatur* (Berlin: Malik, 1930);

Sinclair, *Alkohol* (Berlin: Malik, 1932).

Elias Canetti has been awarded the highest literary prizes and has been acclaimed by a small group of writers and scholars, but he has never been widely recognized by the reading public. His oeuvre includes outstanding writing in all major genres except poetry. At the time that Canetti was awarded the 1981 Nobel Prize for Lit-erature his one novel, *Die Blendung* (The Blind-ing, 1936; translated as *Auto-da-Fé*, 1946), was de-scribed as "a single fundamental metaphor for the threat exercised by the mass-man within our-selves"; his major theoretical work, *Masse und Macht* (1960; translated as *Crowds and Power*, 1962), an investigation of "the origin, composi-tion and reaction patterns of mass movements," was called "a magisterial work by a polyhistor"; and his three plays, *Komödie der Eitelkeit* (pub-lished, 1950; performed, 1965; translated as *Com-edy of Vanity*, 1983), *Hochzeit* (published, 1964; per-formed, 1965; translated as *The Wedding*, 1986), and *Die Befristeten* (published, 1964; performed, 1967; translated as *Life-Terms*, 1983), were cele-brated for their portrayals of "extreme situa-tions" which provide an insightful examination of Canetti's "unique world of ideas." The Nobel lau-dation praises his other works and concludes: "with your versatile writings, which attack sick ten-dencies in our age, you wish to serve the cause of humanity. Intellectual passion is combined in you with the moral responsibility that . . . is nour-ished by mercy."

Canetti's parents, Jacques and Mathilde Arditti Canetti, were descendants of Sephardic Jews who had been driven out of Spain during the fifteenth-century Inquisition. Both parents were educated in Vienna; when they returned to their home, Rutschuk (now Ruse, Bulgaria), then a thriving trading center on the Danube River, Jacques entered his father's profitable wholesale grocery business. But the couple had been smit-ten by the theater in Vienna, and Jacques might have become an actor if his family had allowed it. Mathilde's interest in dramatic literature would become an influential part of the education of Elias Canetti, who was born on 25 July 1905.

The language of the Sephardic Jews was Ladino, a dialect made up of Spanish and Hebrew. In addition to the Ladino spoken at home, Canetti regularly heard Bulgarian, Hebrew, Turkish, Greek, Albanian, Armenian, Romanian, and Russian from the family's servants, the customers in his father's store, and people in the streets of Rutschuk. The parents usually spoke German, especially if they did not want Canetti and his two younger brothers to know what they were saying. His exposure to so many languages and dialects undoubtedly contributed to Canetti's highly sensitive acoustic perception and his concept of the "akustische Maske" (acoustic mask).

In 1911 the family moved to Manchester, England, where the father joined his brother-in-law's business. There Canetti added English to his linguistic repertoire and was introduced to literature.

Canetti's father died of a heart attack in October 1912; the following May the mother decided to move to Vienna. On the way the family made a three-month stopover in Lausanne, Switzerland, where Canetti's mother taught him German. He spoke the language fluently when the family arrived in Vienna in the fall of 1913. German was to be the language of all his writings.

World War I and its aftermath made it necessary for the family to move to Zurich. There, in three months, the fourteen-year-old Canetti wrote his first play, "Junius Brutus," a historical tragedy in five acts and 2,298 lines of blank verse. The play, which has never been published, was dedicated and solemnly presented to his mother on Christmas Day 1919. In 1921 the family moved to Frankfurt am Main.

In 1924 Canetti entered the University of Vienna as a chemistry student. During his student days he came under the spell of Karl Kraus, Vienna's great polemicist; he attended almost every public lecture and reading that Kraus gave. Kraus's caricatures of political foes gave Canetti the idea for his "akustische Masken," which are made up of linguistic examples he collected in those years in Vienna. They are a crucial ingredient of his novel *Die Blendung* and the first two plays, *Komödie der Eitelkeit* and *Hochzeit*. He received a doctorate in 1929 but never worked as a chemist.

In February 1934 Canetti married Venetia Toubner-Calderon, whom he had met at his first Kraus lecture. They were among the last Jews to flee from Vienna in November 1938, after the annexation of Austria by Nazi Germany. Following a brief stay in Paris they moved to London in 1939. Canetti's wife died in May 1963. In 1971 he married Hera Buschor; their daughter, Johanna, was born in 1972. For some years Canetti divided his residence between Hampstead in England and Zurich; he currently lives in Zurich.

Canetti was awarded the Grand Prix International du Club Français du Livre in 1949, the Writer's Prize of the City of Vienna in 1966, the Great Austrian State Prize for Literature in 1967, the Georg Büchner Prize in 1972, the Franz Nabl Prize of the City of Graz in 1975, the Orden Pour le Mérite in 1980, the Nobel Prize for Literature and the Franz Kafka Prize in 1981, and the Great Service Cross of the Federal Republic of Germany in 1983. He received honorary doctoral degrees from the University of Manchester in 1975 and the University of Munich in 1976.

In writings and interviews Canetti has repeatedly and forcefully expressed his passion for the drama. It is surprising, therefore, that he has had only three plays published and produced. More may exist, however, since Canetti has mentioned having written others. *Hochzeit* was written in the winter of 1931-1932 and *Komödie der Eitelkeit* in 1933-1934, both in Vienna; *Die Befristeten* was written in London in 1952-1953. The plays had their premieres in reverse order of their writing. *Die Befristeten* premiered in English translation as *The Numbered* on 5 November 1956 at the Playhouse Theatre in Oxford; its German premiere occurred on the Studiobühne (Studio Stage) of the Theater in der Josefstadt in Vienna on 17 November 1967. The other two plays premiered at the Staatstheater (State Theater) in Brunswick, Germany: *Die Komödie der Eitelkeit* on 6 February 1965 and *Hochzeit* on 3 November 1965.

There are various reasons for the long delay between the writing and the publication and first performances of the plays. As with all his writings, Canetti insisted on reworking his plays with great care. Before leaving Vienna he gave several public readings of the first two plays; by the time he might have been ready to have them published and performed, Austria was annexed to Nazi Germany, and it was impossible for a Jewish playwright to find an audience. During the war Canetti gave up the writing of belletristic works to concentrate on his scientific study of crowds and power. It was not until the publisher

Hanser brought out an edition of the three plays in 1964 that Canetti became known in Germany as a playwright. Finally, Canetti was of the opinion that his plays could be received correctly by the public only after a tradition of the theater of the absurd had been established in Germany in the early 1960s.

From time to time Canetti has indicated that he was writing a book on his theory of the drama. Although no such book has been published, three key concepts emerge as the basis of his theory from interviews he has given, from his notes, and from his essays: the "akustische Maske," the "Grundeinfall" (basic idea), and the "Verwandlung" (transformation). The akustische Maske is the unique linguistic structure of a person, the language that person has created, which he or she has completely to himself or herself, and which will pass away with that person. Canetti uses the acoustic mask in his creation of each character in his plays. The mask defines the character.

Canetti insists that it is mandatory that every drama proceed from a completely new Grundeinfall. The play must be so novel in its plot that it presents viewers with a world they have never before experienced; it must also include a variety of unique features so that it illustrates an event that is completely new to the audience.

The notion of the Verwandlung refers to Canetti's belief that the theater is not a place for entertainment but an educational institution. The playwright is to confront the audience with a reality that results in a catharsis. Canetti does not seek to describe or interpret the world; he wants his grotesque and absurd satires to bring about a change—Verwandlung—through confrontation.

Hochzeit has as its Grundeinfall the examination of greed, lasciviousness, and death. The play depicts a cruel and merciless society that seems no longer to have a moral code and is heading toward Armageddon. *Hochzeit* is divided into a prelude in five scenes and the main act, which presents the actual wedding celebration.

The prelude introduces the residents of an apartment house on Gütigkeitstraße (Kindness Street), all of whom are possessed by the goal of owning the house in which they live. The landlady is a shrewd old woman; her granddaughter visits every day to ask to inherit the house, while hoping that the old lady will soon die. Each time the grandmother's parrot hears the word *Haus* (house) he repeats it three times, thereby cawing

the major theme of this scene and of the entire play. Subsequent scenes of the prelude show the other residents—including a pompous schoolteacher and a young couple—trying to cheat the old woman out of her house. The fifth scene takes place in the basement apartment of the janitor, whose wife is lying on her deathbed while he reads the book of Judges from the Bible: blind Samson pulls down the house upon the Philistines, thereby foreshadowing the events of the main act.

The wedding celebrated in the main act centers on a depraved, petit bourgeois family. The bride's father is Oberbaurat Segenreich (Chief Construction Engineer Richlyblessed), who insists in his vanity that everyone acknowledge that he has built not only this solid house but also this fine family. The other members of the family and the wedding party are greedy to possess property and other people and are obsessed with sex. The nymphomaniacal mother of the bride thinks only of copulating with the groom; the bride lusts for three friends of the family; and—representing the crudest form of sexuality—the eighty-year-old family doctor, the erotomaniac and pedophile Dr. Bock (Stud) brags that he has had all the women in the family and at the party. The bride, Christa, summarizes life in this house: upstairs, she says, is the guileful landlady; downstairs, a corpse; and here at this bacchanalian feast she is getting married.

Into this macabre world Horch (Hark), an idealist, introduces a play within the play. He asks what each person would do if the one he or she loves were threatened by imminent danger. A sudden earthquake changes the game into reality; now that everyone could really save the person he or she loves, each does nothing but try to save himself or herself. Cruel, hateful screams cut the silence. The parrot has the last word: "Haus! Haus! Haus!"

The premiere of *Hochzeit* caused a scandal. Spectators were offended by some words, by the way some characters were portrayed, and by the message of the play. The day before the premiere a Brunswick newspaper had printed an anonymous charge that the play was pornographic. Even though a host of writers and critics, including Günter Grass and Theodor Adorno, vouched for the artistic quality of the play, it closed after seven performances.

Hochzeit is considered Canetti's most stageable play. It was successfully performed under the direction of Karl Paryla in 1970 in Cologne

Scene from a 1988 production in Salzburg of Canetti's Hochzeit, *with (left to right) Peter Simonischek as Horch, Anne Tismer as Christa, Stefan Wigger as Dr. Bock, Barbara Petritsch as Pepi Kokosch, and Fritz Lichtenhahn as the druggist Gall (photograph by Winfried Rabanus)*

and was enthusiastically received when Canetti read it later that year at the Schauspielhaus (Playhouse) in Kiel. When the city of Vienna celebrated Canetti's eightieth birthday in October 1985 Hans Hollmann directed *Hochzeit* at the Akademietheater with a distinguished cast.

The Grundeinfall of *Komödie der Eitelkeit* is that the human race would waste away if deprived of its vanity. A government decree intended to eliminate vanity is imposed on the population: the ownership and use of mirrors are prohibited; photographing people is forbidden, and all photographs of people must be destroyed; all movie houses must be closed and all films destroyed. The punishment for violating the decree is long imprisonment or death. The people have been given thirty days to comply with the decree. The play illustrates how various individuals react to the decree; there are two dozen characters representing as many acoustic masks. The teacher Fritz Schakerl (Shaker) is a traditional enforcer of conduct, but he has a severe stutter whenever he is not acting in an authoritative role. It is Schakerl who announces the decree; during the announcement he does not stammer once. S. Bleiss, a photographer, is in the

business of perpetuating vanity. His favorite gimmick is to take pictures of poor newlyweds standing in front of his car, which the couple can pass off as their own when they display the picture. François Fant, a coxcomb, steals all his mother's mirrors and takes them to the carnival, where he smashes them with a ball while watching his reflection in them. Mme Emilie Fant, François's mother, needs the mirrors for her brothel so that her girls can be attractive for her customers. Heinrich Föhn (Hot Air) strolls across the stage, pontificating to his companion Leda Frisch (Fresh) that a self-image of good health provides the individual with a meaningful life.

In the second half of the play each of the characters has come to terms with the decree ten years later. Schakerl is now the powerful chairman of a committee of crime fighters. He has successfully advocated the passage of a law under which the eyes of young girls will be torn out if they look into someone else's eyes to see themselves. Married to one of these girls, Schakerl grows ill and despondent, a victim of mirror sickness, which can only be cured by looking into a mirror. His stammering returns when he obtains one. Bleiss is still perpetuating vanity, going from door to door selling time in front of a mirror at ten schillings for two minutes. Although he is occasionally caught in this illegal venture, Bleiss survives. Mme Fant has established a "Spiegelbordell" (mirror brothel) where almost all the characters of the play pay high prices to sit in front of mirrors and admire themselves. Föhn stands before a full-length mirror in a luxury cabin making pompous and trivial pronouncements. After each proclamation he pushes a button and hears applause, but each time the applause grows weaker until there is none. Becoming demented, he threatens destruction of the establishment in a thundering voice.

In the final scene most of the characters are in Mme Fant's "Spiegelsaal" (Hall of Mirrors). Each is confronted by and recoils from a raging voice that summarizes his or her personality and the untruthfulness of the mask each had created. All raise high mirrors or pictures of themselves, but they never merge into a group; individual vanity prevails.

The reviews of opening night were so negative that the play closed after only eight performances. By and large the reviewers thought highly of the play and placed the blame on the director, Helmut Matiasek, who had set the play in the Nazi period; thus, he had transformed Canetti's play into a commentary on Nazism rather than a general statement on totalitarian systems and had eliminated the catharsis that Canetti had intended. The most successful rendition of the play was the production in Basel in February 1978 under the direction of Hans Hollmann; Canetti said of it: "mehr als 40 Jahre nach dem Entstehen der *Komödie* ist sie nun in Basel zum erstenmal richtig aufgeführt worden" (forty years after the *Comedy* was written it has now been performed correctly for the first time in Basel). What made the Hollmann production so successful was his full comprehension of Canetti's concepts of the akustische Maske and the Grundeinfall.

In *Die Befristeten* the Grundeinfall is a utopian society of the future in which people are no longer tormented by the uncertainty of when they will die. At birth everyone is given a locket containing his birth and death dates and a number that indicates the number of years the person will live. Although everyone knows the information in his or her own locket, it is a crime to reveal it to others. An official called the Kapselan (locketeer) is the only person who can open the

locket at the time of death to confirm the accuracy of the death date recorded there.

The play has three major and twenty minor characters, as well as a chorus. The minor characters have names such as the Die Mutter 32 (The Mother 32), Der Junge 70 (The Boy 70), Zwei junge Herren, 28 und 88 (Two young Men, 28 and 88), Der Mann, Dr. 46 (The Man, Dr. 46), and Der Junge zehn (The Boy 10). The personality and behavior of each person is determined by his or her number. The Mother 32, for example, is unable to persuade her son, the Boy 70, to be cautious while playing because the son knows that he cannot be killed until he is seventy. The Boy 10 is a spoiled brat because he knows that he has only a short life. The fairy-tale concept of living happily ever after is negated when a woman must remind her granddaughter that the latter will live "bis zu deinem Augenblick" (only until your moment). Those with high numbers display a superior and arrogant attitude; those with low numbers behave in an inferior and obsequious manner.

The major characters are Fünfzig (Fifty), Freund (Friend), and the Kapselan. Fünfzig is reluctant to accept the dictatorship of the Kapselan. For many years he has suspected that the lockets were really empty and that the Kapselan was a fraud. He reveals his suspicions to Freund and subsequently to the masses; they follow him joyfully, bringing the downfall of the Kapselan's deceptive system. The masses believe that they will now live forever; but with the death of the first person this dream vanishes. The uncertainty of the time of one's death is worse than the certainty of a preestablished moment of death had been.

Reviews of the premiere performance of *Die Befristeten*—translated by Carol Stewart under the title *The Numbered* and directed by Mionos Volanakis—by the Meadow Players of the Oxford Playhouse Company were positive. The *Times* of London compared Canetti's play with works by Jean Giraudoux and Jean Cocteau: "Into this distinguished repertoire Mr. Elias Canetti's play erupts with a strangely mathematical absorption." The *Oxford* magazine reported that "the writing is forceful and plain, as is the production.... In scene upon scene they build up the delicate web of tension, achieving with truth and economy effects which grip the mind." By contrast, the German-language premiere in Vienna under the direction of Friedrich Kallina on 17 November 1967 was not well received. The critic for *Die Welt*

(The World) thought that "das Ganze ist ein nettes Gedanken- aber kein Bühnenspiel" (the whole thing is an amiable play for the mind but not for the stage).

Canetti has addressed such major issues as greed, power, lasciviousness, freedom, death, the depersonalization of the individual, and the creation of an inhumane mass society. Some critics have used epithets such as "difficult" or "uncomfortable" in describing Canetti. The controversy surrounding performances of his plays might be explained as the result of the public's unwillingness to see itself in such a brutally honest way: its mask is revealed and it does not like what it sees.

References:

Heinz Ludwig Arnold, ed., *Literatur und Kritik*, special Canetti issue, no. 28, third edition (September 1982);

Dagmar Barnouw, *Elias Canetti* (Stuttgart: Metzler, 1979);

Barnouw, "Elias Canetti—Poet and Intellectual," in *Major Figures of Contemporary Austrian Literature*, edited by Donald G. Daviau (New York: Lang, 1987), pp. 117-141;

Kurt Bartsch and Gerhard Melzer, eds., *Elias Canetti: Experte der Macht* (Graz: Droschl, 1985);

Alfons-M. Bischoff, *Elias Canetti: Stationen zum Werk* (Bern & Frankfurt am Main: Lang, 1973);

Manfred Durzak, ed., *Zu Elias Canetti* (Stuttgart: Klett, 1983);

Festschrift, Hüter der Verwandlung: Beiträge zum Werk von Elias Canetti (Munich: Hanser, 1985); translated by Michael Hulse as *Essays in Honor of Elias Canetti* (New York: Farrar, Straus & Giroux, 1987);

Hans Feth, *Elias Canettis Dramen* (Frankfurt am Main: R. G. Fischer, 1980);

Gitta Honegger, "Acoustic Masks: Strategies of Language in the Theater of Canetti, Bernhard, and Handke," *Modern Austrian Literature*, 18, no. 2 (1985): 57-66;

Richard H. Lawson, *Understanding Elias Canetti* (Columbia: University of South Carolina Press, 1991);

Modern Austrian Literature, special Canetti issue, 16, no. 3/4 (1983);

Edgar Piel, *Elias Canetti* (Munich: Beck & edition text + kritik, 1984);

Sidney Rosenfeld, "1981 Nobel Laureate Elias Canetti: A Writer Apart," *World Literature Today*, 56, no. 1 (1982): 5-9;

Ingo Seidler, "Who Is Elias Canetti?," in *Cross Currents: A Yearbook of Central European Culture, 1982*, edited by Ladislav Matejka and Benjamin Stolz (Ann Arbor: University of Michigan Press, 1982), pp. 107-123;

Susan Sontag, "Mind as Passion," in her *Under the Sign of Saturn* (New York: Farrar, Straus & Giroux, 1980), pp. 181-204.

Tankred Dorst

(19 December 1925 -   )

W. Gordon Cunliffe
University of Wisconsin—Madison

See also the Dorst entry in *DLB 75: Contemporary German Fiction Writers, Second Series.*

PLAY PRODUCTIONS: *Die Kurve*, Lübeck, Bühnen der Hansestadt, 26 March 1960;

Gesellschaft im Herbst, Mannheim, Nationaltheater, 2 July 1960;

Freiheit für Clemens, Bielefeld, Städtische Bühnen, 19 November 1960;

Große Schmährede an der Stadtmauer, Lübeck, Bühnen der Hansestadt, 27 September 1961;

Die Mohrin, Frankfurt am Main, Städtische Bühnen, 25 June 1964;

Ludwig Tieck, *Der gestiefelte Kater oder Wie man das Spiel spielt*, adapted by Dorst, Hamburg, Deutsches Schauspielhaus, 18 December 1964;

Thomas Dekker, *Der Richter von London*, adapted by Dorst, Essen, Städtische Bühnen, 27 February 1966;

Wittek geht um, Düsseldorf, Schauspielhaus; Bern, Stadttheater, 26 May 1967;

Toller, Stuttgart, Staatstheater, 9 November 1968;

Kleiner Mann—was nun?, Bochum, Schauspielhaus, 22 September 1972;

Eiszeit, Bochum, Schauspielhaus, 17 March 1973;

Auf dem Chimborazo, Berlin, Schlosspark-Theater, 23 January 1975;

Goncourt oder Die Abschaffung des Todes, by Dorst and Horst Laube, Frankfurt am Main, Schauspiel, 5 May 1977;

Die Villa, Düsseldorf, Schauspielhaus; Stuttgart, Württembergisches Staatstheater, 20 October 1980;

Merlin oder Das wüste Land, Düsseldorf, Schauspielhaus, 24 October 1981;

Ameley, der Biber und der König auf dem Dach, Vienna, Burgtheater, 30 October 1982;

Heinrich oder Die Schmerzen der Phantasie, Düsseldorf, Schauspielhaus, 16 May 1985;

Korbes, Hamburg, Deutsches Schauspielhaus, 28 May 1988;

Grindkopf, Frankfurt, Kammerspiel, 15 December 1988.

Tankred Dorst (photograph copyright by Isolde Ohlbaum)

BOOKS: *Geheimnis der Marionette: Mit einem Vorwort von Marcel Marceau* (Munich: Rinn, 1957);

auf kleiner bühne: versuche mit marionetten (Munich: Juventa, 1959);

La buffonata, music by Wilhelm Killmayer (Mainz & New York: Schott, 1961);

Große Schmährede an der Stadtmauer; Freiheit für Clemens; Die Kurve (Cologne: Kiepenheuer & Witsch, 1962); *Große Schmährede an der Stadtmauer* translated by Henry Beissel as *Grand*

Tirade at the Town-Wall (Montreal: University Press, 1961); *Die Kurve* translated by Beissel as *The Curve* (Montreal: University Press, 1963); *Freiheit für Clemens* translated by George Wellwarth as *Freedom for Clemens*, in *Postwar German Theatre*, edited by Wellwarth and Michael Benedikt (New York: Dutton, 1968);

Die Bühne ist der absolute Ort (Cologne: Kiepenheuer & Witsch, 1962);

Die Mohrin (Cologne & Berlin: Kiepenheuer & Witsch, 1964);

Yolimba, music by Killmayer (Mainz & New York: Schott, 1965);

Die mehreren Zauberer: 7 Geschichten für Kinder (Cologne: Kiepenheuer & Witsch, 1966);

Toller: Szenen aus einer deutschen Revolution (Frankfurt am Main: Suhrkamp, 1968); edited by Margaret Jacobs (Manchester, U.K.: Manchester University Press, 1975); adapted for television by Dorst, Peter Zadek, Hartmut Gehrke, and Wilfried Minks as *Rotmord oder I was a German* (Munich: Deutscher Taschenbuch Verlag, 1969);

Sand: Ein Szenarium, by Dorst and Ursula Ehler (Cologne: Kiepenheuer & Witsch, 1971);

Eiszeit: Ein Stück, by Dorst and Ehler (Frankfurt am Main: Suhrkamp, 1973);

Auf dem Chimborazo: Eine Komödie, by Dorst and Ehler (Frankfurt am Main: Suhrkamp, 1975);

Dorothea Merz, by Dorst and Ehler (Frankfurt am Main: Suhrkamp, 1976);

Klaras Mutter, by Dorst and Ehler (Frankfurt am Main: Suhrkamp, 1978);

Stücke, 2 volumes, edited by Gerhard Mensching (Frankfurt am Main: Suhrkamp, 1978)—comprises in volume 1: Ludwig Tieck, *Der Kater oder Wie man das Spiel spielt*, adapted by Dorst; *Gesellschaft im Herbst*; *Die Kurve*; *Große Schmährede an der Stadtmauer*; Denis Diderot, *Rameaus Neffe*, translated and adapted by Dorst; *Die Mohrin*; Thomas Dekker, *Der Richter von London*, translated and adapted by Dorst; in volume 2: *Toller*; *Sand*; *Kleiner Mann—was nun?*; *Eiszeit*; *Goncourt oder die Abschaffung des Todes*, by Dorst and Horst Laube;

Die Villa: Schauspiel, by Dorst and Ehler (Frankfurt am Main: Suhrkamp, 1980);

Mosch: Ein Film, by Dorst and Ehler (Frankfurt am Main: Suhrkamp, 1980);

Merlin oder Das wüste Land, by Dorst and Ehler (Frankfurt am Main: Suhrkamp, 1981);

Der verbotene Garten: Fragmente über d'Annunzio, by Dorst and Ehler (Munich & Vienna: Hanser, 1983);

Eisenhans: Ein Szenarium, by Dorst and Ehler (Cologne: Prometh, 1983);

Die Reise nach Stettin, by Dorst and Ehler (Frankfurt am Main: Suhrkamp, 1984);

Heinrich oder Die Schmerzen der Phantasie: Ein Stück, by Dorst and Ehler (Frankfurt am Main: Suhrkamp, 1985);

Deutsche Stücke: Werkausgabe, by Dorst and Ehler, 3 volumes (Frankfurt am Main: Suhrkamp, 1985-1986)—comprises volume 1, *Deutsche Stücke*: "Dorothea Merz," "Klaras Mutter," *Heinrich oder Die Schmerzen der Phantasie, Die Villa, Mosch, Auf dem Chimborazo*; volume 2 (1985): *Merlin*, by Dorst and Ehler; volume 3 (1986), *Frühe Stücke: Der Kater oder Wie man das Spiel spielt, Gesellschaft im Herbst, Die Kurve, Große Schmährede an der Stadtmauer, Rameaus Neffe, Die Mohrin, Der Richter von London*;

Grindkopf (Frankfurt am Main: Insel, 1986);

Ich, Feuerbach, by Dorst and Ehler (Frankfurt am Main: Suhrkamp, 1986);

Der nackte Mann (Frankfurt am Main: Insel, 1986);

Korbes: Ein Drama, by Dorst and Ehler (Frankfurt am Main: Insel, 1988).

OTHER: *Das bunte Fenster: Ein Geschichtenbuch*, edited by Dorst (Munich: Juventa, 1959);

Gesellschaft im Herbst, in *Junges deutsches Theater von heute*, edited by Joachim Schondorf (Munich: Langen-Müller, 1961), pp. 223-292;

Denis Diderot, *Rameaus Neffe*, translated and adapted by Dorst (Cologne & Berlin: Kiepenheuer & Witsch, 1963);

Ludwig Tieck, *Der gestiefelte Kater oder Wie man das Spiel spielt*, adapted by Dorst (Cologne: Kiepenheuer & Witsch, 1963);

Die Münchner Räterepublik: Zeugnisse und Kommentar, edited by Dorst (Frankfurt am Main: Suhrkamp, 1966);

"Arbeit an einem Stück," in *Spectaculum 11* (Frankfurt am Main: Suhrkamp, 1968), pp. 329-333;

Sean O'Casey, *Der Preispokal*, translated by Dorst (Berlin: Henschelverlag, 1969);

Hans Fallada, *Kleiner Mann—was nun?*, adapted by Dorst (Frankfurt am Main: Suhrkamp, 1972);

Molière, *George Dandin*, translated and adapted by Dorst (Frankfurt am Main: Suhrkamp, 1977);

Molière, *Drei Stücke*, translated and adapted by Dorst (Frankfurt am Main: Suhrkamp, 1978)—contains *Der Geizige*; *Der eingebildet* [sic] *Kranke*; *George Dandin*;

Thomas Dekker, *Der Richter von London*, adapted by Dorst (Frankfurt am Main: Suhrkamp, 1978);

Molière, *Der Bürger als Edelmann*, translated and adapted by Dorst and Ursula Ehler (Reinbek: Rowohlt, 1986).

SELECTED PERIODICAL PUBLICATIONS—
UNCOLLECTED: "Wie ein Theaterstück in ein Fernsehspiel verwandelt wird," *Theater heute*, 9 (September 1968): 21-23;

"Dorothea—eine Frau, die nichts lernt: Zum zweiten Teil der Merz-Erzählung," *Süddeutsche Zeitung*, 25 May 1976, p. 9.

The willingness of German dramatists to break with the conventional theatrical approach is often associated with ideological commitment. Bertolt Brecht's dramatic techniques, for example, are intended to promote dialectical materialism. Tankred Dorst, however, is a modern playwright free of any urge to pontificate, to teach his audience correct modes of thought; he admits that he shares the general bewilderment. For Dorst a play is a product of collaboration among the writer, the actors, and the director. Since 1971 most of Dorst's dramas have been coauthored by Ursula Ehler, his companion for more than twenty years.

Dorst did not come from a family with a theatrical or artistic background. He was born on 19 December 1925 to Max Dorst, a moderately prosperous factory owner, and Elizabeth Lettermann Dorst in the village of Oberlind, Thuringia. Many of Dorst's coarser characters speak the dialect of the region. After World War II Dorst's birthplace lay just within the Soviet zone of occupation, which later became the German Democratic Republic. Something of Dorst's childhood appears in his novel *Dorothea Merz* (1976), in which the village is called Grünitz.

After a dreamy youth spent writing poetry and wandering in the hills, Dorst suffered the fate of many of his generation: he went straight from the schoolroom into the army in 1942, filled with a desire to sacrifice his life for his country. It was in these circumstances that Dorst ac-

quired that distrust of ideologies characteristic of many survivors of his generation, young idealists sent off to war to defend a bad cause. He was a prisoner of war in Belgium, England, and the United States from 1944 until 1947. After his release he returned to Germany. There he drifted, living by casual work and smuggling goods across the border. He completed his Abitur (school-leaving examination) in 1950, then studied German, art history, and drama in Bamberg and Munich. He never received a university degree.

Dorst gained experience of drama through the student puppet theater, and his early publications were on puppetry. Puppets occur in his drama either literally or metaphorically, in the form of characters caught up in roles imposed on them. Both kinds of puppets are present in *Toller* (1968), in which a poet is forced to pose as a revolutionary leader.

The first play by Dorst to be seen in a theater was *Die Kurve* (performed, 1960; published, 1962; translated as *The Curve*, 1963). The play opens with two puppetlike clown figures, the brothers Rudolf and Anton, reminiscent of Samuel Beckett's celebrated pair in *Waiting for Godot* (1953). The brothers are dressed in ill-fitting mourning; their pretty country cottage is next to a cemetery, and Rudolf is fashioning a cross. The two live by burying drivers killed on a dangerous unmarked bend in the road. Rudolf repairs and sells the cars, while Anton, the useless intellectual, delivers graveside addresses. They save the life of one victim, a high government official, but it turns out that he is carrying ritual letters of complaint written by the brothers after each of the twenty-four accidents. Fearing that he will undertake improvements of the road and put them out of business, Anton stabs him to death without interrupting his sermon. The play is an ironic commentary on society's willingness to accept the heavy casualties and junk-strewn landscape imposed by the automobile.

In Dorst's next play, *Gesellschaft im Herbst* (Autumn Party; performed, 1960; published, 1961), a treasure hunt is organized by a countess in her large, decaying castle. The frantic search, in the course of which the castle is wrecked, was futile from the outset; the countess's late husband had sold the treasure long ago. The chief wreckers are a proletarian gang secretly in the pay of a speculator. The characters are clichés in the manner of Friedrich Dürrenmatt or the commedia dell'arte.

Freiheit für Clemens (performed, 1960; published, 1962; translated as *Freedom for Clemens*, 1968) uses symbolism to attack ideology. A young man imprisoned without apparent cause is so successfully taught by the authorities how to react "correctly" to stimuli that he finally refuses proffered freedom. He thus demonstrates the puppetlike quality of human behavior.

Theatrical symbolism is brought more successfully to life in *Große Schmährede an der Stadtmauer* (performed, 1961; published, 1962; translated as *Grand Tirade at the Town-Wall*, 1961). A poor woman kneels before a wall and naively calls on the emperor to return her husband, a fisherman who has run off to join the army. (The Berlin Wall was completed four months after the play appeared, giving Dorst's theatrical imagery an unexpected immediacy.) Two officers play cruel games with the woman, first bringing out a straw puppet and at last producing a man in a soldier's uniform who claims to be the missing husband; the man is neither a soldier nor the husband. The officers insist that the pair prove that they belong together by enacting scenes from their married life. She sees through the ruse and, realizing that her husband is dead, is willing to accept the imposter. She uses all her ingenuity to carry the scheme through, even involving the officers by assigning brief roles to them. The result is that the man feels constrained by the mere enactment of married life and runs off to enlist as a soldier—repeating, puppetlike, what the original husband had done. The woman is left enraged, lamenting the human situation. She and her husband have tried to lead virtuous lives, she says, but a wall has intervened: why are laws, good will, hope, care, and love worth nothing?

In 1962 a stipend enabled Dorst to stay at the Villa Massimo near Rome. His next plays to appear were adaptations: the thirteenth-century French love story of Nicholette and Aucassin as *Die Mohrin* (The Negress, 1964); Ludwig Tieck's *Der gestiefelte Kater* (1797; translated as "Puss in Boots," 1913) as *Der gestiefelte Kater oder Wie man das Spiel spielt* (The Puss in Boots; or, How the Game is Played; published, 1963; performed, 1964); and Thomas Dekker's Elizabethan drama *The Shoemaker's Holiday* (1599) as *Der Richter von London* (The London Judge; performed, 1966; published, 1978). In Tieck's play "members of the audience" wreck the stage illusions, calling out such remarks as "The first time I've ever heard a cat talking!" Dorst's "spectators," more sophisticated than Tieck's, can accept a talking cat;

Scene from the premiere of Dorst's Der gestiefelte Kater oder Wie man das Spiel spielt *at the Deutsches Schauspielhaus, Hamburg, in 1964 (photograph by Rosemarie Clausen)*

but they complain that the fairy tale lacks profundity. The "author," who has had the hero's role played by a popular sportsman who is an outstandingly clumsy actor, is in despair; the members of the "audience" are still haranguing him as, in the slapstick tradition, the curtain fails to fall. Dorst admired Dekker's play as an early realization of the absurdity of existence. The officer, Lacy, who dodges military service to pursue the mayor's daughter, Rose, is allowed to prosper; poor Ralph, the shoemaker's apprentice, who returns from the war crippled, has lost his girlfriend and is unable to work. It is only through the intervention of Simon Eyre, shoemaker and judge, that this all-too-natural course of events is modified. In 1964 Dorst received the Gerhart Hauptmann Prize of the city of Munich.

No longer content with the closed world of the theater and its effects, in *Toller* Dorst turned to a well-documented historical event, the Munich uprising of 1919 that attempted to establish a soviet republic. The central figure is Ernst Toller, the expressionist poet and dramatist whose moral scruples make him unsuccessful as the leader of a political revolution. The material gathered by Dorst is used in about forty tableaux, including factually documentary scenes (for example, meetings of the provisional government), naturalistic private scenes (such as Toller with his girlfriend Olga, a bourgeois revolutionary), and cabaret scenes. Puppetlike characters (anti-Semitic students with false noses) and real puppets (effigies of capitalists with moneybags brought onstage by political demonstrators) appear. At the conclusion the stage is divided into two levels. On the upper level Toller is tried for treason. Testimonies to his character are delivered ironically by speakers in distorting masks. Toller's statement in his own defense is delivered from a cage and taken from his play *Masse Mensch* (performed, 1920; published, 1921; translated as *Masses and Man*, 1923), which was written in October 1919 during the first months of his imprisonment. The speech reveals the self-dramatization that prompted Toller's failed revolution. Spectators jeer at him, calling out "Schauspieler!" (actor!). He is found guilty and sentenced to five years in prison. On the lower stage an officer of the government forces that crushed the revolt reads names from a list, and at each name a worker is led off to be shot. The relative wordlessness of this procedure undercuts Toller's defensive volubility. The scene continues the contrast established earlier in the play between Toller, running hither and thither in an attempt to avert the shooting of hostages, and the coldhearted professional revolutionary Leviné. Dorst is demonstrating the gap between theater and revolutionary reality.

Toller, with its skepticism about ideologies, went against the grain of the left-wing student activism of the time and was the subject of protests. A television version took its title, *Rotmord* (Red Murder, 1969), from the vocabulary of the Nazis—another anti-ideological gesture on Dorst's part.

Munich awarded Dorst the Tukan Prize in 1969. He spent 1970 as writer in residence at Oberlin College in Ohio. That year he won the Theater Prize of the city of Lisbon and shared the Adolf Grimme Prize for experimental theater with Peter Zadek and Wilfried Manles.

A television scenario, *Sand* (1971), describes the assassination of the playwright August von Kotzebue by a patriotic student, Karl Ludwig Sand, in Mannheim in 1819. Dorst refrains from suggesting any coherent explanation for the deed. In the penultimate scene the onlookers, bewildered, watch while Sand, who has stabbed Kotzebue, tries to stab himself while talking of freedom. The work was the first collaboration between Dorst and Ehler.

Zadek encouraged Dorst to use the cabaret revue technique he had introduced in *Toller* in the stage adaptation of Hans Fallada's Depression-era novel *Kleiner Mann—was nun?* (1932; translated as *Little Man—What Now?*, 1933). Dorst's play was published in 1972, and Zadek directed it at the Bochum theater in the fall of that year. Johannes Pinneberg and his wife Lämmchen suffer wage cuts, unemployment, and a housing shortage in vivid, naturalistic scenes from the novel interspersed with songs and chorus lines in the period mode. Dorst offers no solutions to the problems he depicts; the absence of political or economic discussion in the play irritated some commentators, but the work was popular with audiences.

Dorst's "neutralism" stands out above all in *Eiszeit* (Ice Age, 1973), a play that depicts the Norwegian novelist Knut Hamsun during the last few years before his death in 1952 at ninety-three. He is living in a home for the aged, accused of collaborating with the Germans during the occupation of Norway. But Hamsun's patriarchal beliefs and a convenient forgetfulness allow him to evade a sense of guilt. The old man listens with genuine interest to the accusations of a wartime partisan, Oswald, for he is willing to expand his self-knowledge; Oswald eventually commits suicide. The audience is left with questions rather than with strengthened convictions—for example, should a celebrated novelist be expected to hold enlightened opinions? What has literary standing to do with political integrity? Would the old man have been treated more leniently for a nonpolitical crime?

Dorst brings his own family chronicle into juxtaposition with recent German history in a seven-part cycle, collected in 1985 as *Deutsche Stücke* (German Plays), consisting of plays, a television script, and novels. The period depicted extends from the Weimar Republic to the 1970s. The comedy *Auf dem Chimborazo* (On the Chimborazo, 1975), the epilogue to the whole, was the first part published and performed.

Scene from the premiere of Dorst's Eiszeit *at the Schauspielhaus, Bochum, in 1973: Karl Friedrich as Reich, Peter Kollek as Holm, Werner Dahms as Paul, O. E. Hasse as the old man, and Werner Eichhorn as the bank director (photograph by Hecke)*

The Chimborazo is a comically exotic name, taken from that of an extinct volcano in Ecuador, for a litter-strewn hill in West Germany from which visitors can look over into the other Germany. It is over there that Dorothea Merz, her two sons, and their friend Klara have their roots. Dorothea plans to light a fire on the hill as a signal of hope to those who remained on the other side of the border. The fire, however, never gets lit as family squabbles bring to the surface old lies and disappointed hopes. Dorothea finally tells her family that they have spoiled everything; in this comment there is an oblique reference to German history.

The play *Heinrich oder Die Schmerzen der Phantasie* (Heinrich; or, The Pains of the Imagination, 1985) is set shortly before the Allied invasion and the Soviet summer offensive of 1944. Sixteen-year-old Heinrich, the son of Dorothea Merz, is sent to a naval training school in Stettin (now Szczecin, Poland). He disgraces himself by falling asleep on sentry duty. Not wanting to return home under a cloud, Heinrich hangs around the railway station in Berlin and finally moves in with his mother's brother, Dr. Plinke.

In Plinke's home the provincial Heinrich gets to know a witty, cynical society of actors and demi-mondaines far removed from the conformity to which he is accustomed. The experience strengthens Heinrich so that he claims that he did not fall asleep but was reading a book out of defiance. Plinke is killed in a daylight air raid. At the end of the play a group of silent people, representing the deported victims of the Nazis, makes a final appearance.

Die Villa (The Villa; performed, 1980) takes place shortly before the foundation of the two German states in a villa in Grünitz just within the Soviet zone of occupation. The visitors and lodgers react in differing ways to the new situation. Heinrich regularly crosses the border, smuggling people to the West and cigarettes to the East. The manufacturer Bergk struggles to keep his business going by allaying the suspicions of two officials. His wife, Elsa, detests the new regime. Also living in the villa are an actor, a flirtatious actress, a young communist, and Tilmann, Heinrich's lame brother. Elsa, unable to accompany Heinrich across the border, commits suicide. The thirty-two scenes which refuse to solid-

Scene from the premiere of Goncourt oder Die Abschaffung des Todes, *by Dorst and Horst Laube, at the Schauspiel, Frankfurt am Main, in 1977 (photograph by Maria Eggert)*

ify into a plot reveal an objective attitude to the events depicted.

A fantastic play on the subject of revolution, *Goncourt oder Die Abschaffung des Todes* (Goncourt; or, The Elimination of Death; performed, 1977; published, 1978) is set in the Paris Commune of 1871. As in *Toller*, Dorst—here collaborating with Horst Laube—depicts the hesitations of a bourgeois man of letters. Carrying the spirit of his dead brother Jules on his back, the critic Edmond de Goncourt moves about Paris besieged by the Prussians and encounters the famous (such as Gustave Flaubert) and the obscure. Grotesque scenes include a woman eating roast dog and a young man chopping off his own finger. It is demonstrated that intellectuals are not suited for active political intervention.

For the opening scenes of the long play *Merlin oder Das wüste Land* (Merlin; or, The Wasteland, 1981) Dorst and Ehler used Tieck's 1829 translation of William Rowley's play *The Child Hath Found His Father*, written early in the sixteenth century and published in 1622. Dorst follows Rowley and Tieck in making the search for Merlin's father a crude knockabout farce. A son, Merlin, is born to Hanne; the father turns out to be the devil, who wishes, through Merlin, to liberate humankind, as evil is its natural environment. Merlin is not inclined to obedience and departs

to help King Artus (Arthur) found the Company of the Round Table. The rest of the play seems to confirm the devil's view of humanity. The familiar tales are told: the sword in the stone, Parzival's highly destructive wanderings, Gawain and the Green Knight, the adulterous passion of Ginevra (Guinevere) and Lancelot, and Mordred's hatred of his father, Artus; the story of Tristan and Isolde is brought into the play through a correspondence between Isolde and Ginevra. The utopia of the Round Table fails through criminal violence produced by Mordred's determination to destroy his father and humiliate Ginevra and by Lancelot's uncontrollable passion; the search for the Holy Grail leads to further crimes. The finale is a battle between Mordred and Artus which leaves a gigantic heap of iron and blood—the wasteland.

The kind of utopian existence planned by Gabriele D'Annunzio, the last of the European aesthetes, in which art and life would intertwine, is seen to be illusory in *Der verbotene Garten* (The Forbidden Garden; published, 1982). The poet, seated in his labyrinthine garden overlooking Lake Garda and visited by figures from his past, discovers that his disciples have reduced his life to newsworthy items such as the capture of Fiume and his friendships with Eleonora Duse and Benito Mussolini.

In 1983 Dorst received the literature prize of the Bavarian Academy of the Fine Arts. His and Ehler's short play *Ich, Feuerbach* (I, Feuerbach; published, 1986) presents an aging, once famous actor who had spent seven years undergoing psychiatric treatment. He is unknown to the director's assistant when he appears at the theater for an audition. The director, who knew him well, is not present when Feuerbach arrives; he leaves the theater before Feuerbach has finished reciting, in a style that indicates mounting insanity, a monologue from Johann Wolfgang von Goethe's *Torquato Tasso* (1790; translated, 1861).

Dorst used fairy tales as the basis for two short plays. In *Grindkopf* (Scurfhead; published, 1986; performed, 1988) the king's son rescues the giant Eisehans from captivity. In return, the giant assigns the prince the task of guarding a pure and limpid pool. The prince fails by dipping his hair into the water when he sees his reflection there; the hair turns into gold and has to be concealed, and the prince is given the nickname "Grindkopf" by those who do not know what he is hiding. It is only after a period of performing menial tasks at the court of the bald king that the prince is released by Eisenhans and awarded the hand of the bald king's daughter.

The premiere of *Korbes* (1988) caused some stir in Hamburg on account of stage nudity. In the play, which is based on a Grimm fairy tale, Korbes beats and otherwise mistreats his housekeeper, Betzn. Overnight he goes blind, but he remains so brutal to Betzn that she leaves him. Blinded, the despicable bully is worse than before; he rages at the potato peelings that he slips on. Korbes's daughter, Hannelore, replaces the housekeeper. As the curtain falls, Korbes is thrashing blindly with his stick while his daughter evades his blows and George Frederick Handel's *Brockes Passion* is played. The play, which is terrifying in its incoherent formlessness—Korbes speaks in dialect fragments—demonstrates human aggressiveness, particularly that of men against women.

References:

Reinhard Baumgart, "Parsifal 1982," *Theater heute*, 23 (October 1982): 18-25;

Peter von Becker, " 'Merlin': Magier und Entertainer. Theater als Phantasiestätte. Ein Werkstattgespräch," *Theater heute*, 20 (April 1979): 34-37;

Volker Canaris, "Die Tage nach der Stunde Null," *Der Spiegel*, 34 (29 September 1980): 233-240;

Canaris, "Ein Volkstheater," *Theater heute*, 13 (November 1972): 30-35;

Günther Erken, "Gespräche in der Dramaturgie," in *Spectaculum 35* (Frankfurt am Main: Suhrkamp, 1982), pp. 283-287;

Erken, *Tankred Dorst* (Frankfurt am Main: Suhrkamp, 1989);

Reinhold Grimm, "Spiel und Wirklichkeit in einigen Revolutionsdramen," *Basis*, 1 (1970): 49-93;

Walter Haug, "Merlin oder Das wüste Land," *Arbitrium*, 1, no. 1 (1983): 100-108;

Heinz-B. Heller, "Tankred Dorst," in *Deutsche Literatur der Gegenwart in Einzeldarstellungen*, volume 2, edited by Dietrich Weber (Stuttgart: Kröner, 1977), pp. 77-79;

Klaus Harro Hilzinger, "Theatralisierung des Dokuments? Tankred Dorst 'Toller,' " in his *Die Dramaturgie des dokumentarischen Theaters* (Tübingen: Niemeyer, 1976), pp. 121-123;

Hellmuth Karasek, "Ab ins Tal: *Auf dem Chimborazo*—Berliner Schlossparkaufführung," *Der Spiegel*, 29 (27 January 1975): 105-106;

Thomas L. Keller, "Tankred Dorst's 'Merlin': Its Performance and Its Appeal," *Germanic Notes*, 16, no. 3 (1985): 35-36;

Gerhard Kluge, "Werkimmanente Poetik in zwei Stücken von Tankred Dorst und Martin Walser," *Amsterdamer Beiträge zur neueren Germanistik 16* (Amsterdam: Rodopi, 1983), pp. 69-88;

Rüdiger Krohn, "Die Geschichte widerlegt die Utopie?," *Euphorion*, 78 (1984): 160-179;

Horst Laube, ed., *Werkbuch über Tankred Dorst* (Frankfurt am Main: Suhrkamp, 1974);

Ulrich Müller, "Parzival 1980," in *Mittelalter-Rezeption*, volume 2, edited by Jürgen Kühnel and others (Göppingen: Kümmerle, 1982), pp. 623-640;

William H. Rey, "Der Dichter und die Revolution," *Basis*, 5 (1975): 166-194;

Günther Rühle, "Ein Mann, der nicht Recht haben will," *Frankfurter Allgemeine Zeitung*, 17 January 1975;

Monika Schattenkofer, *Eine Modellwirklichkeit: Literarisches Theater der 50er und 60er Jahre. Tankred Dorst schreibt Toller* (Frankfurt am Main: Lang, 1985);

Ernst Schürer, "Georg Büchners 'Dantons Tod' und Tankred Dorsts 'Toller': Zwei Revolutionsdramen," in *Festschrift für Walter Huder* (Berlin: Medusa, 1982), pp. 187-203;

Botho Strauss, "Geschichte ist nicht, was geschah," *Theater heute*, 9 (1969): 42-44;

Rainer Taëni, *Toller: Grundlagen und Gedanken zum Verständnis des Dramas* (Frankfurt am Main: Diesterweg, 1977);

Frank Trommler, "Ein Schauspieler der Revolution: Tankred Dorst's 'Toller,'" in *Geschichte als Schauspiel*, edited by W. Hinck (Frankfurt am Main: Suhrkamp, 1981), pp. 355-370.

Friedrich Dürrenmatt

(5 January 1921 - 14 December 1990)

Edson M. Chick
Williams College

See also the Dürrenmatt entry in *DLB 69: Contemporary German Fiction Writers, First Series.*

PLAY PRODUCTIONS: *Es steht geschrieben*, Zurich, Schauspielhaus, 19 April 1947;

Der Blinde, Basel, Stadttheater, 10 January 1948;

Romulus der Große, Basel, Stadttheater, 25 April 1949;

Die Ehe des Herrn Mississippi, Munich, Kammerspiele, 26 March 1952;

Nächtlicher Besuch (Nächtliches Gespräch mit einem verachteten Menschen), Zurich, Kammerspiele, 26 July 1952);

Ein Engel kommt nach Babylon, Munich, Kammerspiele, 22 December 1953;

Der Besuch der alten Dame, music by Gottfried von Einem, Zurich, Schauspielhaus, 29 January 1956;

Frank der Fünfte, music by Paul Burkhard, Zurich, Schauspielhaus, 19 March 1959;

Abendstünde im Spätherbst, Berlin Renaissancetheater, 19 November 1959;

Die Physiker, Zurich, Schauspielhaus, 20 February 1962;

Herkules und der Stall des Augias, Zurich, Schauspielhaus, 20 March 1963;

Der Meteor, Zurich, Schauspielhaus, 20 January 1966;

Die Wiedertäufer, Zurich, Schauspielhaus, 16 March 1967;

König Johann, Basel, Stadttheater, 18 September 1968;

Play Strindberg, Basel, Komödie, 8 February 1969;

Friedrich Dürrenmatt (photograph by Margarete Redl-von Peinen)

Urfaust, Zurich, Schauspielhaus, 22 October 1970;

Porträt eines Planeten, Düsseldorf, Schauspielhaus, 10 November 1970;

Titus Andronicus, Düsseldorf, Schauspielhaus, 12 December 1970;

Der Mitmacher, Zurich, Schauspielhaus, 8 March 1973;

Ein Engel kommt nach Babylon: Opera in Three Acts, music by Rudolf Kelterborn, Zurich, Opera House, 5 June 1977;

Die Frist, Zurich, Kino Korso, 6 October 1977;

Die Panne, Wilhelmsbad, 13 September 1979;

Achterloo, Zurich, Schauspielhaus, 6 October 1983.

BOOKS: *Es steht geschrieben: Ein Drama* (Klosterberg & Basel: Schwabe, 1947); revised as *Die Wiedertäufer: Eine Komödie in zwei Teilen* (Zurich: Arche, 1967);

Der Blinde: Ein Drama (Berlin: Bühnenverlag Bloch Erben, 1947);

Pilatus (Olten: Vereinigung Oltner Bücherfreunde, 1949);

Der Nihilist (Horgen: Holunderpresse, 1950); republished as *Die Falle* (Zurich: Arche, 1952);

Das Bild des Sisyphos (Zurich: Arche, 1952); translated by Michael Bullock as "The Picture of Sisyphos," *Mundus Artium,* 1, no. 3 (1968): 53-69;

Der Tunnel (Zurich: Arche, 1952); republished in *Die Panne and Der Tunnel,* edited by F. J. Alexander (London: Oxford University Press, 1967); translated by Carla Coulter and Alison Scott as "The Tunnel," *Evergreen Review,* 5, no. 17 (1961): 32-42;

Die Stadt: Prosa I-IV (Zurich: Arche, 1952);

Der Richter und sein Henker (Einsiedeln, Zurich & Cologne: Benziger, 1952); edited by William Gillis and John J. Neumaier (Cambridge, Mass.: Riverside Press, 1961); edited by Leonard Forster (London: Harrap, 1962); translated by Cyrus Brooks as *The Judge and His Hangman* (London: Jenkins, 1954); translated by Theresa Pol as *The Judge and His Hangman* (New York: Harper, 1955);

Die Ehe des Herrn Mississippi: Eine Komödie in zwei Teilen (Zurich: Oprecht, 1952; revised edition, Zurich: Arche, 1966); translated by Bullock as *The Marriage of Mr. Mississippi,* in *The Marriage of Mr. Mississippi: A Play and Problems of the Theatre: An Essay* (New York: Grove, 1966); German version edited by

Reinhold Grimm and Helene Scher (New York: Holt, Rinehart & Winston, 1973);

Der Verdacht (Einsiedeln, Zurich & Cologne: Benziger, 1953); edited by Gillis (Boston: Houghton Mifflin, 1964); edited by Forster (London: Harrap, 1965); translated by Eva H. Morreale as *The Quarry* (New York: Grove, 1961; London: Cape, 1962);

Ein Engel kommt nach Babylon: Eine Komödie in drei Akten (Zurich: Arche, 1954; revised, 1958); translated by William McElwee as *An Angel Comes to Babylon,* in *An Angel Comes To Babylon and Romulus the Great* (New York: Grove, 1964);

Herkules und der Stall des Augias: Mit Randnotizen eines Kugelschreibers (Zurich: Arche, 1954);

Theaterprobleme (Zurich: Arche, 1955); translated by Gerhard Nellhaus as "Problems of the Theatre," in *Four Plays* (London: Cape, 1964; New York: Grove, 1965);

Grieche sucht Griechin: Eine Prosakomödie (Zurich: Arche, 1955); translated by Richard and Clara Winston as *Once a Greek . . .* (New York: Knopf, 1965; London: Cape, 1966);

Die Panne: Eine noch mögliche Geschichte (Zurich: Arche, 1956); republished in *Die Panne and Der Tunnel,* edited by Alexander (London: Oxford University Press, 1967); translated by Richard and Clara Winston as *Traps* (New York: Knopf, 1960); translation republished as *A Dangerous Game* (London: Cape, 1960);

Romulus der Große: Eine ungeschichtliche historische Komödie (Basel: Reiss, 1956; revised edition, Zurich: Arche, 1958); edited by Hugh Frederic Garten (Boston: Houghton Mifflin, 1962; London: Methuen, 1962); translated by Nellhaus as *Romulus the Great,* in *An Angel Comes to Babylon and Romulus the Great;*

Der Besuch der alten Dame: Eine tragische Komödie (Zurich: Arche, 1956); adapted by Maurice Valency as *The Visit: A Play in Three Acts* (New York: Random House, 1958); German version edited by Paul Kurt Ackermann (Boston: Houghton Mifflin, 1961); translated by Patrick Bowles as *The Visit: A Tragicomedy* (New York: Grove, 1962; London: Cape, 1962);

Komödien (Zurich: Arche, 1957);

Nächtliches Gespräch mit einem verachteten Menschen: Ein Kurs für Zeitgenossen (Zurich: Arche, 1957); translated by Robert D. Macdonald as *Conversation at Night with a Despised Character: A Curriculum for Our Times* (Chicago: Dramatic Publishing Co., 1957);

Der Prozeß um des Esels Schatten: Ein Hörspiel nach Wieland—aber nicht sehr (Zurich: Arche, 1958);

Das Unternehmen der Wega: Ein Hörspiel (Zurich: Arche, 1958); translated by Alfred Schild as "The Mission of the Vega," *Texas Quarterly*, 5, no. 1 (1962): 125-149;

Das Versprechen: Requiem auf den Kriminalroman (Zurich: Arche, 1958); translated by Richard and Clara Winston as *The Pledge* (New York: Knopf, 1959; London: Cape, 1959); German version edited by Forster (London: Harrap, 1967);

Abendstunde im Spätherbst: Ein Hörspiel (Zurich: Arche, 1959); translated by Gabriel Karminski as *Episode on an Autumn Evening* (Chicago: Dramatic Publishing Co., 1959);

Stranitzky und der Nationalheld: Ein Hörspiel (Zurich: Arche, 1959);

Der Doppelgänger: Ein Spiel (Zurich: Arche, 1960);

Friedrich Schiller: Eine Rede (Zurich: Arche, 1960);

Frank der Fünfte: Oper einer Privatbank, music by Paul Burkhard (Zurich: Arche, 1960; revised, 1964);

Die Ehe des Herrn Mississippi: Ein Drehbuch mit Szenenbildern (Zurich: Sanssouci, 1961);

Die Panne: Ein Hörspiel (Zurich: Arche, 1961);

Gesammelte Hörspiele (Zurich: Arche, 1961);

Die Physiker: Eine Komödie in zwei Akten (Zurich: Arche, 1962); translated by James Kirkup as *The Physicists* (London: French, 1963; New York: Grove, 1964); German version edited by Robert E. Helbling (New York: Oxford University Press, 1965); edited by Arthur Taylor (London: Macmillan, 1966);

Die Heimat im Plakat: Ein Buch für Schweizer Kinder (Zurich: Diogenes, 1963);

Herkules und der Stall des Augias: Eine Komödie (Zurich: Arche, 1963); translated by Agnes Hamilton as *Hercules and the Augean Stables* (Chicago: Dramatic Publishing Co., 1963);

Komödien II und frühe Stücke (Zurich: Arche, 1963);

Drei Hörspiele, edited by Henry Regensteiner (New York: Holt, Rinehart & Winston, 1965) —comprises *Abendstunde im Spätherbst, Der Doppelgänger, Die Panne*;

Theaterschriften und Reden, 2 volumes, edited by Elisabeth Brock-Sulzer (Zurich: Arche, 1966-1972); translated by H. M. Waidson as *Writings on Theatre and Drama*, 1 volume (London: Cape, 1976);

Der Meteor: Eine Komödie in zwei Akten (Zurich: Arche, 1966); translated by Kirkup as *The Meteor* (Chicago: Dramatic Publishing Co., 1966; London: Cape, 1973);

Vier Hörspiele (Berlin: Volk und Welt, 1967);

König Johann: Nach Shakespeare (Zurich: Arche, 1968);

Play Strindberg: Totentanz nach August Strindberg (Zurich: Arche, 1969); translated by Kirkup as *Play Strindberg* (Chicago: Dramatic Publishing Co., 1970; London: Cape, 1972);

Monstervortrag über Gerechtigkeit und Recht nebst einem helvetischen Zwischenspiel: Eine kleine Dramaturgie der Politik (Zurich: Arche, 1969); translated by John Wood as "A Monster Lecture on Justice and Law Together with a Helvetian Interlude: A Brief Discussion on the Dramaturgy of Politics," in *Friedrich Dürrenmatt: Plays and Essays*, edited by Volkmar Sander (New York: Continuum, 1982), pp. 263-312;

Sätze aus Amerika (Zurich: Arche, 1970);

Titus Andronicus: Eine Komödie nach Shakespeare (Zurich: Arche, 1970);

Der Besuch der alten Dame: Oper in 3 Akten nach Friedrich Dürrenmatts tragischer Komödie, music by Gottfried von Einem, German text with English translation by Norman Tucker (London & New York: Boosey & Hawkes, 1971);

Der Sturz (Zurich: Arche, 1971);

Porträt eines Planeten (Zurich: Arche, 1971);

Komödien III (Zurich: Arche, 1972);

Gespräch mit Heinz Ludwig Arnold (Zurich: Arche, 1976);

Zusammenhänge: Essay über Israel. Eine Konzeption (Zurich: Arche, 1976);

Der Mitmacher: Ein Komplex. Text der Komödie, Dramaturgie, Erfahrungen, Berichte, Erzählungen (Zurich: Arche, 1976); play republished as *Der Mitmacher: Eine Komödie* (Zurich: Arche, 1978);

Die Frist: Eine Komödie (Zurich: Arche, 1977);

Dürrenmatt: Bilder und Zeichnungen, edited by Christian Strich (Zurich: Diogenes, 1978);

Friedrich Dürrenmatt Lesebuch (Zurich: Diogenes, 1978);

Albert Einstein: Ein Vortrag (Zurich: Diogenes, 1979);

Die Panne: Komödie (Zurich: Diogenes, 1979);

Werkausgabe in 30 Bänden, 30 volumes (Zurich: Diogenes, 1980)—includes final versions of *Romulus, Mississippi, Ein Engel kommt nach Babylon, Der Besuch, Frank der Fünfte, Die Physiker, Herkules, Der Mitmacher*, and *Die Frist*, and the previously unpublished *Untergang und neues Leben*;

Stoffe I-III (Zurich: Diogenes, 1981);

Die Welt als Labyrinth (Vienna: Deuticke, 1982);

Achterloo: Eine Komödie in zwei Akten (Zurich: Diogenes, 1983; revised, 1988);

Die Erde ist zu schön . . . : Die Physiker; Der Tunnel; Das Unternehmen der Wega (Zurich: Arche, 1983);

Minotaurus: Eine Ballade mit Zeichnungen des Autors (Zurich: Diogenes, 1985);

Justiz (Zurich: Diogenes, 1985); translated by John E. Woods as *The Execution of Justice* (New York: Random House, 1989);

Varlin, 1900-1977 (New York: Claude Bernard Gallery, 1986);

Der Auftrag oder Vom Beobachter des Beobachters der Beobachter (Zurich: Diogenes, 1986); translated by Joel Agee as *The Assignment; or, On the Observing of the Observer of the Observers* (New York: Random House, 1988);

Rollenspiele: Protokoll einer fiktiven Inszenierung und Achterloo III, by Dürrenmatt and Charlotte Kerr (Zurich: Diogenes, 1986);

Versuche (Zurich: Diogenes, 1988);

Durcheinandertal: Roman (Zurich: Diogenes, 1989);

Turmbau: Stoffe IV-IX (Zurich: Diogenes, 1990);

Kants Hoffnung: Zwei politische Reden, zwei Gedichte aus dem Nachlaß (Zurich: Diogenes, 1991).

Editions in English: *Four Plays*, translated by Gerhard Nellhaus and others (London: Cape, 1964; New York: Grove Press, 1965)—comprises *Romulus the Great, The Marriage of Mr. Mississippi, An Angel Comes to Babylon, The Physicists*;

Friedrich Dürrenmatt: Plays and Essays, edited by Volkmar Sander (New York: Continuum, 1982).

Friedrich Dürrenmatt was the leading German-language dramatist of the generation after Bertolt Brecht. He dominated German, Austrian, and Swiss repertoires and was familiar to audiences throughout Europe and North and South America. His plays reach everyone; they teem with brilliant ideas and fantastic inventions; and behind the comic-grotesque satire lies a deeply humane, urgently felt philosophical and religious impetus. He wrote not book dramas but plays to be performed. When not directing the plays himself, he regularly participated in their production, revising and rewriting in consultation with actors up to the last moment; if the performance failed to affect the audience as he thought it should, he cast the text in a new version.

His most popular plays, especially *Der Besuch der alten Dame* (The Visit of the Old Lady, 1956; adapted as *The Visit*, 1958) and *Die Physiker* (1962; translated as *The Physicists*, 1963), made him the darling of theater people and critics. But as directing styles changed and texts came to be seen as mere raw material, Dürrenmatt began to complain of inadequate performances of his works. He also found reviewers rejecting his work because it seemed uncommited when compared to the activist message plays and documentaries that began to appear in the late 1960s. Such criticism was particularly galling to Dürrenmatt, who never tired of demonstrating in his plays the untold damage done by ideologies and their true believers.

Dürrenmatt was born on 5 January 1921 in Konolfingen, in the Emmental region of the canton of Bern, Switzerland, to Reinhold and Hulda Zimmermann Dürrenmatt. A sister, Vroni, followed in 1924. His father was pastor of the Konolfingen church, and his grandfather Ulrich Dürrenmatt had been a member of Parliament and a militantly conservative newspaper publisher who was proud to have served ten days in jail for printing a particularly vicious satiric poem on the front page. Father and grandfather left their imprint on "des Pastors Fritzli" (the pastor's boy Fritzli), as he was called by the townspeople, in his intense preoccupation with religion, his conservative cast of mind, and the hard-hitting, Swiftian satire of his plays. The tales his father recounted from classical mythology and the Bible stories his mother told him provided material for many of his major works.

In 1933 Dürrenmatt entered the secondary school in the neighboring village of Großhochstetten; he spent his spare time in the studio of a local painter, who encouraged him to indulge his passion for painting and drawing. He pursued this activity all his life, producing undisciplined, highly dramatic pictures first of natural catastrophes and great battles of Swiss history and later of the Tower of Babel and astronomical phenomena. He was twenty-three before he decided to concentrate on writing stories and plays and to make visual art an avocation.

The family moved in 1935 to the city of Bern, where Dürrenmatt's father was appointed pastor of the Salem Hospital and the deaconess house. Dürrenmatt was enrolled at the Freies Gymnasium, a Christian secondary school, where he lasted two and a half years. A bad student, he was invited to leave. He transferred to a less rigorous private school, the Humboldtianum, from which he regularly played hooky.

In his school years he was plagued by a tyrannical and chaotic imagination. Frequent attendance at the City Theater of Bern, where his uncle, a high government official, had a loge, provided fuel for these fantasies. In 1941 a summer of concentrated work on neglected subjects—he was good at classical languages but had to make up ground in the sciences—equipped him to pass his final exams. Having been rejected by the Institute of Art, he enrolled at the University of Zurich, where for one semester he studied philosophy, literature, and natural science. He then became a student of philosophy at the University of Bern for a semester, tutoring in Greek and Latin to earn pocket money. His studies were interrupted when he was called to military duty. During basic training his bad eyesight became evident when, according to his own account, he began saluting mailmen, and he was assigned to such tasks as lettering identification tags by hand.

In 1942 he returned to the University of Zurich for two semesters, spending most of his time in the company of painters and writing plays and stories. In 1943 he fell sick with hepatitis and returned home to Bern. He spent his final four semesters of university study there, concentrating on philosophy and contemplating the possibility of a doctoral dissertation on Søren Kierkegaard and tragedy.

In 1946 he married Lotti Geißler, an actress. They settled in Basel the following year, at about the time he was completing his first radio play, *Der Doppelgänger* (The Double, 1960), which was turned down by Swiss Radio, and his first drama, *Es steht geschrieben* (It Is Written, 1947). Opening night spectators in Zurich booed the play; but reviewers recognized Dürrenmatt's powerful talent and potential, and he received a cash prize from the Welti Foundation to encourage him to continue writing plays.

Es steht geschrieben is set in Münster during the period 1534 to 1536, when the city was transformed by Anabaptists into their "New Jerusalem" and was then besieged, defeated, and sacked by a coalition of Catholic and Protestant troops. The play is a panoramic, tumultuous *theatrum mundi*, or universal theater, in the seventeenth-century mode, with more than thirty scenes and a large cast. It mixes monologues, crowd scenes, political intrigue, and religious-existential soul-searching. The language ranges from the biblically hymnic to the grotesque; it is

by turns solemn, prophetic, cynical, highly figurative, apocalyptic, and disillusioning. At the center of the action are two starkly contrasting figures: Johann Bockelson, an actor, confidence man, and voluptuary who has himself crowned King David; and Bernhard Knipperdollingck, a wealthy merchant who renounces his earthly goods and, in the final scene, experiences God's grace as his limbs are broken on the wheel. The play can be read as an allegory of Nazism's rise and fall and of the suicidal fanaticism of the Germans under Hitler, or as an expression of deep pessimism over the course of Western history and of anger at the ruling powers' betrayal of the cause of peace and humanity in the sixteenth century as well as at the beginning of the post-1946 Cold War.

Es steht geschrieben is a passionate and immoderate play that poses insuperable problems for directors and actors, and in 1948 Dürrenmatt decreed that rights for its performance would no longer be granted.

Twenty years later, hoping to make it as stageworthy as his recent successes, he reworked it as a comedy under the title *Die Wiedertäufer* (The Anabaptists, 1967). It was received without enthusiasm by audiences. The play includes large chunks of the earlier drama rearranged and reworded in a more obviously artistic way. Dürrenmatt pared away much of the figurative language and pathos and de-emphasized the play's historicity, with the effect that the farce and cruelty of real life are aesthetically transformed into dramatic satire. The religious utopia of Münster created in part 1 and its downfall in part 2 are presented as theatrical events: Bockelson is a second-rate actor who is able to persuade people, because they are so eager to believe, that he is King David; the whole thing is his show, and he is both star and director. In the end he walks away from the sack of Münster to accept an acting job, leaving the Anabaptist fools who took his fictions so seriously to their bloody fate at the hands of mercenaries who lack religious convictions but cannot tolerate the existence of a Christian community where all property is equally shared. The Anabaptists' overwrought imaginations have been fired by Bockelson's mediocre theatrical performance; but in a moment of clarity near the end they recognize that they must believe in their ultimate victory, for otherwise all their suffering will have proven meaningless. In accord with the laws of Dürrenmattian satiric theater, events take the worst imaginable turn: greed, indifference, and unreason are victorious. The last word no longer belongs to Knipperdollingck in his mystical transport but to the one-hundred-year-old bishop of Münster, who comments in despair on this monstrous, unjust world.

When he forbade the performing of *Es steht geschrieben*, Dürrenmatt extended the interdiction, with greater justification, to his second play, *Der Blinde* (The Blind Man; published, 1947, performed, 1948). It had aroused neither outrage nor much interest in its initial production, despite outstanding direction and a fine cast, and was removed from the Basel repertoire after nine performances. Productions at two other theaters fared no better.

Where *Es steht geschrieben* is theater of the world, *Der Blinde* is theater of the mind. It revolves around the duke, whose realm lies in ruins and whose people have been killed by the ravages of the Thirty Years' War. The parallels to the Germany of the late 1940s, three hundred years later, are obvious. The duke is blind and has chosen to live according to the principle of absolute credulity; for if a blind person does not believe everyone, he must doubt everything. His antagonist is Negro da Ponte, who carries out an elaborate plot to disillusion the duke and force him to renounce his faith. Da Ponte's elaborate deceptions—having a whore play the role of an abbess and an inarticulate African native play General Wallenstein—have little effect, and his most sadistic hoax backfires: the corpse he presents to the duke as that of his daughter Octavia is revealed, to the surprise of all, to be in fact Octavia and not, as planned, the body of another. The duke's guilt and remorse—he believes himself responsible for her death—paradoxically move him to reaffirm his Christian faith. The play has not been revived or revised because it would inevitably sink under the weight of its philosophical and theological pretension. Dürrenmatt's study of the works of Kierkegaard, Karl Barth, and Jean-Paul Sartre led him to supply his characters with speeches that are paradoxical, wooden, overly metaphysical, and undramatic.

On 6 August 1947 the Dürrenmatts' first child, Peter, was born. After the failure of *Der Blinde* they could no longer afford to live in Basel; they moved to Schernelz, above the Lake of Biel, where Lotti Dürrenmatt's mother, Frau Falb, had a home. Dürrenmatt was helped financially by friends and anonymous patrons who wanted to foster his talent.

Before the move he had agreed to provide the Basel theater with a play titled "Der Turmbau zu Babel" (The Building of the Tower of Babel); the cast had been selected, and the manuscript had grown to four acts. But mature consideration forced him to destroy it. The play he quickly wrote to fulfill his obligation, *Romulus der Große* (performed, 1949; published, 1956; translated as *Romulus the Great*, 1964), became the first of his enduring theatrical successes. It is a neatly structured, fast-paced, tragicomic piece composed with the theater audience in mind and having at its center the most appealing of all Dürrenmatt's protagonists, the calm, relaxed, clear Emperor Romulus, who bears no relation to the martyrs, cynics, and overwrought ideologues of the earlier plays. It is his humane sanity that makes him great and leads to his downfall.

Romulus has reigned over Rome for twenty years as the play opens. He has been inactive, preferring to breed poultry on his country estate and to ignore the empire's deterioration. This inaction is his calculated way of bringing the Roman Empire, an institution he views as founded on war and inhumanity, to an end. The Goths are marching on Rome, and he hopes to surrender the empire to them and die at their hands. But in the greatest of the play's anticlimaxes and the worst turn of events for Romulus, the Gothic king Odoacer turns out to be his equal in intelligence and humane wisdom, hoping to surrender to Romulus and so keep the history of the Germanic nations from following its foreseeable disastrous and bloody course. The leaders are forced to accept their impotence and live on with the bitter knowledge that human affairs are being guided by the unreason of history.

The play is filled with comic ideas. Through much of it anticlimax and frustration make for laughter, and the encounters between Romulus and the shortsighted, ambitious fanatics and bureaucrats who assume that Rome must be saved provide funny and even heartwarming scenes. There is humor also in the anachronisms of this "ungeschichtliche historische Komödie" (unhistorical historical comedy), even when they are allusions to Nazi and postwar Germany.

Romulus der Große was also produced in Zurich in 1948, and in 1949 it became the first major Dürrenmatt production in Germany when the Göttingen theater performed it. Critics were stingy with praise, objecting to the anachronisms and some of the comic effects; but the play became a standard in the German-speaking theater and beyond.

Royalties did not yet amount to much, however, and the Falb household was becoming cramped as the family grew by two daughters: Barbara, born in 1949, and Ruth, born in 1951. Adding to expenses was Dürrenmatt's hospitalization for diabetes. To pay the rent on a house in Ligerz on the Lake of Biel, he turned with great success to writing detective novels. His income, augmented by royalties from radio plays, was great enough to make possible the purchase in 1952 of a house above the city of Neuchâtel in which he lived until his death.

Dürrenmatt had completed the manuscript for *Die Ehe des Herrn Mississippi* (1952; translated as *The Marriage of Mr. Mississippi*, 1966) in 1950, only to have it rejected by Swiss theaters. In 1952, however, Hans Schweikart, manager of the Munich Kammerspiele (Intimate Theater), directed the premiere, establishing Dürrenmatt in Germany as an avant-garde dramatist.

The play opens with the cliché of a political assassination carried out by men in trench coats, after which the victim stands up and notes that his death actually takes place at the end of the drama. His long monologue is one of several with which Dürrenmatt interrupts the action, breaks theatrical illusion, provides exposition, and lets his characters criticize the play itself. The stage setting, too, is designed to break illusions. Everything takes place in one room, furnished in bad taste with decorations in styles from Gothic to art deco. In the course of the play these objects are destroyed, with the exception of the coffee table set for two at center stage. Seated at this table State's Attorney Florestan Mississippi proposes marriage to Anastasia. He has murdered his wife because of her infidelity and knows that Anastasia has murdered her husband—by pouring him poisoned coffee at this table—for the same reason. His fanatical and distorted sense of justice tells him that the hell of this marriage will be fitting punishment for both of them.

Mississippi has set new records for the implementation of the death penalty and has chosen as his life's goal the institution of a perfect system of justice in the form of the Law of Moses. To match him Dürrenmatt introduces the fanatic Marxist Frédéric René Saint-Claude, who is killed at the beginning of the play and is later to be eliminated a second time, and Count Bodo von Übelohe-Zabernsee, medical missionary and

fool in Christ, fanatic in regard to Christian charity and self-sacrifice. The utopian schemes of these three allegorical figures with their outlandish names are defeated when they encounter the real world. The nemesis of the three true believers, Anastasia, is an amoral femme fatale who goes to her death reaffirming her lies about her love and fidelity. Another of Dürrenmatt's memorable inventions, she is the modern counterpart of the whore of Babylon and of the medieval church's emblematic Dame World, beautiful face-on, but ugly and diseased when viewed from behind. Diego, the unscrupulous and opportunistic minister of justice, the only character to survive, emerges all-powerful from the chaos of revolution. Dürrenmatt demonstrates the bankruptcy of today's dominant ideologies by showing their adherents to be destructive fools and by giving them speeches that, in their pompous clichés and hyperbole, expose the senselessness of the doctrines. Through Anastasia and the course of affairs, the three fanatics learn that what they have done and said is without meaning or effect.

The play was praised by critics; but the next common undertaking of Dürrenmatt, Schweikart, and the ensemble of the Munich Kammerspiele, *Ein Engel kommt nach Babylon* (performed, 1953; published, 1954; translated as *An Angel Comes to Babylon*, 1964), did not measure up to the first. Productions in Düsseldorf, Zurich, and Vienna fared no better, and the premiere of the revised version in Berlin in 1957 was also a failure.

God's gift of perfect beauty and divine grace, the angel Kurrubi (Cherub), is sent to Earth to become the companion of the poorest mortal in Babylon. Things take the worst imaginable turn when her mission leads her to King Nebuchadnezzar, who, working to carry through his social reforms, is going about disguised as a beggar and falls in love with her. The paradoxical point is that Nebuchadnezzar, for all his wealth and power, is spiritually the poorest of the poor and the lowest of mortals. Kurrubi's overwhelming presence destroys all order in Babylon, and her marriage to the king is seen as the sole way to restore it. But she cannot marry a king, and he will not renounce his power for her sake. She leaves Babylon, and he, in frustration and rage against a seemingly unjust God, determines to avenge his hurt and disgrace by building the Tower. (A sequel to the drama, never completed, was to show how the Tower comes into being even though all are opposed to it.) The third major figure in this fairy-tale play is the city's last

Scene from a 1954 production of Dürrenmatt's Ein Engel kommt nach Babylon *at the Zurich Schauspielhaus, with Walter Richter as Nebuchadnezzar and Gustav Knuth as Akki (photograph by W. E. Baur)*

remaining beggar, Akki, who is the wisest of all Babylonians and would be the richest if he did not continually throw his earnings into the Euphrates. He makes the king, his bureaucratic henchmen, and all civic institutions look ridiculous.

The central figure of *Der Besuch der alten Dame*, the outlandish Claire Zachanassian, is a Fury from hell and the polar opposite of Kurrubi. Contrary to Dürrenmatt's own view, *Der Besuch der alten Dame* is generally regarded as his best-made play. With its simple and sharply pointed dialogue and its compressed, watchlike intricacy it is both a surefire stage success and a literary masterpiece.

Forty-five years before the play opens Claire Zachanassian, then known as Klari Wäscher, lost a paternity suit against Alfred Ill on the basis of perjured testimony by witnesses he bribed. Pregnant and disgraced, she was forced to leave Güllen (the name means liquid manure) and make her living as a prostitute. Since then she has, by marrying men of wealth and influence, become the richest, most notorious, and most powerful woman in the world. She has divorced husbands and taken new ones so often that she has lost count of them. The sole survivor of a plane crash in Afghanistan, she has an artificial leg and a hand made of ivory. She has secretly bought up Güllen's industries, closed them down, and so brought the town to its knees. The play opens with her triumphant return as a putative benefactress of the town. At the end of act 1, after the welcoming ceremony, she does offer the citizens one billion (in an unspecified currency) but imposes a condition: that someone kill Alfred Ill. In the name of humanism and humanity, the citizens indignantly reject the offer. Acts 2 and 3 show, at first in a comic way but with increasingly grotesque gruesomeness, how the Gülleners, precisely because they are only human, succumb to the temptation to live better and buy on credit and must ultimately commit the murder none of them wanted. The rationalizations and devices the townspeople contrive to justify and carry out the act make up the substance of Dürrenmatt's satiric gem.

To compel his audiences to face their own potential complicity, Dürrenmatt removes all possibility of making moral judgments and laying blame on an individual. Claire, with her vengeful misanthropy, is potentially a villain, but toward the end of the play she shows a softer, almost sentimental side; and Alfred Ill, a thoughtless, amoral shopkeeper and Güllen's scapegoat, emerges in act 3 ennobled and ethically transformed by the recognition of his personal guilt.

The climactic scene, in which Ill is sentenced by a vote of the men of the town and killed, is a triumph of satiric writing, presenting in a manner both comic and horrible a travesty of piety, democracy, justice, and Western values, made doubly false by the presence of press and television. Dürrenmatt is savagely castigating Europeans and Americans for their failure to create a just peace after World War II, for drifting into the Cold War, and then for losing their souls to affluence. This dismay and anger over moral depravity and religious indifference informs most of Dürrenmatt's writing after *Der Besuch der alten Dame*. His plays take on a cool, uncompromising, sometimes misanthropic tone; impersonal murderers and their stoically resigned victims speak a language stripped of poetry and rhetorical decoration.

Frank der Fünfte (Frank the Fifth; performed, 1959; published, 1960), written in collaboration with the Swiss operetta composer Paul Burkhard, represents a step in this direction. Owners and employees of the Frank family's gangster bank justify their crimes—no depositor ever gets to withdraw a penny, and those who complain are eliminated—with the excuse that they are committed to escaping the firm and leading a decent life. But all their efforts bind them closer to the institution that they despise and that has become an arena for betrayal and bloodshed. The crushing irony of the conclusion is that the widowed Ottilie Frank, who has desperately attempted to destroy the bank by confessing its criminal nature, must stand by as the government reorganizes and strengthens it and puts it in the hands of her son, Frank VI; it is now all the more pernicious and inhuman because it is run on soulless principles of law and order.

Audiences and reviewers found little to enjoy in the grotesque cruelties of this perverse world—as when the chief of personnel, Egli, is obliged to kill his fiancée for the sake of the company, and she cooperates to spare him another attack of ulcers. Frank V's end—being locked in the vault by his son—is gentle by comparison. The reviews of the Zurich premiere ranged from neutral to negative. Critics looking for leftist political commitment rejected the piece as empty of serious social comment and as a weak imitation of Brecht's *Die Dreigroschenoper* (performed, 1928; published, 1929; translated as *The Threepenny Opera*, 1964), while more conservative reviewers found it in bad taste, blasphemous, and nihilistic. On the other hand, *Frank der Fünfte* reaped nothing but praise in East Bloc countries, particularly Poland and Czechoslovakia. One can only speculate on how members of the Swiss banking industry in the Zurich audience may have felt.

Die Physiker has been second only to *Der Besuch der alten Dame* in its theatrical success in both the East and the West. Its premiere starred Therese Giehse, the original Claire Zachanassian, as Fräulein Doktor Mathilde von Zahndt; Dürrenmatt dedicated the text to Giehse and created the part for her.

Comedy, murder mystery, spy drama, love story, and a play about the problems presented by nuclear technology, *Die Physiker* is couched in straightforward language that fits its taut Aristotelian structure. Dürrenmatt artfully lures his audience into the trap of enjoying what seems a heartwarming happy ending, only to show it to be mere wishful thinking and a misperception of the hard truth that events will always take the worst imaginable turn.

The nuclear physicists of the title are patients in Dr. von Zahndt's private sanatorium, each pretending to be insane. Johann Wilhelm Möbius is the scientific genius of the age; the other two, affecting to take themselves for Albert Einstein and Sir Isaac Newton, are undercover agents of the superpowers and are competing for Möbius's formulas. They fail in their mission because he has destroyed his papers; all three, in an outburst of guilt and altruism, solemnly agree to go on pretending to be insane, spend their lives in the sanatorium, and so save the world from nuclear destruction. These heroics are shown to be deluded when Dr. von Zahndt reveals herself to be a megalomaniac madwoman and boasts that she has copied the crucial formulas, giving her the power to rule the world. To make sure that the physicists can do nothing to stop her she turns the sanatorium into a high-security prison. All the physicists' careful planning, artful dissembling, and high-mindedness, and even the murder each had to commit to try to keep his identity secret, are meaningless.

In 1963 appeared *Herkules und der Stall des Augias* (translated as *Hercules and the Augean Stables*, 1963), Dürrenmatt's stage adaptation of his

1954 radio play of the same title. The transfer from one medium to the other did not make for good theater; the growing mountains of manure are not a problem on the radio but are hard to reproduce onstage, and spectators will not stand for frequent, lenghty narrative expositions. The play's burlesque of myth, realistic and sometimes anachronistic topical detail, poetry, criticism of Swiss provincialism, and flat sermonizing did not combine well.

To the original radio play Dürrenmatt added new scenes and characters, a depressing conclusion, and many ingenious theatrical ideas, indicated in lengthy stage directions. The premise is that the life of a national hero is much harder than one thinks. Hercules is no match for the caution and vacillation of King Augeas's administration: because official permission is never granted, the Augean stables never get cleaned, and Hercules is reduced to joining the circus to make ends meet. The most poignant consequence is that, owing to their inertia, the people of the Kingdom of Elis forfeit their one opportunity to bring order and beauty to their land: they cannot imagine a life without manure.

In *Der Meteor* (1966; translated as *The Meteor*, 1966), a mix of farce and *danse macabre*, the Nobel Prize-winning playwright Wolfgang Schwitter is twice declared dead by medical authorities and resurrected. This situation dismays Schwitter, who is eager to die; elicits reactions ranging from the jubilation of Pastor Lutz to the rage of Schwitter's son; and leads to the demise of seven other persons. Audiences were kept breathless by the pace of the play's action and its surprise twists. On a seemingly endless hot, sunny midsummer day visitors climb the stairs to the stuffy garret where Schwitter starved as a young artist and where he has chosen to try to die after failing to do so in the hospital. He is irascible and says unexpected and hurtful things to those who confront him; it seems that the resurrected behave in an unfettered, demonic way, bringing out the worst in others. A bitter exchange between father and son is followed by the act 1 finale, in which Schwitter orders Auguste Nyffenschwander, wife of the garret's present tenant, to make love to him while her husband pounds on the locked door. Act 2 begins with the obsequies beside his bier, after which Schwitter sits up, takes off the chin support, and drinks brandy and smokes cigars while the just and the unjust continue to die around him. In the play's final scene, a manic variant of the open-ing one, the Salvation Army, playing and singing the Hallelujah Chorus, comes to Schwitter's bedside led by Major Friedli, who brings Schwitter's anger to the exploding point by solemnly pronouncing that he is called to eternal life. Schwitter curses all life in the vilest imaginable way, throttles the major, and runs off as darkness falls.

The Zurich premiere and the two major German productions that followed were successes, and *Der Meteor* was played soon thereafter on the major stages of the world, bucking the growing trend toward documentary political activism. The play offers one magnificent role in its central character and several challenging secondary ones. Most critics admired Dürrenmatt's imaginative power, even those who did not know what to make of the final scene: one thought it a failed effort at profundity, others found it anticlimactic, and a few objected to the irreverence toward the Salvation Army.

In late 1967 Dürrenmatt became comanager with Werner Düggelin at the Basel Stadttheater (City Theater). The collaboration continued until April 1969, when, after a long and severe illness and because of disagreements with the Basel administration, he withdrew. After that he declined to accept a position with responsibilities of that sort, being content to sit on the board of directors of the Zurich theater and occasionally to direct a production of his own work.

König Johann (1968), based on William Shakespeare's *The Life and Death of King John* (circa 1595), transforms a historical play chronicling events of the thirteenth century into a comedy dealing with power politics within any system, be it feudalism, communism, capitalism, or Cold War maneuvering. Dürrenmatt shows how the machinery functions at the top and refers only in passing to the thousands who are slaughtered for the benefit of royal houses, the church, or other institutions.

Dürrenmatt's title figure is not the weak and cruel monarch of the original, thanks to the influence of Philipp the Bastard—who, again like his high-living Shakespearean counterpart, is a clear-eyed reformer urging his king to see reason. Each of their combined efforts to improve the world backfires as it elicits reaction from entrenched powers, and Johann finally pronounces his own death sentence by proclaiming the birth of an heir. With the king poisoned and replaced by an infant, the lords of the realm are free to pillage and kill. Dürrenmatt's point, as in many of

Scene from a 1967 Berlin production of Dürrenmatt's Der Meteor, *with Peter Brogle, Leonard Steckel, and Ellen Schwiers (photograph by Ilse Buhs)*

his plays, is that even those who see and understand are powerless to alter the catastrophic and bloody course of history, for any action they take only makes matters worse.

Dürrenmatt used Shakespearean blank verse, eliminated some characters, tightened up the action, shortened and eliminated speeches, and changed characters and motivations. Under his hand the drama becomes transparent and compelling to modern audiences, applicable to any historical situation. To transform Shakespearean tragedy into Dürrenmattian comedy he added ludicrous situations and farcical stage business. Deals are made while characters are being shaved or sitting in bathtubs; Johann crawls under the covers with the cardinal to escape the cold of an unheated English castle, illustrating the German figure of speech "unter einer Decke stecken" (to be under the same blanket—that is, in cahoots—with someone). Audiences and reviewers greeted the premiere enthusiastically.

Dürrenmatt's other Shakespeare adaptation, *Titus Andronicus* (1970), was a failure. The audience booed during the performance, and critical rejection was unanimous. Shakespeare's play includes episodes of such unmitigated horror—mutilation, rape, murder, and cannibalism—that some scholars have argued that it must be attributed to a lesser playwright. Dürrenmatt has made the play even more shocking by condensing the five acts into nine scenes, thereby eliminating the lamentations of the victims and their loved ones and leaving only the brutality. At the close of the final scene, in which Tamora has been served her two sons in a meat pie and five murders of vengeance have been committed, Alaric, King of the Goths, a figure added by Dürrenmatt, provides a bitter commentary on the brevity and meaninglessness of human existence that replaces the optimistic closing lines delivered by Lucius in Shakespeare's play.

Dürrenmatt's most successful adaptation was *Play Strindberg* (1969; translated, 1970), subtitled *Totentanz nach August Strindberg* (Dance of Death, after August Strindberg) and based on part 1 and the end of part 2 of Strindberg's *Dödsdansen* (Dance of Death, 1901). The piece has been played on major stages in Europe and

America. Using a rough translation and keeping the key dramatic situation of two people trapped in the hell of their marriage, Dürrenmatt strips the original of all psychology, pathos, and philosophizing. He transforms the action into a cooled-down, ritualistic combat between Alice and Edgar played on an arena stage and divided like a boxing match into rounds, each beginning and ending with a bell. As codirector of the premiere Dürrenmatt worked closely with the cast and made revisions on the basis of their experience at rehearsals. The play is a challenge for actors: the speeches are seldom longer than five words, and frequent pauses give the actors the chance to fill the gaps with inventions of their own. It seems painfully difficult for Alice, Edgar, and their guest Kurt to keep their conversations from foundering on a gratuitous insult, indifference, or boredom. Dürrenmatt's text is filled with ideas for stage business—Alice's needlepoint, card games, piano playing, dancing, painting fingernails, building a house of cards, telegraphy—that often seem incommensurate with the words spoken. The effect of burlesque artificiality is heightened by the formal announcement of title and number for each round. There is a photo album scene, a visit scene, and two laughably insipid philosophy scenes. Edgar suffers a stroke and lacks the power of speech for the last four rounds, but his wife fluently translates his babbling into phrases he has earlier used over and over. *Play Strindberg* seems to be an expression of unmitigated misanthropic malice; but it is, at the same time, quite funny, particularly if the performers have a good sense of timing.

Like *Play Strindberg*, *Porträt eines Planeten* (Portrait of a Planet; performed, 1970; published, 1971) has a tone of heartless ferocity. The play is framed by opening and closing scenes set in a timeless infinity. Four gods, one of them hard of hearing, note with total detachment in the first scene that a once stable sun is turning into a supernova and in the last scene that it has disappeared. Inside this frame Dürrenmatt presents, with no blackouts, curtains, or intermission, a series of vignettes showing that life on Earth is doomed because the sun is exploding and because its inhabitants are governed by the death instinct; in Dürrenmatt's words, the play is a dance of death within a dance of death. At the outset a group of European women are trying to wean cannibals from human flesh to the meat of animals through sexual bribery, only to have a shipwreck defeat their efforts. Further sketches, delimited by slight changes in costume or the introduction of new props and all played by the same eight actors, deal with genocide, racial hatred, the Vietnam War, the drug culture, and two astronauts stranded on the moon whose dying words are of interest to the government only if they can be exploited in the promotion of a grandiose Mars program. Everything under this sun is futile and perverse: soldiers die in vain in the jungle, families squabble over nothing, and the earth is on the verge of annihilation.

Porträt eines Planeten is subverted *theatrum mundi* in radically abbreviated form. Its twenty-five scenes give the impression of a comprehensive panorama of human life, but its curt diction and impersonality of tone convey a message that is the opposite of seventeenth-century theater of the world: human nature is incurably perverse and human events are governed by chance and unreason. It is this nihilistic pessimism, unleavened by comedy, that put off audiences and critics at the premiere in Düsseldorf and again in Zurich, where Dürrenmatt himself directed a revised version.

In 1972 the Zurich Schauspielhaus offered Dürrenmatt the position of managing director. He declined and simultaneously resigned from its board of directors on the grounds that he was occupied with a new play, *Der Mitmacher* (The Accomplice; performed, 1973; published, 1976).

In mood *Der Mitmacher* is even bleaker than its predecessor. Rather than universal and cosmic, it is theater at its most spare and hermetic, set in a cell-like chamber deep underground in Manhattan, where the central figure, Doc, lives and works. The remaining characters, all with monosyllabic names such as Boss, Cop, Ann, and Joe, call on him, introducing themselves and providing exposition at length to the audience and then engaging in dialogues as terse and telegraphic as any Dürrenmatt has written. All these people are caught up in the operation of a business somewhat like Murder Incorporated. In the course of the play all are killed except for Doc, the accomplice, who suffers the most severe punishment: he must go on living in the worst of all conceivable worlds, stripped of human dignity and servicing the mass-producing death machine he invented and installed. The others were annihilated while trying to stop it; on the other hand, Doc's escape attempts have only trapped him more firmly, like a fly on flypaper.

A biochemist and intellectual, even though he reads comic books, Doc has a grudge against the world that moves him to offer the firm his services and his invention, the necrodialysator, which eliminates the dead bodies that have been creating a pollution problem and threatening the company with bankruptcy. The machine dissolves and flushes away the cadavers and so opens the way for an increased volume of business. The company is treated like any other business by the government because everyone up through the Supreme Court is on the take. The world of *Der Mitmacher* is several shades darker than the one Claire Zachanassian saw operating on the principles of a brothel; in his later years Dürrenmatt viewed prostitution and procuring as honest professions in contrast to the absolute corruption of modern society. In the end the company, like Frank VI's rehabilitated gangster bank, becomes so essential to the nation's social and economic health that it must be nationalized.

Doc's workshop is sparsely furnished and glaringly illuminated by neon lights. Twice the audience hears recorded strains of Vivaldi, but the main sound effect is a repeated flushing noise. The most prominent props are the crates in which the bodies are delivered. Toward the end the refrigerating system stops functioning while corpses accumulate. As these decompose, the stage becomes a stinking charnel house, attracting flies and rats, a far worse place than Güllen or the Augean Stables. Doc survives, but to do so he has had to necrodyalize both his beloved, Ann, and his son, Bill.

Reviews of the Zurich premiere and of the Mannheim performance eight months later commended the cast but found the play disappointing, some making the obvious comparison with the more humane Samuel Beckett. The Zurich production was plagued by disagreements between its director—the Polish filmmaker Andrzej Wajda, whose German was not strong—and the author. Wajda ultimately withdrew; Dürrenmatt replaced him shortly before the first performance, which proved incomprehensible to the audience. In addition, Boss delivers some lines scourging the hypocrisy of intellectuals—and, by implication, of reviewers—which called forth an ovation on opening night but did little to improve Dürrenmatt's strained relationship with the critics.

On 20 November 1975 Generalissimo Francisco Franco, the Spanish dictator, finally succumbed after his death had been held at bay for weeks by the efforts of thirty doctors so that the transfer of power could take place without civil war. These events provide the framework for Dürrenmatt's *Die Frist* (The Moratorium, 1977), in which he comments on the lust for power, the medical profession, the Church, the Holocaust, the use and abuse of television, and feminism in a manner that is at once farcical, mythical, and grotesque.

The drama is haunted throughout by the unseen presence of the Generalissimo and by the ground bass of his groans carried over a loudspeaker as doctors perform a heart transplant and a stomach resection without anaesthesia. The action is dominated by Exzellenz, the chief executive, who bears a strong resemblance to Henry Kissinger. In part 1, set in the throne room that has been the Generalissimo's office, Exzellenz outmaneuvers the secret service thanks to his tactical acumen and sense of realpolitik. Part 2 takes place in the same room, which has been totally transformed by the installation of medical devices and television control apparatus with monitors and technical directors. The second part, which deals with the general's death, is a triumph of theatrical ingenuity and satiric imagination, mixing European Cup soccer and the rite of supreme unction, the dying process and its exploitation as a media event, farcical family bickering and the battle for power between two dynasties. Like so many of Dürrenmatt's talented politicians, Exzellenz checkmates himself in the end. As he dies, he sees to it that Dr. Goldbaum—a concentration camp survivor, Nobel laureate patterned after Andrey Sakharov, and one of two decent persons in the play and therefore not the ideal candidate—is made head of the new government. Exzellenz's dying words of advice, that if Goldbaum does not become inhuman, then the country will become even more monstrous than it is, offer little hope.

Even more unsettling is the play's finale, which belongs to the Immortals, the most fantastic and grotesque of all the drama's inventions. These bloated, Furylike figures, dressed in tattered costumes taken from a Goya painting, are the Generalissimo's female ancestors. They have haunted the background throughout the play, carrying off a cameraman and trying to kill the heiress to the throne. These metaphysical, man-hating hags, resembling the Graeae of Greek mythology, pronounce their curses on everything male, including God the Father, in a rhymed line form reminiscent of the last choruses of Johann Wolfgang von Goethe's *Faust II* (1832) and ending with a vicious travesty of the concluding Cho-

Scene from the 1977 Zurich premiere of Dürrenmatt's unsuccessful play Die Frist, *with (foreground, left to right) Werner Kreindl as Exzellenz, Heinrich Trimbur as Goldbaum, and Wolfgang Schwarz as Arkanoff (photograph by Rabanus)*

rus Mysticus, distorting Goethe's hymn to the feminine principle into the nihilistic proclamation that the feminine aspires only to eternity and sterility—whereupon they collapse and die, and the curtain falls.

The premiere in Zurich and a second production in Basel not long after pleased neither audiences nor reviewers. The director Kazmierz Dejmek, not fluent in German and working with a weak cast, presented an unimaginative mise-en-scène in Zurich; and in Basel, Hans Neuenfels, a believer in directorial theater, distorted the text, using it as an occasion to realize his idiosyncratic theatrical conceptions.

On 16 January 1983 Dürrenmatt's wife Lotti died. In October of that year he met Charlotte Kerr, a former actress who had become a filmmaker and journalist; they were married on 8 May 1984. Together they made a four-and-a-half-hour film titled *Porträt eines Planeten: Von und mit Friedrich Dürrenmatt* (Portrait of a Planet: By and with Friedrich Dürrenmatt), a documentary about Dürrenmatt at work and at leisure, broad-cast on German television on 26 December 1984.

Dürrenmatt's final drama, *Achterloo* (1983) —the title is a place-name from a children's rhyme—underwent four revisions, the definitive one prepared especially for the 1988 Schwetzingen Festival. It is Dürrenmatt's last word and his most ambitious play, an intricately woven, all-encompassing, fantastic work in the *theatrum mundi* tradition. The characters are inmates of a psychiatric hospital for whom the play serves as therapy. From this narrow base it reaches out, as patients assume various identities, to cover Western history since 1300; the conclusion goes back as far as Old Testament times. To keep this profusion from flying apart, Dürrenmatt bases the plot on events in Poland on 12 and 13 December 1981, when, to prevent the Solidarity labor union from challenging the communist system, to keep Soviet tanks from invading Poland, and to avert any consequent American retaliation, Prime Minister Wojcieck Jaruzelski declared a national emergency and installed a military government. The patient dressed as Napoleon plays Jaruzelski, a master political tactician like Exzellenz in *Die Frist*. He makes the best of a bad situation, maintains the status quo, and spares the world a nuclear war by exploiting the corruption and delusions of the opposing powers. Two patients costumed as Karl Marx represent the Soviets, while "Benjamin Franklin" stands for the United States, "Jan Hus" for Lech Walesa, "Cardinal Richelieu" for Josef Cardinal Glemp, and "Georg Büchner" for Dürrenmatt; another patient plays Joan of Arc. Thus, the Cold War, nuclear warfare, the Roman Catholic church's political activity, Marxism, capitalism, and feminism are allegorically linked to the French Revolution, the persecution of the Huguenots, and the Reformation. Both Büchner and Dürrenmatt have given eloquent expression to a deeply pessimistic view of human history; the play's Büchner-Dürrenmatt figure, who has spent most of his time at a desk writing the play as it goes along, takes this sense of despair and futility to heart. Exiting for the last time he announces that he will write nothing more.

The play's concluding episode is the most visionary, tantalizing, and depressing of all, because it is a parable of the defeat of love by the instinct of aggression. The patients costumed as Joan of Arc and Napoleon reenact the Old Testament story in which Judith, the Israelite heroine, wins the love of the Babylonian general Holofernes and then, according to plan, decapitates him. Just as it seems that the *Achterloo* couple has broken the spell of the historical archetype that calls for blood revenge, just as they seem ready to let their love lead to peace between nations, he unaccountably throws her to the ground, and she shoots him in the back. Then, for the first time in a Dürrenmatt theater-of-the-world play, the normally obligatory figure of God appears on stage. The woman who has been playing Cardinal Richelieu, now attired in a dinner jacket, announces that she is God and that she has died. Hers is the play's last line: "Ich war der Liebe Gott," a double entendre meaning either "I was the dear God" or "I was the God of love."

In 1988 Dürrenmatt announced his decision to abandon the theater. He died at his home on 14 December 1990. *Der Besuch der alten Dame* and *Die Physiker* are still among the most frequently performed plays in Germany, showing that vintage Dürrenmatt continues to be successful. It remains for perceptive directors, players, and critics to help audiences appreciate his later work.

Dürrenmatt won the Literature Prize of the City of Bern for *Ein Engel kommt nach Babylon* in 1954; the Radio Play Prize of the War Blind for *Die Panne* in 1957; the Prix Italia for *Abendstunde im Spätherbst* and the Literature Prize of the *Tribune de Lausanne* for *Die Panne* in 1958; the New York Theater Critics' Prize for *The Visit* and the Schiller Prize from the city of Mannheim in 1959; the Great Prize of the Swiss Schiller Foundation in 1960; the Grillparzer Prize of the Austrian Academy of Sciences in 1968; the Great Literature Prize of the Canton of Bern and an honorary doctorate from Temple University in 1969; honorary membership in Ben-Gurion University, Israel, in 1974; the Buber-Rosenzweig Medal of the German Coordinating Council for Christian-Jewish Cooperation and honorary doctorates from the University of Nice and Hebrew University in Jerusalem in 1977; the Great Literature Prize of the City of Bern in 1979; an honorary doctorate from the University of Zurich in 1983; the Carl Zuckmayer Medal of the State of Rheinland-Pfalz in 1984; the Bavarian Prize for Literature (Jean Paul Prize) in 1985; the Premio Letterario Internatione Monello (Sicily) for *Justiz*, the Georg Büchner Prize of the German Academy for Language and Literature, and an honorary Schiller Memorial Prize from the State of Baden-Württemberg in 1986; the International Prize for Humor and Satire, "Hitar Petar," awarded by the Bulgarian International Museum of Humor and Satire, Gabrovo, in 1987; and the Prix Alexei Tolstoi for his total oeuvre from Association internationale des Ecrivains de Romans Policiers in 1988.

Interviews:

Horst Bieneck, *Werkstattgespräche mit Schriftstellern* (Munich: Deutscher Taschenbuch Verlag, 1965), pp. 120-136;

Violet Ketels, "Friedrich Dürrenmatt at Temple University: Interview," *Journal of Modern Literature*, 1, no. 1 (1971): 88-108;

Heinz Ludwig Arnold, *Friedrich Dürrenmatt im Gespräch mit Heinz Ludwig Arnold* (Zurich: Arche, 1976);

Dieter Fringeli, *Nachdenken mit und über Friedrich Dürrenmatt: Ein Gespräch* (Breitenbach: Jeger-Moll, 1977);

Fritz Raddatz, "Ich bin der finsterste Komödienschreiber, den es gibt: Ein *Zeit*-Gespräch mit Friedrich Dürrenmatt," *Die Zeit*, 23 August 1985, pp. 13-14.

Bibliographies:

Elly Wilbert-Collins, *A Bibliography of Four Contemporary German-Swiss Authors: Friedrich Dürrenmatt, Max Frisch, Robert Walser, Albin Zollinger* (Bern: Francke, 1967);

Johannes Hansel, *Friedrich Dürrenmatt: Bibliographie* (Bad Homburg: Gehlen, 1968).

References:

Armin Arnold, *Friedrich Dürrenmatt* (Berlin: Colloquium, 1969);

Arnold, ed., *Zu Friedrich Dürrenmatt: Interpretationen* (Stuttgart: Klett, 1982);

Heinz Ludwig Arnold, *Querfahrt mit Dürrenmatt* (Göttingen: Wallstein, 1990);

Arnold, ed., *Friedrich Dürrenmatt I*, second edition (Munich: Beck, 1980);

Arnold, ed., *Friedrich Dürrenmatt II* (Munich: Beck, 1977);

Gottfried Benn, Elisabeth Brock-Sulzer, Fritz Buri, Reinhold Grimm, Hans Mayer, and Werner Oberle, *Der unbequeme Dürrenmatt* (Basel & Stuttgart: Basilius, 1962);

Brock-Sulzer, *Dürrenmatt in unserer Zeit: Eine Werkinterpretation nach Selbstzeugnissen* (Basel: Reinhardt, 1968);

Brock-Sulzer, *Friedrich Dürrenmatt: Stationen seines Werkes* (Zurich: Arche, 1960);

Edson M. Chick, *Dances of Death: Wedekind, Brecht, Dürrenmatt and the Satiric Tradition* (Columbia, S.C.: Camden House, 1984), pp. 107-133;

Mark E. Cory, "Shakespeare and Dürrenmatt: From Tragedy to Tragicomedy," *Comparative Literature*, 32 (Summer 1981): 253-273;

Donald Daviau, "Justice in the Works of Friedrich Dürrenmatt," *Kentucky Foreign Language Quarterly*, 9, no. 4 (1962): 181-193;

Daviau, "The Role of *Zufall* in the Writings of Friedrich Dürrenmatt," *Germanic Review*, 47 (November 1972): 281-293;

Peter Demetz, *Postwar German Literature: A Critical Introduction* (New York: Schocken, 1972), pp. 147-162;

Edward Diller, "Aesthetics and the Grotesque: Friedrich Dürrenmatt," *Wisconsin Studies Contemporary Literature*, 7 (Autumn 1966): 328-335;

Diller, "Friedrich Dürrenmatt's Chaos and Calvinism," *Monatshefte*, 63 (1971): 28-40;

Diller, "Friedrich Dürrenmatt's Theological Concept of History," *German Quarterly*, 40 (May 1967): 363-371;

Bodo Fritzen and Heimy F. Taylor, eds., *Friedrich Dürrenmatt: A Collection of Critical Essays* (Normal, Ill.: Applied Literature Press, 1979);

Heinrich Goertz, *Friedrich Dürrenmatt: Mit Selbstzeugnissen und Bilddokumenten* (Reinbek: Rowohlt, 1987);

Robert B. Heilman, "Tragic Elements in a Dürrenmatt Comedy," *Modern Drama*, 10 (May 1967): 11-16;

Robert E. Helbling, "The Function of the 'Grotesque' in Dürrenmatt," *Satire Newsletter*, 4 (Fall 1966): 11-19;

Sigrun Gottwald, *Der mutige Narr im dramatischen Werk Friedrich Dürrenmatts* (New York: Lang, 1983);

Urs Jenny, *Friedrich Dürrenmatt* (Velber: Friedrich, 1965);

Gerhard Knapp, *Friedrich Dürrenmatt* (Stuttgart: Metzler, 1980);

Knapp, ed., *Friedrich Dürrenmatt: Studien zu seinem Werk* (Heidelberg: Stiehm, 1976);

Knapp and Gerd Labroisse, eds., *Facetten: Studien zum 60. Geburtstag Friedrich Dürrenmatts* (Bern: Lang, 1981);

Jan Knopf, *Friedrich Dürrenmatt* (Munich: Beck, 1980);

Moshe Lazar, ed., *Play Dürrenmatt* (Malibu, Calif.: Undena, 1983);

Hans Mayer, *Dürrenmatt und Frisch: Anmerkungen* (Pfullingen: Neske, 1963);

Erna K. Neuse, "Das Rhetorische in Dürrenmatts *Besuch der alten Dame*: Zur Funktion des Dialogs im Drama," *Seminar*, 11 (November 1975): 225-241;

Murray B. Peppard, *Friedrich Dürrenmatt* (New York: Twayne, 1969);

Eli Pfefferkorn, "Dürrenmatt's Mass Play," *Modern Drama*, 12 (May 1969): 30-37;

Ulrich Profitlich, *Friedrich Dürrenmatt: Komödienbegriff und Komödienstruktur: Eine Einführung* (Stuttgart: Kohlhammer, 1973);

Hans-Jürgen Syberberg, *Zum Drama Friedrich Dürrenmatts: Zwei Modellinterpretationen zur Wesensdeutung des modernen Dramas* (Munich: Uni-Druck, 1974);

Timo Tiusanen, *Dürrenmatt: A Study in Plays, Prose, Theory* (Princeton: Princeton University Press, 1977);

Hans Wagener, ed., *Friedrich Dürrenmatt, Romulus der Große: Erläuterungen und Dokumente* (Stuttgart: Reclam, 1985);

Kenneth S. Whitton, *Dürrenmatt: Reinterpretation in Retrospect* (New York: Berg, 1990);

Whitton, *The Theatre of Friedrich Dürrenmatt: A Study in the Possibilities of Freedom* (Atlantic Highlands, N.J.: Humanities Press, 1980);

Peter Wyrsch, "Die Dürrenmatt-Story," *Schweizer Illustrierte*, no. 12 (18 March 1963): 23-25; no. 13 (25 March 1963): 23-25; no. 14 (1 April 1963): 23-25; no. 15 (8 April 1963): 23-25; no. 16 (15 April 1963): 37-39; no. 17 (22 April 1963): 37-39.

Papers:

Friedrich Dürrenmatt's papers are at the Schwizerische Literaturarchiv (Swiss Literature Archive) in Bern. The Reiss AG, Theaterverlag, Zurich, has an archive of reviews of his works and other materials.

Günter Eich
(1 February 1907 - 20 December 1972)

Steven D. Martinson
University of Arizona

See also the Eich entry in *DLB 69: Contemporary German Fiction Writers, First Series.*

PLAY PRODUCTION: *Die Glücksritter: Lustspiel nach Eichendorff in fünf Bildern*, Berlin, Preußisches Theater für Jugend in the Schiller-Theater, 20 December 1933.

BOOKS: *Gedichte* (Dresden: Jess, 1930);

Der Präsident: Neuen Szenen (Baden: Merlin, 1931);

Die Glücksritter: Slngspiel in fünf Akten (Berlin: Chronos, 1933);

Das festliche Jahr: Ein Lesebüchlein vom Königswusterhäuser Landboten, by Eich and Martin Raschke (Oldenburg: Stalling, 1936);

Katharina: Erzählungen (Leipzig: List, 1936);

Abgelegene Gehöfte (Frankfurt am Main: Schauer, 1948);

Untergrundbahn (Hamburg: Ellermann, 1949);

Träume: Vier Spiele (Frankfurt am Main: Suhrkamp, 1953)—includes *Geh nicht nach El Kuwehd!*;

Botschaften des Regens: Gedichte (Frankfurt am Main: Suhrkamp, 1955);

Zinngeschrei: Hörspiel (Hamburg: Hans-Bredow-Institut, 1955);

Die Brandung vor Setúbal (Hamburg: Hans-Bredow-Institut, 1957); enlarged as *Die Brandung vor Setúbal; Das Jahr Lazertis: Zwei Hörspiele* (Frankfurt am Main: Suhrkamp, 1963); edited by Robert Browning (New York: Harcourt, Brace & World, 1966); translated by Michael Hamburger as *Journeys: Two Radio Plays. The Rolling Sea at Setúbal; The Year Lacertis* (London: Cape, 1968);

Allah hat hundert Namen: Ein Hörspiel (Wiesbaden: Insel, 1958);

Stimmen: Sieben Hörspiele (Frankfurt am Main: Suhrkamp, 1958)—includes *Festianus, Märtyrer*;

Der Stelzengänger (Zurich: Spektrum, 1960);

Die Mädchen aus Viterbo: Hörspiel (Frankfurt am Main: Suhrkamp, 1960); edited by Peter Prager (London: Macmillan, 1962; New York: St. Martin's Press, 1962);

Ausgewählte Gedichte, edited by Walter Höllerer (Frankfurt am Main: Suhrkamp, 1960);

Unter Wasser; Böhmische Schneider: Marionettenspiele (Frankfurt am Main: Suhrkamp, 1964);

Zu den Akten: Gedichte (Frankfurt am Main: Suhrkamp, 1964);

In anderen Sprachen: Vier Hörspiele (Frankfurt am Main: Suhrkamp, 1964);

Anlässe und Steingärten: Gedichte (Frankfurt am Main: Suhrkamp, 1966);

Fünfzehn Hörspiele (Frankfurt am Main: Suhrkamp, 1966)—comprises *Geh nicht nach El Ku-*

Günter Eich (photograph by Wolgensinger)

wehd!; *Träume*; *Sabeth*; *Die Andere und ich*; *Blick auf Venedig*; *Der Tiger Jussuf*; *Meine sieben junge Freunde*; *Die Mädchen aus Viterbo*; *Das Jahr Lazertis*; *Zinngeschrei*; *Die Stunde des Huflattichs*; *Die Brandung vor Setúbal*; *Allah hat hundert Namen*; *Festianus, Märtyrer*; *Man bittet zu läuten*;

Festianus, Märtyrer (Stuttgart: Reclam, 1966);

Kulka, Hilpert, Elefanten (Berlin: Literarisches Colloquium, 1968);

Maulwürfe: Prosa (Frankfurt am Main: Suhrkamp, 1968);

Gedichte; *Prosa*; *Horspiele* (Zurich: Diogenes, 1969);

Ein Tibeter in meinem Büro: 49 Maulwürfe. Prosa (Frankfurt am Main: Suhrkamp, 1970);

Nach Seumes Papieren (Darmstadt: Bläschke, 1972);

Günter Eich: Ein Lesebuch (Frankfurt am Main: Suhrkamp, 1972);

Gesammelte Maulwürfe (Frankfurt am Main: Suhrkamp, 1972);

Semmelformen, drawings by Sven Knebel (Zurich: Brunnenturm-Presse, 1972);

Gesammelte Werke, 4 volumes, edited by Ilse Aichinger, Susanne Müller-Hanft, Horst Ohde, Heinz F. Schaftroth, and Heinz Schwitzke (Frankfurt am Main: Suhrkamp, 1973; revised, 1989); edited by Karl Karst, Joachim W. Storck, and Axel Vieregg (Frankfurt am Main: Suhrkamp, 1991);

Gedichte, selected by Aichinger (Frankfurt am Main: Suhrkamp, 1973);

Günter Eich, selected by Bernd Jentzsch (Berlin: Neues Leben, 1973);

Tage mit Hähern: Ausgewählte Gedichte, edited by Klaus Schumann (Berlin: Aufbau, 1975);

Aus dem Chinesischen (Frankfurt am Main: Suhrkamp, 1976);

Marionettenspiele (Frankfurt am Main: Suhrkamp, 1976);

Der 29. Februar: Ein Märchen (Frankfurt am Main: Insel, 1978);

Günter Eich: Ein Lesebuch, edited by Müller-Hanft (Frankfurt am Main: Suhrkamp, 1981);

Günter Eich, edited by Storck (Marbach: Deutsche Schillergesellschaft, 1988).

Editions in English: *Modern German Poetry. 1910-1960*, edited by Michael Hamburger and Christopher Middleton (London: MacGibbon & Kee, 1962; New York: Grove, 1964);

Contemporary German Poetry: An Anthology, edited by Gertrude C. Schwebell (Norfolk, Conn.: New Directions, 1964);

"Darmstädter Rede / Darmstadt Address," translated by Hamburger, in *German Writing Today*, edited by Middleton (Harmondsworth, U.K. & Baltimore: Penguin, 1967);

Günter Eich, translated by Teo Savory (Santa Barbara, Cal.: Unicorn, 1971);

German Poetry 1910-1975: An Anthology, edited by Hamburger (New York: Urizen Books, 1976; Manchester, U.K.: Carcanet New Press, 1977);

Four German Poets: Günter Eich, Hilde Domin, Erich Fried, Günter Kunert, edited and translated by Agnes Stein (New York: Red Dust Press, 1980);

Valuable Nail: Selected Poems of Günter Eich, translated by Stuart Friebert, David Walker, and David Young (Oberlin, Ohio: Oberlin College, 1981).

TELEVISION: *Böhmische Schneider*, Norddeutscher Rundfunk, 12 September 1961.

RADIO: *Leben und Sterben des großen Sängers Enrico Caruso*, Berliner Mittelwellensender, 9 April 1931;

Ich lerne Chinesisch, Funk-Stunde Berlin, 26 January 1933;

Günter Eich liest eigene Prosa, 15 February 1933;

Aus dem Leben des Abenteurers Münchhausen, Funk-Stunde Berlin, 26 February 1933;

Till Eulenspiegel, 10 April 1933;

Die Glücksritter: Nach Eichendorff, Deutschlandsender, 25 May 1933;

Dinkelmann und sein Glück, Deutschlandsender, 31 May 1933;

In den Staub mit allen Feinden Brandenburgs!: Das Werk des Großen Kurfürsten, 22 June 1933;

Eine Geburtstagsfeier für Herrn von Münchhausen, Reichssender, 3 September 1933;

Museum für schwarze Kunst und Zauberei, 7 September 1933; rebroadcast as *Vom Teufel und seiner Großmutter: Ein merkwürdiges und doch freudiges Spiel*, 5 November 1933;

Eine Stunde Lexikon: Ein Traumspiel, Mittelwellensender, 21 September 1933;

Brandenburgs Adler über Afrika: Großfriedrichsburg—des Großen Kurfürsten preußische Kolonie. Eine Hörfolge, Mittelwellensender, 26 September 1933;

Deutscher Kalender: Oktober. Ein Monatsbild vom Königswusterhäuser Landboten, Deutschlandsender, 4 October 1933;

Reise ins Schlaraffenland, 3 December 1933;

Lustiges Lumpenpack, Deutschlandsender, 14 December 1933;

Das Raritäten-Kabinett: Ein Spiel um ein paar schöne Schallplatten, Westdeutscher Rundfunk, 28 January 1934;

Ich träumt' in seinem Schatten: Szenen um deutsche Volkslieder, by Eich, Sigmund Graff, and August Hinrichs, Deutschlandsender, 6 February 1934;

Münchhausen erzählt von seinen Abenteuern, 22 March 1934;

Taugenichts-Tagediebe: Die bunte Welt der Landstraße nach alten Schwänken und Erzählungen von Eichendorff, Hebel und Hamsun, Reichssender, 28 April 1934;

Gespräche am Strande: Ein kleiner Ostseeführer, Reichssender, 1 August 1934;

Weg über die Heide: Zum heutigen 20. Todestag von Hermann Löns, by Eich and Ernst Löns, Reichssender, 26 September 1934;

Antiquitäten: Ein Schallplattengespräch, Süddeutscher Rundfunk, 15 October 1934;

Von einem, der auszog, das Gruseln zu lernen . . . Ein fröhlicher Abend mit guten und bösen Geistern, Deutschlandsender, 27 December 1934;

Des Lebens Überfluß, Mitteldeutscher Rundfunk, 28 January 1935;

Das Spiel vom Teufel und dem Geiger: Eine Ballade um Niccolo Paganini, by Eich and A. Artur Kuhnert, Reichssender, 3 February 1935;

Schritte zu Andreas: Ein funkischer Versuch, Reichssender, 5 February 1935;

Das kalte Herz: Märchenoper für den Funk, music by Mark Lothar, Deutschlandsender, 24 March 1935;

Der Fischer und sine Fru, Reichssender, 30 April 1935;

Mutter und Kind: Hörfolge, Reichssender, 12 May 1935;

Gebt Acht auf MacDown, by Eich and Kuhnert, Reichssender, 26 June 1935;

Kapelle Wolf heult oder die Macht der Musik: Ein lustiges Funkspiel, 21 August 1935;

Straßen hin und her . . . Ein herbstlicher Bilderbogen, Reichssender, 21 September 1935; rebroadcast as *Landstraßen im Herbst: Hörfolge von G. Eich*, 26 October 1938;

Nanuks Glück und Ende: Eine Moralität in 8 Kapiteln, Reichssender, 30 September 1935;

Die Tasche des Landbriefträgers Döderlein: Ein winterlicher Bilderbogen, Reichssender, 26 January 1936;

Künstlerpech: Ein musikalisches Funkspiel, by Eich and Kuhnert, Reichssender, 7 March 1936;

Die Weizenkantate, Deutschlandsender, 11 May 1936;

Fährten in die Prärie: Ein Spiel aus der untergehenden Welt Old Shatterhands und Winnetous, Reichssender, 11 July 1936;

Ove Ekelund, *Ein Mann kämpft gegen seinen Traum: Ein Hörspiel aus dem Schwedischen*, translated by Robert Dinesen, revised by Eich, Reichssender, 16 November 1936;

Der seltsame Gast: Ein neuer Totentanz in 6 Bildern, Reichssender, 22 November 1936;

Krusemann: Ein Querschnitt durch den Roman von. H. W. Seidel, Deutschlandsender, 14 March 1937;

Die Welt auf Schienen! Eine Funkfantasie über die Eisenbahn, by Eich, Kuhnert, P. Althaus, and Horst Lange, Deutschlandsender, 4 June 1937;

Der große Krebs im Mohriner See und andere Geschichten um märkische Gewasser, Reichssender, 14 July 1937;

Der Märkische Kalendermann sagt den neuen Monat an, Reichssender, 3 August 1937;

Radium: Ein Hörspiel nach Motiven des Romans von Rudolf Brunngraber, Reichssender, 22 September 1937;

Rührende und tolldreiste Geschichten um Liebe: Für den Funk umgedichtet, Reichssender, 4 October 1937;

Altdeutsche Geschichten von Liebe und Tod: Szenen, Erzählungen, Balladen und Lieder aus "Des Knaben Wunderhorn" mit alter deutscher Musik, Reichssender, 21 January 1938;

Wenn die Kartoffelfeuer rauchen: Ernsthaftes und Spaßiges um ein Knollengewächs, Reichssender, 30 September 1938;

Geliebte Heimat: Havelland: Eine Fontanesendung, Reichssender, 29 December 1938;

Das Kuriositäten-Kabinett: Sechs lebende Bilder gestellt von G. Eich mit Musik von Schallplatten, Reichssender, 5 January 1939;

Der Tod an den Händen, Deutschlandsender, 6 January 1939;

Alles dreht sich, alles bewegt sich, Reichssender, 15 February 1939;

Der vielbeschriebne Kuckuck, Reichssender, 28 May 1939;

Balthasar Neumann: Hörszenen um den bedeutenden deutschen Baumeister, Deutschlandsender, 18 June 1939;

Junger Rhabarber, Reichssender, 28 June 1939;

Aufruhr in der Goldstadt, Deutschlandsender, 8 May 1940;

Die Glückschuhe: Nach Motiven eines Märchens von Andersen, Bayerischer Rundfunk, 29 March 1948;

Geh nicht nach El Kuwehd!, Bayerischer Rundfunk, 21 July 1950;

Das Diamantenhalsband: Nach Maupassant, Süddeutscher Rundfunk, 6 August 1950;

Ein Traum am Edsin-gol, Süddeutscher Rundfunk, 14 September 1950;

Balthasar Neumann: Schulfunkhörspiel, Bayerischer Rundfunk, 5 December 1950;

Die gekaufte Prüfung, Nordwestdeutscher Rundfunk, 20 December 1950;

Weizen, Hessischer Rundfunk, 12 March 1951;

Träume, Nordwestdeutscher Rundfunk, 19 April 1951;

Sabeth . . . oder die Gäste im schwarzen Rock, Süddeutscher Rundfunk, 14 June 1951;

Reparaturwerkstatt Muck, Südwestdeutscher Rundfunk, 19 June 1951;

Fis mit Obertönen, Süddeutscher Rundfunk, 1 July 1951;

Unterm Birnbaum: Nach Fontane, Hessischer Rundfunk, 3 September 1951;

Verweile, Wanderer, Süddeutscher Rundfunk, 18 November 1951;

Die Andere und ich, Süddeutscher Rundfunk, 3 February 1952; revised version, Hessischer Rundfunk, 12 March 1962;

Blick auf Venedig, Südwestdeutscher Rundfunk, 27 May 1952;

Der Tiger Jussuf, Nordwestdeutscher Rundfunk, 15 August 1952;

Die Mädchen aus Viterbo, Südwestdeutscher Rundfunk, 10 March 1953;

Das Jahr Lazertis, Nordwestdeutscher Rundfunk, 15 January 1954;

Beatrice und Juana, Südwestdeutscher Rundfunk; Bayerischer Rundfunk; Radio Bremen, 4 May 1954;

Der sechste Traum, Bayerischer Rundfunk, 26 May 1954;

Allah hat hundert Namen, Südwestdeutscher Rundfunk; Bayerischer Rundfunk; Radio Bremen, 18 June 1954;

Der Toupetkünstler: Nach Ljeskow, Hessischer Rundfunk; Stuttgart, Süddeutscher Rundfunk, 13 September 1954;

Zinngeschrei, Nordwestdeutscher Rundfunk, 25 December 1955;

Der letzte Tag, by Eich and Ilse Aichinger, Bayerischer Rundfunk; Südwestdeutscher Rundfunk; Radio Bremen, 31 January 1956; rebroadcast as *Lissabon*, Süddeutscher Rundfunk, 26 November 1961;

Elisabeth Tarakanow: Nach Reinhold Schneider, Hessischer Rundfunk; Radio Bremen, 16 February 1956;

Die Brandung vor Setúbal, Norddeutscher Rundfunk; Bayerischer Rundfunk; Hessischer Rundfunk, 30 April 1957;

Omar und Omar, Norddeutscher Rundfunk, 25 August 1957;

Festianus, Märtyrer, Norddeutscher Rundfunk; Bayerischer Rundfunk, 16 October 1958;

Die Stunde des Huflattichs (II), Bayerischer Rundfunk; Norddeutscher Rundfunk, 11 November 1958; revised version, Norddeutscher Rundfunk, 18 November 1964;

Die Mädchen aus Viterbo (II), Hessischer Rundfunk; Süddeutscher Rundfunk, 8 June 1959;

Blick auf Venedig (II), Norddeutscher Rundfunk; Bayerischer Rundfunk, 27 April 1960;

Meine sieben jungen Freunde, Norddeutscher Rundfunk; Bayerischer Rundfunk, 9 November 1960;

Der Tiger Jussuf (II), Bayerischer Rundfunk, 20 March 1962;

Der konfuse Zauberer: Nach Nestroy, Bayerischer Rundfunk; Norddeutscher Rundfunk, 24 June 1962;

Man bittet zu läuten, Norddeutscher Rundfunk; Bayerischer Rundfunk, 15 November 1964;

Zeit und Kartoffeln, Südwestdeutscher Rundfunk; Hessischer Rundfunk; Norddeutscher Rundfunk, 5 October 1972.

OTHER: Willi Fehse and Klaus Mann, eds., *Anthologie jüngster Lyrik 1927*, includes poems by Eich, as Erich Günter (Hamburg: Enoch, 1927), pp. 30-37;

"Wind über der Stadt," in *Almanach der Dame: Fünfzig ausgewählte Gedichte* (Berlin: Propyläen, 1934), pp. 26-27;

"Chinesisch: Beitrag zur Sprachkenntnis," in *Das Fünfminuten-Lexikon*, edited by Gerhard Bahlsen (Frankfurt am Main: Schauer, 1950), pp. 65-68;

"Fis mit Obertönen," in *Hörspielbuch II* (Hamburg: Europäische Verlagsanstalt, 1951), pp. 71-113;

"Aus dem Chinesischen," translated by Eich, in *Lyrik des Ostens: China*, edited by Wilhelm Gundert, Annemarie Schimmel, and Walther Schubring (Munich: Hanser, 1952);

Die Andere und ich, in *Hörspielbuch III* (Frankfurt am Main: Europäische Verlagsanstalt, 1952), pp. 11-52;

"Rede vor den Kriegsblinden," in *Gestalt und Gedanke: Ein Jahrbuch* (Munich: Bayrische Akademie der schönen Künste, 1953), pp. 37-41;

"Der Stelzengänger," in *Im Rasthaus—32 Erzählungen aus dieser Zeit*, edited by Walter Karsch (Berlin: Herbig, 1954), pp. 71-77;

"Aus dem Ungarischen," translated by Eich, in *Im Frührot: Gedichte der Ungarn*, edited by Clemens and Sophie Dorothee Podewils (Munich: Hanser, 1957);

"Züge im Nebel," in *Moderne Erzähler*, edited by Wilhelm Grenzmann (Paderborn: Schöningh, 1957), pp. 21-31;

"Trigonometrische Punkte," in *Mein Gedicht ist mein Messer*, edited by Hans Bender (Munich: List, 1961), pp. 23-24;

"Das und so möchte ich schreiben: Thesen zur Lyrik," in *Lyrik und Rezeption: Das Beispiel Günter Eich*, by Susanne Müller-Hanft (Munich: Hanser, 1972), p. 136.

SELECTED PERIODICAL PUBLICATIONS—
UNCOLLECTED: "Unter Wasser," *Akzente*, 7 (1960): 50-81;

Zeit und Kartoffeln, *Baster Nachrichten*, 3 February 1973.

Though Günter Eich began and ended his career writing pieces for the theater, he is best known for his radio plays. He was born on 1 February 1907 to Otto Eich and Helene Heine Eich in Lebus an der Oder in the eastern German province of Brandenburg. He was the second of two sons. Eich's father, an accountant, served as a tax consultant after moving the family to Berlin in 1918. Eich completed his secondary education in Leipzig in 1925 and then began the study of sinology at the University of Berlin and in Paris. In his first year of university study in Berlin, Eich wrote his first poems; some of these poems were included by Willi Fehse and Klaus Mann in their important anthology of 1927 under the pseudonym Erich Günter. Eich changed his area of study to economics and business and moved to the University of Leipzig in 1927. His interest in the Far East remained keen, however, and he took up the study of Chinese at the Sorbonne in Paris in 1929.

After returning to Germany in 1929 to study economics at the University of Berlin, Eich completed his first radio play in collaboration with Martin Raschke. In 1930 his first collection of poetry, *Gedichte* (Poems), appeared. In 1931 he joined the circle of authors, including Elisabeth Langgässer and Peter Huchel, working for the Dresden literary periodical *Die Kolonne* (The Column). Most of his work was published here and in the *Neue Rundschau* (New Review). Within a short time he gave up his academic pursuits and became a free-lance writer, writing mostly for the major medium of the time, the radio. On 22 June 1940 he married Else Anna Burk, a singer, but it was an unhappy marriage. Eich was living in Berlin at the outbreak of World War II.

Though Eich never documented, and even refused to discuss, his experiences during the war, it is known that he served as a courier in the German Air Force. By 1940 he was a noncommissioned officer. He was captured by the American armed forces in 1945 near Remagen. On his release he settled in Geisenhausen, near Landshut. His wife died shortly after the war.

In 1947 Eich was one of the founding members of Gruppe 47 (Group 47). Another member was the gifted Austrian writer Ilse Aichinger. They were married in 1953, and for the next twenty years Aichinger served as Eich's first reader and best critic. They had two children, Clemens and Mirjam. In 1962 Eich traveled to Japan, India, Canada, and the United States. Following several moves around southern Germany, the Eichs took up residence in 1963 in Groß-Gmain near Salzburg, Austria. In 1965 Eich received the Munich Grant Prize for Literature; in 1968 he was awarded the Friedrich Schiller Memorial Prize of the City of Mannheim. Both prizes were awarded for his radio plays. Eich died on 20 December 1972.

Eich's world was less visual than auditory; he once remarked that the world is to be assimilated not so much through the eye as through the ear. The Hörspiel (radio play) lent itself well to some of Eich's earliest themes, such as sleep, death, and the dividing line between reality and nonreality.

Eich once commented that the dream is a dialogue with oneself; many of his radio plays involve dreams and nightmares, including his first, *Ein Traum am Edsin-gol* (A Dream at Edsin-gol). The play was published in *Die Kolonne* in 1932 but not performed until 1950. At the end of this drama Ludwig stands alone in the desert, cut off from European society; but he cannot escape the guilt of his murder of his neighbor Bernhard. Ludwig still wishes to appropriate Bernhard's wife and possessions. The last sound in the play—the closing of a door—represents the author's response to the character's quest.

Eich's first completed play for the theater was *Der Präsident* (The President; published, 1931); no information is available as to whether it was ever performed. The play is about a business tycoon, George Kalkar, who is constantly in search of more power. He is betrayed by his former wife, Yvonne, and supported by a young girl, Alice, a would-be lover and protector. In the final scene Kalkar stands alone in a forest in the cold northland surrounded by hungry, howling wolves. A sense of disorientation, deceit, and death pervades the play. Nature is depicted as a nightmare, thus dispelling romantic images of harmony between nature and human beings. Eich's comedy *Die Glücksritter* (Soldiers of Fortune, 1933) is a reworking of Joseph Freiherr von Eichendorff's 1841 novella of the same title. As in Eich's radio plays, it is the fine line between appearance and reality, truth and lie, and the endless word games that are most conspicuous in his dramas. At times the reader becomes lost in the rich denotations and connotations of Eich's language.

The radio play *Schritte zu Andreas* (Steps to Andreas; broadcast, 1935; published in Eich's *Gesammelte Werke* [Collected Works], 1973) underscores the impossibility of knowing where one's life will lead. When Andreas calls out Kathrin's name in the dark, she asks if she is dreaming and if anyone is there. Kathrin follows the voice she hears. Death's footsteps parallel her steps to Andreas, and both characters grow fearful. The dramatic action is initiated by the characters' desperate desire to find union in love before being overpowered by death. In the end, Death proves more powerful than love; there is no "Liebestod" (love-death).

Fährten in die Prärie: Ein Spiel aus der untergehenden Welt Old Shatterhands und Winnetous

(Tracks in the Prairie: A Play from the Perishing World of Old Shatterhand and Winnetou; broadcast, 1936; published in Eich's *Gesammelte Werke*), one of Eich's most intricately woven radio plays, shatters romantic notions of the American West. Chief Winnetou's attempt to unite all Indians to rise up against the white man in one last battle is doomed by the introduction of technology, symbolized by the Iron Horse. Furthermore, against Barimu's view of perpetually flowing water as representing Nature in which all things work together, the onetime artist Patt sees something much different in the river: everything, he says, the sky as well as the earth, seems to be dying. One theme of the play, then, is the irrevocable passing of time.

Patt's lament that everything was somehow different before is countered by Tschomboq's recollection that before the intrusion of the white man, one Indian tribe had fought another. Thus, nothing has changed: one enemy has simply been replaced by another. This twofold criticism of the romanticization of the past and of the technological dehumanization of the present is one of Eich's most profound themes.

In *Radium* (broadcast, 1937) the unemployed poet Julien Chabanais decides to become an advertising agent for the radium industry so that he can afford radiation treatments for his cancer-stricken wife. But when he returns from the interview at which he has secured the job, he learns that she has just died. The sinister truth is that only the rich can afford the treatment. Chabanais's boss, Cynac, has a nightmare in which he is haunted by an army of skeletons of former employees he has thrown out into the street; the scenes in which Cynac's nightmare is presented reflect Eich's indebtedness to expressionist drama. The nightmare seems at first to have had a beneficial effect: Cynac appears to be a changed man. He contemplates the possibility that there was something wrong with his life. But he decides that it is too late to believe in anything; he has become the capitalist-turned-nihilist. The play ends with Cynac's remark that he does not like being reminded of unpleasant things.

Eich's radio plays demonstrate again and again that life entails guilt. His involvement with the Nazi radio system no doubt led to the recurrent use of this theme. He was never officially taken into membership in the Nazi party, although he did apply.

Eich received the Gruppe 47 prize for his radio play *Geh nicht nach El Kuwehd!* (Do Not Go to El Kuwehd!; broadcast, 1950; published, 1953). In this play the listener is led unsuspectingly into a nightmare. Mohallab, a wealthy merchant, is making his way to Damascus. Outside El Kuwehd, a beggar warns him not to enter the city. Giving in to the enticements of a young maid who invites him to the house of her lady, Mohallab is captured and sold into slavery. The nightmare ends as he is about to be hanged. When he awakens and is again confronted by a maid extending the same invitation, he follows her anyway.

Eich's best-known play, *Träume* (Dreams; broadcast, 1951; published, 1953), consists of five dream sequences and includes some of his best poetry. A sense of dread pervades the work. The increasing intensity of the acoustic level of the play together with the anxieties expressed by the characters suggest impending doom. The theme of *Träume* is the rejection of reality. In the first dream, for instance, two couples trapped in a railroad car decide to close the hole through which a more brilliant reality than the one they know makes its appearance. In the end, the dialogue is drowned out by the noise of the destruction of the train. If there is to be any salvation, it is in the acceptance of reality.

Die Andere und ich (The Other Woman and I, 1952), for which Eich won the Radio Play Prize of the War Blind, is one of his most sophisticated radio dramas. Ellen, an American on vacation in Italy with her family, gradually assumes the identity of the Italian girl Camilla to the point of losing herself in that persona. As Camilla, she lives through almost forty years of experiences within a few moments of actual time. Social and ecological problems are explored, including the unhealthy seashore environment of the village of Comacchio, poverty, murder, and the frustrations of daily work. In a moment of reflection Ellen realizes that she cannot be free by living out someone else's life.

Festianus, Märtyrer (Festianus, Martyr, 1958) concerns the afterlife of Festianus, who was devoured by lions in the Coliseum. The play begins with the main character in Heaven, questioning why some of his friends were sent to Hell. Allowed to descend into Hell in search of his friend Laurentius, he finds an autocratic police state. He sends Laurentius back to the loveless splendor of Heaven and remains with the sick and the poor in Hell.

In the 1960s Eich received two outstanding awards for his work on the radio play. The first of these came in 1965 with the Munich Grant Prize for Literature. The second was the coveted Friedrich Schiller Memorial Prize of Mannheim, awarded to Eich on 9 November 1968.

In Eich's last radio play, *Zeit und Kartoffeln* (Time and Potatoes; broadcast, 1972; published, 1973), Ottilie is tormented by the very thought of potatoes, which remind her of railroad cars and wartime persecution. As in *Die, Andere und ich*, time operates on two levels: Ottilie converses with two Seumes, Johann Gottfried Seume, the eighteenth- and early-nineteenth-century writer, and Eberhard Dieter Seume, the owner of the potato wagon. In the end, she consumes two bottles of vermouth and commits suicide.

References:

Heinrich Georg Briner, *Naturmystik; Biologischer Pessimismus; Ketzertum: Günter Eichs Werk im Spannungsfeld der Theodizee* (Bonn: Bouvier, 1978);

Glenn R. Cuomo, *Career at the Cost of Compromise: Günter Eich's Life and Work in the Years 1933-1945* (Amsterdam & Atlanta: Rodopi, 1989);

Willi Fehse, "Wie Günter Eich zum Rundfunk gekommen ist," *Rufer und Hörer*, 7 (1953): 524-530;

F. M. Fowler, "Günter Eich," in *German Men of Letters*, volume 4, edited by Brian Keith-Smith (London: Wolff, 1966), pp. 89-107;

Marlies Goß, *Günter Eich und das Hörspiel der fünfziger Jahre: Untersuchung am Beispiel Träume* (Frankfurt am Main, Bern, New York & Paris: Lang, 1988);

Eloa Di Pierro Heise, *Günter Eich: A Poetica da Busca* (São Paulo: Universidade de São Paulo, 1980);

Werner Klose, "Chiffren der Wirklichkeit im Hörspiel Günter Eichs," *Der Deutschunterricht*, 18 (March 1966): 68-78;

Michael Kohlenbach, *Günter Eichs späte Prosa: Einige Merkmale der Maulwürfe* (Bonn: Bouvier, 1982);

Egbert Krispyn, *Günter Eich* (New York: Twayne, 1971);

Ruth Lieberherr-Kübler, *Von der Wortmystik zur Sprachskepsis: Zu Günter Eichs Hörspielen* (Bonn: Bouvier, 1977);

Peter Märki, *Günter Eichs Hörspielkunst* (Frankfurt am Main: Akademische Verlagsgesellschaft, 1974);

Susanne Müller-Hanft, ed., *Über Günter Eich* (Frankfurt am Main: Suhrkamp, 1970);

Peter Horst Neumann, *Die Rettung der Poesie im Unsinn: Der Anarchist Günter Eich* (Stuttgart: Klett, 1981);

Klaus-Dieter Post, *Günter Eich: Zwischen Angst und Einverständnis* (Bonn: Bouvier, 1977);

Larry Richardson, *Committed Aestheticism: The Poetic Theory and Practice of Günter Eich* (New York, Bern & Frankfurt am Main: Lang, 1983);

Heinz Schafroth, *Günter Eich* (Munich: Beck, 1976);

Siegfried Unseld, ed., *Günter Eich zum Gedächtnis* (Frankfurt am Main: Suhrkamp, 1973);

Heinrich Vormweg, "Dichtung als Maul-Wurf," *Merkur*, 23 (January 1969): 85-87;

Albrecht Zimmermann, "Das lyrische Werk Günter Eichs: Versuch einer Gestaltanalyse," Ph.D. dissertation, University of Erlangen, 1965.

Papers:

Günter Eich's literary estate is administered by the Suhrkamp publishing firm in Frankfurt am Main. Most of his papers are at the Deutsches Literaturarchiv (German Literature Archive) in Marbach am Neckar. Other important papers are at the Bayerische Staatsbibliothek (Bavarian State Library) in Munich. Additional materials are in the central archives of Süddeutscher Rundfunk (South German Broadcasting), Stuttgart.

Marieluise Fleißer

(22 or 23 November 1901 - 2 February 1974)

Donna L. Hoffmeister
University of Colorado

See also the Fleißer entry in *DLB 56: German Fiction Writers, 1914-1945.*

PLAY PRODUCTIONS: *Fegefeuer in Ingolstadt*, Berlin, Junge Bühne am Deutschen Theater, 24 April 1926; revised version, Wuppertal, Die Wuppertaler Bühnen, 30 April 1971;

Pioniere in Ingolstadt, Dresden Junge Bühne in der Dresdner Komödie, 25 March 1928; revised version, Munich, Residenztheater München, 1 March 1970;

Der starke Stamm, Munich, Münchner Kammerspiele, 7 November 1950; High German version, Cologne, Köhlner Kammerspiele, 2 March 1974;

Der Tiefseefisch, Berlin, Schloßparktheater, 7 September 1980.

BOOKS: *Fegefeuer in Ingolstadt* (Berlin: Arcadia Theaterverlag, 1926);

Ein Pfund Orangen und neun andere Geschichten der Marieluise Fleißer aus Ingolstadt (Berlin: Kiepenheuer, 1929);

Mehlreisende Frieda Geier: Roman vom Rauchen, Sporteln, Lieben und Verkaufen (Berlin: Kiepenheuer, 1931); revised as *Eine Zierde für den Verein: Roman vom Rauchen, Sporteln, Lieben und Verkaufen* (Frankfurt am Main: Suhrkamp, 1975);

Andorranische Abenteuer (Berlin: Kiepenheuer, 1932);

Karl Stuart: Trauerspiel in fünf Akten (Munich: Desch, 1946);

Avantgarde: Erzählungen (Munich: Hanser, 1963);

Abenteuer aus dem englischen Garten: Geschichten (Frankfurt am Main: Suhrkamp, 1969);

Gesammelte Werke, 4 volumes, edited by Günther Rühle (volumes 1-3, Frankfurt am Main: Suhrkamp, 1972; volume 4, Frankfurt am Main: Suhrkamp, 1989)—volume 1, *Dramen*, includes *Pioniere in Ingolstadt* (1968 version), *Der starke Stamm, Der Tiefseefisch*;

Stücke (Berlin: Henschel, 1976);

Marieluise Fleißer in 1970

Ingolstädter Stücke: Fegefeuer in Ingolstadt; Pioniere in Ingolstadt (Frankfurt am Main: Suhrkamp, 1977);

Ausgewählte Werke, edited by Klaus Schumann (Berlin: Aufbau, 1979);

Der Tiefseefisch: Text; Fragmente; Materialien, edited by Wend Kässens and Michael Töteberg (Frankfurt am Main: Suhrkamp, 1980);

"In die Enge geht alles": Marieluise Fleißers Gang in die innere Emigration. Fragment "Walper," Skizzen und zwei Briefe aus dem Nachlaß, edited by Eva Pfister (Berlin: Friedenauer, 1984).

SELECTED PERIODICAL PUBLICATIONS—
UNCOLLECTED: "Schwabing," *text + kritik*, 64 (1979): 1-2;

"Alles auf dem Rücken von meinem Stück," *Frankfurter Allgemeine Zeitung*, 2 April 1983, p. 23.

Marieluise Fleißer was one of the most talented female dramatists writing in German in the twentieth century. Such eminent theater critics of the Weimar Republic as Herbert Ihering, Alfred Kerr, and Kurt Pinthus praised her early work. Her two plays of the Weimar period are widely viewed as key sociohistorical literary documents depicting the mentality and behavior that later facilitated Adolf Hitler's election victories in the provinces. She was a collaborator of Bertolt Brecht, who credited her *Pioniere in Ingolstadt* (Combat Engineers in Ingolstadt; performed, 1928; published in her *Gesammelte Werke* [Collected Works], 1972) as the play that contributed most to his theory of epic theater. The same play, which was the most scandalous production on the German stage of the 1920s, inspired the career of Rainer Werner Fassbinder, the maverick director of New German Cinema. Her plays, along with those of Ödön von Horváth, gave rise to the socially critical Volksstücke (folk plays) of Fassbinder, Franz Xaver Kroetz, and Martin Sperr that were popular in Germany in the late 1960s and the 1970s. Fleißer's work is also an important topic in feminist literary criticism. All of these accomplishments arise from a corpus of only one thousand pages, which includes five plays, a novel, thirty-three short stories, and sixteen essays. Her thematic scope is also limited; she focuses microscopically on one Bavarian town and on a relatively small cast of women and men, the latter modeled after her father and the other men in her life: Brecht; Hellmut Draws-Tychsen, a writer of travelogues and her fiancé from 1929 to 1932; and Josef Haindl, a tobacco-store owner and champion swimmer whom she married in 1935 in the hope that he could protect her from fascism. Despite her literary importance in the 1920s and the 1970s, she was forgotten and impoverished for most of her career. Only shortly before her death on 2 February 1974, at seventy-two, did she begin to earn more than twenty thousand marks a year. Her works were out of print from 1932 to 1963; only one of her plays was produced between 1929 and 1966; her works have not been translated into English; it took nine years to sell the first edition of her collected works, published in 1972 with a printing of only three thousand copies. Such are some of the extremes of success and failure in the life and work of this astonishing woman.

Luise Marie Fleißer was born to Heinrich Fleißer, a merchant, and Anna Schmidt Fleißer on 22 or 23 November 1901 in Ingolstadt, a provincial town in Bavaria whose spiritual life was dominated by the stern moral principles and endless prohibitions of Catholicism. In *Fegefeuer in Ingolstadt* (Purgatory in Ingolstadt, 1926), her first and best play, she gives expression to the anguish her rigidly moralistic upbringing caused her.

Fleißer enrolled at the University of Munich in 1919. An anecdote suggests what a contrast Munich must have been to the sheltered convent boarding school she had attended in Regensburg: while carrying her on his shoulders during a carnival party, Lion Feuchtwanger is said to have introduced her to Brecht as the woman with the most beautiful bosom in Munich. She refused the prudent course of working toward a teaching degree, preferring Arthur Kutscher's drama seminars. The guilt she felt for defying her father's expectations prevented any wholehearted, consistent rebellion on her part and also helps explain her subservience to men thereafter. On Feuchtwanger's advice she changed her name to Marieluise; switched from expressionism to the Neue Sachlichkeit (New Objectivity) in vogue in the 1920s; and, to her later regret, burned many of her early stories and essays. Writing became her way of rebelling against her subservience to men and her sense of inadequacy.

Fleißer wrote what would later be called *Fegefeuer in Ingolstadt* in secret in 1924 without the interference of her male mentors, Feuchtwanger and Brecht; later that year her father called her back home from school. In directing the premiere Brecht took liberties with the text, downplayed the work's religious emphasis, and changed its title from "Die Fußwaschung" (The Foot-Washing), an allusion to the ritual in Saint John's account of the Last Supper. From Brecht, Fleißer learned to express social criticism more incisively and had professional opportunities she might not have had otherwise; but something was destroyed in her when she accepted his advice, because she never wrote anything quite as good as her first play.

In *Fegefeuer in Ingolstadt* Olga Berotter, an intelligent, headstrong girl home on vacation from boarding school, has become pregnant as the result of an affair with Pepe, her tutor in Latin, who in the meantime has taken up with someone else. She must keep her pregnancy a secret from everyone—including her family, whose members

Fleißer in Berlin in 1927

are embroiled in endless squabbles, spying, and recriminations. Olga finds an ally in Roelle, a smelly, pimply fellow with a bloated neck, who is devoted to her. Both have a capacity for selflessness and generosity, but their fear of being ostracized by their peers calls forth the worst in them. Roelle rescues her when she attempts to drown herself and offers to pay for an abortion; at other times, however, he speaks maliciously about her and spits on her in the presence of others. He is a liar, thief, blackmailer, and Christ figure all in one. When Olga realizes that Roelle is as helpless as she is and can offer no protection, she turns on him. The play ends with Roelle's complete breakdown and Olga's return to her loveless family and their sadomasochistic games. Fleißer uses the ordinary speech patterns of the petty bourgeoisie and occasional Bavarian regionalisms to portray the myopic concerns and low self-esteem of her beleaguered teenage charac-

ters. Glibness of tongue is a survival tactic in the world she depicts. What makes the play so absorbing is its combination of precise sociological observation and poetically compressed language to evoke an ambience of irrationality, vulnerability, and anger. Catholicism as presented in the play is a corruption of genuine religion in its narrow insistence on sexual morality and decorous behavior. The play, which has been called elusive, fascinating, and shattering, was long neglected. After its single Sunday-morning matinee performance in 1926, it was not performed again until 1971. Today it elicits enthusiastic responses, no matter how different the productions are from one another. It also lends itself to a variety of interpretations, from analyses of its Volksstück qualities to new-left explorations of the protofascist conditions it depicts and discussions of its portrayal of women.

Ingolstadt had been a fortress and garrison

for centuries and was proud of its military history. In 1861 there were 12,750 soldiers and 7,193 civilians there; in 1914 three regiments and two battalions were stationed in the town. In 1927 Fleißer described to Brecht how soldiers had once again invaded the town in 1926 to engage in a public works project. Brecht set Fleißer to work on a play about the interactions between soldiers and civilians, especially sexual liaisons. Fleißer came up with a straightforward, episodic play, *Pioniere in Ingolstadt*, that was much to Brecht's liking. When its premiere in Dresden in 1928 had an indifferent reception, Brecht took matters in hand to prevent the same thing from happening in Berlin in 1929. For this production the Theater am Schiffbauerdamm had a stellar cast, including Lotte Lenya, Hermine Körber, and Peter Lorre, and used all the innovative techniques that had been developed by the director Erwin Piscator—film, songs, slogans, and pictures. A film about tourist attractions in Ingolstadt was shown before the play began, for instance. Brecht emphasized the work's antimilitaristic stance, which was mild compared to other plays of the period; added off-color remarks about female anatomy and sexually transmitted diseases; and introduced risqué actions (a girl loses her virginity in a crate as it rocks rhythmically on the stage). The ensuing scandal instigated by Brecht had enormous repercussions for Fleißer's personal and professional life, although, once Brecht's salacious additions were cut by order of the police, *Pioniere in Ingolstadt* had a successful run of forty-two performances. The right-wing press indicted Fleißer for writing what they called Jewish-Bolshevist gutter trash that vilified German womanhood. The press was especially incensed that the play had been written by a woman. Ingolstadt was, of course, indignant about the blight on its reputation. Upset by the public maligning and Brecht's co-optation of her play, Fleißer broke with him shortly after his marriage to actress Helene Weigel on 10 April 1929. Fleißer was publicly attacked many times during the next dozen years and again in the late 1960s and early 1970s; because of the play the Nazis burned her books and forbade her to publish more than six short newspaper articles a year. As late as 1967 a newspaper article warned Fleißer never to write about the combat engineers again. But in 1967, more than ten years after Brecht's death and at the suggestion of Weigel, who wanted the play performed in East Berlin, Fleißer once again set to work on it. She created new

characters, doubled its length, and accentuated the political and military criticism in ways she felt Brecht had wanted her to do originally; she did not, however, use his salacious additions of 1929. Ironically, the play's second premiere, in Munich on 1 March 1970, was booed for being too tame.

The play depicts, in all its versions, exploitation and power struggles in civilian and military life. Unertl terrorizes his maid, Berta, for not washing the dishes well enough and tells his son, Fabian, in her presence, to use Berta to get sexual experience. Berta, whose romantic illusions are poignantly naive, falls in love with the soldier Korl, a Casanova type (modeled on Brecht) who uses women for his sexual pleasure. Korl feels put upon by his superiors and vents his aggressions by mistreating women. Berta's friend Alma, another domestic, becomes a prostitute. Conflicts arise between the townsfolk and the soldiers, especially when the young men notice how the soldiers have taken over all the women. Conflicts within the military cost a sergeant his life. The play shows how militaristic the civilian mentality and practices were in the Weimar Republic, thus illuminating the conditions that led to the rise of fascism. The strength of the play remains, however, its precise satire of intimate relations between men and women.

Der Tiefseefisch (The Deep-Sea Fish; published in *Gesammelte Werke* [Collected Works], 1972; performed, 1980), written right after Fleißer's break with Brecht, portrays the relationship between Fleißer and her fiancé, Draws-Tychsen, and the fierce competition between Draws-Tychsen's circle and that of Brecht's. Draws-Tychsen was the strict antipode to Brecht in his literary stance, but his treatment of women was equally brutal and egocentric. Fleißer portrays in detail his tyrannical and misogynistic behavior, irrationality, and possessiveness, and candidly describes how her masochism, dependency, and feelings of guilt bound her to him. She satirizes his pretensions of being spiritually "deep" by comparing his eyes to those of a deep-sea fish. Fleißer also satirizes Brecht as a writer of the new age who uses plagiarism and American methods of mass production; and she makes fun of the group of second-rate women writers—Elisabeth Hauptmann, Margarete Steffin, and Ruth Berlau—who assisted Brecht in his work. Gesine, the character based on Fleißer, rebels against her dependency on men and finally walks out, vowing that she will never let herself be devoured again. The play was scheduled for performance in

Scene from Bertolt Brecht's 1928 production of Fleißer's Pioniere in Ingolstadt *at the Theater am Schiffbauerdamm in Berlin*

1930, but Fleißer withdrew it when Brecht objected. She added a fourth act in 1972; it was this version that was performed for the first time in 1980.

Between 1937 and 1944 Fleißer wrote a mediocre historical play, *Karl Stuart* (published, 1946), about Charles I of England. It has a conventional structure and stilted language and promotes the values of inner freedom, loyalty, and self-sacrifice. As an apologia for a king who scorned democracy, it had no chance of being performed on the postwar stage, when Germany was turning to democratic structures. It must be viewed as an anachronism stemming from the Hitler years, when Fleißer was isolated from the literary world, overworked in her husband's business, and generally harried by his opposition to her writing. She had a couple of nervous breakdowns during this time and had reason to fear being taken to a concentration camp.

Fleißer's last play, *Der starke Stamm* (Of Sturdy Stock; published in *Gesammelte Werke*, 1972), which she wrote in 1944-1945, has a traditional four-act structure and robust dialogue, unlike the loosely connected episodic scenes and lyrically compressed language of *Fegefeuer in Ingolstadt* and *Pioniere in Ingolstadt*. Its premiere—under the direction of Hans Schweikart in Munich in 1950, with Therese Giehse in the leading

role, Balbina—was popular because its earthy, innocent, and comical elements offered the kind of entertainment audiences wanted in the troubled postwar years. Its successful run of 104 performances at the Schaubühne am Halleschen Ufer in Berlin in 1966, with Ruth Drexel as Balbina, attracted interest for its critical perspective on patriarchal family structures and exploitative business practices in the provinces. This socially conscious interpretation, the one Fleißer had intended, led to her rediscovery and to a renewed appreciation of her writing.

When Fleißer updated the play for its performance in Munich in 1950, she injected into it the shady business deals prevalent immediately after the currency reform in Germany. She also included a religious hoax of 1949 in which people made pilgrimages to Heroldsbach to see the Virgin Mary. The various devious, conniving, and self-seeking characters in the play are alert to every opportunity for making money fast. Balbina, the main character, has all kinds of gimmicks for taking advantage of other people. An image of her manipulative ways is presented when she coddles a hen as she prepares to wring its neck; like the hen, Balbina's victims are no match for her. Aiming to marry the well-to-do Bitterwolf, her brother-in-law, she moves in on the day of his wife's funeral, involves him in her

Fleißer receiving the Bavarian Distinguished Service Medal from Minister of Public Worship and Education Hans Maier in 1973 (dpa)

dubious lottery-ticket business, gets him into debt, and has her mother demand money that he owes her. Bitterwolf distrusts Balbina and marries his young maid, partly because he has made the girl pregnant and partly to take revenge on Balbina. The girl, for her part, is after his money. The bailiff demands that Bitterwolf pay his debts, forcing him to pawn all his merchandise and begin anew. Because of her lottery machines Balbina spends time in jail, where she hatches a scheme to swindle people on the basis of their religious gullibility. In the end Bitterwolf's son, Hubert, is the sole heir of a rich uncle whose wealth has been a source of fascination for everyone throughout the play.

Fleißer's work is not grounded in a conscious politics. She started with herself and her relations with men and, through her uncompromising analyses of behavior, mapped out some of the principal social mechanisms in force during her generation. In her plays the patriarchal family controls but does not nurture. Like Franz Kafka, she is fixated on father figures. She does not reject socially defined roles for men and women nor does she voice feminist alternatives. As she grew older her female characters also matured and became more assertive, but their pres-

ence or absence remained a matter of indifference to her male characters. The pattern of Fleißer's personal life, with its oscillation between prominence and anonymity, rebellion and retreat, is evoked by these women characters; their vivid assertions of self are inseparable from a sense that failure is an absolute given. Her ability to share her sense of failure makes her writing significant today.

Bibliography:

Gabriele Schnabel and Michael Töteberg, "Auswahlbibliographie zu Marieluise Fleißer," *text + kritik*, 64 (1979): 88-93.

Biography:

Sissi Tax, *marieluise fleißer: schreiben, überleben. ein biographischer versuch* (Basel: Stroemfeld / Frankfurt am Main: Roter Stern, 1984).

References:

Peter Beicken, "Weiblicher Pionier: Marieluise Fleißer—oder Zur Situation schreibender Frauen in der Weimarer Zeit," *Die Horen*, 28 (Fall 1983): 45-61;

Susan L. Cocalis, " 'Weib ist Weib': Mimetische Darstellung contra emanzipatorische Tendenz in den Dramen Marieluise Fleißers," in *Die Frau als Heldin und Autorin: Neue kritische Ansätze zur deutschen Literatur*, edited by Wolfgang Paulsen (Bern & Munich: Francke, 1979), pp. 201-210;

Cocalis, "Weib ohne Wirklichkeit, Welt ohne Weiblichkeit: Zum Selbst-, Frauen- und Gesellschaftsbild im Frühwerk Marieluise Fleißers," in *Entwürfe von Frauen in der Literatur des 20. Jahrhunderts*, edited by Irmela von der Lühe (Berlin: Argument, 1982), pp. 64-85;

Walter Dimter, "Die ausgestellte Gesellschaft: Zum Volksstück Horváths, der Fleißer und ihrer Nachfolger," in *Theater und Gesellschaft: Das Volksstück im 19. und 20. Jahrhundert*, edited by Jürgen Hein (Düsseldorf: Bertelsmann, 1973), pp. 219-245;

Karl-Heinz Habersetzer, "Dichter und König: Fragmente einer politischen Ästhetik in den Carolus Stuardus-Dramen bei Andreas Gryphius, Theodor Fontane und Marieluise Fleißer," in *Theatrum Europaeum*, edited by Richard Brinkmann and others (Munich: Fink, 1982), pp. 291-310;

Donna L. Hoffmeister, *The Theater of Confinement: Language and Survival in the Milieu Plays of Marieluise Fleißer and Franz Xaver Kroetz* (Columbia, S.C.: Camden House, 1983);

Ruth-Ellen B. Joeres, "Records of Survival: The Autobiographical Writings of Marieluise Fleißer and Marie Luise Kaschnitz," in *Faith of a (Woman) Writer*, by Joeres, Alice Kessler-Harris, and William McBrien (Westport, Conn.: Greenwood Press, 1988), pp. 149-157;

Wend Kässens and Michael Töteberg, " . . . fast schon ein Auftrag von Brecht: Marieluise Fleißers Drama *Pioniere in Ingolstadt*," in *Brecht Jahrbuch* (Frankfurt am Main: Suhrkamp, 1976), pp. 101-119;

Kässens and Töteberg, *Marieluise Fleißer* (Munich: Deutscher Taschenbuch Verlag, 1979);

Susanne Kord, "Fading Out: Invisible Women in Marieluise Fleißer's Early Dramas," in *Women in German Yearbook: Feminist Studies and German Culture*, volume 5, edited by Jeanette Clausen and Helen Cafferty (Lanham, Md., New York & London: University Press of America, 1989), pp. 57-72;

Friedrich Kraft, ed., *Marieluise Fleißer: Anmerkungen, Texte, Dokumente* (Ingolstadt: Donau Courier Verlag, 1981);

Ralph Ley, "Beyond 1984: Provocation and Prognosis in Marieluise Fleißer's *Purgatory in Ingolstadt*," *Modern Drama*, 31 (September 1988): 340-351;

Ley, "Liberation from Brecht: Marieluise Fleißer in Her Own Right," *Modern Language Studies*, 16 (Spring 1986): 54-61;

Ley, "Outsidership and Irredemption in the Twentieth Century: Marieluise Fleißer's Play *Fegefeuer in Ingolstadt*," *University of Dayton Review*, 19 (Summer 1988): 3-41;

Jeanne Lorang, "Marieluise Fleißer, Brecht et les drames d'Ingolstadt (1924-1929)," *Revue d'Allemagne*, 11 (January-March 1979): 22-45;

Günther Lutz, *Die Stellung Marieluise Fleißers in der bayerischen Literatur des 20. Jahrhunderts* (Frankfurt am Main, Bern & Cirencester, U.K.: Lang, 1979);

Hannes S. Macher, " 'Ich schreibe Leben—aus Betroffenheit': Marieluise Fleißer: Pioniere in Ingolstadt," in *Handbuch der Literatur in Bayern: Vom Frühmittelalter bis zur Gegenwart: Geschichte und Interpretation*, edited by Albrecht Weber (Regensburg: Pustet, 1987), pp. 539-549;

Moray McGowan, *Marieluise Fleißer* (Munich: Beck, 1987);

Egon Menz, "Der 'Tiefseefisch' von Marieluise Fleißer: Zu seiner Berliner Aufführung," *Monatshefte*, 73, no. 3 (1981): 135-139;

Marsha Elizabeth Meyer, "Marieluise Fleißer: Her Life and Work," Ph.D. dissertation, University of Wisconsin—Madison, 1983;

Gerd Müller, *Das Volksstück von Raimund bis Kroetz* (Munich: Oldenbourg, 1979);

Helmut F. Pfanner, "Die Provinzliteratur der zwanziger Jahre," in *Die deutsche Literatur in der Weimarer Republik*, edited by Wolfgang Rothe (Stuttgart: Reclam, 1974), pp. 237-254;

Eva Pfister, "Der Nachlaß von Marieluise Fleißer," *Maske und Kothurn*, 26 (1980): 293-303;

Pfister, " 'Unter dem fremden Gesetz': Zu Produktionsbedingungen, Werk und Rezeption der Dramatikerin Marieluise Fleißer," Ph.D. dissertation, University of Vienna, 1981;

Patricia Preuss, "Ich war nicht erzogen, daß ich mich wehrte: Marieluise Fleißer und ihr Werk in der Diskussion um weibliches Schreiben," *Germanic Review*, 62 (Fall 1987): 186-193;

Friedhelm Roth, "Volkstümlichkeit und Realismus? Zur Wirkungsgeschichte der Theaterstücke von Marieluise Fleißer und Ödön Horváth," *Diskurs*, 6/7 (1973): 77-104;

Rainer Roth, ed., *Der starke Stamm: Volksstück. Materialien und Arbeitshilfen* (Munich: Manz, 1985);

Ursula Roumois-Hasler, *Dramatischer Dialog und Alltagsdialog im wissenschaftlichen Vergleich: Die Struktur der dialogischen Rede bei den Dramatikerinnen Marieluise Fleißer ("Fegefeuer in Ingolstadt") und Else Lasker-Schüler ("Die Wupper")* (Frankfurt am Main & Bern: Lang, 1982);

Günther Rühle, *Materialien zum Leben und Schreiben der Marieluise Fleißer* (Frankfurt am Main: Suhrkamp, 1973);

Peter Schaarschmidt, "Das moderne Völksstück," in *Theater und Gesellschaft: Das Volksstück im 19. und 20. Jahrhundert*, edited by Jürgen Hein (Dusseldorf: Bertelsmann, 1973), pp. 201-217;

Angelika Spindler, "Marieluise Fleißer: Eine Schriftstellerin zwischen Selbstverwirkli-chung und Selbstaufgabe," Ph.D. dissertation, University of Vienna, 1980;

Barbara Stritzke, *Marieluise Fleißer: Pioniere in Ingolstadt* (Frankfurt am Main & Bern: Lang, 1982);

text + kritik, special issue on Fleißer, 64, edited by Heinz Ludwig Arnold (October 1979);

Michael Töteberg, "Ein Mißverständnis," *Merkur*, 31, no. 7 (1977): 698-700;

Töteberg, "Die Urfassung von Marieluise Fleißers *Pioniere in Ingolstadt*," *Maske und Kothurn*, 23 (1977): 119-121;

Gisela von Wysocki, "Die Magie der Großstadt—Marieluise Fleißer," in her *Die Fröste der Freiheit: Aufbruchphantasien* (Frankfurt am Main: Syndikat, 1980), pp. 9-22.

Papers:
Marieluise Fleißer's papers are in the Stadtarchiv (city archive) at Ingolstadt, Bavaria.

Max Frisch
(15 May 1911 - 4 April 1991)

Ehrhard Bahr
University of California, Los Angeles

See also the Frisch entry in *DLB 69: Contemporary German Fiction Writers, First Series.*

PLAY PRODUCTIONS: *Nun singen sie wieder: Versuch eines Requiems*, Zurich, Schauspielhaus, 29 March 1945;

Santa Cruz: Eine Romanze, Zurich, Schauspielhaus, 7 March 1946;

Die chinesische Mauer: Eine Farce, Zurich, Schauspielhaus, 10 October 1946; second version, Berlin, Theater am Kurfürstendamm, 28 October 1955; third version, Hamburg, Schauspielhaus, 26 February 1965; fourth version, Paris, Jeune Théâtre National des Théâtres de l'Odéon, 8 November 1972;

Als der Krieg zu Ende war: Schauspiel, Zurich, Schauspielhaus, 8 January 1949; revised version, Freiburg, Städtische Bühnen, 8 May 1965;

Graf Öderland: Ein Spiel in zehn Bildern, Zurich, Schauspielhaus, 10 February 1951; second version, Frankfurt am Main, Städtische Bühnen, 4 February 1956; third version, Berlin, Schiller-Theater, 25 October 1961;

Don Juan oder die Liebe zur Geometrie, Zurich, Schauspielhaus; Berlin, Schiller-Theater, 5 May 1953; revised version, Hamburg, Schauspielhaus, 12 September 1962;

Biedermann und die Brandstifter: Ein Lehrstück ohne Lehre, Zurich, Schauspielhaus, 29 March 1958;

Die große Wut des Philipp Hotz, Zurich, Schauspielhaus, 29 March 1958;

Andorra: Stück in zwölf Bildern, Zurich, Schauspielhaus, 2 November 1961;

Biografie: Ein Spiel, Zurich, Schauspielhaus, 1 February 1968; revised version, Ludwigshafen, "Das Ensemble," Theater im Pfalzbau, 15 October 1984;

Triptychon (in French translation), Lausanne, Centre Dramatique de Lausanne, 9 October 1979; (German-language premiere) Vienna, Akademietheater, 1 February 1981;

Jonas und sein Veteran, Zurich, Schauspielhaus, 19 October 1989.

Max Frisch in 1948 (photograph by Marie-Agnes Schürenberg)

BOOKS: *Jürg Reinhart: Eine sommerliche Schicksalsfahrt. Roman* (Stuttgart: Deutsche Verlags-Anstalt, 1934); revised as *J'adore ce qui me brûle oder Die Schwierigen: Roman* (Zurich: Atlantis, 1943); revised as *Die Schwierigen oder j'adore ce qui me brûle* (Zurich: Atlantis, 1957);

Antwort aus der Stille: Eine Erzählung aus den Bergen (Stuttgart & Berlin: Deutsche Verlags-Anstalt, 1937);

Blätter aus dem Brotsack (Zurich: Atlantis, 1940);

Bin oder die Reise nach Peking (Zurich: Atlantis, 1945);

Marion und die Marionetten: Ein Fragment (Basel: Gryff-Presse, 1946);

Nun singen sie wieder: Versuch eines Requiems (Klosterberg & Basel: Schwabe, 1946; edited by W. F. Tulasiewicz and K. Scheible, London: Harrap, 1967); translated by David Lommen as *Now They Sing Again*, in *Contemporary German Theatre*, edited by Michael Roloff (New York: Avon, 1972);

Tagebuch mit Marion (Zurich: Atlantis, 1947); enlarged as *Tagebuch 1946-1949* (Frankfurt am Main: Suhrkamp, 1950); translated by Geoffrey Skelton as *Sketchbook 1946-1949* (New York: Harcourt Brace Jovanovich, 1977);

Santa Cruz: Eine Romanze (Klosterberg & Basel: Schwabe, 1947);

Die chinesische Mauer: Eine Farce (Klosterberg & Basel: Schwabe, 1947; revised edition, Frankfurt am Main: Suhrkamp, 1955); translated by James L. Rosenberg as *The Chinese Wall* (New York: Hill & Wang, 1961); German version revised (Frankfurt am Main: Suhrkamp, 1972);

Als der Krieg zu Ende war: Schauspiel (Klosterberg & Basel: Schwabe, 1949; edited by Stuart Friebert, New York: Dodd, Mead, 1967);

Graf Öderland: Ein Spiel in zehn Bildern (Berlin: Suhrkamp, 1951); revised as *Graf Öderland: Eine Moritat in zwölf Bildern* (Frankfurt am Main: Suhrkamp, 1963; edited by George Salamon, New York: Harcourt, Brace & World, 1966);

Don Juan oder Die Liebe zur Geometrie: Eine Komödie in 5 Akten (Frankfurt am Main: Suhrkamp, 1953);

Stiller: Roman (Frankfurt am Main: Suhrkamp, 1954); translated by Michael Bullock as *I'm Not Stiller* (London & New York: Abelard-Schumann, 1958; New York: Random House, 1962);

Herr Biedermann und die Brandstifter: Hörspiel (Hamburg: Hans Bredow-Institut, 1955); adapted for the stage as *Biedermann und die Brandstifter: Ein Lehrstück ohne Lehre. Mit einem Nachspiel* (Frankfurt am Main: Suhrkamp, 1958; edited by Paul Kurt Ackerman, Boston: Houghton Mifflin, 1963; London: Methuen, 1963); translated by Bullock as *The Fire Raisers: A Morality without a Moral with an Afterpiece* (London: Methuen, 1962); translated by Mordekai Gorelik as *The Firebugs: A Learning Play without a Lesson* (New York: Hill & Wang, 1963);

Achtung: Die Schweiz. Ein Gespräch über unsere Lage und ein Vorschlag zur Tat, by Frisch, Lucius Burckhardt, and Markus Kutter (Basel: Handschin, 1955);

Die neue Stadt: Beiträge zur Diskussion, by Frisch, Burckhardt, and Kutter (Basel: Handschin, 1956);

Homo faber: Ein Bericht (Frankfurt am Main: Suhrkamp, 1957; edited by Ackermann and Constance Clarke, Boston: Houghton Mifflin, 1973); translated by Bullock as *Homo Faber: A Report* (London & New York: Abelard-Schumann, 1959; New York: Random House, 1962);

Ausgewählte Prosa (Frankfurt am Main: Suhrkamp, 1961; edited by Stanley Corngold, New York: Harcourt, Brace & World, 1968);

Andorra: Stück in zwölf Bildern (Frankfurt am Main: Suhrkamp, 1961; edited by H. F. Garten, London: Methuen, 1964); translated by Bullock as *Andorra: A Play in Twelve Scenes* (New York: Hill & Wang, 1964; London: Methuen, 1964);

Stücke, 2 volumes (Frankfurt am Main: Suhrkamp, 1962);

Mein Name sei Gantenbein: Roman (Frankfurt am Main: Suhrkamp, 1964); translated by Bullock as *A Wilderness of Mirrors* (London: Methuen, 1965; New York: Random House, 1966);

Zürich-Transit: Skizze eines Films (Frankfurt am Main: Suhrkamp, 1966);

Biografie: Ein Spiel (Frankfurt am Main: Suhrkamp, 1967; revised 1968); translated by Bullock as *Biography: A Game* (New York: Hill & Wang, 1969);

Öffentlichkeit als Partner (Frankfurt am Main: Suhrkamp, 1967);

Erinnerungen an Brecht (Berlin: Friedenauer Presse, 1968);

Dramaturgisches: Ein Briefwechsel mit Walter Höllerer (Berlin: Literarisches Colloquium, 1969);

Rip van Winkle: Hörspiel (Stuttgart: Reclam, 1969);

Der Mensch zwischen Selbstentfremdung und Selbstverwirklichung, by Frisch and Rudolf Immig (Stuttgart: Calwer, 1970);

Wilhelm Tell für die Schule (Frankfurt am Main: Suhrkamp, 1971);

Glück: Eine Erzählung (Zurich: Brunnenturm-Presse, 1972);

Tagebuch 1966-1971 (Frankfurt am Main: Suhrkamp, 1972); translated by Skelton as *Sketch-*

book 1966-1971 (New York: Harcourt Brace Jovanovich, 1974; London: Methuen, 1974);

Dienstbüchlein (Frankfurt am Main: Suhrkamp, 1974);

Montauk: Eine Erzählung (Frankfurt am Main: Suhrkamp, 1975); translated by Skelton as *Montauk* (New York: Harcourt Brace Jovanovich, 1976);

Stich-Worte, selected by Uwe Johnson (Frankfurt am Main: Suhrkamp, 1975);

Zwei Reden zum Friedenspreis des Deutschen Buchhandels 1976, by Frisch und Hartmut von Hentig (Frankfurt am Main: Suhrkamp, 1976);

Gesammelte Werke in zeitlicher Folge, 6 volumes, edited by Hans Mayer and Walter Schmitz (Frankfurt am Main: Suhrkamp, 1976);

Triptychon: Drei szenische Bilder (Frankfurt am Main: Suhrkamp, 1978); translated by Skelton as *Triptych: Three Scenic Panels* (New York: Harcourt Brace Jovanovich, 1981);

Der Mensch erscheint im Holozän: Eine Erzählung (Frankfurt am Main: Suhrkamp, 1979); translated by Skelton as *Man in the Holocene: A Story* (New York: Harcourt Brace Jovanovich, 1980);

Erzählende Prosa 1939-1979 (Berlin: Volk und Welt, 1980);

Stücke, 2 volumes (Berlin: Volk und Welt, 1980);

Blaubart: Eine Erzählung (Frankfurt am Main: Suhrkamp, 1982); translated by Skelton as *Bluebeard* (New York: Harcourt Brace Jovanovich, 1984; London: Methuen, 1984);

Forderungen des Tages: Porträts, Skizzen, Reden 1943-1982 (Frankfurt am Main: Suhrkamp, 1983);

Gesammelte Werke in zeitlicher Folge: Jubiläumsausgabe in 7 Bänden, 7 volumes, edited by Hans Mayer and Walter Schmitz (Frankfurt am Main: Suhrkamp, 1986);

Novels, Plays, Essays, edited by Rolf Kieser (New York: Continuum, 1989);

Schweiz ohne Armee? Ein Palaver (Zurich: Limmat, 1989);

Schweiz als Heimat?: Versuche über 50 Jahre, edited by Walter Obschlager (Frankfurt am Main: Suhrkamp, 1990);

Der Aufruf zur Hoffnung ist heute ein Aufruf zur Widerstand (Saint Gall: Erker, 1991);

Tagebücher, 2 volumes (Frankfurt am Main: Suhrkamp, 1991).

Editions in English: *Three Plays*, translated by Michael Bullock (London: Methuen, 1962)—comprises *The Fire Raisers, Count Oederland, Andorra*;

Three Plays, translated by James L. Rosenberg (New York: Hill & Wang, 1967)—comprises *Don Juan; or, The Love of Geometry*; *The Great Rage of Philipp Hotz*; *When the War Was Over*;

Four Plays: The Great Wall; Don Juan; or, the Love of Geometry; Philipp Hotz's Fury; Biography, A Game, translated by Bullock (London: Methuen, 1969).

OTHER: Robert S. Gessner, *Sieben Lithographien*, annotations by Frisch (Zurich: Hürlimann, 1952);

Markus Kutter and Lucius Burckhardt, *Wir selber bauen unsere Stadt: Ein Hinweis auf die Möglichkeit staatlicher Baupolitik*, foreword by Frisch (Basel: Handschin, 1956);

Bertolt Brecht, *Drei Gedichte*, afterword by Frisch (Zurich, 1959);

"Nachruf auf Albin Zollinger, den Dichter und Landsmann, nach zwanzig Jahren," in Albin Zollinger, *Gesammelte Werke*, volume 1 (Zurich: Atlantis, 1961), pp. 7-13;

Teo Otto, *Skizzen eines Bühnenbildners: 33 Zeichnungen*, texts by Frisch, Kurt Hirschfeld, and Oskar Wälterlin (St. Gallen: Tschudy, 1964);

Alexander J. Seiler, *Siamo italiani/Die Italiener: Gespräche mit italienischen Arbeitern in der Schweiz*, contribution by Frisch (Zurich: EVZ, 1965), pp. 7-10;

Gody Suter, *Die großen Städte: Was sie zerstört und was sie retten kann*, preface by Frisch (Bergisch-Gladbach: Lübbe, 1966);

Andrei D. Sakharov, *Wie ich mir die Zukunft vorstelle: Gedanken über Fortschritt, friedliche Koexistenz und geistige Freiheit*, translated by E. Guttenberger, postscript by Frisch (Zurich: Diogenes, 1969);

Adolf Hitler, *Mein Kampf: Mit Zeichnungen von Clement Moreau*, preface by Frisch (Munich: Neue Galerie, 1974);

"Why Don't We Have the Cities We Need?," in *The Aspen Papers: Twenty Years of Design Theory from the International Design Conference in Aspen* (New York: Praeger, 1974), pp. 41-46;

"Büchner-Preisrede 1958," in *Büchner-Preisreden 1951-1971* (Stuttgart: Reclam, 1981), pp. 57-72.

SELECTED PERIODICAL PUBLICATIONS—
UNCOLLECTED: "Was bin ich?," *Zürcher Student*, 10 (1932/1933): 9-11;

"Kurzgeschichte," *Neue Zürcher Zeitung*, 28 May 1934, pp. 513-514;

"Vorbild Huber: Ein novellistischer Beitrag," *Zürcher Illustrierte*, no. 35 (31 August 1934): 1103, 1104-1106; no. 36 (7 September 1934): 1136-1137, 1139; no. 37 (14 September 1934): 1162-1163;

"Ist es eine Schande?," *Neue Zürcher Zeitung*, 9 September 1934;

"Ausflug aus der Zeit: Skizze," *Neue Zürcher Zeitung*, 7 April 1935;

"Prag, die Stadt zwischen Ost und West," *Neue Zürcher Zeitung*, 30 April 1935, p. 5; 7 May 1935, p. 6 ; 20 May 1935, p. 6;

"Ein Roman, zweimal besprochen," *Neue Zürcher Zeitung*, 22 November 1940;

"Blätter aus dem Brotsack: Neue Folge," *Neue Zürcher Zeitung*, 23 December 1940, p. 5; 25 December 1940, p. 2; 27 December 1940, p. 4; 29 December 1940, p. 1; 30 December 1940, p. 4;

"Die andere Welt," *Atlantis*, no. 1/2 (1945): 2-4;

"Über Zeitereignis und Dichtung," *Neue Zürcher Zeitung*, 22 March 1945, p. 7;

"Stimmen eines anderen Deutschland? Zu den Zeugnissen von Wiechert und Bergengrün," *Neue Schweizer Rundschau*, 13 (1945/1946): 537-547;

"Death is so permanent," *Neue Schweizer Rundschau*, 14 (1946/1947): 88-110;

"Kleines Nachwort zu einer Ansprache von Thomas Mann," *Zürcher Student*, 25 (1947): 57-59;

"Drei Entwürfe zu einem Brief nach Deutschland," *Die Wandlung*, 2 (1947): 478-483;

"Judith: Ein Monolog," *Die Neue Zeitung*, 25 August 1948, p. 3;

"Friedrich Dürrenmatt: Zu seinem neuen Stück 'Romulus der Große,'" *Die Weltwoche*, 6 May 1949, p. 5;

"Orchideen und Aasgeier: Ein Reisealbum aus Mexico. Oktober/November 1951," *Neue Schweizer Rundschau*, 20 (1952/1953): 67-88;

"Unsere Arroganz gegenüber Amerika," *Neue Schweizer Rundschau*, 20 (1952/1953): 584-590;

"Begegnung mit Negern: Eindrücke aus Amerika," *Atlantis*, 26 (1954): 73-78;

"Brecht als Klassiker," *Dichten und Trachten: Jahresschau des Suhrkamp Verlages*, 5 (1955): 35-37;

"Brecht ist tot," *Die Weltwoche*, 24 August 1956, p. 5;

Die große Wut des Phillip Hotz: Sketch, in *Hortulus*, 8 (1958): 34-62;

"Öffentlichkeit als Partner," *Börsenblatt für den deutschen Buchhandel*, 14 (1958): 1331-1334;

"Das Engagement des Schriftstellers heute," *Frankfurter Allgemeine Zeitung*, 14 November 1958, p. 8;

"Erinnerungen an Brecht," *Kursbuch*, 7 (1966): 54-79;

"Politik durch Mord," *Die Weltwoche*, 26 April 1968, pp. 49, 51;

"Die Schweiz als Heimat! Dankrede für die Verleihung des Großen Schillerpreises," *Nationalzeitung Basel*, 19 January 1974, pp. 1, 6;

"Notizen von einer kurzen Reise nach China 28.10-4.11.1975," *Der Spiegel*, 30 (9 February 1976): 110-132;

"Ohnmächtiger Poet," *Süddeutsche Zeitung*, 1 September 1981;

"Wohnen mitten in der Stadt," *Tages-Anzeiger*, Zurich, 7 September 1984;

"Weinprobe," *Zeit-Magazin*, 22 February 1985;

"Protest von Frisch und Dürrenmatt: Zur Chilenen-Ausweisung," *Tages-Anzeiger*, 1 November 1985;

"Gruß eines Tintenfisches aus der Schweiz," *Tintenfisch*, no. 25 (1986): 8-9;

"Am Ende der Aufklärung steht das Goldene Kalb: Max Frischs Rede an die Kollegen, gehalten an den 8. Solothurner Literaturtagen im Rahmen einer Geburtstagsfeier," *Weltwoche*, 15 May 1986;

"Hat die Hoffnung noch eine Zukunft," *Die Zeit*, 26 December 1986;

"Votum in Moskau," *einspruch: Zeitschrift der Autoren*, no. 2 (1987): 1;

"Wort zum Sonntag (5 May 1987): Zum Asylgesetz," *Die Wochenzeitung* (Zurich), 3 April 1987;

"'America' über alles?: Lesung zur Verleihung des Neustadt-Preises," *Die Wochenzeitung* (Zurich), 22 May 1987.

German drama during the 1950s would be unthinkable without the works of Max Frisch and Friedrich Dürrenmatt; the lack of postwar drama in West Germany was made up for by these two Swiss playwrights between 1945 and 1960. They were the best qualified to fill this vacuum because they were writing in German and were so close to the situation in postwar Germany, yet they were not politically compromised by previous accommodation with the Nazi regime. Furthermore, they had stayed in close contact with the development of modernist drama—in particular German exile drama, which had found a haven at the Zurich Schauspielhaus (Playhouse). Plays by exiled dramatists such as Bertolt Brecht, Ferdinand Bruckner, Ödön von Horváth, Friedrich Wolf, and Carl Zuckmayer had been produced there during the 1930s and 1940s, and some of the best German actors and directors had found employment in Zurich after 1933. The Zurich Schauspielhaus was thus an ideal place for young dramatists to learn their trade. Dürrenmatt and Frisch made use of the opportunity offered to them in the 1940s, and they found inspiration for their own works from the plays produced at the Schauspielhaus. By the 1960s Frisch and Dürrenmatt were internationally recognized dramatists whose plays were translated into many languages and performed in many countries. Although Frisch became increasingly disappointed with the inertia of the technical apparatus of the theater and neglected drama in the 1970s and 1980s in favor of prose, he never abandoned it.

Frisch was born in Zurich on 15 May 1911 to Franz Frisch, an archictect, and Lina Wildermuth Frisch. His mother's family had immigrated to Switzerland from Württemberg, Germany. Frisch studied German literature at the University of Zurich from 1931 until his father died in 1933; he then left school and became a freelance journalist, writing mainly for the *Neue Zürcher Zeitung* (New Zurich Newspaper). In 1936 he took up the study of architecture at the Eidgenössische Technische Hochschule (Federal Institute of Technology) in Zurich. After receiving his degree in 1941 he opened an architectural office. He married Gertrud Anna Constance von Meyenburg in 1942; they had three children. In 1944 Frisch was invited to assist at rehearsals and write for the Schauspielhaus. After World War II, in which he served as a gunner on the Swiss border, Frisch won an architectural competition for a public outdoor swimming pool in Zurich, the Freibad Letzigraben, which was built from 1947 to 1949. The first play he wrote, *Santa Cruz*, was performed in 1946 and was published in 1947; his first play to be performed and published was *Nun singen sie wieder* (performed, 1945; published, 1946; translated as *Now They Sing Again*, 1972). They were followed by *Die chinesische Mauer* (performed, 1946; published, 1947; translated as *The Chinese Wall*, 1961).

Santa Cruz is a dream play. Santa Cruz is not a geographical place but a realm of dreams and self-fulfillment. Its opposite is a castle in a wintry European landscape that stands for reality,

marriage, and renunciation. Past and present are synchronized in the dream action of the play. An adventurer and a cavalry officer court the same woman; she opts for marriage and reality but cannot give up her dreams. Neither can her husband, whose alter ego is the adventurer. Only when the adventurer within him dies can the officer and his wife find peace in their life in the castle. Frisch's first play shows the influence of Hugo von Hofmannsthal and Paul Claudel.

Nun singen sie wieder, subtitled *Versuch eines Requiems* (Attempt at a Requiem), deals with war crimes and the vain hope of a moral change. After ordering the shooting of twenty-one hostages, Karl deserts from the army and hangs himself. His wife and child perish in an air raid. The members of the enemy air force are killed in action. The dead celebrate their symbolic requiem with bread and wine. They are committed to a change in spirit, but the survivors do not hear their message. Their deaths will have been in vain unless the audience listens to the song of the hostages, who died singing. Frisch's stage directions specified that scenery was to be present only to the extent that the actors needed it; in no case was it to simulate reality. The impression of a play on a stage was to be preserved throughout. Showing the influence of Thornton Wilder's *Our Town* (1938), the play fails as a Zeitstück (play dealing with current events) because neither time nor place is defined.

Die chinesische Mauer, revised in 1955, 1965, and 1972, is a farce. Its subject is the endless cycle of human self-destruction. The construction of the Great Wall of China around 200 B.C. is an allegory for the atomic bomb. Anachronism is the main principle of the play; the characters include "Der Heutige" (Today's Man), Romeo and Juliet, Napoleon Bonaparte, Christopher Columbus, Don Juan, Pontius Pilate, Brutus, Philip of Spain, Cleopatra, Emile Zola, and Ivan the Terrible. Instead of traditional dramatic conflict, there is a constant exchange of quotations, referring to events of the past. Even with his knowledge of history, Der Heutige cannot stop the cycle.

In 1948 Frisch met Brecht, whose theory of the epic or anti-Aristotelian theater would continue to exercise considerable influence on Frisch's dramatic production until the early 1960s. Frisch's fourth play, *Als der Krieg zu Ende war* (When the War was Over, 1949), is set after the fall of Berlin in 1945. Agnes, a German woman, plans to kill a Soviet colonel while her German husband hides in the cellar. Although nei-

Scene from a 1955 production at the Zurich Schauspielhaus of Frisch's Die chinesische Mauer *(photograph by W. E. Baur)*

ther understands the language of the other, the colonel and Agnes overcome prejudice and fall in love. When the colonel learns that Agnes's husband had participated in the massacre of Jews in the Warsaw Ghetto in 1943, he leaves rather than arresting her husband as a war criminal. Brecht wanted Frisch to take a stand in favor of the Soviet "liberation" of Germany, but Frisch considered the conflict between humanity and inhumanity the main theme of the play.

Frisch spent 1951 and 1952 in the United States and Mexico on a Rockefeller grant. His next two plays were *Graf Öderland* (1951; translated as *Count Oederland*, 1962) and *Don Juan oder Die Liebe zur Geometrie* (1953; translated as *Don Juan; or, The Love of Geometry*, 1967). *Biedermann und die Brandstifter* (1958; translated as *The Fire Raisers*, 1962), first written as a radio drama, is one of Frisch's most provocative plays.

Graf Öderland, which underwent two revisions after its premiere in 1951, was a failure because it does not provide convincing motivation for the protagonist's actions. An ambitious state prosecutor changes into an ax murderer with romantically anarchistic notions. But as he overthrows power in order to be free, he is taking over the opposite of freedom: power. Finally the revolutionary takes over as dictator of a new government. At the end Öderland desperately wants

to wake up from the nightmare of murder and anarchy he has created. Frisch expressly rejected an interpretation of the play as an allegory about Adolf Hitler or a critique of modern democracy.

In *Don Juan oder Die Liebe zur Geometrie* Don Juan is an intellectual in search of his identity. He tries to escape his destined role as a seducer by loving geometry more than women, but the power of the myth catches up with him. He stages his death and descent into hell so as to escape to his first love, geometry. This escape is denied to him, but he experiences his own hell after he marries Miranda, a former prostitute. He becomes a prisoner in his own castle: he cannot leave the castle because he would then have to live as Don Juan again. He ends up as a henpecked husband and father, reading about his own legend in the 1630 version by Tirso de Molina.

Biedermann und die Brandstifter, subtitled *Ein Lehrstück ohne Lehre* (A Didactic Play without a Lesson), is the first of Frisch's parable plays. Biedermann is not an individual but a type: the businessman who combines pleasant behavior with ruthless brutality in order to succeed in the capitalist world; he is an opportunist and a coward. Because of lack of courage Biedermann allows two suspicious vagrants to camp in his attic, even though there have been newspaper reports about arsonists disguised as peddlers asking for a place to sleep. The vagrants store gasoline barrels in Biedermann's attic and openly handle detonators and fuses in front of him. He cooperates because he does not want to make them his enemies. On the other hand, he has no scruples about driving his employee Knechtling to suicide, because he has nothing to fear from Knechtling. Concerned only with saving himself and his house, Biedermann serves the arsonists a sumptuous dinner; in the end he provides them with the matches they use to set his house on fire. Biedermann and his wife perish in the flames. A chorus of firemen provides commentary in a parody of Greek tragedy. In 1959 Frisch added a "Nachspiel" (epilogue) showing Biedermann and his wife in hell, unchanged and as foolish as ever. Frisch rejected any political interpretation of his "didactic play" as an allegory of the Nazi burning of the Reichstag in 1933 or the Communist takeover of Czechoslovakia in 1948. Unlike Brecht, who wanted to change the world with his theater, Frisch did not believe in the revolutionizing effect of the stage. Also, in spite of the absurd aspects of the plot, Frisch did not want his play to be understood as theater of the absurd. Denouncing Eugène Ionesco and his followers, Frisch declared in 1964 that a public that finds satisfaction in absurdity would be a dictator's delight.

Die große Wut des Philipp Hotz (The Great Madness of Philipp Hotz, published, 1958) is a "Schwank" (slapstick farce) that premiered together with *Biedermann und die Brandstifter* in 1958. The conventional stereotype of the intellectual who is unable to act, Philipp Hotz attempts to break out of the prison of his daily life by locking his wife in a closet, destroying the furniture that symbolizes the bourgeois existence from which he wants to escape, and enlisting in the French foreign legion. Hotz even fabricates an adultery that he has not committed. All his efforts to be taken seriously end in failure. Rejected by the foreign legion because he is nearsighted, he returns to his wife and home and the routines of his daily life.

In 1958 Frisch was awarded the Georg Büchner Prize by the German Academy of Literature in Darmstadt, the Literature Prize of the City of Zurich, and the Veillon Prize of Lausanne. In 1959 he was divorced from his first wife. In 1961 he moved to Rome. That year he had his greatest success on the stage with *Andorra* (published, 1961; translated, 1964). The twelve scenes of *Andorra* are linked by statements made by various characters as they step out of the action of the play to give accounts of their deeds and motivations from a witness box in the foreground of the stage. With the exceptions of Andri and Barblin, the characters are mere types without names. Andri is a young man who is thought to be a Jew who was rescued from persecution by the Schwarzen (Blacks) across the frontier and adopted by the local teacher. Andri is, however, the teacher's illegitimate son by the Señora, a woman from across the border. Although he is not Jewish, the prejudices of his social environment impress on Andri the supposedly Jewish characteristics that he finally accepts, even after he learns of his non-Jewish origin. When he falls in love with Barblin, who—unknown to him—is his half sister, Andri believes that his foster father objects to the affair because he is Jewish. Andri perishes as a Jew when the Schwarzen invade Andorra and take him away, while Barblin's head is shaved because she is considered the Judenhure (Jew's whore). Nobody offers any resistance to the invasion by the Schwarzen. Everybody is guilty, including the

teacher, who invented the pious lie of adopting a Jewish child instead of confessing to his illegitimate son; he hangs himself in the schoolroom. The Andorra of this play has nothing to do with the actual state of this name; Frisch said in his notes to the play that Andorra is the prototype of a society ruled by prejudice and fear. There are unmistakable allusions to Switzerland and its relationship to Nazi Germany, even though Frisch stressed in his stage directions that, for example, in the uniform of the Schwarzen any resemblance to the uniforms of the past should be avoided. *Andorra* was criticized for "obscuring rather than analyzing the aberration of anti-Semitism" and of minimizing the Holocaust.

In 1965 Frisch moved to the Ticino, in southern Switzerland. That same year he received the Schiller Prize of Baden-Württemberg. His comedy *Biografie: Ein Spiel* (published, 1967; translated as *Biography: A Game*, 1969) was first produced in 1968. The play, whose subtitle means both "A Play" and "A Game," is introduced by a "Registrator" (chronicler), who reads the stage directions at a lectern. Kürmann, a professor of psychology, wants to start his life over again, like an actor repeating a scene during a rehearsal. He is convinced that he knows exactly what he would do differently. The Registrator and Kürmann's wife Antoinette agree to let him repeat the scene, but it leads to the same result. All other attempts to change the outcome of his life also fail: he is invariably confronted by death from cancer within seven years. Kümann is limited by his own identity; any particular scene of his life could have been different, but Kürmann cannot adopt a different personality. As Frisch said in his notes to the play, the theater grants an opportunity that reality denies: to repeat, to rehearse, to change.

In 1969 Frisch married Marianne Oellers; the marriage ended in divorce a few years later. After traveling to Japan he was a guest lecturer at Columbia University in New York in 1970-1971. In 1974 he received the Great Schiller Prize of the Swiss Schiller Foundation and became an honorary member of the American Academy of Arts and Letters and the National Institute of Arts and Letters. In 1975 he traveled to China. He received the Peace Prize of the German Book Trade in 1976. His *Triptychon: Drei szenische Bilder* (translated as *Triptych: Three Scenic Panels*, 1981) was published in 1978 and premiered in 1979. *Triptychon* consists of three loosely connected scenes dealing with a common theme, that of death. The first scene deals with the embarrassment caused by the death of a seventy-year-old man; the second is a conversation among the dead, who find eternity banal; the last scene deals with the insoluble relationship between a man and his dead lover.

In November 1989 there was to be a referendum on the abolition of the military. Frisch had been a critic of the Swiss army and its ideology since 1974, when he attacked the Swiss arms industry, Swiss resistance to the immigration of political refugees, and the concept of defense by withdrawal behind an Alpine Maginot Line in his *Dienstbüchlein* (Service Booklet). His extended dialogue *Jonas und sein Veteran* (Jonas and His Veteran), which premiered in 1989, and his pamphlet *Schweiz ohne Armee? Ein Palaver* (Switzerland without an Army? A Palaver), published the same year, were Frisch's contribution to the debate on the future of the Swiss army. *Jonas und sein Veteran* consists of a ninety-minute conversation between a Swiss army veteran of 1918 and his grandson Jonas, who faces the alternatives of army service or civil disobedience and emigration. Neither alternative appeals to the young man, who is more interested in a career in computer science. His grandfather is of no help, because his advice consists of historical reminders of Swiss failures and sarcastic analyses of the army as part of Swiss folklore, as an elite unit to protect Swiss capitalism, or as a prop to shore up Swiss national identity. The dramatic dialogue discusses alternatives but does not provide a conclusion. Passages from Frisch's *Dienstbüchlein* are quoted at great length by the grandfather. The proposal to abolish the military was defeated; but it was supported by 35.6 percent of the voters, forcing the army to consider reforms.

In 1989 Frisch was awarded the Heinrich Heine Prize of the City of Düsseldorf. He died in Zurich on 4 April 1991. Although he wrote extensive notes and suggestions for staging his plays, Frisch never provided a comprehensive theory of drama. He questioned the didactic effectiveness of Brecht's epic theater, doubting that anyone would ever change his or her viewpoint as a result of a stage performance. What Frisch had in common with Brecht was his rejection of attempts to imitate reality; the audience is never supposed to forget that what is happening on the stage is make-believe. Throughout his career Frisch was concerned with reminding his audience that his plays were not representations of the world but of our consciousness of the world.

Letters:

"Briefwechsel zwischen Karl Schmid und Max Frisch," in *Unbehagen im Kleinstaat*, by Schmid (Zurich: Artemis, 1977), pp. 255-268.

Interviews:

Gody Suter, "Max Frisch: 'Ich habe Glück gehabt.' Von *Nun singen sie wieder* bis zu *Andorra*," *Weltwoche*, 3 November 1961;

Alfred A. Häsler, "Wir müssen unsere Welt anders einrichten: Gespräch mit Max Frisch," in his *Leben mit dem Haß: Gespräche* (Reinbek: Rowohlt, 1969), pp. 40-46;

Peter André Bloch und Bruno Schoch, "Gespräch mit Max Frisch," in their *Der Schriftsteller und sein Verhältnis zur Sprache, dargestellt am Problem der Tempuswahl* (Bern: Francke, 1971), pp. 68-81;

Rolf Kieser, "An Interview with Max Frisch," *Contemporary Literature*, 13 (Winter 1972): 1-14;

Heinz Ludwig Arnold, "Gespräch mit Max Frisch," in his *Gespräche mit Schriftstellern* (Munich: Beck, 1975), pp. 9-73;

Rudolf Ossowski, ed., *Jugend fragt—Prominente antworten* (Berlin: Colloquium, 1975), pp. 116-135;

Jon Barak, "Max Frisch Interviewed," *New York Times Book Review*, 19 March 1978, pp. 3, 36-37;

Peter Rüedi, "Die lange Ewigkeit des Gewesenen: Max Frisch schrieb ein Stück vom Tod, das nicht gespielt wird," *Deutsche Zeitung*, 21 April 1978, p. 15;

Heinz Sichrovsky, " 'Da müssen sie einfach lesen lernen!' Max Frisch über sein jüngstes Stück *Triptychon* und ein paar Probleme, die er mit dem Theater hat," *Deutsche Bühne*, 3 (1981): 16-17;

Fritz Raddatz, "Ich singe aus Angst—das Unsagbare: Ein Zeit-Gespräch mit Max Frisch," *Die Zeit*, 17 April 1981;

Stephan Bosch, "Max Frischs neue Welt," *Schweizer Illustrierte*, 4 May 1981;

Georges Waser, " Jedes Wort ist falsch und wahr: Der Schweizer Schriftsteller über den Sinn des Schreibens, sinnlose Geschichten, die Wahrheit und den Tod," *Rheinischer Merkur/ Christ und Welt*, 2 October 1981.

Bibliographies:

Alexander Stephan, "Max Frisch [1934-1988]," in *Kritisches Lexikon zur deutschsprachigen Literatur*, edited by Heinz Ludwig Arnold,

Frisch in 1991 (photograph by Renate von Mangoldt)

volume 3 (Munich: Edition text + kritik, 1978), pp. A-Z8;

"Selected Bibliography [1934-1986]," *World Literature Today*, 60 (Autumn 1986): 549-551.

References:

Heinz Ludwig Arnold, ed., *Max Frisch* (Munich: Edition text + kritik, 1975);

Hans Bänziger, *Dürrenmatt und Frisch*, sixth edition (Bern: Francke, 1971);

Bänziger, *Frisch und Dürrenmatt: Materialien und Kommentare* (Tübingen: Niemeyer, 1987);

Bänziger, *Zwischen Protest und Traditionsbewußtsein: Arbeiten zum Werk und zur gesellschaftlichen Stellung Max Frischs* (Bern: Francke, 1975);

Thomas Beckermann, ed., *Über Max Frisch I* (Frankfurt am Main: Suhrkamp, 1971);

Begegnungen: Eine Festschrift für Max Frisch zum siebzigsten Geburtstag (Frankfurt am Main: Suhrkamp, 1981);

Marianne Biedermann, *Das politische Theater von Max Frisch* (Lampertheim: Schäuble, 1974);

John T. Brewer, "Max Frisch's *Biedermann und die Brandstifter* as the Documentation of an Author's Frustration," *Germanic Review*, 46 (March 1971): 119-128;

Michael Butler, *Frisch: Andorra*, Critical Guides to German Texts, 2 (London: Grant & Cutler, 1985);

Butler, *The Plays of Max Frisch* (London: Macmillan, 1985);

Erna M. Dahms, *Zeit und Zeiterlebnis in den Werken Max Frischs: Bedeutung und technische Darstellung* (Berlin: De Gruyter, 1976);

Peter Demetz, "Max Frisch," in his *Postwar German Literature: A Critical Introduction* (New York: Schocken, 1970), pp. 112-125;

Demetz, "Max Frisch: The Last Romantic," in his *After the Fires: Recent Writing in the Germanies, Austria, and Switzerland* (San Diego & New York: Harcourt Brace Jovanovich, 1986), pp. 293-312;

Martin Esslin, "Max Frisch," in *German Men of Letters*, edited by Alex Natan, volume 3, second edition (London: Wolff, 1968), pp. 307-320;

Wolfgang Frühwald and Walter Schmitz, eds., *Max Frisch: Andorra/Wilhelm Tell: Materialien, Kommentare* (Munich: Hanser, 1977);

Heinz Gockel, *Max Frisch: Drama und Dramaturgie* (Munich: Oldenbourg, 1989);

Peter Gontrum, "Max Frisch and the Theatre of Bertolt Brecht," *German Life and Letters*, 33 (January 1980): 163-171;

Gontrum, "Max Frisch's *Don Juan*: A New Look at a Traditional Hero," *Comparative Literature Studies*, 2 (1965): 117-123;

Klaus Haberkamm, "Die alte Dame in 'Andorra': Zwei Schweizer Parabeln des nationalsozialistischen Antisemitismus," in *Gegenwartsliteratur und Drittes Reich: Deutsche Autoren in der Auseinandersetzung mit der Vergangenheit*, edited by Hans Wagener (Stuttgart: Reclam, 1977) pp. 95-110;

Tildy Hanhart, *Max Frisch: Zufall, Rolle und literarische Form: Interpretationen zu seinem neueren Werk* (Kronberg: Scriptor, 1976);

Walter Hinck, "Abschied von der Parabel: Frisch," in his *Das Moderne Drama in Deutschland* (Göttingen: Vandenhoeck & Ruprecht, 1973), pp. 170-180;

Ferdinand van Ingen, "Max Frischs Don-Juan-Komödie im Rahmen des Gesamtwerks," in *Einheit in der Vielfalt: Festschrift für Peter Lang zum 60. Geburtstag*, edited by Gisela Quast (Bern: Lang, 1988), pp. 249-269;

Manfred Jurgensen, *Max Frisch: Die Dramen* (Bern: Francke, 1968);

Jurgensen, ed., *Frisch: Kritik-Thesen-Analysen* (Bern: Francke, 1977);

Hellmuth Karasek, *Max Frisch* (Munich: Deutscher Taschenbuch Verlag, 1976);

Gerhard P. Knapp, ed., *Max Frisch: Aspekte des Bühnenwerks* (Bern: Lang, 1979);

Knapp and Mona Knapp, *Max Frisch: Andorra* (Frankfurt am Main: Diesterweg, 1980);

Wulf Koepke, *Max Frisch* (Columbia: University of South Carolina Press, 1991);

Hans Mayer, *Über Friedrich Dürrenmatt und Max Frisch*, second edition (Pfullingen: Neske, 1977);

Doris F. Merrifield, *Das Bild der Frau bei Max Frisch* (Freiburg: Hecksmann, 1971);

Carol Petersen, *Max Frisch*, translated by Charlotte LaRue (New York: Ungar, 1972);

Jürgen H. Petersen, *Max Frisch* (Stuttgart: Metzler, 1978);

Gertrud B. Pickar, *The Dramatic Works of Max Frisch* (Frankfurt am Main & Bern: Lang, 1977);

Gerhard F. Probst and Jay F. Bodine, eds., *Perspectives on Max Frisch* (Lexington: University Press of Kentucky, 1982);

Peter Ruppert, "Brecht and Frisch: Two Theaters of Possibility," *Mosaic* 15, no. 3 (1982): 109-120;

Albrecht Schau, ed., *Max Frisch: Beiträge zur Wirkungsgeschichte* (Freiburg: Becksmann, 1971);

Walter Schmitz, ed., *Frischs Don Juan oder die Liebe zur Geometrie* (Frankfurt am Main: Suhrkamp, 1985);

Schmitz, ed., *Materialien zu Max Frischs Biedermann und die Brandstifter* (Frankfurt am Main: Suhrkamp, 1979);

Schmitz, ed., *Über Max Frisch II* (Frankfurt am Main: Suhrkamp, 1976);

M. E. Schuchmann, *Der Autor als Zeitgenosse: Gesellschaftliche Aspekte in Max Frischs Werk* (Frankfurt am Main & Bern: Lang, 1979);

Eduard Stäuble, *Max Frisch: Gesamtdarstellung seines Werks*, fourth edition (Saint Gall: Erker, 1971);

Horst Steinmetz, *Max Frisch: Tagebuch; Roman; Drama* (Göttingen: Vandenhoeck & Ruprecht, 1973);

Alexander Stephan, *Max Frisch* (Munich: Beck, 1983);

Adelheid Weise, *Untersuchungen zur Thematik und Struktur der Dramen von Max Frisch*, Göppinger Arbeiten zur Germanistik, 7 (Göppingen: Kümmerle, 1975);

Ulrich Weisstein, *Max Frisch* (New York: Twayne, 1967);

Ernst Wendt and Walter Schmitz, eds., *Materialien zu Max Frischs Andorra* (Frankfurt am Main: Suhrkamp, 1978);

Monika Wintsch-Spieß, *Zum Problem der Identität im Werk Max Frischs* (Zurich: Juris, 1965);

Athur Zimmermann, ed., *Max Frisch* (Bern: Pro Helvetia, 1981).

Papers:

Max Frisch's papers are in the Max Frisch Archives, Eidgenössische Technische Hochschule (Federal Institute of Technology), Zurich.

Curt Goetz
(17 November 1888 - 12 September 1960)

Wolfgang D. Elfe
University of South Carolina

PLAY PRODUCTIONS: *Nachtbeleuchtung: Drei Grotesken*, Berlin, Deutsches Künstler-Theater, 2 November 1918; revised as *Nachtbeleuchtung: Fünf Grotesken*, Berlin, Deutsches Künstler-Theater, 14 February 1919;

Menagerie: Vier Übungen, Berlin, Deutsches Künstler-Theater, 26 February 1920;

Ingeborg, Berlin, Theater am Kurfürstendamm, 8 October 1921; translated and adapted by Arthur Richman as *Isabel*, New York, Empire Theatre, 13 January 1925;

Vom Lieben und Lachen, Vienna, Modernes Theater, 17 April 1924; as *Die tote Tante und andere Begebenheiten: Drei Einakter*, Berlin, Kammerspiele des Deutschen Theaters, 1 October 1924;

Der Lampenschirm: Kein Stück in drei Akten, Berlin, Kammerspiele, 19 January 1925;

Hokuspokus oder Was wollen wir spielen? Komödie (Ein Vorspiel und drei Akte), Stettin, Kammerspiele, 8 February 1927;

Der Lügner und die Nonne, Hamburg, Thalia-Theater, 7 December 1929;

Zirkus Aimée: Operette, music by Ralph Benatzky, Basel, Stadttheater, 5 March 1932;

Dr. med. Hiob Prätorius, Facharzt für Chirurgie und Frauenleiden: Eine Geschichte ohne Politik nach alten aber guten Motiven neuerzählt, Stuttgart, Landestheater (Kleines Haus), 31 December 1932;

It's a Gift, by Goetz and Dorian Otvos, New York, Playhouse, 12 March 1945; German version, *Das Haus in Montevideo*, Zurich, Schauspielhaus, 31 October 1946;

Nöel Coward, *Heitere Geister*, translated by Goetz, Zurich, Schauspielhaus, 8 November 1945;

Nichts Neues aus Hollywood, Hamburg, Schauspielhaus, 12 October 1956;

Alte Möbel, Vienna, Akademietheater, 12 May 1958; as *Miniaturen*, Berlin, Renaissance-Theater, 17 November 1958.

BOOKS: *Die Rutschbahn: Schwank in drei Akten*, by

Curt Goetz in 1923 (*photograph by Edith Barakovich*)

Goetz and Heinz Gordon (Berlin: Bloch, 1919);

Menagerie: Vier Übungen (Berlin: Oesterheld, 1920)—comprises *Der Spatz vom Dache, Die Taube in der Hand, Der Hund im Hirn, Der Hahn im Korb*;

Nachtbeleuchtung: Fünf Grotesken (Rostock: Hinstorff, 1921)—comprises *Nachtbeleuchtung, Lohengrin, Tobby, Minna Magdalena, Der fliegende Geheimrat*;

Ingeborg: Eine Komödie in drei Akten (Rostock: Hinstorff, 1921);

Der Lampenschirm: Kein Stück in drei Akten (Berlin: Oesterheld, 1923);

Die tote Tante und andere Begebenheiten: Groteske (Rostock: Hinstorff, 1924)—comprises *Der Mörder: Eine ärgerliche Begebenheit; Das Märchen: Eine kitschige Begebenheit; Die tote Tante: Eine erbauliche Begebenheit;*

Hokuspokus: In drei Akten. Mit einem Vor- und Nachspiel (Rostock: Hinstorff, 1927); revised as *Hokuspokus: Komödie in vier Akten* (Berlin: Herbig, 1953);

Der Lügner und die Nonne: Ein Theaterstück in drei Akten (Rostock: Hinstorff, 1929);

Dr. med. Hiob Prätorius, Facharzt für Chirurgie und Frauenleiden: Eine Geschichte ohne Politik nach alten aber guten Motiven neuerzählt (Rostock: Hinstorff, 1934); revised as *Dr. med. Hiob Prätorius, Facharzt für Chirurgie und Frauenleiden: Eine Geschichte in sieben Kapiteln. Neufassung* (Berlin: Herbig, 1952); revised as *Dr. med. Hiob Prätorius: Die tiefgründige Komödie in ihrer Bühnen - und Filmfassung,* edited by Valérie von Martens (Ebenhausen: Voss, 1978);

Gesammelte Werke, 3 volumes (Berlin: Published by the author, 1937);

Tatjana: Eine Legende (Zurich: Artemis, 1946);

Die Tote von Beverly Hills: Roman (Berlin: Herbig, 1951);

Gesammelte Bühnenwerke (Berlin: Herbig, 1952);

Das Haus in Montevideo oder Traugotts Versuchung: Eine Komödie im alten Stil über Moral, Versuchung und Belohnung der Tugend in vier Akten frei nach der "Toten Tante" (Berlin: Herbig, 1953);

Miniaturen: Die Rache; Herbst; Die Kommode (Berlin: Herbig, 1958);

Die Memoiren des Peterhans von Binningen (Berlin: Herbig, 1960);

Die Verwandlung des Peterhans von Binningen: Der Memoiren zweiter Teil, by Goetz and von Martens (Stuttgart: Deutsche Verlags-Anstalt, 1962);

Sämtliche Bühnenwerke (Stuttgart: Deutsche Verlags-Anstalt, 1963);

Wir wandern, wir wandern . . . : Der Memoiren dritter Teil by Goetz and von Martens (Stuttgart: Deutsche Verlags-Anstalt, 1963);

Viel Spaß mit Curt Goetz, edited by Fritz Fröhling (Freiburg im Breisgau: Hyperion, 1964);

Dreimal täglich: Rezepte (Stuttgart: Deutsche Verlags-Anstalt, 1964);

Carneval in Paris: Eine seltsame Begebenheit (Stuttgart: Deutsche Verlags-Anstalt, 1966);

Herz im Frack: Geschichten zwischen Schein und Sein, by Goetz and von Martens, edited by Fritz

Fröhling (Stuttgart: Deutsche Verlags-Anstalt, 1966);

Viermal täglich: Weitere Rezepte (Stuttgart: Deutsche Verlags-Anstalt, 1968);

Napoleon ist an allem schuld (Stuttgart: Deutsche Verlags-Anstalt, 1968);

Ergötzliches, by Goetz and von Martens (Freiburg im Breisgau: Hyperion, 1974).

OTHER: Jacques Deval, *Towàrisch: Komödie in 4 Akten,* adapted by Goetz (Berlin: Bloch, 1935);

Noël Coward, *Nach Afrika,* translated by Goetz (Zurich: Europa, 1951);

Coward, *Unter uns Vieren,* translated by Goetz (Zurich: Europa, 1951);

Coward, *Heitere Geister,* translated by Goetz (Zurich: Europa, 1951); republished as *Fröhliche Geister: Eine unwahrscheinliche Komödie in drei Akten* (Berlin: Bloch, 1966);

Franz and Paul von Schoenthan, *Der Raub der Sabinerinnen: Schwank in vier Akten,* adapted by Goetz (Berlin: Bloch, 1955).

Curt Goetz was a well-known stage and movie actor, director, and playwright. His plays—he wrote only comedies, mostly drawing-room comedies—enjoyed great success in their time and are still popular. He also translated works of like-minded authors, such as Noël Coward, into German.

Goetz was born on 17 November 1888 in Mainz to Bernhard Alexander Heinrich Werner Goetz, a Swiss citizen, and Selma Rocco Goetz, a German. His father died when Goetz was less than a year old. The family then moved to Halle, where Goetz's mother managed a nursing home from 1890 to 1906. Goetz's plan to become a physician, like his Swiss grandfather, had to be abandoned for financial reasons. He left the gymnasium at the completion of the tenth grade and moved to Berlin to take acting lessons from Emanuel Reicher, but money problems cut his training short. In 1908 he was hired as an actor by the Stadttheater (City Theater) in Rostock. After a year he accepted a position at Intimes Theater in Nuremberg. To work in Berlin, the undisputed cultural center of Germany, was the dream of every actor and actress from the provinces, and in 1911 Goetz moved to the Kleines (Little) Theater in Berlin directed by Victor Barnowsky. During the 1913-1914 season Goetz transferred to the newly opened Lessing-Theater, which was also directed by Barnowsky. Goetz married Erna Nitter in 1914; they were divorced in 1917. In the 1920s Goetz had contracts with other theaters in Berlin: the Theater am Kurfürstendamm, directed by Eugen Robert; the Deutsches (German) Theater, directed by Max Reinhardt; and the Komödienhaus (Comedy House), directed by Barnowsky.

After Goetz established himself as an actor, he began to write plays. For Goetz, writing was not an escape from the stage; rather, writing and acting were closely linked. When he said of his plays, "Lauter gute Rollen, geschrieben von einem Schauspieler für Schauspieler!" (Nothing but good parts. Written by an actor for actors!) he gave a somewhat immodest but largely accurate characterization. He wanted the actors to look good on the stage and to be liked and admired by the audience. His goal was not to shock, to provoke, or to teach, but to entertain. He often wrote the leading roles with himself in mind as the actor, and after 1923 he wrote his plays in such a way that he and his second wife could appear together in the major parts.

Goetz's *Menagerie: Vier Übungen* (Menagerie: Four Exercises, 1920) consists of four one-act plays. *Der Spatz vom Dach* (The Sparrow [Falling] off the Roof) is a dialogue about divine justice between a prison chaplain and a young man who—as it turns out—has been wrongfully sentenced to two years in jail for seducing a minor. The vain, conceited, self-satisfied, and pompous chaplain proclaims that nothing happens contrary to God's will, that not even a sparrow will fall off the roof without God wanting it that way. The well-mannered, intelligent, and highly articulate young man gives an impressive display of rhetorical fireworks, showing the absurdity of the chaplain's assertions and thereby shaking his smugness. *Die Taube in der Hand* (The Dove in the Hand) is about two married couples who are good friends. The wives learn that their husbands had decided by lot which woman each would marry. Intent on finding out who "won" and who "lost," each woman tries to get the truth from the other's husband. In the process, each participant falls in love with the friend's partner. In the end, however, the marriages and the friendships survive. In *Der Hund im Hirn* (The Dog on One's Mind) the young, vivacious wife of a professor falls in love with another man. The professor devises an elaborate scheme to win back his wife by making her lover confess and, in the process, look ridiculous. As an author who wishes to entertain, Goetz does not question the value system of his time: the professor is successful, articulate, ra-

tional, and intellectually superior to his wife; the wife is playful, excitable, flirtatious, and slightly irrational in a charming way. *Der Hahn im Korb* (The Rooster in the Basket) takes place in a studio where a film of *Hamlet* is being produced. All kinds of problems occur during the filming, including that of making a rooster crow at the appropriate moment. (Goetz had acted in several movies and had directed one by the time he wrote the play.) Here, as in many of his later plays, Goetz uses German dialects with comic effect: his Hamlet, for example, switches back and forth from lofty Shakespearean speech to a crude Cologne patois.

Nachtbeleuchtung (Night Light, 1921) is a collection of five one-act plays that were first performed in Berlin in 1918 and established Goetz's reputation as a master of the one-act genre. In the title play a capricious theater director who is used to giving orders (apparently modeled after Barnowsky), a painfully shy playwright who tries in vain to be heard, and a cocky actor meet late one night at the actor's apartment to discuss the staging of the playwright's drama. Since the apartment is dark—the power company has turned off the electricity because of long-overdue bills—the three sit in the stairwell of the apartment building. They have to turn on the stairwell light every couple of minutes because it automatically goes off after a certain interval to save energy. The conversation centers on the question whether the actor should present a lengthy monologue on the stage after he has shot himself in the head. As in many of Goetz's plays, the characters' witticisms and wisecracks make them entertaining but psychologically implausible. In *Lohengrin* two businessmen have just discovered that their company is facing bankruptcy. While they are deliberating as to what they should do, a stranger appears. He turns out to be a master burglar and embezzler who has come with a rescue plan. After telling the businessmen uncannily accurate details about their business and their private lives, he suggests that they hire him as a cashier. Before the insolvency becomes known, he will disappear with a huge sum of money—a sum that in reality does not exist—so that the insolvency will have a plausible explanation and can be made good by the insurance company. The stranger's impeccable manners stand in comic contrast to his lowly profession. The businessmen are contrasting and exaggerated characters: one is intelligent, worldly, and unscrupulous, while the other is slow, fearful, dull, and awkward. In

Tobby, a wealthy aristocrat, Harry, learns from his faithful servant Tobby that his wife is having an affair with his friend, who is visiting them. Harry, who remains composed and well-mannered even under the most trying circumstances, actually aids his wife and his friend in their "secret" escape. *Minna Magdalena* deals with petit bourgeois prejudice, a frequent topic in Goetz's works. Minna Sack, a servant of a professor, is believed to be pregnant. The alarmed professor and his wife arrange for a meeting with the young woman's petit bourgeois father and cautiously try to enlighten him about his daughter's supposed condition. The play, which is full of funny misunderstandings, exposes society's prejudices against unmarried motherhood and suggests what might happen to Minna if she actually were pregnant; but Goetz never allows his audience or readers to get upset or depressed. As is often the case in Goetz's works, comic effects result not only from the situation but from language: in *Minna Magdalena* there is a comic contrast between the father's simple, earthy, uneducated Saxon dialect and the highly complicated, abstract language of the professor. The main character in *Der fliegende Geheimrat* (The Flying Privy Councillor) is an arrogant but incompetent physician. One day, Herr Mors—Death—shows up at the doctor's office to fetch him. The physician convinces Death that it would be in the latter's interest to let him continue his bungling medical work on earth.

Ingeborg (1921; translated as *Isabel*, 1925) centers on a love triangle. Two men are in love with Ingeborg: her husband, who is an independently wealthy scholar, and their houseguest, a writer. The question is which of the evenly matched competitors will be the winner, but Goetz purposely leaves the outcome vague. There is little action; it is the elegant, witty conversation, filled with aphorisms, puns, and wisecracks, that is at the heart of the work. One of the many indications of the emphasis on language is that the butler is called Herr Konjunktiv (Mr. Subjunctive) because all of his verbs are in the subjunctive mood, making his speech excessively polite. It was during a guest performance of *Ingeborg* in Vienna in 1923 that Goetz met the Austrian actress Valérie von Martens; they were married later that year.

Der Lampenschirm: Kein Stück in drei Akten (The Lampshade: No Play in Three Acts, 1923), a farce in which the actor Hans Karl and a friend are trying to write a drama that has neither a theme nor a plot, consists of a series of loosely connected episodes that take place at Karl's apartment. Karl's condescending treatment of his landlady, an uneducated woman with limited intelligence, reveals that Goetz's seemingly nonpolitical play is, in fact, highly political in that it supports the status quo. Written at a turbulent time in German history when the rigid class system was being challenged, this and Goetz's other plays present it as given and unalterable that there are masters and servants, educated and uneducated people. Goetz often makes fun of the stupidity, vulgarity, and ignorance of the lower classes, thereby appealing to his audience's class consciousness and satisfying its feelings of superiority.

Goetz's next work, *Die tote Tante und andere Begebenheiten* (The Dead Aunt and Other Events, 1924), consists of three one-act plays. In *Der Mörder: Eine ärgerliche Begebenheit* (The Murderer: An Annoying Event) one of Goetz's favorite themes, the love triangle, reappears. At an elegant hunting lodge a woman is waiting for her husband and a close friend to return from a hunting trip. More and more circumstantial evidence accumulates that the husband may have killed the friend out of jealousy. At times the play has a nightmarish, surrealist quality; but it ends happily, as practically all of Goetz's plays do. In *Das Märchen: Eine kitschige Begebenheit* (The Fairy Tale: A Tawdry Event) an unhappy English lord falls in love with a beautiful young Gypsy and is thus saved from suicide. There is suspense to the very end as to whether the Gypsy has murder or love on her mind when she comes to the lord's castle one night. In *Die tote Tante: Eine erbauliche Begebenheit* (The Dead Aunt: An Edifying Event) Traugott Nägler's straitlaced, rigid, middle-class moral code is severely tested when he learns that his sister in South America has willed her fortune to his oldest daughter, provided that the daughter becomes the mother of an illegitimate child before her seventeenth birthday. Many years previously Nägler, a schoolteacher who rules his family with strict military discipline, severed all ties to his unmarried sister when she became pregnant. Even though he has denounced her all these years for her moral failure, the thought of getting her wealth is too tempting. In a hilarious scene he suggests to his daughter's uncomprehending boyfriend that it might be all right if they had a baby before their marriage. There is finally a somewhat contrived denouement, and the oldest daughter claims the inheritance. The question as to how a person's moral code stands up to the pressures of temptation could be the subject of serious drama, but Goetz makes sure that his aim of providing entertainment is not jeopardized.

In 1925 Goetz, a Swiss citizen by birth, purchased a house on Lake Thun in Merligen, Switzerland. The *New York Times* characterized his next play, *Hokuspokus* (1927), as "without question the most entertaining mystery play that Germany ever turned out." Agda Kjerulf is accused of having murdered her husband, Peer Bille, a circus-performer-turned-artist, who has disappeared during a boat trip. The high point of the play is the intellectual and rhetorical brilliance displayed by the prosecutor and the defense attorney, who, on the basis of the same evidence, have come to opposite conclusions. Agda is a woman of such beauty and charm that every man who meets her, including the judge, falls in love with her. In the end Peer reappears, and Agda's legal problems are over. *Hokuspokus* is amusing and intelligent; as the *New York Times* said, it is "a mystery drama for those who do not like to check their brain in the cloakroom." The play's commercial success enabled Goetz to form his own ensemble of actors and actresses that toured the German-speaking countries performing, for the most part, his works.

Der Lügner und die Nonne (The Liar and the Nun, 1929) begins with a prologue that satirizes trends in the German theater and lays down Goetz's own artistic goals. In an encounter between a playwright and a clairvoyant, the latter predicts the kind of play the writer is going to write during his vacation in the Swiss mountains. It is not going to be about politics and ideology; it will not take place among criminals, nor will it deal with prostitution. Rather, it will be a play about decent people in which no obscene language will be used. The clairvoyant further predicts that it will be an "Unterhaltungsstück" (entertaining, amusing play). When the ambitious writer indicates that entertainment might not be enough, the clairvoyant replies: "Ich weiß nicht, was Sie gegen ein Unterhaltungsstück haben!—Wenn sich die Leute den ganzen Tag über Politik, Krachs, Betrug und Stunk geärgert haben, dann wollen sie sich abends im Theater unterhalten" (I don't know what you have against an entertaining play!—After the people have been upset all day about politics, economic disasters, dishonesty and unpleasantness, they want to have a good time in the evening). In the play itself, Charly, the illegitimate son of a cardinal, himself becomes the father of an illegitimate child.

The mother of the child, a waitress, abandons the baby on the doorstep of a convent, where it is found by Angela, a novice. Angela wants to keep the child; believing that it will be taken from her, she tries to commit suicide by jumping into the river and is saved by Charly. The two fall in love and want to get married. The abbess objects, and the case is turned over to the cardinal. The cardinal is a humane and unorthodox clergyman who defends love—physical as well as spiritual—as a gift of God.

Dr. med. Hiob Prätorius, Facharzt für Chirurgie und Frauenleiden: Eine Geschichte ohne Politik nach alten aber guten Motiven neuerzählt (Job Prätorius, M.D., Specialist in Surgery and Gynecology: A Nonpolitical Story Based on Old but Proven Themes Told Anew; performed, 1932; published, 1934) consists of six loosely connected scenes. In scenes 1 and 6, which constitute the frame of the play, Sherlock Holmes and Dr. Watson are trying to solve the case of Dr. Prätorius and his wife, who have died under mysterious circumstances. There is a comic contrast between the brilliant master detective and his much slower friend. Scenes 2 through 5 are flashbacks to the life of Dr. Prätorius, a "superman" who can deliver extemporaneous speeches that are intellectual and rhetorical masterpieces; females, including his patients from ages eight to eighty, fall in love with him; he is an accomplished researcher and a fabulously successful, though unconventional, physician. His success leads to envy and accusations of wrongdoing, and Prätorius has to appear before a review board at the university. He is cleared of all charges. That evening, he and his wife die in a car accident on their way to the opera. But even that sad event is portrayed humorously: Prätorius hits a tree because he is laughing so hard about a witty remark of his wife. *Prätorius* was written in 1932, the worst year of the Great Depression in Germany, a time of near civil war when democracy was being challenged by extremists of the Left and the Right; but the play is strangely untouched by that turbulence. To the extent that criticism can be heard at all, it is directed in a general and always humorous way against envy, greed, and stupidity.

Not becoming directly involved in the political and ideological disputes of the time enabled Goetz—unlike many other writers and actors—to continue to work in Germany after the Nazis gained power in 1933. In addition, his Swiss citizenship gave him a feeling of freedom and security. He gave guest performances with his ensem-

Goetz with his second wife, Valérie von Martens, in the premiere of his operetta Zirkus Aimée *in Basel, 1932*

ble and continued his film work in Germany throughout the 1930s. After the exodus of so many talented artists, the Nazis welcomed the presence of a gifted and well-known person such as Goetz, who provided much-needed entertainment without trying to destabilize the regime. An example of such entertainment is the film *Napoleon ist an allem schuld* (It's All Napoleon's Fault; produced, 1938; published, 1968), for which Goetz functioned as writer, director, and star. An eccentric English lord who is a respected Napoleon scholar meets an attractive orphan girl at a congress of historians in Paris. Her adoption by the lord leads to comic misunderstandings and problems with his jealous wife. In the end, peace and harmony are restored. Obviously, the totalitarian state had no reason to be afraid of such a film.

Finally, disgusted by developments in Germany and worried about the imminent war, Goetz and his wife decided to leave Europe.

They arrived in New York City in February 1939 and moved on to Los Angeles, where Goetz became a screenwriter for Metro-Goldwyn-Mayer (MGM). But Hollywood was difficult for him: he was handicapped by his insufficient mastery of the English language; he found it difficult to get used to the modern production methods of the American movie industry, especially the teamwork and the division of labor; and he was not treated with the respect and admiration to which he had gotten accustomed. Goetz, who did not get screen credit for a single movie while working at MGM, soon left the company, bought a chicken farm in Van Nuys, and devoted himself to his literary work. He revised *Hokuspokus* and *Prätorius* to create more tightly knit plots and to remove elements that were dated or "too German." He also worked his one-act play *Die tote Tante* into the full-length *Das Haus in Montevideo oder Traugotts Versuchung: Eine Komödie im alten Stil über Moral, Versuchung und Belohnung der Tugend in vier Akten frei nach der "Toten Tante"* (The House in Montevideo; or, Traugott's Temptation: A Comedy in the Old Style about Morality, Temptation and the Reward of Virtue, in Four Acts, Based on "The Dead Aunt"; published, 1953). *Das Haus in Montevideo* was the only play Goetz managed to have performed during his American years. It was staged, without much success, on Broadway in March and April 1945 under the title *It's a Gift*, with Goetz and Martens in the leading roles. Not having the constant contact with the stage that he had had in Germany, Goetz turned to fiction in California, writing two short novels with American settings: *Tatjana: Eine Legende* (Tatjana: A Legend, 1946), the story of an obsessive love between an older man and a precocious, artistically gifted girl, and *Die Tote von Beverly Hills* (The Dead Woman from Beverly Hills, 1951), a murder mystery about a nymphomaniac. Goetz's America is, for the most part, a caricature where clichés abound, especially the contrast between the refined, sensitive, and cultured European exile and the boorish, materialistic American. During his California years Goetz also translated Coward's play *Blithe Spirit* (1941) into German as *Heitere Geister* (published, 1951); the play premiered at the respected Schauspielhaus (Playhouse) in Zurich on 8 November 1945.

Goetz and his wife returned to Europe in August 1946. On 31 October *Das Haus in Montevideo* premiered at the Schauspielhaus in Zurich, beginning the second phase of an illustrious career. Goetz established a new ensemble, and as soon as conditions in postwar Germany permitted he resumed his tours. In addition, he became involved in filmmaking again: he wrote the scripts for several film versions of his plays, and in the 1949 film version of *Prätorius* and the 1953 film version of *Hokuspokus* he and Martens played the leading roles. Goetz also got some belated recognition from Hollywood: he sold the movie rights to *Prätorius* to 20th Century-Fox, and a film, *People Will Talk*, that was based on the play was produced in 1951 with Cary Grant in the leading role.

In 1958 Goetz had three one-act plays published and produced under the title *Miniaturen* (Miniatures). In the first play, *Die Rache* (Revenge), Goetz combines his favorite topic, the love triangle, with a crime story. A lawyer is threatened by a former lover of his late wife who believes that the woman killed herself because of her supposedly unhappy marriage to the lawyer. The lawyer remains calm, composed, and witty

Goetz in the role of Dr. Traugott Nägler in a 1951 production of his play Das Haus in Montevideo

as he enlightens his rival about the true nature of his wife, who had many lovers. The tempestuous and passionate love between the lawyer and his wife is recalled in highly melodramatic fashion. *Herbst* (Autumn) is filled with the melancholy of old age, nostalgia for happier times, and regret about missed opportunities. A slightly senile but charming retired theater director strikes up a conversation with a lady on a park bench at a spa. He talks of the best time of his life, when he was in love with a beautiful young dancer; he wanted to marry her, but differences in social rank and age caused him to break off the relationship. The lady on the bench is the dancer; she does not tell him who she is because she does not wish to take anything away from his beautiful memories. The nostalgia for the "good old days" of imperial pre-World War I Germany probably appealed to Goetz's audiences in the 1950s. *Die Kommode* (The Chest of Drawers) takes place in a small town in Saxony before 1914. The director of the court theater shows up unexpectedly at the home of one of his employees to tell him that his talented daughter should become an actress. The petit bourgeois family of the employee is flattered and tries to impress the distinguished visitor, but all their attempts to look and act respectable fall apart when an elderly aunt who is living with them dies during the visit and a quarrel ensues among the relatives over who will inherit her chest of drawers. The ending, which is pure farce, serves as a humorous counterbalance to the somewhat melancholy endings of the other two plays.

Sämtliche Bühnenwerke (Collected Plays, 1963) contains two previously unpublished works. *Nichts Neues aus Hollywood: Ein vergeblicher Versuch zu übertreiben. In drei Akten* (Nothing New from Hollywood: A Futile Attempt to Exaggerate. In Three Acts; performed, 1956) is inspired by Goetz's experiences in the American film metropolis. Its main characters are a famous screenwriter and an actress whose passionate love for one another is complicated by jealousy. A birthday party for the screenwriter allows Goetz to present Hollywood society as characterized by shallowness, lack of refinement, greed, crass materialism, egocentricity, a strict hierarchical structure based on income, and brutal business practices. Two European exiles in the play provide a contrast to the Americans. Goetz's intense dislike of Hollywood prevents his play from being as entertaining as most of his other works.

The three one-act plays of *Seifenblasen* (Soap Bubbles) are framed by a prologue and an epilogue. In the prologue a theater director (Goetz gives him the name of his former boss, Victor Barnowsky) and a critic are deliberating as to what should be done to avert the bankruptcy of the theater when a man and woman enter the theater office, identify themselves as an American dramatist and his wife, and force the director and critic at gunpoint to listen to a reading of the man's three one-act plays. *Die Barcarole*, the first of the three plays, takes place in a theater on a night that *Hamlet* is being performed. During the intermission an actor is playing the barcarole from Jacques Offenbach's *The Tales of Hoffmann* (1881) on the piano; the other actors believe that something horrible will happen whenever this music is played and tell stories about their experiences. When enough suspense has thus been generated the actors playing Hamlet, the king, and Ophelia perform an impromptu play in rhymed verse dealing with a love triangle. It is obvious that "Hamlet" suspects "Ophelia" of having an affair with the "king" in real life and is terribly jealous. The play combines witty, frivolous playfulness and frightening seriousness, but in the end nothing horrible happens. In *Ausbruch des Weltfriedens* (Outbreak of World Peace) the British prime minister calls the ambassadors of major nations to a meeting at which a Dutch inventor tells them about his new invention: a Good Will Satellite that emits rays that cause humans to be happy, peaceful, and good. The diplomats' negative reaction becomes irrelevant when the satellite begins to operate. In no time bureaucratic pettiness, mistrust, and aggressiveness are gone. It is typical of Goetz that he avoids taking sides in the ideological battles of his time. *Die Bärengeschichte* (The Bear Story) is closely related to *Nichts Neues in Hollywood*. A screenwriter and his actress wife are hosting a birthday party in Hollywood at which the entire film industry appears to be present. The hosts are tired of Hollywood and are planning to retire to their house in the Black Forest; but when one of the movie executives, fascinated by the host's idea for a new film, makes him and his wife a fabulous offer, the couple decides to remain in Hollywood. The play portrays the kind of success that eluded Goetz and his wife during their years in California. In the epilogue to *Seifenblasen* the director is delighted with the plays and promises to stage them; the couple reveal that they are actually Germans who pretended to be Americans to further their chances of acceptance. In the 1950s interest in foreign, especially American, literature was strong in Germany as a result of the country's cultural isolation during the National Socialist period.

Goetz wrote three volumes of memoirs: *Die Memoiren des Peterhans von Binningen* (The Memoirs of Peterhans von Binningen, 1960), *Die Verwandlung des Peterhans von Binningen: Der Memoiren zweiter Teil* (The Transformation of Peterhans von Binningen: Second Part of the Memoirs, 1962), and *Wir wandern, wir wandern . . .* (We Wander, We Wander . . . , 1963). The second and third volumes were finished by Martens and published posthumously. The memoirs, which consist mainly of humorous anecdotes, are of limited interest to a reader who is interested in factual information about the author's life and work. They are written for the same purpose as all of Goetz's other works: to provide light entertainment.

In 1955 Goetz moved to Schaan, Liechtenstein. In 1958, the year of his seventieth birthday, he was made a member of the Academy of

Arts in West Berlin and awarded the Gutenberg Medal of the city of Mainz, and Prince Franz Joseph II of Liechtenstein bestowed on him the title of Professor, a great honor in German-speaking countries. He died in Grabs, Switzerland, on 12 September 1960 and was buried in Berlin, the city of his greatest triumphs.

References:

Sibylle Appel, *Die Funktion der Gesellschaftskomödie von 1910-1933 im europäischen Vergleich: Dargestellt an Beispielen aus Deutschland, England, Frankreich und Österreich-Ungarn bzw. Österreich und Ungarn* (Frankfurt am Main, Bern & New York: Lang, 1985);

Wolfgang Drews, "Curt Goetz," in *Jahresring: Beiträge zur deutschen Literatur und Kunst der Gegenwart* (Stuttgart: Deutsche Verlagsanstalt, 1961), pp. 314-318;

Wolfgang D. Elfe, "Curt Goetz," in *Deutsche Exilliteratur seit 1933*, part 1: *Kalifornien*, edited by John M. Spalek and Joseph Strelka (Bern & Munich: Francke, 1976), pp. 259-267;

Angelika Knecht, "Curt Goetz," Ph.D. dissertation, University of Vienna, 1970;

Valérie von Martens, ed., *Das große Curt Goetz-Album: Bilder eines Lebens* (Stuttgart: Deutsche Verlagsanstalt, 1968);

Horst Fuchs Richardson, "Comedy in the Works of Curt Goetz,'" Ph.D. dissertation, University of Connecticut, 1975;

Günter Scholdt, "'Timeo Danaos et dona ferentes' oder Die alte Dame kommt aus Montevideo: Zur Dramaturgie Friedrich Dürrenmatts und Curt Goetz," *Deutsche Vierteljahresschrift für Literaturwissenschaft und Geistesgeschichte*, 50 (1976): 720-730.

Papers:

The literary estate of Curt Goetz is divided among the Stiftung Deutsche Kinemathek (German Film Foundation), Berlin; Goetz's last residence, Fürst Johannes-Straße 73 in Schaan, Liechtenstein; and the office of the executor of his estate, Dr. Ernst Schmerschneider, Vienna.

Günter Grass
(16 October 1927 -   )

Sigrid Mayer
University of Wyoming

See also the Grass entry in *DLB 75: Contemporary German Fiction Writers, Second Series.*

PLAY PRODUCTIONS: *Hochwasser,* Frankfurt am Main, Neue Bühne, 19 January 1957;
Onkel, Onkel, Cologne, Bühnen der Stadt Köln, 3 March 1958;
Beritten hin und zurück: Vorspiel auf dem Theater, Frankfurt am Main, Neue Bühne, 16 January 1959;
Noch zehn Minuten bis Buffalo, Bochum, Schauspielhaus, 19 February 1959;
Stoffreste, music by Aribert Reimann, Essen, Stadttheater, February 1961;
Die bösen Köche, Berlin, Schiller-Theater, 16 February 1961; translated as *The Wicked Cooks,* New York, Orpheum Theater, 21 January 1967;
Mystisch—barbarisch—gelangweilt, Düsseldorf, Kammerspiele, 1963;
Goldmäulchen, Munich, Werkraumtheater, July 1964;
Die Plebejer proben den Aufstand, Berlin, Schiller-Theater, 15 January 1966; translated as *The Plebeians Rehearse the Uprising,* Rhode Island, Theatre Company of Boston, 7 September 1967;
The World of Günter Grass, adapted by Dennis Rosa, New York, Pocket Theatre, 26 April 1966;
Davor, Berlin, Schiller-Theater, 14 February 1969; translated as *Uptight,* Washington, D.C., Kreeger Theatre, 22 March 1972;
Die Vogelscheuchen, music by Reimann, Berlin, 1970.

BOOKS: *Die Vorzüge der Windhühner* (Berlin & Neuwied: Luchterhand, 1956);
Die Blechtrommel: Roman (Darmstadt, Berlin & Neuwied: Luchterhand, 1959); translated by Ralph Manheim as *The Tin Drum* (London: Secker & Warburg, 1962; New York: Pantheon, 1963);

O Susanna: Ein Jazzbilderbuch. Blues, Balladen, Spirituals, Jazz, German text by Grass, pictures by Horst Geldmacher, music by Hermann Wilson (Cologne & Berlin: Kiepenheuer & Witsch, 1959);
Stoffreste: Ballett in einem Akt, music by Aribert Reimann (Berlin: Bote und Bock, 1960);
Gleisdreieck (Darmstadt, Berlin & Neuwied: Luchterhand, 1960);
Katz und Maus: Eine Novelle (Neuwied & Berlin: Luchterhand, 1961); translated by Manheim as *Cat and Mouse* (New York: Harcourt, Brace & World, 1963; London: Secker & Warburg, 1963);
Hundejahre: Roman (Neuwied: Luchterhand, 1963); translated by Manheim as *Dog Years* (New York: Harcourt, Brace & World, 1965; London: Secker & Warburg, 1965);
Hochwasser: Ein Stück in zwei Akten (Frankfurt am Main: Suhrkamp, 1963);
Die Ballerina (Berlin: Friedenauer Presse, 1963);
Onkel, Onkel: Ein Spiel in vier Akten. Mit neun Zeichnungen des Autors (Berlin: Wagenbach, 1965);
Rede über das Selbstverständliche (Neuwied & Berlin: Luchterhand, 1965);
Dich singe ich, Demokratie (Neuwied & Berlin: Luchterhand, 1965);
Die Plebejer proben den Aufstand: Ein deutsches Trauerspiel (Neuwied & Berlin: Luchterhand, 1966); translated by Manheim as *The Plebeians Rehearse the Uprising: A German Tragedy* (New York: Harcourt, Brace & World, 1966; London: Secker & Warburg, 1967);
Ausgefragt: Gedichte und Zeichnungen (Neuwied & Berlin: Luchterhand, 1967);
Der Fall Axel Springer am Beispiel Arnold Zweig: Eine Rede, ihr Anlass und die Folgen (Berlin: Voltaire, 1967);
Über meinen Lehrer Döblin und andere Vorträge (Berlin: Literarisches Colloquium, 1968);
Über das Selbstverständliche: Reden, Aufsätze, offene Briefe, Kommentare (Neuwied: Luchterhand, 1968);

Günter Grass (photograph by Marianne Fleitmann)

Briefe über die Grenze: Versuch eines Ost-West-Dialogs, by Grass and Pavel Kohout (Hamburg: Wegner, 1968);

Geschichten, as Artur Knoff (Berlin: Literarisches Colloquium, 1968);

örtlich betäubt: Roman (Neuwied: Luchterhand, 1969); translated by Manheim as *Local Anaesthetic* (New York: Harcourt, Brace & World, 1970; London: Secker & Warburg, 1970);

Die Schweinekopfsülze (Hamburg: Merlin, 1969);

Freiheit: Ein Wort wie Löffelstiel [by Grass]; *Gegen Gewalt und Unmenschlichkeit* [by Paul Schallück]: *Zwei Reden zur Woche der Brüderlichkeit* (Cologne: Schäuble, 1969);

Theaterspiele (Neuwied: Luchterhand, 1970)—comprises *Hochwasser*; *Onkel, Onkel*; *Noch zehn Minuten bis Buffalo*; *Die bösen Köche*; *Die Plebejer proben den Aufstand*; *Davor*; *Davor* translated by Manheim as *Max: A Play* (New York: Harcourt Brace Jovanovich, 1972);

Demokratie und Sozialismus 1971, by Grass, H. P. Tschudi, and A. Schmid (Bern: SPS, 1971);

Gesammelte Gedichte (Neuwied: Luchterhand, 1971);

Aus dem Tagebuch einer Schnecke (Neuwied: Luch-

terhand, 1972); translated by Manheim as *From the Diary of a Snail* (New York: Harcourt Brace Jovanovich, 1973; London: Secker & Warburg, 1974);

Der Schriftsteller als Bürger—Eine siebenjahresbilanz (Vienna: Dr. Karl Renner-Institut, 1973);

Mariazuehren; *Hommageàmarie*; *Inmarypraise* (Munich: Bruckman, 1973); *Inmarypraise* translated by Christopher Middleton (New York: Harcourt Brace Jovanovich, 1973);

Liebe geprüft: Sieben Gedichte mit sieben Radierungen (Bremen: Schünemann, 1974); translated by Michael Hamburger as *Love Tested: Seven Poems with Seven Etchings* (New York: Harcourt Brace Jovanovich, 1975);

Der lesende Arbeiter; *Bildungsurlaub: Zwei Reden vor Gewerkschaften*, Schriftenreihe der Industriegewerkschaft Druck und Papier, No. 23 (Bonlanden: Weinman, 1974);

Der Bürger und seine Stimme: Reden, Aufsätze, Kommentare (Darmstadt & Neuwied: Luchterhand, 1974);

Radierungen 1972-1974 (Berlin: Galerie Andre, Anselm Dreher, 1975);

Mit Sophie in die Pilze gegangen: Gedichte und Lithographien (Mailand: Grafica Uno, 1976);

Der Butt: Roman (Darmstadt & Neuwied: Luchterhand, 1977); translated by Manheim as *The Flounder* (New York: Harcourt Brace Jovanovich, 1978; London: Secker & Warburg, 1978);

Die bösen Köche: Ein Drama in 5 Akten. Mit 5 Reproduktionen nach Radierungen des Autors (Stuttgart: Reclam, 1978);

Denkzettel: Politische Reden und Aufsätze (Darmstadt & Neuwied: Luchterhand, 1978);

50 erfolgreiche Musterreden für betriebliche Veranstaltungen, Jubiläen, Betriebsversammlungen, Trauerfälle und andere Anlässe: Mit Benutzungshinweisen und Zitatenschatz (Kissing: WEKA, 1978);

Zeit-Gespräche, 2 volumes, by Grass, Fritz J. Raddatz, and others, edited by Raddatz (Frankfurt am Main: Suhrkamp, 1978-1982);

Das Treffen in Telgte: Eine Erzählung (Darmstadt & Neuwied: Luchterhand, 1979); translated by Manheim as *The Meeting at Telgte* (New York: Harcourt Brace Jovanovich, 1981; London: Secker & Warburg, 1981);

Die Blechtrommel als Film, by Grass and Volker Schlöndorff (Frankfurt am Main: Zweitausendeins, 1979);

Werkverzeichnis der Radierungen (Berlin: Dreher, 1979-1980);

Kopfgeburten oder Die Deutschen sterben aus (Darmstadt & Neuwied: Luchterhand, 1980); translated by Manheim as *Headbirths; or, The Germans Are Dying Out* (New York: Harcourt Brace Jovanovich, 1982);

Aufsätze zur Literatur (Darmstadt & Neuwied: Luchterhand, 1980);

Danziger Trilogie (Darmstadt & Neuwied: Luchterhand, 1980)—comprises *Die Blechtrommel, Katz und Maus, Hundejahre*; translated by Manheim as *The Danzig Trilogy* (San Diego: Harcourt Brace Jovanovich / New York: Pantheon, 1987);

Nachruf auf einen Handschuh: Sieben Radierungen und ein Gedicht (Berlin: Galerie Andre, Anselm Dreher, 1982);

Zeichnungen und Texte 1954-1977: Zeichnen und Schreiben I, edited by Anselm Dreher (Darmstadt & Neuwied: Luchterhand, 1982); translated by Hamburger and others as *Drawings and Words 1954-1977: Graphics and Writing I* (San Diego: Harcourt Brace Jovanovich, 1983);

Bin ich nun Schreiber oder Zeichner? (Regensburg: Schürer, 1982);

Kinderlied (Northridge, Cal.: Lord John Press, 1982);

Ach Butt, dein Märchen geht böse aus: Gedichte und Radierungen (Darmstadt & Neuwied: Luchterhand, 1983);

Die Vernichtung der Menschheit hat begonnen: Rede anläßlich der Verleihung des Feltrinelli-Preises am 25. November 1982 (Hauzenberg: Pongratz, 1983);

Widerstand Lernen: Politische Gegenreden 1980-1983 (Darmstadt & Neuwied: Luchterhand, 1984);

Radierungen und Texte 1972-1982: Zeichnen und Schreiben II, edited by Dreher (Darmstadt & Neuwied: Luchterhand, 1984); translated by Hamburger and others as *Etchings and Words 1972-1982: Graphics and Writing II* (San Diego: Harcourt Brace Jovanovich, 1985);

Nachdenken über Deutschland: Stefan Heym und Günter Grass diskutierten am 21. November 1984 in Brüssel (Berlin & Brussels: Dorothea Hartung und Anton Regenberg Goethe-Institut Brüssel, 1984);

Geschenkte Freiheit: Rede zum 8. Mai 1945 (Berlin: Akademie der Künste, 1985);

Die Rättin: 3 Radierungen und 1 Gedicht (Homburg: Beck, 1985);

In Kupfer, auf Stein (Göttingen: Steidl, 1986);

Die Rättin (Darmstadt & Neuwied: Luchterhand, 1986); translated by Manheim as *The Rat* (San Diego: Harcourt Brace Jovanovich, 1987);

Werkausgabe in zehn Bänden, 10 volumes (Darmstadt & Neuwied: Luchterhand, 1987)—comprises volume 1, *Gedichte und Kurzprosa*; volume 2, *Die Blechtrommel*; volume 3, *Katz und Maus*; *Hundejahre*; volume 4, *örtlich betäubt*; *Aus dem Tagebuch einer Schnecke*; volume 5, *Der Butt*; volume 6, *Das Treffen in Telgte*; *Kopfgeburten oder Die Deutschen sterben aus*; volume 7, *Die Rättin*; volume 8, *Theaterspiele* includes *Beritten hin und zurück: Vorspiele auf dem Theater*, translated by Michael Benedikt and Joseph Goradza as *Rocking Back and Forth* in *Postwar German Theatre*, edited by Benedikt and George E. Wellwarth (New York: Dutton, 1967), pp. 261-275; volume 9, *Essays, Reden, Briefe, Kommentare*; volume 10, *Gespräche*;

Hundert Zeichnungen 1955-1987, edited by Jens Christian Jensen (Kiel: Kunsthalle zu Kiel und Schleswig-Holsteinischer Kunstverein, 1987);

Radierungen, Lithographien, Zeichnungen, Plastiken, Gedichte (Berlin: Kunstamt, 1987);

Die Gedichte 1955-1986 (Darmstadt: Luchterhand, 1988);

Zunge zeigen (Darmstadt: Luchterhand, 1988); translated by John E. Woods as *Show Your Tongue* (San Diego: Harcourt Brace Jovanovich, 1989);

Calcutta: Zeichnungen (Bremen: Kunsthalle Bremen, 1988);

Alptraum und Hoffnung: Zwei Reden vor dem Club of Rome (Göttingen: Steidl, 1989)—comprises "Globale Industrialisierung—Entdeckungen und Verluste des Geistes," by Tschingis Aitmatow; "Zum Beispiel Calcutta," by Grass;

Skizzenbuch (Göttingen: Steidl, 1989);

Wenn wir von Europa sprechen: Ein Dialog, by Grass and Françoise Giroud (Frankfurt am Main: Luchterhand, 1989);

Meine grüne Wiese: Kurzprosa (Zurich: Manesse, 1989);

Deutscher Lastenausgleich: Wider das dumpfe Einheitsgebot. Reden und Gespräche (Frankfurt am Main: Luchterhand, 1990);

Tierschutz: Gedichte (Ravensburg: Maier, 1990);

Deutschland, einig Vaterland? Ein Streitgespräch, by Grass and Rudolf Augstein (Göttingen: Steidl, 1990); translated by Krishna Winston and A. S. Wensiger as *Two States—One Nation?* (San Diego: Harcourt Brace Jovanovich, 1990);

Ein Schnäppchen namens DDR: Letzte Reden vorm Glockengeläut (Frankfurt am Main: Luchterhand, 1990);

Schreiben nach Auschwitz: Frankfurter Poetik-Vorlesung (Frankfurt am Main: Luchterhand, 1990);

Totes Holz: Ein Nachruf (Göttingen: Steidl, 1990);

Gegen die verstreichende Zeit: Reden, Aufsätze und Gespräche 1989-1991 (Hamburg & Zurich: Luchterhand, 1991);

Vier Jahrzehnte: Ein Werkstattbericht, edited by G. Fritze Margull (Göttingen: Steidl, 1991);

Unkenrufe: Eine Erzählung (Göttingen: Steidl, 1992).

Editions in English: *Selected Poems*, translated by Michael Hamburger and Christopher Middleton (New York: Harcourt, Brace & World, 1966; London: Secker & Warburg, 1966);

Four Plays, translated by Ralph Manheim and A. Leslie Willson, introduction by Martin Esslin (New York: Harcourt, Brace & World, 1967; London: Secker & Warburg, 1968)—

comprises *Flood*; *Mister, Mister (Onkel, Onkel!* in British edition*)*; *Only Ten Minutes to Buffalo*; *The Wicked Cooks*;

New Poems, translated by Hamburger (New York: Harcourt, Brace & World, 1968);

Speak Out! Speeches, Open Letters, Commentaries, translated by Manheim and others (New York: Harcourt, Brace & World, 1969; London: Secker & Warburg, 1969);

Poems of Günter Grass, translated by Hamburger and Middleton (Harmondsworth, U.K.: Penguin, 1969);

In the Egg and Other Poems, translated by Hamburger and Middleton (New York: Harcourt Brace Jovanovich, 1977; London: Secker & Warburg, 1978);

The Flounder: Written and Illustrated by Günter Grass, 3 volumes, translated by Manheim (New York: Limited Editions Club, 1985);

On Writing and Politics 1967-1983, translated by Manheim (San Diego: Harcourt Brace Jovanovich, 1985; London: Secker & Warburg, 1985).

RADIO: *Zweiunddreißig Zähne*, Süddeutscher Rundfunk, 1959;

Eine öffentliche Diskussion, HR-Frankfurt, 4 November 1963;

Goldmäulchen, Hessischer Rundfunk, 1963.

OTHER: *Die bösen Köche*, in *Modernes deutsches Theater 1*, edited by Paul Pörtner (Neuwied & Berlin: Luchterhand, 1961), pp. 5-72;

Ingeborg Bachmann, *Ein Ort für Zufälle*, drawings by Grass (Berlin: Wagenbach, 1965);

Heli Ihlefeld, ed., *Anekdoten um Willy Brandt*, foreword by Grass (Eßlingen: Bechtle, 1968);

H. Schreiber and F. Sommer, *Gustav Heinemann: Bundespräsident*, foreword by Grass (Frankfurt am Main: Fischer, 1969);

E. Jäckel, ed., *Deutsche Parlamentsdebatten*, volume 3: *1949-1970*, foreword by Grass (Frankfurt am Main: Fischer, 1971);

Wolfgang Mieder, ed., *Mädchen, pfeif auf den Prinzen! Märchengedichte von Günter Grass bis Sarah Kirsch*, contributions by Grass (Cologne: Diederichs, 1983);

Erwin Lichtenstein, *Bericht an meine Familie: Ein Leben zwischen Danzig und Israel*, afterword by Grass (Darmstadt & Neuwied: Luchterhand, 1985);

Der Traum der Vernunft: Vom Elend der Aufklärung, foreword by Grass (Darmstadt & Neuwied: Luchterhand, 1985);

Der Traum der Vernunft: Vom Elend der Aufklärung. Zweite Folge, foreword by Grass (Darmstadt & Neuwied: Luchterhand, 1986);

Karsten Schröder, *Egon Bahr*, foreword by Grass (Rastatt: Moewig, 1989).

Günter Grass, although best known for his fiction, has also had a significant career as a playwright. Some of his most original plays were conceived between 1953 and 1959, before the publication of his best-selling novel *Die Blechtrommel* (1959; translated as *The Tin Drum*, 1962).

Grass was born in Danzig (now Gdansk, Poland) on 16 October 1927 to middle-class parents, Willy and Helena Knoff Grass. He attended school until 1944, when he was drafted into the military. He was wounded near Cottbus in 1945 and ended the war in an American prisoner-of-war camp in Bavaria. After his release the not yet eighteen-year-old Grass worked in a potash mine. In 1946 he found his parents and sister, who had left Gdansk and were living in miserable refugee conditions in West Germany. Grass decided to become a sculptor; he found the academy of fine arts in Düsseldorf partially destroyed and closed, but he entered into an apprenticeship as a stonemason for a local cemetery. A Franciscan shelter for students and old people was his home until 1951. Throughout this time he was constantly writing poetry and drawing. In 1948 he began attending classes at the Düsseldorf academy; he also traveled through France and Italy. He went to Berlin on 1 January 1953 to find a new art teacher; what he actually found there was his personal "tone" in poetry. The result was his first book of poems and drawings, *Die Vorzüge der Windhühner* (The Advantages of Windfowl, 1956). His 1954 marriage to a ballet dancer, Anna Schwarz, led him to write three ballet librettos around this time. The ballet *Die Vogelscheuchen* (Scarecrows), written in 1957, was included in Grass's novel *Hundejahre* (1963; translated as *Dog Years*, 1965) but was not performed until 1970.

In 1955 Grass had won third prize in a poetry contest. This award led to an invitation by Hans Werner Richter to take part in the readings of Gruppe 47 (Group 47), a workshop for writers, whose prize he won in 1958 for a reading from the manuscript for *Die Blechtrommel*. Some of the more prestigious awards that followed in the decades to come were the French literature prize for the best foreign book for *Die Blechtrommel* in 1962, the Georg Büchner prize in 1965, the Fontane prize in 1968, the Alexander Maiakowsky medal and the international literature prize Viareggio in 1978, an honorary doctorate from Harvard University in 1976, the Feltrinelli Prize in 1982, and the Premio Grinzane Cavour in 1992. In 1978 Grass, in connection with the Berlin Academy of Arts and Letters, endowed the Alfred Döblin prize. In 1976, together with Heinrich Böll and Carola Stern, he founded the journal *L'76*; it is now published as *L'80*. In 1978 he was divorced from Anna Grass; he married the organist Ute Grunert in 1979.

The stylistic and thematic parallels between Grass's early drawings, poems, metal sculptures, and plays are striking. The world of "things," of objects, holds fascination for him and comes alive as if independent of the human realm. This world comprises animals, such as birds, toads, snails, and zebras, and artifacts, such as dolls, trumpets, and spoons. The human figures, where they occur, are subordinated to the world of objects.

Grass's one-act play *Beritten hin und zurück* (performed, 1959; published, 1987; translated as *Rocking Back and Forth*, 1967) was written in 1954. The play is subtitled *Vorspiel auf dem Theater* (Prelude in the Theatre) in allusion to the "Vorspiel auf dem Theater" of Johann Wolfgang von Goethe's *Faust I* (1808). A theater director, a playwright, and an actor are trying to use the clown Conelli to inspire a new kind of play, but the clown cannot be separated from his rocking horse, Ingeborg. Try as they might to attune the clown to their ideas, the three fail to interrupt his rocking or to enter his world, in which objects and animals replace persons. After various attempts at plot construction fail because Conelli insists that people are rabbits playing dead, that the actor's wife is a mouse hiding in bed, and that a zebra is the perfect piano player, the playwright is forced to return to the initial situation of the clown on his rocking horse. This scenario might lead to the lynching of the clown by the masses; the last act would show his funeral. At this point the clown spurs his horse to full rocking speed lest they be late for the funeral: the cemetery gates might be closed, he says, and the people unable to place their wreaths; they might miss the party afterward and the performance for children at five o'clock. Here the director and playwright consult their watches with worried expressions. Grass's rejection of fashionable avant-garde theater is apparent in this experiment, as is his renunciation of the usual dramatic action. In retrospect, the clown obsessed with the rocking rhythms of his toy horse can be perceived as a forerunner of Oskar Matzerath, obsessed with the rhythmic language of his tin drum in *Die Blechtrommel*.

A quality of stasis or lack of "action" also characterizes the two-act play *Hochwasser* (performed, 1957; published, 1963; translated as *Flood*, 1967) written in 1955. The play is paralleled by a poem of the same title in *Die Vorzüge der Windhühner*. But while the speaking persona of the poem is simply "wir" (we), the play consists of seven characters representing an older and a younger generation, plus a couple of rats. The stage is divided into the three levels of a house: the cellar, a room, and the flat roof. The owner of the house is Noah; his generational counterpart is Betty, his sister-in-law. The younger generation consists of Noah's son and daughter, the daughter's fiancé, and the son's friend Kongo. An official damage assessor steps out of a grandfather clock in the last scene of the play. The play shows the typical reactions of the residents of the house to the flood. Noah and Betty's reaction focuses on the past, its memories, and objects such as the photo albums and an inkwell collection they move up from the cellar. For them the flood is a mere transitional stage to a future that will be like the past. In anticipation of this future Betty sews parasols while the rain continues and the water rises to the rooftop. Meanwhile, the men of the younger generation make plans to go to the North Pole to experience their dream of ice. Temporarily involved in a love affair with her brother's friend, only the daughter is enchanted by the present: she wants to lose herself floating in the flood and resents all reminders of the past or portents of the future. Thus, the flood causes no changes in their behavior or aspirations; the world following the great flood will be as hopelessly doomed as the one that preceded it. An outside perspective on this world is provided by the rats Strich (Point) and Perle (Pearl). They have taken shelter on the roof, where they comment on and imitate human behavior. As in the poem "Saturn" in *Gleisdreieck* (Three Rail Junction, 1960) and in the 1986 novel *Die Rättin* (translated as *The Rat*, 1987), the rats in *Hochwasser* are juxtaposed with the dove, the false messenger of peace at the end of the Great Flood. Some of the parallels between this early play and the 1986 novel inspired a new production of *Hochwasser* in Germany.

Onkel, Onkel (Uncle, Uncle; performed, 1958; published, 1965; translated as *Mister, Mis-*

ter, 1967) was written in 1956. The play consists of four independent acts, each with a prologue and a title: "Die Grippe" (Influenza), "Der Kuckuck" (The Cuckoo), "Die Primadonna" (The Prima Donna), and "Onkel, Onkel." These four acts are strung together by the protagonist Bollin, called "ein Systematiker" (a Systematizer), an obsessive-compulsive mass murderer.

In the first three acts "Systematiker" Bollin is prevented from carrying out his crimes by three unsuspecting victims. In "Die Grippe" Sophie, a sixteen-year-old patient under whose bed he is hiding, warns him insistently of the dangers of infection. In "Der Kuckuck" a forester who has been lured into a pit by Bollin starts lecturing two mischievous children—and, incidentally, his would-be murderer—about the local species of conifers. The prima donna is only too happy to crown her career by being murdered—in the presence of a photographer—in a gilt bathtub, but she drives the murderer away with her arias and love proposals. In the last act the children, who call Bollin "Onkel," talk him out of his watch, his pen, and his revolver and shoot him dead playing with the gun. It has been suggested that Grass is saying that society fosters criminality. Yet the murderer himself becomes a pathetic figure, frustrated in each encounter with a potential victim; only by stabbing and shooting Sophie's doll Pinkie can he prove himself superior. As a "Systematiker" he feels obliged to educate himself about the dangers of infection, about the local forests, and about opera; yet for all his statistics he is doomed to fall victim to the craftiness of a couple of street children. The play is an indictment of the relentless bureaucratic system, with its rigid adherence to statistics and occupational norms. The neglected street children, on the other hand, with their lack of concepts and stubborn insistence on "things," slip through the holes in the system.

In 1957 Grass wrote the one-act play *Noch zehn Minuten bis Buffalo* (performed, 1959; published, 1970; translated as *Only Ten Minutes to Buffalo*, 1967), a favorite of student theaters. The title is derived from a nineteenth-century ballad by Theodor Fontane in which John Maynard, the helmsman of a burning ship crossing Lake Erie, saves all the lives except his own. In contrast to the ballad, where time is of the essence—as expressed by the repeated announcements of the "minuten" (minutes) to safety—the central object in Grass's play is a rusty locomotive occupied by the engineer Krudewil and the fireman

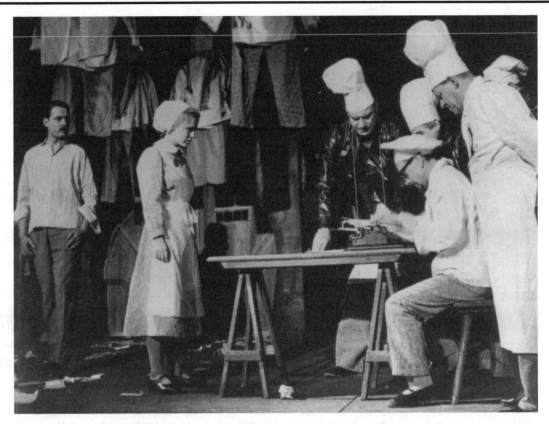

Scene from the premiere of Grass's Die bösen Köche *at the Schiller-Theater in Berlin on 16 February 1961*

Pempelfort. Although they are standing still, they believe themselves to be traveling to Buffalo at high speed, they fear running out of fuel, and they argue and fight. In the foreground of the stage the artist Kotschenreuther paints a picture of a frigate, perceiving the cows in the landscape as sailboats. A cowherd, Axel, is watching him curiously. Each character perceives a different picture in the same scenery. The perspectives come full circle when Krudewil and Pempelfort discover a "Frigate" on the tracks ahead: a huge woman in an admiral's uniform, she is the commander of the sailboat from which they deserted. Frigate now takes over; Krudewil and Pempelfort, miming the rowing of a boat, leave the stage with Frigate commanding from the "stern." The painter, too, leaves the stage when he is informed by Pempelfort that minutes ago he saw another artist painting a frigate. The cowherd climbs into the engine cab, decides to visit Buffalo, and drives the locomotive off the stage while Krudewil's pistol explodes in the smokestack.

The five-act play *Die bösen Köche* (performed, 1961; published, 1972; translated as *The Wicked Cooks*, 1967) ends the first phase of

Grass's work for the theater. It was written in Paris in 1956-1957 while Grass was working on *Die Blechtrommel*. The first American performance took place at the Orpheum Theater in New York in January 1967 under the direction of Vasek Simek; the reviews agreed that the performance was too loud, too violent, and too confusing. In a 1970 student performance at Middlebury College the play was interpreted as an allegory of the Nazi period.

The motif of cooks pervades Grass's graphic and literary work. In the play the cooks' white caps are juxtaposed with black or gray elements. In the first act Petri, the chief cook, produces his underlings: Benny is pushed out of a large trumpet; Grün is born, equipped with two frying pans, from a huge white egg; Vasco is unearthed from a mountain of salt; finally, Stach emerges from a dense snowfall. The cooks, standing under a black canopy, sing "Die Nacht ist voller Köche" (The Night Is Full of Cooks). Herbert Schymanski, nicknamed "der Graf" (the Count), appears in lamplight, preparing to mail a letter. He is supposedly in possession of a unique recipe for a soup popular with the guests of a restaurant owned by someone named Schuster. To keep their jobs the cooks have to get the recipe. But the Count will not reveal it; he only mentions that he adds some gray ashes to a simple cabbage soup, whence it is referred to as gray soup. Vasco has a private conversation with the Count and is therefore regarded suspiciously by the other cooks. He is also the only one with a girlfriend, the nurse Martha. In the second act Vasco is summoned by his dying and domineering aunt, who wants to convert him to orthodox religion. Vasco finds it hard not to count along with the frequent calls of her cuckoo clock. In the third act the cooks resort to extortion to get Vasco to confess, but the Count enters and teases Petri and Grün. Kletterer, a soup kitchen cook, wants to be in on the party the cooks plan for Martha and the Count. The party takes place in the fourth act in the drying room of a laundry. Kletterer, armed with Petri's trumpet, and a mob of his cooks force their way in and threaten the Count. But Vasco exposes the Count as a shy man who is really in love with Martha. A contract is drawn up to let the Count live with her for a while in exchange for the recipe. In the fifth act Martha and the Count return to his country house from a walk, take off their boots, and are washing each other's feet when the cooks, with Kletterer in the lead, climb over the fence. When they demand the recipe the Count explains that he has forgotten it; and anyway no one can cook the same soup twice. The cooks wait outside while the couple think the matter over. Two pistol shots ring out from the house; the Count and Martha have committed suicide. Vasco runs away; the other cooks follow. The chase after the secret recipe has become an end in itself.

The play lends itself to a variety of interpretations. For example, the Count may be seen as an outsider resisting a political system, as a Christ figure, or as the true artist among opportunists. The critical argument with regard to all of Grass's plays from the 1950s revolved for some time around the question whether they were examples of theater of the absurd. Peter Spycher argues convincingly that *Die bösen Köche*, at least, is a poetic allegory rather than absurdist theater.

In 1966 Grass's popularity in the United States led to the production of *The World of Günter Grass* at the Pocket Theatre in New York. Selections from his novels and the scene with the two rats from *Hochwasser* were adapted for the stage by Dennis Rosa, who directed the production. The play included ragtime music by Ryan

Edwards based on Wagnerian themes. Reviews agreed that this staging of Grass's work did him a disservice, while productions of his own plays in America were overdue.

The second phase of Grass's stage works comprises two plays. The four-act *Die Plebejer proben den Aufstand* (1966; translated as *The Plebeians Rehearse the Uprising*, 1967) represents a break with Grass's image-oriented theater of the 1950s and a return to the more traditional German theater of ideas. *Die Plebejer proben den Aufstand* became the most controversial and the most frequently performed and translated of Grass's plays. The play is set on 17 June 1953, during the uprising of workers in East Berlin against higher work norms imposed by the Communist party and East German government. A director, "der Chef" (the boss)—based on Bertolt Brecht—is rehearsing the uprising of the plebeians in *Coriolanus* inside his theater while the actual uprising of the workers is taking place outside. Der Chef and his actors never leave the artificial environment of the theater; all the revolutionary action is reported by workers coming in from the outside in search of support from the man whose lifework had been committed to the workers. The play was misinterpreted by many audiences of the 1960s as a personal attack on Brecht; a close analysis of the text shows, however, that no indictment of the historical Brecht is implied. On the contrary, der Chef is credited with more political foresight than most of the other personae, including the workers whose demands he cannot translate into a manifesto. (The real Brecht wrote a carefully worded letter to the authorities in which he objected to the suppression of the uprising; but only the last sentence of the letter, in which he expressed solidarity with the party, was published.) The conflict attributed to Brecht was in no small measure that of Grass himself as he tried to balance an active political role with his career as a writer and artist.

In Germany, *Die Plebejer proben den Aufstand* was confused, especially by the student Left, with the "documentary theater" prevalent in the 1960s. It appears from the reviews of the first American production of the play by the Theater Company of Boston that in addition to inadequacies of the casting and performance, the main problem for the audience was one of credibility. One question was asked time and again: "Was Brecht like this?" When the first performance in London took place in 1970, however, *The Plebeians Rehearse the Uprising* was described by the *Ob-*

server as "the richest, most complex and sardonic play to come out of Germany in the past decade." The first productions of the play were still too close to the historical facts; as the fictionality of the play increases with time, the universality of its tragic conflict becomes more apparent.

Davor (Before the Act; performed, 1969; published, 1970; translated as *Max: A Play*, 1972) was written at the same time as Grass's novel *örtlich betäubt* (1969; translated as *Local Anaesthetic*, 1970) and dramatizes the middle part of the novel. *Davor* revolves around a student and teacher's arguments over the appropriate means of protest against the Vietnam War. While the student plans a public protest burning of his beloved dog, the middle-aged teacher undergoes dental treatments. The dog, however, is not burned, and the student winds up in the dentist's chair. Although it was unsuccessful at its premiere in Berlin, the play was repeated at theaters throughout the Federal Republic of Germany. A 1972 production of the English version, *Uptight*, in Washington, D.C., was described as "thoroughly entertaining." Although the play is all dialogue and nothing really happens in it, the use of a rock band, bicycles, and other diversions prevented the audience from getting "bogged down in Grass's philosophical complexities," according to the *Saturday Review*.

Grass seems to have been more successful with his theater of ideas than with his early theater of objects. Both phases of his work for the stage were misunderstood in terms of the prevalent contemporary trends, as "theater of the absurd" and as "documentary theater," respectively. Although he has not written a play since *Davor*, and for the most part has kept his distance from the theater (as he announced that he would after *Die bösen Koche* and again after *Die Plebejer proben den Aufstand*), the stage was his first and, for a time, his favorite medium of expression. Some remarks in his book *Zunge zeigen* (1988; translated as *Show Your Tongue*, 1989), where he says that he could be tempted to write a play for the director and the actors of the 1970 Bengali production of *Die Plebejer proben den Aufstand* to be performed in one of Calcutta's three thousand slums, indicate that he might yet return to this medium.

Bibliographies:

George A. Everett, *A Select Bibliography of Günter Grass (From 1956 to 1973)* (New York: Franklin, 1974);

Patrick O'Neill, *Günter Grass: A Bibliography 1955-1975* (Toronto: University of Toronto Press, 1976).

References:

Heinz Ludwig Arnold, ed., *text + kritik 1/1a: Günter Grass*, fifth edition (Munich: Edition text + kritik, 1978);

Arnold and Franz Josef Görtz, eds., *Günter Grass: Dokumente zur politischen Wirkung* (Munich: Edition text + kritik, 1971);

Hanspeter Brode, *Günter Grass* (Munich: Beck, 1979);

Ronald Bryden, "Germany's Tragedy," *Observer* (London), 26 July 1970, p. 24;

Nicole Casanova, *Günter Grass: Atelier des métamorphoses* (Paris: Belfond, 1979);

Gertrude Cepl-Kaufmann, *Günter Grass: Eine Analyse des Gesamtwerkes unter dem Aspekt von Literatur und Politik* (Kronberg: Scriptor, 1975);

Louis Chapin, "World of Günter Grass," *Christian Science Monitor* (Midwestern Edition), 2 May 1966, p. 6;

W. Gordon Cunliffe, *Günter Grass* (New York: Twayne, 1969);

Manfred Durzak, ed., *Interpretationen zu Günter Grass: Geschichte auf dem poetischen Prüfstand* (Stuttgart: Klett, 1985);

Frederic Ewen, "Alas, Poor Bertolt Brecht!," *Nation*, 204 (13 February 1967), 213-214;

Rolf Geissler, ed., *Günter Grass: Ein Materialienbuch* (Neuwied: Luchterhand, 1976);

Franz Josef Görtz, ed., *Günter Grass: Auskunft für Leser* (Neuwied: Luchterhand, 1984);

Ronald Hayman, *Günter Grass* (London: Methuen, 1985);

Henry Hewes, "Distal and Proximal Bite," *Saturday Review*, 55 (20 May 1972): 62-63;

Hewes, "Grass on Brecht," *Saturday Review*, 51 (14 September 1968): 117;

Manfred Jurgensen, ed., *Grass: Kritik—Thesen—Analysen* (Bern: Francke, 1973);

Stanley Kauffmann, "The World of Günter Grass," *New York Times*, 27 April 1966, p. 38;

Alan Frank Keele, *Understanding Günter Grass* (Columbia: University of South Carolina Press, 1988);

Richard H. Lawson, *Günter Grass* (New York: Ungar, 1985);

Irene Leonhard, *Günter Grass* (New York: Barnes & Noble, 1974);

Gert Loschütz, ed., *Von Buch zu Buch—Günter Grass in der Kritik: Eine Dokumentation* (Neuwied: Luchterhand, 1968);

Ann L. Mason, *The Skeptical Muse: A Study of Günter Grass' Conception of the Artist* (Bern: Lang, 1974);

Keith Miles, *Günter Grass* (New York: Barnes & Noble, 1975);

Volker Neuhaus, *Günter Grass* (Stuttgart: Metzler, 1979);

Neuhaus and Daniela Hermes, eds., *Günter Grass im Ausland* (Frankfurt am Main: Luchterhand, 1990);

Julius Novick, "Was Brecht Like This?" *New York Times*, 8 September 1968, p. 11;

Edith Oliver, "Bravo Pour Le Clown," *New Yorker*, 42 (4 February 1967): pp. 93-94;

Patrick O'Neill, ed., *Critical Essays on Günter Grass* (Boston: Hall, 1987);

Henry Popkin, "Mr. Brecht Over a Big Barrel," *Life*, 60 (18 February 1966): 17;

Kurt Lothar Tank, *Günter Grass* (Berlin: Colloquium, 1965); translated by John Conway (New York: Ungar, 1969);

Peter Spycher, "Die bösen Köche von Günter Grass—ein 'absurdes' Drama?," *Germanisch-Romanische Monatsschrift*, 47 (1966): 161-189;

Heinrich Vormweg, *Günter Grass mit Selbstzeugnissen und Bilddokumenten* (Reinbek: Rowohlt, 1986);

Theodor Wieser, ed., *Günter Grass: Portrait und Poesie* (Neuwied: Luchterhand, 1968);

A. Leslie Willson, ed., *A Günter Grass Symposium* (Austin: University of Texas Press, 1971);

Rudolf Wolff, ed., *Günter Grass: Werk und Wirkung* (Bonn: Bouvier, 1985).

Papers:

The Günter Grass Archive is in the Deutsches Literaturarchiv (German Literature Archives) Marbach am Neckar, Germany.

Peter Hacks
(21 March 1928 -)

H. M. Waidson
University of Wales, Swansea

PLAY PRODUCTIONS: *Eröffnung des indischen Zeitalters*, Munich, Kammerspiele, 17 March 1954;

James Millington Synge, *Der Held der westlichen Welt*, translated by Hacks and Anna Elisabeth Wiede, Berlin, Berliner Ensemble, 11 March 1956;

Die Schlacht bei Lobositz, Berlin, Deutsches Theater, 1956;

Der Müller von Sanssouci: Ein bürgerliches Lustspiel, Berlin, Deutsches Theater, 15 March 1958;

Die Kindermörderin, Wuppertal 1959;

Die Sorgen und die Macht, Senftenberg, 15 May 1960; revised version, Berlin, Deutsches Theater, 1962;

Der Frieden, nach Aristophanes, Berlin, Deutsches Theater, 1962;

Die schöne Helena, Berlin, Deutsches Theater, 1964;

Moritz Tassow, Berlin, Volksbühne, 1965;

Polly oder Die Bataille am Bluewater Creek, music by Andre Asriel, Halle, 1966;

Das Volksbuch vom Herzog Ernst oder Der Held und sein Gefolge, Mannheim, Nationaltheater, May 1967;

Amphitryon, Göttingen, 1968;

Margarete in Aix, Basel, 1969;

Omphale, Frankfurt am Main, 1970;

Noch ein Löffel Gift, Liebling?, music by Siegfried Matthus, Berlin, Komische Oper, 1972;

Adam und Eva, Dresden, 1973;

Rosie träumt, Berlin, Maxim-Gorki-Theater, 1974;

Das Jahrmarktsfest zu Plundersweilern, Berlin, Deutsches Theater, 1975;

Die Vögel: Komische Oper nach Aristophanes, Berlin, Oper Berlin, 1975;

Ein Gespräch im Hause Stein über den abwesenden Herrn von Goethe, Dresden, 1976;

Omphale, music by Matthus, Weimar, 1976;

Prexaspes, Dresden, 1976;

Armer Ritter, Göttingen, 1978;

Die Fische, Göttingen, 1979.

Fredegunde, Brunswick, 1982;

Die Binsen, Berlin, 1985;

Peter Hacks

Barby, Halle, 1987;

Musen, Magdeburg, 1987.

BOOKS: *Eröffnung des indischen Zeitalters: Schauspiel* (Berlin: Henschel, 1955);

Das Volksbuch vom Herzog Ernst oder Der Held und sein Gefolge: Stück in einem Vorspiel und 3 Abteilungen (Berlin: Henschel, 1956);

Die Schlacht bei Lobositz: Komödie in 3 Akten (Berlin: Henschel, 1956);

Das Windloch: Geschichte von Henriette und Onkel Titus (Gütersloh: Bertelsmann, 1956);

Theaterstücke (Berlin: Aufbau, 1957)—comprises *Das Volksbuch vom Herzog Ernst oder Der Held und sein Gefolge; Eröffnung des indischen Zeitalters; Die Schlacht bei Lobositz;*

Der Müller von Sanssouci: Ein bürgerliches Lustspiel (Berlin: Henschel, 1958);

Geschichte eines alten Wittibers im Jahre 1637: Eine Moralität (Leipzig: Hofmeister, 1958);

Die Sorgen und die Macht: Historie (Berlin: Henschel, 1960);

Das Turmverlies: Geschichten von Henriette und Onkel Titus (Berlin: Kinderbuchverlag, 1962);

Zwei Bearbeitungen: "Der Frieden" nach Aristophanes; "Die Kindermörderin," ein Lust- und Trauerspiel nach Heinrich Leopold Wagner (Frankfurt am Main: Suhrkamp, 1963);

Der Flohmarkt: Gedichte für Kinder (Berlin: Kinderbuchverlag, 1965);

Stücke nach Stücken (Berlin & Weimar: Aufbau, 1965)—comprises *Der Frieden; Die schöne Helena: Operette für Schauspieler nach dem Libretto von Meilhac und Halévy; Die Kindermörderin; Polly oder Die Bataille am Bluewater Creek. Komödie, nach John Gay;*

Fünf Stücke (Frankfurt am Main: Suhrkamp, 1965)—comprises *Das Volksbuch vom Herzog Ernst oder Der Held und sein Gefolge; Eröffnung des indischen Zeitalters; Die Schlacht bei Lobositz; Der Müller von Sanssouci; Die Sorgen und die Macht;*

Moritz Tassow: Komödie (Berlin: Henschel, 1965);

Der Schuhu und die fliegende Prinzessin (Berlin: Eulenspiegel, 1966);

Lieder zu Stücken (Berlin: Eulenspiegel, 1967; enlarged, 1978);

Amphitryon: Komödie in 3 Akten (Berlin: Eulenspiegel, 1969);

Vier Komödien: Moritz Tassow; Margarete in Aix; Amphitryon; Omphale (Frankfurt am Main: Suhrkamp, 1971);

Der Bär auf dem Försterball (Cologne: Middelhauve, 1972); translated by Anthea Bell as *The Bear at the Huntsmen's Ball* (London: Abelard-Schuman, 1975); translated anonymously as *The Bear at the Hunters' Ball* (Reading, Mass.: Addison-Wesley, 1976);

Die Katze wäscht den Omnibus, by Hacks and Gertrud Zucker (Berlin: Kinderbuchverlag, 1972);

Das Poetische: Ansätze zu einer postrevolutionären Dramaturgie (Frankfurt am Main: Suhrkamp, 1972);

Ausgewählte Dramen, 3 volumes (Berlin & Weimar: Aufbau, 1972-1981)—volume 1 comprises *Columbus oder Die Weltidee zu Schiffe; Die Schlacht bei Lobositz; Moritz Tassow; Amphitryon; Omphale;* volume 2 (1976) comprises *Das Volksbuch vom Herzog Ernst oder Der Held und sein Gefolge; Die Sorgen und die Macht; Margarete in Aix; Prexaspes; Ein Gespräch im Hause Stein über den abwesenden Herrn von Goethe;* volume 3 comprises *Der Müller von Sanssouci; Adam und Eva; Die Fische; Musen;*

Kathrinchen ging spazieren (Cologne: Middelhauve, 1973);

Die Dinge in Buta (Berlin: Berliner Handpresse, 1974);

Lieder, Briefe, Gedichte (Berlin: Neues Leben, 1974);

Die Sonne, by Hacks and Klaus Ensikat (Berlin: Kinderbuchverlag, 1974);

Meta Morfoss: Eine Geschichte (Cologne: Middelhauve, 1975);

Oper (Berlin & Weimar: Aufbau, 1975)—comprises "Geschichte meiner Oper"; *Noch einen Löffel Gift, Liebling?; Omphale; Die Vögel: Komische Oper nach Aristophanes; Versuch über das Libretto;*

Das Pflaumenhuhn (Munich: Betz, 1975);

Adam und Eva: Komödie in einem Vorspiel und 3 Akten (Leipzig: Reclam, 1976);

Das Jahrmarktsfest zu Plundersweilern; Rosie träumt: Zwei Bearbeitungen nach J. W. von Goethe und Hrosvith von Gandersheim (Berlin & Weimar: Aufbau, 1976);

Die Maßgaben der Kunst: Gesammelte Aufsätze (Düsseldorf: Claassen, 1977);

Die Fische: Schauspiel in 2 Akten (Berlin: Henschel, 1977);

Armer Ritter: Ein Kindermärchen in 5 Akten (Berlin: Henschel, 1978);

Das musikalische Nashorn: Gedicht (Berlin: Kinderbuchverlag, 1978);

Sechs Dramen (Düsseldorf: Claassen, 1978)—comprises *Prexaspes, Numa, Adam und Eva, Ein Gespräch im Hause Stein über den abwesenden Herrn von Goethe, Die Fische, Senecas Tod;*

Leberecht am schiefen Fenster: Eine Geschichte (Berlin: Kinderbuchverlag, 1979);

Armer Ritter: Eine Geschichte (Berlin: Kinderbuchverlag, 1979);

Der Mann mit dem schwärzlichen Hintern (Berlin: Kinderbuchverlag, 1980);

Jules Ratte oder Selberlernen macht schlau, by Hacks and Klaus Ensikat (Berlin: Kinderbuchverlag, 1981);

Musen: Vier Auftritte (Berlin: Henschel, 1981);

Pandora: Drama, nach J. W. von Goethe (Berlin & Weimar: Aufbau, 1981);

Die Kinder: Ein Kindermärchen (Berlin: Henschel, 1983);

Essais (Leipzig: Reclam, 1984);

Die Binsen; Fredegunde: 2 Dramen (Berlin & Weimar: Aufbau, 1985);

Maries Baby: Ein Kindermärchen in 2 Aufzügen (Berlin: Henschel, 1985);

Zwei Märchen (Leipzig: Reclam, 1985)—comprises *Der Schuhu und die fliegende Prinzessin, Magister Knauerhase*;

Historien und Romanzen; Urpoesie oder Das scheintote Kind (Berlin & Weimar: Aufbau, 1985);

Kinderkurzweil (Berlin: Kinderbuchverlag, 1986);

Onkel Mo (Berlin: Kinderbuchverlag, 1986);

Liebkind im Vogelnest (Berlin: Neues Leben, 1987);

Der blaue Hund: Bilder zu Versen von Peter Hacks, drawings by Anne Heseler (Frankfurt am Main: Insel, 1987);

Die Gedichte (Berlin & Weimar: Aufbau, 1988);

Schöne Wirtschaft: Ästhetisch-ökonomische Fragmente (Berlin & Weimar: Aufbau, 1989);

Jona: Trauerspiel in fünf Akten, mit einem Essay "Jona, Beiwerk und Hintersinn" (Berlin & Weimar: Aufbau, 1989).

OTHER: Joszef Attila, *Gedichte*, translated by Hacks (Berlin: Eulenspiegel, 1960);

James Millington Synge, *Der Held der westlichen Welt*, translated by Hacks and Anna Elisabeth Wiede (Leipzig: Reclam, 1961);

Carl M. Bellman, *Gedichte*, translated by Hacks (Leipzig: Hofmeister, 1965);

Egon Mathieson, *Der Affe Oswald*, adapted by Hacks (Munich: Parabel, 1971).

Peter Hacks was a leading dramatist in the former German Democratic Republic (GDR). With the possible exception of Heiner Müller, Hacks has probably had a greater impact than any of his East German contemporaries with the number of his plays that have been successfully staged in the Federal Republic of Germany (FRG) and elsewhere. He usually writes comedies in which he frequently introduces verse that is idiosyncratic, fluent, and capable of expressing deep feeling as well as wit and philosophical thought. Some of his plays are based on classical Greek and Roman history and mythology, others on biblical themes and world history. In addition to his plays, Hacks has written a considerable amount of commentary and criticism on his own work

and that of others; a substantial amount of lyrical poetry; and stories and plays for children which were popular in West Germany as well as in East Germany.

Hacks was born on 21 March 1928 in Breslau (now Wroclaw, Poland) to Dr. Karl Hacks, a lawyer of progressive views, and Elly Hacks. He attended school in Breslau until February 1945, when he and his family moved westward with the German retreat before the invasion by Russian troops. The family lived for a time in Dachau, and Hacks completed his school-leaving examination in Wuppertal. In 1946 he entered Munich University, where he studied German literature and drama, philosophy, and sociology. In 1951 he was awarded the doctoral degree; his dissertation was on the drama of the Biedermeier from 1815 to 1840. He began writing for radio and stage, providing scripts for children's radio productions, and won the 1954 Competition for Young Authors of Munich for his stage play *Eröffnung des indischen Zeitalters* (Beginning of the Era of the Indies; published, 1956), which had its first performance on 17 March 1955 at the Munich Kammerspiele. Bertolt Brecht saw this play a few weeks later and invited Hacks and his wife, Anna Elisabeth Wiede, to come to East Berlin. Hacks and Wiede translated John Millington Synge's *The Playboy of the Western World* (1907) as *Der Held der westlichen Welt* (published, 1961) for production by the Berliner Ensemble; the first performance was on 11 March 1956. Hacks accepted a post as resident playwright and producer at the Deutsches Theater.

Eröffnung des indischen Zeitalters is a Marxist historical interpretation of Christopher Columbus's voyage to America: the conquest of a new world is the work of the early bourgeoisie, who thereby initiate a new era. Columbus is a threat to the traditional social order in Spain and Portugal, and his ideas, based on science and humanism, are inimical to the religious establishment of that time. Embedded in the sequence of realistic scenes is a scene which consists of a dream of Columbus's that reveals with hindsight the overall harmful effects of European colonization of the New World.

Two further plays were completed before Hacks left West Germany for East Berlin. *Das Volksbuch vom Herzog Ernst oder Der Held und sein Gefolge* (The Chapbook about Duke Ernst; or, The Hero and His Retinue; published, 1956) is set in the tenth century. Duke Ernst has a series of adventures that he interprets according to knightly conventions; he fails to understand the unscrupulousness and materialistic motivations of the ruling circles. His superior birth enables him to turn to his advantage the situations his clownlike foolishness causes. With a large cast and frequent scene changes, *Das Volksbuch vom Herzog Ernst* was not performed until May 1967, when it was produced at the National Theater in Mannheim. The third play Hacks took with him to East Berlin was *Die Schlacht bei Lobositz* (The Battle of Lobositz, 1956). Ulrich Braeker, the "poor man of Toggenburg," becomes a participant in the Seven Years' War but soon deserts from the Prussian army to return to a peaceful life in Switzerland. Braeker experiences disillusionment because of the cynical attitude of the officers toward the men they command. Braeker has no reason to support the Prussian cause; in fact, it is the defeated Austrians who help him to return to Switzerland. The play's hostility to militarism was particularly relevant at a time when the FRG was introducing conscription.

Unlike the three earlier plays, *Der Müller von Sanssouci* (The Miller of Sanssouci, 1958), which was first performed at the Deutsches Theater on 15 March 1958, is not a large-scale panorama; the play has a small cast, and interest centers on a fairly trivial incident. Hacks's next play affected his career in a decisive way. Up to this point Hacks had given his plays a historical setting, but in response to the offer of a prize by the Henschel Verlag publishing house for the best draft of a drama about life in the GDR he wrote *Die Sorgen und die Macht* (The Anxieties and the Power, 1960); the title is a quotation from Socialist Unity party chief Walter Ulbricht: "Denn wer die Macht hat, hat auch gewisse Sorgen" (For he who has the power also has certain anxieties). Hacks's play had a trial performance at the Deutsches Theater in Berlin; the first public performance was in Senftenberg, where it still aroused official misgivings. After further revision it was again put on by the Deutsches Theater. The play was allowed only a short run in Berlin, and Hacks was compelled to give up his position at the Deutsches Theater. In the play the personal shortcomings of various representatives of factory life account for the poor quality of the coal briquettes produced by the factory. The manager, Melz, is impatient with paperwork; the chairman of the factory trade union, Papmeier, quarrels with Kunze, the party secretary at the factory; Kunze, with his loudness and irritability, causes one worker to take flight to the

Federal Republic, and his dislike of Christianity causes him to withhold a bonus from Clementine Hoffmann; Twardowski, party secretary of the whole industrial complex, fails to treat seriously the complaints from the glass factory about the briquettes. Max Fidorra, the central figure of the play, finally recognizes that quantity should not take priority over quality. Hede Stoll, a member of the indignant work force of the glass factory, gives up her earlier boyfriend—who is given a prison sentence because of his gesture of sympathy with the 1956 Hungarian uprising—and accepts Fidorra's advances. By the fifth act Fidorra fully realizes the need to accept lower wages in order to improve the quality of the briquettes, and he puts forward ideas for hastening production without reducing quality.

Moritz Tassow was completed in 1961 but not performed or published until 1965. It centers on agricultural issues in the fictitious village of Gargentin in Mecklenburg during the summer of 1945. The local estate faces confiscation by the Russian Zone authorities, who will divide the land to encourage individual ownership of farms; the audience, however, would have known that collective farming was to be sponsored by the GDR beginning in 1952. The swineherd Tassow, who was thought to be a deaf-mute, surprises those around him by speaking with striking fluency on the theme of individual self-expression, which he interprets as an anarchic hedonism that refuses to accept authority. He incites the local people to eject the landowner, von Sack, and establishes a collective farm; but his regime neglects to act promptly to take over von Sack's agricultural machinery. Von Sack has ample funds in West Germany and Switzerland and will not suffer from the loss of his estate in Gargentin. Tassow's lifestyle encourages the villagers to be pleasure-seeking and relaxed at a time when hard work is needed for the harvesting and for reorganization after the war. Tassow seduces Jette, the daughter of a local farmer, and abandons her when he leaves; Jochen, a young laborer, will marry her, for the dividing up of the estate will enable him to establish himself as an independent farmer. Tassow will remain outside the stabilizing forces of family life and become a free-lance writer. He is an ostentatious and often overbearing figure. The character with whom the audience is expected to identify is Mattukat, a quiet and trustworthy administrator who, in spite of ill health produced by incarceration in a Nazi concentration camp, is determined to serve the Russian oc-

Scene from the premiere of Der Frieden, *Hacks's adaptation of Aristophanes'* Eirene, *at the Deutsches Theater in Berlin in 1962 (photograph by Dietlinde Krönig)*

cupation force and the people of East Germany. He is a sober man of action who recognizes that even if collective farming will be right in the future, it is inappropriate in 1945. Mattukat's assistant Blasche is, by contrast, petty-minded, self-centered, and patronizing to the local people.

Although Hacks's attempts to present topical and political issues in his plays were unsuccessful, he had success at the same time with adaptations of other dramatists' work. Heinrich Leopold Wagner's 1776 Storm and Stress play *Die Kindermörderin* (The Woman Who Murdered a Child; performed, 1959; published, 1963) lent itself well to Hacks's redrafting; at the end of the play Evchen is allowed to remain alive and to look after her illegitimate child in heroic defiance of social conventions of the time. *Der Frieden* (Peace; published, 1963), adapted from Aristophanes' *Eirene* (The Peace, 421 B.C.), is a comic fantasy: Trygaios is transported on a giant dung-beetle to Olympus, where he negotiates for the return of peace to Athens. Hacks's style in this play is lively and colloquial, and the production by Benno Besson at the Deutsches Theater in 1962 had a long run. John Gay's *Polly* (1729), a sequel to *The Beggar's Opera* (1728), was adapted by Hacks, with music by Andre Asriel. Set in the West Indies, Hacks's *Polly oder Die Bataille am*

Bluewater Creek (Polly; or, The Battle of Bluewater Creek; published, 1965; performed, 1966) presents Polly Peachum as a virtuous, humane heroine who abjures the unscrupulousness of the planters and of MacHeath, the pirate king, to ally herself with the noble-minded Indian prince Cawawkee. Hacks's adaptation of the libretto of Henri Meilhac and Ludovic Halévy's *La belle Hélène* (1865) as *Die schöne Helena* (The Beautiful Helen; performed, 1964; published, 1965), with Jacques Offenbach's music arranged by Herbert Kawan, was also successful.

Margarete in Aix (published, 1971), completed in 1966 and first performed in Basel in 1969, is a large-scale historical play that Hacks considers to be one of his more important works. Margaret of Anjou, the queen of Henry VI of England, was held for five years in the Tower of London during the Wars of the Roses and was released in 1476 after a ransom was paid by the king of France, Louis XI. Hacks's play begins at this point. Margaret is in a state of withdrawal and gloom because of her political defeats and does not appreciate the kindness of her father, King René of Provence. He is a patron of the arts and likes to think well of everyone at his court. René's easygoing rule resembles the commune of Moritz Tassow; it is threatened by

Charles of Burgundy, who is sponsored by Margaret. It would be acceptable to René for Provence to be annexed by Louis XI, thereby ensuring the continuance of a regime of reason and goodwill. Margaret, in a bitter mood, inveighs against her father's intention to allow his kingdom to be taken over by the French monarch. At the grotesque end of the play Margaret dies of anger and shock at the news that Charles the Bold has been killed in battle against the Swiss; but none of the courtiers is willing to make the news of her death public, since King René would then have to cancel a spectacle he had arranged. In addition to the action at a royal political level there are episodes involving troubadours and other representatives of the arts whose life-style is made possible by King René's dream of an artistic utopia.

Hacks's dramatic and poetic theory is expounded in a series of essays he has written, beginning in 1954; sixteen of these essays are collected in *Das Poetische: Ansätze zu einer postrevolutionären Dramaturgie* (The Poetic: Beginnings of a Postrevolutionary Dramaturgy, 1972). In "Die Aesthetik Brechts" (Brecht's Aesthetics) he says that although Brecht is the immediate forerunner of Hacks's aesthetic approach, the older dramatist is now part of the past. The model for a new, forward-looking society is William Shakespeare; contemporary playwrights should look to making the world poetic again, now that the socialist state has been achieved. Shakespeare was valued in late-eighteenth-century Germany for his realism; today we appreciate the poetic brilliance of his language. Hacks hopes that the GDR is about to move into a period comparable to that of Elizabethan England. In "Das Poetische" Hacks contends that the vocabulary of a poetic work of art should avoid elements of the archaic; but it should also not be too new, for the words may not be ready to be used poetically. Brecht's alienation theory is important when the writer is critical of his society, but not when he is living in a state that he regards positively. "Versuch über das Theaterstück von morgen" (Reflections on the Drama of Tomorrow) expounds ideas on classical greatness. With the arrival of the postrevolutionary state, one is in a period of transition where there is movement toward classical perfection. Hacks defines "das Pompöse" (the pompous) as a positive combination of the sensuous with the solemn; classical drama can use theatrical pomp as a celebration of human potentialities. Shakespeare, he argues, wrote classical plays, that is, plays that were positive, dignified, and

large-scale, because he lived during the reign of Elizabeth, when absolutism was acceptable to all social classes. He opposes the theater of the absurd for its being involved in pessimism and decadence, which are features of late capitalism.

Hacks wrote several plays that are classical in their use of Greek mythology or in their portrayal of political intrigue in ancient Rome. *Amphitryon* (published, 1969) was first performed in Göttingen in 1968; the first new play by Hacks to be staged in the FRG since the erection of the Berlin Wall in 1961, it marks the beginning of the reacceptance of Hacks's work in West Germany. The play's lack of topical political reference and its retelling of a myth that had already been given literary treatment by Plautus, Molière, and Heinrich von Kleist would seem to make Hacks's version an unlikely candidate for box-office success. But *Amphitryon* is well balanced and sensitive, full of humor while conveying a serious message. Jupiter impersonates Alkmene's husband Amphitryon while the latter is away at war. After the first appearance on stage of her human husband, Alkmene is confused for a short time, but the final scene offers a solution to the marital confusion which ennobles both Alkmene and Amphitryon: the visit of the god has fired the human couple, especially Alkmene, to become like gods. Hercules' love affair with Omphale, queen of Lydia, in *Omphale* (performed, 1970; published, 1971) deflects him from the labor of destroying the monster Lityernes. Eventually, while dressed as a woman, he overcomes the creature. The work was revived as an opera (1976), with music by Siegfried Matthus. *Prexaspes* (performed, 1976; published, 1978) depicts intrigues and ruthless behavior at the court of King Cambyses of Persia. Hope for a more humane regime is centered on Darios, the heir to Cambyses' kingdom. *Numa* (published, 1978) takes place in the near future, when Italy is a socialist republic. The action, which is full of infighting and deviousness, culminates in a carnival at which the characters are disguised as figures from ancient Rome. *Senecas Tod* (Seneca's Death; published, 1978), a somber play, is concerned with the last day in the life of the Roman man of letters.

In *Adam und Eva* (Adam and Eve; performed, 1973; published, 1976) Hacks turns for the first time to biblical material. Hacks's Lord is amiable and slightly vague, more permissive of human beings making their own choices than was Jupiter in *Amphitryon*. Jupiter was a regal God, whereas the Lord has liberal views. Hacks interprets the Creation story in terms of the philosopher Georg Wilhelm Friedrich Hegel's dialectic: after the thesis of a static Garden of Eden, the antithesis of disobedience (eating the fruit) ushers in the struggles of normal human life, where activity leads ever upwards. As the representative of evil, Satanael has little of the gloomy ferocity of John Milton's Satan in *Paradise Lost* (1667) but is more akin to Johann Wolfgang von Goethe's Mephistopheles in *Faust* (1808, 1832). Satanael may be seen as a Western intellectual mocking and threatening the controlled innocence of the GDR. Stability rather than dynamic mobility appeals to the Lord, who has a trace of complacency reminiscent of Twardowski, the party secretary in *Die Sorgen und die Macht*. Gabriel, the Lord's personal servant and adviser, advocates a merciful attitude to the disobedient couple. Paradise, however, will be closed to human beings from now on. Hacks implies that there is little difference between Christians and Marxists, for both emphasize ethical aspiration.

Hacks has written several plays that relate to Goethe. In *Das Jahrmarktsfest zu Plundersweilern* (The Fair at Plundersweilern; performed, 1975; published, 1976) he expands Goethe's fragment into a lively full-length play. He sees Goethe's work and his own as presenting the contrast and conflict between the bureaucratized Enlightenment and anarchic emotionalism. *Ein Gespräch im Hause Stein über den abwesenden Herrn von Goethe* (A Conversation in the Stein House about the Absent Herr von Goethe; performed, 1976; published, 1978) is a monologue in which Frau von Stein talks to her husband in October 1786. She is embittered by Goethe's secret departure from Weimar and tells of her deliberate refusal to read his writings; in the earlier years of their relationship she was unwilling to say that she was in love with him. A letter from Goethe disappoints her because it does not contain the expected marriage proposal but dwells on the warm weather in Italy. Hacks succeeds in vividly invoking her thoughts, memories, and feelings in this skillfully written monologue. In *Pandora* (published, 1981), an adaptation of Goethe's 1810 play, Epimetheus represents the life of contemplation; his brother, Prometheus, represents the life of action. Epimetheus believes in and longs for Pandora's return to earth; his visionary hopes are compared to the socialist confidence in the advent of a new society. *Musen* (Muses; published, 1981; performed, 1987) is the title of a collection of four one-act plays. In the first, *Charlotte Hoyer*,

Renate Reinecke as Thais and Karin Gregoreck as Roswitha in a scene from the premiere of Hacks's Rosie träumt *at the Maxim-Gorki-Theater in Berlin in 1974 (photograph by Saeger)*

Goethe's cook has been given notice by Frau Goethe but requests an interview with Goethe. This interview upsets the poet's equilibrium and threatens to delay his work on *Faust*. Two of the other plays also center on women who, in various ways, show the egocentricity of male characters to whom they minister. The remaining play in the collection takes place on New Year's Day of the year 2000; two men who have not seen each other for many years renew their friendship.

Rosie träumt (Rosie Dreams; performed, 1974; published, 1976) has as its heroine the tenth-century nun Roswitha of Gandersheim. In this play some Christians are executed and brought back to life; others sell their souls to the devil; prayer saves Rosie from violation. *Die Fische* (The

Fish; published, 1977; performed, 1979) takes place during the war of Mexican independence, in which Austrian interests were in conflict with those of France and the Mexican rebels. The central figure is a scientist who is pursuing research into possible ways of hastening the development of fish into human beings. *Die Binsen* (The Rushes, 1985) is a comedy which is unusually gentle in its approach. The hectic pace of the business world is satirized, while flight to the countryside is shown to have its limitations, too. The action is presumably set in the GDR, which appears as a land that is free from major social and political problems.

Fredegunde (performed, 1982; published, 1985) a five-act blank-verse play, takes place in Paris in 567 A.D., when three brothers are kings of the Franks' empire. No men appear on the stage, however. The action centers on five queens: Fredegunde and Andovera, consorts of King Hilprecht; Galsvintha, a princess from Visigoth Spain whose marriage to Hilprecht is to be celebrated; Galsvintha's sister Brunhilde, who is married to Hilprecht's brother Sigbert; and Ingunde, who is married to Hilprecht's brother Sigbert; and Ingunde, widow of the late monarch Lothar. The newcomer Galsvintha persistently criticizes the court as immoral and soon dies from poisoning. In the final confrontation Fredegunde and Brunhilde fight with axes until Ingunde asserts her authority with a third axe and compels them to pay heed to the latest political argument of the three brother-kings.

Although it is described as a "Trauerspiel" (tragedy), the five-act verse play *Jona* (Jonah; published, 1989) is not without hope for humanity. In the ninth century B.C., Jonah arrives at Nineveh and witnesses the plotting and duplicity that are rampant at the Assyrian court, where power is wielded by the Queen Mother Semiramis. Semiramis masterminds the betrayal of Babylon and a new alliance with the old enemy Ararat; she is also involved in the planning of a battle which is to have a prearranged outcome. Jonah is regarded skeptically by the queen when he declares his intention of bringing down the wrath of God upon Nineveh, but he has a more or less plausible explanation when the divine destruction fails to take place. In his appendix to the play Hacks calls power politics a principal force for evil in the world.

Hacks was one of the most successful playwrights of the former GDR. His achievement is one of quality as well as quantity; his style is daz-

zling, varied, and fluent, and his plays appealed both to the general public and to intellectuals.

References:

Volker Canaris, "Peter Hacks," in *Deutsche Dichter der Gegenwart: Ihr Leben und Werk*, edited by Benno von Wiese (Berlin: Schmidt, 1973), pp. 589-604;

Christine Cosentino, "Geschichte und 'Humane Utopie': Zur Heldengestaltung bei Peter Hacks," *German Quarterly*, 50 (May 1977): 248-263;

Jürgen Gidion, "Paradise Lost: *Adam und Eva* im Mittelpunkt eines Leistungskurses zum Thema Säkularisation," *Der Deutschunterricht*, 76 (1984): 77-86;

Peter Graves, "Utopie in Mecklenburg: Peter Hacks's Play *Moritz Tassow*," *Modern Language Review*, 75 (July 1980): 583-596;

Bernhard Greiner, " 'Zweiter Clown im kommunistischen Frühling': Peter Hacks und die Geschichte der komischen Figur im Drama der DDR," in *Dramatik der DDR*, edited by Ulrich Profitlich (Frankfurt am Main: Suhrkamp, 1987), pp. 344-374;

Dieter Hensing, "*Das Jahrmarktsfest zu Plundersweilen*," *Der Deutschunterricht*, 36, no. 1 (1984): 60-72;

Theo Honnef, " 'Was nie anwendbar war, wird es nicht mehr.' Peter Hacks und die Romantik," *Germanic Review*, 66 (Summer 1991): pp. 122-131;

Franz Hörnigk, "Erinnerungen an Revolutionen: Zu Entwicklungstendenzen in der Dramatik Heiner Müllers, Peter Hacks' und Volker Brauns am Ende der siebziger Jahre," in *Tendenzen und Beispiele: Zur DDR-Literatur in den siebziger Jahren*, edited by Hans Kaufmann (Leipzig: Reclam, 1981), pp. 148-184;

Ruth-Ellen B. Joeres, "Hereinspaziert! Hereinspaziert! Goethe and Hacks at the Jahrmarktsfest zu Plundersweilern," *Germanic Review*, 51 (November 1976): 259-277;

Hermann Kähler, "Ueberlegungen zu Komödien von Peter Hacks," *Sinn und Form*, 24, no. 2 (1972): 399-423;

Gudrun Klatt, "DDR-Dramatik am Beginn der 70er Jahre," *Weimarer Beiträge*, 19, no. 10 (1973): 117-130;

Paul Gerhard Klussmann and Heinrich Mohr, eds., *Die Schuld der Worte. Gert Neumanns Sprachreflexionen. Zum Werk von Peter Hacks. Über Texte von Karl Mickel, Sara Kirsch, Günther Weisenborn, Heiner Muller. Jahrbuch zu Lite-*

ratur in der DDR, volume 6 (Bonn: Bouvier, 1987);

Anna K. Kühn, "Peter Hacks' *Ein Gespräch im Hause Stein über den abwesenden Herrn von Goethe*," *Germanic Review*, 60 (Summer 1985): 91-98;

Horst Laube, *Peter Hacks* (Velber bei Hannover: Friedrich, 1972);

Bernd Leistner, "Zum Schiller-Bezug bei Peter Hacks," in *Selbsterfahrung als Welterfahrung: DDR-Literatur in den siebziger Jahren*, edited by Horst Nalewski and Klaus Schuhmann (Berlin & Weimar: Aufbau, 1981);

Michael Mitchell, *Peter Hacks: Theatre for a Socialist Society* (Glasgow: Scottish Papers in Germanic Studies, 1990);

Thomas di Napoli, "Peter Hacks and Children's Literature of the GDR," *Germanic Review*, 63 (Winter 1988): pp. 33-40;

Rolf Rohmer, "Peter Hacks," in *Literatur der DDR in Einzeldarstellungen*, edited by Hans Jürgen Geerdts (Stuttgart: Kröner, 1972), pp. 454-472;

Judith R. Scheid, *"Enfant terrible" of Contemporary East German Drama: Peter Hacks in His Role as an Adaptor and Innovator* (Bonn: Bouvier, 1977);

Scheid, ed., *Zum Drama in der DDR: Heiner Müller und Peter Hacks* (Stuttgart: Klett, 1981);

Wolfgang Schivelbusch, *Sozialistisches Drama nach Brecht: 3 Modelle. Peter Hacks, Heiner Müller, Hartmut Lange* (Darmstadt & Neuwied: Luchterhand, 1974);

Winfried Schleyer, *Die Stücke von Peter Hacks: Tendenzen—Themen—Theorien* (Stuttgart: Klett, 1976);

Gertrud Schmidt, *Peter Hacks in BRD und DDR: Ein Rezeptionsvergleich* (Cologne: Pahl-Rugenstein, 1980);

Klaus Schumann, "Peter Hacks: *Pandora*—Volker Braun: *Großer Frieden*. Problemfeld Zukunft," *Weimarer Beiträge*, 29, no. 1 (1983): 71-75;

Christoph Trilse, *Peter Hacks: Leben und Werk* (Berlin: Volk und Wissen, 1979);

Hans-Georg Werner, "Ueberlegungen zum Verhältnis von Individuum und Gesellschaft in den Stücken von Peter Hacks," *Weimarer Beiträge*, 20, no. 4 (1974): 31-67.

Peter Handke

(6 December 1942 -   )

Scott Abbott
Brigham Young University

See also the Handke entry in *DLB 85: Austrian Fiction Writers After 1914.*

PLAY PRODUCTIONS: *Publikumsbeschimpfung*, Frankfurt am Main, Theater am Turm, 8 June 1966;

Weissagung and *Selbstbezichtigung*, Oberhausen, Städtische Bühnen, 22 October 1966;

Hilferufe, Stockholm, 12 September 1967;

Kaspar, Frankfurt am Main, Theater am Turm; Oberhausen, Städtische Bühnen, 11 May 1968;

Das Mündel will Vormund sein, Frankfurt am Main, Theater am Turm, 31 January 1969;

Quodlibet, Basel, Basler Theater, 24 January 1970;

Der Ritt über den Bodensee, Berlin, Schaubühne am Halleschen Ufer, 23 January 1971;

Die Unvernünftigen sterben aus, Zurich, Theater am Neumarkt, 17 April 1974;

Über die Dörfer, Salzburg, Salzburger Festspiele, 8 August 1982;

Aeschylus, *Prometheus gefesselt*, translated by Handke, Salzburg, Salzburger Festspiele, August 1986;

Das Spiel vom Fragen oder Die Reise zum sonoren Land, Vienna, Burgtheater, 16 January 1990;

William Shakespeare, *Das Wintermärchen*, translated by Handke, Berlin, Berliner Schaubühne, December 1990;

Die Stunde da wir nichts voneinander wußten, Vienna, Theater an der Wien, 9 May 1992.

BOOKS: *Die Hornissen: Roman* (Frankfurt am Main: Suhrkamp, 1966);

Publikumsbeschimpfung und andere Sprechstücke (Frankfurt am Main: Suhrkamp, 1966)—comprises *Publikumsbeschimpfung, Weissagung, Selbstbezichtigung*;

Begrüssung des Aufsichtrats: Prosatexte (Salzburg: Residenz, 1967);

Der Hausierer: Roman (Frankfurt am Main: Suhrkamp, 1967);

Peter Handke (photograph by Isolde Ohlbaum)

Hilferufe (Frankfurt am Main: Suhrkamp, 1967);

Kaspar (Frankfurt am Main: Suhrkamp, 1967);

Hörspiel (Cologne: Kiepenheuer & Witsch, 1968);

Hörspiel Nr. 2 (Cologne: Kiepenheuer & Witsch, 1969);

Prosa, Gedichte, Theaterstücke, Hörspiel, Aufsätze (Frankfurt am Main: Suhrkamp, 1969);

Deutsche Gedichte (Frankfurt am Main: Euphorion, 1969);

Die Innenwelt der Außenwelt der Innenwelt (Frankfurt am Main: Suhrkamp, 1969); excerpts translated by Michael Roloff as *The Inner-*

world of the Outerworld of the Innerworld (New York: Seabury Press, 1974);

Kaspar and Other Plays, translated by Roloff (New York: Farrar, Straus & Giroux, 1969)—comprises *Offending the Audience, Prophecy, Self-Accusation, Calling for Help, Kaspar*; German version published as *Stücke 1* (Frankfurt am Main: Suhrkamp, 1972)—comprises *Publikumsbeschimpfung, Weissagung, Selbstbezichtigung, Hilferufe, Kaspar*;

Quodlibet (Frankfurt am Main: Verlag der Autoren, 1970);

Die Angst des Tormanns beim Elfmeter: Erzählung (Frankfurt am Main: Suhrkamp, 1970); translated by Roloff as *The Goalie's Anxiety at the Penalty Kick* (New York: Farrar, Straus & Giroux, 1972; London: Eyre Methuen, 1977);

Hörspiel Nr. 2, 3, 4 (Frankfurt am Main: Suhrkamp, 1970);

Wind und Meer: Vier Hörspiele (Frankfurt am Main: Suhrkamp, 1970)—comprises *Wind und Meer, Geräusch eines Geräusches, Hörspiel Nr. 2, Hörspiel*;

Der Ritt über den Bodensee (Frankfurt am Main: Verlag der Autoren, 1970); translated by Roloff as *The Ride across Lake Constance* (London: Eyre Methuen, 1973);

Chronik der laufenden Ereignisse (Frankfurt am Main: Suhrkamp, 1971);

Der kurze Brief zum langen Abschied (Frankfurt am Main: Suhrkamp, 1972); translated by Ralph Manheim as *Short Letter, Long Farewell* (New York: Farrar, Straus & Giroux, 1974; London: Eyre Methuen, 1977);

Wunschloses Unglück: Erzählung (Salzburg: Residenz, 1972); translated by Manheim as *A Sorrow beyond Dreams* (New York: Farrar, Straus & Giroux, 1975; London: Souvenir Press, 1976);

Ich bin ein Bewohner des Elfenbeinturms (Frankfurt am Main: Suhrkamp, 1972);

Stücke 2 (Frankfurt am Main: Suhrkamp, 1973)—comprises *Das Mündel will Vormund sein, Quodlibet, Der Ritt über den Bodensee*;

Die Unvernünftigen sterben aus (Frankfurt am Main: Suhrkamp, 1973); translated by Roloff and Weber as *They Are Dying Out* (London: Eyre Methuen, 1975);

Als das Wünschen noch geholfen hat (Frankfurt am Main: Suhrkamp, 1974); translated by Roloff as *Nonsense and Happiness* (New York: Urizen, 1976; London: Pluto Press, 1976);

Falsche Bewegung (Frankfurt am Main: Suhrkamp, 1975);

Der Rand der Wörter: Erzählungen, Gedichte, Stücke, edited by Heinz F. Schafroth (Stuttgart: Reclam, 1975);

Die Stunde der wahren Empfindung (Frankfurt am Main: Suhrkamp, 1975); translated by Manheim as *A Moment of True Feeling* (New York: Farrar, Straus & Giroux, 1977);

Die linkshändige Frau: Erzählung (Frankfurt am Main: Suhrkamp, 1976); translated by Manheim as *The Left-Handed Woman* (New York: Farrar, Straus & Giroux, 1978; London: Eyre Methuen, 1980);

Das Ende des Fanlierens (Vienna: Davidpresse, 1976);

Das Gewicht der Welt: Ein Journal (November 1975-März 1977) (Salzburg: Residenz, 1977); translated by Manheim as *The Weight of the World* (New York: Farrar, Straus & Giroux, 1984; London: Secker & Warburg, 1984);

Langsame Heimkehr: Erzählung (Frankfurt am Main: Suhrkamp, 1979); translated by Manheim as "The Long Way Around," in *Slow Homecoming* (New York: Farrar, Straus & Giroux, 1985; London: Methuen, 1985);

Die Lehre der Sainte-Victoire (Frankfurt am Main: Suhrkamp, 1980); translated by Manheim as "The Lesson of Sainte Victoire," in *Slow Homecoming*;

Kindergeschichte (Frankfurt am Main: Suhrkamp, 1981); translated by Manheim as "Child Story," in *Slow Homecoming*;

Über die Dörfer: Dramatisches Gedicht (Frankfurt am Main: Suhrkamp, 1981); translated by Manheim as *The Long Way Round: A Dramatic Poem* (London: Methuen Drama, 1989);

Die Geschichte des Bleistifts (Salzburg: Residenz, 1982);

Phantasien der Wiederholung (Frankfurt am Main: Suhrkamp, 1983);

Der Chinese des Schmerzes (Frankfurt am Main: Suhrkamp, 1983); translated by Manheim as *Across* (New York: Farrar, Straus & Giroux, 1986);

Gedicht an die Dauer (Frankfurt am Main: Suhrkamp, 1986);

Die Wiederholung (Frankfurt am Main: Suhrkamp, 1986); translated by Manheim as *Repetition* (New York: Farrar, Straus & Giroux, 1987);

Nachmittag eines Schriftstellers: Erzählung (Salzburg: Residenz, 1987); translated by Manheim as

The Afternoon of a Writer (New York: Farrar, Straus & Giroux, 1989);

Die Abwesenheit: Ein Märchen (Frankfurt am Main: Suhrkamp, 1987); translated by Manheim as *Absence* (New York: Farrar, Straus & Giroux, 1990);

Der Himmel über Berlin: Ein Filmbuch, by Handke and Wim Wenders (Frankfurt am Main: Suhrkamp, 1987);

Das Spiel vom Fragen oder Die Reise zum sonoren Land (Frankfurt am Main: Suhrkamp, 1989);

Versuch über die Müdigkeit (Frankfurt am Main: Suhrkamp, 1989);

Versuch über die Jukebox (Frankfurt am Main: Suhrkamp, 1990);

Noch einmal für Thukydides (Salzburg: Residenz, 1990);

Versuch über den geglückten Tag: Ein Wintertagtraum (Frankfurt am Main: Suhrkamp, 1991);

Abschied des Träumers vom Neunten Land. Eine Wirklichkeit, die vergangen ist: Erinnerung an Slowenien (Frankfurt am Main: Suhrkamp, 1992);

Die Stunde da wir nichts voneinander wußten: Ein Schauspiel (Frankfurt am Main: Suhrkamp, 1992);

Langsam im Schatten (Frankfurt am Main: Suhrkamp, 1992).

Editions in English: *The Ride across Lake Constance and Other Plays*, translated by Michael Roloff and Karl Weber (New York: Farrar, Straus & Giroux, 1976)—comprises *Prophecy, Calling for Help, My Foot My Tutor, Quodlibet, The Ride across Lake Constance, They Are Dying Out*;

Translations: Walker Percy, *Der Kinogeher* (Frankfurt am Main: Suhrkamp, 1980);

Florjan Lipuš, *Der Zögling Tjaž* (Salzburg & Vienna: Residenz, 1981);

Emmanuel Bove, *Meine Freunde* (Frankfurt am Main: Suhrkamp, 1981);

Bove, *Armand* (Frankfurt am Main: Suhrkamp, 1982);

Francis Ponge, *Das Notizbuch vom Kiefernwald und La Mounine* (Frankfurt am Main: Suhrkamp, 1982);

Georges-Arthur Goldschmidt, *Der Spiegeltag* (Frankfurt am Main: Suhrkamp, 1982);

Gustav Januš, *Gedichte* (Frankfurt am Main: Suhrkamp, 1983);

Bove, *Bécon-les-Bruyères* (Frankfurt am Main: Suhrkamp, 1984);

René Char, *Rückkehr stromauf* (Munich: Hanser, 1984);

Marguerite Duras, *Die Krankheit Tod: La Maladie de la Mort* (Frankfurt am Main: Fischer, 1985);

Percy, *Der Idiot des Südens: Roman* (Frankfurt am Main: Suhrkamp, 1985);

Patrick Modiano, *Eine Jugend* (Frankfurt am Main: Suhrkamp, 1985);

Aeschylus, *Prometheus gefesselt* (Frankfurt am Main: Suhrkamp, 1986);

Ponge, *Kleine Suite des Vivarais* (Salzburg & Vienna: Residenz, 1988);

Julien Green, *Der andere Schlaf* (Munich & Vienna: Hanser, 1988);

William Shakespeare, *Das Wintermärchen* (Frankfurt am Main: Suhrkamp, 1991);

Januš, *Mitten im Satz: Gedichte* (Salzburg: Residenz, 1991).

MOTION PICTURES: *3 amerikanische LP's*, screenplay by Handke, directed by Wim Wenders, 1969;

Falsche Bewegung, screenplay by Handke, directed by Wenders, 1975;

Die linkshändige Frau, screenplay by Handke, directed by Handke, Munich, Road Movies Filmproduktion, 1977;

Der Himmel über Berlin, screenplay by Handke and Wenders, directed by Wenders, Berlin, Road Movies Filmproduktion, 1987;

Die Absesenheit, screenplay by Handke, directed by Handke, 1992.

TELEVISION: *Chronik der laufenden Ereignisse*, teleplay by Handke, directed by Handke, WDR, 10 May 1971;

Die Angst des Tormanns beim Elfmeter, WDR, 29 February 1972;

Marguerite Duras, *Das Mal des Todes*, translated by Handke, directed by Handke, ORF, 20 February 1986.

Theatergoers are certain to be shocked by a performance of a Peter Handke play. They may find themselves doing the acting while being cursed from the stage, or they may be subjected to hours of sweet, soporific philosophizing. They may "see" a play that is only words, or they may experience a play without a single word. They may hear mumbled and mixed-up lines meant to elicit subconscious responses, or Handke may give them crystalline oratory. The play may end with a capitalist smashing his head against a rock or with a goddess proclaiming a gentle new age. The play may claim to present no images, or it may be absolutely allegorical. But if the forms cannot be anticipated, the themes remain fairly constant. Handke's plays are all concerned with theater itself, whether by attacking or repeating theatrical conventions; and they all consider language as it enables and inhibits. Handke's plays are disturbing and difficult, not crafted to please huge audiences. And they all, in various ways, circle around the basic question: if our languages, ourselves, and our communities are contingent (as Friedrich Nietzsche, Ludwig Wittgenstein, Martin Heidegger, and Jacques Derrida have suggested), then how and on what basis shall we construct ourselves and our communities? Nonetheless, from the beginning they have attracted directors of the quality of Claus Peymann and Wim Wenders and have played repeatedly in the world's leading theaters. Handke's work has been honored with several major literary prizes, including the Hauptmann Prize in 1967, the Büchner Prize in 1973, the Kafka Prize in 1979, the Vilenica Prize in 1987, and the Grillparzer Prize in 1991.

Just west of the southern Austrian village of Griffen, where Handke was born on 6 December 1942, stands an old monastery church. Maria Siutz Handke, his mother, is buried in its cemetery, as is his stepfather, Bruno Handke. His father and his stepfather were German soldiers, and Handke grew up speaking German. His mother, like most people in the village, was part Slovenian. Even today the church's services and publications are bilingual, and the paintings of the stations of the cross have Slovenian captions. Several of Handke's works, including his novel *Die Wiederholung* (1986; translated as *Repetition*, 1987), are set in Slovenia, and he has translated several works from Slovenian into German.

Handke stood out as a pupil in the village school and won a scholarship to the Catholic boarding school in Tanzenberg. Although he did well in languages and found a friend and mentor in Reinhard Musar, a teacher of German, Handke has often described this part of his life as a nightmare. He transferred to a gymnasium in Klagenfurt for the final two years. From 1961 to 1965 he was a law student at the University of Graz and worked with avant-garde writers affiliated with the Forum Stadtpark. He passed his first examination in law, but when the Suhrkamp publishing house accepted his novel *Die Hornissen* (The Hornets, 1966) he discontinued his law studies.

Handke married the actress Libgart Schwarz in 1966. Their daughter, Amina, was born in 1969, and Handke raised her after he and Schwarz separated in 1972. Handke's *Kindergeschichte* (1981; translated as "Child Story," 1985) describes his efforts as a single father to raise his daughter in Paris.

In 1966 Handke's attack on Gruppe (Group) 47's "new realism" and his insistence that literature is made of language and not of the things language describes made headlines. So did his first play, *Publikumsbeschimpfung* (1966; translated as *Offending the Audience*, 1969), which premiered in Frankfurt am Main under the direction of Peymann. The text of *Publikumsbeschimpfung* begins with rules for the actors. They are told to listen to the litanies of the Catholic church, to listen to "Tell Me" by the Rolling Stones, to watch the Beatles' films, and to observe people-aping monkeys and spitting llamas in the zoo. Next come three pages of directions for setting up the preplay atmosphere expected by the audience: sounds from behind the curtains of scenery being set up, ushers even more formal and ceremonial than usual, protracted dimming of lights, audience members to be refused entrance if not dressed appropriately. When the curtains open to reveal an empty stage and uncostumed actors and the house lights go up, audience members begin to realize that they themselves have been acting in the play. The four actors tell the audience that they will not see the play their theater experiences have led them to expect but a play lacking visual images and action: "Wir sprechen nur" (We will only speak). Nothing will be represented. The stage represents nothing; its emptiness represents no other emptiness. It is simply empty. The audience is the theme, the event. The actors need no tricks, they say, they need not be theatrical.

The speakers repeat themselves, contradict themselves, and talk about repetition and contradiction. They point out the ordered society of theatergoers and contrast it with the stage, where there is no order. They draw attention to the breathing, sweating, swallowing, and blinking of the audience, making them acutely aware of themselves. They describe the events preceding the play: the anticipation, the dressing, the travel, the finding of seats. They discuss the representation of reality in traditional theater: "Es wurde nicht um des Spiels, sondern um der Wirklichkeit willen gespielt" (The play was not played for the play's sake but for the sake of reality). But reality

Scene from the premiere of Handke's Publikumsbeschimpfung *at the Theater am Turm in Frankfurt am Main; from left,*
Ulrich Hass, Michael Gruner, Rüdiger Vogler, and Claus-Dieter Reents (photograph by Günter Englert)

cannot be played, only irreality. When the play points beyond itself it becomes impure.

There are clichéd assessments of the audience's role in the play: "Ihr wart die Entdeckung des Abends. . . . Ihr hattet den Löwenanteil am Erfolg. . . . Euch muß man gesehen haben, ihr Rotzlecker" (You were the find of the evening. . . . You had a lion's share of the success. . . . You were a sight to be seen, you snotlickers). Gradually the positive critical clichés give way to clichéd curses, a contradictory set of epithets: "ihr Saujuden . . . ihr Nazischweine . . . ihr jüdischen Großkapitalisten . . . ihr Proleten . . . Ihr Ewigkeitsfans. Ihr Gottesleugner. . . . Ihr schleichende Pest. Ihr unsterblichen Seelen" (you Jewish swine . . . you Nazi swine . . . you Jewish capitalists . . . you proletarians . . . you fans of eternity. You deniers of God. . . . You creeping plague. You immortal souls). The contradictions show one person's curses to be another's praise, and the curses return to highly stylized praise as the piece ends: "Ihr Damen und Herren ihr, ihr Persönlichkeiten des öffentlichen und kulturellen Lebens ihr, ihr Anwesenden ihr, ihr Brüder und Schwestern ihr, ihr Genossen ihr, ihr werten Zuhörer ihr, ihr Mitmenschen ihr" (You ladies

and gentlemen you, you celebrities of public and cultural life you, you who are present you, you brothers and sisters you, you comrades you, you worthy listeners you, you fellow humans you). The obvious relativity of the clichéd curses and praise raises a basic question: from whose perspective are these values negative and positive? The play also calls into question the values of traditional theater, of traditional audiences, and of supposed meaning beyond the surface, beyond the play, beyond the language of the actors.

Publikumsbeschimpfung was an enormous critical success and still exerts an influence on contemporary theater. Several other "Sprechstücke" (speech-plays), as Handke called them, quickly followed. *Weissagung* (1966; translated as *Prophecy*, 1976) begins with a quotation from Osip Mandelstam: "Wo beginnen? / Alles kracht in den Fugen und schwankt. / Die Luft erzittert vor Vergleichen. / Kein Wort ist besser als das andre, / die Erde dröhnt von Metaphern . . ." (Where to begin? / Everything is out of joint and totters. / The air quivers with comparisons. / No word is better than the other, / The earth resounds with metaphors . . .). The play, spoken by four actors, is a long series of prophetic figures of speech referring back to themselves instead of, as usual, purporting to point beyond themselves; they are signifiers that are simultaneously the signified: "Die Fliegen werden sterben wie die Fliegen. . . . Das Schwein am Spieß wird schreien wie am Spieß" (The flies will die like flies. . . . The pig on the spit will scream as if on a spit). *Weissagung* absolutely refuses to move beyond the "truth" Nietzsche described as "a mobile army of metaphors"; as a result, the play is disconcerting to audiences expecting dramatic action.

Selbstbezichtigung (1966; translated as *Self-Accusation*, 1969), Handke's third Sprechstück, is written for a female speaker and a male speaker. "Ich bin auf die Welt gekommen" (I came into the world), the play begins, and the actors describe their first movements as infants, their first sounds and sights, and then, as they acquire a vocabulary, their socialization: "Ich bin der Gegenstand von Sätzen geworden. . . . Ich bin eine Aneinanderreihung von Buchstaben geworden" (I became the object of sentences. . . . I became a sequence of letters of the alphabet). The speakers describe their subsequent turn from nature to rules and their resulting "Gesellschaftsfähigkeit" (fitness for society). But as the rules lay hold of the speaker, they make a kind of productive "sin" possible. There follow long lists of proudly confessed transgressions: "Ich habe mich geäußert durch Spucken. . . . Ich habe die Waggontür vor dem Halten des Zuges geöffnet. . . . Ich habe in einer Sprache gesprochen, in der zu sprechen volksfeindlich war" (I expressed myself through spitting. . . . I opened the door before the train came to a stop. . . . I spoke in a language defined as inimical to the people). Because of the stultifying effects of society and its languages and rules, this listing of transgression involves a certain heroism, and is, in fact, not self-accusation at all. But then a new list of transgressions begins: "Ich habe die Regeln der Sprache nicht beachtet. Ich habe Sprachverstöße begangen. Ich habe die Worte ohne Gedanken gebraucht" (I failed to observe the rules of the language. I committed linguistic blunders. I used words without thought). The audience expects to cheer at the breaking of grammatical rules, just as it has celebrated the other violations of societal restrictions; but it finds that *these* rules legislate against using language without thought, and that the transgressions involve the speaking of deadening clichés: "Ich habe die Gegenstände tot genannt. . . . Ich habe die Traurigkeit dunkel genannt. . . . Ich habe die

Leidenschaft heiß genannt" (I called objects dead. . . . I called melancholy black. . . . I called passion hot). Thus the speakers accept the strictures of society and confess their sins, revolt against society through the bravado of confession, abjure the language of society as hostile to life, and indirectly praise more "true," nonclichéd language. The message here, that language both inhibits and enables, is one of Handke's central themes. The language of this play has attempted to break into the cycle of society's dominating clichés. And if it has affirmed little, it has at least affirmed its own linguistic activity, an activity that its speakers say has changed them: "Ich bin ins Theater gegangen. Ich habe dieses Stück gehört. Ich habe dieses Stück gesprochen. Ich habe dieses Stück geschrieben" (I went to the theater. I heard this piece. I spoke this play. I wrote this play).

In *Hilferufe* (1967; translated as *Calling for Help*, 1969), another Sprechstück, the unidentified speakers speak sentences, fragments, and words associated with danger or need or question or answer—in short, related to the word *Hilfe* (help): "ein zum tod verurteilter ist entflohen . . . nach dem kochen ist der pilz nicht mehr so giftig . . . unleserliche gesuche werden zurückgewiesen" (a man sentenced to death has escaped . . . after boiling, the mushroom is no longer so poisonous . . . illegible requests will be rejected). Each phrase or word is followed by the response "NEIN" (NO). Finally the question "hilfe?" is asked, and the response is "JA!" (YES!). Handke's notes direct the actors: "die aufgabe der sprecher ist es, den weg über viele sätze und wörter zu dem gesuchten wort HILFE zu zeigen. sie spielen das bedürfnis nach hilfe . . . akustisch den zuhörern vor" (the task of the speaker is to demonstrate the route over many sentences and words to the sought-after word HELP. they play the need for help . . . acoustically, for the audience). As long as the actors are searching for "help," Handke writes, the word has the meaning of the need to find the word. Once the word is finally spoken, however, it has lost that meaning.

The last and longest of the Sprechstücke is *Kaspar* (published, 1967; performed, 1968; translated, 1969). The character of Kaspar, an adult learning language for the first time, is based on the nineteenth-century foundling Kaspar Hauser. He learns to put things in order: "Seit ich sprechen kann, kann ich alles in Ordnung bringen" (Ever since I can speak, I can put everything in order). That this order is arbitrary makes no difference. The discovery that reality can be manipulated by language leads Kaspar to understand metaphor and the arbitrariness of language. Creating order through speech is an ambiguous accomplishment, Kaspar learns; following the intermission, that act of creation becomes oppressive when "die gesellschaftlich Kranken" (the socially sick) are forced, through violence, to fit into the social order. Those who have been brought to order now look for sentences valid for all, straitjacket sentences that ensure peace on earth. Finally, since language has turned out to be an arbitrary system, Kaspar begins to speak in a meaningless chain of statements and words in which each leads senselessly to the next. Kaspar discovers meaning to be both arbitrary and supported by violence. The play suggests that something has been lost—a direct relationship with things, for example—and in admitting that loss the play questions the contingency it has been asserting. *Kaspar* simultaneously argues against the oppression of language and posits, however tentatively, something positive beyond the resulting contingency.

After the Sprechstücke Handke wrote quite a different kind of play, *Das Mündel will Vormund sein* (The Ward Wants to Be the Guardian, 1969; translated as *My Foot My Tutor*, 1976). The title refers to the relationship of dominance and submission. In contrast to the Sprechstücke, which aimed to present only language, in this play not a single word is spoken. The first and last scenes are set in front of a farmhouse, the middle scenes inside the house. Two characters, the ward and the guardian, compete with one another in contests that are won, for the most part, by the guardian. For example, attempting to be higher than one another they jump, climb onto a chair, climb onto a table, and climb onto a chair on the table; the guardian finally wins by hanging from a cord. In another scene the guardian throws bottles and other kitchen items and the ward tries to catch them. He fails repeatedly, and they crash to the floor. Suddenly he catches one; the stage immediately becomes dark, signaling the abrupt, if ephemeral, change in relationship. In the penultimate scene the guardian shows the ward how to use a beet-cutting machine to cut off the tops of beets. As it gets dark on the stage the ward repeatedly tries and fails to sever the top of a beet. When utter darkness rules, nothing is heard but loud breathing that gradually fills the hall; then silence. The play ends as the ward repeatedly reaches into a sack and lets the sand he draws

from it fall into water. The text of the play is written in the first person plural, as if the narrator and readers are members of the audience. The narrator often gives possible audience responses; for example, as to the loud breathing near the end: "ein Röcheln? ein sehr angestrengtes Luftholen? Oder nur ein großer Blasebalg? Oder ein riesiges Tier?" (a death rattle? A very intense inhaling? Or only a bellows? Or a huge animal?). The reader learns things from the directions that cannot possibly be portrayed on the stage: "Tätowierungen auf den Armen sind nicht zu sehen" (tattoos cannot be seen on his arms) or "Hühner sind nicht zu sehen" (There are no chickens to be seen). The latter statement seems to grow out of a stream of consciousness in which a couple of apple seeds have just fallen to the ground—seeds that chickens, had there been any, might have eaten. Early in the play, with the stage dark, breathing like that at the end is heard, and the stage directions describe an Italian spy film in which loud breathing in the dark unnerves an intruder and leads to his death. The narrator says that "dieses Atmen im Finstern ist auch hier gemeint, freilich ohne die Folgen" (this breathing in the dark is meant here as well, although without the consequences). The audience, of course, cannot see this text, nor are they likely to make the same connection the narrator makes here—a connection that may make a difference in interpreting the penultimate scene. When the ward, the guardian, and the ominous beet-cutting machine disappear into darkness from which only the ward reappears, the breathing may, in light of the film reference, suggest the murder of the guardian. But for that meaning to be constructed the theater audience needs more information than it is given.

The premiere of *Das Mündel will Vormund sein*, directed by Peymann, followed a performance of *Selbstbezichtigung* in which the man and woman appeared naked and spoke their lines slowly and monotonously. Before the play even began to approach its end, members of the audience expressed their displeasure so vocally that the actors left the stage. After an intermission the second play began, and still-excited audience members shouted directions to the ward as he picked up toenail clippings and other things for the guardian. Gradually they settled down and responded appreciatively.

Several critical responses to the play refer to earlier statements by Handke about his Sprechstücke that there was nothing to interpret, that an empty stage did not mean anything beyond itself; consequently, the critics argue that this play also points to no meaning beyond itself. Handke, however, has said that "das Stück spiegelt stumm Herrschaftsverhältnisse, zeigt, daß sich Herrschaft auch wortlos ausüben läßt" (the play mutely mirrors relationships of dominance, shows that dominance can also be practiced without words)—a metaphor that most viewers intuit.

Handke's next play was *Quodlibet* (1970; translated, 1976). The title, which literally means "as you like it," refers either to a philosophical or theological disputation or to a multivoiced musical composition in which various melodies are played humorously and simultaneously. The script consists of suggestions of the sorts of words and phrases actors might use to elicit responses from the audience. The actors portray such characters as a general, a bishop, the chancellor of a university, a politician with two Central Intelligence Agency bodyguards, a woman in evening dress, and a woman with a poodle. They murmur half-heard, misunderstood words, random sounds that give rise to Freudian associations on the part of the audience. The play does not depict sex or violence but creates confusion that the audience "resolves" by subconscious associations.

The title of *Der Ritt über den Bodensee* (1971; translated as *The Ride across Lake Constance*, 1973) comes from a story in which a man rides his horse over the ice-covered Lake Constance. On reaching the other side he is told how thin the ice is, and he dies of shock. This story is never told in the play but is related in the stage directions to the epigraph: "Träumt Ihr oder redet Ihr?" (Are you dreaming or are you speaking?). When speaking in a trance, Handke says, we are able to communicate—as least superficially; made conscious of our language, however, we are shocked into miscommunication or silence. With eight characters and a doll, *Der Ritt über den Bodensee* portrays various types of social interaction—love, work, buying, and selling—and the language involved in those interactions. Jannings comes to dominate George after someone suggests that he might be the more powerful of the two, showing that Jannings, too, is constituted by language. Jannings describes the development of language in terms reminiscent of *Kaspar*: "Man hat angefangen, miteinander zu verkehren, und es hat sich eingespielt.... Eine Ordnung ergab sich, und um weiter miteinander verkehren

zu können, machte man diese Ordnung ausdrücklich: man formulierte sie. Und als man sie formuliert hatte, mußte man sich daran halten, weil man sie schließlich formuliert hatte! Das ist natürlich, nicht wahr?" (People began to socialize with one another and it became the rule.... An order resulted; and for people to continue to socialize with one another, this order was made explicit: it was formulated. And once it had been formulated, people had to stick to it because, after all, they had formulated it. That's natural, isn't it?). Relations with things are also dominated by language: " 'Er schlief auf Disteln!' —'Ich kann mich nicht erinnern, so einen Satz jemals gehört zu haben: also kann er gar nicht auf Disteln geschlafen haben!' " ("He slept on thistles!"—"I cannot remember having heard such a sentence: thus he cannot have slept on thistles!").

Handke has said that in this play he wanted to examine both the language of society and the language of the theater. Traditional theater communicates in much the same way as ordinary language, which makes it accessible to audiences, and it is similarly prone to trivialization and exploitation. Handke's theater, however, can only move beyond clichés if it speaks another language—a language largely unfamiliar to the audience; consequently, *Der Ritt über den Bodensee* refuses to deliver a clear message.

In 1970 the novel that first brought Handke a wide readership was published. *Die Angst des Tormanns beim Elfmeter* (translated as *The Goalie's Anxiety at the Penalty Kick*, 1972), the story of a paranoid ex-goalie who begins to read everything as a sign, commits a gratuitous murder, and runs from the police, sold well, was quickly translated into several European languages, and was made into a successful film in 1972 by Wim Wenders. Wenders and Handke had collaborated in 1969 on *3 amerikanische LP's* and would again work together on such films as *Falsche Bewegung* (Wrong Move, 1975) and *Der Himmel über Berlin* (1987; released in America as *Wings of Desire*).

During the late 1960s and early 1970s Handke achieved a certain notoriety in the media. Newspapers titillated their readers with reports of his unorthodox readings at universities, of his brushes with police, and of his relationship with the French actress Jeanne Moreau. Although his works relentlessly questioned the existing social order, political leftists ridiculed him for living in an ivory tower.

Die Unvernünftigen sterben aus (published, 1973; performed, 1974; translated as *They Are Dying Out*, 1975) is a more traditional drama than Handke's earlier plays, with recognizable characters and a plot. Hermann Quitt is a powerful capitalist who exploits his workers and consumers. At the same time, he is a sensitive man who is losing the "rationality" required of a powerful person. The capitalists describe their system, above all, as rational: "Unsere Produkte aber gibt es, und indem es die gibt, sind sie schon vernünftig—sonst hätten wir als Vernunftswesen sie ja nicht aus vernünftigen Rohstoffen in vernünftigen Arbeitsgängen durch vernünftige Menschen erzeugen lassen" (Our products exist and their very existence makes them rational—otherwise we, as rational beings, would not have had them produced in a rational manner from rational raw materials by rational people). Goaded by Kilb, who ridicules the capitalists and their rationality, Quitt abruptly quits the social order that gives him power, shocking even Kilb as he rips off a woman's blouse and spits in his guests' faces. After another character, Hans, reads him Adelbert Stifter's story "Der Hagestolz" (The Old Bachelor, 1850), he is inspired to further revolutionary action. Quitt describes the nineteenth century of Stifter's story as a time when an earlier existing "Weltgefühl" (universal feeling) was already gone, but when there was still a memory of that feeling and a longing for it. Quitt finds his own situation execrable when compared to Stifter's: "wo man früher das Ganze erblicken wollte, sehe ich jetzt nichts als Einzelheiten" (where one once used to see the whole, I see nothing but particulars now). His business dealings have been attempts to hide the fact that he is playing a role that does not even exist, and now that he recognizes that, he says, he will create a new role: he will double-cross his fellow capitalists. But after Quitt has caused chaos in the carefully ordered capitalist system, he finds that he has simply moved out of one role into another. Leaving the rational system of capitalism has not made him the traditional irrational philosopher hearing the voice of his demon or the prophet hearing the voice of God but rather an idiot hearing film titles, lines from popular songs, and advertising jingles. He smashes his head against a rock until he falls senseless to the floor.

From 1973 to 1979 Handke lived in Paris, where he wrote several works, including *Langsame Heimkehr* (1979; translated as "The Long Way Around," 1985), the first volume of an ambitious tetralogy. In part so that his daughter could attend a German-speaking gymnasium, he moved to Salzburg in 1979. His stay there included a personal and working relationship with the actress Marie Colbin, whom he directed in a television version of his 1986 translation of Marguerite Duras's *La Maladie de la Mort* (The Malady of Death, 1982) in 1986.

In Salzburg Handke finished his tetralogy with the prose narratives *Die Lehre der Sainte-Victoire* (1980; translated as "The Lesson of Sainte-Victoire," 1985) and *Kindergeschichte* and the play *Über die Dörfer* (Through the Villages, 1981; translated as *The Long Way Round: A Dramatic Poem*, 1989). Radically different from his earlier work, *Über die Dörfer* premiered at the Salzburg Festival in 1982, where it was directed by Wenders. The first scene of this play is a discussion between Gregor, a writer, and Nova, the spirit of a new age; the second scene is a meeting at a distant construction site between Gregor and his brother Hans, a construction worker; the third is a discussion between Gregor and his sister Sophie about her plan to open her own shop; the fourth scene is a confrontational meeting of all three siblings followed by a philosophical speech by Nova. On one level the question of the play is whether the house inherited by Gregor and inhabited by Hans should be mortgaged to finance Sophie's business. But at bottom, the play is about truth.

After the antitheater of his earlier work, Handke turns in this play to Greek theatrical forms. Two of the scenes take place before the curtain, and the other two, like many scenes in Greek drama that take place in front of a palace, a tent, or a grove, are set in front of a construction site and a cemetery wall. The slow, wordy pace of the play is also patterned on the Greeks, specifically Aeschylus; it is a play of long monologues spoken in elevated language. The repetition of Greek forms; the slow, philosophical tempo; the elevated language; and the appearance of the goddess Nova are not, as some have supposed, a mystical affirmation of the certainties denied in Handke's earlier work. Near the end of the play Hans says: "Es gibt weder Erkenntnis noch Gewißheit. Es gibt nichts Ganzes, und was ich denke, denke ich allein, und was mir allein einfällt, ist nicht Wahrheit, sondern Meinung, und es wirkt keine Weltvernunft, und das gemeinsame Menschheitsziel geht mehr denn je um als Gespenst. . . . Es gibt keine Einheit zwischen oben und unten" (There is neither knowledge nor certainty. There

Libgart Schwarz, as Nova (top), delivers her final pronouncement in the premiere of Handke's Über die Dörfer *at the Salzburg Festival in 1982 (photograph by Winfried Rabanus)*

is nothing whole, and what I think I think alone, and what occurs to me alone is not truth, but opinion, and no world-reason is operating, and the common human goal is circulating more than ever as a specter.... There is no unity between above and below). In response, Nova gives her long speech of comfort. She speaks of gods, for, as she says, "Es gibt dieses Wort [*Gott*], und es ist durch kein anderes ersetzbar" (This word [*gods*] exists, and it is replaceable through no other). She does not mean that gods exist but that, in the language game we have helped create, the word *god* plays an irreplaceable role. Meaning must be created: "vergeßt die Sehnsucht nach den vergangenen heiligen Orten und Jahren. Mit euch ist die heilige weite Welt. Jetzt ist der heilige Tag. Wirkend arbeitend, seht ihr ihn und könnt ihn fühlen.... es gibt in unsrer Menschengeschichte nirgends einen stichhaltigen Trost.... Das übernatürliche ist nicht zu erwarten" (forget the longing for the bygone holy places and years. With you is the holy, wide world. Now is the holy day. Actively working, you see it and can feel it.... there is nowhere in our human history a lasting comfort.... The supernatural is not to be expected). Humans must discover themselves as

gods. Truth will not be found, but neither can we live without it. We must create it as a "Volk der Schöpfer" (people of creators). Gregor returns to his village and discovers the meaning of home, of the land, of the tree at the center—and he decides to give it all up, to keep moving. But he will move slowly and by way of the villages.

In 1986 Handke's translation of Aeschylus's *Prometheus Bound* as *Prometheus gefesselt* (Prometheus Bound; published, 1986), directed by Klaus Michael Grüber, premiered at the Salzburg Festival. In 1987 he left Salzburg to travel in the former Yugoslavia, Greece, Egypt, Spain, and Japan. His translation of William Shakespeare's *The Winter's Tale, Das Wintermärchen* (published, 1991), was staged in Berlin in 1990 by Luc Bondy.

The major original play Handke wrote during this time was *Das Spiel vom Fragen oder Die Reise zum sonoren Land* (The Play [or Game] of Questioning; or, The Journey to the Sonorous Land; published, 1989; performed, 1990). The play, which premiered at the Vienna Burgtheater under Peymann's direction, lasts for more than four demanding hours. There are eight characters in this play, seven of whom are traveling "to

Peter Fitz as the spoilsport, Thomas Holtzmann as the native, Mark Boysen as the actor, Uwe Bohm as Parzival, and Rudolf Buzcolich as the old man in the premiere of Handke's Das Spiel vom Fragen oder Die Reise zum sonoren Land *at the Burgtheater in Vienna in 1990 (photograph by Oliver Herrmann)*

the sonorous land"; the other is a native in various guises who meets them at several points along the way. One of the travelers is the world-praising Mauerschauer, who turns out to be Ferdinand Raimund, the nineteenth-century Austrian author of magical fairy-tale dramas; he is opposed by the cynical Spielverderber (spoilsport), whom the audience finally recognizes as Anton Chekhov. The other travelers are a young actress, a young actor, an old man, an old woman, and a childlike, barefoot Parzival. The pilgrimage is to a land from which, at the play's beginning, a deep, sonorous signal sounds. This tone may come from a place identified near the end of the play as Emmaus (the place where the resurrected Christ revealed himself to two of his disciples); but the play, as one would expect from Handke, is a play of questioning and not of answers. Emmaus turns out to be a ferry and thus serves to convey the travelers along their way, as opposed to being their final destination. Additionally, Emmaus is recognized as plural and not necessarily glorious when the old woman says that "der Billigwohnblock daheim am Ortsrand, wo einem beim Vorbeigehen die Aasfliegen in den Mund schwirren" (the cheap apartment block back home at the edge of the locality, where car-

rion flies swarm into a passerby's mouth) is also called Emmaus. Handke is a studied nonconvert, converted neither to the metaphysical nor to absolute skepticism. His Mauerschauer's repeated declamations approach the metaphysical; he says, for example, "Entdecke ich die Schönheit, macht sie mich für den Augenblick wahr" (when I discover beauty, it makes me, for the moment, true), and "wir haben buchstäblich geglüht vom Ganz-Frage-Sein, und im Himmel oben hat, als Zeichen des uns vorschwebenden Fragens, eine Wolke gestanden" (we literally glowed with Being-Wholly-Question, and in the heavens above, as a sign of the questioning hovering before us, stood a cloud). But in each he pulls back from the transcendence he has approached by referring to fantasy, imagination, a role he plays, or to what he describes as the material here and now. He is constantly aware that he is creating, as opposed to finding, truth. Further relativizing his "truths" are the statements of the Spielverderber; his cynical response to the cloud/sign from heaven is typical: "Warum dann nicht gleich eine Stimme von oben, oder der reitende Bote des Fragekönigs?— Seltsamer Freund: Auch die Zeit deiner Zaubermärchen ist vorbei. Oder?" (Why not then a voice from above, or the riding messenger of the

Question King?—Peculiar friend: The time of your magical fairy tales is also past. Or is it?). But in the back and forth between the two the cynicism of the Spielverderber is also moderated; the opponents even switch sides during one conversation.

Critical responses to the play were sharply divided. "Peter Handke weiß nicht, wie man Stücke schreibt, das heißt, er will es nicht wissen. So tritt uns das Schauspiel selber wie eine Frage entgegen. Wahrscheinlich erwartet es keine Antwort, bestimmt aber Zuneigung" (Peter Handke does not know how plays are written, that is, he does not want to know. Thus the play itself approaches us like a question. Perhaps it expects no answer; certainly, however, sympathy), wrote Benjamin Henrichs in *Die Zeit* (Time). But Peter Iden said in the *Frankfurter Rundschau* (Frankfurt Review): "Die Uraufführung läßt keinen Zweifel mehr zu an der Haltlosigkeit der Texte, deren erhabenes Tönen immer wieder abstürzt in die Platitüde: Was sie als Poesie behaupten, ist süß-saurer Kitsch, hört sich an wie die pubertäre Lyrik von Jünglingen, die zuviel Hölderlin gelesen haben" (The premiere no longer allows any doubt as to the emptiness of those texts whose lofty sounds repeatedly plunge to platitudes: What pretends to be art is sour-sweet kitsch, and it sounds like the pubescent poetry of youths who have read too much Hölderlin).

In a discussion following a performance of the play Handke responded: "Ich hasse alle Leute, die wissen, wie ein Stück geschrieben zu sein hat" (I hate all people who know how a play should be written).

Handke returned to Paris in 1990. In May 1992 his play *Die Stunde da wir nichts voneinander wußten* (The Time When We Knew Nothing of One Another; published, 1992) had its premiere in Vienna, directed by Peymann. Like *Das Mündel will Vormund sein*, it is a play without words. The text is a set of stage directions that describe a public square and the people who pass through it. The light changes in the square. The weather changes. Hundreds of people, played by several dozen actors, move across the square. A sense of randomness and alienation competes with a sense of the fullness and diversity of human existence. Near the play's end the separate characters find kinds of communion with one another, and an old man begins to "speak" in gestures to the group circled around him. It is a moving moment of shared meaning, and, as one would expect with Handke, it does not last. The square becomes once again a place where various figures come and go.

References:

Manfred Durzak, *Peter Handke und die deutsche Gegenwartsliteratur: Narziß auf Abwegen* (Stuttgart: Kohlhammer, 1982);

Raimund Fellinger, ed., *Peter Handke* (Frankfurt am Main: Suhrkamp, 1985);

Herbert Gamper, *Aber ich lebe nur von den Zwischenräumen: Ein Gespräch* (Zurich: Ammann, 1987);

Norbert Honsza, ed., *Zu Peter Handke: Zwischen Experiment und Tradition* (Stuttgart: Klett, 1982);

Manfred Jurgensen, ed., *Handke: Ansätze—Analysen—Anmerkungen* (Bern: Francke, 1979);

Jerome Klinkowitz and James Knowlton, *Peter Handke and the Postmodern Transformation: The Goalie's Journey Home* (Columbia: University of Missouri Press, 1983);

Peter Laemmle and Jörg Drews, eds., *Wie die Grazer auszogen, die Literatur zu erobern: Texte, Porträts, Analysen und Dokumente junger österreichischer Autoren* (Munich: Edition text + kritik, 1975);

Egila Lex, *Peter Handke und die Unschuld des Sehens* (Thalwil/Zurich: Paeda-Media, 1984);

Gerhard Melzer and Jale Tükel, eds., *Peter Handke: Die Arbeit am Glück* (Königstein: Athenäum, 1985);

Manfred Mixner, *Peter Handke* (Kronberg: Athenäum. 1977);

Rainer Nägele and Renate Voris, *Peter Handke* (Munich: Beck, 1978);

Peter Pütz, *Peter Handke* (Frankfurt am Main: Suhrkamp, 1982);

Žarko Radaković, ed., *Književna kritika* (Belgrade), special issue on Handke, 17, no. 1 (1986);

Rolf Günter Renner, *Peter Handke* (Stuttgart: Metzler, 1985);

Michael Scharang, ed., *Über Peter Handke* (Frankfurt am Main: Suhrkamp, 1972);

June Schlueter, *The Plays and Novels of Peter Handke* (Pittsburgh: University of Pittsburgh Press, 1981);

text + kritik, special issues on Handke, 24 (October 1969); 24/24a (July 1971); 24/24a (September 1976); 24 (November 1989).

Christoph Hein

(8 April 1944 -   )

Phillip S. McKnight
University of Kentucky

PLAY PRODUCTIONS: Molière, *Der fliegende Arzt*, translated and adapted by Hein, Berlin, Volksbühne, 11 May 1973;

Vom Furz, translated and adapted by Hein, Berlin, Volksbühne, 11 May 1973;

Vom hungrigen Hennicke, Berlin, Volksbühne, 25 September 1974;

Schlötel oder Was solls, Berlin, Volksbühne, 25 September 1974;

Die Geschäfte des Herrn John D., Neustrelitz, Stadttheater, 21 April 1979;

Cromwell, Cottbus, Theater der Stadt Cottbus, 17 April 1980;

Lasalle fragt Herrn Herbert nach Sonja: Die Szene ein Salon, Düsseldorf, Schauspielhaus, 9 November 1980;

Der Neue Menoza oder Geschichte des kumbanischen Prinzen Tandi: Komödie nach Jakob Michael Reinhold Lenz, Schwerin, Staatliche Bühnen, 29 May 1982;

Die wahre Geschichte des Ah Q, Berlin, Deutsches Theater, 22 December 1983;

Passage, Essen, Grillo-Theater, 25 October 1987;

Die Ritter der Tafelrunde, Dresden, Staatsschauspiel, 12 April 1989;

Ma . . . Ma . . . Marlene: Szenen aus "Horns Ende," Berlin, Maxim-Gorki-Theater, 22 March 1990.

BOOKS: *Einladung zum Lever Bourgeois: Prosa* (Berlin & Weimar: Aufbau, 1980)—includes "Der Sohn";

Cromwell und andere Stücke (Berlin & Weimar: Aufbau, 1981)—comprises *Cromwell*; *Lasalle fragt Herrn Herbert nach Sonja: Die Szene ein Salon*; *Schlötel oder Was solls*; *Der Neue Menoza oder Geschichte des kumbanischen Prinzen Tandi: Komödie nach Jakob Michael Reinhold Lenz*;

Der fremde Freund: Novelle (Berlin & Weimar: Aufbau, 1982); republished as *Drachenblut* (Darmstadt & Neuwied: Luchterhand, 1983); translated by Krishna Winston as *The Distant Lover* (New York: Pantheon, 1989);

Nachtfahrt und früher Morgen (Hamburg: Hoffmann & Campe, 1982);

Das Wildpferd unterm Kachelofen: Ein schönes dickes Buch von Jakob Borg und seinen Freunden (Berlin: Altberliner Verlag, 1984);

Die wahre Geschichte des Ah Q.: Stücke und Essays (Darmstadt & Neuwied: Luchterhand, 1984)—includes *Lasalle fragt Herrn Herbert nach Sonja: Die Szene ein Salon*; "Anmerkungen zu *Lasalle fragt Herrn Herbert nach Sonja: Die Szene ein Salon*";

Horns Ende: Roman (Berlin & Weimar: Aufbau, 1985);

Schlötel oder Was solls: Stücke und Essays (Darmstadt & Neuwied: Luchterhand, 1986)—includes *Cromwell*, "Anmerkungen zu *Cromwell*";

Öffentlich arbeiten: Essais und Gespräche (Berlin & Weimar: Aufbau, 1987);

Die wahre Geschichte des Ah Q; Passage (Berlin: Henschel, 1988);

Der Tangospieler: Roman (Berlin & Weimar: Aufbau, 1989); translated by Philip Boehm as *The Tango Player* (New York: Farrar, Straus & Giroux, 1992);

Die Ritter der Tafelrunde: Komödie (Frankfurt am Main: Luchterhand, 1989)—includes *Die wahre Geschichte des Ah Q, Passage, Britannicus*;

Als Kind habe ich Stalin gesehen: Essais und Reden (Berlin & Weimar: Aufbau, 1990);

Die fünfte Grundrechenart: Aufsätze und Reden (Frankfurt am Main: Luchterhand, 1990);

Bridge Freezes before Roadway (Berlin: Berliner Handpresse, 1990).

OTHER: "Von der Magie und den Magiern," in *Windvogelviereck: Schriftsteller über Wissenschaften und Wissenschaftler*, edited by John Erpenbeck (Berlin: Der Morgen, 1987), pp. 11-34;

"Die Zensur ist überlebt, nutzlos, paradox, menschen- und volksfeindlich, ungesetzlich und strafbar: Rede auf dem X. Schriftstellerkongreß der DDR," in *X. Schriftstellerkongreß der*

Christoph Hein (photograph by Isolde Ohlbaum)

DDR: Arbeitsgruppen, edited by the Schriftstellerverband der DDR (Berlin & Weimar: Aufbau, 1988), pp. 224-247;

Johann Wallbergen, *Sammlung natürlicher Zauberkünste oder aufrichtige Entdeckung vieler bewährter, lustiger, und nützlicher Geheimnisse*, edited by Hein (Leipzig & Weimar: Kiepenheuer, 1988);

"Leserpost oder Ein Buch mit sieben Siegeln," in *Christa Wolf: Ein Arbeitsbuch*, edited by Angela Drescher (Berlin & Weimar: Aufbau, 1989), pp. 398-413;

"Rede am Berliner Alexanderplatz," in *Der Weg zur Demonstration auf dem Alexanderplatz in Berlin*, edited by Initiativgruppe 4.11.89 (Cologne: Kölnische Verlagsdruckerei, 1990), pp. 55-57;

Gustav Just, *Zeuge in eigener Sache*, foreword by Hein (Berlin: Der Morgen, 1990);

"Erinnerung an eine Zeit," in *und diese verdammte Ohnmacht* (Berlin: Basis, 1991), pp. 9-13.

SELECTED PERIODICAL PUBLICATIONS—
UNCOLLECTED: *Die Geschäfte des John D.*, *Theater der Zeit*, 34, no. 6 (1979): 11-13;

"Laudatio auf den Heinrich-Mann-Preisträger Friedrich Dieckmann," *Neue Deutsche Literatur*, 7 (1983): 159-161;

"Massa Sloterdijk und der linke Kolonialismus," *Konkret Literatur* (Fall 1983): 36-41;

"Damit Lessing nicht resigniert: Rede," *Frankfurter Rundschau*, 8 October 1983;

"Das Verschwinden des künstlerischen Produzenten im Zeitalter der Reproduzierbarkeit," *Freibeuter*, 31 (1987): 63-71; 32 (1987): 11-19;

"Literatur und Publikum: Ein Briefwechsel mit Elmar Faber," *Sinn und Form*, 3 (1988): 672-678;

"Die Vergewaltigung," *Neues Deutschland*, 2/3 December 1989, p. 11;

Nachdenken über Deutschland, *Die Weltbühne*, 6 March 1990, pp. 295-298;

"No Sea Route to India," *Time*, 135 (25 June 1990): 68;

"Unbelehrbar—Erich Fried: Rede zur Verleihung des Erich-Fried-Preises am 6. Mai 1990 in Wien," *Freibeuter*, 44 (1990): 24-33;

"Kein Krieg ist heilig. Kein Krieg ist gerecht," *Berliner Zeitung*, 13 February 1991.

Few in the West had heard of Christoph Hein in 1982, when he received the prestigious Heinrich Mann Prize for Literature. Unlike many East German writers who were equally critical of censorship and of the Stalinist regime of the German Democratic Republic (GDR) and who were forcibly expatriated, were compelled to exercise "self-censorship," or simply remained silent, Hein stood out as the country's most eloquent and respected advocate of freedom of speech, press, and artistic expression. Hein established himself as one of the most significant European writers of the late twentieth century with his long novella *Der fremde Freund* (1982; translated as *The Distant Lover*, 1989), which was translated into more than twenty languages within a short time of its publication and became an international best-seller in both Eastern and Western Europe. His controversial play *Die wahre Geschichte des Ah Q* (The True Story of Ah Q; published, 1984), which premiered at the Deutsches Theater in Berlin in 1983, ran for the next six years throughout Europe.

The chief merit of Hein's literary work lies in his relentless search for truth in language. He has said that "Poesie ist keine Sklavenprache" (poesy is not a slave language)—that is, it manifests no tacit agreement with the rulers. He exposes his characters as speakers of "Sklavensprache." He avoids imposing his own attitude on the reader of his prose or the audience at his plays. Social, political, and individual choices, with their various implied consequences, are left open. Hein's plays are a forum in which the audience participates in a continuing dialogue with the author. Hein sought to counteract the spoon-fed dogmatism of the state, which had perpetuated a condition of mental dependency throughout large sections of the population.

Hein was born on 8 April 1944 in Heinzendorf, Silesia (now in Poland), the third of six children of Günther Hein and Lonny Weber Hein. After World War II the family fled the Red Army and took up residence in Bad Düben, near Leipzig, where Hein's father became the town parson and began a long career characterized by resistance to the state's efforts to discredit and suppress religion. From his father, Hein learned resilience, perseverance, and the ability to face adversity without compromising his values. He attended elementary school in Bad Düben from 1950 to 1958, and by the age of twelve he knew he wanted to be a playwright.

Determined that the brightest of his children should not suffer because of his own dedication to his ministry, Günther Hein sent Christoph to join his brother Gottfried at the West Berlin Evangelisches Gymnasium zum grauen Kloster (Evangelical Gymnasium at the Gray Cloister), a humanistic preparatory school which took the sons of East German pastors, doctors, and intellectuals who were not members of the Socialist Unity party.

In 1960 Günther Hein went to East Berlin to lead his church's youth organization. Hein moved in with his parents and commuted to school until August 1961, when the construction of the Berlin Wall forced a decision. Günther Hein was determined to remain in the East with his congregation, and Christoph chose to stay with his family. He was refused entry into the elite preparatory schools, and his application to learn a trade as a cabinetmaker was rejected as well. Between 1961 and 1964 he attended the Vocational School for the German Book Trade, including two years as an apprentice in a bookstore on the Alexanderplatz. In 1964 he began attending evening school at the Volkshochschule (People's High School). He passed his Abitur (school-leaving examination) in 1966 and married Christiane Zauleck in May of the same year.

At the age of nineteen Hein had introduced himself to Benno Besson, a prominent director from Switzerland. Besson had taken Hein under his wing at the Deutsches Theater, and in the 1965-1966 season Hein worked for eight months as the director's assistant without pay, scraping by with honoraria from literary contributions and interviews for weeklies such as *Sonntag* (Sunday) and *Junge Welt* (Young World). Occasionally he picked up ten marks for playing bit parts or forty marks for small singing roles at the theater.

In the summer of 1966 he enrolled at the Cinema College in Babelsberg, but the government ordered the school to invalidate his registration. The intrigues, fictionalized in his short story "Der Sohn" (The Son, 1980), continued when he tried to switch to the College of Theatrical Arts in Leipzig, only to receive a letter of rejection directly from the central Ministry of Culture.

With the birth of his first son, Georg, imminent, Hein moved to Leipzig to be with Christiane and found work as a waiter. Georg was born on 20 October 1966. In January 1967 Hein worked as an assembler in an adding machine factory. In September he finally gained admittance to the Karl-Marx-University in Leipzig. He studied philosophy, but his steadfast adherence to his principles and his biting wit caused an uproar among the faculty and students. After he presented a provocative oral report in 1970, he was advised to change universities or be expelled. He completed his studies at the Humboldt University in Berlin, with a senior thesis on pluralistic logic, in June 1971.

By this time Besson had moved to the Volksbühne (People's Stage) in Berlin, where he and Heiner Müller were leading the venerable theater to its heyday. After Christiane gave birth on 25 October 1971 to their second son, Jakob, Hein went to work as dramaturge and director's assistant at the Volksbühne. He was promoted to house author in 1974.

In his early years at the Volksbühne, Hein translated and adapted Molière's *Le médicin volant* as *Der fliegende Arzt* (The Flying Physician) and the anonymous farce *Du pect* as *Vom Furz* (Of Farts), both of which were first performed on 11 May 1973. His first original plays were both performed at the Volksbühne on 25 September 1974: *Vom hungrigen Hennike* (Hungry Henneke), a short piece for children's theater that questions the heroization of the legendary East German miner Adolf Henneke, was directed by Thomas Valentin; *Schlötel oder Was solls* (Schlötel; or, What's the Use) was directed by Manfred Karge. *Schlötel* was published in 1981 in *Cromwell und andere Stücke* (Cromwell and Other Plays).

Schlötel is set in a factory, but it is not a typical socialist realist work in which solutions to social and economic problems are found by an energetic, heroic worker who then convinces his fellow workers to adopt his ideas. The play examines the conflict of interests between utopian intellectuals and the working class, with its considerably less ambitious needs. The original script portrays Schlötel as a late-1960s radical student who moves from West to East Germany and expects to show the workers what is good for them; in the published version Schlötel is a brilliant sociologist who has just graduated from the University of Leipzig. The new text places more emphasis on the changes brought about by the Neues ökonomisches System (New Economic System), initiated by the Politburo in 1966 to increase productivity.

Schlötel sets out to convince the workers to vote for a system of "Objektlohn" (incentive pay for completed projects), which had been suggested by party leaders. The issue for Schlötel—for which he sacrifices the happiness of his private life with his wife and newborn child—is for the workers to exercise self-determination instead of slavishly accepting the party's orders. But the workers want neither incentive pay, which disrupts the leisurely pace of work, nor emancipation, and they have him fired and banned from the premises. In despair, Schlötel drowns himself in the Baltic Sea. Shortly thereafter, the party decrees the implementation of the incentive pay system. Whether the workers are engaged or apathetic, the party still decides. Hein calls his play a comedy in the vein of J. M. R. Lenz's *Der Hofmeister* (1774; translated as *The Tutor*, 1972). Both plays are replete with humorous dialogue and comic situations, but in each the main character comes to a tragic end while the ruling class continues to do as it pleases.

The West German premiere of *Schlötel*, which was also the first staging of the published version, took place in 1986 in Kassel under the direction of Mathias Fontheim. Many of Hein's references to everyday life in the German Democratic Republic were omitted, and Fontheim's decision to portray Schlötel as a "Storm and Stress" figure undermined the sophisticated intellectual superiority that had lent Hein's character the universal appeal of the idealistic, brooding, and enlightened outsider.

In 1978 Besson and Hein left the Volksbühne due to official harassment over the repertoire. Hein decided to commit himself to full-time writing; by then Christiane had a decent income working on documentary films for DEFA, the East German television consortium. His next stage production was the satirical revue for actors' ensembles, *Die Geschäfte des Herrn John D.* (The Deals of John D., 1979), which premiered on 21 April 1979 in the provincial town of Neustrelitz. The "Drei-Dollar-Operetta" (Three-Dollar Operetta), as it was dubbed by one critic, was favorably reviewed in the West when it was produced at the Vagantenbühne in Berlin in 1983 and at the Theater im Depot in Recklinghausen in 1986 where it was directed by Doris Heliand. The play, which included a medley of American blues, country music, and Dixieland jazz, was a reworking of a 1930 radio play by

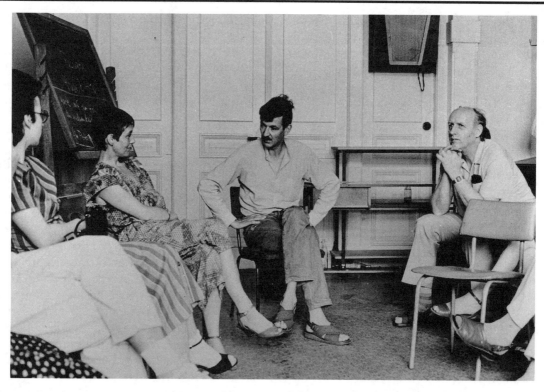

Hein (center) in a discussion with students at the School of Dramatic Arts in Leipzig, circa 1983 (photograph by Viola Vasilieff)

Friedrich Wolf about John D. Rockefeller's monopolization of the oil-refining industry.

In July 1978 *Cromwell*, Hein's first work to be published in the GDR, appeared in *Theater der Zeit* (Theater Times), the monthly theater journal that held the monopoly on all play manuscripts in the country. The historical Oliver Cromwell was a small landowner who was driven by Puritan fundamentalism, which Hein incorporates in the figure of his mother, and was forced into a coalition with the Levellers to prevent the revolution from failing. A faction that arose in the army of the Long Parliament around 1647, the Levellers embodied pure communistic ideals, advocating the leveling of all ranks and the establishment of a more democratic government. It was their influence that pushed Cromwell to execute Charles I in 1649 and to have himself named Lord Protector of the Puritan Republic. Hein's *Cromwell* is sprinkled with anachronisms taken from the French Revolution, czarist Russia, and speeches by Joseph Stalin, and with references to cigarettes, Mauser pistols, Datschas, Red Brothers, Compañeros, and colloquialisms from everyday East German life. The most stunning anachronism is the fate of the Levellers, who are loaded into train cars for the west coast. Ten miles from the Irish Sea the train is stopped, the boxcar

doors are thrown open, and the soldiers are liquidated by forty-three machine guns.

The play was blocked in a dozen other cities before it premiered at the Theater der Stadt (City Theater) in Cottbus on 17 April 1980, directed by Peter Röll. It was cut extensively, and the revisions incorporated references to the Nazis. The West German premiere in Essen on 24 October 1986 went to the opposite extreme by clothing Cromwell's soldiers in East German army uniforms and Cromwell's son in the blue shirt of the Communist Young Pioneers. Han Günther Heyme's version, which premiered on 24 October 1986, focused on the tension between Cromwell's Puritan background, the political impact of the Levellers, and the business interests of Parliament. In 1984 East German productions directed by Klaus Krampe in Gera and by Michael Grosse in Eisenach succeeded in portraying Cromwell's corruption, self-indulgence, and arbitrary exercise of power.

The conflict between public achievement and private values depicted in *Schlötel* and *Cromwell* is the focal point of *Lasalle fragt Herrn Herbert nach Sonja: Die Szene ein Salon* (Lasalle Asks Mr. Herbert about Sonja: The Scene a Salon; published in *Cromwell und andere Stücke*), which Hein described as both a critique and a continuation of *Cromwell. Lasalle fragt Herrn Herbert nach Sonja* is based on the founder of the General German Workers' Union, Ferdinand Lasalle. Hein sets the play in a salon, representative of a stagnating, superficial society. Lasalle, by his own admission, is unable to overcome his own petit bourgeois indulgences and Jewish intellectual background to the point of being able to identify with the workers he purports to represent. His decadence is revealed by his womanizing, which ultimately becomes more important to him than his political program. He dies from a wound to the genitals received in a foolish duel over a woman.

Hein decided to give *Lasalle fragt Herrn Herbert nach Sonja* to a West German theater, and it premiered in Düsseldorf on 9 November 1980, directed by Heinz Engels. It was the first work by Hein to be performed in the West. Aside from antagonizing the West German left, the play was relatively well received. It was more than six years before the play was allowed to be performed in East Germany, opening in Erfurt on 2 February 1987 under the direction of Ekkehard Emig.

Plays that treated alienation or the loss of definitive certainties were virtually nonexistent on the East German stage; thus, when *Die wahre Geschichte des Ah Q* premiered on 22 December 1983—this time not in the provinces but at the Deutsches Theater in East Berlin under the direction of Alexander Lang—it created a sensation. The West German premiere in Kassel, directed by Valentin Jeker, took place a month after the French premiere at the Théatre National de Strasbourg in November 1984. The play went on to be a tremendous success in Paris, Bordeaux, Bern, Zurich, Vienna, Graz, West Berlin, Düsseldorf, Hamburg, Tübingen, Paderborn, Nuremberg, and Wiesbaden.

The play is an adaptation of the Chinese writer Lu Xun's 1921 short story of the same title, a tale of the Boxer Revolution in China in 1911. Hein incorporated dialogue from the story but changed the central character from a village beggar to a self-centered bourgeois intellectual. Ah Q and Wang, intellectuals and self-styled anarchists, are waiting for a revolution which does, in fact, come, but they do not notice it until after it is over. They are locked in a room in a dilapidated building by the Temple Guard, a bureaucrat who follows orders and official policy unquestioningly. Ah Q rapes and kills the nun who has brought them milk soup every Thursday. He is depicted as not quite realizing what he is doing; the analogy to be drawn is the unwit-

ting destruction by bureaucracy of humane values. On two occasions Ah Q addresses the audience. In the first instance he goes into the sixth or seventh row of seats in an attempt to find a single statement that expresses the essence of existence. He stops, returns to the stage, and declares, "ich habe keine Botschaft" (I have no message to give); the audience will have to think of one on its own. The other instance has Wang and Ah Q claiming that they are only performing scenes from the world of bureaucrats and professionals and that the audience members are all bureaucrats.

While the youthful members of the audience responded with glee at the premiere, the bureaucrats and dignitaries invited to the show walked out in protest. Nevertheless, the play ran for six years at the Deutsches Theater, a remarkable run for a contemporary play and strongly indicative of public support in the face of official disapproval.

In the spring of 1987 Hein accepted an invitation from the University of Kentucky to visit the United States. He spent a month traveling with an interpreter under the auspices of the United States Information Agency, visiting dramatists, workshops, and theaters in Virginia, New Orleans, San Francisco, and New York, and a second month conducting workshops and lecturing at the University of Kentucky, Amherst College, New York University, Vanderbilt University, the University of Texas, and UCLA. His return to the GDR was followed by one of his most productive periods, with the publication of many essays, two plays, and the novel *Der Tangospieler* (1989; translated as *The Tango Player*, 1992), which portrays an academic who passes up a chance to become independent and returns to his career under terms that compromise his integrity. It was a bitter commentary on the distortion of the socialist dream by the corrupt Stalinist structure. The two plays were *Passage* (performed, 1987; published, 1988) and *Die Ritter der Tafelrunde* (The Knights of the Round Table, 1989).

Passage is set in the back room of a café in the south of France in 1940. The play depicts the anxiety, hope, and despair of a group of Jewish refugees seeking to get across the border into Spain before the Gestapo closes in on them. When the Gestapo does find them, it causes a break from their lethargic condition of waiting and hoping for the impossible. The catalyst for the existential choices is Hugo Frankfurter—a character based on the critic Walter Benjamin—

Jews crossing the mountains from occupied France into Spain to escape the Gestapo in a scene from the premiere of Hein's Passage *in Essen in 1987 (photograph by Dominique Ecken)*

who stuns the group by poisoning himself as the Gestapo is inspecting their papers. The town's mayor, Paul Joly, who had been protecting the refugees, decides to go to Paris to join the Resistance. The others attempt to escape but are turned back for one more day until the Spanish border opens. The key figure of the play is a seventy-five-year-old retired German officer, Alfred Hirschburg, who is subject to the scorn of the group for his insistence on retaining his identity as a German. In his mind his Jewish origin is of no consequence, and his problems are attributable to a misunderstanding. He breaches the fragile security of the village hideaway by inviting an old comrade in arms to join him. When his friend shows up leading a group of fifteen old Jewish men in traditional caftans who had made a dreamlike trek from Zator, the old duchy of Auschwitz, Hirschburg's historical consciousness is jolted, and his adamant Germanness is transformed. To the awe of the others, Hirschburg leads the old men by night out of the village on a surrealistic trek over the mountains. As the director of the play at the Dresdner Staatsschauspiel (State Playhouse) viewed it, the image of the fif-

teen Jews was a challenge to everyone to contemplate the limits of the possible.

Hein's last play before the end of the German Democratic Republic in many ways predicted the fall of the Communist regime. It showed the stagnation and senility of the older generation and its inability to cope with change. Directed by Klaus Dieter Kirst, *Die Ritter der Tafelrunde* was scheduled to premiere on 24 March 1989 in Dresden. As officials became aware of its content, a controversy ensued about staging it. A "preview" was staged on 24 March and was followed by five or six additional previews, all sellouts. The official premiere took place on 12 April 1989, but the play was performed only once more that season. After the opening of the Berlin Wall, however, the play appeared in theaters all over East Germany and, beginning in Kassel, in many theaters in West Germany as well.

King Artus (Arthur) and his knights represent the old Communist rulers who maintained that history, not they, was mistaken. The knights believe that they must uphold the belief in the Holy Grail even though they have given up hope of ever finding it. Lancelot, who has become editor of an underground newspaper, reports that the people think of their leaders as fools and criminals. Artus's son, Mordret, says that he has no interest in assuming the throne and that he would put the Round Table in a museum. The play ends with Mordret telling Artus that he, Mordret, is going to destroy everything.

A speech Hein gave on freedom of expression at the East German Writers Congress in November 1987 led to the end of censorship in the German Democratic Republic and opened the way to the peaceful revolution of 1989. He was active in the demonstrations, giving speeches and interviews in both East and West. He then worked with the committee established to investigate police brutality during the national celebrations on 7 and 8 October 1989, which preceded the massive November demonstrations and the opening of the Berlin Wall. Hein's hopes for a democratic form of socialism were dashed as the two Germanies were unified under the capitalist system of West Germany. He had once said that if he were to move to the West it would take him years before he could write again; but the West had come to him. Having sold his Bergsdorf farmhouse in 1988, he found a new home near Krakow, an eastern German town near the Polish border, where he could work and collect his thoughts. He has resisted entreaties to enter politics.

Interviews:

"Interview mit Christoph Hein," *Theater der Zeit*, 7 (1978): 51-52;

Gregor Edelmann, " 'Ansonsten würde man ja aufhören zu schreiben . . .' : Interview mit Christoph Hein," *Theater der Zeit*, 10 (1983): 54-56;

Janice Murray and Mary-Elizabeth O'Brian, "Interview mit Christoph Hein," *New German Review*, 3 (1987): 53-66;

Krzystof Joachimczak, "Gespräch mit Christoph Hein," *Sinn und Form*, 2 (1988): 342-359;

Günter Gaus, "Christoph Hein: Gespräch vom 14. März 1990," in *Zur Person*, edited by Gaus (Berlin: Volk und Welt, 1990), pp. 95-114.

Bibliography:

Manfred Behn, "Christoph Hein," in *Kritisches Lexikon zur deutschsprachigen Gegenwartsliteratur*, volume 3, edited by Heinz Ludwig Arnold (Munich: Edition text + kritik, n.d.), n.pag.

References:

Wolfgang Albrecht, "Christoph Hein: Dramatiker und Erzähler," *Deutsch als Fremdsprache: Zeitschrift für Theorie und Praxis des Deutschunterrichts für Ausländer*, 21 (1984): 41-54;

Matthias Altenburg, "Dem Leben kann man nur davonlaufen," *Konkret Literatur* (Fall 1985): 88-89;

Lothar Baier and others, *Christoph Hein: Texte, Daten, Bilder* (Frankfurt am Main: Luchterhand, 1990);

Rudiger Bernhardt and others, "Fur und wider: *Der fremde Freund*," *Weimarer Beiträge*, 9 (1983): 1635-1655;

Brigitte Böttcher, "Diagnose eines unheilbaren Zustands," *Neue Deutsche Literatur*, 6 (1983): 145-149;

Fabrizio Cambi, "Jetztzeit und Vergangenheit: Ästhetische und ideologische Auseinandersetzung im Werke Christoph Heins," in *Die Literatur der DDR: Akten der internationalen Konferenz, Pisa, Mai*, edited by Anna Chiarloni and others (Pisa: Giardini, 1988), pp. 79-86;

Günther Cwordrak, "Ah Q oder was solls," *Weltbühne*, 1 (1984): 26-28;

Jürgen Engler, "Moralität ohne Rückhalt," in *DDR-Literatur '85 im Gespräch*, edited by Siegfried Rönisch (Berlin & Weimar: Aufbau, 1986), pp. 130-136;

Adolf Fink, "Ein Lindenblatt der Verletzlichkeit," in *Deutsche Literatur 1983* (Stuttgart: Reclam, 1984), pp. 134-138;

Bernd Fischer, *Christoph Hein: Drama und Prosa im letzten Jahrzehnt der DDR* (Heidelberg: Winter, 1990);

Fischer, "Christoph Heins *Die wahre Geschichte des Ah Q* (zwischen Hund und Wolf) nach Luxun: Zum komischen Traditionsbezug im Drama der DDR," in *Crossings-Kreuzungen: Festschrift für Helmut Kreuzer*, edited by Edward R. Haymes (Columbia, S.C.: Camden House, 1990), pp. 10-31;

Fischer, "*Drachenblut*: Christoph Heins 'fremde Freundin,' " *Colloquia Germanica*, 21, no. 1 (1988): 46-57;

Fischer, "*Einladung zum Lever Bourgeois*: Christoph Hein's First Prose," in *Studies in GDR Culture and Society 4*, edited by Margy Gerber (Lanham, Md.: University Press of America, 1984), pp. 125-136;

Christoph Funke, "Spiel mit der Geschichte," *Neue Deutsche Literatur*, 10 (1981): 149-152;

Scene from the premiere of Hein's Die Ritter der Tafelrunde *in Dresden in 1989, with (left to right) Rudolf Donath as King Artus, Helga Werner as Jeschute, Joachim Zschocke as Keie, Thomas Stecher as Mordret, and Hanns-Jörn Weber as Parzifal (photograph by Ludwig Böhme)*

Ilse-Marie Gates, "Christoph Heins Novelle *Der fremde Freund*—ein fiktionaler Bericht moderner Kommunikationsschwierigkeiten," *Carleton Germanic Papers*, 18 (1990): 51-73;

Bernhard Greiner, "Bürgerliches Lachtheater als Komödie in der DDR: J. M. R. Lenz' *Der neue Menoza*, bearbeitet von Christoph Hein," in *Die Literatur der DDR: Akten der internationalen Konferenz, Pisa*, edited by Chiarloni and others (Pisa: Giardini, 1988), pp. 329-345;

Antonia Grunenberg, "Geschichte und Entfremdung: Christoph Hein als Autor der DDR," *Michigan Germanic Studies*, 8, nos. 1-2 (1985): 229-251;

Peter Hacks, "Heinrich-Mann-Preis 1982: Laudatio," *Neue Deutsche Literatur*, 6 (1982):159-163;

Klaus Hammer, "Christoph Hein: *Horns Ende*," *Weimarer Beiträge*, 8 (1987): 1358-1369;

Hammer and others, *Chronist ohne Botschaft. Christoph Hein. Ein Arbeitsbuch* (Berlin & Weimar: Aufbau, 1992);

Ursula Heukenkamp, "Die fremde Form," *Sinn und Form*, 3 (1983): 625-632;

Karin Hirdina, "Das Normale der Provinz," *Neue Deutsche Literatur*, 8 (1989): 138-143;

Frank Hörnigk, "*Cromwell*," *Weimarer Beiträge*, 1 (1983): 33-39;

Hörnigk, "*Die wahre Geschichte des Ah Q*—ein Clownspiel mit Phantasie," in *DDR-Literatur '83 im Gespräch* (Berlin & Weimar: Aufbau, 1984), pp. 41-51;

Michael Hulse, "Tumult, Horn and Double Bass," *Antigonish Review*, nos. 66-67 (Summer-Autumn 1986): 247-257;

Siegfried Jäkel, "Das Prinzip des Eklektizismus in Christoph Heins Roman *Horns Ende*," *Jahrbuch für finnisch-deutsche Literaturbeziehungen: Mitteilungen aus der Deutschen Bibliothek*, 21 (1989): 193-201;

Antje Janssen-Zimmermann, *Gegenwürfe: Untersuchungen zu Dramen Christoph Heins* (Frankfurt, Bern, New York & Paris: Lang, 1988);

Klaus Jarmatz, "Vorführung eines dialogischen Prinzips," *Neue Deutsche Literatur*, 9 (1988): 135-140;

Hans Kaufmann, "Christoph Hein in der Debatte," in *DDR-Literature '83 im Gespräch*, pp. 41-51;

Heinz Klunker, "Der Revolutionär endet im Salon," *Theater heute*, 2 (1981): 8-10;

Gabriele Kreis, "In diese Haut wird nichts eindringen," *Konkret Literatur* (Fall 1983): 82-83;

Hartmut Krug, "Ritter von der traurigen Gestalt," *Theater heute*, 7 (1989): 23-26;

Marianne Krumrey, "Gegenwart im Spiegel der Geschichte," *Temperamente*, 4 (1981): 143-147;

Gabriele Lindner, "Ein geistiger Widergänger," *Neue Deutsche Literatur*, 10 (1986): 155-161;

Deitrich Löffler, "Christoph Hein: *Öffentlich arbeiten*," in *DDR-Literatur '87 im Gespräch* (Berlin & Weimar: Aufbau, 1988), pp. 252-258;

Löffler, "Christoph Heins Prosa—Chronik der Zeitgeschichte," *Weimarer Beiträge*, 9 (1987): 1484-1487;

Phillip S. McKnight, "Alltag, Apathy, Anarchy: GDR Everyday Life as a Provocation in Christoph Hein's Novelle *Der fremde Freund*," in *Studies in GDR Culture and Society 8*, edited by Gerber (Lanham, Md., New York & London: University Press of America, 1988), pp. 179-190;

McKnight, "Ein Mosaik zu Christoph Heins Roman *Horns Ende*," *Sinn und Form*, 2 (1987): 413-425;

Georg Menchén, "Verlorene Geschichtlichkeit," *Theater der Zeit*, 5 (1987): 52-53;

Timm Menke, "Der Literat als Politiker: Zur Vorwärtsverteidigung der Kunst in den Essays von Christoph Hein," *Germanic Review*, 64 (Fall 1989): 177-181;

Karl-Heinz Müller, "Wem nützen Ideale?," *Theater der Zeit*, 8 (1980): 12-13;

Heinz-Peter Preußer, *Zivilisationskritik und literarische Öffentlichkeit. Strukturale und wertungstheoretische Untersuchungen zu erzählenden Texten Christoph Heins* (Frankfurt am Main, Bern, New York & Paris: Lang, 1991);

Peter Reichel, " 'En passant': Zitate und Notate zu Christoph Heins *Passage*," *Theater der Zeit*, 5 (1987): 50-53;

Lutz Richter, "Christoph Hein: Auf eine neue Art zum Nachdenken zwingen," *Deutsch als Fremdsprache: Zeitschrift für Theorie und Praxis des Deutschunterrichts für Ausländer*, 24 (1987): 79-89;

Andreas Roßmann, "Der erneuerte Menoza," *Theater heute*, 8 (1982): 42-43;

Roßmann, "Die Revolution als Geisterschiff," *Theater heute*, 3 (1984): 53;

Roßmann, "Die Revolution frißt ihre Ideale," *Theater heute*, 10 (1980): 64-66;

Roßmann, "Kein leichtes Spiel: DDR-Dramatik im Westen," *Deutschland-Archiv*, 12 (1986): 1255-1259;

Dieter Schlenstedt and others, "DDR-Literaturentwicklung in der Diskussion," *Weimarer Beiträge*, 10 (1984): 1589-1616;

Joscha Schmierer, "Das Menschliche, der Mann, der Funktionär und die Frauen," *Kommune*, 3 (1986): 65-68;

Galina Snamenskaja, "Die geistig-seelische Suche im Werk Christoph Heins," *Weimarer Beiträge*, 3 (1990): 506-511;

Erika Stephan, "Christoph Heins Kammerspiel *Passage* im Verständnis des Theaters," in *DDR-Literatur '87 im Gespräch*, pp. 259-272;

Jürgen Stötzer, "Lenz—ein Schatten nur einer ungesehenen Tradition? Aspekte der Rezeption J.M.R. Lenz' bei Christoph Hein," *Zeitschrift für Germanistik*, 9 (1989): 429-441;

Text + Kritik, special Hein issue, 111 (1991);

Hans-Georg Werner and others, "*Der fremde Freund* von Christoph Hein," *Ginkgobaum*, 5 (1986): 34-44.

Günter Herburger

(6 April 1932 -   )

Patricia H. Stanley
Florida State University

See also the Herburger entry in *DLB 75: Contemporary German Fiction Writers, Second Series.*

BOOKS: *Eine gleichmäßige Landschaft: Erzählungen* (Cologne & Berlin: Kiepenheuer & Witsch, 1964); translated by Geoffrey Skelton as *A Monotonous Landscape: Seven Stories* (New York: Harcourt, Brace & World, 1968; London: Calder & Boyars, 1969);

Ventile: Gedichte (Cologne & Berlin: Kiepenheuer & Witsch, 1966);

Die Messe: Roman (Darmstadt & Neuwied: Luchterhand, 1969);

Training: Gedichte (Darmstadt & Neuwied: Luchterhand, 1970);

Jesus in Osaka: Roman (Darmstadt & Neuwied: Luchterhand, 1970);

Birne kann alles: 26 Abenteuergeschichten für Kinder (Darmstadt & Neuwied: Luchterhand, 1971);

Birne kann noch mehr: 26 Abenteuergeschichten für Kinder (Darmstadt & Neuwied: 1971);

Die Eroberung der Zitadelle: Erzählungen (Darmstadt & Neuwied: Luchterhand, 1972);

Helmut in der Stadt: Erzählung für Kinder (Reinbeck: Rowohlt, 1972);

Die amerikanische Tochter: Gedichte, Aufsätze, Hörspiel, Erzählung, Film (Darmstadt & Neuwied: Luchterhand, 1973)—includes "Exhibition oder Ein Kampf um Rom," translated by André Lefevere as "Exhibition; or, A Battle for Rome," *Dimension,* 5, no. 3 (1972): 456-507;

Operette: Gedichte (Darmstadt & Neuwied: Luchterhand, 1973);

Hauptlehrer Hofer; Ein Fall von Pfingsten: Zwei Erzählungen mit einem Nachwort des Autors (Darmstadt & Neuwied: Luchterhand, 1975);

Nüssen und andere Erzählungen (Berlin & Weimar: Aufbau, 1975);

Birne brennt durch: 26 Abenteuergeschichten für Kinder und Erwachsene (Darmstadt & Neuwied: Luchterhand, 1975);

Ziele: Gedichte (Reinbek: Rowohlt, 1977);

Günter Herburger (photograph by Renate von Mangoldt)

Flug ins Herz: Roman, 2 volumes (Darmstadt & Neuwied: Luchterhand, 1977);

Orchidee: Gedichte (Darmstadt & Neuwied: Luchterhand, 1979);

Die Augen der Kämpfer: Roman (Darmstadt & Neuwied: Luchterhand, 1980);

Birne: Die schönsten Abenteuergeschichten für Kinder aus Birne kann alles, Birne kann noch mehr, Birne brennt durch, edited by Herburger, Klaus Roehler, and Daniel Herburger (Darmstadt & Neuwied: Luchterhand, 1980);

Blick aus dem Paradies; Thuja: Zwei Spiele eines Themas (Darmstadt & Neuwied: Luchterhand, 1981);

Makadam: Gedichte (Darmstadt & Neuwied: Luchterhand, 1982);

Das Flackern des Feuers im Land: Beschreibungen (Darmstadt & Neuwied: Luchterhand, 1983);

Die Augen der Kämpfer: Zweite Reise. Roman (Darmstadt & Neuwied: Luchterhand, 1983);

Das Lager: Ausgewählte Gedichte, 1966-1983 (Darmstadt & Neuwied: Luchterhand, 1984);

Capri: Die Geschichte eines Diebs (Darmstadt & Neuwied: Luchterhand, 1984);

Kinderreich Passmoré: Gedichte (Darmstadt & Neuwied: Luchterhand, 1986);

Lauf und Wahn (Ravensburg: Oberschwäbische Verlagsanstalt, 1988);

Kreuzwege (Frankfurt am Main: Luchterhand, 1988);

Das brennende Haus: Gedichte (Frankfurt am Main: Luchterhand, 1990).

MOTION PICTURE: *Tätowierung*, Houwer Film, 1967.

TELEVISION: *Abschied*, Sender Freies Berlin, 1966;

Der Beginn, Sender Freies Berlin, 1966;

Tag der offenen Tür, Westdeutscher Rundfunk, 1967;

Das Bild, Westdeutscher Rundfunk, 1967;

Die Söhne, Westdeutscher Rundfunk, 1968;

Tanker, Westdeutscher Rundfunk, 1970;

Helmut in der Stadt, Hessischer Rundfunk, 1974;

Hauptlehrer Hofer, Sender Freies Berlin, 1975;

Die Eroberung der Zitadelle, Westdeutscher Rundfunk, 1977.

RADIO: *Gespräch am Nachmittag*, Bayerischer Rundfunk, 7 July 1961;

Der Reklameverteiler, Saarländischer Rundfunk, 3 April 1963;

Die Ordentlichen, Saarländischer Rundfunk, 7 June 1965;

Der Topf, Saarländischer Rundfunk, 20 October 1965;

Wohnungen, Radio Bremen, 19 November 1965;

Blick aus dem Paradies, RIAS Berlin, 18 May 1966;

Tag der offenen Tür, Süddeutscher Rundfunk, 25 May 1966;

Das Geschäft, Westdeutscher Rundfunk, 14 January 1970;

Exhibition oder Ein Kampf um Rom, Westdeutscher Rundfunk, 7 October 1971;

Thuja, Westdeutscher Rundfunk, 17 September 1980;

Der Garten, Südwestfunk, 7 July 1984;

Im Zeitsee, Sender Freies Berlin, 1 March 1986.

OTHER: Edouard Dujardin, *Geschnittener Lorbeer*, translated by Herburger (Cologne: Kiepenheuer & Witsch, 1966);

"Saison," in *Aus der Welt der Arbeit*, edited by Fritz Hüser and Max von der Grün (Neuwied & Berlin: Luchterhand, 1966), pp. 270-280;

"Die Verzögerung," in *Porträts*, edited by Walter Karsch (Berlin, Munich & Vienna: Herbig, 1967), pp. 13-19;

"Ende der Nazizeit und andere Gedichte," in *Neue Texte deutscher Autoren*, edited by Martin Gregor-Dellin (Tübingen & Basel: Erdmann, 1971), pp. 152-155;

"Das Allgäu," in *Daheim ist daheim*, edited by Alois Brandstetter (Salzburg: Residenz, 1973), pp. 101-108.

SELECTED PERIODICAL PUBLICATIONS—
UNCOLLECTED: "Das Haus," *Augenblicke*, 1 (1961): 59-61;

"Anderer Abend eines Chauffeurs, *konkret*, no. 5 (1965): 28-29, 32-33;

"Tag der offenen Tür," *Der Monat*, 209 (1966): 59-69;

"Training," *Neue Rundschau*, 78 (1967): 637-644;

"Tanker," *Akzente*, 14 (1967): 455-475;

"Dogmatisches über Gedichte," *Kursbuch*, 10 (1967): 150-161;

"Wider die Fernsehfabriken," *Film*, 5 (1967): 40;

"Eine dritte Revolution: Über Enzensbergers *Kursbuch 9*," *Der Spiegel*, 21 (July 1967): 82-83;

"Landschaft und Vorfahren," *Der Monat*, 222 (1967): 24-30;

"Bankrott der Väter," *Der Monat*, 226 (1967): 5-8;

"Filmklima," *Film*, 10 (1967): 10;

"Die Tätowierung: Filmprotokoll," *Film*, 10 (1967): 45-56;

"Viktor und Bruno: Catch," *konkret*, no. 16 (1969): 40-45;

"Hope," *Kürbiskern*, 1 (1975): 125-138;

"Palimpsest," *Literaturmagazin*, 3 (1976): 191-199;

"Romankapitel: Wieder anfangen," *Literaturmagazin*, 6 (1976): 84-108;

"Gedichte aus Schwaben," *Akzente*, 23 (1976): 135-138.

The radio play became a significant genre in Germany after World War II, before the theaters destroyed in the war were rebuilt. It remains popular today, even though theater productions are now flourishing and television has entered most German homes. Günter Herburger, a writer of novels, critical essays, poetry, and films, began early in his literary career to write radio plays as well. The immediacy of his dialogues and their lack of artifice encourage the listener to identify with his characters.

Herburger was born on 6 April 1932 to Grete Dethleffs Herburger and Adolf Christian Herburger in Isny im Allgäu, a town in southwestern Germany not far from the Swiss border. Herburger's mother is still living; his father, a veterinarian in civilian life, was killed in action in Poland in 1943. After the death of his father, Herburger lived for a time with his grandfather before becoming a scholarship pupil at a Protestant boarding school. He studied piano, painted, wrote poetry, and engaged in sports; but he also became involved in selling black-market cigarettes, and this activity cost him his scholarship. He remained a student at the school, living in a rented room in town. To supplement the little money his mother sent him, he rented the room to fellow students who wanted to spend time with their girlfriends while he went to all-night movies, where, as he has said, he received a second education from American and French films.

Herburger completed his boarding-school education in 1952. From 1953 to 1954 he studied philosophy, Sanskrit, literature, theater, and sociology at the University of Munich and then at the Sorbonne in Paris, but he soon ran out of funds. He worked for some ten years in legal and illegal trades throughout Europe and wrote at night until he became seriously ill from malnutrition. On his recovery he lived for a time in Celle. In 1961 he moved to Stuttgart, where he became a journalist and television editor. His first publication, a journal article, appeared in 1961, and on 7 July of that year his first radio play, *Gespräch am Nachmittag* (Conversation in the Afternoon), aired on Bavarian Radio. From 1962 to 1969 he lived in Berlin. A second play, *Der Reklameverteiler* (The Advertising Distributor) was broadcast by Saarland Radio on 3 April 1963. In 1964 he was invited to become a member of the prestigious writers' organization, Gruppe (Group) 47, and he read his work at a meeting of the group that year in Sigtuna, Sweden. In 1965 he received the Berlin Art Prize "Young Generation," and three of his radio plays were broadcast: *Die Ordentlichen* (Respectable People), *Der Topf* (The Pot), and *Wohnungen* (Dwellings). Since then Herburger has had no difficulty earning his living solely from his writing.

The first of Herburger's radio plays to be published was aired in Berlin on RIAS (Radio in the American Sector) on 18 May 1966: *Blick aus dem Paradies* (The View from Paradise; published, 1981) consists of eleven scenes in which two people, identified only as "er" (he) and "sie" (she), mature from adolescence to old age and death. In scenes 1, 3, 5, 7, 9, and 11 the boy and girl climb to a platform built by the boy in a tree and have their first sexual encounter, surrounded by sounds of birds and animals. A crowd of tourists gathers below, and the boy and girl decide to leave their paradise and make a home in the mountain range in the distance. Among the tourists they recognize themselves as middle-aged; they also see an elderly gentleman whom they both claim as their grandfather. The young people have discussed their grandfathers' idiosyncrasies in detail earlier in the play, but when they inexplicably recognize him below their platform the motif is dropped. The hearer waits in vain for a connection to be made between the grandfather and the couple's later life. It is characteristic of Herburger's writing that, just as in real life, loose ends remain.

The future of the couple is depicted in the even-numbered scenes, and it is as lackluster as the tree-house scenes were bucolic. The adolescents seek privacy in a coal cellar but are chased out by the girl's father. They become parents, quarrel over money, and in scene 8 the girl—who is now a woman—continues to sew as her husband is dragged out of the house by an ambulance driver who insists that he has an order to take the man in for an operation. His suitcase is already packed, the woman announces. In scene 10 the two are dead and buried beside each other in paper clothing. The woman laments that she never had a garden with a high fence, and the man is sorry that he did not travel.

Although absurdist elements appear in all of Herburger's work, his plots are too realistically grounded to be categorized as theater of the absurd. The term *New Sensitivity* that has been applied to his poetry by critics such as Richard Spuler is a more apt, if inexact, label for his drama as well. By *New Sensitivity* is meant an immediacy of communication achieved by eliminating metaphor, using colloquial speech, and paying special attention to everyday objects. This subjective realism is embellished by Herburger with fanciful, sometimes surreal or absurdist sequences.

On 7 October 1971 West German Radio aired Herburger's *Exhibition oder Ein Kampf um*

Rom, which was published in an English translation as "Exhibition; or, A Battle for Rome" in 1972 and in German in 1973. The characters included Herburger, played by himself; Mauricio Kagel, a musician and composer; Ludwig van Beethoven; tradespeople; and a group of sixth-century Italians. Herburger opens the play by calling Kagel on the telephone and proposing that they create a radio play as they speak. Kagel is agreeable, but the conversation soon breaks off. In the next scene Herburger is on the street with a tape recorder questioning passers-by. Kagel's voice returns in a sequence that involves a chauffeur telephoning his employer in the course of being interviewed by Herburger, and Kagel is an intermittent speaker for the rest of the play.

Beethoven introduces himself in several languages, following an excerpt from his Fifth Symphony, which resounds behind Kagel's voice. Several such extraneous speakers are heard before Kagel mentions a sixth-century Italian woman, Amalaswintha, who was killed in a palace intrigue. A play within the play now begins, featuring Amalaswintha, her slaves, and her enemy, the Princess Gothlindis, who kills Amalaswintha by filling her bath with near-boiling water. Kagel and Herburger interrupt this interior play with commentary, and the voices of both men are heard underwater as they try to rescue Amalaswintha from the bathtub. At this point the tape runs out, and the play ends.

According to the preface, the filmscript, *Die amerikanische Tochter* (The American Daughter), published in 1973 but never produced, is a story of guilt and madness exposed unwittingly by a naive American girl as she tries to express her love for her German mother by imitating the hardships the mother endured during World War II. Rita Wayne (to be played, according to Herburger's fanciful casting directions, by Rita Tushingham) has been raised by her father, John Wayne (who is to play himself). Her mother, Christina Opitz (to be played by Kristina Söderbaum), is an industrialist, the widow of the founder of an industrial empire. At the beginning of the film Rita goes to Germany and meets her mother for the first time, because Christina wants to make the daughter her heir. On hearing this news, Luis Opitz (to be played by Luis Trenker), Christina's brother-in-law, decides to marry the girl. Although she is portrayed as a wide-eyed innocent, Rita quickly displays a penchant for knife-throwing: she carries the knife in her blouse and launches it, with a broad smile, at

the dining room wall on her first evening in the Opitz home. Later she slightly injures the family attorney (to be played by Dr. Alexander Kluge), when she throws the knife in his direction. During a tour of one of the family's factories she displays socialist tendencies by talking to the workers and even taking part in their work. After hearing of her mother's youthful meeting with John Wayne, Rita decides to ignore all further efforts to acquaint her with the empire she will inherit. Instead, she revisits places where her mother grew up and starves herself in order to understand how the mother felt when she met the soldier who gave her chocolate and whom she decided not to marry after she became pregnant. (No explanation is given as to how or why Rita wound up in the United States with her father instead of in Germany with her mother.) Rita also visits, with Luis, the prison where he served his brother's sentence for using prisoners as slave labor during the war. She then indulges in an inexplicable escapade with Mark, the family chauffeur (to be played by Mark Spitz) and lover of the family secretary (to be played by Catherine Deneuve), in which the two pose as blind and deaf and beg for money. After this scene Mark rejects Rita and returns to the Opitz estate. The family attorney, dispatched to bring Rita back to her mother, is with the girl on a train in Switzerland when Luis kidnaps her by skiing resolutely beside the train until he finds the right compartment. He leaps into it through the window, pulls the emergency brake, and exits with the girl. She climbs behind him on the skis, and they eventually reach a cabin near the Matterhorn.

Rita is rescued by her father, who has come to Germany to marry Christina. John Wayne shoots Luis. He and Rita tame two wild horses they find in the snow and ride to an estate beside a lake, where the attorney and the secretary are shooting skeet and Christina is out on the lake with Mark. John Wayne takes a motorboat from the dock and pulls up beside them. When he tells Christina that he has killed Luis, she laughs, says he will get nothing from her, and orders Mark to kiss her. John shoots Christina, and Mark leaps into the water. John fires repeatedly, killing Mark and the secretary, who is screaming on shore. Rita then shoots her father. The camera moves from one bleeding body to the next, and the film ends with Rita alone on an empty street, the Matterhorn in the background. The reader may well wonder what America .novies Herburger saw as a boy in the all-night theaters.

In 1972 Herburger campaigned for the German Communist party; he became a member of the Party in 1973. That year he received the Literature Prize of the city of Bremen. In 1979 he was awarded the Gerritt Engelke Prize of the City of Hannover and the stipend "Villa Serpentara." In 1980 he received a year's stipend awarded by the Ministry for Science and Art in Baden-Württemberg, and he received a similar stipend in 1981 from Munich.

Thuja—the title is an Austrian term meaning "tree of life"—aired on West German Radio on 17 September 1980 and was published in 1981. The narrator of the play, Johann Jakob Weberbeck, also narrates the novel trilogy *Flug ins Herz* (Flight into the Heart, 1977), *Die Augen der Kämpfer* (The Eyes of the Fighters, 1980), and *Die Augen der Kämpfer: Zweite Reise* (The Eyes of the Fighters: Second Journey, 1983). In the first scene Weberbeck and two women, each of whom has borne a child by him, are defending the University of Essen from an artillery attack by other women. All three are grievously wounded. In the rest of the play Weberbeck, sitting in the Thuja tree that grows above his family's cemetery plot, converses with various relatives who, like him, are dead. In scene 4 he meets his father, who died when he was a boy, and relives for the father an incident in which a Nazi instructor forced the boy to jump from a height of twenty meters. In scene 7 he looks down on his children, who have come to the cemetery to identify family tombstones. He cries out to them and laments his inability to protect them.

Herburger has lived in Munich since 1969. Herburger's first two marriages, to Brunhilde Braatz and Ingrid Mannstaedt, ended in divorce. Since 1974 he has been married to Rosemarie Leitner. He, has two children: a son, Daniel (born in 1962), from his second marriage, and a daughter, Anna Katrine (born in 1974), from his current marriage.

References:

Peter Bekes, "Günter Herburger," in *Kritisches Lexikon zur deutschsprachigen Gegenwartsliteratur*, edited by Heinz Ludwig Arnold, volume 3 (Munich: Edition text + kritik, 1989), pp. 1-14 J;

Richard Spuler, "Social Criticism and 'New Sensitivity': Günter Herburger's Poetry," *New German Studies*, 7, no. 1 (1983): 31-45.

Wolfgang Hildesheimer

(9 December 1916 - 21 August 1991)

Patricia H. Stanley
Florida State University

See also the Hildesheimer entry in *DLB 69: Contemporary German Fiction Writers: First Series.*

PLAY PRODUCTIONS: *Der Drachenthron*, Düsseldorf, Schauspielhaus, 23 April 1955;

Pastorale, Munich, Kammerspiele, 18 September 1958;

Die Uhren and *Der schiefe Turm*, Celle, Schloßtheater, 18 April 1959;

Landschaft mit Figuren, Berlin, tribüne, 29 September 1959;

Das Opfer Helena, Mainz, Zimmerspiele, 8 October 1959;

Richard Brinsley Sheridan, *Die Lästerschule*, translated by Hildesheimer, Hannover, Landestheater, 5 June 1960;

Die Verspätung, Düsseldorf, Kammerspiele, 14 September 1961;

Sheridan, *Rivalen*, translated by Hildesheimer, Münster, Städtische Bühnen, 18 October 1961;

Carlo Goldoni, *Die Schwiegerväter*, freely translated by Hildesheimer, Berlin, tribüne, 4 December 1961;

Nachtstück, Düsseldorf, Kammerspiele, 28 February 1963;

Das Ende einer Welt, music by Hans Werner Henze, Frankfurt am Main, Kammerspiele, 30 November 1965;

George Bernard Shaw, *Die heilige Johanna*, translated by Hildesheimer, Bielefeld, Städtische Bühnen, 2 January 1966;

Pastorale, Dinslaken, Burghofbühne, 15 January 1966;

Die Eroberung der Prinzessin Turandot, Saarbrükken, Saarländisches Landestheater, 11 September 1967;

Das Opfer Helena; Kammermusical, by Hildesheimer and Hans Dieter Hüsch, music by Gerhard Wimberger, Frankfurt am Main, Theater am Turm, 10 January 1968;

Shaw, *Helden*, translated by Hildesheimer, Cologne, Städtische Bühnen, 15 January 1970;

Wolfgang Hildesheimer (photograph by Renate von Mangoldt)

Mary Stuart, Düsseldorf, Schauspielhaus, 15 December 1970;

William Congreve, *Der Lauf der Welt*, translated by Hildesheimer, Zurich, Schauspielhaus, 18 May 1985.

BOOKS: *Lieblose Legenden* (Stuttgart: Deutsche Verlags-Anstalt, 1952; revised and enlarged edition, Frankfurt am Main: Suhrkamp, 1963; enlarged edition, Frankfurt am Main: Insel, 1989);

Das Ende einer Welt: Funk-Oper, music by Hans Werner Henze (Frankfurt am Main: Frankfurter Verlagsanstalt, 1953);

Paradies der falschen Vögel: Roman (Munich: Desch, 1953);

Die Eroberung der Prinzessin Turandot (Weinheim & Bergstraße: Deutscher Laienspiel Verlag,

1954); revised as *Der Drachenthron: Komödie in drei Akten* (Munich: Desch, 1955);

Ich trage eine Eule nach Athen, und vier andere von Paul Flora illustrierte Geschichten (Zurich: Diogenes, 1956);

Begegnung im Balkanexpreß: Hörspiel (Hamburg: Hans Bredow-Institut, 1956);

Spiele, in denen es dunkel wird (Pfullingen: Neske, 1958);

Herrn Walsers Raben (Hamburg: Hans Bredow-Institut, 1960);

Die Verspätung: Ein Stück in zwei Teilen (Frankfurt am Main: Suhrkamp, 1961); translated by Juliane Kleiboemer as *The Delay*, in *Modern International Drama*, 15, no. 1 (1981): 7-45;

Nocturno im Grand Hotel: Eine Fernseh-Komödie, edited by Karl O. Nordstrand (Lund: Gleerup, 1961);

Vergebliche Aufzeichnungen; Nachtstück (Frankfurt am Main: Suhrkamp, 1963); *Nachtstück* translated by Hildesheimer as *Nightpiece*, in *Postwar German Theater: An Anthology of Plays* (New York: Dutton, 1967), pp. 277-313;

Betrachtungen über Mozart (Pfullingen: Neske, 1963);

Herrn Walsers Raben; Unter der Erde: Zwei Hörspiele (Frankfurt am Main: Suhrkamp, 1964);

Das Opfer Helena; Monolog: Zwei Hörspiele (Frankfurt am Main: Suhrkamp, 1965); *Das Opfer Helena* translated by Jacques-Leon Rose as *The Sacrifice of Helen* (University Park: University of Pennsylvania Press, 1968);

Tynset (Frankfurt am Main: Suhrkamp, 1965);

Wer war Mozart?; Becketts "Spiel"; Über das absurde Theater (Frankfurt am Main: Suhrkamp, 1966);

Begegnung im Balkanexpreß; An den Ufern der Plotinitza: Zwei Hörspiele (Stuttgart: Reclam, 1968);

Interpretationen: James Joyce, Georg Büchner; Zwei Frankfurter Vorlesungen (Frankfurt am Main: Suhrkamp, 1969)—includes *Die Wirklichkeit des Absurden, Das absurde Ich; Das absurde Ich* translated by Patricia H. Stanley as "The Absurd I," *Denver Quarterly*, 15, no. 3 (1980): 92-105;

Mary Stuart: Eine historische Szene (Frankfurt am Main: Suhrkamp, 1971); translated by Christopher Holme as *Mary Stuart*, in *Scripts 3: A Monthly of Plays and Theatre Pieces*, 1 (January 1972): 31-95;

Zeiten in Cornwall (Frankfurt am Main: Suhrkamp, 1971); translated by A. G. Blunden

as "Cornish Times," *Dimension*, 9, no. 3 (1976): 388-415;

Masante (Frankfurt am Main: Suhrkamp, 1973);

Hauskauf: Hörspiel (Frankfurt am Main: Suhrkamp, 1974);

Theaterstücke; Über das absurde Theater (Frankfurt am Main: Suhrkamp, 1975);

Hörspiele (Frankfurt am Main: Suhrkamp, 1975)—comprises *Das Opfer Helena, Herrn Walsers Raben, Unter der Erde, Monolog;*

Biosphärenklänge: Ein Hörspiel (Frankfurt am Main: Suhrkamp, 1977);

Mozart (Frankfurt am Main: Suhrkamp, 1977); translated by Marion Faber as *Mozart* (New York: Farrar, Straus & Giroux, 1982; London: Dent, 1983);

Exerzitien mit Papst Johannes; Vergebliche Aufzeichnungen (Frankfurt am Main: Suhrkamp, 1979);

Marbot: Eine Biographie (Frankfurt am Main: Suhrkamp, 1981); translated by Patricia Crampton as *Marbot* (New York: Braziller, 1983; London: Dent, 1983);

Mitteilungen an Max über den Stand der Dinge und anderes (Frankfurt am Main: Suhrkamp, 1983); translated by Joachim Neugroschel as "Missives to Max," in *The Collected Stories of Wolfgang Hildesheimer* (New York: Ecco Press, 1987);

Endlich allein: Collagen (Frankfurt am Main: Suhrkamp, 1984);

Gedichte und Collagen, edited by Volker Jehle (Bamberg: Fränkische Bibliophilengesellschaft, 1984);

The Jewishness of Mr. Bloom/Das Jüdische an Mr. Bloom (Frankfurt am Main: Suhrkamp, 1984);

Das Ende der Fiktionen: Reden aus fünfundzwanzig Jahren (Frankfurt am Main: Suhrkamp, 1984);

Der ferne Bach: Eine Rede (Frankfurt am Main: Insel, 1985);

Nachlese (Frankfurt am Main: Suhrkamp, 1987);

Die Hörspiele, edited by Volker Jehle (Frankfurt am Main: Suhrkamp, 1988)—includes *Das Ende kommt nie, Die Bartschedel-Idee, Maxine;*

Klage und Anklage: Mit einer Vorbemerkung des Autors (Frankfurt am Main: Suhrkamp, 1989);

Die Theaterstücke, edited by Jehle (Frankfurt am Main: Suhrkamp, 1989);

Mit dem Bausch dem Bogen (Warmbronn: Keicher, 1990);

Gesammelte Werke, 7 volumes, edited by Christiaan Lucas Hart Nibbrig and Volker Jehle (Frankfurt am Main: Suhrkamp, 1991);

Rede an die Jugend: Mit einem Postscriptum für die Eltern (Frankfurt am Main: Suhrkamp, 1991).

Edition in English: *The Collected Stories of Wolfgang Hildesheimer*, translated by Joachim Neugroschel (New York: Ecco Press, 1987).

RADIO: *Das Ende kommt nie*, Nordwestdeutscher Rundfunk, 17 June 1952;

Begegnung im Balkanexpreß, Nordwestdeutscher Rundfunk, 12 February 1953;

Das Ende einer Welt, music by Hans Werner Henze, Nordwestdeutscher Rundfunk, 4 December 1953;

Prinzessin Turandot, Nordwestdeutscher Rundfunk, 29 January 1954; revised version, Süddeutscher Rundfunk, 10 October 1954;

An den Ufern der Plotinitza, Bayerischer Rundfunk, 22 June 1954;

Das Atelierfest, Nordwestdeutscher Rundfunk, 25 May 1955;

Das Opfer Helena, Nordwestdeutscher Rundfunk, 11 October 1955; revised version, Norddeutscher Rundfunk, 12 February 1961;

Die Bartschedel-Idee, Bayerischer Rundfunk and Norddeutscher Rundfunk, 21 February 1957;

Pastorale oder Die Zeit für Kakao, Bayerischer Rundfunk and Norddeutscher Rundfunk, 7 February 1958;

Die Uhren, Süddeutscher Rundfunk, 30 May 1958;

Der schiefe Turm von Pisa, Südwestfunk, 8 September 1959;

Herrn Walsers Raben, Bayerischer Rundfunk and Norddeutscher Rundfunk, 8 March 1960;

Die Lästerschule, Süddeutscher Rundfunk, 12 February 1961;

Rivalen, Südwestfunk, 30 May 1961;

Nocturno im Grand Hotel, Bayerischer Rundfunk and Südwestfunk, 30 December 1961;

Unter der Erde, Bayersicher Rundfunk and Norddeutscher Rundfunk, 14 February 1962;

Nachtstück, Norddeutscher Rundfunk and Sender Freies Berlin, 1 April 1964;

Monolog, Norddeutscher Rundfunk and Südwestfunk, 6 April 1964;

Es ist alles entdeckt: Funkerzählung, Deutschlandfunk, 24 November 1965;

Maxine, Hessischer Rundfunk, Norddeutscher Rundfunk, and Sender Freies Berlin, 8 January 1969;

Mary auf dem Block, Hessischer Rundfunk, Norddeutscher Rundfunk, and Süddeutscher Rundfunk, 6 January 1971;

Hauskauf, Süddeutscher Rundfunk and Westdeutscher Rundfunk, 6 and 9 January 1974;

Biosphärenklänge, Bayerischer Rundfunk, 22 July 1977;

Endfunk, music by Jan Wisse, Radio Hilversum and Westdeutscher Rundfunk, 14 April 1980.

OTHER: *Trials of War Criminals before the Nuremberg Military Tribunals under Control Council Law No. 10: Nuremberg, October 1946-April 1949*, volumes 3-4, edited by Hildesheimer (Washington, D.C.: U.S. Government Printing Office, 1951);

Mozart-Briefe, edited by Hildesheimer (Frankfurt am Main: Suhrkamp, 1975);

"Mein Judentum," in *Mein Judentum*, edited by Hans Jürgen Schultz (Stuttgart: Kreuz, 1978), pp. 264-274;

"Empirische Betrachtungen zu meinem Theater," in *Wolfgang Hildesheimer*, edited by Volker Jehle (Frankfurt am Main: Suhrkamp, 1989), pp. 27-30.

TRANSLATIONS: Frederick Spencer Chapman, *Aktion Dschungel. Bericht aus Malaya* (Frankfurt am Main: Verlag der Frankfurter Hefte, 1952);

Anne Piper, *Jack und Jenny* (Hamburg: Krüger, 1955);

Djuna Barnes, *Nachtgewächs: Roman* (Pfullingen: Neske, 1959);

Carlo Goldoni, *Die Schwiegerväter: Lustspiel in zwei Akten* (Munich: Desch, 1961);

Richard Brinsley Sheridan, *Die Lästerschule: Lustspiel in zehn Bildern* (Munich: Desch, 1962);

Edward St. John Gorey, *Ein sicherer Beweis* (Zurich: Diogenes Tabu, 1962);

Ronald Searle, *Quo Vadis* (Munich: Desch, 1962);

Gorey, *Die Draisine von Untermattenwaag* (Zurich: Diogenes Tabu, 1963);

Gorey, *Eine Harfe ohne Saiten oder Wie man einen Roman schreibt* (Zurich: Diogenes Tabu, 1963);

Gorey, *Das Geheimnis der Ottomane: Ein pornographisches Werk* (Zurich: Diogenes Tabu, 1964);

George Bernard Shaw, *Die heilige Johanna: Dramatische Chronik in sechs Szenen und einen Epilog* (Frankfurt am Main: Suhrkamp, 1965);

Gorey, *Das unglückselige Kind* (Zurich: Diogenes, 1967);

Gorey, *La Chauve-souris Dorée* (Zurich: Diogenes, 1969);

Shaw, *Helden: Komödie in drei Akten* (Frankfurt am Main: Suhrkamp, 1970);

Samuel Beckett, "Wie die Geschichte erzählt wurde," in *Günter Eich zum Gedächtnis*, edited by Siegfried Unseld (Frankfurt am Main: Suhrkamp, 1973);

William Congreve, *Der Lauf der Welt: Eine lieblose Komödie* (Frankfurt am Main: Insel, 1986).

Wolfgang Hildesheimer's first radio play was performed in 1952, the same year his first collection of stories was published. His literary career combined drama with narrative fiction, and the first of several literary prizes he won was for a radio play, *Prinzessin Turandot* (Princess Turandot, 1954), which was later adapted for the stage. In his essay "Die Wirklichkeit des Absurden" (The Reality of the Absurd, 1969), originally a talk given at the University of Frankfurt in 1967, Hildesheimer says that the absurd is an indication of the silent world that refuses to give humanity an answer to its question. By "the world" is meant religious, political, and social institutions; the unanswered question refers to the atrocities that were allowed to happen to the Jewish population of Europe during World War II. Following the Holocaust, people can no longer have faith in governments, institutions, or rules of any kind. All Hildesheimer's work for radio and stage, including the early "thriller" plays, may be considered theater of the absurd, for they all point out the silence of the world.

Hildesheimer was born in Hamburg on 9 December 1916 to Arnold Hildesheimer, a chemist, and Hanna Goldschmidt Hildesheimer. He spent most of his childhood in Berlin, the Netherlands, and Mannheim before he was enrolled in the experimental Odenwald School in Heppenheim in 1930. In 1933 the family moved to England and then, in 1934, to Palestine. Hildesheimer completed his high-school education in Surrey at the Public Heights School and studied drawing, cabinetmaking, and furniture and stage design in Jerusalem until 1937. He continued his studies in drawing and stage design in London from 1937 to 1939. After a year of travel in Europe he returned to Palestine in 1940 to become an English teacher at the British Institute in Tel Aviv, and his first marriage took place about this time. From 1943 to 1946 he served as public information officer for the British government in Jerusalem, and his marriage ended during this period. In 1946 he was appointed a simultaneous translator for the war crimes trials in Nuremberg, and at the conclusion of the trials in 1949 he served as an editor of the proceedings. That same year he moved to the Bavarian village of Ambach am

Starnbergersee to become a free-lance painter; but in 1950 his short stories began to appear in newspapers and journals, and by 1952 his writing career had taken precedence over art. That year a collection of his stories, *Lieblose Legenden* (Loveless Legends), was published, and his first radio play, *Das Ende kommt nie* (The End Will Never Come; published, 1988), was aired.

The "end" referred to in the play is superficially far from tragic; it is merely the end of residence in an apartment building for its middle-class tenants. When an official delivers the eviction notice, the tenants simply pack and wait. Only Martin Roehrich behaves in a mildly independent manner. At the end of the play he has rehung his curtains and unpacked his books; he tells another tenant that nothing is going to happen, but if it does it will be so gradual that it will seem not to be a change. The play reminds one of Germany in the early 1930s, when Jewish residents accepted increasingly repressive orders and finally had to abandon their homes.

Hildesheimer's only novel, *Paradies der falschen Vögel* (Paradise of Dishonest People), was published in 1953, and in the same year he married Silvia Dillman. The couple lived in Munich until 1957, when they moved to Poschiavo, a village in the canton of Graubünden in Switzerland. They have no children of their own, but Hildesheimer's wife has two daughters from a prior marriage.

The radio play *Begegnung im Balkanexpreß* (A Chance Meeting in the Balkan Express Train; performed, 1953; published, 1956) is based on the novel. Following an amorous night in a train headed for Paris, Robert Guiscard, an art forger, falls prey to a conductor who courteously insists that the halted train cannot continue without cash. Guiscard and his companion are deposited not in Paris but in the capital of a Balkan country. Guiscard acquires a fortune by creating paintings that he says are the work of a local painter and convincing the minister of culture that the painter's genius should be exploited. Soon the city is a center of tourism as the home of the artist. When Guiscard becomes greedy and begins forging famous paintings again, a potential extortionist appears. Guiscard extricates himself from this man when the same conductor agrees to uncouple the extortionist's car and leave it on the track as the remaining car, carrying Guiscard and his female companion, continues to Paris.

Hildesheimer's next radio play, *Prinzessin Turandot*, (1954) was published as *Die Eroberung der Prinzessin Turandot* (The Conquest of Princess

Turandot, 1954) and received the prestigious Radio Play Prize of the War Blinded; the work was adapted for the stage as *Der Drachenthron* (The Dragon's Throne, 1955). The clever, ambitious Chinese princess Turandot engages a series of suitors in conversation; as soon as one of them fails to respond or forgets the topic, he is executed. Nineteen princes have lost their lives in this scheme, devised by Turandot and Chancellor Hü so that the aging kings in neighboring countries, having lost their heirs, will offer little resistance to a Chinese invasion. The newest suitor, the Prince of Astrakhan, is an impostor whose identity is discovered by Turandot's slave, Pnina, who was herself a princess before the Chinese conquered her country. This "prince" courted Pnina but disappeared just as she expected to marry him, and she later learned that he had a reputation for courting and leaving princesses. Like Turandot, this man is a clever conversationalist. Pnina reveals his identity after he has won the contest and the princess. Turandot orders him imprisoned. Ten days later the real Prince of Astrakhan arrives, summoned by Hü, to marry Turandot. Turandot orders Hü executed, arranges for Pnina to marry the real prince, and confesses to the false prince that she wishes to share her kingdom with him. They exit to greet their subjects.

The stage play gives Hü, who is Turandot's lover here, a more prominent role. The most important change, however, comes when the false prince refuses Turandot's marriage proposal and announces that he is off to Astrakhan to conquer yet another princess. Turandot must marry the real prince, an energetic but primitive warrior who has already—unknown to her—promised Pnina that she, too, will be one of his wives. This ending leaves room for conjecture about Turandot's future: as the wife of this prince she will probably have little power and no stimulating conversations. Her new husband, as he says, is a man of deeds and not words.

In the radio play *An den Ufern der Plotinitza* (On the Shores of the Plotinitza; performed, 1954; published, 1968) a border war on the shore of the Plotinitza, where Eduard Merlin sits painting, results in his being taken prisoner by the invaders when a female journalist suggests that he may be a spy. On the opposite shore he escapes and meets the daughter of the country's general; her father has contracted to sell her into the harem of a fat, old sultan. Merlin is captured by invaders from the other side and returned to the opposite shore, where he learns that the jour-

nalist has had him declared officially dead; then he is captured again and taken back across the river. He and the general's daughter leave the war zone after he resolves her problem by substituting the journalist for her in the harem of the sultan, who will never know the difference. The daughter soon marries, and Merlin, now a famous "dead" painter, will sell his work as his own agent.

As a radio play, *Das Opfer Helena* (published, 1965; translated as "The Sacrifice of Helen," 1968) was originally aired in October 1955 and revised for a February 1961 broadcast. A stage adaptation premiered in Mainz in October 1959. The play was also presented in a musical version in Frankfurt am Main in January 1968, with a score by Gerhard Wimberger and lyrics by Hans Dieter Hüsch. King Menelaos of Sparta, aware that his wife, Helena—part goddess and the most beautiful woman in the world—seduces all their male guests, declares that once they have rid themselves of Prince Paris of Troy, an unexpected visitor, he will allow no one under the age of seventy to visit them. Helena realizes that Menelaos expects her to seduce Paris and convince him to abduct her so that she may escape her barren future; Menelaos will have an excuse to attack Troy. She decides, instead, to convince Paris to take her to a deserted island where she will teach him the true meaning of love; at the same time, she will avert a war. The love-struck Paris flees with Helena after instructing her daughter, Hermione, to give her father the news that they are on their way to Troy. On the boat Helena tries to coax Paris to change course for the deserted island, but he suddenly drops his smitten facade and announces that it was his plan all along to abduct her and force a war. The Trojan War is described in one sentence, and Helena returns home. She tells Hermione she is now cured, but Hermione misinterprets the remark. Helena does not mean she is cured of flirting but that she no longer has the hope that she can teach a mortal to love. She resigns herself to life with Menelaos and their elderly guests.

Die Bartschedel-Idee (The Bartschedel Idea; published, 1988), based on a story in *Lieblose Legenden*, aired in February 1957. Dr. Florian Geyer, an unscrupulous professor with great contempt for the intelligence of his fellow citizens, invents a man named Bartschedel, a writer of philosophical tragedies and a previously unacknowledged genius. He has a statue erected in honor of Bartschedel and a festival organized to present one of Bartschedel's tragedies, which, of course, Geyer has written. Following the successful festival, a man claiming to be Bartschedel's relative and the only person with access to the dramatist's works visits the minister of culture. The minister consults encyclopedias and archivists and informs the mayor of the deception just as a second Bartschedel relative is announced. The first Bartschedel relative visits Geyer, who is bored with his creation and not only anticipated the arrival of this Bartschedel but expects more Bartschedels to appear. He announces that he and his wife are leaving town.

Pastorale premiered in Munich in September 1958; *Die Uhren* (The Clocks) premiered in Celle in April 1959; and *Landschaft mit Figuren* (Landscape with People) premiered in Berlin in September 1959. These plays were collectively published in 1958 as *Spiele, in denen es dunkel wird* (Plays in Which It Gets Dark). Common elements of the plays are vividly grotesque images and dialogue that is uncommunicative and frequently composed of nonsense responses to practical questions.

Pastorale begins on a sunny afternoon as four well-dressed business and civic leaders—three men and a woman—gather in a meadow to rehearse a song. As a servant performs amusing gymnastics to hold the sheets on the various music stands, the quartet interrupts its practice to quarrel over stock transactions and other business and personal matters. Two of the men collapse and die and darkness falls. The third man and the woman conduct a curiously unloving verbal prelude to a departure that seems to have a romantic goal. Just as they leave, the nurse who had formerly cared for the third man and his dead twin brother arrives with an oversized baby carriage, and the stage grows light again. The nurse and servant embrace, load the lawn furniture onto a wagon, and depart as rain threatens. The dead bodies remain on the brightly lighted stage along with the carriage.

Die Uhren features a bored husband and wife, a glazier who replaces the clear glass in their windows with black panels, and a salesman with a large selection of watches and clocks. It is impossible to communicate with this couple, for they only become animated and responsive when they act out a possible scene between passersby whom the glazier describes from his perch on the ladder. They reveal in this way their disinterest in each other and their lives. When the salesman and the glazier leave together, the man and

woman have no recourse but to imitate the clocks the salesman has left behind, for they cannot see out through their windows. They stand in front of the clocks, then behind them, and finally climb inside two of the clocks. Their imitative ticking brings the play to an end.

Landschaft mit Figuren takes place in an artist's studio. A glazier, who may or may not have been hired by the artist's sleepy wife, Bettina, climbs a ladder, where he remains for most of the play, frequently coming partway down to comment on the action both outdoors and inside. Bettina is upstairs but appears periodically, at first in a nightgown, to complain about the noise. With each successive appearance she wears a different costume but always seems ethereal and helpless. Adrian, the painter, welcomes an elegant middle-aged society woman who wants her portrait painted. Her young lover, Colin, soon arrives, followed by an older gentleman. Adrian arranges them in a group with various props, including a leather gymnastics horse and a cage in which Colin sulks after his attempt to embrace Bettina is rebuffed. Eventually it comes out that Colin helped kill the woman's husband and that the older man is Colin's father. Near the end of act 1 Bettina appears in a riding habit and cracks a whip, and the three quarreling people become rigid and respond silently to her commands. The curtain falls as the glazier continues to set panels in the large window, Adrian calmly paints the group scene, and Bettina watches. In act 2 the frozen figures and the glazier have aged, but Bettina and Adrian remain young. The room is lit by lamps because most of the window panels are now of a violet shade. The glazier announces the arrival of a customer who collects Adrian's work. The customer buys the group portrait after watching the trio act out a scene on the theme of generational conflict, motivated by a music box Bettina cranks. The woman, Colin, and Colin's father are commanded to get into crates, and Adrian and the collector haggle over price with considerable illogic. The crates stand ready for shipment, the glazier and the collector leave, Adrian arranges his studio for the next project, and Bettina goes upstairs, reappearing soon in the nightgown she initially wore. Panes of glass begin to fall from the windows, and the stage is again brightly lit as the curtain comes down to the sound of breaking glass. The suggestion that a repetition of the action will now take place foreshadows Samuel Beckett's *Play* (1963), in which the entire text is actually repeated.

Behind the witty dialogue and grotesque action of the three plays looms an air of deep discontent, even despair, which is accentuated by the darkening of the stage. Hildesheimer has said that his characters reveal the ridiculousness of life in a meaningless world. Theater of the absurd is meant to be an unsettling experience made palatable by the laughter its situations sometimes engender.

The radio play *Herrn Walsers Raben* (Mr. Walser's Ravens; published, 1960) aired in March 1960. Walser, an amateur magician, changes people he finds obnoxious into birds; he has already changed twenty-three relatives into ravens before the play opens, and their cawing is a constant background sound. An aunt arrives with a bodyguard to accuse Walser of murder and to demand a share of his inherited fortune to insure her silence; Walser whispers the magic word, and she, too, becomes a raven. The bodyguard comes in from the next room and reveals that he is a long-missing uncle who also knows the word. He is about to use it on his nephew when the housekeeper enters and saves her employer by using the word, which she has learned over the years, to transform the uncle into a raven. The play ends as Walser and the housekeeper promise to transform each other simultaneously into ravens if the need arises.

The plays collected in *Spiele, in denen es dunkel wird* combine witty dialogue with bizarre stage images; but in his later plays the elegant, pointed dialogue admired by reviewers becomes his primary method for conveying the idea that life is meaningless. *Die Verspätung* (1961; translated as *The Delay*, 1981) is exemplary of Hildesheimer's reliance on verbal rather than visual means to convey absurdity. The "Guricht," a large bird capable of speechlike sounds, never appears but is described by Professor Scholz-Babelhaus, who theorizes that this bird is humanity's closest biological relative. The professor expects to sight the bird from a seat in a dilapidated inn in a village where there is no telephone or post office and only a handful of residents remain. At first he is frantic to make his discovery and report it before his assistant or a rival takes credit for the coup; but he soon confesses that he invented the Guricht because every other discovery he made had already been made by someone else. At the beginning of act 2 he urges the teacher, mayor, and innkeeper to leave town to save themselves before everything collapses. A man drives up and identifies himself as

Scholz-Babelhaus's chief rival, Möllendorf. He leaves, taking the others, before the professor sights a bird that turns out not to be a Guricht. He cannot convince even himself, he says, that he has made a discovery, and he collapses and dies. A casketmaker who has been mumbling throughout the play about a lack of clients begins to sing a song from his infancy; when he turns to look at the dead man the stage darkens. For the premiere production only the professor and casket maker appeared as real people; all other characters wore grotesque masks.

In the radio play "Unter der Erde" (Under Ground; performed, 1962; published, 1975) a husband and wife, as bored as the couple in *Die Uhren*, are the only characters. Working in his garden one afternoon the husband uncovers a huge stone; under the stone is a cave with steps leading into it. He decides to investigate, but his wife refuses to join him. Three weeks later he returns while she is eating dinner; he is transfigured, she says. The next day the wife, curious, clambers down the hole, which has to be uncovered again because she had had it filled in the day after her husband disappeared. Four weeks later she returns, as transfigured as her husband. Then the two go down together, first digging out the opening, which the husband had filled in the day before. Underground they attain a moment of blissful serenity inside a marble-walled palace, but as they explore its rooms the husband sees a patch of sky and realizes that they are in their backyard, and the two climb out of the hole. The last few lines of the play may be interpreted either as an attempt to retain the harmony achieved underground or as a resumption of the civilized hostility that reveals the depth of the couple's alienation.

Nachtstück (1963; translated as *Nightpiece*, 1967) features a limping insomniac with a large supply of sleeping pills and a compulsive need to check the security of his house before medicating himself for sleep. Gun in hand, he checks under the bed one more time as a burglar slides out the other side, climbs across the bed, and attacks the man. The man overpowers the burglar and ties him to a chair with special knots he has invented for such an occasion, but he does not call the police. He wants the burglar to listen to his account of the events that keep him from sleeping. He describes a parade of red-robed cardinals in Rome and a protest march of generals' gray-haired widows in Paris. The telephone rings several times; he refuses to answer, saying it is always a wrong

O. A. Buck as Professor Scholz-Babelhausen in the premiere of Hildesheimer's Die Verspätung *at the Düsseldorf Kammerspiele in 1961 (photograph by Ruthenbeck)*

number, someone either wanting to buy an organ or reciting lists of numbers. The man becomes especially agitated as he describes his feeling that everyone but he understands these numbers. He swallows a quantity of pills as he talks, and the burglar is able to free himself by the time the man collapses. The phone rings again; the burglar answers and has an oddly knowledgeable conversation with someone in America about purchasing an organ. He then places a call and recites the list of numbers written on the insomniac's notepad.

The telephone is more important in the radio play *Monolog* (performed, 1964; published, 1965), which, in spite of its title, involves several anonymous voices giving telephone weather reports, recipes, and religious counsel. The protagonist, another insomniac, talks by telephone to two women named Helga, one who calls him in an error he does not correct and one whom he calls, although he does not want to see her again. He wants to see no one; he wants only to travel beyond the Milky Way to the place where nothing more exists. The play develops the themes of alienation, innocence, and God's silence.

Maxine (published, 1988), another radio play, aired in January 1969. The narrator, who compares himself to a deserter, has come to a rundown hotel at the edge of a desert to escape unexplained pressures in his life. He enters the hotel bar and for most of the play listens to the outrageous but entertaining stories and personal revelations of the drunken Maxine. She cries out for former lovers before passing out. Alain, who is apparently her husband, says that when he, as a priest, heard her confession of a sexual indiscretion, he was inspired to renounce his vow of chastity. He carries her up to bed.

Mary Stuart (performed, 1970; published, 1971; translated, 1972) was produced at the off-Broadway Public Theater in March 1981 in a translation by Christopher Holme; it is, to date, Hildesheimer's only play to be performed in the United States. In the printed text each page consists of two or three columns of simultaneous action and speech. The time is two hours before Mary's execution, and the setting is the execution chamber with its black-velvet-covered execution block at center stage. At the beginning the stage is occupied by the hangman, his assistant, and Mary, who sits pensively on the block. When she refuses to return to her room to dress, her ladies-in-waiting, doctor, pharmacist, secretary, and three menservants gather, bringing the special chair that accommodates her incontinence. They place her on it and begin to dress her, stealing pearls and jewels from the gown as the doctor and pharmacist force her to swallow various medications to keep her sedated. She asks for her pet dogs, but by the time they are brought in she does not notice that they are stuffed; nor does she notice a sex act between her secretary and a lady-in-waiting or the strangulation of the pharmacist by the hangman's assistant at the request of a servant who wants the ring the queen had given the pharmacist. The scrambling society onstage is a microcosm of society at large, where individuals proclaim lofty goals but pursue selfish ends. Mary talks almost continually, recalling her past, giving commands to which the servants pay only lip service, and praying. She pays no heed to the conversations around her, including a grisly exchange regarding the security of her wig. The doctor sees no reason why it should not be nailed down to keep it from coming off when the hangman raises the severed head for all to see. The final event of the play is not the execution but a venomous shouting match between the Anglican minister, who attempts to convert the condemned Catholic sinner, and Mary, whose Latin prayer grows into a shrill scream on the final "amen" before she strides to the block.

The radio play *Hauskauf* (House Purchase; published, 1974) aired in two parts on 6 and 9 January 1974; in a production for Bavarian Radio in August 1974 Hildesheimer played both roles. Most critics assert that the two men in the play—named only A and B—are personifications of the active and passive aspects of a single person. B shows an educated interest in A's mountain-climbing equipment and knows of expeditions A has made to exotic locations; he even has knowledge of the trip A plans with his handmade catamaran to save natives, once he has sold his house. By the end of the twenty-two scenes that take place in and around the house and conversations that reveal a shared pessimism about the progress of mankind, both men say they want the house, an indication of withdrawal—even by the active half of the personality—from a world where the annihilation of humanity and nature is unremitting.

The radio play *Biosphärenklänge* (The Sounds of the Biospheres; performed, 1974; published, 1977) takes place in a living room in which a man tells his wife he has a feeling that something is wrong: he believes the end has begun. She treats his premonition with skepticism, but she begins to change her mind as the silence around them grows. The telephone no longer functions; a luncheon guest does not arrive; no one walks past the house; a dead bird lies on the ground; dogs howl. Suddenly the man says he hears a high-pitched sound like the G of an ocarina. Soon his wife acknowledges the same sound, and it becomes audible to the audience just before what seems to be the end for the man and wife, who can think of nothing to say to each other as final words. The sound grows stronger and breaks off as the play ends.

Hauskauf and *Biosphärenklänge* are fictional representations of Hildesheimer's well-publicized view that humanity is destroying the natural environment. We live in an "Endzeit" (end time), he has said in speeches and newspaper interviews; the damage we are doing to the earth is irreversible. As a result of this view, Hildesheimer stopped writing fiction and became increasingly absorbed in creating collages, pen-and-ink drawings, and watercolors. Hildesheimer explained that writing fiction forced him to contemplate life, but in the making of a collage he contemplated only colors and textures and could exclude time and the real world.

In 1980 Hildesheimer was awarded the Premio Verinna Lorenzon of the province of Cosenza, Italy, for his nonchronological biography *Mozart* (1977). In 1982 he received the Literature Prize of the Bavarian Academy of Fine Arts for *Marbot* (1981), a "biography" of an art critic who never existed. Hildesheimer said that both he and his wife escaped into the nineteenth century during the writing of *Marbot*, and they returned to the present unwillingly. Hildesheimer received an honorary doctorate from the Justus-Liebig University in Gießen in 1982. In 1983 he received West Germany's highest civilian honor, the Great Service Cross of the Federal Republic, and in that same year the longtime resident of Switzerland was granted citizenship in his adopted country. He died on 21 August 1991.

Bibliography:
Volker Jehle, *Wolfgang Hildesheimer: Eine Bibliographie* (Frankfurt am Main: Lang, 1984).

References:

Björn Andersson, *Gestaltung von Entfremdung bei Wolfgang Hildesheimer* (Stockholm: Almqvist & Wiksell, 1979);

Heinz Ludwig Arnold, ed., *Wolfgang Hildesheimer* (Munich: Edition text   kritik, 1986);

Burckhard Dücker, *Wolfgang Hildesheimer und die deutsche Literatur des Absurden* (Rheinfelden: Schäuble, 1976);

Manfred Durzak, "Ich kann über nichts anderes schreiben als über ein potentielles Ich: Gespräch mit Wolfgang Hildesheimer," in his *Gespräche über den Roman: Formbestimmungen und Analysen* (Frankfurt am Main: Suhrkamp, 1976), pp. 271-295;

Martin Esslin, *The Theatre of the Absurd*, revised edition (Garden City, N.Y.: Doubleday, 1969), pp. 224-226;

John Fletcher, "Ionesco, Pinter, Albee and Others," in *The Two Faces of Ionesco*, edited by Rosette C. Lamont and Melvin J. Friedman (Troy, N.Y.: Whitston, 1978), pp. 175-195;

Peter Hanenberg, *Geschichte im Werk Wolfgang Hildesheimers* (Frankfurt am Main: Lang, 1989);

Linda M. Hill, "Absurdity? History? and Magic: Hildesheimer's *Spiele, in denen es dunkel wird*," in *Language as Aggression: Studies in Postwar Drama*, edited by Hill (Bonn: Bouvier, 1976), pp. 61-93;

Volker Jehle, *Wolfgang Hildesheimer: Werkgeschichte* (Frankfurt am Main: Suhrkamp, 1990);

Jehle, ed., *Wolfgang Hildesheimer* (Frankfurt am Main: Suhrkamp, 1989);

Heinz Puknus, *Wolfgang Hildesheimer* (Munich: Beck, 1978);

Dierk Rodewald, ed., *Über Wolfgang Hildesheimer* (Frankfurt am Main: Suhrkamp, 1971);

Patricia H. Stanley, *Hildesheimer and His Critics* (Columbia, S.C.: Camden House, forthcoming 1993);

Stanley, *The Realm of Possibilities: Wolfgang Hildesheimer's Non-Traditional Non-Fictional Prose* (Lanham, Md.: University Press of America, 1988);

Stanley, "Wolfgang Hildesheimer's *Das Opfer Helena*: Another Triumph of the 'They,'" in *From Pen to Performance. Drama as Conceived and Performed*, volume 3, edited by Karelisa V. Hartigan (Lanham, Md.: University Press of America, 1983), pp. 111-120;

Stanley, "Wolfgang Hildesheimer's *Mary Stuart*: Language Run Riot," *Germanic Review*, 54, no. 3 (1979): 110-114.

Papers:

The Hildesheimer Archive is at the Akademie der Künste (Academy of Arts), Berlin.

Rolf Hochhuth

(1 April 1931 -   )

Alfred D. White
University of Wales, College of Cardiff

PLAY PRODUCTIONS: *Der Stellvertreter*, Berlin, Freie Volksbühne, 20 February 1963;

Soldaten, Berlin, Freie Volksbühne, 20 February 1967;

Guerillas, Stuttgart, Württembergisches Staatstheater, 15 May 1970;

Die Hebamme, Zurich, Schauspielhaus; Munich, Kammerspiele; Essen, Städtische Bühnen; Göttingen, Deutsches Theater; Kassel, Staatstheater; Wiesbaden, Staatstheater, 4 May 1972;

Lysistrate und die NATO, Essen, Schauspielhaus; Vienna, Volkstheater, 22 February 1974;

Tod eines Jägers, Salzburg, Festspiele, 11 August 1977;

Juristen, Göttingen, Deutsches Theater; Hamburg, Ernst-Deutsch-Theater; Heidelberg, Städtische Bühnen, 14 February 1980;

Ärztinnen, Mannheim, Nationaltheater, 9 November 1980;

Judith, Glasgow, Citizens' Theatre, 18 October 1984; German premiere, Kiel, Bühnen der Landeshauptstadt, 28 June 1985;

Unbefleckte Empfängnis, Berlin, Schiller-Theater, April 1989;

Sommer 14, Vienna, Akademietheater, 18 December 1990.

BOOKS: *Der Stellvertreter: Schauspiel* (Reinbek: Rowohlt, 1963); translated by Robert David Macdonald as *The Representative* (London: Methuen, 1963); translated by Richard and Clara Winston as *The Deputy* (New York: Grove Press, 1964); German version revised as *Der Stellvertreter: Ein christliches Trauerspiel* (Reinbek: Rowohlt, 1967);

Soldaten: Nekrolog auf Genf. Tragödie (Reinbek: Rowohlt, 1967); translated by Macdonald as *Soldiers: An Obituary for Geneva. A Tragedy* (New York: Grove, 1968; London: Deutsch, 1968);

Guerillas: Tragödie in 5 Akten (Reinbek: Rowohlt, 1970);

Krieg und Klassenkrieg: Studien (Reinbek: Rowohlt,

Rolf Hochhuth (photograph by Peter Peitsch)

1971)—includes "Der Klassenkampf ist nicht zu Ende";

Die Hebamme: Komödie; Erzählungen, Gedichte, Essays (Reinbek: Rowohlt, 1971);

Lysistrate und die NATO: Komödie. Mit einer Studie: Frauen und Mütter, Bachofen und Germaine Greer (Reinbek: Rowohlt, 1973; revised, 1976);

Zwischenspiel in Baden-Baden (Reinbek: Rowohlt, 1974);

Die Berliner Antigone: Prosa und Verse (Reinbek: Rowohlt, 1975);

Tod eines Jägers (Reinbek: Rowohlt, 1976; radio version, St. Pölten: Verlag Niederösterreichisches Pressehaus, 1979);

Eine Liebe in Deutschland (Reinbek: Rowohlt, 1978); translated by John Brownjohn as *A German Love Story* (Boston: Little, Brown, 1980; London: Weidenfeld & Nicolson, 1980);

Tell 38: Dankrede für den Basler Kunstpreis 1976 am 7. Dezember in der Aula des Alten Museums. Anmerkungen und Dokumente (Reinbek: Rowohlt, 1979); translated by Michael W. Roloff as *Tell 38* (Boston: Little, Brown, 1984);

Juristen: Drei Akte für sieben Spieler (Reinbek: Rowohlt, 1979);

Ärztinnen: 5 Akte (Reinbek: Rowohlt, 1980);

Spitze des Eisbergs: Ein Reader, edited by Dietrich Simon (Reinbek: Rowohlt, 1982);

Räuber-Rede: 3 deutsche Vorwürfe. Schiller/Lessing/ Geschwister Scholl (Reinbek: Rowohlt, 1982);

Judith: Trauerspiel (Reinbek: Rowohlt, 1984);

Atlantik-Novelle: Erzählungen und Gedichte (Reinbek: Rowohlt, 1985);

Die Berliner Antigone: Erzählungen und Gedichte (Stuttgart: Reclam, 1986);

Schwarze Segel: Essays und Gedichte (Reinbek: Rowohlt, 1986);

Täter und Denker: Profile und Probleme von Cäsar bis Jünger: Essays (Stuttgart: Deutsche Verlags-Anstalt, 1987);

War hier Europa? Reden, Gedichte, Essays (Munich: Deutscher Taschenbuch Verlag, 1987);

Alan Turing: Erzählung (Reinbek: Rowohlt, 1987);

Unbefleckte Empfängnis: Ein Kreidekreis (Reinbek: Rowohlt, 1988);

Sommer 14: Ein Totentanz (Reinbek: Rowohlt, 1989);

Alle Dramen, 2 volumes (Reinbek: Rowohlt, 1991)—comprises volume 1: *Der Stellvertreter, Soldaten Guerillas, Die Hebamme, Inselkomödie, Entfernte Verwandte*; volume 2: *Tod eines Jägers, Juristen, Ärztinnen, Judith, Unbefleckte Empfängnis, Sommer 14, Hitlers Dr. Faust*.

TELEVISION: *Entfernte Verwandte*, Zweites Deutsches Fernsehen, 17 December 1976.

OTHER: Wilhelm Busch, *Sämtliche Werke und eine Auswahl der Skizzen und Gemälde in 2 Bänden*, 2 volumes, edited by Hochhuth (Gütersloh: Bertelsmann, 1959);

Liebe in unserer Zeit: 32 Erzählungen, edited by Hochhuth (Hamburg: Rütten & Loening, 1961);

Theodor Storm, *Am grauen Meer: Gesammelte Werke*, edited by Hochhuth (Hamburg: Mosaik, 1962);

Die großen Meister: Europäische Erzähler des 20. Jahrhunderts, 2 volumes, edited by Hochhuth (Cologne: Kiepenheuer & Witsch, 1966);

Otto Flake, *Die Verurteilung des Sokrates: Biographische Essays aus 6 Jahrzehnten*, edited by Hochhuth and Fredy Gröbli-Schaub (Heidelberg: L. Schneider, 1970);

Flake, *Das Bild und andere Liebesgeschichten*, selected by Hochhuth (Frankfurt: Fischer, 1971);

Flake, *Schloß Ortenau, Sommerroman, Old Man*, edited by Hochhuth and Peter Härtling (Frankfurt am Main: Fischer, 1974);

Flake, *Die Monthiver-Mädchen*, edited by Hochhuth and Härtling (Frankfurt am Main: Fischer, 1975);

Flake, *Freiheitsbaum und Guillotine: 57 Essays aus 6 Jahrzehnten*, edited by Hochhuth and Härtling (Frankfurt am Main: Fischer, 1976);

Kaisers Zeiten: Bilder einer Epoche. Aus dem Archiv der Hofphotographen Oscar und Gustav Tellgmann, edited by Hochhuth and Hans-Heinrich Koch (Gütersloh: Prisma, 1977);

Flake, *Erzählungen*, edited by Hochhuth and Härtling (Frankfurt am Main: Fischer, 1977);

Joseph Goebbels, *Tagebücher 1945: Die letzten Aufzeichnungen*, introduction by Hochhuth (Hamburg: Hoffmann & Campe, 1979);

Deutsche Erzähler der Jahrgänge 1900-1960, 2 volumes, edited by Hochhuth (Cologne: Kiepenheuer & Witsch, 1981);

Die Gegenwart: 79 deutschsprachige Erzähler der Jahrgänge 1900 bis 1960, 4 volumes, edited by Hochhuth (Munich: Knaur, 1983);

Die zweite Klassik: Deutschsprachige Erzähler der Jahrgänge 1850-1900, 2 volumes, edited by Hochhuth (Cologne: Kiepenheuer & Witsch, 1983).

SELECTED PERIODICAL PUBLICATIONS—
UNCOLLECTED: "Filbinger: 'Der Verurteilte erklärte nichts': Über das Todesurteil gegen den Marinesoldaten Walter Gröger," *Der Spiegel*, 32 (8 May 1978): 140-144;

" 'Der Zynismus ist beispiellos': Über neues Belastungsmaterial gegen den ehemaligen Marinestabsrichter Filbinger," *Der Spiegel*, 32 (12 June 1978): 112-117;

"Bismarck, der Klassiker," *Der Spiegel* (31 July 1978): 44-45;

"Will man das Wahl nennen? Das Spätwerk von Karl Jaspers, wiedergelesen. . . ." *Die Zeit*, 18 February 1983, p. 37;

"Eine Lehre, die vielleicht sehr aktuell ist," *Der Spiegel*, 38 (25 June 1984): 48-53;

" 'Dann wird man Sie ermorden': Die Rohwedder-Szene aus Rolf Hochhuths Drama 'Wessis in Weimar,' " *Der Spiegel*, 46 (1 June 1992): 272-275.

Rolf Hochhuth's plays have received little critical praise: the consensus is that he is incapable of structuring a play, of writing dialogue that is not impossibly wooden, or even of thinking clearly about the kind of aesthetic effect he intends. But whatever their artistic failings, at least three of his plays have had direct social and political consequences of which critical favorites such as Bertolt Brecht or Peter Weiss could only dream. And three have had considerable success with the public, regardless of the critics' strictures, because of their topicality.

Hochhuth was born on 1 April 1931 in Eschwege, east of Kassel, to Hochhuth and Ilse Holzapfel Hochhuth. His father's family had been shoemakers and shoe manufacturers in Eschwege since 1709. After being forced to close his shoe factory in the Depression, in 1932, Hochhuth's father managed his wife's family's wholesale business. The family had liberal leanings in politics, though the young Hochhuth was an unenthusiastic member of the Hitler Youth. He was profoundly influenced by the partition of Germany after 1945, which cut him off from fields and woods he had known as a boy—the border between the two Germanies was four miles from Eschwege. Adolf Hitler's actions determined Hochhuth's early life to such an extent that he ironically calls Hitler his father.

Leaving the Realgymnasium of Eschwege early, he became a bookseller's apprentice in Marburg, Kassel, and Munich. He attended the Universities of Heidelberg and Munich, but did not work toward a degree. An epistolary novel influenced by Thomas Mann's *Buddenbrooks* (1901; translated, 1924), "Victoria-Straße 4" (his parents' address), remained a fragment. A story, "Inventur" (List), likewise unpublished, experimented with narrative form to the point of abolishing it altogether; the largely traditional form of his later works is not due to aesthetic naiveté. Since the age of nineteen he has suffered a slight facial paralysis, which is responsible for his often misleadingly bitter and severe appearance in pho-

tographs. In 1955 he became a reader for the Bertelsmann publishing house and edited one of the most popular collections (1959) of the works of the humorist Wilhelm Busch. In 1957 he married Marianne Heinemann, a former schoolmate whose mother had been guillotined in 1943 as a member of the Schulze-Boysen resistance group. They had two sons and were divorced in 1972. In 1975 Hochhuth married Dana Pavic, a Yugoslavian medical student; they have one son.

Hochhuth's first and best-known play, *Der Stellvertreter* (translated as *The Representative*, 1963; as *The Deputy*, 1964), burst forth in 1963 on a theater world quite unprepared for it and caused a tempest of controversy in Western Europe and North America. Since 1945 various dramatists had dealt with the crimes of the Hitler era, mainly in highly symbolic, mythical, metaphysical ways; in narrative literature a more realistic approach had often been used. But only Günter Grass's *Die Blechtrommel* (1959; translated as *The Tin Drum*, 1962) had attracted mass attention. Hochhuth's play, like all the preceding attempts at "Vergangenheitsbewältigung" (coming to terms with the past), is centered on working out a proper moral response to Nazism.

In 1956 Hochhuth had met a man who had helped with the gassing at Auschwitz. Later, accounts of Auschwitz; of the SS officer Kurt Gerstein, who tried to sabotage the mass murders of Jews; and of the Vatican's attitude to the deportation of Roman Jews became available to him. Starting in 1959 he worked on the play daily, using Gerstein's account; secondary sources, some of which are quoted verbatim in the play; and testimony of witnesses he interviewed in Rome. The play was completed in 1961, but fears of legal action by the Vatican prevented its publication. A prize for promising young authors was awarded for it in 1962, but its future was still in doubt until H. M. Ledig-Rowohlt of the Rowohlt publishing house decided to publish it. Ledig-Rowohlt showed the proofs to the producer Erwin Piscator, who agreed to stage it.

Riccardo Fontana, a young priest informed by Gerstein of the truth about the concentration camps, sees his superiors doing nothing. Armed with a burning desire to save the moral life of the church, he conceives a plan to kill Pope Pius XII and blame the SS for the deed. Recovering from this aberration, he attempts to persuade the pope to condemn the deportation and murder of Jews. When this attempt fails even as Roman Jews are being deported from within the walls of the Vatican, he sacrifices himself at Auschwitz to fulfill the mission of the Vatican which, in his view, the pope as God's "Stellvertreter" on earth has betrayed. The characters in the play fall into four groups. The smallest group consists of Riccardo and Gerstein, who are shocked and outraged by the deeds of the Nazis. The second group, the perpetrators of evil, forms a panorama of human contemptibility. The third, perhaps largest, group of characters are the victims. The fourth group consists of those who see what is going on but close their eyes to the moral aspects and who seem to have no conscience or to subordinate it to some other interest or institution such as church, state, or family. This last group includes Pius XII.

In a 1964 interview with Patricia Marx Hochhuth says that when he asked himself how "the murder of an entire people could take place without the highest moral authority of this earth having a word to say about it," he found that he had to put the pope onstage as "the most meaningful antagonist of Riccardo." The only thinkable attitude of a pope to Nazi excesses is, Hochhuth says, protest and condemnation; the pope's moral leadership could have changed the course of history. Not only the Vatican but also the Allies were quiet about the Holocaust; but above all, Pius was, for Hochhuth, in the position of the fireman who resigns when called to a blaze.

Hochhuth's indignation is suffused with irony. History, he believes, delights in placing an insignificant man in a significant position, giving epochal importance to accidents, destroying the worthy by the agency of the undistinguished. The moral failure of Pius is one that many might share, but it is disastrous because of his position. He acts just like the common soldiers, interchangeable tools of history, who round up the Jews; he shows no vision, no desire to transcend the circumstances in which he is placed. In his stage directions Hochhuth calls for some roles to be played by the same actor, to show how chance determines one's role in history: Pius, for example, is to be doubled with Rutta, a Rhenish industrialist who makes his profit from the slave labor in Auschwitz. But, for Hochhuth, anyone in any social position can rise above circumstances.

The play offers three major scenes of confrontation: of Gerstein with the papal nuncio, of Riccardo with the pope, and of Riccardo with the Doctor; and one touching scene showing the tensions in a Jewish family as they await deportation and vainly hope that conversion to Catholicism

or usefulness to the war effort may save them. Aside from these scenes, the play is largely exposition. High-ranking Nazis discuss their ghastly activities, such as collecting commissars' skulls for anthropological studies of the Slav "subhumans," over a game of skittles in a social club that strikes the horrified spectator as an upholstered, comfortable hell; Gerstein discourses on the self-contradictions of Hitler's racial and expansionist policies; there are long discussions of whether a God who allows Auschwitz can actually exist. The sound of bells in Rome is all-pervading; the Doctor has his own leitmotiv, a screeching circular saw; spilling ink on his fingers, Pius symbolically washes his hands of the Jewish problem. The danger of verging on kitsch is, of course, acute with the use of such trite symbolism. Some critics believe that much of the depiction of Nazism should be omitted as irrelevant to the plot, but Hochhuth is concerned not to let it seem that he is attacking the pope and exculpating the Germans. Hochhuth's exhaustive notes caused the play to be taken as the first of the wave of documentary dramas in Germany in the 1960s, though little of the dialogue is claimed to be authentic. There has been much argument as to whether Hochhuth draws Pius XII fairly. Hochhuth shows Pius as being suddenly confronted with the greatest moral test any man can face and failing because of flaws in his character. Pius is preoccupied both with the need for the papacy to be on the winning side and with the need to protect the church's investments, which could be profitable under Hitler but would be confiscated by Stalin. The welfare of the Jews engages his head but not his heart. Hostile critics find the image of a money-obsessed, emotionally frigid pontiff offensive, but Hochhuth did not mean to be one-sided: one person's monster of insensitivity is another's consummate diplomat. Hochhuth does not doubt that Pius was a man of God; but he is unable to portray this aspect, whereas he is venomously effective in portraying the other aspect, the diplomat—or hypocrite—who, he believes, always won when Pius had to make a difficult decision.

The ending, in which Gerstein and Riccardo almost escape death at Auschwitz, has grave flaws. Riccardo, having worked in the crematorium, has lost his faith. Gerstein attempts to smuggle him out, but the plot is discovered. Gerstein is arrested; Riccardo tries to shoot the Doctor but is shot by a guard, and mutters a prayer as he dies. An alternative final act written for optional stage use is set in Rome, with Riccardo setting out on his last journey as a mere number; in some productions the play ended with the confrontation between Riccardo and Pius. But only Auschwitz, only the meeting of Riccardo and the Doctor, pulls the plot together and makes sense of the forebodings of the early acts. And Auschwitz defies Hochhuth's sense of theater; indeed, he believes that a writer who could present it adequately would be morally frigid. His decision to abandon realism and embrace surrealism and montage is a reaction to the absurdity and horror of the situation, but the scene is an anticlimax when seen on the stage.

In the 1920s Piscator, Germany's leading practitioner of highly technological theater, had made dramatic texts subserve a communist political message. He meant to force the public out of its inertia and produce a reaction that would have effects outside the theater. The pathos, the existentialist élan, the excitement of *Der Stellvertreter* impressed him as soon as he saw the script. But his production was strangely classical, timeless, and psychologically based. Hochhuth's combination of naturalism and surrealism is intended to shock and terrify the spectator; the reduction of characters to types leads to expressionistic vagueness.

Before the first performance, an atmosphere of impending scandal was encouraged by secrecy about the text—broken by the publication of extracts which were then cut from the play as Piscator concentrated on the conflict of the pope and Riccardo and elided much of the sexual horror of Auschwitz. Piscator supplied the equality of conflict that Hochhuth had not provided by weakening Riccardo and strengthening Pius, who was played as a man wrestling with the dilemmas of his position. The final scene was placed in a sort of tunnel with pictures of Auschwitz victims on both sides and other—incongruous—scenic elements. Piscator asked that there be no applause at the end, to mark the seriousness of the subject; but the premiere audience applauded all the same.

However one judges the play in the abstract, there is no denying its effectiveness. Critics noted that where other playwrights gave sophisticated artistic presentations of nothing much, Hochhuth gave a depiction of important subjects that was sneered at by experts but capable of keeping the audience arguing for hours after the curtain fell. One might wish that the theme had been treated more competently, but no other

writer had thought of treating it at all. Hochhuth's main charges against pope and church have not been satisfactorily refuted despite extensive polemics about whether he got the facts right and whether he interpreted them correctly. No other postwar German drama reached out as this one did to influence people who never visited a theater; none achieved such widespread stagings abroad (seventy-three productions in twenty-seven countries). The book, published on the day of the first performance, sold 40,000 copies in three months and 460,000 by 1976. In the seven months after the first publication and performance the publishers received about three thousand reviews, reports, and letters. Public discussions were held in packed halls, and correspondence about the issues raised by the play took place on a remarkably intellectual level for months on end in the *Frankfurter Allgemeine Zeitung* (Frankfurt General Newspaper), a leading right-liberal daily. Much of the discussion, to be sure, left the play itself to one side, addressing matters Hochhuth had not raised, such as whether papal protest would have hastened the end of the Nazi regime. But none of it would have happened without the catalyst provided by Hochhuth.

The first production reached 117 performances in Berlin and then toured to twenty-one cities in Germany; the next season there were thirteen productions in Germany, reaching a total of 504 performances. But it did not stay long in the repertoire. In France the play was even more popular, with 346 performances of Peter Brook's production, but just as ephemeral. Other early productions took place in Sweden and Switzerland. Two English translations appeared, the British one flawed by mistranslations and the American by cuts. The 1964 New York production was criticized for excessive cutting, ineptitude, flat characterization, and patchy acting.

Most German productions, in a bid to preempt Catholic criticism, minimized the scandal intended by Hochhuth as central. Instead, a deeper stumbling block becomes apparent: God's silence about Auschwitz, evoked in the last act, becomes much more serious than the pope's. Nevertheless, by use of religious symbolism the productions assured the spectator of the director's respectability in matters of belief. A darkened stage and sound effects such as church bells and organ music created a pseudosacral atmosphere.

In Rome the play was almost banned. A small club theater was built for the purpose of a

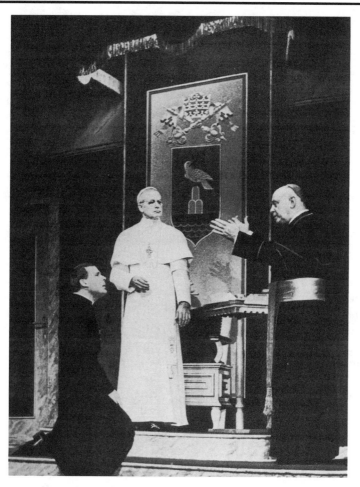

Günter Tabor, Dieter Borsche, and Hans Nielsen in a scene from the premiere of Hochhuth's Der Stellvertreter *in Berlin in 1963*

production, but the actors were driven out and had to give an impromptu performance in the bookshop of the publisher of the Italian edition.

East German television showed a film incorporating four scenes; otherwise, Hochhuth, feeling that to criticize the Vatican was one thing in the West but quite another in an anticlerical state, allowed no East German productions until 1966, when there were three. Passages about the connection of industry and fascism that were generally cut in the West were stressed in East Germany to show that church and business, Hitler's allies, were still active and unreformed in the West.

Even before the first performance the Catholic church, shaken by the threatened loss of its moral credit, considered legal action against Hochhuth for antichurch utterances or for libel of a dead person; then it started a campaign that led to serious public disorder in Basel. On seeing how the Swiss defended his freedom of speech against six thousand Catholic and right-wing demonstrators, Hochhuth moved with his family to

Riehen, near Basel. Articles by Catholics in America accused Hochhuth of anti-Semitism and communism. Three plays were written by clerics defending Pius XII. But in the long run the church had to take Hochhuth seriously, releasing some material prematurely from the Vatican archives and looking more critically at Pius XII, who had up to then been thought a candidate for canonization. Insofar as the Catholic church was a pillar of the West German state and interdependent with the Christian Democratic Union (CDU), the ruling party, the ecclesiastical scandal was also a threat to the government. Even twenty-five years later, in Kurt Waldheim's Austria and Helmut Kohl's Germany, the news of planned performances in Vienna and in Munich (where the play had never before been seen on a publicly subsidized stage) led to protests from the Catholic church and the political right wing and attempts to cancel the productions. The Munich production turned out to have lost all its drama and become a historical debating piece.

In Germany the play was awarded the literary prize of the Junge Generation (Young Generation); in the United States, Hochhuth received a Frederic Melcher Award. Literary critics, glad of a serious political subject to write about, paid much attention to the accuracy of Hochhuth's treatment but had no criteria other than Hochhuth's own historical notes for judging it; such discussions tended to increase the respect paid to his qualities as a self-taught historian. In fact, Hochhuth had worked largely with second- or third-hand sources and works of popularization.

"Der Klassenkampf ist nicht zu Ende" (The Class Struggle Is Not Over), first published in *Der Spiegel* (November 1965), set off a political row during the West German election campaign of 1965 in the course of which the head of government, Ludwig Erhard, described Hochhuth as a "Pincher" (terrier) snapping at statesmen's heels. The ensuing criticisms of Erhard's style of debate and of his intolerance of nonpoliticians intervening in political life probably did the CDU more harm than Hochhuth's original arguments, which were by no means blatantly leftist, but amounted to a plea (accepted in principle, with more or less enthusiasm, by all political parties a little later) for redistribution, for moderation in the capitalist concentration of wealth. As the pope should be moral, so the capitalist should show enlightened self-interest and ensure that the worker gets a share of the prosperity he creates. Rather than radically criticizing the order of Western society, Hochhuth appeals for self-discipline within it.

In his next play, *Soldaten* (1967; translated as *Soldiers*, 1968) Hochhuth tries to do to Winston Churchill, as the man responsible for the bombing of Dresden, what he had done to Pius XII. Two main differences give this play less impact than *Der Stellvertreter*: Hochhuth admires Churchill as he did not Pius XII—having started with the intention of putting Churchill in the dock, he found the character growing in stature and giving convincing arguments; and the historical facts are more subject to dispute. Churchill is seen as strong, rather than as good; Hochhuth admires his strength and his overwhelming desire to act on the world stage. Churchill is one of the few who choose not to adapt to social circumstances; the herd is led by the strongest and most decisive man of action. There is no a priori moral distinction between a Churchill who gets his hands dirty incidentally while leading a just fight and a Hitler whose struggle is unjust from the first. Both are striving to reach the head of

the column by fair or foul means. This attitude earned Hochhuth bitter criticism from those who have a revulsion for murder, whether used as a political weapon or not, and do not believe that the reputation of a recently dead man is enhanced by accusing him of it. Hochhuth, they feel, has not done justice to the complexity or the moral feelings of the historical Churchill; rather, he has created a pseudohistorical monster with similarities to Friedrich Schiller's Wallenstein.

At the center of the play are two British actions of World War II, one general and one specific: the blanket bombing of German cities, rather than military targets, to demoralize the civilian population; and the sabotage of the plane used by the head of the exiled Polish government, Gen. Wladyslaw Sikorski. That the latter actually happened has never been officially admitted or proved beyond reasonable doubt: good arguments have been put forward for seeing the plane crash in which Sikorski died as an accident, while historians doubt whether Sikorski's death brought any advantage to Churchill, who thereafter had to deal with even more intransigent anti-Stalinists. While Churchill's advisers discuss the bombing policy, members of the exiled Polish government attempt to assert their moral rights in the face of the overwhelming political necessity for Churchill not to alienate Stalin. The two themes are linked in that the bombings are also a sop to Stalin on Churchill's part, an alibi to excuse the Western Allies' failure to open a second European front. The play is framed within a fictional postwar celebration of an anniversary of the Geneva treaties laying down rules of land and sea warfare, treaties which, as Hochhuth points out, have never been extended to aerial warfare and were thus not infringed by the bombing of civilians in World War II. An ex-bomber pilot, Dorland, now dying, is the proponent of morality in the frame action, while his son is a cold-war militarist. The father was converted from sinner to angel after being shot down over Germany and forced to help his own victims.

Again Hochhuth includes much peripheral material, resulting in a long play; the text is strewn with brackets marking passages to be cut in performance. A greater unity results from the central position of Churchill throughout, compared with the episodic appearances of Pius XII in *Der Stellvertreter*. Hochhuth's main theme is the tragedy of power. He who fights Hitler has only one virtue, that of fighting Hitler. Getting rid of one's strongest supporters by foul play because they upset one's powerful allies is a revolting and yet admirable act. Even great errors such as the bombing program are historical necessities; their perpetrator embraces them out of the same traits of character that made him the only possible leader against Hitler (Hochhuth provides theoretical, philosophical justifications of this approach in his notes to the play and essays.) Originally Bishop Bell, the outspoken opponent of the bombing policy, was to be a sort of Riccardo to Churchill's Pius XII; but Bell's contribution was purely rhetorical and did nothing to further the action.

Accepted by Laurence Olivier for the National Theatre in London, the English translation, *Soldiers*, caused a controversy in the British press because of its view of Churchill. It was banned by the lord chamberlain, whose office as censor of plays was abolished as a consequence of the affair. Thereafter, the play had its biggest success in London, with 122 performances; the Berlin premiere, directed by Hans Schweikart, had been coolly received and had run for only 50 performances. English-language productions also took place in Toronto, Dublin, and New York. The text sold 123,000 copies over the next ten years. The play had no noticeable effect on the regulation of aerial warfare—a subject close to Hochhuth's heart, for he was shocked by indiscriminate bombing during the Vietnam War. Hochhuth had started writing the play in order to press for the extension of the Geneva conventions to aerial warfare. But the controversies over *Soldaten* did not bring out this aspect. Hochhuth had apparently intended it as a contribution to the attacks on American strategy in Vietnam, but this aspect was little discussed in connection with the play.

In 1968, in response to civil unrest in America, the murders of Martin Luther King, Jr., and Robert Kennedy, the Vietnam War, Richard Nixon's election as president, and the rise in Germany of the extraparliamentary opposition, Hochhuth started work on *Guerillas* (1970). The strength of the two first plays lay in their eliciting reactions of shock from the audience to historical events and the actions of historical personages; the third posits that the audience will be shocked by the undemocratic nature of the United States and will lend its attention to a political gangster drama set in the upper echelons of that society and lacking a foundation in fact. The basic premise, that in a country where money buys power a change of the system can only come from among

the rich and powerful by means of a coup d'état, was worth a dramatic exploration; but the grand scale Hochhuth chooses, the intrusions of theory, the excursions into South America, the melodramatic events and sensational incidents—none of them impossible in the light of what is known about the Central Intelligence Agency but hard to accept in such a concentrated sequence—render the play ineffective.

Twenty years later the events Hochhuth claimed to be inevitable had not happened in the United States, whereas the fabric of the communist world had been rent by unforeseen upheavals. The play's main interest today is as a document of the wave of reevaluation of the United States by German intellectuals at the time of the Vietnam War: having been seen perhaps too rosily as the liberator of 1945, America was seen too bleakly in the late 1960s and early 1970s as aggressive, selfish, and antidemocratic.

Hochhuth founds his drama on a rather eccentric reading of the implications of social facts, notably the lack of a labor party in the United States. Again he focuses on an individual and his tragedy. The hero, Nicolson, is a lawyer and United States senator—and, improbably, a military man and arms company director. Nicolson has gathered around him a group of people dedicated to working covertly for the overthrow of the capitalist domination of the political process in the United States. He intends a coup d'état after the next presidential election to promote the rights, he says, of two hundred million people against the two hundred millionaires who run the country. Through his connections he has infiltrated various security services and parts of the military establishment, and while pretending to work for the CIA in South America is actually sabotaging the American government's attempts to control the continent. Involvement in South America, criticized by his fellow conspirators from the outset, proves his undoing when a talk in the confessional between his wife and the archbishop of San Salvador is overheard by the local forces; Nicolson is cornered by his CIA colleagues and killed.

Critics pointed out that all Hochhuth does is to replace one ruling conspiracy by another. The plot is overloaded with sensational incidents that distract attention from the political analysis. The social injustices by which the audience is supposed to be shocked never appear onstage. Cuba and Nicaragua as examples of mass revolution are disregarded in the interest of the coup d'état theory. Odd details, such as the depiction of Jimmy Hoffa and the Teamsters Union as instruments of progress, jar. The dangers of a coup playing into the hands of right-wing army officers are not seen. The fixation on the great man or savior, cheaply introduced sex, and shallow characterizations were also criticized.

Die Hebamme (The Midwife; published, 1971; performed, 1972) again introduces a reformer who uses a privileged social position together with violence to change matters; but the scale is smaller and the outcome happier. Hochhuth has said that the affluent society can only take social criticism if it is disguised as comedy. A midwife, fleeing from the East before the Russians in 1945, adds to her own identity that of a deceased friend who was a field marshal's widow. For years the supposed Baroness von Hossenbach draws her generous army pension, which the real Sister Sophie uses to the last penny to help the poor victims and outcasts of the West German economic miracle. The events of the play are set off when, shortly before Sophie's retirement, she determines that by fair means or foul the makeshift slum in which these people are housed will be replaced by better conditions. By improper use of a church bank account for which she is a signatory, she opens an old people's home to accommodate some of the homeless; by a trick she gains possession of the keys of new married quarters built for the army and arranges for the rest of the misfits to move into these flats and burn their old shacks behind them.

The political leaders and officials of the town—hollow characters who would be nothing but for their social standing—arrange a series of financial deals to the mutual benefit of everyone except the taxpayers, who do not need to know; avoid the threatened television exposure of the plight in which they have left the underprivileged; and find a fresh building site for the army. Sophie has to confess to arson and extortion to bring about a court hearing in which the facts of the matter can be discussed. She dies—a sentimental touch—with her work accomplished.

Publication of the play did what two television exposés and an article in the magazine *Der Stern* (Star) had not: it secured action for the homeless of Kiel and Kassel. The use of comic accents and puns; the fullness of details in the plot; and the inevitable stage directions and afterword were unpopular with the critics. The shanty dwellers seemed condescendingly portrayed, the ques-

tion of the relation of milieu and character insufficiently treated. That the heroine was shown as a leading member of the rightist party, the CDU, did not ring true, although Hochhuth intended to show that the CDU had lost the social conscience that it had when it issued its first program in 1947 and that there is little difference among political parties but a great difference among the individuals who belong to them. Doubts were expressed as to how a social cause could be furthered by presenting the democratic process as hopelessly corrupt; it was pointed out that the Nazis had made similar criticisms of the Weimar Republic. The heroine is an embezzler and arsonist who causes an accident to prevent the fire brigade from reaching the scene; Hochhuth, critics charged, may believe that there are great altruistic individuals who should be allowed to do such things, but he does not explain how the less altruistic can be kept from emulating such actions for their own ends. In the 1970s, with the rise of terrorism, Germans were becoming quite sensitive about such things. Some thought that Hochhuth should have proposed revision of the political system rather than palliation of its effects by a licensed do-gooder; but a communist heroine would never have gotten five simultaneous premieres in West Germany. *Die Hebamme* was the most performed play of its season and reached 623 performances in West German theaters over three seasons; eighty-eight thousand copies of the book were sold.

Lysistrate und die NATO (Lysistrata and NATO; published, 1973; performed, 1974) is another thesis play, lightened by a humor more appropriate to the subject than that of *Die Hebamme*. The farmers' wives on a small Greek island go on strike, refusing to cook, milk goats, or go to their husbands' beds, because the farmers plan to sell their farms for a NATO base. Such a plan would, the women point out, expose the island to instant Russian attack in case of war. Their preference is for development of a tourist industry. Their leader, Lysistrate Soulidis, is a member of Parliament; conveniently, a rich ex-minister over whom she has a hold resides on the island. During a bacchanal at the local inn the women sleep with a shepherd, a waiter, and the officers sent to assess the island's military suitability—who are then blackmailed into declaring it unsuitable. Hochhuth revised the play under the title *Inselkomödie* (Island Comedy, 1991).

In an essay published with the play Hochhuth justifies the bacchanal as part of a specifically feminine way of doing things, but most critics feel the sexual elements in the play are more redolent of male chauvinism and the indulging of male fantasies than of female liberation. Hochhuth never explains why it is important that the action coincide with the colonels' coup d'état in Athens; indeed, his intention of showing how a Greek island could achieve self-sufficiency and peace and how women could liberate themselves from a patriarchal society seems questionable against such a background. The play received three productions in its first season, running for eighty-three performances in all; but the critics were dismissive of this success; his plays, they said, were increasingly spurned by leading theaters and had found their proper level on the municipal stages, where a philistine audience appreciated their simplicity, clear-cut heroes and villains, and distrust of politicians.

Tod eines Jägers (Death of a Big Game Hunter; published, 1976; performed, 1977) is a dramatic monologue spoken by Ernest Hemingway shortly before his suicide in 1961; some of the material is taken from a fragmentary essay written by the real Hemingway. Reviewing his life and works, Hemingway comes to see the social irresponsibility implicit in much of what he wrote. He is the opposite of Hochhuth's other heroes: he never used his privileged position for social ends but preferred to write for the sake of success and the inflation of his ego. A large window at the back of the stage serves as a screen on which scenes from the writer's past are projected; a black mirror is emblematic of melancholy. The text has several climactic self-examinations interspersed with more mundane material; the dramatic conflict is between the will to live and the wish to die. But Hochhuth's language is too even for the purpose and is more abstract than the real Hemingway's. The effect of the play onstage will depend entirely on the talent of the actor.

In a 1976 speech, published with documentation in 1979 as *Tell 38* (translated, 1984), Hochhuth discusses Maurice Bavaud, a Swiss citizen who was executed by the Gestapo after an attempt to shoot Hitler. Such a person is well suited, Hochhuth argues, to epitomize the message that anyone, given the moral impetus, can try to change history. Hochhuth disregards the evidence that Bavaud was simply mad.

Juristen (Lawyers; published, 1979; performed, 1980) represents a return to the formula of Hochhuth's first two plays. In common with many others, Hochhuth was critical of the fact that no lawyer was ever prosecuted after 1945 for anything he did pursuant to Hitlerian laws, whereas the defense of "only obeying orders" was refused for service personnel. The play could have ended the career of a leading CDU politician, Hans Filbinger, who was then presiding minister of Baden-Württemberg; but Hochhuth let some of his evidence out beforehand in an advance extract published in the newspaper *Die Zeit* (Time) of a narrative work, *Eine Liebe in Deutschland* (1978; translated as *A German Love Story*, 1980). Hochhuth, who had just moved from Basel to Vienna, was sued by Filbinger for five hundred thousand marks in damages.

Eine Liebe in Deutschland concerns a real episode, a love affair between a German woman and a Pole assigned as a laborer in South Germany during World War II. As sexual relations with such workers were forbidden, the woman was sent to a concentration camp, and the man was executed. Hochhuth's description of the willingness in the small town to enforce Nazi regulations is chilling. Among those mentioned in the passages in which Hochhuth comments on the wider issues of that era and the present day is Filbinger, who, as a military lawyer under Hitler—and, even after Hitler, in British prisoner-of-war camps—was party to some sickeningly severe judgments. The publicity surrounding the lawsuit, further revelations about Filbinger's past which accorded ill with the pose of a resistance worker he had adopted since 1960, and his failure to see that he had done anything wrong led the CDU to pressure him to resign from his public offices.

Juristen is much better constructed than *Der Stellvertreter* or *Soldaten*, being based on two interrelated themes: the sins of the fathers under Hitler and the sins of the sons in the Federal Republic. Heilmayer, the presiding minister of a German province (obviously Baden-Württemberg), was a military judge under Hitler. In 1978, at the height of terrorist activity in Germany and Italy, he supports the measures by which any association with communism or participation in left-wing demonstrations around 1968 permanently disqualify a person from public employment. Klaus, a friend of Heilmayer's daughter, Tina, and her common-law husband, Dieter, is fired from his job as a hospital doctor for his single act of opposition to the right-wing press's lies about the unrest of 1968. Meanwhile, Heilmayer attempts to take credit for saving the life of a Polish doctor for whom he advised the death sentence for performing an abortion on a German woman during the war. He becomes federal president after discrediting the previous president by a trick.

The eruption into Tina and Dieter's bohemian flat of the frock-coated, much-decorated minister, fresh from an official function, and his personal guards with their police dogs, riot gear, and guns with telescopic sights is visually effective. Visionary flashbacks to the victims of the Hitler period break up what is otherwise a complete observance of the classical unities.

Juristen is the most consistently effective of Hochhuth's plays and the one with the best chance of standing the test of time as an authentic record of its era. There are, however, such would-be-comic longueurs as the repeated passage across the stage of one of Heilmayer's guards, who has to abandon his post because of diarrhea; and the stress laid in the stage directions on the size of Tina's bosom is embarrassing in its irrelevance. A peculiar effect of Hochhuth's passion for individual rights is that, much against general opinion, he argues that the state should negotiate with terrorist kidnappers to free their victims, whatever the price in cash or political effects.

Though Hochhuth tried not to make Heilmayer just a portrait of the ruined Filbinger, the play, when published, was perceived as a mere tailpiece to a past scandal; few theaters took it up, and their productions varied wildly in competence. The one directed in Göttingen by Günter Fleckenstein with Hochhuth's collaboration brought out strongly the underlying theme: should the lawyer's guide be the perhaps unjust laws in force at the time, or his conscience? That production altered the play's conclusion: in line with their differences of attitude, Tina and Dieter break up. The production in Hamburg directed by Friedrich Schütter with a narrator and photomontages to accompany the mentions of past events was gripping enough to make the spectators in the gallery enthusiastic and those in the stalls uneasy.

Ärztinnen (Women / Doctors, 1980), commissioned by the Mannheim National Theater, takes up the subject of the testing of new drugs and techniques in clinical practice. Hochhuth concentrates on what happens when there is pressure to conduct limited trials so as to make a drug available or a technique publishable for the sake of the profits of the pharmaceutical manufacturer or the am-

bition of the practitioner involved. To make the somewhat rarefied subject fit for the stage, he presents a series of examples in the form of crises affecting the members of a single family; melodramatic situations follow one another in the fashion of a soap opera. Lydia is a doctor who works for a pharmaceutical company. Her warnings that a certain preparation is contaminated go unheeded, and she is then expected to lie on behalf of the firm; she resigns, only to become depressed at the prospect of being jobless at the age of sixty.

Her daughter, Katia, is also a doctor; Riemerschmid, the head of her department and also her lover, hopes to win a professorship by new work on a lung syndrome—much of which will in fact have been done by Katia. But she performs an unnecessary biopsy to get practice in the technique, transforming a serious case into a hopeless one, and is threatened with legal action. Riemerschmid will not protect her; but because his ambition has involved him in politics he is able to procure Lydia a new job, and Lydia, by offering lucrative test contracts, gets a Swedish professor to offer Katia employment in his hospital.

Katia's sixteen-year-old son, Tom, is involved in a road accident; he is unnecessarily treated with a transfusion of artificial blood, enraging Katia, who does not see the similarity with her own previous conduct. He suffers an allergic reaction to the plasma substitute and dies; the doctor treating him is not displeased to have the opportunity for a publication on this reaction. Hochhuth includes a graphic postmortem, for which the stage directions demand the best artificial corpses and fresh pigs' entrails and brains; these props were omitted in the Mannheim premiere but were included in a production by the Berlin Freie Volksbühne (Free People's Stage) and in one directed by Hochhuth at the Ernst-Deutsch-Theater in Hamburg.

The Hochhuthian tendency to black-or-white characterization is avoided by showing the two central figures in their family relationships as well as in their dubious professional lives, but the result is to make the characters inconsistent; the audience can no more bridge the gap between the loving mother and grandmother, on the one hand, and medical corner cutters, on the other hand, than can the characters themselves. All in all, it is one of Hochhuth's less convincing dramatic essays. Its anticapitalist theme made it popular in the East, and it was produced in Moscow and filmed in East Germany.

Judith (1984) takes another stab at the subject of *Guerillas*, with the vague motives of Nicolson and his crew in the earlier play replaced by a specific one. The American president (clearly Ronald Reagan) has ordered the manufacture of chemical weapons; the United States and the Soviet Union have decided that any war between them would be fought in Western Europe, and they do not care about the fate of that region provided that they survive. (There is even a hint that American Jews would not mind punishing Germany with poison gas for Auschwitz.) To avoid the danger that a president who believes in an impending Armageddon may actually order it, he must be assassinated. Judith, the journalist who undertakes this task, first reassures herself of the morality of her aims by visiting a Russian woman who laid a mine for one of Hitler's satraps during the war; that assassination, a historical fact, is also dramatized in a prelude. Judith's brother, a chemist paralyzed by Agent Orange in Vietnam, supplies her with a vial of nerve poison which she looses on the president in the course of an interview in which he shows a cynical disregard of the human consequences of his policies. Though Judith and her Russian counterpart, Jelena, agree that the point of assassination is to send a message of resistance, Judith escapes unsuspected, and the cause of the president's death is officially announced as heart failure.

Rambling, with inconclusive discussions on the ethics of assassination and the interplay of social background and political conviction, and shot through with improbabilities from the world of the cheap thriller, the play also suffers from a parade of Hochhuthian idées fixes such as whether Russian women have underwear (he demonstrates that they do not). Oddly, the feminist potential of the story does not engage Hochhuth's attention. He invokes the tradition of the biblical Judith story, notably its nineteenth-century dramatization by Friedrich Hebbel, and he does his play no good by diverging from it. His Judith, a noted television personality, has no personal or sexual relations with his Holofernes—in fact, the president never appears, and even the murder is offstage. Hochhuth explains that he did not wish to show the murder of a living person, but the upshot is that both the president and the assassin remain colorless—his enormity undemonstrated, her decision to kill him insufficiently motivated.

The Zurich Schauspielhaus commissioned the play but refused to perform it; the Citizens' Theatre in Glasgow premiered it in a production directed by Robert David Macdonald, Hochhuth's old friend and the translator of his first two plays. The play was first done in German in Kiel, where it was directed by Günther Tabor, who had played Riccardo in Berlin in 1963. Although it was heavily cut to get rid of irrelevancies and embarrassments and was helped by documentary films and slides, it was generally found to be a little dull.

Unbefleckte Empfängnis (Immaculate Conception; published, 1988; performed, 1989) is a plea for the acceptance of surrogate motherhood. Though the subtitle, *Ein Kreidekreis* (A Chalk Circle), links the play to the tradition of the conflict of two women over a baby, from Solomon to Brecht, here the biological and the surrogate mother are in agreement against an uncomprehending and hostile world of men. Hochhuth's technique of dividing characters into black and white is still alive. The surrogate mother is Yugoslavian, so that her friendship with the would-be mother can be a touching example of feminine solidarity against the boundaries of national prejudice and class. The plot is sown with diversions such as the surrogate mother's husband's lust for her sister, while exciting pieces of veterinary knowledge are imparted: the play takes place on a farm so that the European Community's different ways of dealing with the breeding of animals and of people can be explored. A discussion of the ethics of surrogacy is rudely ended by a group of feminists with flour bombs and water hoses. In the final scene, a shocking one set in a professional ethics hearing, the defenders of medical morality take an obviously wanted child from a good home, muddy the waters by confusing surrogacy with embryo research, and hound a caring doctor out of the country. But by then the audience has long lost interest. The Berlin director, Heribert Sasse, cut out a whole act but was criticized for cutting too much of Hochhuth's passion and turning the play into a long discussion.

Sommer 14 (Summer 14; published, 1989; performed, 1990) takes up a theme aired in the notes to *Judith*: that the arms race produces war and that there are parallels between the increase of armaments in the 1980s and the growth of the German armed forces before 1914. (Hochhuth participated in demonstrations against the deployment of Pershing missiles in Germany, being photographed in tie and jacket among the scruffy left-wing youth.) The argument is inconsistent—sometimes Hochhuth appears to be blaming Kaiser Wilhelm II's militarism for the

Hochhuth participating in a peace demonstration in Mutlangen on 1 September 1983, the forty-fourth anniversary of the outbreak of World War II (photograph by Michael Schröder/Argus)

war, sometimes he spreads the blame to other countries for forming alliances against the German threat. Hochhuth's painstaking exploration of historical sources is displayed at enormous length—396 pages—but the scenes he chooses to show are arbitrary, their effects in some cases cheap, and the linkage between them is forced. The appearance in various guises of Death, first as the beautiful youth Thanatos of Greek mythology, later as General von Falkenhayn and as a munitions manufacturer's wife, adds a metaphysical dignity to what is really a sordid story of human folly. The play's best scene—equivalent to the pope's decision not to protest in *Der Stellvertreter*— is the Kaiser's belated flirtation with peace, followed, under the pressure of his second-rate advisers, by submission to the logic of events which he himself has set in train, culminating in his appearance on the balcony to give a strangely minor-key speech of encouragement to his people on the outbreak of World War I. The Vienna production was directed by Robert David Macdonald, who cut one particularly irrelevant scene.

Though written much earlier, the fragment *Hitlers Dr. Faust* was published only in the volume *Alle Dramen 2* (All Dramas 2, 1991). This play was to follow the career of Hermann Oberth, the rocket pioneer whose expertise, if called on earlier by the German military, could have helped

Hitler win the war—and whose only regret afterward was that he had not been called on. The scientist or inventor who cannot see beyond the innovative value of his own work and has no sense of the morality of its application is a commonplace of postwar German literature—other examples are May Frisch's *Homo faber* (1957; translated, 1959) and Heinar Kipphardt's *In der Sache J. Robert Oppenheimer: Ein szenischer Bericht* (1964; translated as *In the Matter of J. Robert Oppenheimer*, 1967) —and, judging by the fragment, Hochhuth had little new to contribute to the theme.

Hochhuth's poems have attracted much less attention than his plays, but his stories have achieved some success. *Die Berliner Antigone* (1975) is a variant on the Antigone theme, with elements from *Romeo and Juliet*, set in wartime Berlin. In "Mutterliebe" (Mother Love), in the collection *Atlantik-Novelle* (Atlantic Novella, 1985), a mother is so worried about her sailor son that she uses her contacts to find out the position of the battleship on which he is serving. The data are transmitted by radio, intercepted and decoded by the enemy, and the ship is lost.

Hochhuth is a well-known figure in German theater life for his continual complaints at the small number of plays by contemporary German authors (notably himself) that are being performed. He has pointed out that some major writers have abandoned the stage for the novel because the former did not offer them a living. He has demanded more support for private theaters because subsidized theaters are unlikely to find his uncomfortable subject matter attractive and has called for the establishment of private television stations because German state television is even more directly politically controlled (and thus hostile to him) than the theater. Many theater people dispute his statistics, and most claim that he would have more performances if he wrote something other than dramatized editorials. Certainly, to read through Hochhuth's works from beginning to end is a wearisome business. He has always followed one of his rules for the avoidance of mere propaganda in political drama: to provide moral, not political arguments. But he has had trouble with the other: to have the devils and the saints speak with equal conviction and effect.

Hochhuth's dramas are Zeitstücke (topical plays) like those written in the 1920s by Friedrich Wolf and others, aimed not at eternity but at immediate political effect. The theater should be glad that there is one writer who still thinks that the stage is the right forum for important messages—though he also supplies forewords and stage directions to keep the reader happy. He is a moral rigorist in an era of relativism, and his moral concerns often make him turn the theater into a courtroom or a classroom and the speeches of his figures into pleas or lectures. Hochhuth sees the individual as the irrational element that may overturn or at least hinder the mechanized fantasies of the powerful, and as the central element of life that should not be trampled in the name of abstract ideals or ambitions. Against much modern writing, he puts in a strong plea to see human dignity as linked to free will, to the capacity to refuse to be a tool of evil forces.

Often he praises a great individual; often, on the other hand, it is a victim of history to whom Hochhuth—a militant pessimist in the mold of Georg Büchner or Ludwig Marcuse—provides a memorial. But the greatest effect comes when Hochhuth attacks. He is fascinated by the myth of Sisyphus: one must continue to fight battles for justice, though knowing that there is no qualitative historical progress and that the fight will have to be refought ad infinitum. Twice, with his attacks on Pius XII and on Hans Filbinger, Hochhuth signaled changes of direction in West German society and helped to strip away conspiracies of silence. His plays have been at their most effective when he has seized on a historical cover-up or a social injustice and presented it in a direct and realistic way. Where the German present or recent past is concerned, there is a category of facts that has been given the name "a case for Hochhuth": when the authorities treat a person, or people in general, as expendable, as mere statistics or cannon fodder.

References:

Karl Otmar Freiherr von Aretin, "Das Echo," *Merkur*, 17 (August 1963): 812-820;

Bernd Balzer, *Rolf Hochhuth: Der Stellvertreter* (Frankfurt, Berlin & Munich: Diesterweg, 1986);

Peter Bekes, "Rolf Hochhuth," in *Kritisches Lexikon der deutschen Gegenwartsliteratur*, edited by Heinz Ludwig Arnold (Munich: Edition text + kritik, 1984), n. pag.;

Eric Bentley, ed., *The Storm over The Deputy* (New York: Grove, 1964);

Jan Berg, *Hochhuths "Stellvertreter" und die "Stellvertreter-Debatte": "Vergangenheitsbewältigung" in Theater und Presse der sechziger Jahre* (Kronberg: Scriptor, 1977);

Arnold Blumer, *Das dokumentarische Theater der sechziger Jahre in der Bundesrepublik Deutschland* (Meisenheim: Hain, 1977), pp. 39-103;

Ferdinand Fasse, *Geschichte als Problem von Literatur: Das "Geschichtsdrama" bei Howard Brenton und Rolf Hochhuth* (Frankfurt am Main: Lang, 1983), pp. 178-206;

Jerry Glenn, "Faith, Love and the Tragic Conflict in Hochhuth's *Der Stellvertreter*," *German Studies Review*, 7 (October 1984): 481-498;

Walter Hinck, ed., *Rolf Hochhuth: Eingriff in die Zeitgeschichte* (Reinbek: Rowohlt, 1981);

Reinhart Hoffmeister, ed., *Rolf Hochhuth: Dokumente zur politischen Wirkung* (Munich: Kindler, 1980);

Wolfgang Ismayr, *Das politische Theater in Westdeutschland* (Meisenheim: Hain, 1977), pp. 100-105, 190-226, 336-338, 409-415;

Walter Kaufmann, *Tragedy and Philosophy* (New York: Anchor Books, 1969), pp. 377-394;

Rosemarie von dem Knesebeck, ed., *In Sachen Filbinger gegen Hochhuth: Die Geschichte einer Vergangenheitsbewältigung* (Reinbek: Rowohlt, 1980);

Jenö Levai, ed., *Geheime Reichssache: Papst Pius XII hat nicht geschwiegen. Berichte, Dokumente, Akten* (Cologne: Wort und Werk, 1966);

Patricia Marx, "An Interview with Rolf Hochhuth," *Partisan Review*, 31 (Summer 1964): 363-376;

Moray McGowan, "Nach dem Attentat eine Spritztour . . .," *Theater heute*, 25 (December 1984): 27;

Jacques Nobécourt, *"Le vicaire" et l'histoire* (Paris: Editions du Seuil, 1964);

Franz Norbert Mennemeier, *Modernes deutsches Drama*, volume 2 (Munich: Fink, 1975), pp. 252-262;

Fritz J. Raddatz, ed., *Summa iniuria oder Durfte der Papst schweigen? Hochhuths "Stellvertreter" in der öffentlichen Kritik* (Reinbek: Rowohlt, 1963);

Henning Rischbieter, "Der Fall Hochhuth: Über sein neues Stück 'Guerillas' und die Stuttgarter Aufführung," *Theater heute*, 11 (June 1970): 14-15;

Der Streit um Hochhuths Stellvertreter (Basel & Stuttgart: Basilius Presse, 1963);

Rainer Taëni, *Rolf Hochhuth* (Munich: Beck, 1977); translated by R. W. Last (London: Wolff, 1977);

text + kritik, special Hochhuth issue, 58 (1978);

Hans Albert Walter and W. Dirks, "Hochhuths moralischer Appell," *Frankfurter Hefte*, 19 (1964): 345-352;

Margaret E. Ward, *Rolf Hochhuth* (Boston: Twayne, 1977);

Rudolf Wolff, ed., *Rolf Hochhuth: Werk und Wirkung* (Bonn: Bouvier, 1987).

Papers:

An undated early manuscript for Rolf Hochhuth's *Der Stellvertreter* is at the Erwin Piscator Center, Academy of Arts, Berlin.

Ödön von Horváth
(9 December 1901 - 1 June 1938)

Beth Bjorklund
University of Virginia

See also the Horváth entry in *DLB 85: Austrian Fiction Writers After 1914.*

PLAY PRODUCTIONS: *Revolte auf Côte 3018*, Hamburg, Kammerspiele, 4 November 1927; revised as *Die Bergbahn*, Berlin, Theater am Bülowplatz, 4 January 1929;
Sladek der schwarze Reichswehrmann, Berlin, Lessing-Theater, 13 October 1929;
Italienische Nacht, Berlin, Theater am Schiffbauerdamm, 20 March 1931;
Geschichten aus dem Wiener Wald, Berlin, Deutsches Theater, 2 November 1931;
Kasimir und Karoline, Leipzig, Schauspielhaus, 18 November 1932;
Hin und her, Zurich, Schauspielhaus, 13 December 1934;
Mit dem Kopf durch die Wand, Vienna, Scala, 10 December 1935;
Glaube Liebe Hoffnung, Vienna, Theater am Schottentor, 13 November 1936;
Figaro läßt sich scheiden, Prague, Kleine Bühne des Deutschen Theaters, 2 April 1937;
Ein Dorf ohne Männer, Prague, Neues Deutsches Theater, 24 September 1937;
Himmelwärts, Vienna, Freie Bühne in der Komödie, 5 December 1937;
Der jüngste Tag, Mährisch-Ostrau, Deutsches Theater, 11 December 1937;
Die Unbekannte aus der Seine, Vienna, Studio der Hochschüler in der Kolingasse, 2 December 1949;
Don Juan kommt aus dem Krieg, Vienna, Theater der Courage, 12 December 1952;
Pompeji, Vienna, Theater "Die Tribüne," 6 January 1959;
Rund um den Kongreß, Vienna, Theater am Belvedere, 5 March 1969;
Zur schönen Aussicht, Graz, Vereinigte Bühnen, 5 October 1969;
Mord in der Mohrengasse, Vienna, Burgtheater, 1978.

Ödön von Horváth

BOOKS: *Das Buch der Tänze* (Munich: Schahin, 1922);
Der ewige Spießer: Erbaulicher Roman in drei Teilen (Berlin: Propyläen, 1930);
Geschichten aus dem Wiener Wald: Volksstück in drei Teilen (Berlin: Propyläen, 1931); translated by Christopher Hampton as *Tales from the Vienna Woods* (London: Faber & Faber, 1977);
Italienische Nacht: Volksstück (Berlin: Propyläen, 1931);
Jugend ohne Gott: Roman (Amsterdam: De Lange, 1938); translated by R. Wills Thomas as "Youth without God," in *A Child of Our Time, Being Youth without God and A Child of Our Time* (London: Methuen, 1938); republished as *The Age of the Fish* (New York: Dial

Press, 1939); German version, edited by Ian Huish (London: Harrap, 1974);

Ein Kind unserer Zeit: Roman (Amsterdam: De Lange, 1938); translated by Thomas as "A Child of Our Time," in *A Child of Our Time, Being Youth without God and A Child of Our Time*; republished as *A Child of Our Time* (New York: Dial Press, 1939);

Der jüngste Tag: Schauspiel in sieben Bildern (Emsdetten: Lechte, 1955);

Pompeji: Komödie eines Erdbebens in 6 Bildern (Munich: Sessler, 1960);

Unvollendet, edited by Franz Theodor Csokor (Graz: Stiasny, 1961);

Stücke, edited by Traugott Krischke (Hamburg: Rowohlt, 1961)—comprises *Italienische Nacht*; *Geschichten aus dem Wiener Wald*; *Kasimir und Karoline*; *Glaube Liebe Hoffnung*; *Die Unbekannte aus der Seine*; *Figaro läßt sich scheiden*; *Don Juan kommt aus dem Krieg*, translated by Hampton as *Don Juan Comes Back from the War* (London: Faber & Faber, 1978); *Der jüngste Tag*; *Pompeji*;

Zeitalter der Fische: Drei Romane und eine Erzählung (Vienna: Bergland, 1968)—comprises "Der ewige Spießer," "Jugend ohne Gott," "Ein Kind unserer Zeit," "Der Tod aus Tradition";

Rechts und links: Sportmärchen, edited by Walter Huder (Berlin: Berliner Handpresse, 1969);

Gesammelte Werke, 4 volumes, edited by Huder, Krischke, and Dieter Hildebrandt (Frankfurt am Main: Suhrkamp, 1970-1971)—includes in volume 1 (1970), *Revolte auf côte 3018, Die Bergbahn, Mord in der Mohrengasse, Sladek oder Die schwarze Armee, Sladek der schwarze Reichswehrmann*; in volume 2 (1970), *Zur schönen Aussicht, Rund um den Kongreß, Hin und her, Himmelwärts, Mit dem Kopf durch die Wand, Ein Dorf ohne Männer, Ein Sklavenball*; reprinted in 8 volumes (1972);

Von Spießern, Kleinbürgern und Angestellten, edited by Krischke (Frankfurt am Main: Suhrkamp, 1971);

Glaube Liebe Hoffnung, edited by Krischke (Frankfurt am Main: Suhrkamp, 1973); translated by Hampton as *Faith, Hope and Charity* (London: Faber & Faber, 1989);

Sladek oder Die schwarze Armee: Historie in 3 Akten (11 Bildern), edited by Hildebrandt (Frankfurt am Main: Suhrkamp, 1974);

Italienische Nacht, edited by Krischke (Frankfurt am Main: Suhrkamp, 1974)—comprises *Italienische Nacht, Ein Wochenendspiel*;

Die stille Revolution: Kleine Prosa, edited by Krischke (Frankfurt am Main: Suhrkamp, 1975);

Die Geschichten der Agnes Pollinger: Volksstück in 3 Teilen, edited by Krischke (Eisenstadt: Edition Roetzer / Vienna & Munich: Sessler, 1975);

Ein Lesebuch, edited by Krischke (Frankfurt am Main: Suhrkamp, 1976);

Sechsunddreißig Stunden, edited by Krischke (Frankfurt am Main: Suhrkamp, 1979);

Gesammelte Werke: Kommentierte Werkausgabe in fünfzehn Bänden, edited by Krischke and Susanna Foral-Krischke, 14 volumes published (Frankfurt am Main: Suhrkamp, 1985-　).

OTHER: "Ein Fräulein wird bekehrt," in *24 neue deutsche Erzähler*, edited by Hermann Kesten (Berlin: Kiepenheuer, 1929).

Ödön von Horváth's death in 1938 at the age of thirty-six was a loss for German drama, for the playwright was at the height of an extremely promising career. During the previous fifteen years he had written eighteen plays, as well as three novels and many short prose pieces. While in Paris to discuss plans for a film production he was killed by a branch that fell from a tree under which he had taken refuge during a thunderstorm. His work subsequently sank into oblivion and was not rediscovered until the 1960s. The debate about fascism, as part of Germany's coming to terms with its past, and the student movement of the 1960s led to a focus on the political and social issues treated in Horváth's works.

Horváth's writings portray primarily the lower middle class of blue-collar workers, shopkeepers, and petty government employees, as well as the lower class of prostitutes, pimps, and other shady characters. His focus is on interpersonal relationships, which are most often seen to be conducted for egotistical and materialistic ends. The role of women and male-female relationships in a patriarchal society are also prominent themes, and the playwright's sympathies are clearly with the women. Horváth is a master of dramatic dialogue, and the language that he puts into the mouths of his figures reveals how they use clichés and fixed formulas to mask their true intentions, attempting to blind themselves as well as others. This "Demaskierung des Bewußtseins" (unmasking of consciousness), revealing the hidden agenda behind the patterns of speech and behavior, was Horváth's stated goal and is the salient feature of his oeuvre.

His early works, which were written from a leftist political stance, have often been compared to those of his contemporary Bertolt Brecht. In contrast to Brecht, however, who proffered a Marxist political solution, Horváth suggests no panacea. He remained an observer and analyst. He reached adulthood in the time between the two world wars, when Central Europe was in a period of economic, political, and moral decline. Exposing the degenerate morality and the latent aggressions in a society that was moving toward fascism, Horváth characterized his work as an attempt "möglichst rücksichtslos gegen Dummheit und Lüge zu sein" (to be as ruthless as possible against stupidity and deceit).

Horváth's father, Dr. Edmund Josef von Horváth, was a Hungarian civil servant; his mother, Maria Hermine Horváth, née Prehnal, came from a Hungarian-German family of imperial military doctors. Horváth was born on 9 December 1901 in Fiume (today Rijeka, Croatia) on the Adriatic Sea. Six months later the family moved to Belgrade, where a second son, Lajos, was born in 1903. They moved to Budapest in 1908; when his parents moved on to Munich a year later, Horváth remained in Budapest at an Episcopalian boarding school. He rejoined his family in Munich in 1913 and continued his schooling there at the Kaiser-Wilhelm-Gymnasium. He later maintained that only at the age of fourteen did he write "den ersten deutschen Satz" (his first German sentence).

The family moved to Preßburg (today Bratislava, Czechoslovakia) in 1916 and back to Budapest in 1918. Horváth completed secondary school in 1919 while living with an uncle in Vienna, then enrolled at the University of Munich to study German literature and philosophy. It was about that time that he began writing, although he subsequently destroyed most of his early manuscripts. His first publication was a pantomine, *Das Buch der Tänze* (The Book of Dances, 1922). Since German was the language for all of his literary works, Horváth considered himself a German writer, even though he remained a Hungarian citizen all his life. Historians consider him an Austrian writer, since he was born into the Dual Monarchy and had a close relationship to the Austrian literary and cultural tradition.

In 1924 Horváth moved to Berlin, the center of the cultural and artistic achievements of Ger-

many throughout the 1920s and early 1930s. The director Max Reinhardt and the writer Franz Theodor Csokor were included in Horváth's circle of friends, as were many actors and actresses from the Berlin theaters. Horváth frequently returned to Vienna and Budapest and to Murnau in southern Germany, where his parents had purchased a villa in 1923. He would often remain all day at a coffeehouse in Vienna or Berlin, observing people and listening to them talk while writing at one of the marble-topped tables. He was also attracted to circuses and fairs. Horváth was a brilliant raconteur and a fine mimic with an ear for dialects and a keen sense of humor. Even when he presented them in a humorous light, his sympathies were clearly always with the downtrodden and disenfranchised elements of society.

Written in 1923, *Mord in der Mohrengasse* (Murder on Moor Street; published, 1970; performed, 1978), the only extant play among his early fragments, is indicative of the themes that were to receive fuller treatment later. The action takes place among prostitutes, criminals, and other outcasts, which include Wenzel, the black sheep of the Klamuschke family. When a man is found robbed and murdered on Moor Street, the police trace the crime to Wenzel. They find him at his parental home, where he had returned to hang himself. The desolate family's members are united only by their miserable living conditions, which are accentuated by their inability to communicate with one another.

Zur schönen Aussicht (Hotel Bella Vista; performed, 1969; published, 1970), written in 1927, is set during the depression after World War I. The hotel is a shabby establishment peopled by the male harem of the alcoholic Baroness Ada. The protagonist, Christine, returns to the hotel, where she formerly worked, seeking to marry the member of the harem who fathered her child; but the men band together to extricate themselves from responsibility. The twist comes when Christine reveals that she has inherited a large sum of money, whereupon each of the men wants to claim the previously denied paternity. She walks off, leaving behind the deceived deceivers. Christine is the only one among Horváth's many female figures who is able to emancipate herself from the morally bankrupt milieu.

Revolte auf Côte 3018 (Revolt on Hill 3018; published, 1970), the first of Horváth's plays to be performed, premiered in 1927 at the Kammerspiele (Studio Theater) in Hamburg. The bad press that it drew led the playwright to revise it, toning down the political elements. The revision, *Die Bergbahn* (The Cable Car; published, 1970), was given a premiere in 1929 at the Theater am Bülowplatz in Berlin, where it was received with great enthusiasm. On the basis of that success Horváth was offered a contract and a financial stipend from the Ullstein Publishing Company which lasted through 1932.

Horváth based the work on actual events. Several workers had been fatally injured during the construction of the first cable car line on the Zugspitze; by not halting construction under adverse weather conditions, those in authority had shown a callous disregard for human life. Horváth's play stands in the tradition of socialist workers' drama represented earlier by the works of Gerhart Hauptmann; his play also shows traces of expressionism in the speech of the characters and the melodramatic use of the forces of nature. It is Horváth's only play in which there is a conscious use of dialect, which he later rejected. Horváth designated the work a "Volksstück" (folk play), the genre in which he was to create his greatest achievements.

Sladek der schwarze Reichswehrmann (Sladek, the Black Militiaman; published, 1970) was performed in 1929 at the Lessing-Theater in Berlin, but only in a small matinee production, and it was rejected by critics as too political. It is a documentary drama based on research that Horváth did at the archives of the German League for Human Rights in Berlin. The work of that organization frequently involved investigations of the secret right-wing paramilitary groups who took it into their hands to mete out "justice" during the turbulent times of monetary inflation in the Weimar Republic. On the surface the play is about the rival political factions and their ideological battles; more basically, it shows how an individual can be caught up in historical processes. The play is a series of tableaux that illustrate various stages in Sladek's relationship to the illegal right-wing army and to Anna, his landlady and mistress, who is murdered by the army at his instigation. Sladek's motto is "Man muß nur selbständig denken" (One just has to think for oneself); but his ostensibly original thought is actually a hodge-podge of clichés and inflammatory rhetoric of the political right. Sladek never comes to self-understanding, dying with the vain appeal: "Ich bitte mich als Menschen zu betrachten und nicht als Zeit" (I beg you to think of me as a human being and not as [the representative of] an era)—

but it is as just such a representative that he is most certainly portrayed.

Rund um den Kongreß (All around Congress; performed, 1969; published, 1970), written in 1929, is probably based on two League of Nations congresses held in 1921 to examine prostitution and the white-slave traffic. The play, which bears the genre designation *Posse* (farce), shows prostitution to be an integral part of society that cannot be stamped out so long as it serves the interests of those who claim to be appalled by it.

Horváth's four folk plays are regarded as his greatest achievements. The "Volksstück" had a long tradition in German and particularly in Austrian literature dating back to the eighteenth century, when it was conceived as theater for the common people, as opposed to court theater. But Horváth declared that it was not his intention to revive an old form but to create a new one. It was to be theater for contemporary times, dealing with the problems and cares of the common people, as seen through the eyes of the people. He specified that "die Stücke müssen stilisiert gespielt werden" (the plays must be performed in a stylized way), and he rejected the use of dialect as too naturalistic. With a mixture of realism and irony Horváth exploded the myth of the moral integrity of so-called simple people.

The first of the four major folk plays, *Italienische Nacht* (Italian Night; published, 1961), premiered on 20 March 1931 at the Theater am Schiffbauerdamm in Berlin. The play was a great success, and with it the playwright achieved a breakthrough to fame in the theater world. On the basis of this achievement Horváth was awarded the coveted Kleist Prize, having been nominated by his friend and fellow dramatist Carl Zuckmayer.

The play is set in a small town in southern Germany during the period of the Weimar Republic. It focuses on the Republicans (socialists), who are planning to celebrate an "Italian Night" in contrast to the "German Night" of the Nazis. Whereas *Sladek der schwarze Reichswehrmann* had demonstrated the internal conflicts of the right wing, *Italienische Nacht* shows the self-righteous complacency of the left. The play represents a brilliant innovation in the use of dialogue. The men are seen playing cards, drinking beer, insulting their wives, and exchanging hollow phrases about politics or sex or both at once. Willful ignorance, hypocrisy, and self-deception are abundantly manifest, especially when the characters are trying to impress one another. The mindlessness is particularly evident in the half-digested ideas of the militant idealist Martin and the boorish, banal, self-important talk of the city councilman. Each character follows his own train of thought, drops his cliché or bon mot into the ring, and—just occasionally—says what he is really thinking. Conversation leads to an absurd inflation of language, showing speech to be a mask for concealing true feelings.

Geschichten aus dem Wiener Wald (1931; translated as *Tales from the Vienna Woods*, 1977) represents the culmination of Horváth's literary development. It premiered on 2 November 1931 at the Deutsches (German) Theater in Berlin, directed by Heinz Hilpert, with Carola Neher as Marianne, Heinrich Heilinger as Oskar, and Peter Lorre as Alfred. The production was a great success and brought wide recognition for the playwright.

The ironic title of the play is intended to arouse expectations that will subsequently be destroyed. An idyllic conception of the Vienna Woods, the blue Danube, and cheery Strauss waltzes forms the background for the action, which constitutes a brutally sordid reversal of the illusion. Horváth unmasks not only his characters but also the comfortable myth of Vienna. There are no real villains in the play, for the protagonists all have a recognizable streak of humanity which prevents the audience's total alienation from them; but total identification is also precluded by their hypocrisy and the deceptions they perpetrate on themselves and others.

On a quiet street in the Eighth District of Vienna, suggestive of old-world charm, Marianne lives with her despotic father, "der Zauberkönig" (the Wizard), above their novelty shop. It has never been questioned by anyone that Marianne will marry the boy next door, a butcher named Oskar. He is always correct in his treatment of her, but the primitive, aggressive nature that lies just beneath the surface is suggested by his profession. The engagement party has a bucolic setting in the Vienna Woods, "am Ufer der schönen blauen Donau" (on the bank of the beautiful blue Danube). There Marianne meets Alfred, a suave, unscrupulous drifter. Seeing a way out of her unwanted union with Oskar, she goes off with Alfred. Their romance is short-lived; after the birth of a child he leaves her in a squalid one-room flat. The only employment open to her is as a striptease dancer at Maxim's. A wealthy Austrian-American propositions her; and when she steals the money rather than "earning" it, he calls the po-

lice and she lands in jail. The baby had been entrusted to the care of Alfred's grandmother, who intentionally exposes him to the chill air; the baby contracts pneumonia and dies. With the death of the child, Oskar sees the last obstacle to his "love" for Marianne removed, and he deigns to marry her. His final words as he carries her off, "Du wirst meiner Liebe nicht entgehn" (You won't escape my love), forebode a slow, painful death in a loveless marriage. On her zither, the sinister grandmother plays the Strauss waltz that gave its title to the play.

Kasimir und Karoline (published, 1961) premiered at the Schauspielhaus (Playhouse) in Leipzig on 18 November 1932; it was performed a week later at the Komödienhaus (Comic Theater) in Berlin. Like *Geschichten aus dem Wiener Wald*, it has a setting that arouses certain expectations: all of its 117 scenes are acted out at the Munich Oktoberfest against a background of traditional music, circus entertainment, alcoholic revelry, and general merriment. The uninhibited atmosphere is an ideal setting for unmasking the latent frustrations and repressed savagery of the characters. The play's motto, "Und die Liebe höret nimmer auf" (And love never ends), has a bitter irony: love is here a merry-go-round, part of the entertainment; partners are shown to be as expendable and interchangeable as circus acts or consumer goods. It does not take much to erode Karoline's feelings for her fiancé Kasimir, who has just lost his job as a chauffeur, when she meets Schürzinger, a man of culture and charm who also has money. Karoline's pathetic attempts to return to Kasimir at the end of the play are greeted with disgust by Kasimir and with scorn by Erna, her replacement. Kasimir rejects Karoline's apologies with sententious talk about lying. The cleverness with which the playwright shows the characters' lachrymose emotions to be mainly self-pity precludes identification with either of them.

The last of Horváth's folk plays, *Glaube Liebe Hoffnung* (Faith Charity Hope; performed, 1936; published, 1961; translated as *Faith, Hope and Charity*, 1989), draws its title from 1 Corinthians 13:13. But Horváth changed the order of the biblical elements, implying that "the greatest of these" is not charity but hope. The play was to have been performed in 1932, but because of the Nazi rise to power the premiere was delayed until 13 November 1936 at the Theater am Schottentor in Vienna. The plot is based on a real-life court case. The play opens with Elizabeth at

Daniel Friedrich as Alfred, Hildburg Schmidt as Valerie, and Katalin Zsigmondy as Marianne in a scene from a 1985 Düsseldorf production of Horváth's Geschichten aus dem Wiener Wald *(photograph by Lore Bermbach)*

an anatomical institute, attempting to sell her body for research after her death. Elizabeth has been caught in a vicious circle: having been jailed for working without a permit, which she had not been able to afford, she finds herself in the same hopeless situation on her release. Alfons Klostermeyer, a policeman who had supported her financially and even wanted to marry her, leaves her. Elizabeth has lost faith in herself and the world around her; she has lost the love that she thought she had found; and she has lost her hope for the future. Her last words before she dies, "Da fliegen lauter so schwarze Würmer herum" (There's nothing but black worms flying around), conjure up the horror of the grave. The image also provides a fitting commentary on the people who have surrounded her all her life.

With Adolf Hitler's rise to power in 1933 the theaters in Germany were closed to Horváth. He left Berlin and went to his parents' home in Murnau; when their house was searched by Nazi storm troopers, he went to Austria. In the fall of 1933 he traveled to Budapest to renew his Hungarian passport. On 27 December 1933 he married a singer, Maria Elsner, in Vienna; they separated shortly thereafter and were divorced on 2 September 1934. In place of the female heroines of Horváth's early works, the protagonists of his later plays are most often male. Most of the later plays are comedies, and the language is more ca-

sual and more Austrian than in his works before 1933.

Die Unbekannte aus der Seine (The Unknown Girl from the Seine; performed, 1949; published, 1961) is based on the myth of Undine, the water nymph. In a self-sacrificing gesture, she saves Albert from conviction for a crime he had committed. An epilogue, set in contemporary bourgeois society, presents a humorous, ironic contrast to the preceding mythic phenomenon. Albert, who has become a complacent husband and father, sees the death mask of the mysterious woman, which gives him occasion to ponder. (The death mask of the Inconnue de la Seine was an item commonly found in homes and shops throughout Europe in the early part of the twentieth century.) In the words of the author, the piece is intended to demonstrate "wie die tragischen Ereignisse sich im Alltagsleben oft in eine komische Form kleiden" (how tragic events are often clothed in a humorous form in everyday life).

One of Horváth's wittiest plays is *Hin und her* (Back and Forth; published, 1970), which premiered at the Schauspielhaus in Zurich in 1934. This farce is written for a revolving stage, and it is set on a bridge crossing the river that forms the border between two countries. It deals with the plight of a stateless citizen and shows the idiocies of bureaucracy. Havlicek, the protagonist, is a resourceful character who is able to view his fate with humor, thus precluding pity or pathos. Havlicek carries messages between Konstantin, the border official on one side, and Konstantin's beloved, Eva, the daughter of the border official on the other side. Various other characters arrive, and many humorous episodes take place, including a case of mistaken identity involving the heads of the two states who have a secret rendezvous on the bridge at night. The play is lightweight and has a happy ending. It is only in looking carefully at the primitive chauvinism of the two border guards, and of course at Havlicek's hapless position, that one discerns the existence of a heartless and sinister bureaucracy at work.

Himmelwärts (Heavenward; performed, 1937; published, 1970) is also a humorous piece. The set is a three-tiered vertical structure, reminiscent of that of a medieval morality play. The heaven at the top is characterized by trivia and kitsch rather than mysticism and reverence; and the hell at the bottom resembles a badly organized bureaucracy run by clowns rather than devils. There is a good deal of friendly banter between the two realms. The main action of the play takes place on the middle level, representing earth. Luise sells her soul to the devil for the sake of a career as an opera singer. The devil relents, however, at the end of the play, and Luise reconciles herself to the simple pleasures of life. One can only surmise that Horváth must have written the play with tongue firmly in cheek.

Mit dem Kopf durch die Wand (Beating Your Head against a Wall; performed, 1935; published, 1970), like the previous work, deals with artists' attempts at a breakthrough despite adverse circumstances. The mythical female figure from *Die Unbekannte aus der Seine* is conjured up in séances by artists who are trying to achieve a sensation in the film industry.

In 1935 Horváth moved to Vienna, where he had contact with Zuckmayer, Csokor, and Franz Werfel. In 1936 Horváth was declared persona non grata in Germany. That year he moved to Henndorf, near Salzburg, where he devoted himself to work on two major novels. The year 1937 was, however, a successful one for his dramatic productions, yielding four premieres.

Figaro läßt sich scheiden (Figaro Gets a Divorce; published, 1961) premiered at the Kleine Bühne des Deutschen Theaters (Little Stage of the German Theater) in Prague in 1937. Although based on Pierre-Augustin Caron de Beaumarchais's play *Le Mariage de Figaro* (1784), Horváth's play is set not in the eighteenth cen-

tury but in the 1930s; as Horváth said, the problems of revolution are "zeitlos und in unserer Zeit besonders aktuell" (timeless and particularly topical in our time). After fleeing from Nazi Germany with his master, Count Almaviva, Figaro decides to embark on a new way of life and opens a barber shop. His wife, Susanne, does not go with him, for she cannot abide his "Spießer" (philistine) mentality. After years of separation, in which he becomes a security guard at their former castle and she a waitress in a local bar, they are reunited, for they have continued to love each other. The work suffers from the analogy it suggests between the revolution in eighteenth-century France and the Nazi "revolution" in Germany, which would entail quite different ideological positions on the part of the émigrés. However ambiguous and controversial the politics may be, the human portraits are delightful.

Relations between the sexes receive a humorous treatment in *Ein Dorf ohne Männer* (A Town without Men; performed, 1937; published, 1970), based on a novel by Kálmán Mikszáth. Set in the times of the Turkish Wars, the play contains fairy-tale elements combined with psychological realism in a complicated plot with a happy ending.

Der jüngste Tag (Doomsday; performed, 1937; published, 1955) and his next play, *Don Juan kommt aus dem Krieg* (performed, 1952; published, 1961; translated as *Don Juan Comes Back from the War*, 1978), are the only two of Horváth's later works that he did not designate as comedies. The spark for the tissue of lies and deceit that builds up in *Der jüngste Tag* is a brief kiss that Anna gives Hudetz, the train station attendant. Although intended to arouse the jealousy of Hudetz's wife, it has the effect of causing Hudetz to forget to give the train signal. The express train hurtles past seconds later; it crashes, killing many of the passengers. Hudetz, "ein pflichttreuer Beamter" (an ever-dutiful official), is subsequently dependent on Anna's silence about the true course of events; in an effort to protect him, she testifies falsely that he gave the signal on time. After Hudetz's acquittal, Anna is troubled by her conscience. When she meets Hudetz some months later, Anna's remorse has become so great that it is a threat to him; he then feels forced to kill her. As the play reaches its climax the ghosts of the dead, including Anna, appear to Hudetz. No more masks are possible; the truth must be paid for and lived with. Hudetz must accept a judgment higher than any human one; he says, "Die Hauptsach ist, daß man sich

Veronika Bayer as Erna, Lutz Zeidler as Kasimir, and Gordana Kossanović as Karoline in a 1985 production of Horváth's
Kasimir und Karoline *at the Theater an der Ruhr, Mühlheim (photograph by Thilo Bleu)*

nicht selber verurteilt oder freispricht" (The main thing is that it is not for us to condemn or to acquit ourselves).

Don Juan kommt aus dem Krieg, like the Figaro play, deals with a well-known literary figure; the tone in this case is not humorous but has a deathlike solemnity. Don Juan, the seducer of women, is in search not of love but of perfection, "etwas, was es auf Erden nicht gibt" (something that does not exist in the world). Unlike his literary predecessors, Horváth's Don Juan is portrayed sympathetically, and it is he who is the victim. The war has made him want to be faithful to his fiancée, however much he may have deceived her in the past. Unfortunately for him, his charm bewitches all the women he encounters. Around this sole male figure there are thirty-five female characters in the drama; these roles, however, are to be played by far fewer actresses, the playwright specifies, emphasizing that the search is as repetitious as it is futile. Don Juan goes on searching until he arrives at his fiancée's former home, where he sees a snowman. He dies of yearning, and in the final scene he, too, becomes a snowman facing the prospect of the fires of hell: "Es wird immer wärmer—Adieu, Schneeman" (It's getting warmer all the time—Goodbye, snowman).

Pompeji (Pompeii; performed, 1959; published, 1960) is set at the foot of the rumbling vol-

cano Vesuvius, which erupts at the end of the play. The slave Lemniselenis escapes from her master, and the rest of the play deals with her attempts to get the six hundred pieces of silver needed to buy her freedom. This plot recalls Elizabeth's situation in *Glaube Liebe Hoffnung*; Lemniselenis, however, is well able to handle both her problems and her relationships, and the tone is lighthearted throughout. The volcanic eruption signifies the end of the pagan order and the beginning of the Christian era.

The political situation in Austria became increasingly difficult after the Anschluß, the union of Austria with Germany in 1938. In March of that year Horváth traveled to Budapest and other places where he had previously lived. On 28 May he went to Paris to discuss a cinematic version of his novel *Jugend ohne Gott* with the American film producer Robert Siodmak; Horváth was killed in a storm on the Champs Elysées on 1 June. The funeral, which took place on 7 June at the Saint-Ouen Cemetery in Paris, was attended by many German and Austrian writers living in exile.

Horváth clearly speaks to a modern-day audience, and part of his appeal is his anti-idealistic stance. He uses a popular genre in order to subvert it, to make it tell critical truths. He takes a cynical view of power relationships and shows the subconscious mechanisms at work in the confrontation of egos. The politics of a society are shown to be extensions of the sexual politics that govern personal relationships. His dialogue exposes the shortcomings of language. This manipulative talk presents the civilized veneer that barely masks the underlying libidinal brutality. As he wrote in his preface to *Glaube Liebe Hoffnung*: "Erkenne dich bitte selbst!" (Please recognize yourself!). Audiences see themselves reflected in Horváth's plays, and that recognition accounts for the plays' lasting appeal.

Biography:
Traugott Krischke, *Ödön von Horváth: Kind seiner Zeit* (Munich: Heyne, 1980).

References:
Christopher B. Balme, *The Reformation of Comedy: Genre Critique in the Comedies of Ödön von Horváth* (Dunedin, New Zealand: University of Otago, Department of German, 1985);

Alan Bance, "Ödön von Horváth: Sex, Politics and Sexual Politics," *German Life and Letters*, 38 (April 1985): 249-259;

Bance and Ian Huish, eds., *Ödön von Horváth: Fifty Years On. Horváth Symposium* (London: Institute of Germanic Studies, 1988);

Kurt Bartsch, Uwe Baur, and Dietmar Goltschnigg, eds., *Horváth-Diskussion* (Kronberg: Scriptor, 1976);

Johanna Bossinade, *Vom Kleinbürger zum Menschen: Die späten Dramen Ödön von Horváths* (Bonn: Bouvier, 1988);

Dirk Bruns, "Horváth's Renewal of the Folk Play and the Decline of the Weimar Republic," *New German Critique*, 18 (Fall 1979): 107-135;

Kathy Brzovic and Craig Decker, "The Struggle for Stasis in Ödön von Horváth's *Geschichten aus dem Wiener Wald*," *German Studies Review*, 13 (October 1990): 391-404;

Wilhelm Emrich, "Die Dummheit oder das Gefühl der Unendlichkeit: Ödön von Horváth's Kritik," in his *Geist und Widergeist: Wahrheit und Lüge der Literatur* (Frankfurt am Main: Athenäum, 1965), pp. 185-196;

Jean-Claude François, "Brecht, Horváth and the Popular Theater," *New German Critique*, 18 (Fall 1979): 136-150;

Axel Fritz, *Ödön von Horváth als Kritiker seiner Zeit* (Munich: List, 1973);

Dietmar Goltschnigg, "Das Sprachklischee und seine Funktion im dramatischen Werk Ödön

von Horváths," *Wirkendes Wort*, 3 (1975): 181-196;

Ingrid Haag, "Ödön von Horváth und die 'Monströse Idylle,'" *Recherches Germaniques*, 6 (1976): 154-168;

Dieter Hildebrandt, "Der Jargon der Uneigentlichkeit: Zur Sprache Ödön von Horváths," *Akzente*, 19 (1972): 109-123;

Hildebrandt, *Ödön von Horváth in Selbstzeugnissen und Bilddokumenten* (Reinbek: Rowohlt, 1975);

Hildebrandt and Traugott Krischke, eds., *Über Ödön von Horváth* (Frankfurt am Main: Suhrkamp, 1970);

Huish, *Horváth: A Study* (London: Heinemann, 1980);

Horst Jarka, "Noch nicht entdeckt oder schon wieder vergessen? Das Werk Horváths in den Vereinigten Staaten," *Literatur und Kritik*, 231-232 (1989): 38-52;

Jarka, "Ödön von Horváth und das Kitschige," *Zeitschrift für Deutsche Philologie*, 91 (1972): 558-586;

Jarka, "Sprachliche Strukturelemente in Ödön von Horváths Volksstücken," *Colloquia Germanica*, 4 (1973): 317-339;

Krischke, ed., *Materialien zu Ödön von Horváth* (Frankfurt am Main: Suhrkamp, 1970);

Krischke, ed., *Ödön von Horváth* (Frankfurt am Main: Suhrkamp, 1981);

Krischke and Hans F. Prokop, eds., *Ödön von Horváth: Leben und Werk in Dokumenten und Bildern* (Frankfurt am Main: Suhrkamp, 1972);

Hajo Kurzenberger, *Horváths Volksstücke: Beschreibung eines poetischen Verfahrens* (Munich: Fink, 1974);

Ian Loram, "Ödön von Horváth: An Appraisal," *Monatshefte*, 59 (1967): 19-34;

David Midgley, "Ödön von Horváth: The Strategies of Audience Enticement," *Oxford German Studies*, 14 (1983): 125-142;

Winfred Nolting, *Der totale Jargon: Die dramatischen Beispiele Ödön von Horváths* (Munich: Fink, 1976);

Hartmut Reinhardt, " 'Demaskierung' als moralische Provokation," *Wirkendes Wort*, 3 (1975): 197-214;

Ulrich Weisstein, "Ödön von Horváth: A Child of Our Time," *Monatshefte*, 52 (1960): 343-352;

Benno von Wiese, "Ödön von Horváth," in his *Deutsche Dichter der Moderne* (Berlin: Schmidt, 1975), pp. 592-622;

Krishna Winston, *Horváth Studies: Close Readings
    of Six Plays (1926-1931)* (Bern, Frankfurt
    am Main & Las Vegas: Lang, 1977);

Winston, "Ödön von Horváth: A Man for This
    Season," *Massachusetts Review*, 19 (Spring
    1978): 169-180;

Jack D. Zipes, "Horváths Dramaturgie der Isolie-
    rung," *Literatur und Kritik*, 60 (1971): 591-
    600.

Papers:

The Horváth Archive at the Academy of Arts, Berlin, has Ödön von Horváth's manuscripts, secondary literature, and reviews. Copies of these
holdings are at the library of the University of Wisconsin, Madison, and at the University of Stockholm. Some manuscripts are in the Franz Theodor Csokor estate at the Vienna City Library; the
Manuscript Collection of the Austrian National Library, Vienna; the Schiller Archive at Marbach,
Germany; and the Munich City Library.

Hans Henny Jahnn

(17 December 1894 - 29 November 1959)

Russell E. Brown
State University of New York at Stony Brook

See also the Jahnn entry in *DLB 56: German Fiction Writers, 1914-1945.*

PLAY PRODUCTIONS: *Die Krönung Richards III.*,
    Leipzig, Schauspielhaus, 5 February 1922;

Pastor Ephraim Magnus, Berlin, "Das Theater," 23
    August 1923;

Medea, Berlin, Staatstheater Schauspielhaus, 4
    May 1926;

Der Arzt, sein Weib, sein Sohn, Hamburg, Kammer-
    spiele, 1 April 1928;

Armut, Reichtum, Mensch und Tier, Hamburg, Deut-
    sches Schauspielhaus; Altona, Theater Haus
    der Jugend, 25 July 1948;

Neuer Lübecker Totentanz, Cologne, Studio der Büh-
    nen der Stadt Köln, 16 April 1954;

Thomas Chatterton, Hamburg, Deutsches Schau-
    spielhaus, 26 April 1954;

Der staubige Regenbogen, Frankfurt am Main, Die
    Städtischen Bühnen, 17 March 1961;

Straßenecke, Erlangen, Studiobühne der Universi-
    tät Erlangen-Nürnberg im Markgrafenthea-
    ter, 25 February 1965;

Spur des dunklen Engels, Münster, Städtische Büh-
    nen, 12 December 1969.

BOOKS: *Pastor Ephraim Magnus: Drama* (Berlin: Fi-
    scher, 1919);

Des Buches erstes und letztes Blatt: Drama (Klecken:
    Ugrino, 1921);

Die Krönung Richards III.: Historische Tragödie
    (Hamburg: Hanf, 1921);

Der Arzt; sein Weib; sein Sohn: Drama (Klecken:
    Ugrino, 1922);

Der gestohlene Gott: Tragödie (Potsdam: Kiepen-
    heuer, 1924);

Medea: Tragödie (Leipzig: Schauspiel, 1926);

Perrudja: Roman, 2 volumes (Berlin: Kiepen-
    heuer, 1929);

*Die Einfluß der Schleifenwindlade auf die Tonbildung
    der Orgel* (Hamburg: Ugrino, 1931);

Neuer Lübecker Totentanz (Berlin: Fischer, 1931);

Straßenecke: Ein Ort, eine Handlung (Berlin: Kiepen-
    heuer, 1931);

Armut, Reichtum, Mensch und Tier: Ein Drama (Mu-
    nich: Weismann, 1948);

*Fluß ohne Ufer: Roman in drei Teilen. 1. Teil: Das Holz-
    schiff* (Munich: Weismann, 1949); translated
    by Catherine Hutter as *The Ship* (New York:
    Scribners, 1961); *2. Teil: Die Niederschrift des
    Gustav Anias Horn nachdem er 49 Jahre alt ge-
    worden war*, 2 volumes (Munich: Weismann,
    1949-1950);

Spur des dunklen Engels: Drama (Hamburg:
    Ugrino / Munich: Weismann, 1952);

Hans Henny Jahnn

Klopstocks 150. Todestag am 14. März 1953 (Mainz: Akademie der Wissenschaften und der Literatur, 1953);

Über den Anlaß: Vortrag (Munich: Weismann, 1954);

13 nicht geheure Geschichten (Hamburg: Rowohlt, 1954); translated by Gerda Jordan as *Thirteen Uncanny Stories* (Bern: Lang, 1984);

Thomas Chatterton: Eine Tragödie (Berlin & Frankfurt am Main: Suhrkamp, 1955);

Die Nacht aus Blei: Roman (Hamburg: Wegner, 1956);

Jeden ereilt es (Würzburg: Zettner, 1959);

Aufzeichnungen eines Einzelgängers: Eine Auswahl aus dem Werk, edited by Rolf Italiaander (Munich: List, 1959);

Hans Henny Jahnn: Eine Auswahl aus seinem Werk, edited by Walter Muschg (Freiburg: Walter, 1959);

Die Trümmer des Gewissens—Der staubige Regenbogen: Drama, edited by Muschg (Frankfurt am Main: Europäische Verlagsanstalt, 1961);

Fluß ohne Ufer: Roman in drei Teilen. 3. Teil: Epilog (Frankfurt am Main: Europäische Verlagsanstalt, 1961);

Dramen, 2 volumes (Frankfurt am Main: Europäische Verlagsanstalt, 1963-1965);

Über den Anlaß und andere Essays (Frankfurt am Main: Europäische Verlagsanstalt, 1964);

Perrudja II: Fragment aus dem Nachlaß, edited by Rolf Burmeister (Frankfurt am Main: Heine, 1968);

Ugrino und Ingrabanien: Fragment aus dem Nachlaß, edited by Burmeister (Frankfurt am Main: Heine, 1968);

Werke und Tagebücher, 7 volumes, edited by Thomas Freeman and Thomas Scheuffelen (Hamburg: Hoffmann & Campe, 1974);

Dramen I 1917-1929: Dramen, Dramatische Versuche, Fragmente, edited by Ulrich Bitz (Hamburg: Hoffmann & Campe, 1988).

OTHER: "Entstehung und Bedeutung der Kurvenmensur für die Labialstimmen der Orgel," in *Bericht über den 1. Musikwissenschaftlichen Kongreß der Deutschen Musikgesellschaft in Leipzig vom 4. bis 8. Juni 1925* (Leipzig: Breitkopf & Härtel, 1926), pp. 71-77;

Holloferniges: Märchen aus dem Retköz, translated from Hungarian by Jahnn (Berlin & Zurich: Atlantis, 1940);

Áron Tamási, *Ein Königssohn der Sekler: Roman,* translated from Hungarian by Jahnn (Leipzig: Payne, 1941);

"Mein Werden und mein Werk," in *Hamburger Jahrbuch für Theater und Musik 1948-49* (Hamburg: Toth, 1948), pp. 92-111;

"Vereinsamung der Dichtung: Vortrag," in *Minotaurus: Dichtung unter den Hufen von Staat und Industrie* (Wiesbaden: Steiner, 1953), pp. 247-265;

"Prinzipien der Freien Akademie in Hamburg," in *Neues Hamburg: X. Die Wiederaufrichtung Hamburgs 1945 bis 1955* (Hamburg: Hammerich & Leser, 1956), pp. 58-60.

SELECTED PERIODICAL PUBLICATIONS—
UNCOLLECTED: "Einige Elementarsätze der monumentalen Baukunst," *Kleine Veröffentlichungen der Glaubensgemeinde Ugrino,* 2 (March 1921): 5-46;

"Vincent Lübeck," *Hamburger Nachrichten,* 10 April 1922;

"Die Reglementierung des freien Geistes," *Berliner Börsen-Courier,* 16 December 1926, p. 5;

"Henrik Ibsen und sein Land," *Berliner Tageblatt,* 20 March 1928;

"Die Wurstfinger des Herrn Lehrers," *Die Literarische Welt,* 14/15 (1928): 4;

"Kleine Reise durch Kopenhagen," *Hamburger Fremdenblatt,* no. 231 (22 August 1933): 2;

"Die Insel Bornholm," *Atlantis: Länder/Völker/Reisen,* 3 (March 1941): 101-109;

"Von der Wirklichkeit," *Das Neue: Auswahl zeitgemäßer Stimmen,* 4 (1947): 50-70;

"Was ist vom Menschen zu erwarten?," *Das Neue: Auswahl zeitgemäßer Stimmen,* 5 (1947): 33-55;

"Requisiten des Theaters, zeitgemäße und mutige Worte," *Mindener Tageblatt,* 10 April 1953;

"Kleine Rede auf Hans Erich Nossack," *Sinn und Form,* 2 (1955): 213-219;

"Mozarts zweite Fassung der 'Gärtnerin aus Liebe,'" *Die andere Zeitung,* 4 (26 January 1956): 13;

"Thesen gegen Atomrüstung," *Studenten-Kurier,* 7 (September 1957): 7;

"Der Mensch im veränderten Weltbild," *Blätter für deutsche und internationale Politik,* 12 (20 December 1957): 424-429;

"Freiheit—Frieden—im veränderten Weltbild," *Konkret: Unabhängige Zeitschrift für Kultur und Politik,* 2 (1958): 3;

"Am Schlagbaum vor dem Abgrund," *Vorwärts: Sozialdemokratische Wochenzeitung für Politik, Wirtschaft und Kultur,* 17 (April 1958): 1.

Hans Henny Jahnn wrote plays that bear a strong affinity to those of German expressionism: they deal with such themes as the rejection of civilization for nature; deviant sexual practices; sadistic murderous relations in society and the family; impotence; alienation; and despair. Yet Jahnn, despite his kinship with the expressionists, the early Bertolt Brecht, and such authors as Ernst Barlach and Alfred Döblin, remains a unique, idiosyncratic outsider, whose visions and obsessions were private and pathological.

His plays range from early ecstatic tragedies of doomed adolescents to dramas about artists, protests against racism and nuclear war, and adaptations of Shakespearean historical plays and Greek tragedies. All are marked by those obsessive visions and rituals that are at once a major element of his message and a sign of his personal vulnerability.

Jahnn was born on 17 December 1894 to Elise Petersen Jahnn and William Jahnn in Stellingen, near Hamburg; his father was a ship's carpenter. At a secondary school in Hamburg in

1911 Jahnn met Gottlieb Harms. In the summer of 1913 Jahnn and Harms tried to run away to Iceland; in 1914 they repeated their flight, this time through the countryside of Mecklenburg. They were brought back to Hamburg both times. After graduating from the gymnasium Jahnn and Harms lived together in the village of Eckel. There they began to make plans for a utopian society they called Ugrino.

On 7 August 1915 Jahnn and Harms traveled to Norway to avoid the draft. They settled in the town of Urrland, selected randomly from a map. Jahnn worked on dramas and on the novel fragment *Ugrino und Ingrabanien* (1968) and designed statues and furniture for Ugrino.

Jahnn and Harms returned to Germany at the end of World War I and settled in Eckel. Jahnn's play *Pastor Ephraim Magnus* was published in 1919; for it he won the prestigious Kleist Prize. The Berlin premiere of *Pastor Ephraim Magnus* in 1923 was codirected by two future enemies, Brecht and the right-wing Arnolt Bronnen.

The theology of the Magnus family is a radical revision of traditional Christianity: there is no Trinity; after Jesus' attempts at intimacy with other boys were condemned, he sought women, but they were repelled by his strangeness and intensity. His crucifixion occurred mainly to silence his ecstatic ravings. Jesus was not a god but a sick person in a hostile society.

The old pastor commits suicide and is succeeded as preacher by his son Ephraim. Ephraim; his sister, Johanna; and their halfbrother, Jacob, engage in sexual experiments. Jacob murders his girlfriend during childbirth, then murders another girl and dissects her out of curiosity. He is put on trial and executed; to Jahnn, the punishment reflects the insensitivity of bourgeois society to youthful rebellion, genius, and absolute ideals. Jacob's siblings create a secure grave for him in the catacombs below the cathedral, where they will join him. Johanna and Ephraim, involved in an incestuous relationship, use violence against themselves and each other: Johanna mutilates her own sexual organs; Ephraim lets her castrate, blind, and crucify him; finally, he strangles his already dying sister.

In September 1920 Jahnn founded Ugrino, a utopian community, with Harms and the artist Franz Buse. A large tract of land near Eckel was bought on which to construct the buildings for the utopian community. When Jahnn's mother died, a granite model of a Ugrino building was placed at her grave in Stellingen.

Rainer Frieb, Nikola Weisse, Erwin Wirschaz, and Sieghold Schröder in a scene from a 1979 Bremen production of Jahnn's Die Krönung Richards III. *(photograph by Peter Peitsch)*

Die Krönung Richards III. (The Coronation of Richard III) was Jahnn's first drama to reach the stage; it was published in 1921 and performed in Leipzig the following year. As in William Shakespeare's play, Richard marries the widowed Queen Elisabeth and does away with her adolescent sons. Jahnn eliminates all of Shakespeare's women except Elisabeth and adds fifteen male characters, many of them adolescent boys; Shakespeare's play extends to the death of Richard in battle, while Jahnn's play ends with Richard supreme. Jahnn makes the death of the princes the central event of his play in a lengthy and harrowing scene. Richard instructs Tyrrel and Gurney to bury the two princes alive. Then, he reasons, he will not have killed them; the matter will rest in the hands of God, who is free to rescue them or allow them to die. When an imprisoned page, Paris, finds the princes in the tower and tries to help them, he is killed and placed in one of the two waiting coffins. Gurney and

Tyrrel then bury the two princes together in the other coffin. Thus is created the full Jahnnian burial situation: the adolescent brothers are shielded from the essentially lonely situation of death by sharing a last embrace, their bodies not disfigured by any wound, in a secure coffin deep in the stone cellars of the Tower of London.

In Jahnn's play *Der Arzt; sein Weib; sein Sohn* (The Doctor; His Wife; His Son; published, 1922; performed, 1928) Menke is an obstetrician who believes that only healthy life should be preserved; the weak, deformed, or unhealthy should be allowed to die. Menke contrasts earlier societies and their acceptance of death as a welcome regulator with the present deterioration of society; the decadent modern world is incapable of great achievements like the architecture of the Egyptians. Menke's quest for self-realization and wisdom leads him back to his mountain home to try to regain the love of his wife, Anne; his son, Karl; and Karl's friend, Ulrich. Menke rescued Ulrich from a conventional father's domination and brought him into the family group, and he and Karl are lovers. When Karl declares his sexual love for his mother, Anne suggests the substitution of Ulrich as her sexual partner; it is agreed that Karl will share in the relationship vicariously. In addition to incest and homosexuality, there is reference to bestiality: a minor character, Soter, is brought to trial for sodomy with a horse; he is excused because of Menke's impassioned defense. Anne, having been admitted into the "Egyptian" mystery of incestuous love, accepts death in childbirth as a related mystery, even hastening it by the use of poison. Her death is the signal for the group to assemble in a safe and sacral area, a mountain cave. Menke planned to kill the boys at the same time Anne died; although they refuse ritual death at his hands, the boys destroy one another in a wild love-death orgy.

In 1923 Jahnn and Harms were hired to restore the Jakobi organ of Arp Schnitger in Hamburg, saving it from planned destruction. A publishing house founded by the utopian society, the Ugrino Verlag, began the publication of medieval and baroque music and also published some of Jahnn's works.

Jahnn abandoned the idea of a permanent utopian colony as the German inflation and financial collapse weakened his financial backers. He returned to Hamburg to begin a career in baroque organ restoration. In 1926 he married Ellinor Philips, a teacher of therapeutic gymnastics. Despite his constant extramarital relations with persons of both sexes, the couple remained together until Jahnn's death; their daughter, Signe, named after a girl Jahnn loved and considered marrying in Norway, was born in 1929. Harms married the half-sister of Jahnn's wife, and the two couples lived together for years.

Medea (1926) was Jahnn's first work to find a wide audience: there were several productions of the play, and it received positive critical appraisals. Written in verse, the play is based on the *Medea* of Euripides; but Jahnn transforms the Greek original into a mirror of his own worldview. The two sons of Jason and Medea are transformed from almost silent figures—in Euripides they speak only offstage, while they are being murdered—into articulate, contrasting characters. In the Euripidean model Medea was only a "barbarian" (a non-Greek); Jahnn makes her a "Negerin" (Negress), and the play is full of racism and references to skin color.

The older brother has been given a horse, a symbol of his new manhood, by his father. When the boy takes his first ride he has a violent encounter with Creon's daughter: her stallion—with which she is involved sexually—mates with his mare while he clings to its back. This traumatic event causes him to move from homosexuality to heterosexuality. Creon's daughter's love for her stallion is unparalleled for Jahnn, for whom abnormal sexual patterns are almost always related to male figures: there are no lesbians throughout his work. Even incest or partner-sharing is male-oriented in that it serves to bring two men closer together by means of a woman. The murder of the two brothers by their mother is also unique in that its purpose is revenge against their father; it is not initiated by the youths to achieve unity or to escape an evil or philistine world. The play ends with Medea's palace sinking into the sea with all her servants. All characters die, with the exception of Medea, who returns to the gods, and Jason, whose curse is to remain young and promiscuous but to poison all his lovers.

Harms died in February 1931; he was buried in Nienstedt in a tomb designed by Jahnn. Until Adolf Hitler came to power in 1933 Jahnn served as official organ expert of the city of Hamburg; as such, he was provided a house, the Strohdachhaus in Blankenese. Jahnn tried to found a new political party, the Radikale Demokratische Partei, to serve as a link between the Social Democrats and the Communists. In

Gerhild Didusch as the wet nurse and Barbara Nüsse (in a Nazi leather trench coat) as Medea in a 1989 Düsseldorf production of Jahnn's Medea *(photograph by Lore Bermbach)*

these last pre-Hitler years Jahnn wrote three plays.

Straßenecke (Street Corner; published, 1931; performed, 1965) portrays the life of James, a black American victim of racial injustice. The play is a frame story: in present time James and Alma discuss his social and sexual victimization as various surrealistic figures appear; then a series of flashbacks reenacts important episodes of James's earlier life. At the end present time is resumed, and James is lynched by a racist mob. James has sexual relations with both male and female partners; in each situation he is exploited in a cruel way. Alma's pregnancy with James's child gives a positive note to the otherwise tragic ending: out of death comes a new life.

Jahnn's *Neuer Lübecker Totentanz* (New Lübeck Dance of Death; published, 1931; performed, 1954) is based on the *Lübecker Totentanz* woodcuts of 1463; figures from the woodcuts appear as a chorus. Jahnn introduces a riot in which police clash with unemployed workers and a supernatural figure, der feiste Tod (the fat death), representing the modern death humanity has invented for itself—that of the great wars, poison gas, and social revolution. The playlet has passages of great poetic beauty and is largely free of Jahnn's personal obsessions.

Armut, Reichtum, Mensch und Tier (Poverty, Wealth, Man and Animal), although not published and performed until 1948, was completed in 1933. The first letters of the words in the title combine to form the first word of the title. The bachelor Manao Vinje lives at his Scandinavian mountain farm, cut off from society below during the winter. Manao is sexually involved with his horse, the beautiful mare Falada, and his hired hand, an aggressive and virile youth. The peasants have a fanciful explanation for Manao's love for his horse: they think a beautiful girl or witch is magically confined within its body. Manao turns from his servant and horse to a heterosexual relationship with Sofia, the daughter of a poor shoemaker. Besides her social inferiority and lack of dowry, Sofia is poor in other ways: she is weak and delicate and hardly able to bear a child, whereas the girl Manao had been expected to marry, Anna Frönning, owns her own farm, is robust, and would be an ideal mother. Manao lives with Sofia for a summer, then returns to his isolated farm to await a spring marriage. But Anna eliminates her rival by treachery, murdering Sofia's newborn baby; Sofia is unjustly sent to prison, and Manao reluctantly marries Anna. But when Anna kills Manao's horse in a vain attempt to capture his full allegiance as a lover, Manao acquires a herd of reindeer and moves even higher in the mountains with Sofia, who has been released from prison. Jytte, on a vacation from Denmark, helps nurse Sofia. After Sofia's death Jytte becomes Manao's final mate. She is a synthesis of Anna's health, vitality, and fitness for motherhood and Sofia's openness, honesty, love of animals, and unselfishness.

The Jahnnian death-ritual complex reappears in *Armut, Reichtum, Mensch und Tier* in variant form. Instead of the usual youthful group, the mare and Sofia are put in a single grave, which Manao will share later. The grave, although in the open, is under a great pile of stones; stone is always used in special graves in Jahnn's works. Whereas in the earlier plays the burials took place in secret, being illegal or contrary to Christian practice, here Manao's social position enables him to marshal all the characters, including the supernatural ones (a troll, a mountain spirit, and the ghost of a man who committed suicide), to prepare the grave.

In 1933 Jahnn moved to Zurich. The following year, with the financial support of his friend, the Swiss Germanist Walter Muschg, he was able to buy a farm on the Danish island of Bornholm. After the Germans occupied Denmark he was allowed to continue to live there, being required only to check in periodically with the Gestapo in Copenhagen. During the war years he conducted experiments with hormones from the urine of horses and worked on his novel trilogy, *Fluß ohne Ufer* (River without Banks, 1949-1950, 1961). In 1938 Jahnn was excluded from the list of officially acceptable writers in Germany, although as late as 1940 permission was granted for the publication of the trilogy's first part, *Das Holzschiff* (translated as *The Ship*, 1961), in Leipzig. The work was printed in 1944 but was not distributed until 1949. His translation of a Hungarian novel, *Ein Königssohn der Sekler* (A Prince of the Sekler), by Áron Tamási, was allowed to appear in Germany in 1941. Jahnn was assisted in the translation by Judit Kárász, a young, married Hungarian Jewish woman, whom he persuaded to join his double family—the Jahnns and their daughter and the widow and son of Harms—on Bornholm.

After Bornholm was liberated by the Soviets in 1945, Jahnn's farm was confiscated. The Danish government showed great reluctance to release his assets, regarding him as a citizen of the hated Germany rather than as a refugee from the Nazis. On a trip to southern Germany in 1946 he met the thirteen-year-old Yngve Jan Trede, whom he adopted and sought to develop as a composer and musician. Trede composed baroque fugues and other music for Jahnn's plays. After a stormy relationship with his foster father he married Signe Jahnn and became a music professor in Copenhagen.

Jahnn played an important role in postwar Germany after his return to Hamburg in 1950. Like Brecht and Thomas Mann, he was courted and acclaimed by both East and West. His consistent antibourgeois stance, his pacifism, and his absence from Germany during both world wars overshadowed his unconventional personal life and obsessions. Jahnn was regarded as an opponent of Nazism, even though he had tried to continue his German literary career from Denmark and had never directly opposed German fascism. After the war he was critical of those who had fought Nazism from exile. He was a welcome guest in East Germany, where he was elected to the Academy of Arts. In the West he founded the Free Academy of Arts of Hamburg in 1950 and remained its president until his death.

Spur des dunklen Engels (Path of the Dark Angel; published, 1952; performed, 1969), Jahnn's first drama after an interval of nineteen years, is based on the story of David in I Samuel. To universalize his subject matter, Jahnn offers an alternate set of names for his characters divorced from Biblical associations: Saul, Jonathan, Schmuel (Samuel), Achis, and David are given the alternate names Paulus, Oristan, Eustach, Gottschalk, and Robert. Jahnn also injects many modern objects and ideas into his Old Testament milieu: guns, newspapers, organs and pianos, secret police, border violations, even a "pope" and a Vatican district in the figure of Schmuel and his extrapolitical territory of Rama. The use of these anachronisms is intended to keep the audience detached and objective, in Brechtian epic-theater manner.

The old high priest Schmuel discovers David as a beautiful young herdsman and introduces him to Jonathan. The barefoot shepherd surprisingly reveals himself to be an erudite composer. Jonathan concludes that David is a genius and offers to surrender his right to the throne to him. When David objects that he is not "legitimate," not qualified by birth to become king, Jonathan asks: "Ist nicht Genie der Ausdruck höchster Legitimität?" (Is not genius an expression of highest legitimacy?). Of course, David does show martial skills—he conquers Goliath, becomes a Schillerian robber-chief—and finally does become king. But he continues to compose music throughout the play. (The six musical pieces in the play were composed by Trede. Jahnn stipulates in the introduction that the text of the play should never be published without the music.)

David's erotic relationships are many and varied. He is the "dark angel" of the title, the familiar Jahnnian figure of the irresistible beautiful youth to whom both sexes respond. Jonathan, Saul, the Philistine leader Achis, Jonathan's sister Michal, and two later wives all love him. The pair David and Jonathan is a classic grouping in

Jahnn's work: David, the virile, irresistible youth, contrasts with the older, less attractive, more introspective Jonathan.

Thomas Chatterton (performed, 1954; published, 1955) was the last of Jahnn's plays to be published and performed during his lifetime. It is based on the English boy-poet and literary sensation who took his life in 1770 at age eighteen. The major events of Jahnn's play are taken directly from historical accounts and literary studies. Jahnn adds supernatural figures: a spirit named Aburiel who appears to Thomas throughout, and the ghosts of Bristol citizens from the fifteenth century. The other main area of expansion he permits himself is in Thomas's love relations: he has Thomas move from schoolboy homosexual affairs into a ménage à trois with a girl and a male friend; finally, in London Thomas turns to a promiscuous series of heterosexual affairs, ending in weary distaste for erotic relations of any kind. Like the actual Chatterton, Jahnn's Thomas poisons himself—a favorite method of suicide in Jahnn's work because it avoids disfigurement of the corpse.

In his last years Jahnn wrote and spoke against nuclear armament and war; his last play, *Die Trümmer des Gewissens* (The Ruins of Conscience), addresses this theme. It was published and performed in 1961, two years after the author's death. A certain confusion arose from Jahnn's decision just before his death to change the title to *Der staubige Regenbogen* (The Dusty Rainbow); Erwin Piscator used this title for his production, which premiered in Frankfurt am Main on 17 March 1961. The scene is a secret research center where atomic weapons are being perfected and human experiments are being carried out. It is part of a plan to unleash a global nuclear war against the enemy superpower and the third world, fully expecting the destruction of the home society but with the calculation that enough whites will survive in a great bunker system to regenerate the Caucasian race and ensure its future dominance. Jakob Chervat is the key scientist in this insane project, which is concealed from him by the government agent Sarkis. His son, Elia, is a victim of radiation who wears a turban to conceal his baldness at age eighteen; a sister, born horribly deformed, had to be destroyed. Elia and other young people, including the South American Indian Tiripa, whose tribe was killed to make way for commercial exploitation of an Amazon region, create a secret society to resist the diabolic plan of nuclear war by assassination and sabotage; they are supported by Chervat when he becomes aware of the government's intentions. In a *Hamlet*-like ending Sarkis is killed by the Indian boy, who is himself killed; another youthful rebel is trampled to death. Chervat poisons himself; his wife and the remaining young conspirators must choose between poison and capture and execution. Western society is portrayed as racist, imperialist, and suicidal, and indifferent or hostile to nonwhite peoples, to animals, and to nature. There is a reference to the fate of the whales, an ecological issue that became prominent after the author's death. The play ends without hope as the young people and their scientist ally are destroyed in a futile gesture of rebellion.

Somewhat out of place in this thesis play is Jahnn's usual constellation of young people, sharing homosexual and incestuous erotic relations. Mother-son incest is perceived as a possible danger by a widowed mother, and a conventional outsider is recruited as the sexual partner for a female group member. Jahnn's personal erotic fantasies prevailed to the end of his literary career.

Jahnn died on 29 November 1959 of a heart attack after participating in a student congress against nuclear rearmament at the Freie Universität in Berlin. He was buried near the grave of Gottlieb Harms.

Letters:

Hans Henny Jahnn—Peter Huchel: Ein Briefwechsel 1951-1959, edited by Bernd Goldmann (Mainz: Hase & Koehler, 1974).

Bibliographies:

Jochen Meyer, *Verzeichnis der Schriften von und über Hans Henny Jahnn* (Neuwied & Berlin: Luchterhand, 1967);

Meyer, "Hans Henny Jahnn: Kommentierte Auswahl-Bibliographie zu Hans Henny Jahnn," *text + kritik*, 2/3 (January 1980): 139-153.

Biographies:

Thomas Freeman, *Hans Henny Jahnn: Eine Biographie* (Hamburg: Hoffmann & Campe, 1986);

Elsbeth Wolffheim, *Hans Henny Jahnn, mit Selbstzeugnissen und Bilddokumenten* (Reinbek: Rowohlt, 1989).

References:

Robert F. Bell, "A Woman Scorned. The *Medea* Plays of Euripides, Hans Henny Jahnn, and Jean Anouilh," *Classical and Modern Literature*, 1 (Spring 1981): 177-186;

Walter Blohm, *Die ausserrealen Figuren in den Dramen Hans Henny Jahnns* (Hamburg: Lüdke, 1971);

Russell E. Brown, "Thematic Structure in the Plays of Hans Henny Jahnn," Ph.D. dissertation, Harvard University, 1962;

Richard Detsch, "The Theme of the Black Race in the Works of Hans Henny Jahnn," *Mosaic*, 7 (Winter 1974): 165-187;

Hugo Jakob Eichhorn, "Mythos und Tragik: Hans Henny Jahnns Dramen," Ph.D. dissertation, University of Zurich, 1973;

Wilhelm Emrich, *Das Problem der Form in Hans Henny Jahnns Dichtungen* (Mainz: Akademie der Wissenschaften und der Literatur, 1968);

Hubert Fichte, "Chatterton und Chatterton: Anmerkungen zu Hans Henny Jahnn und Ernst Penzolt," *Homosexualität und Literatur*, 2 (1988): 107-142;

Guenther J. Gerlitzki, "Der mittelalterliche Lübecker Totentanz und der Neuer Lübecker Totentanz von Hans Henny Jahnn: Ein Vergleich," Ph.D. dissertation, New York University, 1959;

Bernd Goldmann, *Hans Henny Jahnn: Schriftsteller, Orgelbauer, 1894-1959* (Mainz: Akademie der Wissenschaften und der Literatur, 1973);

Goldmann, ed., *Hans-Henny-Jahnn-Woche 27. bis 30. Mai 1980. Eine Dokumentation* (Kassel: Stauda, 1981);

Francis S. Heck, "Hans Henny Jahnn: Disciple of André Gide," *Research Studies*, 42 (March 1974): 36-43;

Werner Helwig, *Die Parabel vom gestörten Kristall* (Mainz: Von Hase & Koehler, 1977);

Siegmar Hohl, "Das Medea-Drama von Hans Henny Jahnn: Eine Untersuchung unter besonderer Berücksichtigung des Mythischen," Ph.D. dissertation, University of Munich, 1966;

Erwin Jäger, *Untergang im Untergrund: Die jugendliche Gruppe in den Dramen Hans Henny Jahnns* (Bern: Lang, 1979);

Maria Kalveram, *Die Suche nach dem rechten Mann: Männerfreundschaft im literarischen Werk Hans Henny Jahnns* (Berlin: Argument, 1984);

Siegfried Kienzle, "Hans Henny Jahnn: Szenische und dramaturgische Interpretation," Ph.D. dissertation, University of Vienna, 1962;

Peter Kobbe, *Mythos und Modernität: Eine poetologische und methodenkritische Studie zum Werk Hans Henny Jahnns* (Stuttgart: Kohlhammer, 1973);

Friedhelm Krey, *Hans Henny Jahnn und die mann-männliche Liebe* (Frankfurt am Main: Lang, 1987);

Charles Linsmayer, "Das Todesproblem bei Hans Henny Jahnn," Ph.D. dissertation, University of Zurich, 1973;

Hermann Lober, "Hans Henny Jahnn als Dramatiker," *Die Quelle*, 2, no. 6 (1948): 54-62;

Edgar Lohner, "Akkord ohne Terz: Die Dramen Hans Henny Jahnns," *text + kritik*, 2/3 (January 1980): 4-11;

Lohner, "Hans Henny Jahnn," in *Expressionismus: Gestalten Einer literarischen Bewegung*, edited by Hermann Friedmann and Otto Mann (Heidelberg: Rothe, 1956), pp. 314-337;

Manfred Maurenbrecher, *Subjekt und Körper: Eine Studie zur Kulturkritik im Aufbau der Werke Hans Henny Jahnns, dargestellt an frühen Texten* (Bern & Frankfurt am Main: Lang, 1983);

Hans Mayer, *Versuch über Hans Henny Jahnn* (Hamburg: Hoffman & Campe, 1974);

Dietrich Molitor and Wolfgang Popp, eds., *Siegener Hans Henny Jahnn Kolloquium. Homosexualität und Literatur* (Essen: Die Blaue Eule, 1986);

Walter Muschg, "Hans Henny Jahnn," in his *Von Trakl zu Brecht: Dichter des Expressionismus* (Munich: Piper, 1961), pp. 264-334;

Muschg, "Hans Henny Jahnn: *Armut, Reichtum, Mensch und Tier*," *Fähre*, 2 (1947): 537-540;

Muschg, "Hans Henny Jahnns *Neuer Lübecker Totentanz*," in his *Pamphlet und Bekenntnis* (Olten & Freiburg: Walter, 1968), pp. 362-366;

Hans E. Nossack, "Nachruf auf Hans Henny Jahnn," *Deutsche Literaturkritik der Gegenwart*, 4 (1971): 502-509;

Nossack, "Vorwort zu *Thomas Chatterton*," *Akzente*, 2 (1955): 152-155;

Per Øhrgaard, "Exilautor und/oder Auslandsdeutscher: Hans Henny Jahnns Aufenthalt in Dänemark nach 1933," *text kritik*, 21, supplement (1986): 199-214;

Cornelius Steckner, ed., *Zeitgenosse Hans Henny Jahnn. Ist der Mensch zu retten? Hamburger Literaturtage 1984* (Hamburg: Freie Akademie der Künste, 1985);

Steckner and the Seminargruppe Kulturpolitik, eds., *Ist der Mensch zu retten? Das Leben und Werk Hans Henny Jahnns* (Hamburg: Freie Akademie der Künste, 1984);

Ernst Vogelsang, "Das Bild des Menschen im Werke Hans Henny Jahnns: 3 Analysen," Ph.D. dissertation, Tulane University, 1965;

David M. Weible, "Eros in the Works of Hans Henny Jahnn: A Study of Platonic Influences in Four of the Plays," Ph.D. dissertation, University of Kansas, 1972;

Elsbeth Wolffheim, " 'Nicht verboten, aber auch nicht zugelassen' ": Hans Henny Jahnn im Exil," *Exilforschung*, 4 (1986): 276-290;

Hans Wolffheim, *Hans Henny Jahnn: Der Tragiker der Schöpfung* (Frankfurt am Main: Europäische Verlagsanstalt, 1966).

Papers:

Hans Henny Jahnn's manuscripts, letters, and other documents are in the Staats- und Universitätsbibliothek (State and University Library), Hamburg.

Hanns Johst

(8 July 1890 - 23 November 1978)

Helmut F. Pfanner
Vanderbilt University

PLAY PRODUCTIONS: *Stroh*, Leipzig, Schauspielhaus, 18 September 1915;

Der Einsame, Düsseldorf, Schauspielhaus, 2 November 1917;

Der junge Mensch, Hamburg, Thalia Theater,
13 March 1919;

Der König, Dresden, Schauspielhaus, 20 May
1920;

Propheten, Dresden, Schauspielhaus, 2 November
1922;

Wechsler und Händler, Leipzig, Schauspielhaus,
5 May 1923;

Der Ausländer, Baden-Baden, Städtisches Schauspiel, 15 May 1925;

Die fröhliche Stadt, Düsseldorf, Stadttheater,
19 May 1925;

Marmelade, Ulm, Stadttheater, 10 April 1926;

Thomas Paine, Cologne, Schauspielhaus; Bremen,
Stadttheater; Karlsruhe, Stadttheater; Düsseldorf, Stadttheater, 31 March 1927;

Komödie am Klavier, Düsseldorf, Stadttheater,
24 October 1928;

Der Herr Monsieur, Weissenburg, Freilichtbühne,
July 1932;

Schlageter, Berlin, Staatliches Schauspielhaus,
20 April 1933.

BOOKS: *Die Stunde der Sterbenden* (Leipzig: Verlag der Weißen Bücher, 1914);

Wegwärts: Gedichte (Munich: Delphin, 1916);

Stroh: Eine Bauernkomödie (Leipzig: Verlag der
Weißen Bücher, 1916);

Der Ausländer: Ein bürgerliches Lustspiel (Leipzig:
Wolff, 1916);

Der junge Mensch: Ein ekstatisches Szenarium (Munich: Delphin, 1916);

Der Anfang: Roman (Munich: Delphin, 1917);

Der Einsame: Ein Menschenuntergang (Munich: Delphin, 1917);

Rolandsruf (Munich: Delphin, 1919);

Der König (Munich: Langen, 1920);

Mutter (Munich: Langen, 1921);

Kreuzweg: Roman (Munich: Langen, 1922);

Hanns Johst

Dramatisches Schaffen: Eine Ansprache (Chemnitz:
Gesellschaft der Bücherfreunde, 1922);

Propheten: Schauspiel (Munich: Langen, 1923);

Wechsler und Händler: Komödie (Munich: Langen,
1923);

Lieder der Sehnsucht (Munich: Langen, 1924);

Wissen und Gewissen (Essen: Schlingloff, 1924); enlarged as *Ich glaube! Bekenntnisse* (Munich:
Langen, 1928);

Die fröhliche Stadt: Schauspiel (Munich: Langen,
1925);

Consuela: Aus dem Tagebuch einer Spitzbergenfahrt
(Munich: Langen, 1925);

Der Herr Monsieur, nach Holbergs "Jean de France"
(Munich: Langen, 1926);

246

Briefe und Gedichte von einer Reise durch Italien und die Wüste (Chemnitz: Gesellschaft der Bücherfreunde, 1926);

Thomas Paine: Schauspiel (Munich: Langen, 1927);

So gehen sie hin: Ein Roman vom sterbenden Adel (Munich: Langen, 1930);

Die Torheit einer Liebe: Roman (Munich: Langen-Müller, 1930);

Ave Eva: Erzählung (Munich: Langen, 1932);

Schlageter: Schauspiel (Munich: Langen-Müller, 1933);

Mutter ohne Tod; Die Begegnung: Zwei Erzählungen (Munich: Langen-Müller, 1933);

Standpunkt und Fortschritt (Oldenburg: Stalling, 1933);

Tohuwabohu!, edited by Walth Klöpzig (Bielefeld: Velhagen & Klosing, 1933);

Maske und Gesicht: Reise eines Nationalsozialisten von Deutschland nach Deutschland (Munich: Langen-Müller, 1935);

Kunterbunt, edited by Siegfried Casper (Bielefeld & Leipzig: Velhagen & Klasing, 1938);

Meine Erde heißt Deutschland: Aus dem Leben und Schaffen des Dichters (Berlin: Büchergilde Gutenberg, 1938);

Ruf des Reiches—Echo des Volkes: Eine Ostfahrt (Munich: Eher, 1940);

Erkenntnis und Bekenntnis: Kernsätze aus den Werken und Reden, edited by Georg von Kommerstädt (Munich: Langen-Müller, 1940);

Fritz Todt: Requiem (Munich: Eher, 1943);

Hanns Johst spricht zu dir: Eine Lebenslehre aus seinen Werken und Reden, edited by Casper (Berlin: Nordland, 1944);

Gesegnete Vergänglichkeit: Roman (Frankfurt am Main: Pandion, 1955).

OTHER: *Morgenröte: Ein Rüpelspiel*, in *Das Aktionsbuch* (Berlin: Die Aktion, 1917), pp. 315-327;

"Persönliches," in *Göttinger Musenalmanach auf 1923*, edited by Börries, Freiherr von Münchhausen (Göttingen: Göttinger Universitätszeitung, 1922), p. 88;

"Über Arno Holz," in *Arno Holz und sein Werk*, edited by Ferdinand Avenarius (Berlin: Werk, 1923), p. 35;

"Die Legende vom seltsamen Manne," in *Rückkehr nach Orplid: Dichtung der Zeit*, edited by Martin Rockenbach (Essen: Fredebeul & Koenen, 1924), pp. 106-110;

"Bekenntnis," in *Dichterglaube: Stimmen religiösen Erlebens*, edited by Harald Braun (Berlin: Eckart, 1931), pp. 148-149;

"Der Dichter in der Zeit: Zum Kriegsdichtertreffen 1940," in *Die Dichtung im Kampf des Reiches: Weimarer Reden 1940* (Hamburg: Hanseatische Verlagsanstalt, 1941), pp. 11-14.

SELECTED PERIODICAL PUBLICATIONS—
UNCOLLECTED: "Johann Schuster: Eine Novelle," *Die Aktion*, 5 (1915): 139-141;

"Über Carl Einsteins Negerplastik," *Die Aktion*, 5 (1915): 457-459;

"Timm Kröger," *Das literarische Echo*, 18, no. 17 (1916): 1049-1052;

"Vorahnung des Krieges," *Das literarische Echo*, 18, no. 22 (1916): 1373-1376;

"Goethe und der Expressionismus," *Die neue Rundschau*, 27 (1916): 717-718;

"Leo Sternberg," *Das literarische Echo*, 19, no. 13 (1917): 790-794;

"Persönliches" and "Mutter Lore," *Masken*, 13, no. 4 (1917-1918): 53-57;

"Max Picard," *Die neue Rundschau*, 29 (1918): 716-717;

"Die Proklamation der Arbeitsfreude," *Die Erde*, 1 (1919): 2-3;

"Tragödie der Zeit," *Münchner Blätter für Dichtung und Graphik*, 1 (1919): 14-16;

"Die Welt als Anschauung," *Die neue Rundschau*, 30 (1919): 255-256;

"Resultate," *Die neue Rundschau*, 30 (1919): 1384-1389;

"Wider den politischen Künstler," *Das neue Rheinland*, 1, no. 2 (1919-1920): 33-34;

"Das Drama und die nationale Idee," *Berliner Tageblatt*, 25 October 1922;

"Bekenntnis zur Bühne," *Das literarische Echo*, 25, no. 13-14 (1923): 681-683;

"Shakespeare, die Ardennen und die kleine Schauspielerin," *Orplid*, 1 (1924): 51-53;

"Zu den 'Bemühungen' Thomas Manns," *Hellweg*, 5 (1925): 882;

"Dichtung und Christentum," *Ostwart-Jahrbuch* (1926): 158;

"Zur Freilichtbühne," *Hellweg*, 6 (1926): 353;

"Die Legende eines Herzens," *Orplid*, 3 (1926-1927): 33-38;

" 'Ich glaube!' Bemerkungen zu meinem Bekenntnis-Buch," *Der Bücherwurm*, 13 (1928): 270;

"Spitzbergen," *Velhagen und Klasings Monatshefte*, 43 (1929): 521-528;

"Die Tragödie und die Gestalt," *Zeitwende*, 5 (1929): 147-158;

"Das Theater und die Nation," *Süddeutsche Monatshefte*, 27 (1929): 477;

"Fortschritt und Standpunkt: Eine Ansprache im Südwestdeutschen Rundfunk," *Die literarische Welt*, 8 (1932): 1-2;

"Ein Bild," *Die neue Literatur*, 33 (1932): 247-248;

"Was ist Kulturbolschewismus? Aufgabe der deutschen Bühne," *Die Propyläen*, 30 (1933): 266;

"An die Schriftsteller aller Länder! Aufruf der Union Nationaler Schriftsteller," by Johst and Gottfried Benn, *Völkischer Beobachter*, 1 March 1934;

"Nation und Dichtung," *Wille und Macht*, 4 (1936): 7-14;

"Ansprache zur 4. Weimarer Buchwoche," *Börsenblatt für den deutschen Buchhandel*, 3 November 1937, 866-867.

Hanns Johst took part in the literary movement of expressionism before he turned to the conservative treatment of nationalist themes and finally succumbed to the National Socialists' expectations for political propaganda literature. At first sight, there seems to be little in common between the humanitarian-pacifist sentiments and antibourgeois outcries of Johst's early works and the chauvinistic glorification of heroic militarism and German superiority in his later writings. On closer analysis, however, a common denominator can be discerned in the irrational current that underlies both the metaphysical aspirations of his early protagonists and the anti-intellectualism of his later ones; also, the young Johst's view of the artist's elevated position in society was echoed in the later Johst's call for a leader-artist who would combine the German nationalist state with a new type of cult theater.

Johst's abandonment of individualism for totalitarianism was shared by other expressionist authors; but unlike Bertolt Brecht and Ernst Toller, who turned to the left, Johst (and others, such as Arnolt Bronnen) embraced the political right. Johst did not finish another drama after Adolf Hitler's rise to power, but his plays—with the exception of his early expressionist ones—formed a significant part of the National Socialist repertoire.

Johst's parents belonged to two of the classes that would later flock to Hitler's party: government employees and farmers. His father was an elementary-school teacher, following his own father's profession; his mother was the descendant of a long line of Saxon farmers. Both parents were Lutherans. Johst was born on 8 July 1890 in the small town of Seerhausen. Soon afterward his father died. He was raised by his mother, and he also spent much time on his grandmother's farm. When he was seventeen and a highschool student in Leipzig, he decided to become a missionary. To acquire a practical skill that would help him in this vocation he took a position as a nurse at the Evangelische Heil- und Pflegeanstalt für Epileptische des Rheinlands und Westfalens (Protestant Hospital for Epileptics of the Rhineland and Westphalia) in Bethel, near Bielefeld. Emotionally overwhelmed by the deplorable conditions at the hospital, he soon left and took up the study of medicine in Leipzig; but he later changed his major to philology, which he studied at the universities of Munich, Vienna, and Berlin. For a short time he tried his luck as an actor. When World War I broke out in 1914 he volunteered for military service. His experiences on the western front became the subject of his first play, *Die Stunde der Sterbenden* (The Hour of the Dying, 1914).

This one-scene dialogue expresses the thoughts of several wounded men lying scattered on a battlefield. Although the characters are not distinguished by name or by appearance, they represent different responses to the question of the meaning of suffering. The soldiers include a member of the enemy forces—a Frenchman—and the concern with suffering extends to four-legged creatures (a wounded horse lies on the stage). The only one still living when morning comes is the soldier who has revealed himself as a spokesman for the power of the human will. Thus treating a major theme of German expressionism, Johst also showed himself to be in line with this literary movement with his proclamation of universal brotherhood, his existentialist questioning, and his populating of the stage with types rather than individual characters. Johst's first drama reveals the influences of expressionist forerunners such as August Strindberg and Maurice Maeterlinck, and it was followed by similar, more successful, expressionist plays about the war by authors such as Fritz von Unruh and Reinhard Goering.

There is no evidence that *Die Stunde der Sterbenden* has ever been produced on the stage. Since it was not reprinted after its publication in 1914, National Socialist critics later found it easy either to deny the play's pacifist tendency or to ignore it altogether. But contemporary critics gave it and Johst's following plays, in which the author paid closer attention to the practical conditions of the stage, a favorable reception. Because his first few plays were politically leftist as well as stylistically avant-garde, liberal publishers such as Kurt Wolff, the Leipzig supporter of expressionist authors, and Franz Pfemfert, the publisher of the activist expressionist journal *Die Aktion*, became interested in his works.

Johst's play *Der junge Mensch* (The Young Man; published, 1916; performed, 1919) possesses all the outward signs of an expressionist drama: a youth's revolt against his parents and teachers, nameless types instead of characters, grotesque names for bourgeois teachers (reminiscent of Frank Wedekind's *Frühlings Erwachen* [1891; translated as *Awakening of Spring*, 1909]), station scenes instead of the traditional division into acts (introduced by Strindberg), and unrealistic, ecstatic language. But when the Young Man, who has died between the last two scenes, rises up from the dead in the final scene and climbs back into life over the wall of the cemetery (recalling a scene from Wedekind's play), he renounces his youthful, unrealistic goals and proclaims that he intends to take up a useful occupation. The audience is thus left to believe that the Young Man's earlier revolts were futile and that the lasting power belongs to the society against which the Young Man had tried to rebel. The Berlin theater critic Herbert Ihering averred that the author was making noise in order to hear his own voice and that the play presented no more than an expressionist pose.

Because Johst's one-act play *Morgenröte: Ein Rüpelspiel* (Dawn: A Roguish Play) was clearly antimilitaristic, it was included in Pfemfert's *Das Aktionsbuch* of 1917. Johst lampoons two German professors who review a play within the play, in which the protagonist enriches himself on account of the war and persuades his son to marry a poor girl whom the father has impregnated. The professors disgustedly attribute the play to a "Jude" (Jew) or a "Kaffeehauspessimist" (coffeeshop pessimist), favorite terms of German nationalist propagandists for their scapegoats during and between the two world wars.

The theme of the individual's revolt against society treated in *Der junge Mensch* was repeated by Johst in *Der Einsame: Ein Menschenuntergang* (The Lonely One: A Human Decline, 1917) and *Der König* (The King, 1920). Of the three plays, *Der Einsame* has become the best known because it provided the stimulus for Brecht to write his first play, *Baal* (1922; translated, 1966), in conscious opposition to it. Johst used the mask of the nineteenth-century German dramatist Christian Friedrich Grabbe to express his own frustra-

tions as an expressionist writer who felt misunderstood by the society in which he lived. "*Poeta dolorosus*," the epithet bestowed on Grabbe by Waldmüller, the only friend he has left at the end of the play, became a catchword for expressionist protagonists. Yet despite Grabbe's suffering, which eventually leads to his death, *Der Einsame* is no real tragedy; for nowhere in the play is there any indication that the forces against which the protagonist battles—the illness and early death of his wife, his failure to be understood by his mother, and the mediocrity of his social surroundings—could not be surmounted by a truly great person. Even as a poet, Johst's hero cannot convince anyone that he is the genius that he claims to be. And Grabbe's definition of a hero as "ein vielfaches vom Mörder" (a murderer by multiple degrees) cannot arouse sympathy either among the people who know him or among the play's audience. *Der Einsame* was an ominous forecast of events to come in Germany, when "heroes" like Johst's Grabbe would attain political power. The play remained a popular item of the German stage repertoire until the end of the Third Reich.

In 1916 Johst married Hanne Feder, who was descended from an old patrician family of Nuremberg. The couple had a daughter, Krista. His growing success as a dramatist as well as a poet and prose writer enabled Johst to acquire a farm in the village of Oberallmannshausen on Lake Starnberg in 1918. He did not become involved in the German revolution of 1918-1919, and soon thereafter he joined the ranks of those German nationalists who deplored the shrunken size of the fatherland and opposed the parliamentary system. He proclaimed his new political outlook in essays that were collected as *Wissen und Gewissen* (Knowledge and Conscience, 1924; enlarged as *Ich glaube! Bekenntnisse* [I Believe! Confessions, 1928]). Most significant for the understanding of Johst's political turnabout is the essay "Vom Ethos der Begrenzung" (On the Ethos of Limitation), in which he rejects his liberal past and makes an emotional appeal to the glorification of national values, including the "Muttersprache" (native tongue) and a narrowly defined German literature. This kind of nationalist thinking was, according to Johst, characteristic of all great Germans, with Martin Luther being the greatest of all.

Henceforth Johst's dramas either depict such national heroes or satirize the undermining of what he considered the German mission by

Johst (giving a Nazi salute) and cast members of his play Schlageter *paying tribute to Adolf Hitler, who was in the audience for the play's premiere on 20 April 1933—Hitler's birthday—at the Staatliches Schauspielhaus, Berlin. Actors (left to right) are Maria Koppenhöfer, Albert Bassermann, Lothar Müthel, Emmy Sonnemann (who shortly afterward married Hermann Göring), and Hans Leibelt.*

the Weimar Republic's politicians and business-men. The first play in which a typical German hero occurs is *Propheten* (Prophets; performed, 1922; published, 1923). It centers on the political struggles of Luther, whom Johst depicts as a fighter for German independence.

Another such play—somewhat surprisingly—is *Thomas Paine*, which premiered simultaneously in four German cities on 31 March 1927. Although the hero is an American and most of the action takes place in America (a few scenes are set in Paris), the protagonist is the type of national hero whom Germany, according to Johst, needed during the 1920s because its political efficiency was hampered by a multiparty system and by its economic and political dependence on other countries.

While the historical Paine died in his bed in New York, Johst's protagonist commits suicide by throwing himself into Boston Harbor. He has just returned after a seventeen-year absence, during which he negotiated a French loan for the young American states. On his arrival in Boston he learns that his name has been forgotten by everyone he meets and that the band playing on the dock has not assembled in his honor but to greet a political delegation from England arriving on the same ship. Although such an ending might appear tragic and was so understood by some contemporary critics, Johst did not intend it to be taken that way. The play ends with the singing of the song that Paine once taught his compatriot revolutionaries; and although no one sees any connection between the song and the dead man who has been pulled out of the water, the idea of the revolution lives on in his words. If *America* and *Americans* are replaced with *Germany* and *Germans*, the author's intention cannot be misunderstood: "Nichts wäre Amerika, / Wären wir Amerikaner nicht, / Wir Kameraden, wir!!" (America would be nothing / Without us Americans, / Us comrades, us!!). The stage directions call for the last line to be repeated by those on the stage and then by all members of the cast after the lights have been extinguished. Johst's message was not lost on the people who saw the play performed all over Germany and, after March 1938, in Austria. (An American production in 1930 by the New American Theatre at the Macdougal Playhouse in New York was unsuccessful, and its English-language text by Adolph Klarmann and Helen Schlauch remains unpublished.)

The ending of *Thomas Paine* points to the direction in which Johst wanted drama to develop: the audience was to be emotionally overwhelmed until it spontaneously joined the action on the stage. From this narrowing of the gap between life and theater would result a "Kulttheater" (cult theater) in which national myth and political action would melt into one, and the dramatist and the political "Führer" (leader) would become the same person. This concept stands in contrast to that of Brecht's epic theater, in which the audience also was called into action; but while Brecht wanted to distance his audience from the events on the stage by means of the Verfremdungs-effekt (alienation effect) in order to provoke rational thinking and responsible political action, Johst tried to overwhelm his audience, prevent it from rational deliberation, and turn it into a group of blind followers.

Johst's last drama, *Schlageter*, glorifies a martyr to the National Socialist cause. Fearing that it would be banned by the censors of the Weimar Republic, the author followed his publisher's advice and withheld it from publication until 1933, when it was printed with a dedication to Hitler. The first performance took place at the Prussian State Theater in Berlin on Hitler's birthday, 20 April 1933, under the direction of Franz Ulbrich and with a select cast of actors, among them Alfred Bassermann, Veit Harlan, and Emmy Sonnemann (who later became Hermann Göring's wife), and with the highest National Socialist dignitaries in attendance. At the end of the performance there were a few moments of silence, and then the audience rose to sing the German national anthem and the Horst Wessel Song (the latter, like the play itself, a glorification of an early National Socialist martyr-hero).

The historical Albert Leo Schlageter's alleged heroic qualities can be seriously questioned. He was shot by the French in 1923 after sabotaging French occupation forces in the Ruhr; it has been said that in trying to save his life he betrayed his former comrades. Of course, none of his weaknesses appear in Johst's play, which shows Schlageter as an innocent victim and casts much blame on the "enemies" of the German nation. Beside such external foes as the French, there are the internal enemies, Social Democrats, Communists, and Jews, including the Weimar Republic's leading politicians. Throughout the play

the call for victims and blood is heard as well as such favorite chauvinist clichés as the myth of the invincible German army and of the "stab in the back" as the cause of the Reich's defeat in 1918. The well-known statement attributed to Göring— "When I hear anyone talk of culture, I reach for my revolver"—seems to have originated in this play when Schlageter's financée's brother says: "Wenn ich Kulture höre ... entischere ich meinen Browning " (When I hear the world *cul-ture*, I release the safety on my Browning). The drama ends with an emotional appeal to the audience, as *Thomas Paine* did; this time the German people are called on directly in Schlageter's last words before his execution: "Deutschland!!! / Erwache! Entflamme!! / Entbrenne! Brenn ungeheuer!!" (Germany!!! / Awake! Ignite!! / Take fire! Burn furiously!!).

The impact of this drama on German audiences cannot be overestimated: some forty other theater companies began staging it the day after its premiere, and it was performed in more than one thousand German theaters during 1933. It was also frequently broadcast on the radio and became compulsory reading in German schools. *Schlageter* established its author as *the* dramatist of the Third Reich. He had been president of the National Socialist organization Kampfbund für Deutsche Kultur (Militant Union for German Culture) since 1929. In February 1933 he had been appointed "Dramaturg" (dramatic adviser) to the Prussian State Theater in Berlin (he lost the position five months later after internal squabbles); in the same year he became president of the Deutsche Dichterakademie (Academy of German Poetry). On 8 January 1934 he became president of the Union nationaler Schriftsteller (Union of National Writers), which had been founded as the result of the German writers' secession from the International P.E.N. Club; and in the same month he was made a Prussian state councillor. During 1934 he also became a member of the powerful Reichsschrifttumskammer (Reich Chamber of Literature), and he was made president of the organization in August 1935. On 11 September 1935 he was awarded the Preis der NSDAP für Kunst (National Socialist Workers Party's Prize for Art) at the party's convention in Nuremberg; also in 1935 he was awarded the Wartburg Rose. On the occasion of his fiftieth birthday in 1940 the Goethe-Medaille für Kunst und Wissenschaft (Goethe Plaque for Art and Science) was presented to him by Hitler, and in 1941 he was awarded the Kantate-Dichterpreis (Cantata Writers' Prize) of the city of Leipzig. Johst was a member of the SS with the rank of Obersturmbannführer (brigade leader).

In 1949 Johst was tried by the denazification court in Munich and was classified as a "Mitläufer" (fellow traveler). When he appealed that relatively mild verdict, he was retried and was judged a "Hauptschuldiger" (major offender). He was sentenced to the confiscation of half of his property and three years in prison (for which his time in a work camp during his investigation was counted) and was denied the right to exercise his profession for ten years from 1945. His last book, a novel marked by a conservative style and without any autobiographical references, was published in 1955. Johst died in Ruhpolding, Bavaria, on 23 November 1978.

Bibliography:

"Hanns Johst," in *The Drama of German Expressionism: A German-English Bibliography*, edited by Claude Hill and Ralph Ley (Chapel Hill: University of North Carolina Press, 1960), pp. 84-95.

References:

Siegfried Casper, *Hanns Johst* (Munich: Langen, 1940);

Glenn R. Cuomo, "Hanns Johst und die Reichsschrifttumskammer: Ihr Einfluß auf die Situation des Schriftstellers im Dritten Reich," in *Leid der Worte: Panorama des literarischen Nationalsozialismus*, edited by Jörg Thuneke (Bonn: Bouvier Verlag Herbert Grundmann, 1987), pp. 108-132;

Horst Denkler, "Hanns Johst," in *Expressionismus als Literatur: Gesammelte Studien*, edited by Wolfgang Rothe (Bern & Munich: Francke, 1969), pp. 547-559;

Hans Franck, "Hanns Johst," *Das deutsche Drama*, 4 (1921): 49-55;

Edgar Groß, "Typen des geschichtlichen Dramas der Gegenwart," *Zeitschrift für Deutschkunde*, 42 (1928): 263-268;

Hans Heering, *Idee und Wirklichkeit bei Hanns Johst* (Berlin: Junker & Dünnhaupt, 1938);

Helmut G. Hermann, "Ausgebeutete Amerika-Romantik: Hanns Johst und der 'Parteigenosse' Thomas Paine," in *Amerika in der deutschen Literatur: Neue Welt—Nordamerika—USA*, edited by Sigrid Bauschinger and others (Stuttgart: Reclam, 1975), pp. 315-322;

Xavier Heydet, "Hanns Johst: sa vie, ses œuvres, ses theories sur l'art dramatique," *Revue de l'enseignement des langues vivantes*, 53 (1936): 58-63;

Curt Hotzel, *Hanns Johst: Der Weg des Dichters zum Volk* (Berlin: Freundsberg, 1933);

Arthur Hübscher, "Hanns Johst," in his *Münchner Dichterbuch* (Munich: Knorr & Hirth, 1929), pp. 77-80;

Herbert Ihering, "Der junge Mensch" and "Stroh," in his *Von Reinhardt bis Brecht: Vier Jahrzehnte Theater und Film*, volume 1: *1909-1923* (Berlin: Aufbau, 1961), pp. 163-165, 210-211;

Walter Kordt, "Der Dramatiker Hanns Johst," *Das deutsche Theater*, 1 (1922): 15-30;

Friedrich Märker, "Hanns Johst," *Weimarer Blätter*, 2 (1920): 145-151;

Rudolf Paulsen, "Hanns Johst: Ein Überblick über sein Schaffen," *Weltstimmen*, 7 (1933): 217-221;

Helmut F. Pfanner, *Hanns Johst: Vom Expressionismus zum Nationalsozialismus* (The Hague & Paris: Mouton, 1970);

W. H. Rey, "Die Dialektik der Freiheit im Generationskonflikt der Gegenwart," *Monatshefte für den Deutschunterricht, deutsche Sprache und Literatur*, 44 (1952): 1-12;

J. M. Ritchie, "Johst's 'Schlageter' and the End of the Weimar Republic," in *Weimar Germany: Writers and Politics*, edited by A. F. Bance (Edinburgh: Scottish Academic Press, 1982), pp. 153-167;

Martin Rockenbach, "Hanns Johst," *Orplid*, 4 (1927): 86-93;

Willi Schäferdiek, "Hanns Johst," *Zeitschrift für deutsche Bildung*, 2 (1926): 332-339;

Albert Soergel, "Hanns Johst," in his *Dichtung und Dichter der Zeit*, volume 2 (Leipzig: Voigtländer, 1927), pp. 717-728;

Josef Sprengler, "Hanns Johst, der Dramatiker des Glaubens," *Hochland*, 24 (1926): 215-223;

Hans Sturm, "Hanns Johst," *Das literarische Echo*, 25 (1923): 675-681;

F. C. Weiskopf, "Liebesdienst und Lobgesang: Zu Hanns Johsts Schauspiel 'Schlageter,'" *Neue deutsche Blätter*, 1 (1934): 314-318;

L. A. Willoughby, "Hanns Johst," *German Life and Letters*, 1 (1936-1937): 73-76.

Papers:

Hanns Johst's manuscripts are in the possession of his daughter. They are expected to be turned over to the Deutsches Literaturarchiv (German Literature Archive) in Marbach am Neckar.

Georg Kaiser

(25 November 1878 - 4 June 1945)

Ernst Schürer and Wiebke Strehl
Pennsylvania State University

PLAY PRODUCTIONS: *Der Fall des Schülers Vehgesack*, Vienna, Neue Bühne, 11 February 1915;

Großbürger Möller, Düsseldorf, Schauspielhaus, 20 November 1915; revised as *David und Goliath*, Minden, Stadttheater, 19 March 1922;

Die Bürger von Calais, Frankfurt am Main, Neues Theater, 29 January 1917;

Die Sorina, Berlin, Lessing-Theater, 6 March 1917;

Von morgens bis mitternachts, Munich, Kammerspiele, 28 April 1917;

Die Versuchung, Hamburg, Thalia-Theater, 31 May 1917;

Der Zentaur, Frankfurt am Main, Schauspielhaus, 23 October 1917; revised as *Margarine*, Berlin, Komödienhaus, 4 September 1925;

Die Koralle, Frankfurt am Main, Neues Theater, 27 October 1917;

Rektor Kleist, Königsberg, Neues Schauspielhaus, 26 January 1918;

Das Frauenopfer, Düsseldorf, Schauspielhaus, 23 March 1918;

Drei Einakter: Claudius, Friedrich und Anna, Juana, Frankfurt am Main, Neues Theater; Baden-Baden, Städtische Schauspiele, 21 October 1918;

Der Brand im Opernhaus, Hamburg, Kammerspiele; Nuremberg, Intimes Theater des Stadttheaters; Berlin-Charlottenburg, Kleines Schauspielhaus, 16 November 1918;

Gas, Frankfurt am Main, Neues Theater; Düsseldorf, Schauspielhaus, 28 November 1918;

Hölle, Weg, Erde, Frankfurt am Main, Neues Theater; Munich, Kammerspiele; Berlin, Lessing-Theater, 5 December 1919;

Der gerettete Alkibiades, Munich, Residenztheater, 29 January 1920;

Gas: Zweiter Teil, Brünn, Vereinigte deutsche Theater, 29 October 1920;

Europa, music by Werner Robert Heymann, Berlin, Großes Schauspielhaus, 5 November 1920;

Georg Kaiser

Die jüdische Witwe, Meiningen, Landestheater, 31 January 1921;

Kanzlist Krehler, Berlin, Kammerspiele des Deutschen Theaters, 14 February 1922;

Der Protagonist, Breslau, Lobe Theater, 16 March 1922;

Die Flucht nach Venedig, Nuremburg, Intimes Theater des Stadttheaters, 9 February 1923;

Gilles und Jeanne, Leipzig, Altes Theater, 2 June 1923;

Nebeneinander, Berlin, Die Truppe, 3 November 1923;

Kolportage, Berlin, Lessing-Theater; Frankfurt am Main, Neues Theater, 27 March 1924;

Juana, Nuremberg, Intimes Theater des Stadttheaters, 7 January 1925;

Gats, Vienna, Deutsches Volkstheater, 9 April 1925;

Der mutige Seefahrer, Dresden, Staatliches Schauspielhaus, 12 November 1925;

Der Protagonist, music by Kurt Weill, Dresden, Staatsoper, 25 March 1926;

Zweimal Oliver, Dresden, Staatliches Schauspielhaus; Krefeld, Stadttheater; Hamburg, Thalia-Theater; Karlsruhe, Landestheater; Oldenburg, Landestheater; Mannheim, Nationaltheater; Düsseldorf, Schauspielhaus, 15 April 1926;

Papiermühle, Dresden, Alberttheater; Krefeld, Stadttheater; Aachen, Stadttheater; Leipzig, Schauspielhaus, 26 January 1927;

Der Präsident, Frankfurt am Main, Schauspielhaus, 28 January 1928;

Der Zar läßt sich photographieren, music by Weill, Leipzig, Neues Theater, 18 February 1928;

Oktobertag, Hamburg, Kammerspiele, 13 March 1928;

Die Lederköpfe, Frankfurt am Main, Neues Theater, 24 November 1928;

Zwei Krawatten, music by Mischa Spolianski, Berlin, Berliner Theater, 5 September 1929;

Hellseherei, Stuttgart, Landestheater; Lübeck, Kammerspiele des Stadttheaters; Düsseldorf, Schauspielhaus; Würzburg, Stadttheater; Giessen, Stadttheater; Brieg, Stadttheater; Oldenburg, Landestheater, 19 October 1929;

Mississippi, Munich, Prinzregenten-Theater; Frankfurt am Main, Schauspielhaus; Mainz, Stadttheater; Mannheim, Nationaltheater; Darmstadt, Hessisches Landestheater; Bremen, Schauspielhaus; Kassel, Staatstheater; Magdeburg, Wilhelmstheater; Karlsruhe, Landestheater; Würzburg, Stadttheater; Hamburg, Deutsches Schauspielhaus; Stuttgart, Landestheater; Konstanz, Stadttheater; Oldenburg, Landestheater; Düsseldorf, Schauspielhaus; Dresden, Schauspielhaus, 20 September 1930;

König Hahnrei, Berlin, Staatliches Schauspielhaus, 5 May 1931;

Der Silbersee, music by Weill, Leipzig, Altes Theater; Erfurt, Stadttheater; Magdeburg, Stadttheater, 18 February 1933;

Adrienne Ambrossat, Vienna, Theater in der Josefsstadt, 5 February 1935;

Das Los des Ossian Balvesen, Vienna, Burgtheater, 26 November 1936;

Der Soldat Tanaka, Zurich, Schauspielhaus, 2 November 1940;

Die Spieldose, Basel, Stadttheater, 12 October 1943;

Zweimal Amphitryon, Zurich, Schauspielhaus, 29 April 1944;

Das Floß der Medusa, Basel, Stadttheater, 24 February 1945;

Der Gärtner von Toulouse, Mannheim, Nationaltheater, 22 December 1945;

Klawitter, Brandenburg, Städtische Bühnen, 19 September 1949;

Der Schuß in die Öffentlichkeit, Magdeburg, Städtische Bühnen, 10 December 1949;

Agnete, Mannheim, Nationaltheater, 16 December 1949;

Napoleon in New Orleans, Karlsruhe, Badisches Staatstheater, 28 January 1950;

Rosamunde Floris, Stuttgart, Kammertheater des Württembergischen Staatstheaters, 6 February 1953;

Bellerophon, Saarbrücken, Großes Haus des Stadttheaters, 21 November 1953;

Pygmalion, Munich, Studio Fink, 16 December 1953;

Alain und Elise, Frankfurt am Main, Städtische Bühnen, 1 September 1954;

Das gordische Ei, Marburg, Schauspiel, 21 November 1958;

Rosamunde Floris, Berlin, Städtische Oper, 21 September 1960.

BOOKS: *Hochzeits-Chansons: Verliebte Lautenschläge oder Neue Unterlagen zu alten Vertonungen* (Magdeburg: Friese & Fuhrmann, 1905);

Die jüdische Witwe: Biblische Komödie (Berlin: Fischer, 1911);

Hyperion (Weimar: Dietsch & Brückner, 1911)—comprises *Ballade vom schönen Mädchen*, *La Fanciulla*, *Mona Lisa*;

König Hahnrei: Tragödie in fünf Akten (Berlin: Fischer, 1913);

Hyperion: Die Gabe an die Freunde (Weimar: Wagner, 1913)—comprises *Claudius*, *Mona Nanna*;

Der Fall des Schülers Vehgesack: Eine kleine deutsche Komödie in fünf Akten (Weimar: Wagner, 1914);

Rektor Kleist: Vier komitragische Akte (Weimar: Wagner, 1914); revised as *Rektor Kleist: Tragikomödie in vier Akten* (Berlin: Fischer, 1918);

Großbürger Möller: Ein gewinnendes Spiel in vier Akten (Weimar: Wagner, 1914); republished as *Großbürger Möller: Lustspiel in vier Akten* (Berlin: Fischer, 1915); republished as *David und Goliath: Lustspiel in vier Akten* (Potsdam: Kiepenheuer, 1921);

Der Kongress: Komödie in drei Akten (Weimar: Wagner, 1914); revised as *Der Präsident: Komödie in drei Akten* (Potsdam: Kiepenheuer, 1927);

Die Bürger von Calais: Bühnenspiel in drei Akten (Berlin: Fischer, 1914); translated by Rex Last and J. M. Ritchie as *The Burghers of Calais* in *Five Plays* (London: Calder & Boyars, 1970);

Europa: Spiel und Tanz in fünf Aufzügen (Berlin: Fischer, 1915);

Der Zentaur: Komödie in fünf Aufzügen (Berlin: Fischer, 1916); revised as *Der Zentaur: Lustspiel in fünf Aufzügen* (Berlin: Fischer, 1918); revised as *Konstantin Strobel (Der Zentaur): Lustspiel in fünf Aufzügen* (Potsdam: Kiepenheuer, 1920); revised as *Margarine: Lustspiel in vier Akten* (Potsdam: Kiepenheuer, 1925);

Von morgens bis mitternachts: Stück in zwei Teilen (Berlin: Fischer, 1916); translated by Ashley Dukes as *From Morn till Midnight: A Play in Seven Scenes* (London: Hendersons, 1920; New York: Brentano's, 1922);

Die Versuchung: Eine Tragödie unter jungen Leuten aus dem Ende des vorigen Jahrhunderts in fünf Akten (Berlin: Fischer, 1917);

Die Sorina: Komödie in drei Akten (Berlin: Fischer, 1917);

Die Koralle: Schauspiel in fünf Akten (Berlin: Fischer, 1917); translated by Winifred Katzin as *The Coral*, in *Modern Continental Plays*, edited by S. M. Tucker (New York: Harper, 1929), pp. 469-497; translated by B. J. Kenworthy as *The Coral*, in *Five Plays*;

Gas: Schauspiel in fünf Akten (Berlin: Fischer, 1918); translated by Hermann Scheffauer as *Gas: A Play in Five Acts* (Boston: Small, Maynard, 1924; London: Chapman & Dodd, 1924);

Das Frauenopfer: Schauspiel in drei Akten (Berlin: Fischer, 1918);

Drei Einakter: Claudius; Friedrich und Anna; Juana (Potsdam: Kiepenheuer, 1918);

Hölle, Weg, Erde: Stück in drei Teilen (Potsdam: Kiepenheuer, 1919);

Der Brand im Opernhaus: Ein Nachtstück in drei Aufzügen (Berlin: Fischer, 1919); translated by Katzin as *The Fire in the Opera House: A Nightpiece*, in *Eight European Plays*, edited by Katzin (New York: Brentano's, 1927), pp. 139-186;

Gas: Zweiter Teil. Schauspiel in drei Akten (Potsdam: Kiepenheuer, 1920); translated by Katzin as *Gas, Part II*, in *Modern Continental Plays*, edited by Tucker;

Der gerettete Alkibiades: Stück in drei Teilen (Potsdam: Kiepenheuer, 1920); translated by Bayard Quincy Morgan as *Alkibiades Saved*, in *An Anthology of German Expressionist Drama*, edited by Walter H. Sokel (Garden City, N.Y.: Doubleday, 1963);

Der Protagonist: Einakter (Potsdam: Kiepenheuer, 1921); translated by Hugo F. Garten as *The Protagonist*, in *Tulane Drama Review*, 5, no. 2 (1960); republished in *Seven Expressionist Plays*, edited by Ritchie (London: Calder & Boyars, 1969);

Noli me tangere: Stück in zwei Teilen (Potsdam: Kiepenheuer, 1922);

Kanzlist Krehler: Tragikomödie in drei Akten (Potsdam: Kiepenheuer, 1922);

Der Geist der Antike: Komödie in vier Akten (Potsdam: Kiepenheuer, 1923);

Gilles und Jeanne: Bühnenspiel in drei Teilen (Potsdam: Kiepenheuer, 1923);

Nebeneinander: Volksstück 1923 in fünf Akten (Potsdam: Kiepenheuer, 1923);

Die Flucht nach Venedig: Schauspiel in vier Akten (Berlin: Die Schmiede, 1923);

Kolportage: Komödie in einem Vorspiel und drei Akten nach zwanzig Jahren (Berlin: Die Schmiede, 1924);

Gats: Drei Akte (Potsdam: Kiepenheuer, 1925);

Zweimal Oliver: Stück in drei Teilen (Berlin: Die Schmiede, 1926);

Der mutige Seefahrer: Komödie in vier Akten (Potsdam: Kiepenheuer, 1926);

Der Zar läßt sich photographieren: Opera buffa in einem Akt, music by Kurt Weill (Vienna: Universal-Edition, 1927);

Papiermühle: Lustspiel in drei Akten (Potsdam: Kiepenheuer, 1927);

Der Präsident, Komödie in drei Akten (Potsdam: Kiepenheuer, 1927);

Oktobertag: Schauspiel in drei Akten (Potsdam: Kiepenheuer, 1928); translated by Hermann Bernstein and Adolph E. Meyer as *The Phantom Lover: A Play in Three Acts* (New York: Brentano's, 1928);

Die Lederköpfe: Schauspiel in drei Akten (Potsdam: Kiepenheuer, 1928);

Gesammelte Werke, 3 volumes (Potsdam: Kiepenheuer, 1928-1931);

Hellseherei: Gesellschaftsspiel in drei Akten (Berlin: Kiepenheuer, 1929);

Zwei Krawatten: Revuestück in neun Bildern (Berlin: Kiepenheuer, 1929);

Mississippi: Schauspiel in drei Akten (Berlin: Kiepenheuer, 1930);

Es ist genug: Roman (Berlin: Transmare, 1932);

Der Silbersee: Ein Wintermärchen in drei Akten (Berlin: Kiepenheuer, 1933);

Der Gärtner von Toulouse: Schauspiel in fünf Akten (Amsterdam: Querido, 1938);

Der Schuß in die Öffentlichkeit: Vier Akte (Amsterdam: Querido, 1939);

Rosamunde Floris: Schauspiel in drei Akten (Zurich & New York: Oprecht, 1940);

Alain und Elise: Schauspiel in drei Akten (Zurich & New York: Oprecht, 1940);

Der Soldat Tanaka: Schauspiel in drei Akten (Zurich & New York: Oprecht, 1940);

Villa Aurea: Roman (Amsterdam: Querido, 1940); translated by R. Wills Thomas as *A Villa in Sicily* (London: Dakers, 1939); translation republished as *Vera* (New York: Alliance Book Corp. / Longmans, Green, 1939);

Griechische Dramen (Zurich: Artemis, 1948)—comprises *Zweimal Amphitryon, Pygmalion, Bellerophon*;

Das Floß der Medusa, edited by Walther Huder (Cologne: Kiepenheuer & Witsch, 1963); translated by Ulrich Weisstein as *The Raft of the Medusa*, in *First Stage*, 1 (Spring 1962): 35-48;

Stücke, Erzählungen, Aufsätze, Gedichte, edited by Huder (Cologne & Berlin: Kiepenheuer & Witsch, 1966)—includes *Schellenkönig: Eine blutige Groteske; Napoleon in New Orleans: Tragikomödie in neun Bildern; Die Spieldose: Schauspiel in fünf Akten*;

Werke, 6 volumes, edited by Huder (Frankfurt am Main: Propyläen, 1970-1972)—includes in volume 5 (1972): *Singspiel zum Weihnachtsball am 2.1.1897; Faust; König Heinrich: Ein Bühnenvorgang; Die Pfarrerwahl: Ein hochzeitlich, aber gar ernst und empfindsam Spiel; Ein Feierabend: Skizze; Die melkende Kuh: Tragikomödie; Hete Donat: Drama in fünf Akten; Die Dornfelds: Eine Hauskomödie in drei Akten*; in volume 6 (1972): *Das Los des Ossian Balvesen: Komödie in fünf Akten; Adrienne Ambrossat: Schauspiel in drei Akten; Agnete: Schauspiel in drei Akten; Pferdewechsel; Vincent verkauft ein Bild: Neun Szenen; Das gordische Ei; Klawitter: Komödie in fünf Akten; Der englische Sender*;

Werke in drei Bänden, 3 volumes, edited by Klaus Kändler (Berlin & Weimar: Aufbau, 1979).

Edition in English: *Five Plays*, translated by B. J. Kenworthy, Rex W. Last, and J. M. Ritchie (London: Calder & Boyars, 1971)—comprises *From Morning to Midnight, The Burghers of Calais, The Coral, Gas I, Gas II.*

RADIO: *Der englische Sender*, London, German Programme of the BBC, 26 November 1947.

OTHER: Georg Birnbacher, Lyonel Feininger, Walter Grammatté, Walther Ruttman, and Fritz Schaefler, *Die Fibel*, text by Kaiser and Hans Theodore Joel (Darmstadt: Lang, 1921);

"Wie ich es sehe," in *Das Altenbergbuch*, edited by Egon Friedel (Leipzig, Vienna & Zurich: Wiener Graphische Werkstätte, 1921);

Iwan Goll, *Methusalem oder Der ewige Bürger*, introduction by Kaiser (Potsdam: Kiepenheuer, 1922);

"Photographie Atelier Riess," in *Das Querschnittbuch*, edited by Hermann von Wedderkop (Berlin: Propyläen, 1924), p. 232;

"Über Alexander Moissi," in *Moissi*, edited by Hans Böhm (Berlin: Eigenbrödler, 1927), p. 59;

"Der platonische Dialog," in *25 Jahre Frankfurter Schauspielhaus* (Frankfurt am Main, 1927), p. 96; translated by Bayard Quincy Morgan as "Plato as Dramatist," *Tulane Drama Review*, 7, no. 1 (1962): 188-189.

SELECTED PERIODICAL PUBLICATIONS—
UNCOLLECTED: "Notiz über mein Leben," *Das Programm: Blätter der Münchener Kammerspiele*, 3, no. 14 (1917): 4-6;

"Vorwort zu 'Die Muttergottes,'" *Das Programm: Blätter der Münchener Kammerspiele*, 3, no. 14 (1917): 13;

Die Erneuerung: Skizze für ein Drama, in *Das Programm: Blätter der Münchener Kammerspiele*, 4, no. 2 (1917): 2-4;

"Biographische Notiz," *Das Literarische Echo*, 20 no. 6 (1917): 320;

"Wedekind und seine Zeit," *BZ am Mittag*, 42, no. 60 (1918); republished as "Zum Tode Wedekinds," *Die literarische Gessellschaft*, 4, no. 7/8 (1918): 255;

"Vision und Figur," *Das junge Deutschland*, 1, no. 10 (1918): 314-315;

"Offener Brief an den Herausgeber Hans Theodor Joel," *Die neue Bücherschau*, 1, no. 3 (1919): 1-2;

"Dramatischer Dichter und Zuschauer," *Der Zuschauer: Blätter des Neuen Theaters*, 1, no. 1 (1919): 2-3;

"Mythos," *Theaterzeitung der Staatlichen Bühnen Münchens*, 1, no. 4 (1920): 8-9;

"Europa," *Blätter des Deutschen Theaters*, 7, no. 4 (1920): 5-6;

"Brief über sich selbst: Aus dem Münchener Gefängnis an Max Schach," *Das Tagebuch*, 2, no. 9 (1921): 264-267;

"Ein Dichtwerk in der Zeit," *Blätter des deutschen Theaters*, 8, no. 12 (1922): 92-93; republished as "Ein Dichterwerk in der Zeit," *Masken*, 22, no. 4 (1928): 65-66;

"Der kommende Mensch," *Hannoverscher Anzeiger*, 9 April 1922, p. 9; republished as "Dichtung und Energie," *Berliner Tageblatt*, 25 December 1923, p. 6; translated as "The Energetics of Poetry," *English Review*, 35 (December 1922): 533-537;

"Rezension zu 'Raumsturz' von Fred Antoine Angermayer," *Prager Presse*, 12 April 1922;

"Ein neuer Naturalismus?? Antwort auf eine Rundfrage," *Das Kunstblatt*, 6, no. 9 (1922): 406;

"Die französisch-deutsche Annäherung und die deutschen Schriftsteller," *L'Indépendance Belge* (Brussels), 13 October 1922, p. 1;

"Formung von Drama," *Deutsches Bühnen-Jahrbuch*, 33 (1922): 53;

"Brief an Gustav Kiepenheuer," *Die Tabatière*, 17 January 1923;

"Die Krise des Theaters," *Neue Freie Presse*, 2 March 1923, p. 10;

"Historientreue: Am Beispiel der Flucht nach Venedig," *Berliner Tageblatt*, 4 September 1923, p. 3;

"Der Mensch im Tunnel," *Das Kunstblatt*, 8, no. 1 (1924): 5-6; translated by Eric Bentley as "Man in the Tunnel," *Tulane Drama Review*, 7, no. 1 (1962): 194-195;

"Beitrag," *Volkszeitung Plauen*, 8 March 1924;

"Unreifezeugnis," *Volkszeitung für das Vogtland*," 20 April 1924;

"Brief an Hans Theodor Joel," *Die Kassette* (April 1924): 1;

"Gibt es noch eine Gesellschaft," *Berliner Börsen-Courier*, 25 December 1924, p. 5;

"Bericht vom Drama," *Der Zuschauer: Blätter der Saltenburg-Bühnen*, 2, no. 2 (1925): 1-3;

"Welche Stoffe liefert die Gegenwart dem Dramatiker?," *BZ am Mittag*, 10 December 1925;

"Theater und Publikum," *Berliner Börsen-Courier*, 603 (1925): 21;

"Die zwölf unsterblichen Dichter," *Ostseezeitung* 19 August 1926;

"Georg Kaiser und die Entstehung des deutschen Dramas: Ein Briefwechsel," *Das Stachelschwein*, 1 December 1926, pp. 20-21;

"Wie ein Theaterstück entsteht," *Svenska Dagbladet* (Stockholm), 19 December 1926, pp. 42-43;

"Zu Heinrich von Kleists 150. Geburtstag," *Vossische Zeitung*, 16 October 1927;

"Zur Psychologie des dichterischen Schaffens: Inspiration und Arbeitsweise," *Die literarische Welt*, 4, no. 39 (1928): 4;

"Tendenz im Drama?," *Der Scheinwerfer*, 2, no. 4 (1928): 10;

"Warum ich keine Filme schreibe," *Vossische Zeitung*, 31 March 1929;

"Das Lieblingsbuch meiner Knabenjahre," *Die literarische Welt*, 5, no. 26 (1929): 3;

"Von Magdeburg nach Magdeburg," *Der Querschnitt*, 10, no. 5 (1930): 296-301;

"Brief an Karl Otto," *blickpunkt*, 4, no. 5 (1961): 30.

Georg Kaiser is best known as the leading exponent of German expressionism. Kaiser burst upon the German stage with his play *Die Bürger von Calais*, (published, 1914; translated as *The Burghers of Calais*, 1970) which premiered in Frankfurt am Main on 29 January 1917. During the heyday of expressionism, Kaiser's *Stationendramen* (dramas in "stations"), such as *Von morgens bis mitternachts* (published, 1916; performed, 1917; translated as *From Morn till Midnight*, 1920), and his vision of modern technology in the *Gas* trilogy (1917-1920) were considered the very embodiment of the form and ideas of expressionist drama. But even after the demise of expressionism around 1923 Kaiser's success continued: during the following decade he had the largest number of premieres of any German playwright. He was not only the most widely performed but also the most controversial German playwright during the Weimar Republic, which was cut short in 1933—as was Kaiser's career—when the Nazis silenced all political and cultural dissent. They prohibited the staging of Kaiser's plays because they could not tolerate his antiauthoritarian views and his pacifism. For them he was a prominent representative of the hated Weimar Republic, which they saw as controlled by Jews and Bolsheviks. Kaiser was forced into "inner emigration"; in 1938 he went into exile in Switzerland, where he died in 1945. During those twelve years of isolation Kaiser continued writing, although there was little chance that his new dramas would be staged. He left behind an enormous number of plays as well as novels, poems, and letters. Kaiser's oeuvre mirrors the development of German literature between naturalism and literature in exile—the period from 1889 to 1945. During the 1920s his comedies found a large audience, but today he is remembered mainly for his expressionist plays.

Kaiser was born on 25 November 1878 in Magdeburg, the fifth of six sons of Friedrich and Antonie Anton Kaiser. An energetic and vivacious woman sixteen years younger than her husband, who was forty-nine years old at the time of Kaiser's birth, Antonie Kaiser bore most of the responsibilities for educating her children; as chief agent of the Bavarian Loan Association and the Allianz insurance company, Friedrich Kaiser was on the road most of the time. The Kaisers led a comfortable bourgeois existence. Kaiser's childhood was untroubled by the friction and enmity between father and son that afflicted many expressionists and is an important element in many of their plays, including Kaiser's *Die Koralle* (1917; translated as *The Coral*, 1929). Kaiser never said an unkind word about his father, who apparently did not have the authoritarian tendencies typical of the heads of bourgeois families in Wilhelmian society.

Kaiser entered elementary school in 1885 and the gymnasium three years later. He was a bright but unenthusiastic student and, although he suffered from nervous disorders, a passionate soccer player and bicyclist. He showed an early interest in literature and loved to go to the theater and the opera. He organized a literary club at the meetings of which the members presented their own poetic attempts and read the works of European classical writers as well as modern authors such as Georg Büchner, Henrik Ibsen, Jens Peter Jacobsen, Stefan George, Hugo von Hofmannsthal, Johannes Schlaf, Arno Holz, and Gerhart Hauptmann.

Kaiser developed such an aversion to the gymnasium that he left it in 1895 after attaining his Einjährige (first certificate at the end of the tenth grade) and became an apprentice in a bookshop. Appalled by the tastes of the customers, he left the bookstore in disgust and began a new apprenticeship in 1896 at an import-export firm. To get ahead in this branch of commerce he studied Italian and Spanish; it is not known whether he passed the Handlungsgehilfenprüfung (journeyman's examination). In August 1899 he sailed to Buenos Aires, where he worked as a clerk in the local office of the German electrotechnical company AEG. At night he studied philosophy and started reading the works of Fyodor Dostoyevski. Arthur Schopenhauer's subjectivism and pessimism, Friedrich Nietzsche's call for a revaluation of all values and a new, strong, and independent individual, and the humanism and love for the poor and downtrodden in Dostoyevski's works exerted a lasting influence on Kaiser. His return from South America after two years (not three, as is usually asserted) was occasioned as much by his failing health—he had contracted malaria on a horseback trip across the pampas to the Brazilian border—as by his desire for fame.

After his return to Germany, Kaiser lived with his parents and with his brothers. In 1902 he suffered a nervous breakdown and spent half a year in a sanatorium in Berlin, where he worked in the carpenter shop and in the garden. He also tried to get in touch with the literary circle around Stefan George, but without success. He did not look for a job, since he felt that he would never fit into the world of business. He believed so strongly in his mission as a poet that he accepted financial assistance from his parents and brothers and, after his marriage to Margarethe Habenicht in 1908, from his wife and in-laws as his due. His wife's dowry was substantial, and with it Kaiser bought a house at Seeheim, near Darmstadt; in addition, in 1911 he rented a villa in Weimar, the city of Johann Wolfgang von Goethe and Friedrich Schiller. He maintained that he had to live in beautiful and luxurious surroundings to be able to write. Any doubt as to his ultimate success as a writer he suppressed rigorously.

Although Kaiser deprecates Hauptmann in his letters, it is apparent that he took Hauptmann's work as one of the models for his own early literary attempts. A good example is his sketch *Ein Feierabend* (An Evening; published, 1971), written in 1903, with an epilogue consisting of excerpts from a rather romantic poem by Holz that evokes a peaceful evening in a small town. The poem stands in sharp contrast to the depressing situation in the family of a poverty-stricken bricklayer who, after drinking, has fallen from a scaffold and seriously injured himself. All of the thematic and formal principles of naturalist drama are observed in this dramatic finger exercise. The influence of Holz and Schlaf's *Die Familie Selicke* (The Selicke Family, 1890), of Schlaf's *Meister Oelze* (Master Oelze, 1892), and of Hauptmann's plays is in evidence, as it is in Kaiser's first full-length drama, *Die melkende Kuh* (The Milking Cow; published, 1971), written in 1906. In this play Frau Roland wishes her husband to become the proprietor of the mess hall for the workers constructing the Teltow Canal near Berlin. Frau Roland is ruthless in the pursuit of her goal: she lies, manipulates her husband, blackmails the engineer, and causes the death of her father-in-law in the process. Her plans are defeated when her husband, shaken by his wife's brutality, commits suicide. In naturalistic fashion Kaiser uses dialect in his play, and his characters are determined by their environment. Society is portrayed as corrupt.

Kaiser wrote other plays in the naturalist manner that were not performed until his fame had been established through his expressionist plays. One such play, *Die Versuchung* (Temptation, 1917), written around 1910, is a tragedy dealing with the important naturalistic topic of heredity. The heroine, Karla Axthelm, is inspired by Nietzsche's doctrine of the superman. Since her husband, Albert, drinks wine and smokes cigarettes, she does not want him to be the father of her dream child. She selects for this purpose a wanderer who shuns the decadent cities with their materialism and superficiality and raves about the beauty of nature and the Nordic races. But when she learns that the father of her child does not believe in his own theories, she feels betrayed and defiled and kills herself.

The first plays by Kaiser to be performed were comedies modeled on the works of Frank Wedekind and Carl Sternheim. Nietzsche's vitalistic philosophy, with its praise of the Dionysian elements of life, elevating of instinct above intellect, and attack on the educated but narrow-minded German bourgeoisie, was brought to life in the theater by Wedekind and Sternheim, who espoused the cult of a strong life and attacked the complacency, conventions, and institutions of Wilhelmian society. In Kaiser's plays, however, the Nietzschean vitalism is often countermanded by Schopenhauer's pessimism and nihilism—his denial of the will to live and his wish for salvation in death. Kaiser often presents diametrically opposed ideas in his plays—such as Nietzsche's vitalism and Schopenhauer's pessimism, or compassion for the weak and downtrodden and admiration for the superman—without creating a synthesis.

Wedekind's *Frühlings Erwachen* (1891; translated as *The Awakening of Spring*, 1909) pioneered a topic that became rather fashionable: the attack on the outmoded and repressive school system in Wilhelmian Germany. The students in the play are driven to suicide by the bigoted attitude of

their parents and the hypocrisy and brutality of their teachers. Written in 1905, Kaiser's first play to be performed, *Der Fall des Schülers Vehgesack* (Student Vehgesack's Case; published, 1914; performed, 1915), was clearly inspired by Wedekind's tragedy. But while Wedekind shows his students as victims, Kaiser's pupils are quite able to hold their own. (Kaiser probably learned more about school between 1903 and 1908, during his many stays with his brother Bruno, than he did during his own school days. Bruno, a teacher at Schulpforte near Naumburg, had students boarding with his family.) The play is a coarse and heavy-handed farce, with the stock characters found in most school comedies presented as caricatures. The students are an overworked but boisterous and merry gang; the teachers are well-meaning fools, easily duped by their students; and the teachers' wives are sexually starved and lewd. The teacher Hornemann has neglected his wife to devote all his time and financial resources to his research on Homer's *Odyssey*; she seduces Vehgesack, the student who has been ordered to accompany her on her bicycle rides. When the other lusty wives hear about Vehgesack's sexual prowess he becomes a veritable rooster in a henhouse. Hornemann wants Vehgesack expelled from school, but the principal must avoid scandal because the prince has just announced that his son will attend the institution. To placate Hornemann he finds a different reason for dismissing the student: Vehgesack has written a play, which is strictly forbidden by school regulations. Unfortunately, a publisher already has the manuscript, and, seeing in Vehgesack a new genius, he visits the school. The prince hears about Vehgesack, proclaims him the friend of his son, and extends his special protection to the student: "Es soll der König mit dem Sänger gehen!" (The king shall walk together with the poet!).

Kaiser's second play about school life, the tragicomedy *Rektor Kleist* (Principal Kleist; published, 1914; performed, 1918), written in 1905, focuses on the dichotomy between body and mind, vitality and the intellect; the influence of Nietzsche is dominant. Principal Kleist is a sensitive and intelligent but sickly hunchback who tries to hide his bodily weakness. His rival is the self-assured and vital physical education teacher Kornmüller. The plot revolves around Kornmüller's attempt to find the student responsible for throwing an inkwell against a dormitory wall. He considers Fehse the culprit, while Fehse knows that Kleist had hurled the inkwell at a caricature of himself drawn and pinned to the wall by another student. Kleist privately admits to Kornmüller that he is guilty, but Kornmüller refuses to believe him. Fehse is brought before the faculty and declares his innocence, but Kleist does not own up to his guilt since he fears the ridicule of his colleagues. When Fehse breaks down under the strain and commits suicide after confessing his guilt in a letter, Kleist announces that the culprit has been found and has passed sentence on himself. Because of this cowardly action Kleist is the real villain of the play. He is the perfect example of a Nietzschean intellectual who has recognized the relativity of all values; but he is afraid of this awareness and would prefer to be like Kornmüller, who sees everything as black and white.

In the comedy *Der Geist der Antike* (The Spirit of Antiquity; published, 1923), written in 1905, Professor Nehrkorn, the very picture of the hyperintellectual scientist who lives only for his research, suddenly realizes during excavations in Greece that his life has been one-sided and impulsively decides to start a new and more practical one. His wife, however, recognizes that Nehrkorn has only exchanged one extreme for another and must realize that a healthy balance is necessary. When Nehrkorn's invention, a superior mousetrap, turns out to be a failure, he returns to his profession.

Even more fanatical than Nehrkorn is the main character in Kaiser's grotesque comedy *Der Zentaur* (The Centaur; performed, 1917), written in 1906 and published under this title in 1916, revised as *Konstantin Strobel* in 1920, and republished as *Margarine* (performed, 1925) in 1925. In *Der Zentaur* the narrow-minded and overly conscientious teacher Strobel seems devoid of all common sense. When he learns that the grandmother of his fiancée, Judith, has left them a fortune that will go to a foundation if Judith does not bear a child within one year after their wedding, Strobel naively feels duty bound to prove his masculinity by experimentation. He seduces the servant girl and is delighted when she tells him that she is expecting. Judith's petty-bourgeois father, however, is horror-struck when he hears about Strobel's affair and has his daughter break off the engagement. Strobel's mother is so disgraced by her son's immoral behavior that she dies. Strobel is dismissed from his teaching position. His sense of duty, which had won him the respect of the community, has caused his downfall: he has carried it to extremes without taking feelings and social customs into consideration. In *Konstantin Strobel* Kaiser adds a totally unexpected and grotesque ending: a rich widow hears about Strobel's affair and comes to claim this prize stud for herself; as a teacher Strobel had caused the suicide of her son by his excessive pedantry, and she marries him to have a new child. Practically all reviewers pointed to Sternheim as the spiritual father of this satire; many also noted that the idea was revolting.

Two comedies that were published and staged in 1927 and 1928, when Kaiser was in financial difficulties, were written between his return from Argentina and his marriage. *Papiermühle* (Paper Mill, 1927), written in 1905, focuses on the opportunistic critic Raymond Duchut, who is writing a study of the successful playwright Ernest Ollier. Duchut wants to prove that Ollier's most recent and unusually passionate play, *Francesca da Rimini*, is based on fact. He discovers to his mortification that his own wife, Francine, served as a model for the title character. She spent her vacation with Ollier, and the two have fallen deeply in love. The triangle is resolved when Duchut, who had only married Francine because of her good social connections, relinquishes her to Ollier. *Papiermühle* was treated harshly by the critics. *Der Präsident* (The President; published, 1927; performed, 1928), written in 1906, is also a rather flimsy comedy about an ambitious lawyer who hopes to advance his career by fighting the white-slave traffic but ends up losing his money and his daughter.

In general, Kaiser's comedies that deal with the lives of ordinary people are witty and entertaining; they can be staged successfully if they are played at a fast pace and if the dialogue is pruned carefully. Kaiser tends to be too verbose and to overdo the humor so that it degenerates into farce.

Kaiser's first play to be published commercially rather than privately printed was his "biblical comedy" *Die jüdische Witwe* (The Jewish Widow; published, 1911; performed, 1921). The legend of Judith has been treated by many playwrights, among them Friedrich Hebbel and Johann Nestroy, as a tragedy or comedy. Kaiser portrays Judith as an amoral, strong-willed, modern emancipated woman, much like the heroines of George Bernard Shaw. She is searching for a man since neither her husband, Manasse, a senile and impotent voyeur, nor the weakened defenders of the besieged city are interested in her. In desperation she visits the Assyrian camp. She is attracted to the vital, animal nature of the general Holofernes; but when the intellectual King Nebukadnezar demands Judith for himself, she kills the general, whereupon the horrified king and his army flee in terror. Judith is sent to Jerusalem to become a vestal virgin, and it seems that she will never attain her objective. But the high priest who leads her into the temple is a virile man, and her wish is ultimately fulfilled. The stage in *Die jüdische Witwe*, although still naturalistic, also has a symbolic function. In the first act, for instance, the towering structure of the temple with its huge pillars symbolizes the might of the community and the laws of Jewish society that Judith should obey. Kaiser is here well on his way to expressionist drama.

Another pseudohistorical play by Kaiser in which the language can be called expressionistic in parts is *König Hahnrei* (King Cuckold; published, 1913; performed, 1931). This play reflects the influence of neo-Romantic literature on Kaiser. Neo-Romantic artists tried to escape from the modern world of industry, big cities, social problems, and ugliness into a self-contained haven of art and a cult of aestheticism; the younger neo-Romantics called for a return to nature and for free love. All of Kaiser's works in this genre have either a garden or a room in a castle as their setting. The time is a historical or mythical past, such as ancient Greece, the Middle Ages, or the Renaissance. Three one-act plays, *Claudius* (published, 1913; originally titled *La Fanciulla*, 1911), *Friedrich und Anna* (published, 1918; also published as *Mona Lisa*, 1911, and *Monna Nanna*, 1913), and *Juana* (published, 1918), are linked thematically and stylistically; their topic is love and jealousy. Claudius, the black knight, sallies forth from his castle every night to battle imaginary rivals and loses his wife. Friedrich, on the other hand, overcomes his jealousy: instead of challenging a former lover of his bride to a duel he invites him to dinner because he had made Friedrich's wife happy at a time when Friedrich did not even know her. And Juana, caught between two friends, commits suicide so that they may remain friends and continue to pursue their careers. When the plays were produced in 1918 the critics reacted negatively to their somewhat abstract nature and to the contrived and improbable plots. *König Hahnrei* is the tragedy of King Marke, Isolde's husband. The play is a long monologue in which Marke exposes his jealousy, hatred, and frustration. He refuses to believe what he sees and creates an imaginary world in which he can live happily. While the play's setting and erotic atmosphere and the king's decadent narcissism, introspectiveness, and self-delusion are clearly neo-Romantic, Kaiser's detached attitude, ironic perspective, and tense language turn the medieval legend into a modern play.

In *Europa* (Europe; published, 1915; performed, 1920) the symbolism of color, the stylized movements, and the pantomime are already expressionistic. The play is a satire on the cult of dancing and the Jugendbewegung (youth movement) in Germany. The ending of the play shows that Kaiser was not impervious to the patriotism and militarism that engulfed the peoples of Europe at the beginning of World War I: the warriors carry off the daughter and maidens of King Agenor, whose men have become so effeminate that they cannot defend the country. Thus, Nietzschean Dionysian vitalism triumphs over decadent aesthetic pacifism. With music by Werner Robert Heymann, the play was a great success.

In 1917 *Die Bürger von Calais* caught the attention of critics and the public in war-weary Germany as a call to pacifism and a denunciation of war. The historical background of the play is the siege of Calais by the troops of Edward III of England in 1347, during the Hundred Years' War. An English officer brings an ultimatum: the city will be spared from destruction if six citizens, in sackcloths and with a rope around their necks, turn themselves over to the English king to be executed, bringing the keys to the city with them. Duguesclins, the constable of France, is determined to fight until Calais is destroyed. His opponent is Eustache de Saint-Pierre, a wealthy merchant who pleads for submission to save the rest of the townspeople. His pacifist ethos is taken up by the other citizens. Eustache is the first to volunteer as a hostage, and six other citizens follow his example—making a total of seven, one more than the English demanded.

If Kaiser had wanted to write a historical play to celebrate the heroism of the citizens, the play could have ended there. But he saw the sacrifice as only the first step in the renewal and regeneration of the human being, a central concept of expressionism. Irrationality and the beastly aspects of human nature must be overcome by rational thinking and behavior. Eustache recognizes that the six have volunteered impulsively, that they are not yet ready to act freely, without regret, and from inner conviction. Eustache orchestrates a conversion of their thinking so that a "neuer Mensch" (new human being) will come into existence. One of the seven volunteers will be reprieved, and Eustache keeps the others—and the audience—in suspense to achieve their inner transformation. At the end of the second act the seven draw balls from an urn to determine who is to live and who is to die; but they all draw blue balls. Eustache then informs them that they have until the next morning to consider their decision, and that the one who arrives last at the marketplace shall be free.

In the final act, the other six volunteers arrive at the marketplace before Eustache. They are calm and prepared to die. The assembled citizens accuse Eustache of trying to save his own life when he does not appear. In the midst of their outcry his body is carried onto the stage, and his blind old father announces that he has committed suicide to show them the way. But the six are pardoned by the English king, to whom a son was born during the night. Is this son a reincarnation of Eustache?

By his example and through his teaching Eustache has changed the volunteers; they have become his disciples and will help their fellow citizens establish a kingdom of peace. Eustache has not died in vain, but, like Christ, for the sins of his fellowmen. The secularized religious aspects of the play, such as the last supper of Eustache and the volunteers, the resurrection of Eustache through the birth of the king's son, and the discipleship of the volunteers led critics to refer to the play as a "Verkündigungsdrama" (drama of annunciation) or "Erlösungsdrama" (play of redemption).

The play was influenced by the operas of Richard Wagner: the settings are monumental and the stylized mass scenes have an operatic quality. The play is tightly structured; Kaiser's language is rhythmical and dynamic but rather abstract. With its pathos, this "Ideendrama" (play of ideas) is clearly aimed at the indoctrination of the audience. Through repetitions, parallel constructions, and other rhetorical devices the message is hammered home, and it is further underscored by the setting, the lighting, and the music. The production by Arthur Hellmer at the Frankfurt am Main Neues Theater marked the beginning of the so-called Frankfurt Expressionism.

Großbürger Möller (Bourgeois Möller; published, 1914; performed, 1915), set in a small Danish town, is a tightly constructed comedy after the manner of Sternheim. All members of the Möller family except Sophus believe that they have won eight hundred thousand crowns in the lottery; unfortunately, Sophus has not played the number for the last ten years, instead spending the money collected for the ticket on the musical education of his daughter, Dagmar. He pretends, however, that the money will be coming their way, and all start carrying out their plans as if they were already in possession of the wealth. The brewery owner Magnussen hears about their windfall and sets out to lay his hands on the money. Sophus, however, manipulates him in such a deft manner that in the end everybody has reached his or her goal except Magnussen: he has spent his money in the hope of being richer in the end by eight hundred thousand crowns, only to learn that Sophus's ten-year-old lottery ticket has expired. In danger of becoming the laughingstock of the community, he has to make the best of a bad situation and acquiesce in Sophus's plans. His son Axel, however, is overjoyed, since he loves Dagmar but had vowed never to marry a rich girl. The play has been staged successfully many times.

Von morgens bis mitternachts and two later plays, *Kanzlist Krehler* (Clerk Krehler, 1922) and *Nebeneinander* (Side by Side, 1923), were linked by Kaiser, who called them a trilogy connected by characters but not by plot. The main characters of the three plays—the Kassierer (cashier), the Kanzlist, and the Pfandleiher (pawnbroker)—are men who one day realize that life has passed them by. Their reactions to this realization are so exaggerated that the plays take on tragicomic aspects.

Von morgens bis mitternachts was Kaiser's first Stationendrama; with Reinhard Sorge's *Der Bettler* (The Beggar, 1912) and Walter Hasenclever's *Der Sohn* (The Son, 1914) it is one of the first examples of this genre. In such plays the central character is living a meaningless existence when he suddenly receives an Anstoß (impetus), which leads to his Aufbruch (departure) to a new Ziel (goal). On his Weg (way) to this more or less nebulous goal he goes through many stations led by his vision of a new meaning in life. His action is as much a Flucht (flight) from his past as it is a Marsch (march) to a better future. In the end, the goal eludes his grasp; but the search is more important than the goal. The action of the play is seen through the eyes of the central character; Stationendramen are subjective. The characters are types—they do not have names but carry generic designations such as "Kassierer," "Frau" (wife), "Mutter" (mother), "Tochter" (daughter), "Dame" (lady) that point to their position in the social environment.

In *Von morgens bis mitternachts* the monotonous and machinelike life of the cashier is changed when a beautiful Italian lady comes into the bank to withdraw three thousand marks. He and the bank director consider her an impostor intent on defrauding the bank. This incident is the beginning of a series of events that will lead to the cashier's death. He takes sixty thousand marks and goes to the lady, planning to flee with her to start a new life. But he soon realizes that she is not a confidence woman but a respectable rich widow traveling with her son, an art historian, who needs the money to buy a painting he has discovered. It is too late for the cashier to return to the bank and confess his mistake. Crossing a snowfield, he sees what appears to be a skeleton formed by the bare branches of a tree—a memento mori. But he knows the value of the money he has embezzled and believes that he can master his fate, and he defiantly challenges the Grim Reaper to return at midnight.

The cashier's respectable bourgeois family is disturbed when he returns home earlier than usual. He relates his experience of a rebirth on the snowfield, but the allegory is lost on the family; they are only interested in getting him back into his old image with his slippers, long pipe, and nightcap, the symbolic utensils of the German philistine. When he takes a forceful leave before lunch his old mother becomes so upset that she dies of a heart attack.

The cashier departs from his provincial town and travels to the big city; he leaves the private sphere of workplace and family and enters the public world of sports, politics, amusement, and religion. His next station is a six-day bicycle race where he gets the idea that by betting on the racers he will drive the spectators into unrestrained behavior; he desires to experience passionate life at least vicariously. But the ecstasy of the crowd is cut short when the crown prince appears and the national anthem is played. The cashier leaves the race disappointed: tradition is stronger than vibrant life. He goes to a private room in a cabaret, but his desire for sensual pleasures is disappointed as well. The last stage in his desperate journey is the Salvation Army, where he hears the confessions of various sinners and recognizes them as his own. When he confesses and throws the money into the prayer hall, a wild scramble ensues in which everybody grabs what

he or she can and flees. The cashier's last hope is the Salvation Army girl, but she turns him over to the police for the reward.

Now the cashier has his second vision of death; this time he sees no escape, and he shoots himself. His journey toward redemption and renewal had to remain unsuccessful because he was only looking for self-realization without consideration for anyone else. He was also following his accustomed thought patterns by trying to buy immaterial goods that cannot be purchased. He drew the conclusion that money is worthless and that there is nothing to live for; he did not recognize the purely functional value of money.

Thematically, *Von morgens bis mitternachts* is a Wandlungsdrama (play of regeneration). Although the cashier does not achieve such a regeneration, the audience can learn from his mistakes. This aspect of the play appealed to Bertolt Brecht, who considered Kaiser one of his teachers. The play was successfully produced by the director of the Munich Kammerspiele (Intimate Theater), Otto Falckenberg, on 28 April 1917. It was later performed in many other German theaters and was translated and produced all over the world. A film version was also released.

In *Kanzlist Krehler* the title character is thrown out of his sterile routine when he is given a Monday off following the wedding of his daughter, Ida. Since he has never experienced a free weekday he becomes disoriented; he cannot even find his way home. This experience makes him realize that he is in a rut and is not really alive any more, and it inspires him to try to make a new start: he wants to give up his job and his pension and face the adventures the globe—an important symbolic stage prop—seems to offer. But his wife rejects his ideas and wants him back to normal. She gets support from Krehler's boss, who does not want to lose a valuable employee; he tells Krehler the story of the cashier from *Von morgens bis mitternachts*. Krehler realizes that he is no longer young and that rebirth is impossible, but he does not want to go back to his old life. He turns his desperation and anger against his wife, accusing her of having stolen his life. He wants her to die with him. When she refuses he kills his son-in-law by throwing him off the balcony of a high rise before following him into death. Because of its mixture of naturalistic and expressionistic elements the work did not find favor in the eyes of most critics, who considered it too abstract and contrived.

Sketch by the set designer, Cesar Klein, of the set for the snowfield scene for a 1921 Berlin production of Kaiser's Von morgens bis mitternachts *(Theatermuseum, Munich)*

In the last play in the trilogy, *Nebeneinander*, three plots unfold simultaneously; they are connected only through a letter. The main plot revolves around the pawnbroker and his daughter, who find the letter in a suit that has been pawned. The address has been obliterated, but they read that the intended recipient of the letter, a woman named Lu, is threatening suicide. They try to find her to deliver the letter. In the process they lose their business, and they take their own lives. In the second plot Lu receives a copy of the letter since the man who had written it realized that he left the original in the suit that he took to the pawnbroker. She leaves the city, finds a new life, and finally marries a friend of her sister. In the third plot the man who wrote the letter, Neumann, becomes the director of a film company.

The title and structure of the play are intended to show that society has fallen apart, that people live isolated existences. The play gives dramatic expression to the misery and the economic and moral degradation brought on by a lost war, inflation, corruption, and opportunism. The alienated individual finds no support structure in the lonely crowd, where everybody is intent only on

his or her own survival. The pawnbroker, who has exploited the misery of others, is suddenly transformed into a neuer Mensch and sets out to save a fellow human being. He has experienced a moral rebirth, but people do not understand him. Like the cashier in *Von morgens bis mitternachts* he goes from station to station, but in contrast to the cashier he acts for unselfish and humanitarian reasons. His expressionist passion comes to the same end as that of the cashier, but at least he dies with his daughter and not alone. The Lu plot, on the other hand, has a Hollywood happy ending in the idyllic countryside far from the hectic modern city. For Neumann, the unscrupulous and amoral but witty and vital entrepreneur, the city is the ideal backdrop. His phenomenal rise in the new world of the film is matched in the personal sphere by his conquest of a beautiful film star. Both he and Lu find the happiness they have been looking for. The audience in Berlin wildly applauded the Neumann character; the expressionist era was drawing to a close, and the public was tired of being preached to.

Die Sorina (1917) is a satire in the tradition of Nikolay Gogol and Anton Chekhov on corrupt petty bureaucracy in Russia. The setting is a provincial Russian town, and the plot is predictable. The police inspector Barssukoff courts the famous actress Sorina. He tries to subject her to his will by using his authority to ban all plays with a part she could play. Sorina is saved by the dashing young playwright Barin, who is loved by Barssukoff's wife. In the end the Barssukoffs are duped, and the lovers leave town.

Die Koralle; *Gas* (1918; translated 1924); and *Gas: Zweiter Teil* (1920; translated as *Gas, Part II*, 1929) constitute a trilogy. The principal characters belong to four generations of the family of the Milliardär (billionaire), and the plays cover a period of about seventy years. In *Die Koralle* the protagonist is the billionaire, who rules over a vast industrial empire and ruthlessly exploits his laborers but acts like a philanthropist by endowing hospitals, schools, and convalescent homes. Every Thursday he holds an open house at which people can come and ask for help, which is usually granted. But the billionaire does not want to be reminded of his own poverty-stricken past, and therefore his identical double, his secretary, takes his place. A coral attached to the secretary's watch chain identifies him to the billionaire's bodyguards. Not even the billionaire's children know about this double. For them the billionaire tries to arrange a happy and carefree life to protect them from traumatic experiences such as he suffered on the way to the top. In his children he vicariously experiences a sunny youth without worries. But the billionaire's plans go awry. His son chooses to become a stoker on a steamer and learns about hard work and exploitation, and his daughter decides to serve the needy by becoming a nurse. When his son admits that he almost killed his father because of the latter's brutality in suppressing a workers' protest after an explosion in the mines, the billionaire is deeply shaken and considers suicide; but when he hears about the secretary's happy childhood he shoots him and takes his identity by clipping the coral to his own watch chain. He is arrested and signs a statement that he is the secretary; he has exchanged the secretary's happy past for his own nightmarish childhood and youth, and he is willing to die for this happiness. His last three visitors before the execution—his son, a socialist, and a priest—cannot help him, since joining his son's struggle for a better life or the socialist movement would be as much a betrayal of his philosophy as to believe in God. That philosophy is molded by Schopenhauer's idea that the individual is separated from nature and suffers accordingly; only through abnegation of the will and negation of life will the pain be alleviated and the individual become part of the universe again.

Die Koralle was hailed as a truly expressionist drama, and its powerful poetic language was praised. But while the social concerns of the first three acts were easy to understand, the psychological problems of the protagonist and the complex symbolism of the last two acts confused many critics. Most directors were not yet familiar with the language and style of expressionism, resulting in attempts to present Kaiser's play in a realistic manner.

In *Gas* the billionaire's son now owns his father's factories. He has put his socialist ideas into practice and shares all profits with the workers. The firm's product is gas, a source of energy that has become indispensable for the economies of the world's industrial nations. But it is also potentially destructive, and one day a devastating explosion destroys the main plant and kills many workers. The survivors regard the Ingenieur (engineer) as responsible for the explosion and want him fired before they will return to work. The son thinks that they have become slaves of their machines and have lost their human nature; he wants them to return to a simple life in the country. But the engineer convinces the workers that they cannot turn their backs on industrial progress and become peasants again. They decide to follow him back into the factory, but the billionaire's son has locked them out. At this point the government steps in since it needs gas for the production of weapons. The only hope at the end of the play comes from the daughter of the billionaire's son, who promises to give birth to the New Man.

The protagonist in *Gas: Zweiter Teil* is this New Human Being, the great-grandson of the billionaire, called the *Milliardärarbeiter* (billionaire-worker). He does not own the factories but is a moral leader. The world is now divided into two camps, the *Gelbfiguren* (Yellows) and the Blaufiguren (Blues), who are engaged in an arms race and a war of attrition that can only end in total destruction unless there is a spiritual reorientation of humanity. When the workers proclaim a general strike, the billionaire-worker hopes to convince the enemy to conclude a peace treaty. But the Yellow forces occupy the country and force the workers to return to their soul-killing jobs. In the final act the chief engineer incites the workers to rebellion: he has invented poison gas and urges them to use it against their oppressors even if it means total annihilation. The billionaire-worker urges them to submit and calls for a spiritual renewal, but the masses continue to follow the chief engineer. In desperation the billionaire-worker drops the ball containing the poison gas among the workers, and the world is annihilated.

The isolation and alienation of the characters in the trilogy are expressed through their language. The engineer is concerned with formulas, control stations, machines, and the production of gas, while the capitalists speak of strikes, profits, losses, and meetings. In *Gas: Zweiter Teil* the vocabulary of most of the figures has become extremely limited, consisting of a few basic words. Only the speeches of the protagonists rise above this abstract style and at times even show a lyrical quality. Stage settings and color are used in a symbolic manner; in *Gas: Zweiter Teil* the workers wear either blue or yellow—they have become uniform and have lost their multicolored liveliness.

The theme of these plays is the unpreparedness of the masses for regeneration, an unpreparedness that causes their extinction. It is the enlightened leader who must chart the course for the workers, but they refuse to follow his ideas. Kaiser, whose idea of leadership was based on his reading of the works of Nietzsche never had the faith in the intelligence of the masses that other expressionists professed.

In the *Gas* trilogy Kaiser portrays the inhumanity and injustice of capitalist Wilhelmian society toward the less-privileged classes, and he shows the military-industrial complex of European society that was responsible for World War I. But more important is Kaiser's vision of the dehumanization of an industrial society and the dangers inherent in an unchecked growth of technology. The *Gas* trilogy has remained topical; Fritz Lang's film *Metropolis* (1927) is based on it, and following the atomic accidents at Three Mile Island in Pennsylvania in 1979 and at Chernobyl in the Soviet Union in 1986 there were revivals of the plays.

A group of nine plays by Kaiser can be called "Frauenstücke" (plays about women). They are written for small casts in intimate theaters; the backgrounds are usually artificial settings, such as greenhouses or winter gardens; they are centered around female protagonists who are isolated and live in a fantasy world; and the protagonists do anything to protect the world of their dreams, even commit murder. Kaiser poses the problem of subjective and objective truth, and in most cases the illusion emerges triumphant. The plots revolve around the relationship between a woman and a man, and absolute love and the purity of the woman are seen as the ideal.

In the earliest play in this group, *Das Frauenopfer* (Sacrifice of a Woman, 1918), the wife of Count Lavalette, one of Napoleon's generals, changes places with her imprisoned husband to save him from execution after the fall of Napoleon. He had married her on the orders of the emperor; now, when he sees her sacrifice, he realizes how much she loves him. He eagerly awaits her release so that they may start a new life together. But when they are reunited and she tells him that she had given herself frequently to the guards to buy their silence, he is repelled and calls her a whore. He cannot accept her actions as a sacrifice performed on his behalf, and he wants to return to prison. To rescue him a second time she tells him that she did not save him for love but because she wanted him to become emperor so that she could be empress. He now hates her, and he decides to join Napoleon, who has returned from Elba. His wife disguises herself as her husband a second time and is shot by the gendarmes who are looking for the escaped prisoner. With her dying words she condemns Lavalette because he had never been ready to live only for her as she was ready to suffer and die for him. When Lavalette realizes what she has done for him he can no longer fight for Napoleon. He ends up a lonely man who, however, now has an understanding of true human values. The critics could not make up their minds whether or not the play was an expressionistic work; they objected to the countess's explicit description of a rape; and they found fault with the overly complex and contrived plot and the stilted language. The controversy seems to have kept the play from being forgotten, and by the time it was staged in Berlin in 1923 the critics praised it as one of Kaiser's best dramas.

Der Brand im Opernhaus, (performed, 1918; published, 1919; translated as *The Fire in the Opera House*, 1927) has as its background the burning of the Paris Opera in 1763. The play centers around the orphan girl Sylvette and her husband, who has retired from the decadent life of the rich upper class at the time of Louis XV. He lives isolated with his wife, whom he had married because of her chastity and purity. On the evening of the fire he learns that his wife has led a promiscuous life. When she confesses to her husband after escaping from the fire at the opera house, where she was attending a ball, he refuses to recognize her. He clings to his belief in her purity and pretends that she died in the fire. He orders his servants to bring to his house the body of any woman killed in the fire, which he will then claim to be his wife. But, when the body is identified as the king's mistress by a ring she is wearing, he persuades Sylvette to put on the ring and jump into the flames to purify herself. He wants to go on believing in the purity of his wife.

Hölle, Weg, Erde (Hell, Way, Earth, 1919), based on a sketch by Kaiser titled *Die Erneuerung* (Regeneration, 1917), revolves around an artist's desire to lead the masses in Nietzschean fashion and the expressionist visionary longing for the brotherhood of all mankind. The protagonist, Spazierer, is a wanderer on his "way" from "hell" to "earth." When the friend he is trying to help kills himself, Spazierer tries to press charges against a rich woman who had the means to save him but refused to do so. But nobody takes him seriously. In desperation he stabs a jeweler, considering him responsible for a society that is consumer-oriented instead of stressing human concerns. This act of violence makes people think about social conditions, and when Spazierer leaves prison after serving his sentence for attempted murder he finds a changed world. Now all feel guilty and innocent at the same time since they are all victims of society, and all want to give up their old lives and start anew. After crossing a bridge they arrive on a stony plain, where, under the rays of the morning sun, they are going to build a new society. Even if the road is rocky and the work hard, regenerated humanity will establish paradise on earth. The critics called *Hölle, Weg, Erde* one of Kaiser's weakest dramas; they especially criticized the language, which is mechanistic and impersonal and does not change during the course of the play.

In spite of his success as a playwright and the help of his relatives, Kaiser's debts mounted during and after World War I. His son Dante Anselm had been born in 1914; Laurent followed in 1918; and a daughter, Eva Sybille, was born in 1919. Kaiser's expenses were rising, but he and his wife were not willing to change their lifestyle, and they lost their houses in Seeheim and Weimar in 1918 and were forced to live in rented apartments and later a furnished country house. To meet living expenses Kaiser sold or pawned furniture and art objects.

In *Der gerettete Alkibiades* (1920; translated as *Alkibiades Saved*, 1963), Kaiser questions the tradi-

tional portrayal of Socrates. Since knowledge of the ancient Greek language and Greek history and philosophy were the foundation of a German classical education, Kaiser's view was sharply attacked. The playwright boasted that he had toppled Goethe's and Johann Joachim Winckelmann's interpretation of classical Greece as the land of noble simplicity and serene grandeur. Alkibiades, the ideal of strength and beauty, is contrasted with Socrates, the great thinker. During a battle Socrates saves Alkibiades; Socrates was only in the battle because he stepped on a thorn and could not flee like the others, but he claims that it was his superior intellectual powers that enabled him to save the stronger man. Vitality is discredited. Now Socrates has to hide the fact that it was not his intelligence but the weakness of his body that had induced him to fight. In consequence, he has to invent new philosophical interpretations for all phenomena that confront him. When he is condemned to death he looks forward to it: only in the separation of his soul from his body can he achieve the synthesis of vitality and intellect.

In October 1920 Kaiser was arrested in Berlin and charged with embezzlement. He was transferred to a prison in Munich, where he was examined for weeks in the psychiatric ward. Before the court Kaiser identified himself with Georg Büchner and Heinrich von Kleist, great German writers who had also suffered persecution. He maintained that the laws did not apply to him, that as a genius he stood above the common crowd. He saw himself as an instrument for the creation of great works of art that benefited all of humanity. What he had done was not criminal because he had done it not for himself or his family but for his work, which had to be created at all costs. In February 1921 he was sentenced to a year in prison, but he was released after serving six months—including the time since his arrest— and placed on probation for the remaining half of his sentence. On his release Kaiser settled in Grünheide, a suburb of Berlin.

The conflict between "Schein" (illusion) and "Sein" (reality) that dominates Kaiser's Frauenstücke becomes the main topic in his Künstlerdramen (plays about artists). The first of these Künstlerdramen is the one-act play *Der Protagonist* (published, 1921; performed, 1922; translated as *The Protagonist*, 1960), in which an actor is unable to distinguish between the roles he plays and his real life. His sister is the only one who can call him back to the real world because

Scene from the 1919 Berlin premiere of Kaiser's Hölle, Weg, Erde

he has complete trust in her. One evening after he has acted in a comedy she tells him that she has a lover. The brother, in a good mood from a happy play, wants to meet him. While the sister goes to get her lover, the actor is asked by his patron to perform the role of a jealous husband in another play. When his sister returns he confuses her with his faithless wife in the play and stabs her. In her dying moments she brings him back to reality one last time. He asks his patron not to have him arrested until after that evening's performance, when he will play his part so convincingly that nobody will be able to draw the line between real and feigned madness. The actor had tried to sublimate his incestuous feelings for his sister by turning her into a paragon of virtue and chastity. When she destroyed his idea of her by behaving like a normal woman he killed her and took refuge in madness.

In 1926 Kurt Weill—a student of Ferruccio Busoni, who had revitalized modern opera—set *Der Protagonist* to music. He stayed in Kaiser's home in Grünheide and there met his future wife, Lotte Lenya. The opera was staged successfully in March 1926 at the Dresden Staatsoper.

In prison Kaiser had sketched *Noli me tangere* (Do Not Touch Me; published, 1922). The story of Jesus' betrayal by Judas is presented here in the utmost abstract expressionist fashion; none of the characters has a name. A prison is the place of action, and prisoners 5, 15, and 16 are the main protagonists. 5 was arrested when he tried to steal some carrots because he was hungry; 15 is a well-dressed bourgeois artist; and 16 is the Christ figure. With the arrival of 16 there is one prisoner too many in the cell, which is meant to hold only twelve inmates. The beginning of part 2 shows the prisoners at dinner—a kind of Last Supper. When it is time to sleep, 16 does not have a bed. 16 tries to convince 15 that poets have to set attainable goals and must become part of the people again. 15 offers 16 his bed and in return receives 16's coat. With this exchange a personality change takes place and 15 becomes Christ-like. The change of coat leads to the release of 15, who is mistaken for 16. 5, who has witnessed the exchange, tells the guards the truth for some food. 16 is taken away and punished, and 5 commits suicide. With this play Kaiser repudiates his previous utopian expressionist

Kaiser in 1922

plays. He pleads for a more realistic approach to a better society through love of one's neighbor and decent behavior. It is not sufficient to have a vague idea of the good society; one must also have the means and concrete plans for building this new kingdom. Kaiser's play is so abstract that it is almost unintelligible; it has never been performed.

Gilles und Jeanne (1923) is based on the Jeanne d'Arc legend. The main character is Gilles de Rais, who in the course of the play is transformed into a neuer Mensch. Gilles is erotically obsessed with Jeanne, who rejects him; he therefore causes her death at the stake by accusing her of witchcraft. Later he kills six innocent young women who are presented to him under the pretense that they are Jeanne brought back to life. He defends himself before the same church court that sentenced Jeanne and is acquitted for lack of evidence; but as he leaves he has a vision of Jeanne in her silver armor. He suddenly confesses and, feeling that he has been saved, gladly submits to his execution. Through his confession Gilles has been not only redeemed

but has been elevated above the common people and has become a second Christ. One can consider the play Kaiser's contribution to the mystical trend in expressionism represented by Ernst Barlach. When the play was performed in 1923 and 1924 in Leipzig and Berlin it had mostly negative reviews; the illogical plot and the exaggerated language met with general disapproval.

In the Künstlerdrama *Die Flucht nach Venedig* (The Flight to Venice, 1923) the central figures are the writers George Sand and Alfred de Musset. Musset has left Paris and his lover, George Sand, because he feels exploited by the way she integrates all her experiences, including her love affairs, into her works. He also cannot cope with her bisexual nature, which is expressed in her pseudonym. George Sand, who is desired by men and women alike, follows Musset to Venice, accompanied by a German girl who loves her. Musset confronts George Sand with the accusation that she is exposing his deepest feelings for the whole world to read about. Torn between his love and his revulsion for her, he collapses. George Sand is deeply shaken and wants to prove to herself and to Musset that she can love with total self-abandonment. The young Italian doctor summoned to tend Musset becomes the object of her experiment. She wins him from his English lover, then spends the night with him. In the morning the husband of the Englishwoman arrives to challenge the doctor to a duel, but George Sand convinces him that his wife did not betray him because she was so filled with her new love that the outside world ceased to exist for her. She then tells Musset that she herself experienced this feeling when she slept with the doctor. Musset takes his revenge by asking her to narrate her experiences; the doctor is thus transformed into a literary figure, and when he returns she no longer loves him. George Sand leaves to continue her career, leaving her two lovers behind. The play closes with the doctor's line: "Das Wort tötet das Leben" (The word [literature] kills life).

Kolportage (Colportage, 1924) is a tightly constructed satire on bourgeois life and the literary trends of the time—especially "Trivialliteratur"—set in Sweden. It centers around the exchange of a count's son for the son of a beggar woman to prove that class behavior is not genetically acquired but learned. In the end the once-poor Acke, who is now the noble heir to the Stjernenhö estate, begins a new life with his love, Alice. They depart for America, where there are no class distinctions and everyone can make an honest living. Erik, the count's son has become a wealthy American businessman who is only interested in making his money work for the good of society. The play was successful because the audience enjoyed the humor and the clichés about the arrogant Swedish aristocracy, the wealthy American, and the good-hearted proletarian mother, and because the plot is not as convoluted and contrived as most of Kaiser's others.

With *Nebeneinander* and *Kolportage* Kaiser moved away from his expressionist excesses to a kind of idealistic realism. It is with these plays that he finally conquered Berlin, and they continued to be produced throughout the 1920s. In 1935 the plot of *Kolportage* was used as a scenario for a film titled *Familienparade* (Family Parade). The banning of Kaiser's works two years earlier prevented his name from being mentioned in connection with the film. *Kolportage* experienced a renaissance after 1945.

Gats (1925) focuses on the problem of overpopulation. The Kapitän der Union für weltweiche Kolonalization (captain of the Union for Worldwide Colonization) has been sent out to look for new land for the masses of the unemployed. When he returns he announces that he has found a better solution in the form of a drink called "gats" that induces infertility. In a civilization he discovered in the jungle gats is administered to newlywed couples once a certain population size has been reached. He proposes that the settlers give up the colonization idea in favor of sterilization. But they have dreams of owning land and having families, and they rise in rebellion against the captain and try to kill him. The riots are suppressed by the military, but the captain has to go into hiding. He administers gats to the woman he loves; but when he tells her what he has done, her love turns to hate, and she hands him over to the police. They are not able to protect him and he is lynched by an angry mob. Birth control is a sound idea, but the captain is a radical and megalomanic like most of Kaiser's reformers and does not take human feelings into account. The captain fails to consider that the settlers want children; he also offends the settlers' sense of justice by placing the burden of sterilization on the shoulders of the poor while permitting the rich to have as many children as they wish. Since *Gats* so clearly resembles Kaiser's expressionist plays, most critics compared it unfavorably to these plays. The drama is of interest today, however, because of its topical themes of birth control, overpopulation, and exploitation of the poor by the rich and of the underdeveloped countries by the industrial nations.

In the comedy *Der mutige Seefahrer* (The Brave Seafarer; performed, 1925; published, 1926) three Danish brothers learn that they will inherit the fortune of a schoolmate who has grown rich in America if one of them travels across the Atlantic to visit the dying friend before his end. Lars goes, but his ship is lost with no survivors. The friend regains his health and travels to Denmark to share his wealth with the two surviving brothers and Lars's family. But Lars is alive: he never boarded the ship because of his fear of the ocean. He decides to disappear for good so that his relatives may benefit from the American money. In the end, however, everything turns out happily.

The protagonist in Kaiser's Künstlerdrama *Zweimal Oliver* (Two Olivers, 1926) is an actor who flees the world of reality and takes on a double identity. He is unemployed on the stage but is being paid for playing the lover of a rich woman named Olivia. He cannot tell his insanely jealous wife how he is earning the money. With his problems mounting he withdraws more and more into a dream world. He falls in love with Olivia, and when a rival appears he decides to commit suicide. In reality, however, he shoots his rival and escapes into madness. In an insane asylum he becomes the czar of Russia.

Following the success of *Der Protagonist*, Kaiser asked Weill to write the music for a one-act comic opera titled *Der Zar läßt sich photographieren* (The Czar Has His Picture Taken; published, 1927; performed, 1928). On a visit to Paris the czar goes to a famous photographer to have a portrait of himself made. Meanwhile, a group of Russian conspirators who are looking for a chance to assassinate the ruler have occupied the photographer's studio. One of them, Angèle, takes the photographer's place and hides a gun in the camera. The czar, however, turns out to be a pleasant man and starts flirting with Angèle. She cannot force herself to pull the trigger and is apprehended by the police, who have learned of the plan. Humanity triumphs over politics.

Oktobertag (October Day, 1928; translated as *The Phantom Lover*, 1928) is another of Kaiser's Frauenstücke. Catherine is expecting a child but does not want to reveal the name of the father. In childbirth, however, she screams out the name Jean-Marc Marrien. Her uncle finds the man, a lieutenant from a good family, and questions him about the night Catherine claims to have spent with him. Marrien at first asserts that he does not know her, but she finally convinces him of her love. He agrees to marry her and consider himself the father of the child. The real father, the butcher Leguerche, claims paternity and tries to blackmail the family. Marrien kills him, and he and Catherine retire into a fantasy world.

Kaiser's antimilitaristic play *Die Lederköpfe* (The Leatherheads, 1928) is based on the siege and conquest of Babylon by the Persian King Darius as told by Herodotus. Zopyrus, one of the Persian officers, mutilates himself in such a horrible manner that he has to wear a leather hood at all times. He pretends to desert to the Babylonians, whom he convinces that he has been mistreated by Darius. He distinguishes himself in the defense of the city until he is able to secretly admit the Persians. Darius is so delighted with the success of his "Feldhauptmann" (field commander) that he wants to turn all his soldiers into "Leatherheads." He also promises his daughter to Zopyrus. But she rejects him, telling him that he has forfeited his humanity for military glory. Struck by her accusations, Zopyrus realizes his guilt and sacrifices himself by leading an uprising in which both he and Darius are killed. The play ends with the daughter's appeal to the soldiers to join forces with the townspeople to rebuild the destroyed city. Kaiser's expressionist treatment of Herodotus did not find favor with the audience or the critics; his expressionist pathos, his rather general condemnation of tyranny, and his call for a more humanistic attitude were considered superficial. The Nazis attacked Kaiser for his pacifism. *Die Lederköpfe* played mainly in the provinces.

Hellseherei (Clairvoyance, 1929) is another Frauenstück. With the help of the clairvoyant Sneederhan, Vera wins back the love of her husband, Viktor, an architect who had an affair with a client. In contrast to Catherine in *Oktobertag*, Vera lives in the real world and does not try to flee it. When she is confronted with the truth about her husband's affair by his lover she accepts the facts and takes steps that will prevent further problems. The critics dismissed the play as trite, superficial, and boring.

After finishing the score for *Der Zar läßt sich photographieren*, Weill collaborated with Bertolt Brecht on *Die Dreigroschenoper* (published, 1929; translated as *The Threepenny Opera*, 1964), which became the great Berlin hit of 1928. For his next musical, *Zwei Krawatten*, (Two Neckties, 1929) Kai-

ser turned to Mischa Spolianski, a popular composer. The revue features a love story that includes a winning lottery ticket, an inheritance, and a comparison of Europe and America. Although Jean is successful beyond all dreams in the land of unlimited opportunities and is set to marry Mabel, a rich American heiress, he suddenly remembers Trude, his true love, and returns to her. His loyalty is richly rewarded, since Trude has also just inherited a fortune. The play was a popular success because of the lavish production it received. It featured dancing girls and variety acts and included actors such as Hans Albers and Marlene Dietrich and the dancer Sammy Lewis. The critics did not know whether Kaiser's intent was a parody like *Kolportage* or whether he was simply presenting a Volksstück (folk play). Spolianski's music also came in for criticism, and the lack of political content was noted.

Zwei Krawatten was produced one month before the stock-market crash in 1929. After a peaceful and prosperous interval between 1924 and 1929 the economic situation in Germany deteriorated rapidly, millions of people became unemployed, and Communists and Nazis battled each other in the streets. Kaiser's *Mississippi* (1930), which premiered at sixteen theaters simultaneously, was inspired by a newspaper article which Kaiser had read about a flood that threatened New Orleans; indirectly, it was influenced by the economic crisis. Doris Thompson had divorced her husband, Noel Kehoe, because of his religious fanaticism and his call to Franciscan poverty. Noel's religiously inspired experiment in communal living has been going on for twelve years. He and the other members of the "Bruderschaft der freiwilligen Armut" (Brotherhood of Voluntary Poverty) have rejected greed and materialism and have established a Christian community in the Louisiana countryside, where they grow only enough food for survival. This subsistence farming will lead, Noel hopes, to the starving of the inhabitants of the sinful city of New Orleans and to the overthrow of capitalist institutions in general. When a flood seems to spell doom for New Orleans, Noel is jubilant; but then the governor decides to blow up the dam in the vicinity of the commune to relieve the pressure on the dikes and save the city. Noel tries to sabotage this plan but is shot in the attempt. Dying, he realizes that he had no right to play God. He and Doris, who has rejoined him, perish as regenerated individuals who have rejected violence and reaffirmed their love. The reception of the play was reserved; the

Scene from the premiere of Kaiser's Zwei Krawatten *at the Berliner Theater in 1929*

third act and the ending especially came in for criticism from both ends of the political spectrum, and the transformation of Doris was considered unbelievable. In Oldenburg the Nazis tried to disrupt the performance.

Adolf Hitler was appointed chancellor of the Reich on 30 January 1933. When the Reichstag (parliament building) was set on fire in February the Nazis blamed the Communists; the opposition parties were dissolved and the press was taken over. Since Kaiser had not been politically active his plays could still be produced, and *Der Silbersee* (The Silver Lake; published, 1933) premiered on 18 February 1933 simultaneously in Leipzig, Erfurt, and Magdeburg. In *Der Silbersee* Kaiser alludes pointedly to contemporary events. The songs, especially, reveal Kaiser's antifascist stance, but his message remains the same: the individual must be renewed before society can be changed. The policeman Olim and the unemployed Severin overcome their prejudices and try to help each other. When they are cheated out of their homes and money by two ruthless aristocrats they see no escape other than drowning themselves. But when they reach the Silver Lake they find it frozen over, and they conclude that they are meant to remain alive and continue

their struggle. They wander off into the mist over the lake into an unclear future.

The Magdeburg production was attacked by the Nazis, and Kaiser was notified on 5 May that he had been expelled from the Prussian Academy of Arts. When he approached Gustaf Gründgens, the new director of the Berlin Staatliches Schauspielhaus (state playhouse), about possible productions of his works he was rebuffed by Gründgens's superior, Joseph Goebbels, the minister of propaganda and public enlightenment. Kaiser went into "inner exile" at his home in Grünheide, where he continued to write. Two of his plays were produced in Vienna in 1935 and 1936, but his royalties were meager.

Adrienne Ambrossat (performed, 1935; published, 1972) is based on a story by Guy de Maupassant. Adrienne tries to hide the loss of a borrowed pearl necklace; the truth is revealed when a man with whom she has had an affair comes looking for her. Her husband almost leaves her, but when she is released from prison he is waiting for her so that they may start a new life together. The afflictions they had to endure are a trial from which their love emerges stronger and purer than before. While the Vienna production, with a star-studded cast including Paula Wessely and Ernst Deutsch, was a success, the play itself was criticized for its contrived plot and stilted dialogue.

In the comedy *Das Los des Ossian Balvesen* (The Lottery Ticket of Ossian Balvesen; performed, 1936; published, 1972) Ossian convinces Glynn that he, Ossian, has a moral right to a winning lottery ticket because he had played the number for twenty-four years, while Glynn only played it this year. Ossian realizes, however, that he will have to give up his career and his happy life-style once he becomes a millionaire. He returns the ticket to Glynn, who sends it back to Ossian; he does not want the money, either. It ends up in the wastebasket. Ossian and Glynn are not well differentiated; they act in a similar manner and even use the same arguments in refusing the money. Nevertheless, the play was received favorably when it was produced in Vienna in 1936.

Agnete (performed, 1949; published, 1972), written in 1935, is a Frauenstück. When Heinrich returns from a prisoner-of-war camp in Siberia he learns that he is the father of Agnete's child, which was conceived during Agnete's visit to him in the hospital; Heinrich, in a feverish delirium, did not know that he was making love to the sister of his fiancée, Lena. Agnete had gone there to tell him of Lena's death. Agnete's husband, Stefan, knows that he is not the child's father but loves the boy as if he were his own. When Heinrich demands that Agnete and his child go with him to start a new life in Chile, Stefan is willing to let his wife go but not his son. Unable to leave the boy behind, Agnete stays with her husband, and Heinrich leaves alone. The child represents hope for a better world.

Der Gärtner von Toulouse (The Gardener of Toulouse; published, 1938; performed, 1945), another Frauenstück, has great similarities to *Der Brand im Opernhaus* and *Das Frauenopfer* with their male protagonists who fanatically protect their ideal of female purity. The gardener François marries Janine to obtain a position with Mrs. Teophot; he does not know that his wife once worked in a brothel owned by his new employer. When Mrs. Teophot, after seducing François, tells him about his wife's past, he strangles her. Then he forces his wife to accept the blame for the murder since he believes that she can never atone for her sinful life. François is afraid of his sensuality, which he tries to hide by condemnation and punishment; he shows no sympathy for his wife, who had been forced into prostitution by dire necessity. He ♦n only live in an ideal

Charcoal drawing of Kaiser in 1930 by Joachim Karl Friedrich (Bildarchiv der österreichischen Nationalbibliothek, Vienna)

world, which for him is the greenhouse with its pure plants.

In the summer of 1938 Kaiser traveled to Amsterdam and then to Switzerland. For the remaining seven years of his life he lived in hotels or with friends in Zurich, Montana-Vermala, Morcote, Männedorf, Saint Moritz, and Ascona. Until 1941 he tried to procure a visa for the United States; although his application was supported by Albert Einstein and Thomas Mann, his attempt was not successful.

In *Pferdewechsel* (Changing Horses; published, 1972) written in 1938, the disillusioned Napoleon is on his way into exile on Elba when Marie Roux, the widow of one of his soldiers who perished in Russia, convinces him that he must not succumb to despair since it is not the fame he won in battle but his greatness in defeat that counts. He will remain a model for his followers, and his soldiers, including her husband, will not have died in vain; his creative genius will continue to change humanity for the better. Nietzsche's ideas still held such sway over Kaiser that he did not see the contradiction between the glorification of the great leader and his expressionist belief in equality.

The Künstlerdrama *Der Schuß in die Öffentlichkeit* (The Shot into the Public; published, 1939; performed, 1949) is a detective story set in London. The writer Alan Flanagan has been found shot to death in the woods. The first suspect is his publisher, Unwin, who is in financial difficulties because of huge advances he has made to Flanagan. He was also jealous of Flanagan because the writer was paying too much attention to Unwin's young wife, Helen. After a meeting he had accompanied Flanagan on a walk through the very woods where his body was later found. To top it all off, a gun is found in his possession. As it turns out, however, the murderer is Unwin's bookkeeper, Burns, who had learned about the financial problems of his employer and feared that a bankruptcy would cost him his job; he hoped that the sensational murder would increase the sales of Flanagan's books. He did not commit the murder for selfish reasons but to help his ailing wife. Now that Flanagan's books have become best-sellers, Unwin assures Burns that he will assume all financial responsibilities for his wife. Burns then gladly accepts his punishment.

In Switzerland Kaiser could be more outspoken in his criticism of the Nazis and their allies, the Japanese. In *Der Soldat Tanaka* (Private Tanaka, 1940) the title character is an enthusiastic soldier who venerates the emperor until he finds his sister in a brothel; his parents had sold her to pay the taxes on their home. In a rage, he kills her and his sergeant, who had asked for her services. Condemned to death, he is told that he will be pardoned because of his excellent military record if he begs the emperor for mercy. But Tanaka demands that the emperor apologize to him: he has recognized that the government can only support an army by enslaving the rest of the population, and he knows that some sections of society profit from war while others are exploited. The shots of the execution end the play. *Der Soldat Tanaka* was produced at the Zurich Schauspielhaus, which served as a home for the plays of exiled German dramatists during the Third Reich. The production was successful but was discontinued because of a protest by the Japanese embassy.

Rosamunde Floris (published, 1940; performed, 1953) is yet another of Kaiser's Frauenstücke. Rosamunde and William had a three-

week love affair and then went on with their separate lives. When Rosamunde learns that she is pregnant she tries to seduce Erwin so that she will have a father for her child, but he falls to his death trying to escape from her. She then confronts his family, claiming that she is expecting his child, and his brother, Bruno, breaks off his engagement to marry her. When Bruno's former fiancée finds out who the real father of the child is, Rosamunde kills her and Bruno. Finally she smothers her child because it has begun to look like its father. Now the secret of her pure love for William is safe forever. With the strength of this freedom Rosamunde confesses to a murder she did not commit—that of Erwin—and is sentenced to death. She lives and dies for a subjective reality with its own laws.

In the Frauenstück *Alain und Elise* (Alain and Elise; published, 1940; performed, 1954) Elise, the wife of the wealthy industrialist Dapperre, sits for the painter Alain. Inspired by her beauty he creates a masterpiece and is so elated that he refuses to accept payment for the painting. Elise believes that he has fallen in love with her, and she loves him in return. When she tells Alain about her love he admits that he does not share her feelings. The scorned Elise tells her husband that Alain had kissed her during the painting sessions. He invites Alain to their home and confronts him with the accusation in the presence of Elise. Elise shoots her husband and hands the weapon to Alain, who is arrested and tried for murder. During Elise's testimony Alain realizes that he is responsible for her action since he had aroused her feelings for him. He takes on this responsibility and accepts his life sentence. Like Rosamunde Floris, he finds a new freedom in this acceptance of guilt. He will be deported to Devil's Island, where he will transmute his suffering into art that will save the world. The complicated and illogical plot of this drama is hard to follow, and the paradox of how Alain can save the world by leaving it remains unsolved. The audience is asked to believe that a feeling which originates from the basest of crimes should suddenly acquire a high moral value.

In *Klawitter* (performed, 1949; published, 1972), written in 1940, Ernst Hoff, a proscribed author, has submitted a new play to the Staatstheater under the pseudonym Klawitter. When the play is accepted Hoff has to produce the author, and he is lucky to find one Klawitter in the telephone book. The vulgar and greedy Klawitter is only too happy to cooperate with

Hoff, since he will earn a substantial amount of money. The play is a hit, but when Hoff asks Klawitter for his share of the royalties he is rebuffed. To add insult to injury, his wife becomes Klawitter's mistress. Sitting in a café, the dejected Hoff becomes furious when he hears on the radio that the prize for the best play of the year is presented to Klawitter. He hurls his cup at the radio and is arrested for sabotaging state-approved cultural activities. Contrary to Kaiser's intention, the play does not focus on the policies and actions of the Nazi party; although Hoff's desperate financial situation is certainly the result of Nazi censorship of his plays, he is betrayed by Klawitter, who is not a Nazi. Also, the audience never learns about Hoff's political views or why he is opposed to the Nazis.

Hero worship like that of Marie Roux in *Pferdewechsel* is condemned in Kaiser's *Napoleon in New Orleans* (performed, 1950; published, 1966), written in 1941. Kaiser constructed his play around a legend according to which Napoleon had spent his last years in New Orleans after being abducted from Saint Helena, where a double took his place; according to this legend his grave can still be seen in Louisiana. In actuality, the Napoleon House in the French Quarter was the home of the mayor, Nicholas Girod, an admirer of Napoleon who planned an expedition to Saint Helena to liberate the emperor and bring him to New Orleans; Napoleon died before Girod could realize his plans. The protagonist of Kaiser's play, Baron Dergan, is modeled on Girod. His infatuation with Napoleon is exploited by a criminal gang that sells him fake relics and arranges for Napoleon's "abduction." One of the members then impersonates Napoleon and tells Dergan that he is going to establish a new empire on American soil. He also marries Dergan's daughter Gloria, who adores the emperor. By telling Dergan that he needs weapons for his new army, the false Napoleon swindles him out of all his wealth. When news reaches New Orleans that the real Napoleon has died, Dergan is cruelly awakened from his dreams of conquest and glory. He realizes, however, that he has been justly punished for his unquestioning hero worship. He perishes with his daughter in the flames of his house, which he has set afire. In his last moments he has a vision of a democratic and peaceful America that will be a model for all nations. When Kaiser wrote the play he anticipated immigrating to the United States, where it would be translated and staged. But just as it was completed the United States entered the war and the borders were closed.

In the Künstlerdrama *Das gordische Ei* (The Gordian Egg; performed, 1958; published, 1972), written in 1941, the playwright Abel Oberon and his daughter Marjorie are forced to leave London because Oberon's publisher is demanding a new play that Oberon is unable to write. After hiding out in Scotland they return home to find that a new drama under Oberon's name is playing with great success. Oberon discovers that two students are the authors, but they do not claim the play as their own nor do they ask for royalties. They are idealists whose reward is the enjoyment the drama brings to the audience. Through this lucky turn of events Oberon is freed of all his debts.

Der englische Sender (The English Broadcast; performed, 1947; published, 1972), written in 1941, is based on Heinrich von Kleist's play *Der zerbrochene Krug* (1811; translated as *The Broken Jug*, 1939). Like the village judge Adam, the corrupt and lecherous protagonist of Kleist's comedy, the local Nazi leader Schmutz (Dirt) uses his official position to seduce innocent girls. But Schmutz is such a grotesque figure that he cannot be taken seriously by the audience, and the satire is so heavy-handed that all credibility is lost. When Schmutz learns that some villagers have listened to an English broadcast he threatens dire consequences unless Alma agrees to marry him. To protect the villagers, Alma goes along with Schmutz's plans; but during the wedding his former wife appears and exposes him as a swindler, thief, and bigamist, and he flees into the woods. The play was not produced onstage but was broadcast by the German Programme of the British Broadcasting Corporation.

In *Die Spieldose* (The Music Box; performed, 1943; published, 1966) Paul Chaudraz and his father, Pierre, are poor peasants in Brittanny who wrest a meager living from the soil. Paul has just married Noelle when World War II erupts and he is called up. In the turmoil of the defeat of the French army he is reported killed, and Pierre and Noelle can only find solace by marrying each other. When their child is born they look on it as a replacement for their beloved Paul. But Paul has survived and returns from a German prisoner-of-war camp. When he is told about the marriage he becomes so jealous that he kills his own father. Noelle is horrified and rejects him. Paul now recognizes the enormity of his crime; when he hears that the Germans will execute ten hostages for one of their soldiers killed by a guerrilla unless the killer surrenders, he turns himself in so that the hostages may go free.

The title of *Das Floß der Medusa* (performed, 1945; published, 1963; translated as *The Raft of the Medusa*, 1962) was inspired by Théodore Géricault's painting, but the plot is based on an actual incident in which a ship carrying children from the bombed cities of England to Canada in September 1940 was torpedoed; only a few of the children survived. Allan and Ann are the leaders of the children in the lifeboat. While Allan does everything he can to raise their spirits and improve their chances of survival, Ann insinuates that they will never be rescued because there are thirteen children in the boat. With this evil omen she terrifies the other children and persuades them to throw the youngest child overboard while she distracts Allan so that he cannot interfere. Because of Ann's ability to corrupt the other children, Allan can no longer believe in human goodness: the world is thoroughly immoral, and children are no better than their parents. Allan refuses to be rescued and is shot when a German plane strafes the boat. The play shows marked similarities to *Die Bürger von Calais*: there is a number game, a version of a communion, a lottery, and the self-sacrifice of the protagonist while the other characters are saved. But while the six volunteers in *Die Bürger von Calais* had become regenerated human beings, the rescued children are murderers just like their warring parents.

The last three plays Kaiser wrote are based on classical Greek mythology and are written in blank verse. In *Zweimal Amphitryon* (Twice Amphitryon; performed, 1944; published, 1948) Amphitryon is more interested in power and glory than in his beautiful bride, Alkmene, and he makes war on his peaceful neighbors. Alkmene prays to Zeus to bring him back to her. Zeus is moved by the purity of Alkmene's love and visits her in the form of Amphitryon. Afterward he tells her that she will bear a divine son, Herakles, who will cleanse the earth and establish the Olympic games for the purpose of peaceful contests of strength. Amphitryon must work as a goatherd until he is purified.

In *Pygmalion* and *Bellerophon*, both of which were published in 1948 and performed in 1953, Kaiser is concerned with a topic that took on ever greater importance for him toward the end of his life, the loneliness of the artist. The protagonist of *Pygmalion* is a sculptor; when Athene grants him a wish he asks that his statue, Chaire, come to life. Chaire is a creation of Pygmalion's spirit and embodies perfect aesthetic beauty, and he has fallen in love with her. When Pygmalion and Chaire become lovers in the real world, Pygmalion is sued by his fiancée, Korinna, and by Konon, who had originally ordered the statue. When the jury hears Pygmalion's story they believe he is joking, and he is released; but the judge decides that Chaire must be returned to the brothel from which the people believe she came. Pygmalion is about to commit suicide when Athene intervenes again: she turns Chaire back into stone and returns the statue to Pygmalion. Konon claims her as the work of art he has paid for, and Pygmalion follows Korinna to Korinth. He has come to understand that his works spring not from happiness but from suffering. Pygmalion marries Korinna, but she is not his true love; he remains a lonely man who creates his art to protect himself from life's realities.

The theme of the loneliness of the artist is carried to its logical conclusion in *Bellerophon*. The title character is a musician who was raised by Apollo, the god of music. When he prefers his music over the charms of Anteia, the wife of King Proitos, her pride is hurt. To get revenge, she tells her husband that Bellerophon tried to seduce her. The king sends the young man to his governor, Jobates, with a sealed message that contains instructions to kill him. But Jobates does not immediately look at the letter Bellerophon presents to him. Bellerophon meets Jobates' daughter, Myrtis, a wonderful singer, and falls in love with her. Marriage arrangements are being made when her father finally reads the king's message. He sends Bellerophon to a cave where a dragon lives, but Bellerophon kills the monster. He then searches for his fiancée on his winged horse, Pegasus, and they are united. He and Myrtis are placed among the stars where he will delight the gods with his music. Thus Bellerophon overcomes the difficulties of the artist's life by leaving this world altogether.

In his final years in exile in Switzerland, Kaiser worked on novels that were never completed and wrote lyrical poems. As he did in his last plays, Kaiser bemoans in these poems the fate of the poet in a hostile world.

Following the defeat of the Third Reich in May 1945 Kaiser made plans to found a publishing house in Germany to be called Lenz (Spring). As the newly elected honorary president of the Association of Exiled German Writers in Switzerland, Kaiser intended to promote the work of returning German antifascist writers. But before he could realize his plans he died on Monte Verità in Ascona on 4 June 1945 of an embolism caused by an infected tooth. His body was cremated on 6 June at Lugano, and his urn was interred in the cemetery at Morcote on Lake Lugano.

Letters:

Briefe, edited by Gesa M. Valk (Frankfurt am Main, Berlin & Vienna: Propyläen, 1980);

Georg Kaiser in Sachen Georg Kaiser: Briefe 1916-1933, edited by Valk (Leipzig & Weimar: Kiepenheuer, 1989).

Interviews:

Karl Marilaun, "Gespräch mit Georg Kaiser," *Neues Wiener Journal*, 21 December 1921, p. 4;

Iwan Goll, "Georg Kaiser über Georg Kaiser," *Das Tagebuch*, 5, no. 17 (1924): 573-574;

Hermann Kasack, "Der Kopf ist stärker als das Blut," *Berliner Börsen-Courier*, 25 December 1928;

O. K., "Interview mit Georg Kaiser: Ein Autor, der auf seine Stücke nicht neugierig ist," *Neues Wiener Journal*, 30 October 1930, pp. 6-7.

Biography:

Brian J. Kenworthy, *Georg Kaiser* (Oxford: Blackwell, 1957).

References:

Wilfried Adling, "Georg Kaisers Drama *Von morgens bis mitternachts* und die Zersetzung des dramatischen Stils," *Weimarer Beiträge*, 5 (1959): 369-386;

Arnim Arnold, ed., *Interpretationen zu Georg Kaiser* (Munich: Klett, 1980);

Helmut Arntzen, "Wirklichkeit als Kolportage: Zu drei Komödien von Georg Kaiser und Robert Musil," *Deutsche Vierteljahresschrift*, 36 (1962): 544-561;

Renate Benson, *Deutsches expressionistisches Theater: Ernst Toller und Georg Kaiser* (New York: Lang, 1987);

Heinrich Breloer, *Georg Kaisers Drama "Die Koralle": Persönliche Erfahrung und ästhetische Abstraktion* (Hamburg: Lüdke, 1977);

John O. Buffinga, "From 'Bocksgesang' to 'Ziegenlied': The Transformation of a Myth in Georg Kaiser's *Zweimal Amphitryon*," *German Studies Review*, 9 (October 1986): 475-495;

Rudolf Bussmann, *Einzelner und Masse: Zum dramatischen Werk Georg Kaisers* (Kronberg: Scriptor, 1978);

Susan C. Cook, "Der Zar läßt sich photographieren: Weill and Comic Opera," in *A New Orpheus: Essays on Kurt Weill*, edited by Kim H. Kowalke (New Haven: Yale University Press, 1986), pp. 83-101;

Paul Davies, "The Political and Social Aspects of Georg Kaiser's Drama in the Context of Expressionism," *Revue Frontenac Review*, 14 (1985): 314-336;

Horst Denkler, *Georg Kaiser "Die Bürger von Calais": Drama und Dramaturgie* (Munich: Oldenbourg, 1967);

Bernhard Diebold, *Der Denkspieler Georg Kaiser* (Frankfurt am Main: Frankfurter Verlagsanstalt, 1924);

Manfred Durzak, *Das expressionistische Drama: Carl Sternheim—Georg Kaiser* (Munich: Nymphenburger, 1978);

Anna Margarethe Elbe, *Technische und soziale Probleme in der Dramenstruktur Georg Kaisers* (Hamburg: GEG Druckerei, 1959);

Eric Albert Fivian, *Georg Kaiser und seine Stellung im Expressionismus* (Munich: Desch, 1947);

Max Freyhan, *Georg Kaisers Werk* (Berlin: Die Schmiede, 1926);

H. F. Garten, "Georg Kaiser," in *German Men of Letters*, volume 2, edited by Alex Natan (London: Wolff, 1963), pp. 155-172;

Garten, "Georg Kaiser and the Expressionist Movement," *Drama*, 37 (1955): 18-21;

Garten, "Georg Kaiser Re-Examined," in *Essays in German and Dutch Literature*, edited by William Douglas Robson-Scott (London: University of London, 1973), pp. 41-48;

Werner Geifrig, *Georg Kaisers Sprache im Drama des expressionistischen Zeitraums* (Munich: 1968);

Richard C. Helt and John Carson Pettey, "Georg Kaiser's Reception of Friedrich Nietzsche: The Dramatist's Letters and Some Nietzschean Themes in His Works," *Orbis Litterarum*, 38, no. 3, (1983): 215-234;

Peter Uwe Hohendahl, *Das Bild der bürgerlichen Welt im expressionistischen Drama* (Heidelberg: Winter, 1967);

Walter Huder, "Gedenkwort für Georg Kaiser," *Sinn und Form*, 11 (1959): 257-268;

Huder, "Symbol und Perspektive in Georg Kaisers *Schellenkönig*," *Theater und Zeit*, 10 (June 1958): 13-16;

Erwin Ihrig, "*Die Bürger von Calais*: Auguste Rodins Denkmal—Georg Kaisers Bühnenspiel," *Wirkendes Wort*, 11 (1961): 290-303;

Marianne R. Jetter, "Some Thoughts on Kleist's *Amphitryon* and Kaiser's *Zweimal Amphitryon*," *German Life and Letters*, 13 (1960): 178-189;

Robert Alston Jones, "German Drama on the American Stage: The Case of Georg Kaiser," *German Quarterly*, 37 (January 1964): 17-25;

Klaus Kändler, "Georg Kaiser, der Dramatiker des neuen Menschen," *Wissenschaftliche Zeitschrift der Karl-Marx-Universität Leipzig: Gesellschafts- und Sprachwissenschaftliche Reihe*, 7 (1957/1958): 297-303;

Robert Kauf, "Georg Kaiser hundert Jahre," *Neue Deutsche Hefte*, 159 (1978): 663-666;

Kauf, "Georg Kaiser's Social Tetralogy and the Social Ideas of Walther Rathenau," *PMLA*, 77 (1962): 311-317;

Kauf, "*Schellenkönig*: An Unpublished Early Play by Georg Kaiser," *Journal of English and German Philology*, 55 (1956): 439-450;

Brian J. Kenworthy, *Georg Kaiser* (Oxford: Blackwell, 1957);

Rolf Kieser, *Erzwungene Symbiose: Thomas Mann, Robert Walser, Georg Kaiser und Bertolt Brecht im Schweizer Exil* (Bern: Haupt, 1984);

Hugo F. Koenigsgarten, *Georg Kaiser: Mit einer Bibliographie von Alfred Loewenberg* (Potsdam: Kiepenheuer, 1928);

Koenigsgarten, "Georg Kaiser: The Leading Playwright of Expressionism," *German Life and Letters*, 3 (1939): 195-205;

Rudolf Koester, "Kaiser's *Von morgens bis mitternachts* and Hesse's *Klein und Wagner*: Two Explorations of Crime and Human Transcendence," *Orbis Litterarum*, 24 (1969): 237-250;

Silvia Konecny, "Georg Kaisers *König Hahnrei*," *Zeitschrift für deutsche Philologie*, 97 (1976): 27-35;

Manfred Kuxdorf, *Die Suche nach dem Menschen im Drama Georg Kaisers* (Bern & Frankfurt am Main: Lang, 1971);

Eberhard Lämmert, "Georg Kaiser: *Die Bürger von Calais*," in *Das deutsche Drama vom Barock bis zur Gegenwart: Interpretation*, edited by Benno von Wiese, volume 2 (Düsseldorf: 1960), pp. 305-324;

Rex W. Last, "Kaiser, Rodin and the *Burghers of Calais*," *Seminar*, 5 (Spring 1969): 36-44;

Last, "Kaiser's *Bürger von Calais* and the Drama of Expressionism," in *Periods in German Litera-*

ture II: Texts and Contexts (London: Wolff, 1968), pp. 247-264;

Last, "Symbol and Struggle in Georg Kaiser's *Die Bürger von Calais*," *German Life and Letters*, 19 (1966): 201-209;

Ludwig Lewin, *Die Jagd nach dem Erlebnis: Ein Buch über Georg Kaiser* (Berlin: Die Schmiede, 1926);

Leroy Marion Linick, *Der Subjektivismus im Werke Georg Kaisers* (Strasbourg: Heitz, 1938);

Ian C. Loram, "Georg Kaiser's *Der Soldat Tanaka*: 'Vollendeter Woyzeck'?," *German Life and Letters*, 10 (1956): 43-48;

Loram, "Georg Kaiser's Swan Song: Griechische Dramen," *Monatshefte*, 49 (1957): 23-30;

Arnold Meese, *Die theoretischen Schriften Georg Kaisers* (Fürstenfeldbruck: Loher, 1965);

Willibald Omanowski, *Georg Kaiser und seine besten Bühnenwerke: Eine Einführung* (Berlin, Leipzig & Vienna: Siedentop, 1922);

Wolfgang Paulsen, *Georg Kaiser: Die Perspektiven seines Werkes. Mit einem Anhang: Das dichterische und essayistische Werk Georg Kaisers. Eine historisch-kritische Bibliographie* (Tübingen: Niemeyer, 1960);

Holger A. Pausch und Ernest Reinhold, eds., *Georg Kaiser: Studien zu seinem Werk und Leben* (Berlin: Agora, 1980);

Klaus Petersen, *Georg Kaiser: Künstlerbild und Künstlerfigur* (Bern, Frankfurt am Main & Munich: Lang, 1976);

Petersen, "Georg Kaisers *Rosamunde Floris*: Der Engel mit dem Flammenschwert," *Seminar*, 13 (1977): 13-28;

Petersen, "Mythos in Gehalt und Form der Dramen Georg Kaisers," *Neophilologus*, 60 (April 1976): 266-279;

Petersen, "Das Wort tötet das Leben!: Möglichkeiten des Künstlertums in Georg Kaisers Drama *Die Flucht nach Venedig*," *Colloquia Germanica*, 11, no. 2 (1978): 149-165;

Herbert W. Reichert, "Nietzsche and Georg Kaiser," *Studies in Philology*, 61 (January 1964): 85-108;

Steven P. Scher, "Georg Kaiser's *Von morgens bis mitternachts*: Isolation as Theme and Artistic Method," *Theatrum Mundi: Essays on German Drama and German Literature Dedicated to Harold Lenz on his Seventieth Birthday, September 11, 1978*, edited by Edward R. Haymes, Houston German Studies, 2 (Munich: Fink, 1980): 125-135;

H. J. Schueler, "The Symbolism of Paradise in Georg Kaiser's *Von morgens bis mitternachts*," *Neophilologus*, 68, no. 1 (1984): 98-104;

Ernst Schürer, *Georg Kaiser* (New York: Twayne, 1971);

Schürer, *Georg Kaiser und Bertolt Brecht: Über Leben und Werk* (Frankfurt am Main: Athenäum, 1971);

Schürer, *Georg Kaiser "Von morgens bis mitternachts": Erläuterungen und Dokumente* (Stuttgart: Reclam, 1975);

Schürer, "Verinnerlichung, Protest und Resignation: Georg Kaisers Exil," in *Die Deutsche Exilliteratur, 1933-1945*, edited by Manfred Durzak (Stuttgart: Reclam, 1973): 263-281;

Adolf Munke Schütz, *Georg Kaisers Nachlass: Eine Untersuchung über die Entwicklungslinien im Lebenswerk des Dichters* (Basel: Frobenius, 1949);

Leroy R. Shaw, "Georg Kaiser auf der deutschsprachigen Bühne 1945-1960," *Maske und Kothurn*, 9 (1963): 68-86;

Shaw, "Georg Kaiser (1878-1945): A Bibliographical Report," *Texas Studies in Literature and Language*, 3 (1961): 399-408;

Shaw, *The Playwright and Historical Change* (Madison, Milwaukee & London: University of Wisconsin Press, 1970);

Richard William Sheppard, "Unholy Families: The Oedipal Psychopathology of Four Expressionist Ich-Dramen," *Orbis Litterarum*, 41, no. 4 (1986): 355-383;

M. Helena Goncalves da Silva, *Character, Ideology, and Symbolism in the Plays of Wedekind, Sternheim, Kaiser, Toller, and Brecht* (London: Modern Humanities Research Association, 1985);

Wilhelm Steffens, *Georg Kaiser* (Velber: Friedrich, 1969);

G. C. Tunstall, "The Turning Point in Georg Kaiser's Attitude towards Friedrich Nietzsche,"

Nietzsche Studien: Internationales Jahrbuch für die Nietzsche-Forschung, 14 (1985): 314-336;

Peter K. Tyson, "Georg Kaiser's Breakthrough as an Expressionist in Berlin," *Neophilologus*, 67, no. 4 (1983): 575-581;

Tyson, *The Reception of Georg Kaiser 1915-1945*, 2 volumes (New York, Bern, Frankfurt am Main & Nancy: Lang, 1984);

Ulrich Weisstein, "Was noch kein Auge je gesehen: A Spurious Cranach in Georg Kaiser's *Von Morgens bis Mitternachts*," in *The Comparative Perspective on Literature: Approaches to Theory and Practice*, edited by Clayton Koelb and Susan Noakes (Ithaca, N.Y.: Cornell University Press, 1988), pp. 233-259;

Edith Welliver, "Georg Kaiser's *Kolportage*: Commentary on Class in the Weimar Republic," *Germanic Review*, 64 (Spring 1989): 73-78;

Peter von Wiese, "Georg Kaiser: *Pygmalion*," in *Das deutsche Drama*, volume 2 (Düsseldorf: 1960): 325-337;

Rhys W. Williams, "Culture and Anarchy in Georg Kaiser's *Von morgens bis mitternachts*," *Modern Language Review*, 83 (April 1988): 364-374;

Andrzej Wirth, "Kaiser und Witkiewicz: Der Expressionismus und seine Zurücknahme," in *Aspekte des Expressionismus*, edited by Paulsen (Heidelberg: Stiehm, 1968), pp. 153-164.

Papers:

Manuscripts, letters, and other materials by and about Georg Kaiser are in the Georg Kaiser Archives at the Akademie der Künste (Academy of Arts), Berlin. Duplicates of these materials are in the Georg Kaiser Archives at the University of Alberta, Edmonton, and at the University of Texas, Austin.

Heinar Kipphardt

(8 March 1922 - 18 November 1982)

Erich P. Hofacker, Jr.
University of Michigan

PLAY PRODUCTIONS: *Entscheidungen*, Berlin, Deutsches Theater, 15 March 1952;

Shakespeare dringend gesucht, Berlin, Deutsches Theater, 28 June 1953;

Der Aufstieg des Alois Piontek, Berlin, Deutsches Theater, 12 February 1956;

Die Stühle des Herrn Szmil, Wuppertal, Städtische Bühnen, 29 January 1961;

Der Hund des Generals, Munich, Münchner Kammerspiele, 2 April 1962;

In der Sache J. Robert Oppenheimer, Munich, Münchner Kammerspiele; Berlin, Freie Volksbühne, 11 October 1964;

Joel Brand: Die Geschichte eines Geschäfts, Munich, Münchner Kammerspiele, 5 October 1965;

Die Nacht in der der Chef geschlachtet wurde, Stuttgart, Württembergisches Staatstheater, 15 May 1967;

Die Soldaten, Düsseldorf, Düsseldorfer Schauspielhaus, 17 August 1968;

Sedanfeier: Montage aus Materialien des 70er Krieges, Munich, Münchner Kammerspiele, 2 September 1970;

März, ein Künstlerleben, Düsseldorf, Düsseldorfer Schauspielhaus, 11 October 1980;

Bruder Eichmann, Munich, Residenztheater, 21 January 1983.

BOOKS: *Shakespeare dringend gesucht: Ein satirisches Lustspiel in drei Akten* (Berlin: Henschel, 1954);

Der Aufstieg des Alois Piontek: Eine tragikomische Farce (Berlin: Henschel, 1956);

Der Hund des Generals: Schauspiel (Frankfurt am Main: Suhrkamp, 1963); edited by W. E. Anderson (London: Harrap, 1969);

Die Ganovenfresse (Munich: Rütten & Loening, 1964);

In der Sache J. Robert Oppenheimer: Ein szenischer Bericht (Frankfurt am Main: Suhrkamp, 1964); translated by Ruth Speirs as *In the Matter of J. Robert Oppenheimer* (London: Methuen, 1967; New York: Hill & Wang, 1969);

Joel Brand: Die Geschichte eines Geschäfts (Frankfurt am Main: Suhrkamp, 1965);

Die Soldaten: Nach Jacob Michael Reinhold Lenz (Frankfurt am Main: Suhrkamp, 1968);

Stücke, 2 volumes (Frankfurt am Main: Suhrkamp, 1973-1974);

März: Roman (Munich: Bertelsmann, 1976);

Leben des schizophrenen Dichters Alexander M: Ein Film (Berlin: Wagenbach, 1976);

Angelsbrucker Notizen: Gedichte (Munich: Bertelsmann, 1977);

Der Mann des Tages und andere Erzählungen (Munich: Bertelsmann, 1977);

Zwei Filmkomödien: Die Stühle des Herrn Szmil; Die Nacht in der der Chef geschlachtet wurde (Königstein: Athenäum, 1979);

März, ein Künstlerleben: Schauspiel (Cologne: Kiepenheuer & Witsch, 1980);

Traumprotokolle (Munich: AutorenEdition, 1981);

Bruder Eichmann: Schauspiel (Reinbek: Rowohlt, 1983).

OTHER: " 'Fremd stirbt ein junger Bruder': Späte Erkenntnis," in *Neue deutsche Erzähler*, edited by Michael Tschesno-Hell (Berlin: Aufbau, 1951), pp. 337-362;

"Alphabet des Schmerzes," "In unseren Schlachthöfen zu singen," "Meine Saison im Gefängnis einer verlorenen Zeit," in *Neue deutsche Lyrik* (Berlin: Aufbau, 1951), pp. 61-73;

Deutsche Theater: Bericht über 10 Jahre (Berlin: Henschel, 1957), contributions by Kipphardt;

HAP Grieshaber, *Engel der Psychiatrie*, woodcuts with text by Kipphardt (Düsseldorf: Claassen, 1976);

"Zergliederung einer Verstörung," in *kontext 2*, edited by Marlies Gerhardt and Gert Mattenklott (Munich: Bertelsmann, 1978), pp. 134-146;

"Rapp, Heinrich," in *An zwei Orten zu leben*, edited by Vera Botterbusch and Klaus Konjetzky (Königstein: Athenäum AutorenEdition, 1979), pp. 59-69;

Heinar Kipphardt (photograph by Isolde Ohlbaum)

Aus Liebe zu Deutschland: Satiren auf Franz Josef Strauss, edited by Kipphardt (Munich: AutorenEdition, 1980);

Vom deutschen Herbst zum bleichen deutschen Winter: Ein Lesebuch zum Modell Deutschland, edited by Kipphardt and Roman Ritter (Munich: AutorenEdition, 1981).

SELECTED PERIODICAL PUBLICATIONS—
UNCOLLECTED: "Mitten in diesem Jahrhundert: Gedicht," *Aufbau*, 3, no. 7 (1950): 641;

"Ein Drittel der Erde: Gedicht," *Aufbau*, 4, no. 8 (1951): 748-749;

"Varianten einer Szene," *Theater der Zeit*, 8 (September 1953): 15-23;

"Im Westen wenig Neues: Notizen von einer Reise nach Westdeutschland," *Neue Deutsche Literatur*, 2, no. 11 (1953): 108-115;

"Schreibt die Wahrheit," *Theater der Zeit*, 9, no. 5 (May 1954): 1-5;

"Vom Warencharakter des Wortes," *Wuppertaler Bühnen*, 9 (1961);

"Bruder Eichmann: Protokolle, Materialien," *Kursbuch*, no. 51 (1978): 17-41;

"Die Abweichung hinter Mauern bringen," *Der Spiegel*, 34 (14 April 1980): 231-238;

"Ein Pferd versinkt im Wiesenteich: Ein symbolischer Vorgang, aufgeschrieben von Rapp, Heinrich," *Freibeuter*, no. 3 (1980): 123-124.

The international success of *In der Sache J. Robert Oppenheimer* (1964; translated as *In the Matter of J. Robert Oppenheimer*, 1967) made Heinar Kipphardt a highly regarded writer of documentary drama. In his works in this genre Kipphardt used court records and contemporary social commentaries to convey the substance and ambience of recent judicial hearings of a political nature. His portrayals of persons and circumstances are not meant to be totally objective but to reflect the playwright's own sociopolitical perspective.

Heinrich Mauritius Kipphardt, called Heinar by his parents, was born on 8 March 1922 in Heidersdorf, Silesia (now part of Poland), to Heinrich Kipphardt, a dentist, and Elfriede Kaufmann Kipphardt, a telephone operator. Kipphardt's father's practice was located in neighboring Gnadenfrei, the scene of workers' strikes against industrial mechanization. The boy had a close relationship with his maternal grandmother, who was fond of singing and playing the piano. Within the family he supported his mother against the authoritarianism of his father; he was also accustomed to asserting himself on the playground, and later wrote in his diary: "Prügeleien wurden zu meiner Lieblingsbeschäftigung" (Fighting was my favorite activity). In school he preferred a thrashing by the teacher to practice in penmanship as punishment for misdeeds.

Kipphardt's father, a vociferous anti-Nazi, was sent to the Dürrgoy concentration camp near Breslau in November 1933; later he was sent to Buchenwald. The boy and his mother moved in with his grandmother. Although Kipphardt was able to attend the gymnasium by living with the family of a friend, the social discrimination he experienced as a result of his father's imprisonment made him aware of the impact of political affairs on the life of the average citizen. The choice between obedience to authority and acceptance of personal responsibility for one's conduct would become the central theme in his major dramas.

With the release of Heinrich Kipphardt from Buchenwald in 1937 the family moved to Krefeld in the Rhineland to live with relatives. Denounced in an anonymous letter, the elder Kipphardt was inducted into the army and sent to the front. As a schoolboy, Heinar Kipphardt participated in an amateur theater group. After graduating in 1940 and completing his term of compulsory labor service, he studied medicine in Bonn, Cologne, and Düsseldorf. In 1942 he was drafted and sent to the eastern front. Home on leave early in 1943 he married Lore Hannen. Their daughter Linde was born in March. In 1944 and 1945 Kipphardt received military leaves to study medicine, during which he read works by Georg Wilhelm Friedrich Hegel, Karl Marx, and Friedrich Engels; he also read French and English literature, especially the works of William Shakespeare. When he deserted in 1945 and returned to Krefeld, he found that his father had preceded him there. He resumed his medical studies in Düsseldorf, but, as he had in the gymnasium, he spent much of his time writing and participating in theater groups.

With the collapse of national socialism new dangers seemed to threaten society. Kipphardt was disturbed in particular by the frequent denial of responsibility for the crimes of the past and by the number of people who claimed never to have been members of the Nazi party. Postwar German literature appeared to be taking a sentimental view of the war. Kipphardt rejected the position that art exists apart from life; he believed that an author should not write as a mere observer but should serve as a vehicle of political and social change.

In 1946 Kipphardt passed his preliminary state examination and became a resident physician in the Krefeld city hospital. In the next two years he finished his medical studies. He moved to East Berlin in 1949 and took a position in the psychiatric section of the Charité, the hospital of Humboldt University. He also became editor of the drama section of the *Neue Blätter* (New Pages). In 1950 he became Chefdramaturg (chief drama adviser) at the Deutsches (German) Theater and resigned his position at the Charité. A son, Jan, was born in 1951.

Entscheidungen (Decisions; performed, 1952) depicted typical episodes and individuals from 1933, 1943, 1946, and 1951; scenes set in the latter two years satirized the West German "economic miracle." An episode in which a professor follows orders even though he knows they are given by criminals shows the conflict between obedience to authority and acceptance of personal responsibility. This work was less successful than Kipphardt's later plays, because the characters were types rather than individuals.

In his most successful satiric comedy *Shakespeare dringend gesucht* (Urgently Seeking Shakespeare; performed, 1953; published, 1954), the protagonist, Amadeus Färbel, is not the usual flawless hero of the early socialist stage but an imperfect individual with whom the audience can identify. Färbel is a dramaturge who becomes increasingly annoyed at the poor quality of the manuscripts submitted to him; he says that such plays are like the stomach of a cow, only instead of grass it is ideas and old newsprint that are rechewed. In his frustration Färbel fires the only talented dramatist at his disposal. When he recognizes his error, he tries to rehire the dramatist but must struggle against the opposition of the theater director and the Office for Art, who conceive of the theater as an instrument of moral education and demand ideal stage heroes who are pure and optimistic. Such heroes should not provoke laughter through their mistakes; realistic figures have no place in the theater. This satire showed the predicament of the theater under Stalinistic cultural policies. After changes were made so that the play could pass the East German censors, *Shakespeare dringend gesucht*, with some four hundred performances, became the drama of the season. Kipphardt's achievement was recognized with the National Prize of the

Scene from the premiere of Kipphardt's Shakespeare dringend gesucht *at the Deutsches Theater in Berlin in June 1953,
with Rudolf Wessely as Amadeus Färbel (photograph by A. Pisarek)*

German Democratic Republic.

Der Aufstieg des Alois Piontek (The Rise of
Alois Piontek, 1956), directed by Kipphardt himself at the Deutsches Theater, is a thin and ineffective satire on the West German economic recovery. Piontek, a maker of false diamonds, considers his crimes insignificant in comparison with
the dishonest dealings of people in high places
who prey on the anxiety, stupidity, and poverty
of the masses.

Written in 1957, *Die Stühle des Herrn Szmil*
(The Chairs of Mr. Szmil; performed, 1961; published, 1979) is based on the Russian novel
Twelve Chairs (1928), by Ilya Ilf and Yevgeny
Petrov. The plot concerns the concealment of a
family inheritance in one of thirteen chairs which
were subsequently scattered to the winds. Szmil,
once a baron but now a grouchy official in the socialist society, attempts to track down the valuable chair. The satire demonstrates that there is
no difference between a former member of the
bourgeois society and a citizen living under socialism. *Die Stühle des Herrn Szmil* was intended for performance at the Deutsches Theater but was not released by the censors. It premiered in West
Germany in 1961 but was not successful.

A newspaper campaign in the Socialist

Unity party daily *Neues Deutschland* (New Germany) criticized the repertoire Kipphardt had
announced for the 1959 season at the Deutsches
Theater. His selections and interpretations were
considered bourgeois and too modern; Kipphardt was admonished to produce dialectical propaganda plays. Kipphardt refused to change his
views, and the authorities tried to remove him
from his theater position by offering him a "promotion" to the directorship of the Museum of Hygiene in Dresden. Kipphardt rejected the offer
and moved to Düsseldorf in the Federal Republic, although he hoped an improved political climate would eventually permit his return to East
Berlin. By 1962 the controversy was over, and
Kipphardt was included among the "bourgeois-
humanistic" writers whose works were printed
and performed in East Germany.

Kipphardt received a writer's grant from
the city theater in Düsseldorf for the year
1960-1961 and signed a contract with the
Bertelsmann publishing house. Assured of a liveli-
hood, he moved his family to Munich. On 2
April 1962 his play *Der Hund des Generals* (The
General's Dog; published, 1963) premiered at the
Münchner Kammerspiele (Munich Chamber The-

ater). The play presents fictional events in a documentary manner and employs techniques of the Brechtian theater such as a multileveled stage, a play within a play, and epic presentation. The playwright tried to eliminate an uncritical identification of the audience with the situation depicted and to prevent a judgment based on emotion; instead, following Bertolt Brecht, Kipphardt's goal was critical reflection by the audience. The plot concerns the unnatural response of a general to the death of his dog at the hands of a soldier who was bitten by the animal. In his anger, the general had sent sixty soldiers on a suicidal mission. Brought to trial on a charge of murder seventeen years later, he is acquitted because no direct relationship can be proven between the death of the general's dog and his military orders. The curtain comes down with the statement of the prosecutor, "Rechtsnorm ist Rechtsnorm" (Legal norms are legal norms), followed by the voice of the historian, who views everything in perspective: "Und Mord ist Mord" (And murder is murder).

In 1962 Kipphardt met Pia-Maria Pavel, the wife of Hans Pavel, president of the Drei Masken Verlag (Three Mask Publishing House). Despite the practical and emotional problems involved, they began to share an apartment in 1963.

In Düsseldorf Kipphardt had begun the task of combing through the three thousand typewritten pages of records of the secret investigation of J. Robert Oppenheimer conducted by the American Atomic Energy Commission from 12 April to 14 May 1954. It was under Oppenheimer's direction that the first atomic bomb was produced at the weapons laboratory at Los Alamos, New Mexico; he had remained the senior governmental adviser regarding atomic weapons. But the Atomic Energy Commission had reservations concerning Oppenheimer because in the 1930s his wife and brother had been communists and he himself had been a communist sympathizer. Four years after World War II the Soviet Union had caught up with American atomic research, and in January 1950 the Truman administration decided to develop a hydrogen bomb. The Atomic Energy Commission charged that Oppenheimer had delayed this project and had thus undermined American defense capabilities. The charges were upheld, and Oppenheimer lost his security clearance.

Whereas in *Der Hund des Generals* the moral question could not be decided because of the court's inability to reconstruct the facts, in *In der Sache J. Robert Oppenheimer* Kipphardt shows that the government had a great amount of factual material which it interpreted to its own ends. In both dramas the theatergoer gains the impression that the legal system is in place primarily for the benefit of those in power. Kipphardt selected, condensed, and rearranged the testimony from the thirty-three-day hearing; whereas forty witnesses had appeared before the real board of inquiry, the play presents only six, who represent the viewpoints of others besides themselves. Contrary to Kipphardt's claims, however, research has shown that the transcript of the hearing was not his major source. He appears to have used various popular historical works and to have been more interested in creating a play about the moral dilemma of the scientist in modern times than a factual account of the Oppenheimer hearing.

As the hearing begins, Oppenheimer is full of self-confidence; his connections with communism lie years in the past and have been investigated three times. But his behavior slowly changes, and repeated accusations cause self-doubt to break through the front he has built up. In his efforts at self-defense he must deny having slowed the development of the hydrogen bomb, an action he had considered a moral one. But he is less and less successful in this denial. The dilemma of the scientist who builds a weapon but resists its use becomes ever more apparent.

In der Sache J. Robert Oppenheimer premiered simultaneously under the direction of Erwin Piscator at the Freie Volksbühne (Free People's Stage) in West Berlin and under the direction of Paul Verhoeven at the Kammerspiele in Munich on 11 October 1964 and established Kipphardt's worldwide reputation. Despite the positive image given Oppenheimer, the scientist himself objected to the play. In 1963 he had been rehabilitated, and President John F. Kennedy had presented him with the Enrico Fermi Prize, the highest award conferred by the Atomic Energy Commission. Oppenheimer contended that Kipphardt had made a tragedy out of what had been a farce and, furthermore, had incorrectly interpreted his motives. Oppenheimer also protested the concluding statement his character makes before the commission, which, in fact, had never been made. Some years later, however, the scientist said that he had overreacted and that Kipphardt's play addressed important moral questions. Kipphardt received the

Gerhart Hauptmann Prize in 1964 and the Adolf Grimme Prize in 1965.

In the Third Reich, Adolf Eichmann had directed the transport of European Jews to the concentration camps. Kipphardt's play *Joel Brand: Die Geschichte eines Geschäfts* (Joel Brand: The Story of a Deal, 1965) tells how Brand, an agent of the Jewish organization Waada, negotiated in Budapest with Eichmann for the freedom of one million Jews in exchange for ten thousand trucks for the German army. The Allies, however, rejected the proposal. While the Brand character has few individual traits, Kipphardt's Eichmann is witty, brilliant, and articulate and speaks in five-foot iambic verse. He has a sense of duty and even a code of morality: he requires those who work under him to be above reproach in their financial dealings.

Kipphardt was not permitted to return to East Germany until the Berliner Ensemble announced its intention to perform *In der Sache J. Robert Oppenheimer*; he was permitted to watch rehearsals for its performance at Brecht's old theater on the Schiffbauerdamm. The play opened there on 12 April 1965 in a production considered the equal of Piscator's in West Berlin. In Milan, *In der Sache J. Robert Oppenheimer* was successfully staged using the set of Brecht's *Leben des Galilei* (1955; translated as *The Life of Galileo*, 1963), which had been given shortly before. The Berliner Ensemble also presented the piece as a contemporary example of the "original sin" of Galileo, the scientist who had dared to oppose the common views of his day and had been condemned by the authorities. Using a geological metaphor, a critic said that the case of Oppenheimer was the final morainal deposit of the case of Galileo.

In 1965 Kipphardt and Pia-Maria Pavel purchased an old mill and farmhouse in the village of Angelsbruck, northeast of Munich, where they spent their weekends. The gently rolling landscape there resembles that of Krefeld, Kipphardt's boyhood home. Kipphardt recorded his impressions of Angelsbruck in many poems. At this time he was working on a comedy, *Die Nacht in der der Chef geschlachtet wurde* (The Night the Boss Was Slaughtered; published, 1979), which premiered in Stuttgart in May 1967. A series of satiric and grotesque dream fantasies of the frustrated bank teller Bucksch substitutes for a plot. Bucksch represents the little man who possesses a potential for aggression that, when fueled by prejudice and mobilized by an evil political system, can have dire consequences.

In 1971 Kipphardt and Pia were married; by this time they had two sons, one six years old and the other three. The mill and farmhouse were renovated, and the family, including Kipphardt's parents, moved into the house in the spring of 1972. Kipphardt spent his time in self-examination and in the development of an autobiographical literary figure named Alexander März. The novel *März* appeared in 1976; here März, an author stigmatized by society, becomes schizophrenic and immolates himself in a Christlike crucifixion. His television script *Leben des schizophrenen Dichters Alexander M* (Life of the Schizophrenic Author Alexander M) was published the same year. A stage drama on the same theme, *März, ein Künstlerleben* (März, the Life of an Artist; published, 1980) premiered on 11 October 1980 in Düsseldorf. In this work Kipphardt wished to show that society must accept those who differ from the established norm; individualists should not be forced into one mold. The prologue, which shows a cynical exhibition of schizophrenics before a university psychology class, is the playwright's attempt to make the theatergoer experience the horror to which such persons are subjected. The drama, however, is far less effective than the novel; its techniques are rather conventional, and its characters are schematic and unnatural.

Kipphardt received the Film and Television Prize of the Hartmann Association in 1975 and the Prix Italia, the Literary Prize of the Hanseatic City of Bremen, and a grant for visiting artists from the city of Hamburg in 1976. The former Marxist enjoyed the financial success he had achieved: photographs from the 1950s show the sometime amateur boxer in fine physical condition, but by the late 1970s he had become stout and wore a conspicuous amount of jewelry. A 1980 television documentary showed the pleasure he took in good food, fishing in his own pond, and strolling with his boxer dog.

Adolf Eichmann had been captured in Argentina by Israeli agents in May 1960, tried in Jerusalem, and hanged on 31 May 1962. Kipphardt read more than three thousand pages of informal interviews held before the trial to create the play *Bruder Eichmann* (Brother Eichmann, 1983). A series of scenes gives the substance of conversations Eichmann had with Israeli police officials and other visitors; interspersed are scenes from more recent times in which persons in other situations express attitudes similar to Eichmann's. Several of these scenes are based on a CBS television documentary on preparations by the United States Army for the use of atomic weapons against the Soviet Union; one is taken from a 1982 interview with Israeli general Ariel Sharon in which he demonstrates his lack of concern for the Palestinians; in another, a nightclub comic tells demeaning jokes about Turkish workers in West Germany. When the play premiered at the Residenztheater in Munich in 1983, most of the non-Eichmann scenes were omitted. The title of the play indicates that we are all brothers of Eichmann. By attempting a psychological study of Eichmann and pointing to difficulties he had experienced in his childhood, Kipphardt seems to be seeking understanding for a man who carried out his murderous work in the best of conscience and with a sense of duty.

Kipphardt had completed the manuscript for *Bruder Eichmann* when he was forced to enter the hospital in November 1982. He died on 18 November as the result of cerebral bleeding and was buried at Reichkirchen in Bavaria. He was a member of the PEN-Zentrum of the Federal Republic of Germany and the German Academy of the Performing Arts.

References:

Sigrid Ammer, "Das deutschsprachige Zeitstück der Gegenwart," Ph.D. dissertation, University of Cologne, 1966;

Thomas Anz, "Doch verschlafen hat er nicht," *Frankfurter Allgemeine Zeitung*, 12 December 1981;

Donald A. Borchardt, "The Audience as Jury," *Players*, 50 (Fall-Winter 1974): 10-15;

Helmut M. Braem, "Der Chef als Schlachtvieh," *Die Welt*, 18 May 1967;

Martin Brunkhorst, "Die Rekonstruktion der Vergangenheit bei Heinar Kipphardt," *Deutschunterricht*, 36, no. 3 (1984): 51-59;

Glen R. Cuomo, " '*Vergangenheitsbewältigung*' Through Analogy: Heinar Kipphardt's Last Play *Bruder Eichmann*," *Germanic Review*, 64 (Spring 1989): 58-66;

Helmuth de Haas, "Zwölf Stühle sind zuviel Holz," *Die Welt*, 3 February 1961;

Elisabeth Endres, "Heinar Kipphardts Durchbruch," *Merkur*, 29, no. 339 (1976): 785-788;

Fritz Erpenbeck, "Der Aufstieg des Alois Piontek," *Theater der Zeit*, 11, no. 4 (August 1956): 44-46;

Erpenbeck, "Shakespeare dringend gesucht," *Theater der Zeit*, 8, no. 8 (1953): 57-60;

Anat Freinberg, "The Appeal of the Executive: Adolf Eichmann on the Stage," *Monatshefte*, 78 (1986): 203-214;

Günter Grass, "Abschußlisten," *Süddeutsche Zeitung*, 30 April 1971;

Benjamin Henrichs, "Bruder Eichmann—Vater Eichmann?," *Die Zeit*, 25 February 1983;

Henrichs, "Lehrer ohne Lehre," *Die Zeit*, 26 November 1982;

Georg Hensel, "Kein Mensch wie jeder andere," *Frankfurter Allgemeine Zeitung*, 24 January 1983;

Dieter Hildebrandt, "Die Bombe und die Skrupel," *Frankfurter Allgemeine Zeitung*, 13 October 1964;

Urs Jenny, "Heiner Kipphardt oder: Die Psychologie des faschistischen Menschen," *Theater heute*, 13, special issue (1972): 75-76;

Jenny, "In der Sache Oppenheimer," *Theater heute*, 4 (November 1964): 22-25;

Joachim Kaiser, "Sind Generalslügen dramatisch?," *Süddeutsche Zeitung*, 4 April 1962;

Kaiser, "Von der Brillanz des Bösen," *Süddeutsche Zeitung*, 7 October 1965;

Michael Kowal, "Kipphardt and the Documentary Theater," *American German Review*, 33 (June/July 1967): 20-21;

Barbara Klopke Kuennecke, "Heinrich Kipphardt's *In der Sache J. Robert Oppenheimer*: Sources for the Play," Ph.D. dissertation, University of Oregon, 1976;

Stephan Lohr, " '. . . Literatur, die die Wahrheit nicht beschädigt,' " *Praxis Deutsch*, 11, no. 39 (1980): 54-60;

Clara Menck, "Ein Hund zuviel," *Frankfurter Allgemeine Zeitung*, 14 May 1964;

Peter Morton, "Shakespeare noch immer gesucht," *Die Zeit*, 24 February 1956;

Manfred Nössig, "*In der Sache J. Robert Oppenheimer* von Heinar Kipphardt," *Theater der Zeit*, 20 (16 January 1965): 28-29;

Sjaak Onderdelinden, "Fiktion und Dokument," *Amsterdamer Beiträge zur neueren Germanistik*, 1 (1972): 173-206;

Heinrich Peters and Michael Töteberg, "Heinar Kipphardt," in *Kritisches Lexikon zur deutschsprachigen Gegenwartsliteratur*, edited by Heinz Ludwig Arnold (Munich: Edition text + kritik, 1983);

Marcel Reich-Ranicki, "In der Sache Oppenheimer und Kipphardt," in his *Literarisches*

Leben in Deutschland (Munich: Piper, 1965), pp. 246-250;

Otto F. Riewoldt, *Von Zuckmayer bis Kroetz* (Berlin: Schmidt, 1978), pp. 167-171;

Henning Rischbieter, "Heiner Kipphardt: 'In der Sache Oppenheimer,'" *Theater heute*, 4 (March 1964): 55;

Günther Rühle, "Der Frager," *Frankfurter Allgemeine Zeitung*, 19 October 1982;

Rühle, "Das Leben des schizophrenen Dichters Alexander März," *Frankfurter Allgemeine Zeitung*, 25 June 1975;

Rühle, "Versuche über geschlossene Gesellschaft: Das dokumentarische Drama und die deutsche Gesellschaft," *Theater heute*, 6 (October 1966): 8-12;

Rühle, "Ein Wille und viele Wände," *Frankfurter Allgemeine Zeitung*, 7 October 1965;

Helmut Schödel, "Bruder Eichmann, Bruder Sharon," *Die Zeit*, 28 January 1983;

Hans Schwab-Felisch, "Schade um Lenz," *Frankfurter Allgemeine Zeitung*, 20 August 1968;

Adolf Stock, *Heinar Kipphardt: Mit Selbstzeugnissen und Bilddokumenten dargestellt* (Reinbek: Rowohlt, 1987);

C. Gernd Sucher, "Eine letzte, mißverständliche Warnung," *Süddeutsche Zeitung*, 24 January 1983;

Silvia Volckmann, "Auf ideologischem Schlachtfeld: Heinar Kipphardt, *In der Sache J. Robert Oppenheimer*," in *Geschichte als Schauspiel*, edited by Walter Hinck (Frankfurt am Main: Suhrkamp, 1981), pp. 322-339;

Peter von Becker, "Kein Bruder Eichmann!," *Theater heute*, 24 (March 1983): 1-3.

Papers:
Heinar Kipphardt's papers are in the possession of his former wife, Lore Kipphardt, and his widow, Pia-Maria Kipphardt.

Oskar Kokoschka
(1 March 1886 - 22 February 1980)

Sarah Bryant-Bertail and Susan Russell
University of Washington

PLAY PRODUCTIONS: *Das getupfte Ei*, Vienna, Cabaret Fledermaus, 1907;

Sphinx und Strohmann, Vienna, Cabaret Fledermaus, 29 March 1909;

Mörder, Hoffnung der Frauen, Vienna, Kunstschau, 4 July 1909;

Sphinx und Strohmann, revised version, Zurich, Galerie Dada, 14 April 1917;

Hiob, Dresden, Albert-Theater, 3 June 1917;

Der brennende Dornbusch, Dresden, Albert-Theater, 3 June 1917;

Orpheus and Eurydike, Frankfurt am Main, Frankfurter Schauspielhaus, 2 February 1921;

Mörder Hoffnung der Frauen, music by Paul Hindemith, Stuttgart, Landestheater, 4 June 1921;

Orpheus und Eurydike, music by Ernst Krenek, Kassel, 27 November 1926.

BOOKS: *Die träumenden Knaben* (Vienna: Wiener Werkstatte, 1908);

Dramen und Bilder (Leipzig: Wolff, 1913)—comprises *Hoffnung der Frauen, Sphinx und Strohmann, Schauspiel, Bilderund Zeichnungen*;

Zwanzig Zeichnungen (Berlin: Der Sturm, 1913);

Menschenköpfe (Berlin: Der Sturm, 1916);

Mörder, Hoffnung der Frauen (Berlin: Der Sturm, 1916); translated by Michael Hamburger as *Murderer the Women's Hope*, in *An Anthology of German Expressionist Drama*, edited by Walter H. Sokel (New York: Anchor, 1963), pp. 17-21; translated by J. M. Ritchie as *Murderer Hope of Womankind*, in *Seven Expressionist Plays* (London: Calder & Boyars, 1968), pp. 25-32;

Der brennende Dornbusch: Schauspiel—Mörder Hoffnung der Frauen: Schauspiel (Leipzig: Wolff, 1917);

Hiob: Ein Drama (Berlin: Cassirer, 1917); translated by Sokel and Jacqueline Sokel as *Job*, in *An Anthology of German Expressionist Drama*;

Vier Dramen (Berlin: Cassirer, 1919)—comprises *Orpheus und Eurydike; Der brennende Dornbusch; Mörder, Hoffnung der Frauen; Hiob*;

Oskar Kokoschka in 1909

Der weiße Tiertöter (Vienna: Genossenschaftsverlag, 1920);

Der gefesselte Columbus (Berlin: Gurlitt, 1921);

Variationen über ein Thema (Vienna: Lányi, 1921);

Mörder, Hoffnung der Frauen, music by Paul Hindemith (Mainz: Schott, 1921);

Orpheus und Eurydike, music by Ernst Krenek (Vienna & New York: Universal-Edition, 1925);

Handzeichnungen (Berlin: Rathenau, 1935);

Blumenaquarelle: Sechs mehrfarbige Wiedergaben (Zurich: Rascher, 1948);

Orbis pictus, 2 volumes, texts by Hans Maria Wingler (Salzburg: Galerie Welz, 1951);

Ann Eliza Reed: Erzählung und Lithographien (Hamburg: Maximilien-Gesellschaft, 1952);

Gestalten und Landschaften: Sechs mehrfarbige Wiedergaben (Zurich: Rascher, 1952);

Der Expressionismus Edvard Munchs (Vienna, Linz & Munich: Gurlitt, 1953);

Thermopylae: Ein Triptychon, texts by Kokoschka and Walter Kern (Winterthur: BW-Presse, 1955);

Entwürfe für die Gesamtausstattung zu W. A. Mozarts Zauberflöte, Salzburger Festspiele, 1955/56: Mit einer Einführung von Bernhard Paumgartner, einem Beitrag aus dem Nachlaß von Wilhelm Furtwängler und Bermerkungen des Künstlers (Salzburg: Galerie Welz, 1955); translated by Emil K. Pohl as *Designs of the Stage-Settings for W. A. Mozart's Magic Flute, Salzburg Festival, 1955/56: With an Introduction by Bernhard Paumgartner and a Posthumous Article by Wilhelm Furtwängler, Together with Notes by the Artist* (Salzburg: Galerie Welz, 1955);

Schriften 1907-1955, edited by Wingler (Munich: Langen-Müller, 1956)—includes act 4 of *Comenius*;

Spur im Treibsand: Geschichten (Zurich: Atlantis, 1956); translated by Eithne Wilkins and Ernst Kaiser as *A Sea Ringed with Visions* (London: Thames & Hudson, 1962; New York: Horizon Press, 1962);

Kokoschka, by Kokoschka and Ludwig Goldscheider (Cologne: Phaidon, 1963); translated (London: Phaidon Press, 1963; New York: Phaidon Publishers, 1967);

Handzeichnungen, edited by Ernest Rathenau (New York: Rathenau, 1966);

Kokoschka malt Berlin, edited by Otto Schuster and Willy Fleckhaus (Hamburg: Springer, 1966);

Handzeichnungen 1906-1965, edited by Rathenau (New York: Rathenau, 1966); translated as *Drawings, 1906-1965* (Coral Gables, Fla.: University of Miami Press, 1970);

Bild, Sprache und Schrift: Ein Vortrag, herausgegeben als Sonderdruck zur Feier des l. März 1971 (Frankfurt am Main, 1970);

Griechisches Skizzenbuch, edited by Georg Theodor Ganslmayr (Lucerne: Bucher, 1970);

Mein Leben (Munich: Bruckmann, 1971); translated by David Britt as *My Life* (London: Thames & Hudson, 1974; New York: Macmillan, 1974);

Oskar Kokoschka Handzeichnungen 1906-1969, edited by Rathenau (New York: Rathenau, 1971);

Florentiner Skizzenbuch: Vierundzwanzig Tafeln in der Grösse der Originale, edited by Ganslmayr (Lucerne: Bucher, 1972);

Londoner Ansichten, englische Landschaften (Munich: Brackmann, 1972); translated by Christine Cope as *London Views, British Landscapes* (London: Thames & Hudson, 1972; New York: Praeger, 1973);

Das schriftliche Werk, 4 volumes, edited by Hans Spielmann (Hamburg: Christians, 1973-1976); includes in volume 1, *Comenius* (1972 version); excerpts from act 4 translated by Daria Rothe and Lyn Coffin in *Cross Currents: A Yearbook of Central European Culture: 1983*, edited by Ladislav Matejka and Benjamin Stolz (Ann Arbor: University of Michigan Department of Slavic Languages and Literatures, 1983), pp. 223-230;

Jerusalem Faces (Vaduz: Merlborough Graphics, 1974);

Oskar Kokoschka: Vom Erlebnis im Leben. Schriften und Bilder, edited by Otto Breicha (Salzburg: Galerie Welz, 1976);

Oskar Kokoschka: Frühe Druckgraphik, 1906-1912, edited by Friedrich Welz (Salzburg: Galerie Welz, 1977).

TELEVISION: "Comenius," Zweites Deutsches Fernsehen, 1 March 1975.

OTHER: "A Petition from a Foreign Artist to the Righteous People of Great Britain for a Secure and Present Peace," "On the Nature of Visions," translated by Hedi Medlinger and John Thwaites, in *Kokoschka, Life and Work*, by Edith Hoffman (London: Faber & Faber, 1947), pp. 245-287.

Although Oskar Kokoschka is better known as a painter than a dramatist, his six plays have earned him a place in theater history as one of the earliest writers of German expressionism. His *Mörder, Hoffnung der Frauen* (performed, 1909; published, 1916; translated as *Murderer the Women's Hope*, 1963) is often cited as the first German expressionist play. Intensity of emotion, telegraphic language, color and light symbolism, stark use of gesture and movement, and grotesque imagery, all of which became hallmarks of expressionism, are central to Kokoschka's early plays. Created as gestures of rebellion against what Kokoschka considered the stifling conventions both of the reigning bourgeois morality and of the Viennese Jugendstil (art nouveau) movement, Kokoschka's early plays and paintings aroused much controversy and criticism. In his dramas Kokoschka set out to break down traditional theatrical conventions, particularly the predominant realism, just as in his paintings he sought to break with Jugendstil and its emphasis on decorative stylization.

Kokoschka's father, Gustav Josef Kokoschka, had been a goldsmith in Prague, where he was employed by royalty; but in the economic crisis of the 1880s he was forced to sell his business and move to Vienna, where he survived by repairing watches and selling jewelry. Oskar Kokoschka was born on 1 March 1886 in Pöchlarn, a small town west of Vienna. Since the family was relatively poor, he became a primary breadwinner along with his father and would continue throughout his life to support his two younger siblings and his mother, Maria Romana Loidl Kokoschka. Kokoschka's first play, *Das getupfte Ei* (The Speckled Egg), was performed at the Cabaret Fledermaus in 1907. It was a shadow play performed by puppets with movable limbs made of thin metal sheeting and colored paper; their shadows were projected onto a screen. The text of the play has been lost.

In 1908 Kokoschka enrolled at the School of Arts and Crafts without telling his father, who wanted him to go into a more stable profession. The school's art show of 1908 featured his book *Die träumenden Knaben* (The Dreaming Youths, 1908), an illustrated stream-of-consciousness account of the violent yearnings and poignant frustrations of adolescent sexual desire, and several of his artworks. Although the reviews were not all favorable, the members of the exhibition committee agreed to let Kokoschka stage two plays the next year in the outdoor theater in the garden adjacent to the art museum.

Sphinx und Strohmann (Sphinx and Strawman; published, 1913) and *Mörder, Hoffnung der Frauen* were staged on 4 July 1909. There is little information on this second performance of *Sphinx und Strohmann*, which had already been presented at the Cabaret Fledermaus, but the legend of the shocking effect of the premiere of *Mörder, Hoffnung der Frauen* remains. Kokoschka's description of the event, which appeared in Edith Hoffman's biography, *Kokoschka, Life and Work* (1947), forms the basis for most subsequent accounts. Kokoschka claimed that soldiers in an adjoining barracks, witnessing the violent, erotic, and mysterious actions of the half-naked actors, accompanied by drumbeats, shrill piping, and the fu-

rious catcalls of the audience, stormed the stage; a riot ensued between the soldiers and the audience that required the interference of the police. None of the major Viennese papers reports such a scene, however; the review in the *Neues Wiener Journal* (New Viennese Journal) mentions only the infectious hilarity that greeted the performance, and the *Neue Freie Presse* (New Free Press) observes that the audience greeted the drama with sympathetic good humor.

Kokoschka wrote four slightly different versions of the play, but the plot remains the same. The set is a tower with a large barred door under a night sky. A warrior in blue armor with a bandaged head enters, followed by a group of savage-looking men. A woman in red appears, followed by her attendants. The actors' bodies are painted to depict nerves, muscles, and tendons. The woman is fascinated by the warrior and senses his desire for her. Despite warnings from one of her attendants, she converses with him. The warrior has her branded by one of his men; she wounds him with a knife. He is placed in the tower by his men, who then frolic with the female attendants in the shadows. The woman is obsessed with the warrior and enters the cage. In one version, she pokes his wound maliciously, taunting him. The warrior regains his strength, seemingly draining hers at the same time. As the roosters crow, he tears off the cage door and strides forth with the dawn as she collapses at his feet. The men and women run from him, screaming warnings to the audience: "Der Teufel! Bändigt ihn, rettet Euch, rette, wer kann— verloren!" (The devil! Control him, save yourselves if you can—or all is lost!). The warrior "Wie Mücken erschlägt . . . sie und geht rot fort" (kills them like mosquitoes and leaves red behind); in the final two versions, he "Durch die Feuergasse enteilt" (hastens away through the street of fire) after killing them.

The original version was improvised, based on key phrases and words handed to the actors on slips of paper, after Kokoschka had given them an outline of the action. The first published version appeared, accompanied by a series of line drawings, in the Berlin expressionist magazine *Der Sturm* (The Storm) in 1910. The next version, called simply *Hoffnung der Frauen* (Hope of Women), was published in Kokoschka's *Dramen und Bilder* (Dramas and Paintings, 1913). The third version was a limited edition of one hundred copies printed in Berlin in 1916, and the final version was published in Leipzig in 1917.

Poster drawn by Kokoschka for the premiere of his Mörder, Hoffnung der Frauen *at the Vienna School of Arts and Crafts in 1909*

Most critics interpret the play in terms of the expressionist obsession with the battle between the sexes. For many expressionist writers, this eternal battle signified the war between a higher spiritual essence and a lower animal essence, linked with maleness and femaleness respectively. According to Henry Schvey, the man is the bearer of the spirit, which is enslaved by the body; the woman can only be redeemed by the man's spiritual powers, which she herself is instrumental in suppressing. The title of the play suggests that the woman's only hope is to be murdered and thus spiritually redeemed by the man. The warrior's triumphant exit at the end symbolizes the victory of the spirit over the flesh, since the warrior wears blue armor—the color traditionally associated with intellect, reason, and the spiritual. Most critics claim that the woman's stabbing of the warrior shows her to be by nature unfaithful and cruel, ignoring the fact that the woman acts in self-defense and that it is actually the other men who imprison their leader. Such an in-

terpretation also ignores the role of the chorus in the play, which seems to suggest a different relation between the sexes: the warrior's men and the woman's attendants are cheerful lovemakers, mystified by the tragic conflict between their leaders. In his autobiography, *Mein Leben* (1971; translated as *My Life*, 1974), Kokoschka contrasted the patriarchal relationship between citizen and society, associated with strife and violence, with the matriarchal rule of earlier times. Kokoschka associates patriarchy with the bent toward destruction, Thanatos, which struggles with Eros, the life force associated with matriarchy.

Sphinx und Strohmann also deals with the complexities of sexuality, but on a comic plane. Herr Firdusi's wife, Lilly, has left him for a muscleman. He rails against his situation, then turns to the audience in a Brechtian type of direct address that mocks the conventions of realism: "Wie rührend, wenn ich ein Nasentuch zur Hand nehme, fangen Sie an zu weinen. Warum sehen Sie mich jetzt kühl an, hundert Indifferente gegen einen Aufgeregten. Nur eine Nuance, die den Helden vom Zuschauer unterscheidet. Glauben Sie an einen Bluff? Ich arbeite nur mit Ihrer Intelligenz, Ihren Nerven und den Resultaten unserer gemeinsamen Gespensterromantik" (When I grab my handkerchief you all start to cry, how touching. But why do you look at me now so coolly, one hundred indifferent people against a single desperate person? Only a nuance separates the hero from the audience. Do you believe in a bluff? I am only exploiting your intelligence and your nerves and our mutual romantic interest in ghosts). Lilly returns, dressed in a traditional angel's costume, and literally turns Firdusi's head so that he is unable to see her. Thus Kokoschka turns a common figure of speech into a visual metaphor. Because he is unable to see her, Firdusi proposes to Lilly; he is a little dismayed that his former wife and new fiancée have the same name. He never suspects she is the same person, nor does he notice that she is flirting the entire time with Herr Kautschukmann (Mr. Rubberman), a sexy contortionist wearing a top hat. Firdusi inadvertently hastens this match by introducing himself to Herr Kautschukmann: when he says his name, Firdusi, which sounds like "Führ Du sie" (You take her), Herr Kautschukmann replies, "Großes Vergnügen!" (With great pleasure). At the end of the play Firdusi realizes that he has remarried his own unfaithful wife and dies of shock. Lilly climbs over his body, remarking casually, "Clear away his remains. I will live on without him."

In a second version of the play, published in *Dramen und Bilder*, Kokoschka adds nine wedding guests who appear as painted figures in black suits and top hats on a backdrop with holes for the actors' faces. Although the plot remains basically the same, the second version is a more philosophical inquiry into the implications of the lovers' conflict. It also offers more insight into the wife's motivations. She becomes Anima, the "Weibliche Seele" (Female Soul), who is struggling with desires of her own: "O, wo ist der, der mir wert wär, den als Mädchen ich geträumt, so wie der bewährt kein Mann sich noch vor mir. . . . Von dem einen zu dem andern, muß ich ewig wandern, wandern. [*zu Firdusi*] Guten Tag, Schönster" (Oh, where is the man who is worthy of me, the man I dreamed of as a girl? Oh, no man like that proved himself worthy of me! . . . I am forced to wander and wander eternally, from one to the other. [*To Firdusi*] Hello, handsome). Herr Kautschukmann becomes a doctor, prescribing a cure for Firdusi's lovesickness that leads to his death—this time from suicide, not shock. Kokoschka also adds the character of Tod (Death), who adds his commentary on the action. When Firdusi hears the parrot mimicking the sounds of Anima and Kautschukmann making love, his head snaps back into place as he realizes that he has been tricked into marrying his deceptive wife again. He asks himself, "Wer bin ich?" (Who am I?) and shoots himself, whereupon antlers (the sign of the cuckold) spring out of his head in answer to his query. Because of its nihilistic humor and visual imaginativeness, *Sphinx und Strohmann* was chosen as the first play to be performed at the Dada Gallery in Zurich on 14 April 1917, under the direction of Marcel Janco.

In May 1910 Kokoschka moved to Berlin. While he claimed that he was dismissed from the school as a result of the controversy sparked by the production of *Mörder, Hoffnung der Frauen*, his teacher recalled that his leaving was accompanied by a prize for outstanding achievement. The most likely reason for his departure was the offer of his friend and admirer, the architect Alfred Loos, to arrange commissions for portrait sittings and to attempt to secure funds for an exhibition of his works from the editor of *Der Sturm*, Herwarth Walden. Kokoschka went to work for Walden, and due in large part to his efforts *Der Sturm*, which had originally been a literary and mu-

sical journal, became one of the most influential forums for the visual arts.

By 1911 Kokoschka had tired of the constant struggle for money and moved back to Vienna. He wrote a new play, *Schauspiel* (Play), which was to premiere on 5 June 1913 at the Neue Wiener Bühne; but the authorities banned the production on charges of obscenity while the actors were in dress rehearsal. The play was published in *Dramen und Bilder* (1913) and performed, together with *Mörder, Hoffnung der Frauen* and *Hiob* (1917; translated as *Job*, 1963), at the Albert-Theater in Dresden on 3 June 1917 under its new title, *Der brennende Dornbusch* (The Burning Bush; published, 1917).

In some ways the most enigmatic and highly symbolic of all Kokoschka's plays, *Der brennende Dornbusch* revolves around the conflict between physical and spiritual desires. Mythological, religious, and color symbolism are woven into a mysterious and highly visual story whose slender plot represents stations on the journey from confusion to self-knowledge. The two main characters are unnamed. The dialogue consists for the most part of extended monologues and choral responses. The play's structure resembles a musical composition, consisting of modulated variations of key themes, images and phrases.

In the first scene the woman is alone in her bedroom in the moonlight, waiting expectantly for a man; the audience does not know if he is someone with whom she actually has an assignation or someone she just hopes will come. Her reaction to him is in stark contrast to her attitude toward her drunken lovers in the next room, whom she describes with unflattering nicknames: "Herr Adernrot gab mir einen Backenschlag. Herr Finstergesicht wünschte mir einen guten Tag. Ein Blümchen pflückte mir Herr Lendenkraft, was liegt mir an der gesamten Schlafgenossenschaft" (Mr. Blood-Vessel-Red gave me a slap on the cheek. Mr. Darkface wished me a good day. Mr. Loin-Strength picked me a flower, what do they matter to me, the whole sleeping lot of them). She dreams of being carried off to Heaven, and she sees in the person for whom she waits a rescue from her hopeless existence.

At the end of her monologue, a man from the street below climbs the stairs and enters her room with a candle. As he enters she is singing a song metaphorically describing her predicament: an old man held a bird in a cage all winter; when it was spring the bird could not bear being caged any longer and would not sing for the old man, even though he put a green cloth over the cage's iron bars. When the man comes, the woman asks him: "Mein Singen hieß dich herzuhören? Sahst du mein Gitter offen?" (Does this mean you heard my singing? Did you see my cage open?). He replies that he recognized her genuine hunger for love and came to her. Covering her with a blanket except for her head, he leaves. When she tries to follow him, the wind blows out her candle. He returns, and she symbolically lights her candle with his. Again he covers her with the cloth, this time including her head. Most critics interpret this gesture as his way of instructing her to look inside herself for spiritual renewal; it could also represent the sex act.

When she awakes, her savior has gone. Watching him through her barred window as he runs away from her, she describes their encounter in brutal terms: "Ein weißer Vogel fliegt im Zimmer, hat meine Augen ausgehackt. . . . Ein roter Fisch schwamm durch, hat mein Blut vollgetrunken. . . . Ein Wärwolf rannte aus, hat mein Herz abgefressen . . ." (A white bird flew into the room and hacked out my eyes. . . . A red fish swam through, drank itself full with my blood. . . . A werewolf ran out, gobbled up my heart . . .). One of the lovers goes with her to chase him down, but the man escapes. The scene ends as a Salvation Army choir extols the superiority of heavenly love over earthly passion, which is "ein' Pein, / ein Rosendorn am Pfad / zum Gartentor von Golgotha" (painful, / A rose's thorn on the path / to the garden gate of Golgotha).

The second scene repeats the opening of the first, but this time, instead of being filled with hopeful anticipation mixed with fear, the woman is melancholy. She imagines herself a virgin again and wonders if she can regain her honor through the man. She laments her entrapment in her own body. In the adjoining room, where her other lovers slept before, the man, motionless, sings in a strange tone about a time before time, before creation, before love. Then the earth was formed, beasts devoured humans, and love was violent, painful, and sweet. She becomes weaker and weaker as he sings, and she calls out to him for help. He tells her to remain hopeful, that soon she will leave this place. Her final remark, "schließt über mir Tagesschein" (daylight closes over me), signifies the transition from the night of confusion to the possibilities of a new dawn.

The third scene takes place in a dark wood under a black sky. There is no light except for the reflection from the white ground. The woman, sad and sick, is wandering and wailing as if in labor. She cries out because he is gone and has taken her strength; she feels that she has been led astray and victimized, yet she still desires him.

A chorus of men and women joins her and comments on her plight. At first they consider her simply crazy, but later they try to give her advice as she continues to cry out her despair over losing her lover. Three men of the chorus describe to her three visions of the man: the first two show him suffering (in language linking the man with Christ) as a result of her actions; the third suggests a way for her to escape from her body through identification with the Virgin Mother, who appears in medieval paintings trampling the snake underfoot.

It is the role of the Virgin Mother that the woman chooses to play, and through this role she wins her redemption. When the man from the chorus offers this vision to her, light streams down and the other men and women in the chorus begin to weep and grasp hands, indicating that this is the correct choice. The men of the chorus become reconciled with the women, seeing them no longer as mere physical beings. The chorus ends the scene singing, "Ich glaube an die Auferstehung in mir" (I believe in the resurrection in me). The stage becomes completely dark, and the transformation of the woman becomes apparent as light illuminates a young virgin lying in the place where the woman had been.

The next scene is between the man and the woman. She speaks of her burning desire and begs him to save her through its consummation, but he holds back, indicating his preference for the spiritual over the physical. She is stunned and hurt by this rebuff. Acknowledging her pain, the man explains away his coolness as restlessness. She throws a stone that hits him in the chest, but when he cries out for help she runs to him, exclaiming that she suffers with him. She calls him her husband, and he, recognizing the evil of their actions, cries out, "Warum sind wir nicht gut" (Why aren't we good).

The final scene is the man's deathbed. The woman bows over him in a Pietà-like formation. A mother and child (presumably the Virgin Mother and the Christ Child) walk by. The child pities the suffering sinners, but the mother explains that their pain arose from succumbing to physical desires. A halo forms over the man and woman: through his death (or perhaps his remorse), the two are redeemed. The chorus remarks, "Und so starb ein Mensch, der sich begriffen hat" (And so a person died who understood himself), and chastises them both, saying that though they knew they ought to have behaved differently, they clung to their old ways.

Many critics have interpreted the play as representing the woman's surmounting of her animal nature through the man's martyrdom. The man's refusal to have sex with the woman, according to this reading, incites her rage, which results in her killing him, and her self-fulfillment is achieved only by assuming the role of the Virgin Mary and transforming her physical desire for him into the spiritual love of a mother for her child. Others, such as Regina Brandt, argue that the play is intended to represent the creative process of the artist and the struggle between spirit and flesh.

In April 1912 Kokoschka met Alma Mahler, the widow of the composer Gustav Mahler and the daughter of Emil Schindler, one of the best-known painters of late-nineteenth-century Vienna. Alma's stepfather, Carl Moll, also an artist, introduced her to Kokoschka. Alma wanted to keep her association with Kokoschka secret at first, since it began so soon after her husband's death. Their three-year affair was a stormy one due to Kokoschka's tremendous jealousy, which included resentment of her late husband.

When World War I broke out in 1914 Kokoschka enlisted in the Austro-Hungarian army, largely out of guilt: he knew that others, less well-off than he, would be forced to serve. Loos secured him a position in an elite cavalry regiment. He continued to write to Alma until July 1915, although she seems to have ended their affair the year before. Alma married the architect Walter Gropius in August 1915; Kokoschka received the news about the marriage and about Alma's abortion of their child while he was in the hospital recovering from a bullet wound in the head and a bayonet wound in the side. He was in various hospitals for the next nine months.

When he recuperated he was made a liaison officer at the Italian front, where he was fired on and suffered from severe shell shock. Granted extended leave, he returned to Berlin and then moved to Dresden, where he hoped to secure a professorship at the art academy. In Dresden Kokoschka completed *Hiob* (Job; published, 1917),

an elaboration of *Sphinx und Strohmann* but with a far more cynical tone.

Hiob was first performed in Dresden on 3 June 1917 with Kokoschka as director and set designer and Käthe Richter and Ernst Deutsch in the lead roles; Richter and Deutsch also starred in *Der brennende Dornbusch*, which appeared on the same bill. In May 1919 Kokoschka directed *Hiob* again at Max Reinhardt's chamber theater in Berlin with Paul Graetz as Job and Valeska Gert as the parrot. The public responded in a tumultuous manner comparable to Kokoschka's account of the infamous premiere of *Mörder, Hoffnung der Frauen* in Vienna in 1909.

The play begins with a prologue set in the Garden of Eden. Adam, awakened by God and finding himself wedded to Eve, says, "Mein Gott, hätt er mir nur mein Bein mit Ruh gelassen" (My God, if only he had left my rib in peace). In the main part of the play Hiob, unlike his biblical counterpart, is plagued not by God or Satan but by his unfaithful wife, Anima. When the first act begins the chambermaid tells Hiob that Anima has gone out with a handsome young man and gives him a squawking parrot, which Anima has left behind to comfort him. Hiob is about to fling himself out the bathroom window when a poodle runs inside and, removing his skin, turns out to be Herr Kautschukmann, a psychoanalyst. (In Johann Wolfgang von Goethe's *Faust* [1808], Mephistopheles first appears to Faust in the form of a poodle). Like Herr Firdusi's, Hiob's head is turned when he sees Anima again, and he is thereafter unable to see straight. Kautschukmann pulls out a saw, suggesting decapitation as the best solution to the problem, but Hiob runs away.

In the next act Hiob has fallen asleep from grief on a bench in front of his house. Several young girls tease and flirt with him. Their conversation leads him to attempt suicide by drinking poison. One of the girls grabs the skull and crossbones attached to the bottle of poison and begins to play drums with them, and Hiob flings the bottle at her. He spies the window above him growing rosy and begins to sprout antlers as he tries desperately to enter his house. The antlers then become a clothes tree for the male and female garments cascading out of the rosy window above. Suddenly, the scantily clothed Anima drops from the window and lands on Hiob's head, killing him. Anima's fall like a "reifer Apfel" (ripe apple) represents the fall of Adam and Eve.

The last scene of the premiere of Kokoschka's Hiob *at the Albert-Theater in Dresden in 1917*

The gentlemen in dark suits, who in *Sphinx und Strohmann* were wedding guests, have now become funeral mourners. During their remarks, Hiob's head rolls off his body. Hiob's "losing his head" over Anima also symbolizes the struggle between head and heart, mind and body. At the end of the play Anima returns, munching an apple and referring to herself as Eve. The timeless quality of her seductive capabilities suggests a pessimistic evaluation of the outcome of the war between the sexes.

Kokoschka's next play, *Orpheus und Eurydike* (published, 1919), was written in Dresden in 1917-1918; he claimed that its scenes appeared to him as feverish hallucinations while he recovered from his wounds in 1915. It premiered on 2 February 1921 at the Frankfurter Schauspielhaus (Playhouse) under the direction of Heinrich George.

The play begins with a scene of domestic tranquillity between the lovers. Their serenity is upset by the arrival of the Furies, who have come with the tragic news that Eurydike has been summoned to the underworld by the god Hades. She begs the Furies to allow her one last night with Orpheus, but the couple is too sad and distracted to

enjoy their final hours together. The fate of their love is foreshadowed when Eurydike's ring inexplicably falls from her finger, and she is bitten on the heel by a snake. The Furies, who argue comically with each other in Viennese dialect, dress Eurydike in a shroud and cart her away, thanking Orpheus for his hospitality as they go.

Six years later, Eurydike's handmaid Psyche convinces Orpheus to steal Eurydike back. Orpheus, as instructed by Psyche, neither looks at Eurydike nor mentions her past as he whisks her away from the underworld. They travel through miles of treacherous ice and snow before they reach a shore where a black ship awaits them; they do not know that the ship belongs to Hades. The sailors pray to Amor for wind, but the ship remains grounded. Meanwhile, Eurydike has a horrible dream in which she is carrying Orpheus's child and he wants to throw her overboard. Orpheus, in turn, dreams that she plunged a needle into the heart of the unborn child. This dream is certainly a reference to Alma's abortion of Kokoschka's child.

Orpheus badgers Eurydike into telling him about her past. His jealousy of Hades, the king of the dead, parallels the fierce hatred Kokoschka harbored for Alma's late husband. Seizing her ring, Orpheus sees that their names have been scratched out; all that remains is the Greek phrase *Allos Makar* (Happiness is otherwise). (The phrase is also an anagram of the names Alma and Oskar.) The ring proves to Orpheus that Eurydike has been unfaithful to him, and he tries to throw her overboard. She pleads with him to reconsider and relates the circumstances surrounding her infidelity: she withstood Hades' advances for four years. But by the fifth year, Hades' spell had begun to work on her—the memory of Orpheus and her fear of Hades had completely faded. When Orpheus came to rescue her, Hades agreed to let her go because of her virtue. It was then, out of gratitude, that she finally succumbed to him willingly. After this confession, Eurydike leaves. The last act takes place at their former home. Orpheus has returned to find it in ruins. He sees his lyre among the ashes and sings of his tragedy. A rabble gathers, and an orgiastic riot ensues in which they hang Orpheus for making them sad. A love scene then occurs between Psyche and her lover, Amor (Cupid). Orpheus jumps down from the gallows and argues with a voice he addresses as "Mutter vom Sterben" (Mother of Death), who chastises him for preferring death over life. Then the voice of Eurydike, arising from a rose-colored fog, begs him for forgiveness. Eventually, her spirit appears, covered in veils. She pleads with him to release her from his judgment of hatred against her. Although a heavenly vision of Psyche appears to him, Orpheus refuses to forgive and dances a macabre dance with Eurydike. Seeing that his desire for her has turned to lust, she strangles him. Finally free of him, she exclaims, "Ob es Haß ist, solche Liebe? Dies Verlangen—" (Isn't it hatred, such love? This longing—), and darkness fills the stage.

The epilogue promises a resurrection after this dark night of the soul. Psyche appears on the spot where the spirit of Eurydike was, carrying corn and flowers and Orpheus's lyre. Her lover, Amor, has gone, but she does not despair. She strews the fields with flowers, awakening a chorus of boys and girls who sing of love and peace as Psyche boards Hades' ship and sails away.

Central to the myth of Eurydike and Hades is the concept of regeneration and renewal—the winter that results from Eurydike's descent into the underworld is replaced by the spring of her return. The triumph of the spirit of Eurydike over

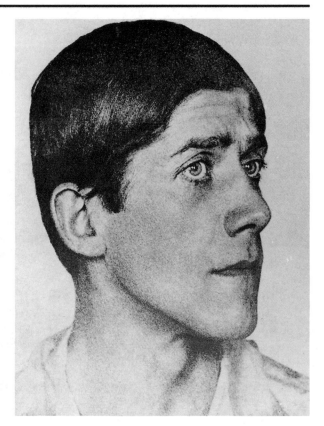

Kokoschka in 1918 (photograph by Hugo Erfurth)

the lust and hatred of Orpheus is echoed in the bounty bestowed by Psyche on the earth. Psyche's retention of Orpheus's lyre suggests the redemptive power of art. Though Orpheus dies, his spirit lives on in the lyre, which continues to sing after he is gone.

Kokoschka's continuing obsession with Alma led him to commission a doll to be made in her likeness in 1919. He sent intimately detailed sketches to the dollmaker and bought expensive clothes and undergarments with which to adorn the doll. Though he was disappointed with its appearance, Kokoschka hired a lady's maid for the doll, painted pictures of it, and took it for carriage rides, to dinner, and to the theater. Eventually he tired of his "Fetisch" (fetish), as he called it, and had a huge party in its honor at which the drunken guests decapitated it and doused it with red wine. The police came to investigate a complaint of a headless, bloodstained "corpse" in his garden. The doll led to a breakthrough in Kokoschka's development as a painter, however: his portrait of it, *The Woman in Blue*, represented a new style for him and advanced his career as a visual artist.

The long-awaited offer from the Dresden Art Academy finally came in 1919. Kokoschka taught there until 1923, when he embarked on a long period of travel and landscape painting.

The seventeenth-century Czech educational reformer, theologian, and last bishop of the Moravian Church John Amos Comenius (Jan Amos Komensky) had been an influence on Kokoschka's thinking, since his father gave him his first book, Comenius's *Orbis Pictus*. Kokoschka moved back to Vienna in 1933, but the growing political unrest in Austria and the increasing threat of a Nazi takeover led him to move to Prague in 1934. There he was invited to paint a portrait of the Czech president, Tomáš G. Masaryk, who, he discovered, was also an ardent admirer of Comenius. In the portrait, Comenius is gazing benevolently over the president's shoulder. Kokoschka encouraged Masaryk to help found a school based on Comenius's ideas where children from all over the world would be educated on humanitarian and democratic principles, without regard for race, nationality, or religion, but Masaryk died before he could implement Comenius's ideas.

After completing the Masaryk portrait in 1936 Kokoschka began writing a play on the life of Comenius. All that exists of this early version is act 4, a scene between Comenius and Rembrandt, who were both in Amsterdam at the end of their lives. In 1972, when Kokoschka rewrote the play, act 4 remained more or less the same. This act, written as a protest against the barbarism of the Nazis, displays his opposition to anti-Semitism and all other forms of discrimination.

A group of artists who had fled Germany moved to Prague, where they published anti-Nazi propaganda. In the summer of 1937 they formed into the Oskar Kokoschka Association. Worried about the fate of some of his paintings in museums in Germany and Austria, Kokoschka contacted a lawyer and art collector in Prague whose daughter, Olda Palkovska, was a law student. The two fell in love.

In 1938 Kokoschka and Olda fled to England, where Kokoschka helped found the Freier Deutscher Kulturbund (Free German League of Culture [FDKB]). The organization helped artists to get into the country, find work, and learn English; published a magazine; and staged plays. By May 1940 the FDKB had branches in many cities and counted more than a thousand Germans and more than a hundred Britons in its membership. Kokoschka and Olda were married on 15 May 1941 in a London air-raid shelter that was the temporary home of the registry office. The Kokoschkas moved to Villeneuve, Switzerland, in 1953. That year Kokoschka established his international School of Seeing in Salzburg, where he taught every summer until 1962.

In 1972 Kokoschka took up *Comenius* (published, 1973) once more for a television film. The play begins in the royal palace in Vienna. The Hapsburg Archduke Ferdinand has been sentenced to death; at the last minute a coup d'état occurs, and he is crowned the new emperor. Ferdinand immediately prepares for war, using money extorted from the Jews by his barber, Shylock. The infamous "Prague Defenestration" of 1618, in which two deputy governors and a royal scribe were thrown out the window of Hradschin Castle, furnishes the justification for Ferdinand's persecution of religious minorities and his subjugation of Bohemia. Act 1 concludes with Drabik, a disciple of Comenius, being tortured while onlookers cheer and a children's choir sings hymns.

The second act begins in Fulnek, a town on the border of Moravia and Silesia, in 1628. Ferdinand has demanded Comenius's arrest, and Comenius has fled his native Bohemia. He has adopted a blind Jewish girl, Hannah, renaming her "Christl" to protect her from pogroms. In his search for protection for himself and his followers Comenius becomes involved with several unscrupulous characters; but his worst misfortune occurs at the end of act 2 when he learns that his protector, Prince Rakoczy, has died from the plague and that Christl, whom he left in the prince's care, has been abandoned. He searches for her for the rest of the play.

In act 3 Comenius is invited by the chancellor of Sweden to reform the Swedish educational system; he incurs the wrath of Queen Christine in 1645, when he attends a conference at Thorn to plead the cause of the Moravian Brethren. The queen dismisses him, and he continues on his solitary way.

The final act opens in Rembrandt's studio. The poverty-stricken Rembrandt, downing schnapps, contemplates the huge mural on his wall that is to become the painting popularly known as *The Night Watch* (its formal title is *The Company of Captain Franc Cocq and Lieutenant Willem van Ruytenburch*). Caring for Rembrandt is his good-natured mistress Hendrikje. Comenius arrives to have his portrait painted and is invited to stay for supper. He seems tired, and he dozes off a few times while Rembrandt talks. Here the

Kokoschka in his studio at Villeneuve, Switzerland, in 1962 (photograph by Marianne Adelmann)

1936 and 1972 versions differ. In the early version Comenius speaks up for understanding between Christians and Jews. A little Jewish girl, named Hannah like the girl Comenius lost years before, enters and asks if it is true, as the Christians say, that she will not go to Heaven because her people killed Christ. Comenius leaves Rembrandt's studio and is stopped by a patrol of soldiers who ask why he is roaming the ghetto without wearing the Star of David. Rembrandt rushes to his defense, but the soldiers drag Comenius off and threaten to come back for Rembrandt. Hannah returns to tell Rembrandt that Comenius has died in the street. As she runs away, Rembrandt cries out to the soldiers, who are dressed in Nazi storm-trooper uniforms, not to trample the child with their boots. Anti-Semitic cries are heard; then Jewish voices join the tumult, calling for justice, humanity, and reason. Rembrandt, alone before his painting, sees Hannah painted in among the boots of the soldiers, as if she were a spirit. He rubs his eyes and calls out to

Hendrikje for schnapps, and asks whose hand painted that little face on his picture.

The intensity of the original fourth act is somewhat diffused in the later version in an attempt to universalize the situation. In this version Comenius, instead of pleading for understanding between Christians and Jews, bursts into a tirade as a result of his failure to reform humanity: "Der Krieg endet nicht mehr! Die Staaten verhandeln ihre Menschen wie Vieh auf dem Schlachthof. . . . Die Welt eine Hölle. . . . Ich glaube, der Mensch wird aussterben nicht anders wie die Riesen und Dynosaurier der Vorzeit, nimmt er nicht Vernunft an" (The war will never end! Nations treat their people like cattle at the slaughterhouse. . . . The world is a hell. . . . I believe humankind will become extinct in the same way as the giants and dinosaurs of prehistoric times if they do not listen to reason). Hannah arrives, this time to bring Rembrandt a kerchief for his birthday and to recite the poem the rabbi gave her to say in the synagogue. Comenius thinks that she is Christl. She tells Comenius she will soon leave the ghetto; her foster father, Shylock, has promised to send her to public school so she can get to know Christians. Comenius leaves and is stopped by soldiers. He tells them he cannot sleep because he has had "wilde Träume vom Frieden, lebenslang. Suche ein Kind, noch immer" (wild dreams of peace, my whole life long. I am seeking a child, as always). They take him away. Alone in his studio, which is dark and smoke-filled, Rembrandt hears Hannah calling his name, and the empty space in the painting brightens until the light fills the room. In the morning the artist awakens to find the figure of Hannah painted in beside the soldiers' boots. He hears her voice announcing that Comenius is dead and that she will accompany him. Her appearance in Rembrandt's painting, she says, is a testimony to Comenius's compassion. The play ends as Hendrikje enters, commenting, "Im Finstern hast du das Bild gemalt. Für mich ist's ein Wunder, schäme mich nicht, es zu sagen" (You have painted the picture in the dark. To me it's a miracle, and I'm not ashamed to say it).

In both versions of the play Rembrandt criticizes the men in the painting, who are supposed to be defenders of freedom but who actually violate human rights: "seht euch diesen Helden an, den Jan Gockelhahn, Kapitän der Cloveniersdoelen, der die Klaue des Freiheitshahnes als Abzeichen trägt. Wagte jemand vor ihmunsere bürgerliche Freiheit ein Funzellicht zu nennen, daß sie den Mechkerern nicht den roten Hahn aufs Dach setzen!" (Look at this hero, Jan Gockelhahn, Captain of the Cloveniersdoelen, who wears the claw of the cock of liberty as a mark of distinction. Let no one dare call our civil rights a dim light in front of him, lest he burn down the houses of those who complain!). It is the inspiration the humanitarian Comenius gives Rembrandt that enables the artist to complete the painting with a dash of light and hope amid the dark hypocrisy of the world around them.

At eighty-six Kokoschka ceased writing plays but continued to paint, despite difficulties with his eyesight. His final years were marked by greater recognition of his accomplishments than he had ever before enjoyed. In 1960 he had been granted an honorary doctorate from Oxford University, finally receiving the attention he felt he had long deserved in his adopted home, and by the time he reached his nineties he was acknowledged throughout Europe as the greatest Austrian painter who ever lived. In 1976 he was awarded an honorary doctorate from the University of Salzburg. He died on 22 February 1980, one week before his ninety-fourth birthday. On his death the Austrian government established an Oskar Kokoschka Prize to be awarded annually in the field of visual arts.

Letters:
Briefe, 4 volumes, edited by Olda Kokoschka and Heinz Spielmann (Düsseldorf: Claasen, 1984-1989).

Biographies:
Paul Westheim, *Oskar Kokoschka* (Potsdam & Berlin: Kiepenheuer, 1918; revised, 1925);
Edith Hoffman, *Kokoschka, Life and Work* (London: Faber & Faber, 1947);
Werner J. Schweiger, *Der junge Kokoschka: Leben und Werk 1904-1914* (Vienna & Munich: Brandstätter, 1983);
Frank Whitford, *Oskar Kokoschka: A Life* (London: Weidenfeld & Nicolson, 1986).

References:
Regina Brandt, *Figurationen und Kompositionen in den Dramen Oskar Kokoschkas* (Munich: UNI-Druck, 1968);
Richard Calvocoressi, ed., *Oskar Kokoschka 1886-1980* (London: Tate Gallery, 1986);
Horst Denkler, "Die Druckfassungen der Dramen Oskar Kokoschkas," *Deutsche Vierteljahresschrift für Literatur und Geistesgeschichte*, 40 (1966): 90-108;
Denkler, "Über Oskar Kokoschkas Dramen," *Jahrbuch der Evangelischen Akademie Tutzing*, 15 (1966): 288-306;
Carol Diethe, *Aspects of Distorted Sexual Attitudes in German Expressionist Drama: With Particular Reference to Wedekind, Kokoschka, and Kaiser* (New York: Lang, 1988);
J. P. Hodin, *Kokoschka, the Artist and his Time* (London: Cory, Adams & Mackay, 1966);
Otto Kamm, "Oskar Kokoschka und das Theater," Ph.D. dissertation, University of Vienna, 1958;
Peter Nicholls, "Sexuality and Structure: Tensions in Early Expressionist Drama," *New Theatre Quarterly*, 7 (May 1991): 160-170;
Daria Rothe, "Kokoschka's *Comenius*," in *Crosscurrents 1983*, edited by Ladislav Matejka and Benjamin Stolz (Ann Arbor: University of Michigan Department of Slavic Languages and Literatures, 1983), pp. 211-221;

Fritz Schmalenbach, *Oskar Kokoschka* (Königstein: Koster, 1967);

Henry Schvey, *Oskar Kokoschka: The Painter as Playwright* (Detroit: Wayne State University Press, 1982);

Hans Maria Wingler, *Oskar Kokoschka: Das Werk des Malers* (Salzburg: Galerie Welz, 1956); translated by F. S. C. Budgen, J. P. Hodin, and Ilse Schreier as *Oskar Kokoschka: The*

Work of the Painter (London: Faber & Faber, 1958);

Johann Winkler, ed., *Begegnung mit Kokoschka* (Pöchlarn: Oskar Kokoschka-Dokumentation, 1973).

Papers:
Manuscripts are at the Oskar Kokoschka Museum and Archive at Kokoschka's birthplace in Pöchlarn and the Stedelijk Museum, Amsterdam.

Erwin Guido Kolbenheyer

(30 December 1878 - 12 April 1962)

Alfred D. White
University of Wales, College of Cardiff

See also the Kolbenheyer entry in *DLB 66: German Fiction Writers, 1885-1913.*

PLAY PRODUCTIONS: *Heroische Leidenschaften*, Düsseldorf, Schauspielhaus, 10 May 1928;

Die Brücke, Düsseldorf, Schauspielhaus, 19 November 1929;

Jagt ihn—ein Mensch!, Düsseldorf, Schauspielhaus; Mannheim, Nationaltheater; Weimar, Deutsches Nationaltheater; Heilbronn, Stadttheater, 31 January 1931;

Das Gesetz in Dir, Düsseldorf, Schauspielhaus; Munich, Residenztheater; Heilbronn, Stadttheater; Dresden, Sächsisches Staatstheater, 14 November 1931;

Gregor und Heinrich, Dresden, Staatsschauspiel, 18 October 1934.

BOOKS: *Giordano Bruno: Die Tragödie der Renaissance* (Vienna: Stern & Rosner, 1903 [i.e., 1902]); revised as *Heroische Leidenschaften: Die Tragödie des Giordano Bruno. In drei Teilen* (Munich: Müller, 1928);

Die sensorielle Theorie der optischen Raumempfindung (Leipzig: Barth, 1905);

Amor Dei: Ein Spinoza-Roman (Munich & Leipzig: Müller, 1908); translated by John Linton as *God-Intoxicated Man* (London: Nicholson & Watson, 1933);

Erwin Guido Kolbenheyer (photograph by Georg Schödl)

Meister Joachim Pausewang: Roman (Munich & Leipzig: Müller, 1910); translated by H. A. Phillips and K.-W. Maurer as *A Winter Chronicle* (London: Lane, 1938);

Montsalvasch: Ein Roman für Individualisten (Munich & Leipzig: Müller, 1912);

Ahalibama: Drei Erzählungen (Munich & Leipzig: Müller, 1913);

Klein-Rega: Eine Kinderstudie (Munich: Callwey, 1914);

Die Kindheit des Paracelsus: Roman (Munich: Müller, 1917);

Wem bleibt der Sieg? (Tübingen: Kloeres, 1919);

Das Gestirn des Paracelsus: Roman (Munich: Müller, 1922);

Der Dornbusch brennt: Ein Flugblatt Gedichte für seine Heimat (Eger: Böhmerland, 1922; revised, 1923);

Ein Gruß vom Wege—Eurem Weg (Rudolstadt: Greifenverlag, 1923);

Drei Legenden (Hamburg-Großborstel: Deutsche Dichter-Gedächtnis-Stiftung, 1923);

Das dritte Reich des Paracelsus: Roman (Munich: Müller, 1926 [i.e., 1925]);

Die Bauhütte: Elemente einer Metaphysik der Gegenwart (Munich: Langen, 1925); revised as *Die Bauhütte: Grundlage einer Metaphysik der Gegenwart* (Munich: Langen-Müller, 1940);

Das Lächeln der Penaten: Roman (Munich: Müller, 1927 [i.e., 1926]);

Paracelsus: Roman, 3 volumes (Munich: Müller, 1927-1928);

Lyrisches Brevier (Munich: Müller, 1929 [i.e., 1928]);

Kämpfender Quell: Karlsbad-Buch (Munich: Müller, 1929);

Die Brücke: Schauspiel in vier Aufzügen (Munich: Müller, 1929);

Aufruf der Universitäten (Groitzsch: Reichardt, 1930);

Jagt ihn—ein Mensch!: Schauspiel in fünf Aufzügen (Munich: Müller, 1931 [i.e., 1930]);

Stimme: Eine Sammlung von Aufsätzen (Munich: Müller, 1931 [i.e., 1930]);

Das Gesetz in Dir: Schauspiel (Munich: Müller, 1931);

Reps, die Persönlichkeit: Roman in einer kleinen Stadt (Munich: Müller, 1932 [i.e., 1931]);

Unser Befreiungskampf und die deutsche Dichtkunst: Rede (Munich: Langen-Müller, 1932);

Weihnachtsgeschichten (Munich: Langen-Müller, 1933 [i.e., 1932]);

Die Begegnung auf dem Riesengebirge: Novelle (Munich: Langen-Müller, 1933 [i.e., 1932]);

Die volksbiologischen Grundlagen der Freiheitsbewegung (Munich: Langen-Müller, 1933);

Deutsches Bekenntnis; Unser Leben: Dichtungen für Sprechchöre (Munich: Langen-Müller, 1933);

Gregor und Heinrich: Schauspiel (Munich: Langen-Müller, 1934);

Der Lebensstand der geistig Schaffenden und das neue Deutschland (Munich: Langen-Müller, 1934);

Neuland: Zwei Abhandlungen (Munich: Langen-Müller, 1935 [i.e., 1934])—includes "Die Dritte Bühne";

Arbeitsnot und Wirtschaftskrise biologisch gesehen (Munich: Langen-Müller, 1935);

Lebenswert und Lebenswirkung der Dichtkunst in einem Volke (Munich: Langen-Müller, 1935);

Völkerverständigung: Ansprache, gehalten im Münchner Rotary Klub (Munich: Rotary Klub, 1935);

Klaas Y, der große Neutrale: Novellen (Munich: Langen-Müller, 1936);

Das Kolbenheyer-Buch, edited by Ernst Frank (Karlsbad: Kraft, 1937);

Wie wurde der deutsche Roman Dichtung? (Munich: Langen-Müller, 1937);

Das gottgelobte Herz: Roman aus der Zeit der deutschen Mystik (Munich: Langen-Müller, 1938);

Wahrheit des Lebens: Worte aus seinen Werken, edited by Rolf Meckler (Munich: Langen-Müller, 1938);

Der Einzelne und die Gemeinschaft; Goethes Denkprinzipien und der biologische Naturalismus: Zwei Reden (Munich: Langen-Müller, 1939);

Gesammelte Werke, 8 volumes (Munich: Langen-Müller, 1939-1941);

Vox Humana: Gedichte (Munich: Langen-Müller, 1940);

Bauhüttenphilosophie: Ergänzende und erläuternde Abhandlungen (Munich: Langen-Müller, 1942);

Die volksbiologische Funktion des Geisteslebens und der Geisterziehung (Vienna: Hölder-Pichler-Tempsky, 1942);

Kindergeschichten (Stuttgart: Verlag Deutsche Völksbucher, 1942);

Zwei Reden: Das Geistesleben in seiner volksbiologischen Bedeutung; Jugend und Dichtung (Munich: Langen-Müller, 1942);

Menschen und Götter: Dramatische Tetralogie (Prague: Orbis, 1944);

Die Philosophie der Bauhütte (Vienna, Berlin & Stuttgart: Neff, 1952);

Gesamtausgabe der Werke letzter Hand: Dichterische Werke, 9 volumes (Lüdenscheid, Gartenberg & Nuremberg: Kolbenheyer-Gesellschaft, 1956-1973);

Gesamtausgabe der Werke letzter Hand: Theoretische Werke, 8 volumes (Lüdenscheid, Gartenberg

& Nuremberg: Kolbenheyer-Gesellschaft, 1956-1978).

OTHER: Johann C. von Grimmelshausen, *Der abenteuerliche Simplizissimus*, abridged by Kolbenheyer (Berlin: Wegweiser-Verlag, 1920); Johannes von Saaz, *Der Ackermann aus Böhmen*, translated by Kolbenheyer, edited by Erich Gierach (Prague: Verlag Volk und Reich, 1943).

In the 1920s Erwin Guido Kolbenheyer was perhaps the leading German historical novelist. His major works, above all the Paracelsus trilogy (1917-1925), had a large readership; but his plays and novels attract little attention today. The plays fall into two groups: dramatic equivalents of his grandiose historical novels and plays on a domestic scale dealing with modern themes. His confidence in his powers as a dramatist was misplaced, though his best scenes show the same sensitivity, commitment, and talent as the best chapters of his novels.

Kolbenheyer was born on 30 December 1878 in Budapest to Franz Kolbenheyer, an architect, and Amalie Hein Kolbenheyer. After Franz Kolbenheyer's death in 1881 his widow returned with Erwin Guido and his sister, Leonie, to Karlsbad (now Karlovy Vary, Czechoslovakia), where her family lived. Kolbenheyer had a private tutor for two years before attending the local school; at eleven he transferred to the Lateinschule (Latin School) in nearby Eger (now Cheb). At the age of fourteen or so he wrote "Nero," an expansive romantic tragedy; the manuscript has been lost. After a year of military service in 1899-1900 he entered the University of Vienna, where he studied philosophy, psychology, history of art, and zoology.

His first mature play, *Giordano Bruno* (1902), was written in 1901-1902. The Italian Renaissance philosopher Bruno sets out to overcome Christian values which have become rigid and life-denying—faith, asceticism, and self-negation—by more modern ones such as rationality, pantheism, and the enthusiastic grasping of sensual and mystical experience. The prologue, conceived as a play in its own right (a planned performance in Prague was foiled when the censor objected to having a drunken monk onstage), shows Bruno fleeing from the morbid atmosphere of the monastery. He arrives at the palace of the Venetian noble Mocenigo, with whose fiancée, Bianca, he falls in love. The jealous Mocenigo betrays the un-

wary Bruno to the Inquisition as a heretic. The pope tries to extract a last-minute recantation; but Bruno, aware that his work will lose influence if he recants, prefers martyrdom and is burned at the stake. Kolbenheyer hints that Bruno had German blood, and that this ancestry was what made him such a liberating thinker.

Written in 1904-1905, *Richter* (Judges; published in 1973 in his *Gesamtausgabe der Werke letzter Hand: Dichterische Werke* [Final Critical Edition of the Collected Works: Literary Works, 1956-1973]) is set in Nördlingen during the witchcraft trials of the 1590s. Martin, the supposed son of Röttinger, a judge who persecutes witches, is in love with Maria Salome Lempin, a superstitious girl. Röttinger orders the arrest of Maria's mother, Rebekka, on charges of witchcraft. The bishop—Martin's real father—refuses to pardon Rebekka. Martin poisons Röttinger; though the latter's evil nature is explained by loneliness and stress, he must die in terror to avenge Rebekka. The functional ethics and grandiose pantheism of Bruno are echoed: a stern sense of what is right and needful for the fulfillment of his mission in life leads Martin to see himself as Röttinger's judge. But Kolbenheyer's treatment is shallow: Röttinger remains a cipher, the theme of justice has no proper ethical framework, and the moral conflict is black and white.

After receiving his doctorate in 1905 Kolbenheyer attended art school; there he met Marianne Eitner, whom he married on 3 April 1906. They settled in Vienna and had two daughters: Christl, born in 1909, and Ulrike, born in 1912. Financial support from his mother allowed Kolbenheyer to devote himself to writing. In three weeks in 1911 he dashed off the comedy *Das Wort* (The Word; published in *Gesamtausgabe der Werke letzter Hand: Dichterische Werke*, 1973), exploring the suppression of parts of the personality. Gröll, a dignified clergyman, lives by the dead word of dogma and represses the artistic and emotional in himself and tries to do so in his son and foster son. But when the boys form an alliance with Gröll's wife, his brother, and his rich patroness Frau von Matthusen, Gröll must finally condone the boys' taking the money intended for their theological and legal studies and using it to study art and music. The humor in the play largely takes the form of references to the ambiguities and pitfalls of words. The Word of God as dead dogma and words as impressive cover for a poor reality are constant themes. Accordingly, the resolution of the play is not in the dialogue but in Gröll's movement from his study to the kitchen, where the rest of the family habitually gathers. In *Das Wort* can be seen the Kolbenheyerian theme of the individual living by his or her own feelings, which are largely influenced by heredity, and his theory that hereditary talents suppressed by environmental influence can reappear in the next generation.

The years 1913 to 1925 were the gestation period of the Paracelsus trilogy, on which Kolbenheyer's reputation rests. The writing of the trilogy was interrupted in 1915, when Kolbenheyer was made an officer in a prisoner-of-war camp for Russians; after the war he moved to Tübingen. In *Die Kindheit des Paracelsus* (The Childhood of Paracelsus, 1917), *Das Gestirn des Paracelsus* (The Constellation of Paracelsus, 1922), and *Das dritte Reich des Paracelsus* (The Third Realm of Paracelsus, 1925) Kolbenheyer produces a great panorama of the German-speaking lands at the time of the Renaissance and Reformation, framed in a mythical conflict between Wodan and Christ—representing the Germanic and the southern European cultures, respectively—and concentrating on the healer and metaphysical thinker who seems to Kolbenheyer to sum up the era. But the pan-European, Christian, and medieval aspects of the thought of the historical Paracelsus are subtly replaced by Germanic, deistic, and rational ones. Kolbenheyer's image of humanity is narrowed by a nationalistic viewpoint.

A volume of biologistic philosophy, *Die Bauhütte* (The Workshop, 1925), followed *Paracelsus*. Kolbenheyer finds a substitute for religion in vitalism: the totality of life, perpetuating itself through species and individuals, is his equivalent of God. The individual is only a vehicle for the vital forces at work in the species, race, people, regional stock, and family; society is determined by biological needs, and free will is an illusion. In *Die Bauhütte* the various biological groupings—species, race, people, and so on—are of equal status. But in later essays Kolbenheyer concentrates increasingly on the Volk (people), which he holds to be the largest group the individual can grasp intuitively. The Volk takes on a life of its own for Kolbenheyer—an intellectual variant of the ideology that was to be responsible for many of the excesses of Nazism. According to Kolbenheyer, the Volk is biologically bound to assert itself; it is impervious to moral ideas. Because Germany is an underprivileged nation, expansion is a natural demand; all Germans must be united in a single

Scene from a performance at the Staatstheater in Berlin of Kolbenheyer's Heroische Leidenschaften, *with Lothar Müthel as Giordano Bruno and Clara Savio as Bianca*

powerful nation-state. Kolbenheyer applied his biologistic thought to literature, drama, politics, and other areas in a series of essays written between 1919 and 1943.

The offer of a belated first performance of *Giordano Bruno* in 1926 led him to revise the play as *Heroische Leidenschaften* (Heroic Passions, 1928). He had four plays in succession directed in Düsseldorf by Louise Dumont, who offered him the post of dramaturge, which he refused. Though popular in Düsseldorf, the plays were only sporadically performed in other theaters. Kolbenheyer refused to sanction performances in Berlin until after 1933 because the sensation-seeking, ephemeral theatrical life of the capital ran counter to his ideals.

In *Heroische Leidenschaften* the abstract idea for which Bruno sacrifices himself is only vaguely religious, and its social implications are unexamined; the way is open for the spectator to give himself up to some equally vague modern ideology, such as Nazism. The actual philosophy of the hero is distorted to bring it closer to Kolbenheyer's own biologism; the plot is structured to bring out stages of Bruno's development in an epic manner. The theory of the philosopher's German descent, suggested in the original play, is accepted here. In a final visionary scene Bruno joins Christ and Socrates.

In *Die Brücke* (The Bridge, 1929), directed by the author at Düsseldorf with Dumont and Wolfgang Langhoff in the cast, generational conflict is dealt with in a conciliatory fashion. The achievements of the older generation are represented by the bridge, a symbol of unity, perhaps even of biological community, built by the older man, Prein. The younger generation is represented by Rübsam, a worker's son. Irritated by Prein's unshakable equanimity, Rübsam makes Prein think his bridge has collapsed by setting off an explosion during a storm, when the bridge cannot be seen from the engineer's office. The young people criticize the shallowness of the science, capitalism, and politics of the older generation but realize that the older people must have had great inner reserves to allow them to survive World War I and its aftermath. The young, conversely, seem irresponsible and rude, but in the end they achieve a due respect for their elders' achievements and will be able to build on them. The plot is melodramatic, the message is vague, and the language is undistinguished, but the premiere ended to considerable applause.

Jagt ihn—ein Mensch! (Hunt Him Down—a Human Being!; published, 1930; performed, 1931) is a futuristic play in which a scientist, Wengert, invents a new fuel. Both capitalists and workers block the introduction of the fuel into general use to avoid economic disadvantages to themselves. Kolbenheyer propagates a vague view of a natural community as superior to the class society. At the end, the unethical capitalists foment violence among the unenlightened workers, and the status quo triumphs over the genius. The wooden characters and dialogue, the lack of a sophisticated grasp of the problems of new energy sources, and the all-too-predictable explosion that kills Wengert's wife have kept the play obscure. Critics were unhappy with the structure of the play, though they admitted its effectiveness on the stage, particularly in the production by Peter Scharoff in Düsseldorf.

In *Das Gesetz in Dir* (The Law in Yourself, 1931) a professor, Bödding, holds that jazz is an atavistic reversion; he is also intolerant of modern dance and attitudes. He holds forth at length about true values—the title is an echo of Immanuel Kant's ethics; has a long argument with the devil, who appears in a hallucination as a man in a dinner jacket and is perhaps a projection of a suppressed side of Bödding himself; and forces Beßmer, who has committed fraud to finance his elopement with Bödding's daughter Sabine, to kill himself. The secrecy of their love proves its shallowness, according to Bödding; it could not stand up to the test of that morality embedded in the individual's genetic makeup. But Sabine, coming to the same conclusion about her elopement as Bödding, has already forced Beßmer to kill her. Bödding claims to have murdered Beßmer and goes off to jail to embark on his penance. The press response to the simultaneous premieres in Düsseldorf, Munich, Heilbronn, and Dresden clearly shows the polarization of public opinion in 1931. The mainstream press found what it could to praise but wished that Kolbenheyer had compressed the action into three acts instead of five; a few dissenting voices damned the play openly and said that—in Düsseldorf particularly—it was a failure disguised only by a claque of the author's friends or by the audience's appreciation of the acting.

Kolbenheyer was elected to the Prussian Academy in 1926 but resigned for political reasons in 1932 and moved to Munich. By 1932, when he received the Goethe Medal, he was an open supporter of National Socialism.

Gregor und Heinrich (1934) is based on the conflict between Emperor Henry IV and Pope Gregory VII in the eleventh century. The pope justifies his desire for power on the grounds of Christian belief, but this belief comes to seem dubious to him. His spirituality and subtlety demonstrate, in Kolbenheyer's biologistic philosophy, the overdevelopment of the Latin race, which from now on must decline. The Germanic emperor makes a tactical self-abasement before the pope at Canossa; but he represents a rising people, and one feels that he has only temporarily given up his claim to unite secular and spiritual authority. The play seemed to connect the Third Reich with the Holy Roman Empire, and audiences discerned current references: Heinrich's stress on a clear delimitation of religious and secular powers refers to the Concordat of 1933, and his attacks on the particularism of the German princes echo Adolf Hitler's impatience with the squabbles of the provinces and the political parties of the Weimar Republic.

The plays Kolbenheyer wrote from 1928 to 1934 form a set of reflections on burning issues

Scene from a 1931 performance at the Residenztheater in Munich of Kolbenheyer's Jagt ihn—ein Mensch! *Grouped on the right are (left to right) Annemarie Holtz as Erna, Otto Wernicke as Dr. Wengert, and Hellmuth Renar as Count Werbestorff.*

of the Weimar Republic: attitudes to technological progress, to modern art, to the generation gap, to religion and philosophy, and to German history and tradition. The conclusions he draws are by no means in tune with current opinions, and the literary and theatrical quality of the plays are not such as to guarantee them continued performance. Yet they do give an insight into one way of approaching vital problems. They contain detailed stage directions stressing that each character is the exponent or bearer of some biologically determined line of development or attitude.

After Hitler took power in 1933 Kolbenheyer courted official suspicion by refusing offices offered him, by expressing independent views, and by rejoining the Prussian Academy but resigning from its governing body when statutes giving it some autonomy were not officially approved. But he also gave lectures in support of Hitler in Britain and France in 1936. Hitler presented him with the Adlerschild des Deutschen Reiches (Eagle Shield of the German Reich) in 1938. His work was officially favored and propagated. He became chairman of the Sudetendeutsche Kulturgesellschaft (Sudeten German Culture Society) and joined the Sudetendeutsche Partei (Sudeten German party); after the annexa-

tion of the Sudetenland, which he supported, his membership in the Sudetendeutsche Partei automatically made him a member of the Nazi party. He thought, however, that the occupation of the rest of Czechoslovakia was a mistake.

During World War II Kolbenheyer wrote the unperformed dramatic tetralogy *Menschen und Götter* (Men and Gods, 1944). It consists of *Mythus*, which features the Norns, Zeus, Wodan, and Jesus; *Eckart*, an interlude in which German mysticism is depicted as the seed of a German religion, and the conflict between the Wodan and Jesus of the Paracelsus trilogy is repeated; *Luther*, in which Wodan forces Martin Luther into a monastic vocation and thus ensures that Germanic strivings will be incorporated into the Christian religion; and *Der Hellweg*, set in World War II, in which the Bible, translated into German by Luther to rescue German religion from Roman domination but itself never truly Germanic, is declared dead, to be replaced by scientific insights—that is, Kolbenheyerian biologism.

In the essay "Die Dritte Bühne" (The Third Theater, 1934) Kolbenheyer seeks a general theory of theater. He insists that the theater belongs to the people, a community seeking art which will cater to its deep emotional needs; it does not belong to the ephemeral audience seeking titillation. He advocates the development of an ensemble working cooperatively, instead of collecting ad hoc casts of stars. Drama is distinguished from other literary genres because in it the individual is shown struggling in opposition to the generality. There are two kinds of art, one born from the senses and offering sensual experience, the other born of ideas and offering the fruits of experience; each kind of author has his own approach and must strive to complement it with the methods of the other. But a third kind of theater is also possible, one in which the spectator does not passively take in either spectacle or ideas but creatively experiences that which is behind the production. While the notion of the completion of the work of art by the recipient is an interesting one, in Kolbenheyer's version it is connected with a totalitarian ideology.

In 1945 Kolbenheyer's house in Munich was requisitioned by the American military government, and he and his wife moved into a summer house lent them by a friend in Schlederloh, south of Munich. Property in Karlsbad that he had inherited from his mother was expropriated by Czech authorities. In 1948 he was prosecuted in a German court for speeches and articles he had written under Hitler; half of his assets were confiscated, and his work was banned from publication for five years. In Schlederloh he wrote *Dreigespräch über die Ethik der Bauhütte* (Three-Way Conversation about the Ethics of the Workshop; published in *Die Philosophie der Bauhütte* [The Philosophy of the Workshop, 1952]), in which he attempts to show that biologism does not preclude metaphysics, ethics, morality, and conscience. In 1952, with compensation funds from the West German government for those who had lost property in the East, Kolbenheyer built a house in a community of Sudeten refugees in Geretsried-Gartenberg. His works were gradually published by the Gesellschaft der Freunde des Werkes von E. G. Kolbenheyer (Society of the Friends of the Work of E. G. Kolbenheyer), founded in 1951. His wife died in 1957. Kolbenheyer died of heart disease on 12 April 1962 in Munich.

Kolbenheyer's best dramatic works are those in which his eye for historical detail and empathy with the thinking of the past were combined with the portrayal of a clash of intellectual attitudes or of power centers: *Heroische Leidenschaften* and *Gregor und Heinrich*. If the conflicts of individual thinker versus orthodoxy and secular versus spiritual power could be separated from racial elements, these plays could be worth reviving. Where Kolbenheyer attempts to write about modern subjects, his characterization and dialogue rarely rise above the pedestrian. He was not equipped to deal with the problems of industrial and urban society, stress and alienation, inequality and exploitation; some critics wonder whether his preference for history was a conscious diversion from these issues. But much in his historical novels shows him to be a master of characterization, empathy, description, structure, argument, and dialogue, and the best scenes of his plays have the same qualities.

Bibliography:

H. Vetterlein, "Kolbenheyer-Bibliographie," *Dichtung und Volkstum*, 40 (1939): 94-109.

Biography:

Ernst Frank, *Jahre des Glücks—Jahre des Leids: Eine Kolbenheyer-Biographie* (Velbert: Blick + bild, 1969 [i.e., 1968]).

References:

Bruno Fischli, *Die Deutschen-Dämmerung: Zur Genealogie des völkisch-faschistischen Dramas und Theaters (1897-1933)* (Bonn: Bouvier, 1976);

Uwe-Karsten Ketelsen, *Von heroischem Sein und völkischem Tod: Zur Dramatik des Dritten Reiches* (Bonn: Bouvier, 1970);

Franz Koch, *Kolbenheyer* (Göttingen: Göttinger Verlagsanstalt, 1953);

Conrad Wandrey, *Kolbenheyer* (Munich: Langen-Müller, 1934);

Alfred D. White, "The Development of the Thought of Erwin Guido Kolbenheyer from 1901 to 1934," D.Phil. dissertation, Oxford University, 1967.

Papers:

The Kolbenheyer Archive, Gartenberg, contains most of Erwin Guido Kolbenheyer's papers and his library.

Else Lasker-Schüler

(11 February 1869 - 22 January 1945)

Michael Knittel
Deep Springs College

See also the Lasker-Schüler entry in *DLB 66: German Fiction Writers, 1885-1913.*

PLAY PRODUCTIONS: *Die Wupper*, Berlin, Deutsches Theater, 27 April 1919;
Arthur Aronymus und seine Väter, Zurich, Schauspielhaus, 19 December 1936;
IchundIch, Düsseldorf, Großes Schauspielhaus, 10 November 1979.

BOOKS: *Styx: Gedichte* (Berlin: Juncker, 1902);
Der siebente Tag: Gedichte (Berlin: Verlag des Vereins für Kunst, 1905);
Das Peter Hille-Buch (Stuttgart & Berlin: Juncker, 1906);
Die Nächte Tino von Bagdads (Berlin, Stuttgart & Leipzig: Juncker, 1907); revised as *Die Nächte der Tino von Bagdad* (Berlin: Cassirer, 1919);
Die Wupper: Schauspiel in fünf Aufzügen (Berlin: Oesterheld, 1909);
Meine Wunder: Gedichte (Karlsruhe & Leipzig: Dreililien Verlag, 1911);
Mein Herz: Ein Liebesroman mit Bildern und wirklich lebenden Menschen (Munich & Berlin: Bachmair, 1912);
Gesichte: Essays und andere Geschichten (Leipzig: Wolff, 1913); enlarged as *Essays* (Berlin: Cassirer, 1920);
Hebräische Balladen (Berlin-Wilmersdorf: Meyer, 1913; enlarged edition, Berlin: Cassirer, 1920); translated by Andri Durchslag and Jeanette Litman-Demeestère as *Hebrew Ballads and Other Poems* (Philadelphia: Jewish Publication Society of America, 1980);
Der Prinz von Theben: Ein Geschichtenbuch (Leipzig: Verlag der Weißen Bücher, 1914);
Die gesammelten Gedichte (Leipzig: Verlag der Weißen Bücher, 1917);
Der Malik: Eine Kaisergeschichte mit Bildern und Zeichnungen (Berlin: Cassirer, 1919);
Gesamtausgabe, 10 volumes (Berlin: Cassirer, 1919-1920);

Else Lasker-Schüler in 1918

Die Kuppel: Der Gedichte zweiter Teil (Berlin: Cassirer, 1920);
Der Wunderrabbiner von Barcelona: Erzählung (Berlin: Cassirer, 1921);

Theben: Gedichte und Lithographien (Berlin & Frankfurt am Main: Querschnitt, 1923);

Ich räume auf! Meine Anklage gegen meine Verleger (Zurich: Lago, 1925);

Konzert (Berlin: Rowohlt, 1932);

Arthur Aronymus: Die Geschichte meines Vaters (Berlin: Rowohlt, 1932);

Arthur Aronymus und seine Väter: Aus meines geliebten Vaters Kinderjahren. Schauspiel in fünfzehn Bildern (Berlin: Fischer, 1932);

Das Hebräerland (Zurich: Oprecht, 1937);

Mein blaues Klavier: Neue Gedichte (Jerusalem: Jerusalem Press, 1943);

Dichtungen und Dokumente: Gedichte, Prosa, Schauspiele, Briefe, Zeugnis und Erinnerung, edited by Ernst Ginsberg (Munich: Kösel, 1951);

Gesammelte Werke, volume 1: *Gedichte: 1902-1943*, edited by Friedhelm Kemp (Munich: Kösel, 1959); extracted and translated by Robert P. Newton as *Your Diamond Dreams Cut Open My Arteries* (Chapel Hill: University of North Carolina Press, 1982); volume 3: *Verse und Prosa aus dem Nachlaß*, edited by Werner Kraft (Munich: Kösel, 1961); volume 2: *Prosa und Schauspiele*, edited by Kemp (Munich: Kösel, 1962);

Sämtliche Gedichte, edited by Kemp (Munich: Kösel, 1966);

Die Wupper: Schauspiel in fünf Aufzügen: Else Lasker-Schüler; Mit Dokumenten zur Entstehungs- und Wirkungsgeschichte und einem Nachwort von Fritz Martini (Stuttgart: Reclam, 1977);

IchundIch: Eine theatralische Tragödie in sechs Akten, einem Vor- und einem Nachspiel, edited by Margarete Kupper (Munich: Kösel, 1980); translated by Beate Hein Bennett as *I and I*, in *The Divided Home/Land: Contemporary German Women's Plays*, edited by Sue-Ellen Case (Ann Arbor: University of Michigan Press, 1992), pp. 137-179;

Gesammelte Werke in acht Bänden, 8 volumes (Munich: Deutscher Taschenbuch Verlag, 1986).

OTHER: "Plumm-Pascha: Morgenländische Komödie," in *Das Kinobuch*, edited by Kurt Pinthus (Leipzig: Wolff, 1914);

"Etwas von mir," in *Führende Frauen Europas: In 25 Selbstschilderungen. Neue Folge*, edited by Elga Kern (Munich: Reinhardt, 1930), pp. 14-29.

Else Lasker-Schüler's reputation is primarily based on her poetry and, to a lesser degree, on her prose. Her dramatic production has re-

mained fairly unknown. Of her three plays, only two were published and produced during her lifetime; the third remains a fragment, is considered almost incomprehensible by some critics, was not published in its entirety until 1970, and was not seen onstage until 1979. Despite this unimpressive record, the plays deserve attention. Their language is deeply imaginative and lyrical, often disturbingly unconventional. Although the plays are not realistic, they are grounded in Lasker-Schüler's experiences. Despite her apparent indifference to politics, she had a keen sense for social conflict and the danger of anti-Semitism. Her last play is a deeply moving though contradictory attempt to deal both with the catastrophe of National Socialism and with her love of German culture, above all its literary tradition. Despite the technical difficulties her plays pose for directors, the most successful stage productions of Lasker-Schüler's dramas have proved the effort to be worthwhile.

Anyone who attempts to write a biography of Lasker-Schüler has to overcome a major difficulty: she fictionalized her life and lived her life as a work of art. As a representative of the neo-Romantic attempt to break down the barriers between "life" and "art," it was natural for her to invent an autobiographical legend that frequently departs from the documented facts. To her, art and life formed a unity that resisted a strict separation of its elements, as she explains in her epistolary novel *Mein Herz* (My Heart, 1912): "Lebe das Leben ja tableaumäßig, ich bin immer im Bilde. . . . Ich sehe also das Leben aus dem Bilde an; was nehme ich ernster von beiden? Beides. Ich sterbe am Leben und atme im Bilde wieder auf. Hurrah" (I live life according to a pictorial arrangement. I am always in the picture. . . . Thus I look at life from the picture; what do I take more seriously? Both. I die from life and I recover in the picture. Hurrah).

The documented facts are that Elisabeth Schüler was born in Elberfeld (today part of the city of Wuppertal) on 11 February 1869, the sixth child of the banker Aron Schüler and Jeanette Kissing Schüler, both of the Jewish faith. Lasker-Schüler's accounts of her childhood emphasize her close relationship with her mother, who had artistic interests and lived, according to her daughter's portrayal, in a world of dreams.

If Lasker-Schüler's information can be trusted, she began suffering from "Veitstanz" (Saint Vitus' dance) at the age of eleven and could not attend public school from then on; instead, she was taught by private tutors—among them her brother Paul, who died in 1882 at the age of twenty. In her essay "Der letzte Schultag" (The Last School Day) in the volume *Konzert* (Concert, 1932) Lasker-Schüler ties her illness to her mother's melancholy: out of fear for her mother, who was alone in a nearby forest during an unexpected thunderstorm, she climbed up the tower of her parents' house to look for her. When she at last saw her mother dejectedly returning, she jumped out of the tower to reach her mother faster; only an awning below saved her from death or serious injury. According to Lasker-Schüler's fictitious account, the fall caused her illness. This invented episode is characteristic of Lasker-Schüler's writing. The tower symbolizes art, which allows the artist a superior view of life; being at the top of the tower, however, also isolates the poet from his or her fellow human beings and entails the danger of not being understood. Second, the view from this elevated position enables the poet to see the inevitable sadness of life: "Auf einmal sah ich meine liebe, liebe Mama so traurig den kleinen Berg herabkommen, so traurig, das vermag meine Hand nicht zu schildern, da müßte ich schon mein Herz aus der Brust nehmen und es schreiben lehren" (Suddenly I saw my dear, dear mommy descend the hill so sadly, so sadly—my hand is incapable of describing it; I would really have to take my heart out of my bosom and teach it to write). These lines can be interpreted as claiming that while art can lead to a profound understanding of the sadness of life, it finds its ultimate limitation in its inability to express this sadness. Written when Lasker-Schüler was in her early sixties, the "tower episode" must also be read as an admission of the poet's lingering doubts about the adequacy of her own poetry as well as of words and images as such.

Lasker-Schüler's first poetry collection, *Styx* (1902), reveals how deeply she was affected by her mother's death in 1890: her loss evokes apocalyptic, catastrophic images. Nonetheless, it is also seen as a new act of creation, which begins a new temporality and hence a new awareness of death: "Wie meine Mutter starb, zerbrach der Mond. Noch einmal trennte Er, der Herr, das Wasser von dem Land" (When my mother died the moon broke into pieces. Once more He, the Lord, separated the water from the land).

In January 1894 Schüler married Dr. Jonathan Berthold Lasker, a Berlin physician and a brother of the world chess champion, Emanuel Lasker. It seems that Lasker-Schüler felt imprisoned by what she considered the bourgeois lifestyle of the marriage. On 24 August 1899 her only child, Paul, was born, but her husband was not the father; Lasker-Schüler never revealed the name of the real father. Before the turn of the century she met the poet Peter Hille, who, unlike her husband, encouraged her creative endeavors. Through Hille she came in contact with many other members of the Berlin artistic community.

Lasker-Schüler's liaison with Hille ended in the spring of 1903, shortly before she was divorced from her husband. In November 1903 she married the composer and writer Georg Levin, who used the pseudonym Herwarth Walden. The following years were overshadowed by worries about money and the failing health of her son. The marriage was undermined by these problems, leading to a separation in 1910 and a divorce in 1912.

During the last, strained years of her relationship with Levin, Lasker-Schüler wrote her first drama, *Die Wupper* (Wupper River; published, 1909; performed, 1919). This multifaceted play combines "naturalistic" features in the Hauptmann tradition with neo-Romantic and symbolistic elements, the influences of art nouveau, and early expressionism. Yet these heterogeneous components form an impressive unity. Lasker-Schüler initially wrote the play's dialogue in the dialect of her hometown, but since few people were able to understand this vernacular she translated it into standard German. The translation, however, is not complete: the characters from the working-class milieu still speak the Wuppertal dialect, or at least a watered-down version of it, while the bourgeois characters use the standard language. Thus, dialect is a device to locate the characters socially.

In *Ich räume auf!* (I Mop Up!, 1925) Lasker-Schüler gives her own romanticized account of how *Die Wupper* came into being: she claims to have written the play in one night. She calls it a "böse Arbeitermär" (bitter workers' tale) that "durch das Gewölbe meines Herzens aus dunkler Erinnerung gepreßt (pressed through the vault of my heart out of dim recollection). By tying together the atmosphere and characters of her hometown, religious bigotry, Protestant sects thriving in the river valley, superstition, crude sexuality, class differences, and social conflicts, she evokes the sad futility of human endeavors and hopes. The characters' aspirations are doomed to fail: they are not in control of their fate. As one of the characters puts it, "Ich hab nix von's Leben, aber es hat mir zum Zeitvertreib" (I don't have anything from life, but it has me as a pastime).

Acts 1 and 4 and the second scene of act 5 are set in the working-class neighborhood of a small factory town on the banks of the Wupper. Dyeing is the main industry, and the stage directions for the fourth act call for a river dyed glowing crimson—one of the play's many strong and eerie expressionistic symbols. Act 2 and the first scene of act 5 are set in and around the old villa of the Sonntag family, who are well-to-do factory owners. Act 3 is set in a fairground, which functions as the play's catalyst and the place where opposite worlds clash.

The proletarian milieu is represented by the slightly senile grandfather Wallbrecker, his daughter Amanda Pius, her son Carl, and Carl's grandmother, the sly and crafty Mutter (Mother) Pius. Carl, an ambitious young man studying for his university entrance examinations, gave up Catholicism—the faith of the lower classes—and intends to become a Protestant pastor. His strongest motivation is the will to leave his modest upbringing behind, but he also has an envious desire to punish all sinners "weil ich sie [die Sünde] nicht genießen kann" (because I can't savor it [sin]). He hopes to marry Marta Sonntag, the frivolous sister of his best friend, Eduard, unaware that Marta is more interested in the opportunistic, morally corrupt Dr. von Simon, the manager of the Sonntag factory. Eduard is the most positive character in the play, yet even he is portrayed as a sickly, idealistic dreamer, naive and out of touch with reality. In contrast to Carl, he converted to Catholicism so that he could flee the world, for which he seems to be too good, and become a monk. His lack of realism is, on the other hand, also seen as the positive quality of a poet: when his snobbish mother criticizes the idealized image he has of his friend Carl Pius, saying, "Du dichtest ihn dir, Eduard" (You're fictionalizing him, Eduard), he half-jokingly replies: "Wie sollte der, der den Himmel verkündet, nicht ein Dichter sein?" (How could he who preaches the word of God not be a poet?).

Heinrich Sonntag, Eduard's older brother, is an unstable individual who, after their father's death, was forced to abandon his military career to take charge of the family business. He gambles, drinks heavily, and seduces working-class girls. One of these girls is Lieschen Puderbach, who is torn between the remnants of her child-

Lasker-Schüler circa 1912. She frequently wore oriental costumes and played a flute during recitations of her poetry.

like innocence and the awakening of her sexuality—a conflict aggravated by the moral rigidity of her fanatically Puritan father.

This ensemble of vulnerable characters is manipulated by the vital Mutter Pius, who is called a "Teufelin" (devil), although in the end she ends up as empty-handed as everyone else. She encourages Carl in his ambitions and persuades him to ask for Marta Sonntag's hand. She makes her fairground booth available to Heinrich Sonntag so that he can be intimate with Lieschen Puderbach. Mutter Pius's concession at the fair is a two-headed child mummy, which she calls Lieschen's twin—an allegory of Lieschen's undecided position between innocence and wantonness.

The merry-go-round of the fair is the main symbol in the play. Its seats, arranged in a double circle, are made up of wooden animals that could never peacefully coexist in real life: a leopard stands next to a lamb, a deer next to a tiger, a lion next to a horse, and so on. Just as this idyll is impossible in the wild, the harmony conjured up by this image is impossible in the human world. A foreshadowing of the destruction of this idyll is the old folk song that the merry-go-round plays: "O du lieber Augustin, alles ist hin, hin, hin . . . " (Dear Augustine, everything's finished . . . "). As act 3 proceeds, the idyll gives way to disillusionment: the fairground turns into a battleground where the drunken workers' resentments collide with the cynical arrogance of their bosses. Toward the end of the act a character says: "Wir wollen den Garten nu reinigen von de Sünde" (Let's now cleanse this garden of sin). The merry-go-round symbolizes the state after the Fall, when everything appears to be the same as it was but is really decayed and saddened. The "diabolical" Mutter Pius—a name of bitter irony—is characterized as "das Karussell, wo wir all drinsitzen" (the merry-go-round in which we all ride).

In act 5 the audience learns that Heinrich has commited suicide after impregnating Lieschen, who enters a reformatory. Mme Sonntag, whose highest interest is the rescue of her family business, brusquely rejects Carl's request for permission to propose to Marta and arranges for Marta to marry Dr. von Simon. Eduard vehemently disapproves of this match. When Mme Sonntag receives a nude photograph of Marta, she assumes that it was sent by the Pius family as an act of revenge and uses it to drive a wedge between Eduard and Carl. Carl, overwhelmed with self-pity, is driven to drink.

Die Wupper portrays a gloomy world without hope. The workers remain divided in their rebellion against the factory owners. Everyone seeks his or her own advantage, but all fail in their endeavors. The driving force behind the characters' actions is their sexuality, which eludes rational control. The only person whose motives are unselfish—and who is, characteristically, also free of sexual desires—is Eduard, but he is too weak and guileless to exert a decisive influence.

Atmosphere is more important in *Die Wupper* than plot. The crucial events, such as Lieschen's seduction and Heinrich's suicide, are not shown; the audience has to gather this information from sparse allusions in the dialogue. There is no crass realism; the lyric tone prevails throughout. Even the three obscene vagabonds,

who, like the chorus of a Greek tragedy, comment on the events, are more comical than shocking. They represent outcasts of society, and so they see things more clearly than the "normal" characters. Yet even one of these vagabonds, Amadeus, succumbs to an illusion when he professes optimism at the outset of the play, "Es gibt noch was hinter de Düsterkeit, wart man, wenn es erst Licht wird" (There is something else behind the gloom; just wait until there is light). The play's end gives the lie to its hopeful beginning.

On 18 January 1911 Lasker-Schüler read *Die Wupper* at the Berlin Neopathetisches Cabaret. The stage premiere of the play took place at the Deutsches Theater in Berlin on 27 April 1919, directed by Heinz Herald. This first production had cubist sets in the expressionist mode by Ernst Stern, with crooked buildings full of nooks and crannies. The director envisioned a combination of naturalism and expressionism; his interpretation emphasized the play's fantastic and magical elements. This production received mixed reviews, but the second production, which opened at the Staatliches Schauspielhaus in Berlin on 15 October 1927, directed by Jürgen Fehling, was an undisputed success. Leading critics, including Alfred Kerr and Herbert Ihering, wrote enthusiastic reviews. Fehling stressed the realistic features of the drama without sacrificing the magical ones. A Cologne production directed by Hans Bauer in the fall of 1958 caused a scandal: the official press of the Catholic archdiocese condemned the play as outdated, obscene, and insubstantial, and on 21 November about a hundred spectators disrupted the performance.

The time after her divorce from Levin was difficult for Lasker-Schüler both psychologically and financially. It was, however, also a time of great creative productivity. She frequently gave readings from her works and tried to make a living for herself and her ailing son by contributing to literary journals and newspapers. In the years before World War I she met artists such as Gottfried Benn (with whom she fell in unrequited love), Georg Trakl, Franz Marc, Alfred Döblin, George Grosz, and Franz Werfel. In November 1913 she traveled to Russia to try to rescue her friend, the anarchist Johannes Holzmann, who had been imprisoned after the failed revolution of 1905. Her efforts came too late: Holzmann died in his cell five months after her intervention. After the war her son developed tuberculosis, and she had to pay for his treatment in an expensive Swiss sanatorium. As his condition deteriorated she took him home to Berlin and took care of him herself. He died on 14 December 1927. The only ray of hope in this gloom was the renowned Kleist Prize, which she received in 1932.

Also in 1932 Lasker-Schüler's narrative *Arthur Aronymus: Die Geschichte meines Vaters* (Arthur Aronymus: My Father's Story) was published. This short piece became the nucleus of her drama *Arthur Aronymus und seine Väter (Aus meines geliebten Vaters Kinderjahren): Schauspiel in fünfzehn Bildern* (Arthur Aronymus and His Forefathers: From My Beloved Father's Childhood Years. Play in Fifteen Scenes; published, 1932; performed, 1936). The play is "epic" in the Brechtian sense—the order of many of the scenes could almost arbitrarily be changed without any major effect on the plot's logic—and it is somewhat Brechtian in its didactic intent. Because of its considerable length and because its cast includes about thirty children and young adolescents, it has not often been produced.

The play is set in the village of Geseke, Westphalia, the birthplace of Lasker-Schüler's father. The historical background is a pogrom that took place there in 1844: a Catholic priest had abused his position as the teacher of a Jewish boy to convert him to Catholicism; after the boy's parents protested, the clergyman circulated an anonymous letter railing against the Catholic church and alleged that it was sent to him by Jews from Geseke. The letter touched off the pogrom, which did not end until the boy's father agreed to his son's conversion to Christianity. Lasker-Schüler reinterpreted these events in such a way that the play became an appeal for religious reconciliation. She also made her own father and his family the main characters.

The play begins with Rabbi Uriel of Paderborn, Arthur's grandfather, receiving a delegation of Jewish merchants who implore him to take action against the resurgence of anti-Semitism and belief in witchcraft. One of the merchants fears that "Unsere Töchter wird man verbrennen auf Scheiterhaufen" (Our daughters will be burned at the stake). The rabbi, however, trusts his friend, Bishop Matthias of Paderborn, who gave him assurances that no danger was imminent. The following scene introduces Arthur Aronymus Schüler, a pert, imaginative, and amusing eight-year-old. The angel of death comes intending to take Arthur away, but after Rabbi Uriel pleads with the angel and offers his own

life instead, the angel relents and leaves Arthur alive. These two scenes reveal the rabbi's wisdom and humanity—he embodies the best traditions of Judaism.

The Catholic chaplain Bernard Michalski, a nephew of the bishop of Paderborn, is a representative of the ideal of tolerance. He has taken a special liking to Arthur and his older sister Fanny. But with all his kindness and good intentions, his love for Arthur remains ambivalent: when he celebrates Christmas Eve with Arthur and two young nieces and the boy, in frolicsome exuberance, steals the glass ball from the top of the Christmas tree, Bernard remarks thoughtlessly: "Aber du willst doch nicht gar ein dreister Judenjunge werden?" (But you surely don't want to become a brash Jewboy?). The remark, regretted by Bernard at once, hurts Arthur deeply.

A target of the mob's witch-hunt is Arthur's other sister, Dora, who suffers from Saint Vitus' dance—an illness that superstition associates with witchcraft. To avert the threat to Dora, the Schülers consider making a donation to the Catholic church in Geseke. Michalski puts forward a different suggestion: to have Arthur Aronymus raised in the Christian faith. Arthur's father rejects this idea: "Ich . . . [und meine Vorväter] pflegten auf *direktem* Wege zu Gott zu gelangen, und ich sollte *Seinem Sohn*—meinen noch unmündigen Sohn auf *Umwegen* zuführen lassen?" (I . . . [and my forefathers] reached God *directly*, but I should let my son, still a minor, be *indirectly* led to *His Son*?). The priest then requests from his uncle, the bishop, an official decree from the church against the witch-hunt directed at the Jews. The bishop's intervention restores the peace between Jews and Christians in Geseke.

The last scene takes place more than a year after these events. Dora has recovered from her illness. Bishop Matthias and his nephew, who has become his assistant in Paderborn, are invited to celebrate Passover with the Schüler family. The scene exists in two slightly different versions: the original one of 1932 and a shortened version used in the Zurich stage production of 1936. The main themes, however, are the same in both versions: unity and reconciliation, friendship between believers of different faiths, and family relationships. In the Zurich version the play ends with the bishop loosely quoting from 1 Peter 1:17: "Gott sieht nicht auf die Person, vielmehr ist ihm in jedem Volke wohlgefällig, wer ihn fürchtet und recht tut" (God pays no regard to the person, but rather he is pleased with those among every people who fear Him and do right).

The play's language is often turgid; some scenes—especially the one in which Michalski and Fanny Schüler intimate their impossible love for each other—are comically mawkish. Given the reality of 1932, Lasker-Schüler's portrayal of anti-Semitism seems overly benign and the message of mutual understanding and respect naive. Similarly, the "Biedermeier" idyll of 1840 offers an insipid contrast to the turbulence of the late Weimar Republic.

A proposed production in Darmstadt was canceled in early 1933. The play was first staged in Zurich during Lasker-Schüler's exile in Switzerland, directed by Leopold Lindtberg, on 19 December 1936. For reasons that are not clear, there were only two performances. The critical response was less than enthusiastic. A second production, staged in Wuppertal during the 1968-1969 season and directed by Hans Bauer, was highly successful; it went on tour and was also shown on West German television. When the Austrian author Peter Handke saw a performance in Berlin, he left the theater during the intermission; the contrast between the "Weihnachtsmärchen" (Christmas fairy tale) and the reality of the Holocaust was unbearable to him.

In April 1933 Lasker-Schüler left Nazi Germany for Switzerland. Her life there was a constant struggle for money, since she was not allowed to work, and for residence permits. In the spring of 1934 she visited Palestine; her account of this trip, *Das Hebräerland* (Hebrew Land), was published in 1937. After her return to Switzerland in July she lived in small hotel rooms in Zurich. Friends noticed signs of paranoia and a general weakening of her mental health. In 1937 she was invited to Palestine for a second time; she spent mid June to the end of August there, reading from her works. In the spring of 1939 Lasker-Schüler had to leave Switzerland for three months to become eligible for a new residence permit. She went to Palestine intending to stay only for a couple of months, but the outbreak of World War II prevented her from returning to Europe. She settled in Jerusalem in a small rented room, which she did not have the money to heat in the winter of 1940-1941. It was during these difficult months, barely capable of typing the manuscript because of the cold, that she wrote her last play: *IchundIch: Eine theatralische Tragödie in sechs Akten, einem Vor- und einem Nachspiel* (IandI: A Theatrical Tragedy in Six Acts, a Prelude and an Epilogue; performed, 1979; published, 1980; translated as *IandI*, 1992).

The play's prelude consists of a monologue given by Lasker-Schüler, who is on her way to the theater with a companion. The monologue—one of many allusions to Johann Wolfgang von Goethe's *Faust I* (1808), here to the "Vorspiel auf dem Theater" (Prelude in the Theater)—sets the lyrical, nonrealistic tone of the play. The poet introduces herself: " . . . Mich führte in die Wolke mein Geschick—/ . . . Für eines Dichters unbegrenzten Traum / Hat wahrlich eure Welt gezimmerte nicht Raum. /. . . Ich führe ja ein höheres Leben— / . . . Und nur mein Vers war keine Illusion!" (. . . My fate has led me into the cloud—. . . / . . . For a poet's unconfined dream your world has not made room. / . . . I lead a higher form of life— / . . . And only my verse was not an illusion!). These words are meant as a summation of Lasker-Schüler's life and work.

The first five acts are set in a theater at a place outside Jerusalem that the stage directions call "Höllengrund" (hell's territory). Lasker-Schüler's Jerusalem is not heavenly; it must remain part of hell because the world is not yet ripe for paradise. The play consists of the dress rehearsal for another play. This complex arrangement mirrors the play's most important motifs: reflection and the ultimate unity of separated, even opposing parts. The scene gathers a colorful and bizarre ensemble of characters. Kings Saul, David, and Solomon, the theater director Max Reinhardt, Lasker-Schüler herself, the American comedy team the Ritz Brothers, critics, and journalists are the audience of the rehearsal. The characters of the play within the play include Dr. Faust, Mephisto, and Marthe Schwerdtlein from *Faust I*; the god Baal; Adolf Hitler, Joseph Goebbels, Hermann Göring, and other Nazi leaders; Marinus van der Lubbe, who was accused of setting fire to the Reichstag building on 27 February 1933; and a scarecrow. At the beginning of the act Lasker-Schüler says that the theme of the play is the unification of the two egos into which she is split. Since this division could not heal in real life, it had to be projected into art. The two egos are represented by "Faust / Goethe" (Lasker-Schüler identifies character and author) and Mephisto. At a deeper level, the poet sees herself as divided by her Jewish heritage, which craves for redemption by God, and her being part of the German culture, which is epitomized by Goethe's drama. But while both the Jews and Faust / Goethe suffer from the limitations of earthly exis-

Scene from the first German production, which took place in Wuppertal in 1968, of Lasker-Schüler's Arthur Aronymus und seine Väter (*Archiv* Theater heute)

tence, Faust /Goethe seeks to overcome these limitations through a pact with the devil. Hence, for Lasker-Schüler, the German culture, in its highest expression, defies the essence of Judaism, which is absolute obedience to God. To reconcile these two halves of her existence, she had to portray Faust /Goethe and Mephisto as God's fallen children, who in the end find their way back to their Father and are saved.

To achieve this goal, the play shows not only Faust /Goethe but also Mephisto yearning for light. Mephisto says: "Und suchte sie [die Lichtung] wie du—denn ich bin, Herre Faust, ein Mensch wie du!" (And I was searching for it [the light], too—for I am, Faust, a human being like yourself !). He and Faust /Goethe represent each culture's good and evil halves, constantly in conflict with each other. But since even the devil is not absolutely evil, the outcome of this struggle is certain: the good will overcome its opposite and will be strengthened by it. Mephisto, after all, roused Faust /Goethe from his "bourgeois" complacency and enabled him to become the artistic genius he is. Since good is more powerful than evil, hell is only a temporary exile from heaven.

The Nazis want to strike a deal with Mephisto: the gasoline monopoly in hell in exchange for the souls of a small town. For Mephisto, the Nazis are vulgar and despicable

upstarts, not on a par with him in the least: "Anspruchsvoller fordert besseren Wein mein Haß—ein edler Haß!" (My hatred, a noble, more demanding one, needs better wine!). When Hitler tries to conquer hell, the Nazi gang perishes in lava streams. Mephisto's evilness is derived from God and hence redeemable; Hitler is the foe of all religions and therefore not redeemable. Only after the downfall of Nazism can Faust / Goethe and Mephisto, the separated halves of one ego, reunite and ascend to Heaven. Lasker-Schüler is expressing her belief in a German-Jewish cultural synthesis in opposition to National Socialism. This synthesis is no longer achieved through Judaism's assimilation into the German culture; rather, the play reinterprets this culture in the light of Judaism.

The final act is set in the garden of an ophthalmologist in Jerusalem. There the poet encounters a scarecrow, an allegory of the expelled, destitute, destroyed Jewish element of German culture. The scarecrow feels homeless and alienated both in Germany and in Palestine. The play ends with the peaceful death of the poet.

Lasker-Schüler read her play at the Jerusalem Berger Club on 20 July 1941; the theologian Martin Buber was in the audience. The play was never published during Lasker-Schüler's life, and the administrator of her literary estate believed

Dedication in the summer of 1989 of the Else Lasker-Schüler Memorial in her hometown, Wuppertal-Elberfeld. The memorial consists of two symmetrical mosaics based on a 1920 photograph of Lasker-Schüler (photograph by Kurt Keil).

the imperfections of the play to be so numerous and so serious that they would destroy Lasker-Schüler's reputation. Therefore he and the editor of the volume containing her posthumous works published only excerpts from the play in 1961. That decision led to a controversy; some critics accused the editor of censorship. In February 1961 the entire fragment was read without permission by students in the Theater A 18 of the Free University of Berlin. Finally, in 1970 the first full publication of the play, with a commentary and a critical apparatus, appeared in the *Jahrbuch der Deutschen Schiller-Gesellschaft* (Yearbook of the German Schiller Society). Any stage production was still prohibited by Lasker-Schüler's executor. While some critics believe the play to be a sad testimony to Lasker-Schüler's declining mental powers, others have called it "unique" and a "mysterious gem." The artistic concept underlying the play is original—it was written before Thomas Mann's *Doktor Faustus* (1947; translated as *Doctor Faustus*, 1948)—but the play's many stylistic weaknesses and its unevenness cannot be overlooked. Some scenes, such as the ones portraying Goebbels's flirtation with Marthe Schwerdtlein,

are in bad taste if not simply silly. When the play's production was finally permitted, however, the premiere in Düsseldorf on 10 November 1979 directed by Michael Gruner and a staging in Wuppertal on 8 December 1979 directed by Hermann Kleinselbeck were impressive successes.

Lasker-Schüler's last publication was a volume of elegiac poetry, *Mein blaues Klavier* (My Blue Piano), in 1943. The following year her health failed rapidly, and she was no longer able to read publicly from her works. She died in Jerusalem on the morning of 22 January 1945 of a heart condition. Reportedly, her last words were: "Mir geht es zu Ende, ich kann nicht mehr lieben" (My end is coming. I can't love any more).

Letters:

Briefe an Karl Kraus, edited by Astrid Gehlhoff-Claes (Cologne & Berlin: Kiepenheuer & Witsch, 1959);

Briefe von Else Lasker-Schüler, 2 volumes, edited by Margarete Kupper, volume 1: *Lieber gestreifter Tiger*; volume 2: *Wo ist unser buntes Theben* (Munich: Kösel, 1969);

Die Wolkenbrücke: Ausgewählte Briefe von Else Lasker-Schüler, edited by Kupper (Munich: Deutscher Taschenbuch Verlag, 1972);

"Was soll ich hier?" Exilbriefe an Salman Schocken, edited by Sigrid Bauschinger (Heidelberg: Stiehm, 1980).

Biographies:

Jürgen P. Wallmann, *Else Lasker-Schüler* (Mühlacker: Stieglitz, 1966);

Erika Klüsener, *Else Lasker-Schüler*, Rowohlts Monographien, 283 (Reinbek: Rowohlt, 1980);

Sigrid Bauschinger, *Else Lasker-Schüler: Ihr Werk und ihre Zeit* (Heidelberg: Stiehm, 1980);

Jakob Hessing, *Else Lasker-Schüler: Biographie einer deutsch-jüdischen Dichterin* (Karlsruhe: Loeper, 1985).

References:

Brigitte Baldrian-Schrenk, "Form und Struktur der Bildlichkeit bei Else Lasker-Schüler," Ph.D. dissertation, University of Freiburg, 1962;

Dieter Bänsch, *Else Lasker-Schüler: Zur Kritik eines etablierten Bildes* (Stuttgart: Metzler, 1971);

Sigrid Bauschinger, "Die Symbolik des Mütterlichen im Werk Else Lasker-Schülers," Ph.D. dissertation, University of Frankfurt am Main, 1960;

Schalom Ben-Chorin, "Else Lasker-Schüler zum 100. Geburtstag," *Almanach für Literatur und Theologie*, 3 (1969): 178-192;

Bernhardt Blumenthal, "Aspects of Love in the Life and Works of Else Lasker-Schüler," Ph.D. dissertation, Princeton University, 1965;

Hans W. Cohn, *Else Lasker-Schüler: The Broken World* (Cambridge, U.K.: Cambridge University Press, 1974);

Fanni Goldstein, "Der expressionistische Stilwille im Werke der Else Lasker-Schüler," Ph.D. dissertation, University of Vienna, 1936;

Werner Hegglin, "Else Lasker-Schüler und ihr Judentum," Ph.D. dissertation, University of Fribourg, 1966;

Clemens Heselhaus, "Else Lasker-Schülers literarisches Traumspiel," in his *Deutsche Lyrik der Moderne von Nietzsche bis Yvan Goll*, second edition (Düsseldorf: Bagel, 1962), pp. 213-228;

Jakob Hessing, "Else Lasker-Schüler und ihr Volk," *Ariel*, 41 (1976): 60-76;

Hans Rudolf Hilty, "Ein nachgelassenes Schauspiel der Else Lasker-Schüler," in his *Jeanne d'Arc bei Schiller und Anouilh* (Saint Gall: Tschudy, 1960), pp. 54-60;

Brigitte Hintze, "Else Lasker-Schüler in ihrem Verhältnis zur Romantik: Ein Vergleich der Thematik und des Sprachstils," Ph.D. dissertation, University of Bonn, 1972;

Johannes Jacobi, "Theater aus dem Geist der Lyrik: *Arthur Aronymus und seine Väter* von Else Lasker-Schüler in Wuppertal," *Tagesspiegel* (West Berlin), 4 October 1968;

Franz Kafka, *Briefe an Felice*, edited by Erich Heller and Jürgen Born (Frankfurt am Main: Fischer, 1967), pp. 296, 306;

Erika Klüsener, "Else Lasker-Schüler: Eine Biographie oder ein Werk?," Ph.D. dissertation, Washington University, 1979;

Angelika Koch, *Die Bedeutung des Spiels bei Else Lasker-Schüler im Rahmen von Expressionismus und Manierismus* (Bonn: Bouvier, 1971);

Werner Kraft, "Else Lasker-Schüler," in *Juden, Christen, Deutsche*, edited by Hans-Jürgen Schultz (Stuttgart & Berlin: Kreuz, 1961), pp. 380-388;

Kraft, "Else Lasker-Schüler (1869-1945)," *Rheinische Lebensbilder*, 5 (1973): 227-242;

Kraft, *Wort und Gedanke: Kritische Betrachtungen zur Poesie* (Bern & Munich: Francke, 1959);

Margarete Kupper, "Der Nachlaß Else Lasker-Schülers in Jerusalem," *Literaturwissenschaftliches Jahrbuch im Auftrage der Görres-Gesellschaft*, new series 9 (1968): 243-283; 10 (1969): 175-230; 12 (1971): 241-291;

Kupper, "Die Weltanschauung Else Lasker-Schülers in ihren poetischen Selbstzeugnissen," Ph.D. dissertation, University of Würzburg, 1963;

Kupper, "Wiederentdeckte Texte Else Lasker-Schülers," *Literaturwissenschaftliches Jahrbuch im Auftrage der Görres-Gesellschaft*, new series 5 (1964): 229-263; 6 (1965): 227-233; 8 (1967): 175-199;

Ruth Lorbe, "Else Lasker-Schüler: Vollmond," in her *Lyrische Standpunkte*, second edition (Munich: Bayerischer Schulbuch Verlag, 1968), pp. 35-45;

Gunter Martens, *Vitalismus und Expressionismus: Ein Beitrag zur Genese und Deutung expressionistischer Stilstrukturen und Motive* (Stuttgart, Berlin, Cologne & Mainz: Kohlhammer, 1971), pp. 116-126;

Fritz Martini, "Else Lasker-Schüler: Dichtung und Glaube," in *Der deutsche Expressionismus: Formen und Gestalten*, edited by Hans Steffen

(Göttingen: Vandenhoeck & Ruprecht, 1965), pp. 5-24;

André Meyer, "Vorahnungen der Judenkatastrophe bei Heinrich Heine und Else Lasker-Schüler," *Bulletin des Leo Baeck Instituts* (Tel Aviv), 8 (1965): 7-27;

Andrea Parr, *Drama als "Schreitende Lyrik": Die Dramatikerin Else Lasker-Schüler* (Frankfurt am Main, Bern, New York & Paris: Lang, 1988);

Heiz Politzer, "Else Lasker-Schüler," in *Expressionismus als Literatur*, edited by Wolfgang Rothe (Bern & Munich: Francke, 1969), pp. 215-231;

Henning Rischbieter, "Wann spielt die *Wupper*?: Überlegungen zum Stück der Else Lasker-Schüler und zu Aufführungen an der Schaubühne und in Darmstadt," *Theater heute*, 17 (August 1976): 29-38;

Georges Schlocker, "Exkurs über Else Lasker-Schüler," in *Deutsche Literatur im 20. Jahrhundert*, volume 5, fifth edition, edited by Otto Mann and Wolfgang Rothe (Bern & Munich: Francke, 1967), pp. 344-357;

Michael Schmid, ed., *Lasker-Schüler: Ein Buch zum 100. Geburtstag der Dichterin* (Wuppertal: Hammer, 1969);

Hans Schwab-Fehlisch, "*Arthur Aronymus und seine Väter* von Else Lasker-Schüler in Wuppertal," *Theater heute*, 9 (September 1968): 35-37;

Wolfgang Springmann, ed., *Else Lasker-Schüler und Wuppertal*, second edition (Wuppertal-Elberfeld: Stadtbibliothek Wuppertal, 1965);

Klaus Weissenberger, *Zwischen Stein und Stern: Mystische Formgebung in der Dichtung von Else Lasker-Schüler, Nelly Sachs und Paul Celan* (Bern & Munich: Francke, 1976).

Papers:

Manuscripts by Else Lasker-Schüler are in the Else Lasker-Schüler-Nachlaßarchiv at the Jewish National and University Library, Jerusalem. The Else Lasker-Schüler Archive is at the public library of Wuppertal-Elberfeld.

Max Mell

(10 November 1882 - 12 December 1971)

Lowell A. Bangerter
University of Wyoming

See also the Mell entry in *DLB 81: Austrian Fiction Writers, 1875-1913.*

PLAY PRODUCTIONS: *Die Pächterin von Litchfield*, Berlin, Kleines Theater, 15 April 1907;

Der Barbier von Berriac, Mannheim, Nationaltheater, 24 November 1911;

Das Schutzengelspiel, Graz, Hof des Grazer Landhauses, 20 July 1923;

Das Apostelspiel, Graz, Rittersaal des Grazer Landhauses, 3 January 1924;

Das Nachfolge Christi-Spiel, Vienna, Burgtheater, 21 January 1928;

Die Sieben gegen Theben, Meiningen, Landestheater, 20 December 1931;

Das Spiel von den deutschen Ahnen, Dresden, Staatstheater, 23 March 1935;

Der Nibelunge Not, Vienna, Burgtheater, 23 January 1944;

Kriemhilds Rache, Vienna, Burgtheater, 6 January 1951;

Jeanne d'Arc, Bregenz Landestheater, 19 July 1956;

Paracelsus und der Lorbeer, Graz, Grazer Schauspielhaus, 14 March 1964.

BOOKS: *Lateinische Erzählungen* (Vienna & Leipzig: Wiener Verlag, 1904);

Die drei Grazien des Traumes: Fünf Novellen (Leipzig: Insel, 1906);

Die Tänzerin und die Marionette (Vienna: Ohwala, 1907);

Jägerhaussage und andere Novellen (Berlin: Paetel, 1910);

Das bekränzte Jahr: Gedichte (Berlin: Juncker, 1911);

Der Barbier von Berriac (St. Veit an der Glau: Schlick, 1911);

Barbara Naderers Viehstand: Eine Novelle (Leipzig: Staackmann, 1914);

Gedichte (Munich: Musarion, 1919);

Hans Hochgedacht und sein Weib (Vienna, Prague & Leipzig: Strache, 1920);

Max Mell

Die Osterfeier: Eine Novelle in Versen (Munich: Musarion, 1921);

Das Wiener Kripperl von 1919 (Vienna: Wiener Literarische Anstalt, 1921);

Alfred Roller (Vienna: Wiener Literarische Anstalt, 1922);

Das Schutzengelspiel (Graz: Moser, 1923);

Das Apostelspiel (Munich: Bremer Presse, 1923); translated by Maude Valerie White as *The Apostle Play* (London: Methuen, 1934);

Morgenwege: Erzählungen und Legenden (Leipzig: Reclam, 1924);

Das Buch von der Kindheit Jesu (Vienna: Rikola, 1924);

318

Schauspiele (Munich: Bremer Presse, 1927)—comprises *Das Nachfolge Christi-Spiel, Das Apostelspiel, Das Schutzengelspiel;*

Das Nachfolge Christi-Spiel (Munich: Bremer Presse, 1927);

Gedichte, mit Holzschnitten von Switbert Lobisser (Vienna: Speidel, 1929);

Die Sieben gegen Theben: Dramatische Dichtung (Leipzig: Insel, 1932);

Anton Wildgans zum Gedächtnis: Gesprochen bei der Gedenkfeier des Burgtheaters am 8. Mai 1932 (Vienna: Gerold, 1932);

Barbara Naderer: Eine Novelle (Leipzig: Insel, 1933);

Das Spiel von den deutschen Ahnen (Leipzig: Insel, 1935);

Mein Bruder und ich: Den Erinnerungen eines alten Wieners nacherzählt (Munich: Langen-Müller, 1935);

Paradiesspiel in der Steiermark (Salzburg: Pustet, 1936);

Das Donauweibchen: Erzählungen und Märchen (Leipzig: Insel, 1938);

Steirischer Lobgesang (Leipzig: Insel, 1939);

Adalbert Stifter (Leipzig: Insel, 1939);

Verheißungen (Leipzig: Reclam, 1943);

Steirische Heimat (Graz: Leykam, 1943);

Gabe und Dank (Vienna: Gallus, 1949);

Das Vergelt's Gott: Ein Volksmärchen (Vienna: Bernina, 1950);

Der Nibelunge Not: Dramatische Dichtung in zwei Teilen (Salzburg: Müller, 1951)—also includes *Kriemhilds Rache;*

In Zauberkreisen: Werden eines Werkes (Graz, Vienna & Munich: Stiasny, 1951);

Gedichte (Wiesbaden: Insel, 1952);

Legenden (Tokyo: Ikubundo, 1953);

Verheißungen: Ausgewählte Erzählungen (Einsiedeln, Zurich & Cologne: Benziger, 1954);

Aufblick zum Genius: Drei festliche Reden (Innsbruck: Österreichische Verlagsanstalt, 1955)—comprises "Zur Lage der Kunst," "Zum Gedenken Schillers," "Adalbert Stifter";

Jeanne d'Arc: Ein Schauspiel (Wiesbaden: Insel, 1957);

Eines Jahres Ewigkeit (Dülmer: Kreis der Freunde, 1962);

Gesammelte Werke, 4 volumes (Vienna: Amandus, 1962); republished as *Prosa, Dramen, Verse*, 4 volumes (Munich: Langen-Müller, 1962);

Der Garten des Paracelsus: Dramatische Phantasie, edited by Lilli Mell (Graz, Vienna & Cologne: Styria, 1974);

Barbara Naderer und andere Erzählungen, edited by Margret Dietrich (Graz, Vienna & Cologne: Styria, 1976);

Spiegel des Sünders: Drei Erzählungen aus dem Nachlaß (Vienna: Österreichische Akademie der Wissenschaften, 1976);

Der Spiegel der Jahreszeiten: Ausgewählte Gedichte, Wien im Jänner 1905 (Graz: Steiermärkische Landesbibliothek am Joanneum, 1976);

Mächte zwischen den Menschen: Erzählungen, edited by Margret Dietrich (Graz, Vienna & Cologne: Styria, 1978);

Herz, werde groß (Graz, Vienna & Cologne: Styria, 1982).

OTHER: *Almanach der Wiener Werkstätte*, edited by Mell (Vienna: Rosenbaum, 1911);

Pope Pius II, *Briefe*, translated by Mell (Jena: Diederichs, 1911);

Österreichische Zeiten und Charaktere: Ausgewählte Bruchstücke aus österreichischen Selbstbiographien, edited by Mell (Vienna: Deutsch-Österreichischer Verlag, 1912);

Österreichische Landschaft im Gedicht, edited by Mell (Vienna: Sesam, 1922);

Ein altes deutsches Weihnachtsspiel, edited by Mell (Vienna: Johannes-Presse, 1924);

Haus- und Volksbuch deutscher Erzählungen, edited by Mell (Leipzig: Staackmann, 1936);

Wolfgang Amadeus Mozart, *Briefe Mozarts*, edited by Mell (Leipzig: Insel, 1937);

Stimme Österreichs: Zeugnisse aus drei Jahrhunderten, edited by Mell (Munich: Langen-Müller, 1938);

Adalbert Stifter, *Gesammelte Werke in sieben Bänden*, 7 volumes, introduction by Mell (Leipzig: Insel, 1939);

Alpenländisches Märchenbuch: Volksmärchen aus Österreich, compiled by Mell (Vienna: Amandus-Edition, 1946);

Franz Grillparzer, *Österreichischer Lebenslauf*, introduction by Mell (Vienna: Dürer, 1947);

Antoni Edward Odyniec, *Besuch in Weimar: Goethes achtzigster Geburtstag. Briefberichte eines jungen polnischen Dichters*, translated by F. T. Bratranek, edited by Mell (Vienna: Pilgrim, 1949);

Peter Rosegger, *Aus meiner Waldheimat: Eine Auswahl*, afterword by Mell (Stuttgart: Reclam, 1953).

Beginning in 1914, when he received the Bauernfeld Prize for the novella *Barbara Naderers Viehstand* (Barbara Naderer's Livestock, 1914),

Max Mell was repeatedly recognized for his contributions to Austrian literature and culture. His awards included the Vienna Literary Prize in 1927, the Grillparzer Prize in 1928 and 1940, the Mozart Prize of the Weimar Goethe Society in 1937, the Austrian State Prize in 1954, and the Austrian Medal of Honor for Science and Art in 1960. The essence of the works for which he was so widely acclaimed lies in their unpretentious yet powerful mediation, presentation, and promotion of things Austrian, extending from the cultural heritage of Vienna to modern rural existence, and in their strong affirmation of the Christian spiritual values he had encountered in his childhood home. Throughout his life Mell devoted himself to the creation of literary art that had the power to encourage, help, comfort, and uplift his fellow human beings.

Born in Marburg an der Drau (now Moribor, Croatia) on 10 November 1882, Mell experienced a variety of immediate influences that shaped his literary personality. Among them were the examples set by his parents—Alexander Mell was a teacher of the blind, while Marie Rocek Mell had a fertile imagination and a fondness for the theater; serious religious training; a warm and happy home life; an early introduction to art and literature; a rigorous humanistic education; and the country environment of his first four years. Although his family moved to Vienna in 1886, he never lost contact with his rural beginnings.

In 1905 Mell received a doctorate in philosophy from the University of Vienna. Around that time he met Olga von Graff, with whom he maintained a platonic but deep friendship for the rest of his life; she had an especially strong influence on the works of his late period. Hugo von Hofmannsthal, whom Mell met in 1907, encouraged, assisted, and collaborated with Mell in many literary undertakings. Their published correspondence provides significant insights into the younger author's life and work between 1907 and 1929, the year of Hofmannsthal's death.

During his early career Mell was more successful as a storyteller and poet than as a dramatist. *Die Pächterin von Litchfield* (The Tenant Farmer's Wife of Litchfield; performed, 1907), a three-act comedy about a tenant farmer, his wife, and a countess who has seduced him, was quickly forgotten. In spite of what Mell saw as a highly successful premiere, *Der Barbier von Berriac* (The Barber of Berriac, 1911), a comedy that depicts the title figure's response to his wife's unfaithfulness,

did not fare much better. After performances in Mannheim, Berlin, and Vienna it disappeared from the stage. As a result, Mell stopped writing plays for almost a decade.

Mell's military service during World War I ended with his illness in 1917. In 1918 he became a literary editor of the newspaper *Wiener Mittag* (Viennese Midday). He resigned in 1922; that same year he declined a position as a producer at the Burgtheater in Vienna.

Mell's success as a dramatist began in 1921 with the publication of *Die Osterfeier* (The Easter Celebration) and *Das Wiener Kripperl von 1919* (The Little Viennese Crèche of 1919). The creation of these and Mell's other early religious plays was stimulated by his recognition of the need for spiritual rejuvenation in a society shattered by the chaos of World War I. The central theme of *Die Osterfeier* and *Das Wiener Kripperl von 1919*, the revitalizing power of faith within the lives of contemporary people, is also the common focus of *Das Schutzengelspiel* (The Guardian Angel Play, 1923), *Das Apostelspiel* (published, 1923; performed, 1924; translated as *The Apostle Play*, 1934), and *Das Nachfolge Christi-Spiel* (The Play About the Imitation of Christ, published, 1927; performed, 1928). All of these works are notable for their realism; the key to their continuing public success lies in their convincing presentation of living human beings rather than artificial figures. From a theatrical point of view, Mell's plays of the 1920s are remarkable for simple staging requirements that permit them to be performed as easily in a village church or schoolroom as on a sophisticated stage.

Written in verse, *Die Osterfeier* has the flavor of a medieval religious play. It presents a simple yet profound situation in which three young Styrian villagers experience a transformation to spiritual maturity. *Das Wiener Kripperl von 1919* has timeless appeal. Against a bleak winter landscape of hunger and pain in postwar Vienna, a streetcar moves through the night, picking up passengers representing the diverse elements of the populace. Each boards the tram with a burden of suffering. All are transformed and renewed when they reach the final station on the line: the stable in Bethlehem.

Das Schutzengelspiel presents the idea that the pure doctrine of Christ is the only fitting basis for people's lives. *Das Schutzengelspiel* never became as popular as *Das Apostelspiel*, but Mell considered it to be his best early play. In *Das Schutzengelspiel* a young woman offends her guardian angel by looking down upon an unwed mother; the angel teaches the young woman humility by requiring her to stand at the church door and beg passing men to marry her. After enduring this trial she is forgiven and finds happiness in marriage. Mell's mastery of language and the richness of his characterizations lend *Das Schutzengelspiel* charm and power, but the direct intervention of the angel reduces the artistic impact of the play. What occurs here is not as compelling as other inner conversions that Mell depicts: faith and love lose some of their meaning when change is imposed from outside. The transformation of the robbers in *Das Apostelspiel* is beautiful because they *choose* not to harm the old man and his granddaughter.

The most popular of Mell's early plays is *Das Apostelspiel*, which combines features of the Christian mystery play with elements of the peasant drama to comment on the power of the Austrian spirit. Based on a Christian legend that Mell read on the wall of Saint John's Chapel in Salzburg in 1912, *Das Apostelspiel* centers on two degenerate soldiers returning from World War I who seek food and shelter in an isolated mountain cottage. Professing to be the apostles Peter and John, they plan to kill the young girl and the old man—her grandfather—who live there. Their plan is thwarted by the child, who questions them about the Bible and their love for Christ. Her naive faith changes the visitors, causing them to leave without harming anyone. Reinhardt's highly successful presentation of *Das Apostelspiel* in Vienna, a year after its premiere in Graz, gave Mell his first breakthrough in a major theater. The popularity of the play increased substantially during the run of a new Burgtheater production directed by Paul Kalbeck in 1937.

Theatrically, *Das Nachfolge Christi-Spiel* is Mell's most powerful early work. The premiere at the Burgtheater under the direction of Franz Herterich, with Raoul Aslan in the leading role, received uniformly positive reviews. During the Turkish wars, robbers enter a castle in Styria, capture its owner, and begin to crucify him. When imperial soldiers intervene and the criminals are sentenced to death, the nobleman pleads for their lives. His request is rejected, and the pious man prays for a miracle to save the lives of the criminals. He collapses and dies as his daughters return home with an image of the crucified Christ. The robbers fall to their knees in response to the image, and the death sentence is lifted.

Under Willy Löhr's direction Mell's first tragedy, *Die Sieben gegen Theben* (Seven against Thebes; published, 1932), premiered in 1931 as part of the centennial celebration of the Meiningen Landestheater (Provincial Theater). Although the author considered it one of his strongest pieces, it was less successful on the stage than the works that followed it. Sources of material include corresponding dramas by Aeschylus, Euripides, and Sophocles; Mell's play, however, is not simply a new treatment of the legend of Polynices' expedition against Thebes but an artistic examination of the fate of Oedipus and his family. Innovations include a Christian Antigone, a linking of the traditional guilt problem with the concept of original sin, and the interpretation of Oedipus in his later years as a symbol for human spiritual blindness. The power struggle between Oedipus's sons, Polynices and Eteocles, results in a war in which the two brothers kill each other. When Kreon assumes power, he has the tyrant Eteocles buried with honor but refuses to give the more humane Polynices the same respect. Their sister, Antigone, buries Polynices in defiance of Kreon's order and comforts Oedipus. She dies in a cavern filled with poisonous vapors rather than beg for her freedom.

Die Sieben gegen Theben is remarkable for its vivid contrasts. In the respective treatments of Eteocles and Polynices, unfeeling brutality is starkly juxtaposed with deep sensitivity. Kreon symbolizes spiritual weakness, injustice, selfishness, and hatred, while Antigone is a model of love, inner strength, mercy, and self-sacrifice. By tempering the tragedy with the idea that the human spirit can employ hope and love to overcome even death, Mell transforms the old material into a play that communicates his own more positive perceptions of mortal existence.

Mell briefly supported Germany's annexation of Austria in 1938 on the basis of cultural and historical considerations. From a political perspective, he soon became disenchanted with the change in Austria's national status. As a result, in 1940 Propaganda Minister Joseph Goebbels objected to Mell's receiving the Grillparzer Prize, and the Nazis banned performance of *Das Spiel von den deutschen Ahnen* (The Play about the German Ancestors, 1935), which, following its successful premiere in Dresden, had had an enormously popular run directed by Herterich at the Burgtheater from February 1936 to October 1938. *Das Spiel von den deutschen Ahnen* represents a return to the pattern of Mell's Christian plays,

Scene from the premiere of Mell's Das Nachfolge Christi-Spiel *at the Vienna Burgtheater in 1928, with Raoul Aslan, on the cross, as the pious castle owner*

but without the religious overtones. Inspired by a German legend about spirits of the dead who return in an effort to comprehend what has taken place, Mell portrays a farmer's struggle to save his patrimony during the Great Depression. When the farmer's wife presses him to sell out, move to town, and buy a tavern, his dead ancestors intervene to prevent the sale of the land. Mell's effective use of language to contrast the worlds of the ancestors and their descendants is especially noteworthy: there is an obvious difference between the "healthy" self-expression of the ancestral spirits and the colorless utterances of the figures from the 1930s. Barbed criticism of the times is also visible when the ancestors force a Nazi, who used a bomb in an assassination and caused the death of an innocent child, to surrender for trial.

Whereas *Das Spiel von den deutschen Ahnen* is Mell's response to the misery of the interwar period, his interpretation of the German epic *Das Nibelungenlied* (circa 1200; translated as *Das Nibelungenlied; or, The Lay of the Last Nibelungen*, 1848) in *Der Nibelunge Not* (The Peril of the Nibelungs; performed, 1944; published, 1951) and *Kriemhilds Rache* (Kriemhild's Revenge, 1951) is an artistic reaction to the turmoil of World War II and its after-

math. The problems of Mell's time are reflected in themes such as deception, betrayal, guilt, and even genocide, while the mood of the two plays mirrors the frustration, bitterness, pain, disappointment, and resignation Mell felt with respect to both the world situation and the personal losses—the devastation of his family's property and the deaths of his brother and mother—that he experienced during the war and the late 1940s.

The premiere of *Der Nibelunge Not* on 23 January 1944 under the direction of Lothar Müthel was greeted as the distress cry of an entire people. By the middle of June it had been performed forty-two times at the Burgtheater. When *Kriemhilds Rache* was staged for the first time seven years later under the direction of Adolf Rott, Mell was praised by the Viennese critic Friedrich Schreyvogel for presenting the eternal senselessness of revenge. *Der Nibelunge Not* focuses on the conflict between Siegfried's wife, Kriemhild, and the wife of Kriemhild's brother Gunther of Burgundy, which arises because they both love Siegfried and because of Siegfried's deceptive participation in Gunther's courtship of Brunhild. Kriemhild's partial knowledge of the latter situation gives her a distorted view of the events and leads her to scorn her rival in an explosive confrontation. This humiliation and Siegfried's rejection of her love lead Brunhild to conspire with Gunther's nobleman-at-arms, Hagen, to kill Siegfried. *Kriemhilds Rache* describes Kriemhild's terrible retaliation against the Burgundians in the court of her new husband, Attila the Hun. When her family comes to visit, Kriemhild, ignoring her brother's request that she forget the past, demands Siegfried's Nibelung treasure and the surrender of Hagen. Gunther refuses, and the Christian king Dietrich von Bern fails in his attempts to avert the disaster. All of the Burgundians are slain; Kriemhild kills Hagen with Siegfried's sword and is slain by one of Dietrich's retainers. Mell's figures are more vital, more complex, and more human than their medieval epic counterparts: Siegfried's deceptiveness causes him to lose much of his heroic stature, Hagen emerges as a noble person motivated only by loyalty to his king, and Dietrich von Bern is the embodiment of Christian ideals.

Jeanne d'Arc (published, 1957), which opened under the direction of Josef Gielen during the Bregenz Festival in 1956, became Mell's greatest international theatrical success. Like other twentieth-century dramatists who have portrayed Joan of Arc, Mell employs documents from the historical trial as the basis for his courtroom scenes; but he places the recorded utterances in new contexts and adds fictional elements that illuminate the heroine's spiritual nature. The main character of the drama is really the fictitious Peter Manuel, an enlightened lawyer who symbolizes modern civilization and who experiences an inner transformation from skeptic to believer because of his encounter with Jeanne. The wife of the man who betrayed Jeanne to the authorities convinces Peter Manuel to help the prisoner. Rejecting Jeanne's supernatural experience as irrational, he urges her to recant. Faced with death at the stake, she gives in; but when her sentence is commuted the lawyer realizes that by recanting Jeanne has rejected her own inner truth. A new encounter with her supernatural guiding voice moves her to retract her recantation and go to her death at peace with herself, leaving Peter Manuel convinced of her divine mission. A major strength of *Jeanne d'Arc* is its simple but beautiful language, which tempers the overwhelming injustice of what takes place. This element, combined with the realistic development of the character, makes the play Mell's masterpiece. Six years after its premiere Mell was saluted during a special meeting of the Austrian Academy of Sciences by Ernst Haeusserman, the director of the Burgtheater. Haeusserman noted that 217 performances of ten productions of Mell's dramatic works had been given at the Burgtheater alone.

After completing *Jeanne d'Arc* Mell spent much of the remainder of his life working on a somewhat Faustian treatment of the sixteenth-century Swiss alchemist and physician Paracelsus (Philippus Aureolus Theophrastus Bombast von Hohenheim). *Paracelsus und der Lorbeer* (Paracelsus and the Laurel; performed, 1964), which premiered in Graz only two weeks after Mell sent the manuscript to the director, was a disaster. The play's failure devastated Mell, and despite years of additional work it was never completed to his satisfaction. It was published posthumously as *Der Garten des Paracelsus* (The Garden of Paracelsus, 1974). This dense philosophical play is interesting primarily for its autobiographical reflection of Mell's relationship with Olga von Graff. Mell died on 12 December 1971.

Although Mell's dramas are deeply personal works, they are also an outgrowth of the European cultural heritage. Austrian Catholicism, Swabian Pietism, Greek tragedy, European humanism, many literary figures, the medieval mystery play, the Austrian peasant play, and more contributed to the theatrical works of one of Austria's most humane modern writers.

Letters:

Hugo von Hofmannsthal/Max Mell: Briefwechsel, edited by Margret Dietrich and Heinz Kindermann (Heidelberg: Lambert Schneider, 1982).

Bibliographies:

Ernst Metelmann, "Max Mell: Bibliographie," *Die schöne Literatur*, 31 (1930): 429-431;

Fritz Fuhrich, "Schriften von Max Mell," in *Almanach für das Jahr 1972* (Vienna: Österreichische Akademie der Wissenschaften, 1973), pp. 291-295.

References:

Alan Best, "The Austrian Tradition: Continuity and Change," *Modern Austrian Writing*, edited by Best and Hans Wolfschütz (London: Wolff, 1980), pp. 23-43;

Christoph Heinrich Binder, *Max Mell: Beiträge zu seinem Leben und Werk* (Graz: Steiermärkische Landesregierung, 1978);

Margret Dietrich, "Max Mell in unserer Zeit," in *Almanach für das Jahr 1972* (Vienna: Österreichische Akademie der Wissenschaften, 1973), pp. 487-501;

William Eickhorst, "Recent German Dramatic Treatments of the Joan of Arc Theme," *Arizona Quarterly*, 17 (Winter 1961): 323-332;

Isolde Emich, *Max Mell: Der Dichter und sein Werk* (Vienna: Amandus, 1957);

Emich, ed., *Licht aus der Stille* (Munich & Vienna: Langen-Müller, 1962);

Hans Jost Frey, " 'Jeanne d'Arc': Ein neues Drama von Max Mell," *Schweizer Monatshefte*, 36 (1956/1957): 488-490;

G. Guder, "Recent Trends in German Drama," *German Life and Letters*, 7 (1953/1954): 28-35;

Clemens Heselhaus, "Max Mell," in *Handbook of Austrian Literature*, edited by Frederick Ungar (New York: Ungar, 1973), pp. 179-181;

Paul Anton Keller, *Dreigestirn* (Maria-Rain: Petrie, 1963);

Dolf Lindner, "Der milde Herbst von Anno 62: Besuch bei dem österreichischen Dichter Max Mell," *Deutsche Rundschau*, 88 (1962): 987-991;

Siegfried Melchinger, "Die Heilige auf der Bühne," *Wort und Wahrheit: Monatsschrift für Religion und Kultur*, 11, no. 2 (1956): 719-721;

Herbert Moser, "Die Gestalt des Paracelsus im Werk von Max Mell," *Blätter für Kunst und Sprache*, 24 (1976): 5-9;

Renée Stahel, *Max Mells Tragödien* (Zurich: Juris, 1967);

Kurt Vancsa, "Das Imitatio-Motiv bei Max Mell," *Unsere Heimat*, 25, no. 5-7 (1954): 130-139.

Papers:

Manuscripts, letters, diaries, and notebooks of Max Mell are in the possession of the Deutsches Literaturarchiv (German Literature Archive) and the Schiller Nationalmuseum in Marbach am Neckar, Germany; the Steiermärkische Landesbibliothek (Styrian Provincial Library) in Graz, Austria; the Österreichische Akademie der Wissenschaften (Austrian Academy of Sciences), the Bundesministerium für Unterricht und Kunst (Federal Ministry of Education and Art), and the Stadtbibliothek (City Library), all in Vienna; the Goethe- und Schillerarchiv in Weimar; the Stadtbibliothek in Munich; and members of the Mell family.

Felix Mitterer
(6 February 1948 -   )

Herbert Herzmann
University College, Dublin
(translated by Hazel Coffey)

PLAY PRODUCTIONS: *Kein Platz für Idioten*, Innsbruck, Volksbühne Blaas, 15 September 1977;

Veränderungen, Graz, Schauspielhaus, 24 October 1980;

Stigma, Telfs, Tiroler Volksschauspiele, 18 August 1982;

Karrnerleut' 83, Telfs, Tiroler Volksschauspiele, 9 August 1983;

Besuchszeit, Vienna, Theater Die Tribüne, 16 April 1985;

Drachendurst, by Mitterer and Anton Prestele, Telfs, Tiroler Volksschauspiele, 7 August 1986;

Die wilde Frau, Innsbruck, Innsbrucker Kellertheater, 16 September 1986;

Kein schöner Land, Innsbruck, Tiroler Landestheater, 12 April 1987;

Verlorene Heimat, Stumm im Zillertal, Zillertaler Volksschauspiele, 27 June 1987;

Heim, Linz, Landestheater, 26 September 1987;

Die Kinder des Teufels, Munich, Schauburg-Theater der Jugend, 8 April 1989;

Sibirien, Telfs, Tiroler Volksschauspiele, 6 August 1989;

Munde, Telfs, Tiroler Volksschauspiele, 3 August 1990;

Ein Jedermann, Vienna, Theater in der Josefstadt, 10 January 1991.

BOOKS: *Superhenne Hanna* (Vienna & Munich: Jugend und Volk, 1977);

Kein Platz für Idioten: Volksstück in drei Akten (Feldafing: Brehm, 1979);

An den Rand des Dorfes: Erzählungen, Hörspiele (Vienna & Munich: Jugend und Volk, 1981);

Der Narr von Wien: Aus dem Leben des Dichters Peter Altenberg. Ein Drehbuch (Salzburg: Residenz, 1982);

Stigma: Eine Passion (Feldafing: Brehm, 1983);

Chryseldis: Bilder 1973-1983; Felix Mitterer: Ein Mär-

Felix Mitterer

chen (Landeck: Edition Galerie Elefant, 1984);

Besuchszeit: Vier Einakter (Munich: Brehm, 1985);

Die wilde Frau: Ein Stück (Munich: Brehm, 1986);

Kein schöner Land: Ein Theaterstück und sein historischer Hintergrund (Innsbruck: Haymon, 1987);

Die Kinder des Teufels: Ein Theaterstück und sein historischer Hintergrund (Innsbruck: Haymon, 1989);

Sibirien: Ein Monolog (Innsbruck: Haymon, 1989);

Verkaufte Heimat (Innsbruck: Haymon, 1989);
Munde (Innsbruck: Haymon, 1990);
Ein Jedermann (Innsbruck: Haymon, 1991).

In the mid 1960s, in the wake of the renaissance of interest in Ödön von Horváth in German-speaking countries, the critical Volksstück (folk play) rose to new prominence. This genre, whose aim is to be intelligible to as many people as possible, has achieved notice through the plays of Martin Sperr, Peter Turrini, Franz Xaver Kroetz, and Felix Mitterer.

Mitterer was born in Aachenkirch, Tirol, on 6 February 1948, to Adelheid Lamprecht, whose husband, a farmer, had been killed in World War II. According to Mitterer, his mother already had "ungefähr" (around) twelve or thirteen children; all he knows of his father was that he was from Romania. Since his mother was too poor to look after this horde of children, Felix was "hergeschenkt" (donated) before his birth to Michael and Juliana Mitterer, farm laborers who later adopted him.

Mitterer traveled with his adoptive parents from one Tirolean farm to another in the 1950s and came to know a world that was, as he recalled looking back, really in the nineteenth century. Like most children of his class, he attended primary school for eight years; it was not intended that he should have more than the absolute minimum of education. Early on, however, he began to read a great deal, without ever receiving any encouragement to do so. His teacher, who was struck by his imaginative essays, arranged for him to attend the teacher training institute in Innsbruck in 1962. After he failed mathematics and Latin in his third year, he left school at the age of seventeen.

A post in the customs office in Innsbruck secured his existence for the next ten years. In the middle of the 1960s he began to write seriously. Although parallels can be drawn between Mitterer's theater and the critical folk plays of Horváth and Karl Schönherr, he became acquainted with their works only some years later. Direct influences must be sought in the peasant farce, which still dominates amateur theater in Tirol. His adoptive mother was an enthusiastic amateur actress, who excelled particularly in the role of the bad wife.

Mitterer's first play, *Kein Platz für Idioten* (No Room for Idiots; published, 1979), into which he inserted much of his own childhood, was originally conceived as a radio play and was

Mitterer in the role of Wastl in a scene from the premiere of his Kein Platz für Idioten *in Innsbruck in 1977*

broadcast by ORF (Austrian Broadcasting) on 21 March 1976. Adapted for the stage, the play, written in Tirolian dialect, had its first performance on 15 September 1977 at the Blaas Folk Theater, an amateur theater in Innsbruck that normally presents crude peasant farces. Because no suitable actor could be found for the role of the mentally handicapped Wastl, Mitterer himself played the part. The production, directed by Josef Kuderna, was a success with the public and was recorded for broadcast by ORF. The author had succeeded in appealing to people who normally stay away from the theater. The play presents the fate of a mentally retarded farm boy. The parents refuse to accept the child, who can hardly speak and will not be able to work. An old man, himself an outsider, adopts the child and achieves some success with his kindhearted education methods. This progress is destroyed when the boy is sent to an institution after sexually molesting a girl, an act he performs through ignorance. Society's rejection of individuals who do not conform to its norms is a theme encountered again and again in Mitterer's works. From autumn 1978 until spring 1979 the play ran at the Die Tribüne theater in Vienna with Mitterer playing Wastl; he also played the role on a tour of South Tirol in autumn 1979 and of Germany in autumn 1980. It has remained his most frequently staged play. For *Kein Platz für Idioten* Mitterer received the 1978 prize of the Provincial Capital Innsbruck for Artistic Production in the dramatic writing category. The artistic and financial success of this play caused Mitterer to give up his job in the customs office. Since 1977 he has been a free-lance writer in Innsbruck.

On 24 October 1980 Mitterer's second play, *Veränderungen* (Changes), commissioned by the Theater in der Josefstadt of Vienna, premiered at the company's guest performance at the Graz Schauspielhaus as part of an annual festival, the Steirischer Herbst (Styrian Autumn). Zoltan Pataky directed. The play takes up a theme that subsequently surfaces again and again: the threat to our quality of life through a false understanding of progress. In this play it is the computerized world of the programmer, Stefan, that threatens to destroy the life of his old-fashioned father-in-law. Although some critics praised the play, most thought the treatment of the issue oversimplistic and clichéd. The author seems to have come to agree with this view; he has banned further productions of the play.

In 1980 Mitterer married the painter Chryseldis Hofer. In the same year his daughter Anna Magdalena was born. She is the only one of his relatives, her father says, that he knows personally.

The following year the Tiroler Volksschauspiele (Tirol Folk Theater Festival) was founded to encourage genuine folk theater, not exaggerated for tourist audiences, to be performed every summer in the city of Hall in Tirol. Mitterer was involved from the start. In the first summer Franz Kranewitter's *Die sieben Todessünden* (The Seven Deadly Sins) was performed; Mitterer wrote "Moritaten" (popular street ballads) to link the seven one-act plays and appeared as a singer. In 1982 the festival moved to Telfs. The reason for the move was a theatrical scandal brought about by Mitterer's play *Stigma* (published, 1983). When the mayor of Hall read the play, he refused to allow this "Schweinerei" (disgrace) to be performed in his

town. The actors declared their solidarity with the author and refused to appear in the other productions intended for the festival. After the committee of the Kongresshalle in Innsbruck, where it had been proposed to move the production, also voted against allowing *Stigma* to be performed, the mayor of Telfs, Helmut Kopp, offered his town as a venue. In the weeks leading up to the production there were protests, threatening letters, bomb threats, and demonstrations by conservative and clerical circles. The author preferred to view the situation positively: where else in the world, he asked, would a whole town become so worked up about a play? The premiere on 18 August went off without incident.

The play is set around 1830. The farm girl Moid gives herself over entirely to the imitation of Christ. Her reaction to the injustice of society, under which she, as a member of the lowest class of the rural hierarchy, suffers particularly, is to develop stigmata. Like a saint, she is atoning for the sins of the world. Her stigmata, even if they are not self-inflicted, as the doctor examining her believes, are a kind of self-punishment for passions she believes to be sinful: her sexual needs and possessive urges. At the same time, her stigmata offer her protection against the lascivious attentions of the farmer's son, the farm hand's unrealistic desire to marry her, and her own temptations. They give her a certain respect, even power, and the area's poor and oppressed look to her for comfort. Although the farmer fears Moid's influence, he does not dare to turn her away from the farm; of course, the money that can be made from the visitors plays a role in his tolerance. Moid's power lasts until the state (the doctor) and the church (the monsignor) render her harmless. She is excommunicated, declared a deceiver and a danger to the public, and is finally murdered. For the most part, Austrian discussion of the play after the first performance concentrated on the purported blasphemy, brutality, and extreme language. Some West German critics, however, recognized the play's quality.

Mitterer's next play, *Karrnerleut' 83* (Traveling People; performed, 1983), is a reworking of Schönherr's folk play *Karrnerleut* (performed, 1904; published, 1905). Mitterer's play received its first performance when the two plays were presented together at the Tirol Folk Theater Festival on 9 August 1983. Schönherr's drama deals with vagrants in Tirol at the turn of the century; since such vagrants do not exist today, Mitterer transforms them into members of the "Nullbock Gene-

A demonstration in Telfs, Austria, in August 1982 to protest the staging of Mitterer's Stigma *there*

ration" (no-hoper generation), idle and apathetic youth. A punk couple passing through a Tirolean village on their way from Berlin to Italy get into trouble with the police. It turns out that the young man is originally from the village, and that the policeman who arrests him is his father. To an extent the play is the story of the prodigal son, although the moral is inverted: the attempted return does not succeed because the conflicts are too great. In December 1983 the Tirol Folk Theater Festival brought the two plays to the Munich Volkstheater. Press reaction there, as at the play's premiere in Telfs, was negative. There was almost unanimous criticism of the play's black and white presentation of events, its clichés, and its melodramatic elements.

In one of four one-act plays published and performed in 1985 under the title *Besuchszeit* (Visiting Hour), *Weizen auf der Autobahn* (Harvesting on the Autobahn), an old farmer cannot come to terms with the fact that his son-in-law, to whom he has signed over his farm, has converted it into a guesthouse with the compensation he received for allowing a highway to be built through his fields. The son-in-law seems to him to be the head of a conspiracy of robots whose aim is the destruction of all worthwhile quality of life. After plowing up the highway one night and sowing wheat on it, and on another occasion spreading dung on the freshly asphalted surface, the farmer is taken to a mental institution. In the end it is not only the old farmer and his world who fall victim to so-called progress; his son-in-law and his daughter also get caught in the wheels of the changes they had longed for when the noise and fumes of the traffic drive away the tourists, and the guesthouse business goes into the red. *Weizen auf der Autobahn* is written for two actors: the old man in the mental institution is visited by his daughter, and it is through their conversation that the audience learns of the events that have taken place. The other three one-act plays follow a similar pattern: in each an incarcerated person receives a visit from the outside. In *Abstellgleis* (Sidetrack) a woman visits her father-in-law, who has been deposited in an old people's home. In *Verbrecherin* (Female Criminal) a man visits his wife, who is in prison after her attempt to murder him. In *Man versteht nichts* (One Who Understands Nothing) a terminally ill woman is visited in the hospital by her husband on several consecutive days, until she finally dies. She never finds out what is wrong with her, and her husband loses his job while she is in the hospital.

None of these "little" people have language adequate to comprehend the economic, political, and social constraints that bind them. The critical events in *Man versteht nichts* remain incomprehensible to both the man and the woman. In their inarticulateness and helplessness, the victims occasionally turn to educated language, which is foreign to them, in the attempt to formulate the inexplicable. Despite the tragedy of such attempts at articulation, there is also something deeply comic about them. When the husband in *Verbrecherin* recapitulates the events that led to his wife's sentencing, for example, he is quoting what was written in the newspapers about the case. For the ruling class, on the other hand, language is a means of securing power. In *Stigma*, the doctor and the monsignor employed Latin as a means of controlling the simple and ignorant population. The letter of notice received by the husband in *Man versteht nichts* talks of "Konjunkturschwankungen" (fluctuations in the economic situation) that "leider zu einer längst fälligen Rationalisierung und zum stufenweisen Abbau der Arbeitskräfteüberkapazität zwingen" (unfortunately make necessary a long-overdue program of rationalization and a phased reduction of the oversupply of labor).

Besuchszeit was first performed on 16 April 1985 by the Tribüne Theater at the Cafe Landtmann in Vienna. After its first performance in the Kammerspiele (Intimate Stage) of the Tiroler Landestheater in Innsbruck on 7 November there was great applause and curtain call after curtain call.

The two plays that had their first performances in 1986 are set in a strange world, apparently far away from today's realities. *Drachendurst* (Dragon Thirst) was written by Mitterer and Anton Prestele for the Tirol Folk Theater Festival. As in the Viennese magic plays of Emanuel Johann Jakob Schikaneder and Ferdinand Raimund, conflicts in the spirit world have effects on human life; the spirits may, of course, be regarded as allegorical figures. The dragon, ruler of the hostile forces of nature and the principle of destruction and death, is hopelessly in love with the doe, the principle of life served by the friendly powers of nature. Any union of these two is impossible; their war must last as long as the world continues. On the human plane, however, a union of opposites, however precarious, is possible through love; such a union is presented in the figures of the rusty-armored knight and dragon killer Niklas and the gentle maiden Martha. Mitterer was attempting here to write a play

for children that would also appeal to adults, and the production in Telfs was successful with the audience. The critics were highly impressed by Kurt Weinzierl's spectacular production, but reactions to the play's text were mixed.

Die wilde Frau (The Wild Woman, 1986) makes use of stories that circulate to the present day in the Alpine region about mysterious female creatures who, when they couple with mortal men, sometimes bring them great good fortune and sometimes ruin. One winter's evening a strange woman comes to a woodcutters' hut, which is occupied by five men of various ages. She remains there for several days. She never speaks; it remains unclear whether she is unable to speak or does not want to. She takes over all the household tasks from the men and is sexually abused by them, each night by a different man. Only the youngest, Wendl, does not take part in this abuse, because he feels an almost religious veneration for the woman. The woman's presence releases suppressed feelings and aggressions in the men, culminating in all the men except the youngest murdering each other. At the end of the play the woman goes away, apparently unaffected by anything that has taken place.

On 12 April 1987 the Kammerspiele of the Tiroler Landestheater gave the first performance of *Kein schöner Land* (There is no more Beautiful Country; published, 1987). The title is an ironic allusion to a Tirolean folk song. The play is based on the life of the tourism pioneer Rudolf Gomperz, who had begun the development of the Tirolean town of St. Anton into a winter-sports resort but was persecuted after the annexation of Austria by Nazi Germany in 1938 because of his Jewish descent; he was finally killed in a concentration camp. His two sons were fanatical members of the Hitler Youth and went on to join the SS. This situation was possible only because Gomperz signed a document in which he claimed not to be the real father of the two boys. Mitterer's play is a liberal treatment of the facts. In the original version the wife and children of Stefan Adler, as the play's hero is called, do not know that he is a Jew until he cannot produce his "Ariernachweis" (proof of Arian race). To make their ignorance plausible one would have to conclude that Adler had concealed his origins long before the Nazi seizure of power; one way of explaining why he would have done so is to recognize the particularly virulent anti-Semitism in Tirol, which existed long before Adolf Hitler, and which was, in Gretl Köfler's words, "Anti-

Christa Porls as Moid and Max Krickl as Seppele in a scene from the premiere of Stigma *in Telfs in August 1982*

semitismus ohne Juden" (Anti-Semitism without Jews), as few Jews lived there. Another explanation would be Adler's desire to assimilate, which was shared by many Jews at that time. Mitterer himself seemed to doubt the legitimacy of using such a dramatic device, and, on the advice of a Jewish friend, changed the text of the play for the Vienna production. Here Adler himself does not know that he is Jewish until he has to produce the Ariernachweis and finds that he cannot.

A highly effective scene is the one in which the father, now a prisoner in the concentration camp, and his son, now an SS man, meet by chance. The son shoots his father out of pity and then kills himself. (The scene encapsulates what actually took place over a longer period of time: Gomperz's older son, Rudolf Gomperz, Jr., was unable to resume a normal life after 1945. He once shot at a photograph of himself in his SS uniform, and in 1966 he shot himself). Immediately after this melodramatic scene, which the audience, as the author intended, takes to be the end of the play, there follows the actual ending. It is in bitterly ironic contrast to what has gone before and is set in the postwar period. The opportunistic mayor, who was first encountered as a partisan of the Engelbert Dollfuss regime and then as

a Nazi, now turns up as mayor again in the newly resurrected Austria. This time he owes his office to the American occupying forces. This chameleon addresses the final words to the audience: "Halten wir zusammen, laßt uns gemeinsam, mit neuem Mut, mit neuer Kraft, mit neuem Schaffensdfrang das neue, das zukünftige Österreich aufbauen!—Ich danke euch!" (Let's stick together; together, with fresh courage, new strength and a new will to create, let us build the new, future Austria!—I thank you!).

That *Kein schöner Land* was such a great success with the public was due to its topicality, apart from its quality as a drama. Discussion had already started about holding a fifty-year commemoration of the Anschluß (annexation of Austria by Nazi Germany). Also, in 1987 and 1988 Austrian President Kurt Waldheim was in the news internationally because of his wartime activities. Reviewers praised the play; there was some criticism of its melodramatics and symbolism, but some critics were of the opinion that such devices were actually to the advantage of a drama in the folk play genre.

Heim (Home) was commissioned by the Linz Landestheater, where it was first performed on 26 September 1987. It is an expansion of

Kärrnerleut' 83 into a full-length drama. As had happened with the shorter play, the press reacted critically to this more detailed treatment of a negative version of the prodigal son parable. There were expressions of shock about the frequent violence—a supermarket branch manager rapes the girl, who has stolen a nightshirt from his store, in the presence of the policeman who turns out to be the father of her boyfriend; the father forces his son at pistol point to declare his filial love. There was also criticism of the simplistic black-and-white treatment of the story, with its good punks and evil authorities.

Verlorene Heimat: Die Zillertaler Auswanderer 1837 (Lost Homeland: The Zillertal Emigrants 1837) was first performed on 27 June 1987 in the village square in Stumm, in the Zillertal, Tirol, where the events depicted in the play had actually taken place 150 years previously. It is intended that the play be produced every ten years in Stumm. This repetition, together with the enormous cast of roughly 150 lay performers, reminds one of a passion play. Mitterer's play depicts the suffering of the Zillertal Protestants, who were expelled from Catholic Tirol in 1837 despite an edict of tolerance that had been in force since the emperor Joseph II's reign in the eighteenth century. Temporal and ecclesiastical authorities unite against a group of people they consider dangerous.

In one of the last great witchcraft trials, which took place in Salzburg from 1675 to 1690, more than two hundred people—most of them children who belonged to groups of beggars—were accused of consorting with the devil and put to death. Some of the fantastical confessions of the accused, which were obtained under torture, are reproduced in Mitterer's play *Die Kinder des Teufels* (The Devil's Children, 1989). In showing the methods of the late seventeenth century of dealing with such social problems as begging, thieving, and poverty, Mitterer again takes the part of the outsiders in society.

Mitterer had a triumphant success with *Sibirien* (Siberia; published, 1989), which premiered on 6 August 1989 at the Tirol Folk Theater Festival in Telfs. It is a monologue by an old man who is handicapped as the result of a hip injury and has been dumped in an old-people's home by his family. There he goes steadily downhill and finally dies. The play's title reflects the emotional coldness experienced by old people in the welfare state.

Mitterer's *Munde* (the name of a mountain in Tirol) was performed at the Tirol Folk Theater Festival in August 1990. His *Ein Jedermann* (An Everyman) was performed in January 1991 at Theater in der Josefstadt in Vienna. It is an updating of Hugo von Hofmannsthal's *Jedermann* (1911; translated as *The Salzburg Everyman*, 1911) in which Jedermann is the director of a big firm, Werke (Good Works) is a Turkish charlady, Mammon is a bank manager, and so on.

In Austria, Mitterer is one of the best-known playwrights of the present day. In 1984 he won the Literature Award of the Ministry for Schools; the Peter Altenberg Prize of the City of Vienna followed in 1986. The province of Styria awarded him the Peter Rosegger Prize in 1988, and in the same year Tirol province awarded him its Art Prize.

References:

Hugo Aust, Peter Haida, and Jürgen Hein, *Volksstück: Vom Hanswurstspiel zum sozialen Drama der Gegenwart* (Munich: Beck, 1989);

Gotthard Böhm, "Erinnern tut not," *Bühne*, 345 (June 1987): 30-31;

Helmut Butterweck, "Einsamkeiten," *Die Furche*, 3 May 1985, p. 19;

Margret Czerni, "Der Abend ging an die Schauspieler: Felix Mitterers 'Heim'—ein unglaubwürdiger Reißer im Western-Stil," *Neues Volksblatt* (Linz), 28 September 1987, p. 9;

Czerni, "Ein Tal erlebt seine Geschichte," *Neues Volksblatt* (Linz), 26 June 1987, p. 11;

Hedy Danneberg, "Es war kein schönes Land," *Volksstimme* (Vienna), 2 June 1987, p. 9;

Bernhard Gajek, "Das Evangelium auf der Bühne: Überlegungen zu drei Volksstücken: Franz Xaver Kroetz' 'Der Weihnachtstod,' Felix Mitterers 'Stigma' und Ludwig Thomas' Magdalena," in *Einheit in der Vielfalt: Festschrift für Peter Lang zum 60 Geburtstag*, edited by Gisela Quast (Bern, Frankfurt am Main & New York: Lang, 1988), pp. 89-100;

Hans Garzaner, "Der Abfall der Gesellschaft," *Arbeiter Zeitung* (Vienna), 12 August 1983, p. 11;

Hans Haider, "Wie das Volksstück sein Publikum erwischt: Presse-Gespräch mit dem jungen Tiroler Schriftsteller und Schauspieler Felix Mitterer," *Die Presse* (Vienna), 28 September 1978, p. 5;

Jutta Höpfel, " 'Besuchszeit': Mitterers Anliegen sind Menschen auf dem Abstellgleis," *Neue Tiroler Zeitung,* 9 November 1985, p. 11;

Höpfel, "Mitterers Elementartheater," *Neue Tiroler Zeitung,* 2 October 1986, p. 19;

Höpfel, "Tirolerische Horror Picture Show entfesselt Urschrei und Spieltrieb," *Neue Tiroler Zeitung,* 9 August 1986, p. 12;

Höpfel, " 'Verlorene Heimat'—die großartige Gemeinschaftsleistung des Zillertales," *Neue Tiroler Zeitung,* 30 June 1987, p. 9;

Oliver vom Hove, "Vom Gipfelkreuz zum Hakenkreuz," *Die Presse,* 16 April 1987, p. 5;

Fritz Kain, "Ein ganzer Knäuel von Greueln," *Volksstimme* (Vienna), 23 September 1987, p. 11;

Erwin Kieser, "Von den Abgeschobenen," *Volksstimme* (Vienna), 18 April 1985, p. 9;

Gretl Köfler, "Die Juden in Tirol," in *Kein schöner Land: Ein Theaterstück und sein historischer Hintergrund,* by Felix Mitterer (Innsbruck: Haymon, 1987), pp. 113-133;

Kurt Langbein, Ernst Schmiederer, Christian Skalnik, Alfred Worm, and Paul Yvon, "Mörderischer Apparat," *profil,* 16 (17 April 1989): 96-105;

Sigrid Löffler, "Ein Experte für die Nichtversicherten," *Theater heute,* 26 (September 1985): 50-52;

Löffler, "A netts Büabl: Felix Mitterer, der Tiroler Volksdramatiker hat Konjunktur. Wiens Großbühnen reißen sich um seine Stücke," *profil,* 5 (29 January 1990): 73-75;

Gerhard Mayer, "Alpensage," *Bühne,* 355 (April 1988): 42;

Gregor Mayer, "Ein Tal spielt seine Geschichte,"

Volksstimme (Vienna), 27 June 1987, p. 9;

Walter Methlagl, "Felix Mitterer: Laudatio anläßlich der Überreichung des Kunstpreises 1988 des Landes Tirol," *Das Fenster,* 44 (1988): 4311-4313;

Bernhard Natter, "Endlich! Jetzt is a Ruah!: Das Bild nationalsozialistischer Ausgrenzungs— und Vernichtungspolitik in Felix Mitterers Theaterstück 'Kein schöner Land,' " *Mitteilungen Brennerarchiv,* 7 (1988): 49-57;

Helmut Schödel, "Schwarzer Vogel Jugend," *Die Zeit,* 21 April 1989, p. 63;

Schödel, "Der verriegelte Himmel," *Die Zeit,* 22 May 1987, p. 65;

Werner Schulze-Reimpell, "Die Schuldfrage bleibt offen: Der Stückeschreiber Felix Mitterer," *Die Deutsche Bühne,* 5 (1986): 34-35;

Franz Schwabeneder, "Barmherzigkeit als Drama: Der Psychotherapeuth Erwin Ringel analysierte in den Linzer Kammerspielen Felix Mitterers 'Stigma,' " *Oberösterreichische Nachrichten,* 5 June 1985, p. 10;

Michael Skasa, "Skandal im Tiroler Theater?— Mitterers 'Stigma' in Telfs (doch) gespielt," *Theater heute,* 10 (1982): 58-62;

Ingeborg Teuffenbach, "Ritter, Drache, Nixe und der Nork: Felix Mitterers neues Bühnenstück," *Tiroler Tageszeitung,* 17 October 1984, p. 14;

Renate Wagner, "Schwierigkeiten mit den Mythen," *Neues Volksblatt* (Linz), 12 February 1987, p. 12;

Arthur West, "Die Frau-Wild ohne Schonzeit: Uraufführung von Felix Mitterers jüngstem Bühnenwerk," *Volksstimme* (Vienna), 28 September 1986, p. 7.

Heiner Müller
(9 January 1929 -   )

Erich P. Hofacker, Jr.
University of Michigan

PLAY PRODUCTIONS: *Zehn Tage, die die Welt erschütterten*, Berlin, Volksbühne, 22 November 1957;

Der Lohndrücker, by Müller and Inge Müller, Leipzig, Städtisches Theater, 23 March 1958;

Die Korrektur, by Müller and Inge Müller, Berlin, Maxim-Gorki Theater, 2 September 1958;

Klettwitzer Bericht, Senftenberg, Senftenberger Theater, 16 November 1958;

Die Umsiedlerin, Berlin, Studentenbühne der Hochschule für Ökonomie, 30 September 1961; revised as *Die Bauern*, Berlin, Volksbühne, 30 May 1976;

Ödipus Tyrann, Berlin, Deutsches Theater, 31 January 1967;

Philoktet, Munich, Residenztheater, 13 July 1968;

Prometheus, Zurich, Schauspielhaus, 18 September 1969;

Drachenoper, by Müller and Ginka Tscholokowa, music by Paul Dessau, Berlin, Deutsche Staatsoper, 19 December 1969;

Weiberkomödie, Magdeburg, Städtische Bühnen, 18 December 1970;

Macbeth, Brandenburg, Brandenburger Theater, 11 March 1972;

Der Horatier, Berlin, Schillertheater, 3 March 1973;

Zement, Berlin, Berliner Ensemble, 12 October 1973;

Herakles 5, Berlin, Schillertheater, 9 June 1974;

Die Schlacht and *Traktor*, Berlin, Volksbühne, 30 January 1975;

Mauser, translated by Betty Nance Weber, Austin, Texas, Austin Theater Group, 3 December 1975; premiere in German: Cologne, Schauspielhaus, 20 April 1980;

Fatzer, Hamburg, Deutsches Schauspielhaus, March 1978;

Germania Tod in Berlin, Munich, Kammerspiele, 20 April 1978;

Die Hamletmaschine, Brussels, Théâtre mobile, 17 June 1978; premiere in German: Essen, 28 April 1979;

Leben Gundlings Friedrich von Preußen Lessings Schlaf Traum Schrei, Frankfurt am Main, Schauspielhaus, 26 January 1979;

Der Bau, Berlin, Volksbühne, 3 September 1980;

Der Auftrag, Berlin, Volksbühne, 16 November 1980;

Herzstück, Bochum, Schauspielhaus, 7 September 1981;

Quartett, Bochum, Schauspielhaus, 7 April 1982;

Verkommenes Ufer Medeamaterial Landschaft mit Argonauten, Bochum, Schauspielhaus, 22 April 1983;

Wladimir Majakowski: Tragödie, Berlin, Schillertheater, 9 September 1983;

the CIVIL warS a tree is best measured when it is down, by Müller and Robert Wilson, Cologne, Schauspielhaus, 19 January 1984;

Anatomie Titus Fall of Rome: Ein Shakespearekommentar, Bochum, Schauspielhaus, 14 February 1985;

Fassung und dramaturgische Einrichtung von Schillers "Wallenstein," Berlin, Schillertheater, 5 April 1985;

Vorspiel zur Winterschlacht, Berlin, Deutsches Theater, 9 May 1985;

Bildbeschreibung, Graz, Vereinigte Bühnen, 6 October 1985;

Die Wolokolamsker Chaussee 1-5, Paris, Théâtre Bobigny, 20 April 1988; premiere in German: Bochum, Schauspielhaus, 10 May 1985.

BOOKS: *Der Lohndrücker*, by Müller and Inge Müller (Berlin: Henschel, 1958);

Zehn Tage, die die Welt erschütterten: Szenen aus der Oktoberrevolution nach Aufzeichnungen John Reeds, by Müller and Hagen Stahl (Leipzig: Hofmeister, 1958);

Die Korrektur (Leipzig: Hofmeister, 1959);

Philoktet; Herakles 5 (Frankfurt am Main: Suhrkamp, 1966);

Sophokles: Ödipus Tyrann. Nach Hölderlin (Berlin & Weimar: Aufbau, 1969);

Heiner Müller (photograph by Liz Schuster)

Geschichten aus der Produktion, 2 volumes (Berlin: Rotbuch, 1974)—includes *Prometheus*;

Die Umsiedlerin oder Das Leben auf dem Lande (Berlin: Rotbuch, 1975);

Theater-Arbeit (Berlin: Rotbuch, 1975)—comprises *Glücksgott, Drachenoper, Horizonte, Weiberkomödie*, "Sechs Punkte zur Oper," "Stellasonett," *Elektratext, Froschkönig*, "Ein Diskussionsbeitrag," "Über den Dramatiker Stefan Schütz," "Ein Brief ";

Stücke (Berlin: Henschel, 1975)—comprises *Der Lohndrücker, Die Bauern, Der Bau, Herakles 5, Philoktet, Der Horatier, Weiberkomödie, Macbeth, Zement; Der Horatier* translated by Marc Silberman, Helen Fehervary, and Guntram Weber as *The Horatian*, in *Minnesota Review*, new series 6 (Spring 1976): 40-50; *Zement* translated by Fehervary, Silberman, and Sue Ellen Case, as *Cement*, in *New German Critique*, 6 (Winter 1979): 7-64;

Die Schlacht; Traktor; Leben Gundlings Friedrich von Preußen Lessings Schlaf Traum Schrei (Berlin: Henschel, 1977); *Die Schlacht* translated by Carl Weber as *The Battle* in Muller's *The Battle: Plays, Prose; Poems*, edited by Weber (New York: PAJ Publications, 1989);

Germania Tod in Berlin (Berlin: Rotbuch, 1977);

Mauser (Berlin: Rotbuch, 1978); translated by Fehervary and Silberman as *Mauser*, in *New German Critique*, 3 (Spring 1976): 122-149;

Der Auftrag; Der Bau; Herakles 5, Todesanzeige (Berlin: Henschel, 1981);

Quartett (Frankfurt am Main: Verlag der Autoren, 1981);

Rotwelsch (Berlin: Merve, 1982);

Herzstück (Berlin: Rotbuch, 1983);

Germania Tod in Berlin; Der Auftrag (Stuttgart: Klett, 1983);

Die Bauern (Die Umsiedlerin oder Das Leben auf dem Lande); Macbeth (Berlin: Henschel, 1984);

Der deutsche Teil von the CIVIL warS, a tree is best measured when it is down, by Müller and Robert Wilson, edited by Schauspiel Köln (Frankfurt am Main: Suhrkamp, 1984);

Shakespeare Factory 1 (Berlin: Rotbuch, 1985)—comprises "Bildbeschreibung," *Wie es Euch gefällt, Waldstück, Macbeth, Wolokolamsker Chaussee 1*;

Gesammelte Irrtümer: Interviews und Gespräche (Frankfurt am Main: Verlag der Autoren, 1986);

Shakespeare Factory 2 (Berlin: Rotbuch, 1989)—comprises *Hamlet, Anatomie Titus Fall of Rome, Wolokolamsker Chaussee 1-5*;

Wolokolamsker Chaussee 1-5 (Berlin: Henschel, 1989);

Jenseits der Nation: Heiner Müller in Interview mit Frank M. Raddatz (Berlin: Rotbuch, 1991);

Kreig ohne Schlacht: Leben in zwei Diktaturen (Cologne: Kiepenheuer & Witsch, 1992).

OTHER: *Quadriga* and *Die Hamletmaschine*, in *Die Hamletmaschine: Heiner Müllers Endspiel*, edited by Theo Girshausen (Cologne: Prometheus, 1978); *Die Hamletmaschine* translated by Carl Weber as *The Hamletmachine*, in *Performing Arts Journal*, 12, no. 4 (1980): 141-146;

Lanzelot, by Müller and Ginka Tscholakowa, music by Paul Dessau, in Dessau's *Opern*, edited by Fritz Hennenberg (Berlin: Henschel, 1976), pp. 89-122;

"Die Form entsteht aus dem Maskieren," in *Theater 1985*, edited by Peter von Becker, Michael Merschmeier, and Henning Rischbieter (Zurich: Orell Füssli & Friedrich, 1985), pp. 88-93.

SELECTED PERIODICAL PUBLICATIONS—
UNCOLLECTED: "Sieg des Realismus," *Neue deutsche Literatur*, 2, no. 11 (1953): 161-163;

"Wohin," *Neue deutsche Literatur*, 4, no. 2 (1955): 98;

"Epigramme über Lyrik," *Neue deutsche Literatur*, 5, no. 8 (1956): 160;

"Die Roten," *Junge Kunst*, 10, no. 1 (1958): 5;

"Gedanken über die Schönheit der Landschaft bei einer Fahrt zur Großbaustelle 'Schwarze Pumpe,'" *Junge Kunst*, 10, no. 1 (1958): 62;

"Klettwitzer Bericht," *Junge Kunst*, 10, no. 8 (1958): 2-8;

"Winterschlacht 1963," *Forum*, 16, no. 6 (1963): 7;

"Fragen für Lehrer," *Forum*, 16, no. 13 (1963): 15;

"Dt 64," *Forum*, no. 11 (1964): 2-3;

"Das Laken," *Sinn und Form*, 17, no. 1 (1966): 767-768;

"Ablehnung eines Stipendium-Angebots des Hamburger Senats," *Eulenspiegel*, 14, no. 4 (1974): 5;

"Author's Preface to *The Horatian*," *Minnesota Review*, new series 6 (Spring 1976): 42;

"Der Vater," *Wespennest*, 17, no. 25 (1977): 36-37;

"Ich wollte lieber Goliath sein," *Die Zeit*, 6 January 1978, p. 30;

"Notate zu 'Fatzer': Einige Überlegungen zu meiner Brecht-Bearbeitung," *Die Zeit*, 17 March 1978;

"Was mich in der gegenwärtigen Lage angeht: Rede zur Verleihung des Dramatikerpreises der Stadt Mülheim," *Frankfurter Rundschau*, 13 September 1979;

"Reflections on Postmodernism," *New German Critique*, 6 (Winter 1979): 55-57;

"Brecht gebrauchen, ohne ihn zu kritisieren, ist Verrat," *Theater heute Jahrbuch*, 21 (1980): 134-136;

"Schreiben aus Schadenfreude ...," *Theater heute*, 23 (April 1982): 1-3;

"Ein Stück Protoplasma: Heiner Müller über Majakowski," *Theater heute*, 24 (September 1983): 30;

" 'Das Vaterbild ist das Verhängnis': Heiner Müller im Gespräch mit Werner Heinitz über Brecht und die Dramatik der Gegenwart," *Theater heute*, 25 (January 1984): 61-62;

"Ich muß mich verändern, statt mich zu interpretieren: Weitere Auskünfte des Autors Heiner Müller," *notate: Informations- und Mitteilungsblat des Brecht-Zentrums der DDR*, 27, no. 3 (1984): 6-7;

"Anatomie Titus Fall of Rome: Ein Shakespeare-kommentar," *Theater heute*, 26 (March 1985): 44-59;

"Russische Eröffnung," *Theater heute*, 26 (July 1985): 17-19;

"Solange wir an unsere Zukunft glauben, brauchen wir uns vor unserer Vergangenheit nicht zu fürchten," *Theater der Zeit*, 41, (1986): 62-64;

"Der Papierkrieger," *Theater heute*, 33 (1992): 1-12.

Asked to describe Heiner Müller, the average theatergoer of 1990 in Frankfurt am Main might have responded that he is a sort of socialist William Shakespeare who would not exist had it not been for the Socialist Unity party (SED) of East Germany and the Prussian monarchy. Since the 1970s he has been widely considered by critics and the public to be the most provocative contemporary dramatist in all of Germany. Many festivals in Western Europe have prominently featured Müller's works—most notably the Frankfurt Experimenta 6, a seventeen-day festival in May and June 1990 in which seventy performances of his dramas were presented by theater companies from Eastern and Western Europe before an audience of twenty thousand. The mayor of Frankfurt pronounced Müller the most important dramatist of the German language; the president of the East Berlin Academy of the Arts declared his works a guarantee of German cultural unity, indicating that when everything else in the former German Democratic Republic (GDR) perishes, Müller's works will remain. The themes of his dramas are not restricted to Germany or to one socioeconomic class but mirror the traumas that concern all peoples; in this respect, he is a universal playwright. A 1983 interview with Müller in the West German newsmagazine *Der Spiegel* (The Mirror) introduced him as the most successful and most internationally esteemed East German playwright since Bertolt Brecht. That same year the Holland Festival in The Hague invited ten acting companies from five countries to present ten plays during a special Heiner Müller Festival. Although the East German government did not permit its companies to attend, the playwright himself directed a performance by another acting company of his version of *Macbeth* (premiered, 1972; published, 1975).

Müller was born on 9 January 1929 to Paul Wilhelm and Elfriede Rudholzner Müller in the small town of Eppendorf in southern Saxony. For the most part, his forebears were day laborers, craftsmen, and farmers. His mother told him of the deprivations of her own childhood, recalling that the salt herring hanging on a string from the ceiling had to feed the family until the next payday. The author's father was an office worker and, in the Weimar Republic, a political activist and minor functionary of the Social Democratic party. Müller's earliest childhood recollection is of brown-shirted Nazi storm troopers breaking into the house on the night of 31 January 1933, beating his father—a small and rather helpless man—and dragging him away. His father attempted to say good-bye to Heiner, but the four-year-old pretended to be asleep. Müller feels that this first act of "treason" has deeply influenced his life and work.

In 1945 Müller was drafted into the Nazi labor force and then into the final military effort. Taken prisoner by the Americans in western Mecklenburg, he escaped after two days and fled to the vicinity of Neubrandenburg—the area of his mother's origin—which was under Soviet occupation. Rumor had it that in the Soviet zone the women were raped and the men murdered; Müller said that he had expected to find the first victims behind the first bushes. Instead, he was fed and assigned to a convoy walking to the next county seat; there he was freed. His father was once again a political functionary in the reestablished Social Democratic party in the Soviet zone.

But after the party's forced fusion with the Communist party he was excluded from the resulting Socialist Unity party because he was repelled by the personality cult of Joseph Stalin. The elder Müller defected to the West in 1952. Years later, when he was asked why, being aware of the injustices perpetrated against his father, he did not follow him to the West, Müller could give no answer except to say that he believed in the Soviet system at that time. He also seems to have wanted to be free of parental influence.

After the war Müller finished his interrupted schooling and received his certificate of graduation. He then spent several years working for libraries and as a clerk in government offices in Neubrandenburg. It was during this time that he began to write poetry and short prose pieces. He also tried his hand at dramatic sketches. Influenced by Bertolt Brecht's *Furcht und Elend des Dritten Reiches* (Fear and Misery of the Third Reich, 1941; translated as *The Private Life of the Master Race*, 1944) and his prologue to *Antigone* (1949), Müller sketched out five brief scenes that he revised over the years and that were eventually published as *Die Schlacht* (performed, 1975; published, 1977; translated as *The Battle*, 1989). The first scene, "Die Nacht der langen Messer" (The Night of the Long Knives), is set on 27 February 1933, the night the Reichstag (parliament building) in Berlin was burned by the Nazis, who blamed the act on the Communists. Two brothers meet; one had been a Communist but became a Nazi for personal protection and gain. Cruelly mistreated and finally superficially accepted by his new comrades, he meets his Communist brother and pleads with the latter to shoot him: "tu was ich nicht kann / Dass ich kein Hund mehr bin, sondern ein toter Mann" (do what I can't do myself / So that I will no longer be a dog but a dead human being). Having done so, the Communist brother says, "Hab ich getötet den Verräter, meinen Bruder, ihn" (I killed him, my brother, the traitor).

The following scene, "Ich hatt einen Kameraden" (I Once Had an Army Buddy) depicts four German soldiers starving in the snow on the eastern front. Driven to cannibalism, one of them says, "Besser drei volle Mägen als vier leere" (It's better to have three full stomachs than four empty ones), and the weakest soldier is shot. "Er war / Unser schwächstes Glied und eine Gefahr / für den Endsieg" (He was / our weakest link and was putting our final victory in jeopardy), says one of the survivors. The sketch closes with the sentimental folk song that gives it its title. Scene 3, "Kleinbürgerhochzeit" (Marriage of the Petit Bourgeoisie), shows a man, his wife, and their daughter as the news comes that Adolf Hitler has committed suicide. "Denk an den Führer: lieber tot als rot" (Think of our leader: rather dead than red), says the man before he shoots his wife and daughter. He turns the inspirational picture of the "Führer" face down when his own turn comes: "Der Starke ist am mächtigsten allein" (The strong man is most powerful when he is alone), he says.

The following scene, "Fleischer und Frau" (The Butcher and His Wife), begins with the butcher changing into his SA (Sturmabteilung [Storm Trooper]) uniform in his shop. An American bomber is shot down; the pilot is murdered by the butcher. Allusions are made that Russians were served as steaks on the home front. The butcher's wife becomes a widow, possibly by her own hand. Here Müller gives the audience a sense of the chaotic conditions of war under which human beings easily become animalistic. The final scene, "Das Laken oder Die unbefleckte Empfängnis" (The Bedsheet; or, The Immaculate Conception) is set in a cellar room in Berlin as the Red Army takes control of the city. Civilians urge a deserting German soldier to take a white sheet outside to hoist in surrender. Stray SS men come upon him and shoot him for treason. A contingent of Russian soldiers returns his body, tosses a loaf of bread to the German civilians, salutes, and leaves. Immediately a struggle for possession of the bread breaks out over the body of the soldier.

At its premiere *Die Schlacht* was followed on the stage by *Traktor* (Tractor; published, 1977). The sergeant in charge of a retreating German army unit orders a field to be mined as the Red Army approaches. One soldier refuses the order, since he knows that in the peacetime soon to follow the field will be needed to plant potatoes. The sergeant orders him to be hanged. In the following scene, which takes place after the war, a farmer asks a tractor driver to plow the field so that it can be planted. The driver refuses, saying that even if half the world cries out in hunger, the field is not worth his life. The farmer cites the example of the self-sacrifice of a comrade who lost his life in the attempt. The tractor driver places greater value on his own welfare than on that of society; Müller characterizes this attitude as one that is responsible for the catastrophes of history. After a long inner struggle, the

driver plows the mined potato field, losing a leg in the process. In the hospital his old doubts return: he is not convinced that the revolution is justified in striding forward over the bones of individuals. The "hero" with the amputated leg overhears the members of the agricultural collective laughing, with full stomachs, about the idiot who filled them.

In the mid 1950s Müller contributed essays and other works to *Neue deutsche Literatur* (New German Literature), a journal sponsored by the Deutscher Schriftstellerverband (League of German Writers [DSV]). He spent the year 1954-1955 working for the DSV; during this time he met and married Ingeborg Schwenkner, a writer who won the Erich Weinert Medal for her radio play *Die Weiberbrigade* (The Women's Brigade; broadcast, 1960).

Müller rejected the usual Communist party prescriptions for writers, such as the crude depiction of the evils of capitalism and the blessings of socialism, as too simplistic to be accepted by the theatergoer. Nor did he accept the approach of "Ankunftliteratur" (arrival literature), which depicted in an often improbable fashion the intellectual and emotional progress of individuals from the political Right to the Left when exposed to the reality of work in a socialist production system. In a series of "Produktionsstücke" (production plays) set in factories, on construction projects, or on collective farms Müller tried to present the problems that might actually be encountered by workers, such as defective equipment, danger, or a shortage of supplies, and to show workers of varying perspectives and backgrounds whom chance had thrown together. In his plays the problems are not all solved and not all the workers are moved to accept the socialist work ethic; but the hope is held out that, in time, more workers might be made to see the desirability of a change in viewpoint. *Traktor* can be considered Müller's first production play, even though it is brief and focuses on only one individual.

In 1957 Müller received a commission to dramatize *Ten Days That Shook the World* (1919), by the American author John Reed, in honor of the fortieth anniversary of the Russian revolution of October 1917. In collaboration with the dramaturge of East Berlin's Volksbühne, Hagen Stahl, he wrote a series of ten scenes that was performed at the Volksbühne in November 1957. This play was the first work by Müller to be seen on the stage.

Der Lohndrücker (The Wage Cutter, 1958), written in collaboration with his wife, is his best-known and most-staged production play. Although the play is set in 1948, the event on which it is based took place in December 1950: the activist bricklayer Hans Garbe repaired a furnace in an East Berlin foundry without first having the smelter cooled down, resulting in a great savings in time and lost production; he completed the dangerous task in only half the time prescribed by the norms and was feted as a "Held der Arbeit" (working hero) in the media, and his deed became the subject of novels and plays. The Müllers' drama assumes the spectator's knowledge of Garbe's accomplishment and concentrates on the activist concept and on the development of a new attitude among the bricklayer's reluctant fellow workers, who feared a raising of the norms (that is, an increase in the work required for base pay). The heroism of Balke, as the Garbe character is called in *Der Lohndrücker* (a Balken is a heavy support beam), is not well received by most of the others, for whom the expected new standards will mean either more work or lower wages. But according to Marxist ideology, under capitalism the worker's primary concern is his own advantage; he does as little as possible for his hourly wage and is unconcerned about the quality of his work. The true socialist, on the other hand, is supposed to put the societal welfare first and willingly make sacrifices to meet the production quota. In the play cynical individuals take advantage of communist slogans of common ownership by taking alcohol and expensive butter from the grocery stand without paying: "Ist doch Volkseigentum" (It belongs to everybody), they say. During the Nazi period Balke had had to denounce Schorn, who is now the Socialist Unity party secretary, to save his own life. To succeed in his repair of the smelter, Balke needs Schorn's help. In a typically laconic exchange Balke asks Schorn whether he can forget what happened back then; Schorn answers simply, "Nein, nie" (No, never). Nevertheless, after a tense pause for reflection the two men put aside personal concerns to work for the advancement of socialism. Other workers concerned about exploitation find that this concept no longer exists; in a factory owned by all, it would amount to self-exploitation, an illogical concept. The play is not a party-inspired hymn of praise to socialism; it shows abuses by management and conflicts among workers who cannot be convinced to change their attitudes. The general tone of the play is positive; it expresses confidence regarding the eventual achievement of socialism in the workplace. Nevertheless, the transition from the old capitalist consciousness will be slow. As the play ends, many workers retain a feeling of hostility against Balke, their "unsolidarischen Kollegen" (uncooperative colleague). In 1959 Müller and his wife received the prestigious Heinrich Mann Prize for *Der Lohndrücker*.

Die Korrektur (The Correction; performed, 1958; published, 1959), on which the Müllers also collaborated, concerns the "Braunkohlenkombinat Schwarze Pumpe" (Bituminous Coal Mine Black Pump), one of the major industrial undertakings of the GDR. Müller considered this one-act play a continuation of *Der Lohndrücker*, showing the progress of the next decade; in the ten years that have passed progress is evident everywhere, from large construction projects to the citizens' diet. Instead of the insecure socialism of 1948, whose existence was frequently imperiled, there is now a firmly anchored social system and system of production. Nevertheless, new kinds of problems make their appearance: because government central planning hinders their production totals, the workers decide to deceive the government by producing quantity instead of quality—just the opposite of Balke's approach in *Der Lohndrücker*. When a poorly constructed foundation collapses, the brigade leader places the fault on an engineer who had also been an engineer under the Nazis. Since the engineer was not at fault, he is defended by another worker; the brigade leader is pressured by the party secretary to apologize to the engineer. The engineer is a member of the old order whom the new order needs.

Müller wrote and rewrote *Die Umsiedlerin oder Das Leben auf dem Lande* (The Resettler Woman; or, Life in the Country; performed, 1961; published, 1975) many times between 1956 and 1961. The protagonist is a woman from one of the old German eastern provinces that had either become Soviet territory or belonged to the western third of Poland after the Soviet Union shifted its borders to take possession of the eastern third of that country. Seven million Germans from this former German territory were forcibly relocated to the GDR or the Federal Republic of Germany after the war. The play paints a detailed panorama of the contradictions of socialist agricultural policy. Presented only once, by student players in September 1961—seven weeks after the erection of the Berlin Wall—the play was immediately closed down by the authorities.

The play consists of fifteen vignettes that sketch the rural development from 1946 until 1960 of an unnamed country that could only be East Germany. The first land reform gives plots from the confiscated farms of the large landowners to individual farmers and workers; with the second land reform, however, the collectivization of the farms takes place at the cost of the individuality and freedom of the individual farmer. One "Neubauer" (new farmer) who had received land under the first reform commits suicide when faced with a state demand for a percentage of his produce and the repayment of debts. The central figure in the play is a peasant woman who comes from the east, makes a new beginning, and is deserted when she becomes pregnant. Together with the wife of the party secretary, also deserted by her husband, she runs her farm cooperatively. A "Mittelbauer" (farmer with fairly extensive land holdings) has the last laugh: as soon as he is forced to join the collective he calls in sick and becomes totally nonproductive. Finally, the much-decorated, wife-deserting party secretary celebrates the victory of socialist production methods and waxes philosophical, declaring that the world will go its way and soon enough we all will die.

In the ensuing party debates Müller was expelled from the DSV in 1961. This measure had severe financial consequences for him: a writer who was not a member of the DSV could not have his plays printed or performed in the GDR. It was only through radio plays, which he wrote under pseudonyms, and the aid of friends that he could survive at all. In 1963 he was rehabilitated and permitted to publish two long poems in *Forum*, the journal of the Free German Youth, for which he received the Erich Weinert Medal.

In 1964 Erik Neutsch's acclaimed nine-hundred-page novel *Spur der Steine* (Track of the Building Stones) recounted the experiences on and off the job of a roving brigade of construction workers. Müller's *Der Bau* (The Construction Project; published, 1975; performed, 1980) is a verse drama in ten scenes based on Neutsch's book. The political and ethical problems which in the novel are presented in long monologues are reduced to brief, vivid lines: the political party comes and goes, we work; the world is a boxing ring, and might makes right; show me a building that is worth a human life; the world is cheap, and a human being is expensive. Müller's drama is a litany of praise to those who worked to build the country. The victims were more important than what their sacrifices had gained. The individual ruined himself for the construction project; every "Richtfest" (topping of a new structure) was a foretaste of a funeral. *Der Bau* was published in East Germany's most respected literary journal, *Sinn und Form* (Content and Form) in 1965. But Müller came under sharp attack at the Eleventh Plenary Session of the Central Committee of the SED in December 1965 for neglecting the dialectics of the development of the GDR. The first secretary of the party, Walter Ulbricht, quoted a line from the play as evidence of the spread of nihilistic, hopeless, and morally subversive philosophies in literature, film, theater, television, and magazines. Other artists indicted at the session included Wolf Biermann, Günter Kunert, and Stefan Heym. As a result of the charges a scheduled production of *Der Bau* in Leipzig was canceled.

The following year the playwright's wife, Inge, who had a history of depression, committed suicide. Müller had been living under this threat for years; he had made reference to it in a poem as early as 1959.

After his condemnation by party officials, performances of Müller's works were banned until 1967. During the ban he made translations and adaptations of various classic plays, including Sophocles' *Ödipus Tyrann* (Oedipus the King; performed, 1967; published, 1969), based on the 1804 translation by the German poet Friedrich Hölderlin, and Aeschylus's *Prometheus* (performed, 1969; published, 1974). In 1966 he completed a play based on Greek mythology, *Herakles 5* (Hercules 5; published, 1966; performed, 1974), which recounts the fifth labor of Hercules. In these plays Müller sought to show that modern class society is just as rife with contradictions, conflicts, and barbarism as the social structures of the ancient world and to stress that the only alternatives are communism or barbarism.

The best known of these plays by "Griechen Müller" (Müller the Greek), as he was frequently called at the time, was *Philoktet* (published, 1966; performed, 1968), an adaptation of a play by Sophocles. *Philoktet* was not permitted to be staged in East Germany until 1979, thirteen years after its completion; but it was performed at the Residenztheater in Munich in 1969 and added considerably to Müller's reputation in the West, even though the degree of stylization and use of metaphorical language make it more a "Lese-Gedicht" (poem to be read) than a play for the stage. A great storm has arisen as the Greek fleet is on its way to attack the Trojans, and the warrior Philoktet is to be sacrificed to pacify the god of the sea. When the party enters the sacred grove, Philoktet is bitten on the foot by a snake. The painful wound causes him to moan constantly; the sacrifice cannot be carried out, because absolute quiet is needed for the sacred rite. In addition, the wound begins to fester and gives off an odor that none can bear. Philoktet is abandoned on the uninhabited island, armed with a wondrous bow whose arrows never miss their target. The lonely and rejected man is filled with hate. Years later, in need of Philoktet's unfailing bow, the Greek general Odysseus sends Neoptolemos to entice him back to Greece. So hostile is Philoktet that he immediately falls upon the visitor; but Neoptolemos's explanation of his mission wins Philoktet's friendship, and he willingly makes the trip. After Troy has been defeated, Neoptolemos stabs the hate-filled Philoktet in the back as the latter struggles with Odysseus. After Philoktet is murdered, Neoptolemos and Odysseus decide that Greece would be best served by reporting him killed by the Trojans. This lie will spur the Greeks to greater efforts.

Müller's adaptation of *Prometheus* opened at the Zurich Schauspielhaus in 1969. By this time he was fully rehabilitated, and in East Germany he was invited to become a dramaturge with the Berliner Ensemble, Brecht's former company at the Theater am Schiffbauerdamm. *Drachenoper* (Dragon Opera; performed, 1969; published, 1975) was written as the libretto for an opera by Paul Dessau. Müller's collaborator on this work was Ginka Tscholakowa, who became his second wife in 1970.

Müller used the prize-winning radio play *Die Weiberbrigade*, written by his first wife, as the basis for his *Weiberkomödie* (Comedy of Women; performed, 1970; published, 1975). In a lighthearted takeoff on *Der Bau*, he again tries to point up problems in production. The members of the women's work brigade tend to overestimate their physical strength, while the men underestimate the same, leading to comic episodes; the stubborn positions taken by both the women and the men are finally worked out. The play was popularly called "*Lysistrata* in socialism."

In 1971 Erich Honecker replaced the aging and rigid Ulbricht as head of state and soon decreed that there were to be no taboos for East German writers who wished to further socialism. Feeling that there was enough distance from the events of the 1950s to write about the conflicts and contradictions in socialism at that time,

Müller expanded some scenes he had written in 1956 and the following years into a full-length play of a different sort than any he had attempted previously. *Germania Tod in Berlin* (Germania Death in Berlin; published, 1977; performed, 1978) gives a sweeping panorama of German history, ranging from Roman battles of conquest in A.D. 9 to the uprising of the workers in Berlin on 17 June 1953. The work is a broad collage in which historical events are sometimes heightened in effect by the poetic language of Greek antiquity; other scenes employ costumed figures reminiscent of vaudeville performers. Figures from various historical periods frequently appear together. *Germania Tod in Berlin* shows the "Aufbauzeit," the time of the building up of East Germany physically, politically, and psychologically and demonstrates the enormity of the heritage of the barbarian past as the experiment in socialism began in Germany. Scene 1, "Die Strasse 1" (The Street 1), briefly describes what Müller considers the greatest misfortune of modern German history: the failure of the general strike and proletarian revolution in Berlin in 1918. "Die Strasse 2" shows the reaction to the proclamation by loudspeaker of the founding of the GDR in Berlin on 7 October 1949. Instead of harmony and enthusiasm a full palette of contradictory, even hostile, attitudes is exposed. "Brandenburgisches Konzert 1" (Brandenburg Concerto 1) is a clownlike performance reciting the familiar story of the successful self-defense of a miller whose mill disturbed the peace of Frederick the Great; the king tried in vain to have it removed. Frederick the Great later wanted to make an example of this case to show his enlightenment, but the miller could not bring himself to play the role of a citizen opposing his sovereign; to him, an attitude of subservience seemed right and proper.

In "Brandenburgisches Konzert 2" even a modern activist cannot free himself from this Prussian heritage of subjugation. In "Hommage a Stalin 1" the German encirclement at Stalingrad represents all wars and warriors of the past; "Hommage a Stalin 2" investigates the effects on those who escaped encirclement. In "Die heilige Familie" (The Holy Family), a mixture of slapstick comedy and black humor, the theatergoer witnesses the birth of the Federal Republic of Germany. Hitler and Joseph Goebbels are the "Erzeuger" (begetters), and the Western Allies, "Die Heiligen Drei aus dem Abendland" (The Three Holy Men from the West), are those who

The "Hommage a Stalin 2" scene from a 1989 production in Bochum of Müller's Germania Tod in Berlin
(photograph by Klaus Lefebvre)

profit: they need this state as a bulwark against the danger from the East. The next scene, "Das Arbeiterdenkmal" (The Workers' Monument), depicts the Berlin uprising of 17 June 1953.

"Die Brüder 1" (The Brothers 1) presents an episode from the annals of Tacitus, the encounter of the brothers Flavius and Arminius at the Weser River. The first serves the Romans, the second is the leader of the Germanic tribe of the Cherusker; one seeks honor, fame, and personal fortune, the other the independence and freedom of his people. Their encounter escalates to warfare in the Battle of the Teutoburg Forest in A.D. 9. "Die Brüder 2" presents a modern encounter of two brothers imprisoned on 17 June 1953 in Berlin. One is a Nazi, the other a Communist who is accused of impeding progress toward socialism. As the Soviet tanks roll through the city, the Nazi beats his brother to death. Before the Communist dies, he tells of a vision of the moral decline of humanity to a state that resembles cannibalism: " . . . und dann zerfleischten sie sich eins das andere. / Zuletzt ersoffen sie im eigenen Blut / Weil es der deutsche Boden nicht mehr fasste" (and then they tore the flesh one from the other / Finally they drowned in their own blood / Be-

cause the German soil could no longer absorb it).

In "Nachtstück (Nocturnal Play) a puppet tries to reach its goal but is prevented from doing so by an external force of which it is not aware. The puppet's disappointment escalates to aggression, which it turns against itself. The result is self-mutilation to the point that it is unable to move. Though totally destroyed, however, the creature is still able to articulate its feelings; and with its cry it forms a mouth that it at first did not possess. It is no longer a puppet, but it is not yet a human being. New energies are generated when the old creation is destroyed.

For the Berliner Ensemble Müller dramatized the Russian novel *Tsement* (Cement, 1925) by Feodor Gladkov as *Zement* (performed, 1973; published, 1975). When the revolutionary hero Tschumalow returns from battle to find his old cement works in decay, the bourgeois engineer Kleist makes it evident that he considers this Promethean figure a symbol of useless effort: "Ihre Sowjetmacht wird die Welt nicht ändern / Tschumalow. Jeder Tag sieht wie der erste aus früh / Dann wird es Mittag und dann kommt die Nacht" (Your Soviet power will not change the world / Tschumalow. Every day looks like the first day / It will be midday early and then comes the night). The final words of the drama challenge the audience to put their energies at the disposal of the Soviet Union.

By this time Müller was readily granted permission to travel outside the GDR. In 1974-1975 he served as writer in residence at the University of Texas at Austin, where he collaborated on the world premiere in English of his "Lehrstück" (didactic play) *Mauser* (published, 1978). An all-female student cast presented the play as an aggressively feminist statement, an interpretation pleasing to Müller.

Mauser is a short play set during the Russian revolution. A chorus, representing the Communist party, tells the character A that he must be shot; he is a professional revolutionary to whom the chorus has given the task of executing enemies of the revolution. The ghost of B now appears; B previously had the task of A, and he had been shot because, out of pity, he had not executed three peasants who were unknowingly enemies of the revolution. A had avoided pity, the error of B. But he had begun killing people just because they were human beings and not primarily because they were enemies. This is his weakness, for which he must be executed. In pronouncing its verdict the chorus says, "Nicht Menschen zu töten ist dein Auftrag, sondern / Feinde. Nämlich der Mensch ist unbekannt" (It is not your task to kill human beings but to kill enemies. You see, the [nature of the] human being is unknown). (The title of the play refers to the German pistol that was a status symbol of the Soviet commissars and professional revolutionaries in the Russian revolution.)

After completing his semester at Austin in 1975, Müller and his wife traveled in the United States and Mexico. What he saw on these travels changed his view of the world. From his new perspective he felt that his plays of even three years earlier read like the texts of a dead author. When he returned to East Berlin in 1975 he became a dramaturge with the Volksbühne, where some of his older plays soon had their East German premieres. Noteworthy was a performance of *Die Bauern* (The Farmers; published, 1975; performed, 1976), a revised version of *Die Umsiedlerin*, whose single performance in 1961 had brought his expulsion from the Writers' League.

Leben Gundlings Friedrich von Preußen Lessings Schlaf Traum Schrei (The Life of Gundling Frederick of Prussia Lessings Sleep Dream Cry; published, 1977; performed, 1979), like *Germania Tod in Berlin*, is a surrealistic collage. It deals with patriotism and the inability of the people to rise up in revolt, attitudes that, in Müller's view, determine the thinking and actions of the present day. In contrast to *Germania Tod in Berlin*, no positive tendencies counter a flood of pessimism; despair seems to have replaced the playwright's fleeting moments of hope. Jakob Paul Gundling was the successor to Gottfried Wilhelm Leibniz as president of the Prussian Academy of Sciences and a member of the "Tabakkollegium" (smoking club), or council, of Frederick II of Prussia (Frederick the Great). In the history books the monarch is presented as enlightened and artistically talented. The first scene of the play is a meeting of the Tabakkollegium at Frederick's castle, Sanssouci, at Potsdam. It demonstrates the relationship between men of intellect and men of political power in an authoritarian state: a declawed and defanged bear pursues Gundling around the table; made to stand still by officers with drawn daggers, Gundling is caught and hugged by the bear. King Frederick comments that the man of intellect has now been made to play the fool; let the people not overestimate the extent of their freedom. Gotthold Ephraim Lessing was a dramatist and a critic of Prussian military might. Lessing received the prestigious position of dramaturge at the new National Theater in Hamburg, but his expectations of being able to use the theater as a school for morality were not to be realized. After some bizarre dreams of Lessing are depicted, the play concludes with his "cry," a furious but impotent protest against his being taken over by the literary historians as a classic writer, as easily consumable cultural goods.

In 1976 the protest poet Wolf Biermann was expatriated from East Germany; Müller was one of the dozen original signers of a letter of mild protest on 16 November. Eventually, many more artists signed, including those of the Berliner Ensemble, and Müller resigned his position there. This conflict between the party and the artists only confirmed his deepened pessimism.

During the final decade of the existence of the GDR Müller often visited the West. He claims that this unusual freedom of movement made him feel guilty even while he enjoyed it. Though the freedom of the West was far greater, Müller says, he experienced everything more acutely in the East.

Faced with a reality full of contradictions, Müller turned his attention to his own reflections, dreams, obsessions, and visions. His more recent plays, particularly *Die Hamletmaschine* (1978; translated as *The Hamletmachine*, 1980), *Quartett* (Quartet; published, 1981; performed, 1982), and *Verkommenes Ufer Medeamaterial Landschaft mit Argonauten* (Ruined Shoreline Medea-Material Landscape with Argonauts; performed, 1983) tend to be monologues in which the playwright clearly states his view of society. His plays are becoming more fragmentary and shorter; the published texts are frequently no more than five to ten pages in length.

Die Hamletmaschine consists of five scenes encompassing one inner monologue, divided into the roles of Hamlet and Ophelia. Each figure represents a different strategy of coping with reality: Hamlet is the intellectual who knows too much and is unable to act; Ophelia has ceased to contribute to her own destruction and is rebelling against woman's traditional role. Ophelia is trying to escape her position as oppressed victim within a patriarchal system dominated by the white male intellectual, represented by Hamlet. Hamlet's opening monologue is a somewhat distorted summary of Shakespeare's tragedy:

FAMILIENALBUM
Ich war Hamlet. Ich stand an der Küste und redete mit der Brandung BLABLA, im Rücken die Ruinen von Europa. Die Glocken läuteten das Staatsbegräbnis ein, Mörder und Witwe ein Paar, im Strechschnitt hinter dem Sarg des Hohen Kadavers die Räte, heulend in schlecht bezahlter Trauer.... Ich stoppte den Leichenzug, stemmte den Sarg mit dem Schwert auf dabei brach die Klinge, mit dem stumpfen Rest gelang es, und verteilte den toten Erzeuger FLEISCH UND FLEISCH GESELLT SICH GERN an die umstehenden Elendsgestalten.
    Die Trauer ging in Jubel über, der Jubel in Schmatzen, auf dem leeren sarg besprang der Mörder die Witwe SOLL ICH DIR HINAUFHELFEN ONKEL MACH DIE BEINE AUF MAMA. Ich legte mich auf den Boden und hörte die Welt ihre Runden drehn im Gleichschnitt der Verwesung....

(FAMILY ALBUM
I was Hamlet. I stood on the shore and talked with the surf BLAHBLAH, at my back the ruins of Europe. The bells tolled, bringing the state funeral, murderer and widow one couple, in the goosestep behind the coffin of the exalted cadaver the counselors, howling in poorly paid

mourning.... I stopped the funeral procession, forced open the coffin with my sword, in so doing the blade broke, with the stump I succeeded and distributed my dead begetter to the miserable people standing around FLESH LIKES FLESH. The mourning turned into jubilation, the jubilation into smacking of the lips, upon the empty coffin sprang the murderer [and] the widow SHALL I HELP YOU UP UNCLE OPEN YOUR LEGS MAMA. I lay down on the earth and listened to the world makes its revolutions in harmony with its decay....)

Die Hamletmaschine is a collage of quotes from works by Müller and others, a monodrama in which the playwright is reeling under the impact of the destructive forces in the world around him; on the other hand, he feels separated from people who work so that they can buy bread and who have no time for philosophical reflection. Remembering the social obligation of his art, Müller recognizes that somewhere bodies are being broken by toil so that he can live in his own filth. Here the stage directions call for a large photograph of Müller to be torn up. In a series of pop images the play shows history to be an endless pattern of destruction, of successive failed revolutions that became counterrevolutions.

Since the mid 1980s the playwright had been working on *Wolokolamsker Chaussee 1-5* (Wolokolamsk Road 1-5); it was performed in 1988 and published in 1989, although individual parts had been printed and performed earlier. The play is in large part in monologue form. Its five parts may be selected and arranged as the director desires; the number of players varies from two to twenty-four. There are few stage directions; time and place are usually left open. The drama is an assortment of recollections by four old German veterans who, sometimes sitting in primitive wheelchairs, reexperience the horrors of World War II. They also recall the events of the early years of the GDR, particularly the workers' uprising of 17 June 1953. One man is blind, another missing a leg, and one had shot himself in the hand in an attempt to avoid the eastern front. Lots are drawn to determine who shall recall a particular experience. None can escape the torment of remembrance: "In meinem Kopf hört der Krieg nicht auf" (In my head the war never ends), says one.

It was only shortly before the popular movement in late 1989 that precipitated the fall of the Berlin Wall that certain more recent plays by

Müller began to be hesitatingly and conservatively produced in the GDR, although they were quite familiar in the West. Particularly cautious was the production of *Leben Gundlings Friedrich von Preußen Lessings Schlaf Traum Schrei* because of its depiction of Frederick the Great, who had only recently been restored to a place of honor under "Prussian socialism." *Germania Tod in Berlin* and *Die Hamletmaschine* were totally banned until 1988. The performance of *Die Schlacht* was permitted when its director made certain that it was misconstrued as pertaining only to West Germany, which, according to the party, was the sole inheritor of fascist ideology. In January 1989 three East Berlin stages were simultaneously performing his plays. In that year the *Times* of London carried an erroneous report that Müller had been nominated for the Nobel Prize. In an almost humorous reflex action, the party promptly conferred on him the GDR National Prize, First Class, for all his work, some of which the East German censors were still banning from print. During the Sixth Workshop of GDR Theater Directors, the disjointed and confused patterns of thought in Müller's recent texts were judged to be a positive attribute; the demand was made for a freer and bolder approach to the production of his works, one more in accordance with his stage directions.

In August 1988 a three-week Heiner Müller Festival was held in West Berlin. It included a symposium and eleven stagings from eight European countries. Müller described these performances as "eine Müller-Vernichtungsmaschine" (a Müller-destroying machine), although the Warsaw Theater's production of *Verkommenes Ufer Medeamaterial Landschaft mit Argonauten* found his favor: Jason and Medea were presented sixfold on the stage. The director's explanation was that Medea is not an individual but a social problem; one cannot find a woman who murders her children and her rival except in tabloid newspapers.

In December 1989 Müller gave *Der Spiegel* an interview titled "Ohne Hoffnung, ohne Verzweiflung" (Without Hope, without Despair) in which he expressed his views on the new freedoms won by the people of the GDR. He considered the reforms "die erste deutsche Revolution von unten" (the first German revolution generated by the masses). Artists, formerly charged by the party with the mind control of the population, should now play as insignificant a role as possible, he said. Toward socialism, he felt ambivalent. Socialism never really existed, he said, but

was an idea of the intellectuals; it was a colonization of the people, a Stalinist concept. Müller agreed that the East Germans were more interested in bringing about capitalism than socialism. Since communists are being removed from power worldwide, the people have a chance to gain back the concept of utopia, "die bisher von den Terroristen verheizt wurde" (which up until now was being senselessly wasted by the terrorists). A people cannot live permanently without the hope of a utopia.

On the other hand, Müller was not in favor of the reunification of Germany; he considered one Germany a boring state of affairs and felt that Europe would be the poorer because one color would be lacking in the quilt. He also knew that his countrymen were offended that West German chancellor Helmut Kohl was stepping in as their new colonial master.

Müller has won many literary prizes. Among them are the Heinrich Mann Prize in 1959, the Erich Weinert Medal in 1964, the *Berliner-Zeitung* Critics' Prize in 1970 and 1976, the Lessing Prize in 1975, the Mülheimer Dramatists' Prize in 1979, the Georg Büchner Prize in 1985, and the Radio Play Prize of Those Blinded in War in 1986. His autobiography, *Krieg ohne Schlacht: Leben in zwei Diktaturen* (War without Battle: Life in Two Dictatorships), was published in 1992.

Interviews:

Horst Laube, "Der Dramatiker und die Geschichte seiner Zeit," *Theater heute*, 16 (1975): 119-123;

"Geschichte und Drama: Ein Gespräch mit Heiner Müller," *Basis: Jahrbuch für deutsche Gegenwartsliteratur*, 6 (1975): 48-64;

Carl Weber, "Heiner Müller: The Despair and the Hope," *Performing Arts Journal*, no. 12 (1980): 135-140;

"Ich scheisse auf die Ordnung der Welt: Interview," *Tip*, no. 7 (1982): 98-109;

Urs Jenny and Hellmuth Karasek, "Deutschland spielt noch immer die Nibelungen: DDR-Dramatiker Heiner Müller über seine Theaterarbeit zwischen Ost und West," *Der Spiegel*, 37 (9 May 1983): 196-207;

Olivier Ortolani, "Die Form entsteht aus dem Maskieren," in *Theater 1985*, edited by Peter von Becker, Michael Merschmeier, and Henning Rischbieter (Zurich: Füssli & Friedrich, 1985), pp. 88-93;

"Ohne Hoffnung, ohne Verzweifelung: Interview mit dem DDR-Dramatiker Heiner Müller in Ost-Berlin," *Der Spiegel*, 43 (4 December 1989): 264-265;

"Es kommen viele Leichen zum Vorschein," *Theater heute*, 30, no. 12 (1989): 4-11;

"Zehn Deutsche sind dümmer also fünf: Gespräch mit dem Dramatiker Heiner Müller," *Neue Rundschau*, 103, no. 2 (1992): 66-78.

References:

Heinz Ludwig Arnold, ed., "Heiner Müller," *text + kritik*, no. 73 (1982);

Hubert A. Arnold, "On Myth and Marxism: The Case of Heiner Müller and Christa Wolf," *Colloquia Germanica*, 21, no. 1 (1988): 58-69;

Verena Auffermann, "Sieger und Mörder, Mörder und Sieger: Heiner Müller forever: Ein Kommentar," *Theater heute*, 31, no. 7 (July 1990): 12;

David Bathrick and Andreas Huyssen, "Producing Revolution: Heiner Müller's *Mauser* as a Learning Play," *New German Critique*, 3, no. 2 (1976): 110-121;

Gerda Baumbach, "Theatralische Qualität poetischer Texte—*Der Bau* von Heiner Müller," *Theater der Zeit*, 33, no. 3 (1978): 50-53;

Alexander von Bormann, "Nämlich der Mensch ist unbekannt: Ein dramatischer Disput über Hamanismus und Revolution," in *Masse Mensch, Die Maßnahme, Mauser: Festschrift für Hermann Meyer* (Tübingen: Niemeyer, 1976), pp. 851-880;

Ellen Brandt, "Trinken, rauchen, sterben. Heinrich Müller in Berlin," *Die Deutsche Bühne*, 60, no. 1 (1989): 10-13;

Helen Fehervary, "*Cement* in Berkeley," in *Brecht-Jahrbuch 1980*, edited by Reinhold Grimm and Jost Hermand (Frankfurt am Main: Suhrkamp, 1981), pp. 206-216;

Fehervary, "Enlightenment or Entanglement: History and Aesthetics in Bertolt Brecht and Heiner Müller," *New German Critique*, 3, no. 8 (1976): 80-109;

Fehervary, "The Gender of Authorship: Heiner Müller and Christa Wolf," *Studies in Twentieth Century Literature*, 5 (Fall 1980): 41-58;

Fehervary, "Heiner Müllers Brigadenstücke," in *Basis: Jahrbuch für deutsche Gegenwartsliteratur*, volume 2, edited by Grimm and Hermand (Frankfurt am Main: Athenäum, 1971), pp. 103-140;

Fehervary, "Introduction to *The Horatian*," *Minnesota Review*, new series 6 (Spring 1976): 40-42;

Gottfried Fischborn, "Intention und Material. Einige Aspekte zu Heiner Müllers *Schlacht* und *Traktor*," *Weimarer Beiträge*, 24, no. 3 (1978): 58-92;

Helmut Fuhrmann, "Where Violent Sorrow Seems a Modern Ecstasy—Über Heiner Müllers 'Macbeth nach Shakespeare,'" *Arcadia*, 12, no. 1 (1978): 55-71;

Theo Girlshausen, *Realismus und Utopia: Die frühen Stücke Heiner Müllers* (Cologne: Prometheus, 1981);

Girlshausen, ed., *Die Hamletmaschine: Heiner Müllers Endspiel* (Cologne: Prometheus, 1978);

Mel Gussow, "Cranking up a Powerful Hamletmaschine," *New York Times*, 5 May 1986, p. H3;

Wolfgang Harich, "Der entlaufene Dingo, das vergessene Floß—Anlaß der *Macbeth*-Bearbeitung von Heiner Müller," *Sinn und Form*, 25, no. 1 (1973): 189-218;

Georg Hensel, "Shakespeare aus der Tiefkühltruhe," *Frankfurter Allgemeine Zeitung*, 20 September 1983;

Jost Hermand, "Braut, Mutter oder Hure? Heiner Müllers *Germania* und ihre Vorgeschichte," in his *Sieben Arten an Deutschland zu leiden* (Königstein: Athenäum, 1979), pp. 127-141;

Hermand, "Deutsche fressen Deutsch: Heiner Müllers *Die Schlacht* an der Ostberliner Volksbühne," in *Brecht-Jahrbuch 1978*, edited by Hermand, John Fuegi, and Grimm (Frankfurt am Main: Suhrkamp, 1978), pp. 129-143;

Jürgen Holtz, "Der Dingo und die Flasche," *Sinn und Form*, 25, no. 4 (1973): 828-847;

Gitta Honegger, "Wilsonmaschine: Robert Wilson inszeniert Heiner Müller in New York," *Die Zeit*, 20 June 1986;

Peter Iden, "Der Hund heisst Woyzeck: Die Verleihung der Akademie-Preise in Darmstadt," *Frankfurter Rundschau*, 21 October 1985;

Hans-Thies Lehmann, "Mythos und Postmoderne—Botho Strauß, Heiner Müller," in *Kontroversen, alte und neue: Akten des VII. Internationalen Germanisten-Kongresses. Göttingen 1985*, volume 10 (Tübingen: Niemeyer, 1986), pp. 249-255;

Martin Linzer, "Historische Exaktheit und Grausamkeit," *Theater der Zeit*, 27, no. 7 (1972): 22-23;

Michael Merschmeier, "Menschen, Tiere, Sensationen: Robert Wilsons *the CIVIL warS*—des Monsterprojekts zweite Etappe im Schauspiel Köln," *Theater heute*, 25 (March 1984): 22-26;

Douglas Nash, "The Commodification of Opposition: Notes on the Postmodern Image in Heiner Müller's *Hamletmaschine*," *Monatshefte*, 81, no. 3 (1989): 298-311;

Ulrich Profitlich, "Über den Umgang mit Heiner Müllers *Philoktet*," in *Basis: Jahrbuch für deutsche Gegenwartsliteratur*, volume 10, edited by Hermand and Grimm (Frankfurt am Main: Suhrkamp, 1980), pp. 142-157, 258-262;

Henning Rischbieter, "Geschichte als Gruselkabinett und als grimmige Ballade," *Theater heute*, 16 (October 1975): 12-15;

Rischbieter, "Ist Heiner Müllers *Germania Tod in Berlin* noch zu spielen—und wie?," *Theater heute*, 30 (March 1989): 26-29;

Rischbieter, "Tötungs-Reigen: *Die Schlacht* von Heiner Müller in Berlin und Hamburg," *Theater heute*, 16 (December 1975): 6-14;

Wolfgang Ruf, "Heiner Müller im Westen: '... rote Fahnen über Rhein und Ruhr,'" *Die Deutsche Bühne*, 60, no. 1 (1989): 14-15;

Günter Rühle and others, "'Experimenta': Heiner Müller in Frankfurt. Müller: DDR-Moderne ins Mausoleum?" *Theater heute*, 31 (July 1990): 7-11;

Axel Schalk, "Heiner Müller's Maschinentheater," *Sprache im technischen Zeitalter*, 18, no. 87 (1983): 242-250;

Judith Scheid, ed., *Zum Drama in der DDR: Heiner Müller und Peter Hacks* (Stuttgart: Klett, 1981);

Wolfgang Schivelbusch, "Optimistic Tragedies: The Plays of Heiner Müller," *New German Critique*, 1, no. 2 (1974): 104-113;

Schivelbusch, *Sozialistisches Drama nach Brecht: 3 Modelle, Peter Hacks, Heiner Müller, Hartmut Lange* (Darmstadt & Neuwied: Luchterhand, 1974);

Helmut Schödel, "Wir sind ein blödes Volk: Ein Heiner-Müller-Tagebuch zur Frankfurter 'Experimenta,'" *Die Zeit*, 8 June 1990, pp. 57-58;

Genia Schulz, "Something is Rotten in this Age of Hope. Heiner Müllers Blick auf die (deutsche) Geschichte," *Merkur*, 33 (May 1979): 468-480;

Marc Silbermann, *Heiner Müller* (Amsterdam: Rodopi, 1980);

Marleen Stoessel, "Mit Dolchen reden: Heiner Müllers *Quartett*," *Theater heute*, 23 (June 1982): 2-4;

Arlene Akiko Teraoka, *The Silence of Entropy or Universal Discourse: The Postmodernist Poetics of Heiner Müller* (New York: Lang, 1985);

B. K. Tragelehn, "Spielweise contra Schreibweise," *Theater der Zeit*, 13, no. 3 (1958): 52-55;

Christoph Trilse, "Heiner Müllers Antike-Fabeln," in his *Antike und Theater heute: Betrachtungen über Mythologie und Realismus, Tradition und Gegenwart, Funktion und Methode, Stücke und Inszenierungen* (Berlin: Akademie, 1975), pp. 93-135;

Betty Nance Weber, "*Mauser* in Austin, Texas," *New German Critique*, 3, no. 8 (1976): 150-156;

Georg Wieghaus, *Heiner Müller* (Munich: Edition text + kritik, 1981);

Wieghaus, *Zwischen Auftrag und Verrat: Werk und Ästhetik Heiner Müllers* (Frankfurt am Main: Lang, 1984);

Franz Wille, "Mühe hat's gemacht: Franz Wille über Heiner Müllers achtstündigen Marathon: "Hamlet" und "Hamletmaschine" im Deutschen Theater, mit Ulrich Mühe," *Theater heute*, 31 (May 1990): 25-28;

Robert Wilson, "Über Heiner Müller: Für heiße Texte braucht man einen kühlen Kopf," *Theater heute*, 26 (December 1985): 30-32.

Robert Musil

(6 November 1880 - 15 April 1942)

Christian Rogowski
Amherst College

See also the Musil entry in *DLB 81: Austrian Fiction Writers, 1875-1913.*

PLAY PRODUCTIONS: *Vinzenz und die Freundin bedeutender Männer,* Berlin, Lustspielhaus, 4 December 1923;
Die Schwärmer, Berlin, Theater in der Stadt, 3 April 1929.

BOOKS: *Die Verwirrungen des Zöglings Törleß* (Vienna & Leipzig: Wiener Verlag, 1906); translated by Eithne Wilkins and Ernst Kaiser as *Young Törless* (London: Secker & Warburg, 1955; New York: Pantheon, 1955);
Vereinigungen: Zwei Erzählungen (Munich & Leipzig: Müller, 1911)—comprises "Die Versuchung der stillen Veronika," "Die Vollendung der Liebe";
Die Schwärmer: Schauspiel in drei Aufzügen (Dresden: Sibyllen, 1921); translated by Andrea Simon as *The Enthusiasts* (New York: Performing Arts Journal Publications, 1983);
Grigia: Novelle (Potsdam: Müller, 1923);
Die Portugiesin (Berlin: Rowohlt, 1923);
Vinzenz und die Freundin bedeutender Männer: Posse in drei Akten (Berlin: Rowohlt, 1924);
Drei Frauen: Novellen (Berlin: Rowohlt, 1924; enlarged edition, Reinbek: Rowohlt, 1968)—comprises *Grigia, Die Portugiesin,* "Tonka";
Rede zur Rilke-Feier in Berlin am 16. Januar 1927 (Berlin: Rowohlt, 1927);
Der Mann ohne Eigenschaften: Roman, 3 volumes (volumes 1 and 2, Berlin: Rowohlt, 1930-1933; volume 3, edited by Martha Musil, Lausanne: Imprimerie Centrale, 1943); translated by Wilkins and Kaiser as *The Man without Qualities,* 3 volumes (London: Secker & Warburg, 1953-1960; New York: Coward-McCann, 1953-1960);
Nachlaß zu Lebzeiten (Zurich: Humanitas, 1936); translated by Peter Wortsman as *Posthumous Writings of a Living Author* (Hygiene, Colo.: Eridanos Press, 1987);

Über die Dummheit (Vienna: Bermann-Fischer, 1937);
Gesammelte Werke in Einzelausgaben, 3 volumes, edited by Adolf Frisé (Hamburg: Rowohlt, 1952-1957);
Das hilflose Europa: Drei Essays (Munich: Piper, 1961);
Aus den Tagebüchern (Berlin: Suhrkamp, 1963);
Theater: Kritisches und Theoretisches, edited by Marie-Louise Roth (Reinbek: Rowohlt, 1965);
Der deutsche Mensch als Symptom: Aus dem Nachlaß, edited by Karl Corino, Elisabeth Albertsen, and Karl Dinklage (Reinbek: Rowohlt, 1967);
Die Amsel: Bilder (Stuttgart: Reclam, 1967); translated by Thomas Frick and Wilhelm Wiegand as *The Blackbird* (Cambridge, Mass.: Simba, 1981);
Sämtliche Erzählungen, edited by Frisé (Reinbek: Rowohlt, 1968);
Three Short Stories, edited by Hugh Sacker (London: Oxford University Press, 1970)—includes *Grigia, Die Portugiesin, Die Amsel;*
Tagebücher, 2 volumes, edited by Frisé (Reinbek: Rowohlt, 1976);
Robert Musil, Drei Frauen: Text, Materialien, Kommentar, edited by Karl Eibl (Munich: Hanser, 1978);
Gesammelte Werke, 4 volumes, edited by Frisé (Reinbeck: Rowohlt, 1978); republished as *Gesammelte Werke in neun Bänden,* 9 volumes (Reinbek: Rowohlt, 1981);
Beitrag zur Beurteilung der Lehren Machs, edited by Frisé (Reinbek: Rowohlt, 1980); translated by Kevin Mulligan as *On Mach's Theories* (Washington, D. C.: Catholic University of America Press/Munich: Philosophia, 1983);
Frühe Prosa und aus dem Nachlaß zu Lebzeiten (Reinbek: Rowohlt, 1988).

Editions in English: *Tonka, and Other Stories,* translated by Wilkins and Kaiser (London: Secker & Warburg, 1965); republished as *Five Women* (New York: Delacorte, 1966)—comprises "Unions": "The Perfecting of a

347

Robert Musil

Love," "The Temptation of Quiet Veronica"; "Three Women": "Grigia," "The Lady from Portugal," "Tonka";

Selected Writings, edited by Burton Pike (New York: Continuum, 1986);

Precision and Soul (Chicago: University of Chicago Press, 1990).

SELECTED PERIODICAL PUBLICATIONS—
UNCOLLECTED: "Das Unanständige und Kranke in der Kunst," *Pan,* 1, no. 9 (1911): 303-310;

"Politisches Bekenntnis eines jungen Mannes," *Die Weißen Blätter,* 1, no. 3 (1913): 237-244;

"Skizze der Erkenntnis des Dichters," *Summa* (1918): 164-168;

Vorspiel zu dem Melodrama Der Tierkreis," in *Der Merkur,* 11, no. 9 (1920): 246-253;

"Das hilflose Europa oder Reise vom Hundertsten ins Tausendste," *Ganymed,* 4 (1922): 217-239;

"Symptomen-Theater," *Der neue Merkur,* 6, no. 3 (1922): 179-186; no. 10 (1923): 587-594;

"Isis und Osiris," *Die neue Rundschau,* 34, no. 5 (1923): 464;

"Der 'Untergang' des Theaters," *Der neue Merkur,* 7, no. 10 (1924): 826-842;

"Ansätze zu neuer Ästhetik: Bemerkungen über eine Dramaturgie des Films," *Der neue Merkur,* 8, no. 6 (1925): 488-506;

"Der Schwärmerskandal," *Tagebuch,* 10, no. 16 (1929): 648-652;

"Literat und Literatur: Randbemerkungen dazu," *Die neue Rundschau,* 42, no. 9 (1931): 390-412.

Robert Musil is not normally thought of as an author with a great affinity for the drama; he is mainly remembered for his narrative works, notably the monumental novel fragment *Der Mann ohne Eigenschaften* (1930-1943; translated as *The Man without Qualities,* 1955). He had only two full-length plays published, as well as a large-scale dramatic fragment. Musil's diaries and notebooks indicate, however, that over the span of about twenty-five years he worked on some ten or twelve dramatic projects, ranging from sketchy scenarios to extensive dialogue drafts. A collection of Musil's reviews and theoretical essays on drama published in 1965 reveals his persistent interest in drama as an art form. Moreover, it can be argued that it is in drama that the shift from the psychological introspection of Musil's earlier writings to the more detached satirical tone of the novel takes place.

Musil was born in Klagenfurt, Austria, on 6 November 1880. After short periods living at Komotau, Bohemia (now Chomutov, Czechoslovakia), and Steyr, Upper Austria, the Musils settled in Brünn (now Brno, Czechoslovakia), where Musil's father, Alfred Musil, became a professor of engineering at the Technical Institute in 1891. Musil's mother, Hermine, née Bergbauer, came from a family of officers in the imperial army. For a while Musil was destined for an officer's career; he attended the military academies at Eisenstadt from 1892 to 1894 and at Mährisch-Weißkirchen from 1894 to 1897 before enrolling at the Vienna Technical Military Academy in 1897. After a few months he abandoned the idea of a military career and enrolled at the Technical Institute at Brünn to study civil engineering. It was around this time that Musil began to write. His notebooks document his emerging interest in the drama; in connection with reading Aristotle's *Poetics*, for instance, he jotted down ideas for some dramatic projects that never came to fruition.

After graduating in 1901 Musil stayed at Brünn for his year of military service. From 1902 to 1903 he worked as a laboratory assistant in mechanical engineering at the Technical University in Stuttgart. The year in Stuttgart brought about a profound reorientation in Musil's outlook: he began work on a novel loosely based on his experiences in the military academies and decided to abandon practical science. At the end of 1903 he enrolled at the University of Berlin to study psychology and philosophy, eventually working on a doctoral dissertation under the renowned theorist of science Carl Stumpf on the Austrian physicist and philosopher Ernst Mach. In 1906 Musil sent the manuscript for a short novel, which had been rejected by several publishers, to the influential drama critic Alfred Kerr for evaluation. Kerr helped Musil revise the text and secured a publisher for the novel, which appeared as *Die Verwirrungen des Zöglings Törleß* (The Confusions of Pupil Törleß, 1906; translated as *Young Törleß*, 1955). He also introduced Musil to the intellectual and literary circles of Berlin.

It was the critical success of *Die Verwirrungen des Zöglings Törleß*, launched by Kerr's uncommonly enthusiastic review of December 1906,

that led Musil to reject offers of academic positions in Munich and Graz on receiving his doctorate in 1908. His career as a free-lance writer was not very successful, however. In 1908 Franz Blei, the editor of the literary journal *Hyperion*, invited Musil to contribute some short narratives. Musil spent the next two years working to the point of exhaustion on two novellas that were published under the title *Vereinigungen* (Unions) in 1911. Both works are to a large extent based on the life of the painter Martha Marcovaldi, née Heimann, whom Musil married in April 1911.

In 1910 Musil moved to Vienna, where his father had secured him a position as librarian at the Technical Institute. The notebooks from the period indicate that Musil attempted to overcome an aesthetic and psychological crisis, brought about by his difficulties in completing *Vereinigungen*, by branching out into drama. A heart ailment forced Musil to take repeated leaves of absence from his library job, including a stay in Rome from September to December 1913. In February 1914 he moved to Berlin, where he joined the editorial board of the prestigious journal *Die neue Rundschau* (The New Review). The outbreak of World War I thwarted this promising start of a literary career. Musil served as an officer in the Austrian army, mainly in the Tirol, where he narrowly survived an artillery attack in September 1915. After a series of severe illnesses he was withdrawn from the front and assigned duties in the press corps in Bozen, Vienna, and Brünn. From 1919 to 1920 he worked in the press archive of the Austrian Foreign Ministry in Vienna.

Around that time Musil wrote *Vorspiel zu dem Melodrama* Der Tierkreis (Prelude to the Melodrama *The Zodiac*), which was published in early 1920. The text combines the fantastic elements of the Viennese "Zauberposse" (magical farce) tradition of Ferdinand Raimund with the pathos of expressionism. It is a series of allegorical scenes in which an unnamed old peddler chases away a woman during a snowstorm so that he can die alone. She leaves, and two of the man's words, *Not* (Misery) and *Tod* (Death), turn into shrouded figures; Not decides to hand the destitute man over to her pimp, Tod. As the man sinks down, he has a series of hallucinations in which his mother appears in three guises—as the Madonna, as his miserable old mother, and as a young girl. The man is then plagued by six of his enemies. Snowflakes dance around the man as he collapses; "Sturm" (Storm) and "Kälte" (Cold) fight over the dying man. Finally, his death is bewailed by his mother. The fate of the man can be seen as a parody of expressionist episodic "station drama" of the type created, for example, by Georg Kaiser and Franz Werfel.

During the summer of 1920 Musil completed his first full-length drama, *Die Schwärmer* (published, 1921; performed, 1929; translated as *The Enthusiasts*, 1983). Musil had been working on this play intermittently since around 1910, when his notebooks indicate that he consulted Kerr's theoretical writings for guidance in the construction of a drama. To a certain extent the play is indebted to the naturalistic model advocated by Kerr. The basic configuration at the outset seems conventional: Regine, the wife of Josef, a high-ranking official in the Ministry of Education, has eloped with her former lover, Anselm. The two are seeking refuge at the house of Regine's sister, Maria, and her husband, Thomas, a former colleague of Anselm's and now a successful academic. New allegiances quickly develop: Anselm is attracted to Maria, while Thomas drifts toward Regine. These new combinations remain ambiguous at the end of the play: it is left open why Maria, despite having been disappointed by Anselm, follows him after he runs away. The rapprochement between Thomas and Regine culminates in what they themselves call an "*Anti*-Liebesszene" (*anti*-love-scene) that helps neither out of his or her isolation and leaves Regine contemplating suicide.

Unlike the plays of naturalistic authors such as Henrik Ibsen and Gerhart Hauptmann, Musil's drama does not adhere to traditional rules of psychological motivation; it never defines the significance of past experiences to the present situation. By means of a successive accumulation of conventional plot elements such as murder threats and intrigues, the motivations for the play's events are pushed further and further back, posing considerable interpretive difficulties. Regine's problem, it turns out, does not revolve around the conflict with her husband or around her wavering between Anselm and Thomas but around the guilt associated with the suicide of her former husband, Johannes. Thomas denounces Josef for hiring a detective to spy on Anselm and Regine yet ends up employing Josef's detective in a counterintrigue against Josef himself. At some point in the past the five "Schwärmer"— Thomas, Anselm, Johannes, Maria, and Regine— had tried to live together in defiance of bourgeois convention. The suicide of Johannes appears to have had a traumatic effect on their endeavor to become "neue Menschen" (new human beings). In their present modes of life—Thomas as the cynical, respectable academic; Anselm as the neurotic philanderer; Maria as the helpless housewife; and Regine as the exalted nymphomaniac—all have betrayed their past communal ideals. For all their intellectual sophistication, they are helpless vis-à-vis their existential dilemmas, frequently resorting to infantile modes of behavior in acting out their conflicts.

The play dispels traditional notions of psychology, for it exhibits no linear developments or easily identifiable causes. Its dialogues are not quasi-realistic imitations of actual conversations but a proliferation of poetic images and apodictic statements of bewildering complexity; the interchange of utterances is akin to a musical score. As melodramatic plot elements accumulate, theoretical discourse pours forth incessantly from the characters' mouths. For this reason, *Die Schwärmer* was widely praised as a literary text—Musil was awarded the prestigious Kleist Prize for it in 1922—yet classified as a "Lesedrama" (reader's drama), too cerebral to be suitable for stage performance. While many critics have tended to view *Die Schwärmer* mainly as an exercise on the way to the monumental *Der Mann ohne Eigenschaften*, Musil always regarded the play as one of his main works.

While serving with the Austrian Army Ministry in Vienna from September 1920 to December 1922 Musil began contributing drama criticism to newspapers in Vienna, Berlin, and Prague. He also wrote several theoretical essays. In "Symptomen-Theater" (The Theater of Symptoms, 1922-1923) and in "Der 'Untergang' des Theaters" (The 'Decline' of Theater, 1924) he formulates his conception of the nature and function of drama. He is outspoken in his disdain for the performance practices of his day, in which the vision of the author is obliterated by adulation of the performers and vacuous sensationalism. To Musil, literature is a means of probing ethical issues with the utmost rigor; he rejects the contention that drama ought to make concessions to the audience. Instead, Musil strives for a combination of an aesthetic experience and a profound existential reorientation. He finds a model for this kind of theater in the work of the Moscow Arts Theater under Konstantin Stanislavsky, whose productions he had seen in 1906 and in 1921. Musil particularly praises the somnambulistic quality of the ensemble playing, rich in nuances, in which the performers, rather than relish-

Elisabeth Schwarz, as Maria, and Joachim Bliese, as Anselm, at table, in a scene from the 1981 Berlin production of Musil's
Die Schwärmer *(photograph by Manfred Neugebauer)*

ing their respective roles, collectively realize the author's vision. Stanislavsky's productions affected Musil profoundly, even though he did not understand a word of Russian. In his reviews Musil tends to lavish praise on dramatic presentations based on what one would not normally regard as texts of great literary merit, such as cabaret performances or Yiddish theater. His concepts of drama are not primarily cerebral but grounded in a utopian notion of the theater as a medium of collective experience.

Musil's second play, *Vinzenz und die Freundin bedeutender Männer* (Vinzenz and the Lady Friend of Important Men, 1924) can be seen as a companion piece to *Die Schwärmer*. Subtitled a "Posse" (farce), it develops further such comical elements of the first play as the detective subplot. It is set in the world of kept women, confidence men, and sexual deviants depicted by Frank Wedekind; when the play was first performed at the Lustspielhaus in Berlin on 4 December 1923 under the direction of Bertold Viertel, with Rudolf Forster in the title role, most critics viewed it as a social comedy on the power of money and sexuality in the tradition of Wedekind, Kaiser, and Carl Sternheim. Characters and situations seem to be based on real-life incidents among Musil's friends, yet the play can be read as a comprehensive critique of social and sexual role-playing.

Vinzenz, a world-weary gambler, is reunited with his former love, Kathi. After fifteen years of separation she now bears the name Alpha, is the wife of the art dealer Apulejus-Halm, and is much admired by various representatives of bourgeois society, the "important men" of the title. Each of the play's three acts features a coup de theatre that highlights the contrived nature of the plot, anticipating some aspects of the theater of the absurd. The play begins with a bizarre marriage proposal at gunpoint as the rich businessman Bärli threatens to kill Alpha and himself should she refuse to leave her husband and marry him. Miraculously, Vinzenz appears and comes to her rescue. In act 2 the lovesick businessman repeats his threat; his second attack on Alpha turns out to be fake, prearranged by Vinzenz to purge Bärli of his passion for her. In act 3 what appears to be a jealous quarrel between Alpha and her friend over Vinzenz is revealed to be a screen test for an alleged film project. As the stage manager of other people's emotions, Vinzenz keeps a playful distance from the erotic desires circulating around him. His reencounter with Alpha fails because she takes him seriously; at the end of the play they part again. Vinzenz decides to become a servant as a means of achieving a semblance of selfhood by imitating somebody else's mode of existence. Sexual domination and social power are of no importance to Musil's protagonist; the play reverses the demonization of sexuality and the social philosophy implicit in the works of dramatists such as

Wedekind and August Strindberg.

For several years Musil and his friend and mentor Blei spent considerable energy trying to arrange a production of *Die Schwärmer*. Various excellent directors, including Viertel and Max Reinhardt, showed an interest, yet all efforts failed. It was not until almost eight years after its publication that the play received its first public performance on 3 April 1929 under the direction of Joe Lherman at the Theater in der Stadt in Berlin. Lherman, a maverick director of an avant-garde theater group, had secured the performing rights through Musil's publisher against the express wish of the author. The production, apparently hastily assembled and underrehearsed, was a critical failure and closed after only ten performances. In an open letter, "Der Schwärmerskandal" (The *Schwärmer* Scandal, 1929), Musil protested against what he regarded as the mutilation of his play.

Failing to find acceptance as a dramatist, Musil concentrated his energies on *Der Mann ohne Eigenschaften*, a project that had been occupying him since about 1918. For a few years he divided his time between Vienna and Berlin, resuming his main residence in Vienna after the Nazi seizure of power in 1933. In June 1935 he gave a speech at the International Writer's Congress for the Defense of Culture in Paris. A year later he suffered a stroke. In July 1938, a few months after the Anschluß (annexation of Austria by Germany), Musil and his wife, who was of Jewish extraction, left Vienna for Switzerland. They lived first in Zurich, then in Geneva. Musil's notebooks of the time suggest that he contemplated revising *Die Schwärmer*, probably in the hope that a new production would alleviate his financial difficulties in exile. Efforts were undertaken to secure the Musils an American visa, but on 15 April 1942 Musil died of another stroke.

Musil's plays were long neglected by critics and public alike. While *Vinzenz und die Freundin bedeutender Männer* received several productions during the writer's lifetime and in the first few years after the war, it has rarely been staged since then. It was not until the 1980s that *Die Schwärmer* attracted considerable attention in the wake of two highly acclaimed productions, at the Burgtheater in Vienna in 1980 and at the Schloßparktheater in Berlin in 1981. The Vienna production, presented without any textual cuts, was televised, while the Berlin production served as the basis for a television film in 1985. Productions at many major theaters have followed, attest-

Scene from a 1957 production at the Städtische Bühnen in Cologne of Musil's 1923 play Vinzenz und die Freundin bedeutender Männer

ing to the public's fascination with this mesmerizingly intellectual play that Hans Neuenfels, the director of the Schloßparktheater production, has hailed as "eins der wichtigsten Dramen des 20. Jahrhunderts, wenn nicht das wichtigste, das die deutschsprachige Literatur bislang besitzt" (one of the most important dramas of the twentieth century if not the most important one that German literature can so far call its own).

Letters:
Briefe nach Prag, edited by Barbara Köpplova and Kurt Krolop (Reinbek: Rowohlt, 1971);
Briefe 1901-1942, 2 volumes, edited by Adolf Frisé and Murray G. Hall (Reinbek: Rowohlt, 1981).

Bibliographies:
Ulrich Karthaus, "Musil-Forschung und Musil-Deutung: Ein Literaturbericht," *Deutsche Vierteljahresschrift für Literaturwissenschaft und Geistesgeschichte*, 39 (1965): 441-483;
Jürgen C. Thöming, *Robert-Musil-Bibliographie* (Bad Homburg: Verlag Dr. Max Gehlen, 1968);

Robert L. Roseberry, *Robert Musil: Ein Bericht* (Frankfurt am Main: Athenäum, 1974);

Wolfgang Freese, "Zur neueren Musil-Forschung: Ausgaben und Gesamtdarstellungen," *text + kritik*, 21/22 (1983): 86-148.

Biographies:

Wilfried Berghahn, *Robert Musil in Selbstzeugnissen und Dokumenten* (Reinbek: Rowohlt, 1963);

David Luft, *Robert Musil and the Crisis of European Culture 1880-1942* (Berkeley: University of California Press, 1980);

Karl Corino, *Robert Musil: Leben und Werk in Bildern und Texten* (Reinbek: Rowohlt, 1988).

References:

Elisabeth Albertsen, "Ea oder *die Freundin bedeutender Männer*: Porträt einer Wiener Kaffeehaus-Muse," *Musil-Forum*, 5 (1979): 21-37, 135-153;

Gerda Ambros, "Robert Musils *Schwärmer*—entfernte Biographien," *Musil-Studien*, 13 (1985): 78-94;

Lisa Appignanesi, *Femininity and the Creative Imagination: A Study of Henry James, Robert Musil and Marcel Proust* (London: Vision, 1973), pp. 116-122;

Helmut Arntzen, "Wirklichkeit als Kolportage: Zu drei Komödien von Georg Kaiser und Robert Musil," *Deutsche Vierteljahresschrift für Literaturwissenschaft und Geistesgeschichte*, 36 (1962): 544-561;

Arntzen, *Zur Sprache kommen* (Münster: Aschendorff, 1983), pp. 257-265;

Lowell A. Bangerter, *Robert Musil* (New York: Continuum, 1989);

Sibylle Bauer and Ingrid Drevermann, *Ethik und Bewußtsein: Studien zu Robert Musil* (Cologne & Graz: Böhlau, 1966): 7-44;

Wilhelm Braun, "An Approach to Musil's *Die Schwärmer*," *Monatshefte*, 14 (1962): 156-170;

Braun, "Musil's Anselm and 'The Motivated Life,'" *Wisconsin Studies in Contemporary Literature*, 8 (Autumn 1967): 517-527;

Braun, "Musil's *Die Schwärmer*," *PMLA*, 80 (June 1965): 292-298;

Braun, "Musil's *Vinzenz und die Freundin bedeutender Männer*," *Germanic Review*, 37 (1962): 121-134;

Braun, "Musil's 'Vinzenz und die Freundin bedeutender Männer,'" *Musil-Forum*, 9 (1983): 173-178;

Bianca Cetti-Marinoni, *Come Si Fa Con un Saggio: Robert Musil e la Genesi degli Schwärmer* (Milan: Angeli, 1988);

Cetti-Marinoni, "'Liebe ist gar nie Liebe'—Zum Verhältnis von Liebesthematik und dramatischer Struktur in Musils Theater," *Studi Tedeschi*, 30 (1987): 1-36;

Cetti-Marinoni, "Verfremdungseffekte bei Robert Musils als Stücke-Schreiber," *Musil-Studien*, 14 (1986): 104-132;

Marianne Charrière-Jaquin, "Musils *Schwärmer*: Lebenskampf? Kartenspiel? Kammermusik?," *Musil-Studien*, 13 (1985): 24-43;

Karl Corino, "*Alpha*—Modell Nr. 2: Bemerkungen zum biographischen Hintergrund von Robert Musil Posse *Vinzenz und die Freundin bedeutender Männer*," *Musil-Studien*, 13 (1985): 95-109;

Chiara De Tullio, "Die *Schwärmer* in der Musil-Literatur. Forschungsbericht." *Musil-Forum*, 15 (1989): 18-38;

Claus Erhart, "Die Zeit der *Schwärmer*," in *Der ästhetische Mensch bei Robert Musil. Vom Ästhetizismus zur schöpferischen Moral* (Innsbruck: Instutut für Germanistik, 1991), pp. 129-230;

Martin Esslin, "Musil's Plays," in *Musil in Focus: Papers from a Centenary Symposium*, edited by Lothar Huber and John J. White (London: Institute of Germanic Studies, University of London, 1982), pp. 23-40;

Dietmar Goltschnigg, "Theoretische und historische Aspekte der Komödie *Vinzenz und die Freundin bedeutender Männer*," in *Robert Musil and the Literary Landscape of his Time*, edited by Hannah Hickman (Salford: University of Salford, 1991), pp. 151-171;

Murray Hall, "Der Schwärmerskandal 1929: Zur Rezeption von Robert Musils *Die Schwärmer*," *Maske und Kothurn*, 21 (1975): 153-186;

Peter Henninger, "La Résistance du Texte: A propos des *Exaltés*," in *Robert Musil: Colloque dirigé par Jean-Pierre Cometti* (Royaumont: Editions Royaumont, 1986), pp. 83-105;

Hannah Hickman, *Robert Musil and the Culture of Vienna* (La Salle, Ill.: Open Court, 1984), pp. 97-132;

Peter Horn, "'Man verkriecht sich hinter seiner Haut.' Zu Robert Musil *Die Schwärmer*," *Acta Germanica*, 20 (1990): 79-105;

Jörg Jesch, "Robert Musil als Dramatiker," *text + kritik*, 21/22 (1968): 26-33;

Lynda J. King, "The New Woman in Robert Musil's Comedy *Vinzenz und die Freundin bedeuten-*

der Männer," *Modern Austrian Literature,* 16 (1983): 23-36;

Monika Meister, "Der Theaterbegriff Robert Musils: Ein Beitrag zur ästhetischen Theorie des Theaters," Ph.D. dissertation, University of Vienna, 1979;

Meister and Paul Stefanek, *"Die Schwärmer* in Wien," *Musil-Forum,* 8 (1982): 137-150;

Egon Naganowski, "Drei Versuche," *Literatur und Kritik,* 66/67 (1972): 321-330;

Naganowski, " 'Vinzenz' oder der Sinn des sinnvollen Unsinns," *Musil-Studien,* 4 (1973): 89-122;

Naganowski, "Robert Musils *Vinzenz,* der Dadaismus und das Theater des Absurden," in *Beiträge zur Musil-Kritik,* edited by Gudrun Brokoph-Mauch (Bern & Frankfurt am Main: Lang, 1983), pp. 63-74;

Naganowski, *"Die Schwärmer* als Bühnenstück," *Musil-Studien,* 13 (1985): 62-77;

Hans Neuenfels, *Robert Musil: Die Schwärmer. Ein Film* (Reinbek: Rowohlt, 1985);

Michael Oczipka, "Die Verwirklichung des 'anderen Zustands' in den Stücken Robert Musils," Ph.D. dissertation, University of Vienna, 1972;

Philip Payne, *Robert Musil's Works, 1906-1924* (Frankfurt am Main, Bern & New York: Lang, 1987);

Thomas Pekar, *Die Sprache der Liebe bei Musil* (Munich: Fink, 1989);

Frederick G. Peters, *Robert Musil: Master of the Hovering Life* (New York: Columbia University Press, 1978);

Burton Pike, *Robert Musil: An Introduction to His Work* (Ithaca, N.Y.: Cornell University Press, 1961);

Wolfdietrich Rasch, "Robert Musils Komödie 'Vinzenz und die Freundin bedeutender Männer,' " in *Das deutsche Lustspiel,* volume 2, edited by Horst Steffen (Göttingen: Vandenhoeck & Ruprecht, 1969), pp. 159-179;

Gilbert Reis, *Musils Frage nach der Wirklichkeit* (Königstein: Hain, 1983);

Annie Reniers-Servranckx, *Robert Musil: Konstanz und Entwicklung von Themen, Motiven und Strukturen in den Dichtungen* (Bonn: Bouvier, 1972);

Christian Rogowski, *Implied Dramaturgy: Robert Musil and the Crisis of Modern Drama* (Riverside, Cal.: Ariadne, 1992);

Rogowski, " 'Lauter unbestimmte Größen': Zu Ingeborg Bachmanns Hörspielbearbeitung *der Schwärmer* von Robert Musil," *Musil-Studien,* 18 (1990): 191-210;

Rogowski, "Seduced Seducers: Strindberg as Intertext in Robert Musil's Comedy *Vinzenz und die Freundin bedeutender Männer,"* *Deutsche Vierteljahrsschrift für Literaturwissenschaft und Geistesgeschichte,* 64 (1990): 549-559;

Marie-Louise Roth, *"Vincent et l'amie des personnalités:* Essai d'interpretation," *Sinn und Symbol,* edited by Karl Konrad Polheim (Bern: Lang, 1987), pp. 433-442;

Michael Scharang, "Musils Dramatik," *Wort in der Zeit,* 11 (1964): 36-45;

Scharang, "Robert Musil—Dramaturgie und Bühnengeschichte," Ph.D. disseration, University of Vienna, 1965;

Scharang, "Robert Musils theatralische Sendung," *Forum,* 137 (1965): 255-258;

Günther Schneider, *Untersuchungen zum dramatischen Werk Robert Musils* (Bern & Frankfurt am Main: Lang, 1973);

Agata Schwartz, "Robert Musil als Dramatiker, Theaterkritiker und—theoretiker," *Fidibus,* 19, no. 1 (1991): 1-65;

Paul Stefanek, "Due poeti in cerca del dramma: Überlegungen zur Dramaturgie Robert Musils und Luigi Pirandellos," *Robert Musil: Nel primo centario della nascita* (Rome: Istituto italiano di cultura, 1981), pp. 63-70;

Stefanek, "Lesedrama?—Überlegungen zur szenischen Transformation 'bühnenfremder' Dramaturgie," in *Das Drama und seine Inszenierung,* edited by Erika Fischer-Lichte, Christel Weiler, and Klaus Schwind (Tübingen: Niemeyer, 1985), pp. 133-145;

Stefanek, "Musils Posse 'Vinzenz' und das Theater der Zwischenkriegszeit," *Maske und Kothurn,* 26 (1980): 249-270;

Stefanek, "Musils Posse 'Vinzenz' und das Theater," *Musil-Studien,* 7 (1981): 111-148;

Stefanek, "Musils Posse 'Vinzenz' und die Tradition der Komödie," *Musil-Forum,* 6 (1980): 25-42;

Norio Tajima, "Die Gestalt des Thomas in den 'Schwärmern' von Robert Musil," *Doitsu Bungaku,* 49 (1972): 39-50;

Jürgen Thöming, "Zu einer Metapher in Musils 'Schwärmern,' " *Musil-Forum,* 7 (1981): 85-97;

Ursula Tiebel, "Robert Musils Wege zum 'Dichter-Theater,' " Ph.D. dissertation, University of Erlangen-Nürnberg, 1978; revised as *Theater von außen: Robert Musil als Kritiker* (Rheinfelden: Schäuble, 1980):

Roger Willemsen, *Robert Musil: Vom intellektuellen Eros* (Munich & Zurich: Piper, 1985);

Christel Zahlmann, "Die Dynamik der Leere: Zu Robert Musils Drama *Die Schwärmer*," in *Phantasie und Deutung*, edited by Wolfram Mauser, Ursula Renner & Walter Schönau (Würzburg: Könighausen & Neumann, 1986), pp. 167-179;

Rosmarie Zeller, "Robert Musil und das Theater seiner Zeit," in *Robert Musil and the Literary Landscape of his Time*, edited by Hannah Hick-man (Salford: University of Salford, 1991), pp. 134-150.

Papers:

The main collection of Robert Musil's manuscripts is in the Österreichische National-bibliothek (Austrian National Library), Vienna. Substantial collections of primary and secondary sources are at the Internationale Robert-Musil-Gesellschaft (Robert Musil Society) in Saar-brücken, Germany, and the Robert-Musil-Archiv in Klagenfurt, Austria.

Hans Rehberg

(25 December 1901 - 20 June 1963)

Jürgen G. Sang
University of Hawaii

PLAY PRODUCTIONS: *Cecil Rhodes*, Bochum, Städtische Bühnen, 8 March 1930;

Johannes Keppler, Wuppertal, Städtische Bühnen, 3 December 1933;

Der Große Kurfürst, Berlin, Staatliches Schauspiel-haus, 30 November 1934;

Der Tod und das Reich, Hessen-Nassau, Gebiet 13 der Hitlerjugend, 1935;

Friedrich I, Leipzig, Altes Theater, 10 April 1935;

Friedrich Wilhelm I, Berlin, Staatliches Schauspiel-haus, 19 April 1936;

Kaiser und König, Hamburg, Staatliches Schauspiel-haus, 27 October 1937;

Der Siebenjährige Krieg, Berlin, Staatliches Schau-spielhaus, 7 April 1938;

Die Königin Isabella, Berlin, Staatliches Schauspiel-haus, 7 April 1939;

Die Preußische Komödie, Darmstadt, Landestheater, 3 March 1940;

Heinrich und Anna, Darmstadt, Landestheater, 30 November 1941;

Gajus Julius Caesar, Breslau, Schauspielhaus, 8 September 1942;

Karl V., Darmstadt, Landestheater, 15 October 1943;

Die Wölfe, Breslau, Schauspielhaus, 1944;

Bothwell und Maria, Karlsruhe, Badisches Staats-theater, 1948;

Heinrich VII, Munich, Residenztheater, 1949;

Elisabeth und Essex, Wuppertal, Städtische Büh-nen, 29 April 1949;

Der Muttermord, Stuttgart, Landestheater, 12 March 1953;

Der Gattenmord, Düsseldorf, Städtische Bühnen, 15 October 1953;

Maria und Elisabeth, Munich, Kammerspiele, 1953;

Königsberg, Duisburg, Stadttheater, April 1955;

Rembrandt, Düsseldorf, Städtische Bühnen, April 1956;

Kleist, Oldenburg, Schloßtheater, 20 December 1958.

BOOKS: *Der Tod und das Reich: Sprechchorspiel* (Leipzig: Strauch, 1934);

Der Große Kurfürst: Schauspiel (Berlin: Fischer, 1934);

Friedrich I.: Komödie (Berlin: Fischer, 1935);

Friedrich Wilhelm I.: Schauspiel (Berlin: Fischer, 1935);

Die goldene Kugel: Schauspiel (Berlin: Althausen, 1936);

Kaiser und König: Schauspiel (Berlin: Fischer, 1936);

Der Siebenjährige Krieg: Schauspiel (Berlin: Fischer, 1937);

Die Königin Isabella: Schauspiel in drei Akten (Berlin: Fischer, 1939);

Die Preußische Komödie: In drei Tagen (Berlin: Fischer, 1940);

Suez, Faschoda, Kapstadt: Drei Hörspiele, edited by the Deutsche Informationsstelle (Berlin: Fischer, 1940);

Heinrich und Anna: Drama (Berlin: Suhrkamp, 1942);

Karl V.: Schauspiel (Berlin: Suhrkamp, 1943);

Heinrich VII.: Schauspiel in drei Akten (Munich: Desch, 1947).

RADIO: *Die Preußische Komödie: Eine Funkdichtung*, Reichsrundfunkgesellschaft, Saal 2, 12 March 1933;

Suezkanal: Eine französische Tragödie, Reichssender Stuttgart, 29 August 1939;

Rembrandt and *Die Nachtwache*, Westdeutscher Rundfunk Köln, 23 April 1956;

Aus dem Leben David Copperfields, 3 parts, Westdeutscher Rundfunk Köln, 15 January-23 February 1957.

SELECTED PERIODICAL PUBLICATIONS—
UNCOLLECTED: "Die Preußische Komödie: Eine Funkdichtung," *Neue Rundschau*, 44 (1933): 721-756;

"Das Reich: Hymnen," *Neue Rundschau*, 46 (1935): 1-8;

"Zum Problem des Theaters," *Programmheft Schauspielhaus am Gendarmenmarkt* (22 April 1936);

"Prolog zu einem Puppenspiel," *Neue Rundschau*, 47 (1936): 113-114;

"Kunersdorf oder Feldherr und König: Ein Hörspiel," *Neue Rundschau*, 47 (1936): 589-604;

"Dem Führer: Am 20. April 1939," *Neue Rundschau*, 50 (1939): 413-414;

"Die Schill'schen Offiziere," *Schulfunk*, 1 (1939-1940): 4-11;

"Der Tod des Dichters Heinrich von Kleist," *Neue Rundschau*, 51 (1940): 555;

"Das Leid," *Neue Rundschau*, 51 (1941): 166;

"Staatsraison und Weltraison. Szene aus dem kommenden Hörspiel Richelieu," *Ruf*, 3, no. 18 (1948): 9-10;

"Ophelia," *Der Kranich*, 9 (1967): 35-36;

Maria und Elisabeth: Tragödie, in *Der Kranich*, 10 (1968): 7-63;

"Wir erwarben gemeinsamen Ruhm . . . Ein Brief Hans Rehbergs an Gustaf Gründgens," *Welt und Wort*, 28 (1973): 164-166.

Hans Rehberg, who started his career as a playwright at the age of twenty-nine, was productive for more than three decades. After 1945 Rehberg's dramatic works were linked to National Socialist (Nazi) ideology. The Nazis, however, had registered the prolific dramatist early on as a controversial figure; when critics prevented Rehberg from rebuilding his career after World War II neither the misgivings of the Nazi regime about him nor Rehberg's theatrical achievements were taken into proper consideration.

Rehberg was born on 25 December 1901 in Posen, the capital of the West Prussian province of the same name (it is now in Poland). Rehberg married Maria Ohly; the couple had six children: Maria, Katharina, Nikolaus, Till, Friedrich, and Hans-Michael. Hans-Michael became a successful stage actor during the 1970s and 1980s. In 1930 Rehberg became a member of the Nazi party.

Rehberg's first play, *Cecil Rhodes* premiered in Bochum on 8 March 1930. It focuses on the tragedy of the idealistic statesman and his obsession with the welfare of the motherland while England pursues its secret imperialist plans. Critics were generally unimpressed with the work.

In *Johannes Keppler* (performed, 1933) the astronomer becomes a tragic hero and is made the sacrificial lamb of conflicting politics of the Catholic emperor Ferdinand II and the Protestant duke of Württemberg. The play focuses on the spiritual instead of the historical life of Keppler. The first of Rehberg's six "Prussian Dramas," *Die Preußische Komödie* (The Prussian Comedy; published, 1940) was broadcast by Berlin Radio on 12 March 1933 under the direction of Edlef Köppen with music written by Hans Klammeier. Rehberg gave the Prussian princes, kings, and courtiers a tragic dimension by portraying their obsession with the Prussian drive to build the state. The play was produced on the stage at the Hesse Landestheater in Darmstadt in 1940. Rehberg's first Prussian drama to be staged, *Der Große Kurfürst* (The Great Elector, 1934), was performed at the Berlin State Theater on 30 November 1934. The Great Elector sacrifices his humanity to his obsession with building a Prussian state. The play reveals the weaknesses, faults, and fears of Prussian rulers. The director, Jürgen Fehling, had the actors speak and gesture with almost surrealistic intensity, elevating the play above any kind of conventional naturalism. Berlin's leading critics praised the performance. The official Nazi newspaper, *Der Völkische Beobachter* (The National Observer) joined the chorus, even though Rehberg had just been thrown out of the party for criticizing a July 1934 government decree legalizing Hitler's murder of Ernst Röhm.

The first performance of Rehberg's next play, *Friedrich I.* (1935), was not given in Berlin. The comedy premiered on 10 April 1935 at the Altes Theater in Leipzig. Detlef Sierck's production did not receive particularly good reviews, but when Heinz Hilpert ventured to produce the play at the Deutsches Theater in Berlin on 30 October 1936 it was successful against all political odds. An excellent cast presented the tragicomic elements even to Rehberg's satisfaction.

Encouraged by this success, Rehberg proceeded to write his next play, *Friedrich Wilhelm I.* (published, 1935). Again, Rehberg dismissed historical facts and emphasized the human elements of the characters. The play premiered on 19 April 1936 at the Staatliches Schauspielhaus in Berlin with Fehling as the director. While the critic Herbert Ihering was impressed by the production, the audiences and some critics were slow to warm to the "un-Prussian" play. Rehberg's plays seemed to promise the glorification of Germanic values, but they actually presented visionary, sometimes expressionistic, interpretations.

Rehberg added another milestone to his Prussian cycle by writing the drama *Kaiser und König* (Emperor and King; published, 1936). It was first performed at the Staatliches Schauspielhaus in Hamburg on 27 October 1937. Apart from the main plot of Friedrich II's and the Austrian empress Maria Theresia's struggle for Silesia, the play shows the conflict of two opposing principles: the rule of the woman as earthmother and the rule of the male as the incarnation of the state.

Der Siebenjährige Krieg (The Seven Years' War; published, 1937) also is not an action-oriented historical drama. But there were enough theatrical elements to lend Friedrich II's epic battle with Austria's General Gideon Ernst, Freiherr von Laudon and the Russian empress Elizabeth fantastic aspects. The first performance of the

play, attended by Hermann Göring, was given at the Staatliches Schauspielhaus in Berlin on 7 April 1938. It was directed by Rehberg's friend and supporter Gustav Gründgens. Although his interpretation of Friedrich as cold and petrified by the power of his will received some criticism, Gründgen's prestige carried the day.

Thereafter, Rehberg turned away from Prussian themes, which had become politically controversial. The first work in this new line of plays, *Die Königin Isabella* (Queen Isabella; published, 1939), premiered on 7 April 1939 under Gründgens's direction. The main characters are weak, eccentric, and haunted persons. The queen is herself haunted by her sacrifices as a woman, the curse of the Plantagenets, and her vision of a unified Spain. The Nazi theater, which increasingly needed demonstrations of dramatic struggles of heroism, could not get much ideological satisfaction from this play, which received fifteen minutes of applause at the curtain.

Rehberg's radio play *Suezkanal* (Suez Canal; broadcast, 1939; published as *Suez*, 1940) demonstrates how Comte Ferdinand de Lesseps's visionary plans were politically exploited. *Suezkanal* was designed to indoctrinate a French audience with mistrust of Britain. In 1941 *Die Weltliteratur* (World Literature), a newspaper affiliated with the SS or *Schutzstaffel* (elite guard), attacked Rehberg for failing to present one decent character in all of Prussia. Rehberg had finally fallen from grace. He stopped writing political radio plays.

Rehberg, who had lived in Sommerswalde from 1931 to 1935 and thereafter in Meckerndorf, moved in 1941 to Ochelhermsdorf in Silesia. There he continued his dramatic work with three plays. *Heinrich und Anna* (Henry and Anne; performed, 1941; published, 1942) deals with England's king Henry VIII and his queen, Anne Boleyn. It is Henry's tragic destiny to live beyond the human measure of good and evil; his kingship is a lonely one. Nazi critics bemoaned the political noncommitment of the play. The tragedy *Gajus Julius Caesar* (performed, 1942) presents a superhuman being, the statesman and genius Caesar, who follows his lone destiny. In *Karl V.* (Charles V; published, 1942; performed, 1943), the weak characterization of Charles, who fails in his quest to win Germany for Spain, was offset somewhat by Rehberg's theatrical effects.

Following public attacks on his works, Rehberg joined the staff of the Supreme Submarine Command as a war correspondent with the rank of lieutenant. On the basis of his experiences he wrote the play *Die Wölfe* (The Wolves; performed, 1944).

The Nazis, searching for a gripping drama about German U-boat mariners, gave Rehberg military leave and sent him on a lecture tour. Dressed in his naval officer's uniform, he gave readings from his unfinished play. But the work did not fulfill the expectations of the Nazis. The daring final scene portrayed the widow of a German officer going insane out of grief and showed a dead soldier commenting on the war and advising the woman to strengthen her will to resist. The play was censored. The sacrilegious treatment of Nazi values such as loyalty, love of fatherland, a hero's death, and Germanic womanhood could not be tolerated. Shortly after this incident all German theaters were closed on 1 October 1944. It is not documented whether Rehberg was discharged from active duty after the propaganda ploy with *Die Wölfe* failed. It is said that he lost all his manuscripts when fleeing from the Russian armies that took Breslau (now Wroclaw, Poland) in February 1945.

With the collapse of the Third Reich, Rehberg and his family trekked from Silesia to the hamlet of Assenshausen in Bavaria. In February 1946 they moved to another Bavarian village, Hohenschäftlarn. After 1945 Rehberg lost no time taking up writing again. *Heinrich VII.* (Henry VII; published, 1947; performed, 1949) goes back to the theme of English history. In 1941 Rehberg had dealt with Henry VIII; here he depicts that king's father, Henry VII.

The first production of a Rehberg play after the war was *Bothwell und Maria* (performed, 1948). This first drama of a three-play cycle dealing with Mary Stuart and Elizabeth I featured the ill-fated love story as the cause of Mary's downfall. In February 1949 and again in July of that year Rehberg's Nazi leanings became a public issue; considered a "Mitläufer" (fellow traveler), he was never able to overcome the odium of having been hailed by Nazi cultural functionaries. But the German theater was still interested in his works, and the second play in the cycle, *Elisabeth und Essex* premiered on 29 April 1949. The play emphasizes the tragic elements of the aging Queen Elisabeth's love for the young rebel. Rehberg concluded the English cycle with *Maria und Elisabeth* (published, 1968), which premiered in 1953 in Munich to mixed reviews. The play reveals human nature behind the façade of political power.

Scene from the premiere of Rehberg's Bothwell und Maria *in Karlsruhe in 1948, with Alexander Golling as Bothwell and Anneliese von Eschstruth as Maria Stuart (photograph by Bauer)*

Rehberg moved to Duisburg in the Ruhr district in 1951. His *Der Gattenmord* (The Murder of the Husband) and *Muttermord* (Matricide) premiered at the Düsseldorf and Stuttgart theatres on 15 October and 12 March 1953, respectively. His treatment of the fates of Agamemnon, Clytemnestra, and Orestes in a contemporary vision of a dehumanized world was rejected by the critics. While the dramatic impact of individual scenes was recognized, the overall treatment appeared chaotic.

Duisburg commissioned Rehberg to write a Festspiel (festival play), *Königsberg*, celebrating the seven-hundredth anniversary of its sister city (which had become Kaliningrad, U.S.S.R., after the war). Rehberg delivered this spectacle about the German colonization of East Prussia without introducing undue nationalistic overtones. The play was successfully performed in 1955 in Duisburg under the direction of Wilhelm Michael Mund, set to music by Günter Raphael, and choreographed by Alexander von Swaine.

True to Rehberg's style, his drama *Rembrandt* (performed, 1956) did not stick to the historical facts. Rembrandt dies lonely and impoverished but is not depicted as a tragic figure. A shortened version of the play broadcast by the West German radio in Cologne was better received by the critics than the theater play.

Rehberg took scenes from an unfinished radio play, "Der junge Kleist" (Young Kleist) and developed them into a full-length drama, *Kleist*, which premiered on 20 December 1958 at the Schloßtheater in Oldenburg. Again, the drama does not reconstruct biographical facts; the last year in the life of the writer Heinrich von Kleist is viewed from various perspectives. While critics such as Bernt von Heiseler and Hans Braun appreciated the drama and Rehberg's work, *Kleist* was unsuccessful. At the time of Rehberg's sixtieth birthday none of his many plays was in the German theater repertoire.

When Rehberg died on 20 June 1963 of heart failure, Germany's leading newspapers published obituaries regretting that a talented dramatist had been denied his proper place on the postwar German stage. A few critics tried to clear Rehberg's name of its Nazi associations. Hopes expressed for a revival of Rehberg's great character dramas have since fallen silent.

References:

Henry Flebbe, "Kaiser und König. Eine geschichtliche Einführung in Rehbergs Schauspiel," *Die Rampe: Blätter des Staatlichen Schauspielhauses Hamburg*, 4 (1937/1938): 37-45;

Joachim Konrad Friesicke, "Der Gegensatz zwischen Vater und Sohn in der deutschen Dramatik von Hasenclevers 'Sohn' bis Rehbergs 'Friedrich Wilhelm I,' " Ph.D. dissertation, University of Munich, 1942;

Otto Friedrich Gaillard, *Hans Rehberg: Der Dichter der "Preußendramen"* (Rostock: Hinstorff, 1941);

Bernt von Heiseler, "Hans Rehberg," in *Gesammelte Essays zur alten und neueren deutschen Literatur* (Stuttgart: Steinkipf, 1966), pp. 145-146;

Herbert Ihering, "Was fordert der Autor vom Kritiker. Stenogramm eines Dialogs mit Hans Rehberg im Rundfunk 1933 über Theater und Rundfunkkritik," in *Literatur und Rundfunk*, edited by Gerhard Hay (Hildesheim: Gerstenberg, 1975), pp. 188-194;

Franz Lennartz, "Hans Rehberg," in *Deutsche Dichter und Schriftsteller unserer Zeit* (Stuttgart: Kröoner, 1969), pp. 546-549;

Hans Werner Richter, "Kortner-Rehberg: Zu Inszenierungs-absichten von Fritz Kortner und dem Stück von Hans Rehberg 'Die Atriden,' " *Die Literatur*, 1 (1952): 1;

Reinhold Schneider, "Preußische Königsdramen. Zu dem Hohenzollernzyklus von Hans Rehberg," *Europäische Revue*, 12 (1936): 992-994;

Hermann Wanderscheck, "Hans Rehberg," in *Deutsche Dramatik der Gegenwart* (Berlin, 1943), pp. 152-159; 316.

Papers:

The best selection of Hans Rehberg's papers is in the Sammlung Badenhop of the Schiller-Nationalmuseum, Marbach. Also, the Zentrum für Theaterforschung (Center for Theater Research) at the University of Hamburg has collected materials on Rehberg. Two scripts of radio plays are in the Deutsche Rundfunkarchiv, Frankfurt am Main; the rest seem to have been lost.

Hans José Rehfisch

(10 April 1891 - 9 June 1960)

Reinhold K. Bubser
University of Northern Iowa

PLAY PRODUCTIONS: *Das Paradies*, Halle, Stadttheater, 14 January 1920;

Der Chauffeur Martin, Mannheim, Nationaltheater, 12 November 1920;

Die Erziehung durch "Kolibri," Düsseldorf, Schauspielhaus, 13 November 1921; revised as *Die Libelle*, Berlin, Renaissancetheater, 19 September 1924;

Wer weint um Juckenack?, Leipzig, Schauspielhaus, 23 February 1924;

Nickel und die Sechsunddreißig Gerechten, Magdeburg, Wilhelmtheater, 18 October 1925;

Duell am Lido, Berlin, Staatliches Schauspielhaus, 20 February 1926;

Razzia, Halle, Stadttheater, 27 October 1926;

Skandal in Amerika, Berlin, Deutsches Künstlertheater, 16 April 1927;

Der Frauenarzt, Frankfurt, Neues Theater, 28 January 1928;

Pietro Aretino, Berlin, Schillertheater, 23 March 1929;

Die Affäre Dreyfus, by Rehfisch and Wilhelm Herzog, Berlin, Volksbühne, 25 November 1929;

Brest-Litowsk, Berlin, Theater des Westens, 10 October 1930;

Sprung über Sieben, Hamburg, Kammerspiele, 26 November 1931;

Der Verrat des Hauptmann Grisel, Bremen, Schauspielhaus; Nuremberg, Intimes Theater, 25 January 1933;

Gentlemen, as Sidney Phillipps, Berlin, Theater Die Komödie; Vienna Deutsches Volkstheater, 20 November 1935;

Wasser für Canitoga, by Rehfisch, as Georg Turner, and Egon Eis, Bochum, Stadttheater, 2 May 1936;

Doktor Semmelweis, Vienna, Volkstheater, 1936;

Der lächerliche Sir Anthony, Vienna, Theater Johanngasse, 1937;

College Boys, Vienna, Johann Strauss Theater, 1937;

The Iron Road, Birmingham, Repertory Theatre, 10 November 1938;

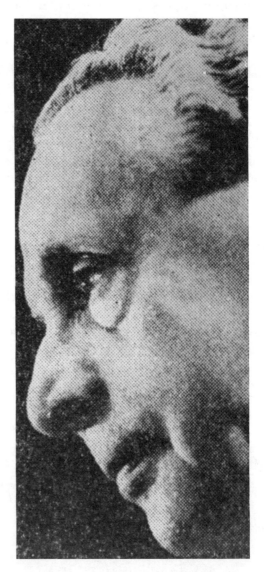

Hans José Rehfisch

Brides at Sea, London, Embassy Theatre, 1943;

Quell der Verheißung, Berlin, Hebbel-Theater, 16 September 1945;

Hände weg von Helena!, Hamburg, Kammerspiele, 6 October 1951;

Die eiserne Straße, Nuremberg, Stadttheater, 10 May 1952;

Lysistrata, Munich, Residenztheater, 4 July 1952;

Von der Reise zurück: Dr. Walters, Cologne, Bühnen der Stadt, 29 October 1952;

Das ewig Weibliche, Berlin, Hebbel-Theater, 17 September 1953;

Strafsache Doktor Helbig, Berlin, Schloßparktheater, 1955; revised, Lübeck, Städtische Bühnen, 1956;

Bumerang, Leipzig, Städtische Bühnen, 26 November 1960;

Verrat in Rom, Leipzig, Städtische Bühnen, 26 November 1961;

Jenseits der Angst, Brunswick, Staatstheater, 20 February 1962.

BOOKS: *Die goldenen Waffen: Tragödie* (Berlin: Reiß, 1913);

Die rechtliche Natur der Enteignung (Berlin: Ebering, 1916);

Heimkehr: Ein Schauspiel in fünf Akten (Berlin: Oesterheld, 1919);

Das Paradies: Eine Tragödie (Berlin: Oesterheld, 1919);

Der Chauffeur Martin: Eine Tragödie in fünf Akten (Berlin: Oesterheld, 1920);

Deukalion: Ein mythisches Drama (Berlin: Oesterheld, 1921);

Die Erziehung durch "Kolibri": Komödie in drei Akten (Berlin: Oesterheld, 1922);

Wer weint um Juckenack?: Tragikomödie in fünf Akten (Berlin: Oesterheld, 1924);

Nickel und die sechsunddreißig Gerechten: Komödie in drei Akten (Berlin: Oesterheld, 1925);

Duell am Lido: Komödie in drei Akten (Berlin: Oesterheld, 1926);

"Razzia!": Eine Berliner Tragikomödie in neun Bildern (Berlin: Oesterheld, 1926);

Pietro Aretino: Schauspiel in drei Akten (Berlin: Oesterheld, 1929);

Der Frauenarzt: Schauspiel in drei Akten (Berlin: Oesterheld,1929);

Die Affäre Dreyfus: Schauspiel, by Rehfisch and Wilhelm Herzog (Munich: Desch, 1951);

Die Hexen von Paris: Roman (Stuttgart: Cotta, 1951);

Oberst Chabert: Schauspiel in drei Akten (Munich, Vienna & Basel: Desch, 1956);

Lysistratas Hochzeit: Roman (Vienna, Munich & Basel: Desch, 1959);

Sieben Dramen (Munich, Vienna & Basel: Desch, 1961)—comprises *Oberst Chabert, Doktor Semmelweis, Die Stunde des Hauptmanns Grisel, Nickel und die sechsunddreißig Gerechten, Wer weint um Juckenack? Verrat in Rom, Bumerang*;

Ausgewählte Werke, 4 volumes, edited by the Deutschen Akademie der Künste zu Berlin (Berlin: Rütten & Loening, 1967)—volume 1: *Dramen*, comprises *Die goldenen Waffen, Wer weint um Juckenack?, Nickel und die sechsunddreißig Gerechten, "Razzia!," Die Affäre Dreyfus, Die Stunde des Hauptmanns Grisel*; volume 2: *Dramen*, comprises *Wasser für Canitoga, Strafsache Doktor Helbig, Oberst Chabert, Doktor Semmelweis, Verrat in Rom, Bumerang*; volume 3: *Die Hexen von Paris: Roman*; volume 4: *Lysistratas Hochzeit: Roman*.

OTHER: *In Tyrannos, Four Centuries of Struggle against Tyranny in Germany: A Symposium*, edited by Rehfisch (London: Drummond, 1944).

The Gebrauchsstück (journalistic play) of the 1920s translates contemporary events into dramatic action. In many instances, this type of play leaves the central questions it raises unresolved. Hans José Rehfisch was a leading author of Gebrauchsstücke. He was a prolific dramatist who became one of the most frequently performed authors during the Weimar Republic and achieved worldwide popularity and success, especially with *Die Affäre Dreyfus* (The Dreyfus Affair; performed, 1929; published, 1951). Many well-known German theater directors, including Max Reinhardt, Leopold Jessner, and Erwin Piscator, staged his plays, and actors such as Fritz Kortner, Marlene Dietrich, Heinrich George, Gerda Müller, and Oskar Homolka vied for roles in them.

Rehfisch was born on 10 April 1891 to Eugen Rehfisch and Hedwig Manczik Rehfisch. His father worked as a physician for the national health insurance plan and developed the electrocardiogram, for which he received the title professor of medicine. Rehfisch graduated from the Leibniz Gymnasium in Berlin in 1909. After studying at the Universities of Berlin, Heidelberg, and Grenoble, Rehfisch received two degrees from the University of Würzburg, one in political science and one in law. His mother, a musician, instilled in him an interest in the theater. After completing his law degree Rehfisch practiced law in Berlin, but he soon abandoned the profession to devote his energies to the theater.

Rehfisch's first play, the unperformed *Die goldenen Waffen* (The Golden Armor, 1913), deals with the fight between Odysseus and Aias (Ajax) over Achilles's armor. A mediator assigns the armor to Odysseus; outraged by this verdict, Aias commits suicide. Aias's tragic hubris lies in the dichotomy between talent and genius: the ordinary talent attempts to exalt himself to the heights of a genius and fails.

Rehfisch wrote *Heimkehr* (published, 1919) in February 1918, when World War I was still raging. Indebted to expressionist dramas, the play deals with the workers movement versus war, the fate of the individual versus that of society, the call for a new awareness versus bourgeois thinking. The protagonist, a German officer, returns home from the war and finds himself face to face with these conflicts. He begins to sympathize with the proletarian movement but cannot sever his strong ties to his capitalist background.

In *Das Paradies* (The Paradise; published, 1919; performed, 1920) a group of people tries to create a utopia in Switzerland. Five men squander their enthusiasm for a new society when they fight over a woman. The play was criticized for its romantic symbolism, nebulous imagery, and snobbish solemnity.

In Rehfisch's tragedy *Der Chauffeur Martin* (1920) the title character kills a pedestrian in an automobile accident. Acquitted of all charges, Martin lashes out at God for allowing the tragedy to happen. He turns into a rebel against all vestiges of God's order in the world. Martin's transformation from a law-abiding citizen into a defiant subversive has been castigated by some critics as being psychologically unconvincing.

Deukalion (Deucalion; published, 1921) recreates the Hellenic myth of the deluge. Pyrrha and Deucalion are spared the wrath of Zeus only to find that their isolation thrusts them into seemingly insurmountable conflicts. Only after Zeus has restored the world and accepted their plea for a new community with other human beings are the conflicts between Pyrrha and Deucalion resolved.

Similar charges have been leveled against Rehfisch's first comedy, *Die Erziehung durch "Kolibri"* (Education by "Kolibri"; performed, 1921; published, 1922). A variation of this comedy appeared in 1924 as *Die Libelle* (The Dragonfly). The comedy recycles themes typically associated with German Biedermeier comedies by such authors as Charlotte Birch-Pfeiffer and Roderich Benedix; middle-class values are examined and ridiculed. A rich uncle bequeaths a house called "Kolibri" to his virtuous nieces and nephews. Gradually, greed erodes their moralistic pretensions.

Wer weint um Juckenack? (Who Weeps for Juckenack?, 1924) opens with Juckenack, a forty-year-old lawyer with a heart ailment, in a state of suspended animation. His maid denounces his callous disregard for his fellow human beings: "Dem waren nur seine Bücher wichtig und seine juristischen Fälle. Gefühl für Menschen hat der nicht gehabt!" (The only thing he cared for were his books and his court cases. He had no feelings for people!). When he recovers, Juckenack decides that he has to fulfill a vision he had when he was unconscious: he noticed that nobody really cared if he expired. He adopts a new motto that he preaches to all who are willing to listen: to practice compassion is more valuable than to carry out the letter of the law. Juckenack helps two young people who are in monetary and legal trouble and receives nothing but ingratitude in return. When Juckenack dies in the end, his bourgeois quest to justify his own existence remains unfulfilled.

Der Frauenarzt (The Gynecologist; performed, 1928; published, 1929) deals with an item in the German penal code, paragraph 218, which prohibited most abortions. Doctors who violated this law faced severe legal penalties and professional ramifications. Rehfisch's Frau von Carlow helped Dr. Fechner reopen his medical practice after he spent a year in prison for performing an abortion. Fechner pledged that he would never again violate the law. Act 2 of the play opens in Fechner's waiting room. Among the women waiting to have abortions is Lotte, who is about to get married but is pregnant by her former fiancé. Fechner abandons his pledge to von Carlow. One of Lotte's acquaintances finds out about her abortion and blackmails Fechner, who flees to India. Reviewers criticized the play for its neutral stance on this sensitive issue and for its lack of dramatic energy.

Die Affäre Dreyfus became an international success. The themes include anti-Semitism, nationalism, injustice, military authority, and political extremism. The play is based on the trial for treason of the French army officer Alfred Dreyfus, the son of a wealthy Jewish textile manufacturer. He was accused of selling military secrets to the German military; the trial was tainted with irregularities, forgeries, and cover-ups. Dreyfus was convicted and sentenced to life imprisonment on Devil's Island; a retrial in 1899 found Dreyfus guilty again, but he was pardoned by the president of France. In a second retrial Dreyfus was found innocent and reinstated in the army. In the play only Colonel Picard gathers enough courage to pierce the tissue of lies. Every legal, political, and historical facet the play presents could be transferred to the Weimar Republic.

Rehfisch continued to write plays based on historical events, but he never again achieved the success that he enjoyed with *Die Affäre Dreyfus*. In 1932 Rehfisch's name appeared on a list of undesirable writers in the Nazi paper *Völkischer Beobachter* (Folkish Observer). He was president of the Association of German Stage Writers and Composers from 1931 to 1933, when he was arrested by the Nazis. After his release in 1936 he went into exile in Vienna, moving to England in 1938. He was sent to Camp Onchan on the Isle of Man and directed theater productions there and in nearby villages. He went to New York in 1945; there he joined Piscator as an instructor in the course on directing at Piscator's Dramatic Workshop, founded in 1939. The Dramatic Workshop was attached to the New School for Social Research, and Rehfisch also worked there as a lecturer in sociology from 1947 to 1949. In 1950 he returned to West Germany and became president of the Verband deutscher Bühnenschriftsteller und Bühnenkomponisten (Guild of German Dramatists and Composers for the Stage).

Although he rewrote many of his plays and remained actively involved in the German theatrical scene after his return from exile, today Rehfisch's name has been almost completely obliterated from the German theater. He receives only occasional mention in literary analyses. Between 1950 and 1960 Rehfisch lived in Hamburg and Munich. He died on 9 June 1960 in Schuls, Switzerland.

Biographies:

Wolfgang Jobo, "Entlarvung eines Zeitalters,"

Neue Deutsche Literatur, 6, no. 6 (1958): 149-152;

Rolf Seeliger, "Gegen die Zerstörung der Vernunft," *Neue Deutsche Literatur*, 8, no. 8 (1960): 158-160;

Claus Hammel, "Klassiker und Zeitgenosse," *Neue Deutsche Literatur*, 9, no. 11 (1961): 148-153;

Hugo Huppert, "Hans J. Rehfisch oder die überwundenen Verführungen," *Sinn und Form*, 23, no. 6 (1971): 1331-1344.

References:

Margret Dietrich, *Das moderne Drama* (Stuttgart: Kröner, 1974);

Manfred Durzak, ed., *Die deutsche Exilliteratur 1933-1945* (Stuttgart: Reclam, 1973);

C. D. Innes, *Erwin Piscator's Political Theatre: The Development of Modern German Drama* (Cambridge: Cambridge University Press, 1972);

Erwin Piscator, *The Political Theatre* (New York: Avon, 1978);

Günther Rühle, *Theater für die Republik, 1917-1933: Im Spiegel der Kritik* (Frankfurt am Main: Fischer, 1967);

Michael Seyfert, *Deutsche Exilliteratur in britischer Internierung: Im Niemandsland* (Berlin: Arsenal, 1984);

Lutz Weltmann, "Zum deutschen Drama: Hans J. Rehfisch," *Die Literatur*, 31 (1928-1929): 131-135;

John Willett, *The Theater of Erwin Piscator* (New York: Holmes & Meier, 1979).

Papers:

Hans José Rehfisch's papers are at the Theaterwissenschaftliches Institut (Theatrical Science Institute) in Vienna and the Deutsche Akademie der Künste (German Academy of Sciences) in Berlin.

Gerhard Roth

(24 June 1942 -   )

Peter Ensberg
Allegheny College

See also the Roth entry in *DLB 85: Austrian Fiction Writers After 1914.*

PLAY PRODUCTIONS: *Lichtenberg,* Graz, Steirischer Herbst, 19 October 1973;

Sehnsucht, Graz, Steirischer Herbst; Basel, Stadttheater, 8 October 1977;

Dämmerung, Graz, Steirischer Herbst, 7 October 1978;

Erinnerungen an die Menschheit, Graz, Steirischer Herbst, 27 September 1985.

BOOKS: *die autobiographie des albert einstein: Roman* (Frankfurt am Main: Suhrkamp, 1972);

Der Ausbruch des Ersten Weltkriegs und andere Romane (Frankfurt am Main: Suhrkamp, 1972)—comprises "Künstel," "Der Ausbruch des Ersten Weltkriegs," "How to be a detective";

Der Wille zur Krankheit: Roman (Frankfurt am Main: Suhrkamp, 1973);

Lichtenberg (Frankfurt am Main: Verlag der Autoren, 1973);

Herr Mantel und Herr Hemd (Frankfurt am Main: Insel, 1974);

Der große Horizont: Roman (Frankfurt am Main: Suhrkamp, 1974);

Ein neuer Morgen: Roman (Frankfurt am Main: Suhrkamp, 1976);

Dämmerung (Frankfurt am Main: Suhrkamp-Theaterverlag, 1977);

Sehnsucht (Frankfurt am Main: Fischer, 1977);

Winterreise (Frankfurt am Main: Fischer, 1978); translated by Joachim Neugroschel (New York: Farrar, Straus & Giroux, 1980);

Menschen, Bilder, Marionetten: Prosa, Kurzromane, Stücke (Frankfurt am Main: Fischer, 1979);

Der stille Ozean: Roman (Frankfurt: Fischer, 1980);

Circus Saluti (Frankfurt am Main: Fischer, 1981);

On the Boarderline: A Documentary Record / Ein dokumentarisches Protokoll (Vienna: Hannibal, 1981);

Bruno Kreisky, by Roth, Konrad R. Müller, and Peter Turrini (Berlin: Nicolai / Vienna: Forum, 1981);

Das Töten des Bussards (Graz: Droschl, 1982);

die autobiographie des albert einstein: Fünf Kurzromane (Frankfurt am Main: Fischer, 1982)—comprises "die autobiographie des albert einstein," "Künstel," "Der Ausbruch des Ersten Weltkriegs," "How to be a detective," "Der Wille zur Krankheit";

Die schönen Bilder beim Trabrennen (Frankfurt am Main: Fischer, 1982);

Lichtenberg; Sehnsucht; Dämmerung: Stücke (Frankfurt am Main: Fischer, 1983);

Landläufiger Tod: Roman (Frankfurt am Main: Fischer, 1984);

Dorfchronik zum "Landläufigen Tod" (Frankfurt am Main: Fischer, 1984);

Erinnerungen an die Menschheit (Graz: Droschl, 1985);

Am Abgrund (Frankfurt am Main: Fischer, 1986);

Der Untersuchungsrichter: Die Geschichte eines Entwurfs (Frankfurt am Main: Fischer, 1988);

Über Bienen (Vienna: Jugend & Volk, 1989);

Im tiefen Österreich Bildtextband (Frankfurt am Main: Fischer, 1990);

Über Bilder: Österreichische Malerei nach 1945: Aus der Sammlung der Zentralsparkasse (Vienna: Jugend & Volk, 1990);

Eine Reise in das Innere von Wien: Essays (Frankfurt am Main: Fischer, 1991);

Die Geschichte der Dunkelheit (Frankfurt am Main: Fischer, 1991).

TELEVISION: *Beobachtungen in Amerika—Ankunft,* South German Broadcasting System, 1976;

Der große Horizont, Austrian Broadcasting System, 13 January 1976;

Sehnsucht, Austrian Broadcasting System, 13 October 1977;

Dämmerung, Austrian Broadcasting System, 23 November 1978;

Menschen in Österreich, Austrian Broadcasting Sys-

Gerhard Roth

tem, 22 October, 29 October, 5 November
1979;

Der stille Ozean, Austrian Broadcasting System, 5
March 1983;

Erinnerungen an die Menschheit, Austrian Broadcasting System, 6 February 1986;

Der Bien, Austrian Broadcasting System, 14 December 1990;

Landläufiger Tod, Austrian Broadcasting System,
27 and 28 March 1991;

Das Geheimnis, Austrian Broadcasting System,
1992.

RADIO: *In Grönland*, Österreich I, 21 September
1977;

Die Unmöglichkeit der Naturwissenschaften, Österreich I, 11 January 1985;

Ein Schneetag, Österreich I, 8 February 1987.

OTHER: "Autorenumfrage: Mittel und Bedingungen schriftstellerischer Arbeit (Gerhard

Roth)," in *Gegenwartsliteratur: Mittel und Bedingungen ihrer Produktion*, edited by Peter R.
Bloch (Bern & Munich: Francke, 1975), pp.
334-336;

"Erste Lese-Erlebnisse," in *Erste Lese-Erlebnisse*, edited by Siegfried Unseld (Frankfurt am
Main: Suhrkamp, 1975), pp. 119-121;

"Czernys Tod (Fragment)," in *Wie die Grazer auszogen, die Literatur zu erobern*, edited by Peter
Laemmle and Jörg Drews (Munich: Edition
text + kritik, 1975), pp. 51-63;

"Eine Art Gast der Gegenwart," in *Wie ich anfing
... 24 Autoren berichten von ihren Anfängen*,
edited by Hans Daiber (Düsseldorf: Claassen, 1979), pp. 239-242.

Gerhard Roth, along with Peter Handke
and the late Thomas Bernhard, is one of the
most important writers in contemporary Austria.
The common theme of his novels and plays is the
isolation of the individual living in an unintelligible world.

Roth was born on 24 June 1942 in Graz, Austria, to Emil Roth, a doctor, and Erna Druschnitz Roth. After completing his Matura (school-leaving examination) in 1961 he studied medicine at the University of Graz. On 16 September 1963 he married Erika Wolfgruber; they have three children: Eva, Petra, and Thomas. The repulsion Roth felt for dissection, combined with the necessity to support his family, caused him to abandon his studies. From 1967 until 1977 he worked at the computing center in Graz before deciding to become a free-lance author. He was divorced in 1986.

Roth was a member of the Graz literary groups Forum Stadtpark (City Park Forum) and Grazer Autorenversammlung (Gathering of Graz Authors). He received the literary stipend from the Styrian government in 1972, the state junior stipend for literature in 1973, the literary prize of the state of Styria in 1976, the prize of the literary magazine of the German SWF broadcasting system in 1978, a stipend from the program for nonresident artists in Hamburg in 1979-1980, the Alfred Döblin Prize in 1983, and the Marie Luise Kaschnitz Prize, the Literary Prize of Vienna, and the *manuskripte* Prize in 1992. He received the Silver Bear at the Berlin Film Festival for the television production of *Der stille Ozean* (1982).

Roth's first play, *Lichtenberg* (1973), is not a biography of the Göttingen eighteenth-century aphorist and professor of mathematics and natural sciences Georg Christoph Lichtenberg. Instead, Roth incorporates isolated passages from Lichtenberg's aphorisms into his own text. Quotations, spoken mostly by the play's main character, the professor, range from one sentence to whole paragraphs in length. Lichtenberg's aphorisms express skepticism toward any kind of systematic cognition; he concentrates on specific details whose connections result in unexpected insights on the part of the reader. Roth's professor follows this lead. He objects to the mechanical systematizing and classifying of human beings and thoughts; he also challenges the orderly and systematic structure of language, proposing instead absurdity, chaos, and a new language based on intuition. According to the professor, quoting Lichtenberg, "die meisten unserer Wörter sind mißbrauchte Werkzeuge, die oft nach dem Schmutz riechen, in dem sie die vorigen Besitzer entweihten" (most of our words are abused tools often smelling like the dirt in which the former owners desecrated them). The play's action centers around a mur-

der case. The professor's next-door neighbor, a widow, has been raped and strangled. The police inspector does little to throw light on the case; the professor tries to find the murderer by performing linguistic experiments on his prime suspect, whom he calls "Objekt" (object). Objekt is a speech-impaired autistic. The professor submits Objekt to a rigorous language test by asking him to say various words; he then takes these words as proof that Objekt committed the murder by associating them with Objekt's alleged actions. For example, he relates the word *Blut* (blood) to the red carpet in the widow's house and the word *Blume* (flower) to the flowers he saw Objekt bring to the widow. Such deductions contradict the professor's avowed principles: the professor is establishing his own rigid interpretive system. Objekt denies the highly questionable conclusions of the professor, who at the end is suspected of the murder himself: the doctor saw him enter the widow's house. The question of who committed the murder is not resolved as *Lichtenberg* comes to a surprising end: Objekt picks up a pistol the professor has carelessly left on the table and kills his torturer.

Roth's second play, *Sehnsucht* (Desire, 1977), is a comedy of manners. The writer Albert Lindberg is unable to form stable relationships with the women he gathers around him. Although vacationing together at the lakeshore, the characters cannot find a common ground on which to communicate. A continuous plot is not developed; Roth presents a series of situations in thirteen scenes that remain unconnected, illustrating the disrupted nature of the relationships. Albert's estranged wife, Katharina, is constantly humiliated by her husband: "Ich bin nichts als ein Fremdkörper und du ignorierst mich" (I am nothing but an alien element and you ignore me). When she asks how their relationship should continue, he replies: "Nichts" (nothing). Ida, Albert's girlfriend, reproaches him for his egocentric way of life: "Du lebst in Deinem Ich wie unter einer Glasglocke. Was kümmert Dich schon ein anderer Mensch, das ist Dir völlig gleichgültig" (You live in your self as though under a bell jar. What is another human being to you, it is all the same to you). Ida leaves with the young actor Philipp, only to return for a final discussion of their relationship; at its end Albert rapes and strangles her. A lonely pharmacist is robbed of his only companion when Albert shoots and kills his dog. Albert justifies his deed by saying: "Es hat mich befreit" (It liberated me).

Helmut Lorin as the professor and Kees Campfens as Objekt in a 1974 production of Roth's Lichtenberg *in Frankfurt am Main*
(photograph by Schwöbel)

Albert's desire is to live in a land "in dem ich die Sprache und die Menschen nicht verstehe. Alles kommt mir abgenützt und unbrauchbar vor. Ich fühle einen Drang, zu zerstören. Nicht sinnvoll zu zerstören, sondern sinnlos irgendwas" (where I don't understand the language and the people. Everything appears used up and useless to me. I feel a destructive urge. Not to destroy meaningfully, but anything meaninglessly). The play was criticized for the abrupt change Albert undergoes from prattler to murderer, a change that is not sufficiently explained. Roth's friend Wolfgang Bauer directed the play in Graz as a burlesque rather than a melodrama; Horst Zankl, the director of the simultaneous premiere in Basel, left out the murder of Ida.

In Roth's third play, *Dämmerung* (Dawn; published, 1977; performed, 1978), the director of a mining company has just been buried, and family members and employees assemble in a restaurant for the obsequies. The order the authoritarian director dictated has vanished, leaving a gap that cannot be filled; conversations overlap or are interrupted. Ferdinand Seitz, the director's son-in-law and successor, is deeply unsatisfied in his private and professional lives. He is trying to dis-

tance himself from his unsatisfying existence; he likes to sit under a chestnut tree, looking off into the distance. Responding to his wife's criticism, he says: "Ich schaue gerne in die Ferne. Was stört dich daran, daß ich in die Ferne schaue? . . . Wo soll ich denn sonst hinschauen? . . . Ich bin nicht dort, wo du bist" (I like to look off into the distance. Why does it disturb you that I look off into the distance? . . . Where else should I look? . . . I am not where you are). Ferdinand blames her for leading a life consisting only of habits; she embodies the life-style he desperately wants to escape. His relationship with Mrs. Wessely, whose marriage is also extremely unhappy, offers no compensation to him; he breaks it off, leaving her in despair and with no purpose in life. An argument between Ferdinand and Dr. Wessely leads to a brawl that has to be stopped by the waiter. The marriage of the lawyer Winter and his wife is a constant competition of mutual humiliation. The short affair between Ferdinand's daughter and the waiter, both of whom remain nameless, offers no hope: the daughter receives no answer from the waiter when she asks if he will go away. *Dämmerung* describes lives void of any hope of change or fulfillment. The play's

Scene from the premiere of Roth's Sehnsucht *in Graz in 1977; left to right: Gerhard Balluch as Albert Lindberg, Peter Uray as Odörfer, Michael Balaun as Philipp Vogel, and Hedda Andreas as Anna Scholz (photograph by Neumüller)*

final words, spoken by the engineer, Blum, confirm the pessimistic perspective: "Das Leben geht weiter. Das ist der einzige Trost . . . " (Life continues. That is the only comfort . . .).

Dämmerung drew heavy criticism. The success of the premiere was credited entirely to the director, Fritz Zecha, and the stage designer, Peter Pongratz. In particular, it was charged, the dialogue in the play reflects the author's inability to convey psychological insights.

Perhaps discouraged by the critical reception of *Sehnsucht* and *Dämmerung*, Roth concentrated on writing prose for seven years. In 1985 his fourth play, *Erinnerungen an die Menschheit* (Recollections of Mankind), was published and performed. Roth dispenses here with any semblance of a plot; the twenty-eight scenes of the play are only loosely connected. A huge red frog appears; two white horses discuss scientific problems; a snake sings; a giant gentian talks; a dog who is a professor gets a shave in a barbershop; food products and dishes fight with each other; mysterious sounds are heard; a mental patient says to his doctor, before opening his wings

and flying off: "Die Menschheit ist nicht die Erkenntnis, sondern der Irrtum. Ein Irrtum löst den anderen ab. . . . Der Erkenntnisdrang führt sich selbst und die Menschen an der Nase herum, leitet sie in die Irre, wie in einem unendlichen Labyrinth" (Mankind is not cognition, but rather error. One error replaces the other. . . . The impulse for cognition fools itself and human beings, misleads them, like in an endless labyrinth). The often highly associative remarks of the characters cannot be explained by applying normal methods of interpretation. Roth emphasizes the illogical and concentrates on fantastic, surrealistic phenomena. Throughout the play there is an obvious distrust of logical, scientific conceptions. Interspersed among the surrealistic scenes are more traditionally composed sequences, all depicting violence. Scenes 5, 13, 19, and 27 describe the execution of a doomed man in the presence of an officer and a priest. The four scenes are identical, with one exception: the role of the priest reading a psalm becomes smaller and smaller until he totally disappears in scene 27. Scene 7 depicts a dying woman who has been raped. A passerby, ignoring her cries for help, lies down on her. After her death he shouts: "Mord!! Verbrechen!! (Murder!! Crime!!). In scene 11 a man, having made love to his girlfriend, tells her of his intention to leave her. She walks into a lake and drowns herself. The man walks away, satisfied with this "solution." In scene 23 three deaf-mutes fight over money; one of them is killed by the other two.

Erinnerungen an die Menschheit received critical praise for its criticism of human reasoning and scientific knowledge. The set, designed by Roth's friend Günther Brus, repeatedly drew applause.

Roth has not written a play since 1985. The dreamworld he created in *Erinnerungen an die Menschheit* also plays an important role in his prose. The novels *Landläufiger Tod* (Common Death, 1984), *Am Abgrund* (On the Abyss, 1986), and *Der Untersuchungsrichter* (The Investigating Judge, 1988) also attempt to escape traditional and systematic orders in language and thought and to open up new surrealistic ways of perceiving reality.

References:

Peter von Becker, "Gewalt in der Idylle: Gerhard Roths 'Sehnsucht' als Beispiel eines dramatischen Genres," *Theater heute*, 11 (1977): 40-44;

Jörg Drews, " 'Haid setzte die Brille wieder auf . . . ': Über Gerhard Roths Bücher," in *Wie die Grazer auszogen, die Literatur zu erobern*, edited by Peter Laemmle and Jörg Drews (Munich: Edition text kritik, 1975), pp. 29-50;

Georg Hensel, "Beifall für den Hund in Basel," *Frankfurter Allgemeine Zeitung*, 11 October 1977, p. 25;

Gerd Jäger, "Wird jungen deutschen Stückeschreibern das Leben zu schwer gemacht?," *Theater heute*, 15 (January 1974): 33-38;

Paul Kruntorad, "Der Regisseur als Autor," *Theater heute*, 19 (November 1978): 52;

Helmut Schödel, "Katastrophen-Klischees: Gerhard Roths 'Sehnsucht' in Basel und Graz," *Die Zeit*, 14 October 1977, p. 48;

Hilde Spiel, "Groteske oder Tiefsinn? Gerhard Roths 'Lichtenberg.' Uraufführung in Graz," *Frankfurter Allgemeine Zeitung*, 23 October 1973, p. 28;

Spiel, "Milde Pfiffe in Graz," *Frankfurter Allgemeine Zeitung*, 11 October 1977, p. 25;

Spiel, "Von den Arten der Sprachlosigkeit: Uraufführung von Gerhard Roths 'Dämmerung' in Graz," *Frankfurter Allgemeine Zeitung*, 9 October 1978, p. 25.

Jura Soyfer

(8 December 1912 - 16 February 1939)

Horst Jarka
University of Montana

PLAY PRODUCTIONS: *Weltuntergang*, Vienna, ABC im Regenbogen, 6 May 1936;

Die Insel der Pinguine. Ein Polarnachtstraum, by Soyfer and Fritz Tann, Vienna, Literature am Naschmarkt, 18 July 1936;

Der Lechner-Edi schaut ins Paradies, Vienna, Literatur am Naschmarkt, 6 October 1936; translated by John Latouche as *Journey to Paradise*, New York, Music Box, 20 June 1939;

Die Botschaft von Astoria, Vienna, ABC im Regenbogen, 27 March 1937;

Vineta, die versunkene Stadt, Vienna, ABC im Regenbogen, 11 September 1937;

Broadway-Melodie 1492, adapted by Soyfer from *Christoph Kolumbus*, by Walter Hasenclever and Kurt Tucholsky, Vienna, ABC im Regenbogen, 20 November 1937.

BOOKS: *Vom Paradies zum Weltuntergang: Dramen und Kleinkunst*, edited by Otto Tausig (Vienna: Globus Verlag, 1947)—includes *Astoria, Kolumbus oder: Broadway-Melodie 1492, Vineta, Der Lechner-Edi schaut ins Paradies, Weltuntergang oder "Die Welt steht auf kein' Fall mehr lang!"*; *Der Lechner-Edi schaut ins Paradies* translated by Horst Jarka as *Eddie Lechner's Trip to Paradise*, in *Modern International Drama*, 4 (Spring 1971): 57-78; *Weltuntergang* translated by Jarka as *The End of the World*, in *Modern International Drama*, 5 (Spring 1972): 61-80;

Von Paradies und Weltuntergang, edited by Werner Martin (Berlin: Verlag Volk und Welt, 1962);

Die Ordnung schuf der liebe Gott, edited by Martin (Leipzig: Reclam, 1979);

Das Gesamtwerk, edited by Jarka (1 volume, Vienna, Munich & Zurich: Europaverlag, 1980; augmented, 3 volumes, 1984).

Editions in English: *The Legacy of Jura Soyfer 1912-1939: Poems, Prose and Plays of an Austri-*

Jura Soyfer, circa 1930

an Antifascist, edited and translated by Jarka (Montreal: Engendra Press, 1977)—includes *Astoria, Vineta*;

"It's Up to Us!": Works of Jura Soyfer, edited and translated by Jarka (Riverside, Cal.: Ariadne Press, 1992).

OTHER: "Dachau-Lied," in *Unser Lied* (London: Verlag Jugend Voran, 1944); translated by John Lehmann as "Song of the Austrians in Dachau," in his *The Age of the Dragon: Poems 1930-1951* (London: Longmans, Green, 1951), pp. 56ff.

Like no other Austrian writing during the interwar period, Jura Soyfer fused passionate political engagement with literary achievement. With his first attempts, agitprop scenes for the Viennese Social Democratic party's political cabarets, he took the side of the working class in the battles between capital and labor during the depression of the early 1930s. After the triumph of fascism over the Austrian Left in 1934 Soyfer wrote for the Viennese Kleinkunst (cabaret theaters). His creative imagination overcame the restraints of censorship and raised his reactions to the political situation to a universal level. Dedicated to the concerns of ordinary people, Soyfer revived the Austrian critical Volksstück (play dealing with the lives of lower-class people) to create a unique kind of drama in which satirical cabaret and revue techniques blended with a lyricism that can be gentle as well as aggressive. Soyfer's plays are documents of the 1930s, but their themes—unemployment, the threatened destruction of civilization, alienation, and colonialism—have retained their validity; his irony, wit, and insights into the contradictions of his time have led to continued performances of his plays in German-speaking areas.

Soyfer was born on 8 December 1912 in Kharkov, Ukraine, to the Jewish industrialist Vladimir Soyfer and Ljubov Brodes Soyfer. Jura and his sister Tamara, five years older than he, had a French governess and enjoyed all the amenities of the Russian upper middle class until the Bolshevik Revolution forced the family to flee. In 1921 they settled in Vienna. There is no record of Soyfer's grade-school education, but in 1923 he entered the Realgymnasium. The son of the Russian industrialist soon became a fervent Austrian socialist; his activities in the Association of Socialist High-School Students gave his literary ambitions purpose and direction. He also joined the collective of the Social Democratic party's Political Cabaret, directed by Robert Ehrenzweig and Victor Grünbaum. Soyfer's agitprop scenes, written for Rote Spieler (Red Players), are simple but effective dramatic allegories of the class struggle. The political tensions and the rise of right-wing forces were also reflected at the University of Vienna, where Soyfer began studying German and history in 1931—the year Josef Nadler, an influential proponent of a racial interpretation of German literature, began teaching there. During the last two years of its existence the *Arbeiter-Zeitung* (Worker Newspaper) regularly published Soyfer's political poems, which displayed a satirical wit

and linguistic virtuosity that made them powerful weapons against fascism and social injustice and also raised them above mere propaganda. Though the caustic language in these poems shows how much Soyfer had learned from the Viennese satirist Karl Kraus, their ideology links him, more than to any other Austrian, to the German satirists Kurt Tucholsky, Franz Mehring, and Erich Weinert.

In the summer of 1932 Soyfer went to Germany as a free-lance journalist. There he became disillusioned with the German Social Democratic party which, adhering to democratic legalism, withdrew step-by-step before Adolf Hitler and his supporters. He returned to Vienna convinced that only force could stop fascism. After Hitler's assumption of power in 1933 he joined the Left opposition in the Austrian Social Democratic party. In February 1934 the political conflict exploded in armed resistance by Austrian workers against fascism. Soyfer was ready to fight, but when he came to the rallying place in his district nobody knew where the weapons were hidden.

With the defeat of social democracy and the triumph of fascism in Austria, Soyfer dropped out of school. For a year and a half he could not get anything he wrote published. Like many young former Social Democrats, he became active in the outlawed Communist party, which, with the moral support of the Soviet Union, promised to oppose fascism more effectively. He also started a novel, "So starb eine Partei" (Thus Died a Party, 1936, 1939, 1974, 1975) as the fragments that survived the war have been titled, analyzing the weaknesses in the party structure that had led to the defeat of the Social Democrats.

Late in 1935 Soyfer started writing dramatic scenes again, but for a new audience, for a different stage, and under various pseudonyms. He wrote for the improvised cabaret theaters in the basements of coffeehouses that were the meeting places of young actors—many of whom had been driven out of Germany—and left-wing intellectuals. In addition to many scenes and sketches now lost Soyfer wrote six plays of which five are still extant. Three of these present the best surviving examples of the new dramatic form developed in those theaters: the so-called Mittelstücke (middle pieces), plays of fifty to sixty minutes duration that were preceded and followed by the usual cabaret numbers. In the two years Soyfer worked for these literally underground stages he became the most radical author for the ABC im Regenbogen, the most radical theater under Fascist censorship.

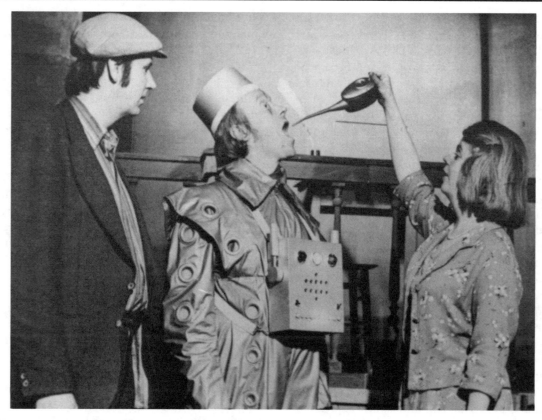

Scene from a 1975 production of Soyfer's Der Lechner-Edi schaut ins Paradies *at the Experiment Theater am Lichtenwerd, Vienna (photograph by Anton Doliwa)*

The apocalyptic title of Soyfer's first play, *Weltuntergang* (performed, 1936; published, 1947; translated as *The End of the World*, 1972), was well justified by political developments in central Europe. Soyfer dramatizes the threat of war as a test situation: how does humanity act in the face of imminent global destruction? In an ironic return to techniques of the nineteenth-century Viennese magical farce, Soyfer opens and ends the play on a supernatural level: the harmony of the spheres is disturbed by humanity, and the heavenly bodies decide to annihilate human life through the impact of a comet. The four weeks that it will take the comet to reach Earth set the amount of time humanity has left to live. A scientist who has invented a machine to divert the comet wages a futile fight against time and stupidity. Life and business go on as usual; in fact, destruction is better business than salvation. Scene after scene confirms the verdict: humanity deserves to be destroyed. And yet humanity is saved in a surprise twist: the comet does not have the heart to destroy the world; he has fallen in love with her in all her contradictions. Soyfer's tragicomic, bitterly satirical global farce ends with

"Das Lied von der Erde" (The Song of the Earth), a passionate declaration of the hope that humanity will choose life over death. The reception of the play was unanimously positive. Soyfer's warning was recognized as the voice of conscience in an inhuman time. History added its own irony: the play was last performed on 11 July 1936, the day Austrian chancellor Kurt von Schuschnigg signed the agreement with Hitler that prepared the way for the Anschluß (annexation of Austria by Germany) two years later.

Soyfer's talent for combining message and entertainment, realism with fantasy, is again apparent in his next play, *Der Lechner-Edi schaut ins Paradies* (performed, 1936; published, 1947; translated as *Journey to Paradise*, 1939). A series of cabaret scenes combining science fiction with poetry and humor with moving lyricism follows an unemployed worker's quest for the reasons behind his plight. When he blames it on technology, the machine he used to work with appears and tells him that it, too, is out of work. Changing into a time machine, it takes him back through the centuries to find the "culprit" who started technology. The trip ends at the gates of Paradise at the moment when humanity is being created, and the worker recognizes that human beings, endowed with the power of decision, are the masters of their own fate. The play ends with the words "Auf uns Kommt's an" (It's up to us), Soyfer's formula against any kind of determinism. Most of the reviews emphasized the comedy at the expense of the serious message, but the play provoked a sermon in Saint Stephen's Cathedral replacing Soyfer's message with "It's up to Jesus Christ."

A practical joke of some young diplomats who opened an embassy in London for the fictitious state Astoria, gave receptions, and handed out medals, inspired Soyfer's *Die Botschaft von Astoria* (The Embassy of Astoria; performed, 1937; published as *Astoria*, 1947; translated as *Astoria*, 1977), a satire on the state as the ultimate abstraction, on the exploitation of utopian hopes for the profit of the few, and on Fascist terrorism that preserves the regime. Soyfer shows the effects of poverty on the masses, their gullibility, their neglect of principles for the sake of a job, their submission to authority. When the main character regrets selling out and tries to expose the pernicious system, he is jeered by the brainwashed mob. Soyfer's first full-length play is also his most many-faceted. Acid satire and gentle, even haunting, dream scenes, moving lyrics and songs of rebellious power such as the "Lied von der Käuflichkeit der Menschen" (Song of People Selling Themselves), situation comedy, and wordplay result in entertaining political theater with a humanist vision. The parallels between Astoria and Fascist Austria were too obvious to escape the censor. *Astoria* had to be revised more than any of Soyfer's other plays and, in spite of an excellent cast, had the shortest run of all.

Vineta, die versunkene Stadt (Vineta, the City under the Sea; performed, 1937; published as *Vineta*, 1947; translated as *Vineta*, 1977) is Soyfer's most unconventional play. A drunken sailor remembers when, as a diver, he was let down to the bottom of the sea and found himself among people who lived an absurd existence outside of time, without memory or history. In strong contrast to the realistic dialogue in Soyfer's other plays, *Vineta* anticipates that of the postwar theater of the absurd. The drama consists in the conflict between the sailor, who attempts to bring the Vinetans back to reality, and the town clerk, an intellectual who knows the truth but does not want to jeopardize his position by enlightening his fellow Vinetans. The clerk founds a school of philosophers, the "Verpes-

Scene from a 1975 production of Soyfer's Vineta *at the Landestheater in Salzburg (photograph by Johann Barth)*

senskreis" (Circle of Oblivionists), and is writing the school's standard work, "Das Vergessen als Denkprinzip reifer Kulturvölker" (Forgetting as a Principle of Thinking for Nations of Advanced Civilization). The sailor, in danger of losing his humanity in the pursuit of a career in a lifeless society, finally saves himself by telling the Vinetans the truth about their unreal existence. Returning to the present, the sailor warns the audience that the engulfing flood may be near and may soon turn the whole world into a Vineta; only a united effort will avert the catastrophe. Soyfer created a surrealist nightmare to awaken his audience to the threat of war.

For Soyfer there was just enough time to write one more play, *Broadway-Melodie 1492* (performed, 1937; published, 1947), an adaptation of *Christoph Kolumbus* (1932), by Walter Hasenclever and Tucholsky. Although the main plot and a fourth of the text were taken verbatim from the source, Soyfer's adaptation surpasses the original as social criticism and political satire. Soyfer presents history from the point of view of ordinary people, colonialism as seen by the colonized. His

Columbus is not heroic; forced to compromise with commercial interests, he sanctions brutal exploitation. Soyfer's condemnation of colonialism evokes associations with Nazi racism; one scene is a prophetic preview of Austria after the Anschluß.

Soyfer never saw his last play on the stage. On 17 November 1937, three days before the premiere, he was arrested in the street; the police had mistaken him for the director of the Communist underground propaganda machine but did not regret their error. Communist literature found in Soyfer's room was reason enough to keep him in jail without trial for three months. In an amnesty for political prisoners Soyfer was released on 17 February 1938. On 13 March, the day after German troops entered Austria, he tried to cross the Swiss border on skis and was arrested. Soyfer was taken to Dachau; his "Dachau-Lied" (Dachau-Song, 1944; translated as "Song of the Austrians in Dachau," 1951) proves that barbarism could not break his spirit. In the fall he was transferred to Buchenwald, where he was assigned to carrying corpses. On 16 February the twenty-six-year-old Soyfer died of typhoid fever. His release papers had arrived shortly before his death.

Friends took his plays with them into exile. They were first published in 1947, but the political climate in Austria after the war was not conducive to a lasting rediscovery. Only in the 1970s was Soyfer recognized as an important playwright of the interwar period. Since then his plays have been successfully performed in studios and on experimental stages in Austria, Germany, and Switzerland. In 1984 a group of young actors in Vienna founded a Jura Soyfer theater group dedicated to his plays and those of other progressive playwrights. The Jura Soyfer Society was founded in 1988.

Letters:

Jura-Soyfer. Sturmzeit. Briefe 1931-1939, edited by Horst Jarka (Vienna: Verlag für Gesellschaftskritik, 1991).

Biography:

Horst Jarka, *Jura Soyfer: Leben—Werk—Zeit* (Vienna: Löcker, 1987).

References:

Jürgen Doll, "La critique de l'Austro marxisme dans 'So starb eine Partei' de Jura Soyfer," *Austriaca*, no. 23 (December 1986): 57-71;

G. F., "Die Renaissance des Jura Soyfer," *Zukunft* (December 1980): 41;

Jean-Claude François, "Comique et satire politique chez Ödon von Horváth et Jura Soyfer," *Austriaca*, no. 14 (May 1982): 153-167;

Eckart Früh, "Jura Soyfer," *Wiener Tagebuch* (April 1981): 22-24;

Ernst Glaser, "Theodor Kramer und Jura Soyfer," *Zukunft* (June 1988): 37-41;

Fritz Herrmann, "Jura Soyfer. Eine politische Einschätzung," *Exil*, 5, no. 1 (1985): 5-21;

Ian Huish, "Paradoxical Optimist. Jura Soyfer. Das Gesamtwerk," *Times Literary Supplement*, 11 October 1985, p. 1152;

Horst Jarka, "Everyday Life and Politics in the Literature of the Thirties: Horváth, Kramer, and Soyfer," in *Austria in the Thirties: Culture and Politics*, edited by Kenneth Segar and John Warren (Riverside, Cal.: Ariadne Press, 1991), pp. 151-177;

Jarka, "Jura Soyfer: A Jewish Writer under Austro-Fascism," *Shofar, Quarterly for Jewish Studies*, 5, no. 3 (1987): 18-27;

Jarka, "Jura Soyfer—A Writer of the Austrian 1930's Only?," in *From Wilson to Waldheim: Proceedings of a Workshop on Austrian-American Relations 1917-1987*, edited by Peter Pabisch (Riverside, Cal.: Ariadne Press, 1989), pp. 125-155;

Jarka, "Ödön von Horváth und Jura Soyfer—Diagnose und Protest," in *Horváths Stücke*, edited by Traugott Krischke (Frankfurt am Main: Suhrkamp, 1988), pp. 84-102;

Jarka, "Politik und Zauberei: Die Stücke Jura Soyfers (1912-1939). Zur oppositionellen 'Kleinkunst' im Wien der dreißiger Jahre," *Modern Austrian Literature*, 5, nos. 1-2 (1972): 96-143;

Calvin N. Jones, "The Dialectics of Despair and Hope. The Modernist Volksstück of Jura Soyfer," *Maske und Kothurn*, 32, nos. 1-2 (1986): 33-40;

Jura Soyfer Gesellschaft, *Die Welt des Jura Soyfer* (Vienna: Verlag für Gesellschaftst + kritik, 1991);

Peter Langmann, *Sozialismus und Literatur: Jura Soyfer. Studien zu einem österreichischen Schriftsteller der Zwischenkriegszeit* (Frankfurt am Main: Meisenheim, 1986);

John Lehmann, *The Whispering Gallery: Autobiography I* (London: Longmans, Green, 1951), pp. 294-302;

Uwe Naumann, "Zwei vom besten Jahrgang," *Konkret*, no. 3 (1981): 42-43;

Alfred Pfabigan, "Jura Soyfer's 'Death of Party,' " in *The Austrian Socialist Experiment. Social Democracy and Austromarxism 1918-1934*, edited by Anson Rabinbach (Boulder & London: Westview, 1985), pp. 169-176;

Thomas Rothschild, "Das Vermächtnis von Dachau. Endlich: Das Gesamtwerk von Jura Soyfer," *Baseler Zeitung*, 31 January 1981; republished in *Frankfurter Rundschau*, 9 May 1981;

Gerhard Scheit, "Der Realismus des Widerstands. Über Jura Soyfer," *Das jüdische Echo*, 38 (October 1989): 213-216;

Scheit, *Theater und revolutionärer Humanismus: Eine Studie zu Jura Soyfer* (Vienna: Verlag für Gesellschaftskritik, 1988);

Rolf Schneider, "Österreichs Büchner? Rolf Schneider über Jura Soyfer: Das Gesamtwerk," *Der Spiegel*, no. 3 (1981): 159-161;

Joachanaan Christoph Trilse, "Jura Soyfer," in *Österreichische Literatur des 20. Jahrhunderts* (Berlin: Yolk und Wissen, 1988), pp. 498-517;

Hans Weigel, "Jura Soyfer," in his *In Memoriam* (Graz, Munich & Vienna: Styria, 1979), pp. 155-162;

Ulrich Weinzierl, "Opfer verlorener Zeiten: Die Wiederentdeckung Jura Soyfers," *Frankfurter Allgemeine Zeitung*, 12 September 1981;

George E. Wellwarth, "Jura Soyfer: An Attempt at Rehabilitation," *American-German Review*, 55, no. 2 (1969): 22-26;

Harry Zohn, "A Poet of Protest," *Jewish Quarterly*, 25 (Winter 1977-1978): 53, 56.

Papers:

Typescripts of works by Jura Soyfer are in the Dokumentationsarchiv des Österreichischen Widerstandes (Documentation Archive of the Austrian Resistance), Vienna.

Martin Sperr

(14 September 1944 -   )

Reinhard K. Zachau
University of the South

PLAY PRODUCTIONS: *Jagdszenen aus Nieder-bayern*, Bremen, Bühnen der Freien Hanse-stadt Bremen, 27 May 1966;

Landshuter Erzählungen, Munich, Münchner Kam-merspiel, 4 October 1967;

Koralle Meier: Geschichte einer Privaten, Stuttgart, Staatstheater, 7 February 1970;

Münchner Freiheit, Düsseldorf, Schauspielhaus, 20 February 1971;

Die Kunst der Zähmung, Bremen, Bremer Theater, 6 June 1971;

Die Spitzeder, Bonn, Theater der Stadt Bonn, 11 September 1977.

BOOKS: *Landshuter Erzählungen* (Berlin: Henschel-verlag, 1968); translated by Anthony Vivis as *Tales from Landshut* (London: Methuen, 1969);

Koralle Meier (Frankfurt am Main: Verlag der Au-toren, 1970);

Der Kunst der Zähmung: Nach Shakespeare (Frank-furt am Main: Verlag der Autoren, 1970);

Der Räuber Mathias Kneißl: Textbuch zum Fernsehfilm (Munich: Piper, 1970);

Münchner Freiheit (Frankfurt am Main: Verlag der Autoren, 1971);

Jagd auf Außenseiter: Jagdszenen aus Niederbayern (Munich: Weissmann, 1971);

Bayrische Trilogie (Frankfurt am Main: Suhrkamp, 1972);

Die Spitzeder (Frankfurt am Main: Verlag der Au-toren, 1977);

Willst du Giraffen ohrfeigen, mußt du ihr Niveau haben: Eine Legende, Prosa, Gedichte, Zeichnun-gen (Munich: Hubert & Klenner, 1979).

TELEVISION: *Mathias Kneißl*, by Sperr and Rein-hard Hauff, West German Television, 20 April 1971;

Adele Spitzeder, West German Television, 19 Sep-tember 1972.

OTHER: *Herr Bertolt Brecht sagt: Kinderbuch*, edit-ed by Sperr and Monika Sperr (Munich: Weissmann, 1970).

In the spring of 1966 West Germany's the-ater scene underwent a major change with the pre-mieres of two plays: Martin Sperr's *Jagdszenen aus Niederbayern* (Hunting Scenes from Lower Ba-varia; performed, 1966; published as *Jagd auf Außenseiter: Jagdszenen aus Niederbayern* [Hunt for the Outsider: Hunting Scenes from Lower Ba-varia], 1971) and Peter Handke's *Publikums-beschimpfung* (published, 1966; translated as *Offend-ing the Audience*, 1971). Each played a major role in moving West German theater away from the prevailing theater of the absurd.

Sperr was born in Steinberg, Bavaria, on 14 September 1944, the son of a teacher. He at-tended school in Wendelskirchen and a Catholic boys' boarding school in Altgasing. His interest in theater was awakened while he was training for a business career at the Siemens firm in Munich. He took acting lessons and played at the Theater 44 in Munich, then went to Vienna in 1962 to en-roll in the Max Reinhardt Seminar. He dropped out after two years due to lack of talent. While working at odd jobs, mainly around the theater, he began his writing career with *Jagdszenen aus Niederbayern*. It was first performed in Bremen in May 1966. His marriage to his first wife, Monika, a writer, was brief (1967-1968). He and his sec-ond wife, Silvia, whom he married in 1968, have a daughter, born in 1971.

Sperr borrowed his idea for a Bavarian "Volksstück" (folk play) from Marieluise Fleißer, who had written plays in the genre in the 1920s and 1930s. The Volksstück normally takes place among common people in the country; dialect the-aters in Germany have a long tradition of show-ing popular "folk" comedies, usually with a trivial plot centering around a love triangle. Sperr made the Volksstück political. He believes that the-ater should not simply reflect reality but should also evaluate it; according to Sperr, the spectator

Martin Sperr with his second wife, Silvia, in 1968

should be able to question the author's representation of reality. He wants to create a critical awareness in the spectator that enables the latter to criticize society. Rather than illustrating his principles with parables, as Bertolt Brecht did in his plays, Sperr tries to convey the rich reality of small-town life in Bavaria. There, he maintains, the need for immediate social change is apparent.

The social behavior uncovered in *Jagdszenen aus Niederbayern* is strongly authoritarian. The play is a study in psychology. Individually, the townspeople are honorable citizens, but as a group they turn into a vicious mob. Those who do not fit in are rejected and suppressed without mercy: the homosexual Abram; the maid Tonka, whom he made pregnant so that he could demonstrate that he belongs to the majority; and Abram's retarded friend Rovo, who commits suicide after being accused of having an affair with Abram. The outsiders desperately long to be normal, and they accept the societal norms that suppress them. Abram is finally chased into the woods by the town's entire population after he stabs Tonka to death.

Sperr's second play, *Landshuter Erzählungen* (performed, 1967; published, 1968; translated as *Tales from Landshut*, 1969), is set in Landshut, Bavaria, in 1958 and shows the West German middle class during the "economic miracle" of the 1950s. Otto Laiper, the owner of an established contracting business, wants to prevent his son, Sorm, from marrying the daughter of his competitor, the newcomer Grötzinger. In a confrontation between father and son Otto suffers a fatal heart attack. Thus, the Romeo and Juliet story comes to a macabre "happy ending." None of the characters is noble or attractive, and Sperr lets them denounce themselves. Sorm says about his future wife: "Und wenn sie Jüdin ist! Na und! Außerdem, so schlimm ists gar nicht. Sie ist nur Halbjüdin" (And that she is a Jew, that's not so bad. She is only a half-Jew). Otto says: "Ich möchte ausdrücklich sagen: Ich habe nichts gegen Juden. Ich hab sogar was dagegen, daß man sie umgebracht hat. Rausekeln allein hätte gereicht" (I want to say: I have nothing against Jews. I don't even like the idea that they were murdered. Running them out would have been

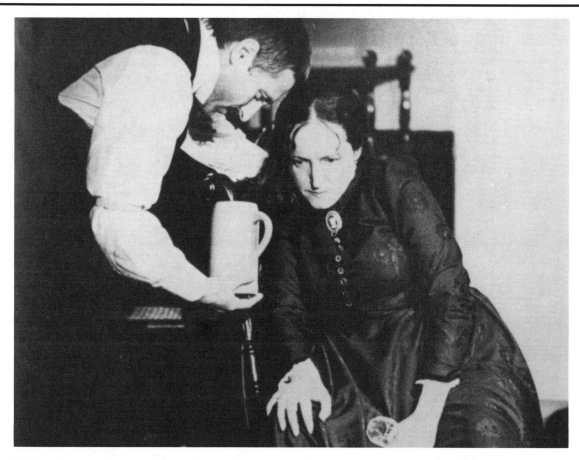

Arnulf Schumacher and Friedericke Weber in a scene from the premiere of Sperr's Die Spitzeder *in Bonn in 1977 (photograph by Detering)*

enough). Even the most positive character in the play, Sorm's brother Glasp, who had attacked his parents' materialism, finally turns into a small-town hypocrite. Many viewers were put off by the lack of positive figures and by the stark naturalism of the play; they complained that the characters are worse off at the end than at the beginning.

The third part of Sperr's Bavarian trilogy, *Münchner Freiheit* (Munich Freedom, 1971), seems trendy and sloppily put together. The play reads like a farce: the Munich brewery family Poschl-Ederer wants to buy up an old neighborhood and rebuild it with expansive office and apartment complexes. The daughter reveals the plans to her leftist friends, who occupy the lobby of the beer factory. The liberal father, whose attempt at mediation fails, commits suicide; the conservative mother succeeds with her business plans. She even passes on a former lover to her returned and changed daughter. As Sperr moved his plots from village to small town to city he tended to subsitute ideology for precise literary representa-

tion. His plays lost what had made them original.

The title character in *Koralle Meier* (1970) is a Bavarian prostitute in the Nazi Germany of the late 1930s. Meier wants to open a vegetable store in her small town but meets fierce resistance from the townspeople. When she helps a Jew escape from Germany, she is denounced to the Nazis and taken to a concentration camp. After being freed by one of her former lovers, she in turn denounces the town's mayor for having a love affair with a Jew. But instead of the mayor, it is Meier who is sent to the concentration camp. In a final outburst just before her death, she attacks the Nazis for their brutality.

In spite of the positive reception of *Koralle Meier*, Sperr switched to the medium of television. He said "Das Theater wird immer mehr zur sterilen Ablage unserer unbewältigten Vergangenheit. Und diese wird so zu einem angenehmen Mittel, die Gegenwart umgehen zu können. Andererseits werden Extremitäten und Perversionen ausgebrütet . . ." (The theater is becoming the sterile depository of our past, and therefore a pleasant way to avoid the present. The theater also tends to indulge in extreme situations and perversions . . .). The television play *Mathias Kneißl* (broadcast, 1971; published as *Der Räuber Mathias Kneißl* [The Robber Mathias Kneißl], 1970) tells in gloomy pictures the story of the Kneißl family, who make their living by petty thievery. "Justice" finally catches up with the family: the mother is put in jail, the father dies during a police raid, and the son, Mathias, escapes into the woods. He is wounded and apprehended by the police, and in the final scene he is on the operating table being fixed up for his execution. In *Mathias Kneißl* the peasants speak a dialect of the Dachau region in Bavaria, while members of the upper class use High German.

The title character in Sperr's television play *Adele Spitzeder* (broadcast, 1972) is the corrupt director of the Dachauer Volksbank (Dachau People's Bank), an emancipated woman who promises her poor investors high returns. Eventually the bank goes bankrupt because it can no longer pay the interest.

On 31 January 1972 Sperr collapsed with a brain hemorrhage, an illness that virtually ended his career as a writer of original works. Afterward he worked at odd jobs—as a cook and in a massage school—returning to acting in 1974. In 1977 he adapted *Adele Spitzeder* for the stage as *Die Spitzeder*. Since 1983 he has been a member of the Münchner Volkstheater (Munich Folk Theater), for which he writes Bavarian adaptations of plays by authors such as William Fitzgerald Kusz, William Shakespeare, Molière, and Karl Wittlinger.

References:
Bernd Anton, "Ein bayerischer Dichter: Zum Theater Martin Sperrs," in *Studien zur Dramatik in der Bundesrepublik Deutschland*, edited by Gerhard Kluge (Amsterdam: Rodopi, 1983), pp. 1-30;

Walter Dimter, "Die ausgestellte Gesellschaft: Zum Volksstück Horváths, der Fleißer und ihrer Nachfolger," in *Theater und Gesellschaft*, edited by Jürgen Hein (Düsseldorf: Bertelsmann, 1973), pp. 219-245;

Rolf Dornbacher, "Martin Sperr: Jagdszenen aus Niederbayern," in *Das deutsche Drama vom Expressionismus bis zur Gegenwart*, edited by Manfred Brauneck (Bamberg: Buchner, 1970), pp. 281-283;

Uta Ganschow, "Martin Sperr 'Landshuter Erzählungen,'" in his *Von Lessing bis Kroetz* (Kronberg: Scriptor, 1976), pp. 180-198;

Wolfgang Ismayr, *Das politische Theater in Westdeutschland* (Meisenheim: Hain, 1977), pp. 385-386;

Hellmuth Karasek, "Die Erneurung des Volksstücks," in *Positionen des Dramas*, edited by Heinz Ludwig Arnold and Theo Buck (Munich: Beck, 1977), pp. 137-169;

Wend Kässens and Michael Töteberg, "Fortschritt im Realismus?," *Basis*, 6 (1976): 30-47;

W. G. Marigold, "Martin Sperr and Franz Xaver Kroetz: New Directions for Left-Wing Playwrights," in *Conference on Twentieth-Century Literature, University of Louisville: Literature and Revolution*, Perspectives on Contemporary Literature, 2 (Lexington: University of Kentucky Press, 1976), pp. 17-23;

Gerd Müller, "Das Volksstück der Gegenwart: Martin Sperr und Franz Xaver Kroetz," in his *Das Volksstück von Raimund bis Kroetz* (Munich: Oldenbourg, 1979), pp. 117-147;

Hans Poser, "Martin Sperr: Bayrische Trilogie— Die Bundesrepublik im Spiegel des Volksstücks," in *Studien zur Dramatik in der Bundesrepublik Deutschland*, pp. 89-105;

Otto F. Riewoldt, "Martin Sperr," in *Kritisches Lexikon zur deutschsprachigen Gegenwartsliteratur*, edited by Arnold (Munich: edition text + kritik, 1978);

Günther Rühle, "Von der Politik zur Rolle: Rückblick auf ein Jahrzehnt (1965-1975)," in his *Theater in unserer Zeit* (Frankfurt am Main: 1976), pp. 233-260.

Botho Strauß

(2 December 1944 -   )

Peter C. Pfeiffer
Georgetown University

PLAY PRODUCTIONS: *Die Hypochonder*, Hamburg, Deutsches Schauspielhaus, 22 November 1972;

Bekannte Gesichter, gemischte Gefühle, Stuttgart, Württembergisches Staatstheater, 2 September 1975;

Trilogie des Wiedersehens, Hamburg, Deutsches Schauspielhaus, 18 May 1977;

Groß und klein, Berlin, Schaubühne am Halleschen Ufer, 8 December 1978;

Kalldewey, Farce, Hamburg, Deutsches Schauspielhaus, 31 January 1982;

Der Park, Freiburg, Städtische Bühnen, 5 October 1984;

Die Fremdenführerin, Berlin, Schaubühne am Lehniner Platz, 15 February 1986;

Besucher, Munich, Kammerspiele, 6 October 1988;

Sieben Türen, Stockholm, Sweden, Stadstheater, 20 November 1988;

Die Zeit und das Zimmer, Berlin, Schaubühne am Lehniner Platz, 8 February 1989.

BOOKS: *Bekannte Gesichter, gemischte Gefühle: Komödie* (Frankfurt am Main: Verlag der Autoren, 1974);

Schützenehre: Erzählung (Düsseldorf: Eremiten-Presse, 1975);

Marlenes Schwester: 2 Ezrählungen (Munich: Hanser, 1975);

Trilogie des Wiedersehens: Theaterstück (Munich & Vienna: Hanser, 1976);

Die Widmung: Eine Erzählung (Munich: Hanser, 1977); translated by Sophie Wilkins as *Devotion* (New York: Farrar, Straus & Giroux, 1979);

Groß und klein: Szenen (Munich & Vienna: Hanser, 1978); translated by Anne Cattaneo as *Big and Little: Scenes* (New York: Farrar, Straus & Giroux, 1979);

Die Hypochonder; Bekannte Gesichter, gemischte Gefühle: 2 Theaterstücke (Munich & Vienna: Hanser, 1979);

Botho Strauß (photograph by Isolde Ohlbaum)

Rumor (Munich: Hanser, 1980); translated by Michael Hulse as *Tumult* (Manchester, U.K.: Carcanet Press, 1984);

Paare, Passanten (Munich: Hanser, 1981);

Kalldewey, Farce (Munich: Hanser, 1981);

Der Park Schauspiel (Munich: Hanser, 1983);

Der junge Mann (Munich: Hanser, 1984); translated by Edna McCown as *The Young Man: A Novel* (New York: Knopf, 1989);

Diese Erinnerung an einen, der nur einen Tag zu Gast war (Munich: Hanser, 1985);

Die Fremdenführerin: Stück in 2 Akten (Munich: Hanser, 1986);

Niemand anderes (Munich: Hanser, 1987);

Versuch, ästhetische und politische Ereignisse zusammenzudenken: Texte über Theater, 1967-1986

(Frankfurt am Main: Verlag der Autoren, 1987);

Besucher: Drei Stücke (Munich: Hanser, 1988);

Fragmente der Undeutlichkeit (Munich: Hanser, 1989);

Kongreß: Die Kette der Demütigungen (Munich: Matthes & Seitz, 1989);

Angelas Kleider: Nachtstück in zwei Teilen (Munich: Hanser, 1991);

Schlußchor: Drei Akte (Munich: Hanser, 1991);

Theaterstücke, 2 volumes (Munich & Vienna: Hanser, 1991);

Beginnlosigkeit: Reflexionen über Fleck und Linie (Munich: Hanser, 1992).

OTHER: Eugene Martin Labiche, *Das Sparschwein: Komödie*, translated by Strauß (Frankfurt am Main: Verlag der Autoren, 1981).

Botho Strauß is one of the leading literary representatives emerging from the student revolution of the 1960s. His sensitive portrayals of the fathers, mothers, and children of the failed upheavals in 1967-1968 and of a Germany saturated with economic success and populated with people in search of some purpose for their efforts have put him in the forefront of today's dramatists and fiction writers. While critics have often labeled Strauß a member of the Neue Sensibilität (New Sensitivity) or Neue Innerlichkeit (New Inwardness), he criticized the introspective nature of these movements from the beginning. Informed by French structuralist and poststructuralist theories, Strauß casts off the notion of a classical subjectivity in favor of a subject defined by his or her position within ideological, literary, economic, and social structures. Radically alone and unable to communicate with his or her surroundings, the subject is the locus of suffering and mourning.

Strauß was born on 2 December 1944 in Naumburg, the son of a consultant in the grocery business. After World War II the family moved to West Germany, where he attended gymnasiums in Remscheid and Bad Ems. He acted in amateur groups while studying drama, sociology, and German literature at the Universities of Cologne and Munich. In 1967 he broke off his studies and joined the staff of the prominent theater journal *Theater heute* (Theater Today). He remained with the publication until 1970, writing articles and reviews that give an early indication of his conception of the stage. At a time when political theater in the Brechtian fashion was all-

pervasive, Strauß criticized it for its trivializing treatment of contemporary issues. Similarly, he discounted Martin Sperr's and Franz Xaver Kroetz's plays, which tried to reestablish "realist" theater in the tradition of Ödön von Horváth and Marieluise Fleißer. Instead, Strauß promoted experimental plays by Peter Handke and Thomas Bernhard, neither of whom was well established at the time, and the theater of the absurd. He stressed that the modern stage should use its techniques to open up new avenues in political thinking rather than focus on subject matter. Strauß was fascinated by the transparency that the theatrical process gained in productions by the Bread & Puppet Theater and the Living Theater that combined all technical and artistic aspects of theater art. He praised them as attempts to free life and art from their mutual estrangement. Strauß's essays on theater have been collected as *Versuch, ästhetische und politische Ereignisse zusammenzudenken* (Essay on the Combination of Aesthetic and Political Events, 1987).

In 1969 Strauß met the brilliant young director Peter Stein. Their friendship and collaboration laid the groundwork for some of the most triumphant theater events of the 1970s. In 1970 Strauß became a dramaturge with Stein at the Schaubühne am Halleschen Ufer in Berlin. Stagings of Henrik Ibsen's *Peer Gynt* (1867) in 1971, Heinrich von Kleist's *Prinz Friedrich von Homburg* (1821) in 1972, and Maksim Gorky's *Dachniki* (Summer Folk, 1904) in 1974, with set designers such as Karl-Ernst Herrmann and actors including Bruno Ganz, Jutta Lampe, and Edith Clever, established the Schaubühne as one of the best theaters in Western Europe.

Strauß's first play, *Die Hypochonder* (The Hypochondriacs; performed, 1972; published, 1979), is a crime and love story with Gothic and melodramatic elements reminiscent of fin de siècle literature. Set in 1901 in Amsterdam, the play is made up of fragments that resist any attempt to mold them into a straightforward story. Throughout the play neither the characters nor the viewers are sure whether the events are real or imagined. While *Die Hypochonder* has some effective moments and earned Strauß the Hannover Drama Award in 1974, it is hardly ever staged.

Bekannte Gesichter, gemischte Gefühle (Well-known Faces, Mixed Feelings; published, 1974; performed, 1975) has a contemporary setting but, again, fin de siècle overtones. A group of middle-aged people living in a hotel in Königs-

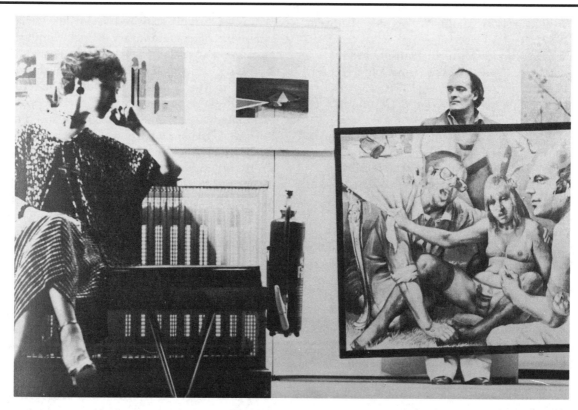

Marlen Diekhoff as Susanne and Hans-Michael Rehberg as Moritz in the final scene of the premiere of Strauß's Trilogie des Wiedersehens *at the Deutsches Schauspielhaus, Hamburg, in 1977 (photograph by Kneidl)*

winter are spending the Christmas holiday discussing their completely inactive lives. Stefan, the owner of the debt-ridden hotel, wants to sell the building to the Interior Ministry and become a bureaucrat; he ends up committing suicide in a freezer. Somewhat reminiscent of Arthur Schnitzler's *Reigen* (published, 1903; performed, 1920; translated as *Hands Around*, 1920), *Bekannte Gesichter* lacks Schnitzler's subtle irony and is overly gloomy.

In *Trilogie des Wiedersehens* (Trilogy of Reunion; published, 1976; performed, 1977) Strauß looks at German society after the student revolution. In the summer of 1975 a group of art lovers gather to preview an exhibit of "capitalist realism" arranged by Moritz, the director of a nonprofit museum. These middle-class people talk eloquently about their psychological problems and amorous quarrels and about political events and aesthetic theories, but they display a vast confusion about the issues that seemed so clear during the upheavals of the 1960s. Everything has become "so unendlich undeutlich" (so infinitely obscure), as one of them says; they know the answers to all problems but are unable to act accordingly. Their visions of grand escapes and

deep feelings become trivial the moment they are put into action: Moritz's flight from the city with a woman ends in a hotel room at the railroad station; two would-be emigrants want to leave Germany because it is "einfach kein fruchtbarer Boden für die großen Gefühle" (just not a fertile soil for grand feelings), but their prospects in Canada lie in the management of a chain of Laundromats. While most of the characters are unable to overcome their passivity, there is one who does act: Kiepert, the chairman of the board of the museum and an influential businessman. He is incensed by the critical nature of the exhibition and threatens to close it down. Kiepert, who only appears briefly onstage with his back to the audience, does not say a word; but his power seems all the greater in contrast to the other characters, who are helpless in the face of the economic and social forces represented by Kiepert.

Trilogie des Wiedersehens was an instant success and was staged within a year in theaters throughout Europe. German critics voted it the Play of the Year. Strauß received a stipend to work at the Villa Massimo, Rome, and the Förderpreis des Schillerpreises (Supporting Award of the Schiller Award). The Schaubühne production of the play, directed by Stein, was broadcast by the ZDF, West Germany's second national television channel. But it was Strauß's next play that established him as one of the most prominent German playwrights of his generation.

Groß und klein: Szenen (1978; translated as *Big and Little: Scenes*, 1979) consists of ten scenes from the life of Lotte, a separated woman in her mid thirties. The play follows Lotte from a package-tour hotel in Morocco through her ordeal of social decline and personal devastation. At first she is eager to establish contacts with other people. She listens to two strangers strolling up and down the terrace at the hotel, longing to become part of the conversation. But all she hears is a long monologue about personal isolation and social estrangement in which the word *Wahnsinn* (insanity) frequently recurs. It is the social insanity bred by the modern "free" world, a world of instant gratification and bureaucracy, of information science and communication networks but no real communication, a world that dehumanizes individuals beyond recognition. As Lotte travels through Germany she meets people who have locked themselves up in a world of drugs or in small rooms, unable to communicate except through intercoms and telephones. Lotte's search for support and human closeness are continuously thwarted; attempts at dialogue end in monologues. In the last scene Lotte, now a bag lady, enters a doctor's waiting room. But she does not suffer from physical illness; her ailment is incurable because it is the ailment of the 1970s in Germany: a general sense of loss and helplessness combined with a search for salvation. While the viewer might be sympathetic toward Lotte, her belief that she is one of the thirty-six just people in the world able to save humanity marks her as a product of the times as much as any of the other characters.

Groß und klein was enormously popular; it was staged in many European theaters, in North and South America, in Africa, and in Australia. During the 1979-1980 theater season it was the most frequently produced play by a contemporary German playwright, drawing more than 160,000 viewers to more than 360 performances in German-speaking countries alone. Stein's production of *Groß und klein* was broadcast on television.

As Strauß's fame grew, he became increasingly reclusive and stopped granting interviews. He lives alone in a sparsely furnished apartment in Berlin; he has never married because, he has

Edith Clever as Lotte in a scene from a 1979 Berlin production of Strauß's Groß und klein *(photograph by Ruth Walz)*

said, living with another person would distract him from his work. In Strauß's writing following *Groß und klein*, this somewhat obsessive attitude has made itself increasingly felt and has been combined with a quasi-religious outlook on the function of the writer. Strauß's reception in the United States has been hampered by such notions, which are often perceived as notoriously Germanic.

Strauß's next play, *Kalldewey, Farce* (published, 1981; performed, 1982), can be considered in conjunction with the simultaneously published *Paare, Passanten* (Couples, Wanderers), a book of vignettes, reflections, and sketches. *Paare, Passanten* is a pessimistic dirge on modernism and on technology-oriented society; it is also a rejection of the Frankfurt School's critical theory, with its emphasis on negative dialectical thinking that was so influential during the student uprising. *Kalldewey, Farce* examines the "Szene" (Scene), the intellectuals and pseudointellectuals who are influential in society. Kalldewey, a fat slapstick figure who utters nothing but obscenities, crashes a birthday party. This stranger, who mysteriously disappears as quickly as he appeared, is heralded by the other characters as a new leader after he vanishes. Because of his absence, he is particularly suited for the projections the characters invest in him as they long for salvation. The feminist movement is represented by "K" and "M," lesbian lovers and psychotherapists. "Die Frau" (the woman) comes to them to seek advice about her love-hate relationship with "Der Mann" (the man). All attempts at mediation and counseling fail; while the relationship does not fall apart, it is never fully realized. Neither can the two lesbians realize their relationship. While they denounce male oppression and ultimately torture the man and literally tear him to pieces, they treat each other with the same lack of care and consideration shown by the heterosexual couple. Strauß received the Mühlheim Drama Award for *Kalldewey, Farce*.

Der Park (The Park; published, 1983; performed, 1984) takes up the theme of art as salvation. The play originated from plans to retranslate William Shakespeare's *A Midsummer Night's Dream* for the Schaubühne. It retains many Shakespearean features, including occasional English sentences. The fairies Oberon and Titania descend on a littered urban park to return beauty and a sense of self to the human race. But they fail in their mission and are stripped of their magical powers by the city dwellers. "Der Streit ist aus, Titania: die Liebe hat verloren!" (The fight is over, Titania: love has lost!), says Oberon. Titania and Oberon age and die among the earthlings, leaving behind nothing but a puckish son who retains a faint longing for the essence of the failed mission.

A return to the roots of Western culture in an attempt to redirect modern life lies at the heart of *Die Fremdenführerin* (The Female Tourist Guide, 1986). Martin, a disheartened schoolteacher, and Kristine, an impish young tourist guide in the ruins of Olympia, begin a love affair. They retreat from the outside world and try to reenact the Adam and Eve story. In the end Martin is stranded as Kristine leaves him for another man.

Besucher (Visitors, 1988) is a collection of three plays. The title play (performed, 1988), a comedy, is a play within a play that changes perspectives continuously so that one is never sure if a scene belongs to the production being rehearsed or to the conflict between the two main

Katja Riemann, Heinz Bennent, and Sibylle Canonica in a scene from the premiere of Strauß's Besucher *at the Kammerspiele, Munich, in 1988 (photograph by Oda Sternberg)*

characters. The conflict is between a famous older actor, defending realistic acting, and a young actor who wants to rid the theater "von den Übeln des kranken Realismus" (of the malady of sick realism). The play includes themes typical of Strauß's writings: reflections on the state of the theater, an ill-fated love story, the loss of culture and human warmth, invectives on television and advertising. At the end, one of the actors wants to stop acting, but of course he is acting as he says so—and the play begins again, letting nobody escape from the never-ending acting of "real" life. The second play, *Die Zeit und das Zimmer* (Time and Room; performed, 1989), is a ponderous, wordy expression of gloom and desperation. The third play, *Sieben Türen* (Seven Doors; performed, 1988), consists of eleven vignettes full of black humor and biting criticism. In one of them a renter complains to the chairman of the real estate company that owns his house that there is a mysterious house within the house. On hearing this news, the chairman breaks down. The message is that individual ownership, responsibility, and accountability have disappeared in today's decentralized social networks, which have been built up in the name of individual freedom and self-fulfillment. In another scene a convict yearns for punishment as the last remaining indicator of individual dignity.

Strauß had two plays published in 1991. *Angelas Kleider* (Angela's Clothes) and *Schlußchor* (Choir Finale) are meditations on the unification of Germany, though neither overtly addresses this topic. In *Angelas Kleider* a woman keeps buying clothes for her hideously ugly daughter. Her attempts to make the daughter more presentable are futile; Angela continues to strike horror in every visitor. The main characters in *Schlußchor* are an architect and a woman real-estate developer; the play deals with the theme of crossing the border between public and private space and the shame and guilt caused by such transgressions.

Strauß's standing as one of Germany's leading dramatists was affirmed in 1989, when he received the prestigious Büchner Prize. It remains to be seen whether he will be able to maintain the high artistic level of *Trilogie des Wiedersehens* and *Groß und klein*, which are still his best plays.

References:

Leslie A. Adelson, "Botho Strauß Pays Tribute to the Bomb: On *Paare, Passanten* and Collective Survival," *German Quarterly*, 57 (Spring 1984): 250-268;

Adelson, *Crisis of Subjectivity: Botho Strauß's Challenge to West German Prose of the 1970's* (Amsterdam: Rodopi, 1984);

Heinz Ludwig Arnold, ed., *text kritik*, special Strauß issue, 81 (January 1984);

Hans-Peter Bayerdörfer, "Raumproportionen: Versuch einer gattungsgeschichtlichen Spurensicherung in der Dramatik von Botho Strauß," in *Studien zur Dramatik in der Bundesrepublik Deutschland*, edited by Gerhard Kluge (Amsterdam: Rodopi, 1983), pp. 31-68;

Martin Rhoda Becher, "Poesie der Unglücksfälle. Über die Schriften von Botho Strauß," *Merkur*, 32 (June 1978): 625-638;

Elke Emrich, " 'Der Mensch verliert das Bild vom Menschen.' Wahnsinn und Gesellschaft in Botho Strauß' 'Groß und klein,' " *Sprache im technischen Zeitalter* (1983): 171-181;

Henriette Herwig, *Verwünschte Beziehungen, verwebte Bezüge: Zerfall und Verwandlung des Dialogs bei Botho Strauß* (Tübingen: Stauffenburg, 1986);

Gerhard vom Hofe and Peter Pfaff, "Botho Strauß und die Poetik der Endzeit," in their *Das Ende des Polyphem* (Königstein: Athenäum, 1980), pp. 109-131;

Dieter Kafiz, "Die Problematisierung des individualistischen Menschenbildes im deutschsprachigen Drama der Gegenwart (Franz Xaver Kroetz, Thomas Bernhard, Botho Strauß)," in *Basis: Jahrbuch für deutsche Gegenwartsliteratur 10* (Frankfurt am Main: Suhrkamp, 1980), pp. 93-126;

Ursula Kapitza, *Bewußtseinsspiele: Drama und Dramaturgie bei Botho Strauß* (Frankfurt am Main: Lang, 1987);

Michael Radix, ed., *Strauß lesen* (Munich: Hanser, 1987).

Ernst Toller
(1 December 1893 - 22 May 1939)

Michael Ossar
Kansas State University

PLAY PRODUCTIONS: *Die Wandlung*, Berlin, Die Tribüne, 30 September 1919;

Masse Mensch, Nuremberg, Stadttheater, 15 November 1920;

Die Maschinenstürmer, Berlin, Großes Schauspielhaus, 30 June 1922;

Bilder aus der großen französischen Revolution, Leipzig, Ausstellungsgelände, 6 August 1922;

Die Rache des verhöhnten Liebhabers, Jena, Freie Volksbühne, 8 May 1923;

Krieg und Frieden: Massenfestspiel, Leipzig, Ausstellungsgelände, 7 August 1923;

Der deutsche Hinkemann, Leipzig, Altes Theater, 19 September 1923;

Erwachen: Massenfestspiel, Leipzig, Auensee, 3 August 1924;

Der entfesselte Wotan, Prague, 29 January 1925;

Hoppla, wir leben!, Hamburg, Kammerspiele, 1 September 1927;

Bourgeois bleibt Bourgeois, Berlin, Lessingtheater, 2 February 1929;

Feuer aus den Kesseln, Berlin, Theater am Schiffbauerdamm, 31 August 1930;

Wunder in Amerika, Mannheim, Nationaltheater, 17 October 1931;

Die blinde Göttin, Vienna, Raimund-Theater, 31 October 1932;

Miracle in Amerika, by Toller and Hermann Kesten, London, Gate Theatre, 1934;

No More Peace!, London, Gate Theatre, 11 June 1936;

Pastor Hall, Berlin, Deutsches Theater, 24 January 1947.

BOOKS: *Die Wandlung: Das Ringen eines Menschen* (Potsdam: Kiepenheuer, 1919);

Der Tag des Proletariats: Ein Chorwerk (Berlin: Verlagsgenossenschaft Freiheit, 1920);

Gedichte der Gefangenen: Ein Sonettenkreis (Munich: Wolff, 1921); revised and enlarged as *Vormorgen* (Potsdam: Kiepenheuer, 1924);

Masse Mensch: Ein Stück aus der sozialen Revolution des 20. Jahrhunderts (Potsdam: Kiepenheuer,

Ernst Toller (photograph by F. A. Swaine, Ltd.)

1921); translated by Vera Mendel as *Masses and Man* (London: Nonesuch Press, 1923); translated by Louis Untermeyer as *Man and the Masses* (New York: Doubleday, Page, 1924);

Die Maschinenstürmer: Ein Drama aus der Zeit der Ludditenbewegung in England in fünf Akten und einem Vorspiel (Leipzig, Vienna & Zurich: Tal, 1922); translated by Ashley Dukes as *The Machine Wreckers* (London: Benn, 1923);

Der deutsche Hinkemann: Eine Tragödie in drei Akten (Potsdam: Kiepenheuer, 1923); translated by Mendel as *Brokenbow* (London: Nonesuch Press, 1926);

Der entfesselte Wotan: Eine Komödie (Potsdam: Kiepenheuer, 1923);

Das Schwalbenbuch (Potsdam: Kiepenheuer, 1924); translated by Dukes as *The Swallow-Book* (London: Oxford University Press, Milford, 1924);

Deutsche Revolution: Rede, gehalten vor Berliner Arbeitern am 8. November 1925 im Großen Schauspielhause zu Berlin (Berlin: Laub, 1925);

Die Rache des verhöhnten Liebhabers oder Frauenlist und Männerlist: Ein galantes Puppenspiel in zwei Akten frei nach einer Geschichte des Kardinals Bandello (Berlin: Cassirer, 1925); translated by Arthur Henderson as *The Scorned Lover's Revenge* in *8 New One Act Plays of 1935*, edited by John Bourne (London: Dickson & Thompson, 1935);

Justiz: Erlebnisse (Berlin: Laub, 1927);

Hoppla, wir leben! Ein Vorspiel und fünf Akte (Potsdam: Kiepenheuer, 1927); translated by Hermon Ould as *Hoppla!* (London: Benn, 1928);

Verbrüderung: Ausgewählte Dichtungen (Berlin: Arbeiterjugend-Verlag, 1930);

Feuer aus den Kesseln: Historisches Schauspiel (Berlin: Kiepenheuer, 1930);

Nationalsozialismus: Eine Diskussion über den Kulturbankrott des Bürgertums zwischen Ernst Toller und Alfred Mühr, Redakteur der Deutschen Zeitung (Berlin: Kiepenheuer, 1930);

Quer durch: Reisebilder und Reden (Berlin: Kiepenheuer, 1930); abridged and translated by Ould as *Which World—Which Way? Travel Pictures from America and Russia* (London: Sampson Low, Marston, 1931);

Wunder in Amerika: Schauspiel in fünf Akten, by Toller and Herman Kesten (Berlin: Kiepenheuer, 1931);

Die blinde Göttin: Schauspiel in fünf Akten (Berlin: Kiepenheuer, 1933); translated by Edward Crankshaw as *The Blind Goddess* (London: Lane, 1934);

Eine Jugend in Deutschland (Amsterdam: Querido, 1933); translated by Crankshaw as *I Was a German* (London: Lane, 1934; New York: Morrow, 1934);

Ausgewählte Schriften, edited by Deutschen Akademie der Künste zu Berlin (Berlin: Verlag Volk und Welt, 1959);

Prosa, Briefe, Dramen, Gedichte (Reinbek: Rowohlt, 1961);

Gesammelte Werke, 5 volumes, edited by John M. Spalek and Wolfgang Frühwald (Munich: Hanser, 1978).

Editions in English: *Seven Plays by Ernst Toller: Comprising The Machine Wreckers—Transfiguration—Masses and Man—Hinkemann—Hoppla! Such Is Life!—The Blind Goddess—Draw the Fires—Together with Mary Baker Eddy, by Ernst Toller and Hermann Kesten. With a New Introduction by the Author*, translated by Edward Crankshaw, Vera Mendel, Ashley Dukes, and Herman Ould (London: Bodley Head, 1935; New York: Liveright, 1936);

No More Peace! A Thoughtful Comedy, translated by Crankshaw (London: Bodley Head, 1937; New York: Farrar & Rinehart, 1937);

Pastor Hall: A Play in Three Acts, translated by Stephen Spender and Hugh Hunt (London: Bodley Head, 1939; New York: Random House, 1939).

SELECTED PERIODICAL PUBLICATIONS—
UNCOLLECTED: "Der kapitalistische Kindermord in China," *Die Weltbühne*, 21 (20 October 1925): 621;

"Arcos Festungshaft," *Die Weltbühne*, 22 (2 February 1926): 173-175;

"The Murder of Gustav Landauer," *Labor Monthly*, 8 (February 1926): 112-114;

"Reportage und Dichtung," *Die literarische Welt*, 2 (25 June 1926): 2-3;

"Max Hölz," *Die Weltbühne*, 23 (1 February 1927): 172-175;

"Ernst Toller in Wien," *Die literarische Welt*, 3 (11 February 1927): 7;

"Der Brüsseler Kolonial-Kongreß," *Die Weltbühne*, 23 (1 March 1927): 325-328;

"Das sozialistische Wien," *Die Weltbühne*, 23 (15 March 1927): 407-409;

"Imperator Noske," *Die Weltbühne*, 23 (29 March 1927): 515;

"Die Erschießung des Gutsbesitzers Heß," *Die Weltbühne*, 23 (3 May 1927): 696-697;

"Gott bei den Beduinen," *Jüdische Rundschau*, 25 May 1927, cols. 1-3;

"Rede auf der Volksbühnentagung in Madgeburg," *Das Tagebuch*, 8 (2 July 1927): 1074;

"Zur Physiologie des dichterischen Schaffens: Ein Fragebogen," *Die literarische Welt*, 4 (28 September 1928): 4;

"Erklärung," *Das Tagebuch*, 10 (14 December 1929): 2196;

"Ernst Toller antwortet auf E. Wollenbergs Angriffe," *Neue Bücherschau*, 7, no. 10 (1929): 543-544;

"Toller über die Literatur in Amerika," *Die literarische Welt*, 6 (17 January 1930): 1;

"Drei Berichtigungen, die berichtigt werden," *Die Linkskurve*, 2 (February 1930): 19;

"Aimee oder die mondäne Prophetin," *Berliner Tageblatt*, 30 March 1930, p. 3;

"Einladung an Dobring," *Die Weltbühne*, 26 (October 1930): 510-511;

"Giftmordprozeß Riedel-Guala," *Die Weltbühne*, 27 (October 1931): 552-554;

"Das neue Spanien I: L'España es Republica," *Die Weltbühne*, 28 (12 April 1932): 550-554;

"Das neue Spanien II: Männer und Frauen," *Die Weltbühne*, 28 (26 April 1932): 622-625;

"Das neue Spanien III: Spanische Gefängnisse," *Die Weltbühne*, 28 (3 May 1932): 667-671;

"Das neue Spanien IV: Spanische Arbeiter," *Die Weltbühne*, 28 (17 May 1932): 749-751;

"Rede in Budapest," *Die Weltbühne*, 28 (June 1932): 853-855;

"Das neue Spanien V: Spanische Miniaturen," *Die Weltbühne*, 28 (21 June 1932): 929-933;

"Erwachtes Ungarn," *Die Weltbühne*, 28 (August 1932): 159-161;

"Schriftsteller stellen sich," *Die Linkskurve*, 4 (August 1932): 2-3;

"The Modern Writer and the Future of Europe," *Bookman*, 85 (January 1934): 380-381;

"Promenade in Seville," *New Statesman and Nation*, new series 7 (14 April 1934): 544-545;

"The Mantilla of Señor Cobos," *Atlantic Monthly*, 153 (June 1934): 727-729;

"Stalin and Wells: A Comment by Ernst Toller," *New Statesman and Nation*, new series 7 (3 November 1934): 614-615;

"The Refugee Problem," *Political Quarterly*, 6 (July-September 1935): 386-399;

"Art and Life: From My Notebook," *London Mercury*, 22 (September 1935): 459-461;

"Ferdinand und Isabella," *Das Neue Tage-Buch*, 4 (25 January 1936): 93;

"A British Free People's Theatre," *New Statesman and Nation*, new series 12 (12 September 1936): 350-351;

"Unser Kampf um Deutschland," *Das Wort*, 2, no. 3 (1937): 46-53;

"Am Sender von Madrid," *Die Neue Weltbühne*, 34 (29 September 1938): 1218-1222;

"Madrid-Washington," *New Statesman and Nation*, new series 41 (8 October 1938): 521-522;

"Pariser Kongreß der Schrifsteller," *Das Wort*, 3, no. 10 (1938): 122-126;

"The Last Testament of Ernst Toller," *New Masses*, 31 (6 June 1939): 1.

From the time he was invited as a young student to attend a conference called by the publisher Eugen Diederichs during World War I until his suicide in 1939, the expressionist playwright Ernst Toller was rarely off the front pages of German or foreign newspapers. His first play, *Die Wandlung* (The Transformation, 1919), performed while its author was in prison for his role in the Munich revolution, was such a theatrical sensation that it prompted public agitation for Toller's pardon—an offer he refused. Toller's works were translated into languages ranging from Bulgarian and Esperanto to Gujarati and Japanese, and his plays were performed in Moscow, Sarajevo, Tallinn, Riga, Copenhagen, Tokyo, London, Paris, Buenos Aires, Helsinki, Urbana, Brooklyn, Berkeley, Princeton, and Poughkeepsie.

Toller was born in Samotschin, Germany (now Szamocin, Poland), on 1 December 1893. His maternal great-grandfather, the first Jew to settle in the town, had been granted certain civil rights under the patronage of Frederick the Great; his paternal great-grandfather, said to have been a man of great wealth, came from Spain. Toller's mother, Ida, née Cohn, and his father, Max, ran a general store. His father ultimately achieved a position of some prominence as a town councillor.

Samotschin was run by a German minority, largely Protestant with an admixture of Jews, in the Catholic province of Posen. Toller found out early that Jews were permitted to make common cause with the other Germans against the Poles but were otherwise scarcely tolerated. When he was sent to the county seat, Bromberg (now Bydgoszcz, Poland), to attend the Realgymnasium, a scientifically oriented high school, he began to write poems and news articles for the local newspaper, the *Ostdeutsche Rundschau* (East German Review). He was an indifferent student, spending his time reading the works of such forbidden writers as Gerhart Hauptmann, Henrik Ibsen, August Strindberg, and Frank Wedekind and spending his money to have term papers written for him by a firm in Leipzig. He sent his first plays to the Bromberg Municipal Theater but received no reply. After a love affair with a local actress, he passed his examinations and went to France in February 1913 to study at the University of Grenoble.

His studies, which concentrated on Fyodor Dostoyevski, Leo Tolstoy and Friedrich Nietzsche, were interrupted by the outbreak of World

War I. Toller took the last train to Germany before the border was sealed. After nearly being attacked by an angry crowd that took him for a spy because of a French label in his hat, he volunteered in Munich for service. After basic training at Bellheim, Toller spent thirteen months in the bloodiest theaters of the war, first at the Bois-le-prêtre and then in the vicinity of Verdun. Finally, just after volunteering for the air corps, Toller was taken ill and was sent to a hospital in Strasbourg. He was discharged from the army on 4 January 1917.

After some weeks in a sanitarium Toller went to the University of Munich to study law, art history, and literature with Arthur Kutscher. Through Kutscher he met some of Germany's leading writers, including Wedekind, Max Halbe, Karl Henckell, Rainer Maria Rilke, and Thomas Mann.

In 1917 Diederichs invited the young student to a conference at Burg Lauenstein, Thuringia, to discuss the form Germany would take after the war. Among the participants were the sociologists Ferdinand Tönnies and Max Weber, the writers Walter von Molo and Richard Dehmel, and the historian Friedrich Meinecke. Toller was disappointed at the wealth of academic analysis of Germany's plight and the dearth of action to do anything about it. He was impressed by Weber, however, and followed him to Heidelberg. There he founded a tiny pacifist group, the Cultural-Political Association of German Students, which was soon destroyed by the army high command: the men were drafted into the army, and the women who were Austrian citizens were deported to Austria. Toller, who was in the hospital at the time, was warned and fled to Berlin.

Continuing his antiwar agitation, Toller wrote to ask Hauptmann to oppose the war publicly; he received no reply. He corresponded with the anarchist Gustav Landauer and made the acquaintance of Kurt Eisner, a pacifist and leader of the left-wing Independent Social Democratic Party. After Eisner was arrested for leading a strike of munitions workers in Munich in January 1918, Toller spoke to the strikers at a mass demonstration, led a delegation to police headquarters to demand Eisner's release, and was himself arrested. Imprisoned in the Leonrodstraße, he wrote the final scenes of *Die Wandlung* and, after his release in May, immersed himself in a systematic study of Marxist and anarchist literature.

Die Wandlung is a "Stationendrama," a series of loosely connected scenes, based on the analogy of the stations of the cross, that mark the spiritual development of the hero. A young Jew, Friedrich, suffers acutely from a sense of being a pariah in his community. To gain acceptance he becomes a fanatical patriot, volunteering to serve in a colonial war. On a desert battlefield he encounters wretched natives who have been mutilated by his comrades, and he begins to realize the truth about the war waged by the fatherland to which he is striving so mightily to belong. He tries to flee his dilemma by volunteering for a dangerous mission, hoping to be killed; instead, he is the only survivor. Friedrich is brought to a hospital, where he hears the nurse speak of God's support of the patriotic cause and hatred of the enemy. Her joy at the news of a defeat that cost the enemy ten thousand lives drives Friedrich to the edge of madness. After the war he becomes a sculptor. He is working on a patriotic statue, desperately trying to salvage his faith, when the sight of a wretched beggar couple causes him to smash the statue in a fit of rage. Having renounced his false faith, Friedrich achieves an insight into more enduring values at a workers' rally. He rejects the chauvinistic platitudes of the reactionaries, but he also speaks against the leftist demagogues who call for the masses to rise up in an orgy of destruction. Slowly his new, positive values evolve as he rejects assaults from his dogmatic mother, his materialistic uncle, and a doctor who considers him insane because of his idealism. Finally his sister shows him the way to a new and different community—that of humankind itself. At a rally in front of the cathedral Friedrich, possessed by the beauty of his vision, eloquently persuades the masses of its truth and necessity. With the call for revolution on their lips, they march confidently into the future.

Toller's mother arranged for his transfer from prison to a psychiatric clinic, from which he was released in the summer of 1918. On 7 November Eisner led a demonstration in Munich from the Theresienwiese to the Landtag (provincial parliament) that ended in the proclamation of a republic with Eisner at its head. On 10 November Toller, who had been ill with influenza in Landsberg, left for Munich, where he was elected to the Central Council of Workers and became vice president of the Bavarian Congress of Councils. The various rightist and centrist forces soon began to regroup, and on 21 February 1919 Eisner, on his way to the Landtag to tender his res-

Toller (center, facing camera) with the sociologist Max Weber (foreground, with hat) at the Lauenstein Conference in 1917

ignation, was murdered. The so-called Council Republic was set up on 7 April; the Majority Socialist government under Josef Hoffmann fled to Bamberg. After a week the government collapsed and was replaced by the Communist Council Republic. The Communists had originally refused to support a government they would not be able to control, arguing that the Council Republic was premature, but they now found conditions ripe. Toller was briefly arrested but was then allowed to lead the artillery of the republic against the Hoffmann forces at Dachau. Ordered to bombard Dachau, Toller realized that with the support of the local populace and farmers the city could be taken without bloodshed. After Toller captured the town he again refused an order, this time to shoot the captured officers.

It was clear to Toller that with one hundred thousand troops marching on Munich from Berlin there was no point in the resistance to the last man that the Communists were demanding. After trying unsuccessfully to prevent the murder of right-wing hostages, Toller went into hiding when the government troops entered Munich on 1 May. He evaded capture for several weeks with the aid of friends, among them Rilke. On 4

June he was betrayed for the ten thousand-mark reward on his head; he was tried and, on 16 June, was sentenced to five years' imprisonment. Undoubtedly the few weeks in hiding saved him from the fate of other revolutionaries, like Landauer, who were shot "while trying to escape."

In prison at Eichstätt and then at Niederschönenfeld, Toller wrote the plays *Masse Mensch* (performed, 1920; published, 1921; translated as *Masses and Man*, 1923), *Die Maschinenstürmer* (1922; translated as *The Machine Wreckers*, 1923), *Der deutsche Hinkemann* (The German Hinkemann, 1923; translated as *Brokenbow*, 1926), *Die Rache des verhöhnten Liebhabers* (performed, 1923; published, 1925; translated as *The Scorned Lover's Revenge*, 1935), and *Der entfesselte Wotan* (Wotan Unchained; published, 1923; performed, 1925), and two volumes of poetry: *Gedichte der Gefangenen* (Poems of Prisoners, 1921) and *Das Schwalbenbuch* (1924; translated as *The Swallow-Book*, 1924).

Masse Mensch is a powerful expressionist play and, in a structural sense, nearly without a flaw. Sonja Irene L. is organizing a general strike against war and capitalism. Her meeting with a

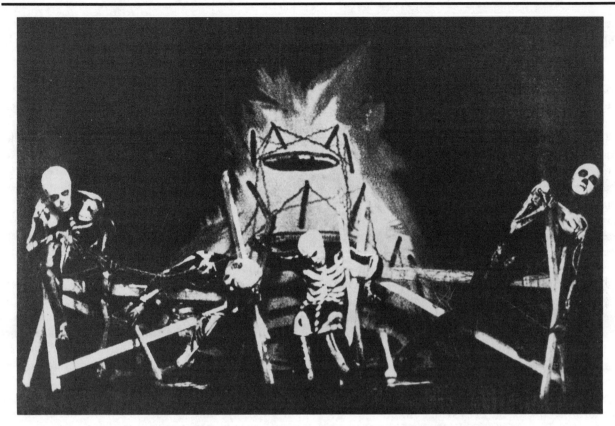

Scene from the premiere of Toller's Die Wandlung, *at Die Tribüne in 1919*

group of workers is interrupted by her husband, a government official, who attempts to dissuade her from her action. When he suggests that she organize charities to help the workers, she tries to explain that she wants to awaken within all humankind a sense of brotherhood. The husband is deaf to her arguments, but she accompanies him home. At another meeting she opposes workers who demand the destruction of the machinery that has put them out of work. Factories and machines, she replies, should be exploited in the service of humanity, not destroyed. She pleads for a strike and eventually persuades the workers. At this point "der Namenlose" (the Nameless One) emerges from the crowd to agitate in favor of a violent uprising that will be brutally suppressed, thereby radicalizing the masses. Sonja is forced to acquiesce in the general wave of emotion, even though in doing so she acts against her conscience. The next morning it is clear that the Nameless One's predictions of defeat were correct. Sonja opposes acts of violent reprisal by the workers; it is only nonviolent spiritual revolution that she can support. The Nameless One rejects this idealism as treason, denounces her as a bourgeois intellectual, and provokes the crowd into

placing her before a firing squad. Just then, counterrevolutionary soldiers surround the hall and arrest the workers. In prison Sonja defines for herself the nature of her guilt in the course of visits from her husband, from the Nameless One, and from a minister. Although she is innocent of the crime of which she has been accused—provoking the workers to violence—in a more profound sense, she tells her husband, she has incurred the guilt attendant on all political action when pure theories must be realized in an imperfect world. The Nameless One urges her to flee, but her escape might result in the death of a guard. This price she refuses to pay, even though by saving herself she could perhaps benefit thousands of workers yet unborn. After unmasking the minister as a servant of a corrupt state she goes to her death, in the process converting two fellow prisoners through her example.

Die Maschinenstürmer is based on the Luddite weavers' uprising at the dawn of the industrial revolution. A prologue introduces the spectator to the misery and suffering of the weavers through a debate in the House of Lords. Lord Castlereagh argues for a bill restricting the right of the workers to organize and providing the death penalty for weavers convicted of wrecking weaving machinery. He is opposed by Lord Byron, who argues that the workers have no legal alternatives and rejects the claim that poverty and exploitation are manifestations of survival of the fittest. The play proper begins when Jimmy Cobbett returns to his native city, Nottingham. He is telling a fairy tale to a group of starving children when he is interrupted by a band of striking workers who are hanging strikebreakers in effigy. He sees that they lack a farsighted leader in their struggle against exploitation and the threat to their jobs posed by the new mechanical looms. He preaches nonviolence and patience to the workers, pointing out that the weaving machinery is here to stay; he also urges the factory owner, Ure, to rehire the workers he has fired. In gaining the trust of the weavers, Jimmy alienates their present leader, John Wible. Wible incites the workers to smash the machinery, thereby providing Ure with an excuse to suppress the revolt with the utmost brutality. Wible convinces the workers that Jimmy, the brother of Ure's foreman, Henry Cobbett, is guilty by association and is therefore a tool of Ure. When Jimmy appears during the ecstatic climax of the workers' destructiveness, he is attacked and killed by them. Wible flees and the revolt is suppressed.

Der deutsche Hinkemann was a popular success, with productions in Leipzig, Hamburg, Frankfurt am Main, Berlin, Stuttgart, Jena, Basel, New York, London, Tartu, Helsinki, Riga, Warsaw, Moscow, Leningrad, Belgrade, Ljubljana, and Buenos Aires; disorders provoked by rightist students caused it to be prohibited in Dresden, Vienna, and Oldenburg. Eugen Hinkemann, emasculated in the war, can no longer endure any form of cruelty; he is repelled when his mother-in-law blinds a goldfinch to make it sing better. Unable to get a job as a laborer, he secretly finds work as a carnival geek, biting through the necks of rats and drinking their blood. In the meantime his wife, Grete, is seduced by Paul Großhahn, a comrade of Hinkemann's. Großhahn takes her to the carnival, where she sees her husband at work. Realizing that his love for her is so great that it causes Hinkemann to abase himself and act against his principles, she breaks off her relationship with Großhahn. Hinkemann goes to a bar patronized by various leftist groups and religious sects, each bitterly opposed to the rest. He asks a doctrinaire socialist how socialism will cure those awful spiritual tortures that result from other than economic

causes. Just then Großhahn, drunk and wounded by Grete's rejection of him, enters and reveals Hinkemann's infirmity to all, maliciously and falsely claiming that Grete finds him ludicrous. Hinkemann rushes out, collapses in a fit of insanity, and is brought home. His insanity dissipates when he looks into Grete's eyes and sees in her a tormented creature like himself, as helpless as he is in a soulless world. He is convinced of her love and repentance but no longer has the strength to go on. Grete, unable to bear Hinkemann's despair, commits suicide.

Der deutsche Hinkemann is the first of Toller's plays that does not deal explicitly with the question of revolution but with human suffering that transcends politics. Eugen Hinkemann's pain is a consequence of passions that will exist under any social structure and that any political system is powerless to eliminate. This darkest of Toller's plays leaves little hope that human beings will be able to follow their better nature even if the exploitative system that forces them to behave brutally to one another to survive is eliminated.

Die Rache des verhöhnten Liebhabers is based on a tale by Matteo Bandello from the sixteenth century. It is a bawdy drama involving rape and cuckoldry, a work totally unrelated to any of Toller's other plays. *Der entfesselte Wotan*, on the other hand, is a satire on the rising nationalist tide. Wilhelm Dietrich Wotan, a barber, exploits the disillusionments of a variety of malcontents in a fraudulent scheme to found a German colony in Brazil. He attracts more and more support for his project until a letter from the Brazilian government reveals that his claims have no basis. Although he is arrested, it is clear that he (like Adolf Hitler after his failed Munich Putsch of 8-9 November 1923) will be dealt with leniently. With all the mordant satire of another chronicler of bourgeois excesses and discontents, Carl Sternheim, Toller sketches the symbiotic relationship between the demagogue Wotan and the reactionaries Schleim and von Wolfblitz, who use him and are in turn used by him.

On 15 July 1924 Toller was released from prison one day early in an effort to forestall demonstrations by his supporters. He began a period of extensive and frequent travel, going to Leipzig in August 1924, to the Middle East in March 1925, to the Soviet Union between March and May 1926, to the United States from October to December 1929, to Spain in the fall of 1931, and to Switzerland in 1933. During this period five of his plays appeared: *Hoppla, wir leben!* (Hoppla,

We're Alive!, 1927; translated as *Hoppla!*, 1929), *Bourgeois bleibt Bourgeois* (Once a Bourgeois Always a Bourgeois; performed, 1929), *Feuer aus den Kesseln* (1930; translated as *Draw the Fires*, 1935), *Wunder in Amerika* (Miracle in America, 1931; translated as *Mary Baker Eddy*, 1935), and *Die blinde Göttin* (performed, 1932; published, 1933; translated as *The Blind Goddess*, 1934).

Bourgeois bleibt Bourgeois, written in collaboration with Hermann Kesten, has never been published. *Wunder in Amerika*, also written with Kesten, is a sort of German dramatic version of Sinclair Lewis's novel *Elmer Gantry* (1927) and is loosely based on the life of Mary Baker Eddy. From Phineas Quimby, Mary Baker learns the efficacy of faith healing, bends it to her own purposes, and founds Christian Science. She marries Asa Eddy, suffers a complicated series of changes of fortune and struggles with a rebellious disciple, and finally dies, pathetically preaching against death to her followers. The play dramatizes the American propensity to follow false gods and false prophets, as well as the perverted values and deafness to true spirituality of Americans. In a trivial kind of way, Mary Baker Eddy belongs to the long series of charlatans and false prophets in Toller's works who delude the masses, at least for a time: Wotan, the Nameless One, John Wible.

Hoppla, wir leben! begins with a prologue in which some revolutionaries are awaiting execution. Among them are Karl Thomas; Eva Berg, a young girl who is in love with Thomas; Albert Kroll; Mutter (Mother) Meller, who faces death with calm dignity; and Wilhelm Kilman, who ridicules a frightened fellow prisoner even though he himself has been able to strike a deal with his captors. Finally, the death sentences are commuted to further imprisonment, whereupon Thomas goes mad and is taken to a mental hospital. Eight years later he is released and visits Kilman, who has become minister of the interior. Kilman is a ruthless compromiser, a tool of the industrial and banking classes ready to engage in any chicanery to prevent worker participation in the upcoming national election, including sending out goons to manhandle Mutter Meller. Eva, who is no longer in love with Thomas, is fired from her job for organizing workers in a chemical plant. Thomas finds work as a waiter at the Grand Hotel, a microcosm for all the depravity and corruption of the Weimar society of the 1920s. He is appalled that his old friends have given up their dreams of a radical transforma-

tion of society, and he determines to assassinate Kilman. Before he can act, Kilman is killed by an anti-Semitic student who regards him as a leftist. Thomas is arrested for the murder and imprisoned along with his former friends. An interview with the psychiatrist convinces him that the world is insane; unable to bear a situation for which he sees no solution, he kills himself. As if to confirm his conclusions, a statue of Kilman is unveiled by the man who hired his assassin.

Feuer aus den Kesseln is based on the mutiny in Kiel in 1917. It closely follows the record of the Reichstag (parliamentary) commission appointed in 1926 to investigate the mutiny; the book version of the play includes an appendix of some sixty pages of documents from the hearings. Toller focuses on a group of sailors on the ship *Friedrich der Große* (Frederick the Great) after the victory at the Battle of Jutland. Their grievances include having to eat rancid food while the officers are well fed, circumscription of their political activities, and inhumane working conditions. When a group of sailors is arbitrarily deprived of shore leave, they go AWOL and are arrested. Their comrades meet in Rüstersiel to support them, but their demands soon grow to a more general call for political action and peace. They set up a committee to look into the complaints about food; they send petitions to a peace conference; they meet with socialist members of the Reichstag; finally, they refuse an order to fight. In the end the members of the committee are tried for mutiny, and two leaders, Köbis and Reichpietsch, are executed. The only suggestions of disloyalty prior to the final act of defiance came from an agent provocateur; Köbis opposed these suggestions and later admitted that the sailors were too stupid and cowardly to do what the prosecution accused them of.

Die blinde Göttin tells the story of a miscarriage of justice. The reprehensible doctor Franz Färber is having an affair with his secretary, Anna Gerst, while his wife, Betty, is bedridden. Just before Betty dies, the maid sees Färber injecting Betty with adrenalin; the maid suspects murder and informs her lover, a municipal court functionary. Officers of the court are more concerned with advancing their careers than with discovering the truth, and Färber and Anna are convicted. After they serve four and a half years of their sentences, Betty's diary is found and reveals that she committed suicide. Färber and Anna are released. Anna realizes that living with Färber would be only a different kind of prison, and she

Scene from a 1921 Berlin production of Toller's Masse Mensch, *with Mary Dietrich as Sonja Irene L.*

leaves him. Like Karl Thomas in *Hoppla, wir leben!*, Anna has been so changed by her imprisonment that it is impossible for her ever again to live unreflectively.

Toller was in Switzerland on a lecture tour on 27 February 1933, the day the Reichstag building was burned; the Communists were blamed for setting the fire. Toller never returned to Germany. On 10 May his books were among the first to be burned by the Nazis in front of the Humboldt University in Berlin. It was the same day he finished writing his autobiography, *Eine Jugend in Deutschland* (A Youth in Germany, 1933; translated as *I Was a German*, 1934). Later that month Toller gave a sensational anti-Nazi address to a meeting of the deeply divided P.E.N. Club in Dubrovnik, Yugoslavia, which resulted in the German delegation walking out. Toller founded an exile P.E.N. chapter in England in 1933 and urged the British government to grant German refugees residence and work permits.

In 1935 Toller married a young actress, Christiane Grautoff. That fall his *Briefe aus dem Gefängnis* (translated as *Letters from Prison*, 1936) was published in Amsterdam. These letters must be read with some caution, since in 1935 Toller no longer had all the documents at his disposal; in some cases he altered and combined letters, in others he disguised or invented the names of recipients to protect people still living in Germany.

The material that he did have had been smuggled out of Germany by his secretary, Dora Fabian, who was imprisoned for her efforts and supposedly committed suicide. In 1936 and 1937 Toller traveled through the United States, Mexico, and Canada, trying to arouse opposition to Adolf Hitler.

Toller's satirical comedy *No More Peace!* (performed, 1936; published, 1937) was published only in English translation. The tiny country of Dunkelstein is about to celebrate the dawn of an age of peace and, at the same time, the marriage of Rahel, daughter of the banker Laban, to Jacob, a Brazilian. Cain, a barber and former soldier, is in love with Rahel and opposes the marriage of a pure-blooded Dunkelsteinian to a Brazilian. Meanwhile, on Mount Olympus, Saint Francis and Napoleon are engaged in a game of dominoes and a dispute about whether humanity's deepest tendencies are bellicose or pacific. Napoleon tests Dunkelstein by sending a telegram declaring war into the midst of the celebration. Although the Dunkelsteinians have no idea who their enemy might be, they immediately mobilize; Cain, with the connivance of Laban, becomes dictator. Total war is declared, marriages with foreigners are forbidden, and Jacob is imprisoned. Saint Francis attempts to undo the harm by sending Socrates to reason with Dunkelstein, but the attempt fails. Finally, Laban blackmails

Cain and restores stability. The play attempts a satirical examination of irrationality, stupidity, shallowness, and materialism, but it fails because of the huge disproportion between the seriousness of its theme and the lightness of the treatment. Toller is attacking the gullibility of the masses and the demagoguery of the National Socialists, but his sharpest barbs are aimed at the ludicrous and ineffectual peace movement. Malcolm Pittock suggests that the play demonstrates how much closer Toller, the former pacifist, was to sharing Napoleon's cynicism than Saint Francis's faith in reason. In the London premiere the role of Rahel was played by Toller's wife.

In 1936 Toller moved to the United States, where he lived most of the time in Santa Monica and wrote film scripts for M-G-M. His final play, *Pastor Hall* (published, 1939; performed, 1947) begins with a dinner to celebrate the marriage of Christine, the daughter of Hall and his wife Ida, to the young scholar Werner Grotjahn, the son of General Paul von Grotjahn, an old family friend. Fritz Gerte, a storm trooper who is in love with Christine, denounces Hall to the Gestapo for currency manipulation. Hall is imprisoned in a camp of which Gerte is the commandant. Although he is forced to watch a fellow scholar being tortured, he refuses to yield to Gerte and is condemned to be tortured himself; but a sympathetic guard allows him to escape. Accompanied by his friend General von Grotjahn, he goes to his pulpit to preach against the Nazi regime. He is arrested and returned to the camp. Most scholars believe that Hall was based on Pastor Martin Niemöller, a former submarine commander and National Socialist who turned against the Nazis to found the Bekennende Kirche (Confessing Church) and was imprisoned in 1937 and again from 1938 to 1945. Wolfgang Früwald and Pittock suggest that Toller is indulging in a kind of self-analysis, wondering whether he would have had the courage evinced by his friend Erich Mühsam—whose courageous resistance and murder are described in the play—had he not fortuitously escaped the Nazis in 1933.

Toller's suicide in New York on 22 May 1939 remains a mystery. Christopher Isherwood has described his depression; discouraged at the obstacles placed in the way of his art in Hollywood, he was seeing a psychoanalyst. Wolfgang Rothe says that he was also depressed about the adultery of his wife, who was not present at the memorial service in New York because she was to appear in a play in Los Angeles. The fact that the re-

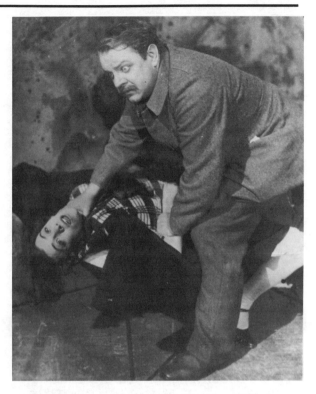

Heinrich George and Helene Weigel in a scene from a 1924 production of Toller's Der deutsche Hinkemann

lief funds he had raised for refugee children on both sides in the Spanish Civil War either fell into the hands of the Fascist dictator Francisco Franco or did not reach their destination because of the collapse of the republic and the impending war in Europe may have played a part. Yet just before his death he had given an impassioned speech to a P.E.N. Club meeting in New York, and on the eve of his suicide he spoke with his friend Ludwig Marcuse about his plans for the future. He died with a ticket to London in his possession.

Letters:

Briefe aus dem Gefängnis (Amsterdam: Querido, 1935); translated by R. Ellis Roberts as *Letters From Prison: Including Poems and a New Version of "The Swallow Book"* (London: Bodley Head, 1936); translation republished as *Look Through the Bars: Letters from Prison, Poems, and a New Version of "The Swallow Book"* (New York: Farrar & Rinehart, 1937);

Jawaharlal Nehru, *A Bunch of Old Letters Written Mostly to Jawaharlal Nehru and Some Written By Him* (London: Asia Publishing, 1960), pp. 205-206, 226, 229-230, 250-251;

Deutsche Literatur im Exil: Briefe europäischer Auto-ren, 1933-1949, edited by Hermann Kesten (Vienna: Desch, 1964), pp. 28-29, 45, 46, 53, 83-84;

Kurt Wolff, *Briefwechsel eines Verlegers: 1911-1953*, edited by Bernhard Zeller and Ellen Otten (Frankfurt am Main: Heinrich Scheffler, 1966), pp. 321-331.

Bibliography:

John M. Spalek, *Ernst Toller and His Critics: A Bibliography* (Charlottesville: Bibliographical Society of Virginia, 1968).

Biography:

Richard Dove, *He Was a German* (London: Libris, 1990).

References:

Rosemarie Altenhofer, "Ernst Tollers politische Dramatik," Ph.D. dissertation, Washington University, 1977;

Francis P. Andersen, "An Analytical Study of Techniques of Persuasion in the Plays of Ernst Toller," Ph.D. dissertation, University of Southern California, 1956;

Richard Beckley, "Ernst Toller," in volume 3 of *German Men of Letters*, edited by Alex Natan (London: Wolff, 1972), pp. 85-104;

Thomas Bütow, *Der Konflikt zwischen Revolution und Pazifismus im Werk Ernst Tollers. Mit einem dokumentarischen Anhang: Essayistische Werke Tollers* (Hamburg: Lüdke, 1975);

Helen L. Cafferty, "Georg Büchner's Influence on Ernst Toller: Irony and Pathos in Revolutionary Drama," Ph.D. dissertation, University of Michigan, 1976;

Cafferty, "Pessimism, Perspectivism, and Tragedy: *Hinkemann* Reconsidered," *German Quarterly*, 54 (January 1981): 44-58;

Richard Allen Cave, "Johnston, Toller and Expressionism," in *Denis Johnston: A Retrospective*, edited by Joseph Ronsley (Totowa, N.J.: Barnes & Noble, 1981), pp. 78-104;

Horst Denkler, "Ernst Toller: *Die Wandlung*," in *Das deutsche Drama vom Expressionismus bis zur Gegenwart: Interpretationen*, edited by Manfred Brauneck (Bamberg: Buchner, 1972), pp. 52-63;

Richard Dove, "Berlin 1919: Zu Ernst Tollers unveröffentlichtem Massendrama," *Germanic Review*, 63 (Summer 1989): 105-111;

Dove, "Ernst Toller, Wilfred Wellock and Ashley Dukes: Some Historical Connections," *German Life and Letters*, 35 (October 1981): 58-63;

Dove, "Fenner Brockway and Ernst Toller: Document and Drama in *Berlin—letzte Ausgabe!*," *German Life and Letters*, 38 (January 1984): 45-55;

Dove, "The Place of Ernst Toller in English Socialist Theatre 1924-1939," *German Life and Letters*, 38 (1984): 125-137;

Dove, *Revolutionary Socialism in the Work of Ernst Toller*, Utah Studies in Literature and Linguistics, 26 (New York: Lang, 1986);

Fritz Droop, *Ernst Toller und seine Bühnenwerke: Eine Einführung* (Berlin: Schneider, 1922);

René Eichenlaub, *Ernst Toller et l'expressionisme politique* (Paris: Klincksieck, 1980);

Robert Elsasser, "Ernst Toller and German Society: The Role of the Intellectual as Critic—1914-1939," Ph.D. dissertation, Rutgers University, 1973;

William R. Elwood, "Ernst Toller's *Masse Mensch*: The Individual vs. the Collective," in *From the Bard to Broadway*, edited by Karelisa V. Hartigan (Lanham, Md.: University Press of America, 1987), pp. 43-50;

Wolfgang Frühwald, "Exil als Ausbruchsversuch: Ernst Tollers Autobiographie," in *Die deutsche Exilliteratur 1933-1945*, edited by Manfred Durzak (Stuttgart: Reclam, 1973), pp. 489-497;

Frühwald and John M. Spalek, eds., *Der Fall Toller: Kommentar und Materialien* (Munich: Hanser, 1979);

N. A. Furness, "Toller and the Luddites: Fact and Symbol in 'Die Maschinenstürmer,'" *Modern Language Review*, 73, no. 4 (1978): 847-858;

Furness, "Toller: *Die Maschinenstürmer*—the English Dimension," *German Life and Letters*, 33 (January 1980): 147-157;

Werner Geifrig, "Ernst Toller—Dichter und Politiker 'Zwischen den Stühlen,'" in *Vergleichen und Verändern: Festschrift für Helmut Motekat*, edited by Albrecht Goetze and Günther Pflaum (Munich: Hueber, 1970), pp. 216-223;

Oskar Maria Graf, "Gedenkrede auf Ernst Toller," *Sinn und Form*, 21 (1969): 897-900;

Stefan Grossmann, *Der Hochverräter Ernst Toller: Die Geschichte eines Prozesses* (Berlin: Rowohlt, 1919);

Peter Heller, "The Masochistic Rebel in Recent German Literature," *Journal of Aesthetics and Art Criticism*, 11, no. 3 (1953): 198-213;

Jost Hermand, "Ernst Toller: Hoppla, wir leben!" in his *Unbequeme Literatur* (Heidelberg: Stiehm, 1971), pp. 128-149;

Nicholas Hern, "The Theatre of Ernst Toller," *Theatre Quarterly*, 2 (January-March 1972): 72-92;

Leroy T. Hopkins, "Ernst Toller's Hörspiel: *Berlin—letzte Ausgabe!*" *Germanic Notes*, 15, nos. 3-4 (1984): 46-67;

Christopher Isherwood, "The Head of a Leader," in his *Exhumations* (New York: Simon & Schuster, 1966), pp. 123-132;

Thomas A. Kamla, "Christianity and the Fatherland: The Problem of Community in Ernst Toller's *Die Wandlung*," *Germanic Notes*, 15, nos. 3-4 (1984): 42-46.

Hermann Kesten, *Meine Freunde die Poeten* (Munich: Donau, 1959);

Alfred Klein, "Zwei Dramatiker in der Entscheidung: Ernst Toller, Friedrich Wolf und die Novemberrevolution," *Sinn und Form*, 10 (1958): 702-725;

Hermann Korte, "Die Abdankung der 'Lichtbringer': Wilhelminische Ära und literarischer Expressionismus in Ernst Tollers Komödie *Der entfesselte Wotan*," *Germanisch-Romanische Monatsschrift*, 34, nos. 1-2 (1984): 117-132;

Eva Lachmann-Kalitzki, "Kindred Spirits: Ernst Toller Seen as Part of a New Spiritual 'Triumvirate,'" *Germanic Notes*, 15, nos. 3-4 (1984): 47-51;

Stephen Lamb, "Ernst Toller and the Weimar Republic," in *Culture and Society in the Weimar Republic*, edited by Keith Bullivant (Manchester: Manchester University Press, 1977), pp. 71-93;

Lamb, "Ernst Toller: Vom Aktisvismus zum humanistischen Materialismus," in *Das literarische Leben in der Weimarer Republik*, edited by Bullivant (Königstein: Athenäum, 1978), pp. 164-191;

Lamb, "Intellectuals and the Challenge of Power: The Case of the Munich 'Räterepublik,'" in *The Weimar Dilemma: Intellectuals in the Weimar Republic*, edited by Anthony Phelan (Manchester: Manchester University Press, 1985), pp. 132-161;

Lamb, "The Medium and the Message: Some Reflections on Ernst Toller's Hörspiel *Berlin—letzte Ausgabe!*," *German Life and Letters*, 37 (January 1984): 112-117;

Fritz H. Landshoff, "Ernst Toller: Eine Radiosendung," *Germanic Notes*, 15, nos. 3-4 (1984): 41-42;

Else Lasker-Schüler, "Ernst Toller," *Emuna*, 4 (1969): 259-260;

Ralph Ley, "The Revolutionist as Poet: The Prison Plays of Ernst Toller," *University of Dayton Review*, 17 (Winter 1985-1986): 15-21;

Andreas Lixl, "Ernst Toller und die Weimarer Republik 1918-1933," Ph.D. dissertation, University of Wisconsin-Madison, 1984;

Katharina K. Maloof, "Mensch und Masse: Gedanken zur Problematik des Humanen in Ernst Tollers Werk," Ph.D. dissertation, University of Washington, 1965;

Werner W. Malzacher, "Ernst Toller—ein Beitrag zur Dramaturgie der zwanziger Jahre," Ph.D. dissertation, University of Vienna, 1959;

Martha Gustavson Marks, "Ernst Toller: His Fight against Fascism," Ph.D. dissertation, University of Wisconsin-Madison, 1980;

Hans Marnette, "Untersuchungen zum Form-Inhalt-Problem in Ernst Tollers Dramen," Ph.D. dissertation, Pädagogische Hochschule Potsdam, 1963;

Franz Norbert Mennemeier, "Das idealistische Proletarierdrama: Ernst Tollers Weg vom Aktionsstück zur Tragödie," *Deutschunterricht*, 24 (1972): 100-116;

Michael Ossar, "Anarchism and Socialism in Ernst Toller's *Masse Mensch*," *Germanic Review*, 51 (May 1976): 192-208;

Ossar, *Anarchism in the Dramas of Ernst Toller: The Realm of Necessity and the Realm of Freedom* (Albany: State University of New York Press, 1980);

Ossar, "Die jüdische messianische Tradition und Ernst Tollers Wandlung," in *Im Zeichen Hiobs: Jüdische Schriftsteller und deutsche Literatur im 20. Jahrhundert*, edited by Gunter E. Grimm and Hans-Peter Bayerdörfer (Königstein: Athenäum, 1985), pp. 293-308;

Mitar Papic, "Ernst Toller auf dem PEN-Kongress in Jugoslawien 1933," *Weimarer Beiträge*, 14, no. 2 (1968): 73-77;

William Macfarlane Park, "Ernst Toller: The European Exile Years 1933-1936," Ph.D. dissertation, University of Colorado, 1976;

Carol Peterson, "Ernst Toller," in *Expressionismus als Literatur: Gesammelte Studien*, edited by Wolfgang Rothe (Bern: Francke, 1969), pp. 572-584;

Ernst Pinner, "Der Dichter Ernst Toller," *Der Jude*, 8 (1924): 784-788;

Erwin Piscator, *Das politische Theater*, revised by Felix Gasbarra (Reinbek: Rowohlt, 1963);

Malcolm Pittock, *Ernst Toller* (Boston: Hall, 1979);

Pittock, *"Die Maschinenstürmer,"* *Durham University Journal*, 35 (June 1974): 294-305;

Pittock, *"Masse-Mensch* and the Tragedy of Revolution,"* *Forum for Modern Language Studies*, 8 (1972): 162-183;

Robert Reimer, "The Tragedy of the Revolutionary: A Study of the Drama of Revolution of Ernst Toller, Friedrich Wolf and Bertolt Brecht 1918-1933," Ph.D. dissertation, University of Kansas, 1971;

Martin Reso, "Gefängniserlebnis und dichterische Widerspiegelung in der Lyrik Ernst Tollers," *Weimarer Beiträge*, 7, no. 3 (1961): 520-556;

Reso, "Der gesellschaftlich-ethische Protest im dichterischen Werk Ernst Tollers," Ph.D. dissertation, University of Jena, 1957;

Reso, "Die Novemberrevolution und Ernst Toller," *Weimarer Beiträge*, 5, no. 3 (1959): 387-409;

Jacqueline Helen Rogers, "Ernst Toller's Prose Writings," Ph.D. dissertation, Yale University, 1972;

Wolfgang Rothe, *Ernst Toller in Selbstzeugnissen und Bilddokumenten*, (Reinbek: Rowohlt, 1983);

Sigurd Rothstein, *Der Traum von der Gemeinschaft: Kontinuität und Innovation in Ernst Tollers Dramen* (Bern: Lang, 1987);

Ernst Schürer, "Literarisches Engagement und politische Praxis: Das Vorbild Ernst Toller," in *Rezeption der deutschen Gegenwartsliteratur im Ausland*, edited by Dietrich Papenfuss and Jürgen Söring (Stuttgart: Kohlhammer, 1976), pp. 353-366;

Paul Signer, *Ernst Toller: Eine Studie* (Berlin: Landsberg, 1924);

Walter Sokel, *Ernst Toller*, volume 2 of *Deutsche Literatur im 20. Jahrhundert: Strukturen und Gestalten*, edited by Otto Mann and Wolfgang Rothe (Munich: Francke, 1967), pp. 299-315;

John M. Spalek, "Ernst Tollers Vortragstätigkeit und seine Hilfsaktionen im Exil," in *Exil und innere Emigration*, edited by Peter Uwe Hohendahl and Egon Schwarz (Frankfurt am Main: Athenäum, 1973), pp. 85-100;

Spalek, "Ernst Toller: The Need for a New Estimate," *German Quarterly*, 39, no. 4 (1966): 581-598;

Spalek, "Der Nachlaß Ernst Tollers," *Literaturwissenschaftliches Jahrbuch der Görres-Gesellschaft*, 6 (1965): 251-266;

Spalek and Wolfgang Frühwald, "Ernst Tollers amerikanische Vortragsreise 1936/37. Mit bisher unveröffentlichten Texten und einem Anhang," *Literaturwissenschaftliches Jahrbuch der Görres-Gesellschaft*, 6 (1965): 267-312;

Margarete Turnowsky-Pinner, "A Student's Friendship with Ernst Toller," *Leo Baeck Institute Year Book*, 15 (1970): 211-222;

Friedrich Vollhardt, "Wer etwas zu sagen hat, trete vor und schweige: Anmerkungen zu einer unbekannten Erklärung Dr. Arthur Schnitzlers (zum Fall Ernst Toller) aus dem Jahr 1919," *Literatur und Kritik*, nos. 157-158 (August-September 1981): 462-473;

Penelope D. Willard, " 'Gefühl und Erkenntnis': Ernst Toller's Revisions of His Dramas," Ph.D. dissertation, State University of New York, Albany, 1988;

William Anthony Willibrand, *Ernst Toller and His Ideology*, Iowa Humanistic Series, 7 (Iowa City: University of Iowa Press, 1945);

Clara Zetkin, "Dem deutschen Dichter Ernst Toller bester Willkommensgruß," *Weimarer Beiträge*, 22, no. 3 (1976): 161-162.

Papers:

Letters, manuscripts, and other materials by and relating to Ernst Toller are at the Akademie der Künste (Academy of the Arts), Berlin; the Staatsarchiv für Oberbayern (Upper Bavarian State Archives); the National Archives, Washington, D.C.; the New York Public Library; the Schiller-Nationalmuseum, Marbach am Neckar, Germany; the private collections of Professor John M. Spalek, German Department, State University of New York, Albany, and of Dr. Harold Hurwitz, Free University of Berlin; the Victoria and Albert Museum, London; and the Yale University Library.

Peter Turrini
(26 September 1944 -   )

Bernd Fischer
Ohio State University

PLAY PRODUCTIONS: *Rozznjogd*, Vienna, Volkstheater, 27 January 1971;

Zero Zero: Ein Kunst-Stück, Vienna, Theater an der Wien, 22 May 1971;

Sauschlachten, Munich, Kammerspiele, 15 January 1972;

Der tollste Tag: Frei nach Beaumarchais, Darmstadt, Landestheater, 26 February 1972;

Kindsmord, Klagenfurt, Stadttheater, 10 March 1973;

Die Wirtin: Frei nach Goldoni, Nuremberg, Schauspielhaus, 24 November 1973;

Josef und Maria, Vienna, Volkstheater, 7 November 1980;

Die Bürger, Vienna, Volkstheater, 27 January 1982;

Campiello: Frei nach Goldoni, Vienna, Volkstheater, 26 September 1982;

Die Minderleister, Vienna, Akademietheater, 1 June 1988.

TELEVISION: *Die Alpensaga*, script by Turrini and Wilhelm Pevny—comprises *Liebe im Dorf* (1976), *Der Kaiser am Lande* (1977), *Das große Fest* (1977), *Die feindlichen Brüder* (1978), *Der deutsche Frühling* (1979), *Ende und Anfang* (1980).

BOOKS: *Erlebnisse in der Mundhöhle: Roman* (Reinbek: Rowohlt, 1972);

Der tollste Tag (Theaterstück): Frei nach Beaumarchais (Wollerau, Vienna & Munich: Lentz, 1973);

Rozznjogd: (Theaterstück): Dialekt- und Hochdeutsche Fassung: Neufassung (Wollerau: Lentz, 1973); translated by Richard S. Dixon as *Chasing Down Rats* (Vienna: Sessler, 1979); German version republished with modern German translation, (Darmstadt: Luchterhand, 1977);

Sauschlachten (Wollerau, Vienna & Munich: Lentz, 1974);

Der Dorfschullehrer, by Turrini and Wilhelm Pevny (Vienna & Munich: Sessler, 1975);

Die Wirtin: Frei nach Goldoni (Vienna & Munich: Sessler, 1978);

Turrini Lesebuch: Stücke, Pamphlete, Filme, Reaktionen etc., edited by Ulf Birbaumer (Vienna, Munich & Zurich: Europaverlag, 1978);

Alpensaga: Eine sechsteilige Fernsehserie aus dem bäuerlichen Leben, 3 volumes, by Turrini and Pevny (Salzburg: Residenz, 1980)—comprises volume 1: *Liebe im Dorf, Der Kaiser am Lande*; volume 2: *Das große Fest, Die feindlichen Brüder*; volume 3: *Der deutsche Frühling, Ende und Anfang*;

Josef und Maria: Theaterstück (Vienna: Frischfleisch und Löwenmaul, 1980);

Ein paar Schritte zurück: Gedichte (Munich: Autorenedition, 1980);

Bruno Kreisky, by Turrini, Konrad R. Müller, and Gerhard Roth (Berlin: Nicolai / Vienna: Forum, 1981);

Die Bürger (Vienna & Munich: Sessler, 1982);

Campiello (Vienna & Munich: Sessler, 1982);

Turrini Lesebuch: Zwei Stücke, Film, Gedichte, Reaktionen, etc., edited by Birbaumer (Vienna: Europaverlag, 1983);

Jugend: Buch zum Film "Atemnot," by Turrini and Käthe Kratz (Vienna & Zurich: Europaverlag, 1984);

Es ist ein gutes Land: Texte zu Anlässen, edited by Christa Binder (Vienna: Europaverlag, 1986);

Die Verlockung, by Turrini and Rudi Palla (Vienna: Europaverlag, 1988);

Die Minderleister (Vienna: Europaverlag, 1988);

Mein Österreich: Reden, Polemiken, Aufsätze (Darmstadt: Luchterhand, 1988);

Müllomania: Ein Drehbuch, by Turrini and Palla (Vienna: Europaverlag, 1988);

Das Plakat: Ein Drehbuch, by Turrini and Palla (Vienna: Europaverlag, 1990).

Edition in English: *The Slackers and Other Plays*, translated by Richard S. Dixon (Riverside, Cal.: Ariadne Press, 1992).

Peter Turrini

Peter Turrini ran away from the rural scene in which he was born but never escaped his roots. He ended up portraying the life of the Austrian countryside and working-class milieu in his plays, television plays, prose, and poetry, becoming one of the most important authors of the 1970s and 1980s to revitalize an old tradition of German and particularly of Austrian theater: the critical folk and village play. His plays depict oppressed proletarians, narrow-minded bourgeois, brutalized farmers, corrupt mayors, and ruthless land developers. What such characters have to tell, and the lives they live, are seldom edifying. Turrini's protagonists may be victims or villains, comical or tragic, or all of these at once; but they always convince their audiences to pay attention to what they have to say.

Turrini was born on 26 September 1944 in Sankt Margarethen, Austria, and grew up in Maria Saal. His mother came from the Austrian province of Styria; his father was a carpenter from Italy. To the other occupants of Maria Saal Turrini was an outsider. Early on, as he explains in *Mein Österreich* (My Austria, 1988), he found escape in the world of literature. After graduating from the gymnasium in Klagenfurt in 1963

Turrini tried to make a living as a woodworker and as a steelworker, occupations that figure prominently in his plays; then he tried his luck as a hotel manager and finally as a copywriter at an advertising agency. Since 1971 Turrini has been a free-lance writer in Vienna. In 1972 he received grants from his home state of Kärnten and the city of Vienna, and in 1981 he received the Gerhardt Hauptmann Prize of the Freie Volksbühne, Berlin. Turrini is a member of the Grazer Autorenversammlung (Writers' Guild of Graz).

Literary fame came virtually overnight in 1971 with the production of Turrini's first major play, *Rozznjogd* (Rat Hunt; published, 1973). A young worker takes his new girlfriend on their first date. The couple arrives at a junkyard in his homemade sports car. The young man takes out his aggressions by hunting for rats, teaching his girlfriend how to handle the rifle. In an attempt to overcome their feelings of alienation and falsehood the two slowly remove all the trappings of civilization—false eyelashes, false teeth, hairpieces, cosmetics, money, and finally clothes. Naked, they engage in an ecstatic and passionate dance in the midst of the junk. At the end they

Gerd Kunath, Markus Boysen, and Oda Thormeyer in a scene from the premiere of Turrini's Die Minderleister *at the Akademietheater, Vienna, in 1988 (photograph by Abisag Tüllmann)*

are shot by two passing rat hunters. Turrini combines the old German tradition of naturalist social drama with the antiestablishment sentiments portrayed in such youth-cult films of the 1960s and early 1970s as *Easy Rider* (1969). Written in dialect, Turrini's play is out to shock the bourgeois audience and to unmask what the playwright considers the repressive capitalism of the 1970s.

Another play written in dialect, *Sauschlachten* (Slaughter of the Sow; performed, 1972; published, 1974), is a parody of the tradition of affirmative and uncritical German folk plays. Valentin, the oldest son of a farmer, refuses to speak; instead, he grunts like a pig. Valentin's father tries everything he can think of to get him to speak, but without success. Finally the frustration of the family, the viciousness of Valentin's half brother, and the intolerance of the villagers lead to cruelty and murder. Valentin is kept in a pig's stall and forced to eat pig's food. The local dignitaries—the doctor, the teacher, the lawyer, and the priest—concur with Valentin's family that whoever speaks like a pig is a pig. In the end Valentin is slaughtered like a swine during a grand ceremony attended by all the notables of the village, and Valentin's mother serves them "pork roast." Turrini confronts the audience with a barbaric cruelty that is meant to represent the

bigotry and intolerance of the Austrian countryside.

Turrini adapted two classical plays that led him away from his rural genre scenes and forced him to attempt character development and more complex plots. Neither *Der tollste Tag* (The Craziest Day; performed, 1972; published, 1973), after Beaumarchais's *Le Mariage de Figaro* (1784), nor *Die Wirtin* (The Innkeeper's Wife; performed, 1973; published, 1978), after Carlo Goldoni's *La Locandiera* (1753), was well received by audiences or critics. Consequently, Turrini became disenchanted with the stage and denounced it as outmoded bourgeois entertainment. He could not continue to write the sort of cynical one-act genre scenes that had initially brought him fame; a further attempt at doing so, *Kindsmord* (Child Murder; performed, 1973), was also unsuccessful. He found a more-engaged style of neorealistic regional literature in writing for television. From 1974 to 1980 he collaborated with Wilhelm Pevny on the six-part series *Die Alpensaga* (The Saga of the Alps; published, 1980), considered by some to be among the best films ever produced for television in German-speaking countries. Almost nine hours long, the series portrays the development of a mountain village from the period of early industrialization around 1900 to the post–World War II years.

The neorealistic style Turrini developed for television proved successful onstage as well. Instead of the parody and irony of his folk plays of the early 1970s, the conflicts of the lower-class protagonists are taken quite seriously in *Josef und Maria* (1980). A night watchman and a cleaning woman spend Christmas night in a closed department store. After many failed attempts at communication and interaction, these two lonely people find their way to intimacy. *Die Bürger* (The Citizens, 1982) attacks Turrini's generation, which controls the levers of power in society but lacks backbone or goals and—most important—has nothing to say. The play takes place at a party in the house of a doctor in his mid forties whose nineteen-year-old son from a previous marriage sees no alternative but to commit suicide. Other characters include the doctor's second wife, who is in her mid thirties; his seventy-year-old father; a Yugoslavian servant; a writer; a director and his wife; an entrepreneur and his wife; a politician; and an Italian actor. Using a tape recorder to play back parts of dialogues or monologues from previous scenes, the drama documents the mindless greed for power, money, and entertainment of the current generation of the bourgeois class. Turrini is suggesting that the bourgeoisie's role as the guarantor of humanistic values has ceased to exist. These Austrian yuppies have become static; there is not one thing they can think of changing. They have also lost their ability to communicate: their language is frozen in empty phrases, and their emotions do not reach beyond their hungry egos.

In *Die Minderleister* (The Underachievers, 1988) the steelworker Hans and his wife, Anna, lose their jobs and, consequently, their house and their dignity. After a personal intervention by Austria's minister for work and science—presented in one of several imaginary and grotesque scenes that employ characters from Hans's and Anna's favorite television shows—Hans finds a new job at his old plant. He is ordered to report any substandard performance by coworkers, but he cannot overcome his scruples. He puts his own name on the list and jumps into the furnace.

Turrini's angry, cynical, grotesque portraits of a cruel and dehumanized country life have given way to more realistic—although sometimes highly stylized—analyses of the decay of the traditional class struggle. Nevertheless, the basic topic of Turrini's dramas and television plays has re-

mained the same: his homeland and the injustices, cruelties, and suffering of its people. At the beginning of his career Turrini called himself a "Heimatdichter" (regional poet) simply to shock those who considered regional literature to be trivial and backward. Now he has accepted the label wholeheartedly and has become an important part of the tradition of critical and enlightening regional literature—in particular of the tradition of the folk play, which has often been declared dead but which has repeatedly managed to renew itself.

Interviews:

Dietmar Schmidt, "Münchener Gespräche mit zwei Bühnenautoren und noch einem," *Frankfurter Rundschau*, 26 February 1972;

Lutz Holzinger, "Die eigene Betroffenheit ist entscheidend," *Kürbiskern*, 4 (1977): 129-134;

Heinz Sichrovsky, "Das Theater ist wie eine realisierte Hoffnung," *Die Deutsche Bühne*, 1 (1982): 12-13;

Hermi Löbl, "Immer ein Voyeur der Wirklichkeit," *Bühne*, 6 (1988): 5-7.

References:

Reinhard Baumgart, "Schlachtplatte, fad und lauwarm," *Süddeutsche Zeitung*, 17 January 1972;

Otto Beer, "Mit Tonband auf Bürgerjagd," *Süddeutsche Zeitung*, 29 January 1982;

Beer, "Weihnachtsmärchen für Senioren: Peter Turrinis 'Josef und Maria,'" *Hannoversche Allgemeine Zeitung*, 26 November 1981;

Annemarie Czaschke, "Ein krachledernes Passionsspiel," *Frankfurter Rundschau*, 18 January 1972;

Wolfgang Drews, "Grausames Abschlachten," *Frankfurter Allgemeine Zeitung*, 19 January 1972;

Erich Emigholz, "Vergnügen schlägt Nachdenklichkeit," *Theater heute*, 3 (1974): 59;

Peter Friedl, "Prominenten-Party," *Theater heute*, 3 (1982): 37;

Dirk Fröse, "Tödliche Party," *Die Deutsche Bühne*, 10 (1982): 29-30;

Jochen Gleiß, "Josef und Maria," *Theater der Zeit*, 4 (1987): 18;

Jürgen Hein, "Das Bild Wiens im Volksstück von Ödön von Horváth bis Peter Turrini," *Literatur und Kritik*, nos. 193-194 (1985): 141-152;

Georg Heinzen, "Ich bremse auch für Tiere," *Konkret*, 12 (1988): 62-64;

Manfred Hölken, "Sie und die Ideologie," *Süddeutsche Zeitung*, 12 January 1984;

Peter Iden, "Die kaltgemachte Komödie," *Theater heute*, 4 (1972): 45;

Elfriede Jelinek, "Der Turrini Peter," *Theater heute*, 12 (1980): 40;

Jürgen Kritz, "Ein Lustspiel in der Sackgasse," *Frankfurter Allgemeine Zeitung*, 29 February 1972;

Paul Kruntorad, "Ein Arbeiter-Faust?," *Theater heute*, 7 (1988): 15-16;

Jutta Landa, *Bürgerliches Schocktheater* (Frankfurt am Main: Athenäum, 1988);

Knut Lennartz, "Josef und Maria," *Theater der Zeit*, 8 (1983): 2;

Sigrid Löffler, "Beruf: Heimatdichter," *Deutsches Allgemeines Sonntagsblatt*, 21 August 1988;

Franz Norbert Mennemeier, "Volkstheater gegen den Strich: Von Marieluise Fleißer bis Peter Turrini," in *Modernes deutsches Drama*, volume 2 (Munich: Fink, 1975), pp. 297-306;

Günther Nenning, "Alpenkönig und Arbeiterfreund," *Neues Forum*, no. 280-281 (1977): 58;

Gerhard Rohde, "Turrinis Kindsmord," *Theater heute*, 4 (1973): 56;

Dietmar Schmidt, "Peter Turrini," *Die Deutsche Bühne*, 7 (1972): 16;

Helmut Schödel, "Der Dichter der Alpen- und der Arbeitersaga: Auf einem Schiff aus Worten," *Die Zeit*, Überseeausgabe 19 (12 May 1989);

Wolfgang Schuch, "Erfolg für Turrini," *Theater der Zeit*, 11 (1988): 50-51;

Uwe Schultz, "Kreuzigung auf dem Klavier," *Stuttgarter Zeitung*, 14 March 1973;

Hilde Spiel, "Denkgeschwätz von links bis rechts," *Frankfurter Allgemeine Zeitung*, 29 January 1982;

Spiel, "Zweimal Rattenjagd," *Frankfurter Allgemeine Zeitung*, 1 February 1971;

Thomas Thieringer, "Wie die Geschichte der Arbeiter eine des Fernsehspiels wurde," *Süddeutsche Zeitung*, 24 November 1987;

Volker Trauth, "Liebeserklärung an kleine Leute," *Theater der Zeit*, 9 (1987): 3-4;

Rainer Wagner, "Im besten Falle Margarine," *Stuttgarter Zeitung*, 28 November 1973.

Martin Walser

(24 March 1927-   )

Heike A. Doane

See also the Walser entry in *DLB 75: Contemporary German Fiction Writers, Second Series.*

PLAY PRODUCTIONS: *Kantaten auf der Kellertreppe*, Stuttgart, Württembergisches Staatstheater, August 1953;

Der Abstecher, Munich, Münchner Kammerspiele, 28 November 1961;

Eiche und Angora, Berlin, Schillertheater, 23 September 1962;

Überlebensgroß Herr Krott: Requiem für einen Unsterblichen, Stuttgart, Württembergisches Staatstheater, 30 November 1963;

Der schwarze Schwan, Stuttgart, Württembergisches Staatstheater, 16 October 1964;

Die Zimmerschlacht: Übungsstück für ein Ehepaar, Munich, Münchner Kammerspiele, 7 December 1967;

Der schwarze Flügel, Berlin, Akademie der Künste, 27 January 1968;

Ein Kinderspiel, Stuttgart, Württembergisches Staatstheater, 22 April 1971;

Ein reizender Abend, Luxembourg, Le Théâtre des Casemats, 10 July 1972;

Das Sauspiel, music by Mikis Theodorakis, Hamburg, Deutsches Schauspielhaus, 19 December 1975;

In Goethes Hand, Vienna, Burgtheater, 18 December 1982;

Ein fliehendes Pferd, Meersburg, Sommertheater, 19 July 1985;

Die Ohrfeige, Darmstadt, Staatstheater, 30 December 1986;

Nero läßt grüßen oder Selbstporträt des Künstlers als Kaiser, Meersburg, Sommertheater, 21 June 1989.

BOOKS: *Ein Flugzeug über dem Haus und andere Geschichten* (Frankfurt am Main: Suhrkamp, 1955);

Ehen in Philippsburg; Roman (Frankfurt am Main: Suhrkamp, 1957); translated by Eva Figes as *The Gadarene Club* (London: Longmans,

Martin Walser (photograph by Isolde Ohlbaum)

1959); translation adapted by J. Laughlin as *Marriage in Philippsburg* (Norfolk, Conn.: New Directions, 1961);

Halbzeit: Roman (Frankfurt am Main: Suhrkamp, 1960);

Lese-Erfahrungen mit Proust (Frankfurt am Main & Berlin: Suhrkamp, 1960);

Hölderlin auf dem Dachboden (Frankfurt am Main: Suhrkamp, 1960);

Beschreibung einer Form: Versuch über Franz Kafka (Munich: Hanser, 1961);

Mitwirkung bei meinem Ende (Biberach an der Riß: Wege & Gestalten, 1962);

Eiche und Angora: Eine deutsche Chronik (Frankfurt am Main: Suhrkamp, 1962; revised, 1963); edited by A. E. Stubbs (London: Harrap, 1973); adapted by Ronald Duncan as *The Rabbit Race*, in *The Rabbit Race; The Detour* (London: Calder, 1963);

Überlebensgroß Herr Krott: Requiem für einen Unsterblichen (Frankfurt am Main: Suhrkamp, 1964);

Der schwarze Schwan: Ein Stück in zwei Akten (Frankfurt am Main: Suhrkamp, 1964);

Lügengeschichten (Frankfurt am Main: Suhrkamp, 1964);

Erfahrungen und Leseerfahrungen (Frankfurt am Main: Suhrkamp, 1965);

Das Einhorn: Roman (Frankfurt am Main: Suhrkamp, 1966); translated by Barrie Ellis-Jones as *The Unicorn* (London: Calder & Boyars, 1971; New York: Boyars, 1981);

Der Abstecher; Die Zimmerschlacht: Übungsstück für ein Ehepaar (Frankfurt am Main: Suhrkamp, 1967); *Der Abstecher* translated by Richard Grunberger as *The Detour*, in *The Rabbit Race; The Detour*;

Theater, Theater: Ein Bilderbuch des Theaters, by Walser and Karl Hargesheimer (Velber: Friedrich, 1967);

Heimatkunde: Aufsätze und Reden (Frankfurt am Main: Suhrkamp, 1968);

Ein Kinderspiel: Stück in zwei Akten (Frankfurt am Main: Suhrkamp, 1970);

Fiction (Frankfurt am Main: Suhrkamp, 1970);

Hölderlin zu entsprechen (Biberach an der Riß: Thomae, 1970);

Aus dem Wortschatz unserer Kämpfe: Szenen (Stierstadt im Taunus: Eremiten-Presse, 1971);

Gesammelte Stücke (Frankfurt am Main: Suhrkamp, 1971; revised, 1987);

Die Gallistl'sche Krankheit (Frankfurt am Main: Suhrkamp, 1972);

Der Sturz: Roman (Frankfurt am Main: Suhrkamp, 1973);

Wie und wovon handelt Literatur: Aufsätze und Reden (Frankfurt am Main: Suhrkamp, 1973);

Das Sauspiel: Szenen aus dem 16. Jahrhundert (Frankfurt am Main: Suhrkamp, 1975; edited by Werner Brändle, 1978);

Jenseits der Liebe: Roman (Frankfurt am Main: Suhrkamp, 1976); excerpt translated by Judith Black as "Beyond All Love," in *New Writing*

and Writers 19 (New York: Riverrun, 1982);

Was zu bezweifeln war: Aufsätze und Reden 1958-1975, edited by Klaus Schuhmann (Berlin: Aufbau, 1976);

Ein fliehendes Pferd: Novelle (Frankfurt am Main: Suhrkamp, 1978); translated by Leila Vennewitz as *Runaway Horse: A Novel* (New York: Holt, Rinehart & Winston, 1980; London: Secker & Warburg, 1980);

Der Grund zur Freude: 99 Sprüche zur Erbauung des Bewußtseins (Düsseldorf: Eremiten-Presse, 1978);

Heimatlob: Ein Bodenseebuch, by Walser and André Ficus (Friedrichshafen: Gessler, 1978);

Wer ist ein Schriftsteller?: Aufsätze und Reden (Frankfurt am Main: Suhrkamp, 1979);

Seelenarbeit: Roman (Frankfurt am Main: Suhrkamp, 1979); translated by Vennewitz as *The Inner Man* (New York: Holt, Rinehart & Winston, 1984);

Das Schwanenhaus: Roman (Frankfurt am Main: Suhrkamp, 1980); translated by Vennewitz as *The Swan Villa* (New York: Holt, Rinehart & Winston, 1982; London: Secker & Warburg, 1983);

Heines Tränen: Essay (Düsseldorf: Eremiten-Presse, 1981);

Selbstbewußtsein und Ironie: Frankfurter Vorlesungen (Frankfurt am Main: Suhrkamp, 1981);

Die Anselm Kristlein Trilogie (Frankfurt am Main: Suhrkamp, 1981)—comprises *Halbzeit, Das Einhorn, Der Sturz*;

Die Zimmerschlacht: Übungsstück für ein Ehepaar (Stuttgart: Reclam, 1981);

Versuch, ein Gefühl zu Verstehen, und andere versuche (Stuttgart: Reclam, 1982);

In Goethes Hand: Szenen aus dem 19. Jahrhundert (Frankfurt am Main: Suhrkamp, 1982);

Brief an Lord Liszt: Roman (Frankfurt am Main: Suhrkamp, 1982); translated by Vennewitz as *Letter to Lord Liszt* (New York: Holt, Rinehart & Winston, 1985);

Gefahrenvoller Aufenthalt: Erzählungen, edited by Klaus Pezold (Leipzig: Reclam, 1982);

Gesammelte Geschichten (Frankfurt am Main: Suhrkamp, 1983);

Goethes Anziehungskraft (Constance: Universitätsverlag, 1983); translated by W. J. H. Burkardt as "Goethe's Magnetism," *South Atlantic Review*, 50 (November 1985): 3-18;

Liebeserklärungen (Frankfurt am Main: Suhrkamp, 1983);

Brandung: Roman (Frankfurt am Main: Suhrkamp, 1985); translated by Vennewitz as *Breakers* (New York: Holt, 1987);

Meßmers Gedanken (Frankfurt am Main: Suhrkamp, 1985);

Ein fliehendes Pferd: Theaterstück (Frankfurt am Main: Suhrkamp, 1985);

Variationen eines Würgegriffs. Bericht über Trinidad und Tobago (Stuttgart: Radius, 1985);

Säntis: Hörspiel (Stuttgart: Radius, 1986);

Die Amerikareise: Versuch, ein Gefühl zu verstehen, by Walser and Ficus (Weingarten: Kunstverlag Weingarten, 1986);

Heilige Brocken: Aufsätze, Prosa, Gedichte (Weingarten: Drumlin, 1986);

Geständnis auf Raten (Frankfurt am Main: Suhrkamp, 1986);

Die Ohrfeige (Frankfurt am Main: Suhrkamp, 1986);

Dorle und Wolf: Novelle (Frankfurt am Main: Suhrkamp, 1987); translated by Vennewitz as *No Man's Land* (New York: Holt, 1989);

Jagd: Roman (Frankfurt am Main: Suhrkamp, 1988);

Die Schamlose, das Glückskind und all die anderen (Munich: Keyser, 1988);

Über Deutschland reden (Frankfurt am Main: Suhrkamp, 1988);

Armer Nanosh: Kriminalroman, by Walser and Asta Scheib (Frankfurt am Main: Fischer, 1989);

Nero läßt grüßen oder Selbstporträt des Künstlers als Kaiser: Ein Monodrama; Alexander und Annette: Ein innerer Monolog (Eggingen: Isele, 1989);

Auskunft (Frankfurt am Main: Suhrkamp, 1991);

Tassilo, 6 volumes (Frankfurt am Main: Suhrkamp, 1991);

Die Verteidigung der Kindheit (Frankfurt am Main: Suhrkamp, 1991);

Das Sofa (Frankfurt am Main: Suhrkamp, 1992).

OTHER: "Ein grenzenloser Nachmittag," in *Hörspielbuch 1955* (Frankfurt am Main: Europäische Verlagsanstalt, 1955), pp. 177-207; revised version in *Spectaculum: Texte moderner Hörspiele*, edited by Karl Markus Michel (Frankfurt am Main: Suhrkamp, 1963), pp. 295-313;

Die Alternative oder Brauchen wir eine neue Regierung?, edited by Walser (Reinbek: Rowohlt, 1961);

"Regie-Erfahrungen mit Weyrauchs Hörspielen," in *Dialog mit dem Unsichtbaren: Sieben Hörspiele*, by Wolfgang Weyrauch (Olten & Freiburg: Walter, 1962), pp. 245-248;

Franz Kafka, *Er: Prosa*, edited by Walser (Frankfurt am Main: Suhrkamp, 1963);

Jonathan Swift, *Satiren*, translated by Felix Paul Greve and others, essay by Walser (Frankfurt am Main: Insel, 1965);

Über Ernst Bloch, edited by Walser (Frankfurt am Main: Suhrkamp, 1968);

Erika Runge, *Bottroper Protokolle*, foreword by Walser (Frankfurt am Main: Suhrkamp, 1968);

Ursula Trauberg, *Vorleben*, afterword by Walser (Frankfurt am Main: Suhrkamp, 1968);

Werner Wolfgang, *Vom Waisenhaus ins Zuchthaus: Ein Sozialbericht*, afterword by Walser (Frankfurt am Main: Suhrkamp, 1969);

Wolfgang Bächler, *Traumprotokoll: Ein Nachtbuch*, afterword by Walser (Munich: Hanser, 1972);

Weyrauch, *Mit dem Kopf durch die Wand*, afterword by Walser (Darmstadt & Neuwied: Luchterhand, 1972);

Ulrich Paetzold and Hendrik Schmidt, eds., *Solidarität gegen Abhängigkeit: Mediengewerkschaft*, foreword by Walser (Darmstadt: Luchterhand, 1973);

Helmut Kessler, *Der Schock*, afterword by Walser (Munich: List, 1974);

"Requiem in Langenargen," in *Auf Anhieb Mord: Kurzkrimis* (Reinbek: Reclam, 1977), pp. 170-200;

Heike Doane, *Gesellschaftskritische Aspekte in Martin Walsers Kristlein-Trilogie*, foreword by Walser (Bonn: Bouvier, 1978);

Die Würde am Werktag: Literatur der Arbeiter und Angestellten, edited by Walser (Frankfurt: Fischer, 1980);

Heinrich Lersch, *Hammerschläge: Ein Roman von Menschen und Maschinen*, afterword by Walser (Frankfurt am Main: Suhrkamp, 1980);

"Was ist ein Klassiker?," in *Warum Klassiker?: Ein Almanach zur Eröffnung der Bibliothek deutscher Klassiker* (Frankfurt am Main: Deutscher Klassiker Verlag, 1985), pp. 3-10.

TRANSLATIONS: D. H. Lawrence, *Das Karusell* (Berlin: Bloch, 1974);

Christopher Hampton, *Herrenbesuch* (Frankfurt am Main: Suhrkamp, 1976);

Mark Medoff, *Die Wette* (Frankfurt am Main: Suhrkamp, 1977);

Edward Bond, *Die Frau*, translated by Walser and Alissa Walser (Frankfurt am Main: Suhrkamp, 1979);

Trevor Griffiths, *Die Party* (Bremen: Litag, 1980);

Molière, *Der eingebildete Kranke*, translated by Walser and Johanna Walser (Bochum: Schauspielhaus Programmbuch, 1983);

Christopher Hampton, *Gefährliche Liebschaften*, translated by Walser and Alissa Walser, in *Theater: Stücke von Achternbusch, Bernhard, Bond, Dorst, Hampton, Kroetz, Wilson*, edited by Rudolf Rach (Frankfurt am Main: Suhrkamp, 1986);

George Bernard Shaw, *Frau Warrens Beruf* (Frankfurt: Suhrkamp, 1986).

SELECTED PERIODICAL PUBLICATIONS—
UNCOLLECTED: "Prophet mit Marx- und Engelszungen: Zum Erscheinen des Hauptwerks von Ernst Bloch in Westdeutschland," *Süddeutsche Zeitung*, 26-27 September 1958;

Erdkunde, in *Kürbiskern*, 1 (1965): 59-72;

"Mythen, Milch und Mut," *Christ und Welt*, 18 October 1968, p. 17;

Wir werden schon noch handeln: Dialoge über das Theater, in *Akzente*, 15 (December 1968): 511-544; translated by A. Leslie Willson as *Acting Is Our Business*, in *Dimension*, 2, no. 2 (1969): 268-323;

"Über das Legitimieren: Ein Gespräch über die Mitwirkung der Intellektuellen beim Auf- und Abbau öffentlicher Meinungen," *text + kritik*, 41-42 (1974): 1-29;

"About Popes," translated by Axel Claesges and Robert Elkins, *Philological Papers*, 24 (November 1977): 1-5;

"Things Go Better with Goethe," translated by Leigh Hafrey, *New York Times Book Review*, 2 March 1986, pp. 1, 35-36;

"George Bush, seine Trainer und der Traum von Amerika," *Die Welt*, 10 December 1988, pp. 6-7.

Martin Walser's works are rooted in specific locations and traditions that reflect conditions in the larger community of contemporary Germany. A deep sense of class origin pervades his work. He believes that Germany has emerged as a society with materialistic rather than democratic principles, and his dramas are contributions to the discussion of Germany's social and political devel-

opment. Among the dramatists confronted with the schism between the theater of the absurd and Bertolt Brecht's epic theater, Walser was the first to strive for a dramatic form unique to the new Germany.

Walser was born on 24 March 1927 in Wasserburg, an idyllic village on the shores of Lake Constance, the second of three sons of Martin Walser, an innkeeper, and Augusta Walser (née Schmid). His parents also operated a small coal business, which eventually became the responsibility of the two older boys. The father, who had failed at several business ventures, died of diabetes in 1938; he left behind several notebooks, which Walser later described as literary attempts to escape his financially precarious existence. Walser's mother was a devout Catholic whose spiritual strength helped carry the family through its recurring financial crises. Early impressions of small-scale retailing and competition, physical labor, and his parents' struggle for survival, along with memories of local choirs and traveling theater groups practicing at the inn, left an indelible mark on his writing and politics. Walser attended the gymnasium in the neighboring city of Lindau from 1938 until 1943, when he was drafted into an antiaircraft unit to defend the home front. In 1944 he was transferred to the labor service, then assigned to an Alpine military unit. He was taken prisoner by the Americans in 1945. After his release he finished his schooling, and he received his diploma in 1946. He enrolled at the University of Regensburg, where the postwar shortage of books and professors steered him toward the student theater. On the recommendation of a friend he transferred to the University of Tübingen in the spring of 1948 to study literature, philosophy, and history but also to perform in the student acting ensemble.

After the monetary reform in June of that year Walser's funds, including a stipend from his home district of Lindau, dwindled. His first short stories, written about this time, reflect the bewilderment of a generation confronted with the nation's devastation and the resurgence of its economic strength. While still a student he accepted a job with the South German Radio in Stuttgart in 1949, progressing quickly from a low-level employee in the entertainment section to reporter and finally to editor of the political division. He married Katharina Neuner-Jehle, also from an innkeeper's family, on 20 October 1950. It was only the casual observation of his professor Friedrich Beißner that Walser had apparently given up on his studies and the fear of disappointing his mother that compelled him to complete his degree in 1951. His dissertation on Franz Kafka was published in 1961 as *Beschreibung einer Form* (Description of a Form).

In Stuttgart, with such notable writers as Alfred Andersch, Helmut Heissenbüttel, and Hans Magnus Enzensberger as his colleagues, Walser's literary career gained momentum. He began to write radio plays, a genre that attracted many struggling writers of the postwar era. Six of these plays were broadcast between 1952 and 1956; one of them, *Kantaten auf der Kellertreppe* (Cantatas on the Cellar Steps), was also staged as a musical in 1953. The plays, which show the influence of the theater of the absurd, existentialism, Brecht, and Eugène Ionesco, give evidence of Walser's finely turned ear for the subtleties of language.

In 1956, feeling that the broadcasting industry had become just another big business, he moved back to Lake Constance to devote himself to his writing. A year later he received the Hermann Hesse Prize for his novel *Ehen in Philippsburg* (Marriage in Philippsburg, 1957; translated as *The Gadarene Club*, 1959).

Walser's first play written for the stage was *Der Abstecher* (performed, 1961; translated as *The Detour*, 1963; published, 1967), a study of exploitation with comic dialogues and satirical characterizations. On a trip from Hamburg to Munich the businessman Hubert makes an unscheduled stop in Ulm, where he hopes to spend the night with his former mistress, Frieda. She, however, is still resentful because he abandoned her when she was pregnant. She is also married now, and her husband, Erich, is as bent on revenge as she. Bound to a chair with his bare feet in a bowl of water, Hubert is awaiting electrocution; but Erich, a train engineer, is no match for the manipulative businessman, and soon both men depart for a night on the town. The disappointed and disdainful Frieda is left behind. This central scene is flanked by two shorter ones depicting Hubert's relationship to his chauffeur, Berthold. Berthold and Erich easily fall prey to their oppressor since they both secretly admire him. The play was an immediate success in both Germanies and in other European countries. During the following years it was performed by fifty-four theater companies, sometimes in conjunction with one of Ionesco's works.

Eiche und Angora (Oak and Angora, 1962; adapted as *The Rabbit Race*, 1963) established Walser's reputation as a dramatist both at home and abroad. Its strength lies in its portrayal of postwar German society's uncompromising pursuit of economic recovery and suppression of its political past. The play begins in 1945, when French troops are about to invade, and all citizens of the small town of Brezgenburg are called on to defend the home front. Alois Grübel, a former communist who has been "cured" of his political unreliability in a concentration camp, is a willing participant. The singing skills he acquired in the camp, along with a proficiency in Nazi jargon, indicate his eagerness to fall into step with his hometown's political metamorphoses. But when the people of Brezgenburg surrender by hoisting white rabbit skins that Alois has sold them, he is accused of being a traitor. He blames the incident on a relapse into his communist past. In 1950 Alois makes a speech commemorating Adolf Hitler's birthday and expressing his surprise at being considered a victim of the Nazi regime. He is sent to an asylum, where he is reeducated to become an anticommunist and a proponent of free enterprise. Ten years later Alois is to be featured in a local singing competition, but first he has to get rid of his foul-smelling rabbits. In anticipation of the great event, Alois kills his animals—only to be told that he will not be singing after all, since his voice is an embarrassing reminder of an "inhumane" past. Enraged, he fastens the bloody skins to the banners decorating the stage and is committed to the asylum again. People like Alois lack in self-esteem and are reverential toward those who dominate their lives. Walser views the unilateral bond between the underprivileged and those of higher social standing as a stubborn link between the feudal and the new democratic Germany. Despite heckling that interrupted the applause on opening night, and some mixed reviews, the play was widely performed throughout Germany; it was also staged in Zurich, Vienna, Edinburgh, and Paris, where it ran for a year at the Théâtre National Populaire. Walser was awarded the Gerhart Hauptmann Prize for it.

Überlebensgroß Herr Krott (The Larger-than-Life Mr. Krott; performed 1963; published, 1964) describes the futile attempts of a capitalist to bring about his own death. Lacking a plot, the play presents a series of satirical scenes in which the growth of Krott's empire is contrasted with his own lifeless existence. Immortal yet devoid of human energy, he is the symbol of an economic system that has outlived its usefulness. With his

Scene from a performance of Walser's Der Abstecher *at the Munich Kammerspiele (photograph by Steinmetz)*

wife and his sister-in-law, who doubles as his mistress, Krott spends his time on the terrace of an exclusive hotel, hovering between life and death. A waiter and his family cater to his every need. Most important, the waiter has taken it on himself to ensure that before any of Krott's foes gain access to the terrace their spirits must be broken. Thus, the capitalist never meets his fate, and the system that benefits only a few will not be overthrown.

Der schwarze Schwan (The Black Swan, 1964) is one of the first German plays to deal with the problem of Germany's national guilt. It also constitutes a break with the Brechtian tradition of political parables with didactic intentions and biting humor. Brecht's condemnation of war, exploitation, and capitalism did not convey the subtle influences on human consciousness, the disclosure of which Walser regarded as the most pressing task of a realistic writer. A young man, Rudi Goothein, has found an incriminating document that bears the name he and his father share and that describes the detailed routine of a concentration camp. Incapable of confronting his father with the evidence of the atrocities, he projects the crimes onto himself in the hope of convincing his father of his own responsibility. But Rudi's insistence on justice is inexplicable to the older Goothein, who feels that he has already paid for his transgressions with a four-year jail sentence. He leaves the son in care of Doctor Liberé, a wartime acquaintance who is now head

of a psychiatric clinic. Liberé, like Rudi, suffers from unexpiated guilt. Although he has long since invented an innocuous past for himself and his family, he has privately condemned himself to a Spartan life like that of a convict. He recognizes Rudi's symptoms but discredits as arrogance his insistence on being responsible for murders committed by others. Undaunted, Rudi pursues the role his father once played; he must know what he would have done under similar circumstances. Prompted by a childhood memory, he claims to be "der schwarze Schwan," who with a quick sign of his thumb decided the fate of new camp arrivals. Dr. Liberé's daughter turns out to be Rudi's former playmate Hedi; she also remembers the SS man called the Black Swan. Rudi decides to shatter his father's and his doctor's construct of an unblemished past. He stages a play in which his fellow patients reenact their experiences in the camps; Rudi portrays Dr. F., the brutal tamer of the inmates. When he ends the play by reading his father's letter, only Liberé and his daughter are shaken; the elder Goothein is secure in the knowledge that he has performed the officially prescribed penance. Rudi atones for his father's crimes by shooting himself.

Walser's most successful drama, *Die Zimmerschlacht: Übungsstück für ein Ehepaar* (The Parlor Battle: Exercise for a Married Couple, 1967), depicts a couple whose facade of a harmonious life is shattered during a few hours of debating whether to go to an engagement party. What en-

Scene from a 1982 performance of Walser's Die Zimmerschlacht, *with Heidemarie Theobald as Trude and Wolfgang Unterzaucher as Felix Fürst (photograph by Klaus Lefebvre)*

tense of marital bliss has vanished. Although their moment of truth occurs in private, their aspirations, hopes, and expectations are nothing but internalized responses to public norms. Both seem to recognize that they have fallen victim to outside domination when they describe themselves at the end of the act as traitors to their marriage. In the second act Felix and Trude are in their early sixties. Felix is involved in an intrigue designed to impress his peers; Trude is acting the jealous spouse. Their relationship has been reduced to role-playing; the search for truth has turned into a game. The private and public spheres are intertwined into an almost impenetrable psychological web. It is this true-to-life complexity, along with skillful use of dialogue, that accounts for the play's popularity. For a decade *Die Zimmerschlacht* ranked third on the list of most-performed plays in the Federal Republic. Staged in many European countries, as well as in Mexico, it brought its author a measure of financial security; he referred to his house on Lake Constance as "Villa Zimmerschlacht."

Walser's belief that twenty years after World War II Germany was still in need of an evolution that would bring it closer to realizing the democracy that it professed to be, along with his strong opposition to the new war in Vietnam, led him to regard the theater as a tool for the political education of the audience. Rather than present an imitation of political events, the stage was to be a place of political interaction in its own right. In *Wir werden schon noch handeln* (published, 1968; translated as *Acting Is Our Business*, 1969), which premiered in 1968 under the title *Der schwarze Flügel* (The Black Piano), all semblance of a plot has disappeared. The actors, who are numbered one through five, debate the functions of their roles and the feasibility of breaking preset patterns of consciousness. The play's intended artificiality, although tempered with spontaneous wit, has caused it to be largely ignored.

Ein Kinderspiel (A Child's Play; published, 1970; performed, 1971) had five productions and fared somewhat better in the reviews. Depicting a failed attempt at murdering a parent, the play is best understood as a reflection on the protest movement of the 1960s.

Walser's *Das Sauspiel* (Pig Wrestling, 1975) is set in Nuremberg in 1526, a time when the Anabaptists, encouraged by Martin Luther's challenge to the Catholic church, set out to fashion their earthly lives according to Christian principles. Luther's religious revolution had also led to

sues is a skillfully choreographed array of sentiments, arguments, and insinuations that reveals both characters with unrelenting wit and logic. The first act opens as Trude and Felix Fürst are getting dressed for a party in honor of one of Felix's fellow teachers and his much younger fiancée. Felix fears that the affair will accentuate his failure not only as a teacher but also as a man, and he tries to convince his wife that it is best to stay home. After several attempts at seduction he admits his fears and intimates that Trude might not fare well in comparison with a younger woman. Trude is not frightened by the prospect, however, nor is she upset by his confession of sexual dissatisfaction. She responds to his every move with ruthless openness until all prethe reformation of local governments; the Nuremberg city council included some of the most enlightened thinkers of the time. Nonetheless, they were unwilling to extend the freedom just gained from Rome to those who might use that same freedom against them. Since the Anabaptists were egalitarians who shunned earthly possessions, the council made a great effort to secure its own wealth and position of power. Walser's play depicts a trial in which an Anabaptist preacher is convicted and executed on the expert advice of an intellectual, Philipp Melanchthon, and his mentor, Luther. Their self-serving judgment is parodied in a "Sauspiel," a contest between blind men attempting to kill a pig, in which a folksinger seeks an advantage over the other competitors by pretending to be blind. The role of intellectuals and artists, which one of the councilmen describes as the creation of beauty in security, had always been the subject of Walser's criticism—even more so after they had failed miserably, in his eyes, at sustaining the progressive mood of the late 1960s. The first production, in Hamburg, was canceled after only a few weeks.

Disheartened by the negative reception of his plays, Walser concentrated for the next seven years on writing novels. He returned to drama with *In Goethes Hand* (1982), his second historical play. Lured to Weimar by his admiration for the great poet Johann Wolfgang von Goethe, Johann Peter Eckermann develops from a young man with literary ambitions into the epitome of selfless devotion as Goethe's private secretary. He recognizes that he is being exploited by his idol, but he remains faithful to Goethe, whose life and poetry he mistakes for the key to his own fulfillment. Although Walser condemns the poet's patronizing exploitation of Eckermann and others, and his allegedly reactionary politics, Goethe is portrayed not as a villain but as a man who effortlessly succeeds in creating his own persona. Walser tempers the complexity of his theme with humor: the incongruity between Goethe's lofty position and the ordinariness of his family life and between Eckermann's timidity and Goethe's savoir faire provides comic moments without forfeiting the profundity of the play.

In 1985 Walser adapted his 1978 novella *Ein fliehendes Pferd* (translated as *Runaway Horse*, 1980) for the newly founded summer theater in Meersburg. Helmut Halm, the model of alienation, has carefully created a facade of compliance with society's demands, behind which he hopes to preserve his true self. While Halm lives in fear of public exposure and humiliation, the physically fit and aggressive Klaus Buch presents himself as the embodiment of those demands. When Halm and his wife meet the Buchs while vacationing at Lake Constance, Buch recognizes Halm as a former classmate. He immediately tries to impress Halm with his accomplishments; Halm, in turn, defends his isolation from the allure of new adventures. The moment of truth comes during a stormy sailing trip when Halm panics and nearly causes Buch to drown. After that, neither Buch's bravado nor Halm's withdrawal into the sanctuary of his inner world can hide their failure to master life or become the men they originally set out to be. Since the narrator's elucidations in the novella are now absorbed into the dialogue, the characters themselves must speak of their fear of failure, temptation, and death in phrases designed to hide those very emotions. This reliance on dialogue alters the mood from that of the novella: the intimacy of prose gives way to quick repartee.

In Walser's play *Die Ohrfeige* (The Box on the Ear, 1986) Karl Mangold, a lathe operator, is laid off due to the financial maneuvering of the factory owner. Ashamed to tell his wife what has happened, he spends his days in a local pub. One day he is challenged to slap the factory owner's face, and he seizes the opportunity to avenge the insult he suffered. The recipient of the blow, however, is not the one he intended but a pompous author who also deserves it. The author suffers a bad fall, which partially paralyzes him but also brings about his social awakening. The monodrama *Nero läßt grüßen oder Selbstporträt des Künstlers als Kaiser* (Nero Sends his Regards; or, Self-portrait of the Artist as Emperor, 1989) is a reflection on the seduction of power and on the poet's vanity and fascination with his own demise.

While Walser's acclaim as a novelist has steadily increased, his efforts to scrutinize public life by exploring the consciousness of the characters on stage have often been rejected. Still, his reputation as one of Germany's most important authors and intellectuals is recognized at home and abroad. He lectured as visiting scholar at Middlebury College and at the University of Texas at Austin in 1973; at Warwick University, England, in 1975; at West Virginia University in 1976; at various colleges and universities in Japan in 1977; at Dartmouth College in 1979; and at the University of California at Berkeley in 1983. His distinctions include an honorary citizenship of Wasserburg, awarded in 1984, and the Grand Order of Merit of the Federal Republic of Germany in 1987. In 1990 he received the Zuckmayer Medallion; the Literature Prize of the Bavarian Academy of Fine Arts; and the Ricarda Huch Prize, which he donated to the reconstruction of the former Frauenkirche in Dresden. He and his wife have four daughters: Franziska, an actress, born in 1952; Katharina, a writer, born in 1957; Alissa, a painter, born in 1960; and Theresia, a singer and actress, born in 1966. The Walsers have lived in Überlingen since 1968.

Interviews:

Hellmut Karasek, "Abschied von der Politik: Hellmuth Karasek unterhält sich mit Martin Walser über dessen neues Stück *Die Zimmerschlacht,*" *Theater heute,* 8 (September 1967): 6-9;

Thomas Beckermann, *Erzählprobleme in Martin Walsers Romanen: Ein Gespräch zwischen Martin Walser und Thomas Beckermann* (Biberach an der Riß: Wege & Gestalten, 1968);

Bettina L. Knapp, "Interview with Martin Walser," *Modern Drama,* 13 (December 1970): 316-323;

Ekkehart Rudolph, "Martin Walser," in *Protokolle zur Person: Autoren über sich und ihr Werk,* edited by Rudolph (Munich: List, 1971): 131-144;

Monika Totten, "Ein Gespräch mit Martin Walser in Neuengland," *Basis,* 10 (1980): 194-240;

Anton Kaes, "Documentation: Porträt Martin Walser," *German Quarterly,* 57 (Summer 1984): 432-449;

Günter Gaus, "Gespräch mit Martin Walser," *Düsseldorfer Debatte: Zeitschrift für Politik, Kunst, Wissenschaft,* 12 (1986): 37-47;

Paul F. Reitze, "Ich werde mich nicht an die deutsche Teilung gewöhnen," *Die Welt,* 29 September 1986;

Reitze, "Es gibt keinen Schriftsteller, der nicht am liebsten Lyriker wäre," *Die Welt,* 30 September 1986;

Michael P. Olsen, "Interview mit Martin Walser," *New German Review,* 4 (1988): 41-55;

Manfred Schell and Reitze, "Mir machen die Menschen in der DDR nur Freude," *Die Welt,* 9 July 1990;

Schell and Reitze, "Die deutsche Einigung ist die Sache von uns allen," *Die Welt,* 11 July 1990.

Bibliographies:

Heinz Sauereßig, ed., *Martin Walser: Bibliographie 1952-1964* (Biberach an der Riß: Wege & Gestalten, 1964);

Sauereßig, ed., *Martin Walser: Bibliographie Beiheft 1952-1966* (Biberach an der Riß: Wege & Gestalten, 1966);

Sauereßig and Thomas Beckermann, eds., *Bibliographie der Werke Martin Walsers 1952-1970* (Biberach an der Riß: Wege & Gestalten, 1970).

References:

Thomas Beckermann, ed., *Über Martin Walser* (Frankfurt am Main: Suhrkamp, 1970);

Otto F. Beer, "In Eckermanns Hand: Walsers Goethe-Stück in Wien uraufgeführt," *Süddeutsche Zeitung,* 20 December 1982;

Günter Blöcker, "Der Realismus X," *Merkur,* 19 (1965): 389-392;

Werner Brändle, *Die dramatischen Stücke Martin Walsers: Variationen über das Elend des bürgerlichen Subjekts* (Stuttgart: Akademischer Verlag Hans-Dieter Heinz, 1978);

Peter Burri, "Kleiner Ritt über den Bodensee," *Frankfurter Allgemeine Zeitung,* 23 July 1985;

Günter Eichler, "Die Ehe als eine fröhliche Hölle," *Spectaculum,* 12 (1969): 296-297;

Gerald A. Fetz, "Martin Walser's *Sauspiel* and the Contemporary German History Play," *Comparative Drama,* 12 (Fall 1978): 249-265;

Eckhard Franke, "Neues Stück von Martin Walser: Schlagfertig—oder runtergehaut," *Theater heute,* 28 (February 1987): 47;

Heinz Geiger, *Widerstand und Mitschuld: Zum deutschen Drama von Brecht bis Weiss* (Düsseldorf: Bertelsmann, 1973), pp. 153-159;

Roger Gellert, "Alois and the Angoras," *New Statesman,* 66 (September 1963): 296-297;

Hermann Glaser, "Martin Walser: *Überlebensgroß Herr Krott,*" in *Das deutsche Drama vom Expressionismus bis zur Gegenwart,* edited by Manfred Brauner (Bamberg: Buchner, 1977), pp. 315-319;

"Der Glückstreffer," *Der Spiegel,* 40 (29 December 1986): 107-108;

Hans-Jürgen Greif, "Martin Walser," in his *Zum modernen Drama* (Bonn: Bouvier, 1973), pp. 7-32;

John Hall, "*The Rabbit Race* and *Detour,*" *Books and Bookmen,* 10 (May 1966): 38;

Joachim Kaiser, "Walsers *Abstecher*—Farce oder

Drama," *Viersener Theaterblätter*, 3 (1965): 23-30;

Hellmuth Karasek, "Bemerkungen über die Zeit und das Zeitstück," *Viersener Theaterblätter*, 3 (1965): 38-42;

Karasek, "Eckermann macht's möglich," *Der Spiegel*, 36 (27 December 1982): 111-112;

Karasek, "Martin Walser: *Der schwarze Schwan*," in *Das deutsche Drama vom Expressionismus bis zur Gegenwart*, pp. 277-280;

Ernst-Günter Kautz, "Ideologiekritik und Grundlagen der dramatischen Gestaltung in Martin Walsers Stücken *Der Abstecher* und *Eiche und Angora*," *Wissenschaftliche Zeitschrift der Humboldt Universität Berlin*, 18 (1969): 93-113;

Hendrik Keisch, "Was vermag Literatur: Deutsche Selbstprüfung im Drama Martin Walsers," *Neue deutsche Literatur*, 14, no. 10 (1966): 175-181;

Paul Kruntorad, "Ehekriege am Bodensee," *Theater heute*, 26 (October 1985): 28-29;

Jens Kruse, "Walsers Eckermann-Stück: Goethe Schelte oder Liebeserklärung?," *Monatshefte*, 79 (1987): 439-448;

Franz Norbert Mennemeier, "Zwischen Groteske und Aktion," in his *Modernes Deutsches Drama*, volume 2 (Munich: Fink, 1975), pp. 275-281;

Rolf Michaelis, "Theater als Blindenanstalt?," *Theater heute*, 17 (February 1976): 7-9;

Werner Mittenzwei, "Zwischen Resignation und Auflehnung: Vom Menschenbild der neuesten westdeutschen Dramatik," *Sinn und Form*, 16 (1964): 894-908;

Gertrud Pickar, "Symbols as Structural Elements in the Dramatic Works of Martin Walser," *Modern Languages*, 54 (1973): 186-191;

Pickar, "Woyzeck and Hamlet Recast in the Twentieth Century—Two of Martin Walser's Dramas," *University of Dayton Review*, 7 (Spring 1971): 61-68;

Ursula Püschel, "Historisches Stück: Kämpfe der Gegenwart," with an interview by Walser, *Theater der Zeit*, 3 (1976): 38-40;

Werner Ross, "Zimmerschlachten," *Merkur*, 23 (1969): 959-971;

Jürgen E. Schlunk and Armand E. Singer, eds., *Martin Walser: International Perspectives* (New York: Lang, 1987);

Wilhelm Johannes Schwarz, *Der Erzähler Martin Walser* (Bern & Munich: Francke, 1971);

Klaus Siblewski, "Martin Walsers *Sauspiel*," in *Deutscher Bauernkrieg: Historische Analysen und Studien zur Rezeption*, edited by Walter Raitz (Opladen: Westdeutscher Verlag, 1976), pp. 190-207;

Siblewski, ed., *Martin Walser* (Frankfurt am Main: Suhrkamp, 1981);

Siblewski and Michael Töteberg, "Martin Walser," in *Kritisches Lexikon zur deutschsprachigen Gegenwartsliteratur*, edited by Heinz Ludwig Arnold (Munich: Edition text + kritik, 1987);

Michael Skasa, "Herr und Hund: Martin Walsers Eckermann-Drama *In Goethes Hand*," *Die Zeit*, 31 December 1982, p. 17;

Rainer Taëni, "Modelle einer entfremdeten Gesellschaft?," *text + kritik*, 41-42 (1974): 57-68;

Taëni, "Versuch einer Gesellschaftskritik durch sprachliche Symbolik," in his *Drama nach Brecht* (Basel: Basilius, 1968), pp. 86-122;

Frank Trommler, "Demonstration eines Scheiterns: Zu Martin Walsers Theaterarbeit," *Basis: Jahrbuch für deutsche Gegenwartsliteratur*, 10 (1980): 127-141;

Klaus Wagner, "Der Elefant auf der Schubkarre," *Frankfurter Allgemeine Zeitung*, 22 December 1975, p. 15;

Anthony Waine, *Martin Walser* (Munich: Beck, 1980);

Waine, *Martin Walser: The Development as Dramatist 1950-1970* (Bonn: Bouvier, 1978);

Ludwig Zerull, "Vom treuen Eckermann zum blutigen Scherzkeks: Dichter inszenieren ihre Stücke," *Theater heute*, 24 (May 1983): 18-23.

Günther Weisenborn
(10 July 1902 - 26 March 1969)

Viktoria Hertling
University of Nevada, Reno

See also the Weisenborn entry in *DLB 69: Contemporary German Fiction Writers, First Series.*

PLAY PRODUCTIONS: *Amerikanische Tragödie der sechs Matrosen von S 4*, Berlin, 16 October 1928;

Die Arbeiter von Jersey, Coburg, 16 February 1931;

Warum lacht Frau Balsam?, Berlin, February 1933;

Die Neuberin, Berlin, Theater am Kurfürstendamm, 24 May 1935;

Die guten Feinde, Bremen, 1 March 1938;

Die Illegalen, Berlin, Hebbel-Theater, 21 March 1946;

Babel, Constance, Stadttheatheater, 1947;

Ballade vom Eulenspiegel, vom Federle und von der dicken Pompanne, Hamburg, Deutsches, Schauspielhaus, 1949;

Drei ehrenwerte Herren, Hamburg, Hamburger Kammerspiele, 1951;

Spanische Hochzeit, Hamburg, Hamburger Kammerspiele, 13 November 1952;

Zwei Engel steigen aus, Mannheim, Nationaltheater, 7 January 1955;

Fünfzehn Schnüre Geld, Hamburg, Thalia-Theater, 30 August 1958;

Walküre—44, Berlin, 16 February 1966.

Günther Weisenborn

BOOKS: *Amerikanische Tragödie der sechs Matrosen von "S 4"* (Freiburg im Breisgau: Reichard, 1928);

Barbaren: Roman einer studentischen Tafelrunde (Berlin: Sieben-Stäbe-Verlag, 1931);

"Warum lacht Frau Balsam?" Schmugglerstück von der deutschen Westgrenze, by Weisenborn and Richard Huelsenbeck (Berlin: Fischer, 1932);

Das Mädchen von Fanö (Berlin: Kiepenheuer, 1935);

Die Furie: Roman aus der Wildnis (Berlin: Rowohlt, 1937); translated by Richard and Clarissa Graves as *The Fury* (London: Hutchinson, 1956);

Die einsame Herde: Buch der wilden, blühenden Pampa, as Christian Munk (Dresden: Heyne, 1937);

Traum und Tarantel: Buch von der unruhigen Kreatur, as Munk (Dresden: Heyne, 1938);

Die Silbermine von Santa Sabina: Roman aus Südamerika, as Munk (Berlin: Curtius, 1940);

Die Illegalen: Drama aus der deutschen Widerstandsbewegung (Berlin: Aufbau, 1946);

Die guten Feinde (Berlin: Aufbau, 1947);

Historien der Zeit, enthaltend die Dramen: Babel, Die guten Feinde, Die Illegalen (Berlin: Aufbau, 1947);

Memorial (Vienna: Desch, 1947);

414

Ballade vom Eulenspiegel, vom Federle und von der dicken Pompanne: Auf dem Theater dargestellt mit Prolog und Chören nach alten Schwänken (Berlin: Aufbau, 1949);

Spanische Hochzeit: Ein kleines Schauspiel (Berlin: Aufbau, 1949);

Die Neuberin: Komödiantenstück (Berlin: Henschel, 1950);

Spiel vom Thomaskantor: Aufzuführen zu Ehre des Meisters aller Musik. Nach alten Berichten verfaßt (Berlin: Henschel, 1950);

Drei ehrenwerte Herren: Komödie (Emsdetten: Lechte, 1953);

Dramatische Balladen (Berlin: Aufbau, 1955);

Der dritte Blick: Roman (Munich, Vienna & Basel: Desch, 1956);

Auf Sand gebaut: Roman (Munich, Vienna & Basel: Desch, 1956);

Das verlorene Gesicht: Die Ballade vom lachenden Mann (Munich, Vienna & Basel: Desch, 1956); revised as *"Lofter" oder Das verlorene Gesicht: Die Theater-Ballade vom lachenden Mann* (Berlin: Henschel, 1959); translated by Gabrielle Bingham as *The Man without a Face* (University Park: University of Pennsylvania Press, 1969);

Göttinger Kantate (Berlin: Arani, 1958);

Fünfzehn Schnüre Geld (Munich: Desch, 1959);

Die Familie von Nevada und ihre Darstellung auf dem Theater (Berlin: Henschel, 1959);

Schiller und das moderne Theater (Düsseldorf: Verband der deutschen Volksbühnenvereine, 1959);

Die Familie von Makabah: Schauspiel (Munich, Vienna & Basel: Desch, 1960);

Der Verfolger: Die Niederschrift des Daniel Brendel (Munich, Vienna & Basel: Desch, 1961); translated by Paul Selver as *The Pursuer* (London: Heinemann, 1962);

Am Yangtse steht ein Riese auf: Notizbuch aus China (Munich: List, 1961);

Theater in China und Europa (Dortmund: Kulturamt der Stadt Dortmund, 1962);

Der gespaltene Horizont: Niederschriften eines Außenseiters (Munich, Vienna & Basel: Desch, 1964);

Theater, 2 volumes (Munich, Vienna & Basel: Desch, 1964)—comprises volume 1, *Dramatische Balladen* (*Das verlorene Gesicht, Die Neuberin, Ballade vom Eulenspiegel, Fünfzehn Schnüre Geld, Das Glück der Konkubinen*); volume 2, *Stücke und Komödien* (*Die Illegalen, Babel, Drei ehrenwerte Herrn, Zwei Engel Steigen aus*);

Die Clowns von Avignon; Klopfzeichen: Zwei nachgelassene Stücke, edited by Heinz D. Tschörtner (Berlin: Henschel, 1982);

Günther Weisenborn, edited by Tschörtner (Berlin: Neues Leben, 1984).

MOTION PICTURE: *Der 20. Juli*, screenplay by Weisenborn, CCC Studios, 1956.

OTHER: *Die Mutter*, by Weisenborn and Bertolt Brecht, in *Versuche*, volume 7, by Brecht (Berlin: Kiepenheuer, 1933); translated by Lee Baxandall as *The Mother* (New York: Grove, 1965);

Ricarda Huch, *Der lautlose Aufstand: Bericht über die deutsche Widerstandsbewegung des deutschen Volkes 1933-1945*, edited by Weisenborn, Walter Hammer, and Guntram Prüfer (Hamburg: Rowohlt, 1953; revised and enlarged, 1954).

SELECTED PERIODICAL PUBLICATIONS—UNCOLLECTED: "General Kundts 'Grüne Hölle,'" *Die Weltbühne*, 1 (1933): 130-132;

"Rede über die deutsche Widerstandsbewegung: Gehalten im *Berliner Hebbel-Theater* am 11. Mai 1946," *Aufbau*, 1 (1946): 571-578;

"Tod und Hoffnung," *Ost und West*, 1, no. 4 (1947): 29-35;

"In memoriam Karl Heinz Martin," *Aufbau*, 4 (1948): 121-123;

"An die deutschen Dichter im Ausland: Gedächnisrede für Ernst Toller," *Der Autor*, 1 (1947-1948): 1-6;

"Aus einer Rede: Gehalten an der Sorbonne in Paris 1951," *Heute und Morgen* (1952): 578-580;

"Erneuerung des Theaters," *Die Literatur*, 1, no. 5 (1952): 2;

"Von den literarischen Fraktionen," *Welt und Wort*, 7 (1952): 39-40;

"Der Troglodyt und die Kultur," *Neue literarische Welt*, 4, no. 12 (1953): 5;

"Von der Wahrhaftigkeit des Realismus," *Neue Deutsche Literatur*, 3 (1955): 122-126;

"Drei Verfahrensweisen der neuen Dramaturgie," *Neue Deutsche Literatur*, 5, no. 7 (1957): 91-95;

"Gespräch mit Günther Weisenborn," *Sinn und Form*, 20 (1968): 714-725;

"An die Jugend," *Sinn und Form*, 23 (March 1971): 289-295.

Little is known about Günther Weisenborn, whose works were translated into eighteen languages, whose plays were performed in many countries, and whose best-selling novels sold more than one and a half million copies. In spite of these successes during his lifetime, there is little scholarly literature available on him. He is remembered primarily for his play *Die Illegalen* (The Illegal Ones, 1946), which was performed in more than one hundred theaters.

Born in the small city of Velbert in the Rhineland on 10 July 1902, Weisenborn finished high school in Cologne in 1922 and enrolled as a medical student at the University of Bonn. In 1924 his first play, *Ole betrog* (Ole Deceived), was accepted for production, but Weisenborn declined the offer and instead agreed to a one-time dramatic reading. Around this time he switched from medicine to the study of literature and philosophy. In 1927 he received his doctorate. That year the Berlin dramaturge Erwin Piscator offered to produce Weisenborn's second play *Amerikanische Tragödie der sechs Matrosen von S 4* (American Tragedy about Six Sailors of Submarine 4; published, 1928). The play premiered on 16 October 1928 with Heinrich George in the lead role, followed by productions in Stuttgart, Oldenburg, and Bonn. Based on a news report about a collision at sea, the play depicts the horror of six American sailors trapped underwater off the coast of New Jersey. One by one they suffocate while a diver, who had earlier tried to convince the sailors to mutiny and not return to their submarine, attempts to rescue them; the diver, too, perishes. The nationalist press took strong offense at the pacifistic play, while the liberal press hailed it as a courageous, though not very poetic, attack on warmongering. The production of his play prompted Weisenborn to move from Bonn to Berlin. It is not known what brought about his brief interlude in Argentina, where he reportedly worked delivering mail to rural areas on horseback. By 1931 he was back in Berlin as the dramaturge for the production of Bertolt Brecht's play *Die Mutter* (performed, 1932; published, 1933; translated as *The Mother*, 1965).

Weisenborn's next play, *Die Arbeiter von Jersey* (Workers of Jersey), premiered in Coburg on 16 February 1931. As the result of radiation poisoning of workers in a watch factory, Blawk and his girlfriend, Joan, lose their jobs and face the possibility of premature death. The plight of the protagonists is symbolic of the situation of all workers. In a series of rapidly changing scenes the protagonists' consciousness progresses from blind fear to active resistance to the system.

Weisenborn's next play, *Warum lacht Frau Balsam?* (Why Does Mrs. Balsam Laugh?), was banned by Joseph Goebbels, the Nazi minister of propaganda, after its premiere performance in February 1933, and one of his novels was publicly burned in May 1933. Until 1945, Weisenborn's novels and plays would appear in Germany under the pseudonym Christian Munk.

Die Neuberin (Mrs. Neuber; published, 1950) premiered on 24 May 1935 at the Theater am Kurfürstendamm in Berlin with Agnes Staub in the role of Caroline Neuber, the eighteenth-century theatrical innovator; the play ran for 265 performances. Depicting the aesthetic debate between the playwright Gotthold Ephraim Lessing and his contemporary critic Johann Christoph Gottsched, Weisenborn takes Lessing's side that theater should be a forum for ethical issues. Weisenborn, like the enlightened Lessing, appeals to reason and hopes to induce an understanding of political reality in his audience. Neuber says at the end of the play: "Die Mächtigen versuchen alles, um durch das Theater rosa Nebel über das Volk zu werfen und mit Witzgirlanden Tatsachen zu kostümieren " (Those in power always try to distract by portraying our misery through rose-colored glasses. They try to dress up reality with jokes).

In 1935 Weisenborn went to New York, where he worked as a newspaper reporter and wrote the novel *Die Furie* (1937; translated as *The Fury*, 1956). On his return to Berlin in 1937 he met the Luftwaffe (air force) lieutenant Harro Schulze-Boysen, who, together with Arvid Harnack, headed the resistance group Rote Kapelle (Red Band). For the next five years Weisenborn was a senior staff member of the state-controlled German radio and, at the same time, a member of the resistance organization.

On 1 March 1938 Weisenborn's *Die guten Feinde* (The Good Enemies; published, 1947) premiered in Bremen. Its central focus is the rivalry between the physicians Robert Koch and Max von Pettenkofer during the later nineteenth century. Both men are portrayed as dedicated scientists who, in spite of their animosity, respect each other and their work.

Fascist propaganda accelerated with the attack on the Soviet Union in 1941. When he was ordered to write the script for a radio broadcast about the supposed assassination of thirty-two thousand physicians in the Soviet Union, Weisenborn added an additional zero to the already inflated number. German radio was thus exposed as a propaganda machine of the worst type. This time Weisenborn got away with this "clerical error." Also in 1941, on the recommendation of the popular actor Heinrich George, Weisenborn became the chief dramaturge at the Schiller-Theater in Berlin. The same year his novel *Mädchen von Fanö* (Girl from Fanö, 1935) was made into a popular motion picture starring Paul Wegener, Brigitte Horney, and Gustav Knuth. Things were going well for Weisenborn. But in 1942 he and his wife were arrested by the Gestapo. Joy Weisenborn was soon released, but Weisenborn was imprisoned in Spandau and then in Moabit. In sharp contrast to the fate of others from the Rote Kapelle, his death sentence was commuted to life imprisonment.

It was during his years in prison that Weisenborn sketched the first scenes of *Die Illegalen*. The play was first performed at the venerable Hebbel-Theater in Berlin on 21 March 1946. Franz Reichert, who had also directed *Die guten Feinde*, was in charge of the production. Appearing ten months after the end of World War II, this play was the first work about the German resistance to be presented onstage. In the program notes Weisenborn said: "Es sitzen hier im Zuschauerraum mutige und gleichgültige Menschen, Flüchtlinge, Heimgekehrte, frühere Hochverräter und heimliche Nazis, wohlwollende Bürger und junge sehnsüchtige Menschen. Es sitzen hier die Witwen des Faschismus neben denen, die guten Willens sind, es sitzen die Übeltäter neben den verzweifelten, die Ermüdeten neben den Hoffnungsbereiten" (Among the audience there are courageous and indifferent people; refugees, returnees from the front, former traitors and secret Nazis; indifferent bourgeois and young hopeful people. There are widows of fascism sitting next to people of good will, villains next to desperate people, those who are exhausted and those who still have hope).

Weisenborn intended the play as a monument for those who perished under fascism. Bulle, a member of a resistance group, is arrested when the Gestapo finds his daughter and has her identify her father by presenting him with a flower. Before he is taken away, Bulle tells her never to forget that her father died for freedom. Walter, another member of the group, lost his father during a strike in Hamburg when he

was a child; his mother does not want him to become friends with Lill, who, she believes, is too involved in politics. "Denk dran, wer die Welt verbessern will, der endet im Schauhaus" (Mark my words, he who wants to change the world will wind up in a mortuary), she says. "Oder in einer besseren Welt" (Or in a better world), Walter replies. Unbeknownst to each other, Walter and Lill belong to the same resistance group: he is in charge of radio broadcasts, and she distributes leaflets. When they discover the truth, they are both relieved and alarmed: personal relationships among group members are discouraged for fear they might endanger one another. Their moments of shared love and tenderness are all too brief: Walter is arrested while transmitting a radio broadcast; to avoid the possibility that he will disclose anything about Lill under torture, he stages an escape attempt and forces the Gestapo to shoot him.

After the war Weisenborn received many honors, and his plays were performed throughout Europe. In 1947 Weisenborn went to Zurich; there he met with Brecht, who had just returned from exile in the United States. While he was in Switzerland, Weisenborn's play *Babel* (published, 1964) premiered in Constance. Set in South America, *Babel* depicts the fierce competition between the fabulously rich "beef-boss" Gamboa and the equally wealthy "wheat kings." Gamboa engages in blackmail, fraud, sabotage, and extortion to eliminate his competitors. His relentless struggle for power seems overstated and unrealistic, and *Babel* had a short theatrical life in postwar Germany.

In *Ballade vom Eulenspiegel, vom Federle und von der dicken Pompanne* (Ballad of Eulenspiegel, of Federle, and of Fat Pompanne, 1949) Eulenspiegel, the wise fool, seeks to raise the consciousness of the early sixteenth-century peasants who, by their disunity, ignorance, and opportunism, lose the battle against powerful feudal lords. The play bursts with witty puns, clever jokes, and surprising twists whereby old proverbs yield new meanings.

Drei ehrenwerte Herren (Three Honorable Gentlemen; performed, 1951; published, 1953) reflects on how quickly the possibilities for change in Germany were lost after World War II. The play deals with a practice that was often employed right after the war: rather than have former Nazis remain in charge, former political prisoners and anti-fascists were entrusted with public offices. A town that is still headed by Nazi support-

Heinrich Cornway as Gamboa in the closing scene of the premiere of Weisenborn's Babel *in Constance in 1947 (photograph by Tschira)*

ers and collaborators is waiting for a former prisoner to arrive and become mayor. Three petty criminals arrive first, and one of them is mistaken for the prospective mayor. The three take charge of the city and its treasury, and during their brief tenure they enact laws promising leniency toward the former Nazis. By the time the real mayor arrives, the old order is back in power.

During the early 1950s the issues that concerned Weisenborn were no longer in fashion; audiences did not want to see plays about fascism. It was not until a decade later that writers such as Rolf Hochhuth and Peter Weiss would have success with plays about the Holocaust.

Consequently, Weisenborn stayed away from this topic in his next plays. His science-fiction comedy *Zwei Engel steigen aus* (Two Angels Descending; performed, 1955; published, 1964) deals with two young female researchers from another planet who land on earth to study its inhabitants. Concluding that the male earthlings are "starke und dumme Troglodyten" (strong and dumb troglodytes) who possess the reasoning capacity of six-year-olds, they return to their own, more civil-

ized world. The play was performed across Germany and in other countries, including Japan.

Weisenborn's *Das verlorene Gesicht* (published, 1956; translated as *The Man without a Face*, 1969) is set in the eighteenth century. The protagonist was kidnapped as a child, and his face was mutilated so he could become a gruesome circus attraction. When he discovers that he is the heir of a rich British aristocrat, he takes revenge on the circus director and leaves his sleazy world. But he is unable to break out of the environment he has known all his life, and he returns to the circus.

After this play, Weisenborn's fame as a playwright waned. Except for the production of his adaptation from the Chinese, *Fünfzehn Schnüre Geld* (Fifteen Strands of Money; published, 1959) in Hamburg in 1959, most of his last plays were unperformed. But his *Walküre—44* (Valkyrie—44) had a positive reception on 16 February 1966 in Berlin. It is a debate in dialogue form about the extent of the German resistance to Nazism: Weisenborn insists that the resistance encompassed all social classes and included more than eight hundred thousand people, of whom more than five hundred thousand were murdered by the Nazis.

Today Weisenborn is virtually unknown; few of his plays have been performed since his death on 26 March 1969, and his novels have practically disappeared. He was not an experimental playwright and did not use nontraditional dramatic techniques. It is likely that his plays will be viewed primarily as documents of the inanities and horrors of Nazism.

Letters:
Einmal laß mich traurig sein: Briefe, Lieder, Kassiber 1942-1943, edited by Joy Weisenborn (Zurich: Arche, 1984).

Bibliography:
Ingeborg Drewitz and Walther Huder, eds., *Günther Weisenborn* (Hamburg: Christians, 1985).

References:
Wilfried Barner, "Über das Nichtvergessen: Günther Weisenborns *Memorial*," in *Exile and Enlightenment. Studies in German and Comparative Literature in Honor of Guy Stern*, edited by Uwe Faulhaber and others (Detroit: Wayne State University Press, 1987), pp. 141-152;

Günther Birkenfeld, "Zur Uraufführung des Schauspiels *Die Illegalen*," *Horizont*, 1, no. 10 (1946): 26;

Ilse Brauer, *Günther Weisenborn* (Hamburg: Christians, 1971);

Detlef Foerster, "Wiederentdeckter Weisenborn: *Die Illegalen* in Rostock und *Die Clowns von Avignon* in Dresden," *Theater der Zeit*, 40, no. 7 (1985): 18-19;

Egbert Höhl, "Die Wiederentdeckung des Menschen: Zu der Berliner und Mannheimer Aufführung von Günther Weisenborns *Das verlorene Gesicht*," *Geist und Zeit*, 1, no. 4 (1956): 150-153;

Walther Huder, "Partisan der Menschlichkeit: Über Günther Weisenborn," *Welt und Wort*, 25 (1970): 45-46;

Walter Pollatschek, "Aufführungsprobleme einer Neuinszenierung. Günther Weisenborns *Die Illegalen* an den Berliner Kammerspielen," *Theater der Zeit*, 16, no. 6 (1961): 15-17;

Marcel Reich-Ranicki, "Günther Weisenborn: *Der Verfolger*," in his *Deutsche Literatur in West und Ost: Prosa seit 1945* (Munich: Piper, 1963), pp. 294-298;

Gerhard Rupp, "Zweiter Weltkrieg im Drama," in *Deutsche Dramen*, edited by Harro Müller-Michaels (Königsstein: Athenäum, 1981), pp. 85-111;

Josef-Hermann Sauter, "Gespräch mit Günther Weisenborn," in his *Interviews mit Schriftstellern* (Leipzig: Reclam, 1982), pp. 69-82;

Hansjoerg Schneider, "Die theatralische Praxis Günther Weisenborns," *Sinn und Form*, 20 (1968): 1508-1516;

Gody Suter, "Weisenborn ad portas! Zu zwei Gegenwartsromanen," *Der Monat*, 9 (January 1957): 73-77;

Gerhard Weissbach, "Günther Weisenborns 'Dramatische Balladen,'" *Aufbau*, 12 (1956): 469-471;

Gertraude Wilhelm, "Günther Weisenborn," in *Handbuch der deutschen Gegenwartsliteratur*, edited by Hermann Kunisch (Munich: Nymphenburger Verlagsanstalt, 1965), pp. 611-612.

Peter Weiss
(8 November 1916 - 10 May 1982)

Ehrhard Bahr
University of California, Los Angeles

See also the Weiss entry in *DLB 69: Contemporary German Fiction Writers, First Series.*

PLAY PRODUCTIONS: *Der Turm*, Stockholm, Studio Stage Stockholm, 1949;

Nacht mit Gästen, Berlin, Schillertheater, 16 November 1963;

Die Verfolgung und Ermordung Jean-Paul Marats, dargestellt durch die Schauspielgruppe des Hospizes zu Charenton unter Anleitung des Herrn de Sade, Berlin, Schillertheater, 29 April 1964;

Die Ermittlung, Berlin (West), Freie Volksbühne; Berlin (East), Deutsche Akademie der Künste, 19 October 1965;

Sangen om Skrapuken, Stockholm, Scala Theater, 26 January 1967; translated from Swedish into German as *Gesang vom lusitanischen Popanz*, Berlin, Schaubühne am Halleschen Ufer, 6 October 1967;

Viet Nam-Diskurs, Frankfurt am Main, Städtische Bühnen, 20 March 1968;

Wie dem Herrn Mockinpott das Leiden ausgetrieben wird, Hannover, Landestheater, 16 May 1968;

Trotzki im Exil, Düsseldorf, Schauspielhaus, 20 January 1970;

Die Versicherung, Essen, Städtische Bühnen, 6 April 1971;

Hölderlin, Stuttgart, Württembergisches Stadttheater, 18 September 1971;

Der Prozeß, Bremen, Theater Bremen; Krefeld, Theater Krefeld, 28 May 1975;

Der neue Prozeß, Stockholm, Kuningl. Dramatiska Teatern, 12 March 1982.

BOOKS: *Från ö till ö* (Stockholm: Bonnier, 1947); translated from Swedish into German by Heiner Gimmler as *Von Insel zu Insel* (Berlin: Frölich & Kaufmann, 1984);

De besegrade (Stockholm, 1948); translated from Swedish into German by Beat Marzenauer as *Die Besiegten* (Frankfurt am Main: Suhrkamp, 1985);

Dokument I (Stockholm, 1949);

Peter Weiss in 1980 (photograph by Isolde Ohlbaum)

Duellen (Stockholm: Tryckeri Björkmans, 1953); translated from Swedish into German by J. C. Görsch as *Das Duell* (Frankfurt am Main: Suhrkamp, 1960);

Avantgardefilm (Stockholm: Wahrström & Widstrand, 1956);

Der Schatten des Körpers des Kutschers (Frankfurt am Main: Suhrkamp, 1960); translated by E. B. Garside and Rosemarie Waldrop as "The Shadow of the Coachman's Body," in *Bodies and Shadows: Two Short Novels* (New York: Delacorte, 1969); translated by S. M. Cupitt as "The Shadow of the Coachman's Body," in *The Conversation of the Three Walkers; and, The Shadow of the Coachman's Body* (London: Calder & Boyars, 1972);

Abschied von den Eltern: Erzählung (Frankfurt am Main: Suhrkamp, 1961); translated by Christopher Levenson as *The Leavetaking* (New York: Harcourt, Brace & World, 1962); translation republished in *Leavetaking; Vanishing Point* (London: Calder & Boyars, 1966);

Fluchtpunkt: Roman (Frankfurt am Main: Suhrkamp, 1962); translated by Levenson as "Vanishing Point," in *Leavetaking; Vanishing Point*;

Das Gespräch der drei Gehenden (Frankfurt am Main: Suhrkamp, 1963); translated by Garside and Waldrop as "Conversation of the Three Wayfarers," in *Bodies and Shadows: Two Short Novels*; translated by Cupitt as "The Conversation of the Three Walkers," in *The Conversation of the Three Walkers; and, The Shadow of the Coachman's Body*;

Die Verfolgung und Ermordung Jean Paul Marats, dargestellt durch die Schauspielgruppe des Hospizes zu Charenton unter Anleitung des Herrn de Sade: Drama in zwei Akten (Frankfurt am Main: Suhrkamp, 1964; revised, 1966); edited by Volkmar Sander (New York: Harcourt, Brace & World, 1968); translated by Geoffrey Skelton and adapted into verse by Adrian Mitchell as *The Persecution and Assassination of Jean-Paul Marat as Performed by the Inmates of the Asylum of Charenton under the Direction of the Marquis de Sade* (New York: Atheneum, 1965; London: Calder, 1965);

Die Ermittlung: Oratorium in 11 Gesängen (Frankfurt am Main: Suhrkamp, 1965); translated by Alexander Gross as *The Investigation: Oratorio in 11 Cantos* (London: Calder & Boyars, 1966); translated by Jon Swan and Ulu Grosbard as *The Investigation: A Play* (New York: Atheneum, 1966);

Nacht mit Gästen: Eine Moritat (Wiesbaden: Offizin Parvus, 1966); republished with *Wie dem Herrn Mockinpott das Leiden ausgetrieben wird* as *Nacht mit Gästen; Wie dem Herrn Mockinpott das Leiden ausgetrieben wird: Zwei Stücke* (Frankfurt am Main: Suhrkamp, 1969);

Sången om Skråpuken (Stockholm: Seelig, 1967); German version published as *Gesang vom lusitanischen Popanz: Stück mit Musik in zwei Akten* (Berlin: Rütten & Loening, 1968); translated by Lee Baxandall as *Song of the Lusitanian Bogey*, in *Two Plays* (New York: Atheneum, 1970);

Vietnam (Berlin: Voltaire, 1967);

Diskurs über die Vorgeschichte und den Verlauf des lang andauernden Befreiungskrieges in Viet Nam als Beispiel für die Notwendigkeit des bewaffneten Kampfes der Unterdrückten gegen ihre Unterdrücker, sowie über die Versuche der Vereinigten Staaten von Amerika die Grundlagen der Revolution zu vernichten (Frankfurt am Main: Suhrkamp, 1967); translated by Skelton as *Discourse on the Progress of the Prolonged War of Liberation in Vietnam and the Events Leading up to It as Illustration of the Necessity for Armed Resistance against Oppression and on the Attempts of the United States of America to Destroy the Foundations of Revolution*, in *Two Plays*; translation republished as *Discourse on Vietnam* (London: Calder & Boyars, 1970);

Der Turm (Stuttgart: Reclam, 1968); translated by Michael Benedikt and Michael Heine as *The Tower*, in *Postwar German Theatre: An Anthology of Plays*, edited by Benedikt and George E. Wellwarth (New York: Dutton, 1967), pp. 316-348;

Notizen zum kulturellen Leben in der Demokratischen Republik Viet Nam (Frankfurt am Main: Suhrkamp, 1968); translated as *Notes on the Cultural Life of the Democratic Republic of Vietnam* (London: Calder & Boyars, 1970; New York: Dell, 1970);

Rapporte, 2 volumes (Frankfurt am Main: Suhrkamp, 1968, 1971);

Dramen, 2 volumes (Frankfurt am Main: Suhrkamp, 1968)—comprises in volume 1, *Der Turm, Die Versicherung, Nacht Mit Gästen, Wie dem Herrn Mockinpott das Leiden ausgetrieben wird, Marat/Sade*; in volume 2, *Die Ermittlung, Lusitanischer Popanz, Viet Nam Diskurs*;

Berichte über die Angriffe der US-Luftwaffe und -Marine gegen die Demokratische Republik Viet Nam, nach der Erklärung Präsident Johnsons über die "begrenzte Bombardierung" am 31. März 1968, by Weiss and Gunilla Palmstierna-Weiss (Frankfurt am Main: Edition Voltaire, 1968); translated by Anna Björkwall and Davis Jones as "*Limited Bombing*" in Vietnam: *Report on the Attacks against the Democratic Republic of Vietnam by the U.S. Air Force and the Seventh Fleet, after the Declaration of "Limited Bombing" by President Lyndon B. Johnson on March 31, 1968* (London: Bertrand Russell Peace Foundation, 1969);

Trotzki im Exil: Stück in zwei Akten (Frankfurt am Main: Suhrkamp, 1970); translated by Skelton as *Trotsky in Exile* (London: Methuen, 1971; New York: Atheneum, 1972);

Hölderlin: Stück in zwei Akten (Frankfurt am Main: Suhrkamp, 1971);

American Presence in South East Asia (Singapore: Island Publishers, 1971);

Die Ästhetik des Widerstands: Roman, 3 volumes (Frankfurt am Main: Suhrkamp, 1975-1981);

Stücke, 3 volumes (Frankfurt am Main: Suhrkamp, 1976-1977);

Aufsätze, Journale, Arbeitspunkte: Schriften zu Kunst und Literatur, edited by Manfred Haiduk (Berlin: Henschel, 1979);

Notizbücher: 1971-1980, 2 volumes (Frankfurt am Main: Suhrkamp, 1981);

Notizbücher: 1960-1971, 2 volumes (Frankfurt am Main: Suhrkamp, 1982);

Der Maler Peter Weiss: Bilder, Zeichnungen, Collagen, Filme, edited by Peter Spielmann (Berlin: Frölich & Kaufmann, 1982);

Peter Weiss: Malerei, Zeichnungen, Collagen, edited by Raimund Hoffmann (Berlin: Henschel, 1984);

Der neue Prozeß: Stück in drei Akten (Frankfurt am Main: Suhrkamp, 1984);

Peter Weiss im Gespräch, edited by Rainer Gerlach and Matthias Richter (Frankfurt am Main: Suhrkamp, 1984);

In Gegensätzen denken: Ein Lesebuch, edited by Gerlach and Richter (Frankfurt am Main: Suhrkamp, 1988).

OTHER: August Strindberg, *Ein Traumspiel*, translated by Weiss (Frankfurt am Main: Suhrkamp, 1963);

Die Versicherung, in *Deutsches Theater der Gegenwart I*, edited by Karlheinz Braun (Frankfurt am Main: Suhrkamp, 1967), pp. 83-146;

Russeltribunalen, edited by Weiss and Peter Limqueco (Stockholm: PAN/Norstedt, 1968); translated as *Prevent the Crime of Silence: Reports from the Sessions of the International War Crimes Tribunal Founded by Bertrand Russell, London, Stockholm, Roskilde* (London: Lane, 1971);

Hermann Hesse, *Kindheit des Zauberers: Eine Autobiographie*, foreword and illustrations by Weiss (Leipzig: Insel, 1974);

Franz Kafka, *Der Prozeß: Stück in zwei Akten*, adapted by Weiss (Frankfurt am Main: Suhrkamp, 1974);

Drei Stücke, translated by Weiss (Frankfurt am Main: Suhrkamp, 1981).

Peter Weiss's play *Die Verfolgung und Ermordung Jean-Paul Marats, dargestellt durch die Schauspielgruppe des Hospizes zu Charenton unter Anleitung des Herrn de Sade* (1964; translated as *The Persecution and Assassination of Jean-Paul Marat as Performed by the Inmates of the Asylum of Charenton under the Direction of the Marquis de Sade*, 1965), generally known as *Marat/Sade*, was the most innovative political drama since the advent of Bertolt Brecht's theater. For the next decade Weiss was the most respected playwright working in the German language.

Weiss was born in Nowawes (today Neubabelsberg), an upper-class suburb of Berlin, on 8 November 1916. In 1918 the family moved to Bremen. Weiss's father, Eugen Weiss, a Czech textile manufacturer, had converted from Judaism to Protestantism; his mother, Frieda Hummel Weiss, was a gentile born in Switzerland and had been an actress before her marriage. The children were raised as Lutherans. In 1929 the family returned to Berlin, where Weiss attended a prestigious gymnasium. In 1933 he transferred to a trade school to learn typing and shorthand. The family immigrated to London in 1934 and to Czechoslovakia in 1936. In 1937 Weiss enrolled at the Academy of Art in Prague, where he was awarded a first prize for one of his paintings. He escaped to Switzerland when German troops occupied the Sudetenland in October 1938. In Switzerland he met Hermann Hesse, who encouraged his painting and writing.

In 1939 Weiss moved to Sweden, where his family had found refuge from the Nazis and his father operated a small textile mill near Göteborg. Weiss worked at the plant as a fabric designer until 1942, then took odd jobs as a lumberjack and farm laborer. In 1944 he married Helga Henschen, a Swedish painter, with whom he had a daughter. In 1945 Weiss became a Swedish citizen. In 1947 Weiss and his wife were divorced. That year he briefly returned to Berlin on an assignment for the newspaper *Stockholms Tidningen* to report on the divided city.

In Weiss's first play, *Der Turm* (performed, 1949; published, 1968; translated as *The Tower*, 1967), the protagonist returns under the name Niente (Nothing) to a society dominated by the Tower. Although he escaped from the Tower into the real world, he has not been able to liberate himself; but his return to the Tower effects his liberation. This existentialist parable presents the individual's isolation in a hostile universe, emphasizing his freedom of choice and responsibility for the consequences of his act. Employed as an escape artist by the circus troupe representing the society of the Tower, Niente is reborn as Pablo. When he liberates himself from a rope that binds him, the Tower disappears.

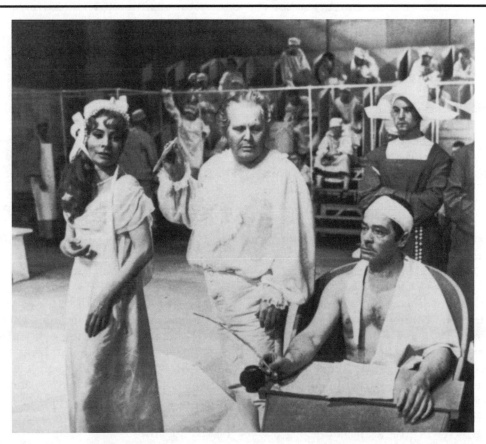

Lieselotte Rau, Ernst Schröder, and Peter Mosbacher in a scene from the premiere of Weiss's Marat / Sade *at the Schillertheater, Berlin, in 1964 (photograph by Harry Croner)*

Die Versicherung (Insurance; published, 1967; performed, 1971), written in 1952, was influenced by German expressionism, Dada, and French surrealism. It is a multimedia production in which film footage runs parallel to the stage performance; action begun by the actors is continued on film, interspersed with commercials and documentary footage of street riots and natural disasters. The play shows the absurdity of bourgeois society's attempts to protect itself by taking out insurance policies against external catastrophes. The breakdown of family relationships, sexual anarchy, experiments with human vivisection, and mass kidnappings trigger a revolution. But the revolution, led by the idle son of a bourgeois family, does not bring change for the better. There is no insurance against anarchy and violence in capitalist society, according to Weiss.

During the 1950s and early 1960s Weiss supervised adult education classes in art and film theory at the University of Stockholm and taught painting as a form of therapy at a prison. Between 1952 and 1960 he made short documentary films and some experimental films that show

the influence of surrealism. His autobiographical novels *Abschied von den Eltern* (Departure from the Parents, 1961; translated as *The Leavetaking*, 1962) and *Fluchtpunkt* (1962; translated as "Vanishing Point," 1966) established him as a writer, and he was invited to the gatherings of the Gruppe (Group) 47, an association of progressive German writers. It was at a meeting of the Gruppe 47 that he presented a recitation of *Marat/Sade*, the drama that would make him internationally famous. The last play of Weiss's early period, *Nacht mit Gästen* (Night with Guests; performed, 1963; published, 1966), employs techniques of the Punch-and-Judy show and Kabuki Theater; it is a one-act play in doggerel verse. While a robber holds his wife and two children as hostages, the husband digs up a chest of gold to ransom his family. A neighbor mistakes the husband for the robber and kills him, the robber stabs the wife to death, and the robber and the neighbor kill each other over the chest of gold. The children discover that the chest contains nothing but turnips.

In 1964 Weiss married Gunilla Palmstierna, a divorced artist and costume designer with two children. She became his collaborator and stage and costume designer for most of his plays.

In *Marat/Sade* Weiss created a type of political drama that was to dominate the stage of the 1960s and 1970s. It was a combination of Antonin Artaud's theater of cruelty, Brecht's epic theater, and the theater of the absurd of Samuel Beckett and Jean Genet.

Marat/Sade is a play within a play, taking place on three levels of time and reality: the murder of Marat by Charlotte Corday in 1793; the depiction of this event in 1808 by the inmates of the insane asylum at Charenton in a performance directed by the Marquis de Sade; and the present-day theatrical presentation of this production, in which the modern audience is addressed with allusions to parallels between the Napoleonic empire and Germany after Adolf Hitler. Sade was, in fact, confined to the asylum at Charenton from 1801 to 1814, and he did direct amateur theatrical productions among the patients for therapeutic purposes; these productions were attended by members of upper-class Parisian society. Marat and Sade never met, but Sade delivered the eulogy at Marat's funeral.

The play revolves around the conflicting positions of Marat and Sade: Marat stands for social change through revolution, while Sade upholds an individualism carried to extremes and claims that human nature never changes. Marat's speeches in the play are authentic quotations from his writings. Weiss thought that Marat's image had been distorted by bourgeois historians because his ideas anticipated Marxism. The figures in the play within the play are represented by mentally ill characters, and their mental illness enables them to speak socially unacceptable truths. When the performance gets out of hand and the inmates begin shouting "Revolution Revolution Copulation Copulation," they are driven back into their cells by the nurses with extreme violence and brutality. The failure of the therapy supports Sade's nihilistic point of view. The complexities of the lesson offered made *Marat/Sade* a milestone in the development of political theater during the 1960s.

There were three seminal productions of the play: the first was the premiere, directed by Konrad Swinarski at the Schillertheater in West Berlin in 1964; the second was directed by Peter Brook with the Royal Shakespeare Company at the Aldwych Theatre in London; the third was directed by Anselm Perten at Rostock, East Germany, in 1965. While Swinarski—who also directed the 1967 film version of the play—favored Sade's point of view, the East German production in 1965 portrayed Marat as the hero and Sade as a decadent libertine. Although this interpretation is not supported by the text, Weiss later declared that any production of his play in which Marat does not emerge as the winner will be mistaken.

In 1964 Weiss attended the trial in Frankfurt am Main of twenty-two former Auschwitz guards for crimes, committed by them or under their supervision, in the infamous German extermination camp in Poland. The trial formed the basis of his next play, *Die Ermittlung: Oratorium in 11 Gesängen* (1965; translated as *The Investigation: Oratorio in 11 Cantos*, 1966). Produced simultaneously in East and West Berlin, *Die Ermittlung* was the first drama to address itself exclusively to the Holocaust. The play includes some of the actual testimony of the witnesses and of the accused at the trial. No attempt is made to present Auschwitz visually on the stage, but its terror is present in the minds of the nine anonymous witnesses for the prosecution, who condense the evidence given by the more than three hundred witnesses at the actual trial. The twenty-two defendants are reduced to eighteen characters who bear the names of the real guards. The accused claim that they were only following orders and that Germans should concern themselves with other things. The verdict is not part of the drama but is left to the audience.

Weiss criticized Portuguese colonialism in Africa in *Gesang vom lusitanischen Popanz: Stück mit Musik in zwei Akten* (performed, 1967; published, 1968; translated as *Song of the Lusitanian Bogey*, 1970) and American involvement in Vietnam in *Diskurs über die Vorgeschichte und den Verlauf des lang andauernden Befreiungskrieges in Viet Nam als Beispiel für die Notwendigkeit des bewaffneten Kampfes der Unterdrückten gegen ihre Unterdrücker, sowie über die Versuche der Vereinigten Staaten von Amerika die Grundlagen der Revolution zu vernichten* (published, 1967; performed as *Viet Nam-Diskurs*, 1968; translated as *Discourse on the Progress of the Prolonged War of Liberation in Vietnam and the Events Leading up to It as Illustration of the Necessity for Armed Resistance against Oppression and on the Attempts of the United States of America to Destroy the Foundations of Revolution*, 1970). *Gesang vom Lusianischen Popanz*, which was originally performed and published in Stockholm as *Sangen om Skrapuken*, uses song, dance, and pantomime to dramatize the involvement of international banks

Weiss (second from left) at a rehearsal for the premiere of his play Die Ermittlung *at the Freie Volksbühne, Berlin, in 1965 with (left to right) the composer Luigi Nono, the director Erwin Piscator, and the set designer Hans-Ulrich Schmückle*

and big business in the brutal suppression of the native uprising in Angola in 1961. The Lusitanian bogey, a symbol of colonial oppression, is toppled at the end of the play, indicating that the liberation from colonialism is near.

The fifteen actors in *Viet Nam-Diskurs* represent historical tendencies and interests, not individuals. The transition from one role to another is effected by a change of a helmet, a shawl, or a piece of jewelry. All figures from the history of Vietnam wear simple black costumes, while the colonialists wear white uniforms. The first part of the play traces the history of Vietnam from 500 B.C. to 1953, the second part from 1954 to 1964. Choreographed movements of the actors indicate geographical and political divisions; in part 2 the action is largely reduced to a chronological sequence of public statements by political figures whose photos are projected onto a screen. The play ends with a chorus stating that the fight will continue.

Weiss did not spare the Soviet system from criticism; in *Trotzki im Exil* (1970; translated as *Trotsky in Exile*, 1971) he takes Stalinism to task. The play was written in celebration of the centennial of Vladimir Ilyich Lenin's birth. Weiss believed that Leon Trotsky's theory of "permanent revolution," for which he was exiled from the Soviet Union and ultimately assassinated, preserved the heritage of Lenin's idea of international revolution. Weiss considered this idea of particular relevance for revolutions in the Third World. The play begins with Trotsky's banishment from the Soviet Union in 1928 and ends with his assassination in Mexico in 1940; there are flashbacks to 1901, 1902, 1903, 1905, 1917, 1921, and 1924. For Weiss, Trotsky is the prototype of the intellectual in exile; Trotsky's writing desk is at the center of all scenes.

Weiss's *Hölderlin* (1971) presents the poet Friedrich Hölderlin as a German Jacobin who escaped into insanity to evade police persecution for his sympathy with the French Revolution.

Richard Münch as Leon Trotsky and Kurt Beck as Lenin in a scene from a 1970 production of Weiss's Trotzki im Exil *at the Landestheater in Hannover (photograph by Kurt Julius)*

Along with Marat and Trotsky, Hölderlin represented for Weiss the prototype of the revolutionary intellectual. The play begins with a student demonstration in support of the French Revolution at the Tübingen Seminary, where Hölderlin studied Protestant theology during the 1790s. The demonstration, reminiscent of the German student movement of the 1960s, is suppressed by the military, and Hölderlin is incarcerated. The next scenes show Hölderlin's progressive alienation as he fails first as a private tutor and then, in the eyes of Johann Wolfgang von Goethe and Friedrich Schiller, as a poet. The second act presents Hölderlin as a revolutionary playwright and finally as a mental patient. Abused by his doctors and wardens, he is haunted by visions of the revolution. In the final scene Hölderlin is visited by Karl Marx. This fictional visit emphasizes the solidarity of all revolutionary writers.

Although *Wie dem Herrn Mockinpott das Leiden ausgetrieben wird* (How Mr. Mockinpott Is Cured of His Sufferings; published, 1969) premiered in 1968, it was written during Weiss's period of dramatic experimentation before 1963. The conventions of the Punch-and-Judy Show,

slapstick comedy, and the theater of the absurd are employed to present the protagonist's self-emancipation from a Kafkaesque predicament. Released from prison, where he was incarcerated for an unknown crime, Mockinpott is driven out of his home by his wife and his former job is denied to him. The government has no explanation for his tribulations. When even God, who appears as a cigar-smoking capitalist, cannot give him a satisfactory answer, Mockinpott realizes that there is no meaning in suffering or any reward for it. He decides to stand on his own feet and to declare his independence.

After a physical breakdown in 1970 due to the disappointing reception of *Trotzki im Exil*, Weiss turned to writing prose. In 1974 he returned to the theater with an adaptation of Franz Kafka's *Der Prozeß* (1925; translated as *The Trial*, 1937). While Weiss's *Der Prozeß* (published, 1974; performed, 1975) was close to the original text of the novel, a second version, titled *Der neue Prozeß* (The New Trial; published, 1984) presents Joseph K. as a victim of modern capitalism: without realizing it, he lends a human face to the ruthless power of capitalism; his humanity is exploited as a cover-up for the machinations of multinational corporations. In March 1982 Weiss and his wife directed *Der neue Prozeß* at the Royal Dramatic Theater in Stockholm; the production was a great success. Weiss died of a heart attack in Stockholm on 10 May 1982. His literary awards included the Charles Veillon Prize in 1963, the Lessing Prize of the city of Hamburg in 1965, the Heinrich Mann Prize of the East German Academy of Arts in 1966, the Carl Albert Anderson Prize in 1967, the Thomas Dehler Prize in 1978, the Prize for Literature of the City of Cologne in 1981, the Prize for Literature of the City of Bremen in 1982, and—posthumously—the Georg Büchner Prize of the German Academy of Language and Literature in 1982.

Like many other modern dramatists, Weiss did not provide a comprehensive theory of drama. He acknowledged that he learned the most from Brecht. Weiss rejected the notion of the theater of the absurd that the world was hopeless and meaningless; he argued in Brechtian fashion that reality could be explained in all its contradictions. Weiss said that the theater stage itself was already an abstraction; naturalistic theater, consequently, was an anachronism. His theater was realistic but never naturalistic.

Biographies:
Otto F. Best, *Peter Weiss* (New York: Ungar, 1976);

Heinrich Vormweg, *Peter Weiss* (Munich: Beck, 1981);

Jochen Vogt, *Peter Weiss mit Selbstzeugnissen und Bilddokumenten dargestellt* (Reinbek: Rowohlt, 1987).

References:
Heinz Ludwig Arnold, ed., *Peter Weiss, text + kritik*, 37 (Munich: Edition text + kritik, 1973; revised, 1982);

Anke Bennholdt-Thomsen and Alfredo Guzzoni, "Peter Weiss' *Marat/Sade* und das Theaterspiel in Charenton," *Zeitschrift für deutsche Philologie*, 102, no. 2 (1983): 221-239;

Otto F. Best, *Peter Weiss: Vom existentialistischen Drama zum marxistischen Welttheater: Eine kritische Bilanz* (Bern: Francke, 1971);

Karlheinz Braun, ed., *Materialien zu Peter Weiss' Marat/Sade* (Frankfurt am Main: Suhrkamp, 1967);

Volker Canaris, ed., *Über Peter Weiss* (Frankfurt am Main: Suhrkamp, 1970);

Peter Demetz, *After the Fires: Recent Writings in the Germanies, Austria, and Switzerland* (New York: Harcourt Brace Jovanovich, 1986), pp. 47-56;

Demetz, *Postwar German Literature: A Critical Introduction* (New York: Schocken, 1970), pp. 125-133;

Manfred Durzak, *Dürrenmatt, Frisch, Weiss: Deutsches Drama der Gegenwart zwischen Kritik und Utopie* (Stuttgart: Reclam, 1972), pp. 243-344;

Roger Ellis, *Peter Weiss in Exile: A Critical Study of His Works*, Theater and Dramatic Studies, no. 37 (Ann Arbor, Mich.: UMI Research Press, 1987);

Donald Freed, "Peter Weiss and the Theatre of the Future," *Drama Survey*, 6 (Fall 1967): 119-171;

Rainer Gerlach, ed., *Peter Weiss* (Frankfurt am Main: Suhrkamp, 1984);

Manfred Haiduk, *Der Dramatiker Peter Weiss* (Berlin: Henschel, 1977);

Karl-Heinz Hartmann, "Peter Weiss: *Die Ermittlung*," in *Deutsche Dramen: Interpretationen von der Aufklärung bis zur Gegenwart*, edited by Harro Müller-Michaels, volume 2 of *Von Hauptmann bis Botho Strauss* (Königstein: Athenäum, 1981), pp. 163-183;

Ian Hilton, *Peter Weiss: A Searching for Affinities* (London: Wolff, 1970);

Wolfgang Kehn, *Von Dante zu Hölderlin: Traditionswahl und Engagement im Werk von Peter Weiss* (Cologne & Vienna: Böhlau, 1975);

Brigitte Keller-Schumacher, *Dialog und Mord: Eine Interpretation des Marat/Sade von Peter Weiss* (Frankfurt am Main: Athenäum, 1973);

Marianne Kesting, "Verbrechen, Wahnsinn und Revolte: Peter Weiss' *Marat/Sade*-Stück und der französische Surrealismus," in *Geschichte als Schauspiel: Deutsche Geschichtsdramen: Interpretationen*, edited by Walter Hinck (Frankfurt am Main: Suhrkamp, 1981), pp. 304-321;

Manfred Kux, "Peter Weiss' *Hölderlin*: Ein dramatischer Versuch, Hölderlin politisch zu verstehen," *Amsterdamer Beiträge zur Neueren Germanistik*, 16 (1983): 225-254;

Ward B. Lewis, "The American Reception of Peter Weiss' *Marat/Sade*," *Maske und Kothurn*, 31, nos. 1-4 (1985): 65-72;

Leslie L. Miller, "Peter Weiss, Marat and Sade: Comments on an Author's Commentary," *Symposium*, 25 (Spring 1971): 39-58;

Fred Müller, *Peter Weiss, drei Dramen: Interpretation* (Munich: Oldenbourg, 1973);

Peter J. Raleigh, "Hölderlin: Peter Weiss' Artist in Revolt," *Colloquia Germanica*, 7 (1973): 193-213;

Erika Salloch, "The Divine Comedy as Model and Anti-model for *The Investigation* by Peter Weiss," *Modern Drama*, 14 (May 1971): 1-12;

Salloch, *Peter Weiss' Ermittlung: Zur Struktur des Dokumentartheaters* (Frankfurt am Main: Athenäum, 1972);

Jürgen E. Schlunk, "Auschwitz and Its Function in Peter Weiss' Search for Identity," *German Studies Review*, 10 (February 1987): 11-30;

Ingeborg Schmitz, *Dokumentartheater bei Peter Weiss: Von der Ermittlung zu Hölderlin* (Frankfurt am Main: Lang, 1981);

Gideon Shunami, "The Mechanism of Revolution in the Documentary Theatre of the Play *Trotzki im Exil* by Peter Weiss," *German Quarterly*, 44 (November 1971): 503-518;

Darko Suvin, "Weiss's *Marat/Sade* and Its Three Main Performance Versions," *Modern Drama*, 31 (September 1988): 395-419;

Gerd Weinreich, *Peter Weiss: Die Ermittlung. Grundlagen und Gedanken zum Verständnis des Dramas* (Frankfurt am Main: Diesterweg, 1983);

John J. White, "History and Cruelty in Peter Weiss's *Marat/Sade*," *Modern Language Review*, 63 (April 1968): 437-448.

Papers:

The papers of Peter Weiss are at the Akademie der Künste (Academy of the Arts) in Berlin.

Franz Werfel
(10 September 1890 - 26 August 1945)

Stephen Shearier
Muhlenberg College

PLAY PRODUCTIONS: *Die Troerinnen*, Berlin, Lessing-Theater, 22 April 1916;

Der Besuch aus dem Elysium, Berlin, Deutsches Theater, 9 June 1918;

Spiegelmensch, Leipzig, Altes Theater; Stuttgart, Württembergisches Landestheater, 15 October 1921;

Bocksgesang, Vienna, Raimund Theater, 10 March 1922;

Schweiger, Prague, Neues Theater, 6 January 1923;

Die Mittagsgöttin, Koblenz, Stadttheater, 1 February 1925;

Juarez und Maximilian, Magdeburg, Stadttheater, 20 April 1925;

Paulus unter den Juden, Bonn, Stadttheater; Breslau, Lobetheater; Düsseldorf, Schauspielhaus Dumont; Cologne, Schauspielhaus; Munich, Prinzregententheater, 30 October 1926;

Das Reich Gottes in Böhmen, Vienna, Burgtheater, 6 December 1930;

The Eternal Road (Der Weg der Verheißung), adapted by William A. Drake, music by Kurt Weill, New York, Manhattan Opera House, 7 January 1937;

In einer Nacht, Vienna, Theater der Josefstadt, 5 October 1937;

Jacobowsky and the Colonel, adapted by S. N. Behrman, New York, Martin Beck Theater, 14 March 1944; German version, *Jacobowsky und der Oberst*, Basel, Stadttheater, 17 October 1944.

BOOKS: *Der Weltfreund: Gedichte* (Berlin: Juncker, 1911);

Wir sind (Leipzig: Wolff, 1913);

Die Versuchung: Ein Gespräch des Dichters mit dem Erzengel und Luzifer (Leipzig: Wolff, 1913);

Einander: Oden, Lieder, Gestalten (Leipzig: Wolff, 1915);

Gesänge aus den drei Reichen: Ausgewählte Gedichte (Leipzig: Wolff, 1917);

Franz Werfel in 1945 (photograph by Trude Geiringer)

Der Gerichtstag: In fünf Büchern (Leipzig: Wolff, 1919);

Der Dschin: Ein Märchen; Gedichte aus Der Gerichtstag; Blasphemie eines Irren; Fragmente (Vienna: Genossenschaftsverlag, 1919);

Die Mittagsgöttin: Ein Zauberspiel (Munich: Wolff, 1919);

Nicht der Mörder, der Ermordete ist schuldig (Munich: Wolff, 1920);

Der Besuch aus dem Elysium: Romantisches Drama in einem Aufzug (Munich: Wolff, 1920);

Spielhof: Eine Phantasie (Munich: Wolff, 1920);

Spiegelmensch: Magische Trilogie (Munich: Wolff, 1920);

Bocksgesang: In fünf Akten (Munich: Wolff, 1921); translated by Ruth Langner as *Goat Song (Bocksgesang): A Drama in Five Acts* (Garden City: Doubleday, Page, 1926);

Arien (Munich: Wolff, 1921);

Schweiger: Ein Trauerspiel in drei Akten (Munich: Wolff, 1922);

Beschwörungen (Munich: Wolff, 1923);

Verdi: Roman der Oper (Vienna: Zsolnay, 1924); translated by Helen Jessiman as *Verdi: A Novel of the Opera* (New York: Simon & Schuster, 1925; London: Jarrolds, 1926);

Juarez und Maximilian: Dramatische Historie in 3 Phasen und 13 Bildern (Vienna: Zsolnay, 1924); translated by Langner as *Juárez and Maximilian: A Dramatic History in Three Phases and Thirteen Pictures* (New York: Simon & Schuster, 1926);

Paulus unter den Juden: Dramatische Legende in sechs Bildern (Vienna: Zsolnay, 1926); translated by Paul P. Levertoff as *Paul among the Jews* (London: Diocesan House, 1928);

Der Tod des Kleinbürgers: Novelle (Vienna: Zsolnay, 1927); translated by Clifton Fadiman and William A. Drake as *The Man Who Conquered Death* (New York: Simon & Schuster, 1927); translation republished as *The Death of a Poor Man* (London: Benn, 1927);

Geheimnis eines Menschen: Novellen (Vienna: Zsolnay, 1927);

Gedichte (Vienna: Zsolnay, 1927);

Neue Gedichte (Vienna: Zsolnay, 1928);

Der Abituriententag: Die Geschichte einer Jugendschuld (Vienna: Zsolnay, 1928); translated by Whittaker Chambers as *Class Reunion* (New York: Simon & Schuster, 1929);

Barbara oder Die Frömmigkeit (Vienna: Zsolnay, 1929); translated by Geoffrey Dunlop as *The Pure in Heart* (New York: Simon & Schuster, 1931); translation republished as *The Hidden Child* (London: Jarrolds, 1931);

Das Reich Gottes in Böhmen: Tragödie eines Führers (Vienna: Zsolnay, 1930);

Die Geschwister von Neapel: Roman (Vienna: Zsolnay, 1931); translated by Dorothy F. Tait-Price as *The Pascarella Family: A Novel* (New York: Simon & Schuster, 1932; London: Jarrolds, 1932);

Kleine Verhältnisse: Novelle (Vienna: Zsolnay, 1931);

Realismus und Innerlichkeit (Vienna: Zsolnay, 1931);

Können wir ohne Gottesglauben leben? (Vienna: Zsolnay, 1932);

Das Geheimnis des Saverio: Novelle (Leipzig: Reclam, 1932);

Die vierzig Tage des Musa Dagh: Roman, 2 volumes (Vienna: Zsolnay, 1933); translated by Dunlop as *The Forty Days of Musa Dagh* (New York: Viking, 1934); translation republished as *The Forty Days* (London: Jarrolds, 1934);

Der Weg der Verheißung: Ein Bibelspiel (Vienna: Zsolnay, 1935); translated by Ludwig Lewisohn as *The Eternal Road: A Drama in Four Parts* (New York: Viking, 1936);

Schlaf und Erwachen: Neue Gedichte (Vienna: Zsolnay, 1935);

Höret die Stimme (Vienna: Zsolnay, 1937); translated by Moray Firth as *Hearken unto the Voice* (New York: Viking, 1938);

In einer Nacht: Ein Schauspiel (Vienna: Zsolnay, 1937);

Von der reinsten Glückseligkeit des Menschen (Stockholm: Bermann-Fischer, 1938);

Gedichte aus dreißig Jahren (Stockholm: Bermann-Fischer, 1939);

Der veruntreute Himmel: Die Geschichte einer Magd (Stockholm: Bermann-Fischer, 1939); translated by Firth as *The Embezzled Heaven* (New York: Viking, 1940; London: Hamilton, 1940);

Eine blaßblaue Frauenschrift (Buenos Aires: Editorial Estrellas, 1941);

Das Lied von Bernadette (Stockholm: Bermann-Fischer, 1941; London: Hamilton, 1941); translated by Lewisohn as *Song of Bernadette* (New York: Viking, 1942; London: Hamilton, 1942);

Die wahre Geschichte vom wiederhergestellten Kreuz (Los Angeles: Pazifische Presse, 1942);

Jacobowsky und der Oberst: Komödie einer Tragödie in drei Akten (Stockholm: Bermann-Fischer, 1944); translated by Gustav O. Arlt as *Jacobowsky and the Colonel: Comedy of a Tragedy in Three Acts* (New York: Viking, 1944); German version, edited by Arlt (New York: Crofts, 1945);

Between Heaven and Earth, translated by Maxim Newmark (New York: Philosophical Library, 1944); German version published as *Zwischen oben und unten* (Stockholm: Bermann-Fischer, 1946);

Poems, translated by Edith Ambercrombie Snow (Princeton: Princeton University Press, 1945);

Stern der Ungeborenen: Ein Reiseroman (Stockholm: Bermann-Fischer, 1946); translated by Arlt as *Star of the Unborn* (New York: Viking, 1946);

Gedichte aus den Jahren 1908-1945, edited by Ernst Gottlieb and Felix Guggenheim (Frankfurt am Main: Fischer, 1946; Los Angeles: Pazifische Presse, 1946);

Gesammelte Werke, edited by Adolf D. Klarmann, 8 volumes (volume 1, Stockholm: Bermann-

Fischer, 1948; volumes 2-7, Frankfurt am Main: Fischer, 1948-1974; volume 8, Munich & Vienna: Langen-Müller, 1975);

Cella oder die Überwinder (Frankfurt am Main: Fischer, 1982); translated by Joachim Neuroschel as *Cella, or, The Survivors* (New York: Holt, 1989);

Das Franz Werfel Buch, edited by Peter Stephan Jungk (Frankfurt am Main: Fischer, 1986).

Edition in English: *Twilight of a World*, translated by H. T. Lowe-Porter (New York: Viking, 1937)—comprises "An Essay Upon the Meaning of Imperial Austria," "Poor People" ("Kleine Verhältnisse"), "Not the Murderer" ("Nicht der Mörder, der Ermordete ist schuldig"), "Estrangement" ("Die Entfremdung"), "The Staircase" ("Die Hoteltreppe"), "Saverio's Secret" ("Geheimnis eines Menschen"), "The House of Mourning" ("Das Trauerhaus"), "The Man Who Conquered Death" ("Der Tod des Kleinbürgers"), "Class Reunion" ("Abituriententag").

TRANSLATIONS: *Die Troerinnen des Euripides* (Leipzig: Wolff, 1915);

Ottokar Brezina: Winde von Mittag nach Mitternacht, (Munich: Wolff, 1920);

Guiseppe Fortunino Francesco Verdi and F. M. Piave, *Simone Boccanegra: Lyrische Tragödie in einem Vorspiel und drei Akten* (Leipzig & New York: Ricordi, 1929);

Verdi and Piave, *Die Macht des Schicksals: Oper in einem Vorspiel und drei Akten* (Mailand: Ricordi, 1950).

OTHER: Vladimir Vasik, *Die schlesischen Lieder des Petr Bezruc*, translated by Rudolf Fuchs, foreword by Werfel (Leipzig: Wolff, 1917);

Guiseppe Fortunino Francesco Verdi, *Briefe*, translated by Paul Stefan, edited by Werfel (Vienna: Zsolnay, 1926); translated by Edward Downes as *Verdi: The Man in His Letters* (New York: Fischer, 1942).

SELECTED PERIODICAL PUBLICATIONS—
UNCOLLECTED: "Die Zukunft der Schule: Eine Entgegnung an Fritz Mauthner," *Berliner Tageblatt*, 27 October 1915, p. 2;

"Die christliche Sendung: Ein offener Brief an Kurt Hiller von Franz Werfel," *Die Neue Rundschau*, 28 (January 1917): 92-105;

"Substantiv und Verbum: Notiz zu einer Poetik," *Aktion*, 7, nos. 1-2 (6 January 1917);

"Die schwarze Messe: Romanfragment," *Genius*, 2 (1920): 255-279;

"Ein Tadelzettel: Entgegnung auf Heinrich Simons 'Steine des Anstoßes in Werfels 'Verdi-Roman,' " *Das Tage-Buch*, 6 (2 May 1925): 639-642;

"Begegnungen mit Rilke," *Das Tage-Buch*, 8, no. 4 (1927): 140-144.

Though scarcely remembered in the United States, where he settled in 1940 and remained until his death in 1945, Franz Werfel was once among the most celebrated European writers in that country. After spawning the expressionist movement with his poetry, Werfel achieved tremendous critical and popular success with his novels and dramas. Admired by readers of German since 1911, his work grew increasingly popular in the United States in the 1930s and 1940s due in part to the burgeoning German-reading exile community, in part to the successful translations of his works, in part to the plays produced in America, and in part to the Hollywood film productions of *Juarez und Maximilian* (published, 1924; performed, 1925; translated as *Juárez and Maximilian*, 1926; filmed, 1938) and *Das Lied von Bernadette* (1941; translated as *Song of Bernadette*, 1942; filmed, 1943). Study of Werfel is warranted by the volume and the former immense popularity of his work. Moreover, anyone interested in drama, prose, or lyric poetry in the German language between 1910 and 1950; in the cross-fertilization of literature and political activism; in the relationship between Judaism and Catholicism; or in questions of religion, culture, aesthetics, and ideology in the Austro-Hungarian Empire will find that Werfel played a central role in all these areas.

The first child of Rudolf Werfel, a glove manufacturer, and Albine Werfel, née Kussi, the daughter of a well-to-do mill owner from Pilsen, Franz Viktor Werfel was born in Prague on 10 September 1890. His Czech nanny, Barbara Simunkova, took him to mass; the young Jewish boy, impressed by the ornateness and solemnity of Catholic services, built altars in his room before which he conducted elaborate ceremonies. This early fascination with the spectacle of the Mass foreshadows his later predilection for theater.

Like many Jewish boys in Prague, Werfel was sent to a school run by the Piarists, an education-oriented Catholic order. Though sickly and a poor pupil, he graduated to the Deutsches

Gymnasium am Graben in 1900. An abysmally poor pupil there also, he was transferred to the Stefansgymnasium. His difficulties in school nothwithstanding, Werfel possessed a voracious appetite for literature and a remarkable memory for musical scores. His love of Karl May's adventure stories would find resonance in several of his dramatic works, and during his later years at the gymnasium he made a name for himself among the denizens of the cabarets with his passionate and unerring recitations of his own lyric poetry and his astoundingly precise recollection of Giuseppe Verdi's arias.

Werfel's problems in school may have served as a boon to his literary creativity. As early as 1904 he began to compose poems for Marianne Glaser, his boyhood love. In 1908, when his pattern of absence from the seventh class began in earnest due to his routine visits to Prague pubs, his first published poem, "Die Gärten der Stadt" (Gardens of the City), appeared in the Viennese daily *Die Zeit* (Time).

Between 1908 and 1912, when he was regularly in the Cafe Arco in Prague with Willy Haas, Ernst Deutsch, Max Brod, Franz Kafka, Johannes Urdizil, and Paul Kornfeld, Werfel conceived an impressive series of poems that, thanks to the encouragement of Haas and Brod, was published in 1911 under the title *Der Weltfreund* (The World Friend). When selections from this volume were reproduced in Karl Kraus's popular journal *Die Fackel* (The Torch), the twenty-one-year-old Werfel's literary career was launched.

During this period Werfel composed his first play, *Der Besuch aus dem Elysium* (The Visit from Elysium; performed, 1918; published, 1920). Consisting of a prologue and one act in prose, the drama was inspired by Werfel's unrequited love for Glaser. One rainy afternoon Hedwig, the wife of a Baurat (member of the Board of Works), is visited by Lukas, who has been presumed dead. Lukas declares his undying love for Hedwig but maintains that by spurning him she motivated him to do great things. The Baurat returns and invites Lukas to stay for dinner. Lukas declines, claiming that he must return to the asphodel fields in Elysium. The content of Werfel's drama, particularly Lukas's despondency and the ways in which he is perceived by others, is typically impressionist; the form, though in some ways conventional, demonstrates Werfel's affinity with certain tenets of expressionist aesthetics.

Written in 1910, *Der Besuch aus dem Elysium* premiered on 9 June 1918 at the Deutsches Theater in Berlin. The director, Heinz Herald, and the set designer, Ernst Stern, faithful to Werfel's incipient expressionist aesthetics, employed stage lighting to establish a milieu situated between dream and reality. There were only two performances in the initial run, but *Der Besuch aus dem Elysium* would be performed at many German theaters by 1945. Not as successful as his later efforts and today virtually forgotten, Werfel's first play is interesting for historians of drama as a link between impressionism and expressionism.

When his father insisted on business training in Hamburg, Werfel responded by flushing valuable company records down the toilet. Forced to return to Prague, he was persuaded by his father to enter the army in 1911. Werfel's commitment to the military was less than completely sincere, and he spent time in custody for pranks and other misdemeanors. The longer his service, the more resolute grew his rejection of established power structures.

After his military training Werfel relocated in December 1912 to Leipzig, where his afternoons were spent in Wilhelms Weinstube with Carl Sternheim, Frank Wedekind, Martin Buber, Kurt Hiller, Else Lasker-Schüler, and Walter Hasenclever. Werfel began to promote his friends' works in 1913 when he and Kurt Wolff founded *Der jüngste Tag* (The Judgment Day); this journal, whose title was taken from one of Werfel's compositions, was to become one of the most important organs of early literary expressionism.

In October 1913 Jakob Hegner, the founder of the Hellau festival theater, suggested that Werfel direct his poetic talents to dramaturgy. Since, like Werfel, Hegner was a Jew interested in Christian themes, he drew Werfel's attention to Euripides, whom he considered to be a forerunner of Christianity. Werfel took up Hegner's suggestion and labored for nearly a year translating and reworking Euripides' *The Trojan Women* as *Die Troerinnen* (published, 1915; performed, 1916).

Werfel notes in his foreword that Troy's collapse stands as a metaphor for the present. The action takes place in "der ewigen Dämmerung" (the eternal twilight), which is interrupted by the horrifying dawn of Troy burning. The stage is divided into two levels connected by a slope. The lower stage, the locus of the tragedy, represents the camp where prisoners of war are kept. The upper stage represents the castle of Troy, where the prologue takes place among gods so oversized that they appear to have the castle at their feet. The play, consisting of eleven scenes in iambic pentameter, was directed by Viktor Barnowsky with set designs by Erich Klossowsky when it premiered on 22 April 1916 at the Lessing-Theater in Berlin; it ran for 14 performances. The first of Werfel's works to be produced onstage, *Die Troerinnen*, made a huge impact during and immediately after World War I. In addition to the initial run, it was performed 73 times through November 1922 and 207 times by 1953. Paul Goldmann, a critic for *Die Neue Freie Presse* (The New Free Press), wrote in his review of 11 May 1916 that Werfel had improved on Euripedes by giving Hecuba the life-affirming closing statement.

At the outset of the war Werfel was pressed into military service. Convincing his superiors that he had both physical and psychological problems, Werfel was assigned to office duty behind the lines and continued his literary activity unabated.

In 1915 Werfel seriously injured his legs by jumping from a cable car. Whether he intended to commit suicide remains an open question, but he rendered himself unsuitable for military service and met Gertrud Spirk, a military nurse who became his first great love since Glaser.

Werfel spent the last years of the war in Vienna working in the War Press Office and frequenting the Cafe Central with Egon Erwin Kisch, Peter Altenberg, Robert Musil, and Franz Blei. Blei introduced Werfel to Alma Mahler Gropius, née Schindler. When the two met, Werfel was still involved with Spirk, and Alma was married to Walter Gropius. The separation from their respective partners was neither quick nor easy. Alma, a pan-Germanist, repeatedly criticized Werfel for his antiwar statements and his choice of literary themes; her virulent anti-Semitism was also a source of discord, since Werfel, though fascinated by Catholicism, was ethnically and culturally Jewish. After satisfying her precondition by renouncing Judaism, Werfel married Alma on 8 July 1929.

Werfel's rejection of Judaism bore consequences in his relationships with his Jewish friends and would return to haunt him during the rise of the Third Reich. He trivialized this decision by saying that he had never abandoned his Jewish essence, but he became further entrenched in the Christian conservative camp.

Werfel's ambivalence, although at times expedient, would protect him from neither his literary peers nor the Nazis. His endorsement of Gottfried Benn's loyalty oath to the government in 1933, for example, would not prevent the Nazis from burning his books.

Werfel wrote most of his major dramas and prose works between 1918 and 1940. The first play of this period, *Spiegelmensch* (Mirrorman; published, 1920; performed, 1921), was dedicated to Alma. Begun in February 1919 and completed a year later, this "Magische Trilogie" (magical trilogy) in verse, which Werfel was invited to read at Max Reinhardt's Deutsches Theater in 1920, consists of three parts and a finale. The action takes place partly in mythical locations, reflecting Werfel's interest in Eastern and Middle Eastern culture. On entering a monastery Thamal is told by the abbot that one should not flee the world but should experience it and struggle with good and evil to reach a higher level of consciousness. Thamal, disgusted by his reflection, shatters the mirror, thereby releasing the "Mirrorman," his alter ego, who awakens his vanity, arrogance, and self-indulgence. He is greeted as a savior in the Land of the Snakes, which is being tyrannized by the evil Ananthas, and he defeats Ananthas in a spiritual battle. Thamal, however, is defeated by his hubris. Ananthas reenters the land, and Thamal is incarcerated. As if all had taken place in a dream, Thamal awakens in the cloister and sees a "höhere Wirklichkeit" (higher reality) in place of the mirror he had shattered. He thus achieves the ultimate self-realization expressed by the abbot at the beginning and in the closing statement of the drama. By gathering experience, both good and bad, and losing himself, Thamal has arrived at a higher level of consciousness. By literally splitting Thamal into the "Ich des Seins" (I of being) and the "Ich der Erscheinung" (I of appearance), Werfel takes up the notion of the dichotomy within the individual, a key theme for impressionists and expressionists alike. In no other play does Werfel deal as cogently with this topic.

Spiegelmensch, which Werfel intended to be a pantomime or a ballet and not a drama at all, premiered on 15 October 1921 at the Altes Theater in Leipzig, directed by Alwin Kronacher with set designs by Alexander Baranowsky; it ran for twelve performances. On the same day it opened at the Württembergisches Landestheater (Provincial Theater) in Stuttgart, directed by Fritz Holl with set designs by Felix Cziossek; there it ran for eighteen performances. The play would run

Scene from the 1921 premiere of Werfel's Spiegelmensch *in Leipzig, with Lutz Altschul as Thamal and Ewald Schindler as the Spiegelmensch*

for a total of seventy-eight performances in several cities by 1926. In Leipzig hurrahs and applause brought the playwright to the curtain several times. Critics praised Werfel's resolution of the Faustian dilemma and noted the influence of Ferdinand Raimund's idea of the "Volksbühne" (people's stage) and of August Strindberg's "Stationenstücke" (station plays).

The title of Werfel's *Bocksgesang* (published, 1921; performed, 1922; translated as *Goat Song*, 1926) is a literal translation of *tragodia*, the Greek word derived from the goat song that is part of the rites of Dionysus. Set in a Slavic landscape at the turn of the nineteenth century, the play is centered around a nameless figure that is half man, half animal. Modeled on Martin Carl Johannes Werfel, the severely malformed boy Alma bore in 1918 after a traumatic labor who died shortly after his birth, this monster is the firstborn of the prosperous farmer Gospodar Milic. The town phy-

sician, a guest at the wedding feast of Gospodar's other son, Mirko, and his bride, Stanja, demands to see the monster, who is kept in a barn because Gospodar believes it to be the product of Satan. The physician returns from the barn shaken and insists that the creature be taken to an institution. Gospodar decides to kill his offspring. Arriving at the barn, however, he discovers that the monster has escaped because the physician had forgotten to lock the stall. A band of indigents led by the student Juvan, Stanja's former lover, engages in an orgy of protest against inequity. They agree to stop the rioting if Stanja will sleep with the monster, whom Juvan has captured; she does so, driving Mirko to suicide. The riot is put down, and Juvan is hanged. A horrifying reality remains to haunt Gospodar: Stanja announces that she is pregnant with the monster's child.

The five-act play in prose premiered on 10 March 1922 at the Raimund Theater in Vienna and ran for ten performances under the director Rudolf Beer, who also designed the sets. By 1924 *Bocksgesang* had run for twenty-seven performances in various cities. Critical response in Germany and Austria was typified by the *Wiener Tagespresse* (Viennese Daily Press), which in its generally favorable review found the play revolutionary but inscrutable. In New York, where Alfred Lunt and Lynn Fontanne played lead roles, *Goat Song* was considered "the event" of the 1925-1926 theater season; the Theater Guild held lectures and discussions in which, at times, more than two thousand people participated. Eugene O'Neill wrote in the *New York Times* on 7 March 1926: "Here is a play which really justifies all one can say by way of enthusiastic praise."

Werfel's next play, *Schweiger* (published, 1922), completed in 1922, premiered on 6 January 1923 at the Neues Theater in Prague and ran for 6 performances under the direction of Leopold Kramer, who also designed the sets. On 14 January 1923 the prose drama began a run of 11 performances at the Landestheater in Stuttgart, directed and with sets designed by Fritz Holl. By 1931 *Schweiger* had been performed 130 times. This tragedy in three acts takes place in a provincial city on three days in 1919: Wednesday, 28 April; Friday, 29 August; and Sunday, 7 September. Prior to his happy seven-year marriage the gentle, generous Schweiger suffered an illness that caused amnesia. All he can recall is that he has not always been a clockmaker and that he has lived in many cities. Schweiger was told by the doctors that he suffered a "Nervenfieber" (nerve fever), yet when his wife asks about his past he answers that his disease was "etwas Okkultisches" (something occult): one day he had "aufgehört zu sein" (ceased to be), and another day he awoke to his present good fortune. So highly regarded that many say he is "zu gut für diese Welt" (too good for this world), Schweiger runs for political office at the townspeople's request. A member of the opposing German Nationalist party, Dr. Viereck, who had treated Schweiger during his illness, decides to undo him by restoring his memory and telling his wife the awful truth that one day he shot from his window at a group of children and killed a ten-year-old boy. Schweiger's wife leaves him. His life and reputation ruined, Schweiger, in an attempt to offset his horrible crime, saves a ship full of children. Believing that he is rid of his past, he declares to his returned wife that they are free to renew their lives and their marriage. He desires a child of his own; but

his wife, who had an abortion during her absence, says that she will not bear the child of a child murderer. When his wife leaves him a second time Schweiger's world collapses. In a fit of lunacy he aims a gun at a crowd of people outside his window. When he realizes what he is about to do, he jumps out the window. His wife, unable to leave him for good, returns moments later to find his lifeless body.

Werfel's treatment of the question of guilt and of the themes of cosmic influences and psychology, although unpopular among critics, met with great success with the public. *Schweiger* was produced in twenty provincial theaters and ran for thirty-eight performances in Berlin. The harshest response to the play came from Kafka, who, along with Arthur Schnitzler, rejected it because he found the main figures "unmenschlich" (inhuman) and the story of Schweiger's psychosis unbelievable. The American reception of the play was similar. The premiere on 23 March of the unpublished translation by Jack Charash at the Mansfield Theater in New York was reviewed unenthusiastically, yet it ran for more than thirty performances and was a great public success.

The least produced of Werfel's dramas, *Die Mittagsgöttin* (The Afternoon Goddess; published, 1919), premiered on 1 February 1925 at the Stadttheater in Koblenz. Directed by Fritz Wilm Wallenborn, who also designed the sets, it ran for one performance. The action of this three-act "Zauberspiel" (magical play) in verse is simple and brief. Mara, the Earth Mother, makes a new man of the disoriented, destitute vagabond Laurentin by giving birth to his son. As a result Laurentin, once a master of evasion, becomes mature enough to find his own course in life. Not a strong play and unfavorably received, *Mittagsgöttin* unmistakably alludes to the playwright's perception of his relationship to Alma Mahler. Werfel said repeatedly in his letters that he felt that Alma had given his life meaning. The story of Mara and Laurentin is also mirrored in the birth of Alma's and Werfel's son in 1918, the year the play was written.

The next play to be produced was *Juarez und Maximilian* (translated as *Juárez and Maximilian*, 1926), which was published immediately on its completion in 1924. This "dramatische Historie in 3 Phasen und 13 Bildern" (dramatic history in three phases and thirteen images) premiered on 20 April 1925 at the Stadttheater in Magdeburg; directed by Adolf Winds, who also designed the sets, it ran for five performances. The

Vienna opening, with Helene Thimig, Wilhelm Dieterle, and Oskar Homolka, took place on 26 May 1925 at the Theater in der Josefstadt. Under Reinhardt's direction and with set designs by Adolf Kunz, this production resulted in sixty curtain calls on opening night and ran for twenty-four performances. Under Reinhardt's direction and with set designs by Ernst Schütte, the play opened on 29 January 1926 at the Deutsches Theater in Berlin. This production, with Ernst Deutsch in the role of Diaz, ran for fifty performances. By 1958 the play had been performed nearly six hundred times in many cities.

The play traces the European imperial intrigue designed to reestablish monarchic control over the Mexican republic, which had gained independence from Spain in 1821. Led by Napoleon III, Mexican monarchists crown Maximilian of Austria emperor in 1865 in an attempt to depose Benito Juárez, the president of the Mexican republic since 1861. Juárez defeats Maximilian, who is executed by a firing squad in 1867. Juárez is never seen onstage; Werfel focuses on Maximilian, who is presented not as a powermonger but as a well-intentioned idealist. Werfel wrote that he believed that Maximilian wanted to improve the lot of the Mexican proletariat.

Juarez und Maximilian established Werfel's international reputation. In 1931 Darius Milhaud used the play as the basis for an opera. There was a plan to make a film of the play in Hollywood; but the adaptation by John Huston, to be directed by William Dieterle, did not materialize. As a result of *Juarez und Maximilian* Werfel was awarded the Grillparzer Prize by the Vienna Academy of Sciences on 15 January 1926 and was elected to the Prussian Academy of the Arts, Poetry Section, on 27 October 1927.

Paulus unter den Juden (1926; translated as *Paul among the Jews*, 1928) is the work in which Werfel most lucidly discusses his lifelong preoccupation with the intersection of Judaism and Christianity. Set in Jerusalem under Caligula, the story of Schaul, the master student of the high priest Gamaliel who becomes Paul, the first missionary of Jesus, treats the moment of the separation of Christianity from Judaism. This "dramatische Legende in sechs Bildern" (dramatic legend in six images) premiered on 30 October 1926 in five cities. At the Prinzregententheater in Munich, directed by Alfons Pape with set designs by Adolf Linnebach and Walter Schröder, it ran for 17 performances; at the Stadttheater in Bonn, directed by Fritz Kranz with set designs by Walter

von Mecus, it ran for 13 performances; at the Lobetheater in Breslau, directed by Paul Barnay with set designs by Harry Wilton, it ran for 15 performances; at the Schauspielhaus in Cologne, directed by Theo Mapes with set designs by Ludwig Sievert, it ran for 26 performances; and at the Schauspielhaus Dumont in Düsseldorf, directed by Gustav Lindemann with set designs by Eduard Sturm, it ran for 24 performances. By 1959 the play had been performed 240 times. Werfel had wrestled with the material and wanted several times to drop the project; it was finished only with the encouragement of such friends as playwrights Schnitzler and Hugo von Hofmannsthal. Werfel's suggestion of the superiority of Christianity to Judaism distressed some of his Jewish colleagues. He responded by claiming that he wrote the play, which was inspired by a trip to Jerusalem in 1925, "als Jude" (as a Jew) who found the moment Paul distanced himself from Judaism catastrophic but interesting, since it bore so many consequences. The play contributed to a high point in Werfel's career: in a poll taken by a popular literary magazine in 1926 he received far more votes than Gerhart Hauptmann, Stefan Zweig, or Rainer Maria Rilke as the most popular contemporary writer in the German language. In 1927 he was awarded the Czechoslovakian State Prize and the Schiller Prize.

Das Reich Gottes in Böhmen (1930; translated as *God's Kingdom of Bohemia*; n.d.) focuses on the Czech reformation that predated Martin Luther by almost one hundred years. Werfel saw the movement led by Jan Hus not as an outbreak of ethnic hatred but as a religious phenomenon. The action of this "Tragödie eines Führers" (tragedy of a leader) is set in Bohemia and Basel between 1431 and 1434; but since the drama was conceived as a metaphor for the contemporary period, the characters speak twentieth-century German. Prokop, leader of the radical Hussites, attempts to realize the Christian ideal of equality by taking property from the lords and giving it to the serfs. Prokop's goal is the establishment of Tabor, the "Gemeinschaft des Kelches" (community of the chalice) free of pope, king, class division, and individual ownership. Due to his megalomania Prokop loses control of his followers and is fatally wounded. Cardinal Julian, who has defeated the Taborites, visits the dying Prokop and acknowledges the similarity of their ideals. The difference between the two is that the Hussite leader is incapable of love. This play, in which religious beliefs conflict with and are finally undermined by worldly interests, is unique in Werfel's oeuvre. He shows here that the problems resulting from economic injustice cannot be overcome without Christian—specifically Catholic—love.

During rehearsals before the premiere Werfel had extensive problems with the director, Albert Heine. Heine emphasized parallels between the theocratic communism of the projected Taborite community and contemporary communism but failed to comprehend sufficiently the play's metaphysical aspects. Squabbles between the playwright and director notwithstanding, the play, with sets designed by Oskar Strand, premiered on 6 December 1930 at the Burgtheater in Vienna, where it ran for thirty performances.

In dealing with the religion-based, antifeudal struggle against Bohemia's high nobility Werfel treats an age-old conflict between fundamentally opposing worldviews. This approach is consistent with his proclivity, also exemplified by *Paulus unter den Juden*, to examine opposites; it is consistent also with the expressionist ideal of pluralism and antidogmatism. Some critics accused Werfel of demonstrating a lack of perspective; the play received positive reviews, however, from Felix Salten and Roaul Auernheimer. A few weeks after the premiere, Schnitzler and Egon Friedell discussed ways to secure the Nobel Prize for Werfel.

Because of the advent of National Socialism in Germany the play was not as frequently produced as others by Werfel. A report in the Nazi paper *Völkischer Beobachter* (National Observer) that Werfel was known as a Czech Jew who not only wrote bad German but made a name for himself by attacking Ludwig van Beethoven and Richard Wagner contributed to the play's suppression until after World War II. Nevertheless, it was performed eighty-one times in various cities by 1959.

The idea for *Der Weg der Verheißung* (1935; translated as *The Eternal Road*, 1936) came from Meyer Weisgal, a Polish theater producer living in the United States, who felt that the danger the Third Reich posed to Judaism required a dramatic treatment of the Old Testament. Werfel accepted the task, unaware of how unwieldy it was to become. The story follows the five books of Moses, the Book of Kings, and the Prophets, adding a contextualizing narrative and amending only where Werfel felt it was necessary to do so for production purposes. The play is set in Israel during a night of persecution. The stage is divided into five levels, and two courses of action

take place simultaneously. The prelude, which establishes the play's context, is set in a synagogue, where a venerable rabbi traces the history of Israel from Abraham to Jeremiah. A member of the community, who whispers that he had nearly forgotten Judaism, is asked by his son, "Warum werden wir verfolgt? Warum hast du mir nichts gesagt?" (Why are we persecuted? Why haven't you told me anything?).

Under Reinhardt's direction, with music by Kurt Weill and set designs by Norman Bel Geddes, the play, in an adaptation by William A. Drake, premiered on 7 January 1937 at the Manhattan Opera House in New York as *The Eternal Road*; Sara Delano Roosevelt, representing the Christian community, and Rabbi Stephen Samuel Wise, representing the Jewish community, were in attendance. Received enthusiastically by critics and public alike, it ran for more than four hundred performances before it was discontinued due to high production costs.

The last major work Werfel wrote in Austria, *In einer Nacht* (During One Night, 1937), takes place in a castle in the mountains near Vienna on Halloween around 1930. Felizitas is unhappy because she married Eduard rather than Gabriel, the man she really loves. Gabriel, who left Europe heartbroken, returns after a long absence and happens to meet Eduard. Aware that his wife is still in love with Gabriel, Eduard invites the visitor to his home to test the two. The love between Felizitas and Gabriel proves to be as strong as ever, but both realize that fruition is impossible, and Gabriel leaves. Eduard accompanies him to the train station and kills him. Gabriel's body is brought back to the castle, and the murder is attributed to bandits. As Felizitas is about to take poison, Gabriel's soul saves her. Through this deed Gabriel's life is renewed, and he shares the future with Felizitas.

This play, in which Werfel returned to the theme of *Der Besuch aus dem Elysium*, was the last Reinhardt produced in Vienna. Under his direction and with set designs by Carl Witzmann, the premiere, with Viennese theatrical and political prominence in attendance, took place on 5 October 1937 at the Theater der Josefstadt; with Thimig playing Felizitas, it ran for thirty-one performances. The popular reception of this play crowned 1937, another high point in Werfel's career, during which he received the Austrian Service Cross for Art and Science for *Höret die Stimme* (1937; translated as *Hearken unto the Voice*, 1938), a prose work.

Alma and Franz Werfel at their home in Beverly Hills, where they settled in 1941

When Nazi Germany annexed Austria in 1938, Werfel was on Capri; he and Alma went into exile in Paris. He was named honorary president of the Austrian PEN Club in 1939. When Germany invaded France in 1940, the Werfels fled to the United States; they settled in Beverly Hills, California. Werfel wrote his last play, *Jacobowsky und der Oberst* (1944; translated as *Jacobowsky and the Colonel*, 1944), in ten days. The play is set in June 1940 between Paris and the Atlantic coast. Among the many fleeing Adolf Hitler are Jacobowsky, a Jew, and Colonel Stjerbinsky, a Polish aristocrat. The colonel, an anti-Semite, learns during his time with Jacobowsky of the real problems besetting humanity. In a manner reminiscent of Gotthold Ephraim Lessing's Enlightenment works, Stjerbinsky sheds his arrogance and biases just as Jacobowsky learns to lose his fear. Based on Werfel's escape from the Third Reich, this "Komödie einer Tragödie" (comedy of a tragedy) shows that ancestral differences dissolve before the common danger of the descent into barbarism.

In a revision by S. N. Behrman the play, under Elia Kazan's direction with set designs by Stewart Chaney, premiered on 14 March 1944 at the Martin Beck Theater in New York. It was so popular in the United States that Gustave O. Arlt's English translation was published as a textbook the same year. Under Franz Schnyder's direction, with set designs by Andre Perottet, it premiered in German on 17 October 1944 at the Stadttheater (City Theater) in Basel. By 1960 it had been performed more than 250 times in many German cities.

Werfel's death on 26 August 1945 was not unexpected; always of frail health, he was preoccupied throughout his life with thoughts of mortality. The furious pace of his productivity was seemingly set to beat the final deadline. While his career had moved ineluctably from peak to peak, Werfel is largely forgotten today.

References:

Gustave O. Arlt, "Franz Werfel and America," *Modern Language Forum*, 36 (March 1951): 1-7;

Eric Bentley, "Franz Werfel's Open Secret," *New Republic*, 114 (18 February 1946): 259-260;

Werner Braselmann, *Franz Werfel* (Wuppertal-Barmen: Müller, 1960);

Horst Denkler, "Franz Werfel," in his *Einakter und kleine Dramen des Expressionismus* (Stuttgart: Reclam, 1968), pp. 280-284;

Irwin Edman, "What Price Mysticism?," *Saturday Review of Literature*, 27 (18 November 1944): 9-11;

Lore B. Foltin, *Franz Werfel* (Stuttgart: Metzler, 1972);

Willy Haas, *Die literarische Welt: Erinnerungen* (Munich: List, 1958), pp. 137-138;

Peter Stephan Jungk, *Franz Werfel* (Frankfurt am Main: Fischer, 1987);

Henry A. Lea, "The Failure of Political Activism in Werfel's Plays," *Symposium*, 22 (Winter 1968): 319-334;

Arthur Luther, *Franz Werfel und seine besten Bühnenwerke* (Berlin: Schneider, 1922);

Alma Mahler-Werfel, *Mein Leben* (Frankfurt am Main: Fischer, 1960);

Helga Meister, *Franz Werfels Dramen und ihre Inszenierungen auf der deutschen Sprachbühne* (Cologne: Philosophische Fakultät der Universität Köln, 1964);

Stephen Shearier, *Das junge Deutschland 1917-1920: Expressionistisches Theater in Berlin* (Bern: Lang, 1988), pp. 39, 143-151;

Harry Slochower, "Franz Werfel and Sholom Asch: The Yearning for Status," *Accent*, 5-6 (1944-1946): 73-82;

Jeremy Smith, *Religious Feeling and Religious Commitment in Faulkner, Dostoyevsky, Werfel and Bernanos* (New York: Garland, 1988);

Walter H. Sokel, *The Writer in Extremis* (Stanford, Cal.: Stanford University Press, 1959);

Richard Specht, *Franz Werfel* (Vienna: Zsolnay, 1926);

Lionel B. Steiman, *Franz Werfel: The Faith of an Exile. From Prague to Beverly Hills* (Waterloo, Ont.: Laurier, 1985);

Annaliese Viviani, *Das Drama des Expressionismus* (Munich: Winkler, 1970), pp. 10-11, 50, 59, 66-67, 71-72, 145-148;

Paul Wimmer, *Franz Werfels dramatische Sendung* (Vienna: Bergland, 1973);

Leopold Zahn, *Franz Werfel* (Berlin: Colloqium, 1966).

Papers:

Manuscript materials of Franz Werfel are at the Schiller-Nationalmuseum in Marbach am Neckar, the University of California in Los Angeles, the University of Pennsylvania in Philadelphia, and Yale University.

Christa Winsloe

(23 December 1888 - 10 June 1944)

Karl Toepfer
San Jose State University

PLAY PRODUCTIONS: *Ritter Nérestan*, Leipzig, Schauspielhaus, 30 November 1930; revised as *Gestern und Heute*, Berlin, Theater an der Stresemannstrasse, 8 April 1931; translated as *Children in Uniform*, London, Duchess Theatre, 7 October 1932; translated as *Girls in Uniform*, New York, Booth Theatre, 30 December 1932.

BOOKS: *Children in Uniform*, translated by Barbara Burnham (London: Gollancz, 1932); republished as *Girls in Uniform* (Boston: Little, Brown, 1933);
Das Mädchen Manuela: Der Roman von Mädchen in Uniform (Leipzig: Tal, 1933); translated by Agnes Neill Scott as *The Child Manuela* (New York: Farrar & Rinehart, 1933); German version republished as *Mädchen in Uniform* (St. Gallen: Allgemeiner, 1951);
Life Begins, translated by Scott (London: Chapman & Hall, 1935); republished as *Girl Alone* (New York: Farrar & Rinehart, 1936);
Passeggiera: Roman (Amsterdam: De Lange, 1938).

MOTION PICTURES: *Mädchen in Uniform*, screenplay by Winsloe and F. D. Andam, Deutsche Filmgesellschaft, 30 November 1931;
Jeunes filles en detresse, screenplay by Winsloe, Globe Films, 1939.

Christa Winsloe in the late 1920s

Christa Winsloe's reputation as a German-language dramatist rests entirely on a single play—which, paradoxically, has never been published in German. This play, commonly but inaccurately known as *Mädchen in Uniform* (Girls in Uniform), reached an international audience in the early 1930s, but not under either of the two titles the author gave it: *Ritter Nérestan* (The Knight Nérestan; performed, 1930) and *Gestern und Heute* (Yesterday and Today; performed, 1931). It was made into a film as *Mädchen in Uniform* (1931) that Winsloe, who collaborated on the

screenplay, repudiated by writing a novelized version under the title *Das Mädchen Manuela* (1933; translated as *The Child Manuela*, 1933). The book has also enjoyed international success, often under the same title assigned to the play and the film. An outstanding example of Neue Sachlichkeit (New Objectivity) in German drama between 1925 and 1932, the play offers a sobering critique of the institutionalization of German militarism in education. But the critique of militarism and pedagogic authority entails a critique of sexual morality: the all-female play dramatizes a

440

tragic and ironic relation between a militaristic ideal of the "heroic" woman and the greater courage required to express a love that is "wrong." It is unique in giving a heroic aspect to lesbian love.

Winsloe was born in Darmstadt on 23 December 1888. She was the daughter of a military officer who expected her to enhance the family fortune through marriage. She studied at the Empress Augusta Academy in Potsdam and then at a Swiss finishing school. But she disappointed her family by deciding to study sculpture in Munich. In 1913 Winsloe married a rich Hungarian sugar dealer and patron of modernist culture, Baron Laci Hatvany. After a honeymoon in Paris the couple settled in Budapest. There Winsloe wrote an unpublished autobiographical novel, "Das Schwarze Schaf" (The Black Sheep), in which an unhappy artist is saved from despair by marrying an idealized man. Toward the end of World War I her husband's relationships with other women, combined with the social turmoil caused by the collapse of the Austro-Hungarian Empire, produced in Winsloe an intense mood of estrangement, isolation, and disillusionment. With the outbreak of the Hungarian Revolution in 1919 she left her husband to embark on an artistic career in Munich.

As Baroness Hatvany she gained easy entry into artistic and intellectual circles, and her articles were published in the Munich press as well as in the popular cultural journal *Querschnitt* (Profile). She wrote another unpublished novel, "Männer kehren heim" (Men Come Home), about a girl who, after being attacked by soldiers, spends the entire war masquerading as a boy in her brother's clothes. Throughout the 1920s Winsloe was known more for her socialite charm than for her artistic achievements. Then, in 1929, she completed *Ritter Nérestan*, which premiered at the Leipzig Schauspielhaus on 30 November 1930. This production was successful enough to inspire a production in Berlin in the spring of 1931 for which Winsloe revised several passages and changed the title to *Gestern und Heute*. The Berlin production was so successful that the director Carl Froelich formed the first employee-owned production company, Deutsche Filmgemeinschaft (German Film Company), to bring the play to the screen. The film, *Mädchen in Uniform*, premiered in Berlin at the end of 1931. By that time the play had attracted the attention of producers in London, where it was produced as *Children in Uniform* in October 1932. The English translation was published under that title the same year. Winsloe never had either German version of the play published and, in spite of its international identity, it has only been published in English as *Children in Uniform* and as *Girls in Uniform* (1933). The failure of the play to appear in print since 1945, while the novel continues to be reprinted, is difficult to explain; possibly publishers assume that the novel represents a more definitive treatment of the themes introduced by the play. But comparison of the play and the novel does not justify this assumption.

The play dramatizes a tragic conflict between old and new codes of sexual morality in an elite school for the daughters of Prussian aristocrats. The protagonist is Manuela von Meinhardis, a melancholy and highly intelligent orphan whose reactionary aunt has placed her in the academy. Early scenes show Manuela's transformation from a shy dreamer into a popular and admired embodiment of feminine boldness. But Manuela is by no means the only character of interest; with a large cast of thirteen students and fifteen adults, all female, Winsloe creates distinct and varied characterizations, several of which achieve considerable dramatic vitality with only a few lines of dialogue. A large emotional and ideological gap separates the school administrators from the students. The old headmistress and her aristocratic cronies remain attached to archaic, pre-1914 militaristic ideals in which "girls are to be taught discipline, order, self-control, and obedience. Those who have not learned to obey can never command." The girls, however, seek knowledge that will prepare them for love rather than duty. Divided by these conflicting sets of interests are the teachers, the nurse, and the seamstress, whose fear of the administrators constrains their ability to show affection to the girls. Fräulein von Bernburg, a teacher whom all the students ardently desire to please, projects toward the girls a maternal feeling that is otherwise absent from their lives. Yet she also possesses an erotic allure: her affection operates as a reward for the bleak discipline the school compels her to demand of the students. She appears aloof yet vulnerable, aristocratic yet humble, mysterious because her motives for teaching in a school in which she is so out of place seem a secret even to herself. As Manuela observes: "I feel she has suffered in some way . . . that . . . there is another side to her quite different from the one she shows us." Manuela's attraction to the older woman grows into a powerful passion. As she prepares for the role of the knight Nérestan in a school production of Voltaire's *Zaïre* (1732), she dreams of being the knight who will set Bernburg free. Her performance is a great success with students, faculty, and administrators. At a party after the play Manuela becomes intoxicated, partly by the punch and partly by the exquisite feeling of love inspired in all the girls by her performance, and she boldly declares her love for the absent Bernburg. Shocked, the headmistress punishes Manuela by isolating her from the other girls and forbidding her any contact with Bernburg. At a secret meeting Bernburg tells Manuela that love between them is impossible and that they must never see each other again. As Bernburg is arguing with the headmistress over the treatment of Manuela and the other students, word arrives that Manuela has leaped to her death from the infirmary window. Although this loss has a deeply transformative effect on Bernburg, it is not clear if Manuela's suicide is enough to change the repressive institution that destroyed her.

Children in Uniform belongs to a tradition in German drama of plays about adolescents in revolt against repressive schooling. Such plays include Frank Wedekind's *Frühlings Erwachen* (published, 1891; performed, 1906; translated as *The Awakening of Spring*, 1909), Arnolt Bronnen's *Die Geburt der Jugend* (The Birth of Youth; published, 1922; performed, 1925), Hanns Johst's *Der junge Mensch* (The Young Man; published, 1916; performed, 1919), Hans Henny Jahnn's *Pastor Ephraim Magnus* (published, 1919; performed, 1923), Georg Kaiser's *Der gerettete Alkibiades* (1920; translated as *Alkibiades Saved*, 1963), Rolf Lauckner's *Wahnschaffe* (The Deformed, 1920), Ferdinand Bruckner's *Krankheit der Jugend* (Sickness of Youth; performed, 1926; published, 1928), and Peter Martin Lampel's *Revolte im Erziehungshaus* (Revolt in the Reform School; performed, 1928; published, 1929). But unlike those works, Winsloe's play does not rely on expressionist aesthetics to develop the relation between individual feeling and institutionalized repression. The play is consistently realistic in that it tells its story through a mass of well-observed details; it avoids the stylistic extravagances of expressionism. But unlike many dramatists of New Objectivity, Winsloe builds dramatic intensity by compressing many characters, actions, and moods into acts rather than by segmenting them into a series of epic episodes. Act 1, which consists of four scenes, depicts the severe and divided milieu of the school on the day Manuela enters it. Act 2, in

three scenes, occurring several weeks later, discloses the beautiful radiance Manuela exudes as a result of her affection for her classmates, her success as an actress, and her love for Bernburg. The brief final act of three scenes concentrates on developing moods of depression, sorrow, despair, anger, and regret. But within each act Winsloe constructs a complex emotional web in which moments of fear, anger, jealousy, repulsion, and remorse contrast dramatically with expressions of gentleness, tenderness, exhilaration, or melancholy. It is rare for a play to offer such a spectrum of emotions. One message of the play is that repression cannot prevent the manifestation of love. Yet love is perverse insofar as its manifestation contradicts and even subverts the ideals which justify the institutions responsible for repression. In the first version of the play, *Ritter Nérestan*, Manuela's expression of love for Bernburg is somewhat more graphic, containing an element of erotic fantasy that is missing from the revised version and that gives Manuela a slightly darker psychological complexion.

The revised version premiered in Berlin on 8 April 1931 at the Theater an der Stresemannstrasse under the title *Gestern und Heute*. Leontine Sagan, a South African, directed the production, which starred Gina Falkenberg as Manuela and Margarete Melzer as Bernburg. During the run Hertha Thiele, who had played Manuela in the Leipzig production of *Ritter Nérestan*, took over from Falkenberg; she would also play Manuela in the film version. The svelte Melzer gave Bernburg distinctively masculine features, such as short-cropped blond hair, jacket, and tie, while Falkenberg's Manuela was darkly feminine. But in the film version, it is Thiele's blond Manuela who assumes masculine qualities, and Bernburg, played by the dark and elegant Dorothea Wieck, projects an enchantingly feminine image. (Wieck was only a year older than Thiele, yet she looks aristocratically "mature" compared to the quasi-androgynous image of adolescence offered by Thiele.) By further contrast, in the Leipzig production of *Ritter Nérestan* a middle-aged, "motherly" actress, Claire Harden, played Bernburg. The film softens the masculinity Thiele bestowed on the role in the stage version; Manuela appears androgynously sleek, while Wieck makes Bernburg seductive by infusing her elegant feminity with a refined military poise.

In October 1932 Sagan directed the London premiere of the play under the title *Children in Uniform*, featuring Jessica Tandy as Manuela and Joyce Bland as Bernburg. Several weeks later the New York production opened under the direction of Frank Gregory as *Girls in Uniform*, with Florence Williams playing Manuela and Rose Hobart as Bernburg. This production ran concurrently with the film version, which had been playing in New York since September.

Critical responses to these productions were enthusiastic and encouraged further productions throughout Germany and in Paris, Budapest, and Riga. The vast majority of published responses came from male writers, who saw the play as an indictment of militarism and reactionary educational ideals; the lesbianism appeared to them as a pathology inadvertently spawned by unhealthy political ideals. More recent feminist evaluations view the play, the film, and the novel as critiques of an oppressive sexual morality; the militarism of the school merely objectifies attitudes toward sexual identity and differences between the sexes that prevail elsewhere in much more subtle ways. But the play suggests that even without the presence of men, the nature of power is such that women will oppress each other. As Bernburg remarks to the headmistress, "Only women can do such terrible things to women!"

Deutsche Filmgesellschaft hired Winsloe and her friend F. D. Andam to write the screenplay for the film version. Sagan was the nominal director of the film, but Froelich closely supervised the direction and appears to have been responsible for deviations from the play that take advantage of the resources of the cinema. The film was an enormous success throughout the world, and some commentators, such as Brooks Atkinson, preferred it to the play. (Later film versions were produced in Mexico in 1950 and in Germany in 1957.) But though it follows Winsloe's story in most details and certainly in spirit, the film departs from the author's intentions in one significant matter: as Manuela is about to leap from the bannister of a high stairwell, the students, at last shaking off their docility, surge toward her; their compassion overwhelms her motive for dying. It is by no means a false or unsatisfying ending, but Winsloe was so unhappy about it that she retold the story in novel form as *Das Mädchen Manuela*. The book differs considerably from the play and the film: male figures appear; Manuela, no longer an orphan, has a complex relationship with her parents; she does not enter the school until halfway through the story; the atmosphere of the school is not especially op-

pressive; the love between Manuela and Fräulein Bernburg is integrated into a detailed description of emotional communication among many other female characters; and Bernburg emerges as a coward. Unable to stand up to the headmistress as she does in the play, Bernburg, out of fear of losing her position, betrays Manuela and causes her death. Whereas Froelich saw Manuela saved by the mass of students, Winsloe's novel (but not her play) suggests that only the courage of a solitary teacher could save her. But the novel lacks the emotional intensity and structural complexity of either the play or the film. After the Nazis assumed power in January 1933 the novel, along with nearly all other literary and artistic works containing homosexual themes, was proscribed. The film, however, was never banned by Nazi censors, possibly because Froelich was for a time president of the party-controlled Reichsfilmkammer (German Film Bureau) and was a successful director of juvenile films throughout the Nazi era. But in America several states, including New York, banned the film because of its "morbid tendency."

In December 1932 Winsloe, who had divorced Hatvany in 1930, met the American journalist Dorothy Thompson at a huge ten-day Christmas party given by Thompson and her husband, the novelist Sinclair Lewis, in Semmering, Austria. After the party Thompson was a guest at Winsloe's Hungarian estate, where the two women conducted a homosexual romance that at first did not seem to interfere with Thompson's marriage. Thompson, deeply enamored of Winsloe's aristocratic sophistication, kept a diary that describes their romance in sometimes startling detail; Vincent Sheean claims that this diary of only a few bold entries is "far more revealing than any other document [Thompson] has left to us." In March 1933 Thompson followed Winsloe to Portofino, Italy; in May, Winsloe, repelled by the Nazism pervading German and Austrian life, accompanied Thompson to the United States and lived with her in New York City and at Thompson and Lewis's farm in Vermont. The two women traveled to Austria in August and returned to Vermont in the spring of 1934. They lived together until early 1935, and Thompson put Winsloe in touch with important persons in New York cultural life. Lewis, however, began to find the arrangement uncongenial, and Winsloe hoped for opportunities in Hollywood. By the summer of 1935 she was living in a bungalow in the Hollywood Hills, where she continued to cor-

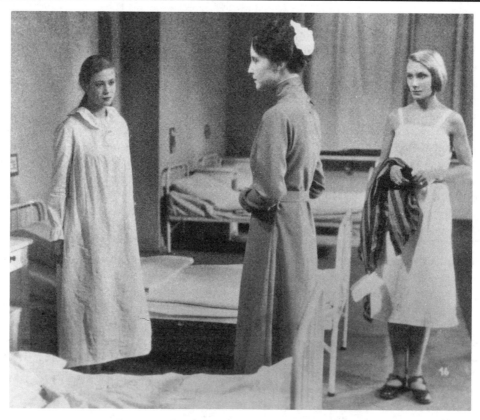

Hertha Thiele (left) as Manuela and Dorothea Wieck as Bernburg in a scene from the 1931 film version of Winsloe's Mädchen in Uniform

respond with Thompson. She completed her autobiographical novel "Das Leben beginnt," which appeared only in English translation as *Life Begins* (1935) and *Girl Alone* (1936). Through her encounters with several men, the heroine discovers that she must choose between artistic and sexual fulfillment and that art and erotic happiness are not adequate substitutes for each other. Winsloe had no success in entering the film industry, nor does she seem to have secured any support from the large German exile community in Hollywood. In late 1935 she returned by ship to Europe and settled in France. Her disappointment with America and her sense of being adrift are evident in her novel *Passeggiera* (Passages, 1938), which describes a disillusioned woman's journey by sea from Los Angeles to Genoa; she is unable to love any of the various men she meets. In Paris the director Georg Wilhelm Pabst invited her to work on the screenplay for *Jeunes filles en detresse* (Girls in Distress, 1939), based on a novel by Peter Quinn. A conventional story about the unhappiness of a girl caused by the impending divorce of her parents, the film enjoyed neither critical nor financial success.

When the Germans invaded France in May 1940 Winsloe could no longer withdraw funds from her German bank; she appealed for help to Thompson, who sent her fifty dollars a month until mid 1942. Living in a small house on the Cote d'Azur, Winsloe wrote a couple of salon comedies, "Der Schritt hinüber" (The Step Beyond) and "Schicksal nach Wunsch" (Destiny According to Desire), and a darker drama, "Aiono," about a Finnish refugee who disguises herself as a man. None of these plays has been published or performed. Meanwhile, she apparently helped some of her Jewish friends escape to Switzerland. As the Germans intensified their presence in the south of France by the end of 1942, Winsloe and her Swiss girlfriend, Simone Gentet, a writer, moved north to Cluny. It is possible that Gentet, described by Winsloe as a drug addict and alcoholic, was—unbeknownst to Winsloe—a spy for the Gestapo. On 10 June 1944 a local butcher named Lambert and four other men, purporting to be members of the French Resistance, "arrested" Winsloe and Gentet, drove them to a forest, and shot them to death. In July 1946 a friend of Winsloe's in Munich, Helen Meier-

Graf, wrote to Thompson to ask for help in clearing Winsloe's name. Thompson enlisted the aid of the French ambassador to the United States, Henri Bonnet, who reported in December that French police files revealed Lambert to have acted from purely criminal motives and that no evidence existed to implicate Winsloe with the Gestapo or any other aspect of Nazism.

References:

Brooks Atkinson, "The Play," *New York Times*, 31 December 1932, p. 10;

Lee Atwill, *G. W. Pabst* (Boston: Twayne, 1977), p. 119;

Richard Dyer, *Now You See It. Studies on Lesbian and Gay Film* (London & New York: Routledge, 1990);

Karola Gramann and Heide Schlüpmann, "Unnatürliche Akte: Die Inszenierung des Lesbischen im Film," in *Lust und Elend: Das erotische Kino*, edited by Gramann and Gertrud Koch (Munich & Lucerne: Bucher, 1981), pp. 70-89;

Gramann, Schlüpmann, and Amadou Seitz, "Gestern und Heute: Gespräch mit Hertha Thiele," *Frauen und Film*, 28 (1981): 32-41;

Mordaunt Hall, "The Screen," *New York Times*, 21 September 1932, p. 26;

Judith M. Kass, "Mädchen in Uniform," in *Magill's Survey of Cinema: Foreign Language Films*, edited by Frank N. Magill, volume 4 (Englewood Cliffs, N.J.: Salem Press, 1985), pp. 1891-1894;

Siegfried Kracauer, *From Caligari to Hitler: A Psychological Study of the German Film* (Princeton: Princeton University Press, 1947);

Rosi Kreische, "Lesbische Liebe im Film bis 1950," in *Eldorado: Homosexuelle Frauen und Männer in Berlin 1850-1950. Geschichte, Alltag, und Kultur* (Berlin: Fröhlich & Kaufmann, 1984), pp. 187-196;

Peter Kurth, *American Cassandra: The Life of Dorothy Thompson* (Boston: Little, Brown, 1990);

Erika and Klaus Mann, *Escape to Life* (Boston: Houghton Mifflin, 1939), pp. 50-51;

Hans Helmut Prinzler, ed., *Hertha Thiele* (Berlin: Deutsche Kinemathek, 1983), pp. 44-51;

Christa Reinig, "Christa Reinig über Christa Winsloe," in *Mädchen in Uniform*, by Christa Winsloe (Munich: Frauenoffensive, 1983), pp. 241-248;

B. Ruby Rich, "*Mädchen in Uniform*: From Repressive Tolerance to Erotic Liberation," in *Re-Vision, Essays in Feminist Film Criticism*, edited by Mary Ann Doane, Patricia Mellencamp, and Linda Williams (Frederick, Md.: University Publications of America, 1984), pp. 100-126;

Marion K. Sanders, *Dorothy Thompson: A Legend in Her Time* (Boston: Houghton Mifflin, 1973);

Margarete Schäfer, "Theater, Theater!," in *Eldorado*, pp. 180-186;

Nancy Scholar, "Maedchen in Uniform," in *Sexual Strategems: The World of Women in Film*, edited by Patricia Ehrens (New York: Horizon Press, 1973), pp. 219-223;

Vincent Sheean, *Dorothy and Red* (Boston: Houghton Mifflin, 1963).

Papers:

Materials related to productions of *Gestern und Heute* and *Children in Uniform* are in the Theaterwissenschaftliches Archiv (Theater Science Archives of the Free University of Berlin; the Deutsches Theatermuseum in Cologne; and the New York Public Library, which also contains a typescript of *Ritter Nérestan*. Winsloe's correspondence with Dorothy Thompson and Thompson's diary about their romance are in the George Arents Research Library of Syracuse University.

Friedrich Wolf
(23 December 1888 - 5 October 1953)

Michael Winkler
Rice University

PLAY PRODUCTIONS: *Das bist du*, Dresden, Städtisches Schauspielhaus, 3 October 1919;

Der Unbedingte, Stettin, Stadttheater, 18 January 1921;

Tamar, Frankfurt am Main, Schauspielhaus, 20 February 1922;

Die schwarze Sonne, Oldenburg, Landestheater, 22 January 1924;

Der arme Konrad, Stuttgart, Württembergisches Staatstheater, 14 February 1924;

Der Mann im Dunkel, Essen, Stadttheater, 1 April 1927;

Kolonne Hund, Hamburg, Deutsches Schauspielhaus, 28 April 1927;

Koritke oder Die Zeche zahlt Koritke, Stuttgart, Kleines Haus des Württembergischen Landestheaters, 5 November 1927;

Cyankali, oder Cyankali Paragraph 218, Berlin, Lessingtheater, 1 October 1929;

Die Matrosen von Cattaro, Berlin, Volksbühne im Theater am Bülowplatz, 8 November 1930;

Tai Yang erwacht, Berlin, Piscator Bühne am Nollendorfplatz, 15 January 1931;

Die Jungens von Mons, Berlin, Berliner Theater, 20 December 1931;

Wie stehen die Fronten, Stuttgart, Gewerkschaftshaus, 6 May 1932;

Von New York bis Schanghai, Stuttgart, Spieltrupp Südwest, 3 September 1932;

Bauer Baetz, Stuttgart, Spieltrupp Südwest, 3 December 1932;

Der gelbe Fleck: Doktor Mamlocks Ausweg (in Yiddish), Warsaw, Kaminski Theater, 19 January 1934; as *Professor Mamlock* (in Hebrew), Tel Aviv, 25 July 1934; as *Professor Mamlock: Ein Schauspiel aus dem Deutschland von heute*, Zurich, Schauspielhaus, 8 December 1934;

Floridsdorf, Toronto, Arbeitertheater des Deutschen Arbeiter- und Farmer-Verbandes, 16 February 1936;

Das trojanische Pferd, Engels, U.S.S.R., Deutsches Staatstheater, 29 December 1936;

Friedrich Wolf as an internee at Le Vernet d'Ariege in France, 1939

Peter kehrt heim, Engels, U.S.S.R., Deutsches Staatstheater, 29 October 1937;

Félix Lope de Vega, *Laurencia oder die Schafsquelle*, adapted by Wolf, Engels, U.S.S.R., Deutsches Staatstheater, 7 November 1937;

Doktor Lilli Wanner, Chemnitz, Städtisches Theater, 2 December 1945;

Beaumarchais oder Die Geburt des "Figaro," Berlin, Deutsches Theater, 8 March 1946;

Patrioten, Cottbus, Stadttheater, November 1946;

Die letzte Probe, Dresden, Vereinigte Volksbühnen, 3 December 1946;

Die Nachtschwalbe, Leipzig, Städtisches Schauspielhaus, 23 February 1948;

Wie Tiere des Waldes, Leipzig, Städtische Bühnen, 1948;

Bürgermeister Anna, Dresden, Staatstheater, 14 October 1950;

Thomas Münzer: Der Mann mit der Regenbogenfahne, Berlin, Deutsches Theater, 23 December 1953;

Das Schiff auf der Donau, Berlin, Maxim-Gorki Theater, 2 February 1955;

Was der Mensch säet . . . , Böhlen, Thomas-Münzer Theater, 6 May 1955.

BOOKS: *Das bist du: Ein Spiel* (Dresden: Kämmerer, 1919); revised as *Das bist du: Ein Spiel in fünf Verwandlungen* (Dresden: Kämmerer, 1920);

Der Unbedingte: Ein Weg in drei Windungen und einer Überwindung (Dresden: Kämmerer, 1919);

Fahrt: Gedichte (Dresden: Kämmerer, 1920);

Die schwarze Sonne: Eine Komödie (Berlin: Rowohlt, 1921);

Elemente: Drei Einakter (Ludwigsburg: Chronos, 1922);

Mohammed: Ein Oratorium, geschrieben im Flandernsommer 1917 (Stuttgart: Chronos, 1924);

Der arme Konrad: Tragödie aus der Bauernrevolte 1514 (Ludwigsburg & Stuttgart: Chronos, 1924);

Das Heldenepos des Alten Bundes aufgespürt und in deutschen Worten (Stuttgart: Deutsche Verlags-Anstalt, 1925);

Kreatur: Roman der Zeit (Hannover: Sponholtz, 1925);

Der Mann im Dunkel: Komödie (Stuttgart: Chronos, 1925);

Der Sprung durch den Tod: Eine Erzählung (Stuttgart: Deutsche Verlags-Anstalt, 1925);

Kolonne Hund: Ein Schauspiel (Stuttgart: Deutsche Verlags-Anstalt, 1927);

Koritke: Ein Schauspiel (Stuttgart: Chronos, 1927);

Kunst ist Waffe: Eine Feststellung (Berlin: Arbeitertheaterbund Deutschlands, 1928);

Die Natur als Arzt und Helfer: Das neue naturärztliche Hausbuch (Stuttgart, Berlin & Leipzig: Deutsche Verlags-Anstalt, 1928);

Schlank und gesund: Ein natürlicher Weg zur Beseitigung heutigen Kultursiechtums, by Wolf and Lisa Mar (Stuttgart: Süddeutsches Verlagshaus, 1928);

Cyankali, § 218: Drama (Berlin: Internationaler Arbeiter-Verlag, 1929);

Herunter mit dem Blutdruck: Die wirksamste Verhütung der Arterienverkalkung und des Schlaganfalls (Stuttgart: Süddeutsches Verlagshaus, 1929);

Schütze dich vor dem Krebs: Seine wirksame Verhütung und operationslose Behandlung (Stuttgart: Süddeutsches Verlagshaus, 1929);

Dein Magen kein Vergnügungslokal sondern eine Kraftzentrale: Durch Selbsthilfe guter Stoffwechsel, gesundes Blut, keine Magen-Darmkrankheiten (Stuttgart: Süddeutsches Verlagshaus, 1930);

Hörspiele (Stuttgart: Deutsche Verlags-Anstalt, 1930)—comprises *SOS . . . Rao Rao . . . Foyn*; *"Krassin" rettet "Italia"*; *John D. erobert die Welt*;

Die Matrosen von Cattaro (Berlin, Vienna & Zurich: Internationaler Arbeiter-Verlag, 1930); translated by Keene Wallis and adapted by Michael Blackfort as *The Sailors of Cattaro: A Play in Two Acts Based on a Mutiny in the Austrian Navy in 1918* (New York, Los Angeles & London: French, 1935);

Der schwache Punkt der Frau: Die wichtigsten Frauenleiden, ihr Wesen, ihre Verhütung, ihre Behandlung (Stuttgart: Süddeutsches Verlagshaus, 1930);

Tai Yang erwacht: Ein Schauspiel (Berlin: Chronos, 1930);

Trotz Tempo 1000 . . . gesund (Radebeul: Madaus, 1930)—comprises *Dein Recht auf Gesundheit*, *Dein Weg zur Gesundheit*, *Die Volks-Gesundheits-Schule*;

Die Jungens von Mons: Schauspiel (Stuttgart: Chronos, 1931);

Bauer Baetz: Ein Schauspiel vom deutschen Bauern anno 1932 (Stuttgart: Schuler, 1932);

Floridsdorf: Ein Schauspiel von den Februarkämpfen der Wiener Arbeiter (Zurich: Oprecht & Helbling, 1935; Moscow: Verlagsgenossenschaft ausländischer Arbeiter in der UdSSR, 1935); translated by Anne Bromberger as *Floridsdorf, the Viennese Workers in Revolt* (Moscow: Co-operative Publishing Society of Foreign Workers in the U.S.S.R., 1935);

Doktor Mamlocks Ausweg: Tragödie der westlichen Demokratie (Zurich: Oprecht & Helbling, 1935; Moscow & Leningrad: Verlagsgenossenschaft ausländischer Arbeiter in der UdSSR, 1935); translated by Anne Bromberger as *Professor Mamlock* (Moscow: Co-operative Publishing Society of Foreign Workers in the U.S.S.R., 1935); German version republished as *Professor Mamlock: Ein Schauspiel* (Berlin: Volk & Wissen, 1952);

Die Nacht von Béthineville: Erzählung (Moscow: Verlagsgenossenschaft ausländischer Arbeiter in der UdSSR, 1936; enlarged edition, Berlin: Aufbau, 1959);

Fort Brimont-Galizyno (Moscow: Verlag für Schöne Literatur, 1936);

Von New York bis Schanghai: Eine politische Revue gegen den imperialistischen Krieg (Engels, U.S.S.R.: Deutscher Staatsverlag, 1936);

Das trojanische Pferd: Ein Stück vom Kampf der Jugend in Deutschland (Moscow: Verlagsgenossenschaft ausländischer Arbeiter in der UdSSR, 1937);

Zwei an der Grenze: Roman (Zürich & New York: Oprecht, 1938);

Gefährlicher Beifall: Erzählungen (Moscow: Verlag sowjetischer Schriftsteller, 1941);

KZ Vernet (Moscow: Verlag Das Internationale Buch, 1941);

Beaumarchais oder Die Geburt des "Figaro": Ein Schauspiel in elf Bildern (Moscow: Meshdunarodnaja Kniga, 1941; Berlin: Aufbau, 1946);

Der Kirschbaum (Moscow: Verlag für fremdsprachige Literatur, 1942);

Der Russenpelz: Eine Erzählung aus Deutschland 1941-42 (Moscow: Verlag für fremdsprachige Literatur, 1942);

Sieben Kämpfer vor Moskau (Moscow: Verlag für fremdsprachige Literatur, 1942);

Heimkehr der Söhne: Eine Novelle (Moscow: Verlag für fremdsprachige Literatur, 1944);

Das Öhmchen: Erzählung (Moscow: Verlag für Schöne Literatur, 1944);

Doktor Wanner: Schauspiel in vier Akten (Berlin: Aufbau-Bühnen-Vertrieb, 1945);

Was der Mensch säet . . . ; Schauspiel in 5 Bildern (Berlin: Aufbau-Bühnen-Vertrieb, 1945);

Dramen, 2 volumes (Berlin: Aufbau, 1946)— comprises volume 1: *Empörung: Der arme Konrad, Beaumarchais, Die Matrosen von Cattaro, Kolonne Hund*; volume 2: *Besinnung: Professor Mamlock, Patrioten, Doktor Wanner, Was der Mensch säet . . .* ; enlarged (1947-1949)—comprises volume 1: *Aufbruch: Das bist du, Mohammed, Tamar, Die schwarze Sonne*; volume 2: *Frauen: Cyankali, Tai Yang erwacht, Die letzte Probe, Laurencia*; volume 3: *Empörung: Der arme Konrad, Beaumarchais, Die Matrosen von Cattaro, Kolonne Hund*; volume 4: *Besinnung: Professor Mamlock, Patrioten, Doktor Wanner, Was der Mensch säet . . .* ;

Lucie und der Angler von Paris: Novellen (Berlin: Aufbau, 1946)—comprises *Lucie und der Angler von Paris; Gaston; Jules; Kiki*; enlarged as *Lucie und der Angler von Paris; Kurzgeschichten und Erzählungen Frankreich 1914/18 und 1939/41* (Berlin: Aufbau, 1949)—includes *Die Nacht von Béthineville, Der verschenkte Leutnant, Lichter überm Graben*;

Die letzte Probe: Romantisches Schauspiel in 9 Bildern (Berlin: Aufbau-Bühnen-Vertrieb, 1946);

Märchen für große und kleine Kinder (Berlin: Aufbau, 1946)—comprises *Das Osterhasenfell, Purzel und Drax, Die drei in Mexiko, Pit Pikus und die Möwe Leila, Der weite Weg*; enlarged (1952)—includes *Der stotternde Kuckuck, Die Biene Cilia und der kleine Franz*;

Die Nachtschwalbe: Dramatisches Nocturno (Berlin: Bote & Bock, 1947);

Vox humana: Verse (Rudolstadt: Greifenverlag, 1947);

Bund Deutscher Volksbühnen: Zeitprobleme des Theaters, die kulturpolitische Situation und die Bedeutung der Volksbühne. Vortrag auf der Gründungstagung des Bundes Deutscher Volksbühnen am 17. Mai 1947 (Berlin: Henschel, 1947);

Wie Tiere des Waldes: Ein Schauspiel von Hetzjagd, Liebe und Tod unserer Jugend (Berlin: Aufbau-Bühnen-Vertrieb, 1947);

Bitte der Nächste!: Dr. Isegrimms Rezeptfolgen. Ein Beitrag zur Deutschen Geschichte und Naturgeschichte (Rudolstadt: Greifenverlag, 1949);

Von der Filmidee zum Drehbuch, by Wolf and others (Berlin: Henschel, 1949);

Bürgermeister Anna: Ein Volksstück (Berlin: Aufbau-Bühnen-Vertrieb, 1950);

So fing es an! Zwei Szenen (Halle: Mitteldeutscher Verlag, 1950);

Bummi: Tiergeschichten für große und kleine Kinder (Berlin: Aufbau, 1951);

Lilo Herrmann: Die Studentin von Stuttgart: Ein biographisches Poem (Berlin: VVN, 1951);

Die Unverlorenen: Zwei Romane (Berlin: Aufbau, 1951);

Ausgewählte Werke in Einzelausgaben, 14 volumes, edited by Else Wolf and Walther Pollatschek (Berlin: Aufbau, 1951-1960)—comprises volumes 1-4; *Gesammelte Dramen* (volume 1: *Mohammed, Das bist du, Tamar, Die schwarze Sonne, Der arme Konrad*; volume 2: *Kolonne Hund, Cyankali, Die Matrosen von Cattaro, Tai Yang erwacht, Die Jungens von Mons*; volume 3: *Professor Mamlock, Floridsdorf, Laurencia, Beaumarchais, Patrioten*; volume 4: *Dr. Lilli*

Wanner, Was der Mensch säet, Wie Tiere des Waldes, Die letzte Probe, Bürgermeister Anna); volume 5: *Zwei an der Grenze*; volume 6: *Die Unverlorenen*; volume 7: *Erzählungen, Kurzgeschichten, Sketche*; volume 8: *Märchen und Tiergeschichten*; volume 9: *Gesammelte Dramen*; volume 10: *Hörspiele und Laienspiele*; volume 11; *Filmerzählungen*; volume 12: *Frühe Romane und kleine Prosa*; volume 13: *Aufsätze über Theater*; volume 14: *Aufsätze*;

Menetekel oder Die fliegenden Untertassen: Roman (Berlin: Aufbau, 1952);

Maxim Gorki: Revolutionärer Romantiker und sozialistischer Realist. Festrede zum fünfundachtzigsten Geburtstag Maxim Gorkis (Berlin: Henschel, 1953);

Thomas Münzer, der Mann mit der Regenbogenfahne: Ein Schauspiel (Berlin: Aufbau, 1953);

Rufe übern Graben: Sketche, Gedichte, Lieder und Fabeln, edited by Peter Korb (Leipzig: Hofmeister, 1955);

Fabeln, edited by Else Wolf and Pollatschek (Berlin: Holz, 1957);

Das Schiff auf der Donau: Ein Drama aus der Zeit der Okkupation Österreichs durch die Nazis (Berlin: Henschel, 1960);

Gesammelte Werke in sechzehn Bänden, 16 volumes, edited by Else Wolf and Pollatschek (Berlin: Aufbau, 1960-1968)—comprises—volumes 1-6: *Dramen* (volume 1: *Mohammed, Das bist du, Der Unbedingte, Die schwarze Sonne, Tamar, Die Schrankkomödie*; volume 2: *Der arme Konrad, Kolonne Hund, Koritke, Vor- und Nachspiel zu "Und das Licht leuchtet . . . ," Cyankali*; volume 3: *Die Matrosen von Cattaro, Tai Yang erwacht, Die Jungens von Mons, Professor Mamlock, Laurencia*; volume 4: *Floridsdorf, Das trojanische Pferd, Peter kehrt heim, Das Schiff auf der Donau*; volume 5: *Beaumarchais, Patrioten, Dr. Lilli Wanner, Was der Mensch säet*; volume 6: *Die letzte Probe, Wie Tiere des Waldes, Bürgermeister Anna, Thomas Münzer*); volume 7: *Hörspiele, Laienspiele, Szenen*; volume 8: *Filmerzählungen*; volume 9: *Vier Romane: Kreatur, Kampf im Kohlenpott, Der Russenpelz, Heimkehr der Söhne*; volume 10: *Zwei an der Grenze*; volume 11: *Menetekel*; volume 12: *Gedichte; Erzählungen 1911-1936*; volume 13: *Erzählungen 1941-1953*; volume 14: *Märchen, Tiergeschichten und Fabeln*; volume 15: *Aufsätze 1919-1944*; volume 16: *Aufsätze 1945-1953*;

Peter kehrt heim: Ein Stück von der deutschen Okkupation der Ukraine 1918 (Berlin: Henschel, 1962).

Edition in English: *Concentration Camp Vernet: Two Stories*, translated by M. S. Korr (Moscow: Mezhdunarodnaya Kniga, 1942).

MOTION PICTURE: *Der Rat der Götter*, Berlin, DEFA, 12 May 1950.

OTHER: Mykola Hurovych Kulish, *Die Beethovensonate: Ein Stück aus der Ukraine 1917*, translated and adapted by Wolf (Berlin, 1932);

Martha Ruben-Wolf, *Abtreibung oder Verhütung*, foreword by Wolf (Berlin: Internationaler Arbeiter Verlag, 1933);

Vsevolod Vital'erič Višnevskij, *Die optimistische Tragödie: Schauspiel in drei Akten*, translated and adapted by Wolf (Moscow: Verlagsgenossenschaft ausländischer Arbeiter in der UdSSR, 1937);

Jean Richard Bloch, *Toulon: Französische Geschichte in drei Epochen*, translated by Friedrich Franz Treuberg, foreword by Wolf (Berlin: Henschel, 1947);

N. Assanov and others, *Sieg des Lebens und andere Erzählungen: Eine Auswahl ernster und heiterer russischer Reportagen*, foreword by Wolf (Berlin: Dietz, 1949);

Pierre Augustin Caron de Beaumarchais, *Der tolle Tag oder Figaros Hochzeit: Drama*, foreword by Wolf (Berlin: Volk & Wissen, 1949);

Volk und Kunst: Monatsschrift des Bundes Deutscher Volksbühnen für Theater, Laienspiel, Volksmusik, Chorwesen und Tanz, edited by Wolf (Berlin: Henschel, 1949);

Alice Lex-Nerlinger, *Die harte Strasse, 1918-1949: Zeichnungen*, explanatory remark by Wolf (Weimar: Mock, 1950).

Friedrich Wolf was most successful and is best known today as a writer of political plays that support communist causes. His plays are Zeitstücke (stage presentations that discuss social issues and provide clear answers); Agitations- und Kampfstücke (productions meant to incite civil disobedience and confrontations with the guardians of the status quo); and Lehrstücke (didactic dramas dealing with public concerns). This type of activist literature constituted a major innovation of German theater during the late 1920s, the waning years of the Weimar Republic. It was hardly ever performed on the stages of theaters his creativity was subordinated to the programs of the organization for which he was a spokesman, and ideological discipline superseded inventiveness. This limitation does not altogether eliminate artistic subtlety or enduring intellectual and emotional relevance from Wolf's plays, but his basic impulse as an artist was to dramatize social injustices in a simplified style that used model situations to press home a few fundamental points.

Wolf was born on 23 December 1888 in Neuwied on the Rhine, the only child of a respected Jewish cloth merchant and tailor, Max Wolf, and Ida Meyer Wolf. He received a humanistic education at the Jewish elementary school and then, from 1899 until 1907, at the Royal Prussian Gymnasium in his hometown. After brief military service in Heidelberg he studied art history and painting at the Kunstakademie (Art Academy) in Munich. In 1908 he made a walking tour of Rome, Venice, and Florence. He studied medicine and philosophy in Tübingen, Bonn, and Berlin; in Berlin he frequently attended plays directed by Max Reinhardt. He contributed to literary journals, notably *Die Jugend* (Youth) and the satirical *Simplicissimus*. He was an enthusiastic reader of the works of Friedrich Nietzsche and a member of the youth organization Wandervogel (Migratory Bird). His Bonn dissertation dealt with cases of childhood multiple sclerosis; his medical practicum was spent in Meißen and Dresden. After his certification as a physician in 1913 and service as a doctor's assistant in Dresden and Bonn, he worked as a ship's doctor on the passenger steamer *Willehad* of the North German Lloyd's Canada Line. At the start of World War I he was sent to the western front; traumatic experiences in the trenches of Flanders, especially at Langemarck in 1916, turned him into a determined opponent of war. Early in 1918 he sought the status of conscientious objector. He assumed the position of chief physician at the military reserve hospital in Langebrück and later moved to Arnsdorf.

Wolf had married Käthe Gumpold on 30 November 1914; they had had two children: Johanna, born in 1915, and Lukas, born in 1919. By the end of the war he had joined the illegal Workers' and Soldiers' Council in Dresden and had become a member of its central committee for Saxony during the November Revolution. He also joined the Independent Social Democratic Party, whose radical politics he represented as a city councilman at Langebrück, his residence after the war. His idealistic activism is further at-

Scene from the premiere of Wolf's Cyankali, *a play that attacks Germany's strict antiabortion law, at the Lessingtheater in Berlin in 1929*

supported by bourgeois subscribers or city and state subsidies. Its audience usually consisted of working-class people who accepted the dramas as re-creations of their daily lives. The messages of these plays are hardly ever complex or ambiguous; they were not intended to transcend their immediate sociopolitical context. Few of Wolf's works exist in a definitive version; practically all of them underwent some rewriting to fit them to specific audiences and circumstances. The more important ones reveal several stages of changing emphasis and shifts in intent. These changes, however, are not reflected in any of the editions of his plays that have been published to date.

Since Wolf's plays would have missed their purpose if they failed to elicit a response of committed solidarity from their audiences, his individual position on any specific issue was less important than his party's policy on that issue. Thus, tested to by his participation in the Dresden Sozialistische Gruppe der Geistesarbeiter (Socialist Group of Intellectuals). His literary work by this time consisted of pacifist poetry, stories, and three dramas. His first play, *Mohammed* (published, 1924), which was never performed, dramatizes an almost mystical awakening that transforms a revolutionary into a practitioner of peaceful resistance who becomes the teacher of a new messianic doctrine of salvation. *Das bist du* (That Is You, 1919) revolves aroung the motif of an individual's new birth and adds the element of the liberating deed as a precondition for spiritual renewal. *Der Unbedingte* (The Absolutist; published, 1919; performed, 1921), rich in messianic symbolism, deals with the confrontation between the bourgeoisie and the working class and makes the poet a leader of the masses in their struggle against capitalist exploitation and against the harmful effects of industrial civilization. A return to the "Erdhaftigkeit" (earthiness) of simple life is proposed as an antidote.

In 1920 Wolf and his family moved to Remscheid in the south of the industrial Ruhr area. He held the position of city physician and was active in community health care, preventive medicine, and social welfare work. His contacts with the impoverished and often revolutionary working class strengthened his political commitments, one practical result of which was his participation in the suppression of a rightist coup d'etat attempted by Wolfgang Kapp and Walther Lüttwitz. His military skill as the leader of a company of striking workers earned him the nickname "Red General of Remscheid." At the end of May 1921 he joined the painter Heinrich Vogeler's Barkenhoff commune at Worpswede near Bremen, remaining there for three months as a doctor and a worker in the peat marshes. While there he wrote the play *Tamar* (performed, 1922; published, 1947). Based on a story in Genesis 38, *Tamar* pits an individualistic young woman against the rigid patriarchal demands of tribal law. *Die schwarze Sonne* (The Black Sun; published, 1921; performed, 1924) is a utopian comedy about life in a primal state ten thousand years in the future.

In November 1921 Wolf moved to Hechingen in Swabia, where he worked as country doctor specializing in homeopathic medicine. After his divorce on 12 December 1921 he married Else Dreibholz, whom he had met in Remscheid. Their two sons—Markus, born in 1923, and Konrad, born in 1926—were to achieve greater

prominence in the German Democratic Republic than their father; the former as the director of the country's security and intelligence service, the latter as its most acclaimed film director. Life among the poor artisans, farmers, and clerks gave Wolf new insights into the plight and political confusions of the rural petit bourgeoisie and the agricultural proletariat—impressions he used to good effect in *Der arme Konrad* (Poor Conrad, 1924), a historical drama about a failed peasants' revolt in Swabia shortly before the Reformation. Extensive research into the history of southwest Germany during the early decades of the sixteenth century, with its wars between the peasantry and their feudal lords, convinced Wolf that that era and his own were periods in which local conflicts preceded a great upheaval—one that he hoped would this time result in a victorious revolution. His play, a first draft of which was finished on 23 August 1923, depicts a rebellion of Swabian peasants who had formed a secret society, "Der arme Konrad." The peasants' Shrovetide play, *Das ehrsame Narrengericht* (The Honorable Fools' Court), which they perform under the direction of their leader, Konz, turns into an armed rebellion against Duke Ulrich. The duke is forced to sign the "Twelve Articles of the Common Man," which are expected to establish a new rule of justice. The peasants envision a return to a primal state of peace and equality, but the duke's treason defeats the revolutionary masses. Their faith in "die große Sach" (the great cause), however, is not vanquished. With this play, written in the stylized language of ordinary people and structured as a paradigm for political action, Wolf found the dramatic form that best suited his purposes. *Der arme Konrad* was performed to great public acclaim, first in Stuttgart and then in several other towns and cities of the southwest where historical reminders of the Peasants' War abound, and it quickly made Wolf's name known throughout Germany. His next play, *Der Mann im Dunkel* (The Man in the Dark; published, 1925; performed, 1927), a satirical social comedy, has three young women start a new life on an island far away from men and civilization.

While he was working on the short novel *Kreatur: Roman der Zeit* (Creation: A Novel of This Time, 1925), Wolf returned to his Jewish roots and also began to study the theories of Karl Marx. He considered his translation of parts of the Old Testament, *Das Heldenepos des Alten Bundes* (The Heroic Epic of the Old Covenant, 1925), as an answer to anti-Semitism. His play

Scene from a 1930 production in Düsseldorf of Wolf's Die Matrosen von Cattaro

Kolonne Hund (Hund's Team, 1927), completed on 4 October 1926, was soon presented on eighteen stages, among them the Hamburg Schauspielhaus in a performance with Gustav von Wangenheim and Hans Otto. Jost Hund, a worker in an agricultural commune much like Vogeler's Barkenhoff, struggles with the industrialist Flint, who has the civic authorities on his side in a violent dispute over access to fresh water. His defeat demonstrates that taking individualistic action against a cohesive system of economic interests is a mistake. *Koritke oder Die Zeche zahlt Koritke* (Koritke; or, Koritke Gets Stuck with the Bill, 1927) likewise shows the defeat of a presumably egotistical proletarian: the porter and waiter Koritke, formerly a member of an athletes' troupe, has adopted Mia, a young woman with artistic abilities. Her biological father, the factory owner Lomm, wants to have her near him in his old age as his office helper. Koritke is forced to renounce his claims to "fatherhood" after a dastardly intrigue instigated by Lomm, but Mia realizes her dream of becoming a celebrated dancer.

Wolf thought of his ideological affiliations—including membership in the Communist party, which he joined in 1928, and in the Bund proletarisch-revolutionärer Schriftsteller (League of Proletarian-Revolutionary Writers)—as extensions of his work as a healer into the realm of or-

ganized politics. *Kunst ist Waffe* (Art Is a Weapon, 1928), a speech he gave at a meeting of the Arbeiter-Theaterbund Deutschlands (Workers' Theater League of Germany) in 1928, clearly formulated his convictions. He applied this dictum effectively in *Cyankali* (Cyanide, 1929), attacking the restrictive antiabortion law in section 218 of the German Criminal Code. Like two other contemporary plays, Hans José Rehfisch's *Der Frauenarzt* (The Gynecologist; performed, 1928; published, 1929) and the medical doctor Carl Credé's *Frauen in Not: § 218* (Desperate Women: § 218), *Cyankali* presents in a highly melodramatic manner the effects of an unwanted (because unaffordable) pregnancy and the strict enforcement of the law against abortion. Wolf, however, rather than appealing to the audience's compassion for the innocent victims, tries to arouse the audience's anger at an injustice. Hete Fent, the twenty-year-old daughter of a worker's widow, changes in eight short scenes from happiness and pride to utter destitution when her lover, Paul, a politically active stoker, loses his job. Poverty forces them to perform an illegal abortion with the help of her mother. Hete and Paul are arrested; seriously ill, Hete pleads for help before she collapses. The play received more than one hundred performances by the Gruppe Junger Schauspieler (Group of Young Actors) at Berlin's renowned Lessing Theater; the group's subsequent tour, beginning in the middle of January 1930, took the play to all major German and some Swiss cities and, starting on 23 April 1930 in Minsk, through the Soviet Union for four weeks. The play caused a public debate of unprecedented intensity and extent. Wolf himself was accused of having performed more than a hundred abortions and was arrested on 19 February 1931 in Stuttgart, where he had opened a practice in 1927. The charges were dropped after mass protests all over Germany, including a huge rally in Berlin's Sportpalast (Sports Palace), on 15 April 1931.

Desperate revolt against arrogant authority and the abuse of legalized privileges is the theme of *Die Matrosen von Cattaro* (The Sailors of Cattaro, 1930), which dramatizes an incident involving the crew of an Austrian cruiser at the end of World War I. Following the example of the Kronstadt uprising in October 1917, the sailors start a revolutionary action; in this case, however, they employ the wrong strategy. Franz Rasch, the mate on the *Sankt Georg*, wastes too much time in fruitless discussions after his initial act of mutiny. The decisions of his sailors' council spoil their first success when trust in the fairness of the authorities replaces self-help; the officers persuade the majority of the sailors to surrender. Rasch and his few comrades soon find themselves isolated. With their arrest the rebellion collapses, and they are executed. The negative ending did not diminish the play's popular success. The Berlin actor Ernst Busch, in the role of Rasch, set the standards for many later performances, all of them on private stages or by actors' collectives who played at political rallies and similar large gatherings. A Russian translation of the play was given more than two hundred performances in Moscow after November 1932, while in Leningrad (today Saint Petersburg) it was shown concurrently on three different stages.

Such acclaim eluded *Die Jungens von Mons* (The Youngsters of Mons, 1931), based on an actual incident that occurred in Britain. A veteran's widow dresses in her husband's uniform to obtain the patriotic support of industrialists as she organizes a gang of hooligans to fight against striking workers. In the end she confesses that her demagogic abuse of nationalist sentiments hurt the cause of her class, and she changes her allegiance with equal belligerence. In *Tai Yang erwacht* (Tai Yang Awakens; published, 1930; performed, 1931) a conciliatory textile worker turns

into a revolutionary and joins the industrial proletariat in their fight against feudal militarism and the exploitation of Chinese workers by colonial investors. While the play offers no more than Wolf's standard fare, its premiere was noteworthy as a collaborative effort between the playwright, the director Erwin Piscator and his actors, and the stage designer John Heartfield.

By this time Wolf had reached the height of his prominence as a propagandist for social causes. His activities included far-flung speaking engagements at which he discussed issues of health legislation and agitated for other changes. Visits to the Soviet Union in March 1931 and in 1932 on the occasion of the fifteenth anniversary of the October Revolution established contacts with Communist functionaries and intellectuals who were to become his protectors, among them Sergei Tretiakov.

In Stuttgart in the spring of 1932 Wolf started his own touring company, Spieltrupp Südwest (Acting Troupe Southwest), which consisted largely of lay actors and former members of an agitprop group, Rote Einheit (Red Unity). Spieltrupp Südwest carried his message of revolution and of resistance to fascism to provincial towns that had fallen on hard times as a result of the world economic crisis after October 1929. Among the plays he wrote for them was *Von New York bis Schanghai* (From New York to Shanghai; performed, 1932; published, 1936), which was presented at a rally of ten thousand Communists in Stuttgart in 1932.

Wolf barely eluded arrest when the Nazi security forces started their coordinated hunt for leftist subversives after the burning of the Reichstag (Parliament) building on 27 February 1933. His play *Bauer Baetz* (Farmer Baetz, 1932), the story of a ruined farmer who cannot prevent the foreclosure of his homestead, was performed only six times. While Wolf was arranging for its staging on 1 March 1933 in Stuttgart, he overheard orders for his arrest and fled the country by way of Austria to Basel, finding refuge with Walter and Margrit Strub, the founders of the Swiss Communist party. In France he was welcomed by Marcel Cachin, secretary of the French Communist party, and Paul Vaillant-Couturier, editor in chief of *Humanité*, the party's principal newspaper. Living in Paris and in Ker Anguilis on the Ile de Bréhat, he finished his play attacking anti-Semitism, *Der gelbe Fleck: Doktor Mamlocks Ausweg* (The Yellow Spot: Doctor Mamlock's Remedy; performed, 1934; published as *Doktor Mamlocks*

Constanze Menz in the premiere of Wolf's Tai Yang
erwacht *in Berlin in 1931*

for rules. His fate is the result of his own wishful thinking at a time when resolute opposition is called for.

In November 1933 Wolf went to the Soviet Union, where he attended the All-Union Congress of Soviet Writers from 17 August to 1 September 1934 at which socialist realism was made the normative program for all Communist writers. In the spring of 1935 he was a speaker at the first Congress of American Writers in New York City, after which he made a lecture tour of the United States. In July 1935 he returned to Moscow, where the Seventh World Congress of the Communist International, meeting from 25 July to 20 August, adopted the policy of popular-front alliances with leftist and humanist forces in the West. His play *Floridsdorf* (published, 1935; translated, 1935; performed, 1936) dramatizes episodes from the workers' uprising in an industrial suburb of Vienna in February 1934. In March 1936 he made a trip through the Scandinavian countries to lecture on the Nazi menace. His play *Das trojanische Pferd* (The Trojan Horse; performed, 1936; published, 1937), written for a youthful Russian audience and using documentary evidence of reports from Germany, shows young Communists working in the anti-Fascist underground. In 1937 Wolf was back in Moscow working on the script for the Soviet film of *Professor Mamlock*. His play *Peter kehrt heim* (Peter Returns; performed, 1937; published, 1962) chronicles the changing political sympathies of a young German soldier in the 1918 Ukraine who discovers his true home alongside the revolutionary peasants and workers.

In January 1938 Wolf went to Paris via Helsingfors after several petitions to become a doctor with the International Brigades in Spain failed to yield satisfactory responses. Like virtually all German and Italian émigrés in France at the outbreak of World War II, Wolf was sent to several primitive internment camps, among them the notorious extradition prison at Le Vernet d'Ariege from September 1939 to October 1940 and an abandoned brick factory, Les Milles, near Aix-en-Provence. During his exile in France he finished a novel about political refugees, *Zwei an der Grenze* (Two at the Border, 1938), and two dramas, *Das Schiff auf der Donau* (The Ship on the Danube; performed, 1955; published, 1960) in 1938 and *Beaumarchais oder Die Geburt des "Figaro"* (Beaumarchais; or, The Birth of "Figaro," 1946) early in 1941. He also worked on several film treatments, one of them dealing with the anti-Nazi Pas-

Ausweg, 1935; translated as *Professor Mamlock*, 1935) in four months. It became a great international success. Mamlock, a highly respected surgeon, a Jew, and a patriotic German with a strong attachment to the pre-1914 Wilhelmine world, refuses an order to vacate his position at a prestigious clinic. In a confrontation with his Fascist adversary, Dr. Hellpach, he insists on a strict separation of politics and medicine, an evasive strategy his wife supports and his son Rolf, an organizer of the resistance, scorns. He is powerless against the machinations of his Jew-baiting opponent, whose threats persuade the clinic's staff to renounce their support of Mamlock. Profoundly disillusioned, Mamlock commits suicide. As he dies he realizes that he should have supported the resistance. Wolf never again invented a character or a dramatic situation that elicited a similar response of reflection and resolve. Mamlock is a man of admirable principles, and for that reason he must give way to those who show no respect

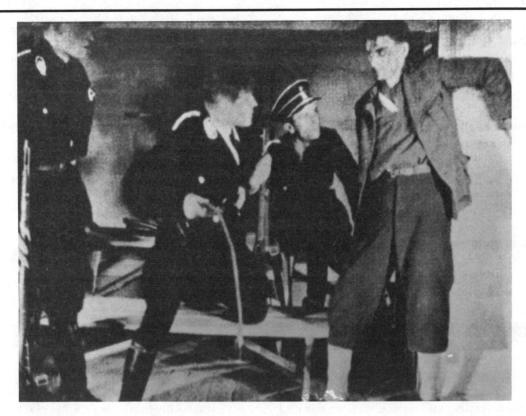

Scene from the production of Wolf's Das trojanische Pferd *that premiered in Engels, U.S.S.R., in 1936*

tor Martin Niemöller, but none was accepted by either a Hollywood or Soviet studio. *Das Schiff auf der Donau* depicts a floating concentration camp on the Danube whose prisoners overcome their divisive self-interests and unite in solidarity against their captors. In *Beaumarchais* the playwright is a perfect revolutionary hero at first, a pragmatic organizer of resistance against privilege and suppression, and an intellectual precursor of 1789. He is a poetic genius whose inspiration is drawn from a close understanding of the people's aspirations and of their natural rights. His play, *Le mariage de Figaro* (1784) as re-created within Wolf's play, is a prelude to revolution in the streets. But the imprisoned Beaumarchais loses confidence in the people's loyalty and becomes a defector from the ranks of the faithful at a time of severe crisis—a timely topic for a Communist author held in captivity in 1940 France.

When the Soviet Union gave Wolf a passport, he was released; after a hasty flight through Italy, Hungary, and the Ukraine with about two hundred other new Soviet citizens, he arrived in Moscow on 18 March 1941. After Germany attacked the Soviet Union on 22 June 1941 he was evacuated, along with most other exiled intellectuals, to Alma-Ata in far eastern Kazakhstan

near the Chinese border. He was recalled to Moscow late in December 1941 to work in the central political branch of the Red Army. He distributed leaflets, made radio broadcasts, and interviewed prisoners of war close to the Stalingrad front, activities for which he was awarded the Order of the Red Star. In July 1943 he was sent to indoctrinate captured German officers, first at Camp 97 near Yelabuga in the Tatar Republic, then at Krasnogorsk, near Moscow. The plays he wrote during this time were two resistance dramas, *Patrioten* (Patriots, 1946) and *Doktor Lilli Wanner* (performed, 1945; published as *Doktor Wanner*, 1945). *Patrioten* is about a French family whose father, a loyal civil servant, advocates peace at any cost, while his son and daughter-in-law want to blow up a railway yard to deny the Nazis an unimpeded flow of trains to the Russian front. *Doktor Lilli Wanner* presents the loyalties of a French doctor who is married to a German surgeon and aids her countrymen, forced laborers in the war industry. Another play, *Was der Mensch säet . . .* (What Man Soweth; published, 1945; performed, 1955), covers the period from 1941 to 1945 and traces the political ideologies of three families.

One of the first exiles to return to Berlin, Wolf arrived on 20 September 1945 and immediately assumed an important role in the cultural reconstruction of the Soviet Zone of Occupation, which became the German Democratic Republic in 1949. His untiring work for various organizations and successful performances of his earlier plays in 1946 and 1947 made him a highly visible spokesman for the new cultural programs and earned him the highest awards. His later plays, however, such as *Die letzte Probe* (The Last Rehearsal, 1946), about Viennese actors at the time of the annexation of Austria by Nazi Germany; *Wie Tiere des Waldes* (Like Animals in the Woods; published, 1947; performed, 1948), about a tragic love affair between a young German deserter and his girlfriend, who kills herself in April 1945 when her father has the boy arrested; *Bürgermeister Anna* (Mayor Anna, 1950), a moderately ribald comedy; and *Thomas Münzer* (1953), about the revolutionary theologian, did nothing to enhance his reputation. He had repeated himself too many times and was considered an anachronism. He served as ambassador to Warsaw from 1949 until 1951. But even before his resignation from the diplomatic service Wolf recognized that he had become more of an ornament than an effective insider in the cultural affairs of his country. He retired to his home in Lehnitz near Berlin and, after several coronary attacks, died on 5 October 1953 of a torn heart muscle.

Letters:

Friedrich Wolf, Wsewolod Wischnewskij: Eine Auswahl aus ihrem Briefwechsel (Berlin: Deutsche Akademie der Künste, 1965);

Briefwechsel: Eine Auswahl, edited by Else Wolf and Walther Pollatschek (Berlin & Weimar: Aufbau, 1968);

Briefe, edited by Else Wolf und Pollatschek (Berlin & Weimar: Aufbau, 1969);

Friedrich Wolf und der Film: Aufsätze und Briefe 1920-1953, edited by Ruth Herlinghaus (Berlin: Hochschule für Film und Fernsehen, 1988).

Biographies:

Walther Pollatschek, *Friedrich Wolf: Sein Leben in Bildern. Text und Bildteil* (Leipzig: Verlag Enzyklopädie, 1960);

Wilfried Adling, ed., *Friedrich Wolf* (Berlin: Deutscher Kulturbund, 1963);

Werner Jehser, *Friedrich Wolf: Sein Leben und Werk* (Berlin: Volk & Wissen, 1968);

Pollatschek, *Friedrich Wolf: Leben und Schaffen* (Leipzig: Reclam, 1974);

Lew Hohmann, *Friedrich Wolf: Bilder einer deutschen Biographie. Eine Dokumentation* (Berlin: Das europäische Buch, 1988).

References:

Gudrun Düwel, *Friedrich Wolf und Wsewelod Wischnewskij: Eine Untersuchung zur Internationalität sozialistisch-realistischer Dramatik* (Berlin: Akademie, 1974);

Gerald A. Fetz, "From *Der arme Konrad* (1923) to *Thomas Münzer* (1953): Friedrich Wolf and the Development of the Socialist History Play in Germany," *German Studies Review*, 10 (May 1987): 255-272;

Klaus Hammer, "Friedrich Wolfs *Beaumarchais*: Im Schnittpunkt zweier Epochen," *Weimarer Beiträge*, 32, no. 7 (1986): 1156-1171;

Hammer, "Weltanschauliche Entwicklung und ästhetische Konzeption Friedrich Wolfs von den Anfängen bis 1929," Ph.D. dissertation, University of Jena, 1984;

Walther Pollatschek, *Das Bühnenwerk Friedrich Wolfs: Ein Spiegel der Geschichte des Volkes* (Berlin: Henschel, 1958);

Ulf-Rüdiger Sacksofsky, "Friedrich Wolfs Dramatik von 1924 bis 1931 und ihre Beurteilung in der Kritik," Ph.D. dissertation, University of Cologne, 1972;

Michael Winkler, "Friedrich Wolf's *Beaumarchais*—A Propaganda Play Nonetheless?," in *Deutsches Exildrama und Exiltheater: Akten des Exilliteratur-Symposiums der University of South Carolina 1976*, edited by Wolfgang Elfe, James Hardin, and Günther Holst (Bern: Lang, 1977), pp. 133-138.

Carl Zuckmayer

(27 December 1896 - 18 January 1977)

Blake Lee Spahr
University of California, Berkeley

See also the Zuckmayer entry in *DLB 56: German Fiction Writers, 1914-1945.*

PLAY PRODUCTIONS: *Kreuzweg*, Berlin, Staatstheater, 10 December 1920;

Terence, *Eunuch*, adapted by Zuckmayer, Kiel, Stadttheater, 1923;

Pankraz erwacht, Berlin, Deutsches Theater, 15 February 1925;

Der fröhliche Weinberg, Berlin, Theater am Schiffbauerdamm, 22 December 1925;

Schinderhannes, Berlin, Lessingtheater, 13 October 1927;

Maxwell Anderson and Laurence Stalling, *Rivalen*, adapted by Zuckmayer, Berlin, Theater in der Königgrätzer Strasse, 1928;

Katharina Knie, Berlin, Lessingtheater, 20 December 1928;

Kakadu-Kakada, Berlin, Deutsches Künstlertheater, 18 January 1930;

Der Hauptmann von Köpenick, Berlin, Deutsches Theater, 5 March 1931;

Kat, by Zuckmayer and Heinz Hilpert, Berlin, Deutsches Theater, 1931;

Der Schelm von Bergen, Vienna, Burgtheater, 21 October 1934;

Bellman, Zurich, Schauspielhaus, 14 November 1938; revised as *Ulla Winblad*, Göttingen, Deutsches Theater, 17 October 1953;

Somewhere in France, by Zuckmayer and Fritz Kortner, New York, Guild Theatre, 7 May 1941;

Des Teufels General, Zurich, Schauspielhaus, 12 December 1946;

Barbara Blomberg, Constance, Deutsches Theater, 30 April 1949;

Der Gesang im Feuerofen, Göttingen, Deutsches Theater, 3 November 1950;

Herbert Engelmann, by Zuckmayer and Gerhart Hauptmann, Vienna, Burgtheater, 10 March 1952;

Das kalte Licht, Hamburg, Deutsches Schauspielhaus, 3 September 1955;

Carl Zuckmayer

Die Uhr schlägt eins, Vienna, Burgtheater, 14 October 1961;

Das Leben des Horace A. W. Tabor, Zurich, Schauspielhaus, 18 November 1964;

Kranichtanz, Zurich, Schauspielhaus, 10 January 1967;

Der Rattenfänger, Zurich, Schauspielhaus, 22 February 1975.

BOOKS: *Kreuzweg: Drama* (Munich: Wolff, 1921);

Der fröhliche Weinberg: Lustspiel in drei Akten (Berlin: Propyläen, 1925);

Der Baum: Gedichte (Berlin: Propyläen, 1926);

Ein Bauer aus dem Taunus und andere Geschichten (Berlin: Propyläen, 1927);

Schinderhannes: Schauspiel in vier Akten (Berlin: Propyläen, 1927);

Katharina Knie: Ein Seiltänzerstück in vier Akten (Berlin: Propyläen, 1929);

Kakadu-Kakada: Ein Kinderstück (Berlin: Propyläen, 1929);

Der Hauptmann von Köpenick: Ein deutsches Märchen in drei Akten (Berlin: Propyläen, 1930); translated by David Portman as *The Captain of Köpenick: A Modern Fairy Tale in Three Acts* (London: Bles, 1932); translated by Carl Richard Mueller as *The Captain of Köpenick*, in *German Drama between the Wars*, edited by George E. Wellwarth (New York: Dutton, 1974), pp. 179-296;

Die Affenhochzeit: Novelle (Berlin: Propyläen, 1932); translated by F. A. Beaumont as "Monkey Wedding," *Argosy*, 23 (March 1938): 53-69;

Gerhart Hauptmann: Rede zu seinem siebzigsten Geburtstag, gehalten bei der offiziellen Feier der Stadt Berlin (N.p., 1932);

Eine Liebesgeschichte (Berlin: Fischer, 1934);

Der Schelm von Bergen: Ein Schauspiel (Berlin: Propyläen, 1934);

Salwàre oder Die Magdalena von Bozen: Roman (Berlin: Fischer, 1935; Vienna: Bermann-Fischer, 1936); translated by Moray Firth as *The Moon in the South* (London: Secker & Warburg, 1937); translation republished as *The Moon Rides Over* (New York: Viking, 1937);

Ein Sommer in Österreich: Erzählung (Vienna: Bermann-Fischer, 1937);

Herr über Leben und Tod (Stockholm: Bermann-Fischer, 1938);

Pro Domo (Stockholm: Bermann-Fischer, 1938);

Carlo Mierendorff: Porträt eines deutschen Sozialisten (New York: Selbstverlag, 1944; Berlin: Suhrkamp, 1947);

Der Seelenbräu: Erzählung (Stockholm: Bermann-Fischer, 1945);

Des Teufels General: Drama in drei Akten (Stockholm: Bermann-Fischer, 1946); translated by Ingrid G. and William F. Gilbert as *The Devil's General*, in *Masters of German Drama*, edited by H. M. Block and R. G. Shedd (New York: Random House, 1962), pp. 911-958;

Gesammelte Werke, 4 volumes (Stockholm: Bermann-Fischer, 1947-1952);

Die Brüder Grimm: Ein deutscher Beitrag zur Humanität (Frankfurt am Main: Suhrkamp, 1948);

Barbara Blomberg: Ein Stück in drei Akten mit Vorspiel und Epilog (Amsterdam & Vienna: Bermann-Fischer, 1949);

Der Gesang im Feuerofen: Drama in drei Akten (Frankfurt am Main & Berlin: Fischer, 1950);

Die langen Wege: Ein Stück Rechenschaft: Rede (Frankfurt am Main: Fischer, 1952);

Ulla Winblad oder Musik und Leben des Carl Michael Bellman (Frankfurt am Main & Berlin: Fischer, 1953);

Engele von Loewen: Erzählungen (Zurich: Classen, 1955);

Das kalte Licht: Drama in drei Akten (Frankfurt am Main: Fischer, 1955);

Fünfzig Jahre Düsseldorfer Schauspielhaus, 1905-1955 (N.p., 1955);

Ein Blick auf den Rhein: Rede, gehalten bei der feierlichen Verleihung der Würde eines Doktor honoris causa der Philosophischen Fakultät der Universität Bonn am 10. Mai 1957. Mit einer Einführungsrede von Benno von Wiese und Kaiserswaldau (Bonn: Hanstein, 1957);

Die Fastnachtsbeichte: Eine Erzählung (Frankfurt am Main: Fischer, 1959); translated by John and Necke Mander as *Carnival Confession* (London: Methuen, 1961);

Ein Weg zu Schiller (Frankfurt am Main: Fischer, 1959);

Gedichte (Frankfurt am Main: Fischer, 1960);

Gesammelte Werke, 4 volumes (Frankfurt am Main & Berlin: Fischer, 1960);

Hinein ins volle Menschenleben, edited by Franz Theodor Csokor (Graz & Vienna: Stiasny, 1961);

Die Uhr schlägt eins: Ein historisches Drama aus der Gegenwart (Frankfurt am Main: Fischer, 1961);

Festrede zum vierhundertjährigen Bestehen des Humanistischen Gymnasiums in Mainz, gehalten am 27. Mai 1962 (Mainz: von Zabern, 1962);

Ein voller Erdentag: Zu Gerhart Hauptmanns hundertstem Geburtstag (Frankfurt am Main: Fischer, 1962);

Eine Weihnachtsgeschichte (Zurich: Arche, 1962);

Geschichten aus vierzig Jahren (Frankfurt am Main: Fischer, 1963);

Three Stories, edited by Derrick Barlow (London: Oxford University Press, 1963)—comprises "Die Geschichte eines Bauern aus dem Taunus," "Die Affenhochzeit," "Die wandernden Hütten";

Das Leben des Horace A. W. Tabor: Ein Stück aus den Tagen der letzten Könige (Frankfurt am Main: Fischer, 1964);

Als wär's ein Stück von mir: Horen der Freundschaft (Frankfurt am Main: Fischer, 1966); translated by Richard and Clara Winston as *A Part of Myself* (London: Secker & Warburg, 1970; New York: Harcourt Brace Jovanovich, 1970);

Meisterdramen (Frankfurt am Main: Fischer, 1966);

Scholar zwischen gestern und morgen: Ein Vortrag gehalten in der Universität Heidelberg anläßlich seiner Ernennung zum Ehrenbürger am 23. November 1967 (Heidelberg: Brausdruck, 1967);

Meistererzählungen (Frankfurt am Main: Fischer, 1967);

Carl Zuckmayer: Eine Auslese, edited by Wolfgang Mertz (Vienna & Heidelberg: Überreuter, 1968);

Memento zum zwanzigsten Juli 1969 (Frankfurt am Main: Fischer, 1969);

Auf einem Weg im Frühling: Erzählung; Wiedersehen mit einer Stadt: Aus dem Stegreif erzählt (Salzburg: Residenz, 1970);

Über die musische Bestimmung des Menschen: Rede zur Eröffnung der Salzburger Festspiele 1970, edited by Max Kaindl-Hönig, with English translation by Richard Rickett and French translation by Martha Eissler (Salzburg: Festungsverlag, 1970);

Stücke meines Lebens: Mit persönlichen Einleitungen des Autors (Frankfurt am Main: Büchergilde Gutenberg, 1971);

Henndorfer Pastorale (Salzburg: Residenz, 1972);

Der Rattenfänger: Eine Fabel (Frankfurt am Main: Fischer, 1975);

Aufruf zum Leben: Porträts und Zeugnisse aus bewegten Zeiten (Frankfurt am Main: Fischer, 1976);

Werkausgabe in zehn Bänden, 1920-1975, 10 volumes (Frankfurt am Main: Fischer, 1976)—volumes 1-2: *Als wär's ein Stück von mir*; volume 3: *Gedichte*; volumes 4-6: *Erzählungen 1-3*; volumes 7-10: *Stücke 1-3*;

Zuckmayer Lesebuch (Frankfurt am Main: Fischer, 1976);

Gedichte (Frankfurt am Main: Fischer, 1977);

Rembrandt: Ein Film (Frankfurt am Main: Fischer, 1980);

Dieser Stadt gehört meine Liebe: 2 Mainzer Reden (Mainz: Carl-Zuckmayer-Gesellschaft, 1981);

Einmal, wenn alles vorüber ist: Briefe an Kurt Grell, Gedichte, Dramen, Prosa aus den Jahren 1914-1920 (Frankfurt am Main: Fischer, 1981);

Austreibung: 1934-1939 (Stuttgart: Reclam, 1983);

Sitting Bull: Ein Indianer-Roman und einige Geschichten (Frankfurt am Main: Fischer, 1984).

Edition in English: *Second Wind*, translated by Elizabeth Reynolds Hapgood (New York: Doubleday, Doran, 1940; London: Harrap, 1941).

MOTION PICTURES: *Schinderhannes*, screenplay by Zuckmayer, directed by Kurt Bernhardt, 1928; released in the United States as *The Prince of Rogues*, 1929;

Der blaue Engel, screenplay by Zuckmayer, Karl Vollmoeller, and Robert Liebmann, Universum Film Aktiengesellschaft, 1930;

Der Hauptmann von Köpenick, screenplay by Zuckmayer, Roto G. P. Film, 1932;

Escape Me Never, screenplay by Zuckmayer, United Artists, 1935;

Rembrandt, screenplay by Zuckmayer, London Films, 1936;

Der Froehliche Weinberg, scenario by Zuckmayer and Kurt J. Brown, Magna Film, 1953; released in the United States as *The Grapes Are Ripe*, 1953;

Der Hauptmann von Köpenick, screenplay by Zuckmayer, Real Production, 1956;

Schinderhannes, screenplay by Zuckmayer, Real Production, 1958;

The Captain from Köpenick, screenplay by Zuckmayer and Helmut Kautner, Gyula Trebitsch Production, 1959.

RECORDINGS: *Als wär's ein Stück von mir*; *Des Teufels General*, read by Zuckmayer, Preiserrecords, PR 3187, 1968;

Ein Stück von mir; *Gedichte*, read by Zuckmayer, Exlibris, EL 12249, 1975.

OTHER: Karl Otto Paetel, *Deutsche innere Emigration: Anti-nationalsozialistische Zeugnisse aus Deutschland*, contribution by Zuckmayer (New York: Krause, 1946);

Ödön Horváth, *Ein Kind unserer Zeit*, commemorative speech by Zuckmayer (Vienna: Berglandverlag, 1951);

Gerhart Hauptmann, *Herbert Engelmann: Drama in vier Akten*, completed by Zuckmayer (Munich: Beck, 1952);

Werner Krauss, *Das Schauspiel meines Lebens: Einem Freund erzählt*, introduction by Zuckmayer (Stuttgart: Goverts, 1958);

Ingeborg Engelsing-Malek, *Amor Fati in Zuck-mayers Dramen*, foreword by Zuckmayer (Constance: Rosgarten, 1960).

Along with Bertolt Brecht and Gerhart Hauptmann, Carl Zuckmayer was one of the most popular and significant German dramatists of the twentieth century. His play *Der fröhliche Weinberg* (The Happy Vineyard, 1925) is given credit for the death of expressionism, and both *Der Hauptmann von Köpenick* (published, 1930; performed, 1931; translated as *The Captain of Köpenick*, 1932) and *Des Teufels General* (1946; translated as *The Devil's General*, 1962) were among the most-often-produced plays of the modern German stage. He brought to the theater a sympathy for the common people and a healthy identification with nature; he could be natural without being "naturalistic." His plays provided superb roles for some of the greatest actors of his time, such as Albert Bassermann, Käthe Dorsch, Käthe Haak, Attila Hörbiger, Werner Krauß, and Paula Wessely. His prose works, while not as successful as his dramas, are still widely read, and his autobiography, *Als wär's ein Stück von mir* (1966, translated as *A Part of Myself*, 1970), presents a vivid picture of Germany from World War I to the 1950s. The taste of the times changed, and Zuckmayer's later plays did not keep pace with the new subtleties of the stage, but he remains a monument to German drama in the twentieth century.

Zuckmayer was born on 27 December 1896 in the village of Nackenheim in the Rhineland into a middle-class family. His father, also named Carl, owned a factory that produced wine-bottle caps. His mother, Amalie Friedericke Auguste Goldschmidt Zuckmayer, was the daughter of a Protestant church councillor who had converted from Judaism. After attending the gymnasium in Mainz, Zuckmayer was caught up in the wave of patriotism at the beginning of World War I and enlisted in the army in 1914. His war service brought him to the rank of lieutenant, but his first poems, which appeared in the journal *Die Aktion* (Action) in 1917, show a pacifistic tendency. Desultory studies at the University of Frankfurt in 1918-1919 and the University of Heidelberg in early 1919—attendance at a single seminar in literary history persuaded him to avoid that area—were followed by a brief marriage to a childhood sweetheart, Annemarie Gans, in 1920 and a short relationship with the actress Annemarie Seidel. The acceptance of his first play, *Kreuzweg* (Crossroad, or The Way of the Cross [the ambiguity is intentional]; published, 1921), for performance in Berlin lured him to that city in the fall of 1920. The play premiered on 10 December; it closed after the third performance. Zuckmayer himself admitted it to be a chaotic and confused piece. The play is a conglomeration of expressionistic themes, lacking any semblance of dramatic motivation or character depiction. The women figures are derivative of Gerhart Hauptmann's more ethereal creations, such as Rautendelein (in *Die versunkene Glocke*; performed, 1896; published, 1897; translated as *The Sunken Bell*, 1898) and Pippa (in *Und Pippa tanzt!*, 1906; translated as *And Pippa Dances*, 1909). The drama offended both conservatives and liberals with its attempt to combine an impossible potpourri of popular themes. Zuckmayer thus received his baptism by fire in Berlin, the most critical center of German drama.

After almost a year's work on a never-completed drama about the Anabaptists in sixteenth-century Germany and a trip to Norway, Zuckmayer received, through the good offices of a friend, the position of Dramaturg (theatrical consultant) in Kiel in the fall of 1922. There his adaptation of Terence's *Eunuchus* as *Eunuch* (performed, 1923) so offended the city council by its obscene allusions that he was summarily dismissed. In the fall of 1923 he became Dramaturg at the Schauspielhaus (Playhouse) in Munich, where he fell under the influence of Brecht. A third failure, *Pankraz erwacht* (Pankraz Awakens), was the result of the Brechtian influence. A lurid piece dealing with incest and murder and supposedly written in a single night in 1923, it premiered in Berlin under the direction of Heinz Hilpert in February 1925. This fiasco disabused Zuckmayer of his delusion that it was his mission to introduce a new epoch in the German theater—which, ironically, was what his next play accomplished.

During a visit to a rich relative Zuckmayer met the Austrian actress Alice von Herdan, whom he married in 1925. Their daughter, Winnetou, was born the following year. In his first flush of marital bliss Zuckmayer completed the play that was to make him a household name. *Der fröhliche Weinberg*, after having been rejected by all fifteen theaters in Berlin, received the distinguished Kleist Prize from the stern and demanding critic Paul Fechter. In spite of the award it was only through the efforts of Julius Elias, the grand old man of the theatrical scene who had taken Zuckmayer under his wing, that the play was accepted for production by Heinz Saltenburg, the director of three large Berlin theaters. Because the play had received the Kleist Prize, Saltenburg, though still convinced it would be a failure, had it shown in his best house, the Theater am Schiffbauerdamm. Not since the uproar over Hauptmann's *Vor Sonnenaufgang* (1889; translated as *Before Dawn*, 1909) had a play elicited such a tumultuous reaction from the German public.

It is a rollicking piece, as redolent with rural atmosphere as the manure heap on which the antihero sleeps off a drunken night, parodying the healthy peasant ethos of "get-my-daughter-pregnant, then-you-can-marry-her (provided that she enjoyed the experience)"—here reversed to have the male prove his virility rather than the female her fertility—and displaying in sympathetic, albeit grossly exaggerated, fashion peasant life in Zuckmayer's hometown of Nackenheim (which did not forgive him until more than two decades later). A vineyard owner, Jean Gunderloch, who, having suffered from a sterile married life, vows that his illegitimate daughter shall have a child-filled marriage. He gets her engaged to a pedantic and effete young dandy; but her true love for a virile boatman wins out, and all ends happily. Even her vapid former fiancé wins an innkeeper's nubile daughter. The dialogue is in the rich dialect of the region, which spares no earthy expression, and the play includes several real Rhine-Hessian folk songs. The action includes a drunken brawl in which militaristic war veterans, peasants, Gunderloch, and prospective purchasers of the vineyard mix it up in true Wild West film style. Parody, satire, and humor combine to produce a shameless comedy in which all could feel themselves to be the butt of the jest. Even the play itself is parodied: at the happy ending, a model of comedy kitsch, where four engagements are celebrated, the old vineyard owner calls out: "All müsse sie sich kriege am Schluß, sonst is das Stück nit gut!" (Everybody has to get everybody at the end, otherwise the play's no good!").

The play is a standard situation comedy, with all the clichés of the genre; but it marked the end of expressionism, bringing the German stage back to the realities of life. The incipient National Socialists attacked the play ruthlessly because, Zuckmayer suspected, he had elicited a true proximity to nature without resorting to the frenetic Blut und Boden (Blood and Soil) nationalism they favored. The bawdy language and humor offended the moralists; students were resentful of the pedantic dandy, who brags about his university days; the army felt that the military had been insulted; and the Jews were upset about a none-too-heroic Semitic figure. Some performances had to have a police cordon around the theater to permit the entry of ticket-holders. But each disturbance contributed to the reputation of the play.

Rather than take immediate advantage of the sensational success of *Der fröhliche Weinberg*, Zuckmayer spent more than a year working on his next play. In the winter of 1922-1923 he had written a scurrilous series of balladlike narratives that he had presented, tongue-in-cheek, as genuine folk ballads, accompanying himself on the guitar or the accordion. Among these narratives was the story of a kind of Robin Hood of the Rhineland, Wilhelm Bückler; known as Schinderhannes, Bückler was a real-life character of the Napoleonic era who had been executed with nineteen of his henchmen. Based on the legends of this popular hero, Zuckmayer's play *Schinderhannes* (1927), like *Der fröhliche Weinberg*, found its roots in the dialect and the soil of the Rhineland, specifically in the Hunsrück.

In the spring of 1926 the Zuckmayers had rented a summer house on the Baltic Sea island of Hiddensee. The property bordered on that of Hauptmann, who was for Zuckmayer "die größte Dichtergestalt des Jahrhunderts" (the greatest writer of the century). *Schinderhannes* owes a great deal to Hauptmann: here, too, there is, as in Hauptmann's *Florian Geyer* (1896; translated, 1929), a folk hero, a revolutionary who by the force of his personality attracts an enthusiastic following but fights the establishment in vain; and here, as in *Die Weber* (published, 1892; performed, 1893; translated as *The Weavers*, 1899), it is the revolutionary anthem of the rebellion that forms the connecting link from beginning to end. Although the play takes place in 1803, when the left bank of the Rhine was occupied by the French, Germany in the 1920s, smarting under the provisions of the Versailles Treaty, could readily identify with the situation of the Napoleonic era. But as is often the case in Zuckmayer's dramas, the success of the play depends on the main character and the extent to which his personality finds resonance in the audience. Although Schinderhannes is a quixotic braggart willing to take on the world, Zuckmayer portrays him in a sympathetic light. When his devoted Julchen, whom he had rejected because of her opposition to his hopeless rebellion, presents him with a child, he naively decides to join the Prussian establishment—not realizing that it will have him executed for his crimes. It is almost with relief that he realizes his error: he cannot be untrue to himself. He goes to his execution triumphantly leading his little band, proud that no fewer than fifteen thousand people have come to witness the event. Produced by the same director as *Der fröhliche Weinberg*, Reinhard Bruck, the play was well received, both for its parallels with the current political situation and for its humorous, earthy flavor. It was twice made into films: first in 1928 under the direction of Kurt Bernhardt, with a scenario by Zuckmayer; and again in 1958 under the direction of Helmut Käutner, with revised dialogue by the author.

In many of his works Zuckmayer treads a narrow path between great literature and kitsch. His love of the common people, his affinity to nature, and his roots in the tradition and language of his Rhenish homeland sometimes take precedence over his literary judgment and taste, and the result is an excessive lyric sentimentality that made many of his plays more popular with the spectators than with the critics. Such a case is his circus drama *Katharina Knie* (published, 1929). Produced in Berlin on 20 December 1928, the play starred Bassermann, whose spectacular performance did much to assure its popular success. The play captures with sympathetic accuracy the atmosphere of the old-time circus, which in the inflationary Germany of 1923 has fallen on hard times. Katharina Knie, daughter of a renowned tightrope performer, wants to break free of her possessive father, and the tradition for which he stands, to marry into the affluent world of the vineyard owners. She is unequal to the challenge. On the death of her father she forsakes her landowner fiancé and takes over the direction of the circus, presumably to gain a reprieve for the dying art form. Structurally, the drama is weak. The little action contained in its last two acts is overshadowed by long, tedious, sermonlike harangues that wallow in lyric sentimentality. The sympathy and deft accuracy with which the circus folk are portrayed, however, gained the play a large following, of which the critics did not form a significant part.

Meanwhile Zuckmayer had entered on a frenzy of productivity in a wide range of genres. In 1926 his collection *Der Baum* (The Tree) had established him as a lyric poet of some note, while *Ein Bauer aus dem Taunus und andere Geschichten*

(A Peasant from the Taunus and Other Stories, 1927) gives further evidence of his often naive belief in the goodness of humanity and of his affinity to nature. He reworked Maxwell Anderson and Laurence Stalling's *What Price Glory* (1924) into *Rivalen* (Rivals), which was produced by Erwin Piscator in Berlin in 1928. The following year brought the trivial children's piece *Kakadu-Kakada* but also the script for the 1930 film *Der blaue Engel* (The Blue Angel) derived from Heinrich Mann's novel *Professor Unrat* (1905; translated as *The Blue Angel*, 1931) and starring Marlene Dietrich. In 1931 Zuckmayer's reworking of Ernest Hemingway's *A Farewell to Arms* (1929) was produced at the Deutsches Theater in Berlin under the title *Kat*. His literary activity was recognized by the Georg Büchner Prize in Darmstadt and the prize for dramatists at the Heidelberg Festival, both in 1929.

By virtually unanimous critical consensus Zuckmayer's best play is *Der Hauptmann von Köpenick*. Based on an actual occurrence in the Wilhelmine Germany of 1906, in which reverence for the army was at an all-time high, the play is a hilarious satire of the militarist mentality. In the real incident an ex-convict, the cobbler Wilhelm Voigt, purchased an army uniform at a costume shop, donned it, commandeered a passing troop of soldiers, led them to the courthouse, took the mayor prisoner, and sent him to Berlin. After arresting the city treasurer and plundering the cashbox of some four thousand marks, for which he left a correct receipt, the bogus captain gave each of his soldiers a mark for a beer and a sausage, then disappeared in a horse-drawn cab. The whole world was convulsed with laughter, including Kaiser Wilhelm II, who reputedly remarked with pride that this episode was an example of German discipline that no other country could emulate. The *New York Times* ran a series of articles on the event, imitating German word order in the reporting.

In Zuckmayer's comedy the actual events comprise only a third of the action. He brilliantly lets the uniform symbolize the military atmosphere, and its progress assumes allegorical proportions. The uniform is first tailored for a newly promoted captain, who must, however, resign his commission because he tried to restrain a drunken soldier while he himself was illegally dressed in civilian clothes. Returned to the tailor, the uniform is purchased by the future mayor of Köpenick, who has just been promoted to lieutenant in the reserves and wants to impress his

Scene from a 1947 Berlin production of Zuckmayer's Der Hauptmann von Köpenick

mother. Years later, he has become too corpulent for the garment; it is returned once again to the tailor, where it serves as a costume for the tailor's daughter. Soiled by spilled champagne, it finds its way to the used-clothing dealer from whom the hero purchases it. The progress of this symbol—from the career officer to the reserve lieutenant who is anything but a soldier, to the status of mere costume, and finally into the hands of a "criminal" who uses it for his own travesty—reflects the fate of German militarism.

Zuckmayer's hero, Voigt, finds himself in a catch-22 situation. Released from prison for a youthful offense, Voigt wishes to work, but to get a job he must have a residence permit, and to get the permit he must show that he has gainful employment. He goes back to jail when he is caught attempting to steal an identity card. Released again ten years later, he buys the uniform and proceeds with the attack on the city hall.

The play premiered on 5 March 1931 at the Deutsches Theater in Berlin under the direction of Heinz Hilpert. It was a great success, but it again brought down on Zuckmayer the wrath of the Nazis. Its popularity was revived at the end of World War II. It has been filmed twice in Germany, in 1932 and in 1956.

After Adolf Hitler came to power in 1933 the production of Zuckmayer's plays was forbidden. His pacifistic views could not be tolerated; moreover, he made fun of Nazi propaganda chief Joseph Goebbels in a public condemnation of the censorship of the 1930 film version of the novel *Im Westen nichts Neues* (1929; translated as *All Quiet on the Western Front*, 1929), by Erich Maria Remarque. The success of *Der fröhliche Weinberg* had provided Zuckmayer with the financial means to purchase a country house near Salzburg, where the family could live in safety—at least during the five years until the Anschluß (annexation of Austria by Nazi Germany).

In spite of the ban on Zuckmayer's plays, *Der Schelm von Bergen* (The Executioner of Bergen) was published in Germany in 1934. It had its premiere at the Burgtheater in Vienna on 21 October of that year under the direction of

Hermann Röbbeling. The play deals with a medieval legend, but its theme of the assertion of individual freedom in the face of an immutable order was pertinent in the Germany of the early 1930s. The order is the static society of the Middle Ages. The empress, who holds the position of highest worldly status, is childless; the executioner is so low on the social ladder that he is excluded from all normal social intercourse, but he is also regarded as a kind of supernatural being, who possesses the arts of healing and magic. The empress appeals to the executioner for help, and the executioner's son furnishes the "Begegnung" (encounter) that enables the empress to become pregnant. At about the same time, his father is injured, forcing the son to assume the odious office. At a court dance the empress's adultery is revealed, but the emperor accepts his illegitimate heir and ennobles the executioner's son. The plot borders on the absurd, but Zuckmayer is able to evoke the illusion of reality.

In 1938 Austria became part of the Third Reich. Zuckmayer was reluctant to leave but was finally persuaded. In his autobiography he describes with exquisite, if hair-raising, humor being removed from the train at the Swiss border to be searched and his winning over the SS officer by showing his Iron Cross and war decorations.

His play *Bellman* had been in the process of being staged in Vienna, with Wessely and Hörbiger in the leading roles, when the Anschluß took place, and the production was canceled. It was produced by Leopold Lindtberg at the Zurich Schauspielhaus on 14 November 1938. But Zuckmayer was so dissatisfied with having burdened the devil-may-care eighteenth-century Swedish vagabond-troubadour Carl Michael Bellman with an inappropriate political plot that he rewrote the play as *Ulla Winblad oder Musik und Leben des Carl Michael Bellman* (Ulla Winblad; or, Music and Life of Carl Michael Bellman). This version was published in 1953 and produced in Göttingen by Heinz Hilpert the same year. Zuckmayer had been interested in Bellman since 1922 and envisioned himself in the figure of this Scandinavian François Villon. The play combines the stagecraft of its author with the personality and original music of Bellman, though the words to the songs are modified somewhat to fit the action of the play. The second version turns around the figure of Bellman's muse and great love, Ulla Winblad. When the play opens, Ulla is lying stark naked in bed in a coun-

try inn, since Bellman has pawned her clothes; he is off to charm a noblewoman out of sufficient funds to meet his present needs. To save Bellman from a debtor's prison Ulla marries a powerful nobleman in the court of the new king, the enlightened Gustav III. The plot involves the murder of the king. There is little dramatic unity, but the music, the skillful handling of the love story, the sheer vitality of the main characters, and Hilpert's successful staging caused even the most critical reviewers to render a positive judgment.

After a year in Switzerland, Zuckmayer immigrated to the United States. The well-known journalist Dorothy Thompson was influential in gaining him admission to the country. After a short stay in New York, Zuckmayer joined other German émigrés in Hollywood, where he received a sinecure from Warner Bros. But the artificiality of life in Los Angeles and the superficiality of his tasks in Hollywood were repugnant to Zuckmayer, to whom nature meant so much. He briefly returned to New York, where he lectured at a dramatic workshop, then leased a dilapidated backwoods farm in Vermont. Although he knew absolutely nothing about farming, by dint of back-breaking labor he was able to make his family self-sufficient.

In December 1941 Zuckmayer read in a newspaper that his friend Ernst Udet, a World War I flying ace and head of the matériel section of the Luftwaffe, had been killed while testing a new airplane. "State funeral," the article concluded. As early as 1936 Udet had told Zuckmayer: "I am a captive of aviation. I can no longer escape it. But someday the devil will take us all." In *Des Teufels General*, produced in Zurich by Hilpert in 1946, Zuckmayer presents an objective but sympathetic picture of a German caught in the web of National Socialism and in the profession to which he is wedded, unable to escape and forced to work for the regime he despises—the very dilemma in which so many German writers, bound by their native language, found themselves ensnared.

The play is set in 1941 in Berlin. There has been sabotage of aircraft matériel, an area for which General Harras—modeled after Udet—is responsible. When Harras's friend, the chief engineer Oderbruch, confesses to being part of a conspiracy responsible for the sabotage, Harras accepts his role as a general of the devil, Hitler, and commits suicide by deliberately flying a test plane with the structural flaw the conspirators

Martin Held and Siegfried Lowitz in a scene from a 1948 production in Frankfurt am Main of Zuckmayer's Des Teufels General *(photograph by Willi Klar)*

have introduced. The ironic last word, pronounced by a Gestapo agent, is "Staatsbegräbnis" (state funeral).

The success of the play largely depends on the personality of Harras: amiable, devil-may-care, bursting with life and wit, he is caught up in the air war while despising its aims. He is unquestionably a self-reflection as well as Zuckmayer's monument to Udet, who had been in a loge at a press ball on the eve of the Reichstag fire in 1933 and, seeing many sporting their wartime decorations in obvious anticipation of the Nazi takeover, had put his own Iron Cross in his pocket and suggested to Zuckmayer that they "moon" the audience in the orchestra below. One cannot help but love Harras, but one must also criticize him for being "the devil's general." According to German law, a bystander who witnesses a crime and takes no step to hinder it also incurs guilt. Harras is his own judge and executioner. The play is condemnation not of the Nazis—they are satirized with gallows humor—but of the "good German" who protested that he had never been a Nazi and had disapproved of Hitler, and re-

fused to accept guilt by association. Ironically, Harras elicited too much sympathy, while the pious Oderbruch was criticized for cold-bloodedly committing sabotage and murder out of his "Christian" convictions. His victims are the sincere if misguided young men whose only guilt was naiveté or a lack of courage to place their lives in jeopardy by revolt.

The play presents a cross section of German society of the time. In addition to Harras, there is Dr. Schmidt-Lausitz, the slimy Gestapo agent, whose name is reminiscent in German or English of *louse*; Sigbert von Mohrungen, director of the office of procurement of raw materials, a member of the old nobility eager to save his skin, if not his honor; young Colonel Eilers, leader of a fighter squadron, celebrating his fiftieth victory in the air, a sincere believer whose naive faith in his country has closed his eyes to reality; and "Pützchen," a nubile and evil superwoman who embodies the new ethos of Nazi feminism. All of these types, vivified by unique personalities, plus many others cavort onstage in the great party celebrating the war hero Eilers that fills the first act. Each of the characters has his or her intrinsic interest, often intensified by a little subplot of his or her own, and the whole spectrum of more than twenty characters, most of whom are onstage at the same time, is handled with consummate artistry. The title of the first act, "Höllenmaschine" (infernal machine), has a dual reference. A listening device is activated in a wall by a waiter, and its ticking becomes audible to the party onstage as well as to the audience; the latter may suspect that it is a time bomb—an infernal machine. And the characters onstage, as a cross section of Nazi Germany, comprise a true machine from hell.

Zuckmayer thought that the play would never be produced, especially in Germany, but it proved to be one of the most popular plays of the century. There were more than five thousand productions—more than two thousand of them in the 1948-1949 season—for the play struck a responsive chord in the vast majority of German hearts. It was filmed with Curt Jürgens in the title role, and Trevor Howard played Harras in London.

Zuckmayer and his wife became American citizens. Together with the exiled actor Fritz Kortner, Zuckmayer wrote an unsuccessful play, *Somewhere in France* (performed, 1941).

At the close of hostilities Zuckmayer was employed by the American military government to make a cultural survey of Germany and Austria.

In Zurich he saw the premiere of *Des Teufels General*, the play he had thought would never be produced. He alternated his residence between Vermont and Europe until he settled in Saas-Fée, Switzerland, in 1958.

In 1949 his drama *Barbara Blomberg* (published, 1949), conceived in Vermont, was produced in Constance under the direction of Hilpert. A historical play about the mother of the illegitimate Don Juan d'Austria, it suffers from too-great length (which Hilpert compressed considerably); tendentious sections that impede the plot; and, in spite of the colorful setting of the revolt of the Netherlands, an unconvincing local color. A strange admixture of humor with tragedy is not always appropriate to the theme. But in spite of its failings, *Barbara Blomberg* is never dull.

Meanwhile the occupation authorities, after long hesitation, had released *Des Teufels General* for production in Germany. It had been sweeping the stage, eliciting not only praise but also avid discussion of the positive side of General Harras and the savage cold-bloodedness of the "Christian" Oderbruch. Possibly as an answer to both sides, Zuckmayer wrote *Der Gesang im Feuerofen* (The Song of the Fiery Furnace; 1950), which premiered in Göttingen on 3 November 1950. The play combines realism with a mythic framework; Hilpert divided the stage into an upper and a lower level for the different levels of the action. Zuckmayer's sources were two newspaper items. One was a report of a massacre in Savoy of a group of young people attending a ball on Christmas Eve; many were members of the French resistance who had been betrayed to the Gestapo by a traitor. The château in which the dance was held was set afire by the Germans, and those who escaped the flames were shot. The other item reported that forty whales had beached themselves on the Florida coast, and most had died. These apparently disparate items are brought together in an apocalyptic pronouncement: " . . . that the time is approaching when the fishes come on to the land—that is the time when Lucifer comes to the earth and no one knows any longer what is good and what is bad." The play opens on the upper, or mythic, level with the accusation of the traitor, Louis Creveaux, before two angels played by actors whose characters will later be killed. On the realistic level the events leading to the massacre and the massacre itself are depicted. In the final scene the traitor's mother holds him in her arms as the angels reappear to intone: "The last judgment remains unknown and unknowable, just as the power that fulfills it."

Hauptmann's widow prevailed on Zuckmayer to finish a play that Hauptmann had left as a fragment at his death in 1946. *Herbert Engelmann* is the story of a soldier returning home from the war who commits a murder, is released for lack of evidence, becomes his own judge, and kills himself. Zuckmayer adheres to Hauptmann's plot but presents a more convincing picture of Engelmann's psychological development. The play premiered in 1952 at the Vienna Burgtheater to mixed reactions from the critics.

Zuckmayer's next play, *Das kalte Licht* (The Cold Light, 1955), was based on the case of the spy Klaus Fuchs, which had recently attracted international attention. Far too long even in the director Gustaf Gründgens's drastic abridgement and burdened with tedious argumentation, the play also suffers from a lack of convincing characters. Zuckmayer tries to combine the problem of the responsibility of the nuclear physicist with the problem of love and trust on the personal level, and on neither level is he persuasive. The fourteen scenes mark the progress of the physicist Kristof Wolters, the Fuchs figure, as a traitor during a period of eleven years. The rather weak motivation for Wolters's treason is his disillusionment when he is interned in Canada by the British as an enemy alien. Then he is involved in the development of the atomic bomb, which culminates in the bombing of Hiroshima in 1945. Great questions plague him: to what extent is a scientist responsible for the consequences of his discoveries? Is one justified in betraying one's country and friends for the sake of sharing knowledge? Is such betrayal an obligation? Wolters at first shares with the Soviets only the discoveries he himself has made and hence regards as his own property. He accepts no money for his treason until it is forced on him. Then he throws it away. On the personal level, he had fallen in love with a Norwegian girl, Hjördis, but she had married Sir Elwin Ketterick, a great British physicist. They are reunited; but she finds a slip of paper containing the time and place of his meeting with an enemy agent, misinterprets it as a personal betrayal, and breaks off their relationship. Instead of answers to the great moral problems, the denouement is instead the death in a fiery auto accident of Sir Elwin, who had come into possession of the slip of paper—the only tangible evidence of Wolters's guilt. But on being assured that Hjördis had not

Hans Peter Thielen as Kristof Wolters and Erich Musil as Thomas Norton in a 1955 Mannheim production of Zuckmayer's Das kalte Licht *(photograph by Adolf Falk)*

betrayed him, he confesses to his treason, while she promises to wait for him for the ten years or so that he will be in prison.

This play marks the beginning of a series of weak attempts. As he grew older, Zuckmayer seemed to become more discursive, more involved in argumentation at the cost of dramatic economy and characterization. His next play, *Die Uhr schlägt Eins* (The Clock Strikes One, 1961), is a lurid and unconvincing attempt to combine the theme of the prodigal son with a critique of postwar Germany's "economic miracle." Probably the worst of his plays, it led the prominent Viennese critic Hans Weigel to announce the end of Zuckmayer as a dramatist to be taken seriously. It is full of trashy clichés, and Zuckmayer's former strong points—the creation of atmosphere and the depiction of convincing and appealing characters—are lacking. Moreover, the picture of postwar Germany is anything but accurate; as Weigel put it, a Wild West tale by Karl May seems like an accurate historical report compared to this alleged German reality.

The trivial one-act *Kranichtanz* (Dance of the Cranes) was written in 1961 but not produced until 1967, when the half-hour playlet culminated a celebration of the author's seventieth birthday at the Zurich Schauspielhaus. Set in a New England farmhouse, the play attempts to convey the local color that Zuckmayer experienced in Vermont; but to an American it is completely artificial. The theme of the prodigal son is tritely presented: Loren, a farmer, is opposed by his renegade son, who marries a model for the sake of a week in Florida with her. The owner of the farm is a strong-willed woman who has inherited it from her former husband along with an alcoholic stepson, Jolly. For the past five years she has been carrying on a love affair with Loren, which she now cuts off for unspecified reasons. When Jolly returns from a drunken hunt and mockingly imitates the mating dance of the crane for her, she picks up his rifle and shoots him. It is possible that this play was intended as the last act of a never-written drama. The critics were polite to the grand old man of the German theater, but the audience reacted with more enthusiasm to Zuckmayer's appearance than to his play.

Zuckmayer's penultimate play also has its setting in the United States. *Das Leben des Horace A. W. Tabor* (The Life of Horace A. W. Tabor, 1964) depicts the rags-to-riches-to-rags story of the nineteenth-century "silver king." Zuckmayer's most resounding failure contains all the clichés about America that are rife in the popular European imagination. The locales are those of the cheap Western film; the language is an unauthentic attempt to portray that of the gold-rush days; and the characters, although in many cases based on real people, do not rise above the level of Hollywood stereotypes (the Chicago gangster, the old prospector, the former Cheyenne medicine man, and so on). The naturalistic tastelessness that tries to reproduce the atmosphere of the "Old West" (such as "Pop" Wyman carrying his money in a scrotum to horrify the saloon girls) seems amateurish after the subtleties of Samuel Beckett, Eugène Ionesco, or Brecht. If it were produced in its original length the play would last more than six hours; even the shortened version Zuckmayer approved must have seemed too long to the director, Werner Düggelin, for he presented an even shorter adaptation. But the play, which spans some twenty years of Tabor's life, suffers from being reduced even slightly, leading critics to remark that the material would have been better suited for a novel.

Zuckmayer's final drama, *Der Rattenfänger* (The Ratcatcher; published, 1975), premiered at the Zurich Schauspielhaus on 22 February 1975, but the theater declared three official premieres to accommodate subscribers, foreign visitors, and critics. After each performance there was a fifteen-minute ovation for the frail author. The play is a sprawling work in two sequences of ten and eleven scenes, respectively, requiring more than ninety actors and extras. Zuckmayer places the story of the Pied Piper into a sociological context in a mythical city where the corrupt patriciate allows the rats to multiply so as to keep the price of flour high. The city is populated by a grotesque and motley collection of the poor, who are hovering on the brink of rebellion. Another motif is that of the generation gap, which causes the children of both the rich and the poor to band together to save the piper from the gallows and then to follow him into voluntary exile over the mountains. The piper falls prey for a short time to a lust for power, indirectly causing the suicide of his beloved Rikke. The venal city regent's jewel-loving wife forces the regent to overwhelm himself with debt; he whines like a dog before her locked bedroom door before going to the whores in the aristocratic bordellos, and she is killed by her two children. There are orgies stimulated by the sniffing of hallucinogenic herbs; Gregorian chants performed by the choirboys and cloister girls; an informer, the baker of the holy wafers, who foments revolution for profit; the "little" executioner entrusted only with the execution of the poor, who, according to custom, must have their arms and legs broken and their intestines torn out before receiving the coup de grace. In all, it is an incredible display, the more astonishing as the product of an aged author.

As the result of a fall, Zuckmayer died on 18 January 1977 in Visp, Switzerland. His wife commemorated events in their lives in her books *Die Farm in den grünen Bergen* (The Farm in the Green Mountains, 1949) and *Das Scheusal* (The Horror, 1972), the charming story of their disreputable dog.

Letters:

Späte Freundschaft in Briefen: Carl Zuckmayer, Karl Barth, edited by Hinrich Stoevesandt (Zurich: Theologischer Verlag, 1977); translated by Geoffrey W. Bromiley as *A Late Friendship: The Letters of Karl Barth and Carl Zuckmayer* (Grand Rapids, Mich.: Eerdmans, 1982);

Carl Zuckmayer an Arnold Jacobius: Briefe aus 24 Jahren (1953-1976) (Mainz: Carl-Zuckmayer-Gesellschaft, 1980);

Zwei Freunde, Carl Zuckmayer und Fritz Usinger: Ein Briefwechsel (1919-1976) (Mainz: Carl-Zuckmayer-Gesellschaft, 1984).

Bibliography:

Arnold John Jacobius and Harro Kieser, *Carl Zuckmayer: Eine Bibliographie 1917-1971* (Frankfurt am Main: Fischer, 1971).

Biographies:

Ludwig Emanuel Reindl, *Zuckmayer: Eine Bildbiographie* (Munich: Kindler, 1962);

Thomas Ayck, *Carl Zuckmayer in Selbstzeugnissen und Bilddokumenten* (Reinbek: Rowohlt, 1977).

References:

Arnold Bauer, *Carl Zuckmayer* (Berlin: Colloquium, 1977);

Ingeborg Engelsing-Malek, *"Amor fati" in Zuckmayers Dramen* (Constance: Rosgarten, 1960; Berkeley: University of California Press, 1960);

Fülle der Zeit: Carl Zuckmayer und sein Werk (Frankfurt am Main: Fischer, 1956);

Barbara Glauert, ed., *Carl Zuckmayer: Das Bühnenwerk im Spiegel der Kritik* (Frankfurt am Main: Fischer, 1977);

Glauert, Siegfried Mews, and Siegfried Sudhof, eds., *Carl Zuckmayer '78: Ein Jahrbuch* (Frankfurt am Main: Fischer, 1978);

Alice Herdan, *Die Farm in den grünen Bergen* (Zurich: Europa, 1949);

Herdan, *Das Scheusal* (Frankfurt am Main: Fischer, 1972);

Marianne Kesting, "Carl Zuckmayer: Zwischen Volksstück und Kolportage," in her *Panorama des zeitgenössischen Theaters: 58 literarische Porträts* (Munich: Piper, 1969), pp. 278-283;

Harro Kieser, *Carl Zuckmayer: Materialien zu Leben und Werk* (Frankfurt am Main: Fischer, 1986);

Rudolf Lange, *Carl Zuckmayer* (Boston: Twayne, 1981);

Wolfgang Paulsen, "Carl Zuckmayer," in *Deutsche Literatur im 20: Jahrhundert*, edited by Otto Mann and Wolfgang Rothe, fifth edition (Munich: Francke, 1967), pp. 332-361;

Sheile Rooke, "Carl Zuckmayer," in *German Men of Letters*, volume 3, edited by Alex Natan

(London: Wolff, 1964), pp. 209-233;

Siegfried Sudhof, "Carl Zuckmayer," in *Deutsche Dichter der Gegenwart: Ihr Leben und Werk* (Berlin: Schmidt, 1973), pp. 64-82;

Hans Wagener, *Carl Zuckmayer* (Munich: Beck, 1983).

Papers:

Many of Carl Zuckmayer's papers, manuscripts, letters, and other documents are at the Deutsches Literaturarchiv (German Literature Archive), Marbach, Germany.

Appendix

The German Radio Play

The German Radio Play

Wulf Koepke
Texas A&M University

Radio created its own literary form, the radio play. Like the stage drama, the radio play can range in quality from mass entertainment to esoteric art; also like the stage drama, it relies heavily on dialogue. There are, however, significant differences that allow the radio play to be considered a different, though related, genre.

Radio broadcasting of texts written originally for other media is called the "reproductive" use of radio. While it is important, it still means the use of material that would exist without radio technology. But there is also a "productive" use of radio; the technology has generated literary forms that would not have existed without it.

While it was at first assumed that radio plays would be dramas acted on an invisible stage, broadcasting stage plays was not very successful. The new genre that began to emerge cut across traditional genres: it had dramatic, narrative, and lyrical features—indeed, it seemed closer to modern forms of narrative than to stage techniques. In the 1920s a distinction was made between a "Sendespiel," a play broadcast by radio, and a "Hörspiel" conceived specifically for the radio. The word *Hörspiel* occurs in Friedrich Nietzsche's *Also sprach Zarathustra* (1883-1892; translated as *Thus Spake Zarathustra*, 1896), but the first commentator who used it in its current meaning was Hans Siebert von Heister in his journal *Der deutsche Rundfunk* (German Radio) in August 1924. Radio plays differ from stage plays by their more rapid and frequent scene changes, by the greater use of sound effects, and by larger emphasis on monologues and narration.

There are three types of broadcasting institutions: state-owned and -operated systems designed to propagate the views of the group in power; publicly financed and controlled systems that are independent of specific governments; and commercial broadcasting systems owned by individuals or corporations and supported by advertising. It is the second type, exemplified by British Broadcasting Corporation (BBC), that, in England and Germany, favored the development of the literary radio play.

The Beginnings

Organized radio broadcasts began in Germany on 29 October 1923 in Berlin. No consensus exists as to which play should be considered the first "real" German radio drama produced; most scholars believe it to have been either *Zauberei auf dem Sender* (Magic at the Radio Station), by Hans Flesch, broadcast on 24 October 1924, or *Spuk* (Phantom), by Rolf Gunold, broadcast on 21 July 1925. As early as 1924 a competition for radio plays was announced, but no prizes were awarded due to a lack of suitable entries. The radio pioneers and enthusiasts were ahead of the writers and the public at large in their appreciation of the potential of the new medium, but writers such as Bertolt Brecht, Walter Benjamin, and Alfred Döblin soon caught on.

The Radio Play Comes into Its Own

In 1929 the first important German conference on the radio play took place in Kassel. By this time the radio play had developed a considerable range in content and form. Friedrich Wolf's *SOS . . . rao . . . rao . . . foyn . . . Krassin rettet Italia* (SOS . . .Krassin saves Italia), broadcast on 8 November 1929 from Berlin, Frankfurt am Main, and Breslau, dramatizes the rescue in 1928 of the crew of the airship *Italia*, which was stranded near the North Pole, by an international effort with the decisive participation of the icebreaker *Krassin* from the Soviet Union. The bias for the Soviet Union and against Fascist Italy is unmistakable, but the humanitarian aspects and the "one world" theme predominate.

The same event is portrayed in a different way by Walter Erich Schäfer in *Malmgreen*, broadcast from Stuttgart in 1929, which consists of the inner monologue of Malmgreen and the voice of the narrator. Dr. Finn Malmgren (Schäfer changed the spelling of the name), a Swedish scientist, was a member of the Italian expedition. After the crash of the airship he and two officers were sent in the direction of Spitsbergen to look for help. Malmgren had a heart condition that he had kept secret to be able to participate in the enterprise, and he died on the way. Schäfer concentrates on the psychological aspects of the drama; he is most interested in the thoughts and feelings of a man's facing certain death.

Ernst Johannsen's *Brigadevermittlung* (Brigade Telephone Exchange), broadcast on 17 October 1929 from Munich, was the most successful radio play of these years; it was rebroadcast by most German stations and translated into several languages. It profited from the uproar created by Erich Maria Remarque's *Im Westen nichts Neues* (1929; translated as *All Quiet on the Western Front*, 1929) and the acrimonious debates on World War I in general. It uses the device of a telephone exchange of an advance artillery unit on the western front to document the absurdity of the meaningless attacks and counterattacks characteristic of trench warfare. The style is strictly realistic, and a few of the soldiers emerge as individual personalities. The play is supposed to be documentary rather than interpretative, typical of the Neue Sachlichkeit (New Objectivity) of the time.

Another extreme and lonely situation was the conquest of the air by the early fliers. Brecht captured the excitement of the first solo transatlantic flight, Charles A. Lindberg's 1927 journey from New York to Paris, in his radio "cantata" *Lindberghflug* (Lindbergh's Flight), broadcast 29 July 1929 with music by Kurt Weill and Paul Hindemith.

The other extreme of formal experimentation is represented by *Schwester Henriette* (Nurse Henrietta), by Hermann Kesser, broadcast on 12 August 1929 from Munich. The entire play is the inner monologue of a nurse who testifies at the trial of a laborer accused of murdering a patient whom she loved and whom she helped to commit suicide. She helps the defendant without revealing her own guilt, and he is acquitted.

A more symbolic, less realistic play has become one of the classics of the genre: Eduard Reinacher's *Der Narr mit der Hacke* (The Fool with the Hoe), broadcast from Cologne on 11 July 1930. In a Japanese fishing village, cut off from the rest of world by a granite cliff from which many travelers have plunged to their deaths, the monk Zenkai appears and undertakes the seemingly impossible task of chopping a tunnel

through the mountain with his hoe. His work and the villagers' reactions are punctuated by the incessant sound of the hoe. After thirty years the tunnel is almost complete. At this point the knight Jitsonosuka appears, and it is revealed that Zenkai had been a samurai and had murdered his master out of wounded pride. Jitsonosuka has killed all of Zenkai's companions in revenge and has finally found Zenkai. Overwhelmed by Zenkai's desire for atonement, however, he destroys his sword and helps Zenkai complete his task. Zenkai dies knowing that he has opened up a new world for the people of the village. The message about overwhelming old hatred and working for peace was especially relevant in the context of 1930.

Hermann Kasack's *Ballwechsel* (Exchange of Balls), broadcast from Berlin on 7 December 1930, uses sophisticated techniques and rhythmic language to portray a tennis match between Red and Green (the names are English, not German), with an underlying drama of rivalry in love. The play, punctuated by the sound of the tennis balls, alternates between the inner voices of Red and Green and the voice of a radio news reporter.

The major event of 1930 was Döblin's adaptation of his novel *Berlin Alexanderplatz* (1929; translated as *Alexanderplatz, Berlin*, 1931), broadcast from Berlin on 30 September 1930. Döblin uses street noises, voices, inner monologues, animation of inanimate objects (such as cars talking to each other), and music. The radio play offers a more complex and upbeat ending than the novel.

More and more writers were attracted by the new medium; some of the major names of the post-World War II radio play emerged before 1933, including Günter Eich, Fred von Hoerschelmann, and Wolfgang Weyrauch. While the emphasis was on re-creating contemporary events in a documentary style, radio also allowed for historical plays and symbolic or allegorical forms.

The Nazi Period

In the late 1920s and especially after 1930 organized groups of listeners and right-wing pressure groups made the appearance of any left-wing writer such as Brecht difficult. The government of Franz von Papen began in 1932 to curtail the freedom of the radio stations. Most of the early organizers of radio-play programming, such as Flesch, Friedrich Bischoff, Ernst Hardt, and Alfred Braun, were dismissed in 1933. Immediately after coming to power the Nazis seized control of the radio stations and transformed the medium into a tool for state propaganda; but they were never quite comfortable with the genre of the radio play and abandoned programming of such plays during World War II, when other countries, such as the United States, were using the form and the services of well-known writers to enhance the war effort.

While the leading administrators of radio stations were dismissed and some were put into concentration camps, programming did not change abruptly. As in other areas, the Nazis tried to adapt forms developed by socialist writers, especially the choral ballad and cantata. The Nazis were mostly forced to reuse previous material—for example, Ernst Wiechert's oratorio *Das Spiel vom deutschen Bettelmann* (The Play about the German Beggar), first broadcast on 31 December 1932 from Leipzig, Berlin, and Königsberg. *Deutsche Passion* (German Passion), by Richard Euringer, broadcast on 13 April 1933 over all German stations, is an oratorio with religious overtones, demonstrating how evil and degraded the Weimar Republic was and predicting that a new age is dawning. After this short-lived movement for choral literature exhausted itself, other forms reemerged, mostly with escapist themes from faraway countries and ages. Until 1935 Harald Braun produced a special series of radio plays by authors such as Eich, Horst Lange, and Peter Huchel.

Hans Rothe's *Verwehte Spuren* (Disappearing Traces), broadcast by the Deutschlandsender in 1935, and based on an actual incident that happened in Paris in 1867, is a mystery play with a faintly political background. Igna Vargas and her mother have come from Brazil to the world's fair in Paris. They have to be accommodated in different hotels. The next day, when Igna goes to meet her mother, the latter has disappeared. Igna eventually learns that her mother has died of the plague and that the authorities claimed ignorance of the matter for fear of frightening away the tourists. Igna finally agrees to keep the secret for the sake of France, her mother's home country. But her faith in humanity is shattered.

The most notable attempt to use the radio play for outright political propaganda may be *Alcazar*, by Robert E. Strunk, the star reporter who covered the Fascist side of the Spanish Civil War. The play depicts the siege of the Alcazar in Toledo, where an outnumbered group of cadets withstood weeks of attacks. The play was broadcast from Breslau on 5 February 1937. The full ex-

tent of such radio-play propaganda has yet to be determined by scholars.

While many exiled German writers worked for Allied radio stations during World War II and produced much narrative material, they wrote few literary radio plays. The most notable example, apart from Brecht's *Lukullus*, which was broadcast from Beromünster, Switzerland, on 12 May 1940, may be *Prozeß der Jeanne d'Arc zu Rouen 1431* (Trial of Jeanne d'Arc in Rouen 1431), by Anna Seghers, broadcast in 1937 by the Flemish network in Antwerp. Seghers's only radio play, it is largely documentary and is based on extensive studies of the trial and execution of Joan of Arc.

The Radio Play from 1945 to the Early 1960s

During World War II and the early postwar period radio was a cultural lifeline and the main source of news in Germany. The Red Cross lists of missing people read over the radio brought thousands of families together after 1945. The Allies consented to a rebuilding of German radio programming along the lines of the BBC, with independent stations financed by monthly user fees. In the 1950s the stations, organized as nonprofit corporations, helped to stimulate cultural life in Germany. They provided much-needed income for authors through readings, lectures, and especially original and adapted radio plays. With a dozen radio stations each needing at least one play per week, good writers had no problem marketing their material. Another reason for the enormous boom of the radio play in the 1950s was its emphasis on individual conflicts and responsibilities and its frequent technique of recalling the past, which coincided with the subdued and inward-looking mood of the population—the often forgotten reverse side of the postwar "economic miracle." The radio play expressed the secret guilt feelings, doubts, and fears of the people. Since the reception of a radio program is "private," as opposed to a theater performance, the radio play was able to catch the Germans alone with their consciences.

Der Held (The Hero), by Volker Starke, broadcast from Hamburg on 20 January 1946, was apparently the first German radio play produced after the war. But it was the production of Wolfgang Borchert's *Draußen vor der Tür* (The Man Outside) in Hamburg on 13 February 1947 that ushered in the new era of the radio play. The story of Corporal Beckmann coming back from a prisoner-of-war camp in Siberia to his native Hamburg and finding no place to stay and the city in rubble is a classic of "Trümmerliteratur" (literature of the ruins) and proved to be one of the outstanding successes of all time. Its staccato rhythms, its shrill, expressionist language, and its less than subtle symbolism made it suitable as mass entertainment. Even today, *Draußen vor der Tür* can still attract audiences.

The primary social function of the German radio play after 1949 was as an antidote to the smugness and complacency of the new materialism in Germany. This function is expressed most vehemently in Eich's *Träume* (Dreams), which was produced in Hamburg on 19 April 1951 and generated a tidal wave of mostly angry reactions. The form of the play is unique. Eich presents five episodes of extreme existential danger as "dreams" of well-to-do bourgeois characters. The dreams take place in different parts of the world, and the dreamers are from five continents. The dream scenes are interspersed with lyrical passages warning of the end of the human race. All the dreams have frightening endings: a total loss of memory, disappearances of explorers in the jungle, people starving in a closed train that never stops, governments preparing the end of the world. The message is to resist, to throw sand into the machinery, not to tolerate oppressive systems whether of the East or the West.

While *Träume* hit the listeners with direct messages and obvious symbolism, the tone of most other plays, especially those by Eich himself, is more subdued. A typical example is Eich's *Die Andere und ich* (The Other Woman and I), broadcast on 3 February 1952 from Stuttgart and Hamburg. An American family vacationing in Italy passes through the fishing village of Comacchio on their way to the beach. Ellen Harland, the mother, sees an old woman waving at her from a house. While swimming, she suddenly goes back in time to find herself in that house in Comacchio as Camilla, an Italian girl cleaning fish and living through the hell of fascism and World War II, always aware that someone is stealing her life. After Ellen is rescued from drowning by her husband she walks to Comacchio—only to learn that Camilla, who had waited for her all her life, has just died. As Eich said in *Träume*, "Alles was geschieht, geht dich an" (Everything that happens concerns you, too): all human lives are intertwined, and there is no escape from responsibility.

Authors who, like Eich, worked predominantly for the radio included Weyrauch,

Hoerschelmann, Peter Hirche, Leopold Ahlsen, and Erwin Wickert. Others, such as Wolfgang Hildesheimer, Friedrich Dürrenmatt, Wolfdietrich Schnurre, Walter Jens, and Marie Luise Kaschnitz, had a shorter period of intense preoccupation with the form. Finally, there were major authors who made single but significant contributions to the genre, such as Ilse Aichinger, Ingeborg Bachmann, Herbert Eisenreich, Siegfried Lenz, Martin Walser, and Max Frisch.

Like Eich, Weyrauch preferred the depiction of extreme situations. His *Die japanischen Fischer* (The Japanese Fishermen), broadcast from Munich on 24 May 1955, dramatizes the plight of Japanese fishermen caught by radioactive fallout from nuclear testing in the Pacific Ocean. The story is narrated by Susushi, the last to die. The play was Weyrauch's greatest international success. Hirche's *Die seltsamste Liebesgeschichte der Welt* (The Strangest Love Story in the World), produced in Hamburg on 10 May 1953, seems far removed from topical themes. It is an imagined dialogue across time, space, and social barriers between a rich young woman and a not-so-young man who was wounded during the war and fired from the factory where he worked. They never meet; they only imagine each other, but they know that theirs is the "real" love. After coming close to meeting when they watch a ballet at the same theater, they drift apart when she marries a rich man and goes on her honeymoon to Italy. The play reflects the emergence of social classes after 1950 and shows that the materialism of the "economic miracle" is unable to fulfill basic human needs.

The shadows of the past, especially the Nazi past, loom large in plays such as *Ahasver*, by Jens, broadcast from Frankfurt am Main on 5 March 1956. At the funeral of a prominent Jewish physician, Albrecht Busch, his friend recalls that Busch's life was that of the Wandering Jew. Dismissed from his university position by the Nazis, he succeeded in private practice in Germany and then in Paris; even when he was in hiding in occupied France, he practiced under an assumed name. His wife, whom he tried to protect by divorcing her, was deported to the German death camps; his two children, however, put down roots in France. An attempt to start again in academic life in Germany after 1945 failed when he could not overcome the hostility of his colleagues, and he retired into private practice once more. He dies a lonely man without a real home.

The number of light comedies among these radio plays is small, but there are quite a few examples of grotesque and black humor. Hildesheimer specialized in the genre. In *Herrn Walsers Raben* (The Ravens of Mr. Walser), broadcast from Hamburg and Munich on 8 March 1960, Walser has the power to transform people—especially unwelcome relatives—into ravens.

While there is no moral lesson in most of Hildesheimer's plays, Dürrenmatt attacked bourgeois hypocrisy. In *Die Panne* (The Breakdown), broadcast from Munich on 17 January 1956, Traps, a traveling salesman, has to spend the night in a small town while his car is being repaired. He is invited to the home of a retired judge, where, during a sumptuous dinner with a retired prosecutor, a hangman, and an attorney, he is tried and found guilty of murder: by telling his boss that the boss's wife was having an affair, Traps has caused him to have a fatal heart attack. But the next morning, while fighting his hangover, Traps shrugs off the experience. The last words of the play indicate that he intends to ruin someone else.

The Radio Play in the GDR

It might have been expected that the East German authorities would build on the established tradition of socialist radio plays and radio cantatas; but it was only in the later 1950s that the dominant themes of socialist realism, especially "brigade plays"—dramatizations of problems in construction and factory work—became a regular feature of radio programs. It was important at that time to win the workers over to socialism and to keep them from leaving the German Democratic Republic (GDR). Heiner and Inge Müller's *Die Korrektur* (The Correction), broadcast in 1957, details the conflicts of an old Communist who fights corruption and sabotage at a construction site and even clashes with the party when it wants to make compromises with hostile engineers. In the end both the hero and the party win: he converts his coworkers to socialism through his upright behavior but comes to understand that he has to bow to party discipline.

In the 1960s, after the Berlin Wall was built and East German society became largely self-contained, emphasis in literature shifted from the heroic feats of socialist reconstruction to the everyday problems of people. Fantastic literature and historical fiction and plays, as well as works in which the "good" (Communist) characters were not always victorious over the "bad" (West-

ern) ones, emerged in the 1970s and 1980s. These developments were reflected in German radio plays in many examples reminiscent of the 1950s in the West, albeit with a more realistic and directly critical bent. In *Scardanelli*, broadcast in 1970, Stephan Hermlin deals with the poet Friedrich Hölderlin's insanity in a collage of scenes with no explicit political message. *Ehrenhändel* (Affairs of Honor), by Günter Kunert, broadcast in 1972, deals with an episode during Heinrich Heine's exile in Paris. Heine, afraid of political persecution from Prussia, is duped by a swindler into believing implausible stories; he emerges as an impractical dreamer, in spite of the justification of his fight against tyranny. The play can be seen as a self-critical questioning of Kunert's situation in the GDR, which Kunert left soon after the play aired.

The realistic play of the 1970s is perhaps best exemplified by *Porträt einer dicken Frau* (Portrait of a Fat Woman), by Günther Rücker, broadcast in 1971. A well-known sculptor wants to model the ugly head of an ordinary fat woman who turns out to be exemplary in her simple humanity. While the play celebrates the virtues of common people who are not involved in politics, it also focuses on the function of art: the sculptor is justified in extracting the inner beauty of this common and even repulsive face.

The "New" Radio Play in West Germany

By the late 1960s the postwar radio play had exhausted itself in West Germany; the major authors, if still active, had turned to other forms. Television replaced radio as the medium for mass audiences, and political activism called for new literary forms. The "new radio play" centered on radical experiments with sounds and language, while the radio play with authentic sounds, or "O-Ton" (Original Sound) play, tried to emulate the documentary theater. It was soon discovered, however, that even the O-Ton play could not guarantee authenticity. A new form of documentary radio play emerged that uses authentic dialogue but places it in a context of reportage, interviews, announcements, songs, and commentaries. Typical topics are social problems such as water and air pollution and unemployment. *Von Gastgebern und Gästen* (Of Hosts and Guests, 1973), by Luca Lombardi and Hans-Günther Dicks, for example, deals with the condition of foreign workers in Germany. Such plays call for action on the part of the audience. The new radio play is overtly subversive: it is the product of the culture industry but extremely critical of it. The new experimental radio play is not meant for mass audiences. In 1968 the Preis der Kriegsblinden (Prize of the War-Blinded), the most prestigious prize for radio plays in German-speaking countries, went to *Fünf Mann Menschen* (Five Pieces Humans), a collage questioning customary language processes and conventional language, by the Austrian poets Ernst Jandl and Friederike Mayröcker. Wolf Wondratschek's *Paul oder die Zerstörung eines Hörbeispiels* (Paul; or, The Destruction of a Radio Example) received the prize for 1969. Wondratschek deconstructs the possibility of a conventional plot; by doing so, paradoxically, he creates a play with more of a plot than the other new radio plays, which remain collages of language processes and radical attacks on conventional language.

In the 1990s German radio has again taken up classical fiction and adaptations of stage plays. Original radio plays tend to be broadcast in late-night time slots for specifically interested listeners. A new form of radio play for broad audiences is waiting to be created.

References:

Margret Bloom, *Die westdeutsche Nachkriegszeit im literarischen Original-Hörspiel*, Europäische Hochschulschriften, series 1, volume 79 (Frankfurt am Main, Bern & New York: Lang, 1985);

Rita von der Grün, *Das Hörspiel im "Dritten Reich": Eine statistische Erhebung und Auswertung entsprechender Daten aus Programm-Zeits chriften ausgewählter Jahrgänge* (Frankfurt am Main: Fischer, 1984);

Roland Heger, *Das österreichische Hörspiel*, Untersuchungen zur österreichischen Literatur des 20. Jahrhunderts, volume 6 (Vienna & Stuttgart: Braumüller, 1977);

Christian Hörburger, *Das Hörspiel der Weimarer Republik: Versuch einer kritischen Analyse*, Stuttgarter Arbeiten zur Germanistik, no. 1 (Stuttgart: Akademischer Verlag Hans-Dieter Heinz, 1975);

Hermann Keckeis, *Das deutsche Hörspiel 1923-1973* (Frankfurt am Main: Athenäum, 1973);

Friedrich Knilli, *Das Hörspiel: Mittel und Möglichkeiten eines totalen Schallspiels* (Stuttgart: Kohlhammer, 1961);

Uwe Rosenbaum, *Das Hörspiel: Eine Bibliographie. Texte—Tondokumente—Literatur*, Studien zur Massenkommunikation, no. 6 (Hamburg: Hans-Bredow Institut, 1974);

Klaus Schöning, ed., *Neues Hörspiel: Essays, Analysen, Gespräche* (Frankfurt am Main; Suhrkamp, 1970);

Schöning, ed., *Neues Hörspiel O-Ton: Der Konsument als Produzent: Versuche—Arbeitsberichte* (Frankfurt am Main: Suhrkamp, 1974);

Schöning, ed., *Spuren des neuen Hörspiels* (Frankfurt am Main: Suhrkamp, 1982);

Heinz Schwitzke, *Das Hörspiel. Geschichte und Dramaturgie* (Cologne & Berlin: Kiepenheuer & Witsch, 1963);

Stefan Bodo Würffel, *Das deutsche Hörspiel*, Sammlung Metzler, volume 172 (Stuttgart: Metzler, 1978).

Books for Further Reading

Adel, Kurt. *Aufbruch und Tradition: Einführung in die österreichische Literatur seit 1945*. Vienna: Braumüller, 1982.

Ammann, Egon, and Eugen Faes, eds. *Literatur aus der Schweiz: Texte und Materialien*. Frankfurt am Main: Suhrkamp, 1978.

Anz, Thomas, and Michael Stark, eds. *Expressionismus: Manifeste und Dokumente zur deutschen Literatur 1910-1920*. Stuttgart: Metzler, 1982.

Arnold, Armin. *Die Literatur des Expressionismus: Sprachliche und thematische Quellen*. Stuttgart, Berlin, Cologne & Mainz: Kohlhammer, 1966.

Arnold, Heinz Ludwig. *Geschichte der deutschen Literatur aus Methoden: Westdeutsche Literatur von 1945-1971*, 3 volumes. Frankfurt am Main: Athenäum-Fischer-Taschenbuch Verlag, 1972.

Arnold, ed. *Deutsche Bestseller—Deutsche Ideologie: Ansätze zu einer Verbraucherpoetik*. Stuttgart: Klett, 1975.

Arnold, ed. *Kritisches Lexikon zur deutschsprachigen Gegenwartsliteratur*. Munich: Edition text + kritik, 1978ff.

Aspetsberger, Friedbert, ed. *Österreichische Literatur seit den zwanziger Jahren: Beiträge zu ihrer historisch-politischen Lokalisierung*. Vienna: Österreichischer Bundesverlag, 1979.

Aust, Hugo, Peter Haida, and Jürgen Hein. *Volksstück: Vom Hanswurstspiel zum sozialen Drama der Gegenwart*. Munich: Beck, 1989.

Bachmann, Dieter, ed. *Fortschreiben: 98 Autoren der deutschen Schweiz*. Zurich & Munich: Artemis, 1977.

Bauland, Peter. *The Hooded Eagle: Modern German Drama on the New York Stage*. Syracuse, N.Y.: Syracuse University Press, 1968.

Baumann, Barbara, and Birgitta Oberle. *Deutsche Literatur in Epochen*. Munich: Hueber, 1985.

Berg, Jan, and others. *Sozialgeschichte der deutschen Literatur von 1918 bis zur Gegenwart*. Frankfurt am Main: Fischer, 1981.

Best, Alan, and Hans Wolfschütz, eds. *Modern Austrian Writing*. London: Wolff, 1980.

Betten, Anne. *Sprachrealismus im deutschen Drama der siebziger Jahre*. Heidelberg: Winter, 1985.

Bloch, Peter R., ed. *Gegenwartsliteratur: Mittel und Bedingungen ihrer Produktion*. Bern & Munich: Francke, 1975.

Blumer, Arnold. *Das dokumentarische Theater der sechziger Jahre in der Bundesrepublik Deutschland*. Meisenheim: Hain, 1977.

Bormann, Alexander von, Frank Trommler, and Horst Albert Glaser, eds. *Weimarer Republik—Drittes Reich: Avantgardismus, Parteilichkeit, Exil*, Deutsche Literatur: Eine Sozialgeschichte, 9. Reinbek: Rowohlt, 1983.

Brauneck, Manfred, ed. *Theaterlexikon: Begriffe und Epochen, Bühnen und Ensembles*. Reinbek: Rowohlt, 1986.

Brauner, Manfred, ed. *Das deutsche Drama vom Expressionismus bis zur Gegenwart*. Bamberg: Buchner, 1970.

Brettschneider, Werner. *Zwischen literarischer Autonomie und Staatsdienst: Die Literatur der DDR*, second edition. Berlin: Schmidt, 1974.

Brinkmann, Richard. *Expressionismus: Internationale Forschung zu einem internationalen Phänomen*. Stuttgart: Metzler, 1980.

Bronner, Stephen Eric, and Douglas Kellner, eds. *Passion and Rebellion: The Expressionist Heritage*. South Hadley, Mass.: Bergin, 1983.

Buck, Theo, and others, eds. *Tendenzen der deutschen Literatur zwischen 1918 und 1945: Weimarer Republik, Drittes Reich, Exil*. Stuttgart: Klett, 1985.

Buddecke, Wolfram, and Helmut Fuhrmann. *Das deutschsprachige Drama seit 1945*. Munich: Winkler, 1981.

Bullivant, Keith, ed. *Culture and Society in the Weimar Republic*. Manchester, U.K.: Manchester University Press, 1977.

Chandler, Frank W. *Modern Continental Playwrights*. New York & London: Harper, 1931.

Chick, Edson M. *Dances of Death: Wedekind, Brecht, Dürrenmatt and the Satiric Tradition*, Studies in German Literature, Linguistics and Culture, 19. Columbia, S.C.: Camden House, 1984.

Daviau, Donald G., ed. *Major Figures of Contemporary Austrian Literature*. New York: Lang, 1987.

Daviau, ed. *Major Figures of Modern Austrian Literature*. Riverside, Cal.: Ariadne Press, 1988.

Demetz, Peter. *After the Fires: Recent Writing in the Germanies, Austria, and Switzerland*. San Diego & New York: Harcourt Brace Jovanovich, 1986.

Demetz, *Postwar German Literature: A Critical Introduction*. New York: Pegasus, 1970.

Denkler, Horst. *Drama des Expressionismus*, second edition, enlarged. Munich: Fink, 1979.

Diethe, Carol. *Aspects of Distorted Sexual Attitudes in German Expressionist Drama: With Particular Reference to Wedekind, Kokoschka, and Kaiser*. Bern: Lang, 1988.

Dietrich, Margret. *Das moderne Drama: Strömungen, Gestalten, Motive*. Stuttgart: Kröner, 1974.

Dube, Wolf-Dieter. *Expressionism*. New York: Praeger, 1973.

Durzak, Manfred. *Das expressionistische Drama: Ernst Barlach, Ernst Toller, Fritz von Unruh*. Munich: Nymphenburger Verlagshandlung, 1979.

Durzak, ed. *Die deutsche Exilliteratur 1933-1945*. Stuttgart: Reclam, 1973.

Durzak, ed. *Deutsche Gegenwartsliteratur: Ausgangspositionen und aktuelle Entwicklungen*. Stuttgart: Reclam, 1981.

Durzak, ed. *Die deutsche Literatur der Gegenwart: Aspekte und Tendenzen*. Stuttgart: Reclam, 1971.

Duwe, Wilhelm. *Ausdrucksformen deutscher Dichtung vom Naturalismus bis zur Gegenwart: Eine Stilgeschichte der Moderne*. Berlin: Schmidt, 1965.

Duwe. *Deutsche Dichtung des 20. Jahrhunderts: Vom Naturalismus zum Surrealismus*, 2 volumes. Zurich: Orell-Füssli, 1962.

Edschmid, Kasimir. *Lebendiger Expressionismus: Auseinandersetzungen, Gestalten, Erinnerungen*. Munich: Desch, 1961.

Emmerich, Wolfgang. *Kleine Literaturgeschichte der DDR*. Darmstadt & Neuwied: Luchterhand, 1981.

Finney, Gail. *Women in Modern Drama: Freud, Feminism, and European Theater at the Turn of the Century*. Ithaca, N.Y.: Cornell University Press, 1989.

Friedemann, Hermann, and Otto Mann, eds. *Expressionismus: Gestalten einer literarischen Bewegung*. Heidelberg: Rothe, 1956.

Garland, Henry B. *A Concise Survey of German Literature*. London: Macmillan, 1971.

Garland, Henry B., and Mary Garland. *The Oxford Companion to German Literature*, second edition, revised by Mary Garland. Oxford & New York: Oxford Univesity Press, 1986.

Garten, Hugh F. *Modern German Drama*. London: Methuen, 1959.

Geerdts, Hans Jürgen, ed. *Literatur der DDR in Einzeldarstellungen*. Stuttgart: Kröner, 1972.

Geiger, Heinz. *Widerstand und Mitschuld: Zum deutschen Drama von Brecht bis Weiss*. Düsseldorf: Bertelsmann, 1973.

Grimm, Gunter E., and Hans-Peter Bayerdörfer, eds. *Im Zeichen Hiobs: Jüdische Schriftsteller und deutsche Literatur im 20. Jahrhundert*. Königstein: Athenäum, 1985.

Grimm, Reinhold, ed. *Deutsche Dramentheorien: Beiträge zu einer historischen Poetik des Dramas in Deutschland*, 2 volumes. Frankfurt am Main: Athenäum, 1971.

Grimm and Jost Hermand, eds. *Die sogenannten Zwanziger Jahre: First Wisconsin Workshop*, Schriften zur Literatur, 13. Bad Homburg: Gehlen, 1970.

Hamburger, Michael. *After the Second Flood: Essays on Post-War German Literature*. New York: St. Martin's Press, 1986.

Hatfield, Henry. *Modern German Literature: The Main Figures in Context*. London: Arnold, 1966; Bloomington: Indiana University Press, 1968.

Hilzinger, Klaus Harro. *Die Dramaturgie des dokumentarischen Theaters*. Tübingen: Niemeyer, 1976.

Hinck, Walter. *Geschichte als Schauspiel: Deutsche Geschichtsdramen: Interpretationen.* Frankfurt am Main: Suhrkamp, 1981.

Hinck. *Handbuch des deutschen Dramas: Vom expressionistischen zum dokumentarischen Theater.* Düsseldorf: Bagel, 1988.

Hinck. *Das moderne Drama in Deutschland.* Göttingen: Vandenhoeck & Ruprecht, 1973.

Hohendahl, Peter Uwe, ed. *Literatur der DDR in den siebziger Jahren.* Frankfurt am Main: Suhrkamp, 1983.

Innes, C. D. *Erwin Piscator's Political Theatre: The Development of Modern German Drama.* Cambridge: Cambridge University Press, 1972.

Innes, *Modern German Drama: A Study in Form.* Cambridge & New York: Cambridge University Press, 1979.

Ismayr, Wolfgang. *Das politische Theater in Westdeutschland.* Meisenheim am Glan: Hain, 1977.

Killy, Walther, ed. *Literaturlexikon: Autoren und Werke deutscher Sprache,* 12 volumes. Gütersloh: Bertelsmann, 1988-1992.

Kluge, Gerhard, ed. *Studien zur Dramatik in der Bundesrepublik Deutschland.* Amsterdam: Rodopi, 1983.

Klunker, Heinz. *Zeitstücke und Zeitgenossen: Gegenwartstheater in der DDR.* Munich: Deutscher Taschenbuch Verlag, 1975.

Knapp, Gerhard P. *Die Literatur des deutschen Expressionismus: Einführung, Bestandsaufnahme, Kritik.* Munich: Beck, 1979.

Koebner, Thomas, ed. *Tendenzen der deutschen Gegenwartsliteratur,* second edition. Stuttgart: Kröner, 1984.

Koebner, ed. *Tendenzen der deutschen Literatur seit 1945,* Kröner, Taschenausgabe, 405. Stuttgart: Kröner, 1971.

Koebner, ed. *Weimars Ende: Prognosen und Diagnosen in der deutschen Literatur und politischen Publizistik 1930-1933.* Frankfurt am Main: Suhrkamp, 1982.

Kracauer, Siegfried. *From Caligari to Hitler: A Psychological History of the German Film.* Princeton: Princeton University Press, 1947.

Krispyn, Egbert. *Style and Society in German Literary Expressionism,* University of Florida Monographs, Humanities, no. 15. Gainesville: University of Florida Press, 1964.

Kröll, Friedhelm. *Gruppe 47.* Stuttgart: Metzler, 1979.

Kunisch, Hermann. *Die deutsche Gegenwartsdichtung: Kraft und Formen.* Munich: Nymphenburger Verlagshandlung, 1968.

Landa, Jutta. *Bürgerliches Schocktheater: Entwicklungen im österreichischen Drama der sechziger und siebziger Jahre.* Frankfurt am Main: Athenäum, 1988.

Langer, Lawrence. *The Holocaust and the Literary Imagination*. New Haven: Yale University Press, 1975.

Lehnert, Herbert. *Geschichte der deutschen Literatur vom Jugendstil zum Expressionismus*, Geschichte der deutschen Literatur von den Anfängen bis zur Gegenwart, volume 5. Stuttgart: Reclam, 1978.

Mandel, Siegfried. *Group 47: The Reflected Intellect*, preface by Harry T. Moore. Carbondale & Edwardsville: Southern Illinois University Press, 1973.

Mann, Otto, and Wolfgang Rothe, *Deutsche Literatur im 20. Jahrhundert*, fifth edition, 2 volumes. Munich: Francke, 1967.

Meixner, Horst, and Silvio Vietta, eds. *Expressionismus—Sozialer Wandel und künstlerische Erfahrung: Mannheimer Kolloquium*. Munich: Fink, 1982.

Motekat, Helmut. *Das zeitgenössische deutsche Drama: Einführung und kritische Analyse*. Stuttgart, Berlin, Cologne & Mainz: Kohlhammer, 1977.

Müller, Gerd. *Das Volksstück von Raimund bis Kroetz: Die Gattung in Einzelanalysen*. Munich: Oldenbourg, 1979.

Müller, Hans Harald. *Der Krieg und die Schriftsteller: Der Kriegsroman der Weimarer Republik*. Stuttgart: Metzler, 1986.

Muschg, Walter. *Von Trakl zu Brecht: Dichter des Expressionismus*. Munich: Piper, 1961.

Nadler, Josef. *Literaturgeschichte Österreichs*. Salzburg: Müller, 1951.

Patterson, Michael. *German Theatre Today: Post-War Theatre in West and East Germany, Austria, and Northern Switzerland*. London: Pitman, 1976.

Paulsen, Wolfgang. *Deutsche Literatur des Expressionismus*. Bern & New York: Lang, 1983.

Paulsen, ed. *Die deutsche Komödie im 20. Jahrhundert*. Heidelberg: Stiehm, 1976.

Paulsen, ed. *Die Frau als Heldin und Autorin: Neue kritische Ansätze zur deutschen Literatur*. Bern & Munich: Francke, 1979.

Phelan, Anthony, ed. *The Weimar Dilemma: Intellectuals in the Weimar Republic*. Manchester, U.K.: Manchester University Press, 1985.

Raddatz, Fritz J. *Zur deutschen Literatur der Zeit*, volume 1: *Traditionen und Tendenzen: Materialien zur Literatur der DDR*. Reinbek: Rowohlt, 1987.

Riewoldt, Otto F. *Von Zuckmayer bis Kroetz: Die Rezeption westdeutscher Theaterstücke durch Kritik und Wissenschaft in der DDR*. Berlin: Schmidt, 1978.

Robertson, John George. *A History of German Literature*, sixth edition, edited by Dorothy Reich. Edinburgh & London: Blackwood, 1970.

Rothe, Wolfgang, ed. *Die deutsche Literatur in der Weimarer Republik*. Stuttgart: Reclam, 1974.

Rothe, ed. *Expressionismus als Literatur: Gesammelte Studien*. Bern & Munich: Francke, 1969.

Rothmann, Kurt. *Deutschsprachige Schriftsteller seit 1945 in Einzeldarstellungen.* Stuttgart: Reclam, 1985.

Rühle, Günther, ed. *Theater für die Republik, 1917-1933: Im Spiegel der Kritik.* Frankfurt am Main: Fischer, 1967.

Scheid, Judith R., ed. *Zum Drama in der DDR: Heiner Müller und Peter Hacks.* Stuttgart: Klett, 1981.

Schrimpf, Hans Joachim, ed. *Literatur und Gesellschaft vom neunzehnten ins zwanzigste Jahrhundert.* Bonn: Bouvier, 1963.

Shearier, Stephen. *Das junge Deutschland 1917-1920: Expressionistisches Theater in Berlin.* Frankfurt am Main: Lang, 1988.

Sloterdijk, Peter. *Literatur und Organisation von Lebenserfahrung: Autobiographien der Zwanziger Jahre.* Munich: Hanser, 1978.

Soergel, Albert, and Curt Hohoff, *Dichtung und Dichter der Zeit,* 2 volumes. Düsseldorf: Bagel, 1961-1963.

Sokel, Walter H. *The Writer in Extremis: Expressionism in Twentieth-Century German Literature.* Stanford: Stanford University Press, 1959.

Spalek, John M., and Joseph Strelka, eds. *Deutsche Exilliteratur seit 1933,* 2 volumes. Bern & Munich: Francke, 1976-1989.

Szondi, Peter. *Theory of the Modern Drama,* translated and edited by Michael Hays. Minneapolis: University of Minnesota Press, 1987.

Trommler, Frank, ed. *Jahrhundertwende: Vom Naturalismus zum Expressionismus (1880-1918),* Deutsche Literatur: Eine Sozialgeschichte, volume 8. Reinbek: Rowohlt, 1982.

Ungar, Frederick, ed. *Handbook of Austrian Literature.* New York: Ungar, 1973.

Viviani, Annalisa. *Das Drama des Expressionismus.* Munich: Winkler, 1970.

Vogelsang, Hans. *Österreichische Dramatiker des 20. Jahrhunderts: Spiel mit Welten, Wesen, Worten.* Vienna: Braumüller, 1981.

Wagener, Hans, ed. *Gegenwartsliteratur und Drittes Reich: Deutsche Autoren in der Auseinandersetzung mit der Vergangenheit.* Stuttgart: Reclam, 1977.

Wallace, Ian, ed. *The Writer and Society in the GDR.* Tayport Fife: Hutton Press, 1984.

Webb, Benjamin Daniel. *The Demise of the "New Man": An Analysis of Ten Plays from Late Expressionism.* Göppingen: Kümmerle, 1973.

Weber, Dietrich, ed. *Deutsche Literatur der Gegenwart in Einzeldarstellungen,* 2 volumes. Stuttgart: Kröner, 1976-1977.

Wiese, Benno von. *Deutsche Dichter der Moderne.* Berlin: Schmidt, 1965.

Wiesner, Herbert, ed. *Lexikon der deutschsprachigen Gegenwartsliteratur.* Munich: Nymphenburger Verlagshandlung, 1981.

Willett, John. *Expressionism*. New York: McGraw-Hill, 1970.

Willett. *The Theater of Erwin Piscator*. New York: Holmes & Meier, 1979.

Willett. *The Theatre of the Weimar Republic*. New York & London: Holmes & Meier, 1988.

Wilpert, Gero von, and Adolf Gühring. *Erstausgaben deutscher Dichtung: Eine Bibliographie zur deutschen Literatur 1600-1960*. Stuttgart: Kröner, 1967.

Zeman, Herbert, ed. *Die österreichische Literatur: Ihr Profil von der Jahrhundertwende bis zur Gegenwart (1880-1980)*. Graz: Akademische Druck- und Verlagsanstalt, 1989.

Contributors

Scott Abbott ....*Brigham Young University*
Ehrhard Bahr ....*University of California, Los Angeles*
Lowell A. Bangerter ....*University of Wyoming*
Beth Bjorklund ....*University of Virginia*
Russell E. Brown ....*State University of New York at Stony Brook*
Sarah Bryant-Bertail ....*University of Washington*
Reinhold K. Bubser ....*University of Northern Iowa*
Edson M. Chick ....*Williams College*
W. Gordon Cunliffe ....*University of Wisconsin—Madison*
Linda C. DeMeritt ....*Allegheny College*
Heike A. Doane ....*Cary, North Carolina*
Steve Dowden ....*Yale University*
Wolfgang D. Elfe ....*University of South Carolina*
Peter Ensberg ....*Allegheny College*
Thomas H. Falk ....*Michigan State University*
Bernd Fischer ....*Ohio State University*
Albert E. Gurganus ....*The Citadel*
James Hardin ....*University of South Carolina*
Viktoria Hertling ....*University of Nevada, Reno*
Herbert Herzmann ....*University College, Dublin*
Erich P. Hofacker, Jr. ....*University of Michigan*
Donna L. Hoffmeister ....*University of Colorado*
Horst Jarka ....*University of Montana*
Michael Knittel ....*Deep Springs College*
Herbert Knust ....*University of Illinois at Urbana-Champaign*
Wulf Koepke ....*Texas A&M University*
Jürgen Koppensteiner ....*University of Northern Iowa*
Ward B. Lewis ....*University of Georgia*
Steven D. Martinson ....*University of Arizona*
Sigrid Mayer ....*University of Wyoming*
Phillip S. McKnight ....*University of Kentucky*
Michael Mitchell ....*University of Stirling*
Michael Ossar ....*Kansas State University*
Helmut F. Pfanner ....*Vanderbilt University*
Peter C. Pfeiffer ....*Georgetown University*
Christian Rogowski ....*Amherst College*
Susan Russell ....*University of Washington*
Jürgen G. Sang ....*University of Hawaii*
Ernst Schürer ....*Pennsylvania State University*
Stephen Shearier ....*Muhlenberg College*
Blake Lee Spahr ....*University of California, Berkeley*
Patricia H. Stanley ....*Florida State University*
Wiebke Strehl ....*Pennsylvania State University*
Karl Toepfer ....*San Jose State University*
H. M. Waidson ....*University of Wales, Swansea*
Alfred D. White ....*University of Wales, College of Cardiff*
Michael Winkler ....*Rice University*
Reinhard K. Zachau ....*University of the South*

Cumulative Index

Dictionary of Literary Biography, Volumes 1-124
Dictionary of Literary Biography Yearbook, 1980-1991
Dictionary of Literary Biography Documentary Series, Volumes 1-10

Cumulative Index

DLB before number: *Dictionary of Literary Biography*, Volumes 1-124
Y before number: *Dictionary of Literary Biography Yearbook*, 1980-1991
DS before number: *Dictionary of Literary Biography Documentary Series*, Volumes 1-10

A

D

E

L

M

O

P

Q

S

Cumulative Index

U

V

W

ISBN 0-8103-5383-0

8892

(Continued from front endsheets)

80: *Restoration and Eighteenth-Century Dramatists*, First Series, edited by Paula R. Backscheider (1989)

81: *Austrian Fiction Writers, 1875-1913*, edited by James Hardin and Donald G. Daviau (1989)

82: *Chicano Writers*, First Series, edited by Francisco A. Lomelí and Carl R. Shirley (1989)

83: *French Novelists Since 1960*, edited by Catharine Savage Brosman (1989)

84: *Restoration and Eighteenth-Century Dramatists*, Second Series, edited by Paula R. Backscheider (1989)

85: *Austrian Fiction Writers After 1914*, edited by James Hardin and Donald G. Daviau (1989)

86: *American Short-Story Writers, 1910-1945*, First Series, edited by Bobby Ellen Kimbel (1989)

87: *British Mystery and Thriller Writers Since 1940*, First Series, edited by Bernard Benstock and Thomas F. Staley (1989)

88: *Canadian Writers, 1920-1959*, Second Series, edited by W. H. New (1989)

89: *Restoration and Eighteenth-Century Dramatists*, Third Series, edited by Paula R. Backscheider (1989)

90: *German Writers in the Age of Goethe, 1789-1832*, edited by James Hardin and Christoph E. Schweitzer (1989)

91: *American Magazine Journalists, 1900-1960*, First Series, edited by Sam G. Riley (1990)

92: *Canadian Writers, 1890-1920*, edited by W. H. New (1990)

93: *British Romantic Poets, 1789-1832*, First Series, edited by John R. Greenfield (1990)

94: *German Writers in the Age of Goethe: Sturm und Drang to Classicism*, edited by James Hardin and Christoph E. Schweitzer (1990)

95: *Eighteenth-Century British Poets*, First Series, edited by John Sitter (1990)

96: *British Romantic Poets, 1789-1832*, Second Series, edited by John R. Greenfield (1990)

97: *German Writers from the Enlightenment to Sturm und Drang, 1720-1764*, edited by James Hardin and Christoph E. Schweitzer (1990)

98: *Modern British Essayists*, First Series, edited by Robert Beum (1990)

99: *Canadian Writers Before 1890*, edited by W. H. New (1990)

100: *Modern British Essayists*, Second Series, edited by Robert Beum (1990)

101: *British Prose Writers, 1660-1800*, First Series, edited by Donald T. Siebert (1991)

102: *American Short-Story Writers, 1910-1945*, Second Series, edited by Bobby Ellen Kimbel (1991)

103: *American Literary Biographers*, First Series, edited by Steven Serafin (1991)

104: *British Prose Writers, 1660-1800*, Second Series, edited by Donald T. Siebert (1991)

105: *American Poets Since World War II*, Second Series, edited by R. S. Gwynn (1991)

106: *British Literary Publishing Houses, 1820-1880*, edited by Patricia J. Anderson and Jonathan Rose (1991)

107: *British Romantic Prose Writers, 1789-1832*, First Series, edited by John R. Greenfield (1991)

108: *Twentieth-Century Spanish Poets*, First Series, edited by Michael L. Perna (1991)

109: *Eighteenth-Century British Poets*, Second Series, edited by John Sitter (1991)

110: *British Romantic Prose Writers, 1789-1832*, Second Series, edited by John R. Greenfield (1991)

111: *American Literary Biographers*, Second Series, edited by Steven Serafin (1991)

112: *British Literary Publishing Houses, 1881-1965*, edited by Jonathan Rose and Patricia J. Anderson (1991)

113: *Modern Latin-American Fiction Writers*, First Series, edited by William Luis (1992)

114: *Twentieth-Century Italian Poets*, First Series, edited by Giovanna Wedel De Stasio, Glauco Cambon, and Antonio Illiano (1992)

115: *Medieval Philosophers*, edited by Jeremiah Hackett (1992)

116: *British Romantic Novelists, 1789-1832*, edited by Bradford K. Mudge (1992)

117: *Twentieth-Century Caribbean and Black African Writers*, First Series, edited by Bernth Lindfors and Reinhard Sander (1992)